Fodor's 92
South
America

FODOR'S TRAVEL PUBLICATIONS, INC.
New York & London

Fodor's South America

Editor: Andrew E. Beresky

Contributors: Joanna Berkman, Hilary Branch, Valerie Brito, Ernesto Fahrenkrog, Jorge Guazzini, Tara Hamilton, Catherine Healy, Edward Holland, Eric Holland, Robert Kaplan, Jenny Keller, Lorrie Kline, Kurt Kutay, Barry Lynn, Peter McFarren, Alexander Miles, Roberta Okey, Jane Onstott, Eduardo Proaño, Tom Quinn, Juliellen Sabalis, Peter Sanches, Rafael Sardà, Alma Schacht, Gabriel Segredo, Kathryn Shaw, Michael Smith, Edwin Taylor, Jim Woodman

Drawings: Michael Conway

Maps: C.W. Bacon M.S.I.A., John Hutchison, Jon Bauch Design, Dyno Lowenstein, Leslie S. Haywood

Cover Photograph: James Holland/Stock Boston

Cover Design: Vignelli Associates

Special Sales

Fodor's Travel Publications are available at special discounts for bulk purchases (100 copies or more) for sales promotions or premiums. Special editions, including personalized covers, excerpts of existing guides, and corporate imprints, can be created in large quantities for special needs. For more information, write to Special Marketing, Fodor's Travel Publications, 201 East 50th Street, New York, NY 10022; or call 800/800–3246. Inquiries from the United Kingdom should be sent to Fodor's Travel Publications, 20 Vauxhall Bridge Rd., London, England SW1V 2SA.

CONTENTS

FOREWORD

South America lies southeast of North America and is bordered by the Caribbean Sea, the North and South Atlantic, the Antarctic, and the North and South Pacific oceans. Distances are great and at first many of the names are new and curious, but a few moments spent studying a map will familiarize you with the coasts, countries, and major cities.

South America is a land of contrasts. The countries differ historically, geographically, ethnically, politically, economically, and culturally. You will also find a variety of languages spoken. Although Spanish is the national language of most South American countries, Portuguese is spoken in Brazil, Dutch in Suriname, English in Guyana, and French in French Guiana.

For the tourist, South America is a land of discovery with new sights, sounds, people, history, ideas, and traditions. You will find uncrowded beaches and hotels, booming metropolises, and ancient cities that date to the beginning of recorded time. You can travel into the depths of the Amazon jungle or visit lands where primitive tribes still exist. You may dance along with Latin rhythms, ski in the middle of July, and enjoy breathtaking scenery.

While every care has been taken to assure the accuracy of the information in this guide, the passage of time will always bring change, and consequently the publisher cannot accept responsibility for any errors that may occur.

All prices and opening times quoted in this guide are based on information supplied to us at press time. Hours and admission fees may change, however, and the prudent traveler will avoid inconvenience by calling ahead.

Fodor's wants to hear about your travel experiences, both pleasant and unpleasant. When a hotel or restaurant fails to live up to its billing, let us know and we will investigate the complaint and revise our entries where the facts warrant it.

Send your letters to the editors of Fodor's Travel Publications, 201 E. 50th Street, New York, NY 10022.

Health Alert. A cholera epidemic, which struck Peru in early 1991, was spreading to the neighboring countries of Ecuador, Colombia, and Chile at press time and was threatening Brazil. The disease has taken more than 1,100 lives and has sickened more than 150,000 in Peru alone. Cholera is spread largely through contaminated water and foodstuffs. Infected people suffer vomiting, diarrhea, and severe, sudden weight loss. The disease is generally treated with rehydration salts and intravenous solutions, but these treatments are not readily available in remote areas. A vaccine gives only brief and incomplete protection and is *not* recommended for travelers. To avoid the disease, you should drink only treated water and eat food that is well cooked and still hot. Ice cubes in drinks should also be avoided. For further information, contact the U.S. Department of Health and Human Services, Public Health Service Centers for Disease Control, Atlanta, GA 30333; tel. 404–332–4559.

SOUTH AMERICA

SOUTH AMERICA

AT A GLANCE

Something for Everyone

by
KATHRYN SHAW

Writer and editor Kathryn Shaw began a long-standing love affair with South America the moment she laid eyes on Rio de Janeiro. Her work as former managing editor of Américas *magazine, published by the Organization of American States, and current editor of* Grassroots Development, *the journal of the Inter-American Foundation, has taken her to South America often—but never often enough, she says.*

Nearly five hundred years after Columbus discovered South America, tourists in the United States are finally waking up to the diverse delights of their neighboring continent. And to many, the magical, mystical sights and sounds of this vast land are a traveler's dream come true.

Once considered too far away for shorter trips (indeed, Moscow is closer to New York than Buenos Aires), the jet age has brought South America's bustling cities and dramatic landscapes within easy reach of U.S. travelers. The media, too, has added to the allure, splashing newspapers, popular magazines, and television screens with images of a world too exciting to go unexplored any longer. Whether it is a temperature-raising Brazilian lambada, an award-winning Argentine film, or a best-selling Colombian

1

novel, North Americans are getting a taste of the variety that South America has to offer—and they want to savor more of the heady brew.

In the wake of so much exposure, increasing numbers of restless vacationers are now exchanging commuter trains, computer screens, and drab, high-rise offices for the fascinating contrasts that await them the moment they arrive in South America. Centuries-old colonial churches with dazzling Baroque façades standing in the shadow of sleek skyscrapers are a common—yet unforgettable—sight throughout the Southern Hemisphere. Smartly dressed socialites in many cosmopolitan cities brush shoulders with Indian women clad in traditional costumes that have changed little since the days of Columbus. In rural areas, shiny new Volvos and BMWs share dusty streets with lumbering oxcarts and men on horseback. Dry gives way to wet as the rainy season begins suddenly, and cold becomes hot within minutes of leaving the highlands for a coastal destination.

Such diversity means that there is literally something, somewhere, for everyone, on any budget, to see and do in South America. Savvy shoppers can spend all day at chic boutiques brimming with bargains in Brazilian gemstones, Argentine leather, or Uruguayan furs, depending on the country. At the same time, handicraft lovers have a choice between the likes of Paraguayan lace, Peruvian textiles, or fine Panama hats (from Ecuador, no less) sold in bustling *mercados,* the New World's answer to chaotic Oriental bazaars. And sun worshippers, those most dedicated of hedonists, can mingle with some of the world's most beautiful people on glittering beaches in posh Punta del Este or Viña del Mar.

The mysteries of ancient Indian ruins such as silent, windswept Tiahuanaco in Bolivia and majestic Machu Picchu in Peru never fail to tantalize amateur and professional archaeologists alike. Nature lovers, too, are astounded when they come nose to nose with friendly sea lions and giant tortoises in the Galápagos Islands, or first hear the mighty roar of Iguaçu Falls—higher and wider than Niagara—as the raging waters plunge over basalt cliffs on the border between Argentina, Paraguay, and Brazil.

The thrills of white-water rafting in the jungles of Peru, deep-sea fishing off the coast of Venezuela, and downhill skiing in the Argentine Andes lure sporting enthusiasts grown tired of Aspen and Vail, while the pristine mountain fastness of the Chilean lake district beckons to hikers and mountain climbers.

Less exhausting pleasures abound for music lovers, whether they prefer a saucy samba in São Paulo, a lively *cumbia* in Bogotá, or the melancholy sound of Andean pan pipes in Quito and La Paz. The entire continent is a gourmet's delight as well, where bounteous Chilean seafood, exotic Afro-Brazilian concoctions, and sinfully succulent Argentine steaks vie for the title of the continent's most delicious regional cuisine.

Indeed, there is so much to see and do in South America that any number of appetites can be satisfied on the same vacation. History buffs, for example, can spend the afternoon touring the summer palace of Brazilian Emperor Dom Pedro II in the mountains just north of Rio after a splendid morning of sunbathing on the beach at Ipanema. Admirers of superb horsemanship, on the other hand, might choose to pass the day at one of Buenos Aires's year-round racetracks, followed by an excellent Argentine wine at dinner and a night of tango in La Boca, the city's picturesque waterfront district.

Few vacation spots could possibly provide better subjects for photographers and artists either, whether they specialize in landscapes, cityscapes, wildlife, or people. It is hard to imagine colors more brilliant, light more intense, or textures more complex than those that meet the eye at every glance. The perfectly shaped cones of Ecuador's volcanoes, the colonial splendor of Lima's churches, the riot of fishing skiffs plying Reloncaví Sound in southern Chile, and the masterpieces of modern architecture in Brasília all beg to be captured on film or canvas. Only that way will friends back home ever believe skies could be so blue, clouds so white, or mountains so majestic.

From bird watchers to beach bums, South America would seem to offer something for everyone. But sometimes those who enjoy it the most do not fit into any category. They are the dreamers, the escapists, the lovers of the unusual, the ones who go with no expectations—and who usually end up being the most richly rewarded.

Different, Yet the Same

How can any one part of the world provide so much for eager travelers to explore? The reasons are as varied as the land itself, beginning with its geography. It is some 4,600 miles from the sultry Caribbean coast of Venezuela to land's end in rugged Tierra del Fuego. Between those two points lie the savannah country of Guyana, the dense jungles of the Amazon Basin, and the endless pampas of Uruguay and Argentina. These natural barriers, together with the great bristling wall of the Andes that runs the entire length of the continent from north to south, kept people in one place for centuries (and still do in many cases). Thus, distinctive regional traits evolved, many of which survive today unscathed by modern times.

Related to the area's geography is its geology. It, too, varies widely from country to country in South America, something that was quickly discovered by fortune-seeking Europeans who governed the territory. Lacking silver or gold, settlers in Paraguay, for example, were left alone to develop a largely agricultural society. On the other hand, thriving colonial cities grew up in places like Lima and Quito, seats of tremendous power based upon the region's staggering mineral wealth.

The Indian population—or lack of it—also makes each area distinct from its neighbors. African food, music, and religion have also left their mark on the Caribbean coast and in much of Brazil, the legacy of black slaves imported to replace less robust native Indian laborers. More recent times have seen waves of Japanese, Italian, and German immigrants who have added their own colorful threads to the vibrant cultural tapestry that makes up South America today.

Despite such sharp contrasts, there are striking similarities that contribute to the flavor of the region as well. The greatest is language, for Spanish became the official tongue in every country save Brazil, where Portuguese is spoken, and the Guianas, where English, French, and Dutch predominate. Spanish and Portuguese priests also spread their Catholicism across the entire continent, although in many areas even today Indians and blacks cling tenaciously to traditional religious practices, calling equally upon pagan and Christian deities as the need arises.

Along with religion, the early Catholic priests stressed family ties, and the tradition of close-knit families became common throughout South America. Whether wealthy apartment dwellers in Caracas, peasant farmers in the Andes, or working-class suburbanites in Buenos Aires, all look to their families for emotional and financial support—as well as for much of their social life. Fortunate indeed is the visitor who makes friends early in his travels and gets invited to their homes for a glimpse at this special side of South America—the one that no guidebook can ever adequately describe.

Dividing Up the Continent

The profusion of countries and cities to choose from might make selecting one destination spot—or even two or three—seem like an impossible
task. The truth is, however, that since the Andes split the continent rather
conveniently into two very distinct regions, making sense of the whole
thing is only half as hard.

There are actually three ranges of mountains that make up the great,
jagged spine of South America, varying between two hundred and four
hundred miles in width and averaging some thirteen thousand feet in
height. Among the loftiest peaks is Argentina's Aconcagua—at 22,834 feet
it is the highest in the Western Hemisphere.

No other part of the world can compare to the spectacular beauty of
the west coast of South America created by this monumental chain of
mountains. From the highlands of Ecuador, Peru, and Bolivia to the headwaters of the mighty Amazon to the gemlike lakes of southern Chile, nature is at its finest. As if inspired by all the splendor, human artists, too,
left marvelous pre-Columbian and colonial treasures for fascinated tourists to behold.

But the majority of the continent lies east of the Andes, and its marvels
are no less alluring. Some of the world's largest and most exciting cities
are found there—Rio de Janeiro, São Paulo, and Buenos Aires—along
with incomparable natural wonders such as Iguaçu Falls and legendary
Amazonia. To many people, the east coast with its beaches and resorts
spells fun, and there is no better place to begin a closer look than in Caracas, the dynamic capital of oil-rich Venezuela.

The Caribbean Coast

Just a few short hours away from the East Coast of the United States,
the sophisticated metropolis of Caracas sprawls east and west along a narrow nine-mile valley, reminding many of Los Angeles. Like that American
city, it has horrible traffic jams—as well as world-class art galleries, hotels,
restaurants, and nightlife. Drawn by its high standard of living, waves of
immigrants from other Latin American countries (as well as Venezuela's
own rural poor) make the city more cosmopolitan every day—and more
congested. As a result, Caracas changes constantly with the construction
of buildings and highways needed to accommodate the ever-increasing
numbers of people and automobiles.

But there are many attractions outside the city for those who prefer
more peaceful pleasures. Mérida, for instance, in the snow-capped Andes
to the west, is the picturesque colonial city of tiled roofs that boasts the
world's highest and longest cable car ride. In four stages, the *teleférico*
rises to the summit of nearby Pico Espejo, a spectacular one-hour ascent.
For those who fancy sunbathing, picture-postcard beaches stretch along
the 1,730-mile coastal ribbon from Maracaibo to Cumaná. Free-port shopping can also be combined with sunning for an added bonus on Margarita
Island in the Caribbean Sea. The Gran Sabana, a tropical highland in Bolívar State, draws many visitors as well. It is there that Angel Falls drops
3,212 feet down the face of Auyantepuy Mountain, making it the world's
highest waterfall. Camping trips upriver to the foot of the falls from the
town of Canaima are very popular with adventurous tourists.

Overshadowed by their booming neighbor, the Guianas sit to the east
of Venezuela like teenage triplets waiting to come of age. Until fairly recently, they were all that remained of European colonial power in South

America. Although the rest of the continent became independent of Spain and Portugal long ago, the British, French, and Dutch held on to their tiny toeholds. Guyana and Suriname finally gained independence in 1970 and 1975 respectively, but French Guiana is still an overseas department of France. Together, the trio comprise an area roughly the size of Sweden. The majority of the population is an unusual mix of Asians and Africans, and the amalgamation of faces, foods, and customs is unequaled elsewhere in South America.

Although challenged by the Dutch, it was the English who ultimately laid claim to modern Guyana, known as British Guiana until its independence. The pleasant capital city of Georgetown was laid out by the Dutch, who placed canals down the middle of wide avenues to remind them of their homeland. Many of the waterways have been filled in, forming tree-lined walks between the streets. But the natural beauty of the interior is by far the country's chief attraction, especially the Rupununi savannah, which is an outdoorsman's paradise.

The only French-speaking country in South America, French Guiana was once known chiefly as the site of Devil's Island, the French penal colony closed in 1953. Today, the French government has ambitious plans for economic development, and tourism is definitely on the agenda. Hunters and explorers should take note, since a river trip through its dense, mysterious forest is hard to match for sheer adventure.

Amazing Brazil

Below the Guianas, Brazil explodes with intoxicating vitality and sensuality. While the raw energy may not be visible to the naked eye, its effects can be seen everywhere—in highways, dams, industrial complexes, and even in the entire capital city of Brasília, which was moved from its idyllic seaside setting into the wilderness in an effort to promote development of the nation's vast interior. Larger than the continental United States, Portuguese-speaking Brazil is the fifth-largest country in the world and occupies half of South America. Its dimensions boggle the mind, as does its incredible potential for future growth.

To most Americans, Brazil is the amazing Amazon, the legendary 4,000-mile-long river and the 750,000,000-acre expanse of tractless jungle, menacing wildlife, and merciless heat through which it flows. Nowhere is that picture more accurate than in Manaus, a river city of some one million inhabitants that sprang up 1,200 miles from the Atlantic during the rubber boom of the nineteenth century. It pulsates again today with commercial activity, and serves as a convenient point of departure for trips into the backwaters of Amazonia.

Rio de Janeiro *is* Brazil to most people, with its spectacular bayside setting, fabulous beaches, skimpy string bikinis, and riotous Carnival celebration. But Brazil goes far beyond its beaches and hedonistic pleasures. It is a fast-paced world of skyscrapers, stock markets, and agro-business carried out in megalopolises like São Paulo and Belo Horizonte. And like the United States, Brazil has welcomed emigrés from all over the world—Lebanese, Eastern European, German, Italian, and Japanese. In return, they have applied their knowledge and skills toward helping to transform their adopted homeland into a major industrial nation.

Brazil's greatest treasure, however, is perhaps one of its least well known. Far away from crowded condominiums and rush hour traffic jams, camouflaged until the very last minute by a canopy of forest green, lies Iguaçu Falls. These awesome cataracts—some 300 separate falls in all—thunder over a two-and-a-half-mile-wide precipice on the border between

Brazil and Argentina. Though Iguaçu is off the beaten path, over a million tourists visit it each year. None go away disappointed. Beginning at the top of a hill crowned by the luxurious rose-colored Hotel das Cataratas, a walkway twists down the side of the gorge, affording views of the rushing cascades that become more magnificent at every turn. Myriad rainbows large and small dance in clouds of mist, and thousands of butterflies in glittering jewel tones chase each other about like playful puppies, alighting affectionately on passersby. Mimicking giant dragonflies, helicopters hover in the air as well, offering passengers a breathtaking bird's-eye view of the watery wonderland.

The Land of Gauchos and Guaraní

Ultimately, the fertile farmlands of southern Brazil become the gently rolling hills and grasslands of Uruguay, the second smallest country in South America. Ninety percent of the land is used for grazing, and Uruguayans are justifiably proud of their fine beef cattle. The country's beaches, too, are among the best in the southern part of South America. Without even leaving Montevideo, Uruguay's gracious capital, visitors can sample more than a half a dozen that fringe the city's sparkling waterfront. But surely the most fashionable beach is located 85 miles to the east at Punta del Este, a haven for well-heeled vacationers from many foreign countries, especially nearby Argentina. Often called the Riviera of South America, this famous resort is also a popular site for international conferences and movie festivals.

Visitors should be sure to include an excursion to Colonia Suiza, originally a Swiss settlement. The most remarkable aspect of Uruguay for most travelers, however, is surely its people. Well educated yet unpretentious, industrious yet relaxed, the Uruguayans differ sharply in manner from the more worldly Argentines living just on the other side of the River Plate.

But before rushing on to explore the vast reaches of Argentina, the world's eighth-largest country, a look at landlocked Paraguay is certainly in order. Visitors to this largely undiscovered and unspoiled land enter a world where time and tradition have stood still for generations. Only recently, with the construction of Itaipú Dam (a joint venture with Brazil that produced the world's largest hydroelectric plant) has the nation begun to emerge from the nineteenth century. While this means that it may be short on extravagant facilities for tourists, it is long on charm and authenticity missing today in many other parts of South America.

Some would say Asunción is a provincial capital, and its pleasures are indeed simple ones—a stroll through the Botanical Gardens, a leisurely lunch at an outdoor cafe, or an afternoon of shopping for ñandutí, the country's uniquely beautiful and intricate spiderweb lace. The real Paraguay, however, is found in the countryside, where motorcycles and portable radios are just now starting to compete with oxcarts and traditional polca music in the hearts and minds of the rural people. The country's original inhabitants were the Guaraní Indians, and nowhere else did the Spaniards actually marry comely Indian maidens the way they did in Paraguay. The result was a blending of European and Indian traits to a degree unknown elsewhere in the hemisphere. But when it came to language, the people's preference for Guaraní prevailed, and the government actually recognized it as an official language along with Spanish.

Mission ruins near Encarnación are another impressive reminder of the Guaraní legacy. It was there that Jesuit priests converted the Indians and organized a unique communal society. Several of the lovely missions, abandoned when the Jesuits were expelled in 1767, are being restored today under the auspices of international organizations.

Leaving Paraguay at Encarnación and crossing the river into Argentina brings one suddenly back into the twentieth century, if not the twenty-first. This is the continent's second-largest country, and the scenery—ranging from the snowy heights of the Andes in the west to the flat grassy pampas along the Atlantic coast—is spectacular. Such stunning visual effects, combined with romantic notions of handsome gauchos dancing the seductive tango, create a mystique that has been lost on few foreigners. These stereotypes fade immediately, however, when visitors take their first walk along Buenos Aires's classy Calle Florida, sit down to tea in an elegant *confitería,* or attend an opera at the world famous Teatro Colón. The *Porteños,* as residents of Buenos Aires are called, are as educated, sophisticated, and urbane as anyone on earth. Their cosmopolitan city never sleeps—or so it seems. Dinner is often eaten at midnight, and the streets are still full of people when one leaves the restaurant at 2 A.M. Some 42 theaters, 200 movie houses, 150 parks, and an untold number of museums and galleries provide pastimes for a population in perpetual motion.

Although most residents of Buenos Aires are curiously out of touch with life in the country's provinces, no tourist should leave Argentina without visiting the wine country of Mendoza, the ski resort of Bariloche, or the Valdez Peninsula where thousands of enormous seals bask on pebbled beaches. The pace is slower, the people more open, and the culture easier to appreciate away from the capital city's constant commotion.

Charming Chile

Leapfrogging the colossal Andes, a capsule tour of South America's west coast begins in Chile, which—like Argentina—immediately strikes the visitor as very cosmopolitan. Due to an influx of European immigrants in the nineteenth century, German and Italian surnames are quite common for Chileans, many of whom converse easily in German, English, or Spanish. They are a handsome, stylish people known for their openness and hospitality.

This 2,650-mile-long ribbon of a country averages only 110 miles in width. From north to south it cuts across five distinct ranges of soil and climate, producing a variety of exceptional scenic attractions. In the arid north is the Atacama Desert, so dry that in some areas no rain has ever been recorded. Next come the copper mines and rich nitrate deposits, followed by the fertile central valley where Santiago, the capital city, is located. The beautiful lake and forest region is below that, with outstanding fishing and skiing. Finally, in the extreme south lies cold, forbidding, windswept Tierra del Fuego.

Known for its award-winning wines and excellent seafood, Chile is also justly famous for the resort city of Viña del Mar, with its wide, white sandy beaches and year-round casino overlooking the Pacific Ocean. Jet-set skiers from the United States and Europe often prefer the championship slopes at Portillo, outside Santiago, where they can schuss during summer months when snows melt in the Northern Hemisphere. Huge, mysterious *moai* statues await tourists looking for a different type of adventure on Chile's Easter Island, the world's most remote inhabited isle.

The Barren, Beautiful Altiplano

Bolivia may share the Andes with its neighbor Chile, but otherwise the two adjoining countries seem worlds apart. Maybe it is because Chile has thousands of miles of Pacific coastline, while Bolivia is completely land-locked. Whereas Chile has been accessible to many different groups of immigrants, Bolivia's isolated population has remained predominantly indigenous. Whereas Chile seems cosmopolitan, Bolivia feels very foreign. And this quite tangible otherworldliness adds to its great appeal.

Visitors are often giddy upon arrival in La Paz, perhaps with relief at having landed safely at the world's highest commercial airport, which is perched just above the world's highest capital city. More likely it is *soroche,* a dizziness caused by the lack of oxygen in the air at 13,000 feet. A pleasant coca-leaf tea (or a tiny pill purchased at any pharmacy) usually solves the problem soon enough and one is ready to explore this land of the Quechua-speaking Indians, descendants of the Inca civilization that disappeared over 1,000 years ago. Not to be missed are the ruins of Tiahuanaco (Tiwanacu), a 50-mile ride from La Paz across the barren yet amazingly beautiful *altiplano,* the high plateau more than 600 miles long and 60 miles wide between two ranges of the Andes. Although the ruins are shrouded in mystery, some researchers believe Tiahuanaco may have been the cradle of American man dating back some 7,000 years. The Bolivian people today still practice ancient customs and traditions, including the use of endearing doe-eyed llamas as beasts of burden.

Making up for having no access to the Pacific Ocean, Bolivia boasts Lake Titicaca, the highest navigable lake in the world. Upon this huge inland sea—100 miles long and up to 50 miles wide—sail sleek modern yachts alongside Indians in their traditional gondola-shaped boats made of *totora* reeds. Crossing the deep-blue lake on a whirring hydrofoil is certainly an unforgettable way to reach the shores of neighboring Peru.

At Puno, on the northwest coast of Titicaca, begins the experience of a lifetime. From there one takes the train to Cuzco, and beyond that to the ruins of magnificent Machu Picchu. Knowledgeable world travelers have said that the scenery on this 11-hour ride surpasses that of the Himalayas. Cuzco itself, once the capital of the Inca empire, is Peru's leading tourist attraction and one of the most interesting cities in the Hemisphere. Although the Spaniards tried to superimpose their culture on the conquered Inca, one gets the impression that they succeeded at best in penetrating only the surface. Symbolically, when the 1950 earthquake struck it felled much of the Monastery of Santo Domingo, which had been built over the ruins of the sacred Temple of the Sun. However, the inner Inca walls that were revealed had withstood the devastating quake.

The three-hour trip by rail from Cuzco to Machu Picchu, while exhilarating, does little to prepare visitors for the marvels of this fantastic hideaway. Thought by many to have been the last refuge of the Inca, it was never discovered by the Spaniards. The maze of temples, houses, terraces, and stairways lay abandoned in lofty solitude until Hiram Bingham, later a U.S. senator, stumbled upon the forgotten city in 1911. Today, along with Iguaçu Falls, Machu Picchu is considered by many to be South America's greatest wonder.

If the gems of Peru's Inca past are locked away on the *altiplano,* then its capital, Lima, is the safekeeper of its colonial treasures. Perhaps no other city in the Americas enjoyed such power and prestige during the height of the colonial era. For an entirely different side of Peru, travelers should also try Iquitos, where the sounds of the Amazon jungle are ever present. Once a difficult journey, efficient air service has now made this region as accessible as the highlands.

Heavenly Highlands

Like Bolivia and Peru, Ecuador also has highlands that can be compared only to Shangri-La. Though a tiny country, it nonetheless claims many of the Hemisphere's most impressive volcanoes. A patchwork quilt of terraced plots in a thousand shades of green covers the lower slopes of these cloud-capped peaks, where corn grows twice as tall as the sturdy peasant farmers who till the fertile soil.

Quito, the nation's capital, lies at the foot of mighty Mt. Pichincha. It is one of the best examples of Spanish colonial architecture anywhere in South America, with winding cobblestone streets, red-tile roofs, and ornately decorated churches typical of many towns in Spain. Just 15 miles outside the city, visitors enjoy having their picture taken as they straddle the Equator at a monument indicating the dividing line between the Northern and Southern Hemisphere.

Ecuador's exquisite handicrafts rival its natural beauty, and they are found in wondrous profusion in market towns throughout the highlands. The coastal region and its bustling port city of Guayaquil also have much to offer, and the most memorable way to get there from Quito is by rail. When in operation, the train maneuvers its way up and down mountain passes by a series of switchbacks on narrow-gauge tracks to reach its destination in the steamy lowlands. Guayaquil is a great commercial center, and also serves as the departure point for planes and ships to the enchanting Galápagos Islands.

In bordering Colombia, this tour comes full circle around the continent. Sometimes called "the corner of South America," it is the only country to have beaches on both the Pacific and Caribbean coasts. As in Ecuador, Colombia's major cities lie in different altitudes, creating very different customs and ways of life. In Bogotá, the capital, at 8,700 feet, there is a formality reminiscent of Spain—not just in the conduct of business and social amenities but also in the Spanish that is spoken, said to be the purest in all of Latin America. However, as one descends 2,000 feet to Medellín, known as "the orchid capital of the world," and another 1,500 feet to Cali, the heart of the coffee country, and then finally to Cartagena at sea level, where there is a strong Afro-Caribbean influence shared with neighboring Venezuela, the atmosphere grows progressively more relaxed and informal. The music, cuisine, costumes, dialects, and attitudes reflect each region, creating a true "potpourri" that is much of the charm of Colombia.

From Pizarro to Pinochet

If the land and peoples of South America are interesting, its history is certainly no less intriguing. Christopher Columbus did not actually set foot on the continent until his third voyage in 1498, when he reached the mouth of the Orinoco River in what is now Venezuela. Both Spain and Portugal were eager to develop overseas empires at that time, and it did not take long for them to send other bold adventurers to explore the territory first charted by Columbus. In 1531, Francisco Pizarro sailed south from Panama with some 180 men and 27 horses. He landed in Peru and by 1533 he had conquered the entire Inca empire, doing in South America what Cortez had done—more easily—in Mexico. One of Pizarro's officers, Pedro de Valdivia, conquered northern Chile and founded Santiago in 1541, giving Spain control of the west coast of the continent from Panama to central Chile.

The Portuguese, meanwhile, were busy on the east coast laying claim to Brazil. Unlike the situation in the rest of South America, the colonization of Brazil was gradual and relatively peaceful. While Spanish conquistadors were seeking the gold of legendary El Dorado, wood was the first natural resource exploited by the Portuguese. Then came sugar, which gave rise to vast plantations along the coast—and to the importation of millions of African slaves to do the backbreaking labor. Afterwards came gold and diamonds, opening up the first land in the interior. Coffee followed, and with it the appearance of planters on the red earth of southeastern Brazil.

Many Spaniards and Portuguese came to South America intending to make a quick fortune and return to Europe as soon as possible. Their expeditions, however, always included farmers and craftsmen who wished to begin life anew in the Americas. What they got instead was an oppressive feudal system that evolved as time passed—along with glittering colonial cities such as Lima, Quito, and Ouro Preto filled with masterpieces of baroque art and architecture. For three centuries South American colonists labored under European rule, but between 1808 and 1823 the New World empires built by Spain and Portugal began to crumble—for many of the same political and economic reasons that led to the revolt of the 13 British colonies in North America.

Although each country had its own revolutionary heroes, two men stand out as leaders in South America's struggle for independence. The first is Venezuelan general Simón Bolívar, a man of tremendous vision, whose courageous battles freed Bolivia, Colombia, Ecuador, Peru, and Venezuela. The second is José de San Martín, the Argentine general who helped win independence for Chile and Peru.

Brazil won its independence from Portugal in 1822 without bloodshed, and changed from colony to monarchy to republic fairly easily.

South America may have been ready for independence in theory, but in practice the newly sovereign nations had little preparation for self-government. Inspired by the American and French revolutions, eager patriots in the Southern Hemisphere also demanded republican forms of government, hoping to follow their example. Unfortunately, most of the newly created republics lacked the broad popular base necessary to enforce their fragile constitutions.

It would be tedious to mention all the revolutions, coups d'etat, and upheavals that have shaken the majority of South American nations since they gained independence. Clearly, down through the centuries from Pizarro to men such as current Argentine president Carlos Menem, and former president of Chile Augusto Pinochet (still the ever-present chief of armed forces), the real power in the Southern Hemisphere has always been vested in its charismatic leaders, rather than in well-intentioned but weak legislation. Things do change, however—even in South America—and recent elections in a number of countries have brought democratic rule (albeit fragile in some cases) to the entire region.

Economic Matters

The political fortune of any leader is forever tied to economics, and South America's heads of state have had particularly rough going in the last few years trying to cope with financial matters. The region blossomed in the 1950s and 1960s, when Latin American resources and potential attracted substantial investment. The oil price boom of 1973–1974 then created huge cash surpluses for oil exporters. Much of it was spent on prestigious industrial projects, and the public debt soared from $20 billion in

1970 to $160 billion in 1980. Given the rosy state of the world's economy at that time, Latin America qualified for new loans while still meeting interest payments on the existing ones. This picture changed drastically in the early 1980s, however, when mounting loans met world recession. Markets for the region's exports dried up and its economies went into the red overnight.

The Latin American debt crisis became a world crisis in August 1982, when Mexico ran out of money and informed its creditors that it could not repay the interest on its loans, much less the capital. It was soon evident that the South American countries of Brazil and Argentina were in serious trouble as well, and Venezuela, Chile, Peru, Colombia, Ecuador, Uruguay, and Bolivia rounded out the list of top 10 debtor nations. Most were forced to renegotiate the terms of their repayments and had to agree to severe austerity measures as a condition of reprieve. This enforced belt tightening has been understandably unpopular with many South Americans, and it threatens to topple delicate democracies.

On the positive side, it has been a time of awakening, of searching for South American solutions to South American problems. There is a growing awareness of the continent's place in the developing world. A solidarity is emerging, one that is more mature than any the great liberator Simón Bolívar could have hoped for, a togetherness seen in commodity cartels, in regional aid programs, and in the unison of voices speaking out on international affairs.

Doing a Little Homework

This then is a quick look at South America, its history and its current economic prospects. Equipped with such information, one can begin to plan a dream vacation—whether it be a whirlwind tour of the continent's most sophisticated cities, a trek through Amazon jungles, or two weeks of uninterrupted bliss basking on the beach in Rio de Janeiro. Carefully choosing one's destination is only part of what it takes to ensure a perfect holiday, however. Doing a little homework never hurts, especially before visiting such new and distant cultures.

Few people go to South America at the drop of a hat. As well as providing for sweet anticipation, the planning period can be an excellent time to brush up one's Spanish. While English is certainly spoken in major cities, Spanish is always preferable—even if badly spoken—to sign language for venturing off the beaten path. Unlike a trip to Africa or Asia, where one would have to pick up several languages to get along, a bit of Spanish or Portuguese is all that is needed in South America to make the traveler much more independent. And there are so many delightful tidbits to be gleaned from taxi drivers, desk clerks, bartenders, and waiters—not to mention people on the street—which are otherwise missed if one must depend on English-speaking guides for every explanation.

Learning as much as possible about South American culture beforehand will also help assure a happy holiday. Something as simple as the dinner hour, which varies greatly from country to country but is almost always later than in the United States, can cause aggravation. However, by being prepared in advance, one can avoid hunger pangs at 10 P.M. by snacking on the delicious pastries often served at tea time. Women traveling alone, especially, should be aware of local customs. In tropical climates, for example, it is quite acceptable for females to wear scanty halter tops. The same is not always true for showing off one's legs, however, and the foreign woman wearing short shorts at the very least invites unpleasant comments. The sight of children begging in some countries often troubles tourists, too. But, if truth be told, many do it partly as a pastime and will break into gleeful smiles when offered a piece of candy or a bright new pencil instead of money.

But the best possible advice for would-be travelers is to leave all their expectations at home, along with television, traffic jams, and the dog or cat. South America *is* a land of pleasant surprises—it is *not* a world where planes, trains, or buses, much less museums, banks, or businesses, operate on Yankee time. Tourists who must have bacon and eggs at precisely 7:30 every morning while reading their favorite newspaper should perhaps consider vacationing in Hawaii. But for those who can do without Dow Jones and the latest baseball scores for a couple of weeks—South America is guaranteed not to disappoint.

PLANNING YOUR TRIP

by
ALMA M. SCHACHT

Alma M. Schacht is president of Unique Adventures, a wholesale tour corporation specializing in Latin America tours. The company also publishes Travel Planner *guides on South American countries for travel agents. Schacht has lived in Colombia and traveled extensively through South America.*

Planning Hints

SOUTH AMERICA OVERVIEW. Before putting together the framework of your South American adventure, we should discuss some vague—even misconceived—notions most North Americans have about the South American continent. First-time visitors generally have no idea of the great size of the continent, and therefore the great distances and varied geography they will encounter.

The continent of South America ranges from north of the equator to the Antarctic Circle. Besides the great changes in latitudes which affect its climate, South America is also a rich fabric of races and cultures. Trying to make broad generalizations about South Americans would be like trying to make sweeping generalizations about North Americans, and similar to saying New Yorkers are like Texans! True, South America was colonized principally by the Portuguese and Spanish; however, the continent has also enjoyed rich contributions from the indigenous Indian races, as well as from other European and Asian immigrants and African slaves. Each country's varied cultural and political history and unique topography make it difficult to speak in terms of South America in broad generalities.

Distance. In an endeavor to help the prospective traveler to South America appreciate the size of this continent and the distances he will be traveling, here are some sample flying times (nonstop) and a comparison of these flying times with other destinations around the world. From **Los Angeles** to *Lima,* 9 hours; *Rio de Janeiro,* 13 hours; *Tokyo,* 15 hours; *London,* 10.25 hours. From **Miami** to *Lima,* 5.5 hours; *Rio de Janeiro,* 8 hours; *London,* 10.5 hours. From **Lima** to *Rio de Janeiro,* 7 hours; *Santiago,* 3.5 hours; *Buenos Aires,* 3.5 hours.

Location (Time Zones). The west coast of the South American continent is roughly aligned with the east coast of North America. In other words, Lima, Peru (west coast) is due south of Miami, Florida and New York, and Rio de Janeiro juts way out in the Atlantic.

Assuming all countries are on standard time, when it is *noon* in New York or Miami it is noon in Bogotá, Colombia, Quito, Ecuador, Lima, Peru, and Santiago, Chile; 1 P.M. in Caracas, Venezuela, La Paz, Bolivia, Asunción, Paraguay, and Buenos Aires, Argentina; 2 P.M. in Brasilia, Rio, and São Paulo, Brazil; 3 P.M. in Recife, Brazil.

Climate. Don't try to apply your own local climates and conditions to South American locations. The most common misconception about the climate and geography of South America is that it is exactly "upside down" from, and opposite to, that of North America. You should not think that the weather on the entire South

American continent is simply the opposite of the particular North American climate you have experienced. To sit in Chicago in June and think that "Because it's summer here, it must be like a Chicago winter right now in South America" is a convenient but misleading notion.

Certain regions in South America do have climates similar to, but reversed from, certain regions in North America. For instance, Puerto Montt, Chile, is almost the same latitude south as Portland, Oregon is north. This whole area has a climate similar to Washington and Oregon states, including snow-capped volcano peaks, etc.

However, because of the range of latitudes that the continent covers, and because of the great variations in altitudes and climatic zones, the traveler is going to encounter several different types of weather within each country. The one thing to remember is that what South America lacks as a climatic season is our harsh winter. At best, we can speak of these countries regionally and give them some regional characteristics:

The Caribbean Coast. The Guianas, Suriname, Venezuela, and Colombia are characterized by sandy coastal beaches and tropical rain forests in the interiors. The entire area is almost equatorial, and the temperatures remain humid, a constant 80° F all year, with the dryest months from July to December.

The Andes Mountains (the mountain range from north to south). Forming the backbone of South America, the Andes Mountains run from central Colombia through central Ecuador, Peru, and Bolivia and then stretch along the frontier between Chile and Argentina. In the north in Colombia, the climate in the mountains is affected by exposure to both the Pacific and the Caribbean trade winds. These mountains are not quite as high as their southern neighbors (the city of Bogotá is just under a mile high) and they enjoy a spring-like climate all year. The higher the altitude, the less spring-like. The dryer months are December, January, and February.

Going south, the Andes become more rugged and are influenced by the Pacific coast currents and trade winds. In Peru, Bolivia, northern Argentina, and Chile, the Andes have a very marked seasonal shift: their "summer" months of December through March are rainy and warmer, with temperatures in the populated valleys reaching the 60s and 70s F, depending on the altitude. Due to the dampness, however, the climate can be quite chilly and penetrating at night. Although the summer is the rainy season, the mountains are still very scenic: the hills and valleys are lush and green, the fields are being tilled and harvested, and the rivers and streams are running full. The countryside is a riot of yellow scotch broom and other wild flowers. The "winter" (June-September) is very dry and cold, with temperatures dipping to freezing at night. The amount of rainfall is negligible, and the unfiltered sun can become quite warm due to the thin air. Be prepared, however, for an abrupt drop in temperatures as soon as the sun sets. The winter assures you of dry, bright, sunny days; however, the fields are lying fallow, the hills and mountains are a dry brown, and the rivers are running low.

Farther South. Now moving farther south to Chile and Argentina, the Andes have a climate very similar to that of the Sierras and Cascades on the Pacific coast of North America, but in reverse. Imagine yourself in San Francisco (which would correspond to Santiago, Chile) and work your way north through the Sierras to the wetter northern mountains of Oregon and Washington (the equivalent of working south from Santiago to Puerto Montt). Continue to Alaska and the climate resembles that of the area in Chile south of Puerto Montt to Punta Arenas in Patagonia, but at opposite times of the year. There are some distinctions, however: the Andes are much higher and more dramatic than our older Sierras and Cascades, their "summer" is dryer, and their "winter" is wetter, as a rule.

The Pacific Coast. The coastal regions of Colombia and northern Ecuador, being equatorial and at sea level, have a lush, subtropical climate. Continuing south, the coast becomes dryer, until reaching Peru, where you encounter the Atacama Desert, the dryest in the world. The Atacama extends the entire coast of Peru and northern Chile to just north of Santiago. The region's climate is tempered by the cold Pacific currents and coastal fog or *garua*. There are two basic seasons: "summer" (December-March), when the sun is hot enough to burn off the coastal fog, is hot and sunny (in Lima it is quite humid); and "winter" (June-September), when the coastal fog and overcast are almost constant and temperatures are cooler. Apply local variables such as altitude (i.e., Arequipa, Peru at 7,000 ft.) and you will have variations on this theme.

From Santiago to the south, apply the same principle as that of working from San Francisco north to Alaska, and you have approximated this beautiful and varied coastal region: First we find the rich central valley of central Chile, then the coastal ranges and pristine beaches, and then, further south, we discover the rivers, lakes, forests, and mountains of the Chilean lake region. Still further south is the broken coastline of Chilean fjords and dense forests, and finally the magnificent glaciers of Patagonia. Reverse the climate from North America and you've got it.

Amazon Basin. From one extreme of coastal Pacific desert, you can cross the mighty Andes and encounter the world's greatest and densest tropical rain forest. This vast tract of jungle encompasses central and southern Suriname and the Guianas, southern Venezuela and Colombia, eastern Ecuador, Peru, and Bolivia, and all of northern Brazil. The Amazon jungle basin contributes over 60 percent of the world's oxygen. Aptly named a "tropical *rain* forest," there is actually a climatic shift between rainy (monsoon) and less rainy months. During the rainy season (December–March) the rivers swell and the Amazon can rise as much as 40 feet. It rains particularly in the late afternoon and at night, and can fall like a wall of water for hours on end. The jungle is flooded and very scenic, and most sightseeing is done by dugout canoe, rather than by foot. During the low water season (June–October) the flood waters recede and jungle tours entail much more walking.

Central Plains. South of the Amazon basin and east of the Andes lie the central plains of South America. In the north they are extensive marshes, swamplands, and forests (not unlike the Everglades) called the *pantanal.* Farther south are the grasslands or *pampas* of Argentina and central Brazil, gradually blending into the rolling green hills and more temperate climate of the coastal ranges on the Atlantic coast.

Atlantic Coast. Boasting some of the most beautiful beaches in the world, most of the South American Atlantic coast is a far cry from our rugged, hostile northern Atlantic coast. Around São Paulo the climate begins to resemble the climate of the Central Atlantic states. The major urban areas (São Paulo, Porto Alegre, Montevideo, and Buenos Aires) enjoy long, warm summers (December–March), lingering autumns, and early springs. None of these cities has the harsh winters of the Atlantic Northeast of the United States and Canada. Their winters are more like Paris or Mobile, Alabama—not as cold as London, or even Atlanta, or Washington, D.C.

WHEN TO GO. March, April, and May are good months just about everywhere in South America and are the off-season for tourism, so you can avoid crowds and higher prices. In the Andes and Amazon you are out of the rainy months but not yet into the less scenic drought of winter or the lower water of the jungle. Winter has not yet come to the southern cities, Rio is not as hot and humid as in January, and the northern coast is balmy all year round.

There are high and low season rates at hotels only in the traditional "resort" areas: Cartagena, Colombia, the coastal resorts of Venezuela, Viña del Mar, Chile, Mar de Plata, Argentina, Punta del Este, Uruguay, and Rio de Janeiro, Brazil. These all have high season rates from December 15 until March 30.

FESTIVALS AND SPECIAL EVENTS. South America is a land of fairs and festivals. Listed below are a great many of the special events regularly scheduled each year. Because most of the continent is Roman Catholic, a great many events are religious holidays and the dates change from year to year. Holy Days and special celebrations are colorful and numerous. All celebrate New Year's, Epiphany (Jan. 6), Easter and Christmas holidays. Spanish-speaking countries celebrate October 12, the anniversary of Columbus's landing in the Bahamas as *el dia la Raza,* "day of the Race."

Also see listing of "Special Events" in the country chapters.

Argentina. May-September Opera season, Buenos Aires; July 9, Independence Day; August 17, General-Liberator San Martin's Birthday.

Bolivia. May 1 (Labor Day); August 6, Independence Day.

Brazil. Carnival (four days before Ash Wednesday); May 1 (Labor Day); September 7, Independence Day; November 15, Anniversary of proclamation of the Republic.

Chile. May 21, Anniversary of Naval Victory at Iquique; June 2–16, Cultural

AVERAGE TEMPERATURE CHART IN ° FAHRENHEIT

		Jan.	Feb.	Mar.	Apr.	May	Jun.	Jul.	Aug.	Sept.	Oct.	Nov.	Dec.
Buenos Aires (Argentina)	Max.	85°	83°	79°	72°	64°	57°	57°	60°	64°	69°	76°	82°
	Min.	63	63	60	53	47	41	42	43	46	50	56	61
La Paz (Bolivia)	Max.	64	64	64	66	66	60	61	62	62	65	67	64
	Min.	43	43	43	40	35	36	34	35	38	40	42	43
Rio de Janeiro (Brazil)	Max.	84	85	83	80	77	76	75	76	75	77	79	82
	Min.	73	73	72	69	66	64	63	64	65	66	68	71
Bogatá (Colombia)	Max.	67	68	67	67	66	65	64	65	66	66	66	66
	Min.	48	49	50	51	51	51	50	50	49	50	50	49
Quito (Ecuador)	Max.	69	69	69	69	69	70	71	71	72	70	70	70
	Min.	46	47	47	47	47	46	44	44	45	46	46	46
Lima (Peru)	Max.	82	83	83	80	74	68	67	66	68	71	74	78
	Min.	66	67	66	63	60	58	57	56	57	58	60	62
Montevideo (Uruguay)	Max.	83	82	78	71	64	59	58	59	63	68	74	79
	Min.	62	61	59	53	48	43	43	43	46	49	54	59
Caracas (Venezuela)	Max.	79	80	81	80	81	80	80	84	82	81	82	80
	Min.	60	62	62	64	66	65	65	65	64	64	62	61

Festival, Arica; August 20, Birthday of Liberator Bernardo O'Higgins; September 18, Independence Day; October, International Fair, Santiago.

Colombia. July, International Trade Fair, Bogotá; July 20, Independence Day; July 24, Bolívar's Birthday; November 13, Independence Day, Cartagena.

Ecuador. May 24, anniversary of colonial Battle of Pichincha, 1822, Quito; June (variable), Corpus Christi Fiestas; July 24, Bolívar's Birthday; August 10, Independence Day; December 6, Anniversary of founding of Quito.

French Guiana. Mardi Gras (variable); July 14, French National Holiday (Bastille Day).

Paraguay. May 1 (Labor Day); May 14–15 Independence Days; June 12, Chaco Peace Day; August 25, Constitution Day.

Peru. June 24, Inca Festival, Cuzco; July 28–29, Independence Days; August 29–30, Feast of Santa Rosa of Lima; September 8, Inca Festival of the Queen; October, Bullfight Fair, Lima; November 1–2, Inca King Festival, Puno.

Uruguay. June 19, Birthday of national hero, José Gervacio Artigas; August 25, Independence Day.

Venezuela. January 1; Carnival, two days in February; Holy Thursday; Good Friday; Easter Saturday; April 19, Declaration of Independence; May 1, Labor Day; June 24, Colonial victory at Battle of Carabobo; July 5, Independence Day; July 24, Liberator Simón Bolívar's birthday; November-February, Bullfight Season; December 17, Bolívar Memorial Day.

Carnival Week. Brazil and most South American countries start Carnival on the weekend preceding Ash Wednesday, usually in February. A word of caution about "carnival-time" visits. Many returning tourists have complained about minimal hotel services where their rooms went uncleaned and the beds unmade for days, many instances of late or no breakfasts and several cases where gas pumps and garage services were closed down. Be prepared for the otherwise orderly system to break down during holiday time.

WHAT IT WILL COST. *Note:* With constant changes in exchange rates the prices in this book are subject to change almost daily. In the individual chapters, attempts have been made to give estimated costs. Most visitors arrive by air, and while some excursion fares are available, the majority of air tickets sold are the standard all-year jet fares.

Cost of a Typical Day: Peru is a popular South American country for international travelers. A day and night in Lima is not typical, of course, for all of South America, but the prices there are very near standard for most capital cities.

Included here is a breakdown of the average tourist's expenses in **Lima** for a day and night:

First-class hotel (one person sharing double-room)	$80
Three meals (including service)	40
Four taxi rides	16
Two drinks (Pisco sours)	3
City sightseeing tour (motorcoach)	16
Laundry (shirt)	1
Dry cleaning	3
Total cost:	$159

The approximate cost per day in other countries, including first-class hotel, meals, transfers, tips, and incidentals (no shopping, of course) would range from $80 to $160 a day.

SOURCES OF INFORMATION. The following information offices, embassies, consulates, and tourist offices may be able to provide you with brochures and information for each country in South America.

In the United States

Argentina: *Argentine Consulate General,* 12 W. 56 St., New York, NY 10019; 212–603–0400. International Trade Market, 2 Canal St., Suite 915, New Orleans, LA 70130; 504–523–2823, 870 Market St., Suite 1083, San Francisco, CA 94102; 415–982–3050. Consulates are located in Baltimore, Chicago, Houston, Los Angeles, Miami, and San Juan.

Bolivia: *Consulate General of Bolivia,* 211 E. 43 St., Room 802, New York, NY 10017; 212–687–0530. Consulates are located in Atlanta, Chicago, Cincinnati, Houston, Miami, New Orleans, St. Louis, San Francisco, San Juan, Seattle, and Washington, D.C.

Brazil: *Brazilian Consulate General,* 630 Fifth Ave., Suite 2720, New York, NY 10111; 212–757–3080. Brazilian Consulates are located in Atlanta, Chicago, Cleveland, Dallas, Houston, Los Angeles, Miami, New Orleans, Norfolk, San Francisco, and Washington, D.C. *Brazilian Tourist Board,* 551 Fifth Ave., New York, NY 10176; 212–286–9600.

Chile: *Chilean Consulate General,* 866 United Nations Plaza, Suite 302, New York, NY 10017; 212–980–3366. Consulates are located in Atlanta, Boston, Chicago, Denver, Houston, Los Angeles, Miami, New York, Philadelphia, San Diego, San Francisco, Washington, D.C., San Juan, and Seattle. *Chilean National Tourist Board,* c/o Lan-Chile, 630 Fifth Ave., Suite 809, New York, NY 10111; 212–582–3254.

Colombia: *Colombian Consulate General,* 10 E. 46 St., New York, NY 10017; 212–949–9898. Consulates are located in Atlanta, Boston, Chicago, Dallas, Detroit, Houston, Los Angeles, Miami, Minneapolis, New Orleans, New York City, St. Louis, San Diego, San Francisco, San Juan, Tampa, and Washington, D.C. *Colombian Government Tourist Office,* 140 E. 57th St., New York, NY 10022; 212–688–0151.

Ecuador: *Consulate General of Ecuador,* 18 E. 41st. St., 18th floor, New York, NY 10017; 212–683–7555. Consulates are located in Atlanta, Boston, Chicago, Dallas, Houston, Los Angeles, Miami, New York, New Orleans, San Diego, San Francisco, and San Juan. *Ecuador Tourist Agency,* c/o Equatoriana Airlines, Airport Executive Tower #2, 7270 N.W. 12 St., Miami, FL 33126; 305–477–0041.

French Guiana: *French Government Tourist Office,* 610 Fifth Ave., New York, NY 10020; 212–757–1125.

Paraguay: *Paraguay Consulate General,* 1 World Trade Center, Suite 1609, New York, NY 10048; 212–432–0733. *Paraguay Consulate General,* 611 Gravier St., Suite 903, New Orleans, LA 70130; 504–522–7424. Consulates are located in Boston, Chicago, Los Angeles, Miami, New Orleans, San Francisco, and Seattle.

Peru: *Consulate General of Peru,* 805 Third Ave., 14th floor, New York, NY 10022; 212–644–2850. Consulate offices are located in Boston, Chicago, Houston, Los Angeles, Miami, New Orleans, New York, St. Louis, San Francisco, Seattle, and Washington, D.C. *Peruvian Tourism Promotion Board,* 444 Brickell Ave., Suite 815, Miami, FL 33131; 305–375–0885.

Uruguay: *Uruguayan Consulate General,* 747 Third Ave., 37th floor., New York, NY 10017; 212–753–8193. Consulates are located in Chicago, Miami, Los Angeles, New Orleans, San Francisco, San Juan, and Washington, D.C.

Venezuela: *Venezuelan Consulate General,* 7 E. 51st St., New York, NY 10022; 212–826–1660. Consulate offices are located in Baltimore, Boston, Chicago, Houston, Los Angeles, Miami, New Orleans, New York, Philadelphia, San Francisco, and San Juan.

In Canada

Argentina: *Argentine Consulate,* 90 Sparks, #620, Ottawa, Ontario. K1P-6A9. Consulate General is located in Montreal. Consulates are located in Edmonton, Montreal, Toronto, and Vancouver.

Brazil: *Brazilian Embassy,* 255 Albert St., Suite 900, Ottawa, Ont. K1P-6A9.

Chile: *Chilean Embassy,* c/o Lan-Chile Airlines, 630 Fifth Ave., Suite 809, New York, NY 10111. Consulate General is located in Montreal.

Colombia: *Colombian Government Tourist Office,* 140 E. 57 St., New York, NY 10022. Consulate is located in Toronto.

Ecuador: *Consulate General,* 2603 Cote Ste. Catherine, Montreal, PQ.

French Guiana: *French Embassy,* 42 Sussex, Ottawa, Suite 309, Ont. K17 2C9.

Peru: *Peruvian Embassy,* 170 Laurier Ave. West, Suite 1007, Ottawa, Ont. K1 P5 V5.

Uruguay: *Uruguay Consulate General,* 1010 Ste. Catherine No. 1300, Montreal, QB H3B-3R7. Consulate is located in Vancouver, BC.

Venezuela: *Venezuelan Embassy,* 320 Queen St., Suite 2220, Ottawa, Ont. K1R 5A3. Consulate General is located in Montreal.

TIPS FOR BRITISH VISITORS. The following embassies and consulates can provide you with **information** you'll need to plan your trip. Be sure, too, to confirm what travel documents are necessary before leaving. Other sources of information are the national airlines of the individual countries you are planning to visit.

Argentina: *c/o Argentine Embassy,* 111 Cadogan Gardens, London SW3 2RH (071–730 4388).

Bolivia: *Embassy of Bolivia,* 106 Eaton Square, London SW1W 9AD (071–235 4248).

Brazil: *Brazilian Embassy,* 32 Green St., London W1Y 4AT (071–499 0877).

Chile: *Chilean Embassy.* 12 Devonshire St., London W1N 2DS (071–580 6392).

Colombia: *The Colombian Embassy,* Flat 3A, 3 Hans Crescent, London 3W1X 0LS (071–589–9117).

Ecuador: *The Ecuadorian Embassy and Consulate,* Flat 3B, 3 Hans Crescent, London SW1X 0LS (071–584 1367).

French Guiana: *French Consulate General* (Visa Section), 6A Cromwell Place, London SW7 ZDQ (071–823–9555).

Paraguay: *The Paraguayan Consulate,* Braemar Lodge, Cornwall Gardens, London SW7 4AQ (071–937 6629).

Peru: *The Peruvian Consulate General,* 52 Sloane St., London SW1X 9SP (071–235–4451).

Uruguay: *The Embassy of Uruguay,* 48 Lennox Gardens, London SW1X 0DL (071–589–8835).

Venezuela: *Venezuelan Consulate General,* 56 Groston Way, London W15LB 7QU (071–387–6727).

Tour Operators. The following tour operators offer packages to most of the South American countries; both multi-center tours and single destination holidays.

Bales Tours Ltd, Bales House, Junction Rd., Dorking, Surrey RH4 3HB (0306–885 991).

Dellstar Travel (South) Ltd., 98 Field End Rd., Eastcote, Pinner, Middx. HA5 1RL (081–868 2968).

Encounter Overland Ltd., 267 Old Brompton Rd., London SW5 (071–370 6845).

Exodus Expeditions, All Saints' Passage, 100 Wandsworth High St., London SW18 4LE (081–870 0151).

Kuoni Travel Ltd., Kuoni House, Dorking, Surrey RH5 4AZ (0306–885 044).

South American Experience, 40 Garden Studios, 11–15 Betterton St., Covent Garden, London WC2H 9BP (071–379–0344).

Thomas Cook Holidays, Thorpe Wood, Box 36, Peterborough, Cambridgeshire PE3 6SB (0733–63200).

HOW TO GO. The traveler to South America may choose a variety of ways to travel—in a group, on a tour, alone on a prearranged itinerary, or in a "plan as you go" form.

In order to save time and money, it is recommended that you contact a professional travel counselor, who will have all the latest details in fares, hotel rates, sightseeing, and interesting local places to dine.

Travel Agents. Travel agents are experts in the increasingly complicated business of tourism. Good travel agents are located everywhere and can save you time and money through their knowledge of important details, thus making it unnecessary for you to waste precious days during your trip trying to obtain tickets and reservations. Unless you have an endless amount of time for your trip and will be traveling on a "plan-as-you-go" basis, it is wise to take advantage of the services of those specialists.

If you wish to merely arrange a steamship or airline ticket or to book a package tour, travel-agent services should cost you nothing. If, on the other hand, you wish to plan an individual itinerary, you must realize that outside of deluxe or first-class hotels, there is very little convenient contact with services in South America. Your travel agent will probably contact one of the South America wholesalers listed below, who can arrange your trip. The services that these wholesalers arrange will be commissionable to your travel agent, and, therefore, will eliminate the necessity of charging you a service charge. You are also sure to be in the hands of operators experienced in handling South America.

To explain the difference between a *travel agency* and a *tour wholesaler* (or tour operator): The retail travel agent helps the client sort out all of the variables involved with their prospective trip—a process called "qualifying" the client and the product—and then contacts the "suppliers," which could be airlines, trains, car rental companies, hotels, and/or tour wholesalers. The wholesaler is organized to handle a high volume of business; many wholesalers specialize in or focus on one particular area of the world or one particular type of special-interest travel. By virtue of their specialization and high volume, the buying power of the wholesaler is much greater than that of the retail agent, and they can better negotiate rates with hotels, sightseeing companies, etc. This savings is passed on to the traveler in the tours that the wholesalers sell through the travel agent and the retail travel agent receives a commission for the representative service they provide.

Your travel agent should not be expected to be an in-depth expert on all destinations around the world; however, he can get in touch with the reputable operators in the business who *are* experts. This service does not cost you more money. Many people think they will save money by bypassing the retail travel agent and contacting the operator (or wholesaler) directly. This is usually not the case, as experienced wholesalers have learned that working through the travel agents saves them time and money. Travel agents screen and field your questions and spend a lot of time qualifying you for your trip before calling the wholesaler, and this, in turn, saves the wholesaler valuable staff and communication time.

In the United States, if you cannot locate a travel agent near your home, contact the *American Society of Travel Agents,* 1101 King St., Alexandria, VA 22314 (703–739–2782); or *A.S.T.A.-West Coast,* 4420 Hotel Circle Court, Suite 230, San Diego, CA 92108 (619–298–5053). In Canada, write to *A.S.T.A.* Chapter President Lise Shearaer, Cabie House of Travel Ltd., 511 W. 14th Ave., Suite 101, Vancouver, BC V5Z 1P5. Any agency affiliated with these organizations is likely to be reliable. The *United States Tour Operators Association* (U.S.T.O.A.), 211 E. 51 St., Suite 12B, New York, NY 10022 (212–944–5727) will send you a list of its members, all of whom are bonded for your protection. (In the last few years, the upheavals in airfares particularly have caused the failure of a number of smaller tour operators, leaving their customers stranded and with no recourse. This cannot happen with U.S.T.O.A. members.)

Qualify Yourself. There are as many different types of trips to South America as there are travelers. However, your trip will probably fall into one of four main categories:

Packaged Group Tour: Also referred to as "Fixed Departure Group Tour Series" or "Group Inclusive Tour" (GIT), these tours are divided into two main categories: "escorted" or "unescorted." Both offer the main advantage of the security of a group for companionship, especially good for people traveling alone. An escorted tour includes the services of an experienced tour escort who accompanies the group throughout and "manages" all of the details of the group's travel, including airport check-ins and arrivals, hotel registrations, etc. A good tour escort will also work well within the group, have a good working knowledge of the destinations, speak Spanish and/or Portuguese, and be able to generally assist the group members along the way. An unescorted tour (group or individual) is also called "locally hosted" and includes the services of a local ground operator and trained guides and "couriers," or transfer agents. Groups are met at each destination by bilingual courier/guides and then are taken on by other agents as the tour moves along. Naturally, a "locally hosted" or unescorted tour will be less expensive than an escorted tour. The concept, however, that group travel to South America saves money is not necessarily correct. The range of packaged group tours can run from very inexpensive "bare bones," unescorted tours with an average land cost (airfare not included) of $50 per person per day (based on sharing a double room), to $200 per person per day for fully escorted tours. The range of prices is influenced by the category of accommodations, the number of guided tours included, the quality of the tour escort (if used), the number of meals that are included (whether meals are on a fixed menu or à la carte, or include alcoholic beverages, etc.), and, finally, the reputation for quality that the particular tour wholesaler has earned. A good travel agent can help you select a reputable tour wholesaler within your price range. Group airfares are rapidly becoming a thing of the past and traveling with a group to South America usually does not give you a break in the airfare.

Following is a list of South America tour wholesalers. Although your travel agent will probably be familiar with these options, you may want to contact some in advance for brochures.

Abreu Tours
317 E. 34th St.
New York, NY 10016
800–223–1580
(212) 661–0555

Amazon/African Explorers Inc.
499 Ernston Rd.
Parlin, NJ 08859
800–631–5650
(201) 721–2929

American Alpine Institute
1212 24th St.
Bellingham, WA 98225
(206) 671–1505

**American Express Travel
Related Services Co. Inc.**
Travel Division
550 Biltmore Way
Suite 1000
Coral Gables, FL 33134
800–327–7737, (FL) 800–432–0909

Bentley Tours
1649 Colorado Blvd.
Los Angeles, CA 90041
800–821–9726
(213) 258–8451

Brazil Expert Travel
3810 Wilshire Blvd., 6th Floor
Los Angeles, CA 90010
800–553–2555
(213) 387–2111

Brendan Tours
15137 Califa St.
Van Nuys, CA 91411
(818) 785–9696

Club Med Inc.
Box 4460
Scottsdale, AZ 85261
800–CLUB–MED
(602) 991–2002

**Continuing Education Abroad/
Peru Tours**
38760 Northwoods Dr.
Wadsworth, IL 60083
800–367–7378
(708) 249–1900

Festival Tours
737 West Oak Ridge Rd.
Orlando, FL 32809
(FL) 800–772–7373
(U.S.) 800–327–2838
(407) 859–5712

Forum Travel International
91 Gregory Lne. #21
Pleasant Hill, CA 94523
(415) 671–2900
(415) 946–1500

Four Winds Travel Inc.
Box 693
Old Greenwich, CT 06870
(203) 698–0944

Galápagos Inc.
7800 Red Rd, #112 .
South Miami, FL 33143
800–327–9854
(305) 665–0841

Hotur
20 E. 53 St.
New York, NY 10022
800–634–6887
(212) 371–8885/7

Inca Floats
1311 63rd St.
Emeryville, CA 94608
(415) 420–1550

Ipanema Tours
9911 W. Pico Blvd.
Suite 580
Los Angeles, CA 90035
800–421–4200
(213) 272–2162

Jetset Tours (N. America) Inc.
1960 East Grande Ave., Room 800
El Segundo, CA 90245
800–453–8738
(213) 651–4050

Journeys International Inc.
4011 Jackson Rd.
Ann Arbor, MI 48103
800–255–8735
(313) 665–4407

Ladatco Tours
2220 Coral Way
Miami, FL 33145
800–327–6162
(305) 854–8422

Marnella Tours
33 Walt Whitman Rd.
#239
Huntington Station, NY 11746
800–645–6999
(516) 271–6969

Marsans International
1680 Michigan Ave.
#1026
Miami Beach, FL 33139
800–432–4056
(305) 531–0444

Melia Travel Service Inc.
450 7th Ave., Suite 1805
New York, NY 10123
800–848–2314
(212) 967–6565

Mountain Travel Inc.
6420 Fairmount Ave.
El Cerrito, CA 94530
800–227–2384
(415) 527–8100

Nature Expeditions Int'l.
Box 11496
Eugene, OR 97440
(503) 484–6529

Olson-Travelworld Ltd.
100 N. Sepulveda Blvd., #100
El Segundo, CA 90245
800–421–2255
(CA) 800–421–5785
(213) 615–0711

Path Tours & Travel
12444 Victory Blvd., #407
North Hollywood, CA 91606
(Western U.S.) 800–843–0400
(CA) 800–521–6215
(818) 980–4442

Portuguese Tours Inc.
321 Rahway Ave.
Elizabeth, NJ 07202
800–526–4047
(201) 352–6112

Questers Tours & Travel
257 Park Ave. South
New York, NY 10010
800–478–8668
(212) 673–3120

Reservation Center Ltd.
844 S. Havana
Aurora, CO 80012
800–525–8588
(303) 341–7612

Rightway Travel Corp.
10935 Camarillo St.
North Hollywood, CA 91602
800–456–7436
(818) 769–9212

Sobek Expeditions Inc.
Box 1089
Angels Camp, CA 95222
800–777–7939
(209) 736–4524

Society Expeditions
3131 Elliott Ave., #700
Seattle, WA 98121
800–426–7794
(206) 285–9400

South American Fiesta Inc.
Box 456
Ridge, NY 11961
800–334–3782
(516) 924–6200

Sunny Land Tours Inc.
166 Main St.
Hackensack, NJ 07601
800–631–1992
(201) 487–2150

Tara Tours
6595 N.W. 36 St. #306A
Miami Springs, FL 33166
800–327–0080
(FL) 800–228–5168
(305) 871–1246

Tessi Travel Consultants, Inc.
133 E. 30th St.
New York, NY 10016
800–223–2178
(212) 481–0111

Tour Arrangements Inc.
82 Washington St.
Marblehead, MA 01945
800–343–3487
(617) 631–8200

Tour Dann International
#7 Penn Plaza
New York, NY 10001
800–524–1100
(212) 244–6616

Travcoa World Tours
2350 Southeast Bristol

Santa Ana Heights, CA 92707
800–992–2003
(CA) 800–992–2004
(714) 476–2800

Travel Plans Int'l. Inc.
1200 Harger Rd.
Oak Brook, IL 60521
800–323–7600
(708) 573–1400

Travel Specialists of Berkeley
2438 Durant Ave.
Berkeley, CA 94704
(415) 548–7000

Unique Adventures
690 Market St., #1100
San Francisco, CA 94104
800–969–4900
(415) 986–5876

United States Travel Consultants
25 S.E. 2nd Ave., #1000
Miami, FL 33131
(FL) 800–228–1092
(305) 358–6017

Victor Emmanuel Nature Tours
Box 33008
Austin, TX 78764
800–328–VENT
(512) 328–5221

Wilderness Travel
801 Allston Way
Berkeley, CA 94710
(415) 548–0420

Prearranged Independent Itinerary. For those of you who thought that you had to take a group tour on a fixed itinerary that could not be modified to suit your plans, or thought you had to just go to South America and "wing" it on your own, there is good news: there is another alternative, which should not cost you more than a packaged group tour. You can book through a good travel agent what is called a prearranged independent itinerary. There are a couple of very good companies that specialize in independent but locally hosted itineraries to South America. These companies specialize in South America, and based on a large yearly volume of business they have been able to negotiate rates for accommodations comparable to any good group tour. Also, due to their specialization, they are competent to handle most requests for special services there. The cost for a customized tour could range from $50–$200 per person, per day (based on two people traveling together, sharing a double room). For more information, contact: *Ladatco Tours Dept. LTR,* 2220 Coral Way, Miami, FL 33145 (800–327–6162 or 305–854–8422), or *Unique Adventures, Inc.,* 690 Market St., #1100, San Francisco, CA 94104 (800–969–4900 or 415–986–4900). In late 1990, Ladatco also began unique air/sea/land cruise packages to principal South American ports including Patagonia, Cape Horn, the Strait of Magellan, and the Chilean Inside Passage.

Unstructured Independent Itinerary. If you have a certain degree of flexibility and time at your disposal, and do not want to be kept on a schedule, then your trip planning might be more on a "plan-as-you-go" basis. You will, however, want a general idea of the area(s) you would like to visit. Depending on the length of time you plan to be traveling, on your budget and your interests, the trip can take on many varied forms.

Short Trips. Recently introduced on the South American travel scene were low cost, short stay, all-inclusive (air, hotel, sightseeing) packages to several countries. At press time Ladacto Tours offers "Flyaway South" programs, whose prices begin at $544 per person for stays of four days/three nights. Those with limited time and limited budgets should explore the current availability of these bargain packages.

Special-Interest Travel.

South America is largely a special-interest destination. Most tourists to South America have a definite purpose or interest in the particular area they choose to visit. Perhaps you didn't even realize you were a special-interest traveler, but if you have a desire to check out some country inns, or have an interesting ceramic or antique collection, then you are a special-interest traveler. Any hobby, intellectual or academic interest, sport, outdoor activity, collection, or special preference in travel style would be considered special interest. There are many special interest tour operators to South America, so many that a comprehensive listing would be too extensive for this publication. It would also be unnecessary, considering that there is an excellent publication that is devoted entirely to this subject: *The Specialty Travel Index*, 305 San Anselmo Ave., Suite 217, San Anselmo, CA 94960, phone (415) 459–4900. Their biannual issues, costing $5 each or $8 for a subscription to both, will give you an exhaustive list of special-interest travel operators worldwide.

Following is a list of some of the most commonly requested special interest tours, and the areas in South America in which they can be best enjoyed.

Hiking and Trekking. This is probably the biggest category in special-interest travel. Most of the hiking and trekking tours are to Peru, while others are to Ecuador and Bolivia. The most popular trip is the Inca Trail Trek from Cuzco to Machu Picchu, which usually takes five or six days. The Cordillera Blanca mountain range around Huaraz, Peru is also popular. There are some extended jungle tours to Peru, either in the Tambopata wildlife reserve (Puerto Maldonado, Peru) on the Madre de Dios River or on one of the tributaries of the Amazon River outside of Iquitos, Peru. The Napo River jungle area is popular in Ecuador. In Bolivia, the "Gold Road" from La Paz to the jungle is popular.

River Running. Oftentimes, a trek will be combined with a river trip. The most popular rivers are the Apurimac, the Colca (Colca Canyon), and the Urubamba River to Machu Picchu, all in Peru. In Colombia there are river trips to the jungle on the Orinoco. None of these trips could be classified as "white water," although there are some rapids. If it's white water you're looking for, the Bio Bio in Chile is a world class river.

Horse-packing. There is a horse-packing program in Chile to the northern Andes, and another offered in Peru, outside of Cuzco.

Fishing–Deep sea. The best deep-sea fishing is on the southern Pacific coast of Ecuador. There is good fishing in northern Peru (Cabo Blanco of Hemingway fame), but little or no touristic infrastructure, so it is difficult to obtain a decent fishing boat.

Fishing–River and stream. For trout fishing, the Chilean/Argentine lake region is world famous and has deserved its fame. For "dorado fish," Paraguay and the *pantanal* of central Brazil are the best. There is no bass fishing in South America.

Archaeology. Again, the center for archaeology is Peru, with additional areas in Bolivia and Colombia. Besides Cuzco, Peru (the capital of the Inca Empire) and Machu Picchu, there are also fascinating pre-Columbian antiquities that pre-date the Incas by hundreds of years. In the south of Peru lie the mysterious Plains of Nazca, and in the north outside of Trujillo is the huge walled city of Chan Chan. In central Peru one finds the remains of the mysterious and ancient Chavin civilization. Outside of La Paz, Bolivia are the impressive ruins of the Tiahuanacan civilization. Southern Colombia is the site for the San Agustin archaeological zone.

Architecture. Brazil is most famous for its innovative and progressive architecture, exemplified by Brasilia, the experimental city in the wilderness. Most cities, with the exception of Buenos Aires, Santiago, and Montevideo, boast wonderful examples of colonial and baroque architecture. Most major cities in South America have at least one structure designed by Eiffel (usually the train station or hippodrome, or both, as is the case in Santiago).

Art. Cuzco, Peru was the center of the colonial school of art, and is now a treasure trove of native colonial art. Quito, Ecuador is also very rich in colonial art, as are La Paz and Sucre, Bolivia. For contemporary art, the primitive art of Bahia, Brazil, is rapidly appreciating in value, not unlike Haitian art 15 years ago. The contemporary artists of Colombia have already been discovered, and many of the artists are in demand worldwide. The art museums and galleries of São Paulo, Brazil are world famous. Many students of art flock to the quaint, baroque colonial towns of Ouro Preto and Congonhas, outside of Belo Horizonte in Brazil, which house the works of "Aleijadinho," or the Little Cripple, an eighteenth-century sculptor whose vivid and expressive work becomes even more incredible when one realizes that he did most of his work with his sculpting tools strapped to his wrists because he suffered from arthritis and leprosy.

Black Culture. The center of the rich Afro-Brazilian culture is Bahia (Salvador). The Afro-American cultures are also very rich on the Caribbean coast of Colombia.

Club Mediterranée. There are two Club Med facilities, one on an island outside of Bahia (Salvador), Brazil, and one outside of Rio de Janeiro.

Flora and Fauna. South America is one of the richest destinations for flora and fauna enthusiasts, from the Galápagos Islands off the coast of Ecuador to the tropical rain forest, the marshlands or pantanal of central South America, and ultimately to the wild lands of the Patagonia peninsula.

See also "Adventure Vacations" chapter.

Roughing It. There are youth hostels in Argentina, Uruguay, Brazil, Peru, Colombia, and Chile. The *International Youth Hostel Handbook,* Volume 2 ($6.95 plus $2.00 postage and handling), lists the hostels and may be ordered from American Youth Hostels, Box 37613 Washington, D.C. 20013–7613 (202–783–6165). For a listing of hostels in Brazil, contact Casa do Estudante do Brasil, Praça Ana Amelia, ZC39, 2000. There are many camping areas in the temperate south, but in tropical areas such as Venezuela, Ecuador and Colombia there are virtually none. However, keep in mind that you may often find adequate lodging in South America for the same small fee usually charged at most American or European camping grounds. Camping information is listed in each of the country chapters.

INFORMATION FOR DISABLED TRAVELERS. One of the newest, and largest, groups to enter the travel scene is the disabled, literally millions of people who are in fact physically able to travel and who do so enthusiastically when they know that they can move about with safety and comfort. Generally these tours parallel those of the non-handicapped traveler, but at a more leisurely pace, with everything checked out in advance to eliminate inconvenience.

For a complete list of tour operators who arrange such travel write to the *Society for the Advancement of Travel for the Handicapped,* 26 Court St., Brooklyn, NY 11242 or phone 718–858–5483. An excellent source of information in this field is the book, *Access to the World: A Travel Guide for the Handicapped,* by Louise Weiss, published by Henry Holt and Co. This book covers travel by air, ship, train, bus, car, and recreational vehicle; hotels and motels; travel agents and tour operators; destinations; health and medical problems; and travel organizations. Another major source of help is the Travel Information Center, Moss Rehabilitation Hospital, 12th St. and Tabor Rd. Philadelphia, PA 19141. And for an international directory of access guides, write to *Rehabilitation International,* 25 E. 21st St., New York, NY 10010 or phone 212–420–1500 for their listing of sources of information on facilities for the handicapped all over the world.

From the U.K.: Britain's major center for help and advice for the disabled traveler is the *Royal Association for Disability and Rehabilitation,* 25 Mortimer St., London W1N 8AB (071–637–5400). It has a library of helpful pamphlets, including the Access guides. The *Air Transport Users Committee,* 103 Kingsway, London WC2B 6QX (071-242-3882), publishes a very useful booklet for disabled passengers entitled *Care in the Air,* available free of charge.

WHAT TO TAKE. This depends entirely on who you are, where you go, and what you do. An executive on a business trip, staying in sleek hotels and attending formal conferences, will hardly pack the same clothes as a college student on vacation, staying in pensions and riding local buses.

If you expect to attend formal or business functions, to be invited out, or to go to concerts or the theater, you will need, as in the United States or Europe, a dark suit and tie for men, and at least one cocktail dress for women. In season, that dark suit can be a summer or a Palm Beach light-weight suit. Black tie and dinner jackets are rare in South America today, and in most capitals and major cities you can hire formal dress, and have it fitted, on 24 hours' notice, if need be. Otherwise, wear what is comfortable and strong, especially if you plan to climb about ruins or be out in villages, countryside, or forest. Sandals may not be practical in muddy or dirty streets.

Men will not have difficulty wearing good sports shirts without ties in most places. Take a couple of ties along anyway. The easiest thing to remember, when packing, is that in South America, as almost everywhere in the world today, you can get what you need locally. In fact, with the assistance of numerous French and Italian designers, and Argentina's excellent wool and leather, it has become a leading center for fashion. You can buy smart, latest-model fashions at reasonable prices. This is also true in other major cities, such as Bogotá, Lima, Santiago, Rio de Janeiro, and São Paulo.

More informally still, if you belong to that large group of tourist who have no formal engagements, you can dress largely to suit yourself. Open-necked sports shirts for men, and pants-suits or short skirts for women, are acceptable. Buenos Aires's top hotel, the 800-room Sheraton, does not seem to mind informal dress in its public rooms, nor does the Plaza place any restrictions, even though it is a favorite with upper-class residents. In Rio de Janeiro, you can wear your bathing suit into most hotels, as they provide separate entrances and elevators for direct access to and from the beach. Women may wear backless, halter-type dresses on hot days, and men may go without jackets.

You can even get by with T-shirts, pull-overs and jeans. Jeans put out by the Argentine subsidiaries of Levi's and Lee's are very popular with all classes, and come in many models. Shorts may be worn in public if they are neither too brief nor too tight, but discretion should be used depending upon the local customs of the residents.

Climate conditions are given for each country of South America in the **Facts at Your Fingertips** sections. See also the temperature chart for major cities earlier in this chapter. A few tips: 1) Cities like Quito, Bogotá, La Paz, and Cuzco can be cold at night because of their altitude, so be sure to bring along a sweater. 2) Most hotels are fitted for 220-volt A.C., though some of the newer ones carry points for 110 volts that will operate U.S. electric razors and other gadgets. You might want to bring a currency converter. 3) Local druggists have preparations for local problems, but you might carry some anti-diarrhea capsules. Most stomach upsets come from over-indulgence—strong seasonings, shell-fish, heavy wines, and lack of rest. Try to eat lightly your first day or two in a new place. 4) When you buy drip-dry clothing, be sure to get dacron-cotton blends in preference to nylon, which can be very hot and damp in the tropics. 5) Finally, your airline allowance is 30 kilos (66 pounds) for First Class and 20 kilos (44 pounds) for Economy—the changeover from weight to size allowances still does not apply to South America. In any case, it makes sense to travel light!

A few additional reminders for your packing checklist would include: suntan lotion, insect repellant, sufficient toothpaste, soap, etc. Always carry an extra pair of glasses, including sun glasses, particularly if they're prescription ones. A travel iron is always a good tote-along, as are some transparent plastic bags (small and large) for wet suits, socks, etc. They are also excellent, of course, for packing shoes, spillable cosmetics, and other easily damaged items.

Imported liquors and tobacco are prohibitively expensive in South America, so you might want to stock up on your favorite brands at duty-free shops in international airports in departure cities. Or try local rums, brandies, wines, and beers. Many are excellent.

HIGH ALTITUDE TRAVEL. Any trip to South America could include exposure to high altitudes: Bogotá lies at about 8,000 feet, Quito at 9,000 feet, Cuzco at 11,000 feet, and La Paz at 12,000 feet. A common misconception is that the elderly cannot go to the high altitudes for health reasons. Age is not necessarily a barrier to travel at high altitudes. Follow the few simple high altitude dos and don'ts. Do not overdo it.

First of all, let's distinguish between altitude sickness, or *soroche* (so-row-chay), and altitude in general as a serious and possibly life-threatening hazard. Anyone with excessively high blood pressure (especially if combined with obesity), respiratory ailments (such as emphysema or asthma), or a history of heart ailments or heart disease, as well as any pregnant woman, should consult a physician *before* traveling to high altitudes, and should probably be advised not to attempt them. Although the altitude might not be life threatening, the discomfort might be unbearable. If you are not sure you can handle the high altitudes, a good suggestion is to plan your trip working slowly up in altitude—for example, go first to Bogotá, Colombia (8,000 feet), then Quito, Ecuador (9,000 feet), and then Cuzco, Peru (11,000 feet). If, at any point along the way you experience altitude sickness, you can change your plans. If you are on a group tour, you can probably "sit out" the rest of the high altitude portions of the trip at a lower altitude (i.e., Lima). If you have booked an independent, pre-planned itinerary, a reputable tour operator should be willing to substitute services at the last minute should you get sick. There might be some cancellation fees, but you would not lose everything you paid. For instance, suppose you are in Quito and realize Cuzco might just be too much. Your local "courier" can telex the tour operator's home office to cancel your trip to Cuzco. Then, when you get to Lima, you can sit down with the local office there and discuss some alternative trips. (By then the tour operator will have advised via telex what credit you have to apply to other travel.) If you are not planning to go to Bogotá or Quito, but do want to go to Cuzco, then you might plan a three- or four-day trip to Arequipa, Peru (about 7,000 feet) and try that altitude first, before going to Cuzco.

It seems that people with high blood pressure suffer from altitude sickness. Consult your doctor before departing.

What is altitude sickness, anyway? Soroche, which is rarely life-threatening, is oxygen starvation to the brain and digestive system, resulting in headache, stomach "queezies," or even nausea. Symptoms may be mild or severe and can attack anyone. Soroche is no respector of age or physical fitness. One of the most important things to remember is that you need to plan a much more leisurely pace when you are at high altitudes. Plan plenty of rest time to allow your body to acclimate. The night before going to a high-altitude destination, do not decide to "party hearty." Avoid coffee or acidic foods, eat low-protein (easier to digest), high-starch foods, and do not overeat or over-indulge. Drink lots of water, avoid carbonated drinks, and take it easy!

PHOTOGRAPHY TIPS. Registration: We recommend that you have all your camera equipment registered with customs before your departure. At the very least, bring along your sales receipts as proof you bought the equipment before arriving in South America.

Film and Filters. After you think you have brought enough film, bring some more! Your unused film can always be kept fresh for a long time in the refrigerator, or sold at the end of your trip to some unfortunate tourist who did not bring enough film. A roll of film in South America will cost you double the price at home, and you cannot be sure it is fresh.

For you "SLR" enthusiasts, Kodachrome film, ASA 64 (for slides) or Kodacolor, ASA 100 (for prints) is recommended for the excellent color rendition. However, it is also a good idea to bring along some Ektachrome or some other "fast" film (with a higher ASA) for use when the sky is overcast. Whatever color film you use, a skylight or haze 2A filter will help cut down on the haze and color shift of high altitudes and the glare of the bright sun reflecting off white adobe buildings, sandy beaches, etc. For black-and-white photography, an orange or yellow filter will bring out the color contrasts in the sky.

Photography in the Andes. The higher the altitude, the greater the proportion of ultraviolet rays in light. Light meters do not read these rays and consequently, except for close-ups or full-frame portraits wherein the reading is taken directly off the subject, photos are likely to be over-exposed. To compensate, shut your lens down one-half to one full stop more than your meter tells you to do, depending on the altitude. Use "bracketing" to assure those especially great shots.

X rays. When you fly, remember that in spite of official claims to the contrary, airport security X-ray machines do in fact damage your photographic films in about

17 percent of the cases. Have your camera and film inspected manually, or pack them in specially lead-lined protective bags available in photo supply stores.

Be Alert. It is important to remember that cameras, being an expensive item here, are worth even more in countries that have high import duties. Too many photographers, unfortunately, have been easy victims of robberies as they stroll through the streets, entranced and distracted. Buy camera insurance if your camera is valuable or if it is not covered under your homeowners insurance policy. Do not pack any valuables, especially camera equipment, in checked baggage. Leaving cameras and lenses in hotel rooms is not recommended.

LANGUAGES. Spanish and Portuguese are the two major languages of South America. Spanish is the official language of Argentina, Bolivia, Chile, Colombia, Ecuador, Paraguay, Peru, Uruguay, and Venezuela. Portuguese is the official language of Brazil. Dutch is the official language of Suriname, French in French Guiana, and English in Guyana.

South America also has many Indian languages and native dialects. Quechua and Aymara are spoken in Peru and Bolivia, respectively. Another interesting example occurs in Suriname, where Dutch is the official language and the inhabitants speak either Dutch, English, Javanese, Hindi, or a Pidgin English called *taki taki.* Guarani is the second official language of Paraguay.

English is understood in the larger cities among the educated classes, particularly in the deluxe and first class hotels. Visitors will have little problem in airports, travel agencies, and leading hotels and restaurants. On the streets, in taxis, etc. sign language and written directions help.

MEDICAL TREATMENT. In most South American countries, there is no shortage of competent, trained, English-speaking doctors. Prescriptions can usually be filled, since all major cities have excellent drugstores and many offer "round-the-clock treatment." When you return home, be sure your medications are in their original labeled bottles to avoid any problems with U.S. Customs. Before leaving, determine whether your health insurance is valid abroad and whether you must obtain receipts for reimbursement.

The *International Association for Medical Assistance for Travelers* (IAMAT) has participating doctors who speak English in every South American country. The organization will send, on request, a booklet listing these physicians. Addresses are: U.S.—IAMAT, 417 Center St., Lewiston, N.Y. 14092; Canada—40 Regal Rd., Guelph, Ontario N1K 1B5; Europe—57 Voirets, 1212 Grand-Lancy-Geneva, Switzerland. Other organizations that provide a similar service are: *The International Health Care Service* (IHCS), 525 East 68th St., New York, NY 10021; *Medic Alert,* 2323 Colorado, Turlock, CA 95381. In the U.K., *Europ Assistance,* 252 High St., Croydon CRO 1NF (081–680 1234), offers an excellent service. The *Association of British Insurers,* Aldermary House, Queen St., EC4N 1TT (071–248 4477), will give comprehensive advice on all aspects of vacation insurance.

Senior citizens may wish to consider the following tips: determine what medical services health/medical insurance will cover outside U.S.; carry an insurance policy identity card; generally, social security Medicare programs do not provide for payment of hospital and medical services outside the U.S.; medication should be packed (ample supply) in original containers along with doctor's prescription; take an extra pair of glasses; enter on passport the name of person to be contacted in case of emergency; if in serious legal, medical, or financial difficulty, contact your embassy or Consulate (addresses are listed in the individual country chapters); if you have allergies, reactions to certain medicines, or other unique medical problems, wear a "medical alert" bracelet.

MONEY. For several years inflation has been a major problem in South America, with notable exceptions in the economies of Venezuela, Colombia, Suriname, and French Guiana. It has been most noticeable in Argentina, Brazil, Peru, and Guyana. Radical devaluations seem to go along with the rampant inflation, including actual changes in the name and value of the currency. In 1986, Argentina devalued the peso and renamed its currency *australes* (plural) or one *austral.* Brazil devalued and changed its currency name from *cruzados* to *cruzados novos* in 1989 and back to its original name *cruzeiro* in 1990. Exchange rates change so quickly that we suggest you check with a bank (Bank of America) or a foreign currency exchange bureau (Deak Perera) for current rates.

As if the currency situation in South America is not complicated enough, there also exist "parallel" exchange rates. This unofficial exchange rate is practiced so openly (except in Chile) that it's not even called a "black market." Although technically illegal, the governments do nothing to stop it, hence the new term, "parallel market." Brazil and Argentina are the two most notable for their "parallel" exchange rates (in Spanish or Portuguese the word is *paralelo*). You can use U.S. dollars (always preferred) as negotiable currency while shopping, etc., and the shop vendors will calculate the price of your purchases in dollars, based on the parallel exchange rate, which can vary as much as 10–25 percent higher than the official rate. The parallel rate is a matter of public information, and everyone will give you almost the exact rate.

Therefore, you need to change very little local money—only what you need for transportation, refreshments, and the like. It is also recommended that you change only a little at a time, because with inflation the rate of exchange gets better every day. Please note that some countries do not allow you to change your money back into dollars, so be conservative with your changing habits.

It has been recommended that you change a small amount of money before you leave on your trip, to get you through the initial airport tips, taxi, porters, and bellhops routine. However, you are going to pay a lot more for this money if you change it ahead of time through a money broker. We recommend that you just stock up on a lot of single dollar bills, and these will be as cheerfully accepted as the local currency for tips, etc. Unless you are arriving at an unusual hour, you can also change money at the airports upon arrival.

Currencies and exchange rates are given in the "Facts at Your Fingertips" section of each chapter.

Credit Travel and Credit Cards. All the major credit cards are accepted in South America, and it is recommended that if you travel with an American Express card, you supplement it with one other major bank card. Vendors very often will not accept American Express if they take one of the other major cards. It is always good to have some "plastic" with you, just in case you need it; however, in those countries where there is a parallel exchange rate, you are much better off exchanging your money on the parallel market and paying your bills in cash. (Your credit card charges will be converted into dollars at the official rate.) The opposite is true for those countries that have high inflation, and let their currency "float" on the free market, so that the official and black market rates are the same. By the time the charge is sent to your credit card company, and then is posted to your statement, you may have gotten an even better exchange rate from when you were there! The credit cards commonly accepted in South America are American Express, Diners Club, Carte Blanche, Visa, and MasterCard.

Traveler's Checks. Traveler's checks are the best way to safeguard your travel funds. Most universally accepted are those of American Express, while those issued by Bank of America and Citibank are also widely used. If not using American Express, make sure that you do use checks drawn on a well-known bank in South America. Verify that the bank is an international concern and that they have branches in the cities you are planning to visit. This is not so much to assure their acceptance but to assure their prompt replacement in case of loss or theft.

The best known and most easily exchanged British traveler's checks are those issued by Thos. Cook & Son and the "Big Four" banks: Barclays, Lloyds, Midland, and National Westminster.

Changing traveler's checks is easiest—if more expensive—at your hotel. If you can afford the extra time, change at banks, and try to avoid doing so on weekends, when the rates are less favorable. In the countries that have parallel exchanges, traveler's checks are also negotiable like cash, although you might find the exchange rate slightly less favorable. Whether on the official or the parallel exchange, the security of having traveler's checks far outweighs the slightly less advantageous exchange rate you get for them.

Note: You do not need your passport to exchange your traveler's checks. A photocopy of your passport and one other picture I.D. (such as a driver's license) is all you need to cash your checks. Keep your airline tickets, passports, extra cash, checks, and jewelry in your safety deposit box at the hotel! Better yet, leave your jewelry at home and wear an inexpensive timepiece.

PASSPORTS AND VISAS. Although U.S. laws do not require a passport for travel in any part of the Western Hemisphere, a passport is required by the laws and regulations of some of the countries concerned. Thus, it is a good idea for travelers to South America to have a valid passport, and most countries there will require an onward or return ticket. See the individual country chapters under "Travel Documents" for specific entry requirements.

The U.S. Government no longer issues family passports. This means that each member of the family must have an individual passport. It is a good idea to have children wear I.D. bracelets listing their names and passport numbers.

Americans. Major post offices are now authorized to process passport applications. You may also apply in person at U.S. Passport Agency offices in various cities; addresses and phone numbers are available under governmental listings in the white or blue pages of local telephone directories. Applications are also accepted at most county courthouses. Renewals (form DSP-82) can be handled by mail provided that your previous passport is not more than 12 years old and was issued after your sixteenth birthday. New applicants will need: 1) a birth certificate or certified copy thereof or other proof of citizenship; 2) two identical photographs two inches square, full face, black-and-white or color, on nonglossy paper, and taken within the past six months; 3) $42.00 (new), $35.00 (renewal); and 4) proof of identity, such as a current driver's license, employment ID card, copy of an income tax return, or governmental ID card. Social Security and credit cards are not acceptable.

You should allow a month to six weeks for your application to be processed, but in an emergency, Passport Agency offices can have a passport readied within 24–48 hours, and even the postal authorities can indicate "Rush" when necessary. If you expect to travel extensively, you may request a 48- or 96-page passport instead of the usual 24-page one at no extra charge. U.S. passports are valid for ten years. If your passport gets lost or stolen, immediately notify either the nearest American Consul or the Passport Office, Department of State, Washington, D.C. 20524. Record your passport's number and date and place of issue separately. It is a good idea to photocopy your passport, before you start your trip. Make three copies; leave one at home, put one in your suitcase, and one in your wallet or purse. This will allow you to leave your passport at the hotel, which is often safer.

Tourist Visas are required of U.S. citizens by Argentina, Brazil, Colombia, French Guiana, Guyana, Suriname, and Venezuela. Holders of valid U.S. passports may usually obtain tourist visas at appropriate consulates within 24 hours of application.

Canadian citizens may obtain application passport forms at any post office; these are to be sent to the Central Passport Office, 125 Sussex Drive, Lester B. Pearson Building, Ottawa, Ontario K1A 0G2. You may apply in person to the province in which you reside. However, a mailed application must be handled by the central office. A remittance of $21 Canadian, three photographs, and a birth certificate or certificate of Canadian citizenship (naturalization papers) are required. Canadian passports are valid for five years and are nonrenewable.

British subjects must apply for passports on special forms obtainable from main post offices or a travel agent. The application should be sent or taken to the Passport Office according to residential area or lodged with them through a travel agent. It is best to apply for the passport at least 6 weeks before it is required. The regional Passport Offices are located in London, Liverpool, Peterborough, Glasgow and Newport. The applications must be countersigned by your bank manager or by a solicitor, barrister, doctor, clergyman or justice of the peace who knows you personally. You will need two full-face photos. The fee is £15; passport valid for 10 years.

Note: Passport and visa information should be confirmed with the consulates of the countries you plan to visit prior to departure.

HEALTH CERTIFICATES. The U.S. Public Health Service advises the following inoculations for travelers to South America: tetanus for travelers to the northern third of South America; typhoid for an extensive trip around South America. All countries in South America strongly recommend yellow fever vaccination, especially for visits outside of the large cities. Travelers should be aware that the incidence of dengue, a viral disease transmitted by mosquitos, has increased in South and Central America over the last few years. Although travelers are considered at low risk for severe dengue infections, extra precautions against mosquito bites are advised. If you intend to visit the Amazon or Iguaçu Falls, plan to take medication against malaria, also transmitted by mosquitos. Check with your doctor or local Health Department for more specific health recommendations before leaving.

CUSTOMS. Customs regulations vary from country to country. See the country chapters for specific information. The following is a general guide of what most of the countries allow you to import: two liters of alcoholic beverages, 400 cigarettes and 50 cigars and 450 grams of tobacco, enough perfume for personal use. Exceptions are noted within each country chapter. There are frequent rigid inspections by customs in other countries of the effects of visitors coming from Peru, Colombia, Ecuador, and Bolivia where illegal marijuana and coca leaf by-products are readily available.

Getting to South America

BY AIR. Are you going to try to see all of South America or two to three countries regionally? If you are going to try to see all of South America, then you should plan on at least two months of traveling, and probably a lot more. In this case, there is no existing airfare that could get you around any more economically than by just buying your air tickets in segments as you go along. However, in purchasing air segments locally, you will incur local sales taxes: Peru—28%; Ecuador—20%; Chile—20%; Bolivia—30%; Argentina—18%; Brazil—10%; Paraguay—18%. In some countries, such as Colombia, there are two fare structures: one in dollars, and one in local currency, which can be lower than the dollar fare. However, air tickets may be purchased in local currency only if the purchaser is a citizen of that country. Additionally, each country has what are called "airpasses." The rules governing these airpasses vary considerably, although they generally permit a certain amount of unrestricted air travel via the national airlines for a given period of time (usually two weeks to 30 days). In some cases, such as Brazil, the airpass cannot be purchased locally. (See "Getting Around South America" later in this chapter.) Therefore you are well advised to purchase the tickets before you leave. Tickets may be issued "open" on non-restricted fares valid for one year. By paying cash and making sure that the air segments are also open as to air carrier you will have the maximum flexibility. The tickets may be reissued if your general plans change. There might be an additional collection, but not necessarily.

If you want to see as much as possible and can travel for 45 days, AeroPeru sells what is called the "South America Travel Spree," which permits unlimited travel on AeroPeru's international routes for 45 days. Any travel within Peru on AeroPeru would cost only $25 per sector. AeroPeru flies to most countries in South America from Lima, Peru, so your trip might entail many back and forth trips to Lima. AeroPeru has sales offices in Miami, New York, and Los Angeles. For information and reservations, call toll-free in the U.S.A., Alaska, Hawaii, and Canada 800–255–7378. At press time, the "Travel Spree" rates were: from Miami—$909 high season, $759 low season; from New York—$1,149 high, $999 low; from Dallas—$1,149 high, $999 low; from Los Angeles—$1,209 high, $1,059 low; and from San Francisco—$1,279 high, $1,129 low.

If you are planning to visit only two or three countries regionally in South America, then there is a greater variety of airfares to choose from. However, a good rule of thumb is that the longer you wish to be away, the lower the number of stops you can make. If you can restrict yourself to 30 days' travel you can usually find an airfare that permits several stops along the way to your furthest destination and back. The second rule of thumb is that your best fares require travel to be exclusively on that one carrier offering the fare. Therefore, when planning your trip, you should first contact the different airlines and familiarize yourself with their routes (all of the airlines have route maps), then choose the airline(s) whose routes best encompass those destinations you wish to cover, and then do some airfare shopping among them.

Airfares to South America are constantly changing. Look into all of the promotional fares available, after you have narrowed your field based on your plans. Unfortunately, there is no inexpensive "no frills" type of air service to South America.

Following is an attempt to outline the complex airfare situation to help you narrow your choices:

Charters. This is the cheapest but least flexible way to travel to South America. There are a couple of charter operators, principally to Rio de Janeiro, although occasionally they will offer charters to Buenos Aires or Lima. The charters are strictly to a single destination, do not offer stopovers en route, and are for a fixed, limited length of time. The charters can, however, usually offer an air and land package tour for about the same price as the lowest available airfare alone via scheduled airlines. The charters are not operated via regularly scheduled airlines, therefore, service is limited, legroom cramped, and schedules changeable.

"APEX" Fares. These fares are cheaper, but are also single destination fares. The advantage to these fares is that they do permit long stays (usually 60–90 days, and in some cases, such as Peru, 150 days), but do not permit stops anywhere else. The fares also require a minimum stay, usually about 21 days.

Group Airfares. The group airfares to South America are just about all gone, with the one notable exception of the GROUP 10 (GV10) airfares to Rio. These fares are offered by Varig and Pan Am out of New York, Miami, and Los Angeles and anyone can book into them. The airlines "consolidate"; that is, they block 10 seats on every flight that the tour wholesalers can sell into, so that the group departure is guaranteed. The airfare does require that it be sold in conjunction with a minimum land package of $18 per day, but you have a choice of many different tour wholesalers' packages to choose from. The fares permit a maximum stay of 14 days, plus one day of travel, and permit two stopovers on the way. Sample Group 10 airfares: Miami/Rio—high season $899, low season $679; New York/Rio—high $999, low $799; Los Angeles/Rio—high $1,120, low $955; Toronto or Montreal/Rio—high $1,060, low $873.

High season is June 15–Aug. 15 and Dec. 1–31. Fares are subject to a $100 surcharge each way during Carnival in Brazil.

Varig Brasilian Airlines has the most flexible packages for these fares, primarily because it has the best route structure to Brazil. Besides a simple round trip to Rio (with a stopover in Iguassu Falls permitted at no extra charge), Varig also has the following tours available for the same Rio GV10 airfare: Miami/Salvador (Bahia)/Rio/Miami;   Miami/Manaus/Rio/Miami;   Miami/Salvador/Rio/Manaus/Miami. For more information on these tours, contact Varig or Pan Am tour desks or local sales offices (see airline listing below).

Individual Tour Basing Fares (ITX): This is a very economical fare system, considering the amount of flexibility allowed. It usually permits a maximum of 21 days' travel with two stopovers on the airlines' routing, plus your final destination, at no additional charge. Up to two additional stopovers are available at $50 each. The fare does require that you purchase a minimum specified amount of land arrangements (i.e. either a packaged tour or a prearranged independent tour). The fare requires travel all on one airline, with the very notable exception of this fare to Buenos Aires on Eastern, which can be on Varig Airlines on the return from Buenos Aires, taking in Iguassu Falls and Rio de Janeiro en route.

Sample Tour Basing Fares

Miami/Lima/Cuzco: $459
NYC/Lima/Cuzco: $659
LA/Lima/Cuzco: $721
Miami/Buenos Aires: $940 high season, $782 low
New York/Buenos Aires: $1,040 high, $925 low
Los Angeles/Buenos Aires: $1,120 high, $1,029 low
Toronto or Montreal/Buenos Aires: $1,099 high, $999 low
Vancouver/Buenos Aires: $1,299 high, $1,199 low.

30-Day Excursion Fares. These fares are more expensive than the ITX fares, but they have two important advantages. First, they permit a maximum stay of 30 days (versus 21) and permit 4 stopovers (two in each direction to and from your furthest point, with each additional stopover costing $30). Second, they permit you to fly on as many different airlines as necessary to complete the trip.

There is a host of other fare groupings, ranging from full-fare economy (generally used by business travelers), to business class, first class, and "sleeper class." All of these fares, and the restrictions that govern them, are constantly changing, depending on the time of year (peak, low, or "shoulder" periods), on how heavy the competition is at any given moment, and on how well-traveled a particular route is. The advantage of an independent booking at a full economy rate is that you may be able to add additional stopovers at no extra charge. Here, again, the rules vary and change frequently. Similarly, you are more likely to be able to change your reservations as you go when flying regularly scheduled major airlines. Be sure to check with airlines and travel agents for the restrictions on fares.

The majority of direct flights to various points begin in Miami, with increasing service out of New York and Los Angeles. There is also service out of Montreal, Toronto, and Vancouver. Rio de Janeiro, Lima, Buenos Aires, Panama, Bogotá, and Caracas are all served nonstop out of New York and Miami.

Caracas: Pan American, Viasa, and LAN-Chile out of New York and Miami; Varig out of Miami.

Bogotá: Avianca Airlines out of New York, Miami, Chicago, and Los Angeles; Ladeco Airlines out of Miami.

Quito: Ecuatoriana Airlines from New York, Miami, Chicago, and Los Angeles.

Guayaquil: Same as Quito, plus Ladeco from Miami.

Lima: AeroPeru from Miami; LAN-Chile Airlines from New York; Canadian Pacific out of Toronto; Varig Brasilian Airlines out of Los Angeles.

Santiago: LAN-Chile Airlines out of New York and Miami; Ladeco and Pan American out of Miami.

Buenos Aires: Varig Brazilian Airlines out of New York, Miami, and Los Angeles; Ladeco out of Miami.

Rio de Janeiro and São Paulo: Varig Brazilian Airlines out of New York, Miami, and Los Angeles; and Pan American out of New York and Miami.

Manaus and Belem: Varig Brazilian Airlines out of Miami.

BY SEA. By and large there is very little ocean-going passenger service left to any part of the world these days, and South America is no exception. What there is has largely polarized between passenger-carrying freighters on the one hand and cruise liners on the other. The steady progress of containerization has cut into the freighter facilities available. Alco Steamship Co., for example, formerly an important carrier of tourists to the southern continent, now has no passenger service whatsoever. In 1985 we saw the termination of some of the last passenger/freighter service to South America when Delta Steamship was bought out and her beautiful "Santa" ships taken off the cargo routes to South America.

On a cruise you get a very pleasant vacation in a floating luxury hotel, and brief tastes of several countries by way of their major port cities. Below is a list of some cruise services available to South America, followed by sources of information on freighter travel. However, in view of the constant changes in cruise itineraries, it is recommended that you contact your local travel agent, who can provide you with the most up-to-date information and make all arrangements—for the same price you would pay if you made the arrangements yourself.

More and more cruise lines stop regularly at La Guaira, Venezuela, Cartagena, and San Andres Island, Colombia.

Chandris, Inc., 900 Third Ave., New York, NY 10022 (212–223–3003), has sailings in fall and winter from San Juan that call at La Guaira, Venezuela. In Britain: 5 St. Helen's Place, London EC3A 6BJ (071–588 2598).

Cunard, Ltd., 555 Fifth Ave., New York, NY 10017 (800–221–4770), has the *Cunard Countess* sailing year-round from San Juan with a stop at La Guaira, Venezuela. Now operating the *Sagafjord,* she has one world cruise which calls at Buenos Aires, Montevideo, Rio de Janeiro, Salvador, and Belém before returning through the Caribbean to Ft. Lauderdale; this 15-day cruise may be booked as a segment of the world cruise. The *Sagafjord* also offers two Amazon River cruises a year, one from Ft. Lauderdale to Belém and up the Amazon to Manaus (14 days) and a second returning from Manaus to Ft. Lauderdale (13 days). The *Vistafjord* is scheduled to stop at both Cartagena, Colombia, and La Guaira, Venezuela, on the ship's 14-day winter cruises out of Port Everglades, FL. The *Sagafjord* includes several South American ports on its annual World Cruises, sailing in early January also from Port Everglades. Additionally, the same ship calls at Cartagena on transcanal trips to the West Coast of the U.S. Sailings are from Fort Lauderdale on the Atlantic. In Britain: 35 Pall Mall, London SW1 5LS (071–930 4321); in Canada: One Dundee Street, Toronto, Ont. M5G 2B2.

Royal Caribbean Line, Inc., 903 South America Way, Miami, Fl 33132 (305–379–4731) puts La Guaira, Venezuela, as a regular port of call for its *Nordic Prince* which sails on alternate Saturdays from Miami year-round (14-day cruises). Sun Viking has 11-day cruises that stop in La Guaira. In Britain: 35 Piccadilly, London, W1V 9PB (071–434 1991).

Royal Viking Line, 95 Merrick Way, Coral Gables FL 33134 (305–447–9660), has some 48/51 day cruises out of New York/Fort Lauderdale that stop in Rio. There are also some sailings from Los Angeles/San Francisco that stop in Cartagena, and reverse from west to east coast and vice versa. In Britain: 3 Vere St., London W1M 9HQ (071–734–0773).

Sitmar Cruises/Princess Cruises, 10100 Santa Monica Blvd., Los Angeles, CA 90067 (213–553–1666). Ordinarily the *Dawn Princess* and the *Sky Princess* sail out of Fort Lauderdale with a call at Cartagena, Colombia on its Caribbean runs, most of the year with some exceptions. Another Sitmar liner, the *Fair Princess,* sails from Los Angeles to Mexico and the Caribbean in the winter and spring. The *Sky Princess* and *Dawn Princess* have also begun service from San Juan to Manaus, Brazil, with 4 ports of call on the Amazon River. The *Star Princess* also offers cruises in the Caribbean. In Britain: c/o Equity Cruises, 77–79 Great Eastern St., London EC2A 3HU (071–729 1929).

Freighter Travel. This is a whole specialized field in itself, too large to be covered in detail here. It can be very rewarding if you have an open schedule. A great number of banana boats, tramp steamers, and tankers also cross the Caribbean bound for South America from Tampa, New Orleans, and Texas ports. Their schedules and prices often depend on where their cargo takes them. A good travel agent can track down the right ship for you. Freighter travel is adventurous, relaxing, and often very inexpensive—it's well worth investigating. The cost factor can be particularly attractive because what you get, if your schedule permits, is in fact a leisurely cruise at reasonable rates, whereas going on a cruise liner you will pay more a day for comparable accommodations because you are paying for a whole extra infrastructure of entertainment that you may neither need nor want.

Staying in South America

GENERAL CUSTOMS. Latin Americans value small courtesies, and it is worthwhile spending some time on the social traditions that are observed in South America. First, it is important to remember that the pace of life is much slower in South America, and Latins cannot comprehend a situation so pressing that one overlooks simple courtesies. Remember to take the time to greet "good morning" or "good afternoon" and the like, accompanied by a smile, with every social encounter—from the front desk clerk at your hotel to your tour guide. The human touch is always something that takes precedence over expediency in South America. For those of you who are planning business in South America, this lesson could make you a winner. Plan twice as much time to conduct your business as you would elsewhere. Let your prospective business associates get to know you; take time to listen and get to know them. Most important, let them be the one to say "let's talk business."

The handshake in Latin America is universal, among both men and women. Men and women shake hands upon meeting and departure; women will also offer a kiss on the cheek to men and women with whom they are on more friendly terms. In Brazil, it's a kiss on both cheeks if you are anything more than first time acquaintances.

WOMEN TRAVELING ALONE. Women traveling alone in South America almost universally comment on the gallant deference with which they were treated by Latin men. This is not necessarily due to any "double standard" in which women are kept on pedestals; it is more due to the fact that South Americans would never want to violate a code of courtesy and conduct that would apply to both sexes. It is also due to the fact that South Americans value more subtle communication, and such overt shows of "appreciation" would not be decorous.

Women traveling alone in South America should not expect overt demonstrations of appreciation, provided their behavior and/or dress is likewise subtle and decorous. Short-shorts and abbreviated tops are acceptable for beach or pool-wear, but not for street-wear. Follow your own judgment, based on what you would wear, do, or say in your own home environment, and you will usually be correct. If you do engage in flirtatious behavior, be prepared for the typical Latin man to take your flirtation seriously.

There are other concerns for the woman traveling alone in South America: Will she meet congenial people along the way? Will she be considered unusual? This is a totally subjective question, and depends largely upon the individual's ability to interact with others. A woman traveling alone might be regarded with curiosity and possibly admiration, but not with censure. The genuine friendliness that one encounters in South America, both among tourists and natives alike, is the greatest draw for tourism, and a woman traveling alone can expect to encounter congenial company all along the way.

Here are some hints which might help you get over that initial adjustment period. Select first class or even tourist class hotels, rather than deluxe, as they are usually smaller and more casual and thus promote communication and interaction among guests. If you have a choice between a private car tour or a motorcoach tour, take the motorcoach, which will give you more opportunity to meet people. Nighttime dining and entertainment could loom as a lonely prospect if it were not for the natural friendliness of the people. If you are alone, it is recommended that you keep pretty much to your hotel restaurant and cocktail lounge. You could dine alone outside of your hotel at better restaurants; however, women in South America do not frequent singles bars alone if they do not want to be misunderstood.

HOTELS. If you want to stay in deluxe or first class hotels, then you have good access to information. Chain hotels (i.e., Sheraton, Intercontinental, Hilton, and Holiday Inn Crowne Plaza) all have reservation and information services. Independent hotels are usually members of a hotel representation firm wherein you can obtain information and rates. Good companies of this type are LEADING HOTELS 800–223–6800, LARC HOTELS (Latin America Reservation Center) 800–327–3573, and SRS (Steigenberger Reservation Service) 800–223–5652 (also in Europe and around the world).

If tourist class or budget accommodations are what you want, you are going to have difficulty obtaining advance information or reservations. These hotels generally do not pay the fee to work through a hotel representation firm, so the only means to contact them is by writing to them, which can be laborious. Most travel agencies or tourist information bureaus are not able to provide more than lists of names and addresses. A travel agency is never going to receive a commission from a budget hotel, and will probably want to levy a service charge if you want them to make your reservations.

South American hotels will surely satisfy even the most fastidious visitor, particularly in their attitude to service. "No" just does not exist in the vocabulary. A smile and a courteous request will get the impossible in South America, and a gratuity is only optional.

FOOD AND DRINK. Dining in South America is an experience. One has never really tasted charcoal-broiled steak until dining with the gauchos of Argentina and Uruguay. Their *parrillada* is a giant-sized serving of half-a-dozen grilled meats that is delicious. Argentina's *asado,* roasted meat prepared on an open fire, is equally as memorable.

The seafood of South America is just as succulent—whether one enjoys Venezuela's tiny oysters and clams (with a dash of sweet lemon) on the beach at Macuto or sits beside the brilliant sea with the smart set in Viña del Mar sampling delicate steamed shrimp and perfect white wine.

In Chile, the *langostinos* (baby crawfish) are also long remembered. Peru offers *seviche*—raw fish marinated in a spicy pepper, onion, and lemon sauce that makes the perfect snack after a day seeing the sights. (See warning about cholera epidemic in Foreword.)

Brazilians enjoy *feijoada completa*—a masterly blending of rice, black beans, and a variety of smoked pork. Also in Brazil, don't fail to sample *vatapa*—a heavy fish and shrimp combination spiced with peppers and paprika. Brazilian seafood is tops on the continent and is reasonably priced. The most varied and tasty cuisine in Brazil is found in Bahia.

For the adventurous, there's Bolivia's really hot *aji* pepper, the sharp Indian curry dishes of Guyana, or the traditional 20-course, spicy Dutch *rijsttafel* in Suriname. On the not-to-miss list also put Colombia's *ajiaco,* a thick potato soup.

Prices vary from very reasonable to about the same as in most U.S. or English restaurants. In the smaller cities, three good meals in the best restaurants normally run from $5 to $6 a day. In the larger cities and capitals, three good meals in the best places will normally run from $35 to $60 daily.

In the more out-of-the-way places, food can be a real bargain. A filet mignon charcoaled on an outdoor grill and served in a garden under the bright evening sky of Asuncion can be enjoyed for as little as $4 (U.S.) Conversely, a mediocre dinner in one of the better restaurants in La Paz can run close to $10.

It's hard to set an average, but with $70 a day you'll normally dine royally in South America. Lima, Caracas, Buenos Aires, Santiago, Bogotá, Rio and São Paulo have the best restaurants and finest food, and also higher prices than the smaller cities. Bahia (Salvador), Brazil and Cartagena, Colombia are, however, in a class by themselves with a heavy Afro influence in their cuisines and with a superabundance of fresh seafood, fruit, and vegetables.

Drinking is also an adventure. Chilean wine is rapidly gaining world renown— and rightly so. The wines from Chile's central region are second to none anywhere in the world. Argentine and Brazilian vintners have also made spectacular progress in the quality of their wines in recent years. Peru's *Pisco,* a brandy made in the Ica valley, is the central ingredient of the potent, delicious Pisco Sour. Colombia's excellent *Medellin Añejo* rum (which sells at the Bogotá airport tax free shop for about U.S. $2.50 a bottle) is outstanding. Uruguay's barley beer is one of many excellent, very inexpensive beers in South America. European immigration to South America brought some master brewers to the continent and you'll appreciate their labors after a long walk in the sun along Punta del Este's perfect, endless beach. Brazilian beer is especially good; draft beer is called "chopp." *Cachaça* is low-priced Brazilian rum, marvelous when mixed with fresh fruit juices in ice-cold *batidas.*

And when you celebrate with the "bubbly" in South America you may do it with Chile's or Argentina's excellent, inexpensive champagne.

TIPPING. Tipping is always optional and is rendered only with good service; however, if the service has been good, you will want to tip and so the following guidelines might help. First of all, in most countries, with the exception of Chile, a 10 percent service fee is included in all hotel charges and restaurant charges. In Chile it may seem that service is added, but the 20 percent "IVA" which you see on your bills is a value added tax, not a service charge. Therefore, if service has been very good, it is acceptible to leave an additional 2–5 percent of the bill as an extra gratuity. It is not expected that you tip chambermaids in hotels where 10 percent service is added to the hotel bill; however, it is courteous and will be appreciated if you leave a tip when your chambermaid has run extra errands for you. (Some hotels have service stations on each floor that are attended 24 hours a day, and you can ring for extra pillows, towels, water, etc., at any time.)

Luggage receives a minimum of $.25 U.S. per bag at airports, and $.50 per bag at hotels. Tour guides receive a minimum of $.50 per person, and a driver $.25 per person for a half day tour and double that for a full day tour.

Small tips for taxi drivers and other services are *usually* accepted in most cities. However, in several places where tipping is not the custom, such as Chile, foreign visitors are often astonished to see their tip politely refused.

In the writer's opinion, the traveler is often overly concerned with tipping enough or too much. Bear in mind that South Americans are people with delicate sensibilities, and such concern with tipping might offend them. In some cases a tip is almost expected, but in most cases, a show of gratitude is the most important thing to remember.

Somewhat related to tipping is the delicate subject of bribing. Bribes do exist, but this system is not as widespread as one would think. Sometimes a traveler encounters an uncooperative agent or official; however, the lack of cooperation could be due to a language barrier and/or the traveler's attitude, which might have been discourteous. Regardless, you might run a greater risk by trying to bribe a public official in some countries with strict regulations against this.

DRINKING WATER AND MILK. The best general rule is to drink bottled water in South America. Many of the public water systems date almost to Colonial times and are not 100 percent safe. Be sure to ask for bottled water (it is usually in your hotel room when you arrive). There are several excellent mineral waters bottled in South America that make drinking bottled water a pleasure rather than a hardship.

Note: In the past few years there have been complaints of tourists drinking bottled water and getting sick anyway. When medical authorities traced the problem they found out the bottled water was "fake." Try to drink aerated mineral water, which is harder to tamper with. Another healthful and natural alternative is "coconut water." Soft drinks and beers are made from fresh, unpolluted spring water. *Mate,* South American tea, is especially popular in Argentina, Brazil, Uruguay, and Paraguay. It is most refreshing served cold with lemon juice. Major coffee producers include Brazil, Colombia, Ecuador, and Peru. All export to U.S. and European markets, but South Americans themselves prefer a darker "espresso" roast. Brazilian *"cafezinhos,"* served in tiny cups, are daylong pick-me-ups.

Pasteurized milk is available in almost every major city in South America. The one rule to remember is to have the bottle opened at your table. Yogurt is also available.

ELECTRICAL CURRENT. It varies from country to country in South America. Most of the top hotels have transformers for current and adapters for plugs for guests with foreign electric razors, slide projectors, etc. Specifics are listed in each chapter.

READING MATERIAL. English-language newspapers and magazines are for sale in all leading South American cities. With the fine jet schedules to South America, there is little delay in receiving airmail editions of newspapers. International editions of news magazines are on sale in all of South America's leading hotels.

Daily English-language newspapers are published in Buenos Aires, Bogotá, Rio, Georgetown, Lima, and Caracas. Bookstores with international publications are plentiful and worth a visit.

MAIL, TELEGRAPHIC SERVICES, AND TELEPHONES. Major hotels will hold mail for arriving guests. Another possibility is to have the mail forwarded to the local American Express office or agency. General Delivery in most of South America is not recommended for visitors. Telegraphic service is available everywhere. Many hotels have cable facilities.

In some South American countries *fichas* (tokens) are needed to operate the phones. These can be purchased from the hotels or in local shops. Countries utilizing this method are Argentina, Brazil, and Chile.

In Uruguay, one must deposit a 10-centavo coin to get a dial tone and in Venezuela one must deposit a *medio* (25 *centimos* coin) to use the phone.

International telephone dialing to the U.S. is available in Brazil and Venezuela by dialing 00 and in the French Antilles (Fr. Guiana) by dialing 19 + 1 + U.S. country code followed by the desired U.S. area code and number.

If your hotel is not equipped for International dialing to the U.S., cut your telecommunications costs by: 1) using your U.S. telephone credit card; 2) placing calls collect; or 3) using telephones at Post Offices or special telephone centers located at railway stations and airports.

Stamps are available through the Post Office and at major hotels in all countries.

SHOPPING. Shopping is one of South America's prime attractions. From the antique Colonial silver in the quaint shops of Quito and Lima to Paraguay's dainty lace and the curious native handicrafts of Suriname, the South American visitor will find an endless array of irresistible shopping bargains. Brazil is famous for semiprecious stones, such as aquamarine, tourmaline, topaz, amethyst, and garnet, and there are magnificent jewelry shops in Rio de Janeiro. With the exceptions of French Guiana, all the countries in this book are included in the customs exemption scheme of the GSP (Generalized System of Preferences), which is explained later in this section under "Customs Returning Home." Many *locally made* products, if acquired in their country of origin, can be brought into the U.S. entirely free of duty without affecting the regular $400 basic exemption.

CONVERTING METRIC TO U.S. MEASUREMENTS

Multiply:	by:	to find:
Length		
millimeters (mm)	.039	inches (in)
meters (m)	3.28	feet (ft)
meters	1.09	yards (yd)
kilometers (km)	.62	miles (mi)
Area		
hectare (ha)	2.47	acres
Capacity		
liters (L)	1.06	quarts (qt)
liters	.26	gallons (gal)
liters	2.11	pints (pt)
Weight		
gram (g)	.04	ounce (oz)
kilogram (kg)	2.20	pounds (lb)
metric ton (MT)	.98	tons (t)
Power		
kilowatt (kw)	1.34	horsepower (hp)
Temperature		
degrees Celsius	9/5 (then add 32)	degrees Fahrenheit

CONVERTING U.S. TO METRIC MEASUREMENTS

Multiply:	by:	to find:
Length		
inches (in)	25.40	millimeters (mm)
feet (ft)	.30	meters (m)
yards (yd)	.91	meters
miles (mi)	1.61	kilometers (km)
Area		
acres	.40	hectares (ha)
Capacity		
pints (pt)	.47	liters (L)
quarts (qt)	.95	liters
gallons (gal)	3.79	liters
Weight		
ounces (oz)	28.35	grams (g)
pounds (lb)	.45	kilograms (kg)
tons (t)	1.11	metric tons (MT)
Power		
horsepower (hp)	.75	kilowatts
Temperature		
degrees Fahrenheit	5/9 (after subtracting 32)	degrees Celsius

CLOSING HOURS. Naturally, opening and closing hours vary from city to city and country to country. The best rule to follow is to remember many shops close for the customary two or three hours Latin luncheon. Plan your shopping between 10 A.M. and noon and 3 P.M. and 6 P.M. and you'll find stores open in every country. However, shops usually are closed on Saturday afternoon and all day Sunday.

In the larger cities, many of the big department stores are now staying open during the lunch hours. In Buenos Aires, for example, the larger stores now open at 9 A.M. and don't close until 7 P.M.

Business hours and holidays are given in each country chapter.

SPORTS. South America is a sportsman's paradise, both for participant and spectator. Hunting, fishing, swimming, hiking, horseback riding, horseracing, tennis, polo, boxing, golf, and baseball are the standard favorites of South America.

In addition, the continent offers visitors thrilling sports seldom seen elsewhere in the world. *Soccer* takes on a new meaning in South America. Anyone fortunate enough to witness a soccer match in Rio de Janeiro's Maracanã Stadium will never forget the sheer spectacle of the day. Rio's Maracanã stadium is the world's largest, seating 200,000, and regularly hosts soccer's most brilliant stars. South American enthusiasm for the game often runs to near madness.

Bull fighting and *Jai Alai* are also South American favorites. The world's top bull fighters annually visit Colombian, Peruvian, Venezuelan, Ecuadorian, and Bolivian *"plazas de toros."* Jai Alai, the world's fastest game, has traveled from Spain's Basque country to South America, with some variation, and is becoming a betting favorite of Latins.

Skiing is important in Argentina, Chile, and Bolivia. Ecuador is a great place for hiking, climbing, and wildlife watching, especially in the Galápagos Islands.

SECURITY. *A word of warning. Never* wear flashy jewelry (especially necklaces, rings, bracelets or watches) on beaches or even on the street in such cities as Rio, São Paulo, Lima, and Bogotá, which are notorious for young hoodlums who snatch and run. It is also wise to use the hotel safe for valuables, including travelers checks and money you do not need for the day. Use the same precautions for cameras and lenses and beware the street marauders who snatch handbags and cameras while on foot or zooming by on motorcycles.

Unfortunately, South America's democracies or "semidemocracies" seem to have higher street crime rates than the police states or dictatorships. In all cases, however, any attempt to deal in "black markets" for currency or drugs is a most dangerous undertaking and to be avoided at all costs.

Political turmoil and the dangers it presents are of great concern to travelers, but these are precisely the subjects it is most difficult to give definite advice about. It is important to remember that each country must be considered individually. Occasionally there are eruptions of demonstrations, but isolated incidents of political activity should be kept in perspective; very rarely do they pose any danger to the tourist. Curfews are often imposed at times of increased activity. At presstime the state department had issued travel advisories pertaining to Colombia and Peru. Do check on the security situation and any special travel documents needed in the countries you plan to visit prior to departure. Although political situations often do not affect tourists, travelers are encouraged to register at their embassy upon arriving in some South American countries. Do research the situation in your country or countries of destination with your travel agent and the appropriate consulates before departure.

Getting around South America

If you have a lot of time, a limited budget, and are not too fussy for creature comforts, you can conceivably travel around South America overland via public buses and trains. You will encounter difficulties if you try to cross the continent. The interior consists of the largest tropical rain forest in the world in the north, the incredibly rugged Andes Mountains, vast marshes and swamps called *pantanal* in the central interior, and extensive grasslands and arid plains. The populated areas traditionally are located near the coasts and in the mountain valleys and that is where you will find roads and fairly adequate commercial transportation.

RAIL TRANSPORTATION. Paul Theroux set out to travel from Boston to Buenos Aires entirely by train. He never accomplished his goal, but ended by writing a humorous book entitled *The Old Patagonia Express,* which told the hilarious tale of his frustrated attempts to do it. Though his book is not a travel guide, it is highly recommended reading for any prospective traveler to South America, especially for those who want to travel by rail, as one would in Europe. The realities of travel in South America are put into proper perspective while at the same time revealing some of the unexpected delights.

Generally speaking, the trains in Colombia, Chile, Argentina, and Brazil are of a better quality than those in other South American countries. Accurate rail schedules are very difficult to obtain; however, surprisingly enough, *Cook's Timetable* is fairly accurate, although not absolutely dependable.

In theory, there does exist an "Amerailpass" similar in concept to the Eurailpass. However, the various national railways are in discord as to revenue sharing, and ticket vendors, travel agencies, and railroad employees are in total disagreement over the governing rules of the pass. In other words, you will find yourself with a rail pass that is so full of contradictions that many times it will not be honored.

The following are some rail segments that you might want to consider:

Ecuador. *Quito to Guayaquil:* Almost the entire south of Ecuador was washed away in 1983 when the climates of both North and South America were temporarily affected by the shifting of the "El Niño" current in the Pacific Ocean. Torrential rains in northern Peru and southern Ecuador caused roads and railways to be washed away. The roads have been restored; nevertheless, the railway in Ecuador is intact only from Quito to Riobamba. Reconstruction is under way. (See the Ecuador chapter for information on the Quito/Riobamba trip.)

Peru. *Cuzco/Machu Picchu/Cuzco:* One of the most famous train rides in South America, this trip can be done round trip from Cuzco in one day, but two days is recommended with an overnight at the government-owned Hotel Turistas Machu Picchu. It is next to impossible to get a reservation at the hotel without going through a travel agent, who in turn will book a package through one of the tour operators. The hotel will not answer letters, telexes, or requests through the airlines. Due to the high demand for the hotel's limited space (only 37 rooms), it will confirm space to known local agencies; the reservation must be pre-paid within 10 days of confirmation, and is non-refundable. An alternative just a short distance away in a town called Aguas Calientes is the youth hostel, which charges about $7 a bed. (All rooms with four beds, bathrooms down the hall. If you want a private room, you must pay for all four beds.) Reservations are suggested for this as well.

Lima/Huancayco/Lima: Not as popular as the other train excursions in Peru, this trip was covered in the popular PBS series "Great Rail Trips of the World." The trip, like Machu Picchu from Cuzco, is strictly a round-trip excursion overland from Lima. The railway terminates in Huancayo, and to go overland from Huancayo to Ayacucho or overland to Cuzco is virtually impossible. Many people have still tried (including this writer and Paul Theroux), and have found the roads impassible (mostly due to fallen trees, mudslides in the rainy season, and rock slides in the dry season). In all cases the frustrated traveler eventually turns back to Huancayo, takes the train back to Lima and flies to Cuzco. The 10-hour train operates in either direction daily except Saturdays, and departs either Lima or Huancayo at about 7 A.M. Most travelers plan their trip to Huancayo to coincide with the Saturday Indian market.

Puno to Arequipa or vice versa: The only feasible way of traveling from Lima to Cuzco overland would be via either *colectivo* or bus from Lima south along the coast to Nazca. Then, on the following day one continues east via colectivo or bus from Nazca to Arequipa. On the third day, one can take the train from Arequipa to Puno (Lake Titicaca) and on the fourth day the train south from Lake Titicaca to Cuzco. This would be recommended only for the very flexible and heartiest of travelers, and cannot be prearranged.

Peru/Bolivia. *Cuzco to La Paz or vice versa:* There is an all-day, 10-hour train from Cuzco to Puno, Peru, on Lake Titicaca (or vice versa). After at least an overnight in Puno you can take either the hydrofoil (Crillon Tours) or the catamaran (Transturin), for crossing Lake Titicaca to Bolivia (which takes about six or seven hours, including lunch) and then motorcoach to La Paz (two hours). Of the two, the catamaran is less expensive though just as dependable and comfortable. The trip can also be made in reverse. These services may be booked through a travel agent. There is also motorcoach service all the way from Puno to La Paz which is much more economical but cannot be booked in advance.

There is train service throughout Bolivia as well as from La Paz to Santiago, Chile, and Mendoza, Argentina. On the international sections you can even book sleeper accommodations. Still, bear in mind that the trains and the rail beds are very old and poorly maintained. Also, the trains are frequently shut down during the rainy season (roughly December through March or April). The famous train from La Paz to Arica, Chile is presently not operating.

Chile. *Santiago to Puerto Montt or vice versa:* Known as "El Rapido," this diesel train departs Santiago daily at about 6:00 P.M. and arrives the following day in Osorno at about 10 A.M. and in Puerto Montt at about noon. This is a very popular and economical way to travel into the Chilean lake region, famed for its spectacular scenery. The alternative is a two hour flight for about $100. The first part of the train trip traverses the broad and fertile Chilean central valley, which, although somewhat scenic, after a few hours becomes somewhat tedious. This is just fine, because by then it's bedtime. By morning (about 8 A.M.) the train starts entering the scenic mountain and lake region of the south. El Rapido also runs daily from the south to Santiago, departing Puerto Montt at about 4 P.M. and arriving in Santiago at about 11 A.M. the following day; however, it is not as highly recommended for scenery, as you will be traveling at night through a good part of the scenery in the south.

The train cars date from the 1930s and the sleeper car has the original mahogany woodwork and brass fixtures. The train has a diner and club car available to passengers in first class (recliner seats) or sleeper class. Although old and shabby in spots, the train is clean, the service is attentive (but no English is spoken) and though the food is not gourmet it is fresh and acceptable. Sleeper class may be booked in either pullman booth or private compartment with a sink but not with private bathroom facilities. The train also has an auto car, so you can take your car with you for about $50. First class on the train would run about $8 per person, a pullman berth about $18, and a sleeper compartment about $40, accommodating two persons. The train may be booked in advance through a travel agent, who can also book a package tour. It should be booked in advance during the summer vacation season, about December through March. Otherwise, you stand a pretty good chance of making a reservation in Santiago through any of the local travel agencies.

From Puerto Montt you can continue on a unique trip via a combination of bus/boat/bus/boat/bus/boat/bus, crossing a necklace of pristine lakes rimmed by virgin forests, waterfalls, and ice-cream cone snow-capped volcano peaks to San Carlos de Bariloche (Bariloche for short), in Argentina.

Argentina. *Bariloche to Buenos Aires or vice versa:* The "Old Patagonia Express" runs from Bariloche to Buenos Aires or vice versa, and is equally scenic in either direction. The train departs Bariloche on Mondays at about 12:30 P.M. and on Tuesdays and Fridays at 10 A.M., and arrives in Buenos Aires at 8:14 P.M. the following day. The train operates from Buenos Aires to Bariloche on Wednesdays, Saturdays, and Sundays, departing at 8:20 A.M. and arriving at about 6 P.M. the following day. The most scenic part of the trip occurs while traversing the Andes Mountains around Bariloche, and, as you can see by the timetable, this part of the trip is during daylight hours in both directions. The very tedious part (crossing the pampas or extensive grasslands of central Argentina) occurs during both daylight and nighttime hours regardless of the direction and lasts for about 20 hours of the 32–34-hour trip. Like the trains in Chile, the trains in Argentina, though old, are clean, service is accommodating, and the food is good.

Brazil. Although the trains are good in Brazil, the bus system is better. The main point to remember is that Brazil is larger than the continental United States, and only slightly smaller than the territorial United States. To contemplate travel overland in Brazil, either by bus or train, is as considerable an undertaking as a tour around the United States, including Alaska and Hawaii.

CRUISES IN SOUTH AMERICA. There are many special cruises within South America; though most of these are round-trip excursions from a given port. With a few exceptions, there are no cruises in South America that would take you from one point to another to enhance an ongoing itinerary. The two exceptions are:

Enasa has regular sailings on the Amazon River between Belém and Manaus (seven days) and Manaus to Belem (six days). Minimum category is about $450 per person, double for an inside cabin. Very little English is spoken. The M/V *Tuna* has weekly sailings on the Rio Negro out of Manaus. The four-day/three-night cruise is currently $499 per person, based on double occupancy.

Either of these two programs may be booked through Unique Adventures, Inc. or Ladatco Tours. (See "How to Go.")

The M/V *Amazonas* has weekly sailings from Leticia, Colombia, on the Amazon River to Iquitos, Peru, or vice versa. The M/V *Amazonas* departs every Saturday, arriving in Iquitos on Tuesday. It departs Iquitos every Wednesday, arriving in Leticia on Saturday. The four-day/three-night cruise in an air-conditioned cabin costs an expensive $495 per person or $250 per person without air-conditioning, both based on double occupancy. There is same-day air service connecting Leticia with either Manaus, Brazil, or Bogotá, Colombia, and Iquitos with Lima, Peru.

BUS SERVICE WITHIN SOUTH AMERICA. While service is good on major highways and prices are low, schedule and tariff books are not distributed outside of the local area. Schedules and fares change constantly, and there is little or no cooperation between lines. The cost is determined by the route taken.

Bus service is available in South America over practically every road shown on a map. In the interior, you're apt to find crowded trucks with plank seats and few comforts. On the other hand, excellent buses run regularly between major capitals and oceanside resorts.

In Argentina, Pluma Bus Company operates international connections, especially to Brazil, and is a good bus system for domestic travel.

In Bolivia there are direct buses to Puno, Peru, from La Paz on Transturin; luxury service is about $20.

In Brazil there is direct bus service to Rio, São Paulo, and Salvador, which is available through Pluma Bus Line. Other lines serve Brasilia, Bêlo Horizonte, Porto Alegre and other cities.

The Chilean Government operates a hotel chain, HONSA (Agustinas 1301, Santiago), which has 12–15-day bus tours for the thrifty minded.

Peru has regular bus and colectivo services from Lima to the most important centers on the coast and sierras. Colectivos carry up to five passengers and charge fares higher than those on regular buses.

In Uruguay, bus service is first-class. There are two companies: Onda (Plaza Libertad 912333) and COT (Plaza Independence).

Venezuela has long-distance buses that are air-conditioned and quite comfortable. Buses leave Caracas for all the main towns in Venezuela from the Nuevo Circo Terminal on Avenida Bolivar Esteb, off Avenida Fuerzas Armadas off Avenida Bolivar.

BY CAR. For the first-time traveler to South America, traveling by your own car is not recommended, since road conditions and facilities are not as developed as those in North America or Europe.

However, for those experienced travelers who have a knowledge of Spanish and Portuguese, and want to travel by car, it is essential to have a reliable, fairly new car, preferably of a well-known make, for which spare parts are available in South America. Good repair facilities are available; gasoline and oil can be obtained everywhere, but high-test premium gasoline is hard to come by except in the capitals. Use tires with tubes and take extra tubes along. Consult your automobile dealer about what spare parts to carry and be sure to take a towing cable, hand pump, pressure gauge, and tube repair kit.

For border crossings, beside car registration and license, you'll need about 25 passport-size photos and a *Carnet de Passages en Douane.* See the consulates or embassies of specific countries for details.

Car Rentals. Most major South American cities have local or international Rent-A-Car Services. Avis has extensive operations throughout the continent and there are several good local car-rental services in various cities. Hertz and National are also well represented. Budget has offices in Chile (Santiago), Ecuador (Guayaquil and Quito), and in Venezuela (Caracas, Margarita Island, Puerto Ordaz, Barcelona, Puerto La Cruz, and Maracaibo).

Prices will vary according to area and the type of car you rent, but unlimited mileage and some form of insurance are usually included in the price. You will have to budget for local taxes and for the price of gasoline.

Leaving South America

DEPARTURE TAXES. Almost all South American countries charge a departure tax, which is subject to change without notice. Taxes may be paid in U.S. currency unless indicated otherwise. The amounts are given in the "Facts at Your Fingertips" sections of individual country chapters.

CUSTOMS RETURNING HOME. American residents who are out of the U.S. at least 48 hours and have claimed no exemption during the previous 30 days are entitled to bring in duty-free up to $400 worth of bona fide gifts or items for their own personal use.

The duty-free allowance is based on the full fair *retail* value of the goods. You must now list the items purchased and *they must accompany you when you return.* So keep all receipts handy with the detailed list, and it is obviously wise to pack the goods together in one case. Every member of a family is entitled to this same exemption, regardless of age, and their exemptions can be pooled. Minors do not receive exemptions on alcohol and tobacco.

One liter of alcoholic beverages and up to 100 non-Cuban cigars may be included in the exemption if you are 21 years of age or older. You may bring in up to 200 cigarettes for your personal use. Alcoholic beverages in excess of one quart are subject to customs duty and internal revenue tax.

Only one bottle of certain perfumes that are trademarked in the United States (Lanvin, Chanel, etc.) may be brought, unless you get written permission from the manufacturer to bring more. Other perfumes are limited by weight or value.

You do not have to pay duty on art objects or antiques provided that they are over 100 years old, so be sure to ask the dealer for a certificate establishing the age of whatever you buy. Remember, however, that many countries regulate the removal of cultural properties and works of art, and that in recent years the trade in pre-Colombian art everywhere in the Americas has come under very severe regulation subject to criminal penalties if violated.

Under the GSP (Generalized System of Preferences) plan some 2,800 items from *developing* countries may be brought into the U.S. duty free. The purpose of this is to help the economic development of such countries by encouraging their exports. In South America, GSP countries are: Argentina, Bolivia, Brazil, Chile, Colombia, Ecuador, Guyana, Panama, Paraguay, Peru, Suriname, Uruguay, and Venezuela. Because the lists are reviewed annually, write to Department of the Treasury, U.S. Customs Service, Washington, D.C. 20229, and ask for the latest edition of the leaflet, *GSP & the Traveller.*

Do not bring foreign meats, fruits, plants, soil, or other agricultural items into the United States. It is illegal to bring in foreign agricultural items without individual permission because they can spread destructive plant or animal pests and diseases. For more information, read the pamphlet *Customs Hints,* or write to Quarantines, Department of Agriculture, Federal Center Bldg., Hyattsville, MD 20782, and ask for Program Aid No. 1083, entitled "Traveler's Tips on Bringing Food, Plant and Animal Products into the United States."

Register (including serial numbers) with U.S. Customs your furs, jewelry, watches, rings, cameras, tape recorders, and other merchandise that might be mistaken as items purchased abroad. If not, obtain a registration at the U.S. Customs office at your departure airport. Otherwise, you may have to pay duty and then file for a refund once you can provide proof of purchase in the U.S.

British subjects returning to Britain: You may bring home (1) 200 cigarettes or 100 cigarillos or 50 cigars or 250 grams of tobacco; (2) two liters of table wine and, in addition, (a) one liter of alcohol over 22% by volume (most spirits) or (b) two liters of alcohol under 22% by volume (fortified or sparkling wine); (3) 60 milliliters of perfume and ¼ liter of toilet water; and (4) other goods up to a value of £32.

Canadian residents: In addition to personal effects, people 16 years and older may bring in the following articles: a maximum of 50 cigars, 200 cigarettes, 2 pounds of tobacco, and 1.1 liters of wine or liquor, provided these are declared to customs on arrival. The total exemption is $300, and unsolicited gift mailings may be up to $40 in value. Canadian customs regulations are strictly enforced; you are recommended to check what your allowances are and to make sure you have kept receipts for whatever you have bought abroad. For complete details ask for the Canadian Customs brochure "*I Declare.*"

ADVENTURE VACATIONS

by
KURT KUTAY and JENNY KELLER

Kurt Kutay, a freelance writer living in Seattle, has guided adventure trips in South America for more than 10 years. Jenny Keller is a professional travel writer living in Seattle.

The New World holds the same fascination and attractions for modern-day adventure travelers as it did for early explorers. The Andes Mountains, which divide the entire continent from north to south, are the longest range in the world; the Amazon basin spans nine countries and contains the greatest expanse of rain forest on earth, habitat for an immense diversity of plants and animals. You can follow in the footsteps of Spanish explorer Francisco de Orellana where he crossed the Andes to discover the Amazon, or you can hike and explore the Galapagos Islands where Charles Darwin formulated his theories of evolution. You can join a dig to unearth relics of past civilizations or escape the tourist centers and discover indigenous cultures in various stages of assimilation into modern civilization.

Today trekking in the Andes, Amazon jungle expeditions, and other off-beat travel opportunities in South America have become more available, thanks to the development of facilities in remote areas and tour services catering to the fit and adventurous. The safety record of established tour operators is excellent, although travel to remote areas in South America is subject to delays, inconveniences, and risks. Few trips to South America go entirely as planned; this is particularly true of adventure trips. Adventure vacations are commonly split into soft and hard adventures.

A hard adventure requires a substantial degree of physical participation, although you don't necessarily need technical skills or athletic abilities. In most cases previous travel experience in developing countries is recommended but not required; a doctor's approval may be needed as well. In a soft adventure the destination itself, rather than the means of travel, is often what makes it an adventure. Although a day's activity might include easy rafting or hiking you can usually count on a hot shower and warm bed at night.

Far more adventure-tour operators exist than can be listed in this chapter. Most are small and receive little publicity outside their local areas, so contact the relevant country's tourist office if you have a specific area of interest. Below are the addresses of the major adventure-tour operators mentioned in this chapter. In addition, some local tour operators are listed in the "Facts at Your Fingertips" sections of the appropriate chapters.

Above the Clouds Trekking (Box 398, Worcester, MA 06102; tel. 508–799–4499, fax 508–797–4779).

Adventure Associates (13150 Coit Rd., Suite 110, Dallas, TX 75240; tel. 800–527–2500 or 214–907–0414, fax 214–783–1286).

Adventure Center (1311 63rd St., Suite 200, Emeryville, CA 94608; tel. 415–654–1879).

Amazon Tours and Cruises (1013 S. Central Ave., Glendale, CA 91204; tel. 800–423–2791 or, in CA, 800–477–4400, fax 818–246–9909).

American Alpine Institute (1212 24th St., Bellingham, WA 98225; tel. 206–671–1505).

Andean Treks (65 Prentiss St., Cambridge, MA 02140; tel. 617–864–1422, fax 617–864–2303).

Anglers Travel Connections (3220 W. Sepulveda Blvd., Suite B, Torrance, CA 90505; tel. 800–624–8429 or 213–325–9628).

Big 5 Expeditions (2151 E. Dublin-Granville Rd., Suite 215, Columbus, OH 43229; tel. 800–541–2790 or 614–898–0036).

Brazil Nuts (79 Sanford St., Fairfield, CT 06430; tel. 800–553–9959 or 203–259–7900, fax 203–259–3177).

CanoAndes Expeditions (37–12 75th St., 3rd floor, Queens, NY 11372; tel. 800–242–5554 or 718–446–8577).

Close-Up Expeditions (1031 Ardmore Ave., Oakland, CA 94610; tel. 415–465–8955).

Earthquest (Box 1614, Flagstaff, AZ 86002; tel. 602–779–5415).

Earthwatch (680 Mount Auburn St., Watertown, MA 02272; tel. 617–926–8200, fax 617–926–8532).

Ecotour Expeditions (Box 1066, Cambridge, MA 02238; tel. 800–688–1822 or 617–876–5817).

Expediciones Andinas (Box 66, Riobamba, Ecuador, tel. 962845).

Explorandes (Bolognesi 159, Lima 18, Peru; tel. 46–9889, fax 45–4686).

Far Horizons (Box 1529, 16 Fern La., San Anselmo, CA 94960; tel. 415–457–4575).

Field Guides, Inc. (Box 160723, Austin, TX 78716; tel. 512–327–4953).

Fits Equestrian (2011 Alamo Pintado Rd., Solvang, CA 93463; tel. 800–666–FITS or 805–688–9494).

Focus Tours (Rua Grao Mogol 502s/223, Sion 30 330, Belo Horizonte, MG Brasil Embratur 07367–00–41–1; tel. 223–0358).

4th Dimension Tours (1150 N.W. 72nd Ave., Suite 250, Miami, FL 33126; tel. 800–343–0020 or 305–477–1525).

Frontiers (Box 959, Pearce Mill Rd., Wexford, PA 15090; tel. 800–245–1950 or 412–935–1577).

Hanns Ebensten Travel (513 Fleming St., Key West, FL 33040; tel. 305–294–8174).

Inca Floats (1311 63rd St., Emeryville, CA 94608; tel. 414–420–1550, fax 415–420–0947).

International Expeditions (1776 Independence Ct., Birmingham, AL 35216; tel. 800–633–4734).

Joseph Van Os Photo Safaris (Box 655, Vashon Island, WA 98070; tel. 206–463–5383).

Lihué Expediciones (Belgrano 262, #104, San Isidro (1642), Buenos Aires, Argentina; tel. 747–7689, fax 112206).

Linda Novick International Art Institute (42 Abeel St., Kingston, NY 12401; tel. 914–331–3179);

Lost World Adventures (1189 Autumn Ridge Dr., Marietta, GA 30066; tel. 800–999–0558 or 404–971–8586).

Magri Turismo (Casilla 4469, La Paz, Bolivia; tel. 341201, fax 005912).

Metropolitan Tours (Box 310, Quito, Ecuador; tel. 593–256–0050, fax 593–256–4655).

Mountain Travel (6420 Fairmount Ave., El Cerrito, CA 94530; tel. 415–527–8100 or 800–227–2384, fax 415–525–7710).

Oceanic Society Expeditions (Fort Mason Center, Bldg. E, San Francisco, CA 94123; tel. 415–441–1106.

Overseas Adventure Travel (345 Broadway, Cambridge, MA 02139; tel. 800–221–0814 or 617–876–0533, fax 617–876–0455).

Peaks and Places (Box 622, Avon, CO 81620; tel. 303–949–5479).

Quest Nature Tours, represented by Worldwide Adventures, Inc. (920 Yonge St., Suite 747, Toronto, Ont. M4W 3C7; Canada; tel. 800–387–1483 or, in Toronto, 416–963–9163).

Questers Tours (257 Park Ave So., New York, NY 10010; tel 800–468–8668 or 212–673–3120, fax 212–473–0178).

RioAndes (Box 1614, Flagstaff, AZ 86002; tel. 602–779–5415).

Rod and Reel Adventures (3507 Tully Rd., Modesto, CA 95356; tel. 800–356–6982 or 209–524–7775).

Safaricentre (3201 N. Sepulveda Blvd., Manhattan Beach, CA 90266; tel. 800–223–6046 or 213–546–4411).

Sobek Expeditions (Box 1089, Angels Camp, CA 95222; tel. 800–777–7939).

Society Expeditions (3131 Elliott Ave., Suite 700, Seattle, WA 98121; tel. 800–548–8669).

Southern Cross Expeditions (Bowling Green Station, Box 1228, New York, NY 10274; tel. 800–359–0193).

Southwind Adventures (1861 Camino Lumbre, Santa Fe, NM 87505; tel. 505–438–7120).

Turtle Tours (Box 1147, Dept. SP, Carefree, AZ 85377; tel. 602–488–3688).

University Research Expeditions Program (University of California, Berkeley, CA; tel. 415–642–6586).

Victor Emanuel Nature Tours (Box 33008, Austin, TX 78764; tel. 800–328–VENT or 512–328–5221).

Wilderness Travel (801 Allston Way, Berkeley, CA 94710; tel. 800–247–6700 or 415–548–0420).

Wildland Adventures (3516 NE 155th, Seattle, WA 98155; tel. 800–345–4453 or 206–365–0686, fax 206–363–6615).

Wings, Inc. (Box 31930, Tucson, AZ 85751; tel. 602–749–3175).

Woodstar Tours, Inc. (908 S. Massachusetts Ave., DeLand, FL 32724; tel. 904–736–0327).

AMAZON CRUISES

Spanning 4,200 miles, the Amazon River is the longest river in the world. From its source in southern Peru, the river encompasses western Brazil, eastern Peru and Ecuador, southern Colombia, and northern Bolivia. The basin drained by the river and its more than 1,000 tributaries comprises the last great wooded wilderness of its kind on earth, a vast natural laboratory with over half the world's species of birds and thousands of species of mammals and plants. Though the Amazon basin's primary rain forest is a fast-disappearing natural resource, the Amazon River remains a vital reservoir for plants, animals, and peoples found nowhere else on earth. The arteries of transportation in this enormous region—the size of the continental United States—are the rivers, streams, canals and oxbow lakes that crisscross its surface. Therefore, the best way to see the Amazon is by boat, from a luxury cruise expedition with all the amenities to a low-budget adventure in native dugout canoes. Traditional riverboat cruises, with private or shared cabins, are also quite popular.

BRAZIL

Season: Year-round.

Locations: Manaus, upper Amazon, Rio Negro, Belem.

Cost: From $2,990 for eight-day and from $4,750 for 17-day luxury expedition cruises, and from $1,750 for 12-day Ecotour expedition.

Tour Operators: CanoAndes Expeditions, Ecotour Expeditions, Society Expeditions.

In Brazil, the Amazonia region covers an area of over 2.7 million square miles, mostly lowland forest. Though there is a small number of large cities, the continental-size floodplain of Amazonia is still almost entirely covered with primitive tropical forest and crossed with great but thinly settled rivers. The scope for adventure here is broad. For luxury expedition cruising, **Society Expeditions** is a good choice for an eight-day cruise along the upper Amazon and Rio Negro. Their ships comfortably accommodate up to 160 passengers. Each stateroom has an outside view, air-conditioning, shower, and toilet. Because the main ships too large to venture off the major waterways, swift go-everywhere Zodiac boats are lowered each day to allow passengers easy access up twisting tributaries. A team of naturalists and specialists accompanies each expedition to provide leadership and conduct seminars. Trips depart in September and October, roundtrip from Manaus. Longer cruises of up to 17 days are also available.

Ecotour Expeditions offers a variety of natural-history trips on a smaller scale (10–15 participants), but trips are perhaps slightly more adventuresome. They also use expedition vessels (60 feet or more in length) on the main rivers and smaller boats with outboard motors to enter the forest directly. Among the ecological zones toured is the *igapo*, or black-water flooded forest. A sample itinerary consists of seven full days' travel on the Rio Negro, where a number of native Brazilians live in tribal houses and practice their customs, with stops in the Analvilhanas Archipelago, the Lago Januari Ecological Park, and Manaus, capital of Amazonas state. Ecotour Expeditions sponsors one- to two-week trips in the Ecuadorian Amazon as well. **CanoAndes Expeditions** is well represented throughout the Brazilian Amazon, with options ranging from six-day round-trip luxury cruises from Belem or Manaus to riverboat cruises along the Rio Negro, as well as lodge-based tours and private exploratory expeditions by Indian dugout canoe to any requested part of the Amazon jungle.

PERU

Season: Year-round.

Locations: Iquitos to Leticia, Pacaya-Samiria National Reserve.

Cost: From $395. for four-day cruise (air-conditioning, private facilities) to $1,090 for eight-day cruise.

Tour Operators: Amazon Tours and Cruises, Oceanic Society Expeditions.

Located on the upper Amazon in northeastern Peru, Iquitos is an ideal jumping-off spot for a jungle adventure. **Amazon Tours and Cruises** offers a range of services from here, including four-day downriver cruises from Iquitos to Tabatinga, Brazil, and Leticia, Colombia, aboard the *Rio Amazonas,* and four-day upriver cruises operating in reverse. Itineraries may be combined for a six-day roundtrip cruise. The vessel has 20 air-conditioned cabins with private facilities and six non-air-conditioned cabins with shared facilities. Three-day cruises between Iquitos and Leticia aboard the *Arca* (of similar design) are also available. Among the many other options available is the *Margarita*, a handsome, two-deck wooden riverboat that departs Sundays on five-night cruises to the rain forest in the Madre Selva area downriver from Iquitos, an ideal area for fishing, birding, and orchid or butterfly collecting. The 68-foot vessel carries 14 passengers in seven compact cabins with shared facilities. Amenities are rustic.

Oceanic Society Expeditions penetrates the world of the Peruvian Amazon on two eight-day expeditions (one in June, one in July) cruising the upper Amazon, Tahuayo, and Ucayali rivers aboard the *Marguerita*. Destination: the Pacaya-Samiria National Reserve, the largest nature reserve in Peru. A high point is the observation of lively pink freshwater dolphins. The itinerary also includes easy nature hikes into the rain forest and a visit to an Indian village to observe traditional customs. Small launches, used for excursions along narrow tributaries, offer excellent bird-watching in the swampy marshlands of the preserve.

AMAZON JUNGLE CAMPING

Because the Amazon River provides an easy and natural access to the jungle, it is a great starting point for Amazon-jungle camping excursions. Transportation is usually provided by expedition boats (typical thatch-roof motorboats), speedboats, and canoes. Passengers can expect to sleep on board in hammocks, at improvised campsites in the jungle, or on sleeping mats in *tambos* (thatch-roof shelters with raised flooring) located deep in the jungle. Since these camping expeditions are more of the rough-and-ready nature they can be tremendously rewarding for the adventure seeker who wants to see the deep rain forest at close range and who enjoys sleeping in the jungle miles from the nearest village and exploring the Amazon backcountry by boat and on foot.

ECUADOR

Season: May–August.

Locations: Amazon basin, the highlands.

Cost: From $1,790 for 16 days, round-trip from Quito.

Tour Operator: Wilderness Travel.
Though a camping expedition to the headwaters of the Amazon is not always easy or comfortable, it certainly gives you a deeper understanding of Amazon ecosystems and culture. Tour guide Randy Borman, an American born in the Amazon to missionary parents, has spent his life roaming the forest trail with Cofan Indian friends—hunting, exploring, and learning the ways of the jungle. He speaks the Cofan language fluently, is an excellent naturalist, and provides a fascinating perspective on jungle lifestyle and survival. **Wilderness Travel**'s 16-day expedition with Randy takes you deep into the forest to meet the Cofans. Daily expeditions are by dugout canoe and include hikes along jungle trails. There are eight nights of jungle camping in communal huts built on stilts; other nights are spent in hotels in the highlands.

PERU

Season: June–August.

Locations: Manu National Park, Iquitos and environs.

Cost: From $1,490 for eight days to $2,390 for 19 days.

Tour Operators: Amazon Tours and Cruises, Oceanic Society Expeditions, Wilderness Travel, Wildland Adventures.

Located in Peru's Amazon basin, Manu National Park is the most undisturbed, biologically rich region on the continent. Protected by unnavigable rivers, impenetrable forests, and the towering Andes, this remote region is now accessible to small groups. In Manu, wildlife flourishes unmolested. Jaguars, rare giant otters, woolly and howler monkeys, and capybara, the world's largest rodent, are only some of the mammals you're likely to see. Squadrons of parrots, including three species of macaw, thrive in Manu; and among the reptiles in strong evidence is the rare black caiman. A marvelous stillness prevails in the rain forest, where you can observe this fascinating wildlife on easy day trips on foot or by dugout canoe and motorized boats. Several tour operators offer Manu as a separate itinerary or in combination with mountain trekking in the highlands. Accommodations include tent camping and jungle lodges.

If you prefer a more comfortable setting, the Amazon Camp and Club Amazonia, operated by **Amazon Tours and Cruises,** offer a good alternative to tents. The camp and club overlook a tree-lined tributary, the Momon River, where the only traffic is the occasional native family making its way by motorboat to the market in Iquitos. Constructed entirely of native material, with thatch roofs and solid-bamboo siding, the camp has 42 screened rooms, each with private facilities but no electricity. The 20 private bungalows of Club Amazonia, located a few miles upstream, provide a base for days of easy sports and mellow activities. Boats are available for day trips or night cruises. A stay at the camp or club may be combined with more rugged Amazon River expeditions that depart from Iquitos to explore the less traveled tributaries of the region. A native guide, expert in the ways of the jungle, accompanies each expedition, along with a boatman and a cook. Basic expedition equipment is provided, including mosquito nets, sleeping mats and sheets, cooking gear and eating utensils, lanterns, and a basic first-aid kit.

BICYCLING

Traveling by bicycle through the rural landscape of South America is a great way to open doors to a more personal connection with local people. When you're on a bike, life is taken at a leisurely pace; you can stop whenever you like to rest or visit. Villages and small towns throughout South America are connected by dirt roads that see few motor vehicles, or even bicycles for that matter. Biking along these roads gives you opportunities to gain insight into a fast-disappearing world.

ECUADOR

Season: May–August, January.

Location: Northern Ecuador highlands.

Cost: From $1,995 for 15 days; includes rural inns and five-star city hotels.

Tour Operator: Andean Treks.

This moderately strenuous inn-to-inn bicycling adventure takes you on a circuit of the 15,000-foot Imbabura Volcano in northern Ecuador's scenic highlands, home to several distinct indigenous groups. Highlights include a visit to the Indian crafts market in Otavalo, biking to a farm in a cloud forest, and pedaling beneath the snows of Cotopaxi Volcano. There are 21-speed off-road bikes for rent, or you can bring your own.

PERU

Season: May–June, October; other departures on request.

Locations: Machu Picchu, Amazon.

Cost: From $1,750 for 16 days. Bikes available for rent.

Tour Operators: Above the Clouds Trekking, Andean Treks.
Peru is a bicyclist's paradise. Cycle amid ancient ruins in the wondrous Sacred Valley of the Incas near Machu Picchu and down into the Amazon rain forest. **Andean Treks'** moderate bike adventure includes six nights' camping, one night at Machu Picchu, and a canoe expedition in Manu National Park. **Above the Clouds Trekking** offers a 16-day tour including five days bicycling from the ancient Incan capital of Cuzco down to the Urubamba River and up to the village of Tres Cruces. Here you can leave your bike behind and end the trip with a four-day trek along the Inca Trail to Machu Picchu. There's a support truck to carry gear.

VENEZUELA

Season: Year-round.

Locations: Merida, Trans-Andean Highway, Sierra Nevada National Park.

Cost: From $890 per week. Includes hotel/inn accommodations, meals, vehicle support, guide services. Bike rental available at $100 per week.

Tour Operators: Lost World Adventures, Safaricentre.
The Venezuelan Andes are a treat for mountain bikers seeking breathtaking scenery and plenty of sunshine. This mountainous region is crisscrossed by scenic roads and trails that provide excellent routes, ranging from tropical cloud forest to highlands. If you want a greater challenge, high unpaved passes lead to secluded mountain lagoons and picturesque villages. When you've had enough pedaling, ascend Pico Espejo on the world's highest and longest aerial cable car. Two-week tours include the Andes, Venezuela's eastern Caribbean coast, and the Gran Sabana.

BIRDING TOURS

From the grasslands of the Pantanal and Llanos to the marshes and savannas of the pampas, and from coastal rain forests and montane cloud forests to the steaming jungle of the Amazon Basin, South America offers a remarkable diversity of bird life. Countless species of birds, delightful weather, superb scenery, comfortable accommodations, and some of the world's finest naturalists and ornithologists combine to make for once-in-a-lifetime vacations in this birder's paradise.

ARGENTINA

Season: October–December.

Locations: Northern Argentina: Chaco, northern Andes; southern Argentina: the pampas, Patagonia.

Cost: From $2,495 to $4,250 for 17–20 days, and $4,695 for 32 days.

Tour Operators: Field Guides Inc., Victor Emanuel Nature Tours.

Dominated in the west by the towering Andes and in the center and east by the vast expanse of the chaco woodland and coastal area, northern Argentina holds one of South America's most interesting concentrations of bird life. The birds of the pampas in southern Argentina are also extraordinary. Ponds, marshes, and grasslands are the natural habitats of immense numbers of birds, including greater rheas, waterfowl, swans, red shoveler, and a host of others. On the Patagonian coast, most tours explore both the renowned Valdes Peninsula and Punta Tombo. The coastline here teems with seabirds, and chances are good for viewing marine mammals, as well. Punta Tombo is the site of a colony of some one million Magellanic penguins. The Patagonian desert scrub also harbors scores of Darwin's rheas, elegant crested tinamous, guanacos, and a number of small birds. Birding tours include the grasslands around Rio Grande, the forests of the far south at Ushuaia, and the shores of the Beagle Channel. From a boat on the channel, numerous seabirds, including a variety of albatrosses, petrels, cormorants, gulls, and waterfowl, can be seen. **Victor Emanuel Nature Tours** range from 11 to 17 days and promise to be among the most comprehensive natural-history tours conducted in the country. For longer but similar itineraries, **Field Guides Inc.** offers an 18-day northern Argentina tour and a 17-day southern Argentina tour. These may be combined for a total of 32 days. With either company you can expect comfortable, quaint accommodations with world-class ornithologists and naturalists as your guides.

BRAZIL

Season: Year-round.

Locations: The pampas, Pantanal, Itatiaia National Park, Amazon Basin.

Cost: From $950 for six days to $4,250 for 20 days.

Tour Operators: Field Guides, Inc.; Turtle Tours; Victor Emanuel Nature Tours; Wings, Inc.

In southeastern Brazil, bird habitats range from coastal rain forest and wet pampas to montane cloud forest and plateau grassland. This region has long been isolated from the mainstream of Amazonian evolution by the dry areas of central Brazil, and many distinctive species of birds have evolved. Such breathtaking birds as the red-billed curassow, bare-throated bellbird, and banded cotinga have their last stronghold here, and small birds abound in the rain forests. Midway between Rio de Janeiro and Sao Paulo is Brazil's second-highest mountain, in beautiful Itatiaia National Park. The road up the mountain winds through lush cloud forest and dark tunnels of giant bamboo, where restless flocks of colorful tanagers forage and secretive antbirds skulk. A family-run inn here invites longer stays for extensive birding in the area. Many companies offer tours through these regions and through Brazil's Pantanal, a vast area of seasonally flooded grassland considered by some naturalists to be the most stunning spectacle of the Americas. The Pantanal teems with waterbirds and landbirds, including the spectacular hyacinth macaw, the largest parrot in the world.

ECUADOR

Season: Year-round.

Locations: Quito, Mt. Pichincha, Rio Napo, Amazon.

Cost: From $1,995 for two weeks to $4,745 for four weeks.

Tour Operators: Quest Nature Tours, Field Guides Inc.

This bird-watcher's haven has a remarkable diversity of habitat: the steaming Amazonian rain forests in the east, the lush temperate and subtropical forests on the slopes of the Andes, the paramo grasses and marshes above timberline. Each region is home to its own variety of birds—hummingbirds, the gigantic Andean condor, bush-tyrants, brush finches, and others in higher elevations and the zigzag heron, harpy eagle, Salvin's and nocturnal curassows, among others, in the jungle.

A pleasant addition to any tour is a visit to La Selva Lodge on the Rio Napo, one of the premier destinations in Amazonia for birding and jungle explorations. Among three tours offered by **Field Guides Inc.** is a memorable 12-day exploration of the Galapagos, where birds live that are found nowhere else on earth, such as the flightless cormorant.

VENEZUELA

Season: December–February.

Location: The Llanos.

Cost: From $2,575 for 16 days.

Tour Operators: Field Guides Inc., Lost World Adventures, Quest Nature Tours, Victor Emanuel Nature Tours, Woodstar Tours.

A trip to Venezuela should include a visit to the vast expanse of savanna known as the Llanos. While there, many visitors choose to stay at Hato Pinero. This huge private ranch has been in the same family for nearly 40 years, during which no hunting was permitted, allowing a fabulous cross-section of habitats and wildlife to thrive. Birds are especially abundant here. Among those you may see are seven species of ibis, herons, the primitive-looking hoatzin, and many raptors. Even yellow-knobbed curassows and the elegant sunbittern are easy to spot, as are scarlet macaws; noisy thorn birds and a host of smaller birds abound in the forests adjacent to the ranch.

CULTURAL TOURS

Many travelers to South America are motivated by the archaeological heritage preserved here in religious sites, fortresses, terraces, and tombs. Others seek the living legacy of cultural expression found in local art and handicrafts, created by South American artists from traditions dating to the earliest human settlements in the Andes. Still others are drawn to experience the cultures of South America's rapidly vanishing indigenous tribes. Conserving these cultures is important: embedded in the fabric of so-called primitive societies are centuries-old secrets for living harmoniously with nature. For all these interests, South America offers a stimulating variety of culturally oriented adventure tours.

CHILE AND EASTER ISLAND

Season: February.

Locations: Santiago, Easter Island.

Cost: From $2,295 for 12 days (Easter Island land cost only) to $3,195 for 17 days (Chile and Easter Island, land only). Approximate round-trip airfare from Miami via Santiago to Easter Island is $1,500.

Tour Operators: Far Horizons, Hanns Ebensten Travel, Sobek Expeditions.

Despite its remote location in the Pacific Ocean, 2,300 miles west of Chile, wind-swept Easter Island continues to draw hundreds of visitors each year to its unique open-air archaeological museum. Nearly 1,000 stone statues, or *moai,* stand gazing with brooding eyes over the island's gently rolling hills, and hundreds of perplexing petroglyphs stand out from their rock surfaces. Sites to visit here are numerous: Hangaroa village, where all 2,000 inhabitants of Easter Island live; Rano Raraku, the quarry where the massive moai were carved and many unfinished giants remain;

Tongariki, site of stunning petroglyphs; the ancient village of Orongo, where the Festival of the Bird Man was held each spring until the 1860s and now famed for its hundreds of intricate petroglyphs; and Vaihu, with its many large moai. The **Far Horizons** 18-day discovery tour, led by archaeologist Dr. Georgia Lee, offers the most extensive exploration of the island. **Hanns Ebensten Travel** offers a cushy 10-day tour, including five days on the island and three in Santiago. **Sobek Expeditions** has a more rugged four-day adventure by foot and jeep; boats to the island depart every Wednesday from Santiago.

ECUADOR

Season: April–September.

Locations: From Quito to Cuenca, Ecuadorian Amazon.

Cost: From $1,455 for 15 days; watercolor workshop from $2,189; jungle trip to Jivaro Indians from $1,550 for 16 days.

Tour Operators: Linda Novick International Art Institute, Turtle Tours, Wildland Adventures.

Traveling by private vehicle from Quito to Cuenca, on **Wildland Adventures'** comprehensive cultural tour of Ecuador, you will visit several remote Indian markets and handicraft centers, stopping frequently to view (and perhaps buy) weavings, pottery, handwoven rugs and baskets, ceramics, and wood carvings. On short, nonstrenuous treks, you can also explore significant archaeological ruins, including Ingapirca, the main Incan ruin in Ecuador. Between treks, accommodations are in hacienda-style inns near small towns; on trek, large three-person tents are used. If you would like to study painting in exotic and colorful locations, painter and art teacher **Linda Novick** holds watercolor workshops each March in Cuenca.

For a different kind of cultural tour deep in the Ecuadorian Amazon, **Turtle Tours** takes visitors by jeep, small plane, foot, and balsa canoe into the heart of the jungle to live among the Jivaro Indians for six days. Due to their isolation, these Indians have been able to maintain many of their customs and rituals, including head shrinking, an intricate rite once performed on the remains of humans, but now done only on those of monkeys. You can join your Indian hosts in fishing, jungle treks to thermal waterfalls, and canoe trips to neighboring villages. Monthly departures (except March and April) include hotels, meals, guides.

PERU

Season: May–October; Sipan, year-round.

Locations: Cuzco, Pitumarca, Chincheros, San Blas, Urubamba, Lima, Sipan.

Cost: $1,425–$1,925 for up to 18 days; Sipan, from $1,294 for 10 days, including airfare from Miami, lodging, and most meals.

Tour Operators: Andean Treks, Earthquest, 4th Dimension Tours.

It's been called the most spectacular archaeological event in the past half century—and it occurred as recently as 1988, in Sipan, Peru. Here archaeologists unearthed a sealed, pre-Incan tomb to find treasures of pure gold: ornate headdresses and masks, exquisite jewelry, and intricately sculpted figures. This priceless trove is on permanent display at the Bruning Museum in Sipan. It is also featured on a 10-day archaeological tour sponsored by **4th Dimension Tours,** with departures from Lima on Sundays. Highlights include some of Peru's other ancient ruins: among them, the adobe city of Chan-Chan, the Pyramids of the Sun and Moon, and the Pyramids of Tucume.

The tradition of backstrap weaving goes back 5,000 years, to the earliest human settlements in the Andes. It has continued to this day, absorbing outside influences but still true to the ancient traditions. **Andean Treks** offers a hands-on encounter of this living tradition, taking you to meet weavers in highland villages where the tradition remains strong. One night is spent in a native home, others in four-star hotels. **Earthquest** has a 14-day tour featuring Peru's finest weavers and spinners, instruction in looms, techniques, preparing natural dies, and preparing and spinning alpaca. For ceramics enthusiasts Earthquest also offers a two-week tour that focuses on the traditional designs of the pre-Inca and Inca cultures. The tour includes demonstrations (by local craftsmen) of clays, glazes, and techniques.

VENEZUELA

Season: Year-round, but temperatures are generally more pleasant May–November.

Location: Amazonian rain forest.

Cost: $1,250 for six days and five nights, including round-trip flights from Caracas, hotel/camp accommodations, meals in Indian village, guide, and equipment.

Tour Operator: Lost World Adventures.

The rare chance to observe and interact with indigenous Indians of the Amazonian rain forest is not for the average tourist. Previously available only to a select few explorers, anthropologists, and missionaries, the **Lost World Adventures** tour is still limited (six to a group) to those with serious ecological and anthropological interests. Conditions in these remote locations are extremely primitive: participants sleep in hammocks hung in rustic dwellings and eat local fish and game. Wilderness experience and a high degree of cultural sensitivity are required.

FISHING

Some of the most diverse fishing in the world is found in South America. Anglers can pursue rainbow, brown, brook, and Dolly Varden trout in the Andes of Chile and Argentina. The northeastern portions of Argentina and the entire Amazon basin offer a smorgasbord of freshwater opportunities, from golden dorado and peacock bass to catfish weighing well over 100 pounds. In Venezuela and Ecuador the saltwater aficionado will find plenty of year-round action for billfish and other species.

ARGENTINA

Season: December–April.

Locations: Tierra del Fuego, Patagonia.

Cost: From $1,590 for six full days fishing.

Tour Operators: Anglers Travel Connections, Frontiers.

For anglers Argentina is the southern hemisphere's Alaska, offering world-class brown- and rainbow-trout fishing on clear streams. **Frontiers** offers Argentine angling in three select regions: San Martin de los Andes, Esquel and Los Alerces Park, and Tierra del Fuego. Visited individually or in combination, each area provides an unforgettable trout-fishing experience. In the Rio Grande of Tierra del Fuego, trophy sea-run browns, a rare and coveted prize, abound. **Anglers Travel Connections** conducts expeditions to Patagonian waters, where wild browns and rainbows are found in greater numbers and in significantly larger sizes than in the United States. Group size is limited to six or eight. Early reservations are recommended.

VENEZUELA

Season: Year-round. Consult individual operators for peak seasons.

Locations: Throughout Venezuela.

Cost: $1,400–$2,600 for seven nights. Shorter or longer stays are available.

Tour Operators: Anglers Travel Connections, Rod and Reel Adventures.

In recent years Venezuela has gained a reputation for world-class bonefishing, at El Gran Roque Island. Guri Lake has also established itself as the world's premier place for peacock bass, and Rio Chico offers options for tarpon and snook. **Rod and Reel Adventures** coordinates angling holidays to all of these destinations and others throughout South America. **Anglers Travel Connections** has its own style of "exotic angling adventures," including combination fresh-and-saltwater packages for the best of both worlds, from budget to luxury; custom trips are available.

HORSEBACK RIDING

A horseback trip can be a challenging and rewarding way to explore the rugged beauty of South America. Many kinds of horseback adventures are available to suit your riding ability, stamina, and yen for roughing it. The ultimate trip is one on which you ride to a new location each day and set up camp for the night. These "progressive" trips are ideal for covering the most-scenic features of the region. They are frequently offered in scheduled-date departures but may also be arranged on a custom basis for small groups.

ARGENTINA

Season: Year-round.

Locations: Pampas, Entre Rios region, northern Patagonia, Argentina wine country, the Andes.

Cost: From $705 for seven days to $2,040 for 18 days, including camping, meals, and accommodations in first-class hotels.

Tour Operator: Fits Equestrian, Southern Cross Expeditions.

It takes some traveling to appreciate a country this large, and **Fits Equestrian** has covered all of it with a variety of itineraries at all skill levels. On one end there's a basic seven-day trip, covering traditional gaucho *estancias* (cattle ranches) in the Entre Rios region; at the other extreme is an 18-day tough-adventure tour on which you will ride 11 days on steep mountain trails through the Andes (expect few comforts on this trip).

Southern Cross Expeditions offers two 11-day horseback riding adventures: "Gaucho Trails in the Andes," October–May, starts in the wine country, follows a trail to the south wall of Mt. Aconcagua, and on to the dense woods of the Lake district. "Gaucho Trails in the Pampas," May–October, takes travelers through the lush Ibera marshlands, where birdlife and wildlife are abundant. Riders become guests of the gauchos (cowboys) on private ranches, where they may be asked to take part in farm activities.

CHILE

Season: November–March.

Locations: Andes.

Cost: $1,980 for 13 days, 12 nights (including six nights' camping).

Tour Operator: Fits Equestrian.

Four to seven hours riding per day takes you at a leisurely pace across the Andes from west to east, all the way to the Argentina border. Only basic riding ability is required, although there is some rough terrain.

VENEZUELA

Season: Year-round.

Locations: Merida, El Tisure, Mucuchies.

Cost: Up to $890 for eight days. Includes hotel/inn/camp lodging, meals, horses, and experienced guide.

Tour Operator: Lost World Adventures.

With **Lost World Adventures,** you can ride on Venezuela's high mountain plateaus, or *paramos,* into the heart of charming Andean villages off the beaten path. Riding elevations range from 5,000 to over 12,000 feet. Horses are small but of sturdy local stock, well-adapted to Andean altitude and trail terrain. Both riding and camping experience are recommended.

MOUNTAINEERING

Mountaineering is a hard adventure that can demand all the strength you possess. But despite its discomforts, strenuous exertion and unpredictable hazards, the sport offers enormous rewards: a surge of self-confidence, the thrill of achievement, and exhilaration at reaching a mountain's summit. There are few better arenas for mountain climbing than South America. From the summit of Argentina's towering Aconcagua Mountain to the volcanic peaks of Ecuador, from Venezuela's Andean regions to Bolivia's Cordillera Real range, South America offers some of the finest and most varied mountaineering challenges in the world. Climbers can find services to outfit and guide them into almost any part of South America's mountain ranges.

ARGENTINA

Season: December–March.

Location: Aconcagua Mountain, Patagonia.

Cost: Aconcagua, from $2,250 for 23 days; Patagonia, $1,480 for 13 days.

Tour Operators: American Alpine Institute (AAI), Andean Treks.

About 2,500 feet higher than Alaska's Mt. McKinley, Argentina's Mt. Aconcagua is the highest peak in the Western Hemisphere. When climbed by the Polish Glacier on its eastern face, the route taken by **Andean Treks,** the ascent provides high-quality ice climbing. Routes range from grueling scrambles to severe technical challenges, making this a strenuous, high-altitude ascent for experienced mountaineers only. **American Alpine Institute,** a well-established outfit spearheading new climbs around the world, offers alpine climbs amid the spectacular towers of Patagonia, including a 13-day expedition to the Fitzroy Peak area in February and a 13-day expedition to the Torres del Paine area in March.

BOLIVIA

Season: April–September.

Locations: Lake Titicaca and the Bolivian altiplano, Cordillera Real range.

Cost: From $590 for six days to $1,160 for 13 days. Includes lodging in hotels and tents, meals on climbs, equipment for groups.

Tour Operator: American Alpine Institute.
Though the Cordillera Real of Bolivia offers some of the continent's finest and most varied alpine climbing, it is probably the least known and least scaled range among comparable mountain groups. This is due to the country's remoteness and relatively low rate of traditional tourism. If you prefer climbing in wilderness areas, the Cordillera Real provides an unparalelled opportunity. **American Alpine Institute** has a series of climbing programs here, ranging from sub-alpine day hikes to advanced climbs for experienced mountaineers only. Climbers are required to acclimatize for at least six days before participating in the institute's most strenuous programs, ideally spending the majority of their time between 10,000 and 12,000 feet. To round out their offerings, AAI sponsors a short expedition to the summit of 21,201-foot Nevado Illimani, the highest peak in Bolivia's Cordillera Real. Groups are small.

ECUADOR

Season: November–February.

Locations: Cotopaxi, Illiniza, Chimborazo, El Altar, Antisana; Galapagos.

Cost: $1,540 for 14 days; from $450 for four-day Antisana climb. Includes lodging, meals while in mountains, climbing equipment. Galapagos costs vary with boat and length of trip.

Tour Operator: American Alpine Institute.
The Andes of Ecuador are comprised of two parallel and impressive chains of peaks, rising dramatically from Pacific coastal lowlands on the west and even more abruptly from the Amazon Basin on the east. Most of Ecuador's mountains are of volcanic origin, but although some retain the classic cone shape of a newly formed peak others are broad and complex, with scores of distinct routes and a range of challenges for the climber. The **American Alpine Institute** offers 14-day programs to climb three of the finest peaks of the Andes: 19,348-foot Cotopaxi, 17,260-foot Illiniza, and 20,703-foot Chimborazo, the highest peak in The Cordillera Real. Climbers can also join an optional four-day extension to ascend 18,715-foot Antisana. The approach to this exotic and seldom-climbed peak presents excellent photo opportunities and wildlife viewing. Both of these itineraries can also be followed by a seven-day exploration of the Galapagos Islands by motor launch. Groups are kept small, either three to five climbers with one guide or six to 10 climbers with two guides. Climbing instruction is provided.

PERU

Season: May.

Locations: Cordillera Vilcanota, southern Peru.

Cost: Varies with size of group.

Tour Operator: Andean Treks.
Intermediate climbers seeking high-altitude ice- and snow-climbing experience to improve their mountaineering skills can join an **Andean Treks** climber's workshop in the Vilcanota range of southern Peru. Included are expert instruction, strenuous high-altitude mountaineering, an attempt on 21,000-foot Nevado Ausangate, southern Peru's highest summit, 15 nights camping, and three-star hotels. The program lasts 22 days and begins and ends in Cuzco.

VENEZUELA

Season: Year-round, but the most favorable weather is November–May.

Locations: Merida, Mucuchies, Mt. Toro, Pico Espejo, Pico Bolivar.

Cost: $690 for six days and five nights. Includes hotel/camp accommodations, meals, guide/instructors, and equipment.

Tour Operator: Lost World Adventures.

If you are in excellent physical condition, **Lost World Adventures** offers an exhilarating six-day "Ultimate Andes" trekking and climbing trip that culminates with an ascent of Pico Bolívar, Venezuela's highest peak, at 16,427 feet. Rock-climbing and mountaineering techniques are taught by experienced, English-speaking guides.

NATURE STUDY

The rain forests of the Amazon come first to mind when one thinks of exploring the natural history of South America. And well they should; the Amazon basin extends into all but two countries on the continent. But the natural history of South America is much more than this vast and diverse ecosystem; it includes the isolated table mountains of Venezuela; the rugged Chaco region of Paraguay, Andean glaciers; tablelands and cloud forests, the driest desert in the world on the coasts of Peru and Chile; and the Antarctic environment of Tierra del Fuego. In planning your natural-history trip decide if you want to focus on one particular region for an in-depth exploration or if you would rather experience a variety of ecosystems over a wider area on one trip. Consider being led by a local guide. Many locals are not only trained biologists and skilled guides, but they add a unique cross-cultural dimension to your experience. Small group tours (15 persons) are the best way to see wildlife.

ARGENTINA

Season: October–February.

Locations: Valdes Peninsula, Iguazu Falls, Patagonia.

Cost: $2,000 for 17-day tour.

Operators: Oceanic Society Expeditions, Sobek Expeditions, Wildland Adventures.

Argentina offers a vast array of natural-history experiences, from the tropical forests surrounding Iguazu Falls in the north to the Antarctic environment of Tierra del Fuego, and the Andes Mountains to the Patagonian steppe. One of the most exciting areas with the greatest concentration of wildlife is the Valdes Peninsula on the south Atlantic coast. **Oceanic Society Expeditions,** which specializes in marine natural-history trips, offers an in-depth, 11-day trip to the peninsula region. Trips in October–November feature close-up observation of mating penguins, killer whales feeding on young penguin, southern elephant seals battling for territory, and a wealth of birds and land mammals. **Sobek Expeditions'** South Atlantic Wildlife trip visits the Valdes Peninsula and Tierra del Fuego. **Wildland Adventure's** Argentina Wildlife Odyssey includes both of these plus a visit to the tropical rain forests of Igazu Falls, for a comprehensive natural-history overview.

BRAZIL

Season: Year-round.

Locations: Pantanal, Atlantic Coast, Iguazu Falls.

Cost: From $100 per day for package nature tour.

Operators: Brazil Nuts, Focus Tours, Questers Tours.
The Pantanal, the world's largest wetlands, lies in the center of South America. Unlike the dense rain forests of the Amazon, this marshy grassland makes an ideal place for wildlife observation; during the rainy season (October through March) flooding forces animals to congregate in high areas. Backcountry travelers in the Pantanal will see a spectacle of colorful tropical birds, caimans (alligators), anteaters, capybaras (large rodents), and possibly tracks of the elusive jaguar. **Focus Tours,** a highly respected nature-tour ground operator in Brazil, specializes in the Pantanal and provides qualified naturalist guides who are sensitive to the environment. Their services are available only to preformed groups. **Questers Tours,** which works with Focus Tours in Brazil, offers several innovative, top-quality natural-history tours, one of which includes the Pantanal, Atlantic rain forests, and highland plateaus of central Brazil. **Brazil Nuts** has the widest range of lodge-based Pantanal safaris.

ECUADOR

Season: Year-round.

Location: Galapagos.

Cost: From $900 to $3,000.

Operators: Adventure Associates, Inca Floats, Metropolitan Tours, Wilderness Travel, Wildland Adventures.
For more than 150 years the Galapagos Islands have excited the interest of scientists and nature travelers. This barren, volcanic archipelago is habitat for some of the world's most bizarre animals and plants. Two-thirds of the resident birds and most reptiles at this showcase of evolution are found nowhere else in the world. Traveling throughout the archipelago you can observe first hand the unusual physical and behavioral characteristics that plants and animals have developed, through the evolutionary process of natural selection, to adapt to the unique environment of each island. Since the wildlife in Galapagos National Park never developed a fear of humans you can approach them for close-up photography and observation. One- and two-week cruise itineraries begin in Baltra or San Cristobal. Two-week trips, such as **Wilderness Travel's** "Ultimate Galapagos," are conducted in vessels ranging from cruise ships holding about 100 passengers to small yachts with a capacity of 12 or fewer. Individual space is available on both size vessels through many companies, or you can charter your own yacht for a private group. The trip includes a rigorous but rewarding three-day climb up the Alcedo Volcano. **Inca Floats** has the most departures, along with high-quality natural-history programs. **Adventure Associates** represents **Metropolitan Tours,** the largest Ecuadorian tour operator brokering space on large ships and small yachts alike. **Wildland Adventures** offers an 11-day cruise itinerary on small yachts that includes a visit to Quito and optional extensions to the Andes and Amazon. An advance deposit (six months to a year) should be made for the best boats, dates, and guides.

VENEZUELA

Season: November–March.

Locations: Venezuelan Highlands, Llanos, Guayana Highlands.

Cost: From $1,500 to $3,000 for 15-day tour.

Operators: International Expeditions, Lost World Adventures, Questers Tours, Safaricentre.

Venezuela, which earned its name ("Little Venice") from early Spanish explorers who were reminded of Venetian waterways by Lake Maracaibo, is a surprisingly new destination for adventure and natural history travel. On its Venezuela natural-history tour, **Questers Tours** explores all the major biogeographical regions. The Caribbean coastline and surrounding mountains and plateaus, known as the Venezuelan highlands, are home to an abundance of wildlife. On the flat savannahs and marshes of the Llanos, formed by the Orinoco River basin, more animals, including caimans, capybaras, howler monkeys, and a diversity of birds, are observed. The tour also penetrates the largely uninhabited Guayana Highlands of Bolívar state, a region of mountainous tablelands, luxuriant rain forests, rivers, and spectacular waterfalls, including Angel Falls, the world's highest waterfall. **Lost World Adventures** has a variety of nature and adventure tours with more departures than any other company specializing in natural-history tours to Venezuela. For example, the company's "Auyan-Tepui Natural History Trek to the Guayana Highlands" is a challenging ascent through the cloud forests to the top of a gigantic sandstone massif, or *tepuis,* one of many that dominate this bizarre landscape.

OVERLAND SAFARIS

There is no faster way to immerse oneself in a number of cultures and landscapes than by an overland trip in special vehicles designed to cross the toughest desert, jungle, and mountain areas. On such an adventure you journey far from the beaten path to explore a South America seldom seen by the average tourist. Camping is the most common way to spend the night, though you may prefer to stay in lodges, inns, and hotels occasionally. You'll be expected to help with tenting, cooking, and with pulling the vehicle out of a ditch in more remote spots, if necessary. A camaraderie evolves on these long-distance trips that often sparks long-term friendships. Flexibility and adaptability are the key.

Season: Year-round.

Locations: Throughout South America.

Cost: From $2,940 for nine weeks to $4,330 for 13 weeks. Consecutive Adventure Center itineraries may be combined at a slightly reduced cost.

Tour Operators: Adventure Center, Safaricentre.

Adventure Center specializes in cross-continental overland trips, covering as much of South America's culture, history, and geography as possible in one extended adventure tour. Itineraries run from one to three or more months and range from Ecuador to the Patagonia region of Argentina, encompassing also the highlights in Peru, Bolivia, Chile, and Paraguay. You travel through mountains, steaming jungles, endangered rain forests, flat grasslands, and desert. You visit lost kingdoms and bustling modern cities and meet with gauchos, Amazon Indians, and highland peoples. **Safaricentre** operates shorter, yet still well-rounded three-week overland adventures along the Inca Real in Peru; two-week jeep safaris in Venezuela; and three-week trips to Argentina, Bolivia, and Chile.

PHOTO SAFARIS

From toucans, caimans, and monkeys in the subtropical jungles of the north, to penguins, sea lions, and elephant seals along the subantarctic coasts, South America presents enough natural and wildlife diversity to keep a nature photographer happy. For many travelers the best way to take advantage of this diversity is to join a photo safari, with scouting and complex logistical details already taken care of. The tours listed below are all led by professional photographers who enhance the trip with instruction and valuable hands-on tips.

ARGENTINA

Season: March.

Locations: From Iguazu Falls to Tierra del Fuego.

Cost: From $3,244 for 21 days, including accommodations, meals, transportation, guide services, and admissions within the trip.

Tour Operators: Close-Up Expeditions, Lihué Expediciones.
This tour focuses in on Argentina's landscapes and animals with an action-packed itinerary designed for wildlife- and nature photographers. The itinerary was developed by **Close-Up Expeditions** in cooperation with **Lihué Expediciones** of Buenos Aires, specialists in Argentine natural history, to provide photographers easy access to private wildlife preserves, ranches, and research centers where wildlife is plentiful. Don Lyon, chief guide of Close-Up Expeditions, along with an Argentine naturalist, lead the way into the heart of Argentina's ecological zones. Transportation is by plane, private van, and minibus. Even the drivers are professional photographers, with backgrounds in photo instruction. Hotel accommodations are comfortable. Groups are kept small to allow for flexibility to react to changing light conditions and serendipitous events along the way.

GALAPAGOS

Season: Year-round.

Locations: Islands of the Galapagos Archipelago.

Cost: From $550 for four days/three nights to $1,200 for eight days/seven nights.

Tour Operator: Big 5 Expeditions.
The untamed beauty and enchantment of the Galapagos Archipelago are celebrated. Remote, removed, untouched, it is a veritable paradise for wildlife photographers, as well as botanists, biologists, and naturalists. There are frigate birds and blue-footed boobies. Prehistoric iguanas clamor over stark lavascapes. Sea lions, fur seals, and 500-pound tortoises seem to be suspended in time. Exceptionally rewarding for photographers is the rare opportunity to approach many of these animals closely, since they have remarkably little fear of people. **Big 5 Expeditions** offers nature-photography tours on four- and five-day itineraries (which may also be combined for up to eight days) aboard the *Galapagos Explorer.* Built for 150 passengers, the ship carries only 90 to ensure maximum comfort. All cabins are outside, with air-conditioning and private bath. Cruises depart Wednesdays and Saturdays from Quito and Quayaquil, Ecuador.

VENEZUELA

Season: December–January.

Locations: The Llanos, Andes Mountains.

Cost: From $1,995 for 12 days, including lodging, meals, and guide services.

Tour Operator: Joseph Van Os Photo Safaris.
During the dry season an incredible number of animals congregate along the drying lagoons and pools that punctuate the vast grassland known as the llanos. Masses of waterbirds, including spectacular flocks of scarlet ibis and thousands of ducks, gather here, presenting wondrous photo opportunities. In a **Joseph Van Os Photo Safaris** tour much of your stay is at a private ranch, Hato Pinero, where you can also view ocelot and red howler monkeys along with some of the ranch's estimated 75,000 spectacled caiman. The ranch is outfitted with photography blinds and vehicles especially adapted for photographing wildlife. Included in the tour is a trip into the scenic Andes Mountains to photograph villages, people, and broad vistas of the *paramo,* Venezuela's tropical alpine grassland, where some of the most unusual plants in the world grow. There is also the chance to photograph 16,000-foot Pico Bolívar from the top station of the world's highest cable car. Accommodations are at a delightful hotel that dates to the 1640s. Joseph Van Os also sponsors an exceptional 23-day voyage to Antarctica and the Falkland Islands.

SCIENTIFIC RESEARCH TRIPS

Whether your interests lie in helping to preserve the earth's dwindling resources, working on projects that will improve the lives of people in developing nations, or searching for clues to the past at archaeological sites, you're sure to find something to match your interests and utilize your skills among the many scientific-research programs currently being operated throughout South America. Joining a research-expedition team contributes labor and money to the research, and as reward you experience the satisfaction of sharing in the discovery. No prior research experience is necessary to join these trips. Instead, organizations look for people who are interested in learning, want to be part of a team, and have the flexibility and sense of humor needed to meet the challenges of a research expedition. All programs are tax-deductible, as allowed by law.

BRAZIL AND CHILE

Season: February, April, June (one two-week trip offered each month) in Brazil; June, July in Chile.

Locations: Ilha Do Cardoso tropical rain forest, near Sao Paulo.

Cost: From $1,495, including lodging and meals, in Brazil; from $1,295 in Chile.

Tour Operator: Earthwatch.
Not so long ago, dense, magical, fecund rain forests blanketed most of the coast of Brazil. But over time, ever-escalating human development has eliminated more than 95 percent of this virgin territory. One of the last remnants of an Atlantic coastal rain forest lies near the city of Sao Paulo, on Ilha do Cardoso, an island state park. In 1976 a research center was established, and it is from this base that **Earthwatch** teams work in shifts around the clock to assess the island's animals and plants. The work is essential for understanding how this severely threatened

habitat works and how to save what is left of it in other parts of Brazil. Teams search for caiman nests and observe the animals' behavior; record the local habitat; map streams, swamps, and other topographic features; photograph animals and habitats; and enter the data into computers. The island contains a host of habitats, hundreds of tree and bird species, and many threatened species of animals. Lodging is in research-station houses and dorms, which have electricity, water, and flush toilets. On Earthwatch's research trips in Chile you can examine Inca sites in the Lluta Valley, study textiles in the laboratories of the Rarapaca Museum, and excavate shell refuse in the Camarones valley.

ECUADOR

Season: June–July.

Locations: Antisana (Alpine Flora of the Paramo), Maquipucuna Reserve (Rain Forest program and workshops).

Cost: From $1,285 for 2 weeks, from Quito.

Tour Operator: University Research Expeditions Program (UREP).
UREP has a 15-year history of sending research teams of University of California scientists, teachers, students, and others to investigate issues of human and environmental concern throughout the world. Current projects in South America include three environmental-studies programs in Ecuador, including workshops in the field and forest for U.S. and Ecuadorian scientists and educators. On "The Alpine Flora of the *Paramo*" expedition you can assist Dr. Thomas Duncan, director of the U.C.–Berkeley Herbarium, in documenting the plant life found in Ecuador's open grasslands, or *paramo*. Interest in natural history is helpful, as well as high-elevation hiking and camping experience. "Seeing the Forest for the Trees" is a research tour on the western slope of the Andes north of Quito. Here, a 10-square-mile tract of land has been designated as the Maquipucuna Tropical Reserve, a pristine forest that contains a range of colorful plant life. In this project a continuing detailed inventory of plant species is being taken to expedite ecological plans for the area. Previous experience in field botany, biology, or plant ecology is desirable. Accommodations are rustic.

PERU

Season: April–October.

Locations: Amazon River Basin, Inca Trail.

Cost: From $1,690 for one week (includes airfare from Miami) for Amazon Dolphin Project; from $1,295 for 11-day Inca Trail Preservation Trek.

Tour Operators: Oceanic Society Expeditions, Wildland Adventures.
Botos, the largest of river dolphins, are native to the Amazon River basin. There is concern that they, like other river dolphins of the world, are at high risk from burgeoning human use of their environment. **Oceanic Society Expeditions,** the travel affiliate of Friends of the Earth, a conservation organization, was scheduled to begin in July 1991 an annual project to study the botos. Led by world-renowned dolphin and whale expert Stephen Leatherwood, participants on the "Amazon Dolphin Project" are to collect data to use in developing a long-term study focusing on the dolphins' movement patterns, social organization, and behavior in relationship to their environment. The study will amass information necessary for protection and conservation. No special skills, other than knowing how to swim, are required to participate in the project. Headquarters is a jungle lodge with three unscreened cabins and two semiprivate cabins.
Another conservation project in Peru is the "Inca Trail Preservation Trek," cosponsored by **Wildland Adventures,** The Earth Preservation Fund, and local Peruvian conservation organizations. The trek offers participants the opportunity to help preserve the natural and cultural heritage of Machu Picchu National Park.

TREKKING

At the height of the Inca empire, the Andes were crisscrossed by a vast network of Inca roads. They followed valleys and traced impossible pathways through narrow, precipitous terrain. Today remnants of Inca trails and footpaths used by today's indigenous people of the Andes lead adventurous hikers to ancient ruins, spectacular mountain peaks, jungle highlands, and small Indian communities. Trekking usually refers to an organized tour with experienced native guides and cooks who provide food, equipment, and camp services. Porters or pack animals carry gear, leaving trekkers the freedom of hiking with only a light day-pack. Treks are graded according to difficulty in terms of distance, terrain, and elevation. Whether you join an organized trek or arrange your own party it is recommended that you select a group with an experienced local guide when trekking through remote areas.

ARGENTINA AND CHILE

Season: November–March.

Locations: Tierra del Fuego, Patagonia, Lakes District.

Cost: From $1,550 for all-inclusive tour with nine days of trekking to $1,700 for 13 days.

Tour Operators: Earthquest, Lihué Expediciones, Mountain Travel, Southern Cross Expeditions, Wildland Adventures.

Most of Argentina and Chile are situated in high Andean mountains, including the highest peak in the Western Hemisphere, Mt. Aconcagua (22,980 feet). Active local mountaineering clubs and well-established national parks systems in both countries are responsible for the excellent trail systems, campsites, and shelters used by trekkers in this region. Long daylight hours, lasting until 11 P.M. add to the attraction of trekking here. The best trekking focuses on a magnificent area of the southern Andes shared by both countries that is generally referred to as Patagonia in Argentina and as the Lakes District in Chile. Lakes, rivers, glaciers, granite peaks, waterfalls, forests, Indians, gauchos, and an amazing display of fascinating wildlife make this one of the world's great natural wonders. **Mountain Travel** and **Earthquest** jointly offer a 10-day trek around "The Wonderous Towers of Paine." These precipitous walls of glacier-carved peaks protrude a near-vertical 6,000 to 8,000 feet out of rolling grasslands, wild chasms, and deep azure lakes. **Wildland Adventures** has a "Patagonian Wildlands Safari" that combines a series of short treks in Glacier National Park, Torres del Paine, and the Fitzroy massif. Their Tierra del Fuego sail trek, dubbed "the southernmost trek in the world," follows the south Atlantic coast of Tierra del Fuego to Cape Horn. Buenos Aires–based **Lihué Expediciones,** one of the most respected adventure-tour companies in Argentina, has trekking programs throughout that country.

Southern Cross's 13-day treks in February and March start at the Atlantic shores of Patagonia and include a one-day boat trip to Tierra del Fuego for three days of trekking and end in a four-day trek around the glaciers that spill from the continental icecap in Pantagonia.

BOLIVIA

Season: April–September.

Location: Cordillera Real.

Cost: From $100 per day.

Tour Operators: Andean Treks, Magri Turismo, Wildland Adventures.

Bolivia encompasses the most impressive concentration of high-elevation, snow-capped peaks in the Andes; in a 100-mile section of the Cordillera Real the elevation averages over 18,000 feet. The elevation of the *altiplano* (high plains), which lies between the Cordillera Real and Occidental ranges is between 12,000 feet and 12,500 feet. La Paz, the highest capital city in the world, is the base for trekking in Bolivia and the place to acclimatize before heading higher. A recommended highland-trekking itinerary combines a two-day trek over a pre-Inca road, the Takesi, with a three-day, high-elevation trek over two 16,500-foot passes to lakes and glaciers in the heart of the Cordillera Real. The 12-foot-wide paved section of the road is an impressive example of pre-Columbian engineering, featuring stone paving, steps, drainage channels, and retaining walls. The trip is outfitted by **Magri Turismo** but can be booked through **Wildland Adventures.** Llamas and herders are used instead of pack horses. **Andean Treks** also offers several treks in Bolivia, including a llama trek in the Cordillera Real and another in the Islands of the Sun in Lake Titicaca.

ECUADOR

Season: Year-round.

Locations: Central valley, western Cordillera, and eastern Cordillera ranges.

Cost: From $80 per day for complete trekking services, including guide, cook, and transport.

Tour Operators: Above the Clouds Trekking, Expediciones Andinas, Wilderness Travel, Wildland Adventures.

Ecuador is the smallest of the Andean countries yet remains one of the most ecologically and culturally diverse nations in South America. The Andes cross Ecuador from north to south in two ranges. Between them lies the fertile Central Valley, along what German explorer Alexander von Humboldt called "The Avenue of the Volcanoes" because the valley is edged by one of the largest concentrations of volcanoes in the world. Spectacular trekking routes, such as the Mt. Cayambe Amazon Highlands Trek offered by **Wildland Adventures,** lead to high-elevation and glacier-clad volcanic peaks and descend to the tropical highlands of the Amazon basin. Unlike its neighbors, Ecuador has a progressive land-reform policy and a fertile agricultural base that have supported diverse communities of native Indians who wear traditional dress and retain many of their customs. Wildland Adventure's "Andean Highlands Cultural Trek" combines several short treks in the Andean foothills to rural villages and little-known Indian markets, where visitors can mingle with a variety of distinctive ethnic groups. Between treks travelers enjoy hot baths and beds in appealing colonial-style inns. Marco Cruz is one of Ecuador's more experienced climber and trekking guides. Private groups can solicit his services through his company, **Expediciones Andinas.**

PERU

Season: April–October.

Locations: Cordillera Blanca, Cordillera Vilcanota, and Cordillera Vilcabamba.

Cost: From $200 for a four-day trek booked locally to about $1,500 for a complete two-week itinerary in Peru.

Tour Operators: Explorandes, Mountain Travel, Overseas Adventure Travel, Peaks and Places, Southwind Adventures, Wilderness Travel, Wildland Adventures.

Peru, the best-known Andean country for trekking, contains three distinct mountain ranges (cordilleras). The ancient Inca capital of Cuzco lies within the Cordillera Vilcabamba, where Yale archaeologist Hiram Bingham discovered the lost city of Machu Picchu, in 1911. Today the 45-kilometer (28-mile) Inca Trail affords adventurous trekkers the opportunity to reach Machu Picchu as the Incas did, by hiking along the royal road built over 500 years ago. This popular route passes through rare examples of cloud forest over a 14,000-foot pass, before descending into subtropical vegetation. It connects the only standing system of Inca architectural ruins remaining from the ancient empire, including steps, a tunnel, and well-preserved ruins in their natural setting. **Wildland Adventures** offers twice-monthly, two-week "Inca Trail Treks," including stops in Lima, Cuzco, and the Amazon jungle, with a (recommended) overnight stop at the Machu Picchu Hotel. Many U.S.-based adventure-travel companies also offer this popular trek. **Overseas Adventure Travel,** for instance, combines moderate and demanding Machu Picchu treks with whitewater rafting in the Sacred Valley and hikes through the rain forest. Independent trekkers can join with others by booking directly with local trekking outfitters in Cuzco.

The Cordillera Blanca, in northern Peru, features the highest tropical peaks in the world, with snow-capped summits, turquoise glacial lakes, and deep gorges. Trekking routes reveal typical Andean wildlife, including the condor and guanaco, protected within the Huscaran National Park. **Peaks and Places** has three grades of treks in this range, the most difficult of which includes walking 100 miles, gaining and losing 6,000 meters (19,680 feet) of altitude while hiking over nine passes and passing through three small villages.

The Cordillera Vilcanota is the southernmost mountain range in Peru, encompassing the *altiplano,* the highland plateau that stretches south to Lake Titicaca and Bolivia. At an average altitude of 13,120 feet, this remote highland is devoid of trees. Local Quechua Indians herd alpacas and llamas and worship Mt. Ausangate (20,280 feet), the chief *Apu,* or tutelar spirit, of the region. The most popular trek in this region circumnavigates the Ausangate massif over two 15,000-foot passes. **Wilderness Travel** and **Mountain Travel** offer the greatest diversity of trekking programs in Peru. **Southwind Adventures** organizes a "Highland Vistas Trek," which combines several ranges in one itinerary. **Explorandes,** the largest adventure-travel tour outfitter based in Peru, has the widest range of itineraries.

WATER SPORTS

Alternately exhilarating and relaxing, white-water rafting and sea kayaking provide a pace and perspective all their own. A single day of white-water rafting would be an exciting addition to your South American trip, or you could join a multiday rafting or kayaking trip. You don't have to be an expert paddler to enjoy a river adventure, but you should know how to swim. Rivers are rated according to difficulty, and South America has some of the wildest commercially rafted rivers in the world. Generally speaking Class III and IV rapids are rolling to rollicking and suitable for beginners. Many Class V (potentially dangerous) rapids are strictly for the experienced. South America has hundreds of untamed rivers worthy of exploration; those listed below are a sample of favorites.

BRAZIL

Season: August for marathon; year-round for white-water rafting.

Location: Down the Amazon from Manaus to Belem.

Cost: Available upon request for marathon; $85 daily for white-water rafting.

Tour Operator: CanoAndes Expeditions.

In August 1992 **CanoAndes Expeditions** is scheduled to begin annual 22-day marathon kayaking expeditions down the Amazon River—(from Manaus to Belem)—with Piotr Chmielinski, the first man to paddle the entire length of the Amazon. The goal of the marathon, with the cooperation of the International Canoe Federation, is to draw attention to the need for better preservation of the Amazon's rain forest. Participants split into two groups: sport kayakers who race to Belem and others who paddle at their own pace. Both groups cover up to 40 miles per day. Everyone starts together in the morning, with support boats traveling alongside to assist when necessary. The groups meet again in the evening to sleep in support-boat cabins. For white-water enthusiasts there are rapids rated up to Class III on the Paribuna River (outside Rio de Janeiro). CanoAndes also offers one-day trips year-round.

CHILE

Season: December–March.

Location: Bio-bio River, Class IV.

Cost: From $1,950 to $2,390 for 14 days, round-trip from Santiago. Includes lodging, most meals, river equipment, and guide services.

Tour Operators: CanoAndes Expeditions, Sobek Expeditions.

For white-water river-runners the Bio-bio River, Chile's largest, is among the wildest rivers in the world. Since the first descent of Bio-bio, undertaken by **Sobek Expeditions,** in 1978, the river's reputation for unparalleled white-water action has become known to rafters around the world. At the headwaters the gradient is gentle, as the river ripples through soft, rolling countryside. This changes abruptly, however, as metamorphic and granitic gorges pinch the river channel to create challenging and complex white-water sections. These swift rapids demand caution, and you may be required to walk around certain rapids or to portage in low water levels. In 10 days on the river you ride nearly 100 rapids, but there are opportunities to enjoy the scenery and hot springs along the way. There's trout fishing, hiking, lounging on soft beaches, and interaction with the people who live along the river—farmers, cowboys, and Indians. Bio-bio is a first-class river and Sobek provides a first-rate adventure. **CanoAndes Expeditions** trips run 14 days (seven rafting) from Santiago.

Kayakers may also join any of Sobek's raft trips on the Bio-bio. Sobek has kayaks available in Chile, but all accessory gear (helmet, paddle, spray skirt, and kayaking jacket) must be provided by the kayaker. Cost for kayakers is half the rafting price. Special arrangements can be made for groups of kayakers requiring raft support only.

ECUADOR

Season: November–April for rafting; May–August, November for riverboating.

Locations: Quijos River, Class III, IV, and V; Toachi River, Class III.

Cost: From $45 for one day; from $180 for two days/one night (one rafting); from $1,480 for 10 days aboard riverboat.

Tour Operators: CanoAndes Expeditions, RioAndes, Sobek Expeditions.

Ecuador's Quijos River provides challenge and white-water fun for everyone: it has Class III rapids for beginners, Class IV action in a great gorge covered by subtropical cloud forest for the more advanced, and Class V rapids for the experienced. **CanoAndes Expeditions** has two- and three-day river-rafting trips in all classes.

Another great rafting river, the Toachi, races out of Ecuador's highland cloud forest into pure tropical rain forest, flowing through virgin-forest canyons interspersed with small farming villages and Colorado Indian territory. **RioAndes** runs the river regularly, offering one- and two-day paddle-rafting trips. They start at the river's first navigable point below the town of Alluriquin and stop midday for a picnic lunch. Accommodations for the overnight trip are in a nearby hotel. **Sobek Expeditions** offers a more extensive 10-day (Class III) river excursion along the Toachi River, including two days of jungle exploration by riverboat into the homeland of the Cayapas Indians, one of many indigenous tribes surviving along the equator in Ecuador.

PERU

Season: May–August.

Locations: Apurimac River, up to Class V; Tambopata River, up to Class IV.

Cost: From $1,502 for up to 10 days on the Apurimac; from $1,990 for 17 days on the Tambopata.

Tour Operators: Above the Clouds Trekking, CanoAndes Expeditions, Sobek Expeditions.

Starting high in the Andes as a small glacier-fed stream, the Apurimac River, the most distant source of the Amazon River, carves deep canyons among snow-capped peaks. As the Apurimac spills from the highlands into the jungle it presents one of the most spectacular white-water challenges in the world. Class V action keeps you riveted on the river, but when pauses allow there are towering mountain summits and Inca ruins to enjoy. **Sobek Expeditions** offers seven-day river-only rafting/camping trips on the Apurimac from Lima to Cuzco, which may be combined with a trek to Machu Picchu, for a total of 16 days. For the excitement of spending 10 days rafting big rapids (up to Class IV), combined with exploring the lush surroundings and exotic wildlife of the Tambopata Wildlife Reservation, there's a 17-day trip along the Tambopata River with **CanoAndes Expeditions.** Half-day trips to week-long excursions running the rapids of Peru's Urubamba, Maranon, or Santa rivers, are available from **Above the Clouds Trekking.**

VENEZUELA

Season: Year-round.

Locations: Orinoco and Caroni rivers, Classes IV and V.

Cost: From $1,490 for seven days.

Tour Operator: Lost World Adventures.

Orinoco's Ature Rapids in Amazonas Territory and the Caroni River's Nekuima Canyon in the Guayana Highlands give even experienced river rafters a memorable roller-coaster ride on their giant frothy waves. **Lost World Adventures'** skilled river guides lead seven-day rafting expeditions along these formidable rivers. Trip cost includes four days rafting, lodge and camp accommodations, meals, guide services, and equipment.

ARGENTINA

Different yet Familiar

by
CATHERINE HEALY

Catherine Healy has been commuting to Latin America since her first trip to Argentina in 1979 as travel editor of the Los Angeles Herald Examiner. *A freelance writer, she has published two romantic adventure novels,* Private Corners, *featuring speed ski racing in Argentina and Chile, and* Perfect Timing, *about a scientific expedition studying giant tortoises in Galápagos. Her non-fiction work has appeared in* Washingtonian, Town and Country, Cosmopolitan en Español, Américas, *and various National Geographic Society projects.*

The Argentines should rightfully be called our distant cousins, for they are the progeny of the same immigrants who, displaced by the same wars, famines, and industrial upheaval, came to North America. In the geographic equivalent of a land extending from Mexico's Yucatan Peninsula to Ketchikan, Alaska, the uprooted built a new nation. Conceived in liberty and hope, yes. And greed, desperation, religious idealism—all of these, too.

There is much that is familiar in Argentina: Angus cattle, fields of wheat to the flat horizon, oil rigs, ski runs, river deltas, and faces we've seen before, the mix of a melting pot.

Yet nothing is quite the same. Here is a familiarity with curious twists and exaggerations—the unexpected that all travelers seek and too often don't find. Fabled Patagonia is a bleak Nevada with millions of penguins perched on burrows like prairie dogs. Lake Nahuel Huapí at the mountain resort of Bariloche in central Argentina is as blue as Lake Tahoe; but only on the lake's Isla Victoria can you see the surrealistic cinnamon forests of Walt Disney's *Bambi.*

Pine plantations march Georgia-like along red soil, then the ruins of another Jesuit commune appear suddenly—carved red sandstone testimonials to a vast empire that lasted approximately from the time the Pilgrims landed to the U.S. Declaration of Independence, then faded when the Jesuits were expelled by Charles III of Spain. And more. Wild West trains cross trestles at a breathless 12,000 feet. Mendoza, like Carmel-by-the-Sea in California, has tucked itself into a beautiful forest. But Mendoza, a city of 1.2 million, sits on a dry, treeless plain at the foot of the Andes. Hundreds upon hundreds of trees had to be planted by hand, and every tree is irrigated through a canal system first dug by the Incas.

The natural spectacles are often bold. A network of concrete catwalks takes you right into the spray at Iguazú Falls, twice as big as Niagara. When you perch on the cliffs at Lago Argentino, the ground underneath quakes as Perito Moreno Glacier creaks and groans toward you, moving five yards a day and shattering curtains of icebergs in its path.

A journey to Argentina grants the pleasures of surprise, of chic boutiques and unsurpassed steaks, of exploring the tail end of the New World, all worthy reasons to visit. Yet there is a bonus of common roots back in the Old World—Europe, the Middle East, or the Orient. When uprooted North Americans meet uprooted Argentines, they stare into a mirror. Both peoples are educated, most own their houses or condominiums, an increasing number seek the help of psychiatrists in attempting to wrest control of their lives. One mix from the melting pot was acculturated under Protestant-English guidelines, the other under Catholic-Spanish. And now, generations later, most of them would not trade places, neither the Spanish-speaking Welsh with Latin swaggers nor English-speaking Italians whose hands are mute.

Who are the Argentines, and what are they like? When the question was put to a Jewish-Argentine psychoanalyst (who has a cousin in Beverly Hills), he jokingly repeated a stereotype: The typical Argentine is an Italian who speaks Spanish and thinks he's British. That was said before the Falklands/Malvinas War against England in 1982, which doesn't make it any less true today—just not as commonly repeated. (Latin Americans have called the South Atlantic islands "Malvinas" since 1698 when they were named by French sailors.) Beyond that shallow peek is an isolated culture that developed on its own, borrowing and adapting until it dug into the deep topsoil of the pampas and grew.

Some Argentines would argue that they are a hybrid in search of an identity, and others would argue the contrary. With great drama and conviction, with passion and facts, they argue for hours over a cup of espresso, philosophizing about who they are. Philosophizing is the favorite sport of the Argentines; second is flirting; then comes soccer. That ranking, too, is debatable, especially when discussed at a busy sidewalk cafe where at least two of the three sports can be practiced.

The Argentine dedication to flirtation can be devastatingly attractive. Argentine men flirt intelligently, usually harmlessly, with a locked glance and a silent, regretted farewell. Nothing crass, no bottom pinching or verbal hounding. Argentines pride themselves on elegance and sophistication. Tall, handsome men (like their compatriots, Guillermo Vilas and the late Fernando Lamas) use their wit to charm, as do the women.

Life as lived by the Argentines requires stamina. They work regular office hours (9 A.M.–7 P.M.) and put in full evenings, too. Often downtown sidewalks are more crowded at 11 P.M. than during the day. They enjoy movies, operas, ballet, symphony, Gestalt therapy groups, university seminars, talking over dinner, talking over coffee (not cocktails), talking, talking. Life has a patina of drama. People live on the edge, elated by a happy turn of events, despairing over *desastres* (dis-AS-trays)—disasters. Life is a roller coaster, and visitors climb aboard for the ride.

Spanish Colonization

Gold that surpassed the dreams of Midas lay waiting to be plundered in the Inca Empire, an advanced civilization centered in Peru. Docile Indians who used the same word for "duty to the state" as "happiness" were already working in fields and mines. For them, the Spanish Conquest meant merely switching from one master to another. When the conquistadors rode south from the capital of Cuzco, they wanted more gold and more slaves whose souls they could save, only to discover they already had the best of the booty. The history of the Spanish in Argentina is really a story of Peru and the pauper.

For most peoples, the Andes would have been a harsh barrier, but the Incas were a highland nation, used to living in mountain basins whose elevations rival the peaks of the Rockies. When the Incas expanded from central Peru, they reached farther and farther through the *cordillera*. Irrigation systems were developed, crops planted, mines dug, and roads built to distribute the goods.

The Spanish rode down the Inca highways, protected by the mountains on both sides, as the Incas had been. Finally, the road branched. The richer route followed the abrupt western slope into the Atacama. There, in the driest desert on earth, the Incas had mined copper. The Spanish took over. By following oases, the Incas had conquered various Indian tribes midway into the lush Central Valley of Chile, where they had been halted by the fierce Araucanians. Likewise, the Spanish were stopped too.

Other conquistadors followed the eastern road into Argentina and marched to its termination, an Inca fortress at present day Tucumán. Here in Argentina the protective eastern mountains ended. The irrigated oasis of Tucumán was under constant threat from the Abipones, nomadic plains Indians who became more dangerous once they mounted stolen Spanish horses.

With neither gold, silver, gemstones, nor sedentary Indians to labor for them, Argentina held little appeal for the Spanish. It was a hostile backwater that was easily ignored. The preoccupation of the Spanish Crown was how to bring the wealth of the New World home, for no sooner had its first treasure ships arrived than pirates, commissioned by France, stole the next shipment. Spain responded with a rigid system of protection that kept Argentina in thrall for almost 300 years.

Lima, a capital for Spanish America, was established on the Peruvian coast, far enough inland to be secure from marauders. All minerals and goods produced along the Andes had to be carried by mule to Lima. Shipped by armed convoy from the nearby port of Callao to the Pacific Coast of Panama, unloaded, carried overland by mule to the Caribbean shore, they were ultimately convoyed by armada to Spain. Manufactured goods were brought back the same way. When one looks at a map and sees that Buenos Aires is much closer to Europe, one naturally wonders why the Spanish didn't choose the obvious, more convenient port for their trade monopoly.

In fact, as early as 1516, Spanish explorers seeking a more efficient route to the Andean treasure sailed into a 140-mile-wide bay that they mislabeled Rio de la Plata, River of Silver. Not only is the muddy water colored pinkish brown, but the bay didn't lead to mountains of silver either. This is the confluence of two major rivers on the continent, the Uruguay, originating in the red hills of southern Brazil, and the mighty Paraná, which flows from the redder highlands of central Brazil. The delta formed when these two rivers meet is larger than the combined land mass of Holland and Belgium.

Landing on the marshy shore along the Rio de la Plata was difficult for the explorers, for in many places one had to walk a couple of miles through the shallows to reach firm earth. The leader of the first group of conquistadors was killed and eaten by Indians, which further discouraged the Spanish. A few decades later, more explorers sailed up the broad Paraná. Indian attacks thwarted their attempts to make settlements, too, but more frustrating was the river itself. This was no Mississippi, despite its length of 1,827 miles. The Paraná is a wide river that winds through the flat pampas. It floods frequently and its channels are often choked with sandbars. Although tributaries rushing down from the Andes would clear the silt, a peculiarity of Argentine geography is that most rivers sink mid-pampas, disintegrating into bogs.

In 1535, a Spanish expedition maneuvered its boats past the hostile Indians on the Paraná, forked onto the Paraguay River, and stopped at the first hills they found afterwards. They named their village Asunción. The city is now the capital of Paraguay, located on the border with Argentina. And there, higher than the flood plain, they settled, nowhere near Lima, far away from gold, but with the tractable Guarani Indians to till for them. The next expedition to Asunción came overland. So much for the Paraná, the River of Silver, and the pampas, the fertile cornucopia that would make Argentina one of the ten wealthiest countries in the world by the twentieth century.

Still, Argentina was not completely forgotten. Mules by the hundreds of thousands were needed to work the mines and carry the bounty to the ships. Only mules, a strong, sterile cross between female horses and male jackasses, could endure both lowland jungles and highland deserts. In the high altiplano of Peru and Bolivia, where the mines are located at elevations over 12,000 feet, horses couldn't survive. To supply the continual demand for replacements, mules had to be bred on lower pastures. The closest grasslands stretched east from Tucumán to the Paraná River in the Argentina pampas, and a boom in mules and wild cattle (slaughtered for the hides and tallow) quickly followed.

By the end of the sixteenth century, all the important towns of colonial Argentina were established. Trade and travel moved in an annual rhythm that lasted until the final throes of the Spanish Empire 200 years later. In the annual march to Lima, Chilean goods avoided the Atacama Desert, in the same way the Incas had, by crossing a 12,602-foot pass over the Andes into Mendoza, Argentina, and hopscotching up a series of oasis towns to Salta. This Andean city was the trade crossroads for all of southern Latin America because of its situation on the Salado River, the only one in the region that reaches the Paraná. With the rise of Salta, settlers came down the Paraná from Asunción, Paraguay, and established a fort city, which they called Santa Fé, at the junction of the Salado and Paraná. The trail along the Salado became a road, forts were built along the road and the river became the boundary between the herds of cattle and mules and marauding Abipone Indians.

Buenos Aires, farther south near the mouth of the Paraná, was founded
in 1580, and ignored. People of Buenos Aires call themselves *Porteños,*
meaning "from the port." Smuggling was a prime business in the village
of Buenos Aires, but generations of *Porteños* also joined other tradesmen
on the dirt road along the Salado River to Salta for the autumn fair. Every
February and March, Peruvian silver and European finished goods were
traded for wines, cow hides, and mules.

Today, the oasis cities in the Andes retain their colonial charm, with
palm trees and tiled roofs, 400-year-old universities and cathedrals. Independence from Spain shattered the northwest's power. One of the few reminders of the monopoly traffic alongside the Salado River are the highways that were built later. Look at a map. The river flows at an 11 o'clock–
4 o'clock angle. Highways of the pampas are either parallel that axis, or
at right angles to it.

El Libertador

A familiar sight in the main square of every city, town, or large village
is a statue of General José de San Martín on his horse, the liberator of
Argentina, Chile, and Peru. El Libertador's portrait is also displayed in
every state school and on postage stamps. Streets, towns, even railway
lines are named in his memory. In a passionate land where the successful
grand gesture is applauded, San Martín set the standard.

The son of a minor Spanish official in Corrientes, San Martín was educated as an officer in the Spanish army. In 1810, he returned to his homeland to fight for independence. Convinced that the Argentines could not
win through local campaigns unless the Spanish were driven from Lima,
San Martín organized a plan that would have daunted Hannibal and his
elephants in the Alps. For two years the tall, lean general secretly trained
an army in Mendoza. Using mules to drag the cannons, he led 3,000 troops
over the 12,602-foot pass into Chile—almost like climbing Pike's Peak to
go to war. In the valley below, he defeated the Spanish. With the help of
the Chilean navy, San Martín's army sailed to Peru and captured Lima.
The year was 1821, but Argentina was not free until 1853 because the freed
citizens turned on each other in a series of civil wars. But the borders of
the Spanish vice-royalty of Rio de la Plata shrank as Bolivia, Paraguay,
Uruguay, and sections of Chile broke away.

At the same time, the power struggle between the long-established
northwest and upstart Buenos Aires, the new capital, was vicious. Only
the extermination of one side or the other would bring peace, San Martín
(incorrectly) concluded. He left for France where he died 26 years later.
His body was reinterred in the Cathedral in Buenos Aires. Out of the civil
war emerged the first of Argentina's charismatic bloody dictators, Juan
Manuel de Rosas, backed by the landowners and their armies of *gauchos.*

The Anglo-Argentine naturalist and writer W.H. Hudson described
how gauchos slit the throats of their enemies in what is otherwise a gentle
autobiography, *Far Away and Long Ago, a Childhood in Argentina,* published in 1918. Hudson's father taught his children that Rosas ruled them
well. Generally, though, that is a minority view. Most Argentines believe
he was a madman and a killer. International movie audiences have recently seen that view in *Camila,* an award-winning Argentine film about
Camila O'Gorman, the educated daughter of a wealthy family. She fell
in love with a Jesuit who dared whisper against Rosas's atrocities and they
ran away together. For this sin, Rosas had them executed.

He didn't suffer the same fate himself. When Rosas was ousted in 1852,
he slipped away to England, where he lived quietly for the next 25 years.

In 1853, a constitution was drawn up, modeled on the original document for the United States. In the 1860s, while the United States was plunged into civil war, England turned to Argentina for its agricultural products. It was a quick leg up on the competition.

The New Argentina: A Lucky Break

Bright blue, cloudless skies dominate the upper three-fourths of the lithographs behind the coffee shop counter at the Sheraton Hotel in Buenos Aires. More than Big Sky Country, this is Immense Sky. Far below are strips of green dotted with black Angus cattle. Windmills pump water in the riverless land, working constantly, for the shifting wind seldom stops. Juan Sanchez's paintings introduce the extraordinary pampas. The same wind has covered the region with a rich topsoil that rises 985 feet above bedrock in Buenos Aires.

These fertile plains were useless land for centuries after the Spanish Conquest, untameable with primitive farming equipment and controlled by aggressive Indians. In the mid-nineteenth century, however, a jumble of events occurred that changed the world in profound ways. The Industrial Revolution introduced railroads, barbed wire, steel plows that could turn the toughest sod, thrashers, refrigerator ships, and dredges to clear silted harbors. This same revolution upended Europe, displacing millions of peasants from farms. Small wars raged like brush fires and peasant boys were drafted for cannon fodder. At the same time, the potato blight in Ireland and Germany forced millions more to move or starve. Finally, common people were ready to suffer the travails of pioneering.

Where once the vast grasslands of Argentina had been seas of green to hurry across, now they were valuable land. After steel plows and barbed wire subjugated and fenced off the sod, that is. And after British cattle, wheat, and corn flourished and there were railroads to carry the goods to the sea and ports to load them onto ships for Europe.

While the Spanish Crown had forbidden non-Spanish immigration, free Argentina campaigned for settlers. From throughout Europe, people responded, particularly Italians and Spanish. During one decade in the late 1800s, 1.6 million immigrants flooded a sparsely settled Argentina that had previously had fewer than 1.4 million inhabitants. British capital financed the transformation of the grasslands, as it was doing in North America, while national cavalries on both continents massacred the Plains Indians. There the similarities ended. Continuing the old Spanish tradition of dividing the land into great estates, there was no available public land after the Indian Wars (1878–1883). Instead, Argentine officers were awarded estates of 100,000 acres and more. To them, cattle, land, and horses meant wealth and prestige. In those days, wheat was merely a way to gain more pastureland for bigger herds.

Immigrant tenant farmers cleared the tough clumps of pampas grass, plowed into the six-foot topsoil, and planted wheat, sharing the profits with the landowner. By agreement, in the fourth year the tenants planted alfalfa hay for cattle and moved on. But when landowners realized the international market for grains, wheat and corn became staples. Fine-wooled sheep from Australia spread throughout the Patagonian deserts. With steady dredging of the Paraná River, Rosario and Santa Fé became great ports, while Buenos Aires at the delta of the river became the greatest of all. There were years when only New York's trade was greater.

Because Argentina had more flexible restrictions than the United States, immigrants continued arriving. A census in 1906 showed that three out of four people living in Buenos Aires had been born abroad. Later came

Jews fleeing their homelands, then Germans and Italians and their former enemies, Poles, Yugoslavians, and Ukrainians. The British community in Argentina is the second largest outside the Commonwealth. (South Africa takes first place.) Today Chinese and Koreans are coming to arrange alternative citizenships.

Argentina was stunned by the worldwide Depression of the 1930s but in fact probably suffered less than many other developed countries because it was just entering the stage of building its own manufacturing industries and needed construction workers. Yet prosperous calm was cracking under the antiquated economic system. Landed gentry and venture capitalists in the cities had tremendous fortunes while the educated workers and middle class had little access to money or political decisions. Frustration simmered, tango singers lamented the futility of life, and national self-pity waited for a spokesman.

The comings and goings of presidents and political parties (and a brief army takeover between 1930–32) are of relatively little importance in this summary. From 1860 on, Radicals alternated in office with Conservatives until June 1943, when the elected president was ousted by the army. The rock opera *Evita* demonstrated the confusion of the next three years with a game of musical chairs among military officers. At the end of the scene, only Col. Juan Domingo Perón remained. The year was 1946 and Argentina had a new hero, another man of the grand gesture.

The Legacy of Perón

On a recent day, a taxi driver passed with hardly a glance at a political booth bearing posters of the late Juan and Evita Perón. Such sights are common in democratic Argentina, where the Peronist party has retained its popularity. The pessimistic driver was winding up a grim analysis of the economic situation for his North American passenger. Then he shrugged: "We've had over 40 years of bad governments. It's going to take time to change things."

Perón was a popular officer, a ski instructor for alpine army troops, charming, clever, a leader. Perón promised to fulfill Argentina's national destiny. He delivered higher wages, longer vacations, and worker resorts built by newly powerful unions. Argentina exploded with excitement and "bully boys" insured that dissent wasn't heard. Starring at his side was Perón's second wife, Eva Duarte, an illegitimate country girl who slept her way to movie fame. As First Lady of Argentina, she found her supreme role, Glamorous Lady Bountiful. Contributions that she wrested from the rich went to the poor . . . and also to Swiss bank accounts. Adored in life, she was idolized after her death from cancer in 1952. When the military forced Juan Perón from office in 1955, the Vatican was being petitioned to declare sainthood for Evita. Her faithful claimed she had a miraculous power to heal.

Cynical Argentines say the greatest miracle occurred in 1973, when Perón returned to power with another showgirl at his side. This was Maria Estela Martinez, called Isabel, who was named his vice president. In less than a year, he was dead, and the widow Perón became president. It was a convulsive era. Terrorism from the extreme right and left, political kidnappings, uniformed guerrillas roaming the sugar cane plantations in Tucumán—everywhere there was danger. Inflation had passed 2 percent a day when the military took over in 1976, to the relief of most Argentines, who were frantic for security.

Generals and admirals fought terrorism with terror, leaving few of their captives alive to report what happened to them. In all, at least 8,960 men, women and children disappeared, including many who were innocent. One survivor, newspaper publisher Jacobo Timmerman, related his experiences in the best-seller, *Prisoner Without a Name, Cell Without a Number,* later made into a U.S. television movie.

At first most Argentines didn't realize what was happening; they wanted to believe the prisoners were terrorists who belonged in jail. "All civil wars are dirty," people in the farthest corners of the country would insist. "A civil war against subversives is the dirtiest of all."

In other ways, times were good. Those were the go-go years, when the peso was overvalued, giving Argentines the equivalent of 50-cent dollars. And the money kept rolling out. Argentines flocked to Miami, Los Angeles, New York, London, and Hong Kong on buying sprees.

A dream world in which $100,000 could earn $60,000 in annual interest turned into a nightmare. Awareness of the military's atrocities and skimming of foreign loans spread even as the currency crashed. The new peso was valued accurately against the U.S. dollar and the reality was a pittance by comparison. The $7,000 monthly salary of an Argentine executive with a multinational electronics company dropped to $800 a month after two devaluations. Desperate for a diversion, the military junta ordered an invasion of the Falklands/Malvinas Islands in April, 1982, forcing a long-standing claim against England's invasion of the Argentine islands in 1833. Argentina lost the war and official relations between the two countries were severed.

Argentines were humiliated and bankrupt. What was once one of the world's richest peoples, an educated people living in a land of plenty, suffered. *The Official Story,* the 1986 Oscar winner for Best Foreign Film of the Year, is the story of one woman's awakening, of her guilt and fears, and finally, newfound courage. It is the story of her nation. "We'll never be afraid again," is the refrain from a popular song that became the anthem of the transition from a military government to an elected one.

Democracy returned in 1983, with the election of President Raul Alfonsin of the Radical party. Alfonsin's five-year term was notable for the government's prosecution of former military leaders, several of whom were given long prison terms for human-rights violations. (In late 1990, most of the imprisoned leaders and those awaiting trial were pardoned, reopening the old wounds of the 1970s.) Following a brief period of economic stability between 1985 and 1987, inflation returned with a vengeance. 1989 saw prices rise a staggering 4,930 percent.

Despite the economic crisis, Argentina managed in 1989 its first peaceful transfer of power in 60 years, when Alfonsin relinquished his post to the Peronist Carlos Menem, elected by a majority of the popular vote. President Menem, the son of Syrian immigrants, promised to implement free-market policies and lift the heavy hand of the state from the economy.

Menem's policies met with initial success, but the country fell back into hyper-inflation in late 1989. Since March 1990, a strict monetary policy has brought inflation down to more manageable levels; nevertheless, 1990 saw the second-highest inflation in Argentina's history at over 1,200 percent.

The government's austerity measures have brought on a severe recession, but economists have been encouraged by the privatizations of the state phone company and airline. At press time, more money-losing state firms are on the auction block, and Argentines have cause for cautious optimism about the future.

BOLIVIA
Le Quiaca

PARAGUAY

ATACAMA DESERT

Salta   Jujuy

Ascunción   Puerto   Iguazú
Stroessner   Falls

Parana River   12

Tucúman

40   Salado River   12   Posadas

La Rioja   9   Uruguay River   BRAZIL

34

San Juan   Córdoba

Aconcagua

Los
Penitentes   San Luis   Parana   URUGUAY

Portillo   Mendoza   Santa Fe

SANTIAGO   14   MONTEVIDEO

35   RIO PLATA

Les Leñas   BUENOS
AIRES

Santa Rosa   3

Colorado River   Mar del Plata

San Martin   Neuquen   Rio Negro   Bahia Blanca
de los Andes

San Carlos   Viedma
de Bariloche   GULF SAN MATIAS

Puerto Montt   Puerto Madryn   Peninsula
Valdés

Esquel   Trelew

Chubut River   Punta
Tombo

GULF SAN
JORGE

40   **ARGENTINA**

3

Lake
Argentina

El Calafate   N

Fitz Roy   Rio   Malvinas/Falkland Islands
and Paine Tower   Gallegos

Punta Arenas   Strait of Magellan

TIERRA DEL   ■ SKI AREA
FUEGO
SCALE   150 Miles
Ushuaia   0   250 Kilometers

PACIFIC OCEAN

ANDES MTNS

CHILE

ANDES MTNS

ATLANTIC OCEAN

FACTS AT YOUR FINGERTIPS

WHAT IT WILL COST. For years, Argentina has had one of the most volatile economies in the world, a boom-bust seesaw riddled with inflation that sometimes has risen nearly 5 percent a day, under both dictator generals and elected presidents. Given such circumstances, travelers have been hardpressed to guess prices. One year a cup of coffee and two croissants would cost $8.50; six months later two people could sit down in the finest restaurant in Buenos Aires and order a four-course dinner with a superb bottle of wine for less than $8.

Wage and price freezes have not tamed inflation, so at press time Argentina is no longer a cheap destination. It is, however, quite affordable, and many bargains remain for those used to New York and London prices. The most sumptuous dinners, particularly with a French accent, can run as high as $100 per person with wine and tip, but likewise, a slab of rare, wood-grilled sirloin with salad, potatoes, espresso, and a house wine costs about $15 at steak houses in Buenos Aires, and a little less in the hinterlands. Some restaurants are gouging on wine tabs, so protect yourself by checking ahead with the hotel concierge for reasonable prices.

Order only national liquors in bars or you'll pay a tremendous import premium—shopowners get from $75–$100 for a bottle of the all-time Latin American favorite, Johnny Walker Black Label. It's simple enough. Say *"Whiskey nacional, por favor"* or *"Vodka nacional,"* or *"Campari."* Don't ask for "Scotch" or the waiter will bring you Scotch from Scotland. At the better bars, from late in the afternoon on through the northern dinner hour, hard liquor is served with free hors d'oeuvres.

To taxi around the area of Buenos Aires where the action is centered costs $2–$3. Figure $35 for a tango show with a couple of drinks; and $60 for a moderate, well-situated hotel, including taxes, double occupancy.

There are few off-season prices.

SOURCES OF INFORMATION. Argentina's national tourist office does not have offices out of the country. Moreover, Argentine embassies and consulates do not give advice to travelers. In general, airlines that fly to Argentina provide some information on popular destinations like Buenos Aires, the lake district of Bariloche, and Iguazu Falls. Area specialists are another key source. When the latest, very specific information is not easily obtained at home, call a reputable travel agency in Buenos Aires. No-hassle accuracy is well worth the cost.

Aerolineas Argentinas can answer some questions (800–333–0276). The airline has no brochures describing Argentina, but sales offices can give verbal information and mail tour brochures; in London, 071–439–6228.

Airlines that fly to Argentina can be helpful. In general, they are associated with tour operators specializing in Latin America and can refer you to those companies for further information. Check with **American Airlines** (800–832–8383); **Pan Am,** which gives the names of tour operators it uses (800–221–1600); and **Varig** (800–468–2744). Consult the **South American Explorers Club,** Box 18327, Denver, CO 80218 (303–320–0388) about off-track travel. The **U.S. Government Printing Office,** Washington, DC 20402 (202–783–3238) is offering *Background Notes on Argentina* for $1. Another good source is the **Latin America Reservation Center,** Box 1435, Dundee, FL 33838 (800–327–3573).

Américas, the magazine of the Organization of American States, has articles about Argentina and other member countries. For a $15 annual subscription write: Box 973, Farmingdale, NY 11737–0001.

The following Argentine travel agencies located in Buenos Aires are particularly attuned to expectations and eccentricities of English-speaking travelers. **City Service,** Florida 890 (312–8416, Fax 313–9407), the American Express affiliate, is a prominent Anglo-Argentine firm. **Macren Travel,** Florida 734, second floor (322–7998, also the fax number), is small, with impeccable personalized service. Andrew Macfarlane, Macren's president, is well-known by North American travel agents and prepares individual programs depending on particular interests. **Melia,** Florida 826, fourth floor (312–8209, 313–8144, Fax 313–9094) is a Spanish-owned agency, the largest in Latin America. It has offices in New York, Chicago, Los Angeles, San Francisco, Santa Monica, New Jersey, Las Vegas, and Miami (800–327–1515) and in London at 273 Regent St. (499–6493). **Thos. Cook & Son,** 25 de Mayo 195, fifth floor (30–8371), has a branch at the Sheraton Hotel in conjunction with Wagons-lits Turismo and offices in several North American and U.K. cities.

WHEN TO GO. From northern jungles to the glacial south, from the highest peaks in the Western Hemisphere to the beach resorts on the Atlantic, Argentina's climate encompasses it all—in a milder way than equal latitudes in the Northern Hemisphere. Because the southern half is narrower, the oceans moderate temperatures. Avoid July if you can, when month-long school holidays overcrowd popular resort areas. January is the other traditional holiday period for Argentines, the peak of their summer, so accommodations are especially crowded both at beaches and inland resorts.

Buenos Aires: Anytime is good for traveling to the "City of Good Air." Rain falls throughout the year. While humid summer temperatures (Dec.-Feb.) steam over 100-degrees on occasion, *pamperos* barrel up from the south blowing clean air through the city. Smog is not a problem. Winters are cold, blowy, and often frosty, but snow comes only very occasionally—indeed, oranges grow in the city's suburbs.

Iguazú Falls: Red clay jungle with high humidity. About 80 inches of annual rainfall, year round. Good luck dictates whether a traveler arrives in the middle of two weeks of rain or a dry month or two. Summer temperatures (Jan.-Feb.) usually range in the high 90s-low 100s. Winter temperatures (June-Aug.) drop about 10 degrees. The best time to visit is August to October, when temperatures are lower and the orchids are at their peak.

Northwest-Argentina's Colonial region: Here on the dry, eastern slopes of the Andes are deserts, high (12,000 feet) plains, and grand canyons. Summer days are blazing hot while nights are cool; winters are snowy with temperatures ranging from the low 20s to upper 40s. At the foot of the cordillera, irrigation from the Inca Conquest on to modern times has turned areas around Tucumán and Mendoza green and humid. Winter days are chilly, not cold. The rainy period is December through March, averaging about 7 inches a month.

Narrow-gauge tourist trains make their thrilling ascents from Salta and Jujuy only during the dry season from April to November.

Patagonia, the Alpine lake district: Lush rain forests receive more than three times as much moisture (snow and rain) annually than the Amazon, mostly from May to July. Like their counterparts in the Alps and the California Sierra, resort towns like San Martín de los Andes and Bariloche are open all year. Skiers come from July to early September; deer hunters from March 1 to April 15; trout fishermen during the November 15-April 15 season. Nature lovers who like to stroll or boat on mountain lakes prefer late November for spring wildflowers or April, when strands of yellow and red beech transform the dense green forests. Busloads of high school seniors come to Bariloche in December for non-stop graduation celebrating. Summer temperatures can get up into the high 70s, but most of the year, temperatures range from the 30s to the 60s.

Patagonia, the coastal deserts: Right whales, 2,000-pound sea elephants, sea lions, and millions of Magellanic penguins court, mate, and raise their young where bleak shrubland meets the Atlantic. Located on the infamous "Roaring Forties" (as sailors call the southern latitude), Westerlies roar across the Pacific and batter Patagonia throughout the year. Thirty mile per hour winds are common, and 100 mile per hour is not unheard of. Summer daytime temperatures are in the low 80s but can drop suddenly to the 50s; winters hover around the freezing mark.

Whale watching cruises begin in July and continue through November until the whales leave. Winter waters are rough until spring. By then (mid-September) penguins begin returning to their shallow burrows. Chicks hatch in December; adults molt in February; nearly all have swum north for a warm winter by the end of March. Visitors can overlap whales and penguins, but generally not sea lions and elephants. They don't arrive until November and leave (approximately) in March.

Patagonia, the south (including a still-growing glacier and the southernmost town in the world):Windy, milder temperatures than one would expect so close to Antarctica—from the 20s to the 40s in winter, and summers in the 40s and 60s. There is moderate precipitation. Glaciers calve into southern lakes throughout the summer thaw from October to the end of April. The biggest spectacle comes at the end of March when one of the higher lakes ruptures through the blue ice dam of Perito Moreno Glacier, shattering gigantic chunks of ice in its path. But Perito Moreno continues to move forward, blocking the lake again. The breakthrough comes every two or three years—last succeeding in 1988.

Although most visitors visit Tierra del Fuego in the summer, there are some, including cross country enthusiasts, who discover that the inhabitants of Ushuaia don't hibernate from May to September. Some are out fishing for crab, served fresh immediately thereafter in local restaurants.

WHAT TO TAKE. Argentina rode out the blue jean revolution in dark three-piece suits. Until recently, Levis were seen only in the duty-free port of Ushuaia, and in Bariloche when vacationing Brazilians arrived. Summers are surprisingly casual today, although you should remember that Buenos Aires is not a beach city. In downtown Buenos Aires men wear North American–style polo shirts and chinos out to dinner. But given the slightest doubt about formality, be conservative. While few women wear shorts in Buenos Aires, casual clothes in the current fashion are very much the rule.

Winters remain formal, with men in suits and dark wool overcoats. Ties must be worn to the Colón Theater. Many women from the middle classes on up wear fur coats (of varying quality), high boots, and dresses. Gold jewelry continues to be worn publicly, but one needs to be cautious as street robberies have become more commonplace. Fashion in the country follows the Buenos Aires example, with the exception of the resort cities of Bariloche and Iguazu. There, easily packable clothes are more commonly seen.

If you're going to the Andes or Patagonia, take along a windproof, waterproof jacket. Sweaters can be worn underneath on cold mornings and shed later during the day. Also, include a windproof cap to protect your ears.

Note: Inveterate readers should bring books with them. Better to suffer the weight than the local price. However, used paperbacks can be found in a special section of the ABC bookstore in Buenos Aires, Córdoba 685, for around $1 each. Pack a collapsible umbrella, also a high-priced item. If you shoot Kodachrome film, bring extra rolls with you as it is neither sold nor processed in Argentina.

SPECIAL EVENTS. January: *National Beach Festival* at Mar del Plata. *National Folklore Festival* at Cosquín, Córdoba. **February:** Processions on horseback at Humahuaca near Jujuy for *La Candelaria. Indian-influenced carnivals* celebrated in the northwest on the weekend before Ash Wednesday and on the weekend following. Mendoza commemorates *San Martín's crossing the Andes* towards the end of the month, before the wine festival (no fixed date). **March:** *Grape harvest festival* in Mendoza. Fountains of free red wine to drink, queen, and parade in early March. **April:** *Cultural season* begins in Buenos Aires with opening of Colón Theater and multitude of other theaters; the season lasts through November. **May:** *Pilgrimage* to Lujan, near Buenos Aires. **July:** *National Agricultural Show,* international judges, one of the finest in world, last two weeks in July in Buenos Aires. Processions in Salta and Jujuy honor *St. James.* **August:** *Snow Carnival* and *national ski championships* in Bariloche, early August. *Fishing competition* for the fighting, 50–60 pound, golden Dorados in Paso de la Patria, a northeast town along the Paraná River. **September:** *Ski competitions and festivals* in all winter resorts. *National Flower Festival* in Escobar, near Buenos Aires. *Polo season* begins, through mid-December (also March–May). **October:** *Pottery Festival* in La Quiaca, Jujuy Province. *Day of the Islander* in Tigre, the Venice of Buenos Aires. *Welsh singing festival* in Trevelin, a Patagonian mountain town near Esquel. **November:** *Argentine National Polo Championships* in Buenos Aires, last two weeks. Highest goal polo teams in world. *Gaucho festival* in Wild West town of San Antonio de Areco, 80 miles north of Buenos Aires. **December:** *School holidays* begin December 15 and end after the first week in March.

TRAVEL DOCUMENTS AND CUSTOMS. U.S. citizens need a valid passport but do not need a visa for visits up to 90 days. Multiple entries are allowed. For further details, contact any of the following consulate offices: 20 N. Clark St., Suite 602, Chicago, IL 60602 (312–263–7435); 2000 Post Oak Blvd., Suite 1810, Houston, TX 77056 (713–871–8935); 3550 Wilshire Blvd., Suite 1450, Los Angeles, CA

90010 (213–739–9977); 80 S.W. 8th St., Suite 1820, Miami, FL 33130 (305–373–7794/1889); 915 World Trade Center, 2 Canal St., New Orleans, LA 70130 (504–523–2823/6660); 12 W. 56 St., New York, NY 10019 (212–603–0400); 870 Market St., Room 1083, San Francisco, CA 94102 (415–982–3050/3070); and 1600 New Hampshire Ave. N.W., Washington, DC 20009 (202–939–6411).

Canadian citizens need a valid passport. No visa is required for tourists.

No visa is required for citizens of the United Kingdom for stays of up to 90 days. The Argentine Consulate in London is at 111 Cardogan Gardens (584–6494, 589–3104).

Cholera, yellow fever, and typhus vaccination certificates must be presented for travelers coming from infected areas. For current requirements, check with the Argentine consulates.

If you come directly to Buenos Aires by air or ship, you will find that customs officials usually wave you through without any inspection. Foreign bus passengers usually have their suitcases opened, along with all other passengers.

Personal clothing and effects are admitted free of duty, provided they have been used, as are personal jewelry and professional equipment, including portable computers. Travel agents or airlines can make advance arrangements for hunting equipment. Fishing gear presents no problems, but can be easily rented in resort towns.

Two liters of alcoholic beverages, 400 cigarettes, and 50 cigars are not dutiable upon entry. Argentine cigarettes have a different taste than North American, so particular smokers should bring their favorite brands.

GETTING TO ARGENTINA. By air. At the southern end of the continent, Argentina is at the end or beginning of a hundred travel routes that fan out to such places as Easter Island, Tahiti, New Zealand, South Africa, North America, Europe, Asia, and the rest of South America. Travelers from North America and Europe can fly nonstop to Buenos Aires or they can make a loop around the continent, stopping en route.

North American Gateways—*From New York:* Pan Am and American Airlines have connecting flights from cities throughout the U.S., also Aerolineas Argentinas, Ecuatoriana, LAN-Chile, Varig. *From Los Angeles:* Pan Am, American, Aerolineas Argentinas, Ecuatoriana, Varig. *From Miami:* Pan Am, American, Aerolineas Argentinas, Ecuatoriana, LAN-Chile, Lineas Aereas Paraguayas, Lloyd Aereo Boliviano, Varig. *From Toronto:* Canadian Airlines, with connecting flights throughout Canada, Aerolineas Argentinas. *From Montreal:* Canadian Airlines, Aerolineas Argentinas.

European Gateways—*From Amsterdam:* Aerolineas Argentinas, KLM, Varig. *From Frankfurt:* Aerolineas Argentinas, Lufthansa, Varig. *From London:* Aerolineas Argentinas, British Airways. *From Paris:* Aerolineas Argentinas, Air France, Varig. *From Madrid:* Aerolineas Argentinas, Iberia, Varig. *From Rome:* Aerolineas Argentinas, Alitalia, Varig. *From Zurich:* Aerolineas Argentinas, Swiss Air, Varig.

Pacific Gateways—*From Australia or New Zealand:* Aerolineas Argentinas has a polar flight from Sydney and Auckland, or you can take Air New Zealand or UTA to Tahiti, then LAN-Chile to Santiago-Buenos Aires.

Typical flying times: Miami-Buenos Aires, eight hours, nonstop; Los Angeles-Buenos Aires, 15 hours, two stops; Paris-Buenos Aires, 12.25 hours, one stop; Auckland-Buenos Aires, 11.50 hours, one stop.

By sea. Every (South American) summer, the Italian Costa Line repositions two of its ships from the Mediterranean to ply the coastlines of Argentina and Brazil (305–358–7325, ask for Mediterranean desk). Cruises ranging from nine to 30 days are scheduled from mid-December through the end of February. There are no air/sea packages. Passengers have a choice of departing from either Santos (the port of São Paulo) or Rio de Janeiro. *Enrico,* a 16,000 ton, 600–650 passenger ship, makes an annual 24-day swing through the Strait of Magellan to Punta Arenas, Chile, back to Ushuaia, Argentina, and down to Cape Horn. The ship also stops at Puerto Madryn for tours of the penguin and sea elephant reserves and Buenos Aires. *Eugenio,* 30,000 tons and 1,000 passengers, includes Buenos Aires in an itinerary that embraces spirited Salvador da Bahia, where *candomblé* (Brazilian voodoo) and Catholicism mix freely. Costa's ships have been upgraded, and feature Italian crews, friendly atmospheres, average food and accommodations, and cleanliness. These cruises are heavily booked ahead; most passengers are Brazilians and Argentines.

Between October and March, Society Expeditions sends its lecturers and naturalists on a number of voyages around the southern tip of the continent and the Antarctic Peninsula. Journeys are around three weeks on the 100-passenger *Explorer,* the 140-passenger *Discoverer,* and the new 160-passenger *Society Adventurer.* For details contact your travel agent or Society Expeditions, 3131 Elliott Ave., Suite 700, Seattle, WA 98121 (800–426–7794).

Another company, *Travel Dynamics,* operates similar specialist cruises on the 120-passenger *Illiria,* out of Ushuaia, Argentina's southernmost city on the Beagle Channel. Programs run about 14 days and include time in Buenos Aires. For details contact Travel Dynamics, Inc., 132 East 70th St., New York, NY 10021 (800–367–6766).

By bus. Travelers can enter Argentina by bus from Bolivia, Brazil, Chile, Paraguay, and Uruguay. There are numerous types of service, from standard to deluxe, with rest rooms and sleeperette seats. There are clean, modern rest stop facilities throughout Argentina.

Sample times: Rio de Janeiro-Buenos Aires, 50 hours. For budget travelers, savings are substantial. Example: The cheapest round-trip airplane ticket between Rio and Buenos Aires is $300; round-trip on a sleeperette bus is about $80.

By hydrofoil and ferry. Frequent hydrofoils and ferries cross the River Plate between Colonia, Uruguay, and Buenos Aires. Ferries operate between Carmelo, Uruguay, and Tigre, in the northern suburbs of Buenos Aires; also between Montevideo, the Uruguayan capital, and Buenos Aires. One-way fares start at around $20.

By train. In November 1985, rains washed out trestles on the spectacular, narrow gauge tracks between Jujuy and La Paz, Bolivia (described in Paul Theroux's *The Old Patagonian Express*). The bridges have now been rebuilt and the service operates weekly. The equally dramatic trip over the highest section of the Andes, past Aconcagua (elevation 22,834 feet) from Mendoza to Santiago, Chile was suspended a few years ago for lack of passengers. A new line links Asunción, Paraguay, with Posadas in Argentina, through the Paraguayan border town of Encarnación.

By car. Rental cars cannot cross frontiers. However, travelers with their own cars can drive into Argentina from Uruguay, Brazil, Paraguay, or Chile.

CURRENCY. As part of the government's program to turn around the economy, the unstable peso was renamed *austral* (which means southern). But it seems an unstable peso by any other name is still a peso. The economy continues to suffer despite various mini-devaluations. It is impossible to predict what the tourist dollar will buy from one week to the next, but at press time on the free exchange market there are about 6,000 australs to the dollar, 5,200 to the Canadian dollar, and 11,600 to the pound sterling. Dollars are the most flexible form of exchange in Argentina, so residents of other countries should change their currencies to dollars before their journey, even holders of Swiss francs. Be sure the bills are not torn or they won't be accepted.

Foreign currencies are now bought and sold openly and finding out current rates is simple—the *Miami Herald's* Latin American edition (available the same day in Buenos Aires) lists the market rates for every Latin currency. You can change money at your hotel or *Casas de Cambio* (currency exchanges), which have small competitive variations on rates. Some display rates for all major currencies.

Stores will usually allow that day's top exchange rate if you pay for your purchases with (1) U.S. dollars in cash or (2) a personal check drawn on a major U.S. bank account or (3) traveler's checks in U.S. dollars. These are sometimes valued slightly lower because traveler's checks are not as easy to buy and sell as unmarked cash.

American Express, Diners Club, MasterCard and VISA are commonly accepted through the country, although some places accept only one or two of those credit cards.

ACCOMMODATIONS. While Argentina does not have any "super deluxe" hotels when graded against the finest international establishments, it offers far more excellent tourist class hotels than do most countries, both north and south of the equator. Amenities in these hotels are superior: centrally located, 24-hour room service and warm personal attention, central heating, bidets, television, dry cleaning, restaurants. Our selection of hotels in Argentina follows this simple grading system based on price: in Buenos Aires *Super Deluxe,* $140–$180; *Deluxe,* $110–

$140; *Expensive,* $70–$110; *Moderate,* $45–70; *Inexpensive,* $15–$45. Outside Buenos Aires prices in the best local hotel range from $30 to over $100, depending on the popularity of the region for tourists and the quality of the hotel, and moderate range hotels are between $30 and $50 a night. All of these prices are for two people in a double room, with 13 percent tax included. Meals are separate. July holidays and summers can be crowded, so reservations are wise but generally not necessary unless you are going to Bariloche or Iguazú.

Pensions, Bed-and-Breakfasts are seldomly used. Pensions here are very basic accommodations for permanent boarders, and cost about $30–$40 a month; there is no tradition of bed-and-breakfasts.

Motels are generally used for romantic trysts and are rented by the hour. Those that are legitimate motels can be found through the Automóvil Club Argentino's nationwide network of motels. Prices and facilities are inexpensive—about $20 to $25. Make reservations through Automóvil Club Argentino, Libertador 1850 (802–6061).

The **Youth Hostel Association,** Talcahuano 214, second floor, Buenos Aires (45–1001) is open weekdays, 11 A.M.–7 P.M., and provides details on hostels throughout the country.

ROUGHING IT. Private campsites can be found in popular tourist destinations, including on the beach in some areas. Usually they have running water, electricity, and bathroom facilities with toilets and showers. The Automobile Club has campgrounds (see above for address). Provincial tourist offices in Buenos Aires have lists of campgrounds in their regions. Some have telephones and you can make reservations.

RESTAURANTS. Our restaurant grading system has three categories: *Expensive,* $25 and up; *Moderate,* $15–$25; *Inexpensive,* $15 and under. These price ranges are based on the cost of an average three-course dinner for one person and do not include beverages, tax, or tip. In Buenos Aires, the dinner bill can go up to $100 with exuberant à la carte ordering from a French-influenced menu and a bottle of fine Argentine wine. Still, dinner in one of B.A.'s best steakhouses costs about $20 for an *empanada* (meat pie), a large sirloin (*bife chorizo*), French fries, a huge lettuce and tomato salad, flan, coffee, and a half bottle of red wine. Inexpensive food depends on the location of the restaurant, not the type of food. Prices tend to be higher downtown and in Recoleta. Credit cards are usually accepted, but often only one or two of the four common cards: American Express, Diners Club, MasterCard, Visa. It is unpredictable which one(s) will be accepted.

Argentine office hours end at about 7 P.M. Whether dining out or at home, Argentines don't eat until 9 or 10 P.M. on the weekdays—and later on weekends. They survive by pausing for tea and biscuits at about 5 P.M. For rumbling northern stomachs that protest after 7 or 8 P.M., Buenos Aires has *confiterias,* steakhouses, and hotel restaurants that remain open from lunch through dinner. Outside of the capital, however, restaurants usually don't open until 8:30 or 9 P.M.

Argentine Food and Drink. Beef or *bife* (beef-eh), as they say in Spanish, is the tale of Argentina, the golden El Dorado of her economy, the taste that reaches back nearly to her mother's milk. Gauchos spent lifetimes eating native cattle . . . and nothing else.

Somewhere around 50 million Angus and Hereford cattle graze on pampas grasses so nutritious that they aren't fattened on corn for tenderness, but more clover. There is nothing quite like the flavor of lean, tender, three-inch bifes grilled over coals of the *quebracho,* an ax-breaking hardwood from the Chaco. Meats are grilled at an *asado,* not a barbecue. *Picante* (hot) translates as spicy in Argentina, but not "Mexican." If you ask for *chimichurri,* some steakhouses will serve a picante sauce made of garlic, olive oil, vinegar, and loads of cilantro (coriander), a parsley cousin. *Bife de chorizo* is a triple-wide strip sirloin; *bife de lomo* is a filet. *Jugoso* is rare, which is not how the Argentines eat their steak.

Adventurous eaters will want to have a parrillada sizzling in a platter set over a pan of hot coals on their table. The mixed grill includes blood sausage, short ribs, and various pieces of internal and external organs like intestines and udder. Thin slices of *matambre* are a typical beef hors d'oeuvre. It is made by laying out boiled eggs, chunks of ham, and hearts of palm on a flank steak, rolling it into a loaf, soaking it in a marinade, and baking it. And naturally, there are hamburgers. Whether it's a reflection of the economy or a taste acquired from North America, hamburgers now rank high in consumption, along with the beef schnitzel called *Milanesa*.

NOTE: If you don't want salt liberally sprinkled on your meat, salad, and potatoes, say *No use (oo-say) sal, por favor.*

Young goat (*chivito*) is wonderfully succulent; tender porkloin (*matambrito de cerdo*) is crispy outside and served with slices of lemon; sausages come in all shapes, sizes, and ingredients; chicken; fat slices of Provolone cheese sprinkled with oregano; and, occasionally, grilled lamb; are other Argentine treats. Asados are always served with French fries. The shoestring variety are called *papas pai.* Argentine restaurateurs don't seem to know about baked potatoes. To vary the monotony, there are mashed potatoes (*papas puree*), boiled (*papas naturales*), creamed (*papas a la crema*), and marvelously light puffs (*papas soufles*).

The favorite Argentine dessert is not the creme caramel *flan* that is served so often, but *dulce de leche,* milk boiled with sugar, a pinch of soda, and a few drops of vanilla or chocolate. The thick, brownish cream is spread on breakfast toast, baked in cakes, meringues, and tarts, and is eaten alone by the spoonful. It is wonderful with vanilla ice cream.

Asado and Italian cuisine, particularly of Naples and Sicily, are typically found throughout Argentina. Buenos Aires has the heaviest immigrant influence, with Jewish delicatessens, British (especially high tea), French, German, Irish, Cantonese (only mediocre), and Persian haute cuisine, to name a few. Bariloche specializes in chocolates, fondues, and strudels. Lamb asado (*corderito al asador*), king crab (*centolla*), and hot potato salad are popular in Ushuaia, while in the Trelew-Puerto Madryn area, Welsh high teas with seven varieties of rich cakes, and local fish are the favorites—sea trout (*trucha*), sea salmon (*salmón*), white sea bass (*corvina*), and squid (*calamares*).

Indigenous cooking continues to infuence two of the northern areas. In the northeast, near Iguazú, typical Guarani foods are fun to try. *Chipa* is a little hard biscuit made with manioc, eggs, and cheese. (Manioc looks like a yam but tastes more like a white potato.) *Sopa Paraguaya* is a very light pie made with corn, cheese, and eggs. A very local dish is *reviro,* in which dried meat, onions, and spices are fried. In the Tucumán-Salta-Jujuy area, typical food comes from the Incan-Spanish tradition. It is hotter and spicier and soup is the common beginning to a meal. Don't miss *locro,* a hearty soup made of white corn, fat red sausages, potatoes, pumpkin, bacon, pork ribs, and small onions; *empanadas Jujeñas,* a more substantial, Jujuy-style pie made of hand-chopped meat and potatoes; *humita en chala,* mildly spiced corn meal tamales cooked in corn leaves; and *quesillo con miel de caña,* soft cheese covered with the extremely sweet honey of sugar cane.

Argentines make beer, whiskey, scotch (the best brand is Premium), vodka, Campari, rums, and so forth. Of these, only wine is exported.

North Americans will find the Argentine reds a little fuller than California's. European connoisseurs are predicting that Malbec, a red wine unique to Mendoza, will be the wine of the twenty-first century on the world market. The slightly more expensive *Martins* Malbec is just as good as top-of-the-line *Trapiche.* You can trust all lines of these two brands; other fine brands in both reds and whites are *Lopez, Norton, Esmeralda,* and *Weinert. San Felipe* has highly recommended white wines, but its reds don't maintain the quality.

Given the high consumption of beef rather than fish, Argentines understandably drink *vino tinto* (red). For those who prefer *vino blanco* (whites,) leave aside Mendoza and turn north to the colonial crossroads of Salta. Here the Torrontés grape thrives. Whereas it is nearly unusable in its homeland of Spain, in Salta the Torrontés produces a very dry white wine with an overwhelming bouquet. Argentines point out pridefully that this wine is exported to Germany and France.

Rules of thumb for ordering wine: Inexpensive reds are better than inexpensive whites. If you want a fairly good wine at bargain rates, order *vino reserva,* for the cheapest of a winery's fine (*vino fino*) lines.

Dereck Foster, the food columnist of the *Buenos Aires Herald,* listed the following wines as his current favorites—adding that the list is "subjective, personal, and probably controversial." White: Colección Privada Chardonnay (Lavaque), Luigi Bosca Sauvignon, Etchart Chardonnay, Saint Felicien Chenin (Esmerelda), Saint Felicien Chardonnay, Nacari Torrontes, Claire (Flichman), Grand Bourg Chenin, Bianchi Chablis, and Orfila Chardonnay. Red: Etiqueta Blanca (Suter), Weinert

Cabernet Sauvignon '77, Saint Felicien Cabernet-Merlot, Luigi Bosca Malbec, Caballero de la Cepa Cabernet (Flichman), Intimo de Canale, and Finca del Marques (Hiram Walker). Wine by the glass is not available, but a half bottle of *vino reserva* costs only about $5 in a restaurant. A popular summer cooler is *clericot*, a white sangria made with either wine or champagne, strawberry, peaches, oranges, or whatever fruits are in season or suit the mood of the bartender.

TIPPING. Add 10–15% in bars and restaurants, while 5% is enough if the bill runs high. Argentines round off a taxi fare, but there is no need to tip cab drivers, although a few who hang around hotels popular with North Americans act like they expect it. Hotel porters should be tipped at least $1, give the doorman about $.50, and beauty and barber shop personnel should be given about 5%.

BUSINESS HOURS AND HOLIDAYS. Shops are open from 9 A.M.–7 or 8 P.M. Monday through Friday; Saturday from 9 A.M. to 1 P.M. In the Buenos Aires suburbs (with the exception of the large malls like Unicenter and Shopping Soleil) and most places outside the capital, shops close for siesta from around 12:30 P.M. until 3:30 or 4 P.M., opening again until 7:30 P.M. Post offices open 8 A.M.–6 P.M. weekdays, 8 A.M.–1 P.M. on Saturdays; there is a 24-hour telephone and telex service at Corrientes 707; bank hours are 10 A.M.–3 P.M.

Shops, banks, and foreign embassies close on national holidays, but restaurants, bars, movies, and theaters generally remain open. Embassies are also closed on their own national holidays.

National Holidays: Jan. 1 (New Year's Day); Maundy Thursday (optional holiday, some offices closed); Good Friday; May 1 (Labor Day); May 25 (Anniversary of the 1810 Revolution); June 10 (Malvinas Day); June 20 (Flag Day); July 9 (Independence Day); Aug. 17 (Anniversary of San Martín's Death); Oct. 12 (Columbus Day); Dec. 8 (Immaculate Conception); Dec. 25 (Christmas).

TELEPHONES. The direct dialing code for Argentina is 54. The city code for Buenos Aires is 1. The towns and cities most often visited by tourists can be dialed directly. *The northwest, with the Iguazú Falls and Jesuit Missions:* Iguazú, 0757; Posadas, 0752. *The Colonial Northwest:* Salta, 087; Jujuy, 0882; Mendoza, 061. *Patagonia:* San Martín de los Andes, 0972; Bariloche, 0944; Trelew (animal reserves), 0965; Calafate, 0902; Ushuaia, 0901. Argentina is two time zones earlier than Eastern Standard Time. There are daylight saving hours mid-October through March, but only in the provinces of Buenos Aires, Santa Fé, and Córdoba, not the western provinces.

Long distance calls can be made through your hotel telephone system, but they are subject to extra taxes there. To avoid the tax, buy special-sized tokens from Telecom Argentina. The office at Corrientes 707 is open 24 hours.

Pay phones can be found in the streets, public buildings, offices, airports and other transportation terminals, and bars and restaurants. They are orange and operate on tokens called *cospeles* that can be purchased at newsstands, cigarette kiosks, and in restaurants and bars. One *cospel* buys from two to six minutes of time, depending on whether you are calling during prime time (8 A.M.-8 P.M.) or otherwise.

Despite the recent privatization of the telephone organization, service in the capital is highly erratic. Here, a common phone greeting is *equivocado* (E-keev-oh-cado), meaning wrong number. Argentines (who have to live with the frustration) are uncomfortable doing business by telephone. Perhaps the only advantage is that very few restaurants require reservations.

Emergency telephone numbers: City Medical Attention, 34–4001; Burn Wounds Hospital, 923–3022; Coronary Mobile Unit; 107; Dial-a-priest, 84–2000; Fire Department, 23–2222; Police 101; British Hospital, 23–1081.

MAIL. When delivery is normal, i.e. not snowed under with Christmas rush, it takes about seven days for letters to pass between Buenos Aires and the U.S. Stamps for a regular overseas letter cost around $.50. Postcards are sold with envelopes to be mailed as letters.

Rush mail. Federal Express and DHL International deliver in two or three business days in downtown Buenos Aires, take an extra day to deliver to the suburbs and other major cities, and about five business days for outlying towns. Minimum rates are expensive, at least $40. U.S. Express Mail takes three days to Buenos Aires and suburbs, longer to other towns. Minimum rate is about $25.

American Express card holders can have mail sent to Buenos Aires care of American Express, City Service Travel, Florida 890 (fourth floor), 1005 Buenos Aires. (This AMEX affiliate does not handle cash advances, however. You need to go to Banco de Galicia, Juan Perón 415, fourth floor, for this.)

NEWSPAPERS. The *Buenos Aires Herald,* Azopardo 455 (34–8476), is one of the best English-language dailies published in a non-English-speaking country. During the last military regime, *Herald* editors and reporters risked death to write against the disappearances. Available daily in several cities, it offers a good cross-section of international news. Droll, opinionated Argentine columnists romp through fields of national expertise, from food and economy to the importance of straightening the hairs on bull testicles for artificial insemination. Movie, theater, and local events are also included.

If you read Spanish, you can have your pick from half a dozen morning and afternoon papers. The most popular are *La Nación* and *Clarin.*

The *Miami Herald*'s Latin American edition arrives about noon the same day; the *International Herald Tribune* is a day or so late; the *New York Times* arrives two to three days late. Check major hotels and the newsstands on Florida for copies. U.S. weekly news magazines are available from most vendors on the streets, along with an unpredictable mix of other imported magazines, all expensive.

ELECTRIC CURRENT. Argentina runs on 220-volt current and uses the continental European plug. Converter plugs are readily available, however, as are transformers to make your 110-volt gear function. Current is 50 cycle A.C., so that your U.S.A. tape recorder or record player will need special spindles to get the correct "drive."

USEFUL ADDRESSES. The **U.S. Embassy and Consulate** are located in the Palermo Park area, Avenida Colombia 4300. Embassy hours: Mon.–Fri., 9 A.M.–5:45 P.M. The Consulate's public hours are 9 A.M.–noon. A marine guard is on duty 24 hours and for emergencies he will make contact with an Embassy official. Phone numbers are 774–8811/9911/7611. The **Canadian Embassy,** Suipacha 1111, downtown on the corner of Suipacha and Santa Fé. Hours: Mon.–Fri., 9 A.M.–5 P.M. Summer hours are slightly shorter. (312–9081). The **British Embassy** is at Dr. Luis Agote 2412 (803–7070). Hours: Mon.–Fri., 9 A.M.–1 P.M. and 2:30–4:30 P.M.; mornings only in the summer.

National tourism offices are located at Ezeiza, the international airport, and Aeroparque, the domestic airport. Information kiosks are run by the Buenos Aires municipality on Florida between Córdoba and Paraguay (outside Harrods), on Florida at the corner of R.S. Peña; and at the San Martín Cultural Center, Sarmiento 1551. Hours are weekdays 8:30 A.M.–8 P.M. and Sat. 9 A.M.–2 P.M. The central information office, ENATUR, is at Santa Fé 883 (312–2232/5550). Open 10 A.M.–5 P.M.

Argentine travel agencies: See "Sources of Information," above for listings of agencies who are familiar with the needs of North American and British travelers.

Provincial tourist offices in Buenos Aires offer excellent, detailed information. Most have photo albums showing main sights and some hotels in various price ranges. English is spoken, but usually by only one person, and the personnel work in shifts, so call ahead. Don't write ahead for information, as their financial situation precludes free brochures and mail delivery is slow. Further, telephoning for information may be frustrating because many Argentines are reluctant to answer questions over the telephone. Office hours vary, and are often inconsistent with published advice.

Provincial offices are generally centrally located within walking distance: *Buenos Aires,* (The Pampas) Av. Callao 237 (40–7045); *Catamarca,* Av. Córdoba 2080 (46–6891/4); *Cordoba,* Av. Callao 332 (45–6566, 49–4277); *Corrientes,* San Martin 333, fourth floor (394–7432/7390); *Chaco,* (jungle frontier) Av. Callao 322, first floor (45–0961/3045); *Chubut* (Penguin colonies, etc.), Paraguay 876 (311–0428); *Entre Ríos,* Suipacha 844 (312–2284); *Formosa,* B. Mitre 1747 (45–1916/1998); *Jujuy,* Av. Santa Fé 967 (393–1295/3174); *La Pampa,* Suipacha 346 (396–1145/0603); *La Rioja,* Av. Callao 745 (44–1662, 41–4524); *Mendoza,* Av. Callao 445 (40–6683, 49–2580); *Misiones* (ruins of Jesuit empire, Iguazu Falls), Santa Fé 989 (322–

1671/0677); *Neuquen* (San Martin de los Andes), Juan D. Peron 687 (49–6819, 46–9265); *Rio Negro* (Bariloche), Tucumán 1916 (45–9931/7920); *Salta,* Av. R.S. Peña 933 (396–1455); *San Juan,* Sarmiento 1251 (35–5580); *San Luis,* Azcuénaga 1083 (83–3641); *Santa Cruz* (Lago Argentino), Av. Córdoba 1345, fourteenth floor (42–0381/0916); *Santa Fé,* Montevideo 373, second floor (40–1825); *Santiago del Estero,* Florida 274 (46–9398); *Tierra del Fuego,* Santa Fé 919 (322–8855); *Tucuman,* Bartolomé Mitre 836, First Floor (40–2214).

HEALTH AND SAFETY. Water is safe to drink everywhere in Argentina, vegetables are safe to eat, and the streets are generally safe for walking. During the bountiful, go-go years, taxi drivers would hand money back to befuddled newcomers when they overtipped; one curious New Zealander spent 23 minutes observing packages left outside the locked door of the bus station in Bariloche. Regrettably, those days are dead. Now, some taxi drivers in Buenos Aires who wait at hotels frequented by North Americans take advantage of the confusing fare structure. Worse, robbery has become a reality, particularly in the Central Post Office, train, and bus stations. A common method of stealing backpacks or bags involves a squirt of mustard or ketchup on a victim's clothes. The thief distracts with clean-up assistance while an accomplice runs with the bags.

Note: Carry a photo copy of your passport for identification purposes and keep the original in the hotel safety deposit box along with your airline ticket and some cash.

If you are robbed: Visit the nearest police station last. The police are polite, but they do not expect to recover any of the stolen property, they do not speak English, and they do not record details about the crime; reporting to the police is worthwhile *only* for your insurance claims. If you are on a tight schedule, many companies will accept a copy of the report you file with your consulate. *First* go to your hotel. They will pay the taxi and help you make other necessary calls with translation, such as 24-hour hotlines to stop credit card use. By going in person, Visa and Mastercard can arrange cash advances before use of the card is stopped. During banking hours, the approval takes 15 minutes.

Fortunately, purse snatchers usually dump passports, drivers' licenses, and other unsalable items into plastic sacks and leave them on the streets where scavengers pick them up and return them to the embassy. Rewards are usually $15–$20.

Official policy is that only a stolen passport is the concern of the U.S. Consulate. When pressed, consulars will tell you that money can be advanced if you call someone in the U.S. to have his/her bank wire money to the State Department in Washington, DC. Authorization is then cabled to Buenos Aires. Allow a minimum of two days. New U.S. passports require about a day and a half.

Canadian citizens should contact their embassy at once. Cash will be loaned to you—payback to be made in Canada. Temporary, 30-day passports, with no photographs, are issued within 24 hours after personal information is cabled to Ottawa and verified. No visa necessary.

The British Embassy will provide new passports, but will only advance cash in rare circumstances.

For those who need to renew or replace Argentine visas, the Immigration Headquarters is at Avenida Antartida Argentina 1355 (312–8661); hours Mon.–Fri., 12:30–5:30 P.M.

GETTING AROUND ARGENTINA. By air. All medium-sized and larger cities in Argentina have been well served by the jets of *Aerolineas Argentinas,* the national airline, and/or *Austral,* a private domestic competitor. The national carrier, however, was privatized in late 1990 by a consortium mainly made up of the Spanish airline *Iberia* and *Austral,* and at press time it is uncertain how the domestic routes will be allocated under the new ownership. All small remote towns will continue to have regular service on *L.A.D.E.,* commuter-sized airplanes operated by the Argentine Air Force. Another private service is by *CADA,* which offers a limited number of flights but at competitive rates. Like the United States and Canada, Argentina has large, sparsely inhabited areas to cross getting from one destination to another. The journey itself is the experience for some travelers; these should skip ahead to the train and bus section. For others, arriving is the start of adventure. They are naturals for the Visit Argentina pass: 4 coupons $359, 6 coupons $409, or 8 coupons $459. The rules are that all coupons must be used within 30 days of the first flight and you can't stop twice in any city except to connect. You should also note that the majority of city-to-city flights require a connection in Buenos Aires, for which two coupons are necessary. Also note: the domestic and international airports are 38 miles apart. The passes are valid for all seasons, and can be purchased in Argentina with the presentation of a passport and international ticket. While it is not possible to change the routing once the pass has been issued, it is permitted to change flight times and dates. Usually seats are available on domestic flights, even in high season.

By train. In *The Old Patagonian Express,* travel philosopher Paul Theroux stepped on the commuter train in Boston one morning, bound for the end of the line at Esquel, Argentina. Such a trip is now once again possible, with the repair of the high railway bridges near the Bolivian border. Within Argentina, some of the highlights of Theroux's journey are combined in South American tour programs. Sobec Expeditions, for example, Box 1089, Angels Camp, CA 95222 (209–736–4524), offers a 19-day, $3,500 land-cost Patagonian Panorama tour. The tour travels by wood-paneled, brass-railed trains from Santiago, Chile, to Puerto Montt. The Andes are crossed by boat and bus (details later in the chapter).

The *State Railways* have a network of nearly 20,000 miles, making it one of the largest in the world. All name trains, like *El Libertador* to Mendoza, *Rayo del Sol* to Córdoba, and the *Expreso Lagos del Sur* to Bariloche, are diesel-drawn. Many carry uniformed hostesses, have wall-to-wall carpeting, and a movie car in back. Most sleepers are air-conditioned. One of the pleasures of Argentine railways in the past has been the low price—the system operated at a loss of over $1 million a day. At press time, however, several of the lines were being privatized and the future of some services is uncertain. General information for all trains in Argentina is available from Maipú 88 (331–3280). Sample times: Buenos Aires-Bariloche, 31 hours; Buenos Aires-Mar del Plata, the beach resort, five hours.

By bus. Buses link Argentina with its neighbors, and with itself. More luxurious buses than North Americans know (with sleeperette seats like first-class airline seats) travel to the most remote points and more Spartan buses make the same journeys. Long-distance buses leave from a central terminal at the port-end of Retiro, the central train station downtown.

By car. The *Argentine Automobile Association* (Automóvil Club Argentino, Av. del Libertador 1850, 802–6061) offers a plenitude of services that make driving in Argentina easier. ACA operates filling stations, motels, and campgrounds, and handles break-downs and repairs. It also offers fishing licenses, detailed maps, and experts (some who speak English) to help you plan your route. There are special programs in which you do the driving and ACA provides gas coupons and makes your accommodation arrangements according to a fixed itinerary. AAA members from other countries can use the consulting services without charge, but remember your credentials. A branch office is conveniently located at Harrod's on Florida, second floor, turn right (312–4411 Ext. 256). English is not spoken here and service is limited to very basic information and brochures. For detailed advice and bookings, go to the main office.

Rental cars. People who like the freedom and convenience of fly-drive vacations will be pleased to discover that all cities and smaller areas that attract tourists have rental car agencies. When these companies have branches in other towns, arrangements can be made to leave the car and fly on, rather than retracing the journey. National, Avis, and Hertz offices in Buenos Aires can make reservations in other locations; provincial government tourist offices also have specifics on car rental agencies. *National Car Rental,* Esmeralda 1084 (311–3583); *Avis,* Maipú 944 (311–1008); *Hertz,* Esmeralda 985 (312–0787). Car hire is expensive by U.S. standards—about $70 per day for a medium car, including insurance but excluding mileage (about $.50 per kilometer). The weekly rate, including mileage and insurance, is around $650.

SPORTS. World-class soccer, tennis, polo . . . spectators in Argentina have a bonus. So do travelers who would rather swing a racket, mallet, or themselves. The Buenos Aires section has sports details for that city. What follows is a guide to outdoor interests in the country.

Here are some trips available out of the United States:

For premier birding, *Victor Emanuel Nature Tours,* Box 33008, Austin, TX 78764 (512–328–5221 or 800–328–8368) offers two comprehensive, 19-day trips that circle south from a pampas ranch where W.H. Hudson lived to the habitat of the 1,000,000 penguins of Punta Tombo. The tour also explores Tierra del Fuego, and finally searches the Patagonian glacier area for the uncommon Hooded Grebe, first spotted in 1974 and considered by many to be the most beautiful of the family. Each tour can be extended to see the colorful jungle birds near Iguazu Falls and a venture into high Andean deserts, subtropical forests, and shrubby Chaco of the colonial Northwest. Possibilities in the latter include seeing all three types of Andean flamingos, watching Giant Coots built nests, and sighting the rarest of the world's dippers, the Rufous-throated. Victor Emanuel's basic tour is about $2,900 (land cost); extensions total $2,100.

Since 1960, the *New York Zoological Society,* Travel Department, Bronx, NY 10460 (212–220–5085), has worked with Chubut Province on conservation research. The current program is researching the migration of penguins in Punta Tombo. Twice a year, members of the society (which is easily joined) assist the society's field scientists in banding penguins and observing their behavior. Thus laymen can have special privileges and cross the fences that separate penguins from people. The group lives in simple dorms at the penguin reserve. Cost of the popular 18-day trip is $1,700 for the land portion and includes a stop at Iguazú Falls with a naturalist guide. A portion of the expenses is tax-deductible.

Now that tours and cruise ships have discovered the penguins at Punta Tombo, innovative *Wilderness Travel,* 801 Alston Way, Berkeley, CA 94710 (800–247–6700), camps at an isolated penguin colony at Cabo Virgenes, near the Strait of Magellan, on its 24-day, $1,990 (land-cost), expedition through Patagonia. Hike to the base of Fitz Roy where condors soar and guanacos stare back shyly. The still-growing Moreno Glacier at Lago Argentino and Tierra del Fuego are included in the journey.

Two easy sweeps through Patagonia are offered by the classic adventuring company, *Mountain Travel,* 6420 Fairmount Ave., El Cerrito, CA 94530 (800–227–2384 outside California; 415–527–8100 in California). Both tours have optional walking and no camping. Its 15-day, $1,990–$2,090 (land-cost) "Patagonia Adventure" highlights Glacier National Park. "Patagonia Overland" is a 25-day, $2,850–$3,050 (land-cost) ramble by expedition bus with a motor launch ride on Last Hope Sound to view the tidewater glaciers on the coast of southern Chile. *Questers,* 257 Park Avenue South, New York, NY (212–673–3120), concentrates on wildlife in its 22-day, $4,918, Patagonian tour.

Serious hikers and trekkers have long been interested in Aconcagua, the highest mountain in the Western Hemisphere (*see* Mountaineering, below), but the fine attractions are somewhat tempered by overcrowding and, unfortunately, litter. An alternative is the area of Las Leñas, a resort some 260 miles south of Mendoza. From the resort, it is possible to arrange trips of various durations by foot or horseback. Programs cater to all levels of experience. See Skiing, below, for contact addresses.

Trekking Argentina, Paraguay 542, 2nd floor (313–6853), organizes programs that feature either trekking, bird watching, horseback riding, or overlanding—or combinations of all four. The tours range from two to three weeks and cost between $500 and $800 weekly, all inclusive. The agent in New York is CanoAndes, 37–12 75th St., Queens, NY 11372 (800–242–5554); in London, Exodus Expeditions, 9 Weir Rd., London SW12OLT (081–673–0859).

Fishing and Hunting. Giant sea-run brown trout migrate up the Rio Grande River on the island of Tierra del Fuego from early January through the beginning of April. Like salmon, they spawn and then turn back to the icy waters of the southern Atlantic as it nears the Antarctic Ocean. The trout were imported from Europe over a century ago, and they are trout—maddeningly elusive, fighting trout of trophy size. *Frontiers International,* Box 161, Wexford, PA 15090 (800–245–1950 nationwide; 412–935–1577 in Pennsylvania), sends eight fishermen at a time down to the Rio Grande to test their dry-fly wiles against these whopping browns. From the great sea-faring browns to the fast-biting rainbows and browns in the Andean lakes and rivers near San Martín de los Andes and Esquel, fishermen rejoice at their results. They stay on estancias with personable attention or in remote permanent camps, also with attention. Frontiers' hunters specialize in birds—aiming for migrations of big Magellan geese, a dramatic spectacle that far outnumbers the Canadian counterpart up north. Goose hunting is legendary near San Martin and Esquel. Other world-class hunting trips include shooting ducks, partridge, and pigeons along the Paraná River near Goya, a subtropical rice-growing area, and shooting doves in the soybean and sorghum fields near Córdoba in the central Pampas. Hunting trips cost between $275 and $440 a day. Eleven-day trips to fish for seafaring browns are $2,690 and $2,153 for an equal time in the mountains of San Martin and Esquel—a fee that includes one guide for every two anglers. Airfare is not included.

Bird shooting is also becoming popular with visitors to the northern province of Entre Rios, with U.S. groups staying at the Palacio Santa Cándida near Concepción de Uruguay (see Tours in Buenos Aires for details of this hotel).

Mountaineering. Called *alpinismo,* this sport is skillfully organized, very popular, and friendly to strangers who share the joy of wilderness. Early in the century, Latin American students sent to European universities were inspired by the enthusiasm for hiking, skiing, and climbing in the Alps. They brought the new sports home to the Andes. Pockets of aficionados hauled skis up to the heights on mules, or trudged up on foot for the quick run down. Eventually they organized into Club Andinos, a loosely bound umbrella group that includes Chileans and Peruvians. They have built refuges along hiking trails and ski areas. Check in the Buenos Aires headquarters, Rivadavia 1255 (38–1566) on Thursday evenings from 7:30–9:30 P.M. for details on trails and rental equipment available from different clubs. Another source is the Federación de Andinismo, whose permanent office is at Viamonte 1560 (40–7127). Open Mon.–Fri., 3–8 P.M. The Argentine-Chilean Andes include Aconcagua, the highest mountain in the Western Hemisphere at nearly 23,000 feet; only the Himalayas are higher. *Mountain Travel,* 1398 Solano Ave., Albany, CA 94706 (800–227–2384) sends mountaineering groups up the Aconcagua every January.

Skiing. You'll find microclimates of perfect powder in South America, eerie scenery, trails cleared by teams of oxen, and an open friendliness. But to be frank, you are not going to find a better version of the trails you know at home. South American ski areas are minuscule by European and North American standards. The two largest resorts are Las Leñas, which has 35 miles of groomed trails, and Bariloche, which claims about 50 miles of skiable terrain, although the lower, warmer slopes are frequently washed clear of snow by rainstorms.

Two U.S. travel agencies particularly knowledgeable about skiing possibilities: Unique Adventures, a San Francisco wholesaler (800–227–3026 nationwide; 800–227–5227 in California); and Ladatco Tours in Miami (800–327–6162 nationwide; 305–854–8422 in Florida).

In general, South American skiing is located along an 800-mile section of the Andes from Mendoza, Argentina/Santiago, Chile south to Bariloche, Argentina/Puerto Montt, Chile. Ski runs in the north are from 7,500-feet to above 11,000-feet, far higher than the timberline. Here in granite couloirs is champagne powder and sunshine. The Andes are lower in the south, more like the slopes one finds in Oregon. Lakes fill valley floors and the skyline is pierced with volcanoes, some of them alive. Southern snow is heavy, like the "Sierra cement" of California's Lake Tahoe, but the views are spectacular, the land open and undeveloped. From the dry north to the wet south, the resorts are:

Los Penitentes. Located alongside the Pan American Highway that crosses the Andes between Mendoza and Santiago, Chile. The ski runs of Penitentes are on the Argentine side of the wide border between the two countries, while fabled *Portillo* is situated on the Chilean side of the highway. Facilities at both resorts are high above timberline at 10,000-feet elevation. Hours from the nearest tree, Penitentes and Portillo are surrounded by rock, a wide-open garden of colors on the Argentine side—violet, green, orange, pink, red, and black mastiffs—and stunning grays on the Chilean side. Skiers at Penitentes face a vivid rock face across the narrow valley, a rainbow rock larger than the Matterhorn sculpted by the weather to resemble cowled monks (the penitents) climbing a staircase to the sky. From the top of the ski runs, it looks like there is no valley below, and it feels like you are skiing toward a mountain-sized wall of changing color. Penitentes has two double chairs, one T-bar, and four snow-making machines, so powder flurries come regardless of droughts caused by an occasional El Niño year. A 16-room hotel and three small condos are at the base of the area. Reservations should be made through a travel agent. Between Penitentes and Portillo is Christ the Redeemer, a large statue above La Cumbre Pass commemorating peace between Argentina and Chile. Cross-country skiers can helicopter from Portillo to the Christ (elevation: 13,860 feet) and ski down. The height of pleasure comes from the view of 23,000-foot Aconcagua, a vista topped only by the Himalayas. The run home is easy-intermediate. To reach Penitentes you can take one of the frequent buses over the Pan American Highway between Mendoza and Santiago, or use the local buses running out of Mendoza and back. One-way trip takes about 2½ hours. If you are continuing over the pass to Portillo, the staff at the Penitentes Hotel can arrange to flag a bus for you.

Las Leñas is the first major ski development of international consequence to be built in the Andes since Portillo led the way in the early 1940s. Although Las Leñas is located 260 miles south of Mendoza, where the Andes begin to decrease in altitude, the snow here continues to be the coveted champagne powder found only on high, above-timberline slopes. Designed by French experts for an Argentine family, Las Leñas opened in June, 1983. The result of Las Leñas's sophisticated planning is that the opening competitions for men's downhill racing on the 1985 and 1986 World Cup circuit were held there, an honor previously denied any area in South America. Las Leñas has room for around 3,000 guests in six apartment buildings and five hotels, including Piscis, a luxury hotel for 200 with a casino and indoor-outdoor pool. All skiers step directly out of their hotel or apartment and slide over to the lifts. There are 11 runs, a groomed area of 35 miles. The vertical drop is over 4,000 feet. Las Leñas offers guided off-trail downhill skiing and 10 miles of cross-country trails. One-week packages begin at $1,600 and include airfare from Miami. For reservations and information write: Skil International Reservations, 9592 Harding Ave., Miami, FL 33154 (305–864–7545, fax. 861–2895). In Buenos Aires, the address is: Arenales 707 (313–2121).

San Martín de los Andes. A secondary resort in the lake region, about four hours north of Bariloche by bus; 90 minutes by jet from Buenos Aires. San Martín is the loveliest of Latin American ski resorts, with runs meandering through beech forests draped with a chartreuse-colored Spanish moss. The perfect cone of Lanin Volcano punctuates the horizon while in between lies a royal-blue valley laced with finger lakes. Chapelco, as the ski area itself is called, goes from a high of 6,500 feet to a 4,125-foot base. The latter is sufficiently high for the snowpack to remain all season, from the top of the peak to the bottom. Most of the 12 runs are intermediate since this is a resort that caters to Argentine skiers who ski only once a year. San Martín has three ski lifts, a T–bar, and a gondola leading to the back bowls on the mountain, and about five miles of cross-country trails.

Skiing in San Martín was developed by Austral, the domestic airline, several years after it established skiing in Bariloche. Austral built winter-tourism centers as an expansion of their already popular summer and fall holiday programs in these two mountain towns. One-week ski packages, including airfare from Buenos Aires, lift tickets, a double room, breakfast and dinner, cost from around $600 per person.

Bariloche. Partying town on the shores of Lake Nahuel Huapí, with a pleasing mix of Teutonic architecture and Italian levity. For many years Bariloche has been the queen bee of Argentine winter sports. It is often called Brazil-oche because so many Brazilians flood in to enjoy the snow. Although rain often washes snow from the base by mid-August, Bariloche's four bowls are superb through September. Bariloche has eight chairs, three T-bars, seven pomas, and a cable car. Although the first series of runs is on the right side of the mountain and the second set on the left, skiers have full play of the mountain with one lift ticket. Serious skiers with limited funds will like the funky Hosteria Dhaulagiri (60–016) near the lifts. A more adult option is the four-star log hotel, Catedral, with 64 rooms and a number of small condos. The contact is through Buenos Aires: Hotel Catedral, Lavalle 482, fifth floor (393–9048). Most visitors, however, stay in town where there is a surfeit of fondue and fun that blasts on through the night, which is exactly how the Latins like to pace their till-dawn evenings. Bariloche's hand-knit sweaters and freshly made chocolates are known throughout the continent. Bariloche ski packages cost $500–$900 for one week, double occupancy, depending on the accommodations you choose and tour operator you select. These packages include a six-day pass, seven nights in Bariloche, breakfast, and transportation from town to the slopes. For reasonable rates and the full spread of hotels contact: Latin American Reservation Center, Box 1435, Dundee, FL 33838 (800–327–3573). For Aerolineas Argentinas' packages, contact: Optar, Cerrito 1070, eighth floor (312–6376/9). In the U.S., ask Aerolineas (800–327–0276) for names of U.S. agencies with ski packages.

Esquel. A half hour by air from Bariloche, with regularly scheduled flights, if the jets are not blown away; eight hours by bus. The two or three runs are located in a natural cyclone bowl. Fresh powder in Esquel means talcum powder freeze-dried in 40-mph winds on a calm day.The best hotel in Esquel is run by the Plaza of Buenos Aires. The 44-room **Hotel Tehuelche** is in the town at the corner of 9 de Julio and Belgrano (2420).

Ushuaia, Tierra del Fuego. The cross-country center of South America, thanks to enthusiastic Club Andino members who took to the sport in 1980, falling down forested hills in a high valley about 20 minutes from town. Since then, the club has built a small restaurant in Tierra Mayor, and trails lead out through ever-green boxwood, past beaver huts. Skis, poles, and boots can be rented, as can snow cats. For down-hillers, the club has bulldozed a couple of short, fat runs directly above Ushuaia. Club Andino is a volunteer organization. Check with the Tierra del Fuego tourist office, Infuetur, at the Hotel Albatros (23–340) for which member to contact. Hotels are listed in the Tierra del Fuego section, later in this chapter.

Beaches. While Argentina's beaches are not world class, like Punta del Este in Uruguay, the country's scenic Atlantic coast has a collection of neat and tidy towns that turn into frenzied sea-side resorts in the summer. Starting from the north, among the most popular are San Clemente del Tuyú, Pinamar (very fashionable), Villa Gesell (a young crowd for the hectic nightlife), and, the hub of it all, Mar del Plata, some 250 miles from Buenos Aires. A little to the south is the more sedate Miramar. All have broad, sandy bays, mild surf, and an assortment of seasonal attractions. Accommodation ranges from the humble to international standard, and there are plenty of excellent restaurants, particularly for seafood. All the resort areas are easily reached by bus from Buenos Aires (leaving from the depot at Retiro Station); Mar del Plata and Miramar are served by train and Mar del Plata by a shuttle air service, along with many of the smaller resorts which are increasingly served by commuter-type planes. The season runs from mid-December through the end of February, although if you go a little earlier or later you miss the worst of the crowds but still catch the good weather. Travel agents can advise on programs. Most are now recommending a visit to Mundo Marino at San Clemente del Tuyú, a marine park that opened in 1989. There are various exhibits and excellent marine-life shows. The best hotel on the coast is the deluxe Hotel Del Bosque at Pinamar (802–6027 in Buenos Aires).

See also "Adventure Vacations" chapter.

Exploring Argentina

BUENOS AIRES

Few cities are enjoyed as ten million Porteños enjoy theirs. This is the Argentine capital, their center of manufacturing, banking, culture, and intellectualism, the place where they have fun. Ardent enthusiasm rises like balloons in the good breezy air—*buenos aires*—no smog here. Buenos Aires was built on human energy, not natural splendors. If you can take the pace, the pulse is infectious.

Buenos Aires surprises many visitors. California cities display more Spanish heritage than the Argentine capital does. Largely forgotten in the colonial times, Buenos Aires boomed in the nineteenth century when Paris set the tone. As with all Spanish settlements in both Americas, old Buenos Aires was laid out around a central plaza bordered by a fort and armory, city hall, and cathedral of a very common sort. As one sardonic Porteño said, "Them that gives, receives. We didn't have much to give the Spanish—not like Lima or Mexico City—and nothing's about what we got back."

But nouveau Buenos Aires rivaled New York as a port for European trade. Landed gentry with *estancias* larger than some countries hired Parisian architects to design urban villas for when they came to town. Bankers and tradesmen did likewise. Porteños had money to spend, and did they ever! The skyline became rococo. Slate roofs, gargoyled eaves, marble . . . soon central Buenos Aires was as gray as Grenoble. A rosy Italianate palace replaced the fort around the old plaza—a Pink House, like the United States's White House, for the president's offices. The old town hall on the other end of the plaza blocked plans for a grand boulevard leading from the *Casa Rosada* to the new Congress building. Part of it was sacrificed for progress. More grand boulevards followed. Eventually the grandest in the world was cleared. Named the 9th of July Avenue, after the day a national congress declared independence in 1816, this "street" is one city block wide. In fact, Nueve de Julio is so wide that it is divided into three streets by grassy strips.

Even as central Buenos Aires turned Francophile, railroad tracks were laid north along the river to the Paraná delta. Commuters fled to the suburbs, led by British immigrants. Red brick and rose gardens prevailed. Today, the suburbs are brick, while in the downtown area glass office buildings border those done in French ornate style. Elsewhere, most neighborhoods are urban, some low-rises with trees, others an overwhelming jumble of high-rise condominiums. You're not going to find many cardboard shanty towns here like in other Latin American cities, which is not to say that the Argentines don't have many urban problems—they do.

To be blunt: "Buenos Aires is an uncontrollable megalopolis," said President Raúl Alfonsin in 1986, when he began promoting a new national capital on the Patagonian coast. Porteños agree. "Of course B.A.'s uncontrollable," they say with a shrug. "And it's too large and it completely dominates the rest of the country. We love it anyway."

Visitors do too. There are only a few great cities with the advantages that Buenos Aires offers. Despite its size, Porteños have not abandoned the center for satellite cities around the fringe. Near the redesigned Plaza de Armas, now called Plaza de Mayo, are superb restaurants, movie theaters, boutiques, book stores, art galleries, and the elegant pedestrian street, Florida, leading to the city's finest hotels. (Inexpensive and moderate ones are in the center as well.) This is the *barrio* of the wealthy, not the poor, but a cup of coffee at a sidewalk cafe on one of those grand boulevards is less than a dollar.

Most sights you'll want to see, most intimate tango and jazz clubs, shops, polo, soccer, symphonies, folkloric shows—nearly everything—are within walking distance or a $2–$3 taxi ride from your hotel. We, who are too accustomed to fear after dark, don't trust our safety on the sidewalks at first. But watch the Argentines and believe. The streets are jammed at ten, and crowded at midnight; not until two o'clock in the morning do the strollers begin to wear out and go home. This is true in summer and winter, on weekdays . . . but not on weekends. Then the crowds coming out of the final movies at three o'clock are hungry. That's no problem, since many restaurants are still open.

One out of every three Argentines lives in Buenos Aires. They find it irresistible, and you will be at the core of the magnet. However, many travelers stop in B.A. on a circle around South America, arriving from either Machu Picchu or Rio de Janeiro. Keep in mind that those are hard acts to follow for a megalopolis on the flats. So adjust your expectations. Buenos Aires is not another Spanish-speaking sprawl between Tijuana and Tierra del Fuego, nor is it a European copy. It is impulsive in an Argentine sense, meaning that its spirit is absolutely not as gray as its buildings, as we've overheard some tour groups decide at first glance. Buenos Aires is *not* a beach city. It sits alongside a muddy estuary that requires continual dredging. Porteños go to Mar del Plata, Uruguay's Punta del Este, or Rio when they want sand.

And one final reminder. Just about everywhere, the narrow sidewalks are wretched. So be careful when you look up to see the architecture, but do look up. You'll see, Buenos Aires seduces.

Exploring the City

A large notch in the map of Latin America comes where the Paraná and the Uruguay rivers flow into a wide estuary, misnamed the Rio de la Plata (*River of Silver* or *River Plate*). Marshy shallows line the 171-mile shoreline. One of the few natural harbors comes where the small Riachuelo flows into the estuary. Here, about 20 miles south of the Paraná-Uruguay delta, is where the Spanish landed in 1536. Angry Indians forced them to abandon the first Buenos Aires. When the second round of settlers arrived in 1580, they located their central plaza slightly closer to the delta from the mouth of the Riachuelo.

Today, almost everything you'll want to see in Buenos Aires curves along the River Plate between La Boca (the mouth) and Tigre, a suburb on the delta. Our suggestions proceed likewise.

Houses in La Boca—at least those along the little lane, Caminito—are pink, blue, green, and any other brilliant, leftover color from ships in port. This clannish tenement area was settled by Genoese sailors whose descendents stay on proudly. Late Sunday morning, on through the afternoon, artists gather in Caminito to sell their work. (By law, it must be the artist, not a salesperson.) Beloved by artists, musicians, intellectuals, and tourists for its narrow sidewalks and wrought iron grills on colonial windows near-

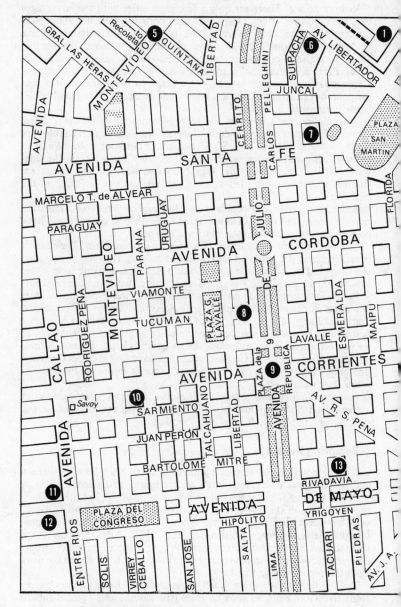

Points of Interest

1) Retiro (Central Train and Bus Station)
2) Sheraton Hotel
3) Plaza Hotel
4) Basilica del Santisimo Sacramento
5) Follow Quintana to the Recoleta District
6) Issac Fernandez Blanco Museum
7) Main Tourist Information Office
8) Colon Theater

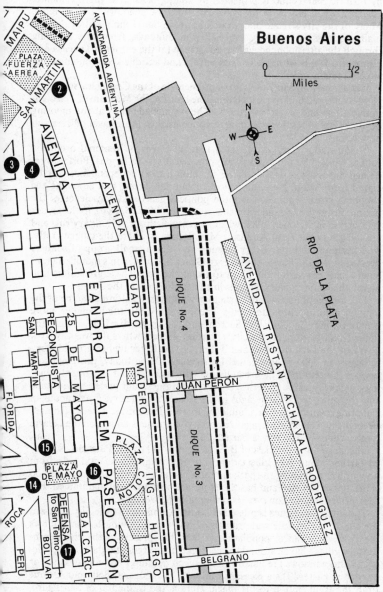

Buenos Aires

9) Obelisk
10) Teatro San Martin complex
11) Confiteria del Molino
12) Palacio del Congreso (National Congress)
13) Café Tortoni
14) Cabildo (Old Town Hall) Museum
15) Cathedral
16) Casa Rosada (Pink House)
17) Follow Defensa to San Telmo

by historic San Telmo is protected by zoning laws. It is more romantic at night, when cracks in the walls fade into the shadows of streetlights. Many of the city's tango and jazz clubs are in San Telmo, but by day the main business is antiques, especially on Sundays, from late morning through the afternoon, when Plaza Dorrego (at the corner of Defensa and Humberto I) fills with dealers and buyers and antique shops on adjoining streets remain open.

Just a hop from San Telmo is the promenade of the Costanera Sur, home of many fine old buildings, including one housing the Museum of Telecommunications and a bird sanctuary. The promenade ends at the mooring of the Frigate Presidente Sarmiento, once used to train naval officers and now a museum.

Conquistador tradition dictated that all towns be centered around a square flanked by the fort and armory, the Plaza de Armas. Porteños renamed theirs Plaza de Mayo after the month when independence was declared from Spain. Here, nine blocks from San Telmo and adjoining the shopping street, Florida, beats the political heart and conscience of the nation. From the first independence hurrah on May 25, 1810, to the joyous celebration in October, 1983, when Argentines threw off military rule and elected President Raul Alfonsin, May Square is where the citizens rally. The tradition endures. Every evening at 7 P.M. a small group of soldiers dressed in the 1813-style uniforms of General San Martín's mounted grenadiers marches across the plaza to lower the flag. These grenadiers also guard the tomb of the General, in the Cathedral on the Plaza.

The cathedral itself is not particularly impressive, although some of the massive paintings are interesting. The interior of the much smaller, more ornate Basilica de Santisimo Sacramento at San Martín 1035, behind the Plaza Hotel, is probably the city's prettiest. Here is where the wealthy wed.

When the very rich fled San Telmo for healthier higher ground, they relocated in what is now called La Recoleta. Even today, this neighborhood is the zenith of fine urban living, with its balconied apartment buildings, sidewalk cafés, galleries, couture boutiques, and pricey restaurants. But the most remarkable sight is the Recoleta cemetery, a necropolis of elaborate mausoleums, a jumble of marble Byzantine, Greek, Roman, French, and Italian extravaganzas. Ask your guide to show you the Duarte tomb, where Eva Perón is buried.

The largest and prettiest of Buenos Aires's 150 parks, Palermo, is located farther along Av. Libertador from Recoleta, a brief taxi ride from downtown. Adjoining the park are the zoo and botanical gardens. The zoo is pretty but not rich and has therefore not been too well maintained. Recent privatization, however, is bringing improvements.

Too often San Isidro is missed by tourists, and more's the pity. Toward the end of a two-mile wide ribbon of single-family suburbs that follows the river, San Isidro, population 80,000, has preserved the eighteenth-century village flavor around the central plaza. Trees line the streets, sidewalks and windows are narrow, and stucco buildings are whitewashed or painted in pastels. It's a pleasant walk past the shops on Belgrano Avenue from the train station to the plaza. Here is the Cathedral of San Isidro, designed in Britain and brought to Argentina brick by brick, back in the early 1890s.

The Paraná Delta is larger than Holland and Belgium combined. With its natural canals, Tigre at the mouth of the delta could be compared with Amsterdam, Venice, or Bangkok. Many of the 40,000 inhabitants live in houses on stilts and send their children to school on bus-boats. On weekends and in the summer, Tigre has a bustle to its waters. Windsurfers, waterskiers, sailors, and canoeists can be seen from the double-decked catamaráns and numerous ferries and launches that leave from the main wharf across from the train station. The summertime stench passes once you leave the docks to explore the luxuriant quiet found further into the delta. (For more details about Tigre and other places of interest, see "Tours," below).

PRACTICAL INFORMATION FOR BUENOS AIRES

GETTING AROUND BUENOS AIRES. From the airport. Most international flights land at Ezeiza Airport, 21 miles from downtown. Bus ($10) or taxi limousine ($40) tickets can be purchased from the well-marked transportation counter in the airport. The bus lets you off at a choice of four central hotels; you can then take a taxi if you're staying elsewhere. Figure about $2 for that—at current prices. To have a car and guide meet you and take you to your hotel costs about $55 for two; arrangements can be made through your travel agent. It will give you a worthwhile orientation to the city, its customs, typical prices, and currency exchanges.

Warning: Ignore taxi drivers who come up to you in the airport; do not take their black and yellow cabs. Some overcharge and there have been reports of robberies.

By bus. A zany, delightful surprise for people who either like to save money or explore local color. Here the *colectivos* may be more colorful than the city. Drivers own the buses and operate through a cooperative. Each route has a color and a number. Ask your concierge for instructions.

By subway. The system is excellent; it is the oldest in South America with the first lines built by the British in 1913. Original art work showing historic scenes of the city highlight some of the stations. Passengers can get on and off to look at no extra charge. The five lines have alphabetical A-B-C-D-E labels; entrances to the stations are marked "Subte" with the letter of the line; tokens cost around 30¢ and can be used throughout the system. The D line goes to the Palermo Park area, Botanical Gardens, the zoo, and the American Embassy nearby. The D line also goes to the city's newest and fanciest shopping mall—Alta Palermo. Get off at the Bulnes station. Maps of the lines and stops are available from the several local tourist offices. One of the kiosks is across from Harrods' on Florida St. (*See* Useful Addresses under "Facts at Your Fingertips," for complete listing.) The subway closes between 1 and 4 A.M.

By train. Go to the northern suburbs, leaving from Retiro, the central station across from the British Clock Tower at the Plaza Fuerza Aera (in front of the Sheraton Hotel). If you buy an *ida y vuelta* (round-trip) ticket to Tigre on the delta, you can stop en route at San Isidro and other interesting suburbs on the route without charge.

By taxi. In central downtown, fares are about $2–$4; out to Palermo-Recoleta, about $6. It has been estimated that there are about 60,000 taxis in Buenos Aires. Consequently, during rush hour it's not difficult to find a cab; nor is it hard in the pre-dawn hours, although then you might want to call a private taxi service for a "remise." These have fixed prices, usually cheaper than taxis for longer trips. Your hotel can help with bookings. Unfortunately, overcharging is common from downtown hotels. Taxis have black bodies and yellow roofs. Meters don't register price; they code the time. The driver tallies the final number against a price sheet. There is a small surcharge for luggage.

Car and chauffeur. This is very convenient, especially for a day's tour of the suburbs or nearby pampas. An approximate price for the day would be around $100, but depends, of course, on the distance you cover. A travel agent or your hotel can make arrangements. Small companies offering this service are: Novas Tour, M. T. de Alvear 474 (313–7316); Remises Paraguay, Paraguay 2380 (961–3245); and Del Plata, Carabelas 295 (35–0749).

Car Rentals. Porteños drive with verve and independence. For the rest of us, it's a guaranteed thrill learning how to negotiate along tremendously broad boulevards where traffic lanes are a state of mind. See "Facts at Your Fingertips" for addresses of some of the major car-rental agencies.

HOTELS. One of the great pleasures of Buenos Aires. Several of the expensive hotels were built for the 1978 World Cup Soccer matches, and have maintained high standards. Hotels of every category are almost all located in a 12-block-by-12-block central area. From rooms that cost $10 a night to ones going for $180, visitors can step out and join the crowds in one of the world's most exciting, nonstop downtowns. Prices are not cheaper for hotels in the outlying areas, so why bother staying out there? All of the hotels listed below are in the city center. See "Facts at Your Fingertips" for definitions of price categories.

Super Deluxe

Alvear Palace, Av. Alvear 1891 (804–4031/45, fax 804–0034). 250 rooms, 50 suites. Built as a luxury apartment complex in 1932, the building was converted to a hotel in 1988. Rooms have no views to speak of, but the fancy Recoleta location makes up for this—the square, cemetery, and a sweep of restaurants are just a block away. Facilities include the excellent Oyster Grill, a traditional tea room, and the Jardin d'hiver coffee shop. A health club and indoor pool will open in 1992.

Sheraton Buenos Aires Hotel and Towers, San Martín 1225/75 (311–6331/9, fax 311–6353). 800 rooms. 24 stories. The city's grandest hotel and the headquarters of Sheraton's South America division. The Sheraton has the broadest range of restaurants and facilities, including a resort-quality swimming pool and tennis courts. Only hotel with good views from all rooms, either the River Plate or the British Clock Tower and park. At the far end of Plaza San Martín. Popular with American businessmen and tour groups.

Plaza Hotel, Florida 1005 (311–5011/29, fax 313–2912). 370 rooms. The city's most gracious, across from the tremendous old trees of Plaza San Martín. Some rooms have great bay windows overlooking the park. Crystal chandeliers, deep red Persian carpets in public rooms, luxurious good taste. Famous grill, more famous international wine cellar. A total refurbishment was completed in 1990; a swimming pool, health club, and health restaurant have been added. The city's finest shops fan out from the Plaza; the president entertains visiting statesmen here.

At press time, two more hotels in the super deluxe category were under construction. Both the **Hotel Park Hyatt** and the **Buenos Aires Inter-Continental** were scheduled to open in late 1991 or early 1992, adding some 700 rooms to the city's total, along with top class restaurants, conference rooms, and health and recreation facilities. The Inter-Continental is located in a new downtown business development on the 800 block of Moreno, just a few blocks south of the central city area. The Hyatt is at the end of the 9th of July Boulevard, at the fringe of the fancy Recoleta neighborhood. Information and reservations can be obtained through Hyatt (800–233–1234) and Inter-Continental (800–33–AGAIN).

Deluxe

Claridge, Tucumán 535 (322–7700, fax 322–8022). 160 rooms. British elegance in public rooms, wood paneling, high ceilings, very Anglo-Argentine. Rooms have recently been redecorated. Good location near the heart of Florida St. There are squash courts, a small gymnasium, and a swimming pool. Popular with North American special interest tour groups.

Libertador Kempinski, Av. Córdoba and Maipù (392–2095/8395/9236). 203 rooms, including 10 suites. Swimming pool on 22nd floor. Modern building and decor, one block from the center of Florida, the walking street. Restaurants, sauna, shops. Guests include international businessmen and European tourists.

Panamericano, Carlos Pellegrini 525 (393–6017/6117). 225 rooms. Lovely big building, conservative, classic decor. Food, service, and cleanliness are all tops. Indoor pool, fitness center, and one of the city's few Japanese restaurants. Near the Colón Theater.

Expensive

Bisonte Hotel, Paraguay 1207 (394–8041, fax 393–9086). 100 rooms. Located on a popular shopping street in the center of the city. The Bisonte has a sunny two-story lobby and a coffee shop overlooking a small park.

Bisonte Palace Hotel, M.T. de Alvear 902 (311–4751, fax 394–9086). 65 rooms. Sister hotel to the Bisonte, sharing the same management and located close by. Consistently good service. There is a coffee shop.

De las Americas, Libertad 1020 (393–3432, fax 393–0418). 150 rooms. On the quieter side of 9th of July, about seven blocks from shops and movies, but near the opera and symphony at the magnificent Colón. The personnel are very attentive, and the coffee shop is small and plain.

El Conquistador Hotel, Suipacha 948 (313–3012/3112/3312). 140 rooms. Excellent, central location. Modern decor uses wood for coziness. Sauna and massages. Cheerful restaurant on top floor for breakfast and quick steak dinners. Piano bar. Popular with Argentine businessmen.

Gran Hotel Colón, Carlos Pellegrini 507 (325–1617, fax 804–1477). 185 rooms, ample suites with private patios. Other rooms are typically small. Swimming pool on the 14th floor. Roof garden club. Located next to the Pan Americano on the busy, super-wide 9th of July boulevard. Wide glass entrance to lobby. Secretarial services and extra telephone lines lure business travelers from outlying areas of Argentina and elsewhere. Also popular with Brazilians.

Principado, Paraguay 481 (313–3122, fax 313–3022). 88 rooms. New for World Cup. Lots of glass, so lots of light. Two-tiered lobby is Spanish colonial with leather couches. Friendly coffee shop on lower level. Two blocks from Florida Street. Many Argentine and Latin American clients.

Moderate

Gran Hotel Dora, Maipú 963, (312–7391). 95 comfortably elegant rooms. A cozy lobby, with a small bar and tea tables. No dining room, but snacks are available. Argentine and European clientele, and often fully booked.

Hotel Crillon, Santa Fé 796 (312–8181/92, fax 312–9955). 96 rooms, across the road from the Plaza San Martín. Has a restaurant, bar, and disco.

Regente Palace, Suipacha 964 (313–6628). 150 rooms, two bars, Small rooms, but pleasant. In the heart of Buenos Aires action. A little bar with a bright breakfast room off the lobby.

Inexpensive

Gran Hotel Orly, Paraguay 474 (312–5344/8). 170 rooms, 10-story building. Only a block and a half from Florida Street. Elegant entrance with marble and brass reception area. Spit-and-polish cleanliness. Bar and coffee shop are open 24 hours. Friends of Porteños from elsewhere in the country stay here—they appreciate quality at most reasonable prices. So do Brazilians.

Rochester, Esmeralda 542 (393–9589/9339). 140 rooms, 20 suites, 24-hour room service. Restaurant serves only breakfast, but there is a snack bar. Simple lobby. Central location for movies and shops, although one side faces a busy street.

Sheltown Hotel, M.T. de Alvear 742 (312–5070/9). 65 rooms. Small lobby with a few tables for breakfast, a television, and leather couches. Right on the main shopping area. Popular with Latin American travelers.

For careful budgeters, there are dozens of small hotels that are cheap, modernized, and clean. They are mostly in the Avenida de Mayo area and are close to the big stores, banks, and government offices. Among the better ones are: **Mundial Hotel,** Av. de Mayo 1298 (37–2031/6). 70 rooms, all with bath and phone. **San Carlos,** Suipacha 39 (40–7021/6). 100 rooms. Bar but no dining room. **Tres Sargentos,** Tres Sargentos 345 (312–6081/5). 60 rooms. Behind Harrod's on a small street only two blocks long. (Between San Martin and 25 de Mayo.) Popular with visiting sports teams. A **Youth Hostel** is at Brazil 675 (362–9133).

Self-Catering Apartments or Service Flats. If you're staying a few weeks or a few months, self-catering apartments provide a home with hotel service—television, phones, maid service, and kitchen. Rates range from $180–$500 or so a week for a one-bedroom.

Downtown apartments include: the **Edificio Suipacha,** Suipacha 1235 (392–6685, 394–7153), one block from the Canadian Embassy on Santa Fé. There are 122 apartments in the building. Shops, provincial tourists, and airlines are neighbors. **Edificio Charcas,** Marcelo T. De Alvear 776 (312–2061), 30 apartments, near the Plaza San Martín. Frequent choice of out-of-towners performing at the Colón. **Aspen,** Esmeralda 933 (313–9011), is popular with U.S. businessmen. In the same popular area is the **Plaza San Martín Suites,** Suipacha 1092 (312–4740), and in Recoleta is the newer **Pigalle,** R.M. Ortiz 1835 (804–4211), which also offers excellent gymnasium facilities.

RESTAURANTS. Dining out is one of the Argentines' favorite pastimes, and a very time-consuming diversion it is, with a three-course dinner ending two or three hours later. No one can linger over an expresso longer than an Argentine, but then few other nationalities enjoy the mental sport of conversation as they do. One consequence is that the restaurant ambience, whether elegant or casual, is a delightful combination of gusto and languidness, fun for all.

Other than the relatively casual, hottest months of summer (December-February), the Argentines dress up to go out. In general, reservations are not necessary and at least one or two of the following credit cards are accepted: American Express, Diners Club, Mastercard, and Visa. Restaurants are open until 2 A.M. or later, weekdays and weekends.

Where tourist magazine, sometimes available from tourist kiosks, includes a list of restaurants. Dereck Foster, the food columnist of the *Buenos Aires Herald,* puts out a booklet called *Guide to Good Eating in the B.A. Area,* available from bookstores, with a substantial glossary of English/Argentine gastronomic terms. Foster's best restaurants are: Catalinas (French seafood and game); Tomo Uno, Lola, La Creole, Friday's, and Chez Michel (French); Broccolino, Robertino, and Marcovaldo (Italian); Gato Dumas (with an emphasis on natural foods); La Terrasse at the Plaza Hotel (a health-oriented menu); Maison Champagne, Sabot, and Brizzi (light Continental); La Cave (Swiss); Colbeh Melahat (Iranian); Genghis Khan (Mongolian barbecue); and the restaurants at the Sheraton, the Plaza, and the Alvear Palace. Every week, Foster and the *Herald* put out a weekend supplement with places to eat and places for shows. Foster's office is behind the Plaza Hotel at San Martín 987, 1st floor (311–8301).

But what about Spanish cuisine in Buenos Aires, visitors might wonder. In general, the native food of the forefathers is scarcer than Szechuan, if you're thinking of paellas and such. Spanish immigrants ate wild beef off the pampas; their half-breed sons were the gauchos of song and legends. Thus, *bife* is the national food, and that is where our restaurant listings begin.

For definitions of price categories, see "Facts at Your Fingertips."

Although our selections include many of the city's most special restaurants, it is by no means exhaustive. Few restaurants in Buenos Aires are bad. A quick steak sandwich (*sandwich de lomito*) at the nearest sidewalk cafe (selected when your feet give out) will likely prove very satisfying.

Typical Argentine: Parrillas and Regional

La Cabana. *Expensive.* Entre Ríos 436 (38–2373). A $3 taxi ride from downtown. For international visitors, the best-known steak house in B.A. and certainly the priciest with full dinners for one plus a half bottle of wine easily nearing $20. Excellent beef, good service, pleasant colonial atmosphere, but equalled (and many claim surpassed) by the other parillas in this section, all of which are more moderately priced. Closed Monday. Lunch noon–3 P.M., dinner 8 P.M.–3 A.M.

A los Amigos. *Moderate.* Costanera Norte (782–9140). Steaks, ribs, and tripes of various sorts. Cool breezes off the River Plate, outdoor and indoor dining. Open every day.

La Caballeriza. *Moderate.* Dardo Rocha 1740, Acassuso (798–1596). Well worth the journey out to the northern suburbs (you'll need to take a taxi from the Acassuso train station), this was a renowned racing stable before being converted into a parrilla restaurant in late 1990. A most pleasant atmosphere in an outdoor courtyard under grapevines, and in indoor converted stables. The staff are young and enthusiastic, and the food and presentation are excellent. Open daily for lunch and dinner.

Las Nazarenas. *Moderate.* Reconquista 1132 (312–5559). Across the street from the Sheraton. Two-story, Spanish colonial with wrought iron, sconces, ferns. Popular lunch stop for Argentine businessmen. For an appetizer, try sliced *matambre,* a stuffed roll of flank steak, or thick slices of grilled Provolone cheese sprinkled with oregano.

Posta El Antiguo Calcagno. *Moderate.* Sante Fe 2411, corner Edison, in the northern suburb of Martinez (798–8156). Founded in 1790 as a stagecoach stop, it is today a general parrilla restaurant with a good price-quality ratio. Open daily for lunch and dinner.

La Tranquera. *Moderate.* Av. Figueroa Alcorta 6464 (784–6119). One of the few asado restaurants that serves kid *(chivito),* the kind that makes you lick your fingers.

Parrilladas with the works—tripes, sweetbreads, etc. Banks of coals and sizzling meat on spits flank the entrance under a pavillion. Keeps the smoke outside. Icy pitchers of *clericot,* the white sangria, are cooling on hot summer nights.

Rio Alba. *Moderate.* Cerviño 4491 (773–9508/5748). Juicy, sweet, lean pork served with lemon slices and shoestring potatoes. Excellent other grills, too. Near the U.S. Embassy and a favorite of that crowd. Noisy during *gringo* hour.

El Ceibal. *Inexpensive.* Las Heras 2265 (83–2707). Food from the northwest part of the country bordering Bolivia and Chile. Carbonada, a stew; locro, a rich, savory soup made with potatoes and corn; and other almost all located in a 12-block-by-12-block central area. From Spanish-Incan specialities.

El Palacio de la Papa Frita. *Inexpensive.* Lavalle 735 (392–1599). Open every day, lunch and dinner. Good beef and general menu.

La Sabrosa Achura. *Inexpensive.* Maza 846 (97–7696). Favorite steak house of the *Herald's* food critic. In particular he praises the parrilladas with sweetbreads, tripe, blood sausages, and the steaks, without question. Down-home atmosphere with the smell (but not smoke) of grilling meats in the air. Open every day.

British Isles

Down Town Matías. *Expensive.* San Martin 979 (312–9844). Near the Plaza Hotel on the ground floor of a modern highrise. Easy to miss the small, indubitably discreet brass sign. Dark, musty and familiar inside. Plain, padded bar stools and wide, wooden bar has been well-polished by tweedy elbows. Flags of local rugby teams adorn the walls. No darts. "That's English," sniffs the bartender, who whips-together an Irish coffee anytime and green beer you know when. Irish stews, kidney pies, and so forth are served only from noon-3 P.M. Most Irish of all, Matías locks up at 10 P.M.

London Grill. *Expensive.* Reconquista 455 (311–2223). Roast beef and Yorkshire pudding, chicken pie, steak and kidney pie, all very tasty. Noon to 11 P.M.

Continental

Blab's. *Expensive.* Florida 325–(394–2873). On the banker and politician's end of Florida. Well-beloved by them for efficient service. Consistently good food, stuffed veal cutlets and sole, for example. Open for lunch only, from noon to 5 P.M.

Clark's. *Expensive.* Junín 1777, Recoleta (801–9502). Sophisticated California style, like its equally *expensive* neighbor, **Harper's** at Junín 1763 (801–7140). Clark's features suckling pig, prawn brochettes, filet mignon à la Clark's; while Harper's, with exposed brick and hanging ferns, has a daily brunch and familiars such as eggs Benedict and beef Stroganoff. Both restaurants are open every day for lunch and dinner.

El Repecho de San Telmo. *Expensive.* Carlos Calvo 242 (362–5473). On the plaza in the oldest part of the city. Low ceilings and crowded tables, an antiquity by B.A. standards. When Argentines say it is more like dining in a museum than a restaurant, they don't mean one of the cafes in North American museums. El Repecho is cozy. Crab and duck are on the menu, along with *bifes.* Unfortunately, it is closed on Sundays during the weekly Sunday antique fair in the plaza. Open dinners only, 8:30 P.M.–1:30 A.M.

La Creole. *Expensive.* Mansilla 2666 (961–7152). Strong on French colonial specialties, along with a good continental selection.

La Mosca Blanca. *Moderate.* (313–4890). Between the Belgrano and San Martín terminals in the main train station (Retiro), across the street from the Sheraton. Don't let the name (White Fly) put you off. A crazy location and an amusing atmosphere. Super huge menu, and huger portions. Open every day from noon-3 A.M.

Ligure. *Moderate.* Juncal 855 (393–4206). Here, above all, service is exemplary— the waiters have a part ownership in the business. Unusual dishes like thistles au gratin, plus standard French fare like steak au poivre, are featured.

Maison Champagne. *Moderate.* Ricardo Rocas 471 (311–1854). Small and attractive, with light, well-prepared food. Excellent local champagnes. Dinner only weekends.

Brizzi. *Inexpensive.* Lavalle 445 (393–5364). Quick service; simple but tasty food. Open for breakfast, serves a good brunch, and closes about 8:30 in the evening.

Sabot. *Inexpensive.* 25 de Mayo 756 (313–6587). Simple, popular foods, no frills. Excellent value. Lunch and dinner Monday to Friday; Saturday, dinner only.

French

Au Bec Fin. *Expensive.* Vicente López 1825 (801–6894). Elegant, superb kitchen, creative menu—delectable prawn mousse and a tartly sweet plum bavarois. Ranked in the *Herald's* top favorites. Reservations suggested. Open every day for dinner only, 8 P.M.–2 A.M.

Catalinas. *Expensive.* Reconquista 875 (313–0182). Chef Ramiro gives a personal touch to a basically French menu where the seafood and game stand out. Quality not price rules here, so go prepared. Closed Saturday for lunch and all day Sunday.

Les Flambeaux. *Expensive.* Juan S. Fernandez 122, San Isidro (765–3745). A French/Swiss selection, with comfortable atmosphere, good service. One of the few top restaurants out in the northern suburbs.

Lola. *Expensive.* Corner of Guido and Junín (804–3410) in the exclusive Recoleta district. This lovely restaurant matches decor, cuisine, and service to perfection. The menu is eclectic but sensible (translated into intelligible English!) and has something for everyone. Good value for the price. Open every day.

Tomo Uno. *Expensive.* Las Heras 3766 (801–6253). Former housewife and amateur chef Ada Concaro went on to prove what a brilliant amateur cook could do. After studies in France, she opened Tomo Uno and quickly set a new standard in Argentina. In general, her kitchen is not experimental, although old favorites like Nicoise salad and ratatouille join specialties like wild boar with chestnuts. Open for lunch and dinner. Closed Sunday.

Chez Michel. *Moderate.* R.S. Peña 2066 (824–7491). Excellent quality and fine selection of foods. Emphasis on Frênch, but some Italian dishes. Good choice of wines, both local and imported. Open Monday to Saturday, dinner only.

El Angel. *Moderate.* Lanusse 550, Beccar (745–5001). Another in the northern suburbs, just past San Isidro. Small, attractive, with excellent cooking in the French traditional style. There is no printed menu—your waiter advises on the daily selection. Dinner only. Closed Sunday.

Friday's. *Moderate.* San Martín 961 (311–5433). Small, intimate restaurant with a very reliable kitchen. Tenderloin scallops with Martini sauce a specialty. Closed Sunday.

Italian

Marcovaldo. *Moderate.* Blanco Encalada (783–0361). Outstanding, authentic antipasti. You can easily make a meal of it. Open for dinner Tuesday to Saturday, and for Sunday lunch. Closed Monday.

Robertino. *Moderate.* Vincente López 2158, Recoleta (803–1460). Glorious northern Italian delectables like cassunzel ampezzani and fileto di vittello served in a charming atmosphere. Very old-world country style, but absolutely elegant. Closed Sunday. Dinner from 8:15 P.M.–1:30 A.M. Reservations suggested.

A'Nonna Immacolata. *Moderate.* Costanera Norte (782–1757). Amusingly wallpapered with out-of-circulation 1,000 peso notes. The money is pale orange, the tablecloths are pink. Superb food in the Italian-American style. Canadians rave about it; Argentines give accolades too. Homemade pasta, Scalope Sorrentina, seafoods. Closed Monday noon.

Broccolino. *Inexpensive.* Esmeralda 776 (322–7652). For many, the best Italian restaurant in town. The variety of pasta dishes is unbelievable,—all different and delicious. The rest of the menu follows suit. Open every day for lunch and dinner.

Others to Try

Gato Dumas. *Expensive.* Roberto Ortiz 1809, Recoleta (44–5828). Continental fare with an emphasis on naturally grown vegetables and herbs lovingly tended and harvested by the restaurant's rather eccentric owner. Open every day for lunch and dinner.

Puerto Marisko. *Expensive.* Demaria 4658, Palermo (773–9051). One of the few restaurants in Buenos Aires specializing in fish and seafood. Traditional nautical decor, good service.

Chinatown. *Moderate.* Juramento 1656, Belgrano, near the Belgrano Station (798–3456). Decorated in the traditional red-and-black pagoda style, with a menu just as lively. In a city not noted for its Chinese cuisine, Chinatown stands out. The Chu family provide personal touches of service.

Colbeh Melahat. *Moderate.* Libertador 13041, in the northern suburb of Martinez (793–3955). Authentic Iranian cuisine in a cozy, delightful atmosphere. Also Pakistani cooking. The only restaurant of its type in Buenos Aires, and well worth the journey out to Martinez. Dinner only. Closed Sunday.

El Figon de Bonilla. *Moderate.* Leandro Alem 673 (312–1457). Good Spanish cooking in a rustic setting. Also a branch in Recoleta.

La Cave du Valais. *Expensive.* Zapiola 1779 (551–4435). Lovely, indulgent amounts of gooey cheese, with capers, boiled potatoes, and an all-you-can-eat raclette. With a fixed price. Fondues and a few other choice specialties. Very cozy, also small and popular. Reservations recommended. Closed Sunday.

Genghis Khan. *Moderate.* Amenabar 2415, Belgrano (784–6860). The only Mongolian barbecue of any standard in Buenos Aires, and this is excellent. Gracious hospitality; value exceeds price. Dinner only.

Los Azahares. *Moderate.* Moreno 1347 (38–0328). Arabian dishes, strong on vegetarian and Oriental fare. Open for lunch weekdays; dinner only on Thursday.

Mora X. *Moderate.* Vicente Lopez 2156 (803–2646). Large and airy, this restaurant is a pleasant mix of traditional wood (in its long bar) and modern Recoleta (stark architecture, greenery), and serves an international selection. Excellent salads. Closed Sunday.

La Esquina de las Flores. *Inexpensive.* Córdoba 1599 (41–4858). Vegetarian restaurant with a health boutique attached. Informal and a good value.

Yin-Yang. *Inexpensive.* Paraguay 848 (311–7798). Naturist, vegetarian, and macrobiotic fare to suit all tastes. Take-away section plus open-air patio and a small shop. The meals are simple but varied, and prepared in the most authentic manner. Closed Sunday.

Hotel Restaurants

El Aljibe in the Sheraton. *Expensive.* San Martín 1225 (311–6565). May be one of the finest places in the world for the single diner; can be *moderate* in price with judicious ordering. Long booths along the walls of comfortable leather offer privacy and room to spread books and newspapers. Sconces and candles give reading light in the midst of a dimmed dining room. Gentle piano and guitar music. Steaks and vegetables (a rarity in B.A.) on a French-influenced menu.

Oyster Grill in the Alvear Palace. *Expensive.* Ayacucho 2025, Recoleta (804–4031). Now one of the city's top restaurants, with the prices to prove it. Food quality lives up to the reputation; emphasis on beef, but also a good international selection. Excellent wine cellar. Reservations requested. Open for lunch and dinner daily.

La Pergola in Hotel Libertador Kempinski. *Expensive.* Maipú and Córdoba (392–2095). Classic French. Rated very highly by local connoisseurs for savor and service. Crêpes de champignons are among the lighter options; pasta and grilled steaks are also available. Open every day from 6 A.M.–1 A.M.

Plaza Hotel Grill. *Expensive.* 1005 Florida (311–5011). Polish on brass, service, decor whispers money, style, power. Traditional gathering place of top executives and politicians. Continental menu, wine list up to other Plaza standards. Specialities include sole, rabbit, and a chestnut mousse. Open for lunch and dinner daily. Lunch 12–4 P.M.; dinner, 8 P.M.–midnight.

Hotel Lancaster. *Moderate.* Córdoba 405 (311–3021). Understated, old European-style hotel, and worthy of mention here because of its outstanding high tea. Lunch and dinner menus are very limited.

La Terrasse. *Moderate.* Plaza Hotel, 2nd floor (311–5011). Very healthy eating; a good variety of low-calorie dishes. Overlooks the hotel's swimming pool and the trees of the San Martin park. Open daily.

Fast Food

Portêno pizzas are an elaborate affair, sometimes with 50 different kinds of toppings—artichokes, seafood, asparagus, chicken—and a choice of crusts. Crispy thin is *a la piedra;* thick and spongy is *de molde.* Pizza is *Inexpensive.* And remember that house wine is sometimes cheaper than Coca cola. A quick walk from the downtown hotels: **Banchero,** Corner of Av. A. Brown and Suarez (La Boca) (21–0711). **Roma,** Lavalle 888 (394–7656). **Los Immortales,** M. T. de Alvear 1234 (42–6124), Lavalle 746, is decorated with pictures of the very-very long departed tango great, Carlos Gardel. **Rigby,** on the corner of Libertad and Paraguay, has an excellent pizza-of-the-house. There is a **Pizza Hut** on Lavalle, between Maipú and Esmeralda.

Hamburgers with French fries and a cola cost about $3. The country-wide **Pumper Nic** chain is the Burger King of Argentina. Downtown locations are: Suipacha 435, Corrientes 1769; Florida 530. **McDonald's** now has outlets in various parts of the city, including the suburb of San Isidro (near the station), on Florida, and in the Unicenter and Alto Palermo shopping malls.

Cafeteria-style restaurants have recently sprung up. Try **Posta Florida,** Florida 291. A full steak or chicken meal with salad and dessert is about $10.

Tearooms and Sidewalk Cafes

An important factor in Argentine social life is the *confiteria,* or tearoom. The Argentine, who has a very light breakfast and dines late, is a steadfast client—particularly at the northern cocktail hour. That's teatime here, although Argentines usually drink coffee or a soft drink. Their custom is to drink wine with food, perhaps inching forward for an aperitif immediately before dinner, and a brandy afterward. Light lunches at a *confiteria* leave travelers full of energy for the afternoon, with cash left over. Open-faced fillet sandwiches, grilled ham and cheese, and *triples* (three-decked clubs spread with ham, cheese, tomatoes, olives, eggs and onion) are typical $2–$3 fare. Sandwiches can be made with croissants *(media lunas).* Salads and dessert are also available. Total bills come to $10 with a small bottle of wine. *Confiterias* abound in the center. Try **Florida Gardens,** 899 Florida, one of the busiest corners of the walking street at the Paraguay St. intersection. Elbow to elbow along the long, crowded bar are expresso and cappuccino sippers—as well as chocolate fans, indulging in the smoothest, richest mousse in the city. (You can sit down and enjoy too.) The oldest *confiteria* is **Gran Café Tortoni,** Av. de Mayo 825, established in 1858. As popular now as then, it is grand, with elaborate, two-story high tin ceilings and a grande dame air. A wonderfully romantic "time machine" evening ends here. Step back in the past with a ride on a polished '30s subway car from the Subte A Line from Plaza de Mayo, headed toward Primera Junta. These wooden cars were state-of-the-art from Britain and surely the most expensive available. Lovingly preserved, the wood flexes with the curves, which you can watch if you sit in the back. The Piedras exit (two stops from Plaza de Mayo) is across the street from Tortoni. Or visit the **Ideal,** at Suipacha 384, near the corner of Corrientes. This is a Buenos Aires landmark, a turn-of-the-century tearoom with a loyal following. There is a piano player, and the high teas are excellent. Another old cafe is the **Confiteria del Molino,** on the corner of Rivadavia and Callao, where politicians have been gathering to argue since the Congress buildings nearby were inaugurated in 1906.

Sidewalk cafes are found mainly on the wide boulevards: the gigantic north-south artery, 9 de Julio, Avenida de Mayo, Córdoba, and Belgrano, one like another, the differences being proximity to the broadest possible view. Argentine's don't loft umbrellas, since these block the view. Instead, awnings provide shade. For people-watching of the Rodeo Drive sort, head for Recoleta. Here are the stylish sidewalk cafes of the city, arranged side-by-side, separated only by hedges in planters.

TOURIST INFORMATION. The National Office of Tourism, ENATUR, Santa Fé 883 (312–2232/5550), is located near the downtown hotels. The hours are limited (10 A.M.–5 P.M.), but information kiosks run by the Buenos Aires municipality can be found along Florida Street *(See* Facts at your Fingertips, Useful Addresses, for locations). The kiosks have English-speaking personnel and city maps, but very few brochures. Sometimes you can find a copy of *Where,* a very useful guide that is published rather sporadically.

TOURS. Most hotels sell the basic tours described below. Your concierge can make reservations. Expect the others in the group to be a cross-section of several countries and the guides multilingual.

The three-hour **city tour** typically includes La Boca, the colorful Italian area at the original port; Plaza de Mayo with the Casa Rosada (Presidential offices); and the Cathedral with General San Martín's tomb. The tours drive along the 9th of July Boulevard, the widest in the world, past the Colón Theater. They stop at the Recoleta cemetery, with its extravagant, original mausoleums (Eva Perón is buried in a plain one), then loop around Palermo Park and the U.S. Embassy. The price is about $13, for a handy inexpensive orientation. On Sundays there are tours of La Boca and San Telmo art and antiques fairs. Three hours, about $13. You can also go on your own for a taxi fare of about $12 round-trip. Other Sunday-afternoon fairs are held in the wealthier plaza of Recoleta, San Isidro, and Tigre.

ENATUR organizes free guided walking tours around various parts of the city, with a different schedule each month. All are only in Spanish. The information booths will provide details.

Night excursions offer either a choice of shows: tango, folkloric, or cabaret (spangled briefs, comics, songs), for about $40, or a *bife* dinner, with bottles of wine and show included, for about $60. **La Plata and Children's City,** a full afternoon for about $18. A nice drive out of the city to La Plata, capital of the province of Buenos Aires. Like Brasilia, La Plata was pre-designed before anyone moved to the new port city; it was founded in 1882. The Children's City has small-scale replicas of the important public buildings in Argentina, some with light fixtures.

You can head easily for La Plata without a guided tour. Trains leave regularly from Constitution Station, the General Roca line; buses leave from the main depot near Retiro Station. The trip takes just over an hour. La Plata is noted for its parks, its gothic cathedral (unfinished), and the once-world-renowned Museum of Natural Sciences.

The River Delta. A popular trip is a drive through the shady riverside suburbs north past Palermo Park up to Tigre for a cruise of the delta. With lunch, the price is $30; the afternoon tour, without food, is $17. Most North Americans skip Tigre, but this is a mistake. The trip is an attractive one and provides some interesting contrasts. Like other delta cities, Tigre uses boat-buses to deliver mail, schoolchildren, commuters, and sometimes groceries up canal-like tentacles of the Paraná River to homes built on stilts.

If you'd rather avoid taking a guided tour, Tigre is the end of the line on the Mitre commuter train (round-trip is about $1) leaving every 15 minutes or so from Retiro Station. Cruise boats depart from a canal parallel to the Tigre station.

Isla Martín García, a granite outcropping with a subtropical climate near the coast of Uruguay, is the St. Helena's of Argentina, where exiled presidents have lived under house arrest. Today Martín García is a bird sanctuary and a trip to the island is really only of interest to naturalists. The military prison is in ruins and tourist facilities are scanty and rather shabby. It is a three-hour journey by a noisy enclosed boat from Tigre, on Tuesday, Thursday, Saturday, and Sunday. Full-day excursions or overnight stays can be arranged through *Cacciola,* Cordoba 762, 2nd floor (394–4115).

Colonia, Uruguay, is a one-hour, $45 round-trip, hydrofoil ride from downtown Buenos Aires (cheaper, but longer, by ferry). A skillfully restored 1700s village that functions today as a beach town, Colonia was the Portuguese thorn in Spain's side during the latter's efforts to gain control of the Rio de la Plata. The historic section of Colonia sits on the tip of a tiny peninsula, about five blocks long and seven blocks wide, and is a short walk from the hydrofoil terminal. (See the Uruguay section of this guide for details of sights and accommodations.)

The Pampas. There are now several opportunities to experience a little of the life of the gauchos. There is a **Fiesta Gaucho at the Estancia Magdalena,** where gallant Sr. Gallo astonishes North Americans with the lively, personalized parties he gives for them. A thoroughbred breeder, Gallo is the fourth generation to live on the family ranch. The full-day program is available on Wednesdays and Sundays and costs around $30. It includes the journey by coach, lunch with folk music entertainment, and fine displays of the horses and gauchos. Book through travel agents.

Another tour, run by **La Cinacina,** a gaucho-style restaurant, is available on Tuesdays and Fridays, and provides a closer look at today's Pampas as well as the life of the gauchos. It includes transport from hotels, a full asado lunch, and a show. The price is around $30, and the personal attention is excellent. You can call 34–1986 or 34–2841 during office hours in Buenos Aires, or **La Cinacina** itself at 0326–2773/2045.

Both the Estancia Magdalena and La Cinacina are in the area of **San Antonio de Areco,** a 1725 stagecoach stop, 80 miles northwest of Buenos Aires. This is a pretty town with a population of 20,000 whose modern homes fit into its gauchoesque motif. The gaucho museum on the outskirts of town is a replica of a ranch house from the 1800s, with a moat for protection from Indians and mini cannons to warn the neighbors of an attack. Much of the furniture comes from the home of the late Ricardo Güiraldes, a local novelist whose *Don Segundo Sombra,* which describes life on an estancia, ranks as a classic. Museum hours are 10–3:15, closed Tues. Areco has several silversmiths of international acclaim.

For an estancia experience in the grand style, you can arrange to stay at **La Bamba,** a 750-acre ranch near San Antonio de Areco where cattle are being fattened and horses are trim and ready to ride. The 150-year-old main house is a sprawling, two-story building with eight of the bedrooms recently converted for guests by long-time owners, the Aldao family. Five of the guest bedrooms have their own bathrooms. There is a swimming pool in the patio. Golf and tennis clubs are available in Areco. Reservations are necessary: Maipu 872, Buenos Aires (322–9707). Cost is around $150 per night for a double, including all meals.

You can reach Areco by the Mitre train line from Retiro Station, by bus from the terminal in the same area, by renting a car and driving yourself, or by organizing a car and driver for a day trip.

On an even grander scale than La Bamba is the **Palacio Santa Cándida,** near the town of Concepción del Uruguay some 190 miles north of Buenos Aires in the province of Entre Rios. Founded in 1847 by General Justo José de Urquiza, who is famous for deposing the dictator Rosas, the opulent mansion (now owned by Urquiza's grandson) is a national historical monument with rooms available for 22 guests. There is also a swimming pool. Apart from the 100 acres of parkland on the estate, with riding, tennis, bird shooting, and various river sports available, sights nearby include the **Palacio San José,** the general's home, and the **Palmar National Park,** noted for rare species of wildlife. Buses run to Concepción del Uruguay from the central terminal in Buenos Aires; a rental car is also a good alternative. Make reservations through a travel agent or with the owners at their home in Buenos Aires: contact Mrs. Helena Zimmermann de Saenz Valiente, Ave. Libertador 2286, 1st floor, Buenos Aires 1425 (802–9364). The telephone number at Palacio Santa Cánida itself is 0442–22–188. Price is around $130 per night for two, including meals. North American guests have been impressed with the warm hospitality and the gracious personal attention of the owners.

A new concept being developed for visitors to Argentina is that of using accommodation in private homes to provide a true experience of Pampas life. Macren Travel (see Sources of Information in the Facts at your Fingertips section) is acting as agent for two estancias that provide accommodation for up to just four people at a time. **Richard and Tessie McLoughlin** have a 350-acre grain and cattle farm 90 miles west of Buenos Aires, near the town of Heavy; farther afield, 255 miles west, is the 2,600-acre **Estancia La Linda Mora** of Michael and Alison Schiele. The ranch features grain crops and beef and dairy cattle. Visitors can join the family and farm life, or enjoy horse-back riding, swimming, and excursions in the area. La Linda Mora is near Arias, in Córdoba, and nearby is the nature reserve of Lago Las Tunas, noted for its flamingos. Macren will arrange transportation, and cost runs to around $130 per night, full board, for two people.

Luján, 40 miles west of Buenos Aires, has the miracle basilica of Argentina. Pilgrims walk here from Buenos Aires to worship at the site where a 17th-century traveler crossing the Luján River bogged down with his oxcart. Legend goes that when he freed his cart, a terra-cotta figure of the Virgin toppled out of the wagon. He put the statue back in the cart, but the oxen wouldn't move forward until he left the Virgin there. He made a small field shrine for the Virgin and finally continued on. The Luján tour by private car lasts eight hours and costs about $100. To go on your own, the Sarmiento Line train leaves every hour from Plaza Once to the Moreno Station where you change trains to Luján. A number of urban bus lines leave Plaza Once at Pueyrredon and Rivadavia, throughout the day. Apart from sightseeing, people head to Luján simply to eat at the L'Eau Vive restaurant, Av. Constitucion 2106, (0323–2774), run by nuns and specializing in trout. Reservations are a good idea.

Special-interest tours can be arranged through travel agencies. This can be efficient and economical for small groups on a tight schedule. See the Sources of Information section, "Facts at Your Fingertips," for a listing of agencies catering to English-speaking tourists.

MUSEUMS. There are about 150 museums in Buenos Aires, covering fine and folkloric art, history, the sciences, and life on the Pampa. Most are government owned, some are private, and hours vary according to the seasons and the whims of custodians. Unfortunately, nearly all of the displays are labeled only in Spanish, although it is sometimes possible to arrange for an English-speaking guide. Here is a selection of the museums most popular with foreign visitors. **Argentine Museum of Natural Sciences,** Angel Gallardo 470 (982–5243). Unique dinosaur fossils abound in Patagonia. If you don't have time to go to the aging museum in La Plata (that once had a worldwide reputation), this is a convenient substitute. Dioramas, geologic displays, birds, and over three million insect specimens are just some of the highlights. Open Tues., Thurs. and Sun. from 2–6 P.M.

Boca Museum of Fine Arts, Pedro de Mendoza 1835, La Boca (21–1080). Contemporary Argentine paintings, sculpture, and figureheads from nineteenth century vessels. Open Wed.–Fri. 8 A.M.–6 P.M.; Sat. 8 A.M.–noon and 2–6 P.M.; Sun. 10 A.M.–6 P.M.

City of Buenos Aires' Museum, Alsina 412, First floor (331–9855). Detailed, intimate history of life in Buenos Aires given in sophisticated displays. Exhibits change every two months. Open Mon.–Fri. 11 A.M.–7 P.M.; Sun. 3–7 P.M.

Isaac Fernández Blanco Museum, Suipacha 1422 (393–6318). A major collection of colonial Spanish-American art housed in a mansion. Open Tues.–Sun. 3–7 P.M.

José Hernández Museum of Argentine Popular Motifs, Av. Libertador 2373 (809–9967). A small gem near the better-known Museum of Decorative Art. Laudable collections from the Indian, Colonial, and Gaucho eras, particularly the latter. Beautiful silver displays. Open Mon.-Fri. 8 A.M.–7 P.M.; Sat. and Sun. 3–7 P.M.

Colón Theater Museum, Tucumán 1161 (35–5414/5/6). Photographs and antique instruments of performers from the long history of the Colón, where Arturo Toscanini first rose from his musician's chair and wielded a baton. It is possible to arrange a tour of the workrooms where new costumes, wigs, shoes, and backdrops are made. Open Mon.–Fri. 10 A.M.–12:30 P.M. and 2–5 P.M.

Museum of Decorative and Oriental Art, Av. Libertador 1902 (801–5988). The ground floor has different private collections of furniture, paintings, and porcelain. Upstairs is the Oriental art. Open Wed.–Mon. from 3–7 P.M.

National Historical Museum, Defensa 1600 (23–6254). Located in the historic district of San Telmo, this 1850s villa has 30 rooms, some decorated with themes from Argentine history. San Martín's uniforms are displayed here. Open Tues.–Fri. 1–7 P.M.; Sat. and Sun. 3–7 P.M.

National Museum of Fine Arts, Av. Libertador 1473 (803–0802). Many rooms of European masters, but best for nineteenth century and contemporary Argentine art. Open Tues.–Sun. 9 A.M.–12:45 P.M. and 3–7 P.M.

National Aeronautical Museum, Av. Rafael Obligado, next to the Aeroparque Airport (773–0665). Outdoor displays of planes from 1940. Open Tues.–Fri. 8 A.M.–noon.

Sarmiento Frigate Museum, Av. Costanera and Viamonte, next to the Yacht Club in the Buenos Aires port (311–8792). A ship that was used to train naval officers. Open daily in summer, otherwise weekends only.

National Railways Museum, Av. Libertador 405, behind Retiro Station (312–5353, Ext. 11306). Over 3,000 items on display, many from early British railway construction and operation. Open Mon.–Fri. 8 A.M.–6 P.M.

La Quinta de Pueyrredon, Rivera Indarte and Roque Saenz Peña, San Isidro (743–0581). The villa of Independence hero Juan Martín de Pueyrredon, it has been maintained as it was during the eighteenth century, completely furnished. Open on Tues., Thurs., Sat., and Sun. 2–6 P.M., closed Jan. and Feb.

SPECTATOR SPORTS. Watching Argentines play **polo** has been compared to seeing the old Bolshoi perform—a virtuosic display of stunning, athletic showmanship. In Buenos Aires, sellout crowds of 20,000 cheer on national heroes like Gonzalo Pieres, a 10-goaler ranked tops in the world. For match information, contact the **Asociación Argentina de Polo,** H. Yrigoyen 636, first floor (331–4646). Seasons run Mar.–May and Sept.–Dec. The best teams compete in the later season.

Soccer matches are played year-round. Passions run when Boca Juniors from the prideful Italian community of La Boca take on their archrivals, River Plate. It's not dangerous in the stands, just a great show. As for the quality of local **tennis** competitions, Guillermo Vilas, Jose Luis Clerc, and Gabriela Sabatini are products of Buenos Aires tennis clubs.

Horse racing. Historians consider the strong thoroughbreds from Argentina one of the factors that favored the British in the South African Boer War. Argentines on spending binges brought the best stock in the world home to breed, and swift Argentine horses were prized throughout the world. But the past forty years of bad economic times have handicapped the thoroughbred breeding industry. It has been a while since Argentine horses defeated all comers in North America and Europe. Still, winners of Argentine competitions are sold for racing up north, their successes being measured by the generations they sire. Several U.S. Triple-Crown champions trace their roots to the pampas.

There are two main tracks in Buenos Aires; check or call the *Herald* for schedules. Generally, races are Wednesday and weekends on the fairly new turf track in the historical suburb of San Isidro, Centenario y Márquez 504 (743–4012). Closer to the city is the dirt track at the traditional Hipódromo in Palermo Park, Av. del Libertador 4499 (772–6021/81).

Boxing and wrestling matches are held in Luna Park, an indoor arena; cricket at the private Hurlingham Club and other Anglo-Argentine enclaves; rugby football on weekends from Apr.–Oct. at the San Isidro Clubs SIC and CASI.

Your best general guide to what's happening where in sports is the *Buenos Aires Herald* (34–8476), which has excellent daily coverage and announcements of local sports events.

PARTICIPANT SPORTS. Fishing: Seventy miles southeast of B.A. at Lake Chascomus, a brackish lake with a series of lagoons. *Pejerrey* (a local catfish), and the aggressive *tararia* that lives in the reeds are stocked by the Hydrobiological Station. Boats, tackles, and bait can be hired on the public pier. Take the Roca line train from Plaza Constitución, changing trains at Glew Station. **Gliding:** *Club Argentino de Planeadores Albatros,* Av. de Mayo 1370, sixth floor (37–5504). Visitors welcome. Gliding is done outside Buenos Aires; equipment is available. Sponsored for many years by the Air Force, Argentine glider pilots have good craft and are active throughout the country. International competitions have been held in the hills near Córdoba, where the wind drafts are challenging. **Golf:** *Public Golf Courses,* Argentine Golf Assoc., Av. Corrientes 538 (394–2743/2972); *Municipal Golf Course,* Tornquist and Olleros, Palermo Woods (772–7576); *Costa Salguero Golf Center,* Av. Costanera and Salguero (805–1216). **Tennis:** *Public Tennis Courts,* Bakerloo, Pampa 1235, Belgrano; Parque Norte, Cantilo and Guiraldes (Costanera Norte) (784–9653); *Parque José Hernández,* Valentin Alsina 1270, Palermo (782–0936). Arrangements can be made through the executive offices at the *Sheraton Hotel* to play tennis on their courts, San Martín 1225 (311–6331). **Squash:** *Olimpia Cancilleria,* also for **racquetball,** Esmeralda 1042 (311–8687); *Posadas Squash Club,* Posadas 1265, seventh floor (22–0548); *Tribunales Squash Courts,* Montevideo 550 (49–8358). **Windsurfing:** On the river at *Parque Norte,* at Cantilo and Guiraldes in Costanera Norte; *El Molino* and *Rocky Point,* both at Elcano and Perú in Acassuso, the suburb before San Isidro. At Acassuso, there have been problems with water pollution.

MUSIC, DANCE, AND STAGE. By any standard of comparison, the Colón Theater, Cerrito 618 (35–5414), is one of the world's finest **opera** houses. Tiered like a wedding cake, the gilt and red velvet auditorium has acoustics that surpass the baroque grandeur. There is a changing stream of imported talent to bolster the local. The Colón is also headquarters for the **National Ballet Company** and for the **National Symphony.** In the summer, the ballet gives open-air performances in Palermo Park. Tickets can be arranged through your hotel concierge. By the way, the famous view of the Colón on 9th of July boulevard is its back side—the entrance faces the trees and fountain of Plaza Lavalle. The whole stage area has recently been renovated.

Some 42 **theaters** are open almost constantly, from those presenting Argentine dramatic works or translations of foreign plays to "revue" theaters with comics who strike out at local political mishaps and choruses notable for the brevity of their costumes. Listings are in the local papers.

Publicly supported dance, mime, puppets, and theater performances are staged at the municipal theater complex, Teatro San Martín, Corrientes 1532 (40–0111/46–5539). Musica e Imagen in the Wilton Palace Hotel Auditorium, Av. Callao 1162 (41–9196) shows excellent films of opera companies like the New York Metropolitan, and other types of performances, summer as well as winter. A new entertainment center is **La Plaza,** Corrientes 1660 (45–7117/7162), an open-air mall with a small outdoor amphitheater and two theaters, along with shops and small restaurants. It offers a variety of shows twice daily (1 P.M. and 9 P.M.) for a nominal fee.

A recent development is the steady growth of **café concerts.** They usually take place in a small salon, often a cellar, and consist of a one-man or one-woman show. A very popular spot with more elaborate, semi-classical shows, is Café Vienés Mozart, Esmeralda 754 (322–3273), which has been featured in *The New York Times.* Viennese whipped creams and other rich specialties are yours to savor while you listen.

You will appreciate the street theater on Florida. Every evening when the crowds are strolling, a host of entertainers appear—an accordionist playing Bach, a magician with live rabbits, folk bands with pounding drums, singers, a harpist, plus pantomime and puppets. All pass the hat.

Movies? International first runs, the powerful films of uncensored Argentine directors, and Italian comedies. There are more than 60 theaters downtown alone, most of them located along two adjoining streets, Corrientes and Lavalle. The *Herald* has a daily list. The names of films are given in Spanish, but the sound tracks of English-language films are left in English, with Spanish subtitles.

SHOPPING. Choice Tierra del Fuego fox in the latest Yves St. Laurent styles, buttersoft leather evening gowns with snakeskin appliques, French designer suits for men at half the price, Calvin Klein briefs, cashmere sweaters, high boots and loafers, briefcases and bags, Marlboro man sheepskin coats . . . international design and Argentine workmanship. While the bargains are not startling (like they were a few years ago when leather jackets cost $50), dollars still buy value, especially if you arrive between seasons. Look for *liquidaciones* signs in the windows—they mean "sale," not "going out of business." Argentine shops have fixed prices, but will often give discounts for cash.

Shop hours are generally from 9 A.M.–7:30 or 8 P.M. By law, prices in the branch shops in the hotels must charge the same rates as in the main stores. Where to look: Calle Florida, the walking street downtown, is classic. The closer you are to Plaza San Martín and the Plaza Hotel, the higher the prices—and in some instances, the better the quality. It's good to look here first, to establish a standard by which you can gauge so-called bargains in factory outlets. Check out **Harrods**—it's no relation to the famous British store although the logo is the same—towards the Plaza San Martín end of Florida. The only good department store you'll find, it's spacious, and, strangely, never crowded. **Downtown Santa Fé** is also good for browsing, along with the avenues in the **Recoleta** neighborhood. The old buildings here are lovely, and the windows have become a showcase of what's best, and most expensive, in Buenos Aires. Sensational art deco items can be found in **San Telmo's** antique shops.

The most luxurious shopping arcade is the galleried **Patio Bullrich,** Av. Libertador 750, near the Recoleta district. This is a collection of very elegant, expensive stores in a lovely old restored building. Here, also, are various cafes, exhibitions, and cinemas, and there are frequently jazz or chamber music concerts in the evenings. Now rivaling Patio Bullrich in style and quality of stores and entertainments is **Alto Palermo,** on the corner of Arenales and Coronel Diaz; (you can take the D subway line and get off at Bulnes).

Leathers

A rainbow of pastels and vivid colors, rough suedes and babyskin soft, the fabulous Argentine reputation with leather is well-deserved, whether cowhide, kidhide, pighide, sheepskin, lizard, snake, or porcupine. From conservative to Miami Vice styles for men, from bikinis to evening gowns for women. **Casa Lopez,** M.T. de Alvear 640 (311–3044), has five locations. **Lofty,** M.T. de Alvear 519 (311–1424), features reversible coats of smooth suede on one side and shiny leather on the other. **Jota U. Cueros,** Pasaje Tres Sargentos 439 (311–0826), specializes in sewing any style or color to your measurements within a few hours.

For briefcases, try **Pullman,** Florida 985 (311–0799). Latest USA Young Lawyer styles, also lightweight leather bags for extra carry-on luggage.

Shoes, boots, and saddles can be found at **Rossi y Carusso,** Av. Santa Fe 1601 (41–1538). Superb riding equipment as well as handbags, clothes, etc. The King of Spain is a patron. Polo equipment and saddles can also be found at **H. Merlo,** Juncal 743 (22–6116), and **La Martina,** Paraguay 661 (311–5963), among others. For men's loafers, try **Guante,** Santa Fé 832 (312–0098) and **Guido,** Florida 704 (322–7548). Made to measure shoes—for women: **Perugia,** Av. Alvear 1866 (802–6340); for men: **López Taibo** Av. Corrientes 350 (311–2132).

Furs

Furs are gorgeous bargains in Argentina, often costing half what the same quality coat would cost in the States. The stub-tailed nutria, a cousin to the beaver, is native to Argentina rivers and lakes. Its long, outer hair is waterproof and a bit harsh to the touch, but the short fur underneath is as soft as velvet. Plucked nutria is most costly. Fox from Tierra del Fuego (Fire Land) is a reddish color, while the Magellanic fox is a more silky, beigy gray. Minks for coats are raised in farms near Mar del Plata, the seaside resort. **Dennis Furs,** Florida 989 (311–8920), is one of the leading fur dealers. Several years ago, the Eisele family began using Yves St. Laurent's designs, label, and unusual fur techniques. Look also at the excellent selections at **Charles Calfun,** Florida 918 (311–1147) and at **Pielycuer,** M.T. de Alvear 529 (313–7640). (You can enter from the Plaza Hotel lobby.)

Jewelry

Precious and semi-precious stones are priced similarly all over Latin America. What varies is the price of the workmanship and the quality. Argentina has benefited from the expertise of French, German, and Italian jewelers who emigrated to Argentina, bringing with them a sophisticated sense of design. **H. Stern,** in the Sheraton, Plaza, and Alvear Palace hotels, is a good place to begin looking at what Argentine designers do with Brazilian stones. One semi-precious stone—known as the Rose of Inca, or Rodocrosita—is found only in Argentina; some of them are as red as rubies. Sculptures of birds in flight from **Cousino,** Paraguay 631, third floor, Suite A (312–2336) are exhibited in the National Museum of Decorative Arts. Among the other top jewelers are: **Guthman,** Viamonte 597 (312–2471); and **Santarelli,** Florida 688 (393–8152).

Sheepskin and Knitwear

Argentina is the third largest exporter of wool in the world. Sheepskin jackets in the **Ciudad de Cuero,** Florida 940, would make the Marlboro man leap off his mount and set in a winter's supply. **Jota U. Cueros,** Tres Sargentos 439 (311–0826), has quick, made-to-order sheepskin clothing in stunning combinations of grey, black, and brown. Two legitimate factory outlets for sweaters that are downtown are: IKS, Paraguay 472 (311–4452) and **Silvia y Mario,** M.T. Alvear 550 (311–4107), with a huge selection of V-neck cashmeres and very elegant, two-piece knit dresses.

Souvenirs

Vico's at the Sheraton (311–6331) has quality gauchoesque items such as *facones* (knives), wide leather belts called *rastas* onto which the gaucho chained his money, and red and black ponchos from Salta. An equally fine selection can be found at **El Altillo de Susana,** M.T. de Alvear 515 (311–1138). There are many other shops on narrow sidestreets off Florida. The best collection of souvenir T-shirts in all sizes is at **Susana Sweaters,** San Martin 1103 (312–8816).

Other Ideas

Some wine experts predict that the taste and properties of the Argentine all-Malbec wine will make it the wine of the 21st century. Carrying bottles home is a heavy, fragile load, but an affordable, special gift. A central liquor store is **Provision Fernández,** San Martín 975 (31–1871). They wrap sets of four bottles in heavy paper with stout carrying string at no charge.

A small arcade on Lavalle, between Maipu and Esmerald, features a dashing selection of lead soldiers, priced from $2–$50.

Browse through a stretch of Antiques stores along Avenida Libertador between the northern suburbs of Acassuso and San Isidro. Serious dealers downtown include: **Galeria Studio,** Libertad 1271; **Zurbaran,** Cerrito 1522 (22–7703); and **Vetmas,** Libertad 1286.

NIGHTLIFE. Let's begin with the basic distinction between the Argentine version of nightlife and ours: They meet for a coffee at 7 *in the afternoon.* For us, a date at 7 P.M. means "I'll meet you at seven *tonight.*"

At first North Americans assume Argentines survive this frenetic pace with *siestas,* but not so. Porteños work the same eight or 10 hours a day that northerners do. The difference is that Argentines refuse to sacrifice pleasure for anything as mundane as sleep. The happy consequence of this habit is a glut of activities at night. The clever traveler can build stamina by slipping in a nap during the *afternoon* lull . . . say from 6:30–8:30 P.M. What follows is by no means an inclusive list, but rather a sampler to whet appetites. Once you are in Buenos Aires, check with your concierge, the *Herald, Where,* or the tourist bureau for the latest updates. The *Herald's* personals encompass escort services and "discreet" masseuses.

Warning: Later in the evening, prostitutes are favored patrons at many of the cabarets and strip tease clubs. Their ploy is as old as the profession—coaxing customers to buy outrageously priced "drinks." Small-time spenders are commonly shocked by $300 tabs—and they have been known to be as high as $1,500—with no recourse but to pay with credit card. Be sure to ask the price of drinks.

Tango, Folkloric Shows

Argentine tango is philosophizing, it is passion. To be more specific: it is embarrassingly emotive, tragic passion, often from men dressed like young, ambitious bank clerks. Which is not to say that tango doesn't captivate non-Spanish speakers, because eventually it does, but that tango is not what we think it is. Argentines sit in tango clubs, sip a drink, and listen to singers. Clubs can be sampled on nightclub tours of the city available through hotels. An easier way to slip into the feeling of tango is to attend a folkloric show. Haunting Andean pipe music from Salta-Jujuy in the north combines with flirtatious handkerchief dancing in the sentimental *zambas.* A few shows dazzle with an extraordinary version of *flamenco,* a "see if you can top this" tapping of heels and backs of heels, ankles, sides of feet accompanied by Cossack leaps and Lash LaRue cracking of whips. The dance came out of the Argentine cavalry during the Indian Wars. And of course, there is a sampling of tango: a serious singer, a passionate, woeful, suffering singer, a virtuoso *bandoneon* star flashing his fingers across double sets of accordion-like buttons. And finally, tango dancers. Currently, the best folkloric performance is at **Casa Blanca,** Balcarce 668 (361–3633). Also good is **Michelangelo,** Balcarce 433 (331–5392), which combines folkloric, tango, and international music in its dinner show. Or try **Taconeando,** Balcarce 725, San Telmo (362–9596/9599). Actress and dancer

Beba Vidart is behind this show, which attracts the biggest names in tango. After the show the audience can tango onto the dance floor themselves. Another way for initiates to vary the music is at **La Casa de Carlos Gardel,** Jean Jaures 735 (962–4265), where there are audiovisual displays on his life. Gardel, with his dark, Tyrone Power looks, died in a plane crash in 1935 at the age of 40. Some claim that Gardel's 1,200 recordings continue to outsell all others in Argentina.

Once you have settled into the mood for an uninterrupted tango, head for **El Viejo Almacén,** at Av. Independencia and Balcarce (362–3503), where the four-hour shows don't begin until 11:30 P.M. or midnight. This is the most famous tango club, set under an illusionary grape arbor with tiny "stars" above. You might also try **Bar Sur,** Estados Unidos 299 (362–6086), also in San Telmo, for spontaneous tango. Bar Sur is also the least expensive.

Jazz

"Hold that Tiger" blasted by trombonists in tails. Jazz in B.A. is treated seriously by the audiences and played enthusiastically by the musicians. Familiar tunes, but this is not New Orleans, it's different and worth exploring. The San Telmo version, with local and foreign groups, can be heard at **Gaelle Jazz Club,** Estados Unidos 465 (361–4685), or **Balcon de La Plaza,** H. Primo 461 (362–1144). **Café Tortoni,** Av. de Mayo 825 (34–4328) has jazz on weekends, and **Patio Bullrich,** Libertador 750, frequently has jazz concerts in the evening. For a combination of jazz and traditional *mate* (an herb tea) drinking, try **Oliverio Mate Bar,** Paraná 328 (542–1537).

Chess and Billiards

Hobbies are a good starting place to meet Argentines, especially those with a universal language. One is chess, which is played in the basement lounge of the **Richmond,** Florida 468 (322–1341). Upstairs, businessmen and newspaper executives eat lunch. Billiards is another friendly option. Upstairs at the **Confiteria Ideal,** Suipacha 384 (396–1081) is a traditional place to pocket balls. Or try **Café Tortoni,** Av. de Mayo 825 (34–4328), where dice-shooters are also welcome.

Dancing

For international dancing that sometimes includes a tango, **Atalaya** on the 23rd floor of the Sheraton (311–6331) has the orchestra, the view, and the elegant spirit to draw full crowds on weekends. Open every night. **Africa,** in the Alvear Palace Hotel, Av. Alvear 1885 (804–4031) and **Mau Mau,** Arroyo 866 (393–6131) appeal to the 25–45-year old crowd, while the popular **Hippopotamus,** in Recoleta, Junín 1787 (802–0500), appeals to adults and a younger crowd, both of the affluent sort. This is also one of the city's most expensive restaurants. Another elegant dining-dancing evening can be spent at **Le Club,** Av. Quintana 111 (22–2565). Porteños never go to discos early—one enthusiastic follower of the "in" scene commented that "Only bobos are seen in discos before 2 A.M." Buenos Aires discos, like discos everywhere, come and go, and places that are frenetically popular one month are "out" the next. Your hotel can advise on current favorites. **Contramano,** Rodríguez Peña 1082 (no phone), is a gay disco.

IGUAZÚ FALLS AND THE JESUIT MISSIONS

A narrow finger of Argentine territory extends up the twisting red Paraná River, north through jungles to its juncture with the Iguazú River. Red sandstone, rusty red as the soil and muddy rivers, is layered with hard black basalt throughout the region. Over time, powerful rivers have trenched through the sandstone, bouncing off platforms of stubborn basalt. Churning water has cut deep canyons in its tumble, cutting through sandstone, then bouncing off newly exposed platforms and tumbling ever farther and farther down.

The most extraordinary geological display in Argentina are the falls on the Iguazú River, 12 miles before it joins the Paraná. That's "falls," 275 of them, a horseshoe of roaring red that is twice as wide as Niagara and higher, too. In a continent of superlatives, Iguazú is special. Just above the plunge, the river is about two miles across. Airborne on spray, rainbows dance 100 feet into the sky. Hundreds of swifts dart in and out of the mists. Quick flashes of color flutter in the tangled gray-green rain forest—home to 25 varieties of butterflies, dark blue ones as big as a man's two hands; orchids; monkeys; parrots; palms; and parasitic vines thick enough for Tarzan to swing on.

We cannot recommend strongly enough that a two-day stop at Iguazú Falls be included in your itinerary. The Brazilian and Argentine National Park Services have coordinated a nearly perfect system of exploring the cascade, but to hike the catwalks over, under, and into the falls, you need time to walk and time to cross international borders.

Three countries meet in this corner of the jungle. The Iguazú River forms the boundary between Argentina and Brazil, while the Paraná River separates those two countries from Paraguay.

Given a few days to spare, Iguazú Falls is a central location from which to see Brazil's gigantic new Itaipú Dam on the Paraná and Argentina's archaeological ruins of San Ignacio Miní. This gutted red sandstone commune was one of 30 utopian villages developed by the Jesuits during the sixteenth-eighteenth centuries. San Ignacio is south along the Paraná River, 39 miles from the provincial capital of Posadas. (See "Practical Information" below for more information on Posadas and the Jesuit Missions.) Argentine and Brazilian tourists usually include a shopping trip into Cíudad del Este (formerly Puerto Stroessner), Paraguay, a cut-rate paradise. Card tables and small shops are crammed with Sonys, Seikos, Chivas Regal, and—the latter are sometimes cheaper than in the United States. In sum, Paraguay's second city is a curiosity.

PRACTICAL INFORMATION FOR IGUAZÚ FALLS AND THE JESUIT MISSIONS

GETTING THERE. There are two Iguazú airports, one on the Argentine side and the other in Brazil. National airliners land in their own country. *Aerolineas Argentinas* and *Austral* fly to Iguazú from Buenos Aires. Aerolineas continues on to Rio de Janeiro and Sao Paulo. *Varig* travels the same route. *Lineas Aeras Paraguayas* has flights to the Brazilian Iguazú from Asunción. Posadas, 200 miles south, is the end of the line for trains; buses converge at the falls from all three countries. The bus trip from Buenos Aires to Iguazú takes 21 hours. Aerolineas Argentinas and Austral fly to Posadas. If you want to join an organized tour, many of the Buenos Aires travel agencies offer two- or three-day inclusive programs.

HOTELS (on the Argentina side). For definitions of price categories see "Facts at Your Fingertips." **Hotel Internacional Iguazú.** *Deluxe.* Parque Nacional Iguazú (20–790). 152 rooms and four suites. Two deluxe hotels face the falls, the five-star, very modern Internacional in Argentina, and the pink colonial-style, four-star Hotel Das Cataratas in Brazil. Half of the rooms in the Internacional have a falls view, as do many of the Brazilian ones. The Internacional has five bars, tennis courts, swimming pool, casino, discotheque, restaurants, and furnished balconies.

Hotel Esturion. *Expensive.* Av. Tres Fronteras 650 (20–020). 122 rooms and eight suites. A fairly new hotel, the Esturion is modern, with polished wood, loads of windows, and balconies. Service is excellent, the food well-prepared, and the swimming pool big. This hotel overlooks the Iguazú River as it joins the Paranà, fairly close to town. It is popular with Argentine tour groups. A Guaraní trio entertains at night, playing a local-style harp and guitars, their voices haunting as nightingales waking at dawn.

Hotel La Cabaña. *Inexpensive.* Av. 3 Fronteras 434 (20–564). Close to town. 18 rooms in delightful bungalows clustered around a beautiful pool complete with an island of flagstone and trees. The mini-island is typical of the Germanic blend of manicured and wild landscaping; the emphasis is on orchids.

CAMPING. Campground Americano: Rt. 12, eight km (five miles) from town on the road to the falls (20–658). Space for 400 campers and tents, a few bungalows, tennis, water, bathrooms.

RESTAURANTS. International cuisine is mixed with Guaraní and Argentine specialties. This is the center of yerba mate and ordinary tea plantations. We think mate tastes like shredded tobacco in tepid water, but aficionados scour health food stores in the northern hemisphere looking for it, and it's fun to try it right on the home front. Give yourself a little ambience and sip mate from a gourd like the gauchos and Guaraní do—through a bombilla, a silver (or tin) straw with a strainer on the end. Regardless of your reaction, bombillas make good souvenirs.

(For more on local dishes such as *sopa paraguaya,* a souffle-like pie of corn cheese and eggs, and definitions of price categories, see "Facts At Your Fingertips.") In general, prices are a couple of dollars lower than in Buenos Aires. The eclectic menu at **La Rueda,** Av. Córdoba 879 (20–955) ranges from pizza to typical Argentine, i.e. beef. For more beef, **El Pilincho,** on Victoria Aguirre.

NIGHTLIFE. Try **El Castillo,** Av. Misiones and Bonpland, or ask your hotel concierge for suggestions.

TOURIST INFORMATION. Tourist Office for the International Zone of Iguazú, Av. Victoria Aguirre 396 (20–800).

WHAT TO SEE. The Falls. Argentina has the falls, while Brazil claims the panorama. Excursions with guides are easily arranged through your hotel, or you can go alone. Allow about four hours to cover the two loops on the Argentine side. Both trails can be managed in a wheelchair. The concrete walks begin just below the Hotel Internacional. A short trail circles around several individual falls from the bottom level, while the three-mile trail is along the upper rim of the falls (remember, there are about 275 of them). Bridges across some of them provide sensational lookout points. The climax is a water-to-face encounter with Devil's Throat, a roaring monster that keeps you humble.

Arrange an excursion to the Brazilian side with your hotel. A full-day option is to visit the falls, Cíudad del Este, and Itaipú Dam. Even if you only want to see the falls, an excursion will simplify things tremendously, particularly if you're staying at the Internacional.

Note: You must have a Brazilian visa if you are a citizen of the United States, Australia or New Zealand.

The only way to reach the other side from Argentina is a 13-mile drive to Puerto Meira, where you catch a ferry for the five-minute ride across the calm-again Iguazú River. From the town of Foz do Iguassu, it's a 19-mile drive to the Brazilian National Park.

Once there, the one-mile loop begins at Hotel das Cataratas. (This one has steps.) Great views, greater views, and then, boom, you reach a large deck at the base of three—*only three!*—gargantuan falls, one of them the now-familiar Devil's Throat. To your left are souvenir shops and hawkers renting rain slickers and hats. Unless you're in a bathing suit—a good idea in the steaming hot summer—you might want to cover up for the next stage—a walk into the falls. Only a little way in, of course, like the swifts you'll see clinging to the sides of drenched boulders, in the water, but not too near the falls. Squint through the mist, then it's back to a mild roar, up an elevator to the top of the falls. A short distance farther along is Puerto Canoas, where the valiant pay to be rowed out to a basalt outcropping at the edge of Devil's Throat.

Ask your hotel about tamer but equally thrilling photo safaris into the jungle. Be sure to lug along your telephoto lens and a tripod. More than 300 species of birds have been identified in this region.

The Jesuit Missions. In the sixteenth century, inspired by Sir Thomas More's *Utopia,* several Catholic orders set about creating new, purer societies away from Europe. Missionaries came to the New World (also to China and Japan) to create humane, higher civilizations. The Jesuits set up their first missions among the Guaraní about 1609. People lived in communal villages, farmed together, and shared what they had, while each family also cultivated a small plot of land of its own. San Ignacio Miní was founded in 1632.

The Indians were inspired to join the Fathers, and with good reason. They were sought by Spanish landowners as laborers and by slave-hunters from São Paulo. To counter such threats, the Jesuits trained their own army of Guaraní to fight the Paulistas. Eventually the Jesuit Empire had huge numbers of cattle, horses, and sheep, and exported great quantities of mate. In short, it became powerful and wealthy. But the Jesuits' more powerful neighbors proved too envious, and began to take action against them. When Charles III of Spain expelled the Jesuits from the New World in 1767, the Jesuit Empire had grown to be larger than France and had a population of 150,000 and more than 30 missions in present day Argentina and Paraguay.

Within five years of the Jesuits' departure, most of the Guaraní had returned to their former life in the forest. (For more details, read *The Epic of Latin America* by John R. Crow.) Today, all that remains of that 150-year social experiment are red sandstone ruins. The roofless walls of San Ignacio Miní are both accessible and fairly well preserved. At its peak, the settlement had 4,356 citizens.

Although excursions can be arranged to San Ignacio from the falls, it is a 14-hour trip, and while the tea, mate, and southern pine plantations are interesting, it is a long drive. If you are traveling on an Aerolineas Pass, another solution would be to fly to Posadas and either arrange an excursion there with an English-speaking guide, rent a car and drive the 39 miles yourself, or take one of the frequent buses. Since information at the ruins is sketchy and in Spanish, a guide is highly recommended.

Posadas. Posadas is a provincial capital with a population of 146,300. It has three car rental companies, including **National,** Bolívar 278 (22–436), and several tourist agencies. Check with the **Tourist Office,** Colón 1985 (30–504) or your hotel. We suggest: **Hotel Libertador,** San Lorenzo 2208 (36–901, 37–601), with 61 rooms, and **Hotel Continental,** Bolívar 314 (38–673, 38–966), which are the best in town. They are centrally located and fit our *inexpensive* category. Farther out in a good residential neighborhood is **Hotel Horianski,** Líbano 725 (22–675), a friendly bed-and-breakfast-type place with style and low rates (less than $15 a night for a double).

THE COLONIAL NORTHWEST

Lights are dim in the peña. Dark-jacketed waiters slip past tables that have been cleared of thick steaks. Many hours later, they'll serve expressos and something sweet to conclude the evening, like *empanadillas de cayote,* sweet turnovers filled with a pumpkin marmalade. But for now the waiters are opening more bottles of local wine. Corks slide out silently, unheard amidst the exuberant music. A guitar, violin, drums, and happy singing combine in a pleasing din. Here at the end of the Inca Empire, flutes and haunting sadness remain. Listeners move to the compelling rhythm. They drum fingers, sing along, and sometimes dance to the very particular music of Salta. Exotic Salta is the birthplace of the *zamba.* Evocative and emotional, the optimistic music sparks a resounding fire until the audience is aflame and strangers no longer sit apart.

Argentines are enamored of their colonial northwest, for it is a region that is different from the rest of the country, more like New Mexico than New England. For more than 250 years, Salta was the center of trade for everyone in southern Latin America. By Spanish decree, all goods had to be exported through Lima and Panama. Only mules could bear the burden of the altiplano and treacherous swamps, and only on the plains east of Salta could mules most conveniently be bred. Every February and March, tradesmen from throughout the empire gathered in Salta, elevation 4,000 feet, to buy and sell. Early wealth built a beautiful trading center, one that illustrates that Spanish design was still very influenced by more than 700 years of Muslim rule. A continuing patina has been added to Salta in recent generations by Syrian and Lebanese immigrants, mostly traders.

Quaint Salta, population 260,000, is a memorable city, its colonial architecture more colorful than that which Californians, for instance, are accustomed to. White-washed walls and red tile roofs are accented with other pastels, while towers and facades are as richly decorated as Granada. In the valley oasis, bougainvillea and palms predominate, but outside, this is an Arizona landscape, with grand canyons, red mesas, and cactus, Indians who sometimes wear the traditional Bolivian bowler hats, and a narrow-gauge, Wild West train ride for tourists.

Throughout the northwest there are adobe villages and interesting cities: Jujuy (who-WHO-ee), the most Indian of Argentine cities; tropical Tucumán, with sugar cane plantations; Córdoba, an industrial center bordered by green hills where woods are fed by spring-fed creeks and German immigrants built chalet hotels. If you have time to wander, each has something to offer. However, if your itinerary is tight, Salta is a charming base from which to explore the region.

PRACTICAL INFORMATION FOR
SALTA AND THE COLONIAL NORTHWEST

GETTING THERE. *Aerolineas Argentinas* and *Austral* fly to Salta and Jujuy from Buenos Aires; Aerolineas flies weekly on to Santa Cruz and La Paz in Bolivia. *Lloyd Aero Boliviano* flies to Salta from four Bolivian cities, including La Paz. **Buses** go from Buenos Aires to Salta, Jujuy, and over the Bolivian border to the capital of La Paz. By bus, it is 24 hours from Buenos Aires to Salta. **Trains** run from Buenos Aires to Tucumán. That part of the journey takes 18 hours. Continuing by bus ride to Salta requires another four-and-a-half hours. An extraordinary journey is by bus (departures are limited; none in summer) from Salta through the Quebrada del Toro, over the volcano peaks of the Andes, and across the Atacama Desert to Antofagasta, Chile, on the Pacific.

HOTELS. For definitions of price categories, see "Facts at Your Fingertips." **Hotel Salta.** *Expensive.* Buenos Aires at Caseros, on the edge of the main plaza (211–011). 86 rooms, recently remodeled. Lovely colonial charm, inside and out. Arches, a carved wooden facade, and an ornate tower blend with the antique mood of the city center. Outdoor pool and air-conditioning. The superb dining room is popular with locals.

Hotel Provincial. *Moderate.* Caseros 786 (218–400). 72 rooms with individual air-conditioning units. Eight-story colonial building with a balcony off the dining room. Central location, plus tennis courts and a swimming pool. Salteños commonly meet at the bar.

Residencial Sandra. *Inexpensive.* Alvarado 630 (211–241). Centrally located, 17 rooms, all with private baths and air-conditioned. Small dining room. Cordial, family atmosphere.

CAMPGROUNDS. There are several in the area. Facilities sometimes include swimming pools, tennis, and volleyball courts. One of the largest is Campo Quijano, about 20 miles from Salta, with 500 tent sites. Check with the tourist office for places close by.

RESTAURANTS. Salta produces a unique white wine that is drier than a vermouthless martini and has a remarkable bouquet. White wine aficionados rave about Salta white; the Germans even import it. (The Japanese buy grape juice.) The

Salta special is made from a finicky Spanish grape, *torrontes,* that is nearly unusable on its home soil, and practically every other place too, except Salta, where the torrontes thrives. The wine is splendid. There are those of us who drink Salta white torrontes with our *bifes.*

All the restaurants listed are *moderate;* expect full meals to run about $10–$15 per person without wine.

Peña Gauchos de Guemes, Uruguay 750 (210–820), has steaks, regional specialties, and folkloric music. It's perched on a hillside overlooking the city. Less intimate but more famous (although the food is rather uninteresting) is **Boliche Balderrama,** San Martín 1126 (211–542), in the center of Salta; it offers music every night. **La Castiza,** Alberdi 134 (213–129) and **La Posta,** España 476 (217–091) are the top steakhouses. The popular **Union Sirio Libanesa de Salta,** San Martín 681 (213–214), requires reservations for its Arabic-influenced menu.

NIGHTLIFE. In Salta, one can actually dance tango at the **Casa de la Cultura,** Caseros 460 (21–5031). There is also a casino: **Sala de Juegos,** Alvarado 651 (217–005); a racetrack; **Hipódromo,** Ruta Nac. 51-km 3, Limache (21–7700), and a dozen discotheques (at last count). A new one is **Quorum,** in the Hotel Colonial (211–236). Check with your hotel about which are currently the most popular.

TOURIST INFORMATION. Salta Tourist Office, (Satour), Buenos Aires 93 (21–1316). Local presidents of international clubs are also sources of information: **Rotary,** Caseros 527 (21–7567); **Lion's,** General Guemes 658 (21–9404).

WHAT TO SEE. Mercado Artesanal, Av. San Martín 2555 (219–195) has high-quality tapestries, wood carvings, ceramics, and beautiful ponchos made by artisans in their workshops here. Open from 10 A.M.–8 P.M.

For gold-gilded ornate, the **Cathedral** and **San Francisco Church,** Caseros 600, are both downtown and open from 7 A.M.–8 P.M. Legend holds that an earthquake suddenly stopped when the statues of Christ and the Virgin Mary in the Cathedral were paraded through the streets on Sept. 13, 1692. The miracle is remembered every September when the images are marched through the streets.

Barrio Guemes is the Beverly Hills of Salta, with colonial and Arabic-style mansions.

The highlight of a Salta visit is the **Train to the Clouds,** a dramatic trip up the deep, weathered canyon, Quebrado del Toro, to the copper mines at San Antonio de los Cobres, elevation 12,475 feet. "Were there many high iron bridges?" a widow from Winnipeg was asked when she returned. "Bridges?!" she retorted. "It seemed like the whole track was built on a bridge." She meant the old-fashioned iron trestles so beloved in cowboy movies. The Spanish word for the narrow-gauge track means "zipper," describing more or less how the train creeps up and around the switchbacks. The Train to the Clouds runs every Saturday from April through November, leaving the Salta train station at 7:30 A.M. and returning about 9:30 P.M. A dining car serves regional food such as empanadas, tamales called humitas, and locro, which is a hearty soup. Information on this trip can be obtained in Buenos Aires from the **Ferrocarriles Argentinos information center,** Maipú 88 (331–3280).

Various Salta excursions are available through your hotel or travel agent, or you can visit the main sights on your own. Cars can be rented in this popular Argentine tourist destination. Of particular interest are the three-hour **city tour;** a 14-hour trip to **Jujuy and the Quebrada de Humahuaca,** the trail used by the Spanish on their way to Bolivia and Peru (you can also take a more extensive, two-day journey the same way); and a 10-hour trip south to **Cafayate,** the center of Salta wine production. Naturally, taste tests are an important part of the latter journey.

MENDOZA: THE PASS CITY

Logic would suggest that the Andes, that oft-described "spine of South America," would be similar in shape from the top of the backbone to the bottom. Instead, it is as if a great hand reached down at latitude 33, and pinched. Here at the chokepoint of the Andes, towering peaks are squeezed even higher. Three summits rise above 22,000 feet, including the giant Aconcagua, elevation 22,834 feet. In contrast, North America's highest peak, Mt. McKinley, is a mere 20,320 feet— *foothills* in this region outreach the Rockies.

Still, consider the effects of a pinch. The distance across the mountains is compacted, making this point a high crossing, but a short one. Consequently, humans have crossed the continental backbone here since time immemorial. Of all mountain passes, this route of the Cuyo, Incas, Spanish, and modern-day Americans is an almighty spectacle. Santiago, the capital of Chile, is on the wet side in the lush central valley; prosperous Mendoza, Argentina, population over one million, sits directly at the base of the Andes on the dry side. In between are rocks and more rocks, some as big as the Matterhorn. There are no trees dotting the landscape here, just a few tattered bushes, a few tufts of grass, and rocks of extraordinary shape and color—orange, pink, violet, green, black, blood red, ruby red, rose red, and crimson, depending on the time of day you see them. In fact, color reigns on the Argentine side, while on the other side of La Cumbre Pass, in Chile, the cliffs are pure, gray granite.

This is a deadly beauty, a rainbow mask painted over an earthquake fault. And yet, because of the quake zone, because eyes bleary of rocks are willing to sacrifice for green trees, Mendoza may be the most beautiful of all oasis cities.

An urban forest planted on a treeless desert, Mendoza is an irrigated monument to survival. The year was 1861 when—once again—an earthquake destroyed the prosperous settlement, 300 years after its founding. Like Californians with a similar, fateful location on a quake belt, Mendocinos rebuilt a safe city. No buildings over three stories could be constructed. (Even today it is a low-rise city.) Sycamores were planted along every sidewalk as a shield from falling rubble. All streets were four-carriages across, wide enough to run into for safety. And for extra safety, every fourth block was made into a park, and more trees were planted. (Deep-rooted trees don't begin toppling until about 7.8 on the Richter Scale.)

Devastating quakes have shaken the region in the subsequent 125 years, but the city has survived. Saplings continue to be planted in the newest suburbs, watered by an enlarged network of small ditches. Unsightly branches are trimmed by city crews. Today, the oldest limbs meet high above the broad streets, arches that refresh both eye and body during the hot summers. Under the dappled sunlight, Mendocinos have spiraled the pleasures of sidewalk cafes. People-watching in a city made wealthy from wine and oil, green shade, and icy pitchers of homemade sangria . . . now there's a triple-headed invitation to sip a while and decide what to see.

PRACTICAL INFORMATION FOR MENDOZA

GETTING THERE. *Aerolineas Argentinas* and *Austral* fly to Mendoza from Buenos Aires, Bariloche, and Córdoba. There are several flights every day from Buenos Aires; flying time is a little less than two hours. Aerolineas flies on to Santiago twice weekly. The Chilean airline *Ladeco* flies into the town of San Rafael. **Buses** of all standards come from Santiago and Buenos Aires, as well as from other Argentine cities. **Trains** from Buenos Aires take 16½ hours and have movie cars, along with sleepers and fine dining. There are no passenger trains over the pass into Chile.

HOTELS. For definitions of price categories see "Facts at Your Fingertips." **Hotel Aconcagua.** *Expensive.* San Lorenzo 545 (24–2450, 24–2321). 160 rooms. It is a prime choice for travelers returning from dusty trips into the mountains, since it has an outdoor pool. It is also air-conditioned. Modern rooms with stylish accents, among them woven bedspreads.

Hotel Plaza. *Expensive.* Chile 1124 (233–000). 86 rooms. Once the luxury hotel of the entire Northwest, the Plaza guards its dignity like an old-fashioned grande dame. Only some rooms are air-conditioned—which can be a trial in the summer—but service in the dining room is both welcoming and excellent.

A number of resort hotels have sprung up around Mendoza, taking advantage of the natural attractions of the area. For example, **Samuay Huasi,** Route 94 near Tunuyán (22–8973), some 75 miles south of Mendoza, is a mountain retreat for skiing in winter and for hiking, horseback riding, and fishing in other seasons. The **Hotel Termas Cachueta,** 20 miles from Mendoza, on the route to Chile, has been built to take advantage of the area's hot mineral waters. Contact addresses are Tucumán 676 in Buenos Aires (322–5672), and Buenos Aires 536 (23–0422) in Mendoza.

CAMPING. There are several campgrounds in the area, some with pools. Check with the Automóvil Club Argentino, Av. San Martín y Amigorena (244–900/1).

RESTAURANTS. The following restaurants are all *moderate* in price. **La Bodega del 900,** Av. de Acceso and Urquiza, Guaymallén (262–773), is popular with visitors and has an international menu. Nightclub show and nice ambience aided by old wine presses on the lower floor. If you're longing for spicy mustard and sauerkraut with your *chorizos* (sausages), the **Club Aleman,** Olmedo 1921, Guaymallen (264–410), will grant respite. Mendoza may be the most Italian city in Argentina. A popular favorite for "home" cooking is **Vecchia Roma,** Av. España 1619 (23–2529), as is **Montecatini,** General Paz 370 (252–111).

NIGHTLIFE. Mendoza's wealth can quickly be seen in the diversions available, including: the **Casino,** 25 de Mayo 1123 (255–862); horse races at the **Hipódromo,** Armani y Montes de Oca in Godoy Cruz (27–2352); nine **movie theaters,** including a drive-in. If you understand Spanish, there are four theaters in the city; if you would prefer to go dancing, at last count there were five **discotheques.** Check with either your hotel or the tourist office for schedules of performances and the type of crowd currently being drawn to the various discos.

TOURIST INFORMATION. Tourist Office, San Martín 1143 (242–800, 242–656).

WHAT TO SEE. Mendoza is a popular destination for Argentine tourists. As a result, there are many organized excursions available through your travel agent or hotel. The most popular are: the **city tour** of Mendoza, which takes three hours and includes Gloria Hill, a park with 50,000 hand-planted trees and an impressive monument depicting San Martín's struggle to cross the Andes and defeat the Spanish. In March, the wine festival is held in the park's amphitheater.

Winery and Countryside. Argentina is the fifth largest producer of wine in the world, and most of the country's wine grows on irrigated pastures around Mendoza. This three-hour tour includes sampling the product at one of 1,400 local wineries and a tour of the oil fields at Lujan de Cuyo.

Crossing the Andes. There are two options here; you can either take a public bus to Santiago, which is an eight-hour journey, or you can take a 10-hour trip into the rock garden, with stops at Puente del Inca, a rainbow arch worn by the bubbling spring waters in the river below, and at Los Penitentes near the Chilean border. Penitentes is a ski area, but during the summer and winter the mountain excursions stop here for chairlift rides to an observation point. Directly across is a wind-carved massif with cowled monks (the penitents) marching up the side. You can easily rent a car and make this trip on your own. Check with your hotel or the tourist office, as there are several agencies.

PATAGONIA

First settled by British immigrants, "Patagonia" still evokes images for us of a wild, remote area, a Timbuktu in English literature, a place of quests and escape. Butch Cassidy, the Sundance Kid, and Etta escaped to Patagonia, and the Welsh came to escape English dominion over their language. The **Patagonia Turistica,** Av. de Mayo 801, 10th floor (334–3700) in Buenos Aires, can provide details on the area's best attractions and facilities.

Whether wandering with your thumb stuck out for a ride or flying from town to town on an Aerolineas Argentinas pass, Patagonia hasn't lost its appeal. An edge is off the remoteness—Argentines and Brazilians are indefatigable travelers—but the wonders continue to be wonderful, the facilities have been upgraded, and there are still places where you can cast a dry fly for a rainbow trout and be completely alone.

Patagonia comprises the bottom third of Argentina, south of the Colorado River on to the Strait of Magellan and beyond, to the island, Tierra del Fuego. The Andes are lower here, with perfect volcanic cones, rain forests, and streams stocked with trout and salmon. Farther south, broad glaciers push out of the mountains and melt into milky green lakes. Lush forests stop abruptly when the mountains reach the flat desert. Millions of sheep live on this shrub land, herded and sheared by a very few people. Farmers irrigate along the few rivers that reach the Atlantic. There is also oil, some aluminum smelting, commercial fishing, and tourism.

Increasingly, these untamed deserts appeal to the Argentine imagination. Is Patagonia their Amazon, a land of untapped wealth? Past president Raul Alfonsin believed so. In a grand gesture worthy of all famous Argentine rulers, he declared that the national capital should be moved to Viedma, about two hours south of Buenos Aires by jet. This town of about 30,000–50,000 people is an irrigated oasis on the bleak Patagonian coast. It sits at the mouth of the Rio Negro, a river whose source is Lake Nahuel Huapi near the Alpine resort of Bariloche. However, it is considered unlikely that Viedma will be Argentina's Brasilia.

Although the region is as close to the South Pole as northern Canada is to the North Pole, Patagonia is a narrow triangle tempered by the oceans on each side, so summers are cool, but winter temperatures hover near the freezing mark, surprisingly high . . . unless you can count the wind chill factor, for the wind down here is capricious—it starts and stops, then twists around to come from another direction. The Roaring Forties, sailors call this southern latitude. Spring breezes blow hardest, from October until December, but they are worth ducking your head into. Patagonia has five world-class sights. From north to south they are: San Carlos de Bariloche, in the lake district, which has a well-deserved reputation as Latin America's favorite mountain resort, with fishing in the summer, deer hunting in the fall, and skiing in the winter; Crossing the southern Andes by boat and bus from Bariloche to Puerto Montt, Chile, or vice versa; penguins, sea elephants, ostrich-like rheas, guanacos, sheep ranches, and Welsh settlements at Peninsula Valdes and Trelew; Glaciers National Park, the spires of Fitz Roy and Paine Tower near Lago Argentino (Lake Argentina), a United Nations' world heritage site; and Ushuaia, the southernmost town in the world, featuring fresh spider crabs, a national park, cross country skiing, and an accessible sheep ranch owned by a National Geographic Society writer/researcher and her husband.

SAN CARLOS DE BARILOCHE

Throughout most of this book, you will read about super high, dry mountains and super humid, malarial jungles. One needs to keep those extremes in mind to understand the deep affection felt by Latin Americans for this gabled Alpine town. Bariloche's altitude of 2,600 feet is low enough for everyone, regardless of heart conditions, and the air is mountain fresh. In town, there is a sweet smell of quaint chocolate *fábricas* (small factories). Geraniums and petunias crowd window boxes and the snowy peaks look close enough to touch. Wildflowers bloom in the lush meadows, and clear streams teeming with trout and salmon tumble over boulders in their rush down to Lake Nahuel Huapí (NAW-well WOP-e). And the winters are mild, with rain more common than snow by the tempering lake.

Often nicknamed Brazil-o-che for the influx of vacationers from the north, Bariloche is one of the five most popular vacation destinations in Latin America. This is the Southern Hemisphere's sophisticated Aspen-Vail-Banff rolled into one, only smaller. Bariloche is a Jackson Hole, sandwiched between craggy granite peaks like the Tetons and a crystalline body of water like Jackson Lake, except it is Swiss-style, not cowboy. Then again, "Bariloche isn't like Switzerland at all," said a hotelier on leave from Geneva to reorganize a local resort. "Everything here is on a grand scale—the mountains, the lake. It's untamed and empty."

Nature may be untamed, but Bariloche is Latin Alpine. Pleasures to be pursued are civilized in a way that occasionally astonishes northerners. Truthfully, our mouths dropped in surprise the first time we waited in a ski lift line behind four women in fur coats and high heels. They were on their way up to the summit for a leisurely lunch on the deck of the restaurant. Wine, wood-grilled steaks, fresh salad that's safe to eat, and beyond their linen-topped table was a panorama of a 40-mile lake bounded by volcanoes. Several hours later, they rode the lift back down, daintily accepting the helping hand of the attendants at the bottom when they disembarked.

Chairlifts at Bariloche start and stop every so often. Perhaps 60 percent of the city's winter visitors don't ski, a figure more typical of France and Switzerland than the United States and Canada, where *skiers* go to ski resorts. Non-skiers are regulars in Bariloche. They come to wear cold weather clothes, for a purpose: to meet men (or women), to restore romance in their marriages, or to be a trifle illicit. They come to gorge on freshly-made chocolate candy, to sip hot chocolate mounded with whipped cream, and to dip juicy slices of local apples into melted chocolate fondue. They dance until three or four o'clock in the morning, sleep through breakfast, and rise for lunch, shopping, a nap, and a midnight dinner. Skiers, on the other hand, make do on a few hours of sleep. No one misses the party—that's a foregone conclusion. This is Latin Alpine, vacation-time with a salsa beat.

All of which can be avoided—and often is by locals who choose to live in Bariloche because they love nature. In off-duty hours, they can be found on the four upper bowls at the ski area (about a half an hour bus ride from downtown), backpacking in the woods, or fishing a favorite stream. If the mood strikes, you can join them for a run, or you can wave "hola" and continue alone in peace.

PRACTICAL INFORMATION FOR BARILOCHE

GETTING THERE. Trains and **buses** arrive from Buenos Aires and other major cities. The bus trip takes 22 hours from B.A.; the train, 30 hours. *Aerolineas Argentinas* and *Austral Airlines* have daily flights, which take two hours from the capital. The private air service *CATA* has flights twice a week. You can also fly to Bariloche from Esquel, twice weekly, or from Trelew, twice weekly.

HOTELS. For definitions of price categories see "Facts at Your Fingertips." Bariloche has an exceptional range of accommodations, from campgrounds, Club Andino refuges in the wilderness, and inexpensive rooms in homes, on up to the pinnacle of elegance, **El Casco,** the one Argentine hotel that international connoisseurs rank as truly *Super Deluxe*.

Other than El Casco, the hotels listed are in Bariloche. There are also the **Hotel Catedral** (*expensive*) and **Hosteria Dhaulagiri** (*moderate*) at the base of the ski mountain. See the section on Skiing in "Facts at Your Fingertips" for more details on these hotels.

El Casco. *Super Deluxe.* About seven miles from Bariloche, west along the lake (22–532, 23–083). Write: Casilla Correo 436. The rate includes half-board, choice of lunch or dinner. 20 rooms, with either lake or mountain views and private balconies (although the pristine effect is slightly marred by the highway and houses on the other side). Everything is first-class, beginning with the service.

Hotel Panamericano. *Super Deluxe.* San Martín 536-70 (25–846/50). 180 rooms; 117 with lake views; 6 suites with living rooms, fireplaces, and terraces. Opened in June, 1987. The Panamericano has 24-hour room service, a swimming pool on the 9th floor, solarium, sauna and massage, baby-sitters, car-rental agency, restaurants, disco, a piano bar, and video movie bar, and ordinary bars. (For information in the U.S., call the Latin America Reservations Center, 800–327–3573 outside Florida; 813–439–2118 in Florida).

Hotel Cascada. *Deluxe.* Av. E. Bustillo, km. 6 (23–046). A short drive from the city on the Huapi Lake shore in a charming wooded setting. 25 rooms, very comfortable facilities. Restaurants, coffee shop, and two bars, plus an indoor pool, tennis courts, and fitness center.

Interlaken Palace Hotel. *Expensive.* Vice Alte. O'Connor 383 (26–156). Used by a number of North American tour operators, so the staff is used to foreign expectations. A modern eight-story building on the shore of the lake. 131 rooms, many with a lake view. Two restaurants, a bar, beauty shop, and boutiques.

Edelweiss. *Moderate.* Av. San Martín 232 (26–165). 102 rooms. Centrally located just up the Civic Center in the middle of the shopping district. 24-hour room service, baby sitters, and laundry service.

Hotel Bella Vista. *Moderate.* Rolando 352 (22–435). 58 rooms. A cozy hotel on a hillside overlooking the town, thus giving truth to its bella (beautiful) vista name. The lobby is comfortable for sitting, with a fireplace and large picture windows. The hotel has lovely gardens, and in the summer, wood fires are stoked for barbecues on the patio.

Hotel Ausonia. *Inexpensive.* J.M. de Rosas 464 (25–402/3). 67 rooms right on the lakefront. A comfortable restaurant. Many repeat Argentine customers who appreciate the location and service.

Other Accommodations and Camping. The municipal tourist office has lists of families who rent rooms. The Automóvil Club Argentino, Av. 12 de Octubre 785 (23–000), has four campgrounds in the area; there are several private ones, but pitching your tent just anywhere that looks inviting is forbidden in much of the area. Reservations are necessary for most types of accommodations during the high seasons of winter (July-August) and summer (December-March). It is critical to book ahead during July, when all of Latin America goes on school holiday, and December, when high school seniors descend on Bariloche from throughout the country to celebrate graduation. Better yet, given a choice, avoid the city during those two months. Rates drop during the spring and fall. The latter season is especially beautiful, for the southern beech puts on a more colorful show than its northern relative, the quaking aspen. Andean beech turn yellow, red, and orange.

RESTAURANTS. German-Swiss-Austrian with a local touch, Italian, fresh game and fish, and the ubiquitous *bife* are specialties here. Beware that appetites are ruined sensationally at **Fenoglio,** Mitre 252 (22–170) and **Chocolatería del Turista,** Mitre 239 (23–124), the two most important of seven chocolate "factories." Most restaurants are *moderately* priced, with dinners costing about $15–$20 per person, including tax. Less expensive meals can be found at confiterias (**Playa Bonita,** Ave. Bustillo, km. 8, 61–067, is a favorite), the hamburger chain, **El Barrilito** near Casita Suiza, and various pizza shops. To name three: **La Andina,** Elflein 95 (23–017), which also has fresh, hot empanadas; **La Andinita,** Mitre 56 (22–257); and **Pizzaiola,** Pagano 275 (26–181).

Casita Suiza, Quaglia 342 (26–111), has a broad menu with the fun of fondue, an Old World skewer on ways to eat beef. Also cheese fondue and sumptuous desserts. **Kandahar,** 20 de Febrero 698 (24–702), serves classic game dishes: wild boar called *jabalí;* venison, the meat of *ciervo* or deer; and trout. The latter are rainbows and browns. The **Hotel Edelweiss** has a very good restaurant, **La Tavola,** especially for trout, the famous morilles black mushrooms, and continental cooking.

NIGHTLIFE. Grisú, J. de Rosas 574 (22–269), was Bariloche's first disco. It's a clever place designed like a mine shaft with romantic amber lanterns in niches and multi-levels. Dancers often alternate between Grisú and neighboring **Cerebro,** Rosas 406 (24–948). Another place that's "in" with the young crowd is the **Paladium,** just around the corner from the Edelweiss Hotel.

TOURIST INFORMATION. Bariloche's **Municipal Tourist Office** (23–022) is in the much-photographed, Germanic-style civic center by the lake. You can't miss it, as one of the main streets passes under its stone arches and the tower is visible from many directions. Hours during the high seasons of summer and winter are from 8:30 A.M.–1 P.M. and 2:30–6:30 P.M. Mon.–Sat. During spring and fall, the office is closed on weekends. **Club Andino,** 20 de Febrero 30 (22–266) has information on hiking trails, refuges, and climbing. Open Mon.–Thurs. 4–10 P.M.

WHAT TO SEE. The region around **Lake Nahuel Huapí.** was declared a national park in 1903, only a couple of decades after second-generation German-Chileans came over the pass from Puerto Montt to open a trading post with the Indians. Thus the tone of Bariloche was fixed—commercial and preservationist at the same time. Many of the residents came from Buenos Aires during the 1960s, seeking fresher air and wilderness, and bringing an urban sophistication to what was once a quaint provincial town. They have made an impact. More than 100 women knit Patagonia wool into pullovers, cardigans, and coats. These sweaters and other local craftsmanship can be found in shops along Mitre and San Martín.

Museo de la Patagonia in the Civic Center is small, but if you are not going further into Patagonia, its taxidermy collection of mounted animals may be the closest you'll get to the fauna of the region. Hours vary.

Excursions are easily available through most hotels. Bariloche's equivalent of a **city tour** departs the city at once for a three-hour drive east along the shore of the lake for a great view of the Volcano Tronador, elevation 11,500 feet. The Thunderer is its name, but it has thundered only one long, ashy belch in the last 20 years. A **chairlift ride** for a view of lakes, volcanos, and the desert plains of Patagonia completes the trip. Another beautiful day trip is to take a steamer to **Victoria Island,** and the Los Arrayanes National Park, where Walt Disney reportedly was inspired by the arrayans for his later movie *Bambi.* These strangely colorful trees have cinnamon-colored bark and deep green leaves. They are indigenous to this island. The eight-hour trip includes lunch at the Victoria Island Inn.

If you are not taking the lake trip over the pass to Puerto Montt, Chile (see the following section for a full description) you are strongly urged to take the day trip on Lake Nahuel Huapí to **Puerto Blest and Lake Frias.**

What about **fishing** in streams and on the lake? Hotels can advise you where you can hire guides, boats, and tackle.

CROSSING THE ANDES FROM BARILOCHE
TO PUERTO MONTT, CHILE

While one can take a bus directly from Bariloche to Puerto Montt, Chile (or vice versa), why hurry across the Andes in 10 hours? The alternative is very special—two days of traveling on boats and buses, cozy mountain hotels, good food, fine wine, and unsurpassed scenery.

The first bus leaves Bariloche mid-morning, taking the paved highway along Lake Nahuel Huapí until it reaches a wharf. Here, a giant arm of water cuts west into the Andes. At the end of the branch is Puerto Blest, a rustic lodge with a large dining room. Because many of the passengers are joyriding to the lodge for lunch and a return to Bariloche, here is the largest of the boats, holding perhaps 100 to 150 tourists. Gulls swoop down for cookies held aloft and fjords are green bulkheads into the white-capped lake, their rocky faces wet with waterfalls.

Odds are nearly perfect that the steamer will head straight into a rainstorm. Puerto Blest is overblessed with rain. Farther along, Argentine National Park guards can tell you that three times as much precipitation falls in this area as in the Amazon.

Typical of Argentine style, lunch in the rainy wilderness is a three-course Italian dinner with a bottle of wine, served by waiters in jackets.

A rusty bus ferries passengers over a crushed black lava road to Lake Frias, where they climb aboard a smaller boat. Camera buffs go amok trying to capture the eerie color of this lake, a phenomenally luminous green almost neon-like in its effect. The scientific explanation is that these mountains are full of copper—when the melting snow carries copper salts down to the lakes, the result is the uncommon hue.

The Argentine customs office is at the opposite end of the lake, while the Chileans have a guardhouse on the other side of Perez Rosales Pass, some distance down the road. Pines are not native to the Andes. The rainforest is a thicket of giant ferns, bamboo, and mossy boxwood trees, all undaunted by the snow. The bus strains up the slippery lava road, over the pass—marked by signs in the forest—and begins its descent.

When you climb out of the bus to go through Chilean customs, turn around for a spectacular view of jagged-toothed Mt. Tronador, a sometimes dormant volcano that is often overlooked in the hurry to see what's ahead.

The hamlet of Peulla sits near the shores of Lake Todos Los Santos. Wooden houses in this German-Chilean enclave have lapped shingles and lace curtains. Cozy rooms in the four-story hotel have flowered quilts. There is a walk through the dripping woods to a sylvan glade. Tradition holds that if you kneel on the carpet of grass and violet and sip from the waterfall, you'll marry within the year.

Lake Todos los Santos is a relatively new lake, formed in 1833 when a severe earthquake separated it from Lake Llanquihue (Yan-KEY-way). (For a vivid description of the quake, read Charles Darwin's report. The young naturalist was ashore from the *Beagle* at the time.) Waters in Todos los Santos are neon green too, but its forested mountains are patched with an occasional clearing. Sometimes one of these farmers rows out to the steamer and puts his wife aboard for shopping in town. Then all is quiet again until suddenly the boat rounds an island and a collective gasp ripples through the passengers. The volcano Osorno, a perfect snowcone, rises directly from the shore, and cameras start clicking. Only Fuji in Japan is more perfect, the Chileans say, modestly, but it is difficult to imagine how anything could be more beautiful.

After a four-course lunch in Petrohue, passengers climb aboard a bus for the trip into Puerto Montt, a German city at the lands-end of Chile. En route, the strange green water tumbles through rapids and over a falls. The bus stops for pictures, then continues around Lake Llanquihue, past farms that the German settlers cleared from the rain forest 130 years ago, past the regimented rose gardens of Puerto Varas, and pulls into a square by Puerto Montt's main hotel, the Perez Rosales.

One option, which must be purchased ahead with your excursion ticket, is to spend an additional day or two at Hotel Ralún (in Puerto Montt, telephone 2100), a 20-room resort offering horseback riding, guided nature hikes, tennis, and sauna. Carved out of virgin forest, Hotel Ralún sits at the tip of a tidal estuary about an hour south of Petrohue. The lobby is built around a waterfall.

PRACTICAL INFORMATION FOR CROSSING THE ANDES

Departures over the Andes are every day Mon.–Sat. during the summer tourist season from Sept. 2–Mar. 31. The rest of the year, the bus-boat excursion operates only on Monday, Wednesday, and Friday. Rates are about $160 including meals. Unique Adventures (800–227–3026) sells Hotel Ralún extensions to travel agents. Daily prices are from $60 for a double, meals are extra, transportation from Petrohue ranges up to $30 round-trip depending on season and number of travelers.

PENINSULA VALDES AND TRELEW

Male sea elephants weigh four tons when they are fully grown. Sprawled on a beach, scratching lazily with five-fingered flippers, they resemble humongous seals. When you walk closer for a better look at their cocker-spaniel-like faces, gravel squeaks under your shoes. A head slowly turns, growling, and suddenly the nose begins to grow. Longer and longer, like Pinocchio caught in a lie. Male sea elephants can produce a trunk at will, a marvelous feat to behold.

Thirteen thousand sea elephants swim north to the gravel beaches of Peninsula Valdes every November to breed and bear their pups. Indeed, the variety and number of sea mammals and birds that breed here ranks this region second only to the Galápagos Islands for travelers in Latin America. In both places, the creatures seem unafraid of humans.

Penguins, whales, Welsh, and the Argentine Navy's home base comprise a curious mix here, drawn here together by one reality: landing along the desert coast of Patagonia is not easy. Plains end abruptly in cliffs at the ocean's edge. A handful of Andean rivers make their way to the Atlantic, where they cut small bays in the escarpment. The tides are ferocious—at the Santa Cruz River, spring tides range up to 48 feet.

The northernmost Patagonian river that reaches the sea is the Chubut. By a fortune of geography, Peninsula Valdes juts into the Atlantic about 60 miles north of the Chubut's mouth. The underbelly of the peninsula is a deep bay where ships can anchor. Traditionally, Puerto Madryn here at Golfo Nuevo and Punta Arenas, Chile, on the other end of the Strait of Magellan are the two primary ports for southern Latin America.

If the long-term plan to relocate the nation's capital succeeds, it will be built about 250 miles north of Puerto Madryn in Viedma. This town is on the mouth of the Rio Negro, but it is not protected by a bay.

Understandably the Spanish tried to settle Golfo Nuevo, beginning in 1550. Twice they failed, ruined by windy desolation and Indian massacres. In a bid for immigrants, the Argentine government persuaded a group of Welsh colonists to settle the Chubut River valley. Miners were lured into agriculture by the promise that they could raise their children speaking

Welsh, not English. Also, they were given 247 acres per couple, good prices on equipment and seeds, and tax breaks.

On July 28, 1865, in the middle of winter, a group of Welsh immigrants landed on the sandy beaches of what is now Puerto Madryn. They struggled on through the cold desert to the Chubut, a small river in a small valley. Unlike the Spanish and the Incas, the Welsh knew nothing of irrigation. The first year they nearly starved. Women wrote in their journals that they feared they were going mad, but by the second year the pioneers had slowly recovered. With water, the brown valley turned green, not as green as the valleys they left behind, but still their children spoke Welsh in freedom, and more Welsh joined them. They built towns along the river: Rawson, the provincial capital, near the mouth; Trelew (meaning town of Lewis), a bustling commercial city where the airport was built; and Gaiman, a red brick village that looked like home. They continued up the river, colonizing the Andes themselves. Esquel and Trevelin are two of the better known towns.

Today, fourth-generation Welsh speak Spanish. Their legacy includes the sweet remnants of high tea and cakes, "foreign" lullabys and hymns in church, and blondes named Jones with flashing dark Italian eyes. The Chubut Valley is unmistakably Argentine.

Normally, this pioneer story would be little known and hardly visited, except for that self-same jutting thumb, Peninsula Valdes, and the (relatively) calm, deep waters of Golfo Nuevo. Animals, too, need a place to anchor.

Every year, about 200 right whales come here to mate and calve. Sea elephants, sea lions, and seabirds like the cormorant and Antarctica dove nest on gravel beaches and sandstone platforms. Occasionally herds of killer whales swim into the bay and cannibalize their right cousins. Eighty miles south of Golfo Nuevo, at Punta Tombo, one million penguins sit on their shallow burrows like prairie dogs. This is a home on the range, where the guanaco and ostrichs roam, along with short-eared *mara,* an oversized rabbit, armadillos, foxes, and millions of sheep.

The breeding grounds have been provincial wildlife reserves since 1965, the outgrowth of an Argentine revulsion at the clubbing of baby seals in other countries. The only threat to the sanctuaries occurred in early 1983, when an admiral governing the province signed a contract with a Japanese company allowing it to kill 100,000 penguins. The skin reportedly made especially supple ladies gloves. But before a single club was raised, the outraged citizens of Chubut Province—with the help of the Argentine Wildlife Foundation—forced the military regime to back down.

Chubut's next challenge is how to protect the animals while giving tourists a feeling of being one with nature. When 750 passengers from a cruise ship descend on a few sea elephants, tourists are the zoo; it's not much better when four or five 40-plus passenger buses and several cars arrive at the same time. By strictly regulating group sizes, policing with licensed naturalist guides, and having lengthy, unfenced trails, the Ecuadorian National Park has protected the mystical atmosphere of Galápagos. Our first visit to Peninsula Valdes and Punta Tombo was equally satisfying, but on a recent trip, we could see that popularity has begun to erode the experience.

Until the Chubut government takes creative action, our suggestion is to schedule your visit during the windy spring in October, before Latin American schools are dismissed and before the summer cruises. A secondary advantage is that you can see all of the creatures then. The penguins will have arrived and the whales won't leave until November.

However, if your itinerary calls for a summer trip, don't hesitate to include Peninsula Valdes. It continues to be an exceptional destination.

PRACTICAL INFORMATION FOR
PENINSULA VALDES AND TRELEW

For years, centrally located Trelew has been the place to see both Peninsula Valdes and Punta Tombo. It has had the only airport and the best choice of hotels. Unfortunately, the prosperous city of 65,000 is not very interesting. Blocky concrete mini-rises predominate. Nearby Puerto Madryn, population 20,000, is a pretty alternative to Trelew, but at press time it was not served by regular flights. Here there are sandy beaches, attractive beachfront hotels with balconies, and campgrounds on the beach. Also, seafood, discos, and a casino are available. A third option is Puerto Pirámides. This small beach community is 60 miles around Golfo Nuevo from Puerto Madryn. Whale-watching boats launch from here, the sea lions are within walking distance, and there is a generally congenial spirit in the evenings. No discos, just a beach, conversation, cheap bottles of pretty good wine, and fresh fish. Also, beef imported from the pampas.

GETTING THERE. *Aerolineas Argentinas* and *Austral* have daily flights to Trelew from Buenos Aires; there are also flights north from Río Gallegos, Rio Grande, and Ushuaia in the south. Buses travel to Trelew and Puerto Madryn from Esquel in the foothills of the Andes. Trelew is also on the main north-south highway between Buenos Aires and Ushuaia.

HOTELS. For definitions of price catagories see "Facts at Your Fingertips." **TRELEW: Hotel Rayentray.** *Expensive.* San Martín and Belgrano (34–702). 80 rooms, nine stories. Considered the best hotel in town; used by many tour groups. Restaurant opens at 8:30 P.M., a half hour earlier than other restaurants in town, a welcome practice after a long dusty day on the road. The National Car desk is in the lobby. **Hotel Centenario.** *Moderate.* San Martín 150 (30–042). 100 rooms, six stories. Modest rooms, but comfortable. Fast bar and restaurant.
PUERTO MADRYN: Hotel Peninsula Valdes. *Expensive.* J.A. Roca 165 (71–292), is the only first-class hotel in the town. 70 rooms, nine-stories. It's near the casino and directly across from the beach.
PUERTO PIRAMIDES: Motel ACA. *Inexpensive.* (72–057). A cheerful white motel with bright yellow roof. The 20 rooms are small, but there is a lively central meeting room and restaurant.

RESTAURANTS. TRELEW: El Quijote, 25 de Mayo 90, has an international menu. **La Cantina,** 25 de Mayo and A.P. Bell, is popular for beef.
PUERTO MADRYN: Seafood is superb at **Club Náutico,** Av. J.A. Roca 790 (71–404), and at **La Caleta,** San Martin 170 (73–804). Figure about $10–$15 per person for dinner in all of the above. **Paris,** 25 de Mayo and R.S. Peña (71–301), has good, inexpensive food.
PUERTO PIRAMIDES: El Salmón, on Acceso Norte, has lovely fresh sea salmon.

NIGHTLIFE. Crazy, a disco at J.A. Roca 775, is in the beach area of Pueta Madryn. Ask at your hotel about other current favorites.

TOURIST INFORMATION. In Trelew, the **Chubut Tourist Office** has an office in the airport and the bus terminal. In Puerta Madryn, the tourist office is at Sarmiento 386 (71–514).

WHAT TO SEE. The usual itinerary for the Chubut area is to be picked up at the airport about noon on the Buenos Aires flight, check into your hotel in Trelew, and then head out to Punta Tombo. This is the penguin's schedule: They arrive in August and houseclean the burrows they've had before. In September they court, a romantic sight with hugging and kissing. In October they mate, usually with the same partner they've had for years. In November they lay eggs and the couples take turns incubating and waddling down to the water to dive for fish. By the end of November, the chicks are born. There's lots of activity on through January while the parents feed their young. In February, the adults begin molting, so they cannot go into the water and feed. Some starve to death before their buoyant feathers grow back. It is a miserable time, with couples patting one another tenderly while they mope together. As fall approaches, they swim north to Uruguay and Brazil for the winter. All of the colony is gone by mid-April.

Once back in Trelew, if you make arrangements for transportation, there's time for a trip to the picturesque village of Gaimen (11 miles away) for Welsh high tea. Our favorite is a chalet called **Ti Gwnyn** near the central plaza.

On day number two, most visitors go to Peninsula Valdes to whale-watch in boats—actually the whales are equally curious about the humans, and they swim right up to the vessels for a closer look. Calves are born in early spring, about August and September, although their schedule isn't as rigid as the penguins. Sea elephants and sea lion rookeries are visited. The pups are pretty well grown by mid-February. And, if arrangements are made ahead of time, you might stop at one of the sheep ranches en route.

LAGO ARGENTINO

Readers are often astonished when we tell them they should allow three full days to see Argentina's Glaciers National Park, not counting travel time to get there. For some travelers, that is the full allotment for Rio or Buenos Aires.

Here at latitude 49, where the southern Andes begin to curl around the end of the continent, mountains are enfolded in permanent mantles of ice. Glacier bays froth in winter tempests, ice battling water for survival and losing. Two hundred miles of rolling plain lie between the Andes and Atlantic. During the Ice Age, glaciers touched both oceans. But now, in a warmer age, the ice has retreated to the mountains, where it licks its wounds in milky green lakes.

All along the foothills in Glaciers National Park, fingers of icy water join Lago Argentino. Each crooked finger is tipped with a glacier calving icebergs. The giant Upsala, withdrawing to the north, is nearly three miles wide and 180 feet high, but world attention focuses on belligerent Perito Moreno, a half-mile-wide bully fighting its way across land and water at a rate of five yards a day.

Perito Moreno is the only growing glacier on earth. In its grind eastward, Perito Moreno has dammed a horseshoe-shaped channel around a headwall that juts out into Lago Argentino. Behind the ice, the blocked lake rises. During spring and summer thaws, the water gnaws on the glacial dam, spitting out larger and larger chunks as it rises. Finally, sometime after the dammed lake is more than 100 feet above its former level, it breaks through. Thunderclaps of exploding ice and the roar of the freed water is a mighty chorus. Great waves splatter against the high peninsula across the way and the earth quakes. On occasion, the waves have swept away sightseers who scrambled down the cliff for a closer view.

This breakthrough occurs late in March—usually—every two or three years. The last icy eruption was in 1988.

Many people watch the glacial spectacle and leave, a regrettable decision, akin to nearing Yosemite and deciding to skip it. As in Yosemite, ice carved its way down canyons, moving mountains of granite as it advanced and fell back. Today, sculpted rock spires like Fitz Roy and the Towers of Paine loom 11,000 feet straight up from the valley floor.

Headquarter town for visiting the spires and glaciers is El Calafate on the southern edge of Lago Argentino. A town of about 4,000 people, Calafate has one paved street, an airport and exists for one reason—tourists.

PRACTICAL INFORMATION FOR
EL CALAFATE AND LAKE ARGENTINA

GETTING THERE. *Aerolineas Argentinas* and *Austral* fly from Buenos Aires to Río Gallegos. L.A.D.E., the **Air Force transport,** flies small planes from Río Gallegos to Calafate, a 50-minute journey. Large, porthole-style windows provide great aerial views. **By bus** from Río Gallegos on the coast to Calafate is a four- or five-hour trip, and well worth the time. It is sometimes possible to cross to Chile by bus from Calafate.

HOTELS. For definitions of price categories see "Facts at Your Fingertips." Calafate has several small hotels with anywhere from 10–42 rooms. Typically, they have central heating, twin beds, stall showers in private bathrooms, and a small restaurant. Room and breakfast costs about $50. Reservations are necessary, as this is a heavily booked area. **Posada Los Alamos,** Moyano and E. Bustillo (91–144) is a new hotel, in the *expensive* category. Newly opened is the **Hostal del Cerro,** Av. Parque Los Glaciares (91–310). Other popular hotels are: **El Quijote,** Gregores 1191 (91–017), 42 rooms, a comfortable gathering room with a fireplace. **Hosteria Kalken,** Tte. Feilberg (91–073), 25 rooms, stone and wooden building on a hill offering a view of the lake and the forests. **Hotel Kau-yatun,** Estancia 25 de Mayo (91–059), 32 rooms, the choice of deluxe travelers, also has horses for hire. **Hotel La Loma,** J.A. Roca (91–016), 32 rooms, built of stucco, has a handicraft shop and private cabins. **Hotel Michelangelo,** Moyano 1020 (91–045/58), 15 rooms, staff is particularly helpful. The **Motel A.C.A.** is at 1 de Mayo (91–004), 15 rooms.

Carital operates 10 rustic cabins about a mile from Perito Moreno glacier, and staying here is an unforgettable experience. Those who've tried it say they feel like they're a million miles from civilization. (If they're Argentine, that translates as 1,736 miles from B.A.) For hot showers, you have to fire up an old wood stove, but the kindling is already chopped, toilets flush, and there is a restaurant. When you step out of your cabin into the woods, you can hear the glacier cracking.

RESTAURANTS. Here in the center of the sheep industry, meals are generally beef and cannellonis. However, **La Tablita,** Coronel L. Rosales and Av. Libertador (91–065), is a barbecue (*parilla*) house featuring lamb. The **Hotel Michelangelo** is touted as having the best of the hotel restaurants, though it is closely rivaled by **La Posta,** in the Posada Los Alamos. For sandwiches and sweets, try the pub/confiteria, **Tio Cacho,** 9 de Julio and Gobernador Gregores.

NIGHTLIFE. At 10:30 P.M. on Saturdays, **Tio Cacho** (see above) has a slide show about the National Park; later Uncle Cacho's becomes the town disco. Even in the wilderness, Argentines don't change their dining and dancing habits. **Don Diego de la Noche,** Libertador, is another popular pub.

TOURIST INFORMATION. The **Tourist Office** is at Coronel Rosales and Av. Libertador. The **Glaciers National Park Office** is also on Av. Libertador.

WHAT TO SEE. Two points cannot be too strongly emphasized. First, transportation is limited, so reserve excursions early—the most secure way is to use a travel agent. Second, the weather and the glaciers are unpredictable. On those occasions when there is too much danger from icebergs, the 85-passenger boat remains docked. Horseback riding or fishing for salmon, trout (browns, rainbows, and brook), and perch are two ways of easing the frustration.

Excursions: There are several one-day options, but three stand out. Sitting on the cliff watching 100-foot stalactites drop from **Perito Moreno** into the lake, plus lunch amidst the thunderous claps of growing glacier versus rising lake, lasts about 8 hours. The boat ride up a northern arm of Lake Argentina to **Upsala Glacier,** a short hike to Onelli Lake and glacier and back to your hotel, takes a long 11 hours. You can arrange an overnight journey if you wish, staying at the Hosteria Refugio Lago Viedma. Lake Onelli is bounded by beech on one side, snowy mountains on the other, and icebergs in between. Part of the trip is by bus, lunch is included, but bring snacks if you get queasy when you go without food for a long time. Likewise, snacks are a good idea on the 11-hour, 220-mile (round trip) bus ride to **Fitz Roy.**

USHUAIA

Great Andean condors—their wings spanning 12 feet, their 30-pound bodies more than a yard in length—circle over the city when the snow begins to fall in Ushuaia. Lights in the duty-free shops glow and joggers pound along the esplanade flanking the Beagle Channel. The southernmost town in the world (population 20,000) is an exciting frontier, summer and winter. Facilities are modern and tourism is organized, yet there is a freshness to the approach, a "Howdy Stranger" attitude that makes a stay here special.

Many Ushuaians are newcomers, lured from La Plata, a secondary port to Buenos Aires on the River Plate, and from Córdoba in the interior. To be frank, the appeal wasn't a love of nature, they'll admit, but a keen desire to make money. Ushuaia is a duty-free port. During the peak of old-fashioned formality elsewhere, when men always wore dark, made-in-Argentina, three-piece suits, Ushuaia's businessmen dashed about in pick-up trucks, wearing jeans and goosedown parkas from the United States. These youthful entrepreneurs and their families work hard and play hard—fishing, rock climbing (unlimited opportunities for this!), cross country skiing, snowmobiling, scuba diving, and beachcombing for whales and dolphins that have been washed ashore.

Unfortunately, most Ushuaians don't speak English, but they've overcome shyness about using charades and similar nouns—esqui (s-SKI) is easy; delfin (del-FIN) for dolphin, estancia (es-TAN-cia) for station, as in an Australian ranch. If you are equally flexible and friendly, they'll use these words to invite you to join them. *Sí, graciás, a mi, me encanta* means, "Thanks, I'd be enchanted to." Remember, Argentines thrill to the grand moment. They are often *encantada,* even the men (*encantado*).

PRACTICAL INFORMATION FOR USHUAIA

GETTING THERE. L.A.D.E., the small Air Force transport planes, fly to Ushuaia from Río Gallegos or Rio Grande. The former is served by *Aerolineas Argentinas* from Buenos Aires. Altogether, the flights take about six hours. **Commercial buses** ferry across the Strait of Magellan and drive south to Ushuaia, but excursion buses can be picked up in Rio Grande, the other town on the island. It is possible to rent a car from either direction, but drop-off fares are high. A note to Australians and New Zealanders: Aerolineas's South Pole flights from Buenos Aires to Auckland and Sydney refuel in Río Gallegos (the Auckland-Buenos Aires flight is nonstop). Some fares allow a stopover, which would allow time to visit Tierra del Fuego and Glaciers National Park.

HOTELS. For definitions of price categories, see "Facts at Your Fingertips." Reservations are necessary during the summer. Accommodations are limited, as Ushuaia is a popular destination for Latin Americans from many countries.

Hotel Albatros. *Moderate.* Maipú 505 (22–505). Recently rebuilt after it was destroyed by fire. 78 rooms. The new hotel meets its old standards as the best in town. Centrally located, the Albatros faces the Beagle Channel. A wall of windows in the restaurant looks out on joggers, raw mountains plunging into the sea, and ships.

Hotel Canal Beagle. *Moderate.* On Maipú at 25 de Mayo (21–117). 56 rooms. It is next door to the Albatros, with a similar view of the channel. Although it is not new, the facilities are modern. Traditionally the two hotels have been ranked number one and number two in town. There is a cozy lobby, restaurant and snack bar, shops, and a travel agency on the premises.

Hotel Ushuaia. *Moderate.* Lasserre 933 (22–024). 60 rooms. Simple, cozy accommodations, and a comfortable restaurant.

Hotel Antartida. *Inexpensive.* San Martín 1600 (21–807). Small hotel (20 rooms) on a hill about a 10-minute walk from the city center. Comfortable rooms, stall showers, steam heat. Friendly, helpful owners are active in the Club Andino.

Other Accommodations and Camping. The tourist office has names of families who rent rooms in their homes. There is a campground at Lago Roca in the national park with showers and a restaurant. For more comfort in the wilderness, try **Hosteria Kaiken** at Lake Fagnano or **Hosteria Petrel** at Lake Escondido (reservations in Ushuaia at 21–421).

RESTAURANTS. Barbecued lamb, *cordero al asador,* is the specialty of **Tolkeyen** restaurant, in a romantic wooded setting a little way out of town. Your hotel can advise on transport. **Tante Elvira,** San Martín between Godoy and Rivadavia (21–982), is the place in Ushuaia to eat crab (*centolla*), either hot or cold. For beef, try **Parrilla Tio Carlos,** Colón 758.

NIGHTLIFE. Consult the staff at your hotel for the current favorites.

TOURIST INFORMATION. Infuetur, in the Hotel Albatros (23–340).

WHAT TO SEE. If they're not swamped with other tourists, the three forest rangers who live at **Tierra del Fuego National Park** are likely to invite you to come along on a nature walk through the woods. What better guides to point out 18-inch high, Great Patagonian Woodpeckers, the oversized, bright green Austral Parakeet with crimson tails, hawks, steamer ducks big as geese, and the tiny, rare Andean Tapaculo, noticeable for its black bills and legs. Gray fox and guanaco have come out of the steppes and into the woods at this national park. On a walk you might chance to spot them, but there's no doubt you'll see the effects of the Canadian beaver.

The 155,000-acre park is 12 miles west of Ushuaia. It can be visited on your own (Ushuaia has rental cars) or with an excursion. Whether you choose freedom or efficiency, you can easily explore Tierra del Fuego. Campgrounds are available in various parts of the island and gasoline can be purchased in the little towns. The **Club Andino,** Solís 50, like its counterpart in the United States, the Sierra Club, has climbing and cross-country ski outings. Also, excursion buses and boats travel to many points of interest.

Among the excursion choices are: A tour of **The Harberton Estancia** and lunch with the family. This sheep ranch (three hours drive from Ushuaia) is the home of Natalie Rae and Tom Goodall, well described in *National Geographic*'s January 1971 article entitled "Housewife at the End of the World." Mrs. Goodall was an Ohio teacher who visited Harberton 25 years ago and married the great-grandson of the founder. Tom Goodall is the grandson of Lucas Bridges who wrote *Uttermost Part of the Earth,* a true account of his family's high adventure in Tierra del Fuego. Natalie Rae Goodall is a self-educated naturalist who has indexed the flora and fauna of the island, sponsored with grants from the National Geographic Society. For details on the ranch tour, contact her in Ushuaia, Sarmiento 44 (22–742).

The **City Tour** lasts two-hours and includes stops at the crab processing plant, the fish breeding farm, and the Territorial Museum, which has photographs and artifacts of the Yaghan Indians and other early settlers in the region. The museum also has a taxidermy room with all species of Fuegoian birds. (If visiting on your own, the museum is located at Maipú and Rivadavia, (22–318). It is open every day from 2–7 P.M.) The **Air Tour** is a 30-minute excursion over the steep valleys and the Beagle channel in planes belonging to the Ushuaia Aero Club. The **Sea Excursions,** of either three or nine hours duration, pass Bird and Seal Islands, Les Eclaireurs lighthouse, and Redonda Island, where guanacos are bred. A naval view ashore is given on the five-hour **Port Brown and Port Almanza** tour. The latter is owned by the Argentine Navy. Check with the tourist office or your hotel for information on these tours.

Rio Grande. A one-day tour by gravel road to a sheep and petroleum port on the island, crossing the Andes en route. The mountains run west–east here, cutting the width of the island. Sheep farms, a meat packing company, lakes, snow-capped peaks, and wild animals entertain. Condors, guanaco, and foxes are commonly seen. Some travelers use this excursion as a way of seeing Tierra del Fuego by land. They either fly into Rio Grande and pick up the bus to Ushuaia, later flying back to Buenos Aires. Or they reverse the procedure. (If you're staying overnight in Rio Grande, be sure you have reservations. Hotels are booked with oilmen.) Shorter excursions go into the mountains and return. The trip to **Escondido Lake** takes three hours; the one to 62-mile-long **Fagnano Lake** lasts six hours and includes sawmills and beaver dams, peat bogs where the Ona Indians hunted guanacos 100 years ago, and lunch in a country inn. The Rio Grande Tourist Office, **Infuetur,** is at the Hotel Los Yaganes (22–372).

BOLIVIA

by
PETER MCFARREN

Peter McFarren, a native of Bolivia and resident of La Paz, has also lived in Cochabamba, Sucre, and the United States. He is a correspondent for the Associated Press in La Paz and a photographer. His photos and articles have appeared in The New York Times, Newsweek, *and the* Wall Street Journal.

Bolivia is a country of superlatives. Landlocked in the western part of the continent, it sprawls over 424,165 square miles and borders Peru on the northwest, Brazil on the north and east, Paraguay on the southeast, Argentina on the south, and both Peru and Chile on the west. It has the highest navigable lake in the world, the highest airport, the highest golf course, the highest ski run, the highest capital, one of the newest and wildest frontiers, one of the oldest ruins, and what is said to be the highest concentration of cosmic rays on earth. Bolivia is also a nation of contrasts, which led a French explorer-scientist to call it the "microcosm of our planet." It has every type of geologically classified land, many types of people, flora, fauna, minerals, and tropical products. Even though Bolivia is known as an Andean nation, nearly two-thirds of the country is located in the tropical lowlands.

Bolivia lies wholly in the tropical zone and experiences every temperature, from the heat of its equatorial lowlands to the Andes' cold. To focus, therefore, on Bolivia's diverse land it is best to start with the inland sea of Lake Titicaca (12,600 feet) and work east. The nation is developing economically and socially in that direction, much as the United States pushed its frontier westward.

Lake Titicaca is a major western boundary between Bolivia and Peru. Stretching some 3,500 square miles, this deep (700 feet in places), clear body of water sprouts a *totora* reed that greatly influences life around the lake. The Aymaras fashion these reeds together into exceptionally strong gondola-like boats to sail on this highest navigable lake in the world. These thick reeds also become floating and inhabited islands. The pliable but durable material breaks loose from lake beds and joins with other matter gradually to form living space for autochthonous tribes. This reed is also used for building simple furniture, for feeding livestock, and for making other useful products.

Lake Titicaca rests on the "altiplano" (high plateau), shaped by the Andes mountain range that hunches along the west coast of South America and slices southeastward through Bolivia. This two-pronged mountain range has formed between its peaks a rambling plain about 85 miles wide and 520 miles long that cuts through southeast Peru and southwest Bolivia. About 40,000 square miles of this bleak, cold, treeless, and windswept plateau lies in Bolivia. However hostile this 30 percent of the nation's land is, it supports 52 percent of the population and houses the major cities. The otherwise impoverished altiplano and its mountain rims are streaked with vast deposits of tin, copper, silver, tungsten, lead, zinc, and other minerals.

For centuries, the Aymaras have clung to this hostile land and have generally resisted efforts to be resettled on the more fertile soil that abounds elsewhere in the country. Their diet consists mostly of a potato-like tuber called "oca" and the nutritious "quinoa" cereal. They also grow some nutritious cereals, and corn, which, when fermented, make an intoxicating brew called "chicha."

The animal life on the altiplano includes the wool-bearing sheep, llama, alpaca, and vicuna, along with the fur-bearing chinchilla and red fox. The fabled vicuna, a rare and very delicate animal, still roams the high regions of the altiplano, but articles made from its scarce fleece are hard to find because the government strictly prohibits its sale. You can, however, obtain rugs, ponchos, and a number of other articles made from llama and alpaca wool.

At the edge of this altiplano, La Paz, the capital of Bolivia, is encased in a basin at an altitude of about 11,900 feet. The discomfort of the thin air is more than repaid by the majestic beauty of the snow-capped mountains that encircle the city. Four of these peaks reach above 20,000 feet.

Spotted along the high mountain shelf southeast of La Paz are several cities whose existence can only be justified by mineral wealth. Oruro is the first city along this high crest, standing at an altitude of 12,200 feet, with a population of 110,700, most of whom are employed in mining. Further south is Potosí, which retains its colonial air and art treasures from an age when the nearby Cerro Rico (Rich Hill) Mountain was one of the first great discoveries of the Spanish conquerors and which pumped the equivalent of some 2 billion dollars into the Spanish treasury. The city (population 113,000) is at 13,340 feet.

These and smaller cities are linked by a railroad from La Paz to Buenos Aires, routed along a fairly level plateau that stretches between the two capitals. Other rail lines at Oruro connect La Paz with Arica, Chile, and Cochabamba, Bolivia's third largest city with 317,000 people. Oruro is the hub of these rail lines. There are also rail connections with São Paulo via Villazón from Santa Cruz.

From this high plane, the land spills off into lush semitropical valleys to the north and east. These valleys, called "yungas," are drained by the Beni River system, which then empties into the Amazon River. This land of present beauty and future development begins about three hours out of La Paz. The mean annual temperature of this healthy area is between 60.8 and 64.6 degrees, while the rainfall is between 27 and 31 inches yearly.

The soil of the altiplano washes into the basins of this region, where citrus fruits, cattle, and other products are raised, many of them going to La Paz. Extensive road-building and river-clearing programs are linking this region with the rest of the nation. Altiplano Indians and others who formerly lived along the routes of these roads have to some extent already been resettled by colonization projects that are introducing many natives to the 20th century. A new route has been constructed to link the High Plateau consumer areas and the productive plain of Beni, which will ensure the incorporation of this jungle area into the economic life of the country.

Cochabamba, Sucre, Tarija, and Caranavi are the major population centers among these fertile valleys. As the center of a colonization area, Caranavi, about 150 miles north of La Paz, has grown from four huts to about 10,000 people. Cochabamba, with an average temperature of 64.6 degrees and situated at 8,570 feet, and eternal sunshine, is described as the best living area in Bolivia. Sucre (population 105,800), still the nation's legal capital, has retained much of its colonial color and charm. Its elevation is 9,184 feet. The 66,900 inhabitants of Tarija are isolated, individualistic, cultured, European, and deeply religious, and have not changed much since declaring themselves an independent republic in 1825.

These valleys spread out into the tropical lowlands that sweep from the Andes foothills in the north to the southeast near Argentina and Paraguay. With much of the land but few of the country's people situated here, this area is said to be Bolivia's future. Most of the area is dense tropical forests, with some rough pasture, swamp, and scrub in the center. Seasonal rainfall is high and the climate is usually hot, except when a cold, Antarctic-based wind from the southern steppes strikes in the tropical east around Santa Cruz. These annoyances are called "surazos," and they strike several times yearly for two or three days.

The northern part of these tropical lowlands was developed in the 16th and 17th centuries by Jesuit priests. The Beni area provided Europe with excellent tropical fruits, nuts, and dried beef. This area fell into decay after the Jesuit priests were expelled and the trails to the outside world disappeared. Today, primitive Indian tribes live in this area and resist contact with the outside world.

The Santa Cruz area has developed rapidly over the last 20 years. Sugar and cotton crops and cattle raising have progressed. Hunters, fishermen, birders, and botanists come to the area and are accommodated in hotels in Trinidad, capital of Beni and the only significant city in the tropical north. Riberalta is another beautiful town in Beni.

The People

Approximately 50 percent of Bolivia's 7.1 million people are descendants of the Aymara and Quechua pre-Columbian indigenous cultures. Twenty percent of the population is mestizo and 25 percent white. Socially, the population is in ferment. The once-stilted social structure of the nation was destroyed by the 1952 social revolution that took political control from a small white oligarchy and passed it to the indigenous majority, under white and mestizo middle-class leadership. Aymara and Quechua people are commonly referred to as "cholos," a somewhat demeaning term applied to these farmers or mine workers. They are also referred to as "campesinos"—peasants—or "mineros"—miners.

This population pattern, like many other things in Bolivia, is changing. Anthropologists have noted that the unique Bolivian ethnic and social composition of the Aymaras and Quechuas now discard some traditional ways, adopt western dress, and extend their diet and consumption habits.

A Short History

Historians usually raise the curtain on Bolivia's history at Tiahuanaco about A.D. 600, although dissenting conclusions date back as far as 7,000 B.C. The Aymara Indians had developed a lesser civilization early at this location between La Paz and the southern end of Lake Titicaca, but the second one was influenced by the Nazca and Chimu civilizations of Peru, and from these mixtures a truly great civilization emerged. It was characterized by great buildings, massive monuments, ornate textiles, skillful pottery, and attractive metalwork.

This flowering civilization began to wither for some unknown reason. When the Quechua-speaking soldiers of the great Inca Empire of Cuzco conquered the area about A.D. 1200, they found the Aymaras about their decaying but still impressive ruins. The Incas held all Bolivia until the arrival of the Spanish conquerors.

In 1535, Diego de Almagro, Francisco Pizarro's partner in conquest, found a site near what is now Oruro. Then four years later Pedro Anzurez found a place later named Charcas (Sucre), which became the Audiencia de Charcas under the Vice royalty of Peru in 1559.

But Bolivia's destiny was shaped in 1545, with the discovery of Potosí and the shadowing mountain of silver: "Cerro Rico." This find stirred great interest back in Spain and inspired a splendor at Potosí that rivaled the pretentious display of Lima. As the vast reserves of silver were shoveled out of the Cerro Rico Mountain, a Crown mint established locally converted the metal into coins for shipment to Spain. For decades, a favorite Spanish description for untold wealth was, "Vale un Potosí (worth a *potosí*).

The autocratic but well-organized social system of the Inca conquest of other indigenous subcultures was destroyed by Spanish colonization. The native population was pushed off fertile plains onto infertile mountainsides or incorporated into a peonage system, despite the Spanish Crown's decree against enslavement. Spanish colonial officials took over the best lands and lived in relative luxury. *Criollos,* people of Spanish ancestry born in the Americas, also lived fairly well but resented their exclusion from high appointive offices dispensed back in Spain.

The *criollos* and the mestizos were the first people in Latin America to sound the cry for liberty from Spanish rule. The first revolutionary movements developed in Chuquisaca, La Paz, and Cochabamba in the summer and fall of 1809. All were suppressed until 1825 when Bolívar in the north and San Martín pressed their simultaneous liberation campaigns along the Andean spine.

General Sucre, one of Bolívar's top leaders, liberated the country at the Battle of Tumulsa on April 2, 1825. Formerly known as Upper Peru, the country was named for Bolívar, the Liberator, in tribute to his leadership in the cause of South American independence. After Sucre set up Bolivia as an independent nation and departed, his top general took over and proclaimed a Peruvian-Bolivian confederation in 1836. General Santa Cruz was defeated by dissident Peruvians 3 years later and the confederation was dismembered.

Independence did little for the people of Bolivia—political control of the nation switched from one greedy group to another. The new Creole rulers lived lavishly from the profits of the vast but ill-used mineral wealth. Bolivia was a republic, but it was not a nation.

For about 161 years after independence, the government changed hands 78 times, often through military coups.

Weak governments made Bolivia vulnerable to the aggressive designs of neighbors. Several border disputes have dominated the nation's history, subtracted one-fourth its territory and left it a landlocked country. Several incidents seemed to work in a pattern—a neighbor would grab a piece of Bolivian territory, then build the loser a railroad. So, Bolivia ended up with several disjointed railroads and without its useful land. When Chile defeated Bolivia and Peru in the War of the Pacific (1879–83), she took Bolivia's Pacific Coast area and built a railroad from La Paz to Arica. When Argentina annexed some of the Chaco area, it too built a railroad connecting the two nations. When Brazil annexed the rich Acre area in 1903, it promised a railroad (not yet completed). But in the Chaco War with Paraguay (1933–35), Bolivia had to surrender a large area without the benefit of a railroad.

But this war was to influence Bolivia's future greatly. Stunned by an embarrassing defeat, young officers and indignant intellectuals began examining the nation's conscience and prescribing solutions. The result was the formation of the National Revolutionary Movement (MNR) that gained power in 1952 and launched the first fundamental reforms in the nation's history.

Social Revolution

Two events have symbolized this revolution and help explain the troubled nature of Bolivia's contemporary history. Returning from the Chaco War with an understanding of the world beyond their immediate misery, some Aymara and Quechua veterans began thinking about the lot of their people and ways to change it. Several veterans in the Cliza Valley, near Cochabamba, organized their fellow men into a union and began joint efforts to build a school. When union members tried to buy this land they had tilled for generations, the planters responded by flooding the valley and destroying the humble homes. Like-minded miners at Catavi on the altiplano fared even worse. Hundreds were shot down by government troops in 1942 while striking for better wages and improved working conditions.

Cliza Valley and Catavi became symbols. The peasants and the miners emerged from the social revolution the two strongest political forces, each armed and functioning as a militia because the traditional army had been destroyed in the 1952 revolution.

The peasants (151,434 family heads were given land titles under the revolution's agrarian reform program) have tended to support the moderate MNR majority. But the miners threw their support to the party's leftist sector. This sector has supported excessive labor demands that have occasionally brought the nation's economy to near disaster and incited political turmoil.

In 1979, after a failed coup, Congress elected the first woman president, Lydia Gueiler Tejada, scheduled to serve until elections slated for 1980. A military coup, however, interrupted the country's democratic evolution again in 1980. In 1982, however, Hernán Siles Zuazo, a former president and co-founder of MNR, came to power and, during his first year as President, took serious action toward placing Bolivia among the continent's few democracies.

In 1985 Siles Zuazo, a leader of the 1952 revolution, turned the government over to Victor Paz Estenssoro, 78. After the 1952 revolution Paz Estenssoro was sworn in as president with Siles Zuazo as his vice president. Paz Estenssoro implemented drastic economic reforms to end an inflation rate running at higher than 24,000 percent, the highest in the world. The peso was devalued by 95 percent, gasoline prices increased 10 fold, and wages were frozen. Surprisingly, there has been very little social unrest. The peso is now stable and hyperinflation has ended and inflation is running at 18 percent a year, the lowest in South America. At the same time, the threat of military coup has evaporated and Bolivia's government is considered one of the most stable in South America.

Elections were held in May 1989, and in August Jaime Paz Zamora was sworn in as the country's 77th president. Democracy is taking a firm hold in Bolivia and the economy is stable. Bolivia remains, however, the poorest country in South America with the highest infant mortality rate.

Bolivia's Rich Earth

From its earliest days, Bolivia's fortunes have risen or fallen with the riches extracted from its bountiful earth. Even before the arrival of the Spaniards, the Incas were already mining the land's precious silver. It was this rich lode that quickly brought conquerors, colonists, adventurers, and prospectors in search of fame and fortune in what became the greatest mining operation in the New World. Known then as Upper Peru, the area quickly prospered and then just as quickly declined as the mines were depleted of the valuable silver. But it wasn't long before those same rich hills in the Eastern Cordillera were found to contain tin, and the country's future course was shaped.

For a while, Bolivia's economy and the welfare of its people were largely dependent on the price of its principal product in the world markets. And to a greater or lesser degree, the same is true today. But now the country is also mining bismuth, zinc, lead, antimony, wolfram and tungsten, as well as tin, gold, and silver; and the prospect of rich natural gas and petroleum deposits are contributing substantially to the nation's economy and helping it to achieve its goal of diversification.

No longer a one-product country, Bolivia is presently expanding its exploration for petroleum. The collapse of the world tin market and the drop in petroleum prices have devastated Bolivia's export economy. Export earnings dropped from 1 billion dollars a year to less than 400 million but in 1990 rebounded to 800 million. Mines are closing and thousands of miners are migrating to the cities and tropical lowlands.

Although mining has been and continues to be, along with natural gas, a chief contributor to the nation's economy, it accounts for less than 10 percent of the gross domestic product and represents less than 2 percent of the labor force. Nevertheless, tin still accounts for close to half of the country's total mineral exports, in spite of the fact that gas production has risen steadily in the past.

Industrially, Bolivia is still running behind economic goals it has set for itself. While manufacturing is changing slowly from handcrafts to industrial goods, the growth in this area has been set back by the lack of facilities and purchasing power. The country still depends in large measure on prices paid for a very limited number of mineral products overseas.

Lately, Bolivia has been cooperating much more effectively with its neighbors and integrating its economy with theirs through its membership in the Andean Common Market and ALADI (Asociación Latinoamericana de Integracion) and development of major rail and gas projects with Brazil.

How to See Bolivia

A visit to Bolivia usually begins in La Paz. After seeing the usual tourist sites around La Paz and the unusual tourist attractions farther north, the Bolivia of the past and future still lies ahead in all its charm and challenge.

A short distance from La Paz is the city of El Alto, which is fast becoming the country's second most populous urban center with 400,000 mainly Aymara-speaking inhabitants who migrated in recent years from the countryside. From El Alto, the road heads to Oruro, a mining center 130 miles southeast of La Paz. The only tourist attraction here is the dance and ceremony performed during the Devil's Festival on the Saturday before Ash Wednesday. This involves an elaborately costumed "bear" and "condor" clearing the way for a parade of similarly costumed dancers led by alternate twosomes of Satan and Lucifer and St. Michael the Archangel and China Supay, the Devil's wife and sexual stimulant. After a leaping and shouting parade through town, the participants crowd into the main plaza and perform dramatic rituals in which virtue, like hero over villain, prevails over sin. A mining theme is woven into the drama, in which the costumes represent a major portion of one's wealth.

Cochabamba is still a city of beauty, eternal spring and sunshine, but it has been caught in the cross fire of Bolivia's political turmoil and economic change. Once the prosperous center of a rich and vast area of plantation agriculture, the social revolution's land reform program has sent many of the old planters into exile or other livelihoods, divided up the big, absentee-owned plantations among peasants, and diverted other peasants to colonization projects in Eastern Bolivia. The most important tourist attraction is the townhouse of Tin Baron Simón Patiño, which has been converted into a museum. The usual market here has the additional attraction of local Indian women with their unusual stovepipe hats. Newly discovered ruins at Incallajta, about 65 miles from Cochabamba, are now open to tourists.

Potosí is nine and a half hours southward by train from Oruro over one of the world's highest railroads, reaching an altitude of 15,809 feet at the junction of Condor. One of the first great cities of the Americas with a population of about 150,000 early in the 17th century, Potosí has retained much of its colonial charm. Twisting, narrow streets pass aging mansions with colonial coats of arms, reminding one that this busy agricultural and mining center was once a majestic city. The city remains in the shadow of "Cerro Rico," which pumped silver into the Spanish treasury in the early colonial period. The "Real Casa de Moneda" (Royal Mint), built in 1542 and rebuilt in 1759, still stands but has been converted into a museum. Some of the old homes and churches have oil paintings of considerable merit. Some 30 churches reflect good examples of Renaissance or Romanesque architecture.

Sucre is still the big oddity of Bolivia. This city, 109 miles northeast from Potosí is the legal capital of the nation, but the Supreme Court Building is the only vestige of what now unofficially belongs to La Paz. La Paz became the "de facto" capital in the wake of the mining boom. Sucre has an interesting display of buildings of both the colonial and republican eras.

Many Latin American revolutionary leaders studied here at one of the oldest universities in Latin America.

La Paz, Oruro, Cochabamba, Potosí, and Sucre are joined by railroad. The only way to get to another important community, Tarija, in the southeast of these upland cities, is by a difficult road or by LAB. This settlement in the rich Guadalquivir River valley was founded in 1574 and has since remained an isolated island apart from the rest of Bolivia. Thus cut off, the people have grown a variety of fine crops for their own consumption, developed an individualism that has made them as much Argentine as Bolivian, produced a supply of skillful farm hands for Argentine agriculture, and formed a pocket of advanced culture apart from the rest of the nation.

Returning to Cochabamba, one can continue eastward into the interior of the nation or take a river trip north to Trinidad. This latter trip involves traveling 120 miles by road to Puerto Chipiriri, on a branch of the large Rio Grande. The boat trip up this river to Trinidad takes four days, and the tourist might later fly back to La Paz or any other part of Bolivia. The alternative of continuing eastward on the Cochabamba-Santa Cruz Highway opens several other interesting possibilities.

The old 315-mile Cochabamba-Santa Cruz Highway demonstrates what 20th-century communication can do for a nation still existing in the 19th century. This highway, completed in 1954 after nine years of construction and a $50 million U.S. Export-Import Bank loan, actually united a nation that was falling apart and shaped an economy that was in serious trouble.

From Cochabamba to Santa Cruz there is a new road that crosses through the Chapare coca leaf producing region. A good part of it is paved, and if you wish, you can begin a river trip on Puerto Villarroel north to Trinidad.

The old Cochabamba-Santa Cruz Highway winds through the Cliza Valley, where the first important modern political movement among Indians began. Spurred by the 1952 social revolution, an indigenous peasant union in the valley community of Ucurena demanded that a planter return land to peasants who had been evicted in the 1930s for union activity. When the planter stalled, these groups began a march on nearby towns, and for a while civil war between rural and urban groups hovered over the nation. Politics are still tense in this valley that someday might symbolize the political awakening of the indigenous population in Central and South America.

Continuing east, the traveler can forget politics and take up geology. In the next 300 miles he will travel through all four of the classified geological areas. First, he will experience the tundra area of the valleys, with its many flowers but no trees. Then comes the rain forest, with its mosses, ferns, and damp, humid climate. Next, there's the desert with pipe-organ cactus, much sand, and little grass. Finally, near Santa Cruz, the tropical jungle breaks out in towering and verdant growth.

"This 311-mile trip is like traveling from Ecuador to Alaska," one geologist remarked after traveling over the road and examining its specimens. Here one finds every temperature zone and practically every kind of vegetation.

Arriving at the frontier community of Santa Cruz, one will quickly see its importance as a commercial and industrial center. Santa Cruz is now the fastest growing city in Bolivia, and its prosperity is apparent in oil fields, cotton plantations, sugar and lumber mills, and its busy airport, now an important arrival and departure point for international flights.

After Santa Cruz the visitor can decide whether to see more frontier or return to La Paz. There is no tourist attraction on the road northward, only an area undergoing rapid economic growth with cattle and tropical farming and intense social change with colonization projects. If a highway survey party cuts a small path through this jungle, colonists will line it immediately and begin tilling its fertile soil. This area is truly a laboratory for economic growth and social development. The center for this area's development is Santa Cruz.

There is still plenty of unexplored frontier in Bolivia. A tourist can travel from Santa Cruz to Corumba, Brazil, by railroad and see unfurled before him the beauty of the tropics, the smell of the jungle and birdlife that at times seems to etch a rainbow in the sky. Over this 406-mile railroad, one passes villages populated by former primitives, some of whom have become civilized only in the past decade. Until several years ago, uncivilized cousins of these residents occasionally attacked the communities with bow and arrow. Now these people have disappeared farther into the jungle brush to avert what they consider the annoyance of modern civilization.

Trees and Birds

Mahogany trees here spread skyward in majestic dimensions, housing communities of many-hued birds. At times, several duplexes or two-room bird dwellings can be seen dangling from a single limb and sometimes a tree will enfold as many as 50 bird nests.

These birds often have several colors arrayed in attractive patterns. When they fly in formations against the late afternoon sky, it is truly something to remember. The many types of parrots (some very talkative) often fly in groups, whereas the many big-beaked toucans usually fly in pairs.

Another interesting tree in the area is a cotton tree, that reaches some 100 feet upward and sprouts a bulb of cottonlike material as large as a cantaloupe and which can be used for making cloth. There is an abundance of other flora that—with the fauna—makes this, the heartland of a continent, something beautiful to see.

In the mid part of the train ride from Santa Cruz to Corumba, an unusual type of topography stretches over about 10 miles. Beautiful mountains rise abruptly like polished stones from what is otherwise level jungleland. These small, stonelike mountains near San José have several colors, which, in the reflection of the noonday sun, provide another-world atmosphere.

Upon reaching Corumba, on the Paraguay River, you can take a steamer down the river to Asunción, Paraguay, or Buenos Aires. By entering Bolivia by rail from Arica, the traveler therefore could continue crossing the continent overland by following the route outlined above. It's rough but rewarding.

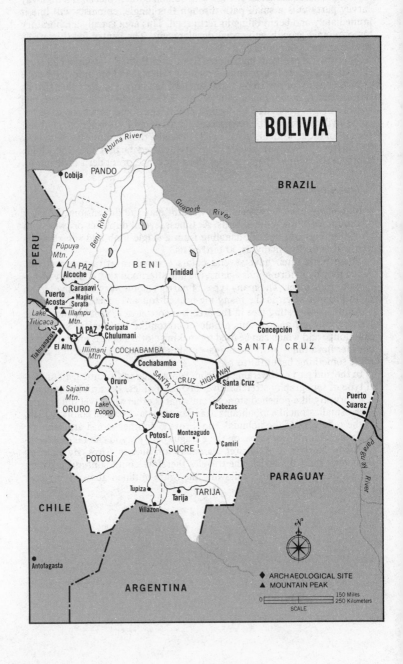

BOLIVIA

BRAZIL

PANDO

Cobija

PERU

Abuna River

Guaporé River

Púpuya Mtn.

LA PAZ
Alcoche

BENI

Trinidad

Puerto Acosta

Caranavi

Mapiri
Sorata

Lake Titicaca

Illampu Mtn.

LA PAZ

Tiahuanaco

El Alto

Illimani Mtn

Coripata
Chulumani

COCHABAMBA

Concepción

SANTA   CRUZ

Cochabamba

SANTA CRUZ HIGHWAY

Oruro

Santa Cruz

Puerto Suarez

Sajama Mtn.

Lake Poopó

ORURO

Sucre

Cabezas

Potosí

Monteagudo

SUCRE

Camiri

POTOSÍ

PARAGUAY

Tupiza

Villazon

Tarija

TARIJA

CHILE

Paraguay River

Antofagasta

ARGENTINA

◆ ARCHAEOLOGICAL SITE
▲ MOUNTAIN PEAK

150 Miles
0 — 250 Kilometers
SCALE

FACTS AT YOUR FINGERTIPS

WHAT IT WILL COST. Bolivia has managed to control an inflation rate that reached 15,000% in 1985. Inflation was running at an annual rate of 18% in 1990, the lowest in South America. As a result, prices have stabilized and the dollar has lost some of its purchasing power. Even so, there are many bargains to be found in Bolivia, especially in handicrafts, silver, and gold. A good meal costs around $7. A moderately priced hotel costs $25 for a double room with private bath.

SOURCES OF INFORMATION. Information on Bolivia is provided at the office of the Consulate General, 211 E. 43rd St., Rm. 802, New York, NY 10017 (tel. 212–687–0530) or at the Bolivian Embassy, 3014 Massachusetts Ave. NW, Washington, DC 20008 (tel. 202–483–4410).

WHEN TO GO. Due to its closeness to the equator Bolivia has every climate and terrain imaginable. Temperature is largely determined by altitude. There is a rainy season that runs from Oct. to Mar. and a dry season that runs from Apr. to Sept. Rains can be heavy in the rainy season but only last an hour or two. During the dry winter season the skies in most of Bolivia are dark blue. In the mountainous regions of the country it is 50° to 70°F under the sun, with temperatures dropping to freezing at night. Carnival takes place in either Feb. or Mar. when the heavy rains are nearly over. If interested in road travel, it's not advisable to travel by land during the rainy season due to deteriorated road conditions.

WHAT TO TAKE. For the city of La Paz and the highlands, woolen sweaters and a windbreaker are recommended. During the day the temperature may reach 70°F. but it drops in the evening. During the rainy season an umbrella or raincoat is necessary. The sun in the mountains is very strong so be sure to bring a good sunscreen and wear a hat. In Santa Cruz, Trinidad, and other tropical regions, light clothing is worn year-round. Jackets are expected at fancy restaurants, but informal clothing should do for most places.

SPECIAL EVENTS. The *Oruro carnival* scheduled for the Sat. before Ash Wednesday, and the *"Pujllay"* carnival in Tarabuco, scheduled for Mar., are important cultural festivals very much worth visiting. Also recommended is the *Fiesta de la Cruz* (Feast of the Cross) that takes place the first weekend in May. In Achocalla, a village located one hour from La Paz, hundreds of area residents dance wearing elaborate costumes and the Aymara Kusillo mask. La Fiesta de la Cruz is also observed in Copacabana and other communities. It is one of the most important feast days. On *San Pedro,* which falls on June 28–29, many villages, among them Achacachi, Curva, Carabuco, and Tiquina, have festivals in honor of San Pedro. The *feast of Santiago,* celebrated July 25, features native dances and processions. *Gran Poder,* celebrated in La Paz late May or early June, has thousands of dancers performing "La Diablada," Morenada, and a host of dances typical of the highland. On *San Juan,* held on June 24, La Paz and other Andean cities are lit up by fires to fend off the cold of winter. Several communities hold celebrations in honor of San Juan. The Alacitas' *fair of miniatures* in honor of the Ekkeko, the Aymara Indian patron of abundance, takes place at the end of January in La Paz. Miniature handicrafts, household goods, houses, vehicles, and figures are sold at the fair. For the opening La Paz residents stock up on miniature pesos and dollar bills and have them blessed at a church with the hope that the year will be plentiful. Alasita fairs also take place in other cities.

Check with the Bolivian Tourist Agency at Edificio Ballivian, Calle Mercado, (tel. 367–463, fax 374–630) for other festivals planned during your visit.

TRAVEL DOCUMENTS AND CUSTOMS. U.S., U.K., and Canadian visitors require passports. Tourist cards are issued at airports or train stations and are valid for 30 days. They can be extended at the immigration office located on the Plaza de Estudiantes in La Paz, tel. 370 475. If you stay longer than 30 days you must stop by the nearest immigration office to get an exit visa. Cigarettes and no more than two bottles of alcohol are allowed. Cameras and typewriters can be brought in without much problem. Be especially careful about what you take out; many tourists who have tried to smuggle out a little bit of cocaine or marijuana have ended up spending years in jail. There is a $12 airport tax on international flights and $1.50 tax on domestic flights.

GETTING TO BOLIVIA. By air. *Lloyd Aereo Boliviano (LAB),* Miami to Santa Cruz and La Paz with connecting flights to other cities. *American Airlines,* Miami to La Paz. *Lufthansa,* Frankfurt to Caracas, Bogota, Lima, and La Paz. *LAB airlines,* Rio de Janeiro and São Paulo to Santa Cruz and La Paz; Buenos Aires to Santa Cruz; Santiago to Arica and La Paz; Panama to Santa Cruz and La Paz; Caracas to Santa Cruz; Asuncion to Santa Cruz and La Paz; Cuzco to La Paz; Lima to La Paz. La Paz is also served by *Varig* from São Paulo and Rio de Janeiro, as well as *Aero Peru* and *Lineas Aereas Paraguayas.* Check with your local travel agent for new schedules and prices to and from La Paz. The new, ultra modern Viru-Viru airport in Santa Cruz opened in 1985. In Bolivia be sure to reconfirm connecting flights.

CURRENCY. The *boliviano* has replaced the *peso* as the official monetary unit of Bolivia. Six zeros have been eliminated from the old peso bills, and new boliviano bills are in circulation.

The official and black market exchange rates are around 3.85 bolivianos to the dollar at press time. Since the government implemented an austerity program, the large disparity that existed between the official and black market rates has been eliminated. It is possible to legally change dollars on the sidewalks of Av. Bolívar and other areas of downtown and El Prado. Money can also be changed at "Casas de Cambio" located throughout La Paz and other cities. Traveler's checks may often be difficult to change unless you have some contact. Hotels base their prices on the official rate, which is revised daily. As of January 1, 1987, the government changed the currency to eliminate the use of six zeros. Dollars can also be used for many transactions. Most hotels and stores now accept VISA, MasterCard, or American Express. Other cards are usually not accepted.

Prices, unless noted otherwise, are in U.S. dollars.

HOTELS. Most Bolivian cities have good to excellent hotel accommodations. Always try and make your reservations in advance for hotels, especially if you're planning on visiting Oruro, La Paz, or Santa Cruz during Carnival. Breakfast is usually not included in hotel rates.

Hotel rates are based on the official dollar exchange rate. Credit card payments are made based on the official rate.

Price ranges given in this chapter are for double occupancy: *Deluxe,* $65 and up; *Expensive,* $30–$60; *Moderate,* $20–$30; *Inexpensive,* under $20.

RESTAURANTS. Restaurants have been classified as follows for dinner for one person, excluding drinks, service charge, tax, or tip: *Deluxe,* $20 and up; *Expensive,* $10–$20; *Moderate,* $5–$10; *Inexpensive,* under $5.

Bolivian Food and Drink. One of Bolivia's little known secrets is its great culinary tradition. Some day the cooking of the Andes should receive the credit it deserves. Corn, potatoes, and *quinoa,* a high protein grain, are native to the Andes. Bolivians have developed thousands of dishes based on these and other products.

Unfortunately, few hotels will provide a good idea of the richness of Bolivian cuisine. Often the best way to be introduced is through Bolivian friends.

For a mid-morning snack, nothing beats "salteña," a hearty stew of beef, peas, potatoes, hard-boiled eggs, olives, and a spicy sauce wrapped in a dough and baked. Served piping hot, it is popular at mid-morning celebrations.

Bolivian soups are second to none. Try a creamy peanut soup with pieces of chick-peas, cabbage, potatoes, and peas, or a pumpkin soup/stew served during Easter with chunks of corn, melted cheese, and fava beans. Also worth trying are "chairo," a hearty soup made with beef, chunks of dehydrated potatoes, fava beans, and potatoes; "sopa de papa lisa," made from small, yellowish potatoes native to the highlands; and "sopa de quinoa," made from the quinoa grain that can also be used in thousands of dishes ranging from granola, bread, stews, casseroles, and puddings.

La Paz and other cities also make an excellent French-style bread. In La Paz the typical bread is known as "marraqueta." Baked early morning and afternoon, the "marraqueta" is tops.

If visiting Sucre, try the chorizos, a pork sausage flavored with green onions, fresh oregano, parsley, nutmeg, garlic, etc. For lunch or dinner be sure not to miss ckocko, a spicy chicken dish flavored with wine and a local corn brew. Also worth trying is fritanga, a pork dish flavored with fresh mint and ground hot red pepper sauce that is accompanied by hominy. For an appetizer or even main dish nothing beats the pastel de choclo or humintas made from ground corn.

In La Paz try the fricasse, a spicy pork and hominy stew served at the Hotel Plaza. If interested in something mild, try the Lake Titicaca salmon trout or excellent grass-fed filet mignon from the Beni or highlands accompanied by one of the 200-odd varieties of potatoes.

In Santa Cruz or Trinidad, try a fresh heart of palm salad or a good juicy steak accompanied by rice with melted cheese and black beans. A delicious accompaniment is fried plantain or yuca.

In terms of fruit it is hard to equal the variety found in Bolivia. Because of the country's proximity to the equator, in Andean cities you will find a wide selection of valley and tropical fruits. Try chirimoya, a green and black-pocketed fruit with a creamy white filling—it makes great ice cream or mousse. Also worth trying are the tumbo, a sweet-acid fruit, orange-colored bananas, and most fruits common to the U.S. and Europe.

Bolivia also has a thriving beer and wine industry. Beer made by Germans or their descendents is superb, as many Europeans and Americans have attested to. Good and flavorful beer is sold throughout the country.

Bolivia's wine industry is based in Tarija, Camargo, and other southern Bolivian regions. Best are Kohlberg Fundador and San Pedro Cavergnet.

Once you've adjusted to the altitude, be sure to try singani, a distilled spirit made from grapes. It is served as a pisco sour or "chuflay," a mixture of "seven-up," singani, and lemon juice.

TIPPING. Restaurants add 11% tax but *not* gratuities to the bill; waiters will expect a 10% cash tip in addition. Taxi drivers do not expect a tip, but for long distances or when hired for long periods in the city, a tip may be given according to the service received. At airports plan on tipping baggage handlers \$.50 for every piece of luggage.

BUSINESS HOURS AND HOLIDAYS. Shops open at 9 or 9:30 A.M., close at noon and reopen at 2:30 P.M., to close again at around 7 P.M. Many shops are also open on Sat. mornings.

Banks open at 9 A.M. and close at 11:30 A.M., reopen at 2:30 P.M. and close at 5 P.M. The post office is open from 9 A.M. to noon and 2:30 until 7 P.M.

National holidays: Jan. 1 (New Year's Day), Monday and Tuesday of Carnival, Good Friday, May 1 (Labor Day), Corpus Christi (movable), Aug. 6 (Independence Day), November 2 (Day of the Dead), Dec. 25 (Christmas).

TELEPHONES AND MAIL. Pay phones exist in many cities and can be used with tokens usually sold nearby. Hotels and ENTEL, the state long-distance telephone company, offer long-distance service. Direct-dial is available from La Paz to many Bolivian cities. Information is 104 in La Paz. The domestic long-distance operator is 101. A long-distance operator can be reached at 356–700.

Mail service is fairly reliable to the U.S. and Europe. Urgent packages can be sent through DHL, Calle Colon, corner of Av. Mariscal Santa Cruz, tel. 379–422; UPS, Ed. Mcal Ballivian of 1209, tel. 350 472; Choice Sky courier Ed. Avenida, Av. 16 de Julio, tel. 328 841, La Paz.

NEWSPAPERS. Bolivia does not have an English-language newspaper but magazines such as *Newsweek* and *Time* are sold in many kiosks and at Amigos del Libro, with branches in La Paz, Cochabamba, and Santa Cruz, which offers a good selection of foreign-language books and magazines (in La Paz, on Calle Mercado). La

Paz has six dailies—*Presencia, Hoy, El Diario, Ultima Hora*, and *La Razon* are sold in the morning, *Jornada* in the afternoon. In Santa Cruz you can purchase *El Mundo o El Deber* and *El Día;* in Cochabamba, *La Opinion* and *Los Tiempos.* Bolivian dailies carry a good amount of foreign news.

ELECTRIC CURRENT. La Paz runs on 220 and 110 current. The rest of Bolivia is 220. Current is 50 cycle A.C.

USEFUL ADDRESSES. The U.S. Embassy is located on the Calle Colon, corner with Mercado. The U.S. consulate at 1285 Calle Potosi (350–120) is open mornings. The Canadian consulate is at Av. Arce 2342 (375–224). The British Embassy is on the Avenida Arce 2732 (329–401).

The tourist information center is in the Mariscal Ballivián Building, 18th Floor, Calle Mercado between Loayza and Colón (367–464, and 358–213).

Useful telephone numbers in La Paz: *Airport information,* 810–122; *Immigration,* 370–475; *Bus terminal,* 367–274; *Police,* 110; *Tourist police,* 367–441.

SECURITY. Due to the continuance of isolated terrorist incidents against U.S. officials and citizens, the State Department recommends that travelers to Bolivia exercise caution. Upon arrival, U.S. citizens should seek the latest travel information and register with the consular section of the U.S. Embassy in La Paz, Edificio Tobia, Second Floor, Calle Potosi, corner of Colon (320–494).

HEALTH AND SAFETY. Despite Bolivia's reputation as an unstable, coup-prone country, it is one of the safest countries to visit in South America. Bolivia has gone through five massive devaluations in as many years, numerous strikes, roadblocks, and marches but during that period not one person has been killed from politically related violence. Since Victor Paz Estenssoro took over Aug. 6, 1985, strikes have decreased and political unrest been reduced to a minimum. Foreign diplomats who have served in other Latin American posts say Bolivia is one of the safest and friendliest countries in the Third World. Bolivia *is* a friendly and hospitable country. Muggings are very rare but be careful of pickpockets, especially on crowded buses or in airports and railroad or bus stations. Be sure to carry your wallet in an inside pocket or body-belt and women should carry their purse close to their bodies.

Water in most cities is treated, but to be on the safe side drink only bottled water and avoid eating salads or raw vegetables in restaurants. Avoid the purchase of cooked food from street stands or in markets.

In the altitude of La Paz, Potosi, and the Altiplano take it easy the first couple of days—avoid alcohol, heavy foods, and too much activity. Drinking coca tea is recommended to help adjust to the altitude. Some of those who've best adjusted to the altitude are the elderly—so don't stay away from La Paz and other highland areas for fear of the altitude.

GETTING AROUND BOLIVIA. By air. *Lloyd Aereo Boliviano,* the national airline, serves most Bolivian cities. To reach tropical cities and towns *Transporte Aereo Militar* (TAM) also provides regular passenger service. During the Dec. to Mar. rainy season flights may be cancelled or delayed due to bad weather.

Lloyd Aereo passengers embarking in Miami should look into a month-long pass for unlimited air travel in Bolivia.

By train. Trains link La Paz with Peru, Chile, Argentina, Potosi, Sucre, Oruro, and Cochabamba. Trains are often delayed, especially during the rainy season. There is also train service between Santa Cruz and Brazil or Argentina.

By bus. There is good bus service between major cities. Crowded buses often serve rural communities. During the rainy season avoid bus travel on unpaved roads, especially the road linking Santa Cruz to Cochabamba. Buses to Oruro and Cochabamba leave regularly. Tickets must be purchased ahead of time for inter-city bus travel. Bus departures are usually on time. Be sure to bring food along.

By boat. Boat service is available from Huatajata on the shores of Lake Titicaca to Copacabana and Puno, Peru. *Crillon Tours, Transturin Trimaran Service, Turismo Balsa,* and *Atlas Tours* offer boat service on the lake. *Fremen Tours* offers boat service on the eastern Bolivian rivers.

By car. In La Paz *Kolla Motor* offers 4-wheel-drive vehicles. *Taxis* can be hired by the hour in front of hotels; they provide service to Lake Titicaca, Oruro, and other regions. In La Paz, *Bolivian Video and Film Rental* offers Toyota four-wheel drive vehicles; tel. 390–700.

In Cochabamba, *Barrons* (22774) provides Toyota jeeps.

FLORA AND FAUNA. Bolivia has a remarkable variety of flora and fauna. In the Andes you will find llamas, alpacas, vicunas, armadillos, condors, etc. To the southeast of La Paz in Comanche there is also the 30-foot-high Puya Raimundi plant that takes one hundred years to flower. In Lake Titicaca there are salmon, trout, Pejerrey, large frogs (with export-quality legs), and a wide variety of birds.

In the tropical part of Bolivia, which covers nearly two-thirds of the country, there is a rich and varied wildlife and fauna. There are monkeys, wild turkeys, pigs, ocelots, piranhas, and alligators as well as several million head of cattle.

See also "Adventure Vacations" chapter.

Exploring Bolivia

LA PAZ

At dawn mist and clouds can be seen rising from the lower valleys until the sun peers from above the Andes and bathes the surrounding hills with hues of red, ocher, and blue. At dusk, as the sun settles on the Altiplano flatlands surrounding the valley of La Paz, a reddish glow envelops the city's greatest landmark, the snowy peaks of the 21,000-foot Illimani Mountain.

With the Andes and deep blue skies as a backdrop, Aymara Indian women, children in tow, sell their wares at roadside market stalls facing tin- and straw-covered adobe homes. Whether landing on the 13,000-foot-high El Alto airstrip or crossing Lake Titicaca by boat, the barren plateau known as the Altiplano is a visitor's first introduction to the city of La Paz.

The Altiplano hides the presence of a thriving metropolis of one million inhabitants that opens up at its edge. Without warning, the plateau breaks and reveals below a deep jagged valley covered with adobe and brick homes clinging to the hillside. Skyscrapers, rising to meet the jagged hills of the valley, cast shadows over adobe, stone, and brick homes, cobblestoned streets and tree-lined plazas that hide rich and colorful traditions growing out of centuries of Spanish conquest, revolution, and Aymara folkore. And only three hours away by car, on the eastern slopes of the Andes, are banana and orange groves.

Before the sun is out, men, women, and children, wearing bowler hats and multilayered skirts known as *polleras,* begin their daily trek by foot or bus to the center of La Paz. By the time the sun has risen, Aymara-speaking vendors are in place in the markets, ready to offer a wide variety of vegetables, fruits, whole pigs, clothing, household goods, and steaming hot coffee.

Aymaras live in the surrounding hills and market areas. Below are the homes and workplaces of a Creole class that has identified itself more with its European forebears than with the Indians who make up 70 percent of the country's population. The city then descends several thousand feet to the neighborhoods of Obrajes, Calacoto, and Irpavi, where diplomats and wealthy Bolivians, including many in the military, live in sumptuous homes.

If you are arriving by plane, it is a good idea to take it easy the first day because of the rarefied air. Those who reach La Paz by crossing the lake from Puno, Peru, however, should be accustomed to the altitude. It is wise to drink and eat lightly at first, but drink plenty of *mate de coca,* a brew made from the coca leaves, to help fend off the effects of the altitude.

To get your bearings and capture some of the color, bustle, and contrasting life-styles found in La Paz, start your visit by taking a walking tour of downtown. With most good hotels located in the center, you'll only be a few blocks from the city's main avenue, Avenida 16 de Julio, better known as El Prado, with its promenade of trees, flowers, and monuments. In the evening it will be jammed with traffic and people returning from work. On Sundays the Prado is filled with families out for a stroll. You will also see old homes, with elaborate iron latticework and balustrades, which managed to survive the 1970s building boom that transformed the skyline of La Paz.

El Prado becomes Avenida Mariscal Santa Cruz going upward. At the upper end of Avenida Mariscal Santa Cruz, before it becomes Avenida Montes, is the San Francisco church, built in 1549. Its stone carved portico shows a fine example of the baroque Spanish architecture, combined with native craftsmanship, that flourished in Bolivia during the sixteenth, seventeenth, and eighteenth centuries. The facade is decorated with carved images of birds of prey, masks, pine cones, and parrots. The church offers one of the finest examples of religious colonial architecture to be seen in South America.

A visitor can spend several days exploring the roads and alleys that branch off from the San Francisco church. Bordering it is the Calle Sagarnaga, lined with dozens of small shops stocked with leather goods, weavings, alpaca sweaters, silver, and antiques. Vendors on the street sell old coins, irons heated with charcoal, silver or pewter ware, and small stone carvings made by the Aymara or Quechua people who inhabit the Altiplano. Sweaters range in price from twenty to fifty dollars, depending on the quality.

Adjacent to San Francisco is a handicraft gallery sponsored by the Catholic church. Open Monday to Friday from 10 A.M. to 1 P.M. and 2:30 to 7 P.M., and Saturday and Sunday in the morning, you'll find weavings, sweaters, and handcrafted Bolivian instruments such as the *quena, zampoña tarka,* and *charango,* a stringed instrument with a backing made from the carapace of an armadillo. At Rumillajta you can purchase these instruments of professional quality for three to thirty dollars. Be sure to ask the vendors, who are young, accomplished musicians, to try them out for you.

A block above San Francisco on the Calle Linares to the right, and especially as you go along until you reach Calle Santa Cruz, you will find Aymara-speaking women wearing the traditional bowler hat offering medicinal cures still used by the *callawayas,* the ancient medicine men who attended the Inca courts and used quinine to cure malaria long before it was adopted by Western medicine. Roadside stands offer herbs for curing rheumatism, stomach pains, etc. Also available are llama fetuses, incense, small bottles with sweet syrups, nuts, wool, copal, and grease—items that are used for white magic ceremonies and to protect a dwelling from evil spirits. For about two dollars you can purchase a bag of offerings to the goddess of the earth, the *pachamama,* and be assured of a bountiful year. Whenever construction on a home begins, these ingredients are burned and the ashes buried in the corner during a ceremony known as the "challa." The Tuesday after Carnival most Bolivians *challan,* or bless their belongings by sprinkling alcohol and streams of colored paper.

The Sagarnaga continues up to market areas, where shoeshine boys, vendors, and peasants offer their wares. Tucked away in courtyards and alleys are *tambos,* where bananas, oranges, and coca leaves are available. Coca leaves, from which cocaine paste is made, are widely used in restaurants as a tea, or chewed by peasants to help fend off the effects of hunger and tiredness.

If walking the streets tires you, take a taxi for about a quarter or a bus for even less up to Buenos Aires avenue. It competes with the downtown business area as the most thriving commercial area of La Paz. On Wednesdays and Saturdays, at least thirty blocks near Buenos Aires are filled with stalls offering contraband goods at low prices.

Above the Buenos Aires are hundreds of workshops that make the elaborate costumes, masks, and trinkets used for the Gran Poder festival, the city's most important folkloric expression. In June thousands of dancers pay homage to the Gran Poder—a god that is a mixture of pagan and Catholic beliefs—in a colorful orgy of dancing, music, and drinking that attracts hundreds of thousands of spectators.

On the Calle Gallardo No. 1080, one block above Buenos Aires, is a small workshop that used to belong to the late Antonio Viscarra, a master maskmaker who devoted sixty-five of his seventy-four years to making elaborate plaster and cloth masks representing the devil, his blue-eyed, blond mistress, and a parthenon of saints, African slaves, and Incas that perform for the Gran Poder, Diablada, and other festivals. Fortunately, his daughter and son-in law Carlos Fuentes carry on this tradition. For around fifteen dollars you can purchase an elaborate horned devil's mask that took a month to make. Or you can purchase beautiful miniature reproductions of larger masks.

After several hours of visiting this area you should be ready for a break. Many *Paceños,* as residents of La Paz are called, take time off at midmorning to eat the salteña, a hearty beef, olive, hard-boiled egg, potato, and pea stew wrapped in a dough that is Bolivia's contribution to haute cuisine. They are sold throughout the city, but be careful where you get them if you want to avoid getting sick. The most delicious ones are served for around 50 cents at the Salteñería Super Salteña on Av. Sanchez Lima and on Calle Socabaya. They are also available in the basement of the Hotel Plaza, the Confitería Arabesque on Calle Loayza corner of Mercado. Salteñas Potosinas and Salteñas Miriam, both on Av. 6 de Agosto, and Filippo Lipi on Plaza Avaroa, are also worth trying.

An alternative mid-morning break is a visit to the popular Cafe La Paz, located on the corner of Ayacucho and Camacho. This quaint old cafe is a hangout for politicians, businessmen, tourists, and labor leaders. It was also Nazi war criminal Klaus Barbie's favorite spot until he was expelled from Bolivia in 1983. They serve the best espresso in town, iced coffee, and lima juice—made from a non-acidy citrus fruit grown in the tropics—and cheese pastries.

Because of the altitude, it is wise to eat the main meal at lunch and have a light supper. A siesta after lunch is enjoyed by many.

An afternoon tour could include a visit to the Galeria Emusa, located on the Prado. The city's most important gallery offers a wide and often beautiful assortment of Bolivian art and sculpture. Emusa is open weekdays 10 A.M. to 1 P.M. and 4 to 7 P.M. Another private gallery to visit is Galeria Arkani on Calle Belisario Salinas which also has an excellent framing shop. Casa de la Cultura (across the street from San Francisco) and Salón Municipal Cecilio Guzmán de Rojas (Calle Colón, between Camacho and Mercado) also have varied art exhibits worth visiting.

Another alternative is to take an all-day tour offered by numerous travel agencies found in La Paz for about $18 (including lunch). Half-day tours will cost around $12. You can also hire a private taxi by the hour.

Heading downhill from the Prado you will pass the university and highrise apartments before reaching the neighborhood of San Jorge and the presidential residence. The road bends and continues downward until it reaches the neighborhood of Obrajes and Calacoto, which are several degrees warmer because of the drop in altitude.

From Calacoto head to La Florida, take the road bordering a river to Aranjuez, cross the La Paz River, and continue toward Mallasa and the

La Paz

Points of Interest

1) Witchdoctor's Market
2) San Francisco Church
3) Mercado Artesanal (handicraft market)
4) Museo Costumbrista
5) Casa de Murillo
6) Municipal Theater
7) Folkloric and Ethnographic Museum
8) National Museum of Art
9) Cathedral
10) Palacio Presidencial
11) Congreso Nacional
12) U.S. Embassy
13) Mercado Camacho
14) National Tourist Office
15) Biblioteca Municipal
16) Museo Tiahuanaco
17) Prehistoric Tiahuanaco Park
18) San Andres University
19) City Tourist Information Center
20) Tambo Quirquincho Museum

Valley of the Moon, named because of the rock and dirt formations that exist there. If you continue eastward, the roads descends to La Palca and other fertile valleys where vegetables and fruits, including peaches, apricots, and plums, are cultivated.

On your way back be sure to visit the square facing the city stadium where a replica of a Tiwanacu courtyard can be found containing authentic stone monoliths and figures that date from the third to twelfth centuries. From there you'll be five minutes away by car from the Plaza Murillo, where the presidential palace and congress are located. Before constitutional rule returned to Bolivia in October 1982, the palace was often guarded by tanks and machine-gun-toting soldiers.

In front of the presidential palace is a statue of former President Gualberto Villarroel. In 1946 a mob attacked the presidential palace, dragged Villarroel to the square, and hung him from a lamp post; a nearby statue commemorates the event. Diagonally across from the presidential palace is congress, which has a visitor's gallery from which you can see democracy at work.

Next to the presidential palace is the cathedral, built in 1835. Facing it on the corner of Calle Socabaya and Comercio is the National Art Museum, which was built in 1775 for a Spanish nobleman and is the finest baroque building in La Paz. The exterior and the courtyard are ornamented with carved floral designs. In the center of the patio is an alabaster fountain surrounded by plants. The three floors of the museum contain some of the painting and scuptural treasures of Bolivia. The first floor is devoted to exhibits of contemporary Bolivian and foreign artists; the second to the colonial works of the grand master of Andean colonial painting, Melchor Perez Holguin and his disciples; and the third to a permanent collection of Bolivian artists. One room is devoted to the sculptures of Marina Nunez Del Prado, whose abstract stone representations of Aymara and Quechua Indians have earned her a worldwide reputation. Art buffs can visit her former home, which now houses an exquisite collection of masks, colonial silverware, and several hundred of her sculptures. The museum is located on Calle Ecuador 2034.

The National Art Museum (tel. 371–177) is open Tuesday through Friday 9:30 A.M. to 12:30 P.M. and from 4 to 7 P.M.; Saturday it is open only in the morning. Admission is about fifty cents, twenty-five cents for students. None of the museums in La Paz offer English-speaking guides.

After leaving the museum take a stroll down the Comercio street and take a right on the Calle Yanacocha until you reach the corner of Ingavi. Around the corner is the Ethnographic and Folklore Museum, a beautiful eighteenth-century structure that is a repository of weavings, masks, feathers, and other objects of Bolivia's great cultural traditions. The museum offers a permanent exhibit on the Ayoreos, an Indian group from the Amazon area of the country, and on the Chipayas, who inhabit the most desolate area of the Altiplano and have maintained a distinct language and culture. Tickets are available for ten cents. It is open Monday through Friday, 8:30 to 11:45 A.M. and 2:30 to 5:45 P.M. On weekends it is open 10 A.M. to noon.

From the museum head up one block, take a left, and go two blocks until you reach Calle Jaen, a narrow, cobblestoned street that houses four museums. They are open Monday through Friday, 9:30 A.M. to noon and 2 to 6:30 P.M., Saturdays and Sundays 10 A.M. to noon. Admission tickets for the four museums can be purchased at the Museo Costumbrista for about a dollar. Saturdays admission is free. Calle Jaen is itself very interesting; as one of the best-preserved colonial streets in La Paz it will give the visitor a glimpse into Bolivia's colorful but often turbulent past.

The Murillo Museum was once the home of the War of Independence hero Don Pedro Domingo Murrillo, after whom the city square is named. In 1810 he was hanged by the Spanish for his anti-crown activities. The colonial-style building houses a handsome collection of Bolivian handicrafts, art, and furniture. If you start to your left, you'll enter a room filled with over forty masks, several of which are the work of Antonio Viscarra or his grandfather. Also shown are miniature representations of some of the traditional dances of the Bolivian highlands and several display cases showing diminutive hats, shoes, furniture, canned foods, and street vendors. The objects are from Alacitas, a traditional fair that takes place for two weeks at the end of January. Bolivia's president and church officials make their yearly pilgrimage to bless over twenty blocks of stands offering candied fruits, sweets, handicrafts, plaster saints and animals, miniature pesos and dollar bills, and local dishes. The day the fair is inaugurated, city residents stock up on thousands of dollars worth of fake bills and miniatures and pray that during the year their wishes will come true.

From the courtyard in the Murillo Museum a stairway leads up to several exhibit halls. In the first room is a collection of silver masks, utensils, peacocks, and saddles that belonged to Bolivia's aristocracy. In other halls are examples of colonial furniture and the room used by Pedro Domingo Murillo.

Farther up the street is the gold museum that houses pre-Columbian gold and silver ornamentations, Inca and pre-Inca ceramics, and a description of Indian metallurgy.

Next to the museum is the Museo Litoral that houses documents, photographs, and paintings relating to the 1867 War of the Pacific when Bolivia lost its outlet to the sea. Bolivia is likely never to forget this loss and stages marches, commemorative events, and international appeals in an effort to recover access to the Pacific.

At the end of the Calle Jaen is the Museo Costumbrista, an elegant colonial-style structure exhibiting ceramic figures representing historical events and local customs. In one case is the Indian guerrilla leader Tupac Katari, who was quartered by the Spanish in 1781 near La Paz. Other displays show the lynching of Murillo in 1810 and the traditional festivities of San Juan, when tens of thousands of fires and fireworks displays light up La Paz on what is said to be the coldest night of the year, June 23. Several cases show popular drinking places, markets, dances, and outings dating to the time when La Paz was a provincial city of less than fifty thousand inhabitants. You'll learn that the first auto made it across the Andes in 1913 and that by 1919 trolleys crisscrossed the city.

A visit to La Paz would not be complete without a visit to a *peña,* where folkloric groups perform first-rate Andean music for tourists and local residents. Worth visiting are Peña Naira, Calle Sagarnaga No. 161, Peña Marko Tambo on the Calle Jaen, La Casa Del Corregidor, Calle Murillo No. 1040, El Guitarrón, Calle Chuquisaca corner Unión, and Cactus, Av. Manco Kapac half a block from Plaza Eguino. Admission costs about five dollars, and they all offer restaurant service. Peñas begin after 9 in the evening and last until past midnight. Be sure to bring a sweater along since after the sun sets the night air becomes brisk. Reservations are recommended.

On a clear night, as you walk back to your hotel or if you head to the Monticulo Park in Sopocachi, you'll see the moon hovering over the eternal snows of the Illimani. The entire canyon up to where it meets the Altiplano is ablaze with street lights, and from the Altiplano above with brilliant stars that sparkle in the clear La Paz sky.

PRACTICAL INFORMATION FOR LA PAZ

GETTING AROUND LA PAZ. By bus. Buses—called micros—serve most city neighborhoods. Fares within the city center are about 30 cents. To outlying neighborhoods fares are higher. Fares are paid as you board the bus. Watch out for pickpockets who may slash purses.

By taxi. Taxis in La Paz will pick up 4 to 5 passengers and follow fixed routes, i.e., down Avenida 6 de Agosto, up Avenida Arce, etc. Fares within the city center are about 25 cents. If traveling to Obrajes or Calacoto, check the fare before boarding. Radio-dispatched taxi service is comfortable and efficient; fares are $2–$4 for trips within the city (call 371111, 369994, 322424–37, 355554, 371137, or 355555). Tourist taxis are also available in front of hotels. They charge an hourly rate of about $5 or according to distance traveled. Be careful you are not overcharged at the airport—an express trip to the city should cost no more than $8. If you share a taxi with four others, expect to pay about $2.

HOTELS. For definitions of price categories, see "Facts at Your Fingertips."

Deluxe

Hotel La Paz (formerly Sheraton), Av. Arce (356–950). 345 rooms, offering a panoramic view of the city and the surrounding Andes mountains. Good for large conventions, conferences. Has an indoor pool, sauna, exercise room. Ten-minute walking distance from Prado.

Hotel Plaza, Av. 16 de Julio (378–300). Elegant, located on the Prado. 165 rooms. Offers sauna, swimming pool, rooms with a view of the Illimani and an elegant rooftop restaurant that serves excellent Lake Titicaca salmon trout, Bolivian dishes—try *fricasse* if interested in something spicy. A gift shop in the basement carries the *Miami Herald*, and Millma sells excellent handicrafts, sweaters, and weavings.

Hotel Presidente, Calle Potosi 920 (367–193). This brand-new hotel, located downtown, has a nightclub, indoor pool, sauna, exercise room. One block from the San Francisco church.

Expensive

Hotel Gloria, Calle Potosí (370010). 79 rooms. Only a block from the San Francisco Church, this hotel offers good accommodations and a rooftop restaurant.

Hotel Libertador, Calle Obispo Cárdenas (343363). 53 rooms. Five-minute walk from the Prado, on a side street.

Moderate

Copacabana, Av. 16 de Julio (352–242). Located on the Prado, across from the Plaza. 64 rooms.

Crillon, Plaza Isabel La Catolica (352–121). 70 rooms. Five minutes by taxi from the center. Once the city's old world hotel.

El Dorado, Av. Villazon (363–403). 64 rooms. Located across from the university. A good bargain—be sure to make reservations.

Sucre, Av. 16 de Julio (355–080). Located on the Prado. Large rooms, snack shop, and restaurant.

Inexpensive

Alem, Calle Sagárnaga 334 (367400). Next to Hotel Sagárnaga, near *peñas* and handicraft shops. Very near San Francisco Church.

España, Av. 6 de Agosto 2074 (354643). 30 rooms. A block from the university and a couple of blocks from El Prado. Price includes breakfast.

Sagárnaga, Calle Sagárnaga 326 (358757). 35 rooms. A few steps from Bolivian handicraft shops and from several *peñas.* Very near San Francisco Church.

RESTAURANTS. For definitions of price categories, see "Facts at Your Fingertips."

La Carreta, *expensive,* Calle Batallon Colorado #32 (355891), offers good steaks. Hotel Plaza offers a cafeteria, the rooftop restaurant **Utama** *(expensive),* and the elegant **Arcon de Oro** *(deluxe).* Good Bolivian food, especially fricasse, sajta de pollo and saice, and lake trout served at the Utama (378311). **La Suize,** *expensive,* Avenida Arce (across the street from the Sheraton), has excellent beef and fondue as well as Swiss specialties. Serves lunch and dinner. Reservations are recommended (353150). Next door, **La Suize Romano,** *expensive,* offers excellent seafood pasta and other dishes (353–150). For some of the best beef dishes in town, try the **Churrasqueria El Arriero,** *expensive,* Casa Argentina, Av. 6 de Agosto 2535. **Refugio Restaurant,** *expensive,* Calle 20 de Octubre and Plaza Abaroa (355–651). **Herradura,** *expensive,* Calle Capitan Ravelo 2341 (324–546), serves great steaks. **Montesano Ristorante Italiano,** *expensive,* Ave. Sanchez Lima 2329 (390–759) offers homemade pastas and good seafood in an elegant setting. **Giorgissimos,** *expensive,* Calle Loayza near corner with Camacho (324456) has good Bolivian and beef dishes. **Chez Lacoste,** *moderate,* Calle 6 de Agosto (324–667), provides a lovely setting for fish and Continental food. **El International,** *inexpensive,* at Calle Ayacucho 206, offers daily fixed menus. **Restaurante Monaco,** Av. Villazon 1958 (365–014), has a fixed menu and a la carte meals. **Cafe La Paz,** *inexpensive,* at Calle Camacho and Ayacucho, has excellent coffee as well as breakfast and tea pastries. For *saltenas,* try **Super Saltenas,** Sanchez Lima and Plaza Abaroa; **El Arabesque,** Loayza and Juan de La Riva; and the **Hotel Plaza snack shop. Cafeteria Verona,** *moderate,* Colon corner with Mariscal Ayacucho, for meals, snacks, and fixed menu lunches. **Quicks,** *inexpensive,* on Plaza Isabel La Catolica, has the best hamburgers in town. **Stefanos,** *moderate,* Aspiazu corner 20 de Octubre, has good pizzas and homemade pastas. **Pizzeria Morelo,** *moderate,* Edificio Santa Teresa, across from the Sheraton (360671), has good pizzas. **California Donuts,** *moderate,* Av. Camacho 1248, good doughnuts, hamburgers, and snacks. **Charlie's,** *expensive,* Plaza Isabel La Catolica, excellent shrimp stew and other dishes. **Pronto,** *expensive,* Calle Jauregui 2248 (one block from Hotel La Paz) good homemade pastas. **Luigi's Pizza,** Av. 20 de Octubre, best pizzas. **Kuchen Stube,** *moderate,* Calle Rosendo Gutierrez, offers delicious German pastries.

USEFUL ADDRESSES AND NUMBERS. Police, 110; **Bus station,** 353510, 352510; **Airport information,** 810 122; **Central train station,** 353510; **Long distance calls,** 356700; **General Hospital,** 376 192.

Tourist Information Center: Mariscal Ballivián Building, 18th floor, on Mercado between Loayza and Colón.

Medical and dental care: house calls are made in Bolivia. *Dr. Ciro Portugal,* Ed Mariscal Ayacucho (360 393). *Dr. Ovidio Suarez,* gynecologist (351501). *Dr. Esperanza Aid* U.S.-trained dentist speaks English (320081). Clinica CEMES, Av. 6 de Agosto (353–465), Clinica del Sur, Obrajes (784–750), and Clinica Rengel, Plaza España (390–792), offer emergency medical treatment. *The Methodist Hospital* on Calle Obrajes 12 (783511).

Exchange houses: *Sudamer,* Calle Colón 256; *América Ltda.,* Av. Camacho 1233; *Cáceres Ltda.,* Calle Potosí, Hotel Gloria; *D'Argent,* Ed. Ballivian, Calle Mercado (across from Amigos del Libro); *Colle Tobias,* Calle Socabaya (across from Ministry of Labor).

Mail, telephone, and telex: Central mail office is located in a new skyscraper on Av. Mariscal Santa Cruz. ENTEL, the national telecommunications company, is located on Calle Ayacucho between Mercado and Camacho. Offers long-distance telephone, telegram, fax, and telex service. Hotel offers same services and mail service. For additional information, dial 104.

TOURS. Crillon Tours, Ave. Camacho 1223 (320222). Runs hydrofoil service on Lake Titicaca from Huatajata to Tiquina, Sun Island, Copacabana, and July (Peru), connecting with further transportation to Puno and Cuzco. Crillon Tours also offers a comfortable hotel and museum about the people who inhabit Lake Titicaca at Huatajata.

Balsa Tours, Ave. 16 de Julio on the Prado (356566).

Transturin, Calle Camacho (363654). Offers bus and boat service to Puno with connections to Cuzco.

Bolivar Travel, Ed. Camara de Comercio, Av. Mariscal Santa Cruz (350 145). **Tawa tours,** Calle Sagarnaga, above Pena and restaurant Naira (329814), offers adventure and trekking tours in the Andes and tropics, where they have their own camps.

Club Andino Boliviano, Calle Mexico 1638 Casilla 5879 (365 065). Offers guided trips to Chacaltaya ski slopes as well as trekking and mountaineering information. For a guide to climb the Andes, contact Bernardo Guarachi, a veteran climber who speaks German.

Fremen Tours, on Plaza Avaroa (376–336), offers river excursions and tours in the Highlands and tropics. Turismo Ensueño, Ed. Ballivian, Calle Mercado, has good service.

Paititi Tours, Calle 20 de Octubre 2668 (329625). Offers excellent organized adventure tours in the Andes, the Altiplano, the jungle, and the valleys. Fully equipped trekking, mountain climbing, boat and jeep trips.

Gaviota Tours, Calle Loayza, Castilla building (351596). Trips to Tiwanacu, Lake Titikaka, Chacaltaya, Yungas, Oruro, and other Bolivian Departments.

Gacela Tours, Hotel Crillon (352121). Arranges tickets and organizes tours to Tarabuco, Tihuanacu, Lake Titikaka, Yungas, and Chacaltaya.

Diana Tours, Calle Sagárnaga 328 (358757). City tours, trips to Tiwanaku, Lake Titikaka, Moon Valley, Chacaltaya, Yungas, Zongo, Puno, Cusco.

MUSEUMS AND CULTURAL CENTERS. Most museums are open Mon.-Fri., 9 A.M.–noon, 2–6 P.M. Sat. and Sun. 9 A.M.–noon. Call ahead to confirm hours.

Museo Costumbrista, Plaza Riosinio at the end of Calle Jaen. Miniature scenes of old La Paz.

Museo Pedro Domingo Murillo, Calle Jaen. Exhibits masks, weavings, miniature handicrafts, silverware, etc.

Museo Nacional de Arte, Plaza Murillo across the street from the Cathedral. Fine collection of colonial paintings and contemporary art.

Museo Tambo Quirquincho, Calle Evaristo Valle. Newly restored colonial structure features mask, art, and handicraft exhibits.

Museo Tiwanaku, Pasaje Tiwanaku behind the Hotel Plaza. This recently restored museum exhibits priceless pre-Columbian artifacts.

Museo de Etnografia y Folklore, Calle Ingavi 916. Permanent exhibit on Chipaya and Ayoreo Cultures.

Museo del Oro, Calle Jaen. Exquisite collection of pre-Columbian gold, silver, and ceramic artifacts.

Goethe Institute, Aven. 6 de Agosto (374453). Cultural programs, lectures, concerts on Bolivian and West German subjects. German library.

Centro Boliviano Americano, Parque Zenon Iturralde (342582). U.S. and Bolivian cultural programs, films, and concerts. Library with U.S. periodicals and books.

Alianza Francesa, Calle Guachalla, corner 20 de Octubre and coffee shop (325022). Bolivian and French cultural programs.

Galeria Emusa, El Prado, 1607 (328931). Best art gallery in town.

Teatro Municipal, Calle Sanjines, corner with Indaburo. Concerts and theater.

Casa de la Cultura. Plaza Perez Velasco. Art exhibits, cultural programs, and concerts.

Galeria Arkani, Calle Belisario Salinas. First-rate art exhibits and framing center.

SHOPPING. For visitors interested in handicrafts, silver and gold jewelry, and fine alpaca ware, La Paz is the place to shop. Galeria Millma in the Hotel Plaza offers beautiful Indian weavings, wall hangings, natural dyed alpaca and cotton sweaters, scarves, and ponchos. It is run by two Americans who are authors of two books on Bolivian weavings. They make most of their alpaca and cotton goods at a workshop located two blocks away on the Calle 20 de Octubre 1824 and a store on Calle Sagarnaga 225. The woolens can also be purchased through the Peruvian Connection catalog. Maderma, Ed. Petrolero, El Prado, offers excellent quality alpaca woolens, books, and souvenirs. Artesanias Bolivianas, Av. Arce (across from Hotel La Paz) sells good, quality handicrafts and alpaca dresses. On the Calle Sagarnaga, Galeria San Francisco next to the church of the same name offers a wide selection of antiques, alpaca goods, weavings, and old coins. Punchay Artesanias, Calle Santa Cruz 156, belongs to a group of musicians. They sell music, weavings, and alpaca sweaters. Schohaus, at Calle Colon 260 (just below the U.S. embassy), offers elegant pewter. Good silver and pewter ware at the Edificio Mariscal Ayacucho, Calle Loayza, and Kings in the Hotel Sucre. Chocoholics should be sure to try the Breick bitter, milk, or milk chocolate sold throughout the city—real chocolate flavor that beats Hershey's. Good chocolate can also be found at **Clavel's** on the Prado.

Film and processing. Slide and black and white film costs 3 to 4 times more than in New York. Fuji and Kodak print film can be bought at bargain prices at the Miamicito—the city's black market. **Foto Linares,** Calle Loayza corner with Juan de la Riva, offers color processing and a good selection of photo supplies and equipment. Best service in town. **Casa Kavlin,** Potosi 1130, sells film and does color processing. **Casa Capri,** corner of Colon and Mariscal Santa Cruz, processes print film. Kodachrome film cannot be processed in South America. **Reifshneider,** Calle Potosí 1316, offers Fuji film, processing, cameras, and equipment repair. **Quipus,** Calle Jauregui 2248, sells postcards, maps, and guides to La Paz and Sucre.

NIGHTLIFE. Nightclubs: Onix, Av. 6 de Agosto 299 (342787). Lively and crowded disco. **Pacha,** Av. 6 de Agosto, Santa Teresa building (350745). **Baccara,** Av. 20 de Octubre 1822 (324039). **Chelzy,** Av. 20 de Octubre 2072. **Forum,** Calle Victor Sanjines, corner Ricardo Mujia. **La Mansion,** Av. Ballivian (Calacoto).

Bars and Pubs: Matheus, on Calle Guachalla corner of Av. 6 de Agosto. Jazz and nice pub setting. **Horno Bar,** Av. 20 de Octubre 2072. Jazz, cozy atmosphere. **Juan Sebastian Bar,** Calle Ecuador 2620. **Rancho Suizo,** Calle Aspiazu (above Calle Ecuador). **Grammofon Bar Lírico,** Calle Belisario Salinas 536. **Dali,** Av. 20 de Octubre (corner of Aspiazu). Modern artsy setting.

Peñas: Bolivian folklore for visitors and locals. All offer restaurant service. **Naira,** Calle Sagárnaga 161 (350530). **Marka Tambo,** Calle Jaén 710 (340416). **La Casa del Corregidor,** Calle Murillo 1040 (363633). **El Guitarrón,** Calle Chuquisaca corner Unión (368050). **Kutimuy,** Calle Murillo 947 (352351). **Los Escudos,** Av. Mariscal Santa Cruz corner with Calle Ayacucho (322028). **Cactus,** Av. Manco Kapac, half a block from Plaza Eguino.

EXCURSIONS FROM LA PAZ

Tiwanacu

Bolivia's most important archaeological sight, Tiwanacu, is located fifty miles to the west of La Paz. It was once the center of one of the most ancient cultures in the Americas. Its monumental stone figures, stone courtyard, and sun gate give a glimpse of a civilization that mysteriously surfaced around 600 B.C. and disappeared around A.D. 1200. Now located twenty miles from Lake Titicaca, it is believed to have once been near the shores of the lake.

There are no guides available at the site, so it is best to take one of the many tours provided by travel agencies in La Paz.

The most imposing monument is the Gate of the Sun, which is thought to be a solar calendar. It is part of an elaborate observatory and courtyard that contain monoliths, the door of the Puma, and a subterranean temple. It lacks the sheer splendor of Machu Picchu, but provides a glimpse into the ancestry of the Aymara people, many of whom still inhabit the area.

Sorata

Legend has it that this charming valley town was the site of the biblical Garden of Eden. The perpetually snow-covered, 22,000-foot-high Illampu Mountain looms over Sorata and the surrounding corn, potato, and wheat fields. The town, once a flourishing commercial center and the gateway to the gold mining region of Tipuani and Mapiri, is laid out in the classic Spanish design, with two well-kept parks and a grid pattern of narrow, cobblestoned streets. Two streams carrying the melt-off from Illampu meet below the village. Sorata, located at 2,450 meters above sea level, is in the temperate zone and is an ideal place to visit for a weekend. During the December to March rainy season it may rain for an hour or two, but normally it is sunny. The remains of elegant estates that once housed rich landowners or gold miners still exist near Sorata.

Located four hours by bus from La Paz or three by private vehicle, Sorata has two comfortable places to stay. The Hotel Prefectural offers private rooms with bathrooms and hot showers, a swimming pool, and a view of the Illampu. To capture a bit of the historic flavor of Sorata, you can stay at the Hostal Casa Gunther, the former residence of a German merchant who became wealthy trading in gold and selling imported crystals, fabrics, and household goods to wealthy gold miners who passed through Sorata en route to La Paz. The hostal offers large bedrooms, clean communal hot showers and bathrooms, and a lovely garden of palm trees and flowers. They also serve upon request a breakfast which includes homemade jams, and a hearty lunch and dinner. For more information on Casa Gunther and Hotel Prefectural, check with travel agencies.

Residents of Sorata make some charming stuffed dolls, wall hangings, and dresses from handwoven wool. These can be found on the main square by asking for Senorita Diana or Artesanias Sorata.

Sorata is the starting point for climbing the Illampu. For the daring, there is an Inca trail that begins near Sorata, crosses the Andes, and drops to the tropical gold mining region of Tipuani. Over a four-day trek you will travel from snow to jungle on a stone-paved Inca highway that crosses crystal-clear mountain streams and lagoons. This trail has been used since the time of the Incas to carry gold, coca leaves, and other products to the highlands. On the trail you are likely to encounter herds of llamas or mules taking potatoes, corn, and other goods to the tropics. For the trip it is necessary to take a sleeping bag, tent, and food supplies, including coca leaves to chew along the way.

Lake Titicaca

If you did not arrive via Lake Titicaca, a trip there is a must. A paved road will take you to the lake, past farming villages and farms where rows of potatoes, barley, fava beans, and quinua are grown. During the October through December planting season a visitor will see Indians using teams of oxen to plow the fields, much as their ancestors did.

An hour-and-a-half after leaving La Paz, you will reach the 13,000-foot-high waters of Lake Titicaca. Totora reed and wooden boats used for fishing or travel are visible from the shore. In Huatajata you can rent a boat and visit Suriki or other islands. Four residents of Suriki built the "Ra Two" for the Norwegian explorer Thor Heyerdahl. Two of the builders have a small souvenir shop in Suriki, an island famous for its totora reed boats and furniture.

If you enjoy seafood you can eat some delicious salmon trout at the Inti Raimi restaurant in Huatajata or at the Hotel Titicaca, which also offers comfortable accommodations and is located between the village of Huarina and Huatajata. Reservations for Hotel Titicaca can be made at the Hotel Libertador in La Paz (355080). In Huatajata, Crillon Tours also offers a first-class hotel, Inca Utama, and has a sunset to sunrise excursion on the Sacred Lake as well as visits to a lovely museum with exhibits on pre-Columbian and contemporary Indian cultures of the Altiplano. Reservations can be made at Av. Camacho 1223, tel. 372970.

Lake Titicaca sprawls for some 3,500 square miles and forms part of the boundary between Bolivia and Peru. The Islands of the Sun and Moon also hold an important place in the history of the Inca civilization. The Island of the Sun has the remains of Inca palaces, gardens, and temples. The Island of the Moon offers a look at the remains of the Temple of the Moon and a great view of the Andes.

If you continue past Huatajata, you will reach the Tiquina crossing. Cars, buses, and trucks are loaded on wooden barges and ferried across the waters en route to the religious sanctuary in honor of the Virgin of Copacabana, also known as the Black Madonna. You can either take a bus from the main terminal in La Paz, hire a private taxi, or go on a tour. During Holy Week throngs of young people spend several days walking to Copacabana to pay homage to the Virgin. On weekends or holidays the main square is jammed with vehicles covered with flowers and colored strips of paper taken to be blessed by the Virgin. On the *Calvario,* a hill overlooking the village and the lake, visitors purchase miniature trucks or homes made from plaster and pray that the Virgin will provide them with a real truck or home during the year.

You can stay at the Hotel Prefectural, located near the lake. Check with travel agencies.

In Copacabana boats are available to take you on a tour of the lake or visit the Inca shrines on the Islands of the Sun and Moon. An hour should cost around five dollars.

The Yungas

In less than three hours you can cross a 15,000-foot-high summit inhabited by condors and llamas and then descend to the tropical Yungas region where bananas, oranges, coca leaves, papaya, and avocados grow. Just to experience the change in temperature and scenery is worth a visit to the Yungas. Buses leave from Flota Yungena on Calle Tejada Sorzano No. 1579 near Mercado Yungas. Visitors can also hire a private taxi or take a tour to the area.

Half an hour past Unduavi the road splits, with the road to the left going to Coroico, Caranavi, and the gold mining region of Tipuani. To the right the road heads toward Chulumani, a picturesque village famous as a vacation place for city residents. Many of the surrounding farmers cultivate coca leaves and fruits. Motel San Antonio and Motel San Bartolome offer comfortable accommodations with private baths. Singles cost eight to ten dollars. San Antonio and San Bartolome have swimming pools.

If you take the road to the left at the crossing, in a little over an hour, traveling over a windy road flanked by thousand-foot precipices on one side and waterfalls on the other, you'll reach Coroico. Near this old village are several communities inhabited by Aymara-speaking blacks, descendants of African slaves brought to work in the mines. The hill overlooking Coroico is called Uchamachi and is said to be the home of Pacha Mama, the goddess of the earth. A good place to eat and stay is the Hotel Prefectural, reached as you enter Coroico.

The road from Coroico continues to Caranavi and to the gold mining villages of Guanay, Tipuani, and Mapiri. In the summer it is quite hot and humid, but worth visiting if you are interested in seeing gold miners working in a wild west environment.

Chacaltaya

One hour from downtown La Paz is Chacaltaya, at 17,000 feet above sea level the world's highest ski slope. On a clear day Chacaltaya offers a breathtaking view of the Altiplano, neighboring peaks, and Lake Titicaca. To check on bus schedules to Chacaltaya call the Club Andino at 324682, or consult with travel agencies.

The ski lodge located halfway up the mountain provides a resting place and snacks for visitors. You will likely be out of breath or possibly feel a bit faint at this extreme altitude, but the fantastic view offsets any discomfort. If you have the energy, you must visit the ice caves located near the slopes. It is advisable to check with the Club Andino for the equipment needed. The Club Andino rents ski equipment at the lodge.

The ski season runs from November to April or May. The Club Andino (324682) provides bus transportation on Sundays and sometimes on Saturdays. Otherwise, hire a jeep or, if weather conditions permit, a taxi in front of major hotels.

The Zongo Valley

A delightful day trip from La Paz is to the Zongo Valley, where the hydroelectric plants of the Bolivian Power Company are located. A four-wheel-drive vehicle is advisable for this trip. Instead of taking the road to Chacaltaya at a fork forty-five minutes from La Paz continue to the Milluni Mine past lagoons that provide La Paz with its drinking water. Continue past the mine and in fifteen minutes the road, bordered by snow peaks and crystal-clear lagoons, starts to wind toward the Zongo Valley. Within an hour you will reach mountain streams that offer good trout fishing. In another hour you will be in the tropics. During the course of twenty miles the road drops from 4,624 meters to 1,480 meters.

COCHABAMBA

Cochabamba is the city of eternal spring. Nestled on the foot of the Tunari and other peaks, this 8,430-foot-high valley city is an important Alpaca handicraft center and vacation spot. With a population of 317,000, Cochabamba competes with Santa Cruz as the second largest city in Bolivia.

The flight from La Paz to Cochabamba in itself makes a trip to this charming city worthwhile. The plane flies alongside the Illimani mountain and other snow-covered peaks. After fifteen minutes in the air from La Paz you can see the tropical lowlands in the distance.

To get a view of the city, take a taxi or walk to the Coronilla mountain. From this monument, which honors women and children who defended the city during the War of Independence, you will see the Tunari mountain and the road to the Chapare, a lush tropical region that has gained world fame as the country's principal cocaine producing region. The trip to Villa Tunari in the Chapare is very worthwhile—the road winds through the mountains and then drops to the tropics. Villa Tunari borders a river that feeds into the Amazon. It is dangerous to venture beyond Villa Tunari, however, unless you do it in an organized boat tour that takes you up the Ichilo River. Check with Fremen Tours (21676 in Cochabamba, 37336 in La Paz). A new paved road that will link Cochabamba and Santa Cruz is now being built that will pass through Villa Tunari.

In the city it is worth visiting the Centro Portales, reached by a five-minute walk from the Hotel Cochabamba. This grand mansion was built by the tin baron Simon Patino, who was originally from the Cochabamba area. He amassed one of the world's largest private fortunes. The mansion was decorated by French designers who used the finest materials money could buy. It now houses a cultural center funded by the Swiss Patino foundation. Patino also built a sprawling estate in Pairumani just above Vinto, a thirty-minute drive out of Cochabamba on the road to Oruro. Check with the tourist office on hours when visits to Portales and Pairumani can be made.

Fifteen minutes after leaving Cochabamba you will encounter dairy farms and villages with centuries-old homes.

If you have a day to spare, hire a car and head out to the Valle Alto. Twenty minutes out of Cochabamba on the road to Santa Cruz, veer to the right by the Angustura dam. In another thirty minutes you'll reach Tarata, an old village with adobe homes and overhanging balconies that has changed very little in recent decades. In December there is a colorful feast with dancers using masks from La Diablada. Check with the Cochabamba tourist office for feast dates. Instead of veering right at the dam, you can also head out to Cliza, Punata, and Arani. These villages are also served by buses that leave from Av. San Martin, near the railway station. The market in Cliza is on Sunday, in Punata on Tuesdays. The Valle Alto is famous for its pottery and dairy products. Small white flags that hang in front of adobe homes indicate the sale of chicha, a fermented corn brew.

For camping, hiking, and fishing, a visit to Mount Tunari is recommended. It is thirty-eight miles from Cochabamba on the road to Morachata-Independencia. The climate is cold but the scenery is spectacular.

Another farming village worth visiting is Quillacollo, located only eight miles from Cochabamba. The Sunday market is very colorful.

If interested in Inca ruins, a weekend trip to Incallajta is a must. A four-wheel-drive vehicle is needed to reach these ruins, which are located seventy-five miles from Cochabamba on the road to Santa Cruz. It is recommended that you take along a guide who knows the road. Two temples and several dwellings remain at Incallajta. Be sure to bring food and warm clothing.

PRACTICAL INFORMATION FOR COCHABAMBA

HOTELS. Hotel Portales, Cochabamba, and Ambassador are the best.
Hotel Portales. *Expensive.* Av. Pando 1271 (43159, 45269). 120 beds. A brand new hotel with swimming pool, suites with Jacuzzis, and two restaurants.
Hotel Ambassador. *Moderate to Expensive.* Calle España (48777). 105 rooms. Considered one of the best in the city. Located three blocks from Plaza 14 de Septiembre.
Gran Hotel Cochabamba. *Moderate.* On the Plaza Ubaldo Anza, better known as the Recoleta (43300). Offers a swimming pool, tennis courts, lovely gardens, and one of the finest restaurants in Bolivia.
Other *moderately* priced hotels include: **Hotel Boston,** Calle 25 de Mayo (28530); **Hotel Colón,** Plaza Colón (48101); **Hotel Emperador,** Calle Colombia (27638); **Hotel Las Vegas,** Calle Esteban Arce (29217).
Inexpensive hotels include: **Hostal Claudia,** Calle Hamiraya (47844); **Hotel Gemas,** Calle Nataniel Aguirre (27683); **Hotel Venecia,** Av. Aroma (26165); **Residencial Brasilia,** Calle Brasil (22107); **Residencial Buenos Aires,** Calle 25 de Mayo (29518); and **Residencial Internacional,** Calle Junín (48304).

RESTAURANTS. Hotel Cochabamba restaurant. *Expensive.* Best in town. Good menu selection.
Restaurant Victor, on the Prado. *Expensive.* Good food but overpriced.
Casa de Campo. Half a block from Plaza de la Recoleta on Calle Aniceto Padilla. *Moderate.* Good Bolivian cuisine and barbeque.
La Estancia. Half a block from Plaza de la Recoleta on Calle Aniceto Padilla. *Moderate.* Excellent beef dishes.

La Huella. Plaza Quintanilla. *Moderate.* Excellent barbeque.

La Suiza, on the Prado. *Moderate.* Fine selection of beef, seafood, and Continental dishes.

Parrillada La Senda. Calle Adela Zamudio 1783 (in the Cala Cala area). *Moderate.* Barbeque and different kinds of beef dishes.

Restaurante Taquina. *Moderate.* At the brewery of the same name. An hour trip toward the mountains, this restaurant with a view of the Cochabamba Valley is open weekends. It serves good beef, lamb, and duck dishes. Their beer is first rate.

TOURIST INFORMATION. Tourist information center on Plaza 14 de Septiembre, in the Prefectura building (23364). Maps of the city and a guidebook sold at Amigos del Libro, Av. Heroines 3712.

Travel agencies in town include: **Exprinter,** Plaza 14 de Septiembre; **Gitano Tours,** Calle Ayacucho (29570); **Delicias Tours,** Av. Heroínas; **Carve Tours,** Av. Heroínas; **Taus,** Calle General Achá; **Viajes Fremen,** Calle 25 de Mayo.

MUSEUMS. Not to be missed is the **Archaeological Museum** located at Calle 25 de Mayo, corner of Heroinas (28090). There are over 25,000 pieces on exhibit.

SHOPPING. Casa Fisher, Plaza Ubaldo Anza (next to Hotel Cochabamba) offers top-quality alpaca sweaters and shawls. **Amerindia,** Av. San Martín 6064, offers hand knitted alpaca goods, coats made of alpaca material, alpaca wool, wool rugs and tapestries, wood carvings, handbags, and leather goods. **Fotrama,** Av. Heroinas near the post office, sells some of the finest alpaca items in Bolivia. **Andea,** Calle Calama, offers alpaca goods and makes the thickest and finest alpaca rugs in Bolivia. Near the railway station is a sprawling black market that sells electronic gadgets, film, cameras, and clothing. Best to go on Wed. or Sat. You can find Kodak and Fuji film for two dollars a roll, video cameras, tape recorders, etc. Facing the railway station is a market that offers fruits, vegetables, handicrafts, handwoven wool blankets, alpaca sweaters, and other goods. Be sure to bargain the prices down.

ORURO

HOTELS. During carnival, hotel reservations must be made months in advance or through a travel agency. The Oruro carnival is one of the finest folkloric festivals in South America. **Hotel Terminal,** at the bus terminal (53209), *moderate.* The best hotel in town. **Hotel Prefectural,** Calle Aldana (60588), *moderate.* Run by the government. For *inexpensive* lodging, **Hotel Lipton,** Av. 6 de Agosto corner Rodríguez (41583); **Hotel Repostero,** Calle Sucre; and **Hostal Osber,** Calle Murguía.

SUCRE

On the cathedral towers of the city of Sucre, sixteen life-size statues keep watch. Twelve of them are the Apostles, and the four figures closest to heaven are, of course, the Saints of Sucre. So runs the story of the Cathedral statues, as told by the residents of this colonial city of 105,800 inhabitants located 420 miles from La Paz. *Sucrenses* have always held a special view of themselves, and the city's colorful history has tended to reinforce it.

Sucre's colonial architecture and museums are a reminder of the history, culture, and tradition that have thrived in this 9,000-foot-high city and influenced a wide region of southern America. Visitors can explore centuries-old churches and museums that exhibit priceless colonial paintings, furniture, and religious figures adorned with gold and jeweled garments. And in March of every year, the traditional folklore of the surrounding Quechua inhabitants comes alive in Tarabuco with one of the most important indigenous festivals in Latin America.

A twenty-minute drive from the airport serviced by modern jets will take you to the city's heart, the Plaza 25 de Mayo. There, veterans of the 1932 war with Paraguay spend their days seated on well-kept benches, watching a parade of students in white uniforms, Quechua peasants offering their wares to tourists, shoeshine urchins, ice-cream vendors blowing their horns, and children playing on the bronze lions surrounding the monument to the great Latin American "Libertador" Antonio Jose de Sucre.

Stately palm and ceibo trees which in August and September bloom with red "gallitos," or little roosters, shield the Plaza from the blazing midday sun that beats down except for brief periods during the November to February rainy season. The sidewalks, bordered by well-groomed trees, are swept before dawn every day with palm branches by Quechua-speaking men and women.

Sucre, founded by the Spaniard Pedro de Anzurez in 1540, is often called "La Ciudad Blanca" (the White City) for its cleanliness and for the houses and churches that are whitewashed every year by government edict, and is referred to as the "City of Four Names"—Charcas, Chuquisaca, La Plata, and Sucre. The intellectual ferment that has characterized Sucre over the centuries comes alive every fall when students return to study at a university founded twenty-four years before Harvard, in 1624. The University of San Xavier was the font of liberal ideas which gave birth to the first cry of independence on the continent.

After you check in at one of Sucre's four comfortable colonial-style hostels or the Hotel Municipal, head for the Plaza, where 1940 Buicks and Studebakers and modern Toyota taxis are available for a quick tour of the city at around four dollars an hour. Because of Sucre's small size, most points of interest are within walking distance from the center.

Wherever you go, you will find that tradition is still an important part of life here. Only three doors from the Plaza on the Calle España, Jaime Soliz still cuts hair with hand clippers and shaves with blades sharpened on leather straps, much as his father, grandfather, and great-grandfather did.

Before making the rounds of museums and Roman Catholic churches and monasteries, spend a few hours walking around to savor a bit of Sucre's past and its remains. Imagine a time when gilded horse-drawn carriages trod through the city's cobblestoned streets carrying women dressed in the latest Parisian fashions, or a time when men in black velvet outfits tailored in Granada or Toledo, Spain, walked the streets followed by their indentured Quechua peasants. Or picture the Plaza before the 1952 revolution that abolished peonage and ended the rule of the Tin Barons, when life in the square reflected the social and professional divisions of the city. Progressives and students gathered on the far side of the Cathedral while doctors, lawyers, and businessmen sat shielded by palm trees opposite the House of Liberty (Casa de la Libertad), where Bolivia was founded and the constitution drawn up. The local blue bloods, descendants of the Spanish and Creole aristocracy once enriched by the silver mines of Potosi or by government posts, sat and conversed on benches lined up adjacent to the Cathedral. Quechua-speaking peasants were relegated to the Plaza's inner circles, unless they were servants attending the children of the well-to-do.

Two blocks from the square on the Calle Nicolas Ortiz is the San Felipe Neri Church built in the seventeenth century. Its size testifies to the power the Roman Catholic church once held in Latin American society. The views from domed roofs and towers, made with bricks bonded with silver from the mining city of Potosi, afford a marvelous panorama of countless churches, said to have numbered one to a block during the colonial period. The extension of the graceful curves of ceramic roofs shield the tiny windows and balconies from the summer rains and piercing winter sun. Porticos, balconies, and archways, visible in the corners of older buildings, are rich in symbolism, depicting mythical gods and Christian effigies. Only the sound of passing vehicles and a television tower on the Sica Sica mountain that overlooks the city remind one of the present. The tourist bureau, located four blocks from the Plaza on Calle Alberto No. 401, can refer you to travel agencies that provide tours to visit the roof and courtyards of San Felipe Neri Church. English-speaking guides are only available through tourist agencies.

If you return to the Plaza by the same street you will face the portals of the baroque-style Cathedral, famous for a Virgin covered by a multimillion-dollar garment endowed with gold, diamonds, emeralds, and pearls donated by wealthy residents during the colonial period, which dates from 1538 to 1825, when the Republic of Bolivia was born.

Adjacent to the Cathedral is a museum displaying colonial paintings, volumes of parchment, and desks inlaid with mother-of-pearl. In the eighteenth and nineteenth centuries musicians performed classical works composed by Creole artists trained by Spanish clergy. These musical manuscripts, preserved at the National Archives on the Calle Espana, have been commercially recorded and bring to life once again the great cultural activity that once took place in Sucre.

A walking tour of Sucre would not be complete without the traditional afternoon tea consisting of ice cream, fruit milk shakes, and pastries. On the Plaza and side streets are several confiterias open for this occasion. Be sure not to miss the delicious *cuñapes,* and cheese pastries served hot at the Confiteria Las Vegas on the Plaza.

If you are in the mood for something religiously sweet head up the Calle San Alberto until you reach Calle Camargo and the Santa Teresa Convent whose nuns until recently spent their adult lives cloistered behind three-foot-thick adobe walls. Between ten and twelve in the morning nuns and novices sell candied figs, oranges, apples, and limes, reciting "Ave María Purísima."

Two blocks from the Plaza on the Calle Calvo you'll reach a small but precious museum adjacent to the Convent of Santa Clara that was founded in 1639. Ensconced within its thick adobe walls is a valuable collection of the works of Melchor Perez Holguin, one of the three most important Latin American colonial painters, and his teacher the Italian painter Bernardo Bitti. They also have on exhibit clerical silver and gold embroidered garments, statuary, furniture, and other items. The museum is open from 9 to 11:30 A.M. and 3 to 5:30 P.M. If you're an early riser, you might enjoy attending the 7 A.M. mass (8 A.M. on Sundays).

As dusk approaches, walk up from the Convent or Plaza toward the eucalyptus-covered Churuquella mountain until you reach the Recoleta Monastery founded in 1601 by the Franciscans. Paintings of religious figures line the hallways around patios and lovely gardens with roses and geraniums in bloom. An adjoining restored chapel still contains intricately carved choir seats that once were occupied by Franciscan monks. Monks offer tours between 9 A.M. and noon and from 3 to 5 P.M. Monday–Friday.

A square with a stone fountain and sun clock borders the monastery and offers a view of the city, with its fifteen colonial churches, whitewashed homes, tiled roofs and parks surrounded by rolling farmlands and ragged mountain peaks that disappear into the horizon. At dusk, the horizon takes on hues of red, orange, and gray that disappear with the advent of darkness, leaving the city lighted by a canopy of stars.

In the early morning you will enjoy a pleasant and lively trip to the colonial-style market located two-and-a-half blocks from the Plaza. There, Quechua women are up before dawn arranging stalls of fresh vegetables, fruits, and canned goods. They are protected from the morning chill by delicately woven capes with abstract animal designs. A dollar will buy you fifty oranges—a great value if you can figure out what to do with them. Vendors at a row of stalls serve fresh vegetables and fruit juices and steaming hot "api," a pungent brew of ground red corn, sugar, cinnamon, and lemon which goes well with freshly fried cheese pastries called "empanadas." Be careful with eating unwashed fruits and vegetables, but hot drinks like api should give you no problem. A command of Spanish words would help in bargaining with the vendors, but with prices so low all you will miss out on is some of the fun of shopping in a Latin American country.

Sucre is best known for its colonial past. There are so many monuments that remind one of its heritage that a selective list will have to suffice. A visit to the "Casa de la Libertad" on the Plaza is a must. This historical museum houses documents and artifacts related to Bolivia's struggle for independence. As you pass through heavy wooden doors and proceed along the hall to the left you will reach a room where the August 6, 1825 Declaration of Independence is on exhibit. In another hall lined with carved pews the Declaration of Independence was signed. Depending on your time and interest you could spend hours examining the many documents and relics of Bolivia's turbulent past.

The Caserón de la Capellanía, on Calle San Alberto near the corner of Potosí, is Sucre's center for tourist development. In this seventeenth-century building you'll find art exhibitions, handicraft shops, workshops. Tourist information is also available here.

The University Museum on Calle Bolívar 698 exhibits fine weavings, archaeological artifacts, and colonial paintings and furniture. You might find especially interesting three mummified bodies that were once buried in a chamber attached to the Santo Domingo chapel. Within hours after they were discovered in the late 1940s the city was rife with rumors of bodies buried alive during the Inquisition and for days thousands stood in line to view the well-preserved bodies of a couple and child. Local residents still talk of torture chambers and of adulterous women forced to ride in the streets bare-chested on mules. According to Don Gunnar Mendoza, the director of the National Archives, wealthy families often built special altars inside churches and then sealed them off after burial.

EXCURSIONS FROM SUCRE

La Glorieta

A ten-minute ride toward the valley of La Florida will take you to "La Glorieta," a grandiose monument to Sucre's past. At the end of the nineteenth century, the wealthy industrialist Don Francisco Argandoña built a miniature estate with Venetian-style canals, lovely gardens, and fountains over which towered an exotic residential palace built in a conglomeration of Moorish, Spanish, and French architectural styles. Doña María Clotilde Argandoña became known as "La Princesa de la Glorieta," a title bestowed by the Pope—for a price—in recognition of her work with abandoned and orphaned children. Today, the canals are gone, the gardens are in ruins, and the grounds are occupied by army cadets. Even so, what remains is a reminder of the vanished splendor of "La Glorieta" and its epoch.

Tarabuco

The most colorful side trip from Sucre is to the town of Tarabuco at a distance of sixty kilometers in the Yamparaez province. The town can be reached on buses provided by tourist agencies or that leave from El Abra. A train-bus leaves every Sunday at 7 A.M. and returns at 2 P.M. The train bus fares are around $1.50. Its Sunday markets attract peasants from the region who are famous for their conquistador-style leather helmets and multicolored handwoven ponchos, "chuspas" (bags for carrying coca leaves and money), "chumpis" (skirts), and musical instruments. The most popular is the "charango," a string instrument whose back is formed by the carapace of the armadillo with hair that is said to grow even after the animal's death.

In March of every year, thousands of peasants from the area of Tarabuco join tourists and Sucre residents in the celebration of the "Pujllay," or carnival, one of the best traditional festivals in Latin America. The event celebrates the Battle of Jumbate which took place on March 12, 1816, when the Indians of the area defeated the Spaniards. Area residents dancing to music played on the "charango," "zampoña," "tokoro," "pinkillos," and bel-spurs; a lively mass sung in Quechua; and the lingering taste of spicy native dishes washed down with the corn brew known as chicha make a visit to the Pujllay a must.

Monteagudo

The road from Tarabuco winds southeast, toward valleys and mountains that gradually take on shades of green and a tropical air. Monteagudo, an eight-hour bus ride in good weather, is a region populated by the Chiriguanos, a sub-group of the Guaranis who inhabit southern Bolivia and Paraguay. Landslides and swollen rivers isolate the region from Sucre during the winter rainy season but in the dry season the frontier town of Monteagudo is readily accessible. The area encompasses vast zones of semitropical virgin land that offer good fishing and adventure. After a few days in this tropical region one can appreciate the fact that years ago Che Guevara fought a losing guerrilla war not far from Monteagudo.

New hotels with private bathrooms and hot showers have opened up.

PRACTICAL INFORMATION FOR SUCRE

HOTELS. Hotel Municipal. On Av. Venezuela 1050 (21216). *Moderate to Expensive.* Elegant hotel, offers comfortable rooms and swimming pool. **Complejo Hotelero Mendez Roca,** Pasaje Argandona (25472). *Moderate.* Offers comfortable cabins with kitchen and private bath.

Several new hostels opened recently that cater to tourists and national visitors, all at *moderate* prices: **Hostal Colonial,** on Plaza 25 de Mayo (24709); **Hostal Libertad,** Calle Arce 99 (23101); **Hostal Sucre,** Calle Bustillos 113 (21411); **Hostal Los Pinos,** Calle Colón 502 (24403); and **Hostal Cruz de Popayán,** Calle Loa 881 (31706). Hostels serve breakfast but usually not lunch or dinner.

For *inexpensive* lodging, **Residencial Bolivia,** Calle San Alberto 42 (24346); **Residencial Oriental,** Calle San Alberto 43 (21644); **Residencial Bustillo,** Calle Ravelo 158 (21560); and **Residencial Charcas,** Calle Ravelo, (23972).

RESTAURANTS. The best in town is **El Solar,** *Moderate.* Calle Bolivar 800 (24341). At this colonial-style restaurant you can dine on delicious, spicy Sucre dishes or on more traditional fare. Be sure to try the singani, a fine grape-distilled liqueur produced south of Sucre in Camargo or Tarija. The **Plaza,** *moderate,* overlooking the main square, offers continental and some local dishes. **Las Vegas,** Plaza

25 de Mayo, *moderate,* offers continental and local dishes. **Piso Cero,** Av. Venezuela 1241, *moderate,* offers Bolivian and continental dishes. For some of the best ice cream anywhere in Bolivia, be sure to visit **Helados Sahara,** a booth near the main park near the Supreme Court. Ask for Tumbo and Guayaba ice cream.

TOURIST INFORMATION. Tourist information center at Caserón de la Capellanía, Calle San Alberto 413 (25994 and 25983). A visit to the San Felipe Neri Church can be arranged through them. University tourist office at Calle Nicolás Ortiz 182 (23763).

Tour agencies include: **Candelaria Tours,** Calle Bolívar 634; **Fremen,** Plaza 25 de Mayo; **Solarsa Tours,** Calle Arenales 212; **Teresita's Tours,** Calle San Alberto 13.

USEFUL NUMBERS. Police, 110; **Bus Station,** 22029; **Train Station,** 31115; **Airport information,** 24445 and 32460; **Long distance calls,** dial 105; **Radio taxi,** 32144, 21414, and 21509. **ENTEL,** the telecommunications office (long distance telephone, telex, and telegram service), at Calle España corner of Urcullo. **Post Office** at Calle Argentina 50.

CULTURAL ACTIVITIES. The Sucre and Tarabuco regions have a thriving indigenous cultural life. On religious feast days processions pass through the streets of Sucre. In Tarabuco, the Pujllay is one of the most colorful festivals in South America. The U.S.- and West German-financed Centro Cultural Masis has been researching and fomenting native cultural expressions in the Sucre and Tarabuco regions. At their center at Calle Bolivar 561 (23403) you can purchase records of their latest European tour and see a nice collection of native instruments. At the Caserón de la Capellania, ASUR has opened a small but exquisite museum devoted to the textile and cultural traditions found in the Sucre area and northern Potosí. A salesroom offers a beautiful selection of textiles that are produced by contemporary artisans who have rescued age-old traditions.

SHOPPING. If you want to purchase weavings and handicrafts, you'll find a fine selection at the **Sala Expo-Venta Artesanal** in the Caserón de la Capellanía, Calle San Alberto 413, at **Artesanías Bolivia,** Calle Argentina 31, and at **Artesanías Candelaria,** Calle Bolívar 634. The best weavings originate in Potolo, Macha, Calcha, and Candelaria. Traditional string instruments at **Gerardo y José Patzi,** on Calle Destacamento 130, 59 and **Trifón Pimentel,** on Calle Junín, 1190. Sucre is also famous for its miniature dolls and fruit baskets made from dough.

POTOSÍ

In 1650, Potosí was the largest city in the Americas, with a population of 160,000, and one of the most important urban centers in the world, renowned for its silver mines, its magnificent colonial architecture, churches glistening with gold, theaters that presented the best of European productions, as well as for its extravagance and vice. In 1553, sixty-seven years before the pilgrims' landing at Plymouth Rock, Potosí was decreed an Imperial City by Charles V, King of Spain.

Today, the echoes of its fabulous colonial past can still be seen in its churches, bearing elaborate baroque facades, private homes with wooden balconies looking over the narrow, winding streets, and a host of fine museums, among them the "Casa de la Moneda," that has served the Spanish Empire as a mint, fortress, and prison since it was first built in 1572.

It is a city of contrasts. Some of the residents, dressed in fine, handwoven wool garments, carry on the cultural traditions of their Quechua Indian ancestors. Others, wearing modern clothing, are the Creole descendants of the Spanish and Indians who were drawn to the city by the silver mines.

They can be seen mingling in the markets, attending mass in the baroque churches, sitting in the city square, or walking the narrow streets of Potosí, bound by an understanding of the Quechua language but separated by class and cultural barriers.

Nestled at the foot of the Cerro Rico (rich mountain) on a 14,000-foot-high plateau surrounded by mountains and valleys that are part of the Andes' eastern edge, Potosí is a must on your visit to Bolivia.

Because of the altitude, it is advisable to take it easy the first day, before making a round of museums, churches, mines, and outlying sights. A drive around Potosí by taxi (about two dollars an hour) is a good initial introduction, especially until one's system is better suited to the rarefied air. You will frequent cobblestoned roads that once carried Spanish royalty and that now barely allow passage of four-wheeled vehicles. Starting at the Plaza facing the Cathedral you can head toward the mountain of Potosí, passing what is left of ninety-odd churches built three or four centuries ago and, farther up, the scattered remains of colonial mining operations. The symmetrical lines of the Cerro Rico, crisscrossed by over 5,000 tunnels, disappear as one approaches, distorted by mounds of rocks and debris accumulated over centuries of mining.

To the left of the Cerro Rico the road heads toward a chain of mountains containing seven lagoons that date to the sixteenth or seventeenth centuries. Water channeled down the mountain once powered rustic silver processing plants built by the Spaniards and their Indian and black slaves. Remains of these stone plants still dot the landscape.

A city of Potosí, with some 110,700 inhabitants, opens up below, bordered by a chain of ocher-colored mountains that contain a few thermal hot springs and legends of wealth, hardship, and intrigue linked to the rise and fall of the city.

Despite the harsh climate, the residents are easygoing and very hospitable. Women wearing multilayered skirts and pilgrim-type hats can be seen walking the streets or selling "tawa tawas chambergos" or "sopaipillas"—delicious sweet pastries typical of Potosí—for around twenty cents. During Corpus Christi the residents of the city, dressed in their best attire, take part in a religious procession. The city streets are lined with women vendors who sell these pastries. The treats are taken home and eaten in the evening with hot chocolate.

It is advisable to drink plenty of "mate de coca" (coca tea) throughout your stay to help fend off the effects of the altitude. It is from this leaf that cocaine is made, but the leaf itself is harmless and a staple at any hotel. After a relaxing first day and early retirement, the visitor should be in good shape to visit the Casa de la Moneda early in the morning. Just off the Plaza 10 de Noviembre, a carved doorway that allowed a horse, mule, or llama to enter opens onto a courtyard where a stone water fountain and a colorful laughing mask built by a Frenchman can be seen. For around fifteen cents a Spanish- or English-speaking guide—if you request one—will give a three-hour tour of the Casa de la Moneda.

This museum, which takes up an entire city block, has walls that in some places are four feet thick. First built in 1572 and then rebuilt between 1753 and 1773, it was established to control the minting of the colonial wealth. The sturdy yet graceful structure is of stone, wooden beams, brick, and domed tiled roofs. One room contains eight-foot-high wooden gears and wheels once operated by Indian and black slaves and used for laminating silver ingots in the process of minting coins. Adjacent to this room are displayed the thousands of coins produced there for the Spanish crown or for several Latin American nations.

The Casa de la Moneda also contains more than 100 colonial paintings and the works of the celebrated twentieth-century Bolivian painter Cecilio Guzman de Rojas. Also worth seeing is an archaeological and ethnographic collection, sculptures, exquisite furniture, and historical artifacts.

A morning at the Casa de la Moneda should test anybody's stamina. A *coca* followed by lunch is advisable. The best place to eat in Potosí is El Mesón, across from the Cathedral on the corner of Calle Tarija and Linares, which offers steaks, soups, and tasty local dishes such as fritanga and asado borracho. If you plan on spending two or three days in Potosí, ask them to specially prepare a traditional and delicious peasant dish called "kala purka," a hearty corn soup served in a ceramic bowl with a steaming-hot volcanic stone in the middle that cooks the soup. Also try the ckocko, a spicy chicken dish served with olives and native corn. For a little over two dollars for most dishes, you should be able to enjoy a delicious lunch in a quiet colonial-style ambience.

A siesta is a custom still enjoyed by many. Since most stores and businesses remain closed until 2:30 or 3 P.M., you won't miss much if you take a brief nap.

An afternoon visit could include a trip to the market on the Calle Bolívar, where you'll be surprised to see a wide variety of tropical fruits that appear out of place at 15,000 feet above sea level.

There are regions in the department of Potosí that produce grapes, peaches, and apples. Oranges and bananas are brought by truck from La Paz or from the south of Sucre. Much of the produce sold at the market comes from surrounding valleys inhabited by Quechua Indians.

Near the entrance to the market on Calle Oruro are several stands that sell elegant local handcrafted silverware. For about ten dollars you can purchase a lovely sugar bowl or a set of serving utensils. You might also find of interest some silver pins made from spoons called "topos." They are still used to fasten the traditional handwoven shawls used by the Quechua-speaking women of the region. Silverware and pewter are also a real bargain.

Silver was the raison d'etre for Potosí, and the residents did not hesitate to make use of it. The sinks and pitchers in the bathrooms of some homes were made from sterling silver. One old-timer recalls attending elegant banquets where the food was served on silver platters and on imported ceramic trays. Some homes were furnished with Persian rugs and English and French pieces that were transported across the Andes from the coastal city of Arica by mule or llama. When the silk or flannel clothing of the well-to-do was soiled, it was simply (or so it seemed) transported by mule or llama back across the Andes and the ocean to France where it was expertly dry-cleaned.

It is said that all the silver mined here could have paved a road from Potosí to Spain. It is not known exactly how much silver was extracted from the Cerro Rico, but it was enough to fill the coffers of the Spanish crown and provide the flowering of painting, music, architecture, and literature in Potosí, Sucre, and the surrounding regions of South America. By the nineteenth century, however, Potosí was in decline as the silver veins became exhausted, leaving only museums and buildings as reminders of the past.

Behind the market is the Church of San Lorenzo, which offers some of the finest examples of baroque carvings in Potosí, if not in all of South America. Elaborate arrangements of flowers, garlands, and mythical and indigenous figures are represented on high relief stone carvings made by Indian artisans. Even though it is closed to the public except for special occasions, it is worth seeing the church's exterior. To get into the court-yard that faces the church you might have to pay the attendant a few pesos.

Four blocks from the imposing San Lorenzo church, on the corner of Calle Sucre and Modesto Omiste, a collection of handmade weavings, belts, ponchos, silverware, and antiques is for sale. The quality ranges from not very good to first-rate, so you have to shop around to make sure you get what you want. For anywhere from twenty to fifty dollars you can purchase lovely weavings that may each take as long as six months to make. The department of Potosí produces some of the finest weavings in Bolivia and, according to weaving experts, in the world. Unfortunately, the finest examples have been exported abroad, and what is now available is not equal.

The narrow Quijarro street a block from the market that leads to the Plaza was designed with bends to break the impact of wind gusts. There are several hatmakers on this quaint old street, among them Antonio Villa Chauarría, house number 1141, who carries on a tradition that is slowly disappearing. During the day, though, with the sun shining, it's a pleasant walk back to the Plaza and to the Santa Teresa Convent located three blocks down from the Plaza on the Calle Chichas. It is only open from 4 to 6 P.M., so you must plan your visit well since it is one of the important museums in Potosí. A donation of around ten cents is requested for a tour that takes about an hour.

After entering the thick wooden doorway of the Santa Teresa Convent, the present will seem centuries away. The small museum within the convent belongs to an order of cloistered nuns and contains a fine collection of colonial paintings, altars, and furniture.

An old wooden turnstile near the entrance is still intact, used since the seventeenth century by nuns to keep their faces safely protected from male visitors. If a male had to enter for any reason, the nuns vanished to a second courtyard, out of sight and sound of the intruders. Even today, if you go there for a tour or to purchase the delicious milk, coconut, and peanut candies on sale for about two dollars a pound, you'll only get to hear their prayers and voices.

This museum offers an interesting, if somewhat morbid, view of a religious life-style that to some extent has adapted itself to the contemporary world. In one room are displayed sharp, star-shaped iron instruments used to inflict pain on the penitent nuns. One blouse is embroidered with wire mesh that has sharp prongs sticking out against the flesh. The fact that they are now museum items indicates, no doubt, that they are no longer of use, although one nun recalled using the artifacts a number of years ago. The same room has leather containers used for transporting sugar from the Santa Cruz region of Bolivia and for storing grains and dry goods.

Adjacent to this room is the dining room, with a main table that contains a skeleton resting on a bowl of ashes, a reminder that "ashes to ashes, we will become." It does not make for the most appetizing place to drop in for lunch.

In the choir room you'll find gold and silver embroidered garments used by the priests, and beneath the wooden floorboards dozens of nuns have been buried. Even in death they were kept isolated from men.

Other rooms contain a valuable collection of colonial paintings, particularly those by Melchor Pérez Holguín, one of three major Latin American colonial painters, and gold-leafed altars that were donated by wealthy residents.

Once you're used to the climate you may want to visit the mines. You can either hire a private taxi or catch the number 5, 7, A, or K buses at the Plaza early in the morning (check with the tourist office for exact time).

After paying about five cents, you will join hundreds of miners as they head up the Cerro Rico to begin the 8 A.M. work shift.

After leaving the center of town, the buses start climbing the Cerro Rico, passing caves and remnants of excavations that began in the sixteenth century and that are still sifted through by independent miners or women. The mountain, resembling a giant anthill, has also served as a tomb for hundreds of thousands of miners.

In the late sixteenth century, the great Inca chieftain, Huainca Capac, ruler of an empire that spread 2,000 miles from Quito, Ecuador, to Chile, visited the mountain of Potosí and ordered that silver found within be made into jewels for his court. But just as his workers were beginning to mine the valuable veins of silver, they heard a thunderous voice that said in Quechua: "Do not dig, it is not meant for you; God has saved it for others." And so it was that shortly thereafter the first contingent of Spanish explorers arrived in this desolate and cold region of Bolivia and established the first Spanish settlement at the foot of Cerro Rico in Potosi. They set in motion a stampede of Spanish adventurers that forever altered the landscape of the region. The Quechua-speaking descendants of Huainca Capac were uprooted from their lands, enslaved, and put to work mining the silver.

In less than twenty minutes, the buses will reach Pailabiri, the principal mining encampment on the mountain. After paying a one dollar entrance fee at the office of the "superintendencia" to the right of the main entrance to the camp, you will be given protective headgear, boots, and lamps. At 8:30 in the morning you will enter the mine on an electric-powered wagon. You'll have a chance to walk through dark and humid tunnels and descend via elevators into mine shafts where the miners work almost naked because of the intense heat. With the silver reserves almost exhausted, tin has become the principal mineral extracted from the mine.

The miners you encounter will be chewing the coca leaf to fend off hunger and exhaustion. A few leaves are also deposited on altars in the name of the goddess of the earth, the "Pacha Mama," the "Tio" or "Supay," the devil responsible for keeping the miners safe—or in peril. The famous carnival festival of Oruro that takes places in February or March of every year centers around the figure of the Tio or Supay, who is the basis for a rich and colorful folkloric tradition that is a mixture of Quechua and Christian religious beliefs.

A week before carnival, a centuries-old ritual is repeated in the mines, when a llama is sacrificed and its blood sprinkled throughout the entrance. This is supposed to evict evil spirits and assure that a rich silver vein will be found.

PRACTICAL INFORMATION FOR POTOSÍ

HOW TO GET THERE. Rail and bus lines offer regular connections from La Paz and Sucre, and thus a chance to see some of Bolivia's varied mountain scenery. **Turismo AndesBus** leaves Potosí for Sucre daily at 7 A.M. and 5 P.M. The trip in comfortable buses takes around five hours. The same schedule applies for the Sucre to Potosí route. One-way fares are about $5. The slow journey (12 hours from La Paz) also gives the visitor a chance to get accustomed to the high altitude.

HOTELS. Several good hostels with private baths have opened in the last few years. Best is **Hostal Colonial**, *inexpensive*, located a five-minute walk from the Casa de la Moneda and main square (24265).**Hostal Libertador**, *inexpensive*, Calle Millares 58 (27877), offers comfortable accommodations with private baths. **Hostal El Tambo**, *inexpensive*, is new with comfortable accommodations. Located in the Zona San Antonio (25186 or 25187).

SANTA CRUZ

Twenty years ago oxen pulled carts through the mud streets of Santa Cruz de la Sierra. In the rainy season, city streets were covered with mud. Only the Plaza was paved. Today, Santa Cruz, at an altitude of 1,460 feet above sea level, has boomed to become a thriving metropolis of at least 529,200 people and the vanguard of Bolivia's economic expansion. Modern office buildings exist side by side with adobe homes with curved tiled roofs. The city has undergone a dramatic transformation in recent years perhaps unlike any other Latin American city.

Santa Cruz, the capital of the rich department of the same name, was founded in 1561 by the Spanish Captain Nuflo de Chavez. Since the department of Santa Cruz borders Brazil on the east, there is a strong Brazilian presence in the area, especially during Carnival. Beautiful women wearing elaborate costumes that are often similar to those seen in the Rio de Janeiro Carnival parade through the streets in a orgy of music, dancing, and drinking. The weekend after Carnival, women with their identities concealed behind masks frequent the city's nightclubs, picking who to dance and have a good time with. It is the day women get back at their unfaithful husbands.

Cruceños, as residents of Santa Cruz are called, are easygoing and friendly. Short sleeves, miniskirts, and sandals are the norm due to the tropical climate. In the evenings or when cold fronts hit the area, a sweater might be necessary. Outdoor restaurants and nightclubs are popular, the nightlife is exciting, and the hotel accommodations are among the best in Bolivia.

A modern airport inaugurated in 1985 now links Santa Cruz with neighboring countries and other Bolivian cities. There are several flights a day connecting Santa Cruz with Cochabamba and La Paz as well as regular service to Trinidad and Sucre. The road between Cochabamba and Santa Cruz is often in terrible condition, so it is best to fly.

Worth visiting is the Santa Cruz zoo, which has a fine selection of native animals and birds in a nicely-designed setting. One should also stop in at the Basílica Menor de San Lorenzo on the main square. The present-day structure was built between 1845 and 1915 on the ruins of a seventeenth-century cathedral. The Cathedral Museum housed in the Basílica has an interesting collection of religious objects, sculptures, paintings, and silver work; many of the items are as much as four centuries old.

On the main square next to City Hall is the Casa de la Cultura Raul Otero Reich. It has cultural exhibits and a permanent show of area handicrafts. If interested in art, be sure to ask for the works of the painter Kuramoto (one of the country's best) and sculptor Marcelo Callau.

The area around Santa Cruz is a real paradise for hunting and fishing, as well as photographic safaris. Check with the tourist information center for arrangements.

PRACTICAL INFORMATION FOR SANTA CRUZ

HOTELS. La Quinta, *deluxe* (42244). Located in a residential neighborhood on Calle Aruma, Barrio Urbari. Offers apartments with private baths, kitchens, restaurant, and swimming pool. Great for families. **Los Tajibos,** *deluxe* (30022). Located a ten-minute ride from downtown on Av. San Martín. Offers beautiful swimming pool, gardens, tennis courts, and large, comfortable rooms. **Gran Cortez,** *moderate* *to expensive* (31234). Good, friendly service and comfortable rooms. Swimming pool. **Hotel Las Palmas,** *moderate to expensive* (30366). Modern, with swimming pool. **Hostal Cañoto,** *moderate* (31052). On Calle Florida. **Hotel Tropical Inn,** *moderate* (46666). On Calle España. **Hotel Bolivia,** *inexpensive* (36292). On Calle Libertad. **Hotel Colonial,** *inexpensive* (33156). On Calle Buenos Aires.

RESTAURANTS. Domenicos, *expensive,* Av. San Martin, Centro Comercial el Chuubi (49616). Offers international cuisine in an elegant setting. **El Arriero,** *moderate,* Av. Cristobal de Mendoza (49315) and a branch at Av. San Martin Equipetrol. Offers excellent Argentine beef. **Brazzery la Boheme,** *moderate,* Calle Rene Moreno 56 (33245) offers French and German food. **Floresca,** Av. Velard, *moderate,* corner of Irala (24453) international cuisine. **La Empalizada,** *moderate,* Barrio Cooper 3, specializes in grills. Excellent food. **Los Patos,** *moderate,* located at Km 2 on highway to Cochabamba (22373). Good duck and beef dishes. **Don Miguel,** *moderate,* on Av. Uruguay, has some of the best beef in town. **Restaurant Nagasaki,** *moderate,* Calle Ingavi 290 (40238), serves Japanese and continental cuisine. **La Pascana,** open-air snack-shop on the main square. **La Buena Mesa,** *moderate,* Cristobal de Mendoza 583 (31284), has good beef dishes. **El Carruaje,** *moderate,* Av. Mutualista next to Grigota movie theater, good service. **El Boliche Creperia,** *moderate,* Calle Beni 222, has excellent crêpes.

TOURIST INFORMATION. Tourist information center at Calle René Moreno 215, corner with Suárez de Figueroa (48644). Travel agencies include: **Condor S.R.L.,** Plaza 24 de Septiembre: **Sudamer Tours,** Plaza 24 de Septiembre; **Tajibos Tours,** Hotel Los Tajibos. Hunting, fishing and safari trips organized at **El Aventurero,** on Calle Libertad 360 (26763). **Airport Information** (181).

SHOPPING. Santa Cruz artisans produce fine handicrafts in wood, ceramics, leather, cotton and straw. For some of the best handicrafts to be found in Bolivia, be sure to visit CIDAC, a cooperative of Santa Cruz artisans that produces export quality ceramics, weavings, and hammocks. If you have time, arrange a visit to a workshop located at Calle Ignacio Salvatierra 407. Try shopping at **Artesanía Boliviana,** Calle Ballivián 17; **Artesanía Inka Products,** Av. Cañoto corner of Landivar; **Artesanía Mon-Atelier, Calle René Moreno 18;** and **Artesanías Nacionales,** Calle Sucre 40.

NIGHTLIFE. Mau Mau, open only during Carnival. Twelve thousand spectators gather for the queen's coronation and shows. Calle 21 de Mayo corner with Andres Ibanes (21867 or 31687). For a drink, **Doña Icha,** bar, on Calle René Moreno 230. **La Cueva del Ratón,** Calle Velasco y La Riva, a hangout for youths. **Tiberio,** Calle Independencia y La Riva, luxury bar. **Paladium,** piano bar and dancing, on Av. Monseñor Santistevan 180. **Mauna Loa,** 3r anillo, entre Av. Paraguazy y Av. Mutualista, for an elegant variety show.

RADIO TAXIS. Cañoto (51320) or Taxi amarillo (33333) have a fleet of taxis.

TRINIDAD AND THE BENI DEPARTMENT

Trinidad, a tropical city of 50,200 established by the Jesuits in the late seventeenth century, is what Santa Cruz was like twenty years ago. Most of the streets are still unpaved, and horses and carts are still a favorite way to travel.

Traditionally, Trinidad has been the center of Bolivia's cattle industry. Cattle were introduced by the Jesuits in 1675. Horses followed, and *beni-anos,* as residents of the Beni are known, became expert horsemen. The Beni is largely made up of fertile grasslands that provide a natural breeding ground for cattle. In recent years farmers using the latest in agricultural technology have diversified into rice farming. Beef is flown from the Beni to La Paz and mining centers on World War II vintage planes. Pilots who fly across the Andes—often without radar—are considered among the best—if not the craziest-in the world.

In many regions of the Beni, indigenous native groups survive as farmers, ranch hands, and artisans. Yucca, rice, bananas, cotton, and sweet potatoes are the most popular crops in the Beni.

Trinidad and the Beni are worth visiting if you are interested in adventure and a change of pace. While Trinidad has excellent hotel accommodations, the rest of the Beni department lacks modern-day comforts—save for some exceptions. Rurrenabaque, for example, is a small village at the western end of the Beni department. Recently the five-star **Tacuara Hostel** has been opened: ideal for its excellent accommodations and beautiful surroundings.

The Beni elite used to send their children to study in Brazil and Europe. Area residents identified more with Brazil and Europe due to the Andes, which separates the region from La Paz and the Bolivian highlands. Today, regular flights and a road usable only during the dry season are opening up the area to tens of thousands of highland settlers.

PRACTICAL INFORMATION FOR TRINIDAD

TOURIST INFORMATION. Prefectural building on Plaza José Ballivián.

SHOPPING. For traditional Beni masks and handicrafts, visit a small shop that faces the cemetery. Also, be sure to try the locally made chocolate bars that make fabulous hot chocolate.

HOTELS. Hotel Ganadero, *moderate-expensive* (21099). This is a modern hotel with a rooftop pool and a view of the tropical city of Trinidad and outlying lowlands. Also recommended in **La Poza del Bato,** a motel-type lodging near the city square. For *inexpensive* lodging, **Hotel Avenida,** Av. 6 de Agosto (20044); **Hotel Bajío,** Calle Nicolás Suárez (20203); and **Hotel Monte Verde,** Av. 6 de Agosto 725 (22750).

RESTAURANTS. Hotel Ganadero offers restaurant (Continental menu) and bar service. **Restaurant Carlitos,** Plaza Ballivián, offers a varied menu. Excellent Beni beef at **El Canchón de Mamita,** Av. Sucre; **Pacumuto,** Calle Nicolás Suárez; and **La Estancia,** Av. Pedro Muiba. Excellent fresh fish and rustic outdoor restaurants can be found on the Mamoré river banks, a few miles from the city. Check with the tourist information center.

BRAZIL

Colossus of the Continent

by
JOANNA BERKMAN and EDWIN TAYLOR

Joanna Berkman, a Boston-based freelance writer, has been a reporter for the Boston Herald, *a social science researcher for Abt Associates in Cambridge, and has taught in the Expository Writing Program at Harvard. She studied Portuguese language and culture at the University of Lisbon and has lived in and written about Brazil.*

Edwin Taylor is an American journalist with more than ten years of experience writing on Brazil. A resident of Rio de Janeiro, Taylor is the editor and publisher of Brasilinform, an English-language information service on Brazil which publishes newsletters. He is also editor of Brazil Travel Update, *the only English-language newsletter on the Brazilian travel trade.*

Brazil is so big and covers so many square miles through all sorts of terrain that it is impossible to make generalizations about what is "typically" Brazilian. From the pine forests and frosts of the south to the steamy cities along the Equator, Brazil is a study in extremes and contrasts.

Because of its peculiar combination of wealth and industrial might in the south, Third World poverty and hunger in the northeast, urban wealth and sophistication in São Paulo and Rio de Janeiro, wildlife preserves in the Pantanal, and aboriginal tribes in the Amazon territories and interior,

177

the Brazilian cultural continuum includes the polar opposites of the societal spectrum, as well as every variation in between.

The struggle between development and conservation, progress and preservation of the past, national pride and openness to the contributions of other countries, is played out here in plain view. The clash of opposites is manifested in almost every phase of life. The Pantanal and the Amazon, acknowledged universally as great natural storehouses of flora and fauna, must contend with the mining and agricultural interests that would deplete or destroy these very resources. Brazilians decry the cultural imperialism of the United States and the power of the International Monetary Fund, yet they listen to American music almost more avidly than to their own and English terms pepper their Portuguese as symbols of imported ideas. Women are beginning to move into the work force and find their own identity outside of traditional roles, yet men are still strongly macho.

Accompanying these modern dilemmas is the romance of the pioneer: Brazil still has a sense of its own frontier because the largely undeveloped interior still *is* a frontier, a kind of continental Alaska within everyone's reach. A new wave of Gold Rush fever has struck, sending thousands of prospectors into the jungle to gamble on striking it rich. Undiscovered Indian tribes and unexplored territory exist to a degree now unimaginable in the United States or Europe.

At the social level, destitute urban slums called "favelas" grow up right next to the most luxurious mansions. Wealthy socialites and movie stars rub elbows with their maids and workers during lavish Carnival parades where everyone participates equally in the magic. Yet, in practical terms, the great divide between rich and poor remains as unbridgeable as ever and Brazil continues to be a nation with very few "haves" and countless "have nots."

These extremes are perhaps the only constants in a nation of coexisting inconsistencies. Regional differences remain profound, providing a set of internal subcultures that with time will no doubt be lost to interstate highways, shopping malls, chain restaurants, and national media. The forces of modernization are hard at work in Brazil, but they must resist the powerful pull of the past and so haven't progressed as far as they have elsewhere. The distinctions and distinctiveness of Brazil still endure.

A Glance at Brazil's History

Brazil was discovered in 1500, just eight years after America. How Columbus missed this giant of the Western Hemisphere and touched down upon little San Salvador remains one of the mysteries of that era. Spain was badly in need of new territories and when they put all their money on Columbus they made a mistake, for Portugal was also in need and backed a sea captain named Pedro Alvares Cabral. The Portuguese king was in a landgrab race for the new colonies with the Spanish rulers, and both of them wanted as much as they could get in the shortest amount of time. There were great things coming out of India that could be sold to fill the royal coffers, later to be converted into ships and arms and manpower to dash across the seas again and grab more land.

When Cabral sighted Brazil he thought that he was seeing India, but upon landing and finding none of the expected Maharajas or a road clearly marked "Cathay," he reasoned that he had discovered someplace new. He thought it was an island and sent out a search party to walk around once and come back again. What Cabral had stumbled upon was, of course, not an island, but the biggest hunk of land to be claimed in the entire New World.

The Tupi natives were friendly, much to everyone's surprise and pleasure; and after celebrating Mass, Cabral left a few men to watch his new country and then hurried back to Portugal.

The Portuguese referred to the new colony as "The Island of Santa Cruz" (Holy Cross); later when their error was discovered they called the new colony "Land of Santa Cruz." But with the coming of merchant ships from the mother country and the vast exporting of a hard wood called "brazil," the people of Portugal began to refer to the place as "The Land of Brazil." From there it was an easy step to calling it simply Brazil.

The Portuguese were interested in trade, and the long coastal lands of their new-found colony were richer agriculturally than anything the Spanish had been able to claim.

Farmers arrived from Portugal to set up huge sugar and spice farms. They plowed from the present-day city of Olinda down almost to Rio. The land was rich, the nights cool, and there was lots of elbow room. But workers were scarce, and imitating their Spanish enemies, they set out to enslave the local Indians.

The natives—there were many different tribes which were being lumped together under the heading "Indian"—were not accustomed to toiling long, hot afternoons in cane or cotton fields and died off rapidly. Some escaped enslavement by fleeing deeper into the jungle. Later, slaves from the bulge of west Africa were brought in. Swooping down along the Guinea coast and as far south as Angola, Portuguese slave traders attacked villages, killed off the weak, and shackled the strong. The trip to Brazil was long and rough and many died on the way, but those that managed to survive the voyage were brave, hardy, and resourceful.

Soon great wealth was flowing to Lisbon, and the Royal coffers were expanding from the raw materials the Portuguese traded with the rest of Europe. So envious were the other land-hungry nations of the era that the Dutch, French, and Spanish all tried to encroach on Portugal's claim. Much of her new wealth was spent in keeping the intruders at bay.

While riches were being reaped from the soil in the northeast, other riches were being dug up in the mountains to the south. No sooner had the present site of Rio de Janeiro been put on the map than thousands of fortune hunters poured through it on the way to the mines of Minas Gerais. Here were what seemed like entire mountains of amethysts, aquamarines, and diamonds waiting to be scooped up. A procession of miners and trouble-makers took over an area many times bigger than Alaska. Wealth made them remember how the nobility had lived back home, and as soon as a miner had enough to live, he wanted to live well. By the boat loads from Portugal came carpenters, stonemasons, sculptors, and painters to build churches, palaces, and cities in the Brazilian wilderness. Up went such architectural treasures as Ouro Petro and Diamantina. There were gas lights and golden horse-drawn coaches in the streets and gem-studded, silver ornaments in the churches. Lace came from Europe to adorn milord's cuffs, and actors and musicians brave enough to make the trip from Portugal had diamonds tossed to them after their performances.

Other men were busy too. A hardy group of adventurous, blood-thirsty crusaders banded together near what is now São Paulo and set out to find more diamond mines and more riches. Carrying the flag of the new colony, these "Bandeirantes" (Flag Bearers) pushed out in all directions, claiming each new step for Portugal. There had been a treaty of Tordesillas signed between Portugal and Spain in the year 1494. It was the idea of Pope Alexander VI, who wanted as little blood spilled in the New World as possible. Both sides agreed to the dividing of the southern continent in a straight line from what is now Belém on the Amazon River to a little east of Porto

Alegre. Everything to the west belonged to Spain, everything to the east to Portugal.

Fortunately for modern Brazil the Bandeirantes knew nothing of this treaty, didn't care, or didn't have a compass. For they spread out over thousands of miles, planting their banner on the banks of the Amazon to the north, Paraná to the south, and on the Paraguayan and Bolivian frontiers to the west. Spaniards, so busy with wars with the Indians, hadn't any idea what was going on in the heart of their lands. When they finally woke up it was too late, for the Bandeirantes had claimed it all for Portugal.

Brazil was ruled from afar by Portugal for many years. When Napoleon captured Portugal, the royal family fled to the new colony. It was like a shot in the arm for the New World. At once the exiled royal family opened the ports of Brazil to trade with some European nations, especially with Napoleon's enemy, England. When the French were defeated, the king, Dom Joao VI, went back to Portugal and left his young son Pedro I to govern. But Pedro had ideas of his own and did away with a number of reforms his father had set up. He proclaimed Brazil's independence on Sept. 7, 1822. As a new nation, Brazil had a long way to go and a lot to learn. So unsure was the nation and so ineptly governed, that after a series of costly wars with Argentina and Uruguay, Dom Pedro I stepped aside in favor of his son Pedro II, who was only five years old. A series of regents then came into power that managed so badly parliament finally decreed Dom Pedro II "of age" when he was just 14.

Then came almost a half century of peaceful and fruitful ruling on the part of the Western Hemisphere's only Emperor (if you don't count the short reign of Maximilian in Mexico), who mingled with his subjects, made a trip to the United States, and declared that he would rather have been a school teacher than an emperor. Under his constant vigilance the nation prospered, trade agreements were signed, an attempt by Argentina to take control was put down. Princesa Isabel freed the slaves on May 13, 1888 by signing the "Lei Auréa," Brazil's Emancipation Proclamation. But a democratic movement was brewing in the military, and in spite of progress and prosperity the army took over and banished Pedro and his royal family back to Portugal. On November 15, 1889, the Republic was born.

Thereafter Brazilian history grows dull with the parade of easily forgettable presidents and minor revolutionaries. There were all sorts of problems that needed to be solved, and very few able men around to solve them. Brazil stuck mostly to what the U.S. was doing politically, while staying close to France for its cultural instruction. Politicians made a number of efforts to gain power at the expense of the nation but the proud giant, in spite of them, kept growing.

Brazil has had very few actual internal wars and has never had a real, bloody revolution à la Spanish-American style. There have been some skirmishes among the gauchos in the south, and once in 1932 the state of São Paulo took on the rest of the nation. It lost.

Getulio Vargas was a strongman who took over in a military coup in 1930. The country was horrified, but soon liked the idea of having one man in charge and did very little except grumble against him. When he was deposed by another military coup in 1945 he sat out his exile on his home ranch in Rio Grande do Sul and prepared for the elections. In 1951 he was elected—legally this time—president of the Republic and right beside him rode his protegé Joao "Jango" Goulart, later to govern the nation. Vargas tried to be more democratic this second time around and supported labor unions and the like, but still that old obstacle, the Latin military, was against him. After a long period of interoffice fights and counter charges, the tired old man put a pistol to his heart and pulled the trigger.

After him came President Café Filho, and then the dynamic spendthrift Juscelino Kubitschek. Kubitschek built Brasilia from a dream into a multimillion dollar reality and put industry and commerce on a fast pace to compete with the rest of the world.

His immediate successor was Janio Quadros, a thin man with a thick moustache who insisted that everything be done exactly his way. He wrote little notes that became law, and tried to squeeze the growing giant of a nation into a special form that he never quite defined. Under some pressure, he suddenly resigned one day in August 1961 and threw the nation as close to a civil war as it has ever come.

The successor to Quadros was leftist-leaning, rabble-rousing Jango Goulart, the old pupil and confidant of Dictator Vargas. The military wanted little of Jango and his friends, and above all did not want the plans and mass platitudes of Vargas back again. In a dramatic ten days, the military kept Jango—on his way home from a trip to Red China when Quadros resigned—out of the capital and virtually a prisoner in his home state of Rio Grande do Sul. Congress hastily voted in a Parliamentary system, drastically curtailing the President's powers, and Jango finally took office, managing to persuade the people to vote the old presidential system back the following year.

Under Goulart the country seethed with strikes and instability. Prices soared to an all-time high and red-tinged politicians were appointed to key positions all over the nation. Goulart himself became swayed by ambitious leftists and many Brazilians feared for their country as never before. Then on March 31, 1964, Goulart was overthrown by the military. As before, the revolt was virtually bloodless, and while Goulart and his family fled into exile in Uruguay, where he died in 1977, the army clamped down and installed one of their own men, General Humberto de Alencar Castello Branco, as president. Again, Brazil had a military government, but this one was different. The Army seized Brazil by the scruff of its neck and shook it—hard. Sweeping reforms paid dividends as inflation began to drop, exports to rise, and overall growth to move out of the red where Jango had left it to a steady 10 percent within 5 years. Hundreds of old-time politicians lost their political rights, and two new parties replaced the countless former ones. In 1967, Castello Branco handed over the presidency to Marshal Costa e Silva, who closed Congress and made things difficult for dissident students and labor leaders. Upon his death in 1969 he was replaced by General Emilio Garrastazu Médici, who continued the Army's reform policy, strengthened the economy, waged war on illiteracy, and initiated bold development plans for the Northeast and Amazon regions.

Médici was succeeded in 1975 by retired General Ernesto Geisel, son of German immigrants and Brazil's first Protestant president. Geisel, who was previously head of the state petroleum enterprise, Petrobrás, maintained most of the policies that brought about Brazil's "economic miracle" and at the same time tried to bring more political liberty and an equitable distribution of wealth. But the petroleum crisis caused problems, and the country's growth slowed from 9.2 percent in 1976 to about 6 percent in 1977 as his government took anti-inflationary measures.

The next president of Brazil, João Figueiredo, a former army general chosen by the military to succeed Geisel, vowed to return the nation to democracy. After taking office in 1979, Figueiredo took the country a long way toward realizing that goal. Press censorship ended, political prisoners were released, and exiles living abroad were able to return without facing arrest or harassment.

Inflation during the Figueiredo government soared, however, hitting 110 percent in 1980.This sudden upward surge forced the Brazilian government to take strong anti-inflationary measures in 1981, which, together with the general economic recession in the western world, produced the country's first negative growth since World War II.

In January, 1985, Tancredo Neves was chosen to be President by the Electoral College, made up of Congress and representatives from state legislatures. Although this was not a direct election by the public, Neves is generally regarded as having been the first popularly elected president following the 1964–1985 military regime because he took his campaign to the people and conducted it as if it *were* a direct election.

A man of advanced age and failing health, Neves fell ill and died before he could take office. After a great outpouring of grief, the nation consolidated behind José Sarney, who assumed the presidency in Neves' stead. The Sarney government, however, was marked by runaway inflation that culminated with a record 1,764 percent in 1989. The government attempted to bring inflation under control with three separate economic programs, each accompanied by a price freeze. Twice the currency was substituted; all, however, to no avail. In December, 1989, Brazilians went to the polls to vote in the first popular presidential election since 1960. The winner was Fernando Collor de Mello, at 40 the youngest president in Brazil's history.

Upon taking office in March 1990, the dynamic Collor instituted the most wide ranging economic reform program in Brazil's history. Inspired by the economic model of the United States, Collor eliminated protectionist barriers and opened Brazil to imports. He ended government price and salary controls, deregulated the economy, and liberalized the exchange policy. The Collor government also instituted Brazil's third monetary reform in five years, replacing the *cruzado novo* with the *cruzeiro*. In his most controversial measure, Collor froze some $40 billion of the assets of companies and the middle class. These funds were placed in blocked accounts to be returned to their owners over a 12-month period starting in September 1991. Through these measures, Collor was able to lower inflation from a peak of 84 percent in March 1990, to 15 percent per month by the end of 1990. At the same time, however, the government's tight money policy pushed the economy into recession.

Brazil Today

When you stop and remember that most Brazilians in the cities have an education that goes only to the eighth grade and that many in the interior who have but three or four years of schooling are considered "educated," you will marvel that anything has been done to improve the country at all.

In spite of these problems, Brazil is making giant strides into the industrialized world. Already its economy ranks as the tenth largest in the world, its gross national product is twice that of Mexico, and Brazilian exports sell so well abroad that they now bring an annual positive trade balance to the country.

Brazil has shown more gains in manufacturing, exports, agricultural, and educational improvements than any other nation in Latin America. Although the desire to put everything off until tomorrow and go to the beach today is always strong, there are many who are doing things for their country.

The population of greater São Paulo is now over 14 million and Rio has around 8 million inhabitants. Industrially speaking, São Paulo is now the heartbeat of the Latin American economy. It has few unemployed, and an intelligent system of social services and public improvements. Across the nation highways are being cut through jungles and over mountains. Twenty-five years ago the road between the two cities was unpaved and impassable during the rainy season. Today there is a double-lane toll freeway, partly financed by U.S. aid. But although highway construction has been a top priority of all post-1964 governments, there are still only about 50,000 miles of paved highway in the whole country, little more than the U.S. had in 1840.

For its manufacturing, Brazil needs power and lots of it. In the past few years the country has been building huge plants in the Paraná River area to service São Paulo, one in the interior of Minas Gerais and two others in the northeast. The mighty Itaipu project, built in partnership with Paraguay, was inaugurated in 1982 and is the largest hydroelectric power plant in the world. Brazil also has its first nuclear power plant operating near Angra dos Reis between São Paulo and Rio. With this energy, Brazil manufactures enough plastics, textiles, automobiles, toys, canned foods, cement, and chemicals to satisfy the home consumer without importing. But some wheat, rubber, petroleum, paper, and machinery for both light and heavy industry must be imported. Economists predict, however, a likelihood of the country becoming self-sufficient in food and many other critical resources in the near future. Brazil hopes enough oil will be discovered offshore to bring self-sufficiency in that area too. Recent discoveries indicate that this once-distant goal may be reached by the end of the century, freeing Brazil from its costly dependency on imported oil.

With respect to health, the government has been busy with the eradication of malaria, yellow fever, denguê, and other mosquito-borne diseases. Efforts have been concentrated in Belém and Manaus to stamp out the dreaded Chagas disease that comes from the bite of little beetles. The Butantan Snake Farm in São Paulo has been doing great work with venoms from snakes, spiders, and scorpions making antidotes for the bites and supplying them free of charge to doctors and interior clinics. Hospitals are being built all over the nation, but the problem of persuading doctors and nurses to leave the big cities to staff them remains. Almost every town has a free clinic that is open day and night for anyone who needs attention; they do everything from setting broken legs to delivering babies.

Many efforts have been made in recent years to update the country's education system on all levels, starting with a nationwide literacy campaign and ending with university reforms. Secondary education has been restructured to stress the practical arts and sciences more heavily than preparation for university; previously, the system turned out a huge surplus of poets and politicians, but too few plumbers, scientists, and computer programmers.

Geographically Speaking

People get set ideas of Brazil's geography either from seeing too many picture postcards or remembering too many Hollywood films. Actually a great part of this enormous nation consists of hilly uplands, plateaus, and low mountains. There is a vast plain that stretches far into the Amazon region and another that spreads out through Mato Grosso and into Bolivia and Paraguay. The Brazilian highlands are some of the oldest geological formations anywhere on earth. These hills are granite and other tough stones that are heavily veined with gold, diamonds, and a variety of semiprecious stones. The Serra do Espinhaço (Spiny Mountains) that run from northern Minas Gerais to Bahia also contain iron ore, gold, and manganese. Here the highest mountain in central Brazil can be found, old Pico da Bandeira (Flag Top), which stands 9,482 feet. Another recently discovered peak in the state of Amazonas is even higher—Neblina (Haze) reaching 9,889 feet. One of the world's largest lava plateaus is to be found in the south of Brazil; termed the Paraná plateau; it is covered with dark, purple-colored soil that is excellent for raising coffee. Along the coast rich deposits of oil have been found.

The eastern side of the Brazilian highland descends abruptly into the sea and has been given the name "The Great Escarpment." There is no coastal plain but a sloping series of steppes that continues far out into the water. All along this there is a series of small rivers and sandy beaches. Wide expanses of white sand reach from way above Recife down past the Uruguayan border. Some beautiful, unspoiled beaches can be found in the far north and the far south. The sands in the states of Paraná and Santa Catarina, for example, are solid and pure. The lack of tourists and year-round dwellers keeps them that way. This combination of sand and escarpment has given Brazil some of the finest natural harbors in the world. Rio is perhaps the best known, but the harbors at Santos, Bahia, Recife, São Luiz, Vitória, and Ilhéus have contributed greatly to the wealth of the nation.

Brazil's rivers are some of the longest and deepest in the world. For scientific study, they've been broken into the three major systems that drain the country's highlands. The first, in the north, is the mighty, almost unbelievable Amazon River, fed by the waters that pour down through jagged peaks, lush jungles, and rich plateaus. Its tributaries sound and look exotic and offer the visitor who is not afraid of discomfort some of the most unforgettable experiences in Latin America. There the great Tocantins and the Araguaia flow. There are the mysterious and unexplored Xingu, the rubber-laden Tapajós and the Madeira. To the far west runs the impressive, and almost unknown, Rio Negro.

The second river system gathers the waters from southwestern Minas Gerais and empties them into the placid yet treacherous Paraná. The water on the western slope of the São Paulo Escarpment flows until it reaches the sea by joining the Rio de la Plata near Buenos Aires.

The almost legendary São Francisco, the largest river wholly within Brazil, is the third system. Beginning in the plateau near Brasilia it flows northward for over a thousand miles until it pours into the sea between the states of Sergipe and Alagoas. Navigable and studded with power plants, the São Francisco has been the main artery to the heart of Brazil for generations.

The vegetation in Brazil varies according to climate and geological conditions. In the Amazon Basin and places along the coast where the rainfall is very heavy, there is a tropical rain forest where broadleafed trees and shrubs grow to gigantic proportions and as many as 3,000 different species of trees have been catalogued within a single square mile. Through these tall shady trees very little sunlight manages to filter down, and consequently the ground is rich in decaying foliage, industrious bugs, and small animals. In the northeast, lack of rain has produced a parched desert of hundreds of square miles, where cattle and humans die together in their search for water. In the south huge stands of pine trees grow wild and are used in the manufacture of paper. There are open prairies that start in São Paulo state and run down into Argentina to form the Brazilian pampas. In the northeast rain forests stand the huge jacaranda trees and the very wood that gave the nation its name, the Brazil tree. The jacaranda is a hard, beautifully grained dark wood almost like mahogany. Most of the fine colonial furniture in the antique shops was made from this wood. Durable yet attractive, it is one of the most sought-after materials in use today.

Sugar, Rubber, and Coffee

That a country as big as Brazil used to be a "one crop" country has always amazed outsiders. "Banana Republics" are usually small islands, not nations as large as the continental United States. Yet until recently, when industrialization diversified the country's economic base, Brazil's entire economy rested on a series of agricultural products the way the American South relied on "King Cotton" before the Civil War.

First there was sugar. It was the earliest crop established on the new lands. The Portuguese crown eagerly awaited the money that sugar gave to the Royal coffers. The climate along the coast, from far below Bahia to way above Recife, was perfect for its growth. It was hot and muggy with abundant rainfall. It added to the nation's prosperity, population, and culture. Then other empire builders like Great Britain and France began to plant and sell sugar on the world market. The Brazilians had to lower their prices and improve their quality to meet the competition. But the English-speaking and the French-speaking peoples preferred their own sugar, put high tariffs on the Brazilian product and almost drove it completely out of competition.

Fortunately rubber was just coming into its own in the Amazon. There were all sorts of uses for rubber in the United States and in Europe. Once it had been discovered that rubber could be vulcanized for longer lasting and more efficient service, there was almost no industry that didn't want and need Brazil's crop. The town of Manaus in the heart of the Amazonian jungle grew to international importance. Jenny Lind came to sing there in a lavish opera house, one of several monumental buildings constructed during the boom years. Supporting all this luxury were thousands of Indian, black, and white day laborers, working deep in the malarial jungles under slavelike conditions. The rubber trees grew wild and had to be worked where they were found. Planting them according to then-popular agricultural precepts produced no rubber at all. Then an Englishman visited the interior and smuggled out a few hundred rubber seeds which he took to Indonesia and cultivated. There the trees flourished, and in seven years Indonesia was competing with Brazil. The Brazilians, proud and overly sure of themselves, refused to lower their prices to meet the new competition. Buyers flocked to Indonesia and almost overnight Brazil was driven out of the rubber market.

The next crop to rise to importance was coffee, first in the State of Rio de Janeiro, then in São Paulo. Coffee had become an important cash crop in southern Brazil, and with rubber out of the way, all energy was devoted to increasing coffee production. São Paulo had the ideal climate of chilly weather followed by warm and rainy days. There was fertile land that was more European in makeup than in Bahia or other places. There was also the added advantage of Italian and German immigrants who wanted to be farmers and raise a cash crop. With everything working smoothly, coffee soon became the most important national product and Brazil depended heavily on it.

Coffee actually built the gigantic industrial city of São Paulo. With the money the growers got from the exports and the taxes the state got from the growers, new industries were started and new ideas tried. There were even many small industries that sprang from the by-products of coffee. The protein in coffee is used to modify certain oils and tars. The carbohydrates are used in the making of cellulose, dyestuffs, and plastics. The coffee bean oil is used in dozens of varied industries. While production has increased elsewhere, particularly in Africa, Brazil remains the world's biggest coffee grower. Surpluses have disappeared, due in part to controls imposed by the International Coffee Agreement.

The Brazilian Heritage

The people of Brazil are a symphony in colors. There are few other nations on earth where such a wide spread of skin tones from whitest white to yellow to tan to deepest black are all grouped under one nationality.

Brazil has long been praised for its alleged lack of discrimination and overt racial prejudice. Although a "black revolution" like that in the United States is unlikely to occur in Brazil, the surface calm is deceptive. There is no discernible feeling of unity among Brazilian blacks or between blacks and mulattoes similar to the organizations of Afro-Americans that brought about the far-reaching social reforms in the U.S. over the past 20 years. There are few, if any, black or mulatto diplomats, judges, or ranking government officials, very few physicians, dentists, college professors, lawyers, or ranking officers in the armed services. In the latter case, a large proportion of enlisted men are black or mulatto but they are commanded by whites.

The mixture that makes up Brazilians began way back in the colonial days when the first Portuguese sailors were left to manage the new land. From the beginning, Portuguese migration to Brazil was almost entirely male. Unlike the British, who migrated to the new world in families, the Portuguese colonizers were men who arrived alone, a situation which encouraged unbridled sexual license, ranging from seduction to rape, first of Indian women and later of African women brought to Brazil as slaves. Miscegenation and cohabitation between white men and women of other races was always practiced openly, and such unions naturally produced children, who, in turn, mated and produced their own offspring. Eventually, both the Catholic Church and the Crown urged such couples to marry. Thus were born the Brazilian people.

In the old plantation houses, it was quite common for the master of the house to have a white wife and a series of slave concubines. All sets of children would be raised together, until the arrival of adolescence and the assumption of adult roles put everyone in their proper places.

Under a benevolent master, a baby of color might be looked upon as an heir by his white father, who might free the mother and allow the son to learn and practice a trade. The father knew that the mother would stay on and work for him and that she needed a place to rear her child, there being no other real alternative for her. After a certain point in the movement toward Abolition, the wombs of slave women were freed (that is, children born to them were free), but the mothers themselves were still considered slaves. There were times when a mulatto son turned out to be smarter, more gifted, or better loved than the master's white sons, and might even be allowed to inherit a share of the plantation upon his father's death. But while acts of munificence like this were thinkable and doable, they should not be wrongly construed. Slavery in Brazil was still a cruel institution, and its legacy continues.

So does the old pattern of interracial and sexual relations. Today, while urban forces are changing many backwoods customs, women are still relatively powerless within the society. White men are frequently paired with women of color, but open liaisons between white women and blacks or mulattoes are rarer and meet with considerable disapproval due to the class differential correlating with race.

Indians and Immigrants

In the center of Mato Grosso and in the Amazonian states, tribes still roam along the watersheds and the deep jungles exactly as they did thousands of years ago. Very little is known of their origins. They seem to have none of the ability that the Indians of Peru or Mexico had in pottery or painting but bear remarkable resemblance to the tall proud Polynesians. Theories abound as to their origin, many people having the idea that they drifted over the Andes from Peru about the same time that other Peruvian Indians were taking boats for the South Seas. Others say they were always in the heart of the jungle and have been flushed out because of the scientific light of the 20th century. Still others hold them as remnants of the original peoples from the lost continent of Atlantis. Whoever they are, and wherever they came from, they make up one of the most interesting segments of the Brazilian population.

Unfortunately, the Brazilian Indian has suffered largely the same fate as has his U.S. and Canadian cousin in being pushed back constantly and falling ready victim to European avarice and disease. Like an endangered species, the natives have been driven from their natural habitat by the encroachment of "civilization." Some die, some opt to enter the mainstream of Brazilian culture, but either way, experts predict their time is limited and they will soon be extinct.

Immigrants make up a large percentage of Brazil's populace. And once they have become established they are considered Brazilian and no longer as "foreigners." Of all countries, Portugal still sends the most immigrants per year. There are a great number of Italians (especially in the industrial São Paulo area) and many Germans and Poles in the rich agricultural south. A very important group of immigrants to Brazil are the Japanese. Many of them came before World War II, and a great many more followed. Because of special treaties signed between Brazil and Japan, they were given land, special farming equipment, and special considerations. What they have managed to do with the land, especially in the Amazon area where they've filled local markets with fruits and vegetables hitherto unknown, is truly impressive.

All of these races and nationalities have managed to get mixed together in Brazil's melting pot, and there is a beneficial national trait of "live and let live" that is commendable. You are unlikely to find people attacking or killing others for purely racial motives. Racial hatred, per se, is difficult to maintain in a nation of mixed genetic inheritance. At the same time, wealth correlates positively with whiteness, resulting in resentments born of economic causes. Although Brazilians do not call this de facto discrimination "racism," there is much tension beneath the friendly surface.

Catholicism and the Church of the Spirits

Brazil is officially a Roman Catholic country. The Holy See in the Vatican likes to boast that it is the "largest Catholic country in the world," and at first glance it may appear to be, for there are beautiful churches and cathedrals ranging from the colonial to the baroque and modern all over the nation. The church owns huge parcels of choice lands in Rio and São Paulo; and in interior towns long-robed fathers and nuns can be seen everywhere. When a president takes the oath of office there is always a priest and a Bible close at hand. Children study catechism, are baptized with the names of saints, and attend Catholic schools. Everybody wears a religious medal or two. Taxi and bus drivers have prints of St. Christopher prominently placed, and in June the two biggest winter celebrations are reserved for St. John and St. Peter. To the tourist, overcome with the gold and gems of Bahia's São Francisco church or the impressive concrete modernism of the cathedral designed by Oscar Niemeyer in Brasilia, Catholicism and allegiance to Rome seem to be everywhere. Actually, much of this is on the surface. The real church for masses of Brazilians is the church of the spirits.

The Portuguese brought their religion all ready made to the new colony and planted it right along with the rows of cotton and sugar cane. The Indians had their own gods whom they worshipped and, even when driven into slavery, refused to relinquish. When the African blacks were beaten and chained aboard stinking slave ships bound for the new world, they may have been forced to leave their families and their possessions behind, but they brought along their gods.

Foremost among them was Iemanjá who was the goddess of the rivers and water. There was also Oxalá who was the god of procreation and harvest. Exú was a wicked spirit who could cause mischief or death. There were others of lesser rank, but all powerful, like Ogun, Oxôssi, Xangó, and Yansan. They arrived in Brazil together with the slaves who, when things were going badly, turned to the gods of their homeland.

The Catholic Church was naturally against this, threatened excommunication to the whites who did not control their slaves' religious practices, and threatened corporal punishment to the slaves themselves if they continued to believe in their old gods. The slaves, most of whom came from the very best and aristocratic native tribes, were smart enough to realize they couldn't fight the priests but would have to compromise. So they took on all the ritual of Rome but didn't take their old gods from the high places.

Many times all they did was give the African god a new Christian name. Thus Iemanjá became the Virgin Mary and was queen of the heavens as well as queen of the seas. Oxalá, already most powerful in Africa, became the most powerful in Rome, Jesus Christ. Exú, full of evil to begin with, became Satan. Ogun became St. Anthony, Obaluayê became St. Francis, Yansan, St. Barbara, and Oxôssi was turned into St. George. On their altars, along with the sacred white feathers, the magical beads and the bowls of cooked rice and cornmeal, were placed plaster statues of the Virgin, Christ, and gleaming crosses. The Roman Church was content to let matters lie, hoping for an eventual dying off of African tradition over the years and a strengthening of Christian beliefs—which hasn't been the case.

Bahia is still the stronghold of the voodoo religion, which they prefer to call "Candomblé." Rio holds second place with its powerful "Macumba" and São Paulo is third with its spiritist doctrine called "Umbanda." Visitors to all three places—as well as almost any small town across the nation—can witness a voodoo ceremony. All it takes is an arrangement with someone who knows the right time and place, and the patience and good manners to sit through the ceremony once you get there.

Rites on the Beach

There is no stranger or more pagan sight in all Latin America than that which takes place on the sands of Copacabana Beach each new Year's Eve, a ceremony that is enacted on every beach along Brazil's extensive coastline. Travelers who have seen things all over the world still stare at this with fascination and disbelief. For under the warm, tropical sky and with the tall modern apartment buildings for a background, literally thousands of voodoo worshippers meet to pay homage to Iemanjá, the goddess of the sea.

The end of the old year is a time for thanksgiving and the beginning of a new year is the time to ask for the things that will make you happy for the next twelve months. From all over the city stream the faithful, determined to start the new year off right. They are of all ages, both sexes, and all colors and economic brackets. Armed with fresh flowers, candles, and *cachaça* (sugarcane alcohol), they invade the beach around ten P.M. and get ready for the stroke of midnight. Some draw mystic signs in the sand. Others lay out a white tablecloth loaded with the gifts that a proud, beautiful woman would like to receive. There are combs, mirrors, lipsticks, hair ribbons, perfumes, and wines. Around this offering they set a chain of lit candles and chant and sing over it. Some of them bring bouquets of flowers with notes asking for special favors tucked in among the blossoms. Even whole spiritist temples show up in full force, with their white costumes, drummers, and altars. They rope off a section of the beach, light candles, and begin to dance. Others bring a live chicken or goat that will be sacrificed to the goddess.

By 11:20 P.M. the six-kilometer-(five-mile-) long beach is a mass of white-dressed bodies and flickering candles. From a distance it looks as if it has been invaded by millions of fireflies. Amid the worshippers, the curious and the tourist may freely wander, if careful not to step on an offering or to offend the goddess in any way.

At exactly midnight, fireworks, sirens, and bells can be heard from all parts of Copacabana, Ipanema, and Leblon beaches. Now the festivity reaches its maximum. Shrieking, sobbing, and singing, the mass of humanity rushes into the water carrying the flowers and gifts for the goddess. Others stay patiently on the shore waiting for the third wave after the stroke of midnight to come up and claim their offering. Be it hypnotic suggestion or whatever, the waves suddenly seem to grow in size and come slapping onto the sand with a new fury. Once the water has carried the gift into the sea, the giver relaxes and goes home, for this means that the goddess was satisfied with the gift and has promised to grant all wishes. If the ocean should throw the offerings back, this is considered an ill omen.

Music

Brazil is one of the world's most musical countries, and talent flourishes in the tropical climate as exuberantly as the exotic creepers that grow two inches a day. Brazil is well known for having invented the samba and bossa nova, but just take a look at the list of "serious" musicians Brazil has also given the world in this century: composers Heitor Villa-Lobos, Claudio Santoro, Camargo Guarnieri, and Marlos Nobre; pianists Guiomar Novaes, Ophelia de Nascimento, Jacques Klein, Roberto Szidon, Joao Carlos Martins, and Nelson Freire; singers Bidu Sayao, Maura Moreira, Maria d'Apparecida, Joao Gibin, and Maria Lucia Godoy; guitarists Eduardo and Sergio Abreu; conductors Eleazar de Carvalho and Isaac Karabtschevsky; early music specialist Roberto de Regina and ballerina Marcia Haydée, to mention only a few.

The four musical centers of Brazil are Rio, São Paulo, Salvador, and Curitiba. Salvador has the best music school, where many rising young composers have learned their trade from a German-influenced faculty; Curitiba presents an annual music festival that puts anything similar in the rest of South America to shame, while both Rio and São Paulo offer a musical season that can match that of many a European capital in quality.

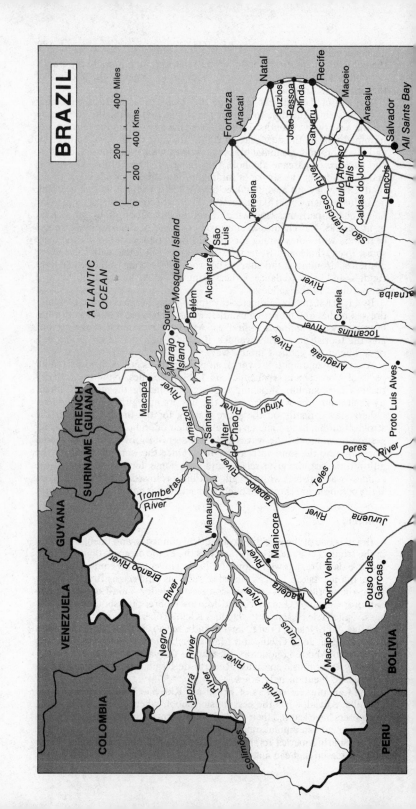

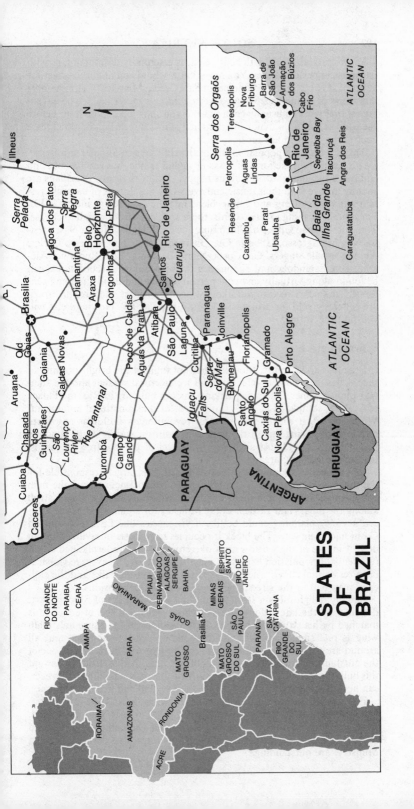

Rio's musical life, like the city itself, is essentially cosmopolitan, with fine musical performances. You never know whom you might discover for yourself at Rio's Teatro Municipal or Sala Cecilia Meireles (a rare example nowadays of a cinema's being converted into a concert hall). One advantage is that you can usually get a ticket if you show up half an hour before the concert, unless a major international star is appearing, in which case book a few days in advance.

There is also the popular music of Brazil, "musica popular brasileira" (MPB), which, in the form of bossa nova and samba, has reached out and embraced the entire world with its happy, vibrant rhythms. Brazilians are equally in love with their music and every city has dozens of bars and restaurants where drums and guitars blend into the hypnotic sounds of MPB. For tourists wishing to buy records, there are plenty from which to choose: Tom Jobim, João Gilberto, Chico Buarque de Holanda, Milton Nascimento, Ney Matagrosso, Gilberto Gil, Gaetano Veloso, and Roberto Carlos. Among female singers, Gal Costa, Maria Bethania, Elba Remalho, Alcione, Tetê Espindola, and Simone are the best-known. Record stores can be found along virtually any commercial district and in all shopping centers. If you see a record you like, ask to hear it first. Records in Brazil are generally sold for around $4.50 for a popular LP. Nowhere else will you find the variety or quality of this exciting music.

Architecture

Brazilian architecture, though it has not fulfilled the bright promise of the thirties, has much to offer both the architectural student and the amateur photographer. The most striking modern building in Rio, the Palace of Culture, completed in 1945, is now protected as a national monument. When started, it was one of the most revolutionary buildings anywhere in the world, being one of the first to be built on *pilotis*—huge concrete pillars that leave almost all the ground level of the site free for patios, plants, and parking areas.

Le Corbusier, a long-time friend of Brazil, was largely responsible for the design, ably assisted by the brilliant Brazilian Lucio Costa, the man who planned Brasilia and the Barra de Tijuca suburb of Rio. Take a stroll among the pillars and gardens of the Ministry for a glimpse of what 20th-century city planning could be like if visionaries like Le Corbusier and Costa had their way. The block it occupies is an oasis of civilized urban delight in one of the world's most overcrowded and underplanned cities. (Students of population explosion may like to study the average Copacabana residential street, where the cars park on the sidewalks and the children play ball in the street, and draw their own conclusions.)

Equally delightful is a stroll around the Rio Museum of Modern Art, designed by the late Affonso Reidy, whose exuberant use of concrete is matched by his structural daring; the whole floor of the Museum's main wing is one single slab without divisions or central supports, and all around are the splendid gardens laid out by Roberto Burle Marx, one of the outstanding landscape gardeners of our time. A disastrous fire swept this building in 1978, but it is being restored. Its artistic holdings, however, can never be replaced and it will take years to find and acquire new ones.

For architects, though, Brasilia is the real thing. Despite its many problems it is here to stay and is a truly great place to visit, wander around, and photograph. The air is fresh and unpolluted, the traffic well organized by Brazilian standards, and many of its buildings, like the new Foreign Ministry, are outstanding.

FACTS AT YOUR FINGERTIPS

WHAT IT WILL COST. For tourists, the anti-inflation program introduced in March 1990 by the government of President Fernando Collor de Mello has meant higher prices. The government's economic program included a currency reform and tight monetary controls. The new currency, the cruzeiro, was thus born in a tight money environment, which immediately increased its worth in relation to the dollar. This has meant that the previous advantage enjoyed by tourists carrying dollars has evaporated and prices have jumped in dollar terms. Top hotels in Rio and São Paulo now go for over $200 a night, double their previous rates, while in the better restaurants diners will pay up to $50 a person. Lower prices are available for both lodging and dining options but, unfortunately, as the price declines so does the quality, often sharply.

Entertainment expenses have also increased but are still not near the levels of New York or London.

You can hear a great concert for $20 or less in a large hall; clubs rarely charge more than a few dollars to get in. Shows sponsored by Funarte, Funarj, Fundação Roberto Marinho, and other arts organizations offer tickets for a dollar or two. If you have a student I.D., further reductions are sometimes available. Bus travel is a fine alternative to the expensive air flights. Brazil has top quality regional bus companies with modern air-conditioned vehicles that crisscross the country on regular and on-time schedules. One warning though: be aware of the distances. Brazil is larger than the continental U.S.

SOURCES OF INFORMATION. Embratur, Brazil's National Tourism Authority, is located in Rio at Rua Mariz e Barros, 13, near Praça de Bandeira (273–2212). In New York, the office of the Brazilian Tourism Board, 551 Fifth Ave., Suite 421, New York, NY 10176, has tourist information. Consult the telephone directory for further information. In Rio, Pan American Airlines, Avenida President Wilson, 165 A, Centro (240–6662) and Varig Airlines, Brazil's national carrier, at Avenida Rio Branco 128 (222–2535) can both provide information on travel in Brazil.

WHEN TO GO. Tropical rains are usually intermittent and allow time for outdoor activities. In some towns the rain comes at a certain time during the day and thus seldom interrupts activities because they are planned around it.

There are festivals, special events, and sporting attractions year round.

Seasons below the Equator are the reverse of the north—summer, December 21 to March 20; winter from June 21 to September 20. Temperatures vary with altitudes—warm along the coast, colder in the highlands.

Rio de Janeiro is located on the Tropic of Capricorn and the climate is just that—tropical. In summer, temperatures can rise to 105°F., although the average ranges between 84–95°F. In winter, temperatures stay in the 70s, occasionally dipping into the 60s. São Paulo, due to its higher altitude, is always cooler than Rio, and the weather fluctuates frequently, even within the same day. Further north where the equator crosses the country, the weather is always hot.

High season in Brazil begins in November and lasts through April, with Carnival as the peak tourist attraction.

Carnival Week. Brazil starts Carnival on the weekend preceding Ash Wednesday. A word of caution about "carnival-time" visits. Tourists have complained about minimal hotel services resulting in their rooms being left uncleaned, the beds unmade for days, and late or no breakfasts. Gas pumps and garage services often close down. Be prepared for the otherwise orderly system to take a holiday during Carnival.

PACKING. Informality is the rule in Rio—fortunately, considering summer (December-March) temperatures occasionally reach a humid 40°C. (104°F.). One seldom sees a tie at Copacabana restaurants or nightclubs. Ironically, jackets and ties are needed in the daytime at some of the better downtown luncheon clubs where bankers and businessmen gather. A hat is needed only on the beach or golf course.

Slacks are acceptable for women. Shorts are worn in beach neighborhoods but not in downtown areas, and bathing suits are about the skimpiest you'll ever see. You will surely see the Brazilian "tanga" (the "string" originated in Rio). In wintertime (summer in the Northern hemisphere), there can be chilly days (in the lower 50s, F.), so a sweater or wrap is a necessity. As a general rule, dress in Rio as you would in Miami, but with seasons reversed.

In São Paulo, weather is cooler and dress is more formal. Temperatures can change rapidly and drastically within a single day, so it's wise to take a jacket or sweater with you wherever you go. Always carry an umbrella in São Paulo. Businessmen often wear suits and ties but not always. Sportswear is enough for a Brasilia sight-seeing trip of a day or two; if you stay longer or have diplomatic contacts, more formal clothing will be needed. But a man will rarely need a dinner jacket in Brazil—unless he wants to swelter at one of Rio's gala Carnival balls rather than wear a costume (a common, simple one consists of bright shirt, Hawaiian leis, captain's cap and shorts).

During winter (May to October), you will need warmer clothing in the South, whereas in Bahia, the North, and Northeast, the climate is humid and tropical year-round. Sun glasses and a light raincoat or umbrella are good items to have along when visiting anyplace in Brazil. Outside Rio and São Paulo, an insect repellent will be needed. Local druggists have preparations for local problems, but you might carry some antidiarrhea capsules and whatever prescription medicines you require.

Dry Cleaning and Laundry. Good service is available in the better hotels. Usually the best dry cleaning and laundry service in Brazil is done in the private plants of such leading hotels as those of the Intercontinental chain. Prices for dry cleaning can be expensive. You might object to the strong odor of the cleaning fluids used. It is better to take clothing that is washable.

SPECIAL EVENTS. January: In Salvador, Bahia, *Festival of the "Boa Viagem"* or the Good Lord Jesus of the Seafarers (1st). A procession of hundreds of small vessels led by a decorated galley to the end of Boa Viagem beach. Lasts four days with samba, capoeira, and dancing, plus feasts of Bahian food. In Salvador, Bahia, *Feast of Bonfim,* the highpoint of which is beautifully-dressed Bahian women cleaning the steps of the Basilica of Bonfim (3rd Sun.). **February:** In Salvador, Bahia, *Festival of Iemanjá.* The holy mothers and daughters begin singing the goddess's praises at the crack of dawn (2nd). **Feb-March:** *Carnival.* In Rio, the year's biggest tourist attraction, but also spectacular in Bahia, Recife, and Olinda. Always 4 days before Ash Wednesday. **March:** *Formula I Grand Prix,* São Paulo. *Holy Week,* Ouro Preto, Minas Gerais. Solemn celebrations in the biggest urban complex of the 18th century considered by UNESCO to be part of the World Cultural Heritage. Religious rites from the baroque and Gold Rush eras. **April:** Ouro Preto, Minas Gerais, *Tiradentes Day* is the centerpiece of the national holiday weekend celebrating the Father of Brazilian Independence, Joaquim José da Silva Xavier, known as Tiradentes because he was a dentist (17th–21st) **June:** *Festas Juninas,* a cycle of celebrations honoring various saints throughout the month. Particularly noteworthy in Paraty, Rio de Janeiro state. *Bumba-Meu-Boi,* São Luis, Maranhão. A festival occurring here and in other cattle-raising areas of Brazil celebrating the religious legend of the slave who kills his master's ox and must resurrect it or be put to death himself. Festivities include street processionals and dancing, begin June 24 and last well into July. *Amazon Folklore Festival,* Manaus, Amazonia. **July:** *Bahian Independence Day* (2nd). **August:** *Brazilian Grand Prix Sweepstakes,* Jockey Club, Rio de Janeiro (1st Sun.). **September:** *Biennial Art Exposition,* São Paulo, S.P. Held every other year in odd years, this is the largest art show in Latin America. Lasts several months. **October:** *Oktoberfest,* Blumenau, Santa Catarina. A celebration by Southern Brazil's large German colony. **November:** *Aleijadinho Week,* Ouro Preto, Minas Gerais. Honoring the great 18th century sculptor whose work has made this area a living art treasure. **December:** *New Year's Eve* celebration, Rio de Janeiro.

TRAVEL DOCUMENTS AND CUSTOMS. Brazil requires tourist visas of all citizens of countries demanding visas of Brazilians. This includes the United States and Canada but not Great Britain.

Americans: Passports and visas–the latter available from the nearest Brazilian Consulate—are required for travel to or in Brazil. A tourist visa, valid for 90 days, is easily obtainable and free. A 2 X 3 inch passport photo, passport, and a round-trip ticket will secure your visa.

Passports must be valid for at least six months from the intended date of arrival in Brazil. Adult passports are valid for 10 years, others for five years. When you receive your passport, write down its number, date and place of issue separately. If it is lost or stolen, notify either the nearest American Consul or the Passport Office, Department of State, Washington, D.C. 20524, as well as the local police.

If a resident alien, you need a Treasury Sailing Permit, Form 1040 C, certifying that federal taxes have been paid; if a non resident alien, Form 1040 NR; apply to your District Director of Internal Revenue for these. You will have to present various documents: (1) blue or green alien registration card; (2) passport; (3) travel tickets; (4) most recently filed Form 1040; (5) W-2 forms for the most recent full year; (6) most recent current payroll stubs or letter; (7) check to be sure this is all! There is an IRS office in the U.S. Embassy in São Paulo. To return to the U.S. you need a reentry permit if you plan to stay abroad more than one year. Apply for it in person at least six weeks before departure at the nearest office of the Immigration and Naturalization Service or by mail to the service, Washington, D.C.

Canadian citizens may obtain application passport forms at any post office; these are to be sent to the Central Passport Office, Dept. of External Affairs, Ottawa, Ontario K1A OG3. You may apply in person to the province in which you reside. However, a mailed application must be handled by the central office. A remittance of $21 Canadian, two photographs, and a birth certificate or certificate of Canadian citizenship (naturalization papers) are required. Canadian passports are valid for five years and are nonrenewable.

British citizens may apply for a passport at any U.K. passport office or British consulate, either by mail or in person. Two photographs, a birth certificate or proof of citizenship (naturalization papers), and £15 are required.

Customs Entering Brazil.

Travelers from abroad may bring duty free to Brazil the following items: clothing, jewelry for personal use, personal books and magazines, cosmetics, and toilet articles. In addition visitors are allowed to bring one camera, hair dryer, electric razor, video camera, cassette player, tape deck, tape recorder, portable radio, and other electronic devices obviously for personal use. Carrying tools or machines obviously intended for work use or electronic items that are out of the ordinary for personal use (e.g. can openers, typewriters, toasters, microwave ovens) will require justification. You must register such items at the Brazilian Consulate before you leave your country of origin, since you must have permission to enter with them and you will be checked as you leave to make sure you haven't sold them. Get everything in writing, and carry receipts with you, especially if the articles are in their original packaging. It is difficult to get personal computers approved. You are, however, allowed to bring in up to $300 worth of presents over and above those items you intend to use personally. Electronic items may be given as gifts up to this monetary limit. You can also bring through customs a maximum of $300 worth of anything you buy at the duty-free shop upon deplaning (in addition to your limit of $300 in goods brought from abroad). Once you pass customs, you may not reenter the duty free shop, so make all purchases beforehand. Regulations are constantly changing, so make sure to ask and hang on to all paperwork. If you are traveling on business, it is the responsibility of your company to arrange the proper documentation. Otherwise, be prepared for a lot of red tape and/or heavy duties.

Health Certificates.

No vaccinations are required to enter Brazil unless coming from an infected area.

Pets need to be vaccinated—inquire at the Brazilian embassy as to what is required for your pet, and do so well in advance.

HOW TO GET THERE. By air.

The majority of flights terminate in Rio, though the national *Varig Airlines* also services São Paulo, Manaus, Brasilia, and other destinations, primarily from Los Angeles, Miami, and New York. *Pan American Airlines* runs daily flights to Rio and São Paulo from these major American cities and *American Airlines* offers daily flights between Miami and Rio. Among the airlines serving Brazil from Europe are *Varig, Aerolineas Argentinas, Air France, British Airways, Iberia, Lufthansa, SAS, Swissair,* and *TAP. Pan Am, Varig,* and *South African Airways* fly to Rio from points in the Pacific and Africa. From the U.S. to Rio and São Paulo there are smooth jet flights on five airlines: from New York, Miami, Los Angeles on *Avianca, Argentine Airlines, American Airlines, Pan American,* and *Varig;* from Dallas-Houston on *Pan American.* From Miami to Brasilia on *Pan American* and *Varig,* to Manaus and Belém on *Varig.*

From London to Rio and São Paulo: *British Airways, Varig* (some flights stop in Bahia), and main European and South American airlines from other principal capitals on the Continent.

From South Africa: *South African Airways* and *Varig* have flights from Johannesburg and/or Cape Town.

From the Pacific, Australia, and New Zealand: *Qantas* through Tahiti to Acapulco and Mexico City, changing for South American desinations, or *LAN-Chile* from Fiji, Tahiti, or Easter Island through Santiago.

From the Orient: *Varig* or *Japan Air Lines* from Tokyo, or other airlines, changing for South America on the U.S. West Coast.

By sea. Passenger accommodation on freighters from the U.S. is offered by *Columbus Lines, Torm Lines Holland-America, Ivaran Lines* and *Moore-McCormack Lines* one-way or round-trip cruises. *Lloyd Brasileiro* and *Brodin Line* call at Rio, Santos, and Paranagua. *Sunline Cruises* at: Rio, Vitoria, Salvador, and Recife. From Europe by: *Lamport and Holt Line Ltd.*

By bus. TEPSA buses connect with several countries and operate within Brazil.

CURRENCY. In March 1990, the newly inaugurated government of President Fernando Collor de Mello launched an economic program designed to stem Brazil's relentless inflation, which was averaging over 2,000 percent a year. As part of this program, a new currency, the cruzeiro, was introduced, the country's third monetary reform since 1986 (the cruzeiro replaced the cruzado novo, which in 1989 had replaced the cruzado, which in 1986 had replaced the original cruzeiro).

To prevent further confusion, the government established parity for the cruzeiro and cruzado novo, which means that both cruzeiro (Cr$) and cruzado novo (NCz$) bills are worth their face value. Although increasingly rare, some cruzado (Cz$) bills are still in circulation; to calculate their value in cruzeiros, just remove three zeros. Under the Brazilian monetary system, there are 100 centavos, or cents, to each cruzeiro, although high inflation has left these centavos virtually worthless.

Brazil has a special floating exchange rate for tourists. Called the tourism exchange, it is available at hotels, banks, travel agencies, and officially authorized currency exchanges (called *casas de câmbio*). In each case, you must present your passport when exchanging currency at the tourism rate. This rate is nearly identical to the black market rate with the obvious advantage that it is entirely legal. Since the tourism exchange was introduced in 1989, there has been no need for tourists to exchange currency on the black market. Credit card companies and hotels all now use the tourism exchange rate, thus guaranteeing tourists the most favorable rate for their currency.

Traveler's checks are the best way to safeguard travel funds, although you will always receive slightly less for them in exchange than for greenbacks. Nevertheless, they are safer. Anyone can change dollar bills, no questions asked. But you must present a passport and sign in the presence of the clerk in order to change traveler's checks. It is advisable to carry the bulk of your money in traveler's checks, and a smaller quantity in bills. Outside of major cities it is more difficult to exchange your traveler's checks than cash.

Prices, unless noted otherwise, are in U.S. dollars.

HOTELS. Although cost is as good an indicator as you're likely to find, the following price categories do not necessarily reflect the quality of every hotel accurately. *Super deluxe* hotels begin at $180 per night; *Deluxe* hotels charge from $125 to $180; *Expensive* hotels range from $80 to $125, *Moderate* hotels range from $40 to $80, and *Inexpensive* hotels are $40 or less. Continental breakfast is generally included in the room rate. While personal inspection of the premises is impossible if you are making reservations from afar, checking out the room in an inexpensive or moderate hotel before you take it is always a good policy. At the expensive and super deluxe establishments, reservations should always be made well in advance, especially during high season and when special events are occurring. Unless you are traveling with a tour during Carnival, you will need to reserve rooms in the best hotels at least a year ahead. Motels in Brazil are not hotels with free parking, as they are in the U.S. Motels are for couples engaging in amorous interludes and are rented out for short periods of time—hours, afternoons, overnight. These establishments are completely legitimate and are not designed to serve the prostitution trade. Many super deluxe hotels in Rio and São Paulo now offer American television programs via satellite dishes.

RESTAURANTS. Our restaurant grading system has four categories: *Deluxe,* $35 and up; *Expensive,* $20 to $35; *Moderate,* $10 to $20; *Inexpensive,* under $10. These prices are for one person and do not include wine, beer, or other drinks, but do include the "coberto" or "couvert," an appetizer course including bread, butter, and, depending on the restaurant, cheese or pâté spreads, olives, quail eggs, crudités, sausage, etc.

Brazilian Food and Drink. It's as hard to find restaurants labeling their food "Brazilian" as it is to find "French" food in France, and most of the best restaurants in Rio and São Paulo are French and Italian. What you find in restaurants not specializing in some other national cuisine is Brazilian food; a typical meal consists of beans, rice, french fries, and beef, chicken, or fish. Brazilians are not fond of vegetables and salads must be ordered separately.

Many Brazilian dishes are adaptations of Portuguese specialties. Fish stews called *caldeiradas* and beef stews called *cozidos* are popular, as is *bacalhau,* salt cod cooked in sauces, or grilled. Dried salted meats form the basis for many dishes from the interior and northeast of Brazil, and pork is used heavily in dishes from Minas Gerais. You will find Brazilian cooking both sweeter and saltier than you are used to, and there are two categories of food called *salgados* (salties) and *doces* (sweets). The first are served as appetizers and snacks in standup "lanchonetes," and the desserts are sold in sweet shops and restaurants. Many "doces" are direct descendents of the egg-based custards and puddings of Portugal and France.

The national dish of Brazil is *feijoada,* traditionally served on Saturdays at lunch. Originally a slave dish, feijoada now consists of black beans, sausage, beef, and pork. It is always served with rice, finely shredded kale, orange slices, and farofa, manioc flour that has been fried with onion and egg.

The cuisine of Bahia is sometimes equated with Brazilian food as a whole, although it is actually best eaten in Salvador, where it originates. *Muqueca* is made out of many kinds of shellfish cooked quickly in a sauce of dendé oil, coconut milk, onions, tomatoes and coriander. Dried shrimp, dende oil, coconut milk, and cashews are the basic ingredients of *vatapá,* and *xinxim de galinha,* which substitutes lime juice for coconut milk to make a sauce for chicken.

From Brazil's southeast comes *churrasco,* or barbecued meats marinated and grilled or roasted over charcoals. Restaurants specializing in meat are called *churrascurias,* which serve either à la carte or "rodizio" (all you can eat) style.

The national drink is the *"caipirinha,"* made of crushed lime, sugar, and *pinga* or *cachaça,* strong liquors made from sugar cane. When whipped with crushed ice and fruit juice, pinga becomes a *batida,* which sometimes includes condensed milk.

Coffee is served black and strong with sugar in demitasse cups and is called *cafezinho.* Coffee is only served with milk at breakfast.

TIPPING. At restaurants and nightclubs, when 10 or 15% is added to your bill, you usually add 5% more. In hotels, 10% is usually added to your bill as a service charge. However, you will find that porters, doormen, elevator operators, and chambermaids are accustomed to getting a small tip for their services, either at the time the service is performed, or when you check out. If a taxi driver helps you with your luggage, a per bag charge of about 35¢ to 50¢ US is levied in addition to the fare. At the barber's or beauty parlor, a 10–20% tip is expected. Cinema and theater ushers do not expect tips. In general, tip washroom attendants, shoeshine boys, etc., about one-third what you would tip at home. At airports, tip the last porter who puts your bags into the cab; they work on a "pool" system and all earnings go into a general kitty.

BUSINESS HOURS AND HOLIDAYS. Opening and closing hours naturally vary from city to city. Rio stores open 9 A.M. to 6:30 P.M., Sat. to 1 P.M. Shopping malls open at 10 A.M. and close at 10 P.M. during the week and at 6 P.M. on Sat. The business day generally begins at 9 A.M. and ends at 6 P.M. although punctuality is not a Brazilian trait. Stores and offices may open later, and frequently stay open until the last customer leaves. Banks open at 10 A.M. and close at 4:30 P.M. Lunch is taken from noon to three, and while businesses in major cities do not close, you may not find who you're looking for.

National Holidays: Jan. 1, New Year's Day; Carnival (always 4 days before Ash Wednesday); Good Friday (Paixão); Easter (Páscoa); April 21, Tiradentes Day (hero of Brazil's independence); May 1, Labor Day (Dia do Trabalho); Corpus Christi; Sept. 7, Independence Day; Oct. 12, Nossa Senhora de Aparecida (Brazil's patron saint); Nov. 2, All Souls (Finados); Nov. 15, Proclamation of the Repúblic; Dec. 25, Christmas (Natal); Dec. 31, New Year's Eve (Ano Novo).

Other dates that are celebrated nationally or locally include: Jan 6, Epiphany (Santos Reis); Jan. 20, São Sebastião (Rio's patron saint); Jan. 25, Anniversary of the founding of São Paulo; Feb. 1, Anniversary of the founding of Rio de Janeiro; Ash Wednesday; Ascension Day (Ascensão); June/July, Festas Juninas commemorating saints' days; Assumption (Assunção de Nossa Senhora); Nov. 1, All Saints Day (Todas os Santos); Nov. 19, Flag Day (Dia da Bandeira).

Note: People usually close up shop early the day before a holiday. Election days, when scheduled, are also considered holidays.

TELEPHONES. All parts of Brazil are connected by Embratel, the national telephone company. Public phones are everywhere and are called "orelhões," or "big ears." These are yellow with the blue phone company logo for local calls, or solid blue for calls between cities ("interurbana"). To use the public phones, you must buy tokens, called "fichas," at newspaper stands or Telerj stations, where you can make long distance calls. Local fichas cost the equivalent of U.S. 2¢, long-distance tokens about U.S. 14¢. It is wise to buy several at a time so that you can insert them in the slot in advance and avoid getting cut off. Unused fichas will be returned when you hang up. To use the public phones, pick up the receiver and listen for a constant dial tone. Drop the ficha into the slot, listen again for a dial tone, then dial. For international telephone calls through an operator, dial "000111." For information on international calls, dial "000333." Operators who assist from these numbers speak English. To make an automated collect intercity phone call within Brazil, dial 9 plus the area code and number. The recipient of your call will hear a recorded message in Portuguese saying "you are receiving a collect call." After the tone, give your name and if the person on the other end does not wish to accept charges, he or she just hangs up to disconnect the call. Telephone numbers in Brazil do not always have an equal number of digits, nor do area codes. This irregularity does not indicate that you have a wrong number. The area code for Rio is 021, for São Paulo 011. Other area codes for all parts of the country are listed in the front of the phone directory.

MAIL. The post office is called "Correios" and is open from 8 A.M. to 5 P.M. weekdays, until noon on Sat. An airmail letter from Brazil to the U.S. and most parts of Europe costs the equivalent of $1.80 for 20 grams. Airmail takes at least 5 days to reach the U.S. from Brazil and vice versa. Brazil has both national and international rapid mail service, the price of which varies according to the weight of the package and the destination.

Major hotels will hold mail for arriving guests. Do not use general delivery to receive mail—have it forwarded to American Express. Telegraphic service is available everywhere from post offices, and many hotels have their own facilities.

NEWSPAPERS. English-language newspapers and magazines are for sale in all leading cities. With timely jet schedules to Brazil, there is little delay in receiving airmail editions of New York and Miami newspapers. International editions of news magazines are on sale in all leading hotels.

Rio's two leading Portuguese newspapers are *Jornal do Brasil* and *O Globo*. In São Paulo, there are six major newspapers in Portuguese: *Folha de São Paulo, Folha da Tarde, Journal da Tarde, O Estado de São Paulo, Diario Popular,* and *Gazeta Mercantil*. Nightly news reports are broadcast on all major television networks in Portuguese.

ELECTRIC CURRENT. Most of the top hotels have transformers for current and adapters for plugs for guests with foreign electric razors, slide projectors, and so on. Usually 110 or 120 volts, AC 60 cycle in Rio and São Paulo.

USEFUL ADDRESSES. In Rio: *Riotur,* Rua da Assembléia 10, 8th and 9th floors, Centro (242–8000): information on tourist events in the city of Rio. Open Mon.-Fri., 9 A.M. to 12:30 and 2 P.M. to 6 P.M. Kiosk at Pão de Açucar. *TurisRio,* Rua da Assembléia 10, 7th and 8th floors, Centro (252–4512); tourist information on the state of Rio de Janeiro. Open Mon.–Fri. 9 A.M. to 6 P.M. *Embratur,* Rua Mariz e Barros, 13, 6th floor, Praça da Bandeira, (273–2212); Brazil's National Tourism Authority, information on all regions of the country. *American Consulate,* Av. President Wilson, 147 (292–7117). *British Consulate,* Praia do Flamengo, 284, 2nd fl. (552–1422). *Canadian Consulate,* Rua D. Gerardo 35, 3rd floor (233–9286). English-speaking doctors can be contacted by calling the U.S. Consulate-General at 292–7117, or by calling the Rio Health Collective for a referral at 325–9300 ext. 44.

In São Paulo: *Paulistur,* the city's Tourism Authority, was abolished. For information, contact the *Secretaria de Esportes e Turismo do Estado de São Paulo,* the state tourism authority, at Praça Antonio Prado, 9, Centro (229–3011) and at Av. São Luis 115, Centro (231–0044). Open Mon.–Fri. 9 A.M. to 5 P.M. Information is also available from the *São Paulo Convention Bureau,* Alameda Campinas 646, 5th floor (289–9397, 284–3099, 251–3858). Open Mon.–Fri. 9 A.M. to 6 P.M.. *American Consulate,* Rua Padre João Manoel, 933 (881–6511). *British Consulate,* Av. Paulista 1938, 17th fl. (287–7722). *Canadian Consulate,* Av. Paulista 854, 5th fl. (287–2122).

HEALTH AND SAFETY. Rio and São Paulo are modern urban centers with good sanitary conditions, but once you get out of the major cities into rural areas, you will be subject to tropical diseases that periodically recur and sometimes reach epidemic proportions: yellow fever, denguê, malaria, and hepatitis are all recent outbreaks. Get inoculations before you go for those illnesses for which there are serums (e.g. yellow fever). Check with your local health authority, the travel clinic at your local hospital, the Department of Immigration, or some other public health outlet to see what you will need. Anyone planning adventure travel of any kind—including fishing expeditions in the Pantanal and trips to the Amazon—should take malaria prophylaxis tablets before traveling in the affected area. Should you contract an illness while in Brazil, try to get it diagnosed and treated while still there, since doctors trained in tropical medicine and pharmaceuticals to treat various ailments are readily available. If this is not possible, be sure to tell your doctor at home where you have been. Most visitors who stay for a few weeks have no problems, but those that do occur are usually the result of overindulgence, unfamiliar foods, or trying to tan too fast. It is always safest to eat only peeled fruit and cooked vegetables, and to be selective with street food vendors and stands. Let overall cleanliness be your guide.

Drinking Water and Milk. The best general rule is to drink bottled water in Brazil. Many of the public water systems date almost to colonial times and are not 100 percent safe. Be sure to ask for bottled water (it is usually in your hotel room when you arrive).

Pasteurized milk is available in every major city. In the north and northeast milk should be boiled before drinking. "Leite Longa Vida," processed milk that does not need refrigeration until it is opened, is sold in cardboard cartons and can be consumed as is.

Medical Treatment. In Brazil there is no shortage of competent, trained, English-speaking doctors. The International Association for Medical Assistance for Travelers (IAMAT), 736 Center St., Lewiston, N.Y. 14092, has participating doctors in every South American country. All speak English. They will send, on request, a booklet listing these physicians, which you can carry on your trip. The booklet takes from 6 to 8 weeks delivery time, so order it well in advance of your trip. English speaking doctors can be located in Rio through the Rio Health Collective, Av. das Américas 4430, sala 303, Barra da Tijuca (325–9300, ext. 44). The RHC operates a free referral service for medical specialists of all kinds, and can provide English-speaking nurse companions and translators if needed. Provides 24-hour service. Elsewhere, consult the American Consulate.

British residents may rely on Europe Assistance, 252 High St., Croydon CRO 1NF, which operates an on-the-spot medical assistance service throughout the world. Note: This service involves a fee.

Pharmaceuticals pose no problem for the visitor. All major cities have excellent drugstores and many offer "round the clock" service.

Safety. Although Brazil has the tenth largest economy in the world, it is a country where 2 percent of the population are very, very rich and the rest are very, very poor. Poverty breeds crime. The tourist who can afford the trip is a millionaire by Brazilian standards, and thus a prime target for crime. Crime is a problem in large cities everywhere, and Rio and São Paulo are no exceptions. To lessen the risk of being assaulted, never wear gold or silver jewelry or watches; carry photographic equipment in a knapsack worn back-to-front; do not carry a bag at all, if possible; avoid trouble spots like the Jardim de Allah, the 553 bus, and the Santa Teresa trolley in Rio, and do not wander around the streets of downtown São Paulo alone at night. Be especially on the lookout for young boys working in groups or with prostitutes. Report crimes at your hotel where the staff will direct you to the proper authorities. To minimize losses in case of assault, carry only as much money as you will need and leave all valuable documents (passports, airline tickets, traveler's checks, etc.) in the safe provided by your hotel.

GETTING AROUND BRAZIL. By air. There are four major commercial airlines (*Varig, Cruzeiro do Sul, Vasp,* and *Transbrasil*), which together fly over 3 billion passenger-miles a year. The airline companies take good care of their planes, have top flight mechanics, and first-class pilots, and crews who refuse to let a plane go up unless they are absolutely certain it is ready to fly. The service is nothing short of excellent and full course meals are the rule rather than the exception, followed always by a cup of black coffee.

Their plane scheduling is fairly imaginative and is designed to meet both passenger needs and the competition. One of the most successful and most used of all the airline services is the popular "air bridge" between Rio and São Paulo. In 1959, the four air companies pooled their forces to set up a system to keep both passengers and planes constantly flowing between the two major cities. The traveler does not even need to buy a ticket and reservations are not accepted in advance. You just show up at the airport and get aboard the next plane. During the rush hours there is a plane leaving every 30 minutes, and every hour on the hour up to 10:30 P.M. The air bridge has been a success since its inauguration, carrying more than 2,000 passengers a day. The cost is about $57 one way. *TAM* and *Rio Sul* also fly between Rio and São Paulo, Mon. through Fri., and do accept reservations.

So successful was the Rio-São Paulo bridge that in 1962 air bridges were inaugurated to Belo Horizonte and Brasilia. The flights are not so frequent, because the distances are greater, but the regular commuters seem more than satisfied. Planes tend to fill up on weekends; book well in advance if you plan to fly anywhere on a Friday, especially to or from Manaus or Brasilia.

If you're planning on doing a good deal of domestic flying in Brazil, you should purchase a Brazil Air Pass, which is sold only outside of the country. This $440 pass gives you unlimited air travel within Brazil for 21 days. All major cities are served, including São Paulo, Manaus, Brasília, Belém, Recife, and Buzios. Given the high price of domestic air travel, the pass is a true bargain. Check with your travel agent before starting your trip.

By rail. Train service between Rio and São Paulo is reasonably comfortable. An overnight trip for two in a private cabin costs about $17; there is a dining car, and your porter can even provide "room service." There is excellent regional service from São Paulo on the Paulista and Sorocabana lines. Most service to other areas of Brazil is inferior to air travel. Travelers save both time and often considerable trouble by avoiding long rail journeys in Brazil.

By bus. With its growing highway network, Brazil can offer comfortable bus travel over most of the country, and even internationally. Unless you're in a tour group, however, you can't book straight through from, say, Montevideo to Rio. Instead, you buy a ticket from one principal city to the next—Montevideo Porto Alegre, then Florianópolis, Curitiba, São Paulo and Rio. But you'll need the hotel room and rest between each long leg anyway. On most-traveled routes, service is frequent and inexpensive. Between São Paulo and Rio (6½ to 7 hours), for example, there is a bus every half hour all day long costing about $15, and night "sleeper" at $30.

Car Rentals. Most major cities have local or international Rent-A-Car Services. Avis, Budget, and Hertz have extensive operations throughout the country, and the top Brazilian car rental firm is Localiza with nationwide operations. Prices in Rio average around $50 a day including insurance and taxes. You will pay more for automatic transmission.

Car rental agencies in Rio at the airport and on Rua Princesa Isabel, Copacabana: *Hertz,* 275–4996; *InterLocadora,* 542–0143 or 275–6546; *VIP's,* 295–0040; *Localiza,* 275–3340.

SPORTS. Soccer, called "futebol" and pronounced foo-tea-ball, is as much a national heritage for Brazilians as wine is for the French and snow for the Eskimo.

The soccer the Brazilians play is a fast game, almost like a ballet, that begins when little boys take their first ball to the beach or into the middle of a vacant lot. You can see them bouncing the ball off their knees, giving a backward kick with a bare foot and sending it to a buddy who butts it with his head. In Brazil as well as the rest of the soccer-playing world, only the goalkeeper is allowed to touch the ball with his hands.

If you like sports at all and are in Rio on a Sunday when two of the major Rio teams are playing each other, you should visit the huge Maracanã soccer stadium. The four main Rio teams are Flamengo (Brazil's most popular team), Vasco (chiefly identified with the Portuguese colony in Rio), Fluminense (the high society team), and Botafogo (the least definable in personality). If you try to go, talk it all over ahead of time with someone at the hotel who can tell you how to get there, when to go, how to buy tickets, and so forth. Unlike baseball, U.S. or Canadian football, rugby, cricket, and the like, soccer is easy to understand even if you've never seen it before. But even if the game doesn't turn you on, the stadium is impressive, and the crowd itself is half the spectacle. Soccer crowds in the British Isles and northern Europe can be extremely surly; and in the Mediterranean and other Latin American countries (as well as most of Brazil), they can be dangerously passionate. But the Maracanã crowd is unswervingly good natured, and the stadium is exceptionally safely constructed, so don't worry about stories you may have read about soccer disasters. For one of the big games between two of the major local teams, large numbers of the rooters bring huge homemade flags, featuring the team's colors in a variety of homemade designs, and they wave these flags when their team comes on the field or scores a goal. Another feature you are not likely to encounter at the World Series or the Super Bowl is that drums start beating in various parts of the stadium well before the game and maintain their tom-tom rhythm without a break right through to the end. All in all, the crowd is one of the most colorful and exciting spectacles in sport. If you go, try to buy the highest-priced reserved seats. If you want to be with "the people" in the "arquibancada," be advisd that it is plain concrete bleachers, so be sure to buy foam rubber pads to sit on before you go into the stadium.

Capoeira and More. Another sport that is purely Brazilian, not to be found anywhere else in the world, is Capoeira. It is a fight, a dance, and a bit of judo all rolled into one. In the early slave days there were constant fights between the blacks, and when the owner caught them at it he had both sides punished. The blacks considered this unfair and developed a smoke screen of music and song to cover up the actual fighting. When a pre-arranged battle was to be fought, the natives brought their "berimbau," a bow-shaped piece of wood with a metal wire running from one end to the other, where there was a painted gourd. Using an old copper coin the player would shake the bow, and while the seeds in the gourd rattled he would strike the taut string. The effect is like background music for a Hollywood monster film. There would be a chorus chanting a fast song and the two fighters would get in the center and slug it out, primarily with their feet. Whenever the master came into view the fighters would do an elaborate pantomime of slashing the air with their fists and kicking out so as to miss their opponent. Over the years this was refined into a sport that is practiced in Bahia and Recife today. Both cities have their champion and there are many *capoeira* houses where the tourist can go to watch these dances. In Salvador (Bahia), they may be seen on any Saturday morning around the Modelo Market. The idea is to swing and kick to the mood of the music but without either man touching the other. The back-bending all the way to the floor, the agile foot movements to stay clear of a gleaming knife, and the strange African music make it a sport that needs great dexterity to play but is fascinating to watch.

Rio has recently become a *hang-glider's* paradise. Taking off from a mountain peak, the colorful kites circle sometimes for hours before landing at the end of Gavea beach, beyond the Inter-Continental and Nacional hotels.

Water-skiing and *underwater diving* are also practiced by sportsmen in clubs all along the coastline. Brazilians are a very club-conscious people, and almost everyone you meet will be a member of something and will be able to take you to his particular club and introduce you around. They love to show off visitors and most clubs can only be entered with a member. Once you are inside you'll find the friendship and generosity for which the Brazilians are famous.

Horse racing is also immensely popular. The Grande Premio Brasil held first Sunday in August highlights the racing season. *Golf* and *tennis* are available in all leading cities. There are two golf clubs in Rio, where you can play by invitation only. *Yachting* is extemely popular in Rio. And there is *surfing* and *windsurfing* on the beaches.

For those who like to *fish,* Brazil can be a surprising wonderland. Many tourists try for some marlin fishing off the coast of Rio, and others go to the magnificent Foz do Iguaçu to try their hand at dorado. In the Amazon River there are monstrous fish called Pirarucú that reach up to 280 pounds each. The nation's rivers and streams are filled with a variety of game fish. No license is needed and no limit set.

If you have a taste for hunting; you're out of luck, because the government outlawed the hunting of big-spotted jaguars, wild boar, fleet-footed jungle deer, moss-backed turtles, and dozens of other animals which were once considered fair game. But a camera safari into the Mato Grosso or Amazon jungles can still be an adventure. Most travel agencies can tailor a program to suit you.

See also "Adventure Vacations" chapter.

Exploring Brazil

RIO DE JANEIRO

Rio de Janeiro has been called the most beautiful city in the world by many experienced travelers. With a natural setting surpassing even Hong Kong and San Francisco, it has everything. There are long stretches of soft sandy beaches and lines of tall palm trees. There are mountains covered with deep green untouched jungle and birds, butterflies, and flowers in profusion. There are great fleecy clouds floating lazily over the ocean, which pushes in cool breezes and an occasional rain storm. There are warm days and cool nights and starlit skies and huge full moons.

What nature has given, the Brazilians have embellished with their own personalities. Along the black and white mosaic promenades walk some of the loveliest women in Latin America. The men, well built and tanned from hours on the beach, add their note of masculine grace. Colonial buildings vie for space with modern air-conditioned skyscrapers. There is music everywhere, from the honking of taxi and automobile horns, to soft singing voices. There is an excitement in the air, curiously mixed with the tropical languor.

But Rio is more than just a beautiful setting. It is a city that boasts its own ballet company, magnificent opera house, and dozens of cultural centers. It is a mecca for artists and enterprising businesspeople. It also calls the international drifter, the expatriate, and the fortune hunter. And in recent years, with the construction of many luxurious hotels, it is South America's tourist capital as well.

São Sebastiao do Rio de Janeiro is 15 miles long and varies from 2 to 10 miles wide. Nestling between the tall green mountains and the deep blue-green sea, the city offers a breathtaking sight, by day or night. During the day the sun plays on the sand and palm trees, and the white buildings with their red tile roofs serve more to ornament the city's natural beauty than to detract from it. At night the city wears strings of glowing lights, giving the impression that strands of diamonds have been lazily entwined around the buildings and the mountains by some benevolent giant.

The most obvious attraction for the visitor is the beach. Just the name Copacabana inspires romantic images, and rare is the tourist who doesn't arrive in Rio and immediately jump into a swimsuit. Rio has 23 different beaches, scattered from the international airport in the north to the other side of the mountains in the south. Most popular are the beaches at Copacabana, Ipanema, and Leblon. There are no bathing fees for any of the beaches. Oceanfront hotels provide cabanas, towels, chairs, umbrellas, and security guards for their guests. Waves at the beach come in hard and fast most of the time, so don't expect to do much swimming, just a lot of splashing. Also be prepared to confront lots of people on the weekends. Take nothing of value to the beach—no cameras, no jewelry, no passports, no airline tickets, and only enough cash in cruzados for a drink or a snack, which you can buy from one of the roving vendors.

Assuming you've had enough sun and that you want to see some of the city itself, a good plan is suggested in the following pages.

Botafogo and Sugar Loaf

Take a taxi or a bus to Botafogo and the Museu do Indio, or the Indian Museum, open Tuesday to Friday from 10 A.M. to 5 P.M. and on the weekends from 1 to 5 P.M. (admission is free). Located in an old home at Rua das Palmeiras 55 (286–8799), it is a storehouse of Indian work (feathers, ceramics, stone, and weaving), as well as a growing archive of films and recordings of the indigenous people's way of life and music.

Close by, at Rua São Clemente 134, is the *Casa Rui Barbosa* (286–1297), former home of one of Brazil's leading citizens of the 19th century. Barbosa, a diplomat and politician, wrote Brazil's first constitution and supported direct elections, abolition, educational reform, federalism, the equality of nations and their right to remain neutral during war. A museum since 1930, Barbosa's house is open to the public from 10 A.M. to 4 P.M. Tuesday through Friday, and from 2 to 5 P.M. on Saturdays, Sundays, and holidays. Hourly guided tours are available.

Next, head for Sugar Loaf, which is right nearby. It is advisable to get there early for there are usually many people who want to make the visit—especially during school holidays, January to March and July. Once you are borne upward you'll have the pleasant sensation of space all around you and a vivid panoramic display of Rio and her natural beauties below. The car makes a half-way stop on Urca mountain, where there is a pleasant restaurant and a small amphitheater that has shows and popular concerts. Starting in 1978, this peak also became the site for a spectacular pre-Carnival ball. You can either linger here or transfer to the next car to go to the top, where you have the city at your feet and can identify the other points of interest that you must see before you leave. It is best to visit Sugar Loaf *before* you visit the Corcovado Christ statute, or you will remember Sugar Loaf only as an anticlimax.

There are taxis waiting at the platform where you will return and ask the driver to take you—slowly—to the Gloria Church (Igreja da Gloria). On the way down Avenida Pasteur you will pass the high-walled Yacht Club (admittance strictly to members only but you can peer over the chain-barred entrance-way) and the pink-painted colonial buildings belonging to the Federal University. Coming out in front of the tunnel of Pasmado, you'll go along Botafogo beach and after going around a bend you'll be in the Flamengo beach district where a major face-lifting has taken place. Here they have built the largest public park in Latin America on land reclaimed from the sea. Every ounce of earth was carted in by truck. The planting was done by master landscape gardener Roberto Burle Marx. Thanks to the Flamengo *aterro,* as it is called, you can now drive to and from Copacabana in a matter of minutes. The park is a delightful place for a late afternoon stroll. You can also explore it by tractor-drawn minitrain, and if you have small children with you, there is a fine playground, and a special space for model aircraft enthusiasts. Be sure to use the overpasses and underpasses to cross the main freeways; accidents are frequent on the *aterro* and just about everywhere else in Rio.

Favorite Church of the Imperial Family

The driver will turn off and climb a steep hill that is lined on both sides with houses harking back to the days of the Portuguese colonials and will let you off in front of the big wooden doors of the Gloria Church. Built in the 18th century, it was the favorite spot of the Imperial Family and contains many fine examples of art from both the Old and the New Worlds. The site of the church was once the hut of a hermit who, in 1671, with the help of two mysterious youths (angels), sculptured a beautiful statue of Our Lady of Glory. Seventeen years later, when the image had been accredited with miraculous powers, the hermit returned to Portugal, taking the image with him. But the ship sank into the ocean, and the statue washed ashore at Lagos, Portugal. In 1924 a copy was enshrined in its place in the Gloria Church. The Brazilians still want the original image returned. On August 15, the church is lit up like a baroque birthday cake and silhouetted against the dark sky and palm trees it is one of the loveliest sights in Brazil.

Walk down the street you drove up and then along the Praça (park) Paris. Laid out by a French architect a good many years ago, it reminds many Parisians of home, with its marble statues, trimmed hedges, reflection pools, and water fountains. On the opposite side of the avenue you'll see the contrast in the ultramodern Monument to the Brazilian Dead of World War II. Brazil sent troops to fight in Italy and suffered heavy losses. Construction of Rio's controversial and long-overdue subway, which tore up much of this area, is now finished. Despite a series of financial crises and floods, the final stations have been completed, linking the downtown area with the edges of the north and south zones of the city.

Museums and Historic Sites

Have lunch in the area, perhaps in the rooftop restaurant of Mesbla, Rio's largest department store, right across the street from the Passeio Público, oldest public park in the city. Filled with tall shade trees, small lagoons and rustic bridges, it is a pleasant place to get out of the sun. It also has its share of tramps and beggars and a large collection of alley cats.

Leave the park by the upper right-hand sidewalk and keep walking right over to Rio's main commercial heartline, Avenida Rio Branco. Walk up Rio Branco Avenue and you will pass the National Library (Biblioteca Nacional at #219/239 Av. Rio Branco, 220–3040; open Monday to Friday from 9 A.M. to 8 P.M., and Saturday from 9 A.M. to 3 P.M. and the Museum of Fine Arts (Museu Nacional de Belas Artes, Av. Rio Branco 199, 240–0160; open Tuesday to Friday from noon to 6 P.M., Saturdays, Sundays, and holidays from 3 to 6 P.M.) on your right and the Municipal Theater (Teatro Municipal, Praça Floriano, 210–2463) on your left. If this theater looks familiar, it is because it is an exact one-quarter scale copy of the Opera House in Paris. If you are here at lunchtime, drop in for an unforgettable meal at the Café do Teatro, downstairs in the opera building. Good cuisine mixes here with an incredible setting, reminiscent of a Cecil B. DeMille Biblical epic. Two blocks farther down the Avenue on the left rises the 34-floor, air-conditioned, glass-paneled Edificio Avenida Central, Rio's first skyscraper.

If you walk through the arcades to the other side of this modern building and look across the street, you'll see the old Convent of Santo Antonio (Igreja do Convento de Santo Antonio, Largo da Carioca, 262–0129/262–1201; the convent was being restored at press time and was not open to the public. Built between 1608 and 1619, it contains, aside from priceless colonial art objects, the tombs of Leopoldina, the first Empress of Brazil, and the Infante Dom Pedro de Bourbon. Beside the convent is the richest little church in Rio, the São Francisco da Penetência (Igreja de São Francisco da Penitência, Largo da Carioca, 5; 262–0197. Closed at press time for restoration work. Its interior is completely hand sculpted and covered in gold foil. It also has a remarkable altar and sacristy. The climb up the hill is worth it.

The former hill of Santo Antonio was removed, its earth used to form the Flamengo *aterro*. The site was transformed into a double avenue bordered by new buildings. These include the cone-shaped Metropolitan Cathedral—still unfinished—the aluminum-block headquarters building of Petrobrás (the government oil monopoly) and, across the avenue, the high-rise headquarters of the National Housing Bank and the glass tower of the National Savings Bank. Behind this modern setting you will see the colonial arches built in 1723 to carry water down to the city.

Go back down Rio Branco, until you come to Rua Ouvidor. There are no automobiles permitted on this street and it buzzes like an overactive beehive.

Five blocks from Ouvidor is Avenida Presidente Vargas. Be careful crossing the street here, because Brazilian drivers are notorious for disobeying traffic lights. To your right is the back entrance of the squat, attractive Church of Candelaria. (Igreja de Nossa Senhora de Candelária, Praça Pio X at the beginning of Getulio Vargas, 233–2324; open Monday to Friday from 7:30 A.M. to noon and 1 to 4:30 P.M.; Saturday from 7:30 to noon, Sunday from 9 A.M. until noon mass is over). The front of the building once overlooked the waters of Guanabara Bay, but the view is now obstructed by buildings and elevated drives. The inside is dark and relaxing after a walk in the sun.

Continuing downward on Rio Branco you will come to Praça Mauá and the beginning of miles of docks that have made the city such an important world trading center. Praça Mauá is peopled by all sorts, with heavy emphasis on foreign sailors. Now take a bus marked Copacabana, Ipanema, or Leblon and go back to your hotel and have a tall, cool drink. You've earned it today.

The Mother of Palm Trees

Another full day could start with an hour at the beach, a shower, and then a visit to the Botanical Garden on Rua Jardim Botânico. Take any bus marked "Joquei" or "Jardim Botânico"—they all run along Rua Jardim Botânico. The garden is one of the best in the world, say noted horticulturalists, and is carefully kept up. Covering an area of 567,000 square meters, there are over 135,000 plants and trees. There are 900 varieties of palm tree alone. Founded in 1808 by the prince regent Dom Joao, there stood near the entrance gate the famous *palma mater* transported from the West Indies and planted by the monarch. There is also a strikingly beautiful avenue of palms that is 740 meters long and contains 134 royal palms. Also be sure and see the bronze fountain dating back to 1820 and the mammoth Victoria Regia water lilies that measure 21 feet around. There is also a peaceful jungle atmosphere, lake and waterfall, a small greenhouse filled with insectivorous plants, including Venus flytraps, and some rare trees from Indonesia, whose huge roots spread atop the ground like writhing cobras.

From there take a taxi to the Laranjeiras Palace, the residence of the governer of Rio. You probably won't be allowed past the guard, but the drive through the Guinle Park and past the luxurious private apartment houses that line it is worthwhile. Now still in your cab, take a quick look at Catete Palace on Rua do Catete, Flamengo. Built of granite and rose-colored marble in 1862 by a wealthy coffee baron, it was purchased 32 years later by the federal government and used as the Foreign Office. Dictator Getulio Vargas, when he returned to power as duly elected President of the Republic, insisted on living there rather than at the other palace where he had been tossed out. It was also at Catete that he killed himself in 1954. The palace, with its magnificent gardens, was converted into the Museum of the Republic when Brasilia was inaugurated. The Museu da República, Rua do Catete, 179 (225–4302), after a lengthy restoration, is open to visitors Tues.–Sun. from noon to 5 P.M.

Now you can have lunch downtown and hop into another cab for a better look at the old aqueduct, over which little trolley cars cross on their way to the lovely residential area of Santa Teresa. You saw these arches from the other side yesterday. Now, however, you will be standing in the Lapa district. The parks and fountains inaugurated in 1975 are on a site that was once the center of Rio's bohemian nightlife and samba. Many of the surrounding buildings have escaped the march of progress; indeed, some have been protected as examples of Rio's architectural history. Look for the Automóvel Club, the Sala Cecilia Meireles concert hall, the National School of Music, and the large white Convent of Santa Teresa, built in 1970 and now the home of a Carmelite order of nuns who have no contact with the outside world.

Now for a visit to one of the most charming corners of the city, the Largo do Boticário just off Rua Cosme Velho. Everyone will tell you it dates from colonial times, whereas in fact only one of its houses dates from earlier than the 1920s. It is a pleasantly shady spot, one of its attractions being an English-owned antique store.

Now comes the treat, Corcovado. You can do one of two things. Continue in your taxi to the top of the mountain, which will give you a slow, unwinding, breathtaking view of all angles of the city, or go to Rua Cosme Velho 513 and take a tiny cogwheel train to the top. Trains leave every half hour and the ride is almost straight up through dense vegetation. When you arrive you'll have to climb a number of stairs to get to the base of the statue. The statue is impressive up close and the view from the top simply indescribable. The statue, inaugurated in 1931, has a height of 120 feet and weighs 700 tons. The head alone weighs 30 tons; each arm weighs 30 tons and each hand 8 tons. The statue was designed by Frenchman Paul Landowski and paid for by contributions of the people of Rio.

The best time to visit the statue is in the late afternoon about one hour before sunset. The effect of the reddening sun against the buildings and the sea far below is stunning. Wait patiently and one by one the lights of the town will start to come on, like fireflies awakening for the evening. Within half an hour the city will be dressed in sparkling diamonds and silhouetted against the dark shapes of Sugar Loaf and the blackening waters of the bay and ocean. **Warning:** The last trolley leaves at 7 P.M. and is always crowded. If you go up in a cab have the driver wait.

You may want to visit the Maracanã soccer stadium, the biggest in the world. Built in 1950 for the World Championship Games, it can hold—and has held—as many as 200,000 people at one time. While the designers looked after the comfort of the spectators, they also considered the players, and there is a wide moat around the field to protect the athletes should they lose.

Within walking distance is the Quinta da Boa Vista and the Museu Nacional, a beautiful old pink and white building that used to be the Imperial Family's Rio palace, in a gemlike setting of landscaped parks, lakes and marble statues. The museum is open from 10 A.M. to 4:45 P.M. every day except Monday and is filled with traces of Brazil's past, both historical and archeological. There are Indian funeral urns, reconstructed fossils, a fine collection of Amazon reptiles and insects, and one of the best collections of birds in the world (264–8262).

Right beside the museum is the zoo. Open Tuesday to Sunday from 9 A.M. to 4:30 P.M., it keeps most of its more important animals in unwalled natural settings. Be sure to note the colorful Amazon macaws as you go in (their squawking for attention will force you to notice them) and the hungry leer on the face of the jungle jaguar. Also don't miss the shaded jungle pool with the colorful red cranes and little white scavenger birds. The monkeys have an island of their own, as do the Amazon boa constrictors and the alligators. Telephone for the Jardim Zoologico is 254–2024.

Now here you need another cab to visit the Church of Penha just as the sun goes down. Perched high atop a mountain, and with 365 steps, it is a favorite place for repentant pilgrims to crawl on their knees. The inside is hung with crutches and silver charms representing parts of the body that were cured, thanks to the intervention of Our Lady of Penha. The view from the top is superb. Igreja de Nossa Senhora da Penha is located on the Largo da Penha, 19, and is open from 7 A.M. to 5 P.M.

The Emperor's Picnic Table

On the fourth day, call another cab and make the voyage to the Tijuca Forest. On leaving Copacabana, you will pass through the neighborhoods of Ipanema and Leblon, climb higher to go around the Two Brothers mountain on Avenida Niemeyer, and go past the Gavea Golf Club in São Conrado. Have your driver stop at the Emperor's Table (Mesa do Imperador). Here is a mammoth concrete picnic table where the Emperor used to bring his royal court to dine. It has an unequaled view of the south zone of the city. Nearby is the Chinese View (Vista Chinesa), which also is impressive.

The forest itself was once part of a private estate belonging to the Baron de Taunay and is studded with exotic trees, thick jungle vines, and a delightful waterfall. Also be sure and see the tiny little Mayrink Chapel with an altar painting by Brazil's famed Candido Portinari. This chapel is very popular with Brazilians and, in spite of its cramped quarters, has seen many society marriages.

Another Side to Rio

Brazil is a country of contrasts in its geography, its peoples, and its economic levels. Though it has a large and rapidly growing middle class it is still a country of the very rich and the very poor.

At first glance the favela slum sections in Rio, nestling into the mountainsides in the south zone, seem to be pastel-painted, enchanted summer cottages with magnificent views of the ocean. Then on closer inspection you can see that there is no enchantment, just bleak despair and resignation. It is not advisable to explore the favelas under any circumstances.

The favelas themselves began back in the year 1897 when soldiers of the new Republic, having put down a revolt of the Monarchists in the state of Bahia, suddenly found themselves without a cause, without money and without a place to live. They had been encamped on a hill they named Favela because of the abundance of a wildflower with the same name. So when they arrived in Rio, they called their first settlement of shacks "favela" too. The soldiers assumed they had the right to any land that wasn't being used, and once their shacks were built there were few politicians willing to incur their wrath by driving them off.

The years from 1920 to 1940 saw the favelas grow alarmingly. Brazil was entering into world trade and needed more coffee, cocoa, and fruit to export. Workers deserted the cities for the farms, cultivating the land

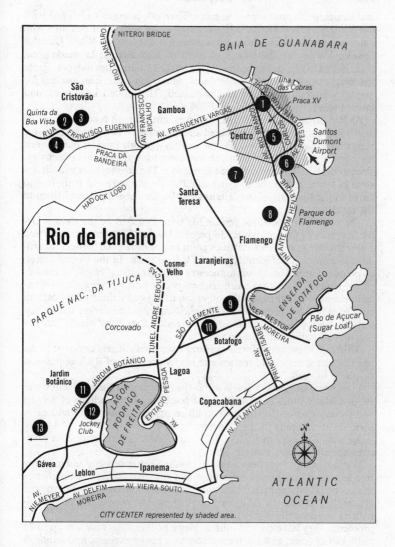

Points of Interest

Botanical Garden (Jardim Botânico) **11**
Casa Rui Barbosa **9**
Candelaria Church (Igreja da Candelaria) **1**
Chacara do Ceu **7**
City Museum (Museu da Cidade) **13**
Indian Museum (Museu do Indio) **10**
Jockey Club **12**
Maracanã Stadium **4**
Museum of Modern Art (Museu de Arte Moderna) **6**
Museum of the Republic (Museu da República) **8**
National Museum (Museu Nacional) **3**
National Museum of Fine Arts (Museu Nacional de Belas Artes) **5**
Zoological Gardens (Jardim Zoologico) **2**

and shipping the produce to the coast. Then prices began to fall and with the fall the workers returned to the cities, along with other peasants who had lost their jobs. They took up residence in the favelas. When Dictator Getulio Vargas set the wheels of industry into motion, he made great promises to the Brazilian people. More flocked to the cities to work. From the north, truckloads of "nordestinos" converged upon Rio, anxious for employment but unlettered and untrained. They found little work and much misery.

As Rio expanded her metropolitan area, cut through roads and erected new buildings, the poor were routed and tenements demolished. Land was plentiful in the far suburbs, but the working groups (maids, bus drivers, washerwomen) could not afford to live away from the centers of activity. Transportation was sporadic and expensive. The free schools and clinics were in town, not in the outlying suburbs. People were not truly free to move to the fresh air of the distant suburbs, for necessity bound them to the favelas.

The racial mixture of the favelas has been classified by the Census Department as 28 percent white, 36 percent black, 35 percent mulatto, and 1 percent Oriental. These statistics point up the difference between Brazilian concepts of racial identity and the U.S. attitude. In the United States, all people of mixed black-white ancestry are regarded as "black," a classification which does not take into account proportions or percentages of racial ancestry. In Brazil, on the other hand, anyone lighter than "café au lait" in skin color is classified as "white," and anyone darker with a discernible trace of European ancestry is mulatto. Brazilian "blacks" are apparently of purely African descent.

Although some major favela eyesores have been entirely removed in the last few years, many still remain and nearly one-sixth of Rio's population still lives in them.

The choice sites in any favela are at the bottom near the road and water supply. Many times there will be just one pump for hundreds of people, and those living at the top have to fill empty cans with water and carry them on their heads to their homes.

As would be expected under such conditions, normal sanitation practices are almost non-existent.

Welfare groups have been active in building better housing and in giving free lessons in mechanics, carpentry, and the manual arts. A number of the poor of Rio have been moved into individual concrete houses, financed originally through the Alliance For Progress but now under projects financed domestically. Unfortunately, while these moves have solved some problems, they have created others. Many ex-favelados now live up to 25 miles out of town, making transportation a heavy expense, and although they are being encouraged to buy their new homes on the installment plan, many cannot afford the low monthly payments and once again face eviction.

Like all pockets of poverty, these hillside slums have become breeding grounds for crime and in recent years Rio's crime rate has soared. Tourists can be prime targets for the legions of pickpockets and purse snatchers. While we do not wish to sound an undue alarm, it is always best to be cautious. Besides the *favela* area, other favorite hangouts for thieves in Rio are the beaches, the Santa Teresa trolley, the Maracanã soccer stadium, and popular tourist attractions such as Sugar Loaf Mountain and Corcovado (here be careful on the train to the top). When visiting any of these spots take only the essentials, no jewelry, as little cash as possible, no large bags, and hold on to your camera at all times. When on the beach watch out for overly friendly kids hanging around your towel. They work in groups and while one distracts you another will be off with your valuables.

Carnival

Though Carnival is celebrated everywhere in Brazil, it is in Rio that the tourist will find its most fantastic expression. Carnival is a fast-moving, mad, unbelievable, music-filled, sleepless time when the entire nation rockets off into orbit and doesn't come back to earth for four days and five nights.

The official season is actually the Saturday night before and the days leading up to Ash Wednesday, but in practice the action starts Friday at 11 P.M. when the first "bailes" (balls) begin. Usually this period falls in February but can also come in March; however preparations are going on months before.

The visitor to Rio will start hearing the strains of Carnival in late December. At first it's nothing more than the gentle throb of drums from the hillside shanty towns, mingled with the ordinary sounds of the city at work. At night the drums get louder and voices are added, chanting a fast, spirited refrain. Soon the visitor notices children parading through the streets, beating on old tamborines, tin cans, or the hoods of parked automobiles. Their naked feet dance in the dust of the streets and the sands of the beach. In front of the hotels they go through the motions of a fast samba looking not only for tips and praise but also for a good time. Then, as the actual season draws closer, their parents and older brothers and sisters will parade through Copacabana in a cacophony of drums, whistles, triangles, and a weird, yelping instrument called the *cuica.* They will actually block the entire avenue, causing traffic to come to a halt while people hang out of their apartment windows and encourage them. The police do nothing to set the flow of cars in motion again, for usually they have left their posts and are dancing right in the midst of the revelers.

Stores that normally sell pens, books, and ink blotters suddenly deck their windows with coils of serpentine streamers and bags of confetti. Fabric shops, their wares spilling out onto the sidewalks, are crowded with men and women buying bright-colored silks and cottons. Other shops sell laces, stiff crinolines, masks, gold and silver chains, and decorated hats. Seamstresses double their prices and sew into the dawn, and all through the city runs an electrifying current of excitement. It affects not only the young but the oldsters as well, not only the Brazilians but the visitors.

Samba Schools Get Ready

This is a good time for the tourist to arrange for a visit to a Samba school, for they are at the peak of their practice sessions and admit anyone who is willing to pay a small admission and sit on a hard bench. The school usually belongs to a certain favela slum, and most of the dancers, nearly all blacks and mulattoes, live right there. They rehearse after work far into the night or on Saturdays and Sundays. For a complete listing of where each samba school is located and/or performing, consult Riotur's monthly *Guide.* Most samba schools are located in the Zona Norte (north side) of Rio. Talk to your hotel concierge about which to attend and transportation arrangements. Alternatively, the Beija Flor Samba school rehearses on weekends for the public in Botafogo near the Estrela do Sul Churrascaria and, off-season, performs at the Concha Verde on Sugarloaf mountain on Monday nights. Each samba school also has a theme. And the rules of the Carnival commission insist that the theme be Brazilian.

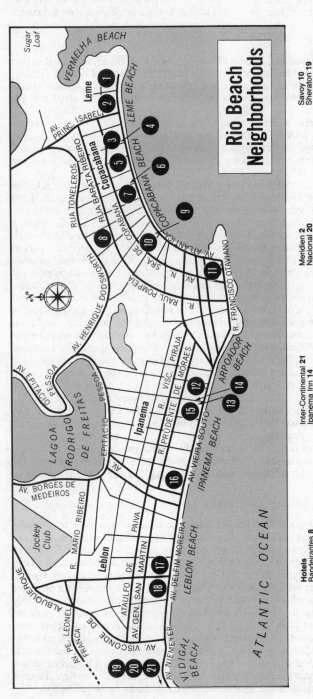

Rio Beach Neighborhoods

Hotels
Bandeirantes 8
California 7
Ceasar Park 13
Copacabana Palace 4
Everest 15

Inter-Continental 21
Ipanema Inn 14
Lancaster 3
Leme Palace 1
Marina Palace 17
Marina Rio 18

Meridien 2
Nacional 20
Olinda 6
Othon Palace 9
Praia Ipanema 16
Rio Palace 11

Savoy 10
Sheraton 19
Sol Ipanema 12
Trocadero 5

Because they live in poverty throughout the year, they want to "act rich" during the throbbing night of glory. A specially written samba and a complete dance routine are also centered around the theme or "enredo." A samba school can have as many as 3,000 people in it, each with his own job to do in the over-all pageant. Each school has a "bateria" or marching band of percussion instruments and drums, some of which number up to 300 men.

Such an organization costs money—in any country—and the members show great ingenuity in scraping up the needed funds. Costumes alone can cost as much as $500 apiece, which is a lot of money to anyone, especially for someone who earns but $80 a month. The top group of samba schools parading Sunday night through Tuesday morning provides the greatest show of the entire Carnival. In 1984, the Rio state government built a modernistic, concrete stadium to serve as permanent home to the samba school parade with top-quality facilities including a special section for foreign tourists to enjoy at ease what is truly an incomparable event, easily the highlight of Carnival. Tickets for this section are sold only to foreign tourists through tour operators and travel agents, and cost around $200. Tickets can be purchased from scalpers for $190 and up. These *cambistas,* as they are called, station themselves around the principal tourist hotels and approach foreign-looking folks.

The parades start around 8 P.M. and end the following morning. Bleacher tickets are sold, at cheaper prices, for the other Carnival nights as well, to parades of "blocos," "frevos," and "great associations." You will have no difficulty getting in to see the "secondary" samba schools fighting to win a place in next year's top parade. You can watch these for nothing, and they are just as authentic.

The schools have their one night of glory as they vie with one another for the top prize offered by the Carnival commission. To win that top prize is just as important for them—and they practice just as hard—as the pennant is for any U.S. baseball team.

Days of Delirium

The city goes insane the weekend before Ash Wednesday. Samba is everywhere. Down from the hills stream the poor of Rio, gaudily bedecked in satins and tinsel, their faces powdered or smeared in paint. Out of swank apartment houses come the rich in their costumes costing many hundreds of dollars, laughing and embracing everyone they meet. Entire streets are blocked off from traffic, and samba bands play 24 hours a day for anyone who wants to dance. And everybody does.

The Carnival Samba has no rigid routine of steps that one must follow. The feet move fast, the body shakes from the hips and the arms are thrown overhead in complete abandon. The music penetrates to the very bones and the Brazilians give themselves to it much as a canoe gives itself to a river's rapids. Tourists seeing this for the first time are aghast; but as their feet start beating out the music, they discover themselves trying some of the steps, and then they, too, are carried by the crowd into the very midst of the laughing, sweating bodies. By this time all reserve is gone, and only hours later, when they have collapsed onto the moonlit beach, do they realize how far away from home they really are. The next day, now bitten by the bug, they go completely native.

Carnival is for everyone. The largely black poor have their street dancing and their parties in wooden-walled, tin-roofed shacks. The middle class give blow-outs in their apartments or visit a friend who has a home in the suburbs with a backyard to expand in. The rich have their parties at their sumptuous homes in the surrounding hills or go to one or all of the fancy dress balls.

These nearly all-white balls give the visitor a true and intimate picture of upper-class, movie-star-struck Brazilians at play. Crowded, hot, reeking with perfume and whisky, they are one never-ending confusion of noise, music, and bare flesh. Tickets should be purchased in advance from hotels or tourist agencies rather than taking a chance of buying them at the door. Most tickets are sold out weeks in advance for the most prestigious balls, but may also be procured from cambistas. Business suits and ordinary dresses are not permitted at the better balls. Men wear shorts and other cool, comfortable clothing. Women wear elaborate, skimpy, sequined costumes which can be purchased in Rio or concocted of bikinis, garter belts, stockings, corsets, and other erotic apparel. Guests of honor are usually Brazilian movie stars, top models, or television personalities. Many costumes competing for prizes and notoriety are extravagant versions of legendary or imaginary "royalty" and represent investments of tens of thousands of dollars.

Carnival's Lavish Balls

One of the most exclusive Carnival balls is the "Hawaiian Night" at the Rio Yacht Club. It is held one week earlier beside the swimming pool under the tall palms—and the pool is where most of the sweating bodies end the night's festivities around dawn.

Each year there is an infusion of new balls as Rio's top showmen compete with each other to turn out the biggest and most lavish carnival ball.

The best balls are held at Rio's showhouse/club, the Scala, Avenida Afrânio de Melo Franco 296, Leblon, 239–4448 (Baile de Gala da Cidade; Grande Gala Gay; Baile do Champagne and Vermelho e Preto) and Monte Libano, Avenida Borges de Medeiros, 701, Leblon, 239–0032 (Night at Baghdad). But every night there are dozens of less expensive balls at other clubs—all open to the public and equally crowded and frenzied. Also popular is the ball held at Pão de Açucar (Sugarloaf), which offers a breezy, spectacular view of the bay along with the elaborate costumes. You will pay from $25 to $55 per person at the more expensive balls; tables for four cost between $200 and $275.

When the dawn of Ash Wednesday finally comes to put an end to the revelry for another year, Rio looks as if it has been attacked by Roman hordes. Sleeping bodies lie everywhere. Drunks sit on curbstones holding their heads. Arabs wander dazedly down the center of the avenue accompanied by exhausted clowns, dishevelled Pierrots, and stumbling African slaves. And while an army of street cleaners starts sweeping up the tons of debris, somewhere a never-say-die Samba band can still be heard playing.

Some advice to the inexperienced attending Carnival balls and processions: Leave your inhibitions at home or at the hotel. Dress lightly. Be sure your shoes or sandals are comfortable. Leave papers and your "14 karat hardware" in the safe! Take along only as much money as you intend to spend and your credit card.

PRACTICAL INFORMATION FOR RIO DE JANEIRO

WHEN TO GO. Almost any time is a good time to visit Rio, for the climate is not that variable and there is something interesting going on almost all the time. The hottest months of the year are Jan. to Mar. when the temperature can rise to a sweltering 104 degrees in the shade. But these months are also the months with the most rain, and even though the rain's cooling effects lessen as the water evaporates, the sudden showers do give pleasant respites. The beaches are heavily populated during these months, and the sun can be unbearably hot for fair-skinned tourists after 10 A.M. The coolest months of the year are July and Aug. when there is occasionally a gray cast to everything and the ocean comes crashing up over the sidewalks and fills the main avenue with sand. At this time Brazilians stay away from the beaches, wear heavy Italian sweaters, and complain of the cold. Visitors from more northern climates find the air comfortable and many even prefer it to the blistering heat of Jan.

Of course the big event in the Rio calendar is Carnival, that impossible spectacle of madness that takes place from Friday night to the morning of Ash Wednesday. Carnival can be as early as the first week in Feb. or as late as Mar. These are the hot months, remember, so come prepared to sweat while you Samba. Make reservations well in advance, at least a year ahead for top hotels, if you are not traveling as part of a package tour.

The cultural year begins in Apr., with stars of international magnitude drawing capacity audiences during concert seasons for performance after performance. This is also the beginning for the artists and the galleries and hardly a week goes by without an important new showing of Brazilian painting or sculpture. Movie houses show many European and American films, but remember that the movies are in their original language with Portuguese subtitles.

GETTING AROUND RIO. From the airport. Vouchers are issued at set prices for taxis at the airport, depending on your final destination. Inside Rio, taxis are the best way to travel. Your hotel can arrange with *Localiza/National* or *Hertz* to rent a Brazilian-made automobile for around $50 a day. Most require a valid driver's license and credit cards. Rio taxis have meters that start at around $.50 as we go to press. Between 10 P.M. and 6 A.M. the number 2 on or above the meter indicates the higher night fare. This fare is also charged for driving you up steep hills, such as to the Corcovado, although some Rio taxi drivers refuse to climb hills. The numbers which register on the meter are keyed to a table which must be affixed to the left rear window. You pay the amount that corresponds to what appears on the meter.

By bus. In general, tourists in Rio should avoid city buses when alternatives such as taxis or comfortable air-conditioned buses are available. The Santa Teresa Trolley should not be used.

You get onto a bus at the rear and leave at the front, paying the conductor as you go through the turnstile. Buses only stop if you pull the cord by the side windows. Most bus fares start around the equivalent of $.25 and it is wise to have change ready since they often have no change at all. So keep plenty of small change handy for bus fares. Air-conditioned buses, called "frescões" (big fresh ones), go to most sections of the city, for a fare that averages $3. You must hail buses from regularly marked stops—they will not stop automatically just because people are standing there. The **Mêtro** from Botafogo to the Zona Norte passes through Centro and is the quickest way to get around downtown.

For a glimpse of the real Brazil in comfort, take an **intercity bus trip.** Deluxe coaches are now available on a few main routes, and bus travel in general within Brazil is fast, reliable and cheap. Book well in advance, however, and check your reservation. The main bus station, known as the Rodoviária Novo Rio, is five minutes from Praça Mauá by taxi.

A **hydrofoil** goes across the bay to Niteroi, or drive across the impressive bridge, paying a toll each way. There are ferries to Paqueta and other islands. You can also take a boat tour of Guanabara Bay, with lunch included.

HOTELS. Hotels in Rio range from sumptuous to simple, with the most luxurious concentrated in Copacabana, Ipanema, Leblon, and São Conrado. The cost of hotel rooms in Rio is directly proportional to the grandeur of the ocean view and the height from which the sea can be seen. Rooms are classified standard, superior, or deluxe as a function of their location within the hotel as well as their size and furnishings. Beachfront hotels are generally more expensive than those with no view of the ocean. Most hotels add 10% service charge to their room rates. For definitions of price categories, see "Facts at Your Fingertips," earlier in this chapter.

Vidigal-Sao Conrado

Super Deluxe

Inter-Continental Rio, Prefeito Mendes de Morais, 222, on Sao Conrado beach (322–2200). Opened its 500 air-conditioned rooms overlooking the beach and golf course in October 1974. Among its many attractions are a brasserie, snack bar, one of Rio's smartest cocktail lounges, lighted tennis courts, discotheque, French and Italian restaurants, swimming pool with underwater bar stools, convention rooms. Convenient parking. Satellite dish.

Sheraton Rio Hotel & Towers, Av. Neimeyer 121 between Leblon and Sao Conrado (274–1122). The only hotel that can claim a near-private beach, with no street to cross to bathe in the Atlantic surf; in addition, it has its own fresh-water pools and two lighted tennis courts. Rio's first luxury-class hotel, 617 rooms, three restaurants, featuring Brazilian and international cuisine, highlighted by the elegant Valentino's, outdoor amphitheater, health club, satellite dish, shops.

Deluxe

Nacional-Rio, Av. Niemeyer 769, also on Sao Conrado beach (322–1000). First to be built in the area, this tower has 520 wedge-shaped rooms, as well as 25 luxury suites and one floor of presidential suites. Three restaurants serve Brazilian and international specialties. Across the lobby is Rio's biggest hotel convention center, theater, shops, heliport.

Copacabana

Super Deluxe

Meridien-Rio, Av. Atlântica 1020 (275–9922). A late 1975 inauguration, this one near the beginning of Copacabana; its 36 floors make it the tallest building on the beach. It counts 552 rooms, including two presidential suites, 130 more in the luxury class and 29 cabanas. Panoramic rooftop restaurant and rotisserie serving international and French cuisine, pool, bars, nightclub, sauna, shops, beauty parlor, satellite dish.

Rio Othon Palace, Av. Atlântica 3264 (521–5522). Opened in 1976, this hotel soars 30 stories above the center of famed Copacabana Beach and combines traditional Brazilian charm with the latest advances in hostelry. Largest in the beach area, it has 606 air-conditioned rooms, two presidential suites and a variety of other luxury suites. Rooftop bar and pool with panoramic view, international restaurants, bars, nightclub, banquet facilities for up to 700, shopping gallery, beauty parlor.

Rio Palace, Av. Atlântica 4240 (521–3232). Most luxurious of all Brazilian-owned hotels. The 416-room facility is at the end of Copacabana Beach in a multi-story shopping complex. Numerous bars, restaurants, nightclubs, meeting rooms, and auditoriums. Two pools, satellite dish.

Deluxe

Copacabana Palace, Av. Atlântica 1702 (255–7070). A Rio landmark, with 400 rooms, 2 restaurants, 24-hour service, a sidewalk cafe with view to the beach on the one side and pool on the other, theater. Recently purchased by the British Orient Express group, the hotel was undergoing a $25 million renovation at press time.

Leme Palace, a posh estabishment at Av. Atlântica 656 (275–8080) in the Copacabana Beach area known as Leme. 194 rooms, good restaurant and sidewalk bar, cozy rooftop bar. Entirely air-conditioned. *H. Stern* store.

Internacional Rio, Av. Atlântica 1500 (295–2323). Rio's newest hotel, Swiss-owned, aimed at the business traveler.

Miramar, Av. Atlântica 3668 (247–6070). Restaurant, rooftop bar, marvelous view.

Rio Atlântica, Av. Atlântica 2964 (255–6332). Newly opened, on the beach.

Expensive

California, Av. Atlântica 2616 (257–1900). Modern rooms, bar, restaurant.

Debret, R. Almte. Gonçalves 5 (521–3332). Air-conditioned, ocean view.
Lancaster, Av. Atlântica 1470 (541–1887).
Luxor, Av. Atlântica 2554 (235–2245). Terrace restaurant.
Olinda, Av. Atlântica 2230 (257–1890).
Ouro Verde, Av. Atlântica 1456 (542–1887). One of 8 hotels in the world that retain the "discreet charm of the small hotels," according to *Fortune* magazine, this 66-room Swiss-owned and -managed jewel enjoys international prestige. Exquisite decor, all-round comfort, and courteous service.
Rio Copa, Av. Princesa Isabel 370. 110 air-conditioned rooms in new hotel on busy street leading to the beach. 275–6644.
Savoy Othon, Av. N.S. de Copacabana 995 (521–8222). 160 rooms. Fine restaurant and bars.
Trocadero, Av. Atlântica 2064. (257–1834). Fine Brazilian restaurant, Moenda.

Moderate

Acapulco, Rua Gustavo Sampaio 854 (275–0022). 120 modern rooms, with a view of the back side of the Merídien across the street.
Apa, Rua República de Peru 305 (255–8112 or 521–1443). Near Copacabana beach.
Bandeirantes Othon, Rua Barata Ríbeiro 548 (255–6252). Located three blocks from the beach; coffee shop and bar.
Biarritz, Rua Aires Saldanha 54 (521–6542 or 521–1443). Near Copacabana beach.
Castro Alves, Av. Copacabana 552 (255–8815). Near Copacabana beach.
Excelsior, Av. Atlântica 1800 (257–1950). 220 rooms, fine restaurant and bar with ocean view.
Martinique, Rua Sá Ferreira 30 (521–4552). Near Copacabana beach.
Plaza Copacabana, Av. Princesa Isabel 263 (275–7722). Near Copacabana Beach.
Toledo, Rua Domingos Ferreira 71 (257–1990). Near Copacabana beach.

Ipanema

Super Deluxe

Caesar Park, Av. Vieira Souto 460 (287–3122). 242 all air-conditioned rooms with TV and refrigerator. Two excellent restaurants, bar, beauty salon, barber shop, sauna, pool. Private security guards patrol beach on foot and with binoculars from hotel roof to protect guests and other bathers from "beach rats" out to relieve them of their valuables. Satellite dish.
Everest-Rio, Rua Prudente de Morais 1117 (287–8282). 22-story hotel has 176 rooms and satellite dish, one block from beach. (Although comfortable, only price range puts this hotel in the super deluxe category.)

Deluxe

Praia Ipanema, Av. Vieira Souto 706 (267–0095). Beachfront.
Sol Ipanema, Av. Vieira Souto 320 (267–0095). Restaurant, bar, beauty parlor, sun deck, and children's pool on roof. Beachfront.

Moderate

Arpoador Inn, Rua Francisco Otaviano 177 (247–6090). At the beginning of the beach. Casually elegant, with 50 air-conditioned rooms and restaurant.

Leblon

Deluxe

Marina Palace, Av. Delfim Moreira 630 (259–5212). Beach hotel, Rio's newest with 165 rooms.
Marina Rio, Ave. Delfim Moreira 696 (239–8844). On the beach beyond Ipanema. Modern new hotel with 69 air-conditioned rooms, bar, restaurant.

Moderate

Carlton, Rua Joao Lira 68 (259–1932). Quiet surroundings.

Downtown

Expensive

Gloria, Rua do Russel 632 (205–7272). In Flamengo not far from the city's center. 730 deluxe and first-class rooms. Fine colonial-style restaurant, bars, pool, terrace with view. Convention center. Overlooking Flamengo Beach.

Moderate

Aeroporto, Av. Beira Mar 280 (210–3253). Near city airport.
Ambassador, Rua Senador Dantas 25 (297–7181).
Ambassador Santos Dumont, Rua Santa Luzia 651 (210–2119). In the Clube de Aeronáutica building downtown.
Center, Av. Rio Branco 33 (296–6677). Opened late 1975. Air-conditioned, with refrigerator-bar in each room.
Flamengo Palace, Praia do Flamengo 6 (205–1552). 60 rooms, opened in 1975.
Grande Hotel OK, Rua Senador Dantas 24 (292–4114).
Novo Mundo, Praia do Flamengo 20 (205–3355). Restaurant, bar. *H. Stern* store.
Regina, Rua Ferreira Viana 29 (225–7280).
São Francisco, Rua Visconde de Inhauma 95 (223–1224). Air-conditioned, restaurant.

Apartment hotels are also available with maid service. The top residential hotels are: **Apart Hotel,** Rua Barata Ribeiro 370; 256–2633. **Rio Flat Service,** Rua Alm. Guilhem 332 (Leblon); 274–7222. **American Flat Service Apart Hotel,** Rua Humaita 244 (246–8070).

Inexpensive

Argentina, Rua Cruz Lima 30 (225–7233).
Florida, Rua Ferreira Viana 81 (245–8160).
Paissandu, Rua Paissandu 23 (225–7270).

RESTAURANTS. Typical Brazilian food is varied, unusual and delicious, but one of the biggest troubles for the tourist is trying to get some of it. Almost all the good restaurants in Rio serve international-type food only and shy away from the home product. The Brazilian wants to eat something different from everyday fare when going out to dine. Try at least one *feijoada, vatapá,* or the mouthwatering *muqueca de peixe.* For definitions of price categories see "Facts at Your Fingertips."

Brazilian

Banana Café. *Deluxe.* Rua Barão da Torre, 368, Ipanema (521–1460). Above the "Alô-Alô" Piano Bar, next to the Club Hippopotamus, and owned by the same entertainment tycoon, this laid-back restaurant offering everything from snacks to gourmet meals has become one of Rio's most "in" eateries. Reservations needed, all credit cards accepted, open for lunch and dinner.
Chale Brasileiro. *Expensive.* Rua da Matriz, 54, Botafogo (286–0897). Traditional colonial setting, Bahian cuisine, waitresses in costume, less spicy food also available. Open for lunch and dinner from 11 A.M. to midnight, accepts major credit cards, reservations advisable on weekends.
Maria Tereza Weiss. *Expensive.* Rua Visconde de Silva, 152, Botafogo (286–3098). Maria Tereza Weiss is Brazil's Betty Crocker and Julia Child rolled into one. Many traditional dishes, plus international selections. Open daily. Major credit cards accepted.
Moenda. *Expensive.* In the Trocadero Hotel, Avenida Atlantica 2064, Copacabana (257–1834). Bahian specialties and traditional cuisine. Open noon to midnight, accepts major credit cards.
Arataca. *Moderate.* Rua Dias Ferreira, 135, Leblon (274–1444). Specializes in

the cuisine of the Amazon state of Pará, including fish from the Amazon River. Open 11 A.M. to 2 A.M., major credit cards accepted, no reservations.

Bar do Arnaudo. *Moderate.* Rua Almirante Alexandrino 316-B, Santa Teresa (252–7246). Typical dishes from Pernambuco, including dried, salted beef with fried manioc, bean dishes, roast kid. Diners are requested not to use the tables as percussion instruments. No reservations, cash only. Open Tues. through Sat. from noon to 10 P.M.; Sun. until 9 P.M.

Seafood

Candido's. *Deluxe.* Rua Barros de Alarcão, 352, Pedra de Guaratiba (395–1630). An hour's drive south of Rio, go for an afternoon-long lunch after the beach. Open Mon.–Fri. noon until 7 P.M. in winter, until 9 P.M. in summer. Sat. until 11 P.M.; Sun. until 8 P.M. You *must* make reservations. Diner's Club accepted.

Quatro Sete Meia. *Deluxe.* Rua Barros de Alaracão, 476, Pedra de Guaratiba (395–2716). Reservations are obligatory at this small, simple seafood restaurant that takes its name from the numbers of its address. Open noon to 5 P.M. Mon.–Thurs., noon to 10 P.M. Fri.–Sun. Cash only.

Barracuda. *Expensive.* Marina da Gloria, Parque do Flamengo (265–3997). An elegant luncheon spot for businesspeople, specializing in shrimp and other seafood. A small bar and piano music at night. Open noon to midnight. Reservations at lunch, all major credit cards accepted.

Grottammare. *Expensive.* Rua Gomes Carneiro, 132, Ipanema (287–1596). Noted for grilled fish and salads. Closed Mon., open for dinner only from 7 P.M. on. Reservations recommended, credit cards accepted.

Sol e Mar. *Expensive.* Avenida Reporter Nestor Moreira, 11, Botafogo (295–1997). Dine on a pier overlooking Guanabara Bay and Sugarloaf. Many Spanish specialties. Open daily from noon. Reservations and credit cards accepted.

Albamar. *Moderate.* Praça Marechal Ancora, 184, Centro (240–8378). In the former Mercado Municipal, a green octagonal building near Praça XV de Novembro. Deviled crab, fish chowder, fish filet in black butter are all recommended. Crowded at lunch but not at dinner. 11:30 A.M. to 10 P.M. Closed Mon. Nice view of Guanabara Bay. No reservations needed, accepts American Express.

Cabaça Grande. *Moderate.* Rua do Ouvidor, 12, Centro (231–2301). Unpretentious Portuguese-style restaurant with steaming fish and seafood stews called *caldeiradas,* generous portions, and good service. Ice cold beer. Noon to 4 P.M. Closed Sat. and Sun. Diners Club and American Express accepted. No reservations, no credit cards.

A Marisqueira. *Moderate & Expensive.* Rua Barata Ribeiro, 232, Copacabana (237–3920) and Rua Gomes Carneiro, 90, Ipanema (227–8476). Broiled and fried fish, fish and seafood stews, many beef and chicken dishes as well. Open 11 A.M. to 1 A.M. No reservations. Credit cards accepted.

Shirley. *Moderate.* Rua Gustavo Sampaio, 610, Leme (275–1398). Be prepared to wait at this small, hidden restaurant featuring seafood and fish prepared Spanish style. No reservations. Open noon to 1 A.M.

Tia Palmira. *Moderate.* Caminho do Souza, 18, Barra de Guaratiba (410–1169). Open for lunch only 11 A.M. to 6 P.M. and closed Mon. Prix fixe menu.

Salads and Vegetarian

Natural. *Moderate.* Rua Barão da Torre, 171, Ipanema (267–7799). Inexpensive daily vegetarian plate includes rice or grain, beans, vegetables, and soup. Also serves chicken and fish, which are more expensive but still extremely reasonable.

Super Salads. *Moderate.* Avenida Armando Lombardi, 601, Barra da Tijuca (399–1026). Prix fixe all-you-can-eat buffet of salads, including meat, fish, chicken, fruits, vegetables, and several hot entrees. Open from noon daily.

Alfaces. *Inexpensive.* Rua Visconde da Graça, 51, Jardim Botanico (294–4391). Fresh, tangy fruit and vegetable salads sold in quantities of 100 grams, cheeses, cold meats, hot baked potatoes with stuffings, desserts. Open 11:30 A.M. to midnight.

Delírio Tropical. *Inexpensive.* Rua da Assembléia 36, Centro (242–6369). Sandwiches, cold cuts, and salad plates for under $5, are well seasoned, fresh, and tasty.

Japanese

Mariko. *Deluxe.* Avenida Vieira Souto, 460, in the Caesar Park Hotel, Ipanema (287–3122). Rio's choicest sushi bar, also serves sashimi and tempura. Open from 6 P.M. to 1 A.M., closed Sun.

Leblon Sushi Bar. *Moderate.* Rua Dias Ferreira 256 (274–1342).

Portuguese

Antiquarius. *Deluxe.* Rua Aristides Espinhola, 19, Ipanema (294–1049). Elegant atmosphere and cozy bar, authentic Portuguese entrees and desserts. Open every day for lunch and dinner, noon to 2 A.M. Reservations accepted.

Churrascurias

Rodeio. *Deluxe.* Avenida Alvorada, 2150, Bloco G, Casa Shopping, Barra da Tijuca (325–6163). A branch of the well-known São Paulo churrascuria, with the same high-quality meats. Open for lunch and dinner from noon to 2 A.M., most major credit cards accepted.

Buffalo Grill. *Expensive.* Rua Rita Ludolf, 47, Leblon (274–4848). Open daily from noon to 3 A.M. Live music, bar. A la carte menu.

Mariu's. *Expensive.* Avenida Atlantica, 290, Leme (542–2393). If you only go to one churrascuria during your stay in Rio, make it Mariu's. Great meats and accompaniments; rodizio. Reservations advisable on weekends and during high season. Open every day, 11:30 A.M. to 1 A.M.; credit cards accepted.

Porcao de Ipanema. *Expensive.* Rua Barão da Torre, 218, Ipanema (521–0999). Rodizio-style service, open every day, 11 A.M. to 1 A.M.

French

Rio's best restaurants are French, both classical and nouvelle cuisine. All tend to be on the high end of the price scale.

Le Bec Fin. *Deluxe.* Avenida Copacabana, 178, Copacabana (542–4097). Over 30 years of classical French cooking. Reservations suggested, all major credit cards accepted, dinner only.

Claude Troisgros. *Deluxe.* Rua Custodio Serrão, 62, Jardim Botanico (226–4542 or 246–7509). Nouvelle cuisine on a "menu confiance"—you don't know what you'll be eating until it arrives, but everything is delicious. Reservations are a must. Open noon to midnight.

Clube Gourmet. *Deluxe.* Rua General Polidoro, 186, Botafogo (295–1097). Nouvelle cuisine, prix fixe menu, and the best wine cellar in town. Comfortable, converted townhouse with/outdoor dining area. Reservations essential. Open for lunch (except Sat.) from noon to 3:30 P.M. and for dinner from 8 P.M. to 12:30 A.M.

Monseigneur. *Deluxe.* Av. Prefeito Mendes de Moraes 222 (322–2200). In the Inter-Continental Hotel. A pleasing mix of modern and traditional French cuisines are served here, coupled with a luxurious setting and the romance of strolling violins. Dinner only, 8 P.M. to 2 A.M. All major credits cards.

Ouro Verde. *Deluxe.* Avenida Atlantica, 1456, Copacabana, in the Ouro Verde Hotel (542–1887). Traditional French cuisine, open noon to midnight, make reservations.

Le Pré Catalan. *Deluxe.* Avenida Atlantica, 4240, Copacabana (521–3232). Located in the Rio Palace Hotel, this restaurant is a must stop for aficionados of gracious and elegant French dining. Lunch from noon to 3 P.M.; afternoon tea from 4 to 6:30 P.M.; and dinner from 7:30 P.M. to midnight. Major credit cards.

Saint Honoré. *Deluxe.* Avenida Atlantica, 1020, Copacabana (275–9922). The Hotel Meridien's pride and joy, this restaurant is overseen by French chef Paul Bocuse and in addition to great food you get a spectacular view of the beach and bay. Prix fixe menu at lunch, noon to 3 P.M.; à la carte at dinner, 8 to 11 P.M. Make reservations. Closed Sun.

Italian

Alfredo's. *Deluxe.* Prefeito Mendes de Moraes 222 (322–2200). In the Inter-Continental Hotel. A branch of the world famous Alfredo's of Rome, and absolute tops in Rio for pasta, especially fettuccine. Make reservations.

Enotria. *Deluxe.* Rua Constante Ramos, 115, Copacabana (237–6705). Classical Italian cuisine made fresh on the premises daily, from pasta to bread. Fine wine selection. Choose from the prix fixe menu of the day. Reservations suggested, closed Sun., dinner only, most credit cards honored.

Le Streghe. *Deluxe.* Prudente de Morais, 129 (Praça General Osório), Ipanema (287–1369). Fine, carefully prepared food, relaxed, sophisticated atmosphere, bar/disco named Caligula for after dinner. Open 7:30 P.M. to 2 A.M., reservations advisable, all major credit cards accepted.

Valentino's. *Deluxe.* Sheraton Rio Hotel & Towers, Avenida Niemeyer, Vidigal (274–1122). Beautifully served nova cucina entrees in an elegant atmosphere with excellent service. Open daily 7 P.M. to 1 A.M.; all major credit cards, reservations accepted.

La Mole. *Moderate.* Avenida Copacabana 552, Copacabana (257–5593) and Rua Dias Ferreira, 147, Leblon (294–0699). A chain of restaurants serving excellent pasta, pizza, and many other choices at reasonable prices. No reservations. If there is a line, you are given a number. All major credit cards.

Pizza Palace. *Moderate.* Rua Barão da Torre, 340, Ipanema (267–8346). Good homemade pasta, pizza, meat, and chicken dishes available in an open, sidewalk cafe setting. No reservations.

International

Rio's. *Deluxe.* Parque do Flamengo (551–1131). American bar with live music, good view of Sugarloaf and the bay. Open daily, noon to 2 A.M.

Un, Deux, Trois. *Deluxe.* Rua Bartolomeu Mitre, 123, Leblon (293–0198). Open daily for dinner, lunch on Sat. and Sun. only. Live music and bar make dinner here a full evening.

Antonio's. *Expensive.* Avenida Bartolomeu Mitre, 297, Leblon (294–2699). Has a faithful following of regulars. Open daily from noon to 2 A.M.

Cafe do Teatro. *Expensive.* Avenida Rio Branco in the Teatro Municipal (262–4164). Marvelous Assyrian decor makes dining here a special experience. Open for lunch only, 11 A.M. to 3:30 P.M., closed Sat., Sun., and holidays.

The Lord Jim Pub. *Expensive.* Rua Paul Redfern, 63, Ipanema (259–3047). A meeting place for English speakers and the foreign community featuring British food, drinking, darts, and afternoon tea, for which you should make reservations. Open Tues. through Sat., 4 P.M. to 1 A.M. and Sun. from 11 A.M. to 1 A.M.; closed Monday. Cash only.

Neal's. *Expensive.* Rua Sorocaba, 695, Botafogo (286–0433). A Manhattan-style bar-restaurant in a renovated townhouse serving American favorites like hamburgers, ribs, and T-bone steaks. Videos of American stars, posters from *New Yorker* covers and New York museum exhibitions. Open until the wee hours, usually around 4 A.M. Lunch weekdays; Sat. and Sun., dinner only, from 7 P.M. on; closed Mon.

Café Colombo. *Moderate.* Rua Gonçalves Dias 32–36, Centro (232–2300). Lunch only in a historic belle époque setting with an aura of the past. Large portions, reasonable prices, good food. No reservations. 8:30 A.M. to 6:30 P.M. weekdays; tearoom only on Sat. until noon; closed Sun.

TOURIST INFORMATION. Riotur, the official tourism agency of the city of Rio, operates information posts in the following locations: Main Office, Rua da Assembléia, 10, 8th and 9th floors, Centro (242–8000). Open Mon.-Fri., 9 A.M. to 12:30 P.M., 2 to 6 P.M. Branches: *Estaçao Rodoviária Novo Rio,* Avenida Francisco Bicalho, 1, São Cristovão (291–5151 Riotur), open 6 A.M. to midnight. *Pao de Açucar,* Avenida Pasteur, 520, Urca, Estação do Teleférico, open from 8 A.M. to 8 P.M. English, French, Spanish, German, Italian, and Japanese are spoken. **TurisRio,** the state of Rio's official tourism bureau, also has main offices at Rua da Assembléia, 10, on the 7th and 8th floors (252–4512), open Mon.–Fri. 9 A.M.–6 P.M. Branches: International Airport, Arrivals, Sections A, B, and C (398–4073/7). Open from 5 A.M. to 11 P.M. Same languages spoken as above.

TOURS. You can easily book a tour around Rio and its environs through your hotel. There are many tour operators licensed by Embratur who cater to tourists in English, Spanish, and other languages. Most tours are by air-conditioned bus, which will pick you up and drop you off at your hotel. Tours are run to Corcovado/Floresta de Tijuca ($17), Pão de Açucar and the Botanical Garden ($18), Petropolis ($20), Petropolis and Teresopolis ($30), downtown and Niteroi Bridge ($13), and various other combinations of these sights. Night and special tours include Rio by Night ($50), Samba Show ($40), football game ($17), Paradise Island Tour around Sepetiba Bay ($36), Macumba, or African Spiritist cult ceremonies ($50), and Buzios/Cabo Frio ($50).

Tour operators offering these itineraries include: **BTR,** Av. Nossa Senhora de Copacabana 330,402 (235–1320). **BrazilRio Viagens e Turismo, Ltda.,** Avenida Copacabana 300A, Copacabana (541–5099). **Ékoda,** Rua México 11, sala 1502, Centro (240–7067). Specializing in service to Búzios. **Gray Line,** Avenida Niemeyer 121, loja T1, São Conrado (central reservations: 274–7146, 294–0393, 294–1196). **Kontik-Franstur,** Avenida Atlantica, 2316A, Copacabana (237–7797). **SulAmerica Turismo,** Av. Copacabana 441, suite 201, Copacabana (257–4732, 236–6947). **Vikings,** Rua Barata Ribeiro, 383, sobreloja, Copacabana (255–9242). **Walpax,** Rua Visconde de Pirajá, 547, suite 725, Ipanema (511–1242).

For a more culturally-oriented approach, the **Projeto Roteiros Culturais,** supported by the Associação Brasileira de Educação (Brazilian Education Association), sponsors guided tours by Prof. Carlos Roquette in English and French, for $20. In-depth explanations are available in tours of Colonial Rio, Imperial Rio, the Botanical Garden, Chácara do Ceu Museum, the Teatro Municipal, and other points of interest. Information is available 24 hours a day at 322–4872, and offices are located at Rua Santa Clara 110, suite 904, Copacabana.

SIGHTS AND MUSEUMS. Rio is divided into the Zona Norte (North Zone), Zona Sul (South Zone), and Centro (Center), and it makes sense to see the points of interest in each zone at the same time. Many of these have already been described in the Rio narrative. The Zona Norte is the poorer section, with the lower economic classes and small individual homes. Away from the breezes of the ocean it can also be sticky hot. But it does have interesting and important spots to visit like the **Church of Penha,** the **Museu Nacional,** in the former Imperial Palace, **Quinta da Boa Vista,** the **Zoo, Maracanã** (the world's biggest soccer stadium), and the **Feira Nordestino at São Cristovao,** held Sun. from 6 A.M. to 1 P.M., a fair which features food and articles from Brazil's Northeast.

The central part of the city is the commercial area, with bustling Avenida Rio Branco and Avenida Presidente Vargas. Here are all of the banks, important department stores, and office buildings. Here also is the **Museum of Modern Art** (Museu de Arte Moderno—MAM), Parque do Flamengo, Avenida Infante Dom Henrique (210–2188), open Tues.–Fri. noon to 6 P.M., Sat. and Sun. 3 to 6 P.M.; the **Museum of Fine Arts** (Belas Artes), Av. Rio Branco 199 (240–0160 or 240–0068), open Tues. through Fri. noon to 6 P.M. and weekends and holidays 3–6; the **National History Museum** (Museu Historico Nacional), Praça Marechal Ancora, near Praça XV; (220–5829), open Tues–Fri., 10 A.M. to 5:30 P.M.; Sat., Sun., and holidays from 2:30 to 5:30 P.M. Partially under restoration and reorganization, the classic **Municipal Theater;** all the old **Congress and Supreme Court buildings** from when Rio was the nation's capital; and an area with movie houses called **Cinelândia.**

Other museums and sights in this area include: **Paço Imperial** (Royal Palace), Praça XV de Novembro, Centro (232–8333). Currently used as an exhibition and concert hall, the Paço Imperial was the site of many historic events, including the signing of the "Lei Áurea," Brazil's Emancipation Proclamation, by Princesa Isabel in 1888. Open Tues. through Sun. from 11 A.M. to 2:30 P.M.; and other days according to ongoing events (check newspaper listings), it also features an exhibit on the archeological research carried out during the building's recent restoration. Gift shop has prints of old Rio, picture calendars, and items sewn from printed fabric inspired by Indian body painting designs. **Aqueduto da Carioca** (Aqueduct), located in Lapa, near Centro, was completed in 1750 and is part of the National Historic Register.

The Santa Teresa trolley tracks run on it. **Museu do Palácio do Itamarati** (Itamarati Museum), Avenida Marechal Floriano 196, Centro (291–4411, ext. 6), temporarily closed for complete renovation. The palace itself is considered one of the best examples of classical architecture in Rio and was built in 1853. After the proclamation of the republic, it was purchased by the Federal Government and served as the President's residence until 1897. Remodeled in 1930, the building now houses a museum with a varied collection of art and artifacts. **Museu Chácara do Ceu,** Rua Murtinho Nobre, 345, Santa Teresa (232–1386) is open Mon. to Fri., noon to 5 P.M. In addition to a beautiful view of Rio from a peaceful garden, this museum offers a select sample of the art collection of Raymundo Castro Mayer, which includes works by prominent European painters and the Don Quixote series by Portinari, considered one of Brazil's great artists. **Museu do Folclore Edison Carneiro** (Edison Carneiro Folklore Museum), Rua do Catete, 181, Catete (285–0891) is open from Tues. to Fri., 11 A.M. to 6 P.M.; Sat., Sun., and holidays from 3 to 5 P.M. Collection includes handcrafts, household and religious objects, musical instruments, and popular literature (broadsides) from all over Brazil. **Museu da Imagem e do Som** (Museum of Image and Sound), Praça Rui Barbosa, 1 (near Praça XV de Novembro), Centro (262–0309), closed for renovation at press time. Varied collection of recordings, photographs, and archives reflecting the life of the city of Rio and Brazilian Popular Music.

The south of Rio is the chic and expensive place to live. Here are the best hotels, restaurants, and beaches. Here is Copacabana, Ipanema, and Leblon. A little farther are Avenida Niemeyer and São Conrado beach, where the newest hotels are located. Here also is the beautiful **Lagoa (lagoon) Rodrigo de Freitas,** the traditional **Jockey Club,** the calm and well-kept **Botanical Gardens, Presidents' and governors' palaces,** and, rising from the bay's blue water, **Sugar Loaf. Museu da Cidade** (City Museum), Estrada de Santa Marinha (Parque da Cidade, Gávea), 322–1328, open Tues. to Sun., noon to 4:30 P.M. Objects illustrating the history of the city are displayed by century, with a special room on the pharmaceutical industry. The **Villa Riso** (for groups with reservations call 322–1444), at Estrada da Gávea 728, São Conrado, operates as a museum, performance space, and concert hall and features employees in colonial dress (à la Williamsburg, VA.) who give a tour of this former fazenda.

Separating the city into north and south districts is the junglelike **Tijuca Forest** with its Emperor's Table, Chinese View, and impressive waterfall. You can visit it via private car, taxi, or bus tour.

BEACHES. Visitors to Brazil are always surprised to see how important the beach is to the Brazilians. Not just for those who live in the coastal cities, but even for those who live deep in the interior. Copacabana Beach or fashionable Ipanema Beach are focal points of life in Rio. The beach permeates the lives of Cariocas the way winter conditions the lives of Canadians. Everyone falls under the influence of the beach, which is cocktail party, college mixer, soccer field, and backyard all in one.

Rio's beaches—all 23 of them—are all public. There are rest rooms, but no private cabanas or changing rooms. You either arrive in your suit at the beach or else you peel off your clothes right there with your bathing suit on underneath. There is no color line drawn, the rich lie on the none-too-clean sand with the poor, as fruit and soft drink sellers walk over them equally. As one upper-crust American tourist once put it: "It is probably the most democratic beach in the world."

The undertow is strong, making swimming difficult, but the waves are prized by surfers. And lifeguards are stationed along Copacabana, Ipanema, and Leblon in numbered *postos,* or posts, which also serve as landmarks by which you can orient yourself.

Brazilians begin their beach life early. It is not at all unusual to see tiny babies in wicker baskets soaking up the sun alongside their bikini-clad mothers. When they get old enough to walk they are usually accompanied by a maid who hovers over them. Once there are able to leave their maids they go to the beach with their friends. The boys learn to play soccer, boys and girls learn volleyball, windsurfing, and surf boarding. Later on, these same children will do their homework on the beach, listen to rock music on the beach, meet a "steady" on the beach, and when the cycle is completed bring their newly born babies to the beach.

Almost anything goes on there. Early in the morning you can see old men still trying to keep young by a sunrise dip or jogging. Muscle boys cavort there. Crooks steal there and politicians even campaign there. Many business deals are closed there too. Often a weary executive will arrange to meet a client at the beach. The client also shows up in a swimsuit and with his briefcase. In spite of the sand, the bugs, and the noise of the shouting people, they manage to get their business done.

There are also many things to buy on the beach. A short list would include Coca-Cola, beer, ripe coconuts, skewered bits of shrimp, peanuts, ice cream, natural sandwiches (ricotta cheese and carrot, tuna or chicken salad on whole wheat), corn on the cob, bright-colored kites, sunglasses, beach umbrellas, and hats and visors to protect you from the sun. The vendors wander among the bathers and call attention to their wares by blowing on whistles, shouting, singing, beating a small drum or whirling a metal rachet that clatters loudly. Keep your eye on your belongings. There may be fast-working kids around, ready to snatch the unguarded purse or camera.

Another annoyance that Brazilians take for granted is the volleyball games that seem to spring up just as you have gotten comfortable and drowsy on the sand. From out of nowhere will appear eight to a dozen young people, their arms loaded down with poles, nets, rope and a leather ball. They plant the stakes, string up the net and mark off their boundaries in a matter of minutes. Brazilians, with a disinclination for trouble, just pick up their towels and move elsewhere; it is the foreigners who get furious and threaten to take on both sides of the team at once. There have been laws passed that say a volleyball game cannot be played in certain sections of Copacabana Beach or started before 2 P.M., but they are frequently ignored.

Apart from Copacabana, Ipanema, and Leblon, which are all close to hotels in the Zona Sul, the best beaches are further south: Barra da Tijica, Recreio dos Bandeirantes, Prainha, and Grumari. For a change, try the beaches on the Ilha de Paqueta, an island in Guanabara Bay which permits no automobiles, only horse-drawn carriages and bicycles. Take a ferry boat (231–0396) or hydrofoil (231–0339) from the Estação das Barcas at Praça XV. Ferries run 5:30 A.M. to 11 P.M. Mon. through Sat. and 7:10 A.M. to 11 P.M. Sun.; the hydrofoils run every two hours from 10 A.M. to 4 P.M. Mon.–Fri. and hourly from 8 A.M. to 5 P.M. on weekends.

SPORTS. Tennis is popular. See the manager of the Rio Country Club or the Caiçaras in Ipanema or the Paissandu Club in Leblon for special permission to play. Only hotels with courts are the Inter-Continental, Sheraton, and Nacional.

Surfing is popular at Copacabana Beach, Ipanema's Arpoador Beach, and at Praia dos Bandeirantes. The sea is rough and dangerous.

Golf hasn't really caught on in Brazil as yet, but the two clubs that exist for it are stunning, beautifully trimmed places in the hills of Gávea. The Gávea Golf Club has many American and English members and a number of foreign firms keep memberships for their executives. The tourist can visit the club and admire the majestic scenery without being accompanied by a club member, but to play you must be invited or have your hotel make reservations for you. The Itanhanga Golf Club is nearby.

Ocean fishing goes on year-round, and if you don't know someone who has a boat you can always rent one at the Marina da Gloria. There are marlin as well as other ocean gamefish awaiting either your hook and sinker or your spear. No license is needed and the fish are so big you won't have to throw any of them back.

Horse racing events are held Mon. and Thurs. nights and weekend afternoons at the Jockey Club. An impressive place with excellent grass and dirt tracks, it runs the best horses in the nation for your pleasure. Betting is not only permitted, but encouraged. The first Sunday in August is reserved for the Grande Premio Brazil, which draws the finest bluebloods from all over Latin America. It is also an occasion for ladies to wear elaborate hats and gowns, and for the top brass, from the President on down, to show up glittering in medals.

Soccer rules supreme in Brazil, and will remain so for years to come. The best players in the world (this is no exaggeration) are on hand to delight the visiting soccer fan. Rio's clubs have top players and any game that has teams like Vasco, Flamengo, Botafogo, or Fluminense can be counted on for plenty of excitement.

Yachting is a major sport in Rio. The Rio Yacht Club in Botafogo is open to members only and gate crashing is not easy. Farther downtown, in front of the Gloria Hotel, is the public Marina da Gloria (205–6447 or 285–2247) where rental boats and equipment are available.

MUSIC AND DANCE. Rio has a solid program of classical music and dance, and offers concerts by visiting performers as well as resident artists. The **Teatro Municipal** Praça Floriano, Centro (210–2463) houses the city's Opera and Ballet companies and is the favored performance space for touring orchestras and dance troupes as well—at Christmas time, the house troupe features the Nutcracker, snowflakes and all, and the Bolshoi performed there in May, 1986. The **Sala Cecilia Meireles,** Largo da Lapa, 47, near Cinelandia (232–9714), frequently features classical music concerts with guest artists and Brazilian music festivals; and the **Sala Sidney Miller** at Rua Araújo Porto Alegre, 80, near the Teatro Municipal (297–6116, ext. 255), runs various jazz and Brazilian popular music series featuring new performers and regional music.

Events sponsored by Funarte, Funarj, Fundação Roberto Marinho, and Fundação Calouste Gulbenkian are consistently high caliber and worth seeking out. Listings of current performances appear daily in *O Globo* and *Jornal do Brasil* in the entertainment section. Programs are scheduled year-round, but the cultural "season" begins during Rio's autumn in April and extends until the end of December.

ART GALLERIES. Rio has a lively art scene, with many openings (listed in the newspaper entertainment section under "Artes Plasticas" and in Riotur's monthly *Rio Guide*), especially during the cultural season, which begins in April and extends through the Brazilian autumn and winter. Galleries and antique stores are concentrated in the Shopping Center da Gávea, Rua Marquês de São Vicente, 52, Gávea; the Shopping Cassino Atlantico, Avenida Atlantica 4240, Copacabana; and the Rio Design Center, Avenida Ataulfo de Paiva, 270, Leblon. Opening and closing hours are idiosyncratic, varying from gallery to gallery and opening to opening. But in the shopping centers, schedules tend to conform with normal business hours. It is best to check the newspaper or call.

In the Shopping Center da Gávea: **AMC,** store 160 (239–8794); **Ana Maria Niemeyer,** store 205 (239–9144); **Art Poster Gallery,** store 214 (259–8147); **Beco da Arte,** store 368 (259–1449), also in Rio Design Center, store 314 (511–1746); **Borghese,** stores 138/139 (274–3245), also in Rio Design Center, store 201 (259–6793); **Bronze,** store 220 (259–7599); **Contorno,** store 261 (274–3832); **Paulo Klabin,** loja 204 (274–2644); **Saramenha,** store 165 (274–9445); **Toulouse,** store 350 (274–4044).

In the Cassino Atlantico: **Aktuel,** store 223 (287–4693); **G.B. Arte,** store 129 (267–3745); **Gauguin,** store 233 (227–4738); **Maria Augusta,** store 131 (227–8461); **Ralph Camargo,** store 112–113 (521–1727); **Rejane,** store 130 (521–1896); **Versailles,** store 109 (247–2185); **Villa Bernini,** store 214 (247–5198).

In the Rio Design Center: **Montesanti,** store 114 (322–3480); **Way,** store 213/214 (259–0394); and **Museum,** store 305 (239–1032).

In Ipanema, on Visconde de Pirajá: **Andréa Sigaud,** no. 207, store 307 (247–2921); **Solo Espaço de Arte,** no. 547, store 213 (274–5847); **Estampa,** no. 82, store 106 (227–2413); **Olivia Kann,** no. 351 store 105 (521–3695).

Elsewhere in the Zona Sul: **Acervo,** Rua das Palmeiras, 19, Botafogo (266–5837); **Solar Grandjean de Montigny,** Rua Marquês de Vicente 225, Gavea (274–9922); **Atelier Hélio Rodriques,** Rua General Dionisio, 47, Botafogo (246–2591); **Bahiart,** Rua Carlos Góes 234, store G, Leblon (239–4599); **Banerj,** Avenida Atlantica 4066, Copacabana (267–3046); **Bonino,** Rua Barata Ribeiro, 578, Copacabana (235–7831); **Centro Cultural Candido Mendes,** Rua Joana Angélica, 63, Ipanema (227–7882); **Claudio Gil,** Rua Teixeira de Melo, 30A, Ipanema (227–3975); **Thomas Cohn,** Rua Barão da Torre 185A, Ipanema (287–9993); **Ibeu,** Avenida Copacabana, 690, 2nd floor, Copacabana (255–4268); **Irlandini,** Rua Teixeira de Melo, 31D–E, Ipanema, (267–7891); **Petite Galerie,** Rua Barão da Torre, 220, Ipanema (287–0231). Also; **Funarte** has several galleries at Rua Araújo Porto Alegre, 80, Centro (297–6116); **Centro Cultural Itaipava,** Avenida Epitácio Pessoa, no number, in front of Parque Catacumba (267–3839); **Centro Cultural Banco do Brasil,** Rua Primeiro de Março, 66 (216–0620). **Galeria de Arte Jean-Jacques,** Rua Ramon Franco, 49, Urca (542–1443); **Francisco Brennand,** R. Marquês de São Vincente, 75, Loja N (274–5943).

SHOPPING. Brazil is considered a "developing country" under the GSP customs exemption plan so many of the things you buy here may be able to enter the U.S. wholly duty free. Get the latest list from the U.S. Customs Service before you go. Precious stones, clothing, and leather goods are all good buys. Most shops will accept traveler's checks and dollars in cash at close to the black market rate.

Gems and Jewelry

Top gem seller is **H. Stern,** who in the last 30 years has built an international organization with branches all around the world, including New York and St. Thomas (V.I.). Their headquarters are on Rua Visconde de Pirajá 490, tel. 274–3447, with branches at Galeão International Airport, downtown Santos Dumont domestic airport, the Touring Club (landing pier), Sheraton, Inter-Continental, Meridien, Othon Palace, Gloria, Nacional, Leme Palace, Copacabana, Marina, and all other principal hotels. They and other leading jewelers offer a one-year guarantee and worldwide service. Stern's has the largest selection in town at reasonable prices, from the low-priced to the extremely expensive. They also let you see their artists at work in the lapidary and jewelry workshops of their headquarters.

Stern's also has stores in these other principal Brazilian cities: São Paulo—Praça da República 242, Hotel Brasilton, Hotel São Paulo Hilton, Shopping Center Iguatemi, Shopping Center Ibirapuera; Brasilia—Hotel Nacional; Salvador—Hotel Othon Palace, Hotel Meridien, International Airport; Manaus—Hotel Tropical, International Airport; Foz do Iguaçu—Hotel das Cataratas, International Airport.

For over thirty years the **Amsterdam-Sauer** Company has been a pioneer in lapidary art and the leading Brazilian specialist in emeralds. The owner, Jules Roger Sauer, is a well-known gemologist who has reactivated some old mines and opened a series of new ones. His company today has its own mining, cutting, designing, and jewelry divisions, as well as shops. Their headquarters are at Rua Mexico 41, downtown. Showcases at the hotels: Leme Palace, Savoy, Ouro Verde, California, Trocadero, Olinda, Lancaster.

Roditi, whose slogan is "The fastest growing jeweler in town," has branches in New York and Geneva. His main showroom is downtown at Av. Rio Branco 39, fifteenth floor. Shops are at Av. Rio Branco 133, Av. Atlântica 1702 (Copacabana Palace), Av. Atlântica 994 (next to Hotel Meridien), Av. Atlântica 2364, Rua Xavier da Silveira 22-A (Rio Othon Palace), and Av. Niemeyer 769 (Hotel Nacional Rio).

Maximino, a traditional jeweler and gemologist, has his head office with a magnificent gem museum downtown at Av. Rio Branco 25, and two branches at Copacabana: Rua Santa Clara 27 and Rua Figueiredo Magalhães 131. A couple of small but outstanding traditional jewelers, all with many years' experience, are **Joalharia Schupp** on Rua Gonçalves Dias 49, which has no branches but owns mines, and **Franz Flohr** on Rua Miguel Couto 23. The late Franz founded the shop back in 1936; his two sons, Gunther, a stonecutter, and Werner, a designer, are the present owners.

Ernani and Walter's ad says "No luxury store," meaning that his prices are highly competitive. His shop is at Praça Olavo Bilac 28, second floor, near the Flower Market. A number of small jewelers are to be found in this neighborhood, such as **Gregory and Sheehan.**

Burle Marx, whose head office is downtown at Pça Mahatma Gandhi 2, sells only at Rua Rodolfo Dantas 6 (next to Copacabana Palace). His specialties are unusually shaped semiprecious stones in one-of-a-kind settings. His necklace and bracelet designs have won prizes. The government often purchases jewelry from him as gifts for visiting dignitaries—the French premier's wife and the Empress of Japan, for example.

A relatively new addition to Rio's gem scene is **Mayer** at Av. Copacabana 291-E, just next to the theater of the Copacabana Palace Hotel. For collector specimens try **Edwin** at Rua Xavier da Silva 19-A behind the Othon Palace Hotel in Copacabana.

Souvenirs

The best way to acquire souvenirs is to windowshop around your hotel on Copacabana, where there are numerous shops, such as **Casa de Folclore, Macumba Souvenir,** and **Liane,** that carry Indian artifacts, butterfly trays, wooden statuettes, stuffed snakes, silverware, etc. Souvenir shops in Copacabana are concentrated along Avenida Copacabana itself, especially between Rua Paula Freitas and Avenida Princesa Isabel, and in Shopping Cassino Atlantica.

For articles made of alligator skin, look for the specialty shop, **Souvenir do Brasil,** on Av. Rio Branco 25. For beautiful leather handbags visit Rozwadowski, Av. Rainha Elizabeth 152, suite 101. **Copacabana Presentes,** Av. Copacabana 331-A, specializes in leather and alligator items, stones, skins, rugs, handbags, and belts. **Copacabana Couros e Artesanatos,** nearby at Rua Fernando Mendes 45, also features alligator goods and has exclusive designs for handmade bags and belts. Although you will see alligator goods for sale, it is against the law in Brazil to hunt the animal. Check to see whether you will be able to bring these goods home with you or into the next country on your itinerary. Brazilian artistic wood carvings and native paintings by **Batista and Mady** are excellent souvenirs; visit their studio on Rua Pacheco Leão 1270 in Ipanema where an appointment may be made to see their works.

Malls

Copacabana and Ipanema are loaded with chic boutiques and shops. To capture the flavor of the city, wandering up and down Avenida Copacabana or Visconde de Pirajá and their cross streets, which constitute the main shopping drag, can't be beat. But there are a number of malls, too, for those short of time or for days when you simply wish to get out of the rain or sun. **Rio Sul,** Avenida Lauro Muller 116, Botafogo, has over 400 shops, including the best stores of the Zona Sul. The biggest and newest mall is **Barra Shopping,** Avenida das Americas, 4666 in Barra da Tijuca. Ask at your hotel about free bus service to these malls. Other malls include:

Casa Shopping, Avenida Alvorada, 2150, Barra da Tijuca, specializing in household items.

Rio Design Center, Avenida Ataulfo de Paiva, 270, Leblon. Interior design and home decoration.

Sao Conrado Fashion Mall, Estrada da Gávea, 899, São Conrado. Built to serve the hotels Nacional and InterContinental.

Shopping Center Cassino Atlântico, Avenida Atlantica 4240, Copacabana. Attached to the Rio Palace Hotel, this mall features art galleries, antique stores, and souvenir shops.

Shopping Center da Gávea, Rua Marquês de São Vicente, 52, Gávea. Notable for leather shops featuring women's clothing and shoes, and galleries.

Malls are generally open from 10 A.M. to 10 P.M. on weekdays, smaller malls until 6 P.M. on Sat. Stores are not open on Sun.

Clothing

Most of the leading shops in Rio are concentrated in Ipanema, but they also have multiple branches in Copacabana and major malls. High fashion, good quality clothing for women can be found at the following Ipanema stores: **Aspargus,** Rua Maria Quiteria, 59 (cotton jersey ensembles and knits); **Krishna,** Rua Garcia D'Avila, 101 (linen and silk suits and dresses); **Maria Bonita,** Rua Vinicius de Morais 149 (linen, cotton, and silk outfits); **Georges Henri,** Rua Visconde de Pirajá 525; **Chocolate,** Rua Visconde de Pirajá 550, entrance on Anibal de Mendonça; **Spy & Great,** Rua Garcia D'Avila 58; **Alice Tapajós** and **Marcia Pinheiro,** both in the Forum de Ipanema, Rua Visconde de Pirajá, 351.

Casual wear for women and teens is available at **Evelyn's,** Avenida Copacabana 471, Copacabana and nine other branches; **Cantao, Smash, Smuggler, Yes Brazil,** and **Toot,** all with branches in Rio Sul. Many boutiques also carry bikinis, but **Bum Bum,** Rua Vinicius de Morais 130 and **Agua na Boca,** Rua Visconde de Pirajá, loja 117, both specialize in swimwear.

Stores carrying clothing for both women and men: **Dijon,** Garcia D'Avila, 110 (and many branches in Rio); **Company,** Garcia D'Avila 56; **Van Gogh,** Visconde de Pirajá 444, loja 101; **Philippe Martin,** Rua Visconde de Pirajá, 338; **Elle et Lui,** Rua Garcia D'Avila, 393; and **Bee,** Rua Visconde de Pirajá 483 (T-shirts for the whole family).

Elegant men's wear at: **Richard's,** Rua Maria Quiteria 95; **Georges Henri,** Rua Maria Quiteria 77; **Eduardo Guinle,** Rua Visconde de Pirajá 514a.

Leather

The Shopping Center da Gávea is the place to go for women's leather clothing. Try **Frankie Amaury.** Also in Gávea Shopping are **Bottega Veneta, Nazaré,** and **Ariella** for fine leather shoes and bags. In Ipanema, **Rotstein** and **Pucci,** both at Visconde de Piraja 371, carry excellent women's shoes, as do the following stores, all on Visconde de Pirajá: **Mariazinha,** no. 365B, **Beneduci,** no. 423B and **Formosinho,** nos. 106A, 135B, 265A, which sells stock ends of export models at amazingly low prices (also a store at Av. N.S. de Copacabana, no. 582). In Rio Sul, **Altemia Spinelli, Birello, Germon's,** and **Sagaro** all have good women's shoes. Two shops in Rio Sul specialize in bags for women: **Victor Hugo** and **Santa Marinella,** both with branches in Ipanema.

Fairs

Popular fairs, selling food, clothing, and household items are held throughout the city every day of the week. In Ipanema, the fair is held on Fri. on Praça Nossa Senhora da Paz; in Copacabana, on Thurs. on Rua Ronald de Carvalho between Avenida Copacabana and Rua Barata Ribeiro. The **Feira Nordestino** is held every Sun. from 6 A.M. to 1 P.M. at São Cristovão in the Zona Norte. You will hear the distinctive twang of Brazil's northeast in the conversation and "frevo" music played there, sometimes by a live band. Food of the region is also available. The **Feira de Antiquidades,** or Antique Fair takes place every Sat. at Praça XV de Novembro, Centro, from 8 A.M. to 5 P.M. **Fierarte craft fairs** take place every Sun. from 9 A.M. to 6 P.M. at Praça General Osório in Ipanema, and on Thurs. and Fri. from 8 A.M. to 6 P.M. at Praça XV de Novembro, Centro.

NIGHTLIFE. Rio's varied nightlife gets started late, around 10 or 11 P.M. and goes until 4 or 5 in the morning, or until the last customer leaves. Shows, concerts, and club performances begin around 9 or 9:30 P.M., sometimes later. Many nightclubs also serve food, and quite a number of restaurants also have live music and dance floors—there is sometimes a fine line between one definition and another.

Samba Shows

Samba Shows are geared specifically to tourists, begin at $20, and consist of dancers (invariably "mulatas," Portuguese for mulatto women), fancy costumes, and dinner. **Scala,** Av. Afranio de Mello Franco, 292, Leblon 239–4448); **Plataforma I,** Rua Adalberto Ferreira, 32, Leblon (274–4022); **Oba Oba,** Rua Humaita 110, Botafogo (246–2146 or 286–9848); **Noites Cariocas,** Pão de Açucar, Morro de Urca (541–3737). The guided tours of Rio by Night generally include one of these Las Vegas style shows, but you can make reservations yourself and go without paying the additional cost of the tour.

Concerts

Tickets range from $10 to $30, more for foreign performers. **Canecao,** Av. Venceslau Braz, 215, Botafogo (295–3044), near Rio Sul, features the best in national and international performers. Seats are at tables or in a gallery, with drinks and snacks available to all. **Scala** (details above) also stages shows of noted performers; **Circo Voador,** Arcos da Lapa Lapa (252–8231), presents top Brazilian popular and jazz artists, and after the concerts you can stay and dance. Limited seating—you may wind up sitting on the dance floor. Musical concerts are also presented in various stadiums, museums and parks around town. Consult newspaper listings and posters for information.

Nightclubs and Bars

O Viro da Ipiranga, Rua Ipiranga 54, Laranjeiras (225–4762), is an important spot for Brazilian popular music. The best places to hear jazz are **Jazzmania,** Ave. Rainha Elizabeth 769, Ipanema (227–2447), and **People Jazz Bar,** Av. Bartolomeu Mitre, 370A, Leblon (294–0547). Cover charges average $10 to $15. Make reservations on weekends, other days access depends on the popularity of the performer. **Mistura Fina Up,** Rua Garcia D'Avila 15, Ipanema (267–6596) also has jazz and popular music. For Rock n' Roll as well as jazz, **New Let it Be,** Rua Siqueira Campos, 260, Copacabana, draws a young crowd. Many other piano and jazz bars cater to professional people with more disposable income. These include **Biblo's Bar,** Av. Epitácio Pessoa, 1484, Lagoa (521–2645), popular with singles; **Banana Café,** Rua Barão da Torre, 368, Ipanema (521–1460); **Caligula,** Rua Prudente de Morais, 129, Ipanema (287–1369); **Un, Deux, Trois,** Av. Bartolomeu Mitre, 112, Leblon (239–0198).

The following are private clubs, but if you're staying at one of the 5-star hotels, you can arrange to be admitted (ask the concierge): **Hippopotamus,** Rua Barão da Torre, 354, Ipanema (247–0351), has dancing, dinner, and music; **Palace Club,** Hotel Rio Palace, Av. Atlântica 4240, downstairs, Copacabana (521–3232).

Discotheques

Discos are called "danceterias" in Brazil, and generally draw a young crowd, playing a good many American and British tunes in addition to Brazilian rock. The biggest in Rio is **Help,** Av. Atlantica 3432, Copacabana (521–1296). Also, **Bali Bar,** Estrada da Barra da Tijuca, 1636, Barra (399–3460), open every night; and **Papillon,** in the Inter-Continental Hotel (322–2200), also open every night of the week.

Dancing to live band music tends to draw a more mature group. **Sobre As Ondas,** Av. Atlantica 3432, Copacabana (521–1296); **Vogue,** Rua Cupertino Durão, 173, Leblon (274–4145); **Vinicius,** Av. Copacabana, 1144, Copacabana (267–1497); **Carinhoso,** Rua Visconde de Piraja, 22, Ipanema (287–3579). **Asa Branca,** Av. Mem de Sá, 17, Lapa (242–7066), also has dinner and shows, closed Mon.

Gafieiras

Asa Branca, described above, is sometimes categorized as a "gafieira," despite its luxuriousness. Most gafieiras are funky dance halls with live Brazilian band music and a heterogeneous clientele not necessarily from the Zona Sul. **Elite,** Rua Frei Caneca, 4, 1st floor, Centro (232–3217), open Fri.–Sat., 11 P.M.–4 A.M., Sun., 9 P.M.–3 A.M.; **Estudantina,** Praça Tiradentes, 79, 1st fl., Centro (232–1149), open Thurs.–Sat.; and **Mr. Merengue,** Rua Raul Pompeia 94, Copacabana (521–0279), open 10 P.M. with Sun. matinees at 4 P.M. All are unpretentious, genuine, and cheap, and cost about a dollar at the door.

Karaoke

Karaoke is a Japanese word meaning "empty stage or orchestra" and has been adopted by Brazilians as a popular form of entertainment. In a karaoke club, the customers are the performers, and a menu of songs is delivered with the food menu. You sing to a back-up tape, with words provided. Good clubs for English speakers: **Canja,** Av. Ataulfo da Paiva, 375, Leblon (511–0484); **Limelight,** Rua Ministro Viveiros de Castro, 51, Copacabana (542–3596); and **Manga Rosa,** Rua 19 de Fevereiro, 94, Botafogo (266–4996).

EXCURSIONS FROM RIO

Like San Francisco or Boston, Rio is close to mountains as well as beautiful beaches on the north and south shores. Three areas outside city limits are of major interest and are only an hour or two away by car.

THE MOUNTAINS—SERRA DOS ORGÃOS

Petrópolis, Teresópolis and Novo Friburgo are popular mountain resorts offering Cariocas a break from the summer heat. Located in the Serra dos Orgãos mountain range north of Rio, these towns were settled by German and Swiss colonists, giving them a decidedly Alpine appearance.

Petrópolis

Petrópolis is a city of considerable historic significance. Emperor Dom Pedro II liked the climate and fresh air of the area so much that he ordered a residence built in 1845 and sent for German emigrants to found a city around it. Today, his former summer palace is the Museu Imperial, Rua da Imperatriz 220 (242–7012), open Tuesday through Sunday from noon until 5:30 P.M. The museum is full of royal memorabilia, including the Imperial Crown, weighing in at 1,720 grams, 639 diamonds and 77 pearls. The House of Santos Dumont, Brazil's father of aviation, Rua do Encanto 124, is open from 9 to 5 Tuesday to Sunday. Brazilians believe that Dumont, after whom the Rio airport is named, was the first to fly—not the Wright Brothers. The Crystal Palace, a great greenhouse at Praça da Confluencia at Rua Alfredo Pacha, was the scene of a gala ball attended by former slaves and Princesa Isabel, after she signed Brazil's emancipation proclamation in 1888. The Catedral São Pedro de Alcântara, Av. 7 de Setembro, holds the earthly remains of Dom Pedro II, the Empress Dona Teresa Cristina and Princesa Isabel. CONDEPE, the city's tourist bureau, is located at Rua Irmãos D'Angelo 48, Sala 204/206 (243–3262). Petrópolis is also a center for cotton jersey ("malha") fashions at bargain prices, concentrated on Rua Teresa. Chartered buses bring shoppers here from all over Brazil on Saturdays, so go midweek to avoid crowds.

Teresópolis

Teresópolis, an hour's drive from Petrópolis past wooded hillsides and lovely homes and farms, belonged at one time to an Englishman named George March. In 1855 he sold his ranch to the government who cut it into lots and encouraged immigration. The town gets its name from the Empress Teresa, the same way Petrópolis took its name from Dom Pedro. The most memorable thing about Teresópolis is the string of mountains it's on, the Serra dos Orgãos, which became a national park in 1939. Here is the 1,692-meter Finger of God pointing straight to Heaven, as well as the Finger of Our Lady, the 1,980-meter Friar's Nose, and the 2,050-meter Devil's Needle. Tallest of them all is The Rock of the Bell, which towers 2,263 meters above sea level. Alpinists climb these mountains every weekend, and if you're interested, ask your travel agent to put you in contact with a group.

Nova Friburgo

Nova Friburgo, farther east in the same mountain range, came into being by command of the Imperial Family, but years before either Petrópolis or Teresópolis (in 1818 to be exact). The man responsible for laying out the city, with its parks and beautiful homes, was the Count of Nova Friburgo. The three main squares are symphonies in marble, eucalyptus, and bamboo. Be sure and visit the park of São Clemente with its pools and wide shaded paths, currently being used as a country club. The *Paço Catete,* former residence of the Count of Novo Friburgo within the park, is being renovated and will eventually function as a museum. The gardens were designed by Glasioux, who also did the Quinta da Boa Vista in Rio. Of special interest in Novo Friburgo is the Cão Sentado (Sitting Dog), which perches atop a promontory reached after a hike of over an hour. The trail is clearly marked, although in disrepair, but the climb is worth it both to see this natural rock formation that looks like sculpture, and to get a good view of the countryside. The city itself sponsors many fairs featuring the immigrant groups that have settled there.

PRACTICAL INFORMATION FOR SERRA DOS ORGÃOS AND PETROPÓLIS

HOW TO GET THERE. Guided bus trips are offered by various tour agencies and the city's sights can be covered in a day, minus shopping. From Rio, public buses leave from Castelo (Praça XV de Novembro) from the Terminal Menezes Cortes, Platform A, leaving every half hour from 11:45 A.M. to 7:30 P.M. (call 224–7577 for information), and every half hour from 5:30 A.M. to midnight from the Rodoviário Novo Rio bus station.

HOTELS. Casa do Sol, Estrada Rio/Petrópolis, 115, Quitandinha, (0242–243–5062)—a huge resort complex, turned condominium, with a lake in front, this is considered a landmark. A travel agent may be able to get you a reservation; **Riverside Parque Hotel,** Rua Hermogêneo Silva, 522, Retiro (0242–242–3704).

TERESÓPOLIS

HOW TO GET THERE. Public buses to Teresópolis leave from the Menezes Cortes terminal in Castelo every half hour from 4:15 to 7:45 P.M., and every half hour from 6 A.M. to 10 P.M. (plus a midnight bus) from the Rodoviário Novo Rio bus station. Call Viação Teresópolis, 233–4625 for information.

HOTELS. Alpina, Av. Pres. Roosevelt 2.500 (742–5252); **Rosa dos Ventos,** Estrada Teresópolis/Friburgo, Km. 22.6 (742–8833); **Sao Moritz,** Estrada Teresópolis/Friburgo, Km. 36 (239–4445 for reservations).

NOVA FRIBURGO

HOTELS. Sans Souci, Rua Itajai, Sans Souci (0245–22–7752); **Park Hotel,** Alm. Princesa Isabel, Parque São Clemente (0245–22–0825); **Mury Garden,** Estrada Novo Friburgo/Niteroi Km. 70 (42–1120; reservations in Rio 220–2234). **Bucsky,** Estrada Novo Friburgo/Niteroi Km. 76.5 (22–5052; reservations in Rio 252–5053). These resort hotels include full meal plans and offer recreational facilities.

THE NORTH SHORE—CABO FRIO AND BÚZIOS

On the coast north of Rio, Cabo Frio has wide white sandy beaches, long enough and hard enough to drive on. It is studded with architectural relics from the colonial days, including forts, a 17th-century Franciscan convent, and an ancient cemetery. All places are open to the public and tourists can wander around undisturbed to their hearts' content. If you like water-skiing or fishing, make friends with someone from Rio who has a boat, or else convince a salty old fisherman that he should rent you his. You might also visit the little fishing village of Barra de São João and watch the men working with their long woven nets. The thatched roof cottages are mixed with modern summer homes of Cariocas who have discovered it as a weekend spot. Seven miles south on the beach is the fishing village of Arraial do Cabo. Here scores of Japanese fishermen live and bring in giant whales during the cold months from June to September.

One of the best beaches is Praia do Peró in Ogiva, a long, empty stretch of white sand perfect for a long walk or run.

PRACTICAL INFORMATION FOR THE NORTH SHORE

Rent a car to get to Búzios; you'll need it to get to the various beaches, and bus service from Rio extends only as far as Cabo Frio.

CABO FRIO

HOTELS. Accommodations in this area are available at pousadas, small, owner-operated inns; **Porto Peró,** Av. dos Pescadores 2002 (0246–643–1395); **Ponta de Areia,** Av. Espadarte 184 (0246–643–2053); **Portoveleiro,** Av. dos Espadartes, 129 (0246–643–3081). Prices depend on high or low season, but range between $50 and $80, not including meals. This area is still simple, casual, and quiet.

BÚZIOS

HOTELS. Búzios, sometimes considered Rio's "Côte D'Azur," is a watering hole for affluent Cariocas and international jetsetters. **Nas Rochas Club,** Ilha Rasa, Marina Porto Búzios (0246–623–1303), occupies its own island and offers a 5-star restaurant, swimming pool, running track, nautical sports, breakfast, dinner and all activities included in the daily rate, beginning at $180. Make reservations in Rio, (021) 253–0001.

In Armação dos Búzios or Centro, comfortable, elegant lodging is available at **Pousada Casas Brancas,** on a hill overlooking Praia da Armação. Casas Brancas is noted for its special breakfasts and warm hospitality, starting at about $100 a night (0246–623–1458). Also, **Pousada La Chimère** on Praia dos Ossos, (0246–623–1460), prices begin at about $60 per night. There are many more pousadas in existence and under construction.

RESTAURANTS. Búzios is noted for great dining. French: **Au Cheval Blanc,** Rua Bento Dantas, Centro. Italian: **Le Streghe,** Rua Bento Dantas 201, a few doors down from **Au Cheval Blanc,** and **Satiricon,** on the road from Centro to Praia dos Ossos. **Adamostor** has excellent seafood (reservations needed here, 23–1162). All of these are *expensive* to *deluxe.* For simpler, *moderate* fare: **Maia** on the beach, Rua José Bento Ribeiro Dantas 275; or **Girau,** Rua Manoel Turíbio de Farias 351. No telephone reservations—Centro is so small, you can drop in and make them in person.

THE SOUTH SHORE—ANGRA DOS REIS AND PARATÍ

Make Angra Dos Reis your headquarters for visiting some of the 300 islands in the Ilha Grande Bay.

The coastal village of Paratí was founded way back in the early 16th century. Its calm, natural little harbor was the perfect jumping off point for adventurers looking for the gold and precious stones in Minas Gerais. For decades the town flourished while it catered to the needs of the miners and helped them spend their money. But the boom calmed down, Santos rose in importance because of its superb harbor, and over the years Paratí was forgotten. Then just a few years ago, the Paulistas rediscovered this colonial village (actually located in Rio de Janeiro state), and the government declared it a national monument whose architectural style must be preserved. Today it is important as a tourist center. Those who have taken the time to visit it come back with glowing tales of baroque churches, charming squares, and an unspoiled old-world charm.

Many artistic and cultural festivals, including the Festa do Divino and the Festas Juninas are held in Angra and Paratí in May and June. The main attraction of Angra is as a point of departure to explore the islands of Sepetiba Bay. Paratí itself is small and can be seen in a day's walking tour.

PRACTICAL INFORMATION FOR ANGRA DOS REIS AND PARATÍ

HOTELS. Angra and Paratí are served by the Frade Hotel chain, which operates the **Hotel do Frade,** the **Portogalo** (Angra) and the **Frade Pousada Paratí** (Paratí). Book in Rio at Rua Joaquim Nabuco, 161, Copacabana (267–7375). The chain sends a bus down from Rio regularly for about $10 to serve its hotels, which offer a full range of recreational activities, including all nautical sports, tennis and cruises around Sepetiba Bay, daily or overnight on a specially fitted yacht. Rooms start at $100, without meals; leisure options are extra, full meal plans available. Close by at the seaside town of Mangaratiba is Brazil's newest Club Med, the **Club Mediterranee Rio das Pedras,** *deluxe* (224–0803; reservations in Rio 297–5337). On the beach with full facilities, pool, tennis, gymnastics, restaurants, bars, and convention center.

OTHER DESTINATIONS

Itacuruçá and Aguas Lindas

Itacuruçá is the take-off point for the saveiro boats that form the second leg of the Island Paradise Tours, offered by a number of tour operators from Rio. A bus picks you up at your hotel, drops you at the boat, and takes you back to Rio at the end of the day. Four hotels are located on tropical paradise islands in this area about 55 miles southwest of Rio. The Jaguanum occupies its own beach on Jaguanum Island, about 30 minutes by launch from the Itacuruçá pier. Luxurious apartments and bungalows, deep-sea fishing. European management. Book in advance in Rio (235–2893), including meals.

Aguas Lindas is in a cove where many of the wealthy have weekend cottages, on the island of Itacuruçá. There are thirty-two rooms and bungalows overlooking the beach. On another side of the island is the Hotel de Pierre with several air-conditioned apartments (call 788–1016 or 788–1560).

Resende

143 kms. from Rio, Resende is an excellent vacation spot in Itatiaia Park. Among its attractions: Agulhas Negras Peak; Penedo, a Finnish settlement; Blue Lake; waterfalls; Agulhas Negras military academy. Best hotels are the Simon, expensive, in the Parque Nacional (52–1122: 240–4508 in Rio); and Cabanas de Itatiaia, moderate (0243–52–1328). Nearby, in Resende itself, the Espigão Palace and the small Avenida are the only choices for lodgings; both are inexpensive.

SÃO PAULO

No matter how well you've studied Latin America and boned up on Brazil, the city of São Paulo will come as a startling surprise. There is nothing like it in any other South American nation, no other place that can come close or that even hints of coming close. It's the richest area in South America, the fastest growing, and the pride of all the Brazilians. Nothing of importance happens in Brazil that doesn't begin in São Paulo. Brasilia may be the country's capital, but politically, economically, and culturally, São Paulo is the number one city in the country, and the largest, wealthiest metropolis in all of South America. Where Rio is beautiful, São Paulo is brilliant. Where Rio is devil-may-care, São Paulo is committed and dynamic. Where Rio is laid-back and lackadaisical, São Paulo is efficient, productive, and propelled by the work ethic.

Paulistanos, as natives of the city are called, work hard, play hard, and demand the very best in shopping, restaurants, and entertainment. Paulistanos are the shrewd, industrious Yankees of Brazil. This mighty headquarters of multinational companies and manufacturing is a craggy concrete center of skyscrapers and astute entrepreneurs. This is where Brazilians come to make it big, for everyone knows that the right place and the right time are here, and the secret ingredients to success are hard work and persistence. This giant city is a magnet for money and talent, drawing the ambitious from all parts of Brazil and all over the world.

São Paulo is a cross between New York and Los Angeles. Like Los Angeles, it sprawls over 589 square miles, is covered by a semi-permanent blanket of smog, and is connected by a giant freeway system. Like New York, skyscrapers dominate the horizon in jagged concrete clusters, the constant din of traffic and construction provides a permanent white noise in the background, and life is lived indoors, at night, in the best, most sophisticated restaurants, nightclubs, and company in all Brazil.

Like their counterparts in New York, Paulistanos have a love-hate relationship with their city. They complain that it is ugly, dirty, and threatening. On weekends, they escape to Guarujá by the sea or Campos do Jordão in the mountains the way New Yorkers flee Manhattan for Long Island or the Catskills. Some say they find it impossible to live here, yet they can't imagine living anywhere else. No other Brazilian city has the tempo, the creative drive, the excitement that comes from the pursuit of excellence.

Most tourists never get to São Paulo, as it is rarely included on a vacationer's itinerary. Yet a visit to Brazil that did not include São Paulo would be like going to the United States without seeing New York—unthinkable. Nevertheless, many settle for the seductions of Rio instead of the superlatives of São Paulo, a mistake São Paulo's 14 million residents have avoided. Seventy percent of São Paulo's inhabitants are descendents of immigrants, most of whom arrived between 1885 and 1914 as part of the great global migration from Europe and Asia to the New World. Another wave of Europeans arrived after the Second World War, while transplants from Brazil's interior and impoverished northeast arrive daily to start new lives. This is Brazil's big apple. Great expectations are what São Paulo is made of. People with dreams to realize come here, work hard, and make it happen. The city is constantly growing—demographers estimate that by the year 2000, São Paulo will have a population of 26 million.

Historically, immense wealth generated by the coffee plantation period positioned São Paulo fortuitously: when the late-blooming Brazilian industrial revolution finally burgeoned during the late 1950s and early 1960s, São Paulo boomed, growing outward from the Centro district in concentric circles of development, forming an accretion of 500 neighborhoods. Little is left from the colonial period except for the determined spirit of the Bandeirantes, hunters for Indian slaves and gold whose hardy expeditions into the interior claimed much of Brazil's territory and countless native lives. The legacy of such ruthlessness and rapid growth is relentless concrete, helter-skelter urban sprawl, a mania for achievement, and an area so rich that it is virtually a country within a country. The costs of industrialization have been as high as the profits—São Paulo also holds the dubious distinction of including within its immediate vicinity Cubatão, generally conceded to be the world's most polluted community.

São Paulo today is a cosmopolitan hybrid, manifesting layers of cultural amalgamation that distinguishes it from the rest of Brazil, where the ethnic stew is made of a different mix. To the original African and Portuguese influences—epitomized by the earthy sensuality of samba and the piety of Catholic tradition—were added the cultural traits of later immigrants, primarily Japanese and Italian. The largest Japanese community outside Japan added its industriousness and pragmatism; the Italians contributed their flair for seizing and enjoying the moment. Simmered together with the universal yearnings of the immigrant, these cultural ingredients produced the Paulistano: responsible, competent, ambitious, free from Anglo-Saxon angst at pleasure, warm and flexible in dealing with people.

The state of São Paulo, whose residents are called "Paulistas," is a fit setting for its active, pulsating, capital city. With some of the richest farmland in Brazil, it supplies almost half the nation's coffee, cotton, fruits, and vegetables. The fertile land is criscrossed by an excellent system of railways and modern highways, which the industries scattered in the small towns use to their advantage.

São Paulo is a cosmopolitan city that owes its progress to people from all nations, the richness of the soil and the temperate climate. It is a never ending source of investigation and amazement on the part of sociologists and a richly rewarding experience to those Brazilians who feel their country is capable of becoming an important world power.

From a sleepy little Jesuit colony founded in 1554 it has grown into a metropolis almost three times the size of Paris, with an industrial district that swallows up mile after mile of surrounding land per annum. There is a violent energy in the air and none of the sentimentality that binds the rest of the nation to the past. For São Paulo there is only the future. The Paulistas like to say that "São Paulo can never stop." And from the way it has weathered every political crisis and change and steered its way through inflation and depression, it looks as if it never is going to stop.

But it is not an inhuman city of robots, concrete, and machines. It is a city of people who have come looking to better themselves from every nation on the globe. They are individuals who desire better living conditions and are willing to work for them. The Paulista asks nothing from anyone. He has two hands and uses them to get what he wants. Sometimes his attitude is rather Texan, in that he thinks the world comes to an end at the state's boundaries. His capital city is self-contained and thrives on the manufacture of textiles, clothes, paper, pottery, chemicals, automobiles, trucks, buses, and steel. His state alone provides one-fourth of the two million new jobs Brazil needs annually to keep unemployment from becoming a severe problem.

The city was first with enough cheap electrical power to handle any industry that was interested in building there. It also offered a direct railway connection to the seaport town of Santos, and its early governors encouraged immigration of industrial workers rather than farmers. Those Europeans who couldn't take the climate of Rio or Bahia thrived in São Paulo, built their homes there, and encouraged their children to stay on and handle the family businesses. The result is that today the city counts a number of millionaire families who are third and fourth generation Paulista, and they are proud to tell the visitor the way their grandparents worked their way up from steerage class to the mansions along Avenida Paulista, which are rapidly being replaced today by ultra-modern bank and office buildings.

The Times Square of Brazil

Probably the best place to "feel" the pulse of the city is right in its heart, the bridge over the vast Avenida Anhangabaú. It leads into the Praça do Patriarca. Just stand there and observe the autos and people hurrying below you in what appears to be organized confusion. This is the Times Square of Brazil, and the bridge you're on is the Viaduto do Cha (tea), named for the product once grown in this valley. The intricately worked bridge farther down the avenue is the Santa Ifigênia, recently spruced up by the city and bathed in golden light at night by the General Electric Co. Now look at the buildings that flank each side of the bridge and note especially the squat white granite, solid looking one that is partly below the bridge and partly above it. It is the Matarazzo Building, former headquarters of one of Brazil's most successful immigrant families. The first Matarazzo came to Brazil as an immigrant and arrived dripping wet when his boat overturned going to the shore. He had lost every one of his possessions. Undaunted but penniless, he started to buy and sell pork fat door to door. Soon he had a small lard company and this he parlayed into a canning factory. Not long afterward there was nothing that he wasn't manufacturing or operating. Today the Matarazzo businesses are run by his granddaughter and grandsons.

Now walk up Rua Barão de Itapetininga across the Praça Ramos de Azevedo along the front of the majestic Teatro Municipal and four blocks to Av. Ipiranga. Here is the center of the man-in-the-streets haunts, with the huge movie theaters, the elegant and well-kept Praça de Republica and the sidestreets leading off to shops and specialty stores. Most of the tourist and souvenir shops are in this area, as well as the airline company offices and better bookstores.

Edifício Italia, tallest building in South America, is situated at the highest point in São Paulo. Visit one of its rooftop bars or restaurants on a clear day or night. Behind it, on Ipiranga, is the graceful, serpent-shaped apartment and office building designed by famed Brasilia builder Oscar Niemeyer, across the street from the São Paulo Hilton. Turning from Ipiranga and walking down São Luiz, which leads to the Hotel Jaraguá, you'll see new office buildings with shops, theaters, and luxury stores that have sprung up in the past few years. São Paulo is like New York in this respect; wherever you look there is an old building coming down and a new one rising in its place.

In 1888 the state government purchased an old farm house and turned it over to a scientist who had some crazy notion that snake serum could be used to save the life of someone bitten by a snake. His first patients were the horses of the Paulista cavalry, and he had 64 snakes to work with. Today the Instituto Butantan, Avenida Vital Brasil 1500, Butantã (873–

7222), the largest snake farm in Latin America, counts more than 70,000 snakes in its collection, as well as thousands of spiders, scorpions, and lizards. The institute extracts their venom regularly and processes it so it can be flown anywhere in the world when it's needed in a hurry. The institute is open Tues.–Sun. and holidays from 9 A.M. to 5 P.M. Be sure to see them milking the snakes between 10 A.M. and 4 P.M. You can take a bus from Praça da Republica or, of course, a taxi, for it's quite a distance from the downtown area.

Within walking distance of the snake farm is the House of the Flagbearer (Casa do Bandeirante), Praça Monteiro Lobato (211–0920). An old ranch house that goes back to the 18th cenury, the building was completely restored in 1954 and decorated with priceless furniture and pottery of the period. Even the outside buildings like the corn crib and the mill are authentic down to the last detail. If you are interested in the antiques of this era, you'll love the place. It's open from Tues. to Sun. from 9 A.M. to 5. There is a guide here. Entrance is free.

Parks, Museums, and Sights

Ibirapuera Park is perhaps the biggest one of its kind in the world. It covers two million square meters, is decorated with natural lakes and rolling, well-watered lawns, and contains ten modern exhibition halls where one thing or another is being shown. The entrance to the park is dominated by a statue containing 36 figures of the pioneers, Indians, and horses who braved the unmapped lands and carved out a new empire. The statue, the work of Frenchman Victor Brecheret, is 50 meters long and has been given the affectionate if irreverent name of "Don't push." Inside the park you'll be able to visit the Japanese Pavilion, which is an exact reproduction of the Katura Palace in Japan and is kept up by donations of the Japanese colony. There is also a windowless dome of cement called the History Pavilion. Here are the museums of Science, Aeronautics, and Technical Arts. In the Pavilion Pereira, the world-famed Bienal art exhibits are held in odd years—the next one is in 1991. The greatest display of contemporary art in Latin America, the show attracts painters from all over the globe who compete for top honors in the art world. The Planetarium is also in this park and is rated the best in South America. Complete, absorbing shows are given each Saturday, Sunday, and holiday 4 to 6 P.M., and on weekdays arrangements can be made ahead for groups. Tickets at the door cost about $2. There is also a radio-telescope (the only one in Brazil) that lets you "listen" to the stars, as well as an interesting corner where telescopes are assembled. (For information call 544–4606.) Take any bus marked Ibirapuera.

Along the banks of the Anhembi River, at the entrance to the São Paulo-Rio Highway, is Anhembi Park, whose exposition hall is the world's largest aluminum structure. The roof is supported by 25 light columns and the hall is illuminated by 200 aluminum globes. Right beside it is a modernistic convention hall seating 5,000 persons. A 453-room hotel is also under construction nearby.

The Zoological Park is located in Avenida Miguel Estafeno, 4241, Agua Funda (276–0811). The largest zoo in South America, it displays over 400 animals and 600 birds. There are few fences or cages and Paulistas dot the lawns on Sunday afternoons with their tablecloths and picnic baskets. It is open daily from 9 A.M. to 6 P.M., and adult admission is about $2.

Near the zoo, on the same avenue at number 3031, is the Jardim Botânico, an orchid farm where there are over 35,000 species. The force of so much beauty is overpowering at times. You may visit the orchids and the zoo by taking a number 546 bus from Praça da Liberdade or Anhangabaú. At press time the orchid farm was undergoing repairs. Call 577–3055 to check if it has reopened to the public.

Just behind the zoo, but requiring a closed car in which to visit it, is the Simba Safari, Av. do Cursino 6338, Vila Morais (946–6249), where lions, camels, monkeys and cheetahs roam free in their own wilderness, and only the visitors are caged. Open from 9 A.M. to 5:45 P.M. Tues. to Sun. in summer, 9 A.M. to 5 P.M. in winter.

If you are interested in collecting stamps or coins, then a must on your itinerary is a visit to the center of downtown Praça da Republica on a Sunday morning. There collectors and dealers traditionally gather to talk, swap, and sell. But today they are outnumbered by "hippies" selling their handicraft—leather goods, furniture, paintings, and trinkets made of glass, straw, and metal.

Three museums should be on your list of musts. The first is the Museu de Arte de São Paulo, Avenuida Paulista 1578 (251–5644). Open Tues. to Fri. from 1 to 5 P.M., Sat. and Sun. from 2 to 6 P.M. MASP has the only collection in South America that shows a panorama of Western art from the Gothic Age to the present. Here hangs Raphael's famed "Resurrection," painted when he was just 17 years old. There is a Rembrandt self-portrait, three Frans Hals, 13 works by Renoir, 10 by Toulouse-Lautrec, and many others. There is a section of 19th-century and contemporary Brazilian painters, a selection of Gobelin tapestries, and a collection of early Italian majolica. The basement houses special exhibits, frequently changed, of art, antiques, glass collections, and other treasures. Frequent traveling and special exhibits, such as a collection of Picasso's prints, enrich MASP's program. Admission fees of about a dollar are charged for these.

The second important museum is the Museu de Arte Contemporánea (571–9610) located in the Pereira Pavillion in Ibirapuera Park. There are over 1,650 works by such modern masters as Kandinsky, Leger, Carrá, Portinari, and various cubists of the pre-World War I era. Open every day but Monday from noon to 6 P.M. Admission is free.

Third is the Museum of Brazilian Art at Rua Alagoas 903 (826–4233). Here are copies of all the monuments and statues in the parks and buildings of Brazil, including copies of the famed Prophets of Aleijadinho. Free admission Tues. through Fri. from 2 to 10 P.M., Sat. and Sun. from 1 to 6 P.M.

Also important are the Museum of Modern Art (Museu de Arte Moderna—MAM), Parque Ibirapuera (549–9688), open Tues.–Fri. 1 to 8 P.M. and weekends 11 A.M. to 5 P.M.; and the Sacred Art Museum (Museu de Arte Sacra), Avenida Tiradentes, 676 (227–7687), large collection of Brazilian art from the colonial period, as well as a beautiful collection of nativity scenes (presépios) on display year-round; open Tues.–Sun. from 1 to 5 P.M.

PRACTICAL INFORMATION FOR SÃO PAULO

WHEN TO GO. The weather information for Rio is also good for São Paulo, except that when it is cool in Rio, it is twice as chilly here. Since the city sits 820 meters (2,665 ft.) above sea level, it is prey to the variable winds that come northward from cold Argentina as well as those breezes coming from muggy Mato Grosso jungles. It is a stimulating climate that does not sap one's energy. There is a continuing series of interesting things like museum openings, art exhibits, industrial fairs, and sports programs. There is always something going on, and the visitor will not have to worry about killing time, in spite of the lack of sandy beaches.

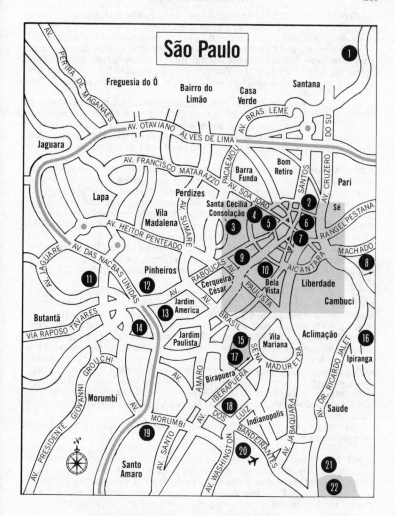

São Paulo

Points of Interest

Butanta Institute (Instituto Butuntã) 11
Botanical Garden (Jardim Botânico) 21
Congonhas Airport 20
Forest Park (Horto Florestal) 1
Jockey Club 14
Marco Zero—City Center 6
Municipal Theater (Teatrô Municipal) 5
Museum of Bixiga's Memories (Museu Memórias do Bixiga) 9
Museum of Brazilian Art (Museu de Arte Brasileira) 3
Museum of Contemporary Art (Museu de Arte Contemporanea) 17
Museum of Religious Art (Museu de Arte Sacra) 2
Parque do Carmo 8
Parque do Ibirapuera 15
Pateo de Colégio—Historic Center 7
Paulista Museum (Museu Paulista "do Ipiranga") 16
Praca da Republica 4
São Paulo Art Museum (Museu de Arte de S. Paulo, MASP) 10
Shopping Center Eldorado 13
Shopping Center Ibirapuera 18
Shopping Center Iguatemi 12
Shopping Center Morumbi 19
Zoological Garden (Jardim Zoológico) 22

HOW TO GET TO SÃO PAULO. Most people visit here after they have been in Rio. The easiest and most comfortable way to come is via the modern, efficient *Ponte Aérea* (Air Bridge), which consists of the constant arrival and departure of airplanes between Rio's Santos Dumont airport and São Paulo's Congonhas field. They leave every half-hour from 6 A.M. till 10:30 P.M. Reservations aren't needed, unless you want a certain plane. You just show up and take the next plane. It is a good idea to book in advance for a weekend flight, especially Friday evening. Tickets: about $57 one way.

In 1985, São Paulo finally inaugurated its long-awaited international airport of Cumbica, in the industrial suburb of Guarulhos, about a 45-minute drive from downtown. Most international flights now land there, although some still use Viracopos in Campinas, just over an hour away. Buses linking Guarulhos airport, Congonhas airport, and Praça da República run about every 20 minutes and cost about $10.

São Paulo can also be reached by first-class buses which leave Novo Rio bus terminal every half hour and make the 253-mile trip in five-and-one-half hours on an excellent highway with one rest stop. *Expresso Brasileiro, Viação Cometa,* or *Itapemirim* will give you more than satisfactory service. The late-night sleeper buses, called "leitos," run about $30 and are extremely comfortable and modern. Regular shuttle buses are half the price of leitos. All buses arrive in São Paulo's Tietè terminal, linked by the Metrô to downtown.

Low-cost trains leave Rio's Central do Brasil railroad station. The sleeper leaves at 11 P.M., arriving in São Paulo about 8 A.M. Not fancy, but clean and comfortable, with a dining car. Sleeper seats and Pullman compartments range from $19 to $48.

GETTING AROUND SÃO PAULO. From the airport. At Congonhas city airport, there are no regular taxis. The red and white airport taxis outside the arrival wing will cost about $10 to your downtown hotel. To take a regular metered cab (many are VW beetles), walk down to the central entrance. Cost: about $6 to city center. The same system of a price table correlated with the figure registered on the meter is used here as in Rio. Avis, Hertz, L'Auto, and Localiza/National rental cars are available, but São Paulo is a difficult city for the nonresident to get around in, due to its size, traffic congestion, and constant road repairs. City buses are cheap, about 40 cents for most fares, but lines are long at rush hours, and, for non-Portuguese speakers, the routes can be confusing. A subway crosses the city from north-south and east-west for 50 cents. It is safe, rapid, comfortable, and convenient, but only serves a small sector of the city.

Tours can be arranged by a local traval agent. See "Tours" later in this Practical Information section.

HOTELS. Booming São Paulo is a city of international businesspeople and their customers; so it is only natural that the city is prepared to take care of them. There are hundreds of good hotels in town, and rates are about what they are for similar accommodations in Rio. Most Paulista hotels serve Continental breakfast free of charge. For a definition of price categories see "Facts at Your Fingertips."

Super Deluxe

Caesar Park. Rua Augusta 1508 (285–6622). On the fashionable shopping street and a few blocks from the U.S. Trade Center and Avenida Paulista business center, offers European personal service—the staff knows you by name. Restaurants, a coffee shop, bars, banquet and small convention facilities, outdoor swimming pool on the roof, and beauty shop. Conservative, for discriminating people. Satellite dish.

Maksoud Plaza. Alameda Campinas 150 (251–2233). One of São Paulo's newest hotels, located one block from the Paulista business district. Acknowledged as one of Brazil's finest hotels. Popular with business travelers, it is deluxe in every sense. Electronic temperature controls in all 420 rooms, room service, TV, and other amenities. Panoramic indoor elevators permit an excellent view of the atrium lobby as they glide to the two squash courts on the top (22nd) floor. American billiards, indoor swimming pool, sauna, VIP Club, convention facilities, as well as shops. Restaurants are *La Cuisine du Soleil* with superb French food, the *Vikings'* Scandinavian smorgasbord, and *Belavista,* the latter open 24 hours a day. Satellite dish.

Mofarrej Sheraton. Al. Santos, 1437 (284–5544). São Paulo's newest deluxe hotel overlooks a beautiful park and caters to business clients with special butler services and facilities for executives, two pools, (one indoor), beautiful lobby piano bar, and São Paulo's newest and best rooftop restaurant and bar. The hotel has quickly jumped into the number-two spot in São Paulo, and is challenging the Maksoud for number one. Satellite dish.

São Paulo Hilton. Av. Ipiranga 165 (256–0033). Popular hotel for conventions and business people. Its 34 stories command a sweeping view of the world's fastest-growing city; four restaurants, five bars, including the *London Tavern* pub-disco restaurant, large convention center and theater. Satellite dish.

Transamerica. Av. Nações Unidos 18591 (523–4511). Opened in 1985, close to downtown with two restaurants, swimming pool, and a convention center. Satellite dish.

Deluxe

Bourbon Hotel. Av. Vieira de Carvalho 99 (223–2244). Small, elegant, comfortable hotel near the Praça da Republica. Good restaurant and service.

Brasilton São Paulo. Rua Martins Fontes 330 (258–5811). Part of the Hilton group, in the center of shopping and downtown, convenient to most everything. A popular hotel for business lunches, international stars; where the action is. Two restaurants, bars, banquet and convention facilities. Satellite dish.

Crowne Plaza. Rua Frei Caneca 1360 (284–1144). Part of the Holiday Inn chain, the hotel has a prime location near the offices and banks of Avenida Paulista. 223 rooms, bar, restaurant, pool, exercise facilities, satellite dish.

Della Volpe Garden. Rua Frei Caneca 1199 (285–5388). A new hotel aimed at the business traveler with 137 rooms, bar and restaurant, complete exercise facilities with indoor track (120 yards), satellite dish.

Eldorado Higienopolis. Rua Marquês de Itú 836 (222–3422). Restaurant, bar and coffee shop. Residential neighborhood. Outdoor swimming pool. Ten-minute walk to downtown commercial area. Sister to the Eldorado Boulevard.

Grand Hotel Ca D'Oro. Rua Augusta 129 (256–8011). "Home away from home." Many American families stay in suites here until their household goods arrive. The owner Fabrizio Guzzoni and his two sons, Eugenio and Aurelio, are always available. This 400-room hotel offers the most to a family with children: tennis court, outdoor swimming pool and children's pool and play equipment. Banquet and convention facilities and one of the best formal Italian dining rooms. The only luxury hotel with kennel. Satellite dish.

Novotel. Rua Ministro Nelson Hungria 450 in the suburb of Morumbi (533–1211). Good for executives visiting factories on the Marginal. Outdoor swimming pool and a view of the city.

Expensive

Augusta Boulevard. Rua Augusta 843 (257–7844). Another modern hotel on this famous shopping street.

Comodoro. Av. Duque de Caxias 525 (220–1211). Close to the bus station. Though in a not-too-desirable location, is popular with theater and sports groups.

Othon Palace Hotel. Rua Libero Badaro 190, Praça Patriarca (239–3277). Strategically located in the center of the financial district. Part of Brazilian chain of Othon hotels, contains the *VIP Bar, The Four Seasons Restaurant,* and the *Swiss Chalet.* Three large rooms for meetings, cocktail parties, and other social occasions. All air-conditioned.

São Paulo Center. Largo Santa Ifigenia 40 (228–6033). Recently redecorated in modern style, adjacent to the heart of the old city. Ifigenia Bridge immediately to the left and within walking distance of the Colegio Patio, founding site of Sao Paulo. 111 air-conditioned rooms. Very popular executive lunch.

Moderate

Osaka Plaza. Praça da Liberdade, 149 (270–1311). Has a good Japanese restaurant.

Samambaia. 7 de Abril 422, at Praça da República (231–1333). Right in the downtown area. Small but excellent service and cuisine.

As in Rio, Apartment Hotels are also available, the top ones being: **Triannon Residence,** Al. Casa Branca 363 (283–0066); **Augusta Park Residence,** Rua Augusta 922 (255–5722); and **The Park Lane,** Rua Carlos Sampaio 157 (285–1100).

RESTAURANTS. Prepare yourselves for some of the finest international eating delights on the continent. It is difficult to choose the best when every one is so good. Your dining should not be confined to the following list, as it is merely the *crème de la crème* of the Paulista restaurants. Look around and experiment. The finest restaurant in São Paulo is generally conceded to be the *Ca D'Oro*. For definitions of price categories, see "Facts at Your Fingertips," earlier in this chapter.

There are literally thousands of restaurants in São Paulo, the gourmet capital of Brazil. Since São Paulo is a city of large immigrant communities which have retained their national cuisines, it's possible to eat any kind of food you have a yen for. In the Oriental Liberdade section, you can find Japanese restaurants in the moderate price range, and less expensive. In Bixiga, the popular name for Bela Vista, dozens of cantinas and bistros featuring pasta, pizza, and other Italian specialties at moderate prices compete for customers. Stroll around these districts, read menus, and feast. By far the largest number of fine restaurants are located in the Jardins district, where you can find anything from a sandwich to a first-class nouvelle cuisine meal.

International

A Biaúca-Jardins. *Expensive.* Avenida Faria Lima, 609, Jardim Paulista (813–1311). Open every day, Sat. for dinner only, Sun. lunch only. One of the most popular bars in the city with live music from 7 P.M. on, modest cuisine but an "in" place.

Manhattan. *Expensive.* Rua Bela Cintra, 2238, Cerqueira Cesar (852–0947). Open for lunch and dinner. A place to see and be seen.

Paddock. *Expensive.* Av. Faria Lima 1541, loja 109 (Cal Center), Jardim Paulistano (814–3582). Some Brazilian dishes in addition to International cuisine. Live music at dinner. Open for lunch and dinner; closed Sun.

La Tambouille. *Expensive.* Avenida 9 de Julho, 5925, Jardim Europa (883–6276). Open 11:30 to 1 A.M. Reservations advised. Leans toward Italian nova cucina, but a variety of classical dishes is also available.

Tatini's. *Expensive.* Rua Batatais 558 (Service Flat St. Paul), Jardim Paulista (885–7601). International cuisine with Brazilian touches. Open for lunch and dinner; closed Mon.

Terraço Italia. *Expensive.* Avenida Ipiranga, 344, 41st floor, Centro (257–6566). A spectacular view of the city from all angles is the biggest attraction here, although the food is well prepared, too. Afternoon tea, live music at night. Open daily from 11:30 A.M. to 3 P.M.

Le Caesar. *Expensive.* Rua Augusta, 1508, Cerquira Cesar (285–6622). Sophisticated spot for businesspeople. Open noon to 3 P.M. and from 7 P.M. to midnight.

Bistrô. *Moderate to Expensive.* Av. São Luis 258/Rua da Consolacão 222, sobreloja (257–1598). Live music in the evening. Open for lunch and dinner until 1 A.M.

French

Le Coq Hardy. *Deluxe.* Av. Adolfo Pinheiro 2518, Alto da Boa Vista (246–6013). Imaginatively prepared dishes with exotic ingredients. Open noon to midnight; dinner only on Sat.; closed Mon.

La Cuisine du Soleil. *Deluxe.* Alameda Campinas, 150, in the Hotel Maksoud, Bela Vista (251–2233). Open Sat. for dinner only, lunch and dinner on weekdays, closed Sun. Superb service and atmosphere in São Paulo's ritziest French restaurant.

Vivaldi. *Deluxe.* Alameda Santos 1437 (284–5544). São Paulo's newest top-quality French restaurant in the Mofarrej Sheraton. Rooftop with spectacular view of the city. Open for lunch and dinner.

L'Arnaque. *Expensive.* Rua Oscar Freire, 518, Cerqueira Cesar (280–0081). Excellent nouvelle cuisine with a Brazilian twist in friendly, comfortable, relaxed surroundings with a sidewalk bar. Open noon to 3 P.M. and 8 P.M. to 1 A.M.

La Cocagne. *Expensive.* Rua Campos Bicudo, 129, Itaim Bibi (881–5177). Open noon to 2:30 P.M. and 7 P.M. to 1 A.M. Closed Sun., Sat.

David's. *Expensive.* Rua Oscar Freire, 913, Cerqueira Cesar (282–2507). Open every day, noon to 4 P.M. and 7 P.M. to 2 A.M. Noted for its popular bar with live music.

Italian

Ca D'Oro. *Deluxe.* Rua Augusta, 129, in the Hotel Ca D'Oro (256–8011). Many consider this the best restaurant in São Paulo in all categories. Make reservations, open daily for lunch and dinner.

Massimo. *Deluxe.* Alameda Santos, 1826, Cerqueira Cesar (284–0311). Closed Mon., open for lunch and dinner the rest of the week. One of the most durable, popular restaurants in the city.

Gigetto. *Moderate to Expensive.* Rua Avanhandava, 63, Centro (256–9804). Open daily for lunch and dinner until 3:30 A.M. During its 50 years in business, it has become a meeting place for journalists, intellectuals, and artists.

Jardim de Napoli. *Moderate to Expensive.* Rua Dr. Martinico Prado 463, Higienópolis (66–3022). Good meats and pastas. Serves lunch and dinner until midnight; closed Mon.

Via Veneto. *Expensive.* Alameda Barros 909, Santa Cecilia (66–7905). Homemade pasta. Open daily until 2 A.M.

Brazilian

Many restaurants and hotels serve the traditional feijoada on Saturdays. In addition, try these restaurants specializing in Brazilian dishes.

Andrade. *Moderate to Expensive.* Rua Artur de Azevedo 874, Pinheiros (64–8644). Specialities from northeastern Brazil are served here. Live music at dinner and at Sun. lunch. Lunch and dinner Tues.–Sat.; lunch only on Sun.; closed Mon.

Bolinha. *Moderate to Expensive.* Avenida Cidade Jardim, 53, Jardim Europa (852–9526). Famous for feijoada, which has been served here daily for almost 40 years. Open 11 A.M. to 1 A.M.

O Profeta. *Moderate.* Al. dos Aicas 40, Indianópolis (549–5311). Live music. Regional cuisine from Minas Gerais. Open 11:45 A.M. to 1 A.M.

Portuguese

Abril em Portugal. *Expensive.* Rua Caio Prado, 47, Centro (256–5160). Dinner only, 8 P.M. to 2 A.M., closed Sun. Live guitar and fado music, dancing after midnight.

Marquês de Marialva. *Expensive.* Rua Haddock Lobo, 1583, Cerqueira Cesar (852–1805). Closed Mon., open for lunch and dinner.

Presidente. *Expensive.* Rua Visconde de Parnaiba 2424, Brás (292–8683). Bacalhua is the specialty here. Open weekdays 11 A.M. to 9:30 P.M.; lunch only on Sat.; closed Sun.

Japanese

Mariko. *Deluxe.* Rua Augusta 1508, in the Caesar Park Hotel (285–6622). Closed Sun.

Suntory. *Deluxe.* Alameda Campinas, 600, Jardim Paulista (283–2455). Closed Sun., overlooks a garden and fish pond.

Komazushi. *Expensive.* Avenida Brigadeiro Luis Antonio, 2050, loja 7, Centro Commercial Paulista (288–5582). Sushi and sashimi specialities. Lunch and dinner; closed weekends and holidays.

There are also dozens of *inexpensive* Oriental restaurants in the Liberdade section, including **Hinodê**, Rua Tomas Gonzaga, 62 (278–6633); **Yamaga**, Rua Tomas Gonzaga, 66 (278–3667), closed Tues; and **Korea House**, Rua Galvão Bueno, 43, upstairs (278–3052), open daily for lunch and dinner.

Churrascurias

Baby Beef Rubaiyat. *Expensive.* Avenida Faria Lima, 533, Jardim Paulistano (813–2744). Open daily for lunch and dinner.

Bassi. *Expensive.* Rua 13 de Maio, 334, Bela Vista (34–2375). Large portions, excellent meat.

Dinho's Place. *Expensive.* Alameda Santos, 45, Paraiso (284–5333) and Avenida Morumbi, 7976, Brooklin Paulista (542–5299).

Rodeio. *Expensive.* Rua Haddock Lobo 1498, Cerqueira Cesar (883–2322). Famous for its excellent barbecued meats.

Other restaurants: For fish and seafood, **St. Peter's Pier,** Alameda Lorena, 1160, Cerqueira Cesar (881–2413), open daily, except Mon., dinner only on Sat.; **La Truite Cocagne,** Rua Campos Bicudo, 153, Jardim Paulista (883–2770); **La Trainera,** Avenida Faria Lima, 511, Jardim Europa (282–5988). For Arab food, **Cedro's,** Rua Oscar Freire 800, Cerqueira Cesar (64–2123).

TOURIST INFORMATION. For information, contact the **Secretaria de Esportes e Turismo do Estado de São Paulo** (Office of Sports and Tourism of the State of São Paulo), Praça Antonio Prado, 9, Centro (229–3011) and the **Delegacia de Turismo,** Avenida São Luis 115, Centro (231–0044). Both are open from Mon. through Fri., 9 A.M. to 6 P.M. Also, the **São Paulo Convention Bureau,** at Al. Campinas 646, 5th floor (289–9397, 284–3099, 251–3858), offers information on the city and is open Mon. through Fri., 9 A.M. to 6 P.M.

TOURS. There are many tour operators in São Paulo sponsoring tours within the state and beyond—inquire at your hotel. For tours of the city of São Paulo, try the "Circuito Cultural," which leaves from and returns to the Shopping Center Iguatemi (Jardim America) on Sundays. Eight distinct itineraries around the city are offered. Call one of the agencies above for more information.

ART GALLERIES. The concentration of affluence in the São Paulo area has created a strong market for art collectors, lovers, and investors. Most of the better galleries are concentrated in Jardins. Check the newspaper for openings, and call for store hours, which vary. **Arte Aplicada,** Rua Haddock Lobo, 1406, Jardim Paulista (64–4725); Applied Art, as the name implies, specializes in well designed objects for practical use and decorations, as does **Deco Galeria,** Rua Franceses 153 (289–7067). **Arte Final Galeria,** Rua Verbo Divino 125 (246–5900), shows paintings, prints, sculptures. **Gabinete de Arte Raquel Arnaud,** Avenida 9 de Julho, 5719, Itaim Bibi (881–9853), contemporary conceptual and geometric sculpture and paintings. **Luiza Strina,** Rua Padre João Manoel, 974A, Cerqueira César (280–2471), modern Brazilian artists. **André Blau,** Rua Estados Unidos, 2280, Jardim America (881–6664), contemporary art. **Chelsea Art Gallery,** Rua Estados Unidos, 1591, Jardim America (852–4218). **Jacques Ardies,** Rua do Livramento, 221, **Villa Mariana** (884–2916), best collection of Brazilian primitives. **Skultura,** Alameda Lorena, 1593, Cerqueira César (280–5624). Modern sculpture in all sizes and materials. **São Paulo,** Rua Estados Unidos, 1454, Cerqueira César (852–8855), contemporary Brazilian artists. **Dan,** Rua Estados Unidos, 1638, Cerqueira César (883–4600). **A Galeria,** Rua Bela Cintra 1533, **Jardim Paulista** (853–2122). **Paço das Artes,** Avenida Europa 158, Jardim Europa (64–1728), alternative art. **Galeria de Arte Uirapurú,** Rua Oscar Freire 213 (852–5410). **O Bode: Arte Popular Brasileira,** Rua Bela Cintra, 2009, Cerqueira César (853–3184), artesanatos (folk art) from the north and northwest.

SHOPPING. As the largest industrial and commercial center of South America, São Paulo offers just about anything you want to buy. There are four major shopping malls in the Zona Sul, open from 9 A.M. to 10 P.M.; **Iguatemi,** Av. Brig. Faria Lima, 1191, Jardim Paulistano (210–1333); **Ibirapuera,** Av. Ibirapuera, 3103, Moema (543–0011); **Morumbi,** Av. Roque Petroni, Jr. 1089, Morumbi (533–2444); **Eldorado,** Av. Reboucas, 3970, Pinheiros (815–7066).

However, the city itself could easily be considered a shopping center, with a number of special streets lined with great shops. Rua João Cachoeira, Itaim, is the city's wholesale clothing center, with many small "confeccões" (factories), some with outlets that sell to the general public. Many, however, are "pronta entrega," and sell only in quantity to buyers. It is best to ask when you have doubts.

The area known as the Quadrilátero dos Jardins, consisting of 28 streets within the perimeter defined by Av. Paulista, Rua Estados Unidos, Brig. Luis Antônio, and Av. Rebouças, has the best of the best: whether you're looking for a great sandwich, French baguettes, or party clothes, you'll find it in this area. Worth special mention are Rua Dr. Mário Ferraz and Avenida Cidade Jardim, both of which feature expensive, fashionable boutiques.

NIGHTLIFE. Surprisingly enough, there are better clubs and bars in São Paulo than you'll find in Rio. The Paulista enjoys going out after a day in the office and seems to have more money to spend on nighttime playing. Like New York, São Paulo has a sophisticated nightlife revolving around food and music. The functions of restaurants, nightclubs, and bars frequently overlap, and the following are general categories. The "in" places change frequently, as one group of friends moves on to a new place and another discovers the former's haunt, but the following have endured.

Bars

Clube do Choro, Rua João Moura 763, Pinheiros (883–3511). Live Brazilian "chorinho" music. Also a restaurant with good Saturday feijoada.

Opus 2004, Rua Pamplona, 1187, Cerqueira Cesar (284–4740). Live jazz music.

Spazio Pirandello, Rua Augusta, 311, Consolação (256–5245). Open 8 P.M. to 4 A.M. Closed Mon. Restaurant and meeting place for artists, journalists.

Supremo, Rua da Consolação, 3473, Consolação (282–6142). Open Tues., Wed., Fri., and Sun., noon to 4 A.M.; Thurs. and Sat. 8 P.M. to 4 A.M. Popular bar and restaurant with Brazil's yuppies, always crowded.

Nightclubs

Baccarat Rock, Rua 13 de Maio 155, Bela Vista (256–2495). Live music for dancing. Open Thurs.–Sat. 9 P.M. to 4 A.M. and Sun., 6 P.M. to midnight.

Calash, Rua Amauri, 328 Jardim Paulista (282–7652). Open daily from 6 P.M. to 2 A.M. Dance floor and soft music.

150 Night Club, Alameda Campinas, 150, in the Maksoud Plaza Hotel, Bela Vista (251–2233). Dance floor, first rate shows with an emphasis on jazz.

Gallery, Rua Haddock Lobo, 1626, Cerqueira Cesar (881–8833). Open Mon. through Sat., from 8 P.M. until the last customer leaves. Dance floor, shows, restaurant. This is a private club—ask your deluxe hotel to arrange a reservation or go with a Brazilian member.

Kyoto, Rua da Gloria, 295, Liberdade (270–5306).

Madame Satã, Rua Conselheiro Ramalho 783, Bela Vista (285–6754). Rock music, video clips. Attracts an exotic crowd. Open Wed.–Sun. from 8 P.M. to 6 A.M.

L'Onorabile Societá, Av. 9 de Julho 5872, Jardim Paulista (282–9855). Private, go with a member or arrange entry through your hotel. Open Tues.–Sun. from 10 P.M.

Saint Paul, Alameda Lorena 1717, Cerqueira Cesar (282–7697). Closed Sun. Mon. and Thurs. are singles' nights, couples only are admitted on weekends, from 9 P.M. to 5 A.M.

Soul Train, Rua Amauri, 334, Jardim Paulista (852–6566). Open daily from 9 P.M. to 4 A.M. Fri. and Sat. couples only are allowed and there is a cover charge.

Ta Matete, Avenida 9 de Julho, 5725, Jardim Paulista (881–3622). Open from 8:30 P.M. to 4 A.M. Closed Mon.

Show Houses

Plataforma 1, Avenida Paulista, 424 (289–5238). Open Mon. through Sat. from 8:30 P.M. to 4 A.M. Variety show with mulatas. Artistic cover charge.

Palace, Avenida dos Jamaris, 213, Moema (531–4062). Open Fri.–Sun. from 10 P.M.

Palladium, Avenida Rebouças, 3970, 3rd fl., Shopping Eldorado, Pinheiros (815–7066). Bar, restaurant, dance floor, and sophisticated non-touristic floor show. Artistic cover charge. Open from 10:30 P.M. Wed. and Thurs., from 11:30 P.M. on weekends.

Danceterias/Discotheques

Paulicéia 22, Rua Pinheiros 473, Pinheiros (883–5038). Popular with university students and journalists. Open 5:30 P.M. to 4 A.M.

Show Days Saloon, Ave. Rebouças 3970, 3rd floor (Shopping Eldorado) (814–9583). Wild West decor; popular with couples.

Up & Down, Rua Pamplona 1418, Cerqueira Cesar (285–1081). Trendy disco with computer-controlled lights and giant TV screens.

Zoom, Rua Dr. Zuquim 311, Santana (299–6696). Two dance floors, three bars; holds 2,000 people. Open Fri. and Sat. 10 P.M. to 4 A.M.; Sun. 3 P.M. to 6 P.M. and 8 P.M. to midnight.

SOUTHEASTERN BRAZIL

The headquarters of Brazil's southeastern region are the cities of Rio and São Paulo, but in both the state of Rio and the state of São Paulo there is an abundance of attractions for the traveler who wants to get away from the big city. The two states combine miles of beautiful beaches with a mountainous region that runs down the coast and is home to numerous mountain resort villages that serve as getaways for the harried Paulistas and Cariocas who want peace and quiet together with mountain air.

THE STATE OF SÃO PAULO

If one cannot understand the "Paulistas" contented "I want to be isolated" attitude from studying their capital city, then it will certainly become apparent when the rest of their domain is seen. The area has everything from sandy beaches to lofty mountain plateaus, from colonial splendor to ultramodern health resorts. To see all of it you need time, much more time than most tourists have to devote to an area. That is one of the problems of visiting Brazil. There is so much to see that it's absolutely impossible to crowd it all in one visit.

The State of São Paulo itself is about the size of Great Britain and Northern Ireland put together, covering 95,800 square miles. Slow to take root (the first colonies founded by the Jesuit fathers were complete failures), São Paulo didn't really start to grow until the coffee plant was introduced in the early 1800s. The product found a ready market, and when in 1847 a landowner near Limeira brought over a colony of Germans to work his fields, the area was on its way at last. The demand for coffee grew and more and more immigrants came from Europe to try their hand with the new plant. From Italy alone came a million people. Portugal sent half a million and Spaniards and Japanese many hundreds of thousands. From the sale of coffee came money enough to start factories, install electrical power, build railways, and clear rich forest land.

Santos is another pride of the Paulistas, for aside from having the biggest dock area in Latin America, it also has a tropical climate and some beautiful beaches. Apart from the basilica of Santo Andre, which faces the beach and the row after row of modern apartment buildings, the city has little to offer the tourist except her beaches. They are different from the ones in Rio, the sand being darker and harder.

The nearby island of Guarujá is lush, green, and lined with towering palm trees—and, increasingly, with high-rises along the ocean. Today, to reach more unspoiled areas you must go north by bus or car, crossing the ferry to Bertioga and beyond (but avoid Sundays and holidays because of long lines). There are some relatively untouched beaches, considering the proximity to Santos and the number of weekend visitors. They offer a pleasant visual and mental change from the hustle of the city. A trip around the island by automobile can be made in an hour, for the roads are paved and in good condition. The best beaches north of Guarujá are Ubatuba, Caraguatatuba, and the romantic island of Ilha Bela.

The coastal village of Paratí was founded way back in the early 16th century. Its calm, natural little harbor was the perfect jumping off point for adventurers looking for the gold and precious stones in Minas Gerais. For decades the town flourished while it catered to the needs of the miners and helped them spend their money. But the boom calmed down, Santos rose in importance because of its superb harbor, and over the years Paratí was forgotten. Then just a few years ago, the Paulistas rediscovered this colonial village (actually located in Rio de Janeiro state), and the government declared it a national monument whose architectural style must be preserved. Today it is important as a tourist center. With the Rio-Santos Highway passing close by, traffic jams became so great that cars are now banned from most city streets. Those who have taken the time to visit it come back with glowing tales of baroque churches, charming squares, and an unspoiled old-world charm. Many houses have been restored by private parties and the tendency is to preserve as much of the original flavor as possible.

São Paulo's mineral water resort area is located in the northeastern part of the state near the border with the state of Minas Gerais. The top resorts, Poços de Caldas, Caxambú and Aquas da Prata, are all within a short distance of one another and some 150 miles from the city of São Paulo. The various spas and hot spring resorts radiate northward into the higher country, away from the capital city. Most of them have a large German or Swiss population and will remind the traveler more of Europe than South America.

The hot springs attract an equal number of visitors, who go there to sit in the warm, swirling (at times rather smelly) water, rather than drink it. Campos do Jordão, Poços de Caldas, and Serra Negra all have dry climates and their waters are famous for treating such diverse ailments as rheumatism, skin diseases, and fatigue. Clean and nicely landscaped, these villages are as pleasant to the eye as they are to the skin.

PRACTICAL INFORMATION FOR THE STATE OF SÃO PAULO

WHEN TO GO. This depends on where you are going. Because of the varying altitude of the state, which ranges from sea level to 9,000 feet, it can be hot in some spots and cold in others at the same time. If you want the seashore, then the months of Dec. to Apr. are the best. But exactly during these months you will be competing with Brazilian tourists for the best hotels in such popular vacation beach towns as Guarujá, Ubatuba, Caraguatatuba, Ilhabela, and Paratí. During Carnival in Feb. or Mar. it is almost impossible to find a hotel room without a reservation well in advance. Those same months will be chilly in the evenings in the mountain resorts but you will have an easier time finding a place to stay. The situation reverses itself during the southern hemisphere winter months from July to Sept., when the bracing temperatures of the mountains attract Paulistas looking for a friendly fireplace to stretch out in front of. For this period, the mountains load up with vacationers while the beaches are often empty.

HOW TO GET THERE. Although the state of São Paulo is large, the concentration of top vacation spots in two areas—the beaches near Santos and the mountains near the border with Minas Gerais—make ground travel the best option. Good highways connect São Paulo with the resort areas and major bus lines serve all of the cities. The Rio-Santos highway runs along some of the most beautiful coastline in Brazil, unfortunately the upkeep of the highway in recent years has not been what it should have been, making the trip more of an adventure than most international travelers are looking for. From the city of São Paulo a winding road leads down the coastal mountains to Santos. A highway link also exists from Santos to the island of Guarujá or you can take the ferry boat (30 cents) at the end of Avenida Almirante Saldanha da Gama, which is the final stop along the Santos beachfront. The boats leave every fifteen minutes or so on a first-come, first-served basis. They handle cars as well as people and the trip takes 15 minutes. On the other side there are buses waiting to transport passengers to the various beaches. A word of warning: the Paulistas love their beaches. On hot weekends in the summer huge lines form for the ferry boats to Guarujá and back and the highway up the mountain to São Paulo from Santos frequently has bumper to bumper traffic on Sun. evenings.

SANTOS

HOTELS. There are hotels and boarding houses on just about every corner. While the beaches of Santos do not compare with those of nearby Guarujá, you can find far cheaper hotels here and then cross over to the quality beaches of the island by ferry. The best bets are: **Mendes Plaza,** *Expensive,* Av. Floriano Peixoto, 42 (37–4243); **Parque Balneario,** *Expensive,* and aging but still respectable hotel from the days when Santos was the prime attraction of the São Paulo seashore. Av. Ana Costa 555 (34–7211); **Fenicia Praia,** *Inexpensive,* Av. Presidente Wilson 184 (37–1955); **Indaia,** *Inexpensive,* Av. Ana Costa 431 (35–7554); **Avenida Palace,** *Inexpensive,* Av. Presidente Wilson 10 (39–7366).

RESTAURANTS. Admittedly the restaurants of Santos would probably never figure on anyone's dining out list. In particular avoid seafood, which tends to be vastly overpriced and of low quality. There are plenty of pizzerias and hamburger spots to satisfy your hunger. Any more serious dining out should be left for the city of São Paulo or a trip on the ferry to Guarujá.

WHAT TO SEE. Even though it has fallen out of favor with Paulistas in recent years, Santos still has the relaxed, friendly air of a beach city. It also has an extensive beach front that can be best appreciated by taking a city bus along the beach in the direction of the neighboring city of São Vicente. Santos is also the largest coffee port in the world, but avoid the temptation of visiting the port area—it is not safe for tourists.

GUARUJÁ

HOTELS. The love affair of São Paulo residents with this island has led to an explosion of hotel construction. The best are: **Casa Grande,** *Deluxe,* Av. Miguel Stefano 999, Enseada Beach (86–2223); **Jequitimar Hotel and Spa,** *Expensive,* Av. Marjory Prado 1100, on the beach (53–3111); **Delphin Hotel Guarujá,** *Expensive,* Av. Miguel Stefano 1295, Enseada Beach (86–2111); **Guarujá Inn,** *Expensive,* Av. da Saudade 170, Enseada Beach (87–2332); **Ferrareto,** *Moderate,* Rua Mario Ribeiro 564 (86–1112); **Gavea,** *Moderate,* Alameda Floriano Peixoto 311 Pitangueiras Beach (86–2212).

RESTAURANTS. There are several fine international restaurants in Guarujá although prices at times run well above the levels of the city of São Paulo. Among the better restaurants are: **Captain's,** *Expensive,* Rua Benjamin Constant, 211 (55–2515); **Rufino's,** *Expensive,* good for seafood, Estrada do Pernambuco 111; **Dalmo o Barbaro,** *Moderate,* on road to Bertioga at kilometer 14.5 (53–3188), seafood; **Restaurante do Joca,** *Moderate,* on the road to Bertioga, km. 12.

WHAT TO SEE. Despite the growing presence of high rise-apartments on the island, Guarujá remains extraordinarily beautiful. To explore the island, rent a taxi and take a trip to the many beaches. Keep your eye out for the spectacular vacation homes built here by wealthy Paulistas.

UBATUBA

HOTELS. The boom in top quality hotels along the São Paulo coast is also visible in this once sleepy beach city. The main hotels are: **Mediterraneo,** *Expensive,* Praia de Enseado (42–0112); **Sol e Vida,** *Expensive,* Praia de Enseada (42–0188); **Solar das Aguas Cantantes,** *Moderate,* Praia do Lazaro (42–0178); **Wembley Inn,** *Moderate,* Praia das Toninhas (42–0198).

RESTAURANTS. Cassino Sol E Vida, *Moderate,* seafood, in Sol e Vida Hotel. Enseada beach (42–0188); **Malibu,** *Moderate,* international food, Saco da Ribeira beach (42–0830).

WHAT TO SEE. This region is overflowing with small, beautiful beaches, both north and south of the city.

CARAGUATATUBA

HOTELS. One of the best resorts along the coast is the **Pousada Tabatinga,** *Deluxe,* on Tabatinga beach, tennis courts and, a rarity in Brazil, a 9-hole golf course (24–1411); **Guanabara,** *Moderate,* Rua Santo Antonio 75 (22–2533).

RESTAURANTS. Top restaurant in the area is the **Pousada Tabatinga,** *Expensive,* in the hotel of the same name, international cuisine (24–1411).

ILHABELA

HOW TO GET THERE. Just south of Caraguatatuba, this island jewel is reached by a ferry boat from the mainland city of São Sebastiao.

HOTELS. Mercedes, *Moderate,* Mercedes Beach (72–1071); **Ilhabela,** *Moderate,* Av. Pedro Paula de Morais 151 (72–1083); **Devisse,** *Moderate,* Av. Almirante Tamandare 343 (72–1385); **Pousada do Capitão,** *Moderate,* Av. Almirante Tamandare 272 (72–1037).

RESTAURANTS. Surprisingly, the island has several fine seafood restaurants: **Deck,** *Moderate,* Av. Almirante Tamandaré 805 (72–1489); **Viana,** *Moderate,* Viana beach at the 3 kilometer mark (72–1089).

AGUAS DA PRATA

HOTELS. This mountain mineral water spa follows the custom of the region—all meals are included in the room rate. The best hotels are: the **Panorama,** *Moderate,* Rua Hernani Gama Correa 45 (42–1511); **Ideal,** *Moderate,* Rua Gabriel Rabelo de Andrade 79 (42–1011); **Parque Paineiras,** *Inexpensive,* on the highway to São João da Boa Vista (42–1411).

AGUAS DE LINDOIA

HOTELS. Best hotel is the new **Nova Lindoia Vacance,** *Moderate,* with tennis courts, Av. das Naçoes Unidas 1374 (94–1191); others are the **Hotel das Fontes,** *Moderate,* Rua Rio de Janeiro 267 (94–1511); and the **Majestic,** *Moderate,* Praça Dr. Vicente Rizzo 160 (94–1811), with tennis courts. Meals included at all hotels.

ARAXA

HOTELS. Famous mineral spa in Minas Gerais near the border with São Paulo. Best hotel is **Grande Hotel,** *Moderate,* Estância do Barreiro (661–2011).

Suggested side trips to springs at Barbeiro, Osario, and Cascatinha Gruta de Monje and Historic Museum of Dona Beja.

CAMPOS DO JORDÃO

HOW TO GET THERE. The most sophisticated and popular of the mountain resorts of São Paulo, Campos can be reached by bus or car from São Paulo or by a short train ride from São Jose dos Campos, one of the state's main cities located on the Rio-São Paulo Highway (Via Dutra).

HOTELS. This picturesque mountain village has become one of São Paulo's top tourist attractions, offering Swiss-style hotels and chalets amidst a setting of tabernacle pines, mountains, and streams. Tops among the hotels are the **Toriba**, *Deluxe,* expensive but worth it, located in a natural park, with meals, included in room rate, better than those served in many international restaurants with good ratings. Av. Ernesto Diederichsen (62–1566); book well in advance, the hotel is a favorite of European residents of São Paulo; **Orotur Garden Hotel,** *Expensive,* meals included, Rua 3 (62–2833); **Vila Inglesa,** *Expensive,* meals included, Rua Senador Roberto Simonsen 3500 (63–1955).

WHAT TO SEE. The natural setting is easily one of the most beautiful in Brazil and no matter how many walks among the pines you take, there will always be something else to see. Horses can be rented and there are many nearby mountains that can be easily climbed. In the month of June the city hosts one of South America's finest classical music festivals and throughout the year there are activities for the guests at the many hotels in the region.

CAXAMBÚ

HOTELS. This popular mineral resort is located just across the border in Minas Gerais. Recommended hotels are: **Gloria,** *Moderate,* Rua Camilo Soares 590 (341–1233); **Palace,** *Moderate,* Rua Dr. Viotti 567 (341–1044); **Grande,** *Inexpensive,* Rua Dr. Viotti 438 (341–1099). All with meals included.

WHAT TO SEE. Recommended side trips to Parque das Aguias, Colina de Santa Isabel. Chacara Rosalan, Chacara das Ucas, São Tome das Letras, Corcovado Morro de Caxambú.

POÇOS DE CALDAS

HOTELS. One of the best known hot springs in Latin America, Poços is also in the state of Minas Gerais. It boasts 37 hotels but try to get into the **Palace,** *Moderate,* with meals, Praça Pedro Sanches (721–3392). Built by the state government, it has up-to-date facilities for the treatment of rheumatism, skin and intestinal diseases. Also the **Minas Gerais,** *Inexpensive,* Rua Pernambuco 615 (721–8686).

WHAT TO SEE. In the vicinity suggested side trips are to Cascata das Antas, Veu de Noiva, Fonte dos Amores, and Morro de São Domingos.

SÃO LOURENÇO

HOTELS. A third well-known Minas Gerais mineral water city. Recommended hotels are: **Primus,** *Moderate,* with meals, Rua Coronel Jose Justino 681 (331–1244); **Brasil,** *Moderate,* Alameda João Laje (331–1422); **Negreiros,** *Moderate,* Rua Venceslau Bras 242 (331–1533).

ATIBAIA

HOTELS. A mountain village 45 miles from the city of São Paulo, Atibaia is most proud of the fact that according to UNESCO it possesses the second healthiest climate in the world, losing out only to Switzerland. It also is home to one of the best mountain resorts in Brazil. The **Village Eldorado,** *Expensive,* Dom Pedro I Highway km 70.5 (484–2533), is an idyllic escape for São Paulo's businessmen.

Other good hotels are **Parque Atibaia,** *Expensive,* Ferñao Dias Highway (484–3744), **Recanto da Paz,** *Moderate,* Av. Jerônimo de Camargo, 10 chalets on a former farm (487–1369). The area surrounding Atibaia is one of Brazil's most popular camping areas.

THE SOUTH

The south of Brazil moves to the same upbeat, quickened pace of the city and state of São Paulo. Here in the states of Rio Grande do Sul, Paraná, and Santa Catarina, the results of heightened economic growth over the last 15 years are clearly apparent. Large, modern cities with efficient public transportation systems coexist with the ruins of colonial times and the natural beauty of one of Brazil's most fascinating areas. In the far south on the borders of Argentina and Uruguay, a mixture of Spanish, Portuguese, German, and Italian cultures has produced the fabled land of the gauchos: the flat pampas grasslands stretching as far as the eye can see, the spirited proud horses, the women in their skirts and multicolored petticoats, the thousands of grazing cattle, the lonely nights, and full moon, and the gaucho lament plucked softly on a guitar. These romantic flatlands have created their own spirit and folklore visible today in the dances, songs, and traditional dress of the region. There are the old mission cities, now in splendid ruin, built by the Jesuits in the 1600s. There is the rich grape-growing area where the best wines in Brazil are produced. And there are vast cattle ranches, source of the succulent beef that has made the gaucho barbecue—the churrasco—a synonym for mouthwatering steaks and sausages throughout Brazil.

While its tentacles stretch into Paraná and Santa Catarina, the color, the legend, the clothes, and the individualism of gaucho country are more closely associated with Rio Grande do Sul. In neighboring Santa Catarina the accent is on beaches and sauerkraut in a state known for its German influence and the beauty of its coastline. Paraná, third state in the region, is home to perhaps Brazil's most spectacular natural wonder, the magnificent Iguaçu Falls.

RIO GRANDE DO SUL

The thriving state capital of Pôrto Alegre, home to 1,300,000 Brazilians, will surprise you. One of the most up-to-date and fastest growing cities south of São Paulo, it has modern buildings, amiable people, and well-stocked shops. Lying as it does at the junction of five rivers, it has become an important shipping port, and much of the state's leather, canned beef, and rice are shipped from here to destinations as far away as Africa and Japan. The Lagoa dos Patos on which the city nestles is the largest freshwater lagoon in South America.

Pôrto Alegre

The old residential part of the city is on high ground with delightful views all around. It is dominated by the Governor's Palace (where soldiers crouched with machine guns both when "Jango" Goulart came back as President in 1961 and when he left in disgrace in 1964). Nearby there are an imposing stone cathedral and two high white towers of an old church called the Lady in Pain. The streets of the city wind in and around and up and down, and one of the best ways to enjoy Pórto Alegre is to get

out and walk; head toward the prisons and the electrical energy plant on
General Salustiano. The huge, green-grassed park of Farroupilha is the
site of a zoo and botanical gardens and on weekends and holidays is also
a setting for folk dancers.

Caxias do Sul

Caxias do Sul is located 70 miles north of Pôrto Alegre along a highway
that also passes through the mountain resorts of Gramado, Canela, and
Nova Petropolis, all within 15 miles of Caxias do Sul.

The best Brazilian wine is produced in the area around Caxias do Sul,
home of Italian immigrants who transported the art from their native land.
Today 28 different companies work at growing, selecting, and bottling the
juices from thousands of tons of grapes grown in this region. In March
the entire city stops work to celebrate the "Festival of the Grapes."

Farmers arrive to show off their products, visitors come from all over
Brazil as well as France and Italy, and regional folk dances are held. There
is also more beef eaten than can be imagined and more wine drunk than
should be. The owners of *Michielon* (Avenida Michielon 136) welcome
visitors to their bottling plant from 7:30 to 11:00 A.M. and from 1:30 to
5 P.M.

The Missions

In the first years of the 1600s, the Portuguese domination of Brazil
didn't go farther south than Laguna in the State of Santa Catarina. Below
this was Spanish territory, and it was here that the Jesuits came from Spain
to build a series of missions. They managed to win the confidence of the
Indians and soon had them making and laying bricks. The Indians stayed
near the missions for protection. Then the Portuguese "flagbearers" from
São Paulo came rushing south. Enemies of the Spanish, they killed the
priests, enslaved the Indians, and destroyed the mission cities. What is left
today—towering walls, delicately curved arches, carved angles and cornices—stands in mute testament to the grandeur that the Jesuits tried to
implant on Brazilian soil. The Cathedral of São Miguel, roofless and over-
grown with grass, is probably the most impressive ruin. There is a museum
beside it with some of the wooden images and iron bells that were salvaged
from the Cathedral. Other ruins, all reachable in one day, are at São João
Velho, São Lourenço das Missoes, and São Nicolau. At this last ruin the
legend still holds that the Jesuits buried a treasure chest before the Portuguese arrived.

All through this area and especially near São Borja, the home of both
Presidents Getulio Vargas and João Goulart, you'll see the gauchos and
their horses. They still wear the bright-colored shirts and neckerchiefs,
the balloon pleated trousers, the creased leather boots, and the flat chin
strap hat. They will stop and talk to you and may even offer a taste of
their chimarrao, the traditional gourd of hot maté tea.

Nova Petropolis, Gramado, and Canela

For a break from the flat pampas of the state there is nothing better
than a visit to the cities of Nova Petropolis, Gramado, and Canela, all
located in the mountains that run down the coastline. Here the spirit of
German and Swiss immigrants is apparent in cozy small hotels and chalets
with fireplaces and surrounded by tall pines in an idyllic natural setting
that inspires long walks and horseback riding. The region is famous for

its homemade chocolate candy and knitted wear. Every weekend in January and February, Nova Petropolis is alive with the Summer Festival and in June and July the Winter Festival repeats the weekend schedule of events.

Gramado, a sophisticated retreat for wealthy Brazilians who maintain vacation homes here, is the site of the Brazilian Film Festival in March. Calm and relaxing, the city is a sedate jewel tucked away amidst mountains and forests. Only four miles away, Canela is a smaller version of the same magical formula.

PRACTICAL INFORMATION FOR RIO GRANDE DO SUL

For definitions of price categories see "Facts at Your Fingertips."

PÔRTO ALEGRE

WHEN TO GO. Try not to come in the winter months from June to Aug.; cold winds from the south whip across the pampas and the temperature drops to the 30s-40s with occasional frosts and snowfall once every 4–5 years. Almost any other time is fine as the temperature is moderate, 70s–80s, and the spring (Oct.–Dec.) is especially enchanting, with the fresh green grass, the new wildflowers, and the young calves and lambs.

HOW TO GET THERE. Pôrto Alegre is connected with the rest of Brazil by daily **flights** via *Varig-Cruzeiro, Vasp,* and *Transbrasil* airlines. There are international flights from Santiago, Chile (Varig), Montevideo, Uruguay (Pluma, Cruzeiro), and Buenos Aires, Argentina (Cruzeiro). **Buses** make connections from Rio, São Paulo, Curitiba, Iguaçu, and Florianopolis. You can take buses throughout the state. Since the land is flat, the highways run smoothly and buses stick to a tight schedule that is bound to please. **Automobiles** can also be rented in Pôrto Alegre and Varig airlines has regular service from the capital to many small towns in the interior that can be explored on foot.

HOTELS. The best in town are: **Plaza San Rafael**, *Expensive*, on Av. Alberto Lins 514 (21–6100), with its 284 rooms, air-conditioning, bar, nightclub, and central location making it the ideal spot while in the gaucho capital. **Center Park**, *Expensive*, Rua Frederico Link 25 (21–5388). **Continental**, *Moderate*, Largo Vespasiano Julio Veppo 77 (25–3233). **Alfred Pôrto Alegre**, *Moderate*, Rua Senhor dos Passos 105 (26–2555). **Alfred Executivo**, *Moderate*, Praça Otavio Rocha 270 (21–8966). **Everest Palace**, *Moderate*, Rua Duque de Caxias 1357 (28–3133). **Embaixador**, *Moderate*, Rua Jeronimo Coelho 354 (28–2211). More modest and with no restaurants are **São Luiz**, *Inexpensive*, Av. Farropos 45 (28–1722); **Metropole**, *Inexpensive*, Rua Andrade Neves 59 (26–1800); and the **Açores**, *Inexpensive*, Rua dos Andradas 855 (21–7588).

RESTAURANTS. It's an ironclad rule that you can't go wrong anywhere in Gaucho country if you eat in the local churrascurias or steak houses. Here you can be sure that the meat is fresh and the rice is fluffy and delicious.

Probably the best beef in all Brazil is served in Pôrto Alegre. In most churrascarias, you slice your own steak off the sizzling skewer, and eat it with a salad of lettuce, tomatoes, and hearts of palm—washing it all down with an inexpensive mug (caneca) of vinho verde. Start with a linguiça (grilled sausage), then move on to filet, picanha, or lombo de porco (pork loin).

There are just too many good spots with this mouth-watering specialty grilling over smoldering charcoal to list all, but start with the **Capitão Rodrigo** (considered the city's best, *Moderate*) in the Plaza São Rafael Hotel, Rua Alberto Bins 514 (21–6100). Next try the **Zequinha**, *Moderate*, Av. Assis Brasil, 1204 (41–8157). Other top steak houses are the **Quero-Quero**, *Moderate*, Rua 24 de Outubro, 171 (22–1934), and the **Moinhos de Vento**, *Moderate*, Rua Dona Laura, 546 (30–5437).

Etruria, *Moderate*, Rua Santo Antonio 421 (21–9132). Regional specialties with folkdance show at **Recanto do Seu Flor**, *Moderate*, Av. Getúlio Vargas 1700 (33–

6512). French and International cuisine, with live music, at **Le Bon Gourmet,** *Expensive,* Av. Alberto Bins 514, in the Plaza São Rafael Hotel (21–6100). German at the **Floresta Negra,** *Moderate,* Av. 24 de Outubro 905 (22–7584).

MUSIC AND DANCE. Performances of the traditional dances and folk songs of Rio Grande do Sul may be seen at the **Teatro de Camara,** Rua da Republica 575, every Mon. evening at 9 or at the **Centro de Tradiçoes Gauchas,** Av. Siqueira Campos, 1184, 5th floor (28–1711), Fri. at 8:30 P.M.

CAXIAS DO SUL

HOW TO GET THERE. By plane, bus, or rental car from Porto Alegre, 80 miles to the south.

HOTELS. Good hotels are: **Alfred Palace,** *Moderate,* Rua Sinimbu 2302 (221–8655); the older **Alfred,** *Moderate,* next door at 2266 (221–8655); **Samuara Alfred,** *Moderate,* 12 miles from downtown on the Parque do Lago (225–2222); **Volpiano,** *Moderate,* Rua Ernesto Alves 1462 (221–4744); **Cosmos,** *Moderate,* Rua 20 de Setembro 1563 (221–4688); **Italia,** *Inexpensive,* Av. Julio Castilhos 3076 (221–7966).

RESTAURANTS. Don Jon, *Moderate,* in the Alfred Palace Hotel, Rua Sinimbu 2302 (221–8655), international cuisine; **Alvorada,** *Moderate,* Rua Os 18 do Forte 200 (222–4637), Italian restaurant; **Gianella,** *Moderate,* Av. Rubem Bento Alves 905 (221–3386), steak house (churrascuria) all you can eat (rodizio) with show.

WHAT TO SEE. This is the capital of the wine country with a strong Italian influence. Some of the wineries have tasting tours. Every three years in February and March the city is host to the Grape Festival, the largest promotional event for Brazil's wine producers.

NOVA PETROPOLIS

HOW TO GET THERE. By bus or rental car, the city is located 60 miles from Pôrto Alegre and 25 miles from Caxias do Sul.

HOTELS. The city has three main hotels, all small and all with excellent views of the countryside: **Recanto Suiço,** *Moderate,* Av. 15 de Novembro 2195 (281–1229); **Veraneio dos Pinheiros,** *Inexpensive,* RS–235 Hwy.; **Veraneio Schoeller,** *Inexpensive,* RS–235 Hwy. (281–1117).

GRAMADO AND CANELA

HOW TO GET THERE. By bus or rental car. The two cities are located 80 miles from Porto Alegre and 40 miles from Caxias do Sul.

HOTELS. The growing fame of these cities as a tourist center plus the publicity given to the Brazilian Film Festival held each year in Gramado has led to a rapid growth of new hotels. Most are medium-sized to small and several offer chalets. All of the best hotels have excellent views from the rooms. The best hotels are: **Laje de Pedra in Canela,** *Expensive,* the largest and most luxurious of the hotels in the two cities, Av. Presidente Kennedy (282–1530); **Serrano,** *Expensive,* Gramado, Av. das Hortênsias 1112 (286–1332); **Ritta Hoppner,** *Moderate,* Gramado, Rua Pedro Candiago 305 (286–1334); **Hotel das Hortensias,** *Moderate,* Gramado, Rua Bela Vista 83 (286–1057); **Gramado Palace,** *Moderate,* Rua D'Artagnann de Oliveira 237 (286–2021); **Grande Hotel,** *Moderate,* Canela, Rua Getulio Vargas 300 (282–1285); **Canto Verde,** *Inexpensive,* Gramado, Av. das Hortênsias 5660 (286–1961); **Alpestre,** *Inexpensive,* Gramado, Rua Leopoldo Rosenfeld 47 (286–1311); **Alpes Verdes,** *Inexpensive,* Canela, Villa Alpes Verdes (282–1162).

RESTAURANTS. The mountain air will whet your appetite, which is just as well since the two cities have several excellent restaurants specializing in international, Swiss, and Italian cuisine as well as the ever present churrascarias. **Saint Hubertus,** *Expensive,* Swiss cuisine, Gramado, Rua da Carriere 974 (286–1273); **Panoramico** in the Hotel Laje de Pedra, *Expensive,* Av. Presidente Kennedy, Canela (282–1530), international cuisine; **Edelweiss,** *Expensive,* German, Rua da Carriere/Rua João Leopoldo Lied, Gramado (286–1861); **Le Petit Clos,** *Expensive,* Swiss, Rua Demétrio Pereira dos Santos 599, Gramado (286–1936); **Bella Italia,** *Moderate,* Italian, Av. Borges de Medeiros 2879, Gramado (286–1207); **Nono Mio,** *Moderate,* steak house, Av. Borges de Medeiros 2070, Gramado (286–1252); **Bela Vista,** *Moderate,* steak house, Av. das Hortênsias 3964, Gramado (286–1359).

WHAT TO SEE. The **natural attractions** of Gramado and Canela are the most compelling sights of the region, although if you happen to be in town in March don't miss the **Brazilian Film Festival.** English-language films are also shown during the festival, but even if the films don't impress you, you'll love the parties. Make hotel reservations well in advance as the cities fill up for the festival. Gramado also offers a **classical music festival** in July. **Hiking paths** are plentiful here and **horses** can also be rented. Ask at your hotel for directions on how to get to the many beautiful viewpoints in the area overlooking canyons and waterfalls.

SANTO ANGELO

HOW TO GET THERE. By car or bus from Pôrto Alegre, a 250-mile trip. By plane from Pôrto Alegre.

HOTELS. Unfortunately there is not much to choose from. All hotels are modest. Best bets are: **Avenida II,** *Inexpensive,* Av. Venâncio Aires 1671 (312–3011); **Maerkli,** *Inexpensive,* Av. Brasil 1000 (312–2127); **Santo Angelo Turis,** *Inexpensive,* Rua Antonio Manoel 726 (312–4055).

WHAT TO SEE. Santo Angelo is the jumping off point for the **Mission Region.** The most interesting and best preserved of the mission ruins is São Miguel, 30 minutes from Santo Angelo. A light and sound show at the ruins gives the history of the mission and the region.

PARANÁ AND SANTA CATARINA

Iguaçu Falls

Paraná is home to one of Brazil's most unforgettable sights, the Iguaçu Falls. Eleanor Roosevelt remarked that: "Iguaçu Falls make Niagara look like a kitchen faucet." The water comes from some 30 rivers and streams from the interior of Paraná, and as it rushes toward the 200-foot precipice, it foams and carries huge trees it has uprooted. The volume of roaring, earth-shaking water has been estimated at 62,000 cubic feet per second. During the flood months of May to July the water plunges over at 450,000 cubic feet per second.

Brazilians and Argentines have each made national parks on their side of the falls and views from both countries are spectacular and different. Your hotel will take care of transportation to the Argentine side and all the necessary customs paperwork. You will be impressed by the Devil's Throat Falls, which must be seen by taking a highly adventurous outboard trip across the rapid currents to a trembling but secure little island. Don't wear your good clothes. The spray of this breathtaking portion of the fall is thrust 500 feet into the air.

On the road to Iguaçu from Curitiba, capital of Paraná, is Vila Velha, a unique region of unusual rock formations carved by wind and water over millions of years.

Curitiba

Curitiba is a busy city of one million inhabitants standing some 3,000 feet above sea level on the plateau of Serra do Mar. For over a century, its bracing climate and picturesque location have attracted immigrants of Slav, German and Italian origin, who have imparted a few European characteristics to its buildings and surroundings. Formerly best known as the center of the *hervamate* industry, it has now acquired much greater importance as the capital of a flourishing and progressive state that derives its economic prosperity from extensive coffee plantations in the north and vast timber forests in the southwest, as well as fertile areas that produce abundant crops of cereals and other foodstuffs. In addition to being the capital of the State of Paraná, it is the headquarters of the Fifth Military Region and therefore the residence of many officers and their families, and there are barracks for infantry and artillery regiments. There is also a modern and well-equipped military air base. The University of Paraná attracts thousands of students from all over the states of Paraná and Santa Catarina as well as from more distant states of the union.

Along the coastline of Paraná are several historical cities from colonial times, the most interesting of which is Paranagua, founded in 1648 and today one of Brazil's most important ports. A three-hour train ride from Curitiba down the coastal mountains to Paranagua is one of the more spectacular journeys in Brazil, with breathtaking views of the coast and mountains at virtually every curve.

Cities of Santa Catarina

In Santa Catarina the accent is decidedly German, with graphic examples of German influence, especially in the architecture and food, found in the cities of Joinville and Blumenau. Blumenau is located in a valley reminiscent of the Rhine region of Germany and has recently carried this association one step further with an Oktoberfest. The state's coastline has the finest beaches in southern Brazil, a fact that is now attracting the residents of São Paulo to the beaches of Santa Catarina. Laguna, a colonial city founded in 1676, in addition to its picturesque narrow streets and colonial architecture, also has the south's best beach resort hotel, the Laguna Tourist Hotel.

Appropriately, for a state known for its beaches, the capital of Santa Catarina, Florianopolis, is an island city with fine beaches on the oceanside.

CURITIBA

PRACTICAL INFORMATION FOR PARANÁ AND SANTA CATARINA

For definitions of price categories see "Facts at Your Fingertips."

HOW TO GET THERE. By air. Daily flights from São Paulo and Rio via *Vasp, Varig-Cruzeiro,* and *Transbrasil.* **By bus.** Served by major bus lines from all of the country's large cities.

HOTELS. Numerous fine hotels here include the newly opened **Hotel Bourbon & Tower,** *Expensive,* Rua Candido Lopes 102 (223–0966); the **Iguaçu Campestre,** *Expensive,* on the BR-116 Highway (262–5313); **Slaviero Palace,** *Moderate,* Rua Sen. Alencar Guimarães 50 (222–8722); **Mabu,** *Moderate,* Praça Santos Andrade 830 (234–2277); **Caravelle Palace,** *Moderate,* Rua Cruz Machado 282 (223–4323);

Deville Colonial, *Moderate,* Rua Com. Araujo 99, downtown (222–4777); **Araucaria Palace,** *Moderate,* Rua Amintas de Barros 73, downtown (224–2822); **Guaira Palace,** *Moderate,* Praça Rui Barbosa 537 (232–9911); **Ouro Verde,** *Moderate,* Rua Dr. Murici 419 (224–1633); **Tibagi,** *Moderate,* Rua Candido Lopes 318 (223–3141); **Tourist Universo,** *Moderate,* Praça Osorio 63 (223–5816); the **San Martin,** *Moderate,* Rua João Negrão near Rua XV de Novembro, 169 (222–5211).

RESTAURANTS. You will find good food in the dining rooms of the better hotels and at the following restaurants (all are *moderate* in price, with the exception of the steak houses and Italian restaurants, which are *inexpensive*): For churrasco (steak)—**Pinheirão Campestre,** Av. Victor Ferreira do Amaral 1010 (262–3711). German foods—**Schwarzwald,** *Moderate,* Rua Claudino dos Santos 63 (223–2585). French and international dishes—**Ile de France,** Praça 19 de Dezembro 538 (223–9962). Italian—**Bologna,** Rua Carlos de Carvalho 150 (223–7102). Also numerous fine restaurants in the Santa Felicidade area, such as the Italian restaurants **Madalosso** (272–1014), and **Veneza** (272–1673), and the steak house **Churrascão Colônia** (335–8686), and the **Chalet Swisse** (273–1223).

WHAT TO SEE. Places of interest include: the **Coronel David Carneiro Museum,** with a unique collection of objects of historical interest and the **Graciosa Country Club.** Also noteworthy are the modern buildings, especially the **Civic Center,** which houses in one homogenous group the **Governor's Palace, State Secretariats, House of Assembly, Treasury, Law Courts,** etc. There are two modern **theaters** (one for plays and revues, one for concerts and ballet) and a **library** in the center of the town.

IGUAÇU FALLS

HOW TO GET THERE. Most tourists arrive by **plane** from, Rio or São Paulo at the Iguaçu airport. There is, however, a land connection also on a paved highway from Curitiba with frequent **buses.**

HOTELS. Varig Airlines-owned **Hotel das Cataratas,** *Moderate,* has good food and there are guides to take you to the falls. It's best to make a reservation with a Rio or São Paulo travel agent or call ahead for rooms (for reservations in São Paulo call 231–5844). Other good hotels are the **Internacional Foz,** *Expensive,* Rua Alm. Barroso, 345 (74–4855); the **Salvati,** *Moderate,* Rua Rio Branco 651 (74–2727), in town, and, out of town headed toward the falls on the Cataratas Highway, the **Bourbon,** *Expensive,* (74–1313); the **Carimã,** *Moderate* (74–3377); **San Martin,** *Moderate,* (74–3030); and **Panorama,** *Moderate* (74–1200).

FLORIANOPOLIS

HOW TO GET THERE. The state capital of Santa Catarina can be reached by air from all of Brazil's major cities as well as by bus.

HOTELS. The best hotels are: **Jurere Praia,** *Super Deluxe,* 58 beach houses for rent with minimal rental period of one week (66–0108); **Maria do Mar,** *Expensive,* Rodovia Virgilio Varzea (33–3009), on the beach; **Diplomata,** *Expensive,* Av. Dr. Paulo Fontes 800 (23–4455), tennis courts; **Florianopolis Palace,** *Expensive,* Rua Artista Bittencourt 2 (22–9633); **Querencia,** *Moderate,* Rua Jeronimo Coelho (22–2677); **Faial Palace,** *Moderate,* Rua Felipe Schmidt 87, downtown (23–2766).

Located on an island with many fine beaches, Florianopolis is a popular spot for camping. Permits are not needed.

RESTAURANTS. Fragata, *Moderate,* seafood, Rua Henrique Veras, (32–0366); **Manolo's,** *Moderate,* international cuisine, Rua Deominda Silveira 156 (33–5462; **Ataliba,** *Moderate,* steak house, Rua Jaú Guedes da Fonseca (44–2364).

BLUMENAU

HOW TO GET THERE. A modern prosperous city of 150,000, Blumenau is served by *Varig* and *Cruzeiro* airlines. The best way to reach the city, however, is by bus from São Paulo. While the highway is not the best in Brazil, it passes through both Blumenau and Joinville, giving you a good look at the German origins of this region, visible in the homes as well as the features of the residents, many of whom are blue-eyed blondes.

HOTELS. Plaza Hering, *Moderate,* Rua 7 de Setembro 818, (22–1277); **Grande Hotel Blumenau,** *Moderate,* Alameda Rio Branco 21 (22–0145); **Garden Terrace,** *Moderate,* Rua Padre Jacobs 45 (22–3544).

RESTAURANTS. In German country there is nothing better than hearty German cuisine. Among the best are: **Frohsinn,** *Moderate,* Morro do Aipim, on top of a hill with a view of the city and surroundings (22–2137); **Moinho do Vale,** *Moderate,* Rua Paraguai 66, along the river that flows through the city (22–3337); **Cavalinho Branco,** *Moderate,* Alameda Rio Branco 165 (22–4300). The city also has a well respected French restaurant, **Le Bon Gourmet,** *Expensive,* Rua 7 de Setembro 818 (22–1277).

JOINVILLE

HOTELS. Like Blumenau a city with a strong tie to Germany, Joinville's top hotels are: **Tannenhof,** *Moderate,* Rua Visconde de Taunay 340 (22–8011); **Anthurium Parque,** *Inexpensive,* Rua São Jose 226 (22–6299); **Joinville Tourist,** *Inexpensive,* Rua 7 de Setembro 40 (22–1288).

RESTAURANTS. For German food, try the **Weinhof,** *Moderate,* international cuisine (in Tannenhof hotel), Rua Visc. de Taunay 340, 11th floor (22–8011); **Bierkeller,** *Moderate,* Rua 15 de Novembro 497 (22–1360); or **Jucalemão,** *Moderate,* Rua Ministro Calógeras 1407 (22–9750).

LAGUNA

HOW TO GET THERE. The state's top beach resort is reached by bus or car on a highway from Florianopolis 75 miles away.

HOTELS. The Laguna Tourist, *Deluxe,* is tops in the region and highly popular with international tourists, on the beach, Praia do Gi (44–0022). Make reservations well in advance. Other fine hotels are: **Itapiruba,** *Moderate,* on the beach, Praia de Itapiruba, BR-101 Hwy. (44–0294); **Lagoa,** *Moderate,* Trevo BR-101 Sul (44–0844). The city also has several fine camping areas.

CENTRAL-SOUTH BRAZIL

To visit Brasilia, Brazil's capital, is more than a step into the future, it's a headlong leap into the 21st century. Rising amidst the scrawny jungle of the high red earth plateau, stands one of the most unusual, most strikingly different, most beautiful cities in the world.

There is nothing outdated about Brasilia. In fact, everything there, architecturally, is far in advance of its time. Like something out of Buck Rogers, the city's administrative buildings spread out along the ground, coil around, then leap up in a shaft of marble to capture the rays of the sun.

It was a city "they" said couldn't be done, but others, more dedicated and more determined, went ahead and did it. With a rare thrust of Brazilian energy, a city rose in just three years, in the very spot where once the jaguar roared.

No trip to this magnificent and confusing country is complete without a visit to this city. It's not quite the same as visiting Italy and not seeing Rome—but almost.

Yet all around this spanking new wonderland of modernity nestles the old Brazil—the land of coffee beans and beef cattle, of palm trees and sluggish rivers, of shoeless peasants and Indians.

While it would be unfair to say that the area neighboring the new capital hasn't progressed with the city, it is a gross exaggeration to say that it has greatly changed. Belo Horizonte, the most important interior city after São Paulo, has taken advantage of the geographical fact that almost everyone and everything traveling by highway to the new capital passes through it. But it was a bustling and prosperous town before Brasilia, as its steel mills and hundreds of factories attest. Goiania, a vibrating little town that has sprung up in the past half century, was doing all right before Brasilia was even thought of. But it, too, has managed to cash in on the boom.

One city in the Belo Horizonte area but far enough away from any national progress not to be tarnished is Ouro Preto. The sleepy, colonial prize still rings with the sound of hooves on its cobblestone streets, the sound of Latin chants coming from its thick walled churches, and the sad plaintive notes of a lover's guitar being strummed beneath a balcony. The city at one time (the 1700s) was a bustling capital state with gold, silver, diamonds, and slaves. But hemmed in by tall, almost impassable mountains, it slowly strangled in the commercial competition of the 20th century. In 1897, it lost its status as capital city of Minas Gerais, and Belo Horizonte came into prominence instead. Preserved by the National Patrimony, it stands as a proud reminder of the glory that was once Imperial Brazil. Here, too, are many works by Brazil's greatest colonial artist, the sculptor Aleijadinho.

BRASILIA

Brazil has had three capitals—Salvador, Rio de Janeiro, and, since 1960, the new city of Brasilia. The reason for the move from Salvador to Rio was that the Portuguese court wanted to be near the center of all the mining and exporting activity. The reason for the move from Rio to Brasilia was that the nation had stagnated for too long along the coast and officials wanted to waken the center of this sleeping giant.

It was not a new idea. As far back as 1808 newspapers were clamoring that Rio was not an adequate place for a capital and were proposing the construction of a city in the interior, where communications could be made with the rest of the country: "Our present capital is in a corner of Brazil and contacts between it and Pará or other far removed states is extremely difficult. Besides, Rio subjects the government to enemy invasion by any maritime power." In 1892, Congress authorized a special expedition to go into the backlands and study the terrain in the center of the nation where "a city could be constructed next to headwaters of big rivers and where roads could be opened to all seaports." After a three-month overland trip, the expedition leaders decided on the planalto area of Goias. They turned in their report and nothing was done with it.

It was not until 1956, when a sharp politician named Juscelino Kubitschek was elected president of Brazil, that the idea became a reality. He needed a campaign platform when he was running for President, and one night at a rally someone shouted to him about building a new capital. Immediately he took up the idea as his own and, as soon as he was installed as President, he set the wheels in motion.

It was a monumental undertaking, one without equal in the modern world. What had to be done was to build a totally new city that would become the center of government for the biggest nation in Latin America—with all the conveniences of light, power, telephones, sewage, housing, streets, police protection, fire protection, schools, hospitals, banks, industry, commerce, ministries, churches, theaters, as well as all the necessary buildings needed by the Congress, Supreme Court, and the President to govern the country.

In the very beginning there was nothing there but scrub trees, red dust, and wild jaguars. President Kubitschek flew there, had Mass said, stayed the night, and set up a long list of work committees. Money came from all over the world in the form of loans and government grants. The Brazilians pushed the button on their printing presses and turned out billions of cruzeiros that inflated their economy as never before.

Very few of the raw materials needed for such a grandiose enterprise could be obtained in Brasilia and had to be contracted from outsiders. Airplanes flew in continually from Rio and São Paulo, loaded with steel bars and bags of cement. The roads to the new capital were still under construction, so all this heavy equipment had to be brought in by air.

Literally thousands of unskilled, uneducated workers, who needed money and were willing to face any hardship to get it, came from the northeast of the nation. They learned fast and worked hard. Living in wooden shacks and working as much as 15 hours a day, they built Kubitschek's dream city.

Back in Rio, opposition to the new capital was loud and heated. Debates in the senate turned into fistfights, and investigating committees were formed to see where all the money was going. Very few people wanted to move to Brasilia and they complained bitterly about the "lack of everything" there. They said their children would not have the proper schools, that they would be unable to pay the high prices that the artificial city was commanding, and that they would be separated from their families and friends. Actually, most of the big politicians were unhappy about being away from the beach and afraid that their investments in Rio apartment buildings and commercial shops would suffer once the city ceased to be the nation's capital. Kubitschek's government countered this with special inducements to civil servants of a 100 percent increase in salary for working in Brasilia, special tax considerations, and an earlier retirement age. He also promised free transportation of government workers and their household effects, commissioned furniture factories to manufacture modern styles to be sold to workers at wholesale costs, and put rentals on new houses and apartments at ridiculously low rates.

"Freetown," where most of the construction workers lived, had grown into a city of over 100,000. It was a rough, sprawling, dirty, vice-ridden place, where anything went as long as there was money to buy it. It was straight out of Hollywood. There were wooden store facades with false second stories. Instead of horses, men parked their jeeps in front of the 101 bars. Two movie houses did a roaring business.

Kubitschek had set the date for the inauguration of the city for April 21, 1960, and in spite of all odds it was ready. The inauguration itself was a memorable day that began with a Mass in the uncompleted cathedral and ended with a fireworks display, during which the name Juscelino Kubitschek burned in letters 15 feet tall.

For all of the troubles and haste that Brasilia generated, it is today a modern, comfortable, functioning capital city. It offers many things of interest to the visitor aside from its architecture and feeling of unreality. It has already started to do what those journalists of 1808 wanted. The area around the capital is being opened and a new era of pioneering and colonization has started. There are roads (the Brazilians call them highways) that stretch outward from the new capital to far off Acre, and upward to the coastal city of Belém, and others under construction will go to Fortaleza and Salvador, Bahia. All along these roads, families are coming in, clearing the land, and raising their children. Little communities are forming, and the poor of the big cities are finding out how much nicer life can be in the country than in a cramped favela slum. It will be a long time before the city really "works" or the interior of the country is really settled—maybe another hundred years—but there is no doubt that Brasilia has kicked off the much-needed social improvement.

In spite of its world fame and the fact that it is the capital of South America's largest nation, Brasilia is still a moderate-sized city, with a population of one million. Tourists can see it all in one day, if pressed for time, or two days if they are interested in the various architectural wonders or in studying more closely the mode of life of a group of people who have been recently uprooted from their original environment.

Most visitors to Brasilia take an early plane from Rio—there are flights from 6:30 A.M. onward—land in Brasilia before noon, take a sightseeing tour around the main buildings, and have lunch at one of the two good hotels; in the afternoon they continue their tour, this time visiting the old "free city," and are delivered to the airport in time to catch a flight back to Rio and dinner.

There is one treat that the linger-awhile type of tourist gets that the one-dayer doesn't. That is to see the city illuminated at night. There is probably no lovelier urban sight in all Brazil than the federal buildings, all white marble with reflecting glass windows, shimmering under dozens of huge, superbly placed spotlights, while the stars shine brightly out of a jungle sky of black velvet. As one old peasant woman told her daughter after she made the trip to the new capital in the back of an open truck: "It looked like I always expected Heaven to look at night. It was difficult to tell where the building lights ended and the stars began. They seemed to be put there to show off the other."

Another thing you'll notice about Brasilia is the sky. It is bluer than the sky in Rio and turns purple. There are always fleecy cloud formations decorating it. Another noticeable item is the red earth of the city. Not unlike the red soil of Georgia, it has stained the bases of the buildings, has tinted the carefully planted grass, and, in a sudden gust of wind, is just as liable to coat your face and clothes with a fine red powder. The earth is very poor in minerals; artistically, it looks as if it had been placed there on purpose for contrast.

Those with only one day to spend should be able to cover the most important points of the city by using this itinerary.

Leaving the airport, take a taxi (if you prefer to drive yourself, there are rental cars available at the airport, too) and watch for the white arrow-shaped signs saying "cidade" (city). If you turn right, take a dip curve, and come up again to where the sign says "Eixo Rodoviario," you will be on the main avenue of the south wing of the city. Along this avenue the luxury apartments are built, and since all rooms have huge plate glass windows onto the street, the Brazilians refer to them as "the Candango's television." The workers do spend a great deal of time looking up into the windows of the senators and ministers who live there. It's cheaper than

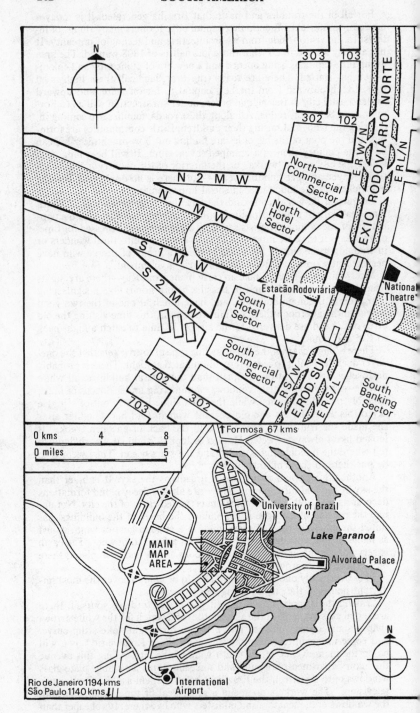

N

303 103

ERW/N

EIXO RODOVIÁRIO NORTE

ERL/N

302 102

North Commercial Sector

N 2 M W

N 1 M W

North Hotel Sector

S 1 M W

S 2 M W

Estação Rodoviária

National Theatre

South Hotel Sector

South Commercial Sector

ERS/W

E. ROD. SUL

ERS/L

South Banking Sector

702

703 302

0 kms 4 8

0 miles 5

↑Formosa 67 kms

University of Brazil

MAIN MAP AREA

Lake Paranoá

Alvorado Palace

N

Rio de Janeiro 1194 kms
São Paulo 1140 kms ↓

International Airport

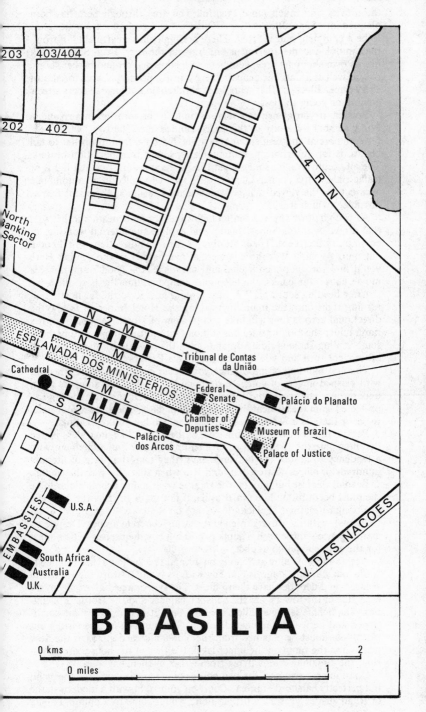

203 403/404

202 402

North Banking Sector

L 4 R N

N 2 M L
N 1 M L
ESPLANADA DOS MINISTÉRIOS
Cathedral
S 1 M L
S 2 M L

Tribunal de Contas da União

Federal Senate
Chamber of Deputies
Palácio dos Arcos

Palácio do Planalto
Museum of Brazil
Palace of Justice

EMBASSIES
U.S.A.
South Africa
Australia
U.K.

AV. DAS NAÇÕES

BRASILIA

0 kms   1   2

0 miles   1

the movies and much more eventful! The area through here has been planned into Super Blocks (Super Quadras) and each block was designed to be a complete unit in itself. There are high-class apartments in front, then middle-income apartment buildings in the rear. Each Super Block has its own shopping area, complete with supermarket and barber shops, etc., as well as a Catholic chapel. There is also a primary school for almost every Super Block, so that school-age children do not have to cross streets coming or going to class.

Brasilia, if you glance at a map, is built in the form of an airplane, a fitting symbol for a city in this space-minded age. The two "wings" are for commercial and residential areas. The fuselage, from propeller to tail blades, is for government, communications, and transportation centers. The city highways are so designed that there are almost no red lights or traffic signs. City planner Lucio Costa's wife was killed in an automobile accident and he vowed that he would make Brasilia as "accident free as possible," which it is.

As you go down this residential highway, turn off beneath another sign that directs you to a Super Quadra and explore the internal workings of community life there. Then, heading in the same direction, you'll come out onto Avenida W3, the commercial main street of the capital. Here you'll find the shops, both chic and mundane, the good restaurants, a movie house, the banks, the telephone company, and the post office.

After heading south on W3, turn around and go to the far north and, turning right onto the main highway by the Hotel Imperial, follow the directional arrows that will take you in front of Hotel Nacional, down a ramp under the monumental bus station (with music, shops, and perhaps some visiting Indians riding up and down the escalators), then make another right turn and you'll be on the Three Powers Square.

The first building of importance you'll pass is the national Cathedral, with clasped fingers of concrete reaching to the sky. Worshippers go in underground and come out to hear Mass in the center under the fingers, protected from the elements by huge panes of glass. Check with your hotel to see if there is a Mass on the Sunday or holiday you're visiting.

Besides the Cathedral, on both sides of the square, like huge glass-plated dominoes, are the 18 various government ministries. Functional, but with a tendency to absorb the hot sun's rays, they take the place of literally hundreds of offices scattered around Rio when that city was the capital.

Beyond the last building on the right is what many people claim to be the most beautiful building in Brasilia, if not in all Brazil—the Ministry of Foreign Relations (Palácio dos Arcos on the map, "Itamaraty" to all residents), with its water garden and soaring concrete arches. Despite its extravagance—those arches support nothing but themselves—it's a must for the amateur photographer.

Across the way, almost floating on air and the shallow reflection pools, is the magnificent Congress building with its twin, 28-story towers where senators and deputies have their offices. The two orange halves, sitting on each side of the towers, are the Senate Chamber and the House of Deputies. The Senate is the smaller, inverted one. It is completely air conditioned and perfectly illuminated within. The building can be visited but permission must be obtained from the blue-uniformed guard at the desk just across the ramp on the upper level. If either of the houses are in session, the Brazilian flag is flying from either of their flagpoles.

Continuing down past the two houses of congress, you'll see the small but perfectly balanced Supreme Court on your right with a modern statue of Blind Justice in front. Further along, you'll come to a plump, oblong cement box, with a huge head of Juscelino Kubitschek in its courtyard; it is the Brasilia Museum.

Directly facing the Supreme Court is probably one of the most beautiful of all the buildings, the Planalto Palace, where the president has his offices. Guided tours can be arranged. Be sure to see the luxurious Hall of Mirrors, where state receptions are held, the severe but lovely room to the right where the President holds open conferences, and the sun-illuminated interior corridors on the second and third floors, where tropical plants grow in profusion.

Head east now, toward the lake, past what seems to be miles of modern lamp posts, until you come to the exclusive Alvorada Palace, official president's residence, at the "propeller" of the airplane. This was the first administrative building ready and the most expensive. Every inch of cement, all the steel girders, the pipes, the glass, tiles, everything had to be flown in, because there was no way to reach Brasilia by land. Beside this jewellike palace is a small circular chapel, where the presidential family attends Mass.

The long, low, burned-out building nearby is the Brasilia Palace Hotel, gutted in a fire in 1979.

After lunch, you will still have some three hours to see the other less important things or to go back for a closer look at what you saw that morning. You could visit the handsome national theater, a pyramid of weathered concrete near the bus station, head off in the same direction for the Yacht Club (where you get an interesting side view of the Three Powers Square), or continue way out on the as yet almost deserted North wing and arrive at the other side of the lake, where many expensive homes have been built or are going up.

For a sharp contrast of a "satellite city" to modern Brasilia—from the "architecture" of a dust town to the year 2,000—take a 20-minute drive beyond city limits to one of the communities settled by the Brazilian builders. You may want to hire one of a group of American guides, right opposite the Hotel Nacional.

If you will have an hour or so before your plane, take a quick look at the wild-west, clapboard satellite town called Free City. Though the bulk of Brasilia's working class now lives far out in the satellite towns of Gama or Taguatinga, the *Cidade Livre* (Free Town) still stands as a monument to those hardy northeasterners who built the 21st-century capital city.

PRACTICAL INFORMATION FOR BRASILIA

WHEN TO GO. The best time is probably the summer, from Nov. to around the middle of Apr. It gets chilly in Brasilia. Because the city is on a high plateau, some 3,500 feet above sea level, and in the direct path of winds from the moist warm jungles as well as those from the colder south, its climate is variable and invigorating. Sweaters at night during the winter months are almost a necessity, and no matter what the season, you'll probably want to sleep under a blanket.

HOW TO GET THERE. There are daily flights from Rio, São Paulo, and Belo Horizonte. Buses also travel the roads connecting these cities with the nation's capital on a daily basis.

HOW TO GET AROUND. Take a taxi. Many people prefer to have a guided tour by one of the registered agencies. If you only have time for a once-around-lightly view of the city, then *Ciclone-Hinterland Turismo* at the Setor Commercial Sul, or *Trips, Toscano, Excelsior,* or *Presmic,* all located in the arcade of the Hotel Nacional, will give you the best service. They have their own cars, usually Brazilian-made Volkswagen "Kombi" station wagons, and their drivers speak English as well as half a dozen other languages. Prices are moderate but a little higher than in Rio for the same service, ranging from $20 to $40.

You might, just for the fun of it, get on any of the buses that leave from the street level platform at the centrally located Highway Terminal ("Estaçao Rodoviaria") and stay on it till it takes you back to the terminal again. No matter which line you take, you'll get odd and interesting angles of the city that other tourists don't catch from the guided tour. But it's best to do this after you've seen Brasilia the regular way, so you can appreciate what you are seeing even more. Bus fares are about 40 cents.

HOTELS. (For definitions of price categories see "Facts at Your Fingertips.") The recent construction of two luxury hotels has brought some relief to Brasilia's chronic shortage of quality hotels. Since the city's founding in 1960, its leading hotel has been the **Nacional,** *Deluxe.* Setor Hoteleiro Sul (321–7575), situated in the heart of the city with an incomparable view of the Congress, Ministries, and the banking section. Ten floors of comfortable apartments with an excellent restaurant where one of the daily specialties is a long smorgasbord table with 100 different dishes to choose from. Now the aging Nacional has been joined by the **Naoum Plaza** and the **Academia de Tenis Resort.** The Naoum is a modern, comfortable, and conveniently located hotel of 200 rooms with pool, bar, and restaurant, *Deluxe,* Setor Hoteleiro Sul, Quadra S, Bloco H/I (226–6494). The Tenis Resort has quickly become Brasilia's most chic hotel, offering 100 apartments and bungalows amidst a park-like setting replete with tennis courts for guests, *Deluxe,* Setor de Clubes Esportivos Sul, Trecho 4, Cj. 5, Lote 1–B (321–3332).

Other good hotels are the **Garvey Park,** *Moderate,* Setor Hoteleiro Norte, Quadra 2, Bloco J (223–9800); **Carlton,** *Moderate,* Setor Hoteleiro Sul, Quadra 5, Bloco G (224–8819); **Eron Brasilia,** *Moderate,* Setor Hoteleiro Norte, Quadra 5, Lote A (321–1777); **Torre Palace,** *Moderate,* Setor Hoteleiro Norte, Quadra 4, Bloco A (321–5554); **Phenicia,** *Moderate,* Setor Hoteleiro Sul, Quadra 5, Bloco J (321–4342); **Aracoara,** *Moderate,* Setor Hoteleiro Norte, Quadra 5, Bloco C (321–9222); **Saint Paul,** *Moderate,* Setor Hoteleiro Sul, Quadra 2, Lote 5 (321–6688); **Bristol,** *Moderate,* Setor Hoteleiro Sul, Quadra 4, Bloco F (321–6162).

RESTAURANTS. Brasilia does have some good restaurants. (For definitions of price categories see "Facts at Your Fingertips.") For good solid Brazilian beef, done "churrasco gaucho" style, pay a visit to the **Churrascuria do Lago** (223–9266) on the banks of the lake, in walking distance of the Hotel Brasilia. Their specialty is a "mixto," which is a little bit of everything, both beef and pork, served with rice, manioc flour, and a special barbecue sauce of raw onions, tomatoes, and vinegar. *Moderately* priced.

A good spot for international cuisine is the **Piantella,** *Moderate,* Comércio Local Sul, 202–B1. A loj. 34 (224–9408) with live music. **Florentino,** *Expensive,* is the favored eatery of the nation's congressmen, where political deals are always in the works. Comércio Local Sul, 402–B1. C loj. 15 (223–7577). The Centro Commercial Gilberto Salomao, where bureaucrats and diplomats of all levels gather nightly, is home to the **Gaf,** *Expensive,* for international cuisine (248–1754), and the **Au Chalet,** *Expensive,* for Swiss (248–2897).

WHAT TO SEE. Everything. The two presidential palaces (the Alvorada where the man in power lives and the Planalto where he works), the twin-towered **Congress building** at the Praça dos Tres Poderes, the domino-placed **Ministry buildings** in the same area, the crown-shaped cathedral at the Eixo Monumental, the national theater also at the Eixo Monumental, the modern spacious apartments, and the bustling—almost small town—atmosphere of the business district. A visit should be paid to the yacht club and the area known as Embassy Row. A visit to the shrine of Dom Bosco is also in order, not just to pay him homage, but to get an over-all, complete view of the city. There are no museums as yet of any importance, nor any special collections. The exteriors of the buildings are more interesting than the interiors (with a few exceptions mentioned already), and don't forget to take note of the way the highways and by-passes have been laid out. Also study the faces of the "candangos," the dusty but courteous immigrant workers who built the city with almost nothing but bare hands and determination.

SPORTS. In Brasilia, there used to be such an exodus of governmental workers, especially such important types as congressmen and ministry directors, that weekend activities were limited. But the city is now developing a social life of its own, even on weekends. The one favorite focal point is the yacht club, on the artificially created Lake Pinheiro. Although open only to members, your travel agent or almost any Brazilian citizen can get you in. There is a nice big pool, a small but more than adequate restaurant, and if you look sad, and wistful, some friendly Brazilian is bound to ask you if you'd like to take a ride on the lake in his "yacht." There are about ten other good social clubs that have also sprouted up—all normally crowded and lively on sunny weekends.

People do **go fishing,** some as far away as on Bananal Island in the surrounding state of Goias. Check with your tourist agent in Brasilia about this and see if they can arrange a two-day trip to the Carajá Indians, who will act as your guides. There is a hotel there; it was called the Juscelino Kubitschek until the latter's political disgrace, whereupon it became John Kennedy. Don't go there without a reservation. Andre Safari & Tours, in the Torre Palace Hotel, specializes in this trip.

MINAS GERAIS—BELO HORIZONTE AND THE HISTORICAL CITIES

The third largest city of Brazil with a population of 1.7 million, Belo Horizonte is an airy modern metropolis nestled into the mountains of Minas Gerais, source of much of Brazil's vast mineral wealth. Although the city is relatively young, celebrating its 90th anniversary in 1987, it is the jumping off point for the fabled historical cities of Minas, colonial-era towns that dot the surrounding mountains and offer visitors a first-hand look at life in Brazil in the 18th century when the gold fields of this region attracted Portuguese adventurers and Catholic priests, a combination that gave birth to the area's famed baroque churches, rich in gold leaf.

But before taking off for a look at its historical surroundings, spend some time in Belo Horizonte itself. There are many things for the tourist to do. One of them is to stroll along the shady downtown streets and watch the new buildings going up all around. Another is to visit the municipal park located in the heart of the business area. Town fathers planned well, for should you become tired of cement and commerce, you can cross over into the well-kept park, with its tree-lined walks, its small lakes, its rustic bridges, and red flowered bushes. There is something going on there almost all the time, and it is a favorite spot for lovers, nursemaids, and photographers.

Another interesting place is the Minas Tennis Club, one of the biggest sports arenas in the state. Extremely modern in design, the gymnasium can hold 10,000 people. Its swimming pool is Olympic size and its separate courts for volleyball, basketball, and tennis have caused favorable comment from many international sports-minded figures.

Just as modern, but much more controversial, is the oddly shaped church at Pampulha, just outside the city. Designed by famed Brasilia builder Oscar Niemeyer, the church, once constructed, was refused consecration by Catholic authorities because both Niemeyer and Portinari (whose frescoes adorn it) were known Communist sympathizers. The battle raged for a number of years until the people of Minas put pressures to bear on the Bishop and the church was blessed.

The Tassini Museum has a collection of maps, crystal, lamps, work tools, photographs, and general miscellanea collected over a 30-year span by one Raul Tassini and donated to the city. It is devoted strictly to objects that figure in the history of Belo Horizonte and the early diamond mining days. Well worth a visit, it is open every day except Monday.

When you have finished with the sights of Belo Horizonte it will be time for you to travel back into the past of this fascinating region. Most trips to the historical cities can be handled on a one-day basis, using Belo as your starting and ending point. Your first trip should definitely be to Ouro Prêto (Black Gold, so-called because of the black coloring of gold in the area caused by iron oxide in the soil). Though still little known outside of the country, Ouro Prêto is one of the most unforgettable tourist attractions in all of South America. It is revered by Brazilians the way Italians revere Venice or the Americans, Williamsburg. Founded in 1711 with the name Vila Rica (Rich Village), it soon became the center of the gold, diamond, and semiprecious stone trading in the colonial era. So much gold came from the hills around Ouro Prêto that the area was named simply "minas gerais" or "general mines."

It became *the* place to live in those days, and the rich built fine houses and palaces, donated gold to construct churches, and hired the very best artists to decorate them. One of the most famous names to come out of this period was a crippled mulatto sculptor called Aleijadinho. The man could do no wrong when he was working with wood or stone, but arthritis turned him into a monster. His facial features became so deformed by disease that he put a sack over his head so that no one could be frightened by his ugliness. His legs refused to coordinate and his fingers and hands became so contorted that his assistants used to tie his hammer and chisel to his wrists with leather thongs so he could work. What he did with the beauty inside him is in evidence in Ouro Prêto and the surrounding area and is part of the rich Brazilian cultural heritage.

The Glorious Churches of Ouro Prêto

The best place to see Aleijadinho's artistry is the Church of São Francisco, located just down the hill to the left from the Praça Tiradentes. Note the twin towers in an almost salt-and-pepper-shaker form. Be sure and inspect the huge soapstone medallion high up over the front door, as well as the intricately carved doorway. Inside, the main altar with cherubic faces, garlands of tropical fruits, and allegorical characters is still fresh with the original paint. Also note the twin soapstone side altars. Just doing one of them is enough for a man to be hailed as a genius, and he did two for this church alone.

His work can also be seen in the impressive Monte do Carmo Church, in whose tall towers hang two bells that weigh 7,000 pounds. The altar dominating the church of São José was also done by Aleijadinho.

There are 11 churches in this one town in the Brazilian hills. If any were in Europe, they would be international "musts" on any tourist itinerary, but hidden away as they are here, they have preserved their charm and offer a new delight to the tourist with spirit enough to come this far to see them.

While in Ouro Prêto, don't fail to take a slow tour of the Museum of Inconfidência. Housed in an impressive baroque building that was started in 1748 and finished in 1846, it was at one time the home of the Municipal Congress. It was here that the first Brazilian rebellion against the Portuguese was started and here that the first rebel, a white-bearded martyr nicknamed "Tiradentes" (tooth puller), was captured, then taken to Rio and brutally executed. The museum is full of clothes, children's toys, slaves' manacles, firearms, books, and gravestones of the turbulent era. Ask for someone who speaks English to give you a guided tour. Admission is free.

Many people stay two days in Ouro Prêto, savoring the winding old streets and the colonial buildings and dodging the donkeys and horses and carts that still move among the automobiles. Ever since 1933, when the entire city became National Patrimony, not a thing has been changed, and it is to the Brazilians' credit that many things have been restored and cleaned up. Tour buses are no longer allowed to transverse the city's narrow streets, in order to preserve the colonial-period buildings. The buses stop outside of the city from where taxis take you into Ouro Prêto. Whether you spend the night or not, try to stay at least until sundown, when you will witness the reflection of the sunset off the city's tiled roofs, the gradual darkening of the surrounding hills and mountains, and finally the cool mist that spreads across the city, evoking a sensation of distant times in Brazil's colonial past. If you decide to remain for a second day, you might hire a taxi and travel a few miles to the sleepy village of Congonhas. The main attraction there is the church of Bom Jesus de Matosinhos, where Aleijadinho sculpted 12 life-sized statues of the Prophets and placed them outside at the front entrance.

These works, breathtaking in their exact details and expressive faces, have been called "a genial mixture of Quasimodo, Beethoven and Michelangelo." Aside from a number of statues inside the church, he did the Stations of the Cross in life-size, using 66 different figures that are housed in six separate buildings. Rarely visited by the Brazilians themselves, these figures are "finds" for the really discriminating tourist.

Aleijadinho, deformed and crippled though he was, got around. His works can be seen in the churches of the nearby town of Mariana and São João Del-Rei. Baroque lovers should also visit the churches of Sabará.

Diamantina took its name from the diamonds that were extracted in great quantities from its soil in the 1700s, and even today the mines still supply gold, iron ore, and rock crystal. It was here also that the famous Chica da Silva, the mulatto slave who captured the heart of the wealthy Portuguese mine owner, lived. He showered her with gold and precious stones, built her a palace with hanging gardens and even transported a sailing yacht overland for her pleasure. Then he turned around and dug her a lake to sail it on.

The city looks very much like it did in the days of Chica. Be sure to note the covered overhanging roofs with their elaborate brackets.

PRACTICAL INFORMATION FOR
BELO HORIZONTE AND THE HISTORICAL CITIES

HOW TO GET THERE. Like the rest of the country, this area is no exception when it comes to distances. Belo Horizonte is 453 miles from Brasilia, 250 miles from Rio de Janeiro, and 360 miles from São Paulo. Ouro Prêto, the living museum city, is a full 75 miles away from Belo, but the people in the state capital consider it "a suburb." And Diamantina (another colonial jewel in the Minas hills), is 180 miles away, but citizens in Belo will calmly tell visitors who have nothing to do for the day, "Why don't you run over and see Diamantina?"

The city of Belo Horizonte is served by all of Brazil's major airlines, and there are daily flights between the city and Rio, São Paulo, and Brasilia. Bus service is also frequent and the roads are good. For trips from Belo to the historical cities, the best bet is by bus or car. The roads in the region are paved and in good condition. There is regular train service between Belo Horizonte and Diamatina. Day tours depart from Belo for all of the colonial cities in the region. Taxis will drive you to Ouro Prêto and back for $45 or so and a regular bus line charges about $4 for the same service.

BELO HORIZONTE

HOTELS. Brasilton Contagem. *Expensive.* Contagem industrial district on a hilltop near Belo Horizonte (396–1100). First Hilton Hotel in Brazil outside São Paulo, the Brasilton Contagem opened early in 1978. Rooms are built around central courtyard with pool and tropical gardens, and all have air conditioning, heat, color TV, well-stocked mini-bars.

Othon Palace. *Expensive.* Av. Afonso Pena, corner Tupis e Bahia (273–3844). Newest, biggest, and most luxurious in the city, with 317 air-conditioned rooms, rooftop pool and bar, international restaurant, coffee shop, sauna, conference facilities for 800 persons. Overlooking trees and lakes of Municipal Park.

Hotel Del Rey. *Moderate.* Pça Afonso Arinos 60 (273–2211). One of the best traditional hotels downtown; 270 air-conditioned rooms, private baths, 24-hour room service.

Normandy. *Moderate.* On Rua Tamoios 212 (201–6166). Service is very good; the rooms large and airy; modern restaurant and bar are fine. Located in the center of the city's business district, it is one of the most popular meeting places. Insist on an outside room.

The Amazonas. *Inexpensive.* On Avenida Amazonas 120 (201–4644). New and small but service is very good. Excellent restaurant on the 11th floor.

Other hotels include the **Wembley Palace.** *Moderate.* Rua Espirito Santo 201, downtown (201–6966); the **Serrana Palace.** *Moderate.* Rua Goitacazes 450, downtown (201–9955); and the **Financial.** *Inexpensive.* Av. Alfonso Pena 571, downtown (201–7044).

Note: The **historical cities region** offers a range of hotels but most are quaint inns and pensions, some rather primitive in their basic comforts.

RESTAURANTS. As in most Brazilian cities, new restaurants are constantly opening with an increasingly international flavor. Tops among Belo's international eateries is the **Tacho de Ouro** in the Othon Hotel, *Expensive* with live piano music, Av. Alfonso Penna 1050 (273–3844). Also good is the **Nacional Club,** *Moderate,* Rua Bernardo Mascarenhas 77 (337–9461). But Minas is also rightfully famous for its own regional cooking, hearty meals perfect for the cool nighttime temperatures in this mountainous state. Specialties are suckling pig and sausages but any pork dish in one of Belo Horizonte's finer restaurants is recommended. A true Minas meal is always accompanied by tutu, a delicious black bean mash. One of the state's traditional dishes, a favorite throughout Brazil, is *tutu à mineira*—sausages, pork and tutu. In Belo, for regional cooking try **Petisqueira do Galo,** *Moderate,* Av. Olegário Maciel 1516 (335–5773); **Chico Mineiro,** *Moderate,* Rua Alagoas 626 in the sophisticated Savassi neighborhood, home to the city's newest and liveliest night spots (273–6027); **Arroz com Feijao,** *Moderate,* Av. do Contorno, 6510, Funcionários (225–0536); and **Nini e Familia,** *Moderate,* Av. Cristóvão Colombo 631, Savassi. Best churrascarias are **Vitelo's,** *Moderate,* Rua Claudio Manoel, 1149 (226–0993); **Minuano,** *Moderate,* Rua Professor Morais 635 (225–3600) and **Carretão Guaíba,** *Moderate,* Av. do Contorno 8412 (337–7566)–not only is the food good here but the way it's served is spectacular, all the steaks and sausages you can eat. Called rodizio or rotation-style, this system has become popular in recent years— the waiters rotate from table to table carrying long skewers heavy with sizzling meat and sausages and stopping only when you say no more. Other conventional churrascarias are **O Laçador,** *Moderate,* Rua Gonçalves Dias 874 (224–3335) and **Grill,** *Moderate,* Av. do Contorno 5671 (221–9368). The best Italian restaurant is **Tavernaro,** *Moderate,* Rua Antonio de Albuquerque 889 in Savassi (221–8283) and for French cuisine try **Cafe Ideal,** *Moderate to Expensive,* Rua Cláudio Manoel 583, Funcionários (226–6019).

NIGHTLIFE. The nightlife in Belo has become concentrated in the Savassi neighborhood, with many outdoor bars, excellent restaurants, and a few night clubs with live Brazilian music. The "in" spots tend to change from season to season but try **Sunset Boulevard,** Av. Getúlio Vargas 1640 (223–9000); and **Era Uma Vez um Chalezinho** (with excellent fondue), Rua Paraiba 1453 (221–2170). All are located in Savassi, where you can't go wrong for nightlife.

OURO PRÉTO

HOTELS. The best hotel is the **Estrada Real,** *Moderate,* located on the highway at the entrance to the city, Rodovia dos Inconfidentes km 87 (551–2122). Like all the hotels in Ouro Prêto this one is small, with 30 rooms and 10 chalets. Other options are **Luxor Pousada,** *Moderate,* Rua Dr. Alfredo Baeta 16 (551–2244) **Gran-**

de Hotel Ouro Prêto, *Moderate,* Rua Senador Rocha Lagoa 165 (551–1488); **Pouso Chico Rey,** *Moderate,* Rua Brigadeiro Mosqueira 90 (551–1274); **Pousada Recanto de Minas,** *Inexpensive,* Rua Manganês, 287 (551–3003); **Colonial,** *Inexpensive,* Travessa Camilo Veloso 26 (551–3133); **Toffolo,** *Inexpensive,* Rua São José 76 (551–1322).

The best **restaurant** in town is the **Taberna Luxor** in the Luxor Pousada, Rua Alfredo Baeta 10 (551–2244).

DIAMATINA

HOTEL. The Tijuco Hotel, *Inexpensive,* is really the only option in the city. Located on Rua Macau do Meio 221 (931–1022), it adheres faithfully to the historical atmosphere demanded by the visitor.

CENTRAL-WEST BRAZIL—THE PANTANAL

While most visitors to Brazil have heard of the country's beautiful Atlantic beaches and the jungle attractions of the Amazon rain forest, few are aware that Brazil is also home to the last major ecological frontier on earth. Known as the Pantanal, this 140,000 square mile area covers a region the size of Holland, Switzerland, and Belgium combined. Once an inland ocean in prehistoric times, the Pantanal today is a giant plain with an average elevation of 400 feet that is cut by the basin of the Paraguay River. Just south of the Amazon watershed, the northern Pantanal is home to the headwaters of the rivers that form the Paraguay Basin. In the rainy season these rivers drain south, forming huge lakes throughout the region with only a few areas left above the level of the waters where the Pantanal's wildlife escapes from the floods. In the dry season, the water level subsides and the Pantanal's incredible variety of wildlife moves out to the now dry plain, accumulating along the banks of the many rivers that cut through the area. The dry season (usually May to September) is the best time to visit the Pantanal, a time of the year when visitors can see thousands of alligators, armadillos, monkeys, the capivara (the world's largest rodent), and if you're lucky the famed onça, the Brazilian jaguar. But the best sights are reserved for those who lift their gaze skywards. As birdwatchers throughout the world have long known, the Pantanal is world-class birding territory where in a single day you can see more species than you ever thought existed.

For those who come to do more than watch the wildlife, the Pantanal is also famed as one of the top fishing areas on the earth. It is practically unbeatable for both variety and quantity of fish. Here you will find the piraracu, at 600 pounds the largest fresh-water fish in the world. Other top eating varieties are the pintado and the pacu and if you've ever wondered what a piranha looks like close up, here is the place to find out.

Unlike the Amazon, the Pantanal is not closed in by jungle; thus, movement here, by river, road, or rail, is relatively unrestricted. In past days the lack of facilities for tourists made a trip to the Pantanal a form of Brazilian safari but today the region has received major investments in tourism infrastructure. Comfortable fishing camps plus small hotels for those who simply want to sit back and enjoy nature watching are now scattered throughout the Pantanal. But while the comfort has increased a sense of adventure still prevails, thanks to the as yet undisturbed natural setting where tranquil rivers with alligators sunning on the banks cut through the vast sedimentary plain, leaving a sensation that you have escaped the modern world and returned to prehistoric times. A trip to the Pantanal is an unforgettable experience.

Exploring the Pantanal

The region has two main gateways, in the north via the city of Cuiaba, capital of the state of Mato Grosso, and in the south by way of the city of Curumba, in the state of Mato Grosso do Sul. These two states contain all of the Pantanal as well as some of the largest cattle ranches in South America. In this area a sense of frontier life still exists, but the region's main cities are expanding quickly. Only ten years ago, Cuiaba was a city where you could see roughened ranch hands walking the streets wearing holsters and packing six-shooters. Today such sights belong to folklore and Cuiaba is a bustling modern city with high rises sprouting up at every downtown corner. The cattle ranches plus an explosion of farming (especially soybeans, of which Brazil today is the world's number two producer, behind the United States) have brought new wealth to the city and region.

Once you've arrived in Cuiaba get in touch with a tour operator, assuming you have not already taken this step in Rio or São Paulo. A guide is highly recommended for the Pantanal. On your first day in Cuiaba either join a tour or rent a van with an English-speaking driver to take you on a drive on the nearby Transpantaneira Highway. The Pantanal in this area is swampy, somewhat like the Everglades in Florida, and the highway is built above the level of the swamps, giving you an excellent view of the region and whatever wildlife is visible. Some tours spend the night in small towns along the highway, returning to Cuiaba the next day. The city itself has few attractions. While it was founded in the 18th century by Portuguese adventurers looking for gold, Cuiaba has preserved little of its heritage. The Indian Museum of the Federal University of Mato Grosso is of interest and Cuiaba is also home to a satellite tracking station maintained by NASA.

On day two, arrange to visit the Chapada dos Guimarães, a mystical rock formation located 40 miles from Cuiaba. This immense geological formation surges to a height of 2,400 feet with lush green forests and spectacular waterfalls as well as curious rock formations carved by the action of the wind over millions of years. The Chapada also possesses a strange magnetic force that reduces the speed of cars, even when they are going downhill.

Now you are ready for a full-scale trip into the Pantanal. From this point on you will have to deal with a travel agency or tour operator to arrange things for you. Most trips last three to four days and several begin with a drive or flight from Cuiaba to the city of Caceres, about 120 miles to the southwest. Here you will take a trip in an outboard motorboat down the Paraguay River for three hours until you reach the Jauru River. Going up the Jauru (always have your camera ready, especially for the birds and alligators), you will soon arrive at the Hotel Fazenda Barranquinho, one of the better hotels in the area, with room for 36 guests. Run by a tourism agency, the hotel provides horses and outboard boats for fishing and trips.

In this hotel, as in other fishing camps and hotels in the Pantanal, you will receive all the assistance you need from the staff to either fish or take trips to see and photograph the wildlife (there is no hunting allowed in the Pantanal). Accommodations tend to be comfortable but modest. Although the Pantanal today is no longer off the beaten track, it still has no luxury facilities for tourists. The food is included in the room rate and most of it comes from the region itself. Besides the fish from the rivers, you will have freshly-baked bread made by the hotel as well as such Pantanal delicacies as monkey meat and piranha soup. Be prepared to take things easy since there is virtually nothing to do at night except rest or talk to the other guests of the hotel. The hotels are isolated and it is not possible to travel from one to another at night since all travel in the Pantanal is by boat.

Similar excursions into the Pantanal are possible via the southern gateway city of Corumba, located on the Paraguay River. If you wish to get an idea of the immensity of this part of Brazil, there is a train ride from the city of São Paulo to Corumba. The one-and-a-half day trip is not known for its comfort but the final ten hours provide a spectacular view of the Pantanal. Once in Corumba, a sleepy river town with little to see, boat trips into the Pantanal can be arranged. For the truly adventuresome there is a two-day trip across the Pantanal on a supply boat that carries food and other necessities to small settlements located in the marshlands. The boat goes up the Paraguay and São Lourenço Rivers, ending the trip at Porto Jofre, the last stop on the Transpantineira Highway. The trip provides an excellent look at the Pantanal and the way its inhabitants live, but life on board is rustic to say the least. There are no cabins and passengers must bring their own hammocks to sleep in. To buy a passage go to the wharves in Corumba.

PRACTICAL INFORMATION FOR THE PANTANAL

WHEN TO GO. The dry season (May to Sept.) is the only time when it is practical to make a trip to the Pantanal. During the rainy season (Oct. to Mar. or Apr.), the Pantanal is mostly under water, which makes visits impossible although you may rent a plane to fly over the region. It is usually hot, except for June and July, and few of the hotels or fishing camps have air-conditioning so dress for warm weather. Also, mosquitoes are a constant nuisance—bring lots of bug spray.

HOW TO GET THERE. Both Corumba and Cuiaba have airports that are served by *Vasp, Varig-Cruzeiro,* and *Transbrasil* airlines. There are also direct buses from São Paulo and Rio that make the trip to the two cities although the journey is long and tiring. The train ride from São Paulo to Corumba will provide you with a view of the booming interior region of the state of São Paulo, easily the most developed area of Brazil.

HOTELS. For definitions of price categories see "Facts at Your Fingertips." In Cuiaba the best hotels are **Eldorado Cuiabá**, *Moderate,* Av. Isaac Póvoas, 1000 (624–4000); **Aurea Palace**, *Moderate,* Av. General Melo 63 (322–3377); **Excelsior**, *Moderate,* Av. Getulio Vargas 264 (322–6322); **Las Velas**, *Moderate,* Av. Filinto Muller 62 (381–1422).

In Corumba there is little to choose from but try **Nacional**, *Moderate,* Rua América, 906 (231–6868); **Pousada do Cachimbo**, *Moderate,* Rua Alan Kardec 4 (231–4833); and **Santa Monica**, *Inexpensive,* Rua Antonio Maria Coelho 345 (231–3001).

For accommodations in the Pantanal, the most recommended options are: **Hotel Fazenda Barranquinho**, *Moderate,* (279–0555 in São Paulo), for fishing and nature watching, near Cuiaba; **Hotel Cabanas do Pantanal**, *Moderate,* fishing and nature trips, northern Pantanal near Cuiaba (321–4142); **Cabana do Lontra**, *Moderate,* fishing and nature trips, in the southern Pantanal near Corumba (283–5843 in São Paulo); **Fazenda Mato Grosso**, *Moderate,* fishing and nature trips, northern Pantanal near Cuiabá, Rua Antônio Dorileo 1200 in Coxipó, Mato Grosso (361–2980, reservations in São Paulo at 227–7991); **Hotel dos Camalotes**, *Moderate,* fishing and nature trips, air-conditioning in the rooms, southern Pantanal near Corumba (383–1224); **Paraiso dos Dourados**, *Moderate,* fishing and nature trips, air-conditioning in the rooms (258–4355 in São Paulo), southern Pantanal near Corumba; **Santa Rosa Pantanal**, *Moderate,* fishing and nature trips, northern Pantanal near Cuiaba (322–0513); **Corumbi, Amazonas, Trans-Tur** and **Santa Isabel** "botels," boats converted into hotels, air-conditioning, southern Pantanal near Corumba (231–3016 in Corumba). All of these hotels have accommodations for 20 to 40 persons.

RESTAURANTS. The best eating in this area is in restaurants specializing in river fish. At the hotels in the Pantanal, fish is the main course and in some cases the only course. In Cuiaba try **Flutuante,** *Moderate,* Rua Santa Baracat (381–5157)—the menu contains a wide choice of the best fish dishes of the region, which should give you a good idea of the flavor of the different species caught in the Pantanal; **Regionalissimo,** *Moderate,* Rua 13 de Junho (next to the Casa do Artesão) (322–3908), regional specialties, live music; **Milano's,** *Moderate,* Ave. Isaac Póvoas, 1331 (321–9597); **Aurea Palace,** *Moderate,* in the hotel of the same name, Rua General Melo 63 (322–3377). In Corumba the best fish restaurant is the **Ceara,** *Moderate,* Av. Rio Branco 580 (231–1930).

TOURS. Getting to the gateway cities of Curumba and Cuiaba is not difficult, but from then on you will need the assistance of professionals to arrange visits to the Pantanal. Most large travel agencies and tour operators in Rio and São Paulo now offer Pantanal packages and you can get in touch with them through your travel agent at home. Plan a Pantanal trip well in advance since hotel space is limited and the best spots are always booked up ahead of time. Some persons, such as bird-watching enthusiasts, may want a special tour package to visit particular areas of the Pantanal. Your best bet in that case would be to get in touch with *Rio Custom Tours,* Travessa Madré Jacinta 25, Rio de Janeiro (274–3217), a Rio tour operator that specializes in Pantanal trips, especially for foreign bird-watchers.

BAHIA

If you have only time to visit two cities in Brazil, make them Rio and Salvador, although, as residents of the latter will quickly add, once you've been to Salvador you won't need to visit Rio. With a rich colonial past evident in its historical churches, forts, and buildings Salvador is known to Brazilians as the most Brazilian of their cities. For this it draws not only upon its history (Salvador was Brazil's first capital) but also upon the colors, tastes, sounds, and aromas of this unique city that mixes old and new, black and white, religion and mysticism. A blend of African, Indian, and European cultures, Salvador moves to its own rhythm, slow and sensual, more at ease even than Rio and blessed with miles and miles of practically untouched beaches. The capital of the state of Bahia, with which it is so closely identified that Salvador is often called Bahia, Salvador is at once South American and African, a mix that makes it unlike any other city in the world.

There are red-tile roofs tacked atop white plaster walls. There are palm trees, baroque architecture, an abundance of churches, and happy carefree people. These are the expectable things. Then there are the thousands of black faces, with bodies swathed in cloth of neo-African styles. There are dishes of hot strange foods prepared nowhere else in the world. There is a strange drum beating voodoo ritual that mingles the best of the African and Christian ideals into a powerful, frighteningly personal religion. There is a fight dance called *capoeira* that originated in Bahia and is only practiced here. There are modern automobiles vying with plodding donkeys. There are sumptuous mansions vying for a place in the sun with mud-thatched shanties.

If you stay there for awhile, you'll find Salvador is not just a city but an entire way of life, where the arts and the human personality are more important than money or political ambitions. The city has been called the "Renaissance of Latin America," because of its attitudes toward beauty and self-expression and the number of artists from all over the nation (and the world) who have gone there for inspiration. But this does not mean that Bahia is all siestas in the sun. Far from it. One glance at the dozens of new office buildings and the hundreds of modern apartments and houses will dispel that idea. It is simply that the Bahianos have found a way to live with the best of both worlds, and, like their hybrid religion, their city has become a surprising, fascinating experience.

SALVADOR

Salvador was the first city the Portuguese built up when they colonized Brazil. That was in 1549. Today this city spreads around the bay of Todos os Santos (All Saints), which is so wide (1,052 square kilometers) it could supposedly hold all the ships in the world. Salvador was built by the early settlers to keep the Spanish, French, and Dutch away from the new colony belonging to King Dom Joao III. The administration buildings and residences were built on the hills, the forts, docks, and warehouses on the beaches. To this day, it is still divided into upper and lower cities. From 1500 to 1815, Salvador enjoyed being the nation's busiest port. The sugar from the northeast and the area surrounding All Saints Bay and the gold and diamonds from the mines in the south all passed through this town. It was a golden age for Salvador when magnificent homes and richly decorated churches were built. Its churches have few rivals anywhere in the world. Thanks to a federal commission called The National Historic and Artistic Patrimony Service, created in 1941, many of the city's old churches are the same today as they were the day they were built. Entire squares, such as Largo do Pelourinho, hundreds of private homes and even the hand-chipped street paving bricks have been preserved and restoration work is still continuing. Salvador counts 97,000 buildings and about 20,000 of them are over 250 years old. Yet there are brand new buildings going up everywhere to meet the living requirements of the progressive citizens of today.

Salvador may be seen, if necessary, in three days but only if you're pressed for time. The city really requires five days at the minimum. Save time for shopping and if possible one extra day to travel into the interior of the state of Bahia.

The first day: By now you've become intrigued by the history of Salvador, so plunge into the Upper City, home to Brazil's best preserved colonial architecture. If you wish to do this on your own it would be best to contact an English-speaking guide either through your hotel or the local tourism authority, Bahiatursa (see "Practical Information" below). Otherwise, there are several local tour operators that can give you an excellent tour of the colonial Upper City and other sights in Salvador in air-conditioned mini-buses with English-speaking guides. For those of you on your own, start out at the downtown Praça da Sé. Remember, you should dress casually because of the heat but don't wear bermudas or swimming wear as some churches will not let you in. To the left of the Praça is the Archbishop's Palace, built in the 18th century and today used as the Catholic Law School. On the other side of the Tourist Office is the 18th-century Holy House of Mary church. Walking up Guedes de Brito Street, you'll see Saldanha Palace with its impressive gateway. The School of Arts and Crafts is there now. As you walk up Bispo Street you'll pass São Damasco Seminary, built in 1700, and will come to a little square and the Church of São Francisco Convent. It is one of Brazil's most famous and undoubtedly one of the most beautiful in the world. Hand carved in every nook and cranny and then covered with shining gold, it is so impressive that

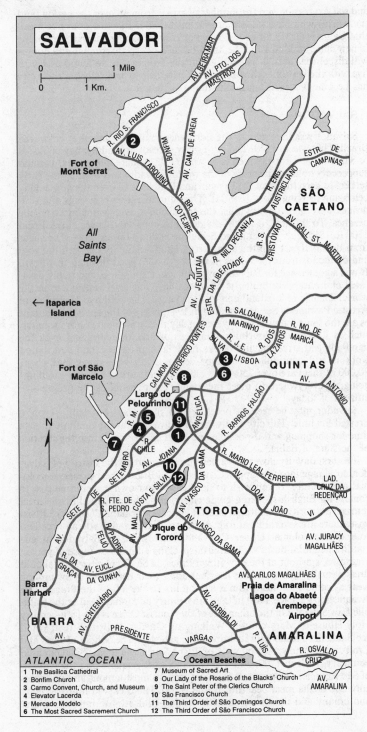

SALVADOR

0 _____ 1 Mile
0 _____ 1 Km.

AV. BEIRA MAR
AV. PTO. DOS MASTROS

R. RIO S. FRANCISCO

**Fort of
Mont Serrat**

AV. LUIS TARQUINO
AV. BONFIM
AV. CAM. DE AREIA

AV. BR. DE COTEJIPE

ESTR. DE CAMPINAS

**SÃO
CAETANO**

R. ENG. AUSTRICLIANO
AV. GALL ST. MARTIN

*All
Saints
Bay*

AV. JEQUITAIA
R. NILO PEÇANHA
ESTR. DA LIBERDADE

R. CRISTÓVÃO
R. S.

← **Itaparica
Island**

R. SALDANHA
MARINHO
R. MQ. DE MARICÁ

R. J. E.
R. DOS LAZAROS

**Fort of São
Marcelo**

AV. FREDERICO PONTES
CALMON
SILVA
LISBOA

QUINTAS

3
6

AV. ANTONIO

N

R. M.
**Largo do
Pelourinho**
8
11
ANGÉLICA
5
4
9
1
R. BARROS FALCÃO

R. CHILE
7
AV. JOANA
10
12
R. MARIO LEAL FERREIRA
AV. SETE DE SETEMBRO

AV. MAL. COSTA E SILVA
AV. VASCO DA GAMA
AV. DOM JOÃO VI

R. FTE. DE S. PEDRO

LAD. CRUZ DA REDENÇÃO

**Dique do
Tororó**
AV. VASCO DA GAMA
TORORÓ

R. P. PADRE FEIJÓ
R. DA GRAÇA
AV. EUCL. DA CUNHA

AV. JURACY MAGALHÃES

AV. CENTENÁRIO
AV. CARLOS MAGALHÃES

**Barra
Harbor**

**Praia de Amaralina
Lagoa do Abaeté
Arembepe
Airport** →

BARRA
AV. PRESIDENTE VARGAS
AV. GARIBALDI
P. LUIS

AMARALINA

ATLANTIC   OCEAN   **Ocean Beaches**

R. OSVALDO CRUZ

AV. AMARALINA

1 The Basílica Cathedral	7 Museum of Sacred Art
2 Bonfim Church	8 Our Lady of the Rosario of the Blacks' Church
3 Carmo Convent, Church, and Museum	9 The Saint Peter of the Clerics Church
4 Elevator Lacerda	10 São Francisco Church
5 Mercado Modelo	11 The Third Order of São Domingos Church
6 The Most Sacred Sacrement Church	12 The Third Order of São Francisco Church

many tourists stay around all day just watching the play of light on the walls. It is especially beautiful during a High Mass. The image of St. Peter of Alcantara on the lateral altar on the right is so well done that church authorities had a battle with Emperor Dom Pedro II, because he wanted it for his private chapel. Only the men may visit the blue-tiled cloisters of the monastery; women must be content to peer through the grillwork. There are Franciscan fathers there who will show you around. When you leave drop some money into the poor box, for the church does an impressive job three times a day supplying warm meals for the poor. Right next door is the church of the Third Order of São Francisco. Inside there is a room that is worth seeing full of life-size statues. The intricate facade was carved in 1703 but hidden for many years by a thick coat of plaster. It was a major art find when it was uncovered recently. Now to the square of Terreiro de Jesus with the 16th century Basilica Cathedral, the church of the Third Order of São Domingos (1731), and the church of St. Peter of the Clerics. From here, up Alfredo de Brito Street you come to the architectural spectacle of the Largo do Pelourinho. It was here that thousands of slaves were chained together, then sold on that platform on the right side of the street. Note the typical old balconies, the tiles and the people who look as if they've stepped from a Debret engraving. The streets that lead into the Largo, all narrow and cobblestoned, contain several fine shops for the purchase of the region's delicate lace work—blouses, dresses, table cloths, etc. Walk slowly down to Taboão Square where five streets cross and then up the Ladeira do Carmo. Now take a quaint flight of steps that leads to the Church of the Passo and continue to the top of the street. Here the Carmo Convent and the Church of the Third Order of Carmo stand side by side. The church is famed for its image of the crucified Christ. To enter the convent, you have to know the way. Beside the biggest door in the room hangs a cord. Pull it and from somewhere inside a smiling guard appears to escort you about. Be sure and tip him when you leave. Going up the Ladeira do Carmo, there is a corner of blue-tiled houses.

Tell the driver to take you to Baixa do Sapateiro, a street filled with shops and private homes that time has somehow forgotten. Afterward look at the Convent of the Desterro (1678), where the sisters have a well-deserved reputation as candy makers. It is Brazil's oldest and most beautiful convent. Go up Avenida Joana Angelica to the Tororó steps. Below them lies the Dique, an artificial lake made in the 17th century as part of the city's defense system. It is also considered by followers of candomblé, the African religion brought to Brazil by the slaves, to be the bay of Oxum, a river nymph who is the god of beauty and good fortune. At night presents are left on the banks of the Dique for Oxum. Also, no one swims in the Dique—these are sacred waters.

For the night of your first day in Salvador visit one of the many bars with live Brazilian popular music. Salvador is the birthplace of many of Brazil's top singing stars, such as Gilberto Gil, Gal Costa, Caetano Veloso, and Maria Bethania, and in the city's nights spots you can listen to their songs and those of the other giants of samba and bossa nova. Nightlife is centered in the Barra neighborhood, along the beach of the same name. For your first night try Bistro 507 or Bistro do Luis in nearby Rio Vermelho.

The second day should be devoted to beaches and outdoor scenery. Rent a car and driver for the day and tell the driver to go *slowly* towards the Lagoa do Abaeté. The first impressive building you will pass is the white columned University Rectory. If you wish you may go in to see the blue tiles and the reconstructed auditorium. On the beachfront drive, called the Orla, you will see the results of the boom in tourism in Salvador in recent years. Anxious to compete with Rio, the city government has land-scaped the beach area for a total of some 15 miles, turning this area of white sand beaches into one of the most beautiful beach drives in Brazil. Along the beach there are kiosks where you can savor a cold drink while you sample a seafood snack Bahia-style. (Although Bahian food has a reputation for being hot, in fact it is merely well-spiced. The hot sauces are served separately and if you wish to taste them, do so with caution. They are not really needed, though. Bahian food, especially seafood, is delicious and easily stands on its own, without the sauces.) Along the drive you will be impressed by the vast quantity of coconut palms as well as the little boys selling fresh coconuts.If you stop for one, watch how deftly a boy can nick off the top with his knife. The milk is warm and sweet. Ask him to split open the coconut and then go on and eat the soft white meat with your fingers. You will pass famed Itapuã Beach with its tall coconut trees and finally reach the lagoon. Brazilian composers have written dozens of songs about this strange inland lake with its contrast of white, white sand and black, black waters. Native women wash their clothes here, and there are some good restaurants in the area for lunch or a cooling drink. Take your bathing suit too, for you might like to sample one of the beaches on the way going or coming.

Once you've finished with the lagoon go back to the beaches and follow them out into the newest area where hotels and restaurants are now sprouting. The beaches here are even better than the stretch between Barra and Itapuã. Running on north of the Quatro Rodas Hotel are the beaches of Barra do Jacuípe, Itacimirim, Arembepe, Guarajuba, and Praia do Forte, where once a year great sea turtles return to lay their eggs. The drive is refreshing and the highway is flanked by coconut palms and white sand dunes. At Arembepe you'll find the remnants of a 1960s colony of hippies once frequented by rock stars Janis Joplin and Mick Jagger. Stop for lunch at Guarajuba and afterward continue on to Praia do Forte, which is quickly becoming the most popular beach in the Salvador area—it also boasts the ruins of Brazil's only haunted castle.

For your second evening you should consider one of the three basic nighttime activities that all first-time visitors to Salvador should take in. First is a capoeira exhibition, where, at the best Salvador academy in Brazil, you will witness the fascinating capoeira dance-fight. At first glance it looks like an involved dance, with the two men rotating around a small space flinging their legs into the air and seemingly just missing each other's heads with their feet. In reality, though, capoeira was invented as a karate-like fight—and was often a fatal one. The slaves were not permitted by their masters to fight between themselves but by disguising their struggle as a dance they were able to resolve their disputes. Thus capoeira is accompanied by the strange-sounding berimbau, a curving stick with a carved-out gourd at its base and a single chord running from top to bottom which is stroked by the musician. Together with drums, this musical background slowly builds up with the tempo of the dancers until you become hypnotized by the flying bodies in front of you and the eerie mystical sounds of the drums and the berimbau. Although in today's capoeira no blows are struck it is easy to imagine the force of the dancers' legs and feet should they strike their mark.

If you decide to leave capoeira for another evening, you may opt for a night of black magic, a candomblé ceremony. Candomblé is another example of how the African slaves fought to preserve their own culture in the new world. Prohibited from practicing their native religions, the slaves pretended to worship the saints of the Catholic Church but in reality for each saint they substituted one of their native gods. Over the centuries the Catholic priests grew to accept the fact that for many of the worshipers who filled the churches, the symbols of Catholicism were also symbols of candomblé. This duality of worship continues to exist today with the exception that while once it was banned by the church, today it is accepted and even extolled as an example of the blending of races and cultures in Salvador. Known as the most deeply religious of Brazilian cities, Salvador has 166 churches but it also has 4,000 candomblé temples. Bahians say: it's better with both—if one doesn't work, the other will.

Several of the candomblé temples allow tourists to witness their ceremonies and there is rarely a week that goes by without at least one celebration for one of the many African gods. Each god has his or her counterpart in the Catholic religion and each also wears a special color and dresses and dances in a specific manner. Thus when a particular god is being honored candomblé followers will wear his color that day—even to work. You can arrange to visit a temple through your hotel or a tour operator. Remember not to take photos unless the permission of the Mae do Santo (priestess) is given. Be prepared to be separated from your friends once you arrive there. They will tell you where to sit and it's always men on one side and women on the other. There is nothing to be frightened of either, but don't be surprised to see the Brazilian beside you suddenly become "possessed" by spirits, fall onto the ground, roll his eyes, and then dance in a contorted, uncomfortable position. When you leave (sometime after midnight) show your appreciation by placing some money at the feet of the chief drummer.

One more thing you should be aware of. While most foreigners naturally associate candomblé with the voodoo ceremonies of the Caribbean, there is a major difference between the two. Unlike voodoo, candomblé is not aimed at producing bad luck for your enemies. Followers are forbidden to use the spirits convoked by the ceremonies to perform evil deeds. Candomblé is to be used only to produce positive results for the worshiper. There are no dolls with pins sticking out of them in candomblé.

Finally, if you don't feel you're ready for a night of either candomblé or capoeira, why not try a mixture of both as well as a sample of other Bahian dances and folklore? There are four restaurants and one theater in Salvador that offer Bahian folklore shows at night where examples of capoeira, candomblé, and the many other dances of the region are presented (see "Practical Information" below). All are good but the restaurants have the advantage of also offering you a sample of Bahian cuisine. The combination of food and folklore is the perfect match for a Bahian night.

The third day: Now you'll visit the other end of the city on the Itapagipe peninsula. If you leave about 9 A.M. from the Praça da Sé the car will go down commercially busy Rua Chile to Castro Alves Praça, then down the Ladeira da Montanha (where many accidents have happened when the brakes didn't hold) and reach the lower city. That big column of white cement rising to the upper city is the Lacerda elevator and is used to join the two levels of Salvador. Imagine if you had to walk up and down those steep hills every time! Taking Avenida Frederico Pontes, you'll pass the attractive Fort of Lagartixa and the Noble House of Jequitaia built in the 18th century and now used as an army officers' school.

Ask your driver to go to the Bonfim church, and on the way you'll pass the 18th-century Archbishop's summer palace, which is connected to the Penha church by a very interesting passageway. Now at Bonfim church, you are really in Bahia, for this church is the city's main sanctuary. It is not ornate or covered with gold, just a simple building with years of tradition among the faithful. It is said that the Lord of Bonfim never fails anyone and the room of miracles looks as if that might be so. Here you'll see wooden, silver, and plaster reproductions of parts of the human body hanging on the walls. These are there in gratitude for cures worked through prayers to the Lord of Bonfim. Almost always the cures are said to be miracles, as the many inscriptions indicate. It is here, on the Thursday before the third Sunday in January, that thousands of black women dressed in their colorful regional dress and carrying pottery jugs with flowers and water come to symbolically wash down the church steps. It is one of the most time-honored festas in Bahia. There is a spectacular view from atop this hill.

Back in the car, go to the Fort of Mont Serrat, named for the great shrine of the Black Virgin in Spain at Montserrat, near Barcelona. Its white walls rising from the seacoast, this 16th-century building looks like a giant bird ready for flight. There is the Mont Serrat Church nearby with its renowned carving of the Repentant St. Peter. If the church is closed, call the guard who lives at the back, and even though he grumbles, he'll show you the tiny jewellike interior. A tip calms him down amazingly. Now you can go to the Cacao Institute, where pictures and graphs tell the story of the chocolate industry from the planted seed to the finished foil-wrapped bar. More than $100,000,000 of cocoa is exported annually from Bahia's ports. Now you are ready for a visit to the Mercado Modelo. Recently reconstructed following a 1983 fire, the market is a Salvador tradition. Here in row after row of stalls you will find the best handicrafts of not only Bahia but all of northeastern Brazil. Although there are many fine shops specializing in specific products all over Salvador, the market has the advantage of bringing everything together in one place. Take your time and comparison shop. You will find the same quality handicrafts in several stalls but the prices are not always the same. Be prepared to bargain. The best price is seldom the first price. Many of the merchants now accept credit cards. Now take a boat at the Cairu docks for a quick look at the Fort of São Marcelo right in front of the market in the bay. It was built in 1650 and kept invaders away. Then it was used as a prison and now serves more for curiosity than anything else. Back in your car, go to the lovely Museum of Sacred Art on Ladeira de Sodré. You'll be impressed with the tiles and the silver altar. It is unquestionably the most beautiful museum in all Brazil. Then, if there is still time, visit the Museum of Bahian Art at Av. 7 de Setembro 2340.

On this night, if you have not done so as yet, treat yourself to a Bahian meal. Most Bahian dishes are fish-based, with shrimp a favorite not only of the cooks but also of the customers of the city's better restaurants. The ingredients that add that special taste and rich coloring to Bahian food are coconut milk, peanuts, cashews, and dendé (palm) oil. The city's universally recognized best restaurant for traditional Bahian cooking is Casa da Gamboa, where you can't go wrong. The top seafood restaurant in the city is Bargaço. Either one will give you an excellent idea of what Brazilians mean when they say that only in Bahia can you find real Brazilian cooking.

Excursions from Salvador

If by now you have realized that three days is just not enough for Salvador, then you'll have time for one of the city's most pleasant day trips. The All Saints Bay is not meant simply to be seen but also to be experienced. In colonial times, Bahian-made boats called saveiros were used to transport goods back and forth between the city of Salvador and the outlying sugar plantations spread around the bay. Several of these boats have now been converted into modern schooners by wealthy Bahians and a few of them are rented out to tourist groups. Pioneer in this area and still the best is LR Turismo, one of Salvador's top tour operators. If you are traveling in a group it should be no problem arranging a day's outing on the bay. If you are alone you will have to try to hitch a ride on somebody else's tour. If you want, you can rent the boat for yourself but be ready to pay a stiff price, at least $200.

The bay is filled with small islands but most boat trips stop at the largest of them, Itaparica. The island is a tropical paradise with beautiful white sand beaches on the ocean side. There are a few good hotels, and Club Mediterranee has established its only Brazilian club on the island. Looking back across the bay to Salvador gives you the best view available of the city. The day-long cruise on the bay is a delightful experience but if you want to spend less time on the water there is a launch that leaves from in front of the Mercado Modelo and in 45 minutes takes you to Itaparica where you can explore the island, then return by the same launch to Salvador. Either way, you shouldn't leave Salvador without having crossed the bay.

For a fifth day you should try to get outside of the city and into the country. Either by renting a car, taking a bus or joining a tour, you can make a lovely day out of an excursion to the nearby colonial city of Cachoeira. At one time the capital of the state, Cachoeira is considered by the citizens of Salvador to be the state's best example of colonial times. Founded in the 18th century, Cachoeira was the center of the booming sugar cane industry that made Bahia the wealthiest state of Brazil during the colonial period. Its richly decorated churches with beautiful ornaments and images show the affluence of the era. On the road to the city you will see sugar cane and cocoa plantations and some tours offer a visit to a distillery that produces cachaça, a potent Brazilian drink that is produced from sugar cane. The area also raises tobacco and the best cigars in Brazil are made here. You can visit an old cigar factory where the women who work there still hand-roll the cigars.

Carnival Bahia-Style

If by chance or good planning you happen to be in Salvador during carnival, you will witness one of the truly great spontaneous festivals on the face of the earth. Unlike Rio de Janeiro, where street carnival has been slowly fading away, replaced by the samba school parades and club balls, in Bahia 90 percent of the party is on the street, day and night. There is no starting gun for carnival in Salvador but it seems that everyone realizes at the same moment that it is time to begin the celebration. The result is what will first appear to the uninitiated visitor to be pure pandemonium. The streets are packed with jumping bodies, chasing after giant sound trucks from which comes a nonstop ear-shattering flood of carnival music, some live from bands atop the trucks and some on tape. However it is presented you cannot help but hear it, even if you are 10 miles away.

The trucks, called trio electricos or electronic trios (although there can be anywhere up to a half dozen musicians and singers on board at any given moment), are Salvador's own contribution to Brazilian carnival legend. No one can tell you exactly how this tradition started but clearly it is here to stay. After you have overcome your first shock, you should try gingerly to mix with the crowd. You will soon discover that the normally friendly and outgoing Bahians are ten times as much during carnival. Before you know it you'll be swept along with the moving throng, jumping and laughing with all of them without the slightest idea of what is happening. This is the special joy of carnival in Bahia—spontaneous, uninhibited, and pure fun. Leave your inhibitions back in the hotel room.

Center stage for Salvador's carnival is the Praça Castro Alves at the start of Rua 7 de Setembro. If you saw it on a normal working day you would never believe the amount of people that can be squeezed into it for carnival. Even more difficult to understand is how these people can go on dancing and jumping all day and most of the night.

But while Salvador's carnival is far more of a participatory event than that of Rio there are also parades to be seen. The most impressive is that of the Afroxés, particularly the Filhos de Gandhi. Afroxé is the sacred music of candomblé and around this theme several large associations have been formed to take part in carnival. They parade through the city's streets dancing to the Afro-Brazilian beat of percussion instruments. The most striking are the Filhos de Gandhi (the sons of Gandhi), an all-male Afroxé with thousands of members, all of whom dress in white tunics and turbans. The turbans, worn in candomblé ceremonies and also by the elderly Bahian women you see in the city selling Bahian food on the sidewalks, are a result of the Moslem influence on the African slaves who were brought to Brazil. The passage of the long white file of the Filhos do Gandhi is always a moving experience and one further example of the mystical air that pervades the life of Salvador.

PRACTICAL INFORMATION FOR SALVADOR

WHEN TO GO. Because of its consistently warm climate, almost any time of the year is a good time to visit Salvador. But there are certain events that will make this attractive city even more interesting if you plan your trip to coincide with them.

January 1 has the celebration of Our Lord the Good Jesus of the Navigators. Hundreds of boats float offshore, decorated with flags and streamers. Later, there are exhibitions of drum beating and capoeira fighting. January 1, Festa de Nosso Senhor dos Navigantes takes place at Monte Serrat. On January 6, Festa dos Reis is celebrated in all parts of the city.

February 2 is devoted to Iemanjá, the goddess of the sea, who is also the Virgin Mary. In Rio Vermelho and Itapoan, celebrants make offerings all along the shores, and boats are gaily decorated. Festa de Rio Vermelho, in honor of Saint Anne, is held two Sundays before Carnival. Carnival itself is celebrated as in Rio and all business stops for four days. Must be experienced to be believed.

May 10 has the procession of St. Francis Xavier, a feast day in honor of the city's patron saint, held since 1686.

In *June,* twelve days after Holy Ghost, there is a Christian procession. At the same time candomblé worshippers hold services to Oxosse, the African God of the Hunt. Festa de Santo Antonio, a religious feast, takes place in June, while the 24th has the Festa de São João, a popular festival with local dances, entertainment and fireworks. On *June* 29 a twelve day and night candomblé celebration honors all the gods.

July 2 is devoted to the heroes of Brazil's fight for independence. Aside from parades, there are folklore dances and candomblé ceremonies.

On the second Sunday in *September* is held an impressive procession to the sea of Our Lady of Monte Serrat, while on the 27th the twin gods Cosme and Damião are honored with banquet tables loaded with rich regional cooking.

October, all month long, is devoted to the African gods Exú, Iabás, Ogum, Omulu, and Oxum.

December 4 is the Festa de Santa Barbara. Three days of festivities at Saint Barbara's Market, Baixa dos Sapateiros. *December* 8 has the celebration of Conceiçao de Praia, held in front of Our Lady of Conceição Church and includes candomblé, capoeira and folksingers. *December* 13: Festa de Santa Lucia, in front of the Pilar church.

HOW TO GET THERE. Salvador's 2 de Julho airport was classified as one of Brazil's international fields in 1975 and today there are regularly scheduled flights to and from Asuncion, Paraguay (*Aerolineas Paraguayas*): Frankfurt (*Lufthansa*); Lisbon (*Varig* and *Air Portugal*); Madrid (*Iberia*); and Paris (*Air France*). From Rio there are daily 90-minute flights (round trip costs about $275). There are also frequent flights from Brasilia and, of course, cities in the Northeast. Alternatives are driving or taking a 27-hour bus trip ($40 one way, or $88 on a "deluxe sleeper") up the good highway from Rio, or calling on one of the cruise or cargo ships that stops here.

HOW TO GET AROUND. Buses are overcrowded, dirty, and never on schedule. Taxis are plentiful and cheap, but bargain first if you're going to use one by the day. You should be able to make a deal for around $30 to $40. There are tourist agencies with cars for hire at $20 to $30 for the day, and your hotel can usually supply you with a limousine and an English-speaking driver. But the best way to see most of the city is just to get out and walk around the old streets. Nothing will happen to you. You're a lot safer in the back streets of Bahia than you are in New York or London. You can charter a native schooner for a day's cruise of the bay for $27 to $40 per person, from either *L.R. Turismo* at Av. Sete de Setembro 3959 (248–3333) or *Panorama Turismo,* Rua Marquës de Caravelas 110 (240–3266). Both have group rates for the bay trips and L.R. Turismo offers excellent tours of the old city during the day.

HOTELS. Outside Rio, Brazil's biggest spurt in construction of tourist-type hotels has taken place in Bahia. The Quatro Rodas Salvador is an excellent luxury hotel located near the beach on Rua Pasargada. Other top hotels are the Meridien and Othon Palace, which opened in 1976 and 1975. Alternate choices are the charming little (33 rooms) Galeão Sacramento on Itaparica Island or the 164-room beachfront Salvador Praia. Itaparica Island also offers the Club Mediterranee in a secluded setting with nonstop activities. For definitions of price categories see "Facts at Your Fingertips."

Deluxe

Club Mediterranee (833–1141). The first Club Med in Brazil is located on Itaparica, the largest and most scenic of the many islands in Salvador's bay. The club follows the general style of Club Meds worldwide, with every type of activity imaginable. Reservations must be made in advance and can be made at offices in Rio (224–0803) or São Paulo (813–7311).

Meridian Bahia, Rua Fonte do Boi 216 (248–8011). Overlooking the ocean, 30 minutes from the airport, 15 minutes from downtown Salvador, deluxe class, 502 rooms including 2 deluxe suites, 77 suites, and 27 cabanas. Conference and banquet facilities. Congress hall equipped with audio-visual aids and for simultaneous translation; 5 meeting rooms. Panoramic restaurants and bars at the top. Discothéque, beauty parlor, sauna, solarium, sea- and fresh-water swimming pools, tennis, marina, boutiques.

Salvador Praia, Av. Presidente Vargas 2338-Ondina Beach (245–5033). Pool, bar, restaurant, convention rooms. Mural by famous Brazilian painter Caribé and sculpture by Mario Cravo dominate the lobby.

Expensive

Bahia Othon Palace, Av. Presidente Vargas 2456 on Ondina Beach (247–1044). Built in a "Y" shape, with all 301 rooms facing the ocean. Swimming pool, nightclub, convention hall, sauna, and everything you'd expect in a modern new hotel. Pride of the Othon chain and one of Brazil's best.

Enseada das Lajes, Av. Oceanica, 511 (237–1027). Another new beachfront hotel with pool, bar, and restaurant.

Grande Hotel de Barra, Rua Forte de São Diogo 2 (247–6011). Beachfront at harbor entrance. Calm waters for swimming. Air-conditioned.

Hotel da Bahia, Praça 2 de Julho 2 (321–3699). 277 rooms, air-conditioning, 2 pools.

Marazul, Av. 7 de Setembro 3937 (235–2110). On the beach, this fine new hotel has a pool and one of Salvador's best restaurants.

Quatro Rodas Salvador, Farol de Itapua on Itapua Beach (249–9611). This hotel is the latest addition to the Quatro Rodas chain, the best in the northeast. It has two excellent restaurants, an ocean-view rooftop nightclub, beach, pool, and a bar on the banks of a manmade lagoon. The hotel also possesses several tennis courts and an auditorium where many of Brazil's top singing stars perform. Like the other Quatro Rodas hotels in the northeast, the Salvador hotel also has a satellite dish for live reception of American television programs.

Moderate

Bahia do Sol, Av. 7 de Setembro 2009 (247–7211). 84 rooms.
Bahia Praia, Av. Presidente Vargas 2483 (247–4122). 40 rooms, restaurant.
Belmar, Av. Otavio Mangabeira 3345 (371–2424). 48 rooms, pool, restaurant.
Galeão Sacramento, on Itaparica Island (833–1021). In the island's village known as Mar Grande, this small (33 rooms) hotel is new and spectacular. One of the best small hotels in Brazil. Pool, beach, bar, and restaurant.
Hotel do Farol, Av. Presidente Vargas 68 (247–7611). Close to the beach, pool, restaurant.
Itapoan Praia, Rua Dias Gomes 4 (249–9988). 72 rooms with pool and restaurant.
Mamelucos, Praia de Ipitanga 33 km. (378–1175). 30 cabanas on the beach. Swimming pool, tennis court.
Ondina Praia, Av. Presidente Vargas 2275, across from Ondina Beach (247–1033). Modern, with pool, bar, and restaurant.
Pituba Plaza, Av. Manoel Dias da Silva 2495 (248–1022). 114 rooms.
Praia do Sol, Av. Otavio Mangabeira (371–3004). 84 rooms, pool, restaurant.
Praiamar, Av. 7 de Setembro 3577 (247–7011). 171 rooms, close to the beach, pool, and restaurant.
Vela Branca, Av. Antonio Carlos Magalhaes 585, on Pituba Beach (359–7022). Modern, motel-type accommodations with bar, restaurant, pool.
Vila Velha, Av. 7 de Setembro 1971 (247–8722). 98 rooms.

Inexpensive

Barra Turismo, Av. 7 de Setembro 3691 (245–7433). 60 rooms.
Paulus, Av. Otavio Mangabeira 165 (248–5722). 77 rooms, pool, bar.
Pelourinho, Rua Alfredo de Brito 20 (321–9022). Restaurant. Located in historical old city.
Praia da Armação, Av. Otavio Mangabeira (371–2722). 58 rooms, restaurant.
Solar da Barra, Av. 7 de Setembro 2998 (247–4917). 18 rooms.
Villa Romana, Rua Professor Lemos de Brito 14 (247–6522). 52 rooms, pool, and restaurant.

RESTAURANTS. If you want to sample local dishes ask for: *Acaraje,* dumplings with bean mash; *vatapa,* a fish stew; *caruru,* a type of shrimp creole; *ximxim de galinha,* chicken cooked with peanuts and coconut; *muqueca de peixe,* fish creole; *camaroes a baiano,* shrimp creole; *frigadeira de camarao,* spicy shrimp omelette; *efo,* an herb cooked with dried shrimp, traditionally served during candomblé religious services; *sarapatel,* a stew of pork heart, lungs, kidney and liver in blood sauce—not for the weak of stomach; *cocada,* a dessert made of coconut; *quindins,* an egg and coconut dessert. Remember all Bahian dishes are spicy and the chile peppers and sauces are extremely hot. The leading alcoholic drink is called "a batida."

Besides the typical regional food, Salvador is also famed for seafood dishes in general. Northeast Brazil is one of the best parts of the world for fresh and tasty seafood.

For definitions of price categories see "Facts at Your Fingertips."

For regional food the best is **Casa da Gamboa,** *Expensive,* Rua Newton Prado 51, (321–9776). Also good are: **Maria de São Pedro,** *Moderate,* Mercado Modelo, 1st floor (242–5262); **Agdá,** *Moderate,* Rua Orlando Moscoso 1 (231–2851); **Arroz- de Hauçá,** *Moderate, Rua Professor Sabino da Silva 598 (247–3508);* **Ondina,** *Moderate,* Alto de Ondina (245–8263); **Velhos Marinheiros,** *Moderate,* Av. da França, (243–9860); **Iemenja,** *Moderate,* Av. Otavio Mangabeira, (231–5770); **Xeiro Verde,** *Moderate,* Av. Otavio Mangabeira 929 (248–5158); **Senac,** *Moderate,* Largo do Pelourinho 13/19 (242–5502).

Don't fail to try a *muqueca mixta* (mixed seafood dish) at the **Lampião,** *Expensive,* at the Bahia Othon Palace, or almost any dish at the **Forno e Fogão,** *Moderate,* at the Pousada do Carmo. **Solar do Unhão,** on the shoreline of Av. do Contorno and *Expensive*, was originally a slaves' quarters in the 18th century, and is worth a visit (245–5551).

For international cuisine, try: **Chaillot**, *Expensive*, international, Av. Presidente Vargas 3305 (237–4621); **Le Saint Honore**, *Expensive*, French nouveau cuisine at the Meridien Hotel (248–8011); **Bernard**, *Expensive*, also French, Rua Gamboa da Cima 11 (245–9402); **Le Mignon**, *Expensive*, French food, Rua Almirante Marques de Leão 475 (245–6479); **Cidade do Salvador**, *Moderate*, international, at the Quatro Rodas Hotel (249–9611); **Porto Seguro**, *Moderate*, international, the Salvador Praia Hotel, Av. Presidente Vargas 2338 (245–5033); **Di Liana**, *Moderate*, Italian, Estrada do Coco, near the airport, (378–1088); **Don Giuseppe**, *Moderate*, pizza, Av. Otávio Mangabeira 74 (248–6049); **Il Forno**, *Inexpensive*, a good pizzeria, Rua Marques de Leão 77 (247–7287). The Barra neighborhood, center of Salvador nightlife, has several pizzerias and snack restaurants.

For seafood: **Bargaço**, *Deluxe*, Rua P Quadro 43 (231–5141), excellent seafood, many Bahian recipes, near the convention center; **Enseada das Lajes**, *Moderate*, in the hotel of the same name (237–1027); **Frutos do Mar**, *Moderate*, Rua Alm. Marques de Leão 415 (245–6479).

While fish dishes are the top attraction in Salvador, if you want a break, the best churrascaria (steak house) is **Baby Beef**, *Moderate*, Av. Antonio Carlos Magalhães, near the Iguatemi Shopping Center (244–0811). Also **Roda Viva**, *Moderate*, Av. Otavio Mangabeira (348–3839).

USEFUL ADDRESSES. *U.S. Consulate,* Av. Antonio Carlos Magalhães (358–9166). In addition to the consulate there is a *U.S. Information Service Office* in the Edificio Casa Blanca Av. Sete de Setembro 333. *The American Society of Bahia,* tel: 8–0073. *Police;* Radio Patrol: Dial 190. *Medical facilities:* Pronto Socorro, tel: 5–0000.

Bahiatursa (Bahia State Tourist Board) has several information booths at the airport, bus terminal, and Mercado Modelo, among others. Its main information center is on Praça Tomé de Souza (241–4333).

WHAT TO SEE. Spread out over the length and breadth of this intriguing city are dozens of things that belong on your itinerary. The most important are: Agua de Meninos market, steep streets of Pelourinho, and Baixa dos Sapateiros, the Praça Terreiro de Jesus artisans market Sundays, the Lacerda elevator between the city's upper and lower levels, the harbor filled with multicolored sail fishing boats, the lighthouses and the old forts, the churches with special emphasis on São Francisco and Bonfim, the museums of Modern Art and Sacred Art, the beaches with the fishermen and their nets, the lagoon of Abaeté, the artists at work, a capoeira fight, and most definitely a candomblé ceremony.

Candomblé is the term adopted in Brazil for a religion of African origin. In Salvador, these cults have been preserved in almost original form and are a vital part of the culture. Ceremonies honoring the various divinites, called "orixas," are held in temples called "terreiros." These consist of a large room or outdoor area for public ceremonies, with various smaller rooms or huts, one for each "saint" or orixá. Visitors may attend the public ceremonies, which are usually held on Sun. nights around 8:30 P.M. Some of the most important "candomblé" terreiros are: Federação de Culto Afro-Brasileiro, Rua Carlos Gomes 17, 2nd floor (321–0145); Bogum, Ladeira de Bogum 35; Menininha do Gantois, Alto de Gantois 23; Olga de Alaketo, Av. Alasketo 69. Call Bahiatursa for information on how to get to the temples and what god is being celebrated. It is always best to be accompanied by a guide and most tour operators offer a visit to a candomblé temple.

MUSEUMS. Museu de Arte da Bahia, located at Av. 7 de Setembro 2340, closed at press time for restoration. Ceramics, chinaware, ornamental tiles, antique furniture. **Museu de Arte Sacra,** Rua do Sodre 276. Open Mon. through Fri., 9:30 to 11:30 A.M. and 2 to 6 P.M. An outstanding collection of figures of saints and other religious art. **Museu Carlos Costa Pinto,** Av. Sete de Setembro 2490. Open Wed. to Mon., 2:30 to 6:30 P.M; Sat.–Sun. 3 to 6 P.M.; Sat.–Sun. 3 to 6 P.M. Antique furniture, Baccarat crystal, jewelry, china, silverware, and paintings. Also collection of "balangandãs" (silver charms). **Museu de Arte Moderna,** at the Solar Unhão. Open Tues. to Sun., 1 to 5 P.M. Expositions of paintings only when announced—no permanent collection. **Museu do Carmo.** Located in the Convento do Carmo. Open every day 8 A.M. to 12 noon, 2 to 6 P.M. Vestments and other religious art objects. **Museu do Reconcavo Wanderley de Pinho** open Tues.–Sun. 9 A.M. to 3 P.M. About an hour's drive from the city, not far from the port of the Industrial Center of Aracatu. Engravings, old maps, historical notes. **Museu da Cidade,** Rua Gregório de Matos, 40, open Mon.–Fri. 8 A.M. to 12 noon, 2 to 6 P.M.; Sat. 8 A.M. to noon, has an interesting collection of figures of Orixas or deities venerated in the *Candomblé* rites with their costumes and weapons; also the world's largest collection of ceremonial women's headgear of African origin.

SPORTS. Salvador has miles of beautiful beaches. The cleanest and most attractive tend also to be the most distant, located beyond the district of Pituba. Because it is ideal for children, "Pla-K-For" is a favorite of Americans. This beach, like others, is reached by city bus. With luck you may see fishermen pulling in their big nets at beaches named "Praia Chega Nego," across the Aero Club, "Piatã" and "Itapoã."

Capoeira, originally an African way of fighting with the feet, was developed in the days when slaves were forbidden to use their fists to carry weapons. Now it is preserved in a very acrobatic form of dance, accompanied by the typical instrument known as the "berimbau," tamborines, drums and other percussion instruments. Shows are given by the following "schools" under the direction of the Master, whose name the school bears: *Mestre Bimba,* Rua Francisco Muniz Barreto 1, 1st floor, Terreiro de Jesus; *Academia de Capoeira Angola,* Largo de Santo Antonio (Sto. Antônio Além do Carmo Fort); *Associação de Capoeira Orixás da Bahia,* Rua Carlos Lopes 51, Maçaranduba. Days and hours vary, so consult Bahiatursa.

ART GALLERIES. Escritorio de Arte da Bahia (245–6933) and **Noguerol** (237–2025), both at the Salvador Praia Hotel, Av. Presidente Vargas 2338. **Kennedy Bahia,** Av. Otávio Mangabeira (248–0819), sells tapestries. **Núcleo de Arte do Desenbanco,** Av. Magalhães Neto (231–2322) and **Cavalete,** Rua Paciência 149 (247–9194).

Many artists in Bahia maintain exhibits at their studios, although getting in touch with them can be difficult. Ask at the galleries about visiting a particular artist. **Carybe,** Rua Medeiros Neto 9, Brotas. Drawings and paintings. **Fernando Coelho,** Parque Florestal, Brotas, Rua Waldemar Falcao. Paintings. **Floriano Teixeira,** Rua Ilheus 33, Rio Vermelho. Paintings. **Hansen-Bahia,** Jardim Jaguaripe, Piata. Woodcut engravings. **Jenner Augusto,** Rua Bartolomeu de Gusmao 7, Rio Vermelho. Paintings. **Mario Cravo Jr.,** Rua Caetano Moura 39, Federacao. Sculptures in metal and plastic. **Mirabeau Sampaio,** Rua Ary Barroso 12. Sculptures and drawings. **Walter Sa Nenezes,** Av. Tiradentes, Roma. Paintings.

SHOPPING. The most typical souvenirs of Bahia are the "balangandães" (singular "balangandã"), a cluster of silver or alloy gourds, fruit and figas, formerly worn by slaves. Also typical are the many items carved from "jacaranda," the Brazilian rosewood. For these try: **Gerson Artesanato de Prata Ltda.,** ground floor of the Convento do Carmo. **Penitenciaria do Estado,** Lemos Britto (State Prison), located in Mata Escura do Retiro, accessible by car or taxi only. All prices are clearly labeled at the **Instituto Maua,** Av. Sete de Setembro 261, while bargaining is widely practiced at other places. For antiques, wooden figures of saints, furniture, etc., walk along Rua Ruy Barbosa off Avenide Setembro, near the Cinema Guarani and the "A Tarde" building. Especially reliable are: **Casa Moreira,** Rua Visconde do Rio Branco 1, behind the City Hall, **Jose Pedreira,** Alameda Antunes 7, Barra Avenida, or any number of shops along Rua Ruy Barbosa, roughly between numbers 30 and 65. The modern **Shopping Center Iguatemi,** with all types of shops and restaurants, is well worth a visit. It is located at Largo da Mariquita 3 in the Rio Vermelho district.

NIGHTLIFE. The folklore of Bahia is rich and varied and Salvador has several fine folklore shows which will give you a good idea of what to expect should you later decide to visit a candomblé ceremony or a capoeira show. The best folklore show is at the **Solar do Unhao** restaurant, where you will also be treated to a delicious meal. Av. Contorno (245–5551), daily, with the show starting at 9 P.M. (confirm time). Other nightclubs and restaurants with folklore shows are: **Senac,** a vocational school for waiters and cooks that has a fine combination of good, inexpensive food, a folklore show, plus exhibits of Bahian artists; Largo do Pelourinho 19 (321–5502); **Tenda dos Milagres,** restaurant with show, Av. Amaralina 553 (248–6058); **A Moenda,** restaurant with show, Rua P. Quadra 28 (231–7915); **Teatro de Ondina,** show, Alto de Ondina (247–4599).

Bahia is also home to some of the best Brazilian popular music and there are several small bars and nightclubs, especially in the Barra neighborhood, with live music—samba and bossa nova. The best for live music are: **Bistro 507,** Av. Sete de Setembro 507 (Barra); **Clube 45,** Rua Barão de Sergy 196 (Barra); **Bistro do Luis,** Rua Conselheiro Pedro Luis **48; Casquinha de Siri,** Av. Otavio Mangabeira, 37 (Piatã); **Clube 45 Pub,** Rua Barão de Sergy, 196 (Barra). Besides Barra, the nearby neighborhoods of Rio Vermelho and Pituba also have several fine bars with live Brazilian music, most of them located along the beach.

In Salvador as throughout Brazil, nightlife usually starts with a beer and conversation at an outdoor cafe. The top meeting places are **Berro d'Agua,** Rua Barão de Sergy 27-A (Barra); **Manga Rosa,** Rua Cezar Zama 60 (Barra); **Graffiti,** Rua Odorico Odilon 41 (Rio Vermelho); and **Bar 68,** Largo da Santana 3 (Rio Vermelho).

THE STATE OF BAHIA

For the moment tourism in the state is centered in Salvador, with day trips possible to the historical city of Cachoeira and the beaches north of the city. Beyond these two areas, any trips must be at least overnight. The best attractions are the Paulo Afonso Falls along the São Francisco River, the southern Bahia city of Ilheus, capital of the cocoa market of which Bahia is the world's second largest producer, and the highlands area of Lençois.

Paulo Afonso, besides the beautiful falls of the same name, also offers a look at an inland area of Brazil that is now being turned from desert into fertile farmland thanks to a massive irrigation project. The São Francisco River, Brazil's second largest after the Amazon, is to the country what the Mississippi is to the United States in terms of history and legend. Until the 1970s it was possible for tourists to book passage on the river boats that still ply the São Francisco, passing through most of the Northeast. Now, however, there is only one remaining boat trip for tourists, close to Paulo Afonso, which travels down the river on a day trip, passing through the locks in the area of the Paulo Afonso Falls and hydroelectric project. For information check with L.R. Turismo in Salvador. (See *How To Get Around* under "Practical Information for Salvador.")

In Ilheus, besides the city's beaches, which are not quite as good as those of Salvador, the city is also a living monument to Brazil's greatest fiction writer, Jorge Amado, one of the giants of Latin American literature, whose best known novel *Gabriela* was set in this city.

Lençois, in the mountainous area of the Chapada Diamantina, was the diamond capital of Brazil in the 19th century. The region is now a mountain getaway for the residents of Salvador. Besides the beautiful scenery and cool mountain air, the memory of the city's past importance is preserved in its homes and buildings.

PRACTICAL INFORMATION FOR STATE OF BAHIA

For definitions of price categories see "Facts at Your Fingertips."

PAULO AFONSO
260 miles north of Salvador

HOTEL. Grande Hotel de Paulo Afonso. *Moderate.* The best hotel in the city with restaurant, bar and pool (281-1914).

ILHEUS
240 miles south of Salvador

HOTELS. This city of 145,800 has three good hotels: **Transamérica Ilhéus Resort and Fishing,** *Expensive,* Estrada para Canavieiras, Km 77 (212–1122); **Ilheus Praia,** *Moderate,* bar, restaurant, and pool, Praça Dom Eduardo (231–2533); **Pontal Praia,** *Inexpensive,* bar, restaurant, and pool, Av. Lomanto Jr. 1358 (231–3033).

LENCOIS
240 miles west of Salvador

HOTEL. Pousada de Lençois. *Moderate.* Rua Altina Alves 747 (334–1102).

THE NORTHEAST

The area known as the Northeast begins in Bahia and extends to the edge of the Amazon in the north, taking in that part of the nation that bulges out into the Atlantic Ocean up north. In addition to Bahia the region is composed of the states of Sergipe, Alagoas, Pernambuco, Paraiba, Rio Grande do Norte, Ceará, Piaui, and Maranhão. Although they are all part of the same region, the other states differ markedly from Bahia in that they have little of the African influence that makes Bahia so distinct. North of Bahia, the influence is predominantly European. With the passage of the centuries, however, even this influence has diminished and today the Northeast of Brazil has its own culture and characteristics, born of the geographical and climatic peculiarities of this region.

The main one of these is the tendency of the region to alternate between drought and flood. The arid interior area, known as the sertão, is prone to periodic droughts, which have driven many of its residents to the cities of the south in search of employment. The last, and worst, of these droughts ended after a five-year run in 1984. And when the rains come, they come in torrents—in 1985–86 the same area that had been stricken by drought was subject to massive flooding. Despite its problems, however, the interior of the Northeast may yet prove to be a vital food-producing area for Brazil. The success of irrigation projects in Bahia has encouraged the government to invest its money plus funds from the World Bank in a multi-billion dollar irrigation project for the rest of the Northeast in an effort to make the desert bloom.

But while the inland area of the Northeast is one of the poorest and most backward in Brazil, the coastal region is fertile and safe from drought. For the tourist this combination offers some of the most picturesque sights in Brazil. There are the jangada fishing boats, little more than balsa-wood rafts with a single sail, that brave the Atlantic with lone fishermen aboard, forts and churches, literally hundreds of miles of uninterrupted virgin beaches, women weaving fine lace, leather-clad northeastern cowboys who yearly face the searing heat of the interior, clay sculptors, and finally, for aficionados, the best shrimp, lobster, and seafood eating that you will find anywhere in the Americas.

Away from the state capitals, most located along the coast, you will find it rough going, but the recent discovery of the Northeast by European tourists—mainly the Germans, Swiss, French, and Austrians—has led to a building spree of hotels and restaurants of international quality on the coast. Here, mainly in the cities of Maceio, Recife, Fortaleza, and São

Luis, you will discover an enchanting combination of warm weather, excellent beaches (the ocean water temperature in the Northeast is warm year-round), good hotels, and top quality restaurants, all at prices that today make the Northeast one of the great bargain destinations in the world.

Maceio

The present boom city in northeast tourism is Maceio, capital of the state of Alagoas. The state has long been famous for its 150-mile coastline, which the experts claim has the finest beaches in Brazil. Until recently, however, there was little in the way of basic comforts to greet the international tourist. Fortunately, things have changed, with new hotels already built and others on the way.

Like the other major coastal cities of the Northeast, Maceio combines its colonial past with the beauty of its natural setting. This is a place to relax and take it easy, enjoying the beaches and taking long walks through the city. On the mainland side of the city are several large, beautiful lakes which can be visited by taxi. This is a good outing for lunch as there are several fine restaurants along the Mundau lake. The best beaches are just north of the city's limits and it is here also that the newest hotels have been built. Colonial buildings and churches can be seen in the center of the city around the Praça Dom Pedro II, a public square.

Recife

North of Maceio is the state of Pernambuco, whose capital Recife is also the true capital of the Brazilian Northeast. The sixth largest city in Brazil, with a population of 1.5 million, Recife is a vibrant metropolis whose spirit is halfway between the modern cities of the south and the more traditional centers of the Northeast, a combination of old and new that makes the city both an example of the past and a window on the future. If you have time for only one stop in the Northeast, make it Recife.

Known as the Venice of Brazil because it is built on three rivers and connected by a host of bridges, Recife got its name from the reefs that line the coast and make the city's most popular beach, Boa Viagam, also one of the more unusual bathing spots in Brazil.

In the morning, when the tide is in, the waves come up almost to the road, then as the tide recedes, the rocks of the reefs slowly appear. Depending on the time of the day, individual swimming pools are formed, fish flap around the bathers, and the hidden rock formations dry into odd colors in the afternoon sun.

Another sight to see along this beach is the departure (about 6 A.M.) or the return (about 2 P.M.) of the *jangadas,* those crude, log rafts with the beautiful sails that local fishermen take out onto the high seas. Many stories and legends have been written about them, and they are as dangerous as they look. Only an expert navigator and swimmer should try one. It looks easy for the sunburnt men of Recife, but they have been working on them all their lives.

Boa Viagem for the residents of Recife is what Copacabana and Ipanema beaches are for Rio's citizens—the center of social life. On the weekends the beach is packed and at night the many restaurants, bars, and sidewalk cafes turn Boa Viagem into a glittering center of nightlife, the top spot in the Northeast for a night on the town.

Recife and Pernambuco were at one time part of the Dutch colonial empire until the Portuguese from the south of Brazil drove them out. The influence of the two European colonial powers is evident in the city's many fine churches. In the downtown area of Recife is the convent and church of Saint Anthony with the famed Gold Chapel, a baroque design covered in gold leaf and one of the most important and beautiful examples of religious art in Brazil. Other colonial-era churches in the center of Recife are the Church of the Blessed Sacrament, built in 1753, the Basilica of Our Lady of Carmo (1687), the Cathedral of the Clergymen of Saint Peter with the adjoining Saint Peter's Courtyard, where there are bars, restaurants, antique and handicraft shops (these three churches are all located on Av. Dantas Barreto), and the Basilica of Our Lady Penha (1656), on Rua da Penha. While you are downtown you should also visit the Cinco Pontas Fort, built by the Dutch in 1630 and today home to the city museum, and the Pernambuco Culture Center, built as a prison in the 19th century but now the best regional crafts center of the Northeast, offering a multitude of shops (located in the former prison cells) showing the wares of the region as well as performances of northeastern dances and music.

But the best of the old Northeast is preserved in the ex-colonial capital of Olinda, today a suburb of Recife, a half hour from downtown. In recent years Olinda has enjoyed a renaissance, taking on a life of its own after it was declared a world historical monument by UNESCO. Built on a series of hills overlooking the ocean, Olinda is remarkably well preserved, with its narrow, winding streets snaking up and down the hills and offering at every turn spectacular views of the ocean and Recife in the distance while up close you see the historical past of the Northeast in the colonial churches and homes of Olinda.

The city was built by the Dutch during their brief turn at running Pernambuco in the 1600s. Many of the houses still have the original latticed balconies, heavy doors, and pink stucco walls, evoking the colonial period. Residents of the city are forbidden to change its architecture or to construct any new buildings that would not be compatible with the colonial motif. The result is a beautiful, compact city where the white, pink, and red of the homes and tile roofs stand against the rich green of the heavily landscaped hills and the blue of the ocean below. Give yourself plenty of time to explore Olinda by foot and if you can don't miss the sunset from here. You won't forget it.

The top attractions in Olinda are the Church of Our Lady Carmo, built in 1588; the Convent of Our Lady Neves (1585), the first Franciscan church in Brazil; the Seminary of Olinda (1584), the Cathedral (1537), with an extraordinarily beautiful view; the Pernambucan Museum of Sacred Art; the Misericordia Church (1540), the best preserved and most impressive of Olinda's churches; the Ribeira Market, where handmade goods are sold; the Museum of Contemporary Art housed in an 18th century building; and the São Bento Monastery (1582), the first law school in Brazil. The highest point in Olinda, the Alto da Sé, is also the city's social center. Here, by day, several stands sell regional art and handicrafts, while at night on the weekends the square is packed with young people from Recife and Olinda and tourists attracted by the convivial nature of the milling crowds moving back and forth between several small bars that open at night on top of the hill.

At Alto da Sé, and also at the downtown Culture Center, you will notice small clay statuettes for sale. Almost all of these are made in the interior town of Caruaru, considered the leading handicrafts center of South America. Reached by daily bus or special taxis on Wednesdays and Saturdays, the days of the fair, the trip is well worth it. Not only will you be able to see a very colorful interior market place, but you'll be able to rub elbows with the leather-clad cowboys of the harsh, dry region, see the way the people live on the parched soil, and be entertained by strolling musicians and dancers. Allow one full day for this.

Near the Recife-Olinda area is the historical city of Igarassu, which among its colonial buildings numbers the oldest church in Brazil, the Church of Saints Cosme and Damião. Also worth a visit is the island of Itamaracá, famed for its beaches and site of a fort built by the Dutch. Both Igarassu and Itamaracá can be visited in day trips from Recife or Olinda.

Farther away but just as interesting is the interior city of Nova Jerusalem, a replica of the city of Jerusalem of Biblical times that has been constructed to serve as an immense open air theater where, every Easter, the Northeast is home to one of the world's more remarkable passion plays. Nova Jerusalem is located 30 miles from Caruaru and is a must if you decide to visit the famous Caruaru fair; plan on spending the night in Caruaru. While in Nova Jerusalem you should also visit the Statue Park, where Northeastern artists have sculpted lifesize granite statues of typical and historical figures of the region.

Parties are also a part of the Northeastern lifestyle—the two biggest blowouts in the region are Carnival and the saints days during the month of June. For Carnival, Olinda has acquired a reputation as fun capital of the Northeast. Each year through its narrow streets thousands of revelers dance all day and all night, performing the frevo, a regional dance that requires its performers to defy both gravity and human endurance. In the month of June on the days of the most popular saints, block parties are held throughout Recife, where a traditional dance called the quadrilha, similar to American square dancing, is performed.

João Pessoa and Natal

North of Recife is the city of João Pessoa, capital of the state of Paraiba and another site of fine beaches. The city has one of the best hotels in the region, the Tambaú, part of the excellent Tropical hotel chain owned by Varig Airlines. Beyond João Pessoa is the city of Natal, capital of Rio Grande do Norte. Besides warm water and good beaches, Natal is also known for its miles of sand dunes that run along the ocean.

Fortaleza

Capital of the state of Ceara, this city of 1.8 million, fifth largest in Brazil, has fallen on hard times lately, the result of the region's most recent drought which drove thousands of impoverished tenant farmers from the interior into the city. Because of this Fortaleza has not yet been able to live up to its tourism potential, but there is no question that in the near future the city will be making its name known outside of Brazil. The reason for this is that even in hard times, Fortaleza has excellent attractions—fine beaches and even better ones located nearby, the best lobster fishing and eating in Brazil, and the top lace industry in the country. The city is also on its way to becoming a world-class fashion center, thanks to the combination of abundant raw materials and cheap manpower. These two factors have already permitted Fortaleza fashion designers to challenge their big city rivals in Rio and São Paulo and today one of Brazil's most important fashion fairs takes place annually in Fortaleza in April.

Due south of Fortaleza on the coast is the city of Aracati, Ceara's most famed lace center where you will see little girls just three years old learning to thread a needle and unravel snarled thread, as well as aging grandmothers almost blind from the years of close, delicate labor. Close to Aracati are Ceara's best beaches, most notably Canoa Quebrada, with white sand dunes and crystal clear turquoise waters. This area is still little explored for tourism, a fact that complicates visits but also guarantees the survival for the moment of an area of rare primitive beauty.

São Luis

The last major city along the coast of the Northeast, São Luis, capital of the state of Maranhão, is also the poorest. While this does not detract from the beauty of its beaches, the biggest in the region, it has unfortunately complicated efforts by local officials to preserve the city's historical heritage. Many of the colonial buildings in the old part of the city, some of them still covered with 18th century French and Portuguese tiles, are today in desperate need of preservation, a fact recognized by local authorities who are, sad to say, handcuffed by a lack of funds. For that reason what is one of the largest areas of colonial buildings in Brazil is slowly wasting away. For the time being, however, it is still worth taking a walk through the old town, where you will see the colonial homes and buildings with their colorful tiles (all buildings in São Luis today have these tiles but most of them were added recently to maintain the colonial spirit of the city; only the historical buildings still have Portuguese and French tiles from the 18th century), as well as wrought iron balconies.

The city of São Luis is located on an island; on the mainland is another colonial relic, the city of Alcantara, today a national monument where the colonial ruins are maintained. Access to Alcantara, 15 miles away from São Luis, is by boat or private plane since the only road link is a precarious dirt strip that can take up to a day's journey. Boats leave daily from downtown São Luis but these are primitive fishing boats suitable only for the adventuresome. A catamaran also makes the trip and is far more comfortable and reliable, although the trip is made only with groups (contact Baluz Turismo at 222–6658).

São Luis is known for its folklore presentations, which are considered the most authentic of the Northeast. The principal one is called bumba-meu-boi, an involved dance drama which reenacts a folk tale with colorfully costumed dancers. The same dance is performed throughout the Northeast but São Luis in particular is famed for the beauty of the costumes of the dancers. The city is also home to the Tambor de Mina, a voodoo ceremony that has generated a dance-ritual called Tambor de Criolo. These African religious rites were brought from the Caribbean by slaves and are the only ones in Brazil that are similar to the voodoo ceremonies of Haiti in their use of dolls and pins.

PRACTICAL INFORMATION FOR THE NORTHEAST

WHEN TO GO. The weather in the Northeast is good all year long, with the temperature and humidity increasing as you go north, nearing the equator and the Amazon. The rainy season usually begins in Apr. and continues through June, although in São Luis there is daily rainfall starting in Sept. Rains in the Northeast tend to be torrential and can lead to flooding in the downtown areas of the cities, so if possible avoid the rainy season. The best time to come is between Jan. and Apr.; for Carnival the top location is Recife-Olinda. Although the sea breeze keeps the temperatures of the coastal cities at pleasant levels, in the interior areas of the Northeast it can get extremely hot.

HOW TO GET THERE. The capital cities are all served by Brazil's major airlines, *Varig, Vasp, Cruzeiro,* and *Transbrasil.* The highways along the coast are also good up to Fortaleza. From Fortaleza to Sao Luis, however, you are better off flying, as the road connections are poor. Buses serve the entire region and bus transportation is the most popular way of travel from one capital to another. Recife has an international airport and receives charter flights from Europe and Canada plus regularly scheduled flights from Miami *(Varig)* and Lisbon *(Air Portugal).* For the adventuresome there is a highway that cuts through the jungle between Brasilia and Belem offering a fascinating look at the backlands of Brazil, including the state of Maranhao in the Northeast. There are daily buses in both directions and the trip takes three days. Comfort is minimal.

MACEIO

HOTELS. New and the best hotel in town is the **Jatiuca,** *Expensive,* Rua Lagoa de Anta 220 (231–2555). 96 rooms on the beach with pool, tennis court, restaurant and bar. Second best and also new is the **Luxor,** *Expensive,* Av. Duque de Caxias 2076 (221–9191), near the beach, pool, restaurant and bar. Other good hotels are the **Pajuçara Othon,** *Moderate,* Rua Jangadeiros Alagoanos 1292 (231–2200), with pool, restaurant, and bar; **Beira Mar,** *Moderate,* Av. Duque de Caxias 1994 (221–0101), pool, restaurant, and bar; **Enseada,** *Moderate,* Rua Antonio Gouveia 171 (231–4726), pool and bar; **Ponta Verde Praia,** *Moderate,* Av. Alvaro Octacilio 2933 (231–4040), pool, restaurant, and bar.

RESTAURANTS. Accompanying the arrival of tourism in Maceio has been the opening of several fine restaurants with excellent options for regional as well as international dishes. The best restaurants for northeastern seafood dishes are: **Restaurante das Alagoas,** *Moderate,* in the Hotel Jatiuca (231–2555); **Lagostao,** *Expensive,* Av. Duque de Caxias 1384 (221–6211) for lobster; **Restaurante do Alipio,** *Moderate,* Av. Alípio Barbosa 321 (221–5186); **Bem,** *Moderate,* Rua Joao Canuto da Silva 21 (231–3316); **Peixada da Rita,** *Moderate,* Rua Antonio Baltazar (291–1110), simple but excellent. For international cuisine try: **Forno e Fogao** in the Hotel Luxor, *Expensive,* (221–9191); **Fornace,** *Expensive,* Av. Robert Kennedy 2167 (231–1780), on the beach; **Seandro's,** *Expensive,* Av. Fernando Lima 554 (221–3164), live music, dancing. **Gstaad,** *Moderate,* Av. Robert Kennedy 2167 (231–1780), good for fondue.

RECIFE

HOTELS. Most of the top hotels in Recife are located along Boa Viagem beach, although the beach area of next-door Olinda has the new Quatro Rodas Hotel, best in the area. In Boa Viagem the newest and best is the **Recife Palace,** *Deluxe,* Av. Boa Viagem 4070 (325–4044), owned and run by the same people who have Rio's excellent Rio Palace Hotel, with French restaurant and discotheque, on the beach; **Miramar,** *Deluxe,* Rua dos Navegantes 363 (326–7422), 120 air-conditioned rooms, swimming pool, bar, restaurant, and nightclub; a new Sheraton, the **Petribu Sheraton,** *Deluxe,* was scheduled to open in mid-1991, Av. Bernardo Vieira de Mello 1624 (361–4381), 200 rooms, convention center, pool, tennis courts, restaurant and bars, on the Piedade Beach; **Boa Viagem,** *Moderate,* Av. Boa Viagem 5000 (341–4144), beach-front, pool, bar, and restaurant; **Casa Grande e Senzala,** *Moderate,* Av. Conselheiro Aguiar 5000 (341–0366), bar and restaurant; **Castelinho Praia,** *Moderate,* Av. Boa Viagem, 4520, Boa Viagem, (326–1186); **Internacional Othon Palace,** *Moderate,* Av. Boa Viagem 3722 (326–7225), pool, restaurant, and bar; **Jangadeiro,** *Moderate,* Av. Boa Viagem 3114 (326–6777), on the beach, pool, bar, and restaurant; **Novotel Chaves,** *Moderate,* Av. Bernardo Vieira (361–1318), beach-front, bar, pool, and restaurant; **Park,** *Moderate,* Rua dos Navegantes 9 (325–4666), pool, bar, and restaurant; **Pousada do Vale,** *Moderate,* Estrada de Aldeia km. 7 (271–1010), resort hotel with sports facilities, horseback riding, pool and small lake; **Recife Praia,** *Moderate,* Av. Boa Viagem 9 (325–0522), pool, satellite dish; **Savaroni,** *Moderate,* Av. Boa Viagem 3772 (325–5077), on the beach, pool, bar, and restaurant; **do Sol,** *Moderate,* Av. Boa Viagem 978 (326–7644), bar, restaurant and pool, on the beach; **Coral,** *Inexpensive,* Av. Conselheiro Aguiar 4000 (325–3205), bar, restaurant, and pool; **Praiamar,** *Inexpensive,* Av. Boa Viagem 1660 (326–6905), on the beach. **Saveiro,** *Inexpensive,* Av. Conselheiro Aguiar 4670 (325–3424); **Vela Branca,** *Inexpensive,* Av. Boa Viagem 2494 (325–4470), restaurant, on the beach; In Olinda: **Quatro Rodas Olinda,** *Deluxe,* Av. Jose Augusto Moreira 2200 (431–2955), a top quality resort hotel on the beach with pool, tennis, two restaurants, bar, and nightclub. Best hotel in the area. Has a satellite dish for live reception of American television programs. Also **Marolinda,** *Moderate,* Av. Beira Mar 1615 (429–1699); **14-Bis,** *Inexpensive,* Av. Ministro Marcos Freire 1414 (429–0409).

RESTAURANTS. Lobster and other seafoods are the highlight of Recife dining. Tops is a restaurant called, appropriately, **Lobster,** *Moderate,* Av. Rui Barbosa 1649 (268–5516). Other fine seafood restaurants are: **Canto da Barra,** *Moderate,* Av. Bernardo Vieira de Melo 9150 (361–2168); **Costa do Sol,** *Moderate,* Av. Bernardo Vieira de Melo 8036 (361–1495); **Pra Vocês,** *Moderate,* Av. Herculano Bandeira, 115 (361–1495). For regional cooking, which in addition to lobster, shrimp, and fish includes manioc, tapioca, jerky, cornmeal dishes, chicken and sausages, try **Mucama,** *Moderate,* Av. Conselheiro Aguiar 5000 (341–0366); **Serido,** *Moderate,* Rua José Osorio 270 (227–1087); **Lapinha,** *Moderate,* Praça Boa Viagem 16, (326–1914); **O Buraco de Otilia,** *Moderate,* Rua da Aurora 1231 (231–1518); **Edmilson,** *Moderate,* Av. Maria Irene 311 (341–0644); **Recanto Picuí,** *Moderate,* Praça do Derby 353 (222–0014).

International cuisine is also well represented in Recife with the restaurant of the **Recife Palace Hotel,** *Expensive,* for fine French nouveau cuisine; **Tasca,** *Expensive,* Portuguese, Rua Dom José Lopes 165 (326–6309); **da Nonna,** *Moderate,* for Italian food, Rua Cap. Temudo 198 (224–0093); **Costa Brava,** *Moderate,* international, Rua Barao Souza Leao 698 (341–3535); **Maia's,** *Moderate,* Rua Engenheiro Domingos Ferreira, 5782 (326–2922); **La Fondue,** *Moderate,* Swiss, Rua Des. Joao Paes 186 (326–8659). For steak, the best are **Marruá,** *Moderate,* Rua Ernesto de Paula Santos 183 (326–1656); **O Laçador,** *Moderate,* Rua Visconde de Jequitinhonha 138 (326–3911). The top spot for pizza is the **Pizza Pazza,** Av. Conselheiro Aguiar 2348 (326–5365).

In Olinda the best restaurants are: **Vila d'Olinda,** *Moderate,* regional and seafood in the Quatro Rodas Hotel; **L'Atelier,** *Moderate,* French, Rua Bernardo Vieira de Melo 91 (429–3099); **Mourisco,** *Moderate,* seafood, Praça Joao Alfredo 7 (429–1390); **Rei da Lagosta,** *Moderate,* seafood, specializing in lobster, Av Beira Mar 1255 (429–1565).

NIGHTLIFE. Recife is easily the hot spot of the northeastern night, with the action centered on Boa Viagem beach and in Olinda. In Boa Viagem, the most popular nightspots are crowded side by side on Avenida Boa Viagem, the street that runs alongside the beach. Here you will find a wide variety of bars and sidewalk cafes that serve as the meeting places of Recife at night. In Olinda the same function is performed by the Alto da Sé, located at the highest point of the hills of the colonial city, overlooking Olinda and Recife in the distance. The crowds begin gathering in the afternoon on Sat. and Sun. and the party doesn't stop until the wee hours. At Alto da Sé there are small bars, some with live music, plus tables scattered around the sidewalks where strolling vendors sell beer and snacks. The souvenir salesmen who work here during the day also stay around for the nightlife, creating a delightful bohemian mix, with artists pushing their paintings in the midst of the throngs moving constantly up and down the streets. The Northeast is also blessed with its own lively forms of popular music and folkdances but, unlike Salvador, Recife does not yet have a good restaurant-nightclub with folk shows. There is, however, an excellent dance troupe called the **Pernambucan Folk Dance Ensemble,** which has performed in Europe and the United States. Made up of young residents of Recife, the ensemble performs on the weekends at the theater of the Recife Convention Center. The lively one-hour show will give you a good idea of the variety of songs and dances that exist in the Northeast. With this in hand you should then head for what is called a forró, a nightclub that specializes in Northeastern song and dance. The best is the **Cavalo Dourado,** Rua Carlos Gomes 390. Loud and lively, forrós are Recife's answer to the fact that Carnival only comes once a year.

SHOPPING. Recife has several handicraft centers where you can find high quality leather goods, excellent ceramics, and fine lace, all at good prices. The largest handicraft center in the city is the **Casa da Cultura de Pernambuco** (Pernambuco Culture Center) at Cais da Detenção downtown. There are a multitude of shops selling products from throughout the state plus a theater, museum, and snack bars. Close by at Praça Dom Vital is the **São Jose Market.** Another downtown crafts center is the **Patio de São Pedro** with several shops, bars, and regional restaurants.

On Sat. and Sun. starting at 1 P.M. a handicraft fair is held in the Boa Viagem Praça or square on the beach of Boa Viagem. In Olinda, the **Alto da Sé** and the **Ribeira Market** also offer a fine selection of handmade goods from the Northeast.

JOÃO PESSOA

HOTELS. Best here is the **Tambaú**, *Expensive*, 110-room circular hotel built into the sea at Av. Almirante Tamandaré 229 (226–3660). Two others with swimming pools are the **Tropicana**, *Moderate*, on Rua Alice de Azevedo (221–8444), and—on Cabo Branco (White Cape) 10 kilometers from town—the **Casa de Repouso O Nazareno**, *Inexpensive*, (228–1442). Or try **Manaira Praia**, *Moderate*, Av. João Mauricio, 1737 (226–1550).

RESTAURANTS. For seafood try **Badionaldo**, *Moderate*, Rua Vitorino Cordoso (228–1442); **Peixada do João**, *Moderate*, Rua Coração de Jesus 147; **Elite**, *Moderate*, Av. João Mauricio 33 (226–3000); **Marinas**, *Moderate*, Av. Cabo Branco 5100 (226–5734).

NATAL

HOTELS. Several new hotels have recently opened along Natal's beachfront. Recommended are **Novotel Ladeira do Sol**, *Moderate*, Rua Fabrício Pedrosa 915 (221–4204); **Parque da Costeira**, *Moderate*, Via Costeira at the 7 kilometer mark (222–6147); and **Vila do Mar**, *Moderate*, Via Costeira at the 5-kilometer mark (222–3755). Acceptable downtown hotels are the **Luxor**, *Moderate*, Av. Rio Branco 634 (221–2721); the **Sambura**, *Inexpensive*, Rua Professor Zuza 263 (221–0611); and the **Tirol**, *Inexpensive*, Av. Alexandrino de Alencar 1330 (221–3223). There are also the **Jaraguá Center**, *Moderate*, Rua Santo Antonio 665, downtown (221–2355), bar and restaurant; the **Natal Mar**, *Moderate*, Via Costeira 8101 (219–2121), on the beach, pool, bar and restaurant.

RESTAURANTS. The best bets are: **Raizes**, *Moderate to Expensive*, Av. Campos Sales, 609 (222–7338); **Carne Assada do Lira**, *Moderate*, Rua Mipibu, 657 (222–9937); **Peixada Arabiana**, *Moderate*, Av. Engenheiro Roberto Freire 9036 (236–3005).

FORTALEZA

HOTELS. Most comfortable for the tourist are **Esplanada Praia**, *Expensive* (224–8555), the **Imperial Palace**, *Expensive*, (244–9177), and the **Beira Mar**, *Expensive* (244–9444), on Av. Pres. Kennedy in the Meireles district, or the **Colonial Praia**, *Moderate*, on Rua Barao de Aracati in the same area (211–9644). Closer to town is the **Iracema Plaza**, *Moderate*, Av. Pres. Kennedy 746 (231–0066). Downtown the best is the 12-story **Savanah**, *Moderate*, Rua Major Facundo 411 (211–9966). Others nearby are the **Magna Praia**, *Moderate*, Av. Aquidabã 1002 (244–9311) on the Iracema beach; **Samabaia**, *Moderate*, Av. Heraclito Graça 57 (211–9299); **Excelsior**, *Inexpensive*, Rua Guilherme Rocha 172 (211–0233).

RESTAURANTS. One of the best in town is at the **Ideal Club**, (224–9300), *Moderate*, on the beach. Old-world charm, with white columns and dark carved wooden balcony overlooking a grove of palm trees. The restaurant is part of the ultra chic Ideal Country club. Another private club with a good restaurant is the marble **Nautico Beach Club**, *Moderate*, Av. Aboliçao 2727 (244–9300).

Other good international restaurants: **Sandra's**, *Expensive*, Av. Engenheiro Luis Vieira 555 (234–6555); **Panela**, *Moderate*, at the Iracema Plaza hotel (231–0066); the **Iate (Yacht) Clube**, *Moderate*, Av. Matias Beck 4813 in Mucuripe. For seafood, try the following, all on Av. Pres. Kennedy along the beach: **Alfredo**, 4616, *Moderate* (224–2711); **Peixada do Meio** 4632, *Moderate* (224–2711). **Trapiche**, 3956, *Expensive* (244–4400).

In general the best hotels and restaurants in Fortaleza are located along the Meirelles beach on Av. President Kennedy. Bars and outdoor cafes are also here for nightlife. The nearby Praia do Futuro beach is being developed now for tourism and will offer some fine new hotels, restaurants, and bars in the near future. Unfortunately the remainder of the city has suffered greatly from the recent economic problems of the state resulting from the last drought and today has little to offer except some rather depressing scenes of abject poverty.

SHOPPING. Fortaleza is famed for its lace work and here you will find intricate hammocks, lace blouses, tablecloths, and beautifully embroidered skirts, all at incredibly low prices. The best shopping areas are Central de Artesenato, Av. Santos Dumont 1500 and the Centro de Turismo, downtown at Rua Senador Pompeu 350, open all day Sat. and until 1 P.M. on Sun.

SÃO LUIS

HOTELS. Easily the best hotel in the city is the **São Luis Quatro Rodas,** *Expensive,* Praia do Calhau (227–0244), located on the best beach in São Luis, with swimming pool, tennis courts, bar-nightclub, and one of the finest seafood restaurants in all of Brazil. Highly recommended as a getaway spot for complete relaxation. Other hotels are: **Vila Rica,** *Expensive,* Praça Dom Pedro II 299 (232–3535), downtown with pool, bar, and restaurant; **São Francisco,** *Moderate,* Rua Dr. Luis Serson, 77 (227–1155), pool, bar, and restaurant; **Panorama Palace,** *Moderate,* new, Rua dos Pinheiros (227–0067), pool, bar, and restaurant.

RESTAURANTS. Victor, *Moderate,* Quatro Rodas Hotel, excellent seafood, try their many varieties of white fish, all marvelous; **Ricardão,** *Moderate,* Praia do Aracaji, for lunch; **Solar do Ribeirão,** *Moderate,* Rua do Ribeirão 141 (222–3068), famed for shrimp dishes.

THE AMAZON

The Amazon region has figured so prominently in novels and films that few people who come to see it don't have some preconceived notion of what they will find. Most often they expect an impenetrable jungle, herds of animals, flocks of swooping birds, and unfriendly Indians. In reality, there is little groundcover vegetation, the trees range from 50 to 150 feet in height, little animal life can be spotted, and the birds nest in the tops of the high trees.

Francisco de Orellana, a Spanish Conquistador, sighted the river in 1541 and was so taken by the size that he called it Rio Mar, the River Sea. Exploration was slow and arduous, and as explorers forged their way through unknown territory, they encountered and fought what they thought was a race of women warriors, whom they called Amazons. Whether they actually believed they were face to face with something out of pagan mythology is not known; but it is easy to imagine that they felt the name "Amazon" and its implications were pointedly appropriate to this hostile land, and this name came to refer to the entire region.

Most of the Amazon basin has been explored and charted. The river itself is 3,900 miles long, the second longest river in the world, and has 17 tributaries each over 1,000 miles long plus over 50,000 miles of navigable trunk rivers. Ocean-going vessels can travel 2,700 miles upriver to Iquitos, which is still about 600 miles from the origin of the river.

About one-third the world's oxygen is produced by the vegetation, and one-fifth the fresh water in the world is provided by the Amazon. Although there are over 18,000 plant species in the basin, the extremely heavy rainfall leaches the soil of its nutrients and makes organized cultivation extremely impractical. Although poor in agricultural possibilities, the

Amazon is rich in among other products, gold, diamonds, lumber, rubber, oil, and jute.

American travel firms began to make it more accessible in 1956. The region is now becoming increasingly open to tourism. Such cities as Belém, Manaus, Santarem, and Porto Velho in Brazil, Leticia in Columbia, and Iquitos in Peru, are easily reached by air and offer fine hotels, good food, excellent services, and fascinating sightseeing.

The main attraction in the Amazon is the jungle. It extends into nine countries of South America—French Guiana, Suriname, Guyana, Venezuela, Ecuador, Peru, Bolivia, Colombia, and Brazil. Most of these countries have developed tourism facilities—most of them new—enabling the visitor to explore the basin in reasonable safety and comfort. However, as it is a primitive area, many tourist facilities call for "roughing it."

Belém

The city of Belém is the gateway to the Amazon, 90 miles from the open sea. Ultra-modern highrises dot the horizon, mingling with older red-tile-roofed buildings.

Belém was the first center of European colonization in the Amazon. The Portuguese settled here in 1616, using the city as a jumping off point for the interior jungle region and also as an outpost to protect the mouth of the Amazon River. A river port with access to the sea, Belém developed over the years into the major trade center for the Amazon. Like the upriver city of Manaus, Belém rode the ups and downs of Amazon booms and busts, alternately bursting with energy and money and slumping into relative obscurity. All of this is evident in the architecture of the city where colonial structures survive along with rubber-era mansions and ostentatious monuments to the civic spirit of past magnates. This is most evident in the "old city" where you will find the Our Lady of Nazare church with its ornate interior replete with carrara marble and gold, the former city palace, the Laura Sodre palace and the Bolonha Palace, the latter three examples of works by European architects brought to the city by the rubber barons.

While here, walk to the Praça da Republica, faced by the Municipal Theatre, to see the Victorian marble statues. The theatre is the third oldest in Brazil. Nearby is the handicrafts center run by the state tourism office, Paratur. In this daily fair you will find wood, leather, and straw objects plus handmade Indian goods and examples of the region's colorful and distinctive pottery, called marajoara.

Stop in the Goeldi Museum; in addition to an extensive collection of Indian artifacts and excellent photographs, there is a zoo with many local animals in their natural surroundings. In the Jungle Park, a large area of virgin forest has been preserved and traversed by trails, which lead to reflection pools with huge water lillies. Also worthwhile is the Agricultural Institute, where rubber and Brazil nut trees are cultivated. Or, delve into history with a visit to an old rubber plantation.

Although Belém today is a bustling, modern city, the influence of the Amazon river and jungle remains strong. Despite its international airport, the city still depends heavily on the river for contact with the outside world. The highway to Brasilia was built to end Belém's isolation from the rest of the country but it is still a seasonal highway, subject to periodic closures because of heavy rains and flooding along the route. Its main value to the city is in providing land access for farm products and manufactured goods from the south. Buses also ply the highway but the four-day trip is only for the adventuresome.

Because of its heavy dependence on the river, the port of Belém is today, as it was 300 years ago, an active trade and business center. Here you will find the Ver-o-Peso market (literally "see the weight," a colonial-era salespitch that has survived the passage of time). Dozens of boats of all types and sizes line up at the dock to unload their wares or haul on board Amazon goods destined for other ports. The market is a confusion of colors and voices with vendors offering medicinal herbs, regional fruits, miracle roots from the jungle, alligator teeth, river fish (both stuffed and for eating) and good luck charms for the body and soul. Short on cleanliness but long on local color.

The port of Belém itself is best seen by boat. Paratur operates a sternwheeler that provides tours of the port and nearby islands. The oldtime river boat, with a bar on board, leaves from the Praça do Pescador at 9 in the morning on Saturdays and Sundays, returning at noon. Two private firms, Ciatur and Neytur, also conduct river tours, leaving from the pier at the Novotel Hotel daily. Both of these tours include a stop along the river with a short hike through the jungle. You can also arrange a boat trip to Jaguar Island, with its luxuriant vegetation and array of bird life. A small river cuts through the island; a short boatride provides interesting insight into the lifestyle of the islanders.

Marajó

Just north of Belém and reached by boat or plane is the island of Marajó, larger than Denmark. The island has two distinct zones of vegetation—forest and grassy plains—and is famed for its herds of water buffalo. The island is a vast unspoiled tribute to the abundance of the Amazon region. Its only city, Souré, also has excellent river beaches. The trip to the island takes 6 hours by boat or 30 minutes by plane and if you decide to stay the night, make sure to choose the Pousada Marajoara located on the riverfront and designed in the form of an Amazon indian village, just right for capturing the spirit of this unique part of the world. While on the island, try out the distinctive local cuisine with such delicacies as buffalo steak and desserts made with buffalo milk.

In general, dining in the Amazon is as different as everything else in the region. Besides buffalo, you will have the opportunity to eat piranha fish, armadillo, wild Amazon duck and a wide variety of river fish with such exotic indian names as *tucunaré, pirarucú, tambaquí, curimatá, jaraquí,* and *Pacú* (beware of anyone offering you alligator or turtle—the killing of both is against the law). For dessert try some of the region's tropical fruits, found only in the Amazon, such as *cupuacu, graviola, taperebá, pupunha, biribá, bacabá, burití, abio,* and *acaí.*

Macapá

North from Marajó is Macapá, an Amazon river city of 95,000 and capital of the territory of Amapá. The city, one of only five in the world that lies directly on the equator, is 40 minutes flying time from Belém. Like Belém, Macapá was an Amazon outpost established by the Portuguese to develop the region and keep out invaders from Europe. To this end, the Portuguese built their largest fort in Brazil in the city. Its remains are today one of Macapá's main tourist attractions.

The top attraction, however, is provided by nature. Called the pororoca, this extraordinary natural wonder occurs when the incoming ocean tide crashes against the outflowing waters of the Amazon. The violent meeting produces churning waters and waves that reach 15 feet in height. The most remarkable aspect of the pororoca, however, is the sound that results. For nearly an hour before the final meeting of the waters, the air is filled with what sounds like a continuous crack of thunder, gradually building in intensity. At the end, the rushing ocean waves sweep into the forest along the river banks. The intensity of the pororoca is at its greatest during the months January to May when the Amazon is in flood stage. It is truly one of the most unforgettable sights in South America.

Santarem

Throughout modern times, the Amazon has been a magnet for adventurers and dreamers. First wood, then rubber and today gold have served as the lures for thousands of would-be millionaires seeking to carve their fortunes out of the jungle. Many have left behind rusted monuments to their dreams. The most noteworthy of these is Fordlandia, an Amazon boondoggle envisioned by Henry Ford who poured millions of dollars into a vast rubber plantation destined to supply him with the raw material for the tires of his cars. The scheme failed and today its remains can be seen in the jungle some 40 miles outside of Santarem, a city of 100,000 on the Amazon between Belém and Manaus. Santarem is now enjoying unprecedented growth due to the latest Amazon boom cycle, this time built around gold strikes that have been made in the region starting in 1981. Originally settled by former soldiers of the Confederacy following the Civil War, Santarem boasts names like Higgins and MacDonald. The Tropical Hotel Santarem offers superior accommodations and arranges local boat trips on the Amazon and its tributaries.

The Brazilian shipping company, Enasa, is now operating two catamaran-style vessels between Belém and Manaus with a stop at Santarem. They boast 53 double and 8 quadruple air-conditioned cabins with private baths plus a small pool, bar, dining room and discotheque. The twice-monthly sailings are usually on Fridays from Belém arriving in Manaus the following Thursday. Departures from Manaus are on Friday arriving in Belém on Wednesday.

Manaus

A sprawling city of nearly one million, built in the densest part of the jungle, Manaus has re-established its role as the key city of the Amazon basin after years of dormancy (the long-hoped-for expansion of the Amazon basin did not attain the desired results despite the inauguration of seasonal road connections with Belém and Brasilia). Vestiges of Manaus' opulent rubber boom days still remain; the famous Opera House, completed in 1910, where Jenny Lind once sang and the Ballet Russe once danced, has recently been restored to its former splendor. The building is adorned with French ironwork and houses works of art and chinawear—seemingly out of place in the jungle. For further insight into the rubber boom period, visit a rubber plantation.

The Custom House and Lighthouse were imported piece by piece from England and reassembled alongside the floating dock, built especially to accommodate the annual 40-foot rise and fall of the river.

Contemporary Manaus is a combination of modern highrise buildings scattered among lower, older stucco structures. Still, the city has more than its share of hotels, restaurants, and unusual sights. Wander through the City Market Building, where caged animals and parrots are offered for sale alongside exotic fruits and vegetables.

For shopping, try the Credilar Teatro, an imposing edifice of native red-stone and glass. Or, taxi to the suburb of Cachoeirinha to see the Little Church of the Poor Devil (Pobre Diablo) built by one poor laborer; it's only 12 feet wide and 15 feet long. While in the suburbs, stop at the Salesian Mission Museum to see a complete documentary of the now vanished "Floating City"; also, visit the Indian Museum operated by the same order.

For natural beauties, plan a trip to Taruma Falls and, of course, a boat ride beginning on the Rio Negro that detours onto a small tributary that is completely covered by a green umbrella of giant trees and vines. Birdlife is abundant in this region and with luck, you might spot a scampering monkey high in the trees. The fascinating end to the voyage cruises is the "Wedding of the Waters," where the coffee-brown Amazon and the inky-black Rio Negro meet and continue for miles toward the Atlantic before intermingling.

The Upper Regions

The upper reaches of the Amazon River are generally more interesting than the lower portions because the upper river is only one-half mile wide and the channel flows close to either shore most of the time. Indian life is far more evident.

There is weekly tour/cruise service on the upper Amazon between Iquitos, Peru and Leticia, Colombia. Reconstructed especially for cruising on the Amazon, the M/V *Rio Amazonas* sails from its home port of Iquitos each Wednesday and arrives in Leticia Saturday morning; return sailings depart Leticia Saturday afternoons and arrive in Iquitos Tuesday mornings. Sailing times in both ports are coordinated with air service to/from Bogotá, Manaus, Iquitos and Lima.

The *Rio Amazonas* carries 55 passengers in 16 air-conditioned twin cabins with private bath and 10 non-air-conditioned twin/triple cabins with community bath facilities at half the cost. All meals, twice-daily shore excursions, lectures and films on the flora, fauna, and Indian life are all included in the cruise cost. Shore excursions are not duplicated on the in-depth roundtrip cruise, six nights from Iquitos back to Iquitos.

PRACTICAL INFORMATION FOR THE AMAZON

For definitions of price categories see "Facts at Your Fingertips."

WHEN TO GO. Since the Amazon Valley lies close to the Equator, winter and summer in the usual sense do not occur. High humidity is common only in the deep jungle, not in the cities or on the river. Average temperature is 80°F. Nights are always cool. Rainy Season—December to June (high water). Dry Season—July to November (low water). Travel in both seasons is good.

HOW TO GET THERE. From USA: Gateway is Miami, via *Lloyd Boliviano, Varig, Faucett,* and *Suriname Airways, Avianca* and *Aeroperu.*

From S.A. to Manaus: *Varig, Cruzeiro, Vasp, Lloyd Boliviano.* To Belém: *Varig, Suriname Airways, Vasp,* and *Cruzeiro.* To Leticia: *Avianca* and *Cruzeiro.* To Iquitos: *Faucett, Aero Peru,* and *Cruzeiro.*

WHAT TO TAKE. Light summer clothing. Drip dry shirts and khaki slacks for the men. Cotton dresses for the ladies or skirts and blouses. Pants and pantsuits for women are also acceptable. All shirts and blouses should be long-sleeved. All colors may be worn with the exception of green. Very comfortable shoes are a must, and sneakers or tennis shoes will come in handy. In addition, for its jungle tours, *Amazon Explorers* has the following suggestions and comments: (1) Rubber boots (high) for walk through the jungles. A must. (2) Hat or head cover. Flashlight—

since electricity is limited. (3) Insect repellent (for overnight trips a mosquito net will be supplied). (4) Knife, scissors, first aid kit, toilet paper, sewing kit, sunglasses. (5) Camera and *plenty* of film. Plastic bags to store exposed film. (6) All medications as needed. (7) Walking stick if needed will be supplied. (8) For fishermen: please bring variety of hooks and line. (9) Binoculars—good quality binoculars for bird and animal watching—500 varieties of tropical Amazon birds are constantly around you. (10) As the life on the Amazon is much more relaxed and primitive than anywhere else in the world, you must be prepared for constant changes, delays, or cancellations of flights or steamers according to the moods of the river. Should such changes occur while traveling, your guide will notify you immediately and make new arrangements accordingly.

HOTELS. Once a wilderness area as far as hotel accommodations were concerned, the Amazon has now thoroughly acceptable, even luxurious, lodging. For definitions of price categories, see "Facts at Your Fingertips."

BELÉM

Deluxe

Hilton, Av. Pres. Vargas 882, Praça da Republica (223–6500). Finest hotel in town, all rooms with private bath, air-conditioning; 2 bars and 2 restaurants.

Moderate

Equatorial Palace, Av. Braz Aguiar 612 (241–2000). One of the best in the city, with a bar, pool, and restaurant; the rooms have bath, air-conditioning, telephone, TV, and refrigerator.

Excelsior Grao Para, Av. Presidente Vargas 718 (222–3255). Rooms have bath, air-conditioning, and telephone; bar and restaurant.

Novotel, Av. Bernardo Sayao 4804 (229–8011). 121 air-conditioned rooms near Rio Guama.

Regente, Av. Governador Jose Malcher 485. (224–0755). Rooms with private bath, air-conditioning, and TV.

Vila Rica Belém, Av. Julio Cesar 1777 (airport) (233–4222). Rooms have private bath, air-conditioning, telephones, and TV; bar, restaurant, and pool.

Inexpensive

Central, Av. Presidente Vargas 290 (222–3011).

Sagres, Av. Gov. Jose Malcher 2927 (228–3999). 136 rooms, all air-conditioned, TV, bar, restaurant, and pool.

Vanja, Rua Benjamin Constant 1164 (222–6688). Rooms with private bath, air-conditioning, and telephone.

MANAUS

Deluxe

Tropical, (Estrada da Ponta Negra (238–5757). Built and operated by Tropical Hotels, a subsidiary of Varig, on good beach overlooking the Rio Negro. 341 air-conditioned rooms, swimming pool, excellent restaurant, night club. About 10 minutes from the new airport and 45 minutes from town. Best buy.

Expensive

Amazonas, Praça Adalberto Valle (234–7679). Located in the center of the city, this 10-story building has 182 air-conditioned apartments and two elevators. All rooms have private bath, hot and cold water, and television. Permanent buffet service. Swimming pool.

Novotel, Av. Mandii, 4 (237–1211). Newest in town. 168 air-conditioned rooms in commercial section.

Moderate

Hotel Imperial, Via Getulio Vargas 277 (233–8711). 100 air-conditioned rooms, TV and bar in every room.

Lord, Rua Marcílio Dias 217/225 (234–9741). In the center of the city, this 6-story hotel has 105 apartments all with private bath, hot and cold water, and telephone. Restaurant.

Monaco, Rua Silva Ramos, 20 (232–5211). 112 air-conditioned rooms with private bath, color TV, and pool. Downtown area.

Inexpensive

Central, Rua Dr. Moreira 202 (232–7887). Centrally located, this 50-room, 3-story hotel has air-conditioning, private baths, and telephones.

Flamboyant, Av. Eduardo Ribeiro (234–0696). Mid-town, the 23 rooms all have private bath and telephone. Bar and swimming pool. Near the Opera House.

Nacional, Rua Dr. Moreira 59 (233–0537). Also downtown, this small hotel has 16 rooms with private bath.

Rei Salomao, Rua Dr. Moreira 119 (234–7374). In the center of the city, these 28 apartments have air-conditioning, private bath, and telephone.

SANTAREM

Moderate

Tropical, Av. Mendonca Furtado 4120 (522–1533). Offers 120 air-conditioned rooms with refrigerators. One of finest hotels in the region.

Inexpensive

Uirapuru, Av. Adriano Pimental 140 (522–5881). A small hotel with local flavor but not all rooms have air-conditioning.

MACAPÁ

Moderate

Novotel, Av. Eng. Azarias Neto 17, on the river, downtown (222–1144). Restaurant, bar and tennis court. New and very good. By far the best in town.

Inexpensive

Amapaense Palace Hotel, downtown. Av. Tiradentes (222–3366). Old and no frills.

MARAJÓ

Moderate

Pousada Marajoara. Located on the river in the island's capital city of Souré. (741–1287). The only hotel that can be recommended on the island. Fortunately it's very good, built in the form of an Amazon indian village. Best meals on the island are in the hotel's restaurant.

RESTAURANTS. The favorite local dish is *pato no tucupi,* which is duck in yellow soup with a herb that tingles all the way down the throat and long after it's in the stomach. For definitions of price categories, see "Facts at Your Fingertips."

BELÉM

For international food try **Augustus,** *Moderate,* Av. Almirante Barroso 493 (226–8317); or the **O Teatro,** *Expensive,* at the Hilton (223–6500).

Avenida, *Moderate,* on Av. Pres. Vargas 882 (223–4015), offers good regional food in comfortable surroundings. Also for Amazon specialties, **à em Casa,** or **O Outro,** at Av. Gov. José Malcher 982 and 247 (223–1212); and **Circulo Militar,** Praça Frei Caetano Brandão (223–4374). All *Moderate.*

For barbecue, **Gaucha,** *Moderate,* Av. Governador Jose Malcher 2731 (226–8427) and **Na Brasa,** *Moderate,* Av. Nazaré 124 (225–4541).

Other specialties: Japanese food at **Miako**, *Moderate*, Rue 1 de Março 766 (223–4485) and Portuguese food at **Casa Portuguesa**, *Moderate*, Rua Senador Manoel Barata 897 (223–4871).

MACAPÁ

The best restaurants in the city are the **Novotel**, *Moderate*, Av. Eng. Azarias Neto 17 (223–1144), in the hotel of the same name, international cuisine, and **Peixaria**, *Inexpensive*, Av. Mãe Luzia 84 (222–0913) for fish.

MANAUS

River fish is the main meal at Manaus's restaurants, with the top specialties being the *pirarucu*, and *tucunaré*. While the fish are always fresh, the cooks of Manaus have not yet mastered the art of preparing them, with a few exceptions. The best are **Caçarola**, *Moderate*, Av. Manués, 188-A (233–3021); **Panorama**, *Moderate*, Boulevard Rio Negro, 199 (624–4626); **Piauí**, *Moderate*, Rua Dr. Moreira 202 (234–2133) and **Caravelle**, *Moderate*, Av. 7 de Setembro 1043 (234–1154). The Hotel Tropical has a fine international restaurant, the **Tarumã**, *Expensive* (238–5757).

HOW TO GET AROUND. There are regular plane services that take you into Belém, the capital of the State of Pará on the mouth of the Amazon River. To get to Manaus, the capital of the state of Amazonas, you must go by plane. *Cruzeiro* flies Manaus/Tabatinga/Iquitos and return twice weekly; Tabatinga is one mile from Leticia by taxi. *Varig* and *Vasp* fly from Rio and Brasilia to Manaus, as well as to Belém and Paramaribo. Varig-Cruzeiro and Vasp also fly from Belém to Macapá and Santarem. The same airlines offer flights from Rio, São Paulo, Brasilia, Belo Horizonte and Porto Alegre to Macapá.

Enasa operates two catamaran-style vessels between Belém and Manaus with a stop at Santarem, usually twice a month. Sailings are usually on Fridays from Belém, arriving in Manaus the following Thursday. Departures from Manaus are on Fridays, arriving on Wednesday in Belém. Rates per person are $595 for an outside cabin and $495 for an inside double cabin. For reservations, contact Gran Para Tourismo, Ave. Presidente Vargas #679, Belém, Pará, Brazil.

TOURS. There are three options for river and port tours in Belém: the **Paratur sternwheeler** leaves Praça do Pescador every Saturday and Sunday at 9 A.M. for a three-hour tour. Tickets can be bought at any travel agency or at the Paratur offices in Praça Kennedy (224–9633). Tickets also can be bought upon boarding. **Ciatur** provides daily tours leaving from the pier at the Novotel Hotel. Tickets may be bought at the pier or at the Ciatur offices, Av. Presidente Vargas 645 (228–0011). **Neytur** also offers daily tours leaving from Novotel's pier at Av. Bernardo Sayao 4804. Neytur's offices are located at Rua Carlos Gomes 300 (224–2469).

For **river tours** in Macapá, Santarem, and Manaus, check at hotels—in Macapá at the Novotel Hotel, in Santarem at the Tropical, and in Manaus at the Tropical, Amazonas, Novotel, and Lord hotels. Several tour operators in Manaus now offer overnight stays in the jungle in so-called **jungle lodges** or aboard boats. Before you go, however, check at one of the hotels mentioned above or with the local tourism authority, **Emamtur**, Av. Taruma 379 (234–5983). Some of these arrangements are more adventurous than most travelers want. There are also river boats that carry passengers and cargo throughout the region. While romantic in appearance, they are definitely not for tourists. The boats are old and many of them are unsafe.

SPORTS. Most popular sport in this area is *fishing*. *Selvatour* (234–8984) provides all services in Manaus. They are experts at arranging jungle expeditions.

SHOPPING. The streets of Belém have a number of shops that sell jungle items; but remember that live animals or birds may not be imported into the U.S. Skins of protected animals such as alligators or crocodiles, or shoes/handbags or other articles made of these skins, are also not allowed into the U.S. and will be confiscated by the U.S. Customs. The Paratur handicrafts fair is located at Praça Kennedy near the Praça da Republica.

Manaus, a free port, has hundreds of shops, stocked with goods from all over the world. *House of the Hummingbird,* which is owned and operated by Richard Melnyk, features rare and unusual artifacts handcrafted by Indians, Caboclos (half-breeds) and regional artisans. Will ship anywhere without service charge.

NIGHTLIFE. Though they are not abundant, this region does have nightclubs, at least in the larger cities like Manaus. The disco at the Tropical Hotel, *O Uirapuru,* is the hottest spot and the *Star Ship,* on Rua Constantino Nery, has a show and dancing. Manaus also has a casino. While supposedly illegal, this does not seem to bother the local authorities. Ask for directions at your hotel.

CHILE

The Atacama, Andes, Antarctica

by
JIM WOODMAN

Jim Woodman is editor and publisher of Latin Travel Review, *the newspaper of Latin America's travel industry. For the past 26 years he has been a frequent visitor and traveler throughout Chile and has been twice decorated by the Chilean government for his work in tourism.*

Visitors will receive a warm welcome from Chileans, who are intensely patriotic and unceasing in their efforts to insure visitors share their opinion that Chile is the best country in the world. Foreign tourists who visit Chile come mainly from Argentina and Brazil.

Modern air travel has broken down the barriers that once isolated Chile from the rest of the world: the snow-capped Andes mountains on one side, and 5,000 miles of Pacific coast on the other. The first European invaders were the Spanish "Conquistadores," by whom the purely Indian population was forced farther and farther south, fighting fiercely as they went.

This fighting spirit of the Araucanian Indians most probably accounts for the fact that the majority of Chileans are of Spanish descent; in the early days few of the Chilean Indians intermarried with the Spanish, unlike the softer-natured Indians of Peru. Even today, although a quite notable Indian strain runs through some sectors of the working classes, mixed Spanish and Indian blood is rare in the middle and upper classes.

Spanish and Indian are not the only Chilean races. In the battles for independence, the Chileans' leader was named O'Higgins; their Navy was formed by Cochrane. The last three presidents were Alessandri (Italian origin) and Frei (Swiss), and Allende's mother was named Gossens. The former military junta included members named Pinochet and Matthei. Thinking casually of Santiago shops and factories, the names of Küpfer, Haddad, Bercovich, Luchetti, and Mackenzie come easily to mind. They are all Chileans.

A Brief History

In northern Chile, not far from the great Chuquicamata copper mine, villages of some pre-Inca civilization have been unearthed in their entirety. But no record of who these people were survives. The Incas came later, extending down as far as central Chile and bringing their civilization with them. The native Chilean Indians, the Chango coastal race, the Araucanians, the Onas (the last living Ona died early in 1975), and the Alacalufes and Yaghans of the south were all of inferior civilization. It was the cooking fires of the Alacalufes that caused sailors to name the southern tip of Chile "Tierra del Fuego" (Land of Fire).

The first European to see Tierra del Fuego was Hernando de Magallanes (Magellan in English), who sailed in 1520 through the straits that bear his name today.

Around 1535, an expedition under Don Diego de Almagro started down from Cuzco in Peru on the inevitable search for gold and silver. He reached Santiago—after tramping heedlessly over the copper deposits, which are Chile's mainstay today, and returned empty handed. A further optimist, Don Pedro de Valdivia, a captain under Pizarro, also led an expedition. He reached the central zone and in 1541 founded the city known as Santiago del Nuevo Extremo at the foot of a small hill called Huelen (pain) by the Indians. Today this hill is a park in the center of modern Santiago and is called the Santa Lucia Hill. There for all to read is a stone facsimile of Pedro de Valdivia's letter to his king, praising this new territory and urging the king to send settlers.

His second expedition in 1549, was aimed principally at suppressing the Araucanian Indians; but he was captured and, under the orders of Caupolican, their chief, put to death. An avenging mission under Garcia Hurtado de Mendoza fought its way much further south and in turn captured and executed Caupolican. A story of the Spaniards' war against the Indians is told in a famous poem "La Araucana" by Alonso de Ercilla y Zuñiga.

Life under the rule of the Viceroyalty in Lima progressed slowly, developing a farming colony whose coast was forever at the mercy of raiding English and French pirates. Restive under this regime, the criollos (Spaniards born in Chile) began to long for independence, and their first Junta de Gobierno was formed on September 18, 1810, a date still celebrated in Chile as Independence Day.

When in the following year Jose Miguel Carrera was nominated president, the Viceroy sent an army to crush the upstart "Chileans." Fighting continued until 1818 when an army under the Argentine general San Martin and Bernardo O'Higgins won the final victory.

O'Higgins became Director Supreme, but he got into difficulties as ruler and finished his life in voluntary exile. He was succeeded by Ramón Freire. Still the country remained divided and chaotic until around 1830, when Diego Portales won the battle that ended what was virtually civil war. Portales was shot in a military uprising in 1837, but his victory left Chile tranquil until 1879, a quiet broken only by Chile's brief alliance with Peru against the Spaniards, which led to the bombardment of Valparaiso, after due warning, by the Spanish Navy.

The Pacific War

For some time there had been wrangling with Bolivia over the rich guano deposits and later over the nitrate fields in the Atacama desert. Chileans began to work these deposits under the most grievous conditions and the burden of a ruinous tax. Threatened by Bolivia with embargo of the factories, the Chilean government took a hand, and in February 1879 the Chilean army landed at Antofagasta and captured the town. The War of the Pacific had begun. Peru allied herself with Bolivia, and the fighting continued for four angry years, until Chile finally emerged victorious in 1883. Chile acquired the Bolivian provinces of Antofagasta and Tarapaca and the Peruvian provinces of Tacna and Arica. Chile later (1929) returned Tacna to Peru, but retained Arica. The 1883 treaty cost Bolivia her sea coast; an outlet corridor is sporadically being negotiated by Chile, Bolivia, and Peru.

The nitrates brought great wealth to Chile but not political stability. In 1891, there was another civil war, this time between pro-Congress and pro-presidential factions. The former won, and the president (Balmaceda) committed suicide.

The elections of 1970 ushered in sweeping reforms in Chilean politics and life. The Marxist Unidad Popular party, headed by Salvador Allende Gossens, embarked on an ambitious program to restructure the entire Chilean economy. Policies included tax reform, land redistribution, an overhaul of the banking system, and nationalization of major industrial concerns, including the American copper giants Kennecott and Anaconda.

Mismanagement of social programs and violence by pro-Allende extremists alienated many Chileans, and opposition to the regime was strident, particularly among the country's elites and armed forces. In September 1973, the heads of the Army, Navy, and Air Force, aided by Chilean *carabineros* and backed secretly by the CIA, staged a gory coup. In the course of widespread torture and execution of Unidad Popular supporters, Allende was killed; the insurgents claimed, not very plausibly, that he had committed suicide.

A four-man military junta—*los Generales,* as they are called in Chile—ruled the country until 1989, when a new president and a new Congress were elected by popular vote. Chile today enjoys a stable political climate under their traditional democratic system. With the healthiest and most dynamic economy in Latin America, the country has succeeded at attracting a good amount of foreign investment.

The Economy Today

Chile is still the world's greatest producer of natural nitrates and their by-product, iodine. The nitrates are coming into their own once again as petroleum-based synthetic fertilizers experience heavy cost increases. In all, Chile heads the list of mineral producers in Latin America with two-thirds of the total, including copper, coal, iron, gold, silver, oil, manganese, lithium, and sulphur.

Forestry products—pulp, logs, sawn wood, and manufactured goods—constitute the second largest export item.

Wine is both a consumer product and an export item. Certainly the Chileans consume plenty, but France is one of Chile's chief wine customers. It is a product worthy of the attention of the most critical and experienced wine fancier.

All this suggests that Chile definitely falls into the category of a "developing country" and, indeed, it has not been unscathed by the debt crises which beleaguer most Latin American nations. Yet, the country continues developing, and so does its middle class, including politicians, industrialists, artists, professional men and women, engineers, scientists and doctors. Women have equal opportunity in Chile and rise to high posts in the central administration, education, and business.

Arts and Artists

Thus, it comes as no surprise that one of the two most important poets was a woman: Nobel prize winner Gabriela Mistral, the pen name of a former provincial school teacher, Lucila Godoy. The other Chilean Nobel Prize was awarded to Pablo Neruda (whose real name was Neftali Reyes), who came home to die in 1973 from his ambassadorial post in Paris.

Chilean artists have exhibited in several of the world's capitals: Juan Francisco Gonzalez, Alfredo Valenzuela, Camilo Mori, Roberto Matta, and sculptors Nicanor Plaza and Rebeca Matta. Among internationally known musicians are violinist Alfonso Montecinos and pianists Rosita Renard and Claudio Arrau, the latter recognized as one of the best living interpreters of Beethoven.

The Way of Life

Chile is European in character, population, and culture. Chileans are by nature friendly and traditionally give a hearty welcome to foreign visitors.

Chileans are family oriented. Most entertaining is done in homes with family and friends. The best place to see Chileans on holiday is during the summer months of January and February when everyone who possibly can goes to one of the immensely popular Pacific coast resorts.

In winter the ski resorts are the destination and from June through October one will find the affluent Chilean on the slopes.

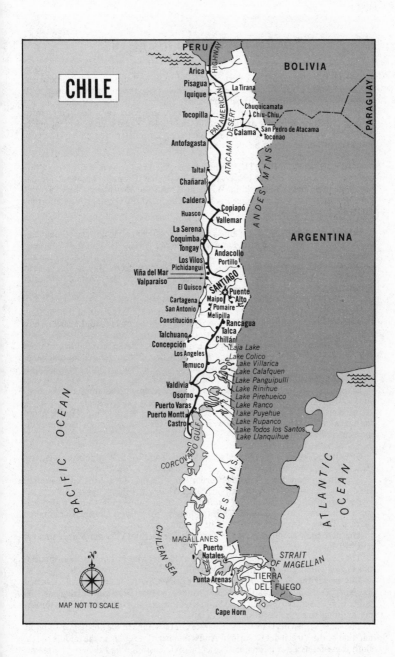

CHILE

PERU
Arica
Pisagua   La Tirana
Iquique
                    Chuquicamata
Tocopilla   Chiu-Chiu
            Calama
                San Pedro de Atacama
                Toconao
Antofagasta

Taltal
Chañaral
Caldera
Huasco   Copiapó
            Vallemar
La Serena
Coquimba   Andacollo
Tongay   Portillo
Los Vilos
Pichidangui
Viña del Mar
Valparaiso   El Quisco   SANTIAGO
                        Puente
            Maipo   Alto
Cartagena   Pomaire
San Antonio Melipilla
Constitución   Rancagua
Talchuano   Talca
Concepción Chillán
Los Angeles   Laja Lake
Temuco   Lake Colico
                Lake Villarica
                Lake Calafquen
Valdivia   Lake Panguipulli
Osorno   Lake Rinihue
Puerto Varas   Lake Pirehueico
Puerto Montt   Lake Ranco
Castro   Lake Puyehue
                Lake Rupanco
                Lake Todos los Santos
                Lake Llanquihue

BOLIVIA

PARAGUAY

ANDES MTNS.

ATACAMA DESERT

PAN-AMERICAN HIGHWAY

ARGENTINA

PACIFIC OCEAN

CORCOVADO GULF

ANDES MTNS.

ATLANTIC OCEAN

CHILEAN SEA

MAGALLANES
Puerto
Natales   STRAIT
                OF
                MAGELLAN
Punta Arenas   TIERRA
                DEL FUEGO

Cape Horn

MAP NOT TO SCALE

FACTS AT YOUR FINGERTIPS

WHAT IT WILL COST. A first-class hotel room in Santiago will run between $70 and $80 for a double room, and a moderately-priced meal for two around $30. Single rooms outside Santiago cost from $20 to $30 for respectable, clean accommodations. Single meals run from $3 to $6. There are good car rental companies throughout Chile. A couple driving within Chile today would average $35 for meals and $45 for lodging per day. In a car averaging 20 miles to the gallon, the cost to travel 100 miles would be about $11 (with insurance).

SOURCE OF INFORMATION. For information on all aspects of Chile the Chilean National Tourist Office SERNATUR is invaluable. They offer excellent, factual travel planning free for the asking. Write: SERNATUR, Providencia 1550, Santiago, Chile. In the U.S., the airlines LAN–Chile and LADECO can provide information and brochures on travel in Chile.

WHEN TO GO. Because of Chile's unique geography, almost every climate can be found within its boundaries. Santiago's pleasant climate is similar to Southern California's, except that it has more rain. When to go depends on whether you want to ski or to fish for trout and swim. The cold season is from May to Oct.; warm weather is from Oct. to Apr. The high tourist season along the coast and at beach resorts runs from about Dec. to Mar.

WHAT TO TAKE. The visitor must remember that Chile is south of the equator, that the ski season is during the Northern Hemisphere summer, and that swimming and fishing season is when the northern countries are freezing.

Unless visiting the Antarctic, expect temperate weather. From Santiago to the south, however, waterproof clothing is needed due to year-round unpredictable rains. Santiago and Viña del Mar have rainy spells in winter; with the exception of coastal areas, the former has no rain in summer.

Briefly, city wear is much the same as for any temperate country. For women, suits and dresses, slacks and pants suits; for men, suits and ties.

In resort areas, sports clothes are acceptable during the day, and a suit is usual for men at night. Women shouldn't wear shorts in the cities, although they are common in resort areas.

SPECIAL EVENTS. The Santiago, Valparaiso, and Viña del Mar *opera, theater,* and *ballet season* runs from April to November.

The International Song Festival (February) in Viña del Mar is truly international. Held in a magnificent natural amphitheater. Mainly for the young.

An *industrial and agricultural exhibition* held in Santiago in October also features some very fancy riding by Chilean "huasos" (cowboys) and the Carabineros "Green Team," a cossack-type exhibition riding group.

The two main *horse races* of the year are the Derby (Viña del Mar, January) and "El Ensayo" (Santiago, October).

The *national golf championship* is held in Viña del Mar in January, and international golf events continue through March.

July brings the *Feast of the Virgen del Carmen,* patron saint of Chile's armed forces. After the decisive battle for Chile's independence, Bernardo O'Higgins ("the father of the country") promised to build a temple on the site in Maipú. The imposing building was completed only in 1975.

The same Virgen del Carmen is celebrated in La Tirana in the north near Iquique, and that of the Virgen del Rosario in Andacollo near La Serena in the middle north. Both these feasts have in common oriental-style costumes and dancing by teams, which practice all year to oriental-sounding music played on strange traditional instruments. The origin of this touch of the East is unknown. These very picturesque ceremonies, which last a week starting on July 16, command audiences of over a hundred thousand visitors from all over the world, who camp on the hillsides.

September 18th is *Independence Day*, and on September 19th the armed forces stage their big parade in the Parque O'Higgins, attended by the President and ministers and diplomatic corps. For the country in general, *"El Dieciocho"* (the 18th) is mainly a drinking holiday, with much red wine and Chicha (a fermented grape drink which tastes innocent but isn't) accompanied by "empanadas."

World speed-skiing championships are held occasionally in Portillo. The world speed skiing record was broken on the Portillo slopes.

Association football season is from early spring right through summer, with a break in January and February. The twice yearly contests between the two major universities, called "Clasicos," feature an elaborately produced show on the field before the games.

In January is the *International Horsemanship Championship* in Viña del Mar, where some first-class riding can be seen. Chileans usually carry off the honors, although the show is international.

TRAVEL DOCUMENTS AND CUSTOMS. Passports are required of all visitors except nationals of Argentina, Brazil, Uruguay, and Paraguay, who need only their national identity cards. Visitors under 18 may be included on their parents' passports, but if traveling alone they need both individual passports and authorization from their legal guardians. Visas are not required except for citizens of African countries, stateless persons, and citizens of countries with which Chile has no diplomatic relations. Carriers will supply the obligatory Tourist Card, valid for 90 days and renewable up to 180 days. This must be handed in upon leaving the country. Onward or return passages should be confirmed as soon as possible after arrival. A smallpox vaccination certificate is no longer required for new arrivals to Chile.

Tourists may bring in personal belongings, 400 cigarettes, 400 grammes of tobacco, 50 cigars, two open bottles of perfume, two liters of alcoholic beverages, and gifts. On leaving the country, they may take souvenirs and handicrafts not exceeding $500 in value.

Health Certificates are not required for entry into Chile.

There is a $12.50 **airport tax** payable upon departure.

GETTING TO CHILE. By air. *American, Pan Am, LAN-Chile,* and *Ladeco* offer direct service from Miami to Santiago. *Ladeco* offers direct service from Miami to Arica. Also *Avianca, Ecuatoriana, LAB, LAP,* and *AeroPeru* serve Santiago from the USA. *Canadian Pacific* offers service from Canada via Mexico.

From Europe, there is *Air France* from Paris; *Alitalia* from Rome; *Iberia* from Madrid; *KLM* from Amsterdam; *Lufthansa* from Frankfurt; *Swissair* from Geneva and Zurich; and *Varig* from London, Frankfurt, Paris, and Madrid. *LAN-Chile* also flies to Madrid and to Easter Island and Tahiti for connections to Australia and the Far East.

By sea. Chile can be reached by boat through any of its major seaports. Principal point of arrival is Valparaíso, one of the busiest ports on the Pacific Coast. The steamship companies reaching Chile are many and their services varied, but some of the most important ones are *Compañia Sud Americana de Vapores* from New York and the main ports of Europe; *Delta Line,* from the United States via the Panama Canal; and *Royal Netherlands S.S. Co.* from Rotterdam and Le Havre.

By train. From La Paz, Bolivia, there are railways to Arica.

By road. The Pan American Highway enters Chile through Arica. The Chilean portion is entirely paved, but a few poor stretches remain. TEPSA buses come to Chile from as far north as Ecuador.

CURRENCY. Local currency is the peso. Banking hours are from 9 A.M. to 2 P.M., Mon. through Fri. All banks have a foreign exchange section, but some work only in dollars. There is no obligation to exchange foreign currency for pesos upon arrival. At press time the exchange rate was approximately 340 pesos to the dollar.

Prices, unless noted otherwise, are in U.S. dollars.

HOTELS. Chile offers excellent accommodations that meet high international standards. Several hotels in Santiago and throughout the country rate a luxury classification. In all regions of Chile, whatever hotels may lack in facilities is more than made up by comfortable, homey atmosphere. Chile's famous hospitality is particularly evident in the provinces, where it is not uncommon to see the owner or the manager sit down to dinner with the guests.

The real problem with hotels is not in their quality but in their quantity. Many truly marvelous places in Chile are almost unknown because the facilities for people to visit them simply do not exist. Progress has been slow in this sense.

Chile's Tourist Department has bestowed its luxury classification on a few hotels in the country. As these are scattered, almost any region will have at least one. Some of them, as much because of their natural setting as their architectural beauty, are fabulous. The *Hotel Portillo,* for instance, is located at the famous ski resort and between June and September offers some of the world's most beautiful snowscapes, plus a beautiful frozen-over lagoon.

Throughout this chapter hotels have been classified according to price for double occupancy accommodations as follows: *Deluxe,* $85 and up; *Expensive,* $60–$85; *Moderate,* $35–$60; *Inexpensive,* below $35. Hotels in the provinces are generally *moderate* to *inexpensive.* Hotels are all EP and with 18 percent tax over quoted rates. Resort areas have reduced tariffs during the off-season (mid-Mar. to mid-Nov.). Advance bookings are essential in the resort areas.

RESTAURANTS. Traditionally, the Chilean is a homebody. Entertaining is done in the home. For this reason, Santiago was, until a few years ago, a very difficult town to paint red. The normal hour to begin dinner, either at home or in a restaurant, still remains 9–9:30 P.M., or later.

The tourist can find plenty of amusements, no matter how long his stay. Of course, most of this activity is centered in Santiago, but Viña del Mar and Valparaiso have their own fine offerings, especially in the busy summer season. In all three cities there is a noticeable lack of nightclubs; most places offer fine meals as well as opportunities to dance, and many have their own floorshows. The price ranges, given for a complete meal for one person, are: *Expensive,* $20 and up; *Moderate,* $15–$20; *Inexpensive,* below $15. A meal at dining/dancing restaurants, nightclubs, and discotheques runs anywhere from $5–$35. A service charge is no longer added to the bill in restaurants, but a tip is expected for good service (10 percent is customary).

Chilean Food and Drink. Chile is a cosmopolitan country, and this is strongly reflected in her food and drink. Santiago, for instance, is filled with French, Chinese, Italian, and Spanish restaurants, among those offering other international cuisines. But the real charm of wining and dining in the capital—or in any of Chile's cities— lies in the great quantity of foods and beverages that are typically Chilean.

There are a number of typical dishes that generally go over well with visitors. The highly flavorful dishes are for the most part rather simple to prepare and can be made back home fairly easily.

At the head of the list comes the *Empanada.* A very unsuitable translation would be meat pie, but at least that gives some sort of idea. Inside a flour pastry shaped like a small turnover goes a combination of meat and onions cut into small pieces, hard-boiled egg, raisins, and olives. The "pie" is baked in a hot oven until the crust is somewhat hardened and is generally served with red wine as the first course of a meal. It can also be made using chicken or fish as the staple ingredient.

Humitas are made from corn—the first of the season, since it must be tender. The corn is ground into a paste, seasoned, then wrapped in corn husks. These small bundles are then placed in a pot of boiling water for almost an hour. Separate the husks, and you have a Chilean dish, rather like the Mexican tamales but seldom so highly seasoned.

Pastel de Choclo (freely translated as "corn pie") is something of a cross between an Empanada and a Humita. The same *pino* (small pieces of meat, onions, raisins, and boiled egg) used in the Empanada are placed in an earthenware oven dish and topped with pieces of chicken and ground corn. The mixture is baked until the corn is brownish in color, then served hot.

The *Cazuela de Ave* is a kind of souped-up soup. It contains rice, corn, green beans, chicken, carrots, pumpkin, salt, and a number of herbs. After the mixture is boiled, it is served piping hot, often as the second course of a Chilean luncheon after the Empanada. Known as a common man's dish, it is often served in the best households as well.

Bife a lo Pobre is the name for a steak poor Chileans used to eat, but these days it would be difficult for a poor man to afford one. (Some have suggested the name be changed to *Bife a lo Rico.*) It is a big steak with fried potatoes and onions, and a pair of fried eggs is placed on the top of the steak when served.

The *Parrillada* contains a selection of meat grilled over hot coals. In most restaurants, the Parrillada is served on its own small grill, so that the heat is conserved as the diner makes his selection. Ordinarily accompanied by fried potatoes and some kind of salad, the Parrillada is a very popular and tasty dish. But a word to the squeamish eater: if you are not prepared to eat parts of a cow you had no idea were edible, you had better pass up the Parrillada and stick to a conventional *Filet* or *Entrecot* (T-bone).

Curanto is not so much a dish as a complete dinner. In Santiago, it is made in pots and served in some restaurants, but this is hardly authentic. In the southern region of Chile around Puerto Montt and especially on Tenglo Island, which faces Puerto Montt, the Curanto is prepared in a very different way. A hole is dug in the ground and stones placed in the bottom. Fires are lit on top of the stones. When they are red hot, the wood and ashes are swept away and the food, in sacks, is placed on top of the stones. Wet sacks go atop the food sacks, and on the wet sacks go several layers of earth and grass to conserve the heat inside. After several hours the "oven" is opened and the feast begins. The food inside the sacks is a rather mad combination of peas, pork, seafood, potatoes, and any number of other ingredients. But the result is incredibly tasty—and unforgettable.

Also common, especially in the countryside, is *Pan de Horno,* a country bread baked in an earthen oven. *Sopaipillas* (fried pumpkin patties) are very popular, especially on rainy days. And *Pan de Pascua* (fruitcake) is in almost every household at Christmastime.

Chile's seacoast (the longest in the world) naturally offers an immense variety of seafoods. And the list would be much longer if the Chileans so wanted, as there are many kinds of fish that are simply ignored by the population.

Best known of the *mariscos* (shellfish) are the huge lobsters from Juan Fernández Islands, among the best in the world. But equally enjoyable are the *centollas* (king crabs with spotted scales). These are found in the south and are especially famous around Punta Arenas.

Abalone are common—and good—throughout the country; so are sea urchins, clams, prawns, and giant mussels *(choros).* In the north, freshwater prawns grow to the size of small lobsters.

Chile's world-famous grapes are the base of its four most popular drinks. First, of course, is wine itself. Then comes *Pisco,* a powerful liquor distilled from grapes and most often seen in the *Pisco Sour Cocktail.* Grapes are also used to make *Chicha,* a medium-brown sweet beverage somewhat reminiscent of apple cider with added punch. The last, and most powerful, is *Aguardiente,* which translates literally into "fire water."

Chilean wines are world famous, and the fame is well deserved. As was already mentioned, countries like France, Canada, and the United States import Chilean wines of the better qualities. A bottle of good quality costs about $3.

The variety of Chilean wine is extremely wide. At the bottom of the scale are the common wines (which are of a remarkably good quality), normally consumed at home and in bars.

At the other end of the scale are the excellent high-quality table wines used on special occasions. Such well-known types as Cabernet, Borgoña (Burgundy), Rhin, and Pinot are a common sight on Chilean tables or in bars and restaurants. Due to the confusion from having some 20 well-known brands of wine, each of these with its individual classifications, the tourist would perhaps be best advised to decide on *tinto* (red) *or blanco* (white) and let the waiter supply the details. Or, if one wants to go *a la chilena,* he can just ask for *vino de la casa* (house wine).

Chileans boast of their wines, and they drink them in quantity. You would do well not to try to drink glass for glass with a Chilean, for the odds are that he has been drinking since childhood. From the time they are very young, children are given a little wine and water with their meals; the water is gradually eliminated as they grow older. Thus by the time they reach maturity, they are not only connoisseurs but have also acquired a considerable immunity to the alcoholic content.

Pisco is made only in Chile and Peru. It is colorless and has a slightly sweet smell and a very distinctive taste. In all its forms it looks and tastes innocent—but beware, for it never is. Commonest probably is the cocktail *Pisco Sour,* made with *pisco,* lemon juice, and sugar shaken together in ice and then made frothy by the addition of beaten egg white. A mixture of *pisco* and vermouth is called a *Pichuncho.* Also, dry ginger ale is used to make a long *pisco* drink.

Right after the grapes are in—around May—and during the September Independence Day celebrations, a favorite drink is *chicha,* a fermented grape-juice drink. Like *pisco,* this innocent looking, slightly sweet beverage has a kick of a mule.

Aguardiente is the most alcoholic of the four national drinks. Distilled from grapes and ordinarily clear in color, it also comes as a kind of brandy, *Armañac.* *Aguardiente* is the drink responsible for the fact that Chilean teatime goes under the name *las once.* Among the many legends told about the origin of this custom, this is one of the most interesting. In colonial days the men and women used to gather to have tea in the afternoon. The men would soon get bored with such a "lifeless" drink and slip off one by one to the kitchen pantry to uncork the bottle of *Aguardiente.* When someone noticed the absence and asked about it, the tolerant wife would explain, "Oh, he's having his *once." "Once"* in Spanish means eleven, and *Aguardiente* has eleven letters.

Aguardiente is also the base for one of the most popular drinks in the country, *Cola de Mono* (monkey's tail). Made with *Aguardiente,* coffee, milk, sugar, cinnamon, and egg yolk, it is served in most Chilean homes during the Christmas season but can also be found in some downtown bars throughout the year.

Beer is one of the drinks consumed in largest quantities in the country, perhaps because of the large German element in the population. Very popular because of its low price, beer can be found in many types throughout the country. Generally considered superior are the Condor Royal Guard, and Escudo brands in bottled beer and the draft beer *(schop).* Imported canned beer is available almost everywhere.

Also locally manufactured are a number of other liquors. The Chilean version of London Gin is quite good; locally made vodka is acceptable. Whisky sold under local trademarks is imported and bottled in Chile and is not unpalatable. However, almost all import restrictions have been lifted, and customs duties lowered, so that practically all brands of Scotch whisky are available at around $7 a bottle. In Chile, it is possible to find most of the soft drinks well known throughout the world, such as Coca-Cola, Pepsi Cola, Orange Crush, Ginger Ale, Orange Fanta, plus a number that are strictly Chilean: Bilz, fruit juices in bottles *(Nectar de Fruta),* and several brands of mineral and soda waters.

TIPPING. Restaurants and bars no longer add service charges to the bill, but waiters expect a 10 percent cash tip when service is good. City taxi drivers do not expect a tip, but for long distance or hire for long periods in the city, a tip may be given according to the service received. Taxis in the city are metered.

BUSINESS HOURS AND HOLIDAYS. Shops are open from 10 A.M. to 7 P.M., Sat. from 10 A.M. to 2 P.M. Post office, 9 A.M. to 4:30 P.M.; closed Sat. Banking hours are from 9 A.M. to 2 P.M. Mon. through Fri.

National Holidays. The following legal holidays are observed in Chile: January 1; Holy Week; May 1; May 21; August 15; September 11, 18, and 19; October 12; November 1; December 8; December 25.

TELEPHONES AND MAIL. Internal telephone service in Chile is automatic and fairly efficient. International service via satellite is excellent. Santiago is directly south of Boston, Massachusetts, so that the time of day in Chile is the same as in the Eastern zone of the U.S. There are public phones which cost 30 pesos. Telex and telefax are available. There are several international cable services.

Mail services to all parts of the world are good, but incoming deliveries are often slow. Don't use sea mail, since delays are enormous. Hotels will mail your letters.

NEWSPAPERS. There is no daily English-language newspaper published in Chile. However, Miami and New York airmail editions of current papers are widely available.

The leading Chilean daily newspapers are: *El Mercurio, La Tercera de la Hora, La Segunda,* and *La Nacion.*

ELECTRIC CURRENT. Chile runs on 220 volt current and uses European-style connection plugs. Major hotels in Santiago, however, have dual outlets and 110 volt converters are available at leading hotels throughout the country.

USEFUL ADDRESSES. Embassy of United States, Agustinas 1343, 5th Floor (71–01–33); **U.S. Consulate,** Merced 230 (71–01–33); **British Embassy and Consulate,** Avenida Concepcion 177, 4th Floor (223–9166); **Embassy of Canada,** Av. Ahumada 11, 10th Floor (696–2256).

Sernatur (government tourist office), Providencia 1550 (696–0474).

Automobile Club, Vitacura 8620 (212–5702).

LAN-Chile Airlines, Agustinas 640 (632–3442); **American Airlines,** Huérfanos 1199 (71–30–04); **Pan American,** Av. Libertador Bernardo O'Higgins 949, 23rd floor (71–09–19); **Ladeco,** Huérfanos 1157 (698–2233).

SECURITY. At press time the State Department recommended that U.S. citizens exercise caution when traveling in Chile. Travelers should be aware that bombings and other violent acts directed against Mormon churches and/or other institutions identified with the United States continue to occur. On arrival in Chile, U.S. citizens should seek the latest travel information and register with the consular section of the Embassy, Merced 230, Santiago (710–133). Nevertheless, Chile is essentially a safe country to visit. The national police force, the Carabineros, are well organized and effective crime fighters.

Visitors, however, should stay in central areas and avoid outlying poorer sections of town. The rule here as everywhere is, use your common sense.

GETTING AROUND CHILE. With its long coastline, obviously the best way to see Chile should be by boat, but unfortunately the coastal lines are not basically passenger ships and don't offer much in the way of amenities. A trip south through the canals is really worth the trouble, though. Contact Naviera Magallanes, Miraflores 178, piso 12, Santiago.

Transportation between Santiago and the Valparaíso area, including Viña del Mar, is excellent and there is a good road. Buses run frequently, and collective taxis are available all day. There is also frequent bus service to the coast villages and towns to the south and north of Valparaíso.

Looking northward, La Serena is a town likely to attract the visitor. There are frequent buses along the Pan American Highway. There are bus services—frequent in summer, less so in winter—to the local places of interest, and there is a delightful little railway up the valley to Rivadavia, via Vicuña, Gabriela Mistral's birthplace. If you think you may be late for the down service after your visit, tell the driver, and he'll probably wait for you.

There are buses to Copiapo, the mining district and attractive town.

Antofagasta, the largest town in the north, can be reached by road, air or sea.

For the northern towns, use *LADECO* (this is an abbreviation for "Linea Aerea del Cobre," or Copper Airline, which was formed primarily to serve the copper mines of the north).

To Iquique, travel by bus or plane.

Finally, sitting right on the Peruvian border is Arica, served by *LADECO* and *LAN-Chile* and frequent buses (which provide a fascinating ride—although rather tiring after 1,500 miles—over the desert). The valleys behind Arica have very little transport, and almost the only way to see them is by rented car.

Going south from Santiago, Talca is on the main rail route and on the Pan American Highway bus routes. It is also united with Argentina by way of a road through the Vicente Perez Rosales Pass. The Lagoon is reached by paved roads, and there are bus and car services.

Bus service connects Constitución with the capital, and rail service links it with Talca. It is possible to arrive in private plane by landing at Quivolgo.

Chillán is connected to Santiago by bus and train and airplane service. Side trips to the ski slopes and thermal baths can be made by train part way and then by car (50 miles east of Chillán; the beautiful and scenic road is 70 percent paved).

Concepción can be reached by land, sea, and air with well-established services in all three systems. The airport is Carriel Sur. The State Railway has a Santiago-Concepcion run, and the bus service is quite good. The road is paved all the way. Steamships on their way to Puerto Montt and Punta Arenas stop at Talcahuano.

The State Railways Information Bureau on Avenida Arturo Prat in Temuco can give the current complete information on the many excursions possible from this city. As a general rule, the starting point for all of them is Temuco.

Many of the lakes are in the province of Valdivia, and most excursions start from there. A road connects Valdivia with San Martín de los Andes, Argentina, and the Pan American Highway links it with Santiago. Las Marías and Pichoy are the airports, and a branch of the Santiago-Puerto Montt railroad goes there. For the most part, it's a bit difficult to make such arrangements on your own. To get to Lake Ranco, for example, several train combinations are necessary. This, combined with the difficulty of getting reservations in season, makes it almost imperative for the tourist to let a travel agency help him to see the south. There is good bus service from Santiago but, again, only to the principal cities.

As is the case of Valdivia, there is excellent transportation to Osorno and to Puerto Montt by train or bus. But to get from these centers to the lakes themselves is more complicated. Some taxis take passengers where there are no local buses, but this varies from city to city and lake to lake. For this reason, it is always best to consult a travel agent before heading south. They know the ins and outs to unravel what might otherwise become too complicated. Many times private planes are used to simplify the trips.

Boat service to Easter Island and Robinson Crusoe Island is infrequent and unreliable. TAXPA private airline (Nueva York 53, Room 102) operates nonscheduled service to Robinson Crusoe and Transportes Aereos Robinson Crusoe operates regular flights twice a week from October to March (Agustinas 1173, Santiago). For Easter Island, LAN-Chile makes twice-weekly stops outward bound to Tahiti, and the same on its return flights to Chile. Transportation is also available to tour the island.

Punta Arenas has boat and air contact with the rest of Chile. The boats leave from Valparaíso or Puerto Montt, and LAN-Chile and LADECO fly daily from Santiago to Pres. Ibañez del Campo airport, run by the Chilean Air Force. For excursions within and outside the city, contact the efficient Turismo Comapa, Independencia 840 (225–505).

Two excellent 79- and 150-passenger cruise ships, the M/N *Skorpios I* and *II,* offer weekly six-day cruises south from Puerto Montt to the impressive glacier at Lake San Rafael. The trip through southern Chile's canals and islands is a sightseeing spectacular. Cruises start at $650, everything included. This is one of Chile's best kept travel secrets and one of South America's best travel experiences.

There are almost 150 tourist agencies in Chile, 78 of them in Santiago. Many specialize in different parts of the country. Hotels will put the visitor in touch with the appropriate agency and make recommendations.

All major rental car franchises are in Chile, roads are well-maintained and well-policed, and there are regular security checks.

SPORTS. Chileans participate in almost every sport common to countries in the Western Hemisphere. Without spectacular success, but with plenty of enthusiasm, Chile has been represented at the Olympic Games (summer and winter), the World Championship of Football (soccer), riding championships, international athletic meets, and a host of other competitive events, especially tennis.

All of Chile is crazy for football (soccer). Chileans have happily seen their soccer teams grow from adolescence to maturity in a short time.

While Football is King, there are other sports in which Chile has an outstanding record. Recently its participants won the South American Riding Championship, and Captain Larraguibel still holds the world record in high jumping. Chile was a finalist in the 1976 Davis Cup championships.

Skiing. With the abundance of mountain ranges come an abundance of places to ski (June to September), such as the ski resorts of Farellones, Lagunillas, and Portillo and the new Ski Center with a ski lift in the south of the slopes of the Villarrica Volcano. Portillo, located five hours by train from Santiago, is the country's ski capital and boasts fine accommodations, several chairlifts and tows, and a six-mile run. Other smaller runs are located as close as 32-miles from Santiago, Swiss and Austrian ski pros operate Chile's ski schools.

The biggest skiing news in Chile is Valle Nevado, the most ambitious ski resort ever planned in South America. Located 40 miles from Santiago, Valle Nevado opened the first eight of its planned 50 ski lifts in June 1988 amid 22,000 Andean acres of slopes. Here virgin runs stretch as long as 10 miles and climb as high as 17,908 feet. Information from: Valle Nevado, Gertrudis Echeñique 441 (480–839) or Gray Line Ski Tours: Box 1001, Santiago (698–2164).

New ski facilities are now well organized throughout Chile. Outside the Santiago area the most popular resort is Chillán, located 50 miles from the city of Chillán, featuring an 102-room hotel, thermal baths, four large open-air swimming pools fed by volcanic springs, and five ski runs, the largest served by a 8,202-foot double-chair lift. Also popular is the ski center at Villarrica Volcano. Here a new 1800-foot chairlift offers wide-open descents set against the spectacular backdrop of the Chilean lakes below with a massive smoking volcanic cone above. A 36-room Refugio-Hosteria is located at the base of the lift. Scores of excellent hotels are available to skiiers in nearby Pucon and Villarrica.

A new ski center is also under development on the slopes of Osorno Volcano, 37 miles from Puerto Varas. Two lodges can now accommodate 150 persons. A 1,968 foot T-bar lift is in operation.

Fifty miles from Temuco, on the slopes of the Llaima Volcano, is the Llaima ski resort in the Los Paraguas National Park, so named because of the lovely snow-covered trees that resemble umbrellas. Two lodges can accommodate about 170 guests, and there is a mile-long ski lift. Here you can ski year round.

Water Sports. Beaches and lakes all through the country give ample opportunities for every water sport from skin diving to water skiing. Boating is another favorite pastime with Chileans and visitors, and there are facilities for deepsea fishing in the north, at Tocopilla and Antofagasta (Mar./Sept.) Skin diving is good along the whole coast.

Chile is a fisherman's paradise. A license is required, which may be obtained from the "Club de Pesca y Caza" (Rod and Gun Club) in any city.

In the north there's deepsea fishing all year round for tuna, bonito, swordfish, black marlin, striped marlin, and shark. In the central valley are found brown trout and pejerrey. The really good rainbow trout fishing is in the south, where a 10-pound fish is a little fellow.

For fishing tours down south, trout fishing enthusiasts can now arrange angling expeditions on a comfortable six-birth motorboat to remote northern Patagonia (south of Puerto Montt). For information contact Puma Fishing, Pedro de Valdivia 0169, Santiago. Also the Rod and Gun Club secretary can be helpful if you're interested. The same club will arrange for licenses to hunt quail, partridge, snipe, doves, rabbits, ducks, and others.

Spectator Sports. A number of country clubs and stadiums allow visitors to participate in or watch such sports as basketball, tennis, volleyball, golf, horseback riding, track events, hockey, polo, rugby, and bowling. Many of the resident foreigners belong to country clubs where all sports are practiced.

In sports spectacles, football again occupies the top spot. The Football Association organizes many international games in which the most famous teams of the world have come to play, though they have never found it easy to beat the Chilenos. These matches, as well as most other sporting events, are held in the state-owned National Stadium, with a seating capacity of 80,000. The World Basketball Championship took place there, as did part of the World Football Championship of 1962. Much of the national competition in football takes place in the stadium each year, and important swimming, tennis and track events are usually held there.

Horse Racing. Horse racing fans have plenty of opportunities to enjoy the sport. In Santiago there are two race tracks, the *Hipódromo Chile,* open Saturdays and every other Wednesday, and the *Club Hípico,* open Sundays and the other Wednesday. Races normally start at 2 P.M. In Viña del Mar, races are held at the Sporting Club, open all day on holidays.

See also "Adventure Vacations" chapter.

Exploring Chile

SANTIAGO

"Santiago," as Chileans are often heard to say a bit critically, "is Chile." And they are very right. Santiago is not only the capital politically, but economically, and culturally as well.

Not that there is no activity outside the big city. Such cities as Valparaíso (principal port on the Pacific coast), Viña del Mar (the Pacific coast's most fashionable vacation spot), and Concepción (home of a fine university and center of the steel and coal mining industry) cannot be bypassed so easily. Nor can Arica in the far north, Punta Arenas in the far south, and many other cities in between.

But Santiago is the center of it all. The government reduced former extreme centralism by establishing 12 "Regions" with considerable local power, and Congress was moved to new quarters in Valparaíso. Still, most government agencies and principal offices are in the capital; thus, headquarters of the biggest industries and companies are too. By sheer weight of the population, now over 4 million, Santiago is also the center of cultural life and boasts three of South America's top educational institutions: the University of Chile (state-run and the largest), the Catholic University (private), and the University of Santiago.

The tourist's interest in Santiago is centered around the many activities and natural beauty. The Andes form an inspiring backdrop and there are many hills within the city itself. The downtown area is one of Latin America's busiest, its streets overflowing with people rushing about shopping or tending to their businesses. However, this city seems to suffer more than a normal amount of air pollution during the colder months, April through mid-September, most probably produced by an excessive number of public buses. Luckily, the new government has decided to face the problem.

The main downtown street is called Avenida Bernardo O'Higgins, or, more simply, the *Alameda*. Once a branch of the Mapocho River, it was later dried up and converted into a modern, wide thoroughfare. Right downtown on this main street stands Santa Lucía Hill, an amazing example of what can be done with an unappealing area. The hill is regarded as the birthplace and bulwark of Santiago, as it was here Don Pedro de Valdivia founded the city and from here Don Casimiro Marcó del Pont, the last Spanish governor, defended the city from attacks by Independence-seeking Chilenos. Mapuche Indians had earlier dedicated it to the God of Pain (Huelén) and Christians erected on its summit the very first hermitage and the first Cross of the Conquest.

National hero Bernardo O'Higgins first had the idea of using the hill as a cultural attraction when he tried to build an observatory and a parthenon atop it. But decades were to pass before historian, politician, writer, and great patriot Don Benjamín Vicuña Mackenna made the dreams of O'Higgins come true. From 1872 to 1874, he directed the work by convicts which transformed the hill from an eyesore to the lovely, unique park it is today.

The hill is a kind of living museum, since two fortresses constructed by Marcó del Pont still remain: one, the Castillo González, overlooks the "Alameda" and provides a wonderful view of the city from its main terrace; and the other, Castillo Hidalgo, now houses the Popular Arts Museum in what were once the dungeons. Many claim Santa Lucia is one of the loveliest parks in the Americas.

San Cristóbal Hill

Santa Lucia, at 240 feet above street level, is small in comparison to San Cristóbal Hill. Usually the first sight to impress a visitor to Santiago, this hill is 1,200 feet high and adorned with a statue of the Virgin Mary, France's gift to Chile. At night the big statue is flooded with lights and can be seen from almost any point of the city. San Cristóbal is within easy walking distance from downtown, four blocks across the Mapocho River. The best way to reach San Cristóbal's summit is by the cable car that offers a 6,646-foot ride to a terrace, where there is a small café, many gardens, and walkways. The ride is the best sightseeing trip in Santiago and the cable car leaves every 14 seconds. This means there is seldom a line and no waiting, even on holidays.

The view is absolutely marvelous. Set aside a couple of hours and get to the top just before sunset; then wait to watch the lights begin to twinkle on until the whole city stretched out before you becomes a giant birthday cake. Needless to say, this place is a favorite spot for lovers.

A third of the way up San Cristóbal is the city zoo, which can be reached by car, funicular, or, for hiking enthusiasts, walking. The animals are kept in places very similar to their natural habitats, taking advantage of the hill's mountainlike appearance. Especially interesting is the zoo's collection of typically Chilean animals and birds.

There is also the very attractive Tupahue swimming pool surrounded by lawns and gardens.

In the same group of hills to which the San Cristóbal belongs is the Pirámide, so called because of a small monument there honoring Don Manuel de Salas, one of Chile's founding fathers. The monument was erected by British merchant John O'Brien, who sided with the South American colonies and joined General San Martín's forces to fight the Spanish. He became San Martín's principal collaborator and lived many years in Chile, his second country. Because he used to live in what is now Pirámide del Salto del Agua, he decided to dedicate a monument to the man who had been kind enough to give him the place. San Martín himself used to go there after fighting to rest his nerves and restore his energies.

At the foothills of San Cristóbal, the bohemian and picturesque Bellavista district can be a delightful experience, thanks to its moderately priced restaurants with local atmosphere, small theaters, art galleries, and live music.

But once you are off the hills and back downtown, a logical place to start your tour of the center is La Moneda, the Presidential Palace. The Palace was designed by Joaquín Toesca and completed in 1805. It now houses the Ministry of Interior and the Foreign Affairs Ministry, as well as the presidential offices. On two sides of it are tall buildings housing governmental offices, the postal and telegraph building, and the *Hotel Carrera*. One plaza behind La Moneda (toward the Alameda) has a statue of former President Arturo Alessandri Palma, and another in front of it (on Moneda Street) is now Constitution Plaza and site of the ceremony of the changing of the Palace Guards.

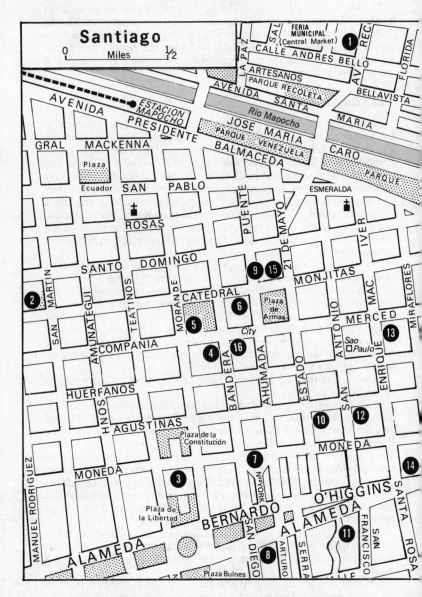

Points of Interest

1) Recoleta Franciscana Church
2) Church of Santa Ana
3) Palacio de La Moneda
4) Tribunales de Justicia
5) Congreso Nacional
6) Cathedral
7) Church of Augustinas
8) Universidad de Chile
9) Post Office
10) San Augustin Church
11) San Francisco Church
12) Municipal Theater
13) La Merced Church
14) Biblioteca Nacional
15) Museo Historico

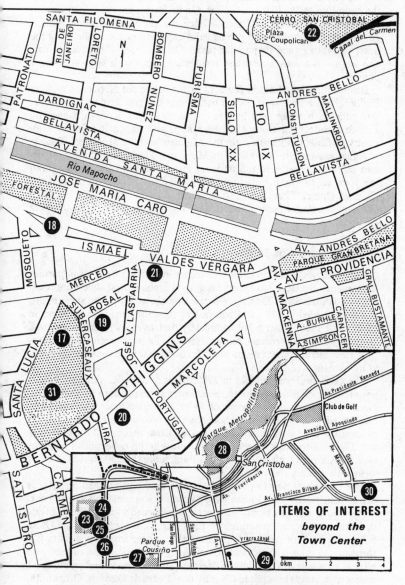

16) Museo Precolombino
17) Museum of Popular Arts
18) Museo de Bellas Artes
19) Church of Vera Cruz
20) Clinica Universidad Catolica
21) U.S. Embassy
22) Zoological Garden
23) Quinta Normal

24) Museum of Contemporary Art
25) Museum of Natural Science
26) Universidad de Santiago
27) Club Hipico
28) Virgen del San Cristobal
29) Estadio Nacional
30) Prince of Wales Country Club
31) Cerro Santa Lucia

Five blocks from La Moneda, as you walk away from the Alameda, is the main square, the Plaza de Armas. On its fringes are the relic-filled Cathedral, the sprawling Central Post Office, and the Municipality of Santiago. Delightful cobblestoned promenades closed to motor traffic cross the heart of Santiago and its popular plaza. On two sides of the plaza—east and south—is a commercial and residential center with large apartment houses.

Behind the Cathedral, on Bandera Street, is the old National Congress Building. Since the newly elected parliament has relocated to Valparaíso, this building is being used by one of the ministries. It was designed by French architect Ambroise Henault, who is also responsible for the University of Chile headquarters on the Alameda and the Municipal Theater at Agustinas and San Antonio. The Municipal Theater is the most important cultural center, and top national groups perform there throughout the year, as do international attractions like the Bolshoi Ballet and the Chinese Opera. There are also performances by the Ballet Nacional Chileno, the Philarmonic Orchestra of Santiago, and the brilliant Opera Nacional.

The Churches of Santiago

As a Catholic country, Chile's churches are among its most important monuments. Santiago has many, ranging in architectural style from modern to colonial. Santo Domingo, located on the street of the same name, was inaugurated in 1771 and was one of the most beautiful churches in Chile until 1963, when a fire completely destroyed its interior and roof. Only the stone walls remain, but its style can still be appreciated from outside. Reconstruction has begun and the church has been declared a national monument.

The Cathedral was finished in 1788. Most of its relics and holy figures are of Jesuit origin, brought to the country or made here by that order. Notable are the wooden figure of Saint Francis Xavier and the 17th-century silver lamp weighing more than 50 pounds. In the sacristy, full of furniture several centuries old, is a magnificent painting of the Last Supper. The monstrance is the most striking piece in this collection of religious objects. Adorned with emeralds and rubies, more than 30 pounds of silver went into making the vessels.

The Church of San Francisco, begun in 1568 and finished in 1618, is of a style inspired by the Italian Renaissance. It was constructed with enormous stones, and practically no mortar was needed to unite them. Inside it, in the cloister, are paintings by Juan Zapata, a member of the Quito School of the 17th century. Separating the cloister from the sacristy is a three-leaved door with evident Renaissance inspiration, and in the main altar is an image of Our Lady of Mercy; carved of wood and standing 11 inches high, it was brought to Chile by Don Pedro de Valdivia. Other notable images are those of Saint Francis of Assisi, founder of the order that lives in the adjoining monastery; Saint Michael, dating from 1594; and the Christ of La Caña, brought from Lima in 1630.

Other churches worth a visit are San Agustín, Agustinas and Estado Streets; La Merced, at Compañía and McIver; Santa Ana, Cathedral and San Martín; Recoleta Dominica, seven blocks from Mapocho Train Station on Recoleta Street; and Recoleta Franciscana, at the beginning of Recoleta Street.

Santiago's Museums

Worth a visit is Chile's *Museo Historico Nacional,* Plaza de Armas 951, which offers a complete presentation of Chile's history. San Francisco Church, Londres 4, has a good collection of religious art. The *Museo Precolombino,* Bandera 305, has an excellent archaeological collection. The *Fine Arts* Museum at one side of the lovely Parque Forestal offers permanent exhibitions of the works of Chilean artists and several interesting shows throughout the year. For the mechanically minded, there is an aviation museum and a vintage car museum.

PRACTICAL INFORMATION FOR SANTIAGO

GETTING AROUND SANTIAGO. By Metro. Santiago's modern Metro is one of the world's finest subway systems. Visitors will find the two main lines run to most major sites and areas they want to visit. The subway is well organized, immaculately clean, and one of the city's showcases. Fares are very inexpensive (less than 20 cents) and service operates from 6:30 A.M. to 10:30 P.M. On Sat. and Sun., they run from 7:15 A.M. to 11:30 P.M.

By car. Hertz, Avis, and National have agencies in Santiago. Hertz has locations throughout Chile. Rates are expensive. Sample rate: a Suzuki costs approximately $200 a week plus 18% tax and insurance. For brief stays in Chile, the visitor's home license is sufficient; for longer stays, bring an international license. All firms require a major credit card.

By bus. Intercity buses are good and comfortable, and some have bar and toilet facilities. Chileans travel mostly by bus, because buses are cheaper and run more frequently than the railroads do.

The State Railways offer acceptable service to the South in "automotor saloons," with bar service and music.

For many out-of-town runs—Viña del Mar, for instance—there are collective taxis which make quick excursions at modest rates.

HOTELS. Santiago offers a wide range of hotels in every price category. Leading hotels include the new Crowne Plaza, Sheraton San Cristobal, and the traditional downtown Carrera. Ask the National Tourist Board (Providencia 1550) for their *Practical Guide to Santiago,* in English, which includes hotels. For definitions of our price categories see "Facts at Your Fingertips."

Deluxe

Carrera. Teatinos 180 (698–2011). Facing Plaza de la Constitución and La Moneda Palace, right downtown. 324 recently decorated rooms—singles, doubles, and suites—all with private bath and telephone. Air-conditioned.

Crowne Plaza Holiday Inn. Bernardo O'Higgins 136 (381–042). Has 304 rooms and features pool, tennis courts, playground, bars, nightclubs, and reception, banquet, and convention facilities. Conveniently located downtown.

Plaza San Francisco Kempinski. Av. Bernardo O'Higgins 816 (393–832). Recently opened with 110 elegant and modern air-conditioned rooms, the hotel features pool, bar, snack bar, convention facilities, and large parking garage. Good international restaurant. Located in front of Colonial San Francisco Church and within walking distance of important downtown landmarks.

Sheraton San Cristobal Hotel and Towers. Av. Santa Maria 1742 (274–5000). 350 rooms with bath, TV, air-conditioning. In elegant residential district, 10 minutes by taxi from downtown. Good international, local specialties in restaurant. Superb mountain views. Cocktail lounge. Pools, shops.

Expensive

El Conquistador. Miguel Cruchaga 920, and Estado (696–5599). A first-class hotel in the very heart of the business, shopping, and entertainment center. 133 single and twin-bedded rooms and suites, all with private bath and telephone. Good international cuisine, grill room, coffee shop, and American bar.

Galerias. San Antonio 65 (384–011). 162-room hotel located downtown at the corner of Moneda. The Gallerias is popular with commercial travelers.

Hostal Del Parque. Merced 294 (392–694). New apartment hotel featuring 30 apartment suites with kitchenette. It is located beside the U.S. Consulate. A European-style exclusive residence.

Manquehue. Esteban dell 'Orto 6615 (220–9269). In exclusive Las Condes area. New 23-room hotel with quiet two-floor setting beside park. Small swimming pool, bar, sauna, restaurant. Beautiful all-wood interior.

Río Bidasoa. Vitacura 4873 (242–1525). In elegant Vitacura area with 30 rooms, swimming pool, bar, restaurant, telephone, and color TV. Ideal for executives.

Tupahue. San Antonio 477 (383–810). Modern building. Downtown. 207 double and twin rooms, all with private bath, completely carpeted, air-conditioned. Music, telephone, and TV. Dining rooms and self-service cafeteria, grill. Music bar. Temperate swimming pool.

Moderate

Hotel de Don Tito. Huérfanos 578 (391–987). Small hotel with 6 suites, 8 twins, 8 singles. Bar. Homey atmosphere.

Foresta. Victoria Subercaseaux 353 (396–262). Excellent location facing Santa Lucia Hill. 40 suites. Spanish dining room, bar, tea room, conference room.

Gran Palace. Huérfanos 1178, 10th floor (712–551). 72 rooms, some suites, in modern new building, all with private bath and telephone. Grill, American bar, roof terrace garden. Room service and valet service at all times. Transportation to and from railway stations, bus stations, airport. Garage for parking.

Libertador. Bernardo O'Higgins Ave. 853 (394–213). Good location, on the Alameda facing old San Francisco church. 115 rooms, each with phone, radio, bath. Restaurant, laundry, and room service. In the same building: beauty parlor and Turkish baths for ladies.

Panamericano. Huérfanos and Teatinos (723–060). Two blocks from the Moneda Palace on Teatinos Street, 90 rooms with private baths, all looking toward the street facing the magnificent Andes. All rooms with telephone and radio. Room service. Bus service. Garage. Good bar.

Santa Lucia. Huérfanos 779 (398–201). 65 rooms with private baths and telephones occupying three floors of modern downtown building. One- or two-bedroom suites with living room and kitchenette. Monthly rates available. Terrace Restaurant and Winter Garden Restaurant serve good meals. Room service, laundry, shoe shine, beauty parlor, and parking facilities.

RESTAURANTS. For definitions of price categories see "Facts at Your Fingertips."

Deluxe

Aquí está Coco. Among the finest in town for seafood specialties. Wine-tasting "cave," international atmosphere. La Concepción 236.

La Cascade. Excellent French food. Fairly *expensive,* but worth it. Ave. Francisco Bilbao 1947.

Coco Loco. An elegant seafood restaurant. Rancagua 0554.

Puerto Marisko. Fine seafood and nice atmosphere. Isidora Goyenechea 2918.

Expensive

Aji Verde. Traditional Chilean dishes and Latin American music, within picturesque Bellavista district. Constitución 284.

Bali Hai. Polynesian atmosphere, Easter Island show. Av. Colon 5146.

Caleta Los Leones. Shellfish specialties. Los Leones 195.

Canto del Agua. Seafood and international cuisine. Nueva de Lyon 0129.

Chez Henry. Chilean and international cuisine. Portal Fernandez Concha 962, downtown.

Don Carlos. Argentine steakhouse with tango entertainment. Sebastian Elcano, corner of Colón.

Le Due Torri. Very good Italian cuisine. International atmosphere. Isidora Goyenechea 2908.

Enoteca. In San Cristobal. Hilltop. A super view of Santiago, city of glass walls. Excellent music and fine food. A special place downstairs for learning about vineyards and to taste the finest wine, *piscos* of the North and South zone.

La Estancia. International food, excellent steak, folkloric music. Las Condes 13810.

Maistral. French, Chilean, international cuisine. Exclusive and *expensive*. Air conditioning. Spanish, English, French, German, Italian spoken. Mosqueto 485.

El Otro Sitio. Peruvian specialties. Antonia Lope de Bello 53.

Moderate

Los Adobes de Argomedo. Good restaurant to sample Chilean specialties with nightly folklore show. Downtown. Argomedo 411.

Canta Gallo. 150-year-old beautiful building with the "Comilona a la Chilena" (eat all you want at a *reasonable* price) every Mon. and Fri. Show with typical Chilean music. Av. Las Condes 12345.

Da Carla. Excellent Italian food downtown. MacIver 577.

Casablanca. International cuisine and U.S.-style luncheon buffet. Nightly show. Holiday Inn Crowne Plaza Hotel.

Giratorio. Elegant new restaurant featuring international menu. Located on 16th floor, the restaurant revolves slowly for panoramic view of Providencia. Nva. Providencia 2250.

Munchen. Excellent service and best German food in Santiago. El Bosque 204.

El Villorrio. Downtown restaurant with typical Chilean specialties. San Antonio 676.

Inexpensive

Casa de Cena. Bargain-priced Chilean and international food. Almirante Simpson 20.

El Naturista. Natural foods. Moneda 846.

Los Buenos Muchachos. Chilean specialties and folkloric entertainment. Cumming 1031.

TOURIST INFORMATION. Chile's energetic National Tourist Office (SERNATUR) maintains helpful offices in the city's international airport and at its new building in Providencia 1550 (251–7469). City brochures and maps are available free.

TOURS. Three excellent tour companies offer sightseeing and special interest tours (to wine cellars, vineyards, ski resorts, and rural areas). Leading tour operators are Cocha Turismo, Latour, and Sportstours.

Cocha Turismo, Agustinas 1173 (698–3341), Santiago.

Latour, Suite 602, Agustinas 1476 (727–918).

Sportstours, Teatinos 333, 10th Floor (696–8832).

MUSEUMS. Worth a visit is Chile's *Museo Historico Nacional,* Plaza de Armas 951 (381–411), which offers a complete presentation of Chile's history. San Francisco Church has a good collection of religious art. The new *Museo de Arte PreColombino,* Bandera 361 (717–284), and *Museo de Bellas Artes,* Parque Forestal (330–655), are also well worth visiting. For the mechanically minded, there is an aviation museum and a vintage car museum. Museums are open Tues. through Sat. from 10 A.M. to 6 P.M.; Sun. and holidays 10 A.M. to 1 P.M.

SHOPPING. Because Chile is considered a developing country, you can bring many of the locally made products that you buy there into the U.S. duty free under the GSP plan, as explained in *Facts at Your Fingertips,* earlier in this volume.

There are today almost no import restrictions in Chile, and the shops are well stocked with imported goods of all kinds. Most brands of American cigarettes are available everywhere, and a few English, at an average price of $1 per pack of 20 cigarettes.

Among Chilean goods, the excellent textiles are worth mentioning. For "typical" items, colorful hand-woven ponchos are a good buy, also vicuña rugs, and—although perhaps a little heavy for air travel—there is excellent artisan copper work.

Chilean stones have achieved much popularity abroad, and there are many "rock shops" in the city and suburbs selling quality work in lapis lazuli, Chilean jade, amethyst, agate, onyx, and others.

There are enormous price differences from shop to shop, so it is as well to look around before buying. In some of the smaller shops it is still possible to bargain for a lower price, but not in the big department stores. Take a slow wander through the many arcades *(pasajes)* in the city center and in Providencia, which has become a big shopping area.

Best shopping bargains for Chilean crafts and art can often be found at the government operated CEMA shops. The main CEMA store is located in Santiago at Portugal 351.

NIGHTLIFE. Discos are the center of Santiago's nightlife. Most popular spots are: **Gente,** Apoquindo 4900; **La Scala,** Cerro San Cristobal; **Casamila,** Alvaro Casanova 298-A; and **Disco Brass,** Hotel Crown Plaza.

We recommend that those visitors who want entertainment in the Chilean capital choose one of the many popular restaurants offering folklore shows. These include **Los Buenos Muchachos, Aji Verde,** and **Los Adobes de Argomedo.**

There are no casinos in Santiago.

EXCURSIONS FROM SANTIAGO

From Santiago it is easy to reach many other interesting cities and areas in Chile.

Las Vertientes is 40 minutes away by car in the direction of San José de Maipo through Puente Alto. The nearby Maipo River offers an extra attraction.

Or go to El Arrayán, located on the banks of the Mapocho River on the road to the Farellones ski resort. It is only 20 minutes from downtown Santiago by car, and buses and *liebres* (small buses) also make the trip. Hostería El Arrayán has a swimming pool for guests and offers a magnificent view of the mountains and rivers. The crisp mountain air is wonderful. On the road to El Arrayán are several restaurants, some of them rather rustic. In the Las Condes area is La Estancia, which features Chilean music and singing, as well as good food.

Continuing on the same road you will reach Farellones, 30 miles from Santiago and some 7,400 feet above sea level. It has six ski lifts, one of them a chair lift rising all the way to the top of Colorado Hill—10,664 feet above sea level. The fields of Farellones and Colorado have acquired a well-deserved international fame, and many competitions are held there during the skiing season—from the last of May through mid-October. Accommodations are good, if somewhat scarce. There are 75 *refugios* (guest houses), 15 belonging to clubs and 60 in private hands. A store rents all the necessary equipment, and there are several snack bars. Transportation is pretty good during the whole season, with a daily service of buses, cars, and trucks. It's a fine weekend or one-day trip.

Three miles farther up on the road are the La Parva slopes, very popular with Santiaguinos. La Parva has three poma lifts, one over a mile long, and several chairlifts to some of the most challenging slopes. There is a small restaurant for the public, but most visitors lodge at nearby Farellones.

Lagunillas ski fields are farther along the same road to Las Vertientes. There the fields are good and the accommodations adequate. Several clubs and private *refugios* take guests. There is a chair lift about a mile long, and Lagunillas offers several long ski trips, some of which must be taken with a guide. Transportation to Lagunillas is by car and bus in a two-hour trip.

On the road into the Andes is the mountain town of El Volcán, from which many mountain hikes can be taken, and farther up Lo Valdes, practically the Andes themselves. Nearby are the Morales Thermal Baths, 6,000 feet above sea level (58 miles from Santiago, 8 from El Volcán). The baths are supposedly good for respiratory ailments, as is the climate.

The Central Valley has its own share of attractions. The town of Maipo, where the great Battle of Maipo took place, has a museum, a monolith commemorating the battle, and a temple to the Virgin of Carmen built after O'Higgins' promise. A Parthenon of the Heroes pays homage to the men who took part in the famous independence battle. Maipo also has a good swimming pool with a good restaurant; the top rodeo of the year is held there with competitors from all over the country.

About 37 miles southwest from Santiago, near Melipilla, is the town of Pomaire, well known for its pottery and ceramics. The craftsmanship has been handed down for countless generations, and collectors of original folkloric art will find many pieces worth taking home. The trip is best made by car. Pomaire pottery can also be found in Santiago's central market and at many art stores.

Two full-day excursions increasingly popular with visitors are the Monaco's Country Day Tour, a delightful Chilean-style house and farm only one half hour from downtown with a large swimming pool, horseback riding, country lunch, open bar, and a homey atmosphere; and the tour to Los Lingues, a historic colonial ranch-hacienda built in 1710 and located 78 miles from Santiago. Los Lingues features Chilean equestrian exhibitions and excellent food and drink.

Santiago province has many beach resorts: San Antonio is a busy seaport and seafood center; Cartagena is a very popular vacation spot. Others are San Sebastián, Las Cruces, Isla Negra, El Tabo—all with beautiful beaches and agreeable climates. El Tabo has a white sand beach; from there to the north they are yellow-white, to the south grey-white. El Quisco is one of the best beaches of the region, and in summer it is heavily populated with Santiaguinos and tourists. Algarrobo has extremely peaceful waters because a big rocky island just off the coast breaks the waves. The sea here is as peaceful as a pond, and for this reason it is a top spot for yachting, skin diving, and water skiing. Transportation to and from this area is excellent, especially during summer. A train services Cartagena, and buses reach every other town in the area, which is crowded in summer.

Special mention is due to Rocas de Santo Domingo beach resort, located in the same area south of San Antonio. The road to the resort passes through Llo-Lleo, with its wonderful climate, and Tejas Verdes. Before arriving in Santo Domingo, one must cross a bridge stretching more than a mile over the Maipo River. The town has marvelous gardens and houses, and a splendid golf course. A small hotel, the Piedra del Sol, offers five seaside cabins.

Other beach resorts are located in the nearby province of Aconcagua. Papudo, Zapallar, Maitencillo, and Marbella are all easily reached by bus or car; the trip to Papudo, the most distant, takes about three hours.

The world-famous ski resort of Portillo, site of the 1966 world Ski Championships, is also in Aconcagua province. Located at 9,300 feet above sea level, Portillo boasts ski slopes more than 2,000 feet long, plus ice-skating rinks. Classes for novices in both ice-skating and skiing are given by champions from the U.S., France, Austria, and Chile. The winter sports season begins in June and lasts through September. The natural beauty of Portillo is further enhanced by Laguna del Inca, 300 feet from the *Hotel Portillo*. During winter it becomes a skating rink, and during summer it is a sailing and fishing spot.

Portillo has first-class facilities. With several ski lifts and two chair lifts, the snazzy six-floor *Hotel Portillo* (231–3411 in Santiago) is easily the best resort of its kind on the continent. Transportation is provided by tourist bus or private car. Travel agencies will help make arrangements during the season.

VALPARAISO AND THE COAST

The tourist arriving in Chile by ship may well think that his first view— the many hills surrounding the port with houses miraculously clinging to their sides—cannot be surpassed by anything else in the country. And the visitor who has arrived by air or by way of Los Andes will be equally surprised when he takes the trip to Valparaíso and its nearby sister, Viña del Mar.

Valparaíso, also known as Valpo, is divided into two sections: the hills section and the "basin" section, which serves as the commercial center. Each of the hills is like an individual city, and the twisting streets that go up and down them will enchant any tourist. The view from these hills over the bay and on to Viña is one of the most striking in all of Chile.

The taste of the port is found in its twisted streets next to the Mercado, with its myriad bars, underground taverns and sailor hangouts. The cultural life of the port is as busy as its maritime one and centers around the Arturo Prat Naval School, Beaux Arts Museum, Severín Public Library, Naval History Museum, Catholic University of Valparaíso, branches of the University of Chile, and the Technical University Federico Santa María, one of Latin America's most outstanding. Valpo's poets and writers have enriched Chilean literature since the beginning of the republic.

Valpo's historical spots are many. Among the most important is the Mirador O'Higgins, located in Alto del Puerto. This spot offers the best view, and for this reason it was used by General O'Higgins when he saw the Chilean Navy off to aid Peru in its War of Independence with Spain. Another spot is Cerro Los Placeres, where Diego Portales may have been murdered.

Valparaíso's beaches take a back seat to those of Viña. The principal, most central one is Las Torpederas, surrounded by plazas and gardens. From there a tour can be taken around the various fishing towns, and another to visit such places as the Paseo Rubén Darío, a beautiful wooded area with paths and benches; the park of Playa Ancha, and the Playa Ancha football stadium. A bit more time is required to visit such spots as the Quebrada Verde Park. There is also the historical field of Placilla, where the Revolution of 1891 was decided and the fate of President Balmaceda sealed. After defeat, he took his life.

Viña del Mar, 10 minutes further up the coast from Valpo, is a true gem—"The Pearl of the Pacific." Its natural beauty is a year-round attraction, and in the summer a flurry of activity makes the place even more enjoyable. A series of beaches—some almost downtown—draw thousands of sun worshippers daily in the summer.

El Recreo, the first beach after leaving Valparaíso, is wide and comfortable, with terraces full of vacationers and a seawater swimming pool. It is followed by Caleta Abarca, with a view of the port and surrounded by beautiful gardens and walkways. Other beaches are spotted along the 10-mile coastal road connecting Viña with Concón, and whether the vacationer prefers crowded beaches with many activities or isolated spots inhabited only by the visitor and nature, he can find either extreme—and anything in-between—in the Viña area.

But Viña's charm takes in far more than its beaches. The city is set amidst a forest, and man's hand has been used to complement the marvelous work done by Nature. Modern buildings that form the city's skyline gracefully combine with the more traditional chalets and even castles. Here the President of Chile has his rustic Summer Palace on Cerro Castillo (Castle Hill). Wide, well-designed avenues, such as the Avenida de la Marina, lined on one side by palm trees and apartment buildings and on the other by the *estero,* an inlet of the sea with multiple bridges and illuminated fountains decorate the city.

The abundance of flowers have given Viña the name, "The Garden City." Aside from the thousands of private gardens, tourists may visit the Quinta Vergara, an old mansion converted into a park with huge, beautifully kept gardens and walkways. Here during the summer, many outdoor cultural events are held, among them the annual Song Festival. Other lovely parks include the Plaza Vergara, in the heart of town, and the Plaza Mexico, with its lighted fountains.

Places to visit include the Municipal Theater, offering top dramatic and ballet presentations; the Benjamín Vicuña Mackenna Municipal Library; the Academy and Museum of Fine Arts in the Quinta Vergara; the Valparaíso Sporting Club, one of Chile's best racing tracks; Sausalito Stadium, set amid the forest on the banks of El Tranque lake; and the Granadilla Country Club, with magnificent golf course. Viña is small and friendly enough that the tourist will have no trouble finding his way from one spot to the next.

But *the* place to visit in Viña is the Municipal Casino. Gamblers can while away their money (or make a pile) at roulette or baccarat *(punto y banca)* in elegant surroundings during the high season, September 15 to March 15, from 5 P.M. to 5 A.M.; from 5 P.M. to 2 A.M. in low season. And for nongamblers, the Casino has a full-scale nightclub and boite with top national and international acts, excellent food and drink, and plenty of dancing space. Funds from the Casino have contributed much to making Viña the clean, attractive, progressive city it is.

In Viña take advantage of the *victorias,* horse-drawn carriages that are found everywhere. They are fun for drives along the shore road and through the quiet shaded streets, and they are less expensive than cabs. (In Viña, as in many other Chilean cities, taxicabs have no meters. Be careful not to get taken; ask *cuánto* before leaving.)

Around Valparaíso and Viña del Mar are a number of towns in Chile's Central Valley. Quillota, as Charles Darwin said, is a bit of the tropics installed in Chile. It is considered to be a place to go for a rest, and its fruits are exported to the rest of Chile. Other towns in the area are Limache, Olmué, Quilpué ("City of the Sun"), and El Granizo. Algarrobo, a small town 50 miles south, has become a very popular middle-class vacation spot, boasting small sailing boats, and good seafood restaurants and hotels. Villa Alemana is famous as a rest spot. La Calera is an important fruit-growing area.

PRACTICAL INFORMATION FOR THE COAST

VALPARAISO

HOTEL. Prat Hotel, *Moderate,* 1443 Condell St. (253081). 60-room commercial hotel in city center.

RESTAURANT. Restaurante Bote Salvavidas, *Moderate,* Muelle Prat. Specializes in seafood and shellfish.

VIÑA DEL MAR

HOTELS. Miramar. *Deluxe.* Caleta Abarca (664–077). A 122-room remodeled hotel is now Viña's most outstanding. Located right on the ocean, this modern hotel offers full facilities plus a spectacular view and the city's finest location.

Oceanic. *Deluxe.* Recently opened, this beautiful 24-room seaside hotel provides good service and a wonderful view of the Pacific Ocean. On the way to Reñaca.

O'Higgins. *Expensive.* Arlegui Street (882–016), facing Plaza Francisco Vergara, beside the sea inlet called the estero. Near Municipal Casino, beach. Elegant and comfortable. 300 rooms and apartments with baths and phones. Charming Winter Garden. Reception and convention facilities. Top-quality restaurant specializing in international cuisine, grill room and boite with orchestra, American bar. Room and valet service, laundry at all times, beauty parlor, barber shop, swimming pool, terraces and gardens. Garage and service station.

San Martin. *Expensive.* San Martín and Siete Norte Streets (972–548). 120 rooms with private bath and telephone, some with view of the ocean. Large sitting room with huge windows overlooking Avenida Peru and the Pacific. Only three short streets from the Casino. American bar with highly skilled barman. Room service, laundry, shoe shine, messenger service. Restaurant and snackbar.

Alcazar. *Moderate.* Alvárez Street 646 (685–112). Comfortable old hotel with new ultramodern addition of separate cabins, 75 rooms with private bath and telephone, restaurant and bar. Room service and laundry. Garage and parking lot. Well located, only one block from train station and two blocks from downtown Viña.

Holiday Motel. *Moderate.* Angamos 367 (970–623). Comfortable 42 unit motel with swimming pool in nearby Renaca.

RESTAURANTS. Anastasia. *Expensive.* Beautiful beachfront restaurant in nearby Reñaca. Excellent food in the top-floor dining room; ground-floor snack bar and sophisticated shops.

Armandita. *Expensive.* Sumptuous Argentine-style steaks on individual grills. One block from Hotel San Martin.

Chez Gerald. *Expensive.* Good French cooking; dancing; two outdoor terraces; good bar. Ave. Peru, corner of 6 Norte.

San Marcos. *Moderate.* Good Italian food, next door to Armandito, above.

CASINOS. Municipal Casino, the biggest of the casinos, is open daily, year-round. Large gambling salons, full-size cabaret and boite with Chile's best dance bands. Saturday evening there is also a show in the main dining room.

THE NORTH

To the north of Santiago lies the great Atacama, the driest desert in the world. Endowed with a special beauty all its own (sunset on the Atacama is a wonder, with the sands taking on a thousand different tones), it is also spotted with oases all the way up to the northern border.

LA SERENA

The first major city to the north—and one of the most charming—is La Serena, more than 300 miles from Santiago. The region is famous for its climate and fruits, and ex-President Gabriel González Videla, a native son, gave the city great impetus by rebuilding many of its public buildings in a picturesque Spanish style. Its plazas contain well-designed gardens, and flowers can be seen almost everywhere. Big trees along Francisco de

Aguirre Avenue lend their shadows and their ancient beauty, and two hills, the Santa Lucía and the Cerro Grande, provide excellent views of the city and the sea. La Serena also has an archeological museum, located in the great mansion of Count Villaseñor, highlighted by a collection of art by the Diaguitas Indians.

Near La Serena is the Cerro Tololo Observatory, second in the world in the size and sophistication of its equipment. This observatory and two others, Las Campanas and La Silla, are located here to take advantage of the region's extraordinary air conditions: more days of sunshine than anywhere else, no cloud cover day or night, and the air is totally smog free. Astronomers declare the site unequaled for atmospheric clarity.

La Serena's well-known beaches are El Faro, which takes on a festive look during holidays; Punta Teatinos; Las Cuatro Esquinas; and Caleta del Arrayán. Four miles from the city by paved road is the Balneario de Peñuelas, with its extraordinary view, cabins, and restaurant service. A nearby racetrack and airfield complete the picture.

Coquimbo is La Serena's seaport, and near it is La Herradura, with a hotel, several motels, and caves where Sir Francis Drake is believed to have hidden treasure. Nearby Vicuña is the birthplace of Chile's Nobel Prize poetess Gabriela Mistral, and she is buried (according to her wishes) in Monte Grande. Andacollo, another of the region's attractions, has colorful religious celebrations that attract about 100,000 believers and tourists yearly. Tongoy, a beach resort, is well known for its delicious seafoods. Also well known are the beach resort of Los Vilos and the beach at Pichidangui (both farther south along the coast).

PRACTICAL INFORMATION FOR LA SERENA AND ENVIRONS

HOTELS. For definitions of price categories see "Facts at Your Fingertips."
Bucanero. *Expensive.* Av. Costanera (312–231). Located at La Herradura, near La Serena's seaport of Coquimbo. Seascapes in view from the private balconies. Excellent restaurant and bar.

Cabañas Mistral. *Expensive.* Located at nearby La Herradura, these 12 new, tasteful cabins feature 1 or 2 bedrooms, dining room, kitchenette, and bathroom. The swimming pool and beautiful restaurant overlook the protected bay and its excellent beach.

Hotel Francisco De Aguirre. *Expensive.* Cordovez 210 (212–351). La Serena's largest hotel, a modern three-story building with 73 double rooms with private baths. Large sitting room, bar, restaurant, sauna, pool, and boite. Large terraces surrounded by gardens. Ample facilities.

Jardín del Mar. *Expensive.* Avenida del Mar (312–823). Recently opened beautiful motel with excellent accommodations, comfortable 4- 6-bed cabins, and magnificent gardens surrounding large pool. Each cabin features TV, bath, bedroom, sitting room, kitchenette, and terrace.

Cabinas De Peñuelas. *Moderate.* American-style motel four miles from La Serena by paved road. The motel has several cabins located by the sea, each with sitting room, bedroom, bath, and terraced garden. Each cabin accommodates six people. The Casino provides excellent restaurant service. The view is magnificent. Water skiing and skin diving in the temperate sea.

Hosteria Vicuña. *Moderate.* 35 miles from La Serena by paved road. 14 recently renovated double rooms with private baths, dining room, bar, sitting room, terrace, swimming pool. Vicuña is a quiet city with a wonderful climate and is near the "Termas de Toro" (Bull Thermal Baths).

Turismo Ovalle. *Moderate.* Located at one corner of the plaza in the city of Ovalle. Comfortable rooms—13 singles and 19 doubles—with dining room, bar, tea room, large sitting room. Thirty miles from the excellent beach of Tongoy, well known for seafood and temperate waters.

COPIAPÓ

Copiapó, another 150 miles to the north, was one of Chile's most important cities during the fat years of the last century. Most of the cultural life of the country was centered in it, and Santiago, compared to Copiapó, was practically a provincial city. The Southern Hemisphere's first railroad and the country's first public lighting service, technical education system, and state school were all in Copiapó. All the bills were paid by the mining revenues, especially from the silver mines of Chañarcillo, which were discovered by the famed Juan Godoy.

North of Copiapó are the two-mile-apart seaports of Chañaral and Barquito, from which the copper production of nearby Potrerillos and El Salvador is shipped. The latter is at an elevation of 7,800 feet. Some 15,000 people live there. Vallenar, south of Copiapó, is near the iron ore field of El Algarrobo, one of the most important in the country. Huasco is Vallenar's port, 30 miles away, and is famous for its wines and its *pisco,* as well as for its seafood. Caldera is 52 miles northwest of Copiapó; in 1851 the first railway in the hemisphere was built between these two cities. The main activity of this port is the loading of minerals.

PRACTICAL INFORMATION FOR COPIAPÓ

HOTELS. For definitions of price categories see "Facts at Your Fingertips." **Diego de Almeyda Hotel.** *Expensive.* O'Higgins 656 (2075). Facing the plaza of the important mining center of Copiapó. 30 double rooms with private baths, several sitting rooms, ample gardens, dining room-restaurant, bar, card room, tea room.

Hosteria De Chañaral. *Moderate.* Miller No. 268. Also at seaside, a modern building with 9 single and 10 double rooms, all with private bath and a view of the Pacific. Terraces, dining room-restaurant, bar. Chañaral is an important embarkation port for iron ore, nitrate, and copper.

Hosteria Puerta del Sol. *Moderate.* Wheelwright No. 750, at seaside. Seven double rooms with private baths, dining room-restaurant, bar, sitting room in new building. Caldera is 53 miles from Copiapó by paved road running through the Pampa Salitrera (nitrates). A picturesque place, considered the beach resort of Copiapó.

Hosteria Vallenar. *Moderate.* Alonso de Ercilla 850. Modern two-story building surrounded by terraces, gardens, ponds. 19 double rooms with private baths, big sitting room, bar, dining room, restaurant. Vallenar is an important mining city.

ANTOFAGASTA

The province of Antofagasta, still further north, is renowned because, for 360 days of the year, it has the highest solar intensity in the world. Its geysers (of Tatio) attract many tourists, and like the rest of the north it is chiefly desert and mountain ranges. Famed archeological zones such as Pucará are in the region. The capital city of the province is also named Antofagasta, center of copper and nitrate mining activity. The city is an important railway center through which pass the international lines to La Paz, Bolivia, and Salta, Argentina. Much of Bolivia's international commerce passes through Antofagasta, according to the treaty signed after the War of the Pacific.

Antofagasta is a progressive city. Its beautiful plazas and parks are a tribute to man's conquest of the desert. The Plaza Colón has a big Westminster Clock donated by the British residents, and the Spanish and Yugoslavian communities have also contributed monuments and adornments for the city's beautification.

For sports enthusiasts, Antofagasta has a fine Sporting Club, tennis courts, a golf course, and an Automobile Club. Deepsea fishing is a favorite sport, but requires arrangements made by a travel agent.

Best-known beaches are the Balneario Municipal, the Isla de la Chimba (also known as Guamán), and La Portada, where just offshore the action of the waves over the centuries carved a hole in a rock, leaving an arch that looks like a doorway *(portada)*, from which the name is derived. On the city's highest hill is painted an enormous anchor, which greeted the arrival of the steamship *Peru* in 1886, one of the first to arrive in Antofagasta Bay.

Calama, 136 miles northeast of Antofagasta, is a desert oasis located more than 6,000 feet above sea level. Its *Calemeño* wine has become quite famous, as have its melons and sweet corn. Its chinchilla farms provide luxury furs.

A few miles north of Calama is Chuquicamata, the largest open pit copper mine in the world, and the nitrate plants of Maria Elena and Pedro de Valdivia. Also near Calama is *Dupont* explosives factory, which supplies most of the explosives used in Chilean mines.

The province features the additional seaports of Tocopilla (north of Antofagasta) and Taltal (south of Antofagasta). Through Tocopilla goes much of the nitrate from the pampas and the copper from the Chuquicamata mine. It has some very good beaches (Punta Blanca and Caleta Bay, the latter with seawater swimming pool) and is famous as a site for deepsea fishing. Swordfish and black marlin abound in its waters.

Throughout the area are many ancient towns lost among the salt and the desert sand, some truly prehistoric and others reminders of the golden days of nitrate. Sixty miles southeast of Calama is San Pedro de Atacama, where the late Jesuit priest Alfred le Paige of Belgium worked for many years uncovering secrets of the Atacameño Indians. Father le Paige worked for over a quarter of a century to found the now internationally famous archeological museum. Many scholars come to Chile with the sole purpose of visiting it; one of its distinguished guests was ex-King Leopold of Belgium. An old church adds to the touristic and historic value. The town is also the best jump-off point for an excursion to the large and impressive Atacama Salt Lake.

Only 22 miles from San Pedro is Toconao, rich in archeological treasures, such as the legendary *Camino del Inca*. It provides a superb view of the Láscar Volcano.

Chiu-Chiu is 23 miles from Calama. The baptismal basin in its parish dates from 1557, and documents found there go back to 1611. Also nearby is the town of Pukará de Lassana, which means desert fortress—which it was. The geysers of Tatio in the same area shoot astounding hot water columns in the midst of the scorched plains.

PRACTICAL INFORMATION FOR ANTOFAGASTA

HOTELS. For definitions of price categories see "Facts at Your Fingertips." **Topotel Calama.** *Expensive.* Camino Aeropuerto 1392 (212–208). This beautiful new hotel features 60 rooms facing an interior patio with swimming pool, sauna, health club, restaurant and piano bar.

Turismo Antofagasta. *Expensive.* Balmaceda 2786 (224–710). A five-story luxury hotel with all the necessary comforts. 108 double rooms with private baths and magnificent view of the Pacific. Large hall, bar (American bar facing sea), terrace with gardens, swimming pool (with outdoor restaurant), big dining room opening onto terrace, internal gardens, boite, beauty parlor, barber shop, shops inside the hotel. Good service. The hotel owns boats and private transportation.

Hosteria Calama. *Moderate.* J.J. La Torre No. 1521. 14 rooms opening onto terraces, sitting room, dining room-restaurant, and bar. Calama is 140 miles from Antofagasta and very near Chuquicamata, the largest open pit copper mine in the world.

Hosteria San Pedro De Atacama. *Moderate.* A comfortable, recently improved inn in the town where time seems to have stopped at the beginning of the colonial period. San Pedro de Atacama is full of incredible archeological treasures, and a famous museum has been built for the mummies found there and for the ceramics and Indian art of the area. The town is 60 miles from Calama.

Hosteria Tal Tal. *Moderate.* Esmeralda 671. Paved road from Antofagasta to the south leads to Taltal. At seaside, with 10 double rooms, each with private bath. Terrace facing the sea, sitting room, dining room-restaurant, bar. Near Taltal is the Chiu-Chiu Lagoon, over 900 feet deep, where legend claims some of the Inca treasures were sunk. Chiu-Chiu is still a colonial town in its way of life and its architecture.

Hosteria Tocopilla. *Moderate.* Decorated with contemporary art, it has 14 rooms with private baths and faces the sea. Beautiful gardens flank the inn, which also has three very comfortable sitting rooms, a dining room-restaurant, and a bar. The inn is half a mile from Tocopilla by paved road. Tocopilla embarks nitrate from nearby deposits. Deepsea fishing is famous in Tocopilla; swordfish and tuna are sought by fishing fans from many parts of the world.

IQUIQUE

Patriotic Chileans have a special place in their hearts for the northern port city of Iquique. It is not because of the battle won, as in the case of Arica or Maipo, but because of the battle lost at sea by Arturo Prat during the 1879 War of the Pacific. The war was just beginning on May 21, 1879, when the great warship *Huáscar* of the Peruvian Navy arrived at Iquique accompanied by a smaller warship. Two small wooden ships under the command of Captain Arturo Prat were Chile's only defense. But Prat fought the giant enemy until his own craft was practically broken in half. When the ships collided, Prat and a few of his followers jumped aboard the enemy ship, only to die under the bullets of Peruvian guns. But his heroic gesture fired up the whole country, and this fervor continued until the war ended in victory for Chile.

Iquique was a great nitrate seaport; now it is the center of the country's rapidly growing fishing industry, and oil drilling is also underway in the region. The city offers the tourist much local color. Many plazas seem to defy the desert with their gardens, the best known being Plaza Arturo Prat. Here is a famous clock tower and the Casino Español, an artistic imitation of the Alhambra Palace in Spain. Iquique also has an archeology and anthropology museum with a collection of mummies unearthed in the desert surrounding the city. The *mercado,* with all kinds of local and imported merchandise, is a favorite tourist spot and is surrounded by many popular restaurants with local, Peruvian, and Asiatic dishes. Today, Iquique is a free port.

Iquique's beaches attract large crowds almost year round. Cavancha has a beautiful street running beside it and is very close to town. The Balneario Municipal is four miles away, Playa Blanca eight miles and Piedras Buenas twelve miles. It also offers fine opportunities for fishing, and several national and international records have been set here.

Iquique's Pica Valley, 85 miles from the city, is famous for its lemons, grapes, oranges, "guayabas," and mangos. It was discovered in 1536 by Captain Ruy Díaz. Don Pedro de Valdivia was also in the valley when he made his conquering expedition in 1540. The church and bell tower of Matica, near Pica, were built about this time. North of Pica Valley is Mamiña, 72 miles from Iquique and famous for its thermal baths. The Pampa del Tamarugal, 186 miles long and 25 to 30 miles wide, is named after the "Tamarugo," a small but hardy spiked bush that grows on it. A wooded area is developing. La Tirana, a fresh oasis with an annual religious celebration, is situated on the pampa.

On the coast 60 miles north of Iquique is the small port of Pisagua, known as the land without winter. The bay, surrounded by high hills, has very quiet waters, the natural setting forms a kind of overcoat over the whole village.

PRACTICAL INFORMATION FOR IQUIQUE

HOTELS. For definitions of price categories see "Facts at Your Fingertips." **Hosteria Cavancha.** *Expensive.* Los Rieles 250 (21158). Three minutes south from Iquique City near Cavancha Airport. 32 double rooms with private bath. Beautiful gardens with terraces facing the Pacific. Private seashore. Modern. Excellent typical and international cuisine. Laundry and garage-service station.

Hotel Arturo Prat. *Expensive.* Anival Pinto 695 (21414). In downtown Iquique, at one corner of the Plaza de Armas, 25 singles and 26 doubles, each with private bath. Big sitting room, dining room, bar, and covered and open-air gardens where meals are served. Boats available for fishing and water skiing. Nearby are the Mamiña Thermal Baths, with a great medical reputation.

Hotel Chucumata. *Expensive.* Balmaceda 850 (236–55). Beautiful resort complex with 42 rooms looking over gardens and terraces with swimming pool, open-air restaurant, and bar. Located a few meters from the beach, in one of the best areas of Iquique.

ARICA

One of the world's highest railroads, the International Railway, operates from the far northern city of Arica to La Paz, Bolivia. (Two round trips are offered weekly in summer, and once or twice a month during the rest of the year.)

Among the city's attractions are the Vicuña Mackenna Park, the Juan Noé Park (named after the doctor who fought malaria in the Azapa Valley), the Church of San Marcos, designed by French architect Gustave Eiffel and declared a national monument, and the University of Tarapaca Anthropological Museum.

Sports fans have the Carlos Dittborn Stadium, named after the late organizer of the World Football Championship in Chile in 1962, a race track, polo fields, a golf course, and a swimming pool. The beaches are beautiful, with wonderfully temperate waters, and you can swim at night at La Lisera, a mile from town, and at Chinchorro and Miramar on the northern side of the city.

Arica also has a gambling casino and several of the best hotels, bars, restaurants, and boites in the country.

The valleys around Arica are true oases in the desert. Lluta Valley, about 10 miles from Arica, is a center of cotton, corn, wheat, and tomatoes. Some agricultural produce comes out of the Chaca and Camarones valleys. Putre, on the Arica Altiplano, has 500 inhabitants living in 100-odd houses. Parinacota looks like a ghost town, with its ancient church and closed houses. And the magnificent 18,000-foot Payachatas Volcano, with the Chungará and Cotacotani lagoons at its foot, makes an impressive sight.

Nearer Arica is the livelier Azapa Valley, with its olives and other tropical fruits. Sugar cane is also found in some of these valleys, which now and then break up the dry and almost tragic monotony of the forbidding northern desert.

In the valley there are still vestiges of ancient hamlets, geoglyphs, and pre-Spanish cemeteries. About 30 minutes by car up the valley from Arica is the small but excellent San Miguel de Azapa archaeological museum with displays of well-preserved mummies, now believed to be the world's oldest—8,000 years old, they predate Egyptian mummies by 3,000 years.

PRACTICAL INFORMATION FOR ARICA

HOTELS. For definitions of price categories see "Facts at Your Fingertips."
Hosteria Arica. *Deluxe.* Facing sea, Morro de Arica (231–201). 60 double rooms with private baths. Also offers motel-type cabins. Dining room, sitting room, bar. Terraces and covered gardens overlooking the Pacific. Private beach.

Saint Gregory. *Deluxe.* 67 rooms including 8 suites and 14 cabins, some rooms with air conditioning. On the Azapa Valley, 10 minutes from downtown Arica. Pleasant gardens, swimming pool, tennis, squash, international restaurant, its own car rental service, piano bar, and jacuzzi.

Azapa Inn. *Expensive.* Gmo. Sanchez (242–612). Suites with kitchenette, refrigerator, private baths, terraces and tropical park. Boite, bar, elegant swimming pool.

El Paso. *Expensive.* Modern in design, surrounded by tropical parks and gardens. Located a mile from the city of Arica by paved road. 40 double rooms with private baths. Sitting room, dining room, bar, large comfortable terraces.

Hotel Savona. *Inexpensive.* 28 rooms. Clean, well-run hotel in city center.

CASINOS. Casino Municipal de Arica is open throughout the year. It offers baccarat, roulette, and Black Jack. There are also a good restaurant and a late-night cabaret. There is also a casino in Coquimbo (Casino de Juegos de Coquimbo) open all year.

SOUTH OF SANTIAGO

The provinces south of Santiago are mostly agricultural and there are fewer tourist attractions until the lake region is reached. Several thermal baths are spotted along the way, among them the Cauquenes, 12 miles from Rancagua by car or bus; Del Flaco, in the province of Colchagua and 56 miles from the city of San Fernando, because of the altitude not recommended for weak hearts; and Mondaca, in Talca province, off-limits for heart cases. Another 22 recommended thermal baths stretch from near Iquique in the north all the way to Aysén in the south and are said to have remarkable healing powers.

At Rapel, some 80 miles from Santiago, a 30-mile-long lake has been formed by the backdp from a hhdroeleccric dam. Chib lake hab become very popular for fishing, sailing, swimming, and water skiing.

TALCA

The first important city on the southern trek is Talca, 150 miles from Santiago. Situated on the River Claro, Talca is in the middle of grape, wine, wheat, and cattle country. The town has a golf course, polo field, swimming pools, clubs, and theaters.

The Laguna del Maule is 90 miles from Talca. It offers good rainbow trout fishing; however, the fish are small by Chilean-lake standards. Boating, sailing, and other water sports may be enjoyed here, although temperatures tend to be rather low because of the altitude. Near the lake is the Altos de Vilches summer resort, with a hotel that is open from October through March. Several thermal baths are in the area, the best of them being Panimávida, 35 miles by road. Other impressive sights are La Mina, with an inn for visitors; the small Maule Lagoon, just before the big one;

Las Balustradas, overlooking a 900-foot cliff; the 180-foot Maule Falls and the Penitentes, an incredibly beautiful sight with mountains, lava formations, and exuberant vegetation.

PRACTICAL INFORMATION FOR TALCA

HOTELS. For definitions of price categories see "Facts at Your Fingertips." **Plaza.** *Expensive.* 1 Poniente 1141 (31515). Talca's finest, in a three-story building facing the Plaza de Armas. Large sitting room, dining room, private supper room, bar on the first and second floors. 70 rooms with bath. Near Talca is Constitución, a famous beach resort, and 90 miles away by paved road is the Laguna de Maule, located near the Argentina border.

Hotel Marcos Gamero. *Expensive.* 1 Oriente 1070. New 32-room hotel now considered best in city. Good restaurant and bar.

CONSTITUCIÓN

Constitución, a port some 60 miles from Talca, has fine bathing beaches and is known as a summer resort. It is surrounded by pine-covered hills, and the coast is noted for its unusual rock formations and peaceful waters ideal for almost all water sports. There is a yearly Carnival Maulino in February, with a masked ball and a Venetian promenade down the Maule River.

PRACTICAL INFORMATION FOR CONSTITUCIÓN

HOTELS. Hosteria Constitución. *Expensive.* Freire 315. The inn is located on the banks of the Maule River and is surrounded by gardens. The bar has large windows and a terrace overlooking the river; the cozy dining room has a fireplace, terrace, and small tables from which you can see the view. The sitting room also has a fireplace, plus a glass roof. 19 rooms with private baths, all looking on the magnificent Maule. Constitución is famed for its large beaches, clean and peaceful waters, and rock formations.

CHILLÁN

Next stop on the southern tour is Chillán. One section, Chillán Viejo, retains much of its colonial air; the house where Bernardo O'Higgins, liberator of Chile, was born still stands. The other has avenues and all the comforts of the 20th century. Among its attractions is the Mexico School decorated by world-famous Mexican muralist David Alfaro Siqueiros. The Cathedral is ultramodern and the plazas and parks beautiful. The "mercado" is also a tourist attraction with its many regional products, among them ceramics and pottery from Quinchamalí and other nearby towns. The mountains surrounding Chillán are among the most striking the tourist will see in Chile.

Leaving the city, near Recinto, one may visit the Cueva de Los Pincheira, huge caves in which the Pincheira brothers used to hide after their cattle stealing raids. A series of pottery-making towns—Quinchamalí, Colliguay, Huechupin, Cuca, Chonchoral, and Confluencia—offer collectors original creations of the famous black pottery.

Some 58 miles from Chillán at the altitude of 5,400 feet are the Chillán ski slopes, and near the slopes are the mineral springs that make the area famous, with a complete hotel.

PRACTICAL INFORMATION FOR CHILLÁN

HOTELS. Hotel Isabel Riquelme. *Expensive.* Constitucion 576 (223–664). Sitting rooms, smoking room, big dining room, private supper rooms, bars. Big comfortable bedrooms, with a sitting room on each of the three floors. Two singles and 58 doubles with private baths. Chillán offers thermal baths and nearby ski slopes, plus the interesting crater of the Chillán Volcano. Located in the center of Chillán.

CONCEPCIÓN

Concepción, capital of the province by the same name, is an important city for industry, culture, and tourism. As an industrial center it boasts the Huachipato steel plant, coal mines, and textile plants in Tomé and Chiguayante. Nine miles away is the sister city and port of Talcahuano, also the principal naval port of the country and the main port for timber export. Its intellectual life is centered around the University of Concepción, financed by contributions and by a twice-a-month National Lottery. The tourist attractions are many: in the center, the historical Cerro Amarillo (Yellow Hill) offers a very good view of the town; the central plaza is lovely; the modern campus of the University is the only real university city in Chile; Cerro Caracol, 300 feet high, offers a grand view of the valleys and the great Bío-Bío River, the largest in Chile. Across the river is San Pedro, with beautiful forests and lagoons. In the largest lagoons boating and other water sports are practiced. The principal beaches are Las Escaleras, reached by stairs carved in rock; Ramuntcho, named after one of the novels by French writer Pierre Loti who visited the place in 1875; and La Desembocadura del Río, one of the most striking places for the visitor who goes there for the first time. Near this beach is the Pedro del Río Zañartu Museum, located on a farm and featuring local and Araucanian art objects.

La Planchada Fort is maintained by the city as a landmark. For two centuries this fort defended Concepción.

Only 19 miles from Concepción is the textile center of Tomé, famous for its products of exceptional quality. Tomé also has good beaches and other attractions.

Near the port of Talcahuano is the Quiriquina Island, where the Naval School has an establishment for its students, as well as the giant Huachipato steel plant. Seventeen miles from Concepción is Coronel, which with Lota shares the leadership in the country's coal production. The Lota mines extend for several miles under the sea. In Lota is the famous Parque de Lota. In the Gulf of Arauco is the Island of Santa María, and in the same area is the beach resort of Laraquete, a seven-mile golden-sand beach about an hour by car from Concepción.

PRACTICAL INFORMATION FOR CONCEPCIÓN

HOTELS. Araucano. *Deluxe.* Caupolican 521 (229–944). Elegant and comfortable hotel in the heart of the city. 300 apartments with bath and phone. Furnished in Spanish-Araucanian style. Swimming pool. Restaurants with excellent meals. Disco, shops. Room service, laundry, garage, and service station.

Alborada. *Expensive.* Barros Arana 457 (228–226). 40 rooms, recently renovated; very good service. Centrally located.

THE CHILEAN LAKE REGION

Laja Lake

The fabulous Chilean lake region begins in Los Angeles, some 320 miles south of Santiago, where the Laja Lake is located. The most famous sight in the Los Angeles region is the Laja Falls, probably the most inspiring scenery in the country. The Falls start at the Laja Lake, are 4,500 feet high, and cover 48 square miles. The Antuco Volcano is reflected in the lake, and every year fishing competitions are held there. Fifteen miles north of Los Angeles, the Laja River, which flows from the lake, drops some 200 feet to form the Laja Falls, or Salto del Laja. This region is famous for its views, and there are four volcanoes: the Antuco, the Copahue, the Tolhuaca, and the Collapén.

Temuco and Lake Villarrica

Almost 200 miles farther south, after the Araucanian center at Temuco, is one of Chile's loveliest and most famous lakes, the Villarrica. Its 66 square miles of waters change colors throughout the day. Viewed from the lake, the nearby Villarrica Volcano is an awesome sight. On the banks of the Villarrica are the internationally known vacation spots of Pucón and Villarrica, with luxury hotels and ample opportunities for fishing and water sports. A legend says that if a small *morro* (hill) near the lake is visited by a recently married couple the lake becomes furious. So honeymooners had best watch out.

Valdivia

Next in line, in the province of Valdivia, is the beautiful Lake Panguipulli, whose name means "puma hill" in English. There is a small and very good privately owned hotel ("hosteria"). Excursions can be made from the *Hosteria Cancahuasi* (ex-Rainbow Fly Club), a good fisherman's hotel in Chan Chan. Also in Valdivia are the Lake Pirihueico, closer to the border with Argentina and with a hotel on its bank offering excursion services; Lake Calafquén, offering excellent fishing but no hotel; Lake Riñihue, with two lovely hotels, connected with Panguipulli by the truly beautiful Enco River, down which a one-day fishing excursion can be made; Lake Ranco, with 23 islands well known for its excellent fishing (fish up to 18 pounds have been taken from the lake) and a game deer hunting private island. Hostería Riñinahue is considered to be one of the best fishing spots in the lake district and offering the most beautiful scenery imaginable as well.

Osorno

The province of Osorno holds forth even greater wonders. The first lake, Puyehue, contains some wonderful islands filled with native birds and has marvelous waterfalls and a big, good hotel for tourists. Near the lake are the Puyehue Thermal Baths, considered by many the finest hot springs establishment in all of South America. The fishing is, again, superb. Further south, Lake Rupanco, a bit nearer to the city of Osorno has top fishing and famous hot springs, but unfortunately tourist facilities are limited.

On to the south in the province of Llanquihue is the biggest of them all: Lake Llanquihue. Near Puerto Montt, and with marvelous Puerto Varas on its banks, Llanquihue measures 320 square miles and in some parts is 1,500 feet deep. Its waters are deep blue, and it is the scene for many water sports and some very good fishing. The lake is surrounded by some of the world's most beautiful volcanoes, especially the Osorno, with its eternally snow-capped peak. The sight is absolutely breathtaking.

Osorno Volcano also lends its majestic presence to Lake Todos Los Santos, also known as Esmeralda—the first name because it was discovered on All Saints' Day, the second because of the emerald color of its waters. Theodore Roosevelt described this lake as the most beautiful he had ever seen, and most tourists must agree.

Motorboats operate on the principal lakes of this region—Esmeralda, Llanquihue and Ranco—and most of the hotels on their banks organize excellent excursions.

More Than Lakes

Of course, the lake region offers more to the tourist than spectacularly beautiful views. Many of the cities mentioned have an individual charm that makes each of them worth a good, slow visit.

Valdivia, with its Calle-Calle River full of boats, was founded by Don Pedro in 1552 and is an important and busy province. The climate is humid, and beautiful lakes, woods, beaches, and rivers surround the cities. Along the waterways are countless little cool, green islands. One recommended side trip is to Llifén, on the banks of Lake Ranco, with a marvelous hotel complete with airstrip.

Frutillar, a charming lake resort to the Lago Llanquihue, is worth a visit, especially during its "semanas musicales" (classical music festival) held every summer from the end of January to the first third of February. It is renowned for its Germanic atmosphere.

Osorno is one of the many cities inhabited by great numbers of German descendants whose forefathers colonized the region. Here the German language is used almost as much as Spanish. Even road signs and menus are printed in German in some places, and its wonderfully organized streets look like a bit of old Europe. Among the many interesting excursions (besides those to the lakes) is the Antillanca ski resort (4,200 feet above sea level), 62 miles from Puyehue. The very good 150-room hotel, run by Club Andino de Osorno, provides services winter and summer, including restaurant, disco, sauna and health club, bar, outside heated pool, and game and video rooms. The skiing facilities include 4 lifts for 12 slopes, first-aid center, ski school, and ski rental. At the foothills of Antillanca volcano, the wonderful Puyehue National Park is worth a visit.

The city of Puerto Montt from which the trip through the zone of canals begins, is famous for its seafoods and its seaport. It also has Isla de Tenglo with its famous *curantos*. Nearby is Maullín, with its lovely river.

PRACTICAL INFORMATION FOR THE LAKE REGION

HOTELS. For definitions of price categories see "Facts at Your Fingertips."
LAJA FALLS. Hosteria Salto del Laja. *Expensive.* Veritably beside the Laja Falls, this modern, very comfortable inn is designed to provide its guests with a beautiful view without ever leaving the motel. A bar, dining room, and swimming pool add to the visitors' comfort.

LOS ANGELES. Mariscal Alcazar. *Expensive.* This modern building located in the center of the city features a sitting room with fireplace, dining room opening onto terrace, bar, 25 double rooms with private baths. Near the city are the famous Laja Falls (120 feet high), a beautiful natural attraction.

TEMUCO. Nuevo Hotel La Frontera. *Deluxe.* Bulnes 726 (36190). Luxurious 55-room hotel with swimming pool, solarium, conference room, bar, dining room. Located downtown.

LAKE VILLARRICA. Antumalal. *Deluxe.* 2 km from Pucón (441–011). One of Chile's most fabulous, on the banks of Lake Villarrica. Famous for its views and its service, it has been visited by such personalities as Queen Elizabeth, Prince Philip, and Barry Goldwater. The hotel organizes fishing and hunting trips for its guests. 20 rooms with private baths. Located on a small hill surrounded by forests.

Gran Hotel Pucon. *Expensive.* Holpzafel 190 (441–001). Located on the banks of Lake Villarrica with an overwhelming view of some of the world's most beautiful scenery. Sitting room, bar, dining room, private supper room, game room, tennis courts, terraces overlooking the lake, large gardens, "pergolas" (summer houses), and docks on the lake. Offers water skiing, horseback riding, hiking, excellent fishing, and hunting. Hotel has boats and transportation facilities for guests. 130 rooms, all with private bath.

Motel Yachting Club Villarrica. *Expensive.* San Martin 802 (441–191). On the banks of the lake, with broad gardens. Swimming pool, sauna. Boats for fishing and yachts.

VALDIVIA. Hotel Villa del Rio. *Expensive.* Av. España 1025 (216–292). On bank of Calle Calle River near city center. 50 rooms, yacht basin, gardens, restaurant, bar.

Pedro de Valdivia. *Expensive.* Carampangue 180 (212–931). Modern building surrounded by gardens, with large sitting room, dining room, magnificent bar. The hotel is decorated with beautiful murals and has an elegant boite, 85 double rooms with private baths. The city is famous for its beauty, located on the banks of the Calle-Calle River. Several picturesque towns along the river can be reached by boats leaving Valdivia. The region is also famous for its forests.

LAKE CALAFQUEN. Hosteria Calafquen. *Expensive.* On the banks of the lake bearing the same name, this inn is of rustic design and offers almost every tourist comfort. Three floors and a bar, dining room, sitting room, terraces. Three single rooms and 50 doubles, each with private bath. The region offers unlimited opportunities for good fishing, hunting, and water sports. From the inn the tourist can reach San Martín de los Andes in Argentina.

OSORNO. Hotel del Prado. *Expensive.* Cochrane 1162 (235–020) has become Osorno's best. Four blocks from the city center on the corner of Cochrane and Bilbao Sts. 20 rooms, color TV, bar, dining room.

Hotel Waeger. *Moderate.* Cochrane 816 (233–721). 25 rooms, restaurant, good downtown location.

LAKE PUYEHUE. Gran Hotel Termas de Puyehue. *Expensive.* (231–1004 in Santiago). Located on the banks of Lake Puyehue, the hotel has thermal baths. The building is modern with many extras: swimming pool with hot thermal water, tennis courts, riding stables, boats for fishing and water skiing. 100 single and double rooms. Near the hotel is the Salto del Pilmaiquén (Pilmaiquén Falls) and the Antillanca Volcano, with famous ski slopes.

Nilque Motel. *Expensive.* (234–960 in Osorno). Located on the shores of Lake Puyehue is one of Chile's finest resorts. Forty attractive cabins line the private beach. Activities include boating, fishing, and horseback riding. Rodeo complex as well as full facilities for children. It is probably Chile's premier family resort.

Refugio Antillanca. *Moderate.* (727–812 in Santiago). A short 12 miles from Puyehue, on the Antillanca Volcano ski slopes. Newly constructed accommodations for more than 100 skiers in twins, triples, and quads. Bar, disco, dining room.

PUERTO VARAS. Hotel y Cabanas del Lago. *Expensive.* (232–291). A good lake-shore hotel with 40 doubles featuring private bath, TV, charming decoration with local wood, and a fantastic view over Lake Llanquihue and its breathtaking Volcan Osorno. Best hotel in area. Near casino, resort facilities.

Hotel Licarayen. *Moderate.* San Jose 114 (232–305). A very charming hotel, personally run by its owner, on the lake shore with a marvelous view. 10 rooms in the old yet cozy wing and 12 rooms in the new wing which includes one magnificent suite.

Hotel Bellavista. *Moderate.* (232–520). Excellent new tourist-class hotel (opened 1988). 30 lake-view rooms with private baths. Restaurant, bar, very good location.

BEYOND THE LAKES

PUERTO MONTT AND CHILOÉ

For those with a pioneer spirit, the boat trip from Puerto Montt is highly recommended. The boat leaving Puerto Montt makes the run of the ports and touches scores of fishing villages. The region is not well developed to receive tourists, but the trip is unforgettable. The trip takes about 10 days and visits a great variety of picturesque towns, passing dozens of small islands so covered in vegetation that they seem to be plants sprouting from the water. Sailors and those living in the area call them *maceteros* (flower pots). The fishermen who populate the area will be seen around the hundreds of canals—a hardy people living amidst beautiful but cruel natural surroundings.

On the big Island of Chiloé are two towns with tourist accommodations: Ancud and Castro. Ancud, the capital of the province, is four hours from Puerto Montt by boat, or 1½ hours by car and ferry. The bay of Ancud is famous for its beauty, and the many attractions include the Cerro Caracoles, from which the panorama of the city and its surroundings can be seen. Near Ancud is the fort of San Antonio, the last Spanish stronghold in the War of Independence, as well as La Máquina (the machine), so called because there the first mechanized timber mill in South America was installed in 1828. Other attractive places are the thermal baths in Llanchahué across the bay of Ancud, and such spots as Faro de Aquí, Faro de Punta Corona, Mar Brava, and Chacao.

Castro is located on the banks of the Castro Canal and surrounded by small islands and towns. As all ships going or coming in the southern region must stop there, its commercial and maritime life is very important. Of special attraction in the area are the towns of Huillinco, Queilén, Quellón and Chonchi, the latter with a small wooden church.

Some of the best kept secrets in South America are the spectacular fjord cruises in Chilean Patagonia, operating from Puerto Montt and Chiloé to the magnificent San Rafael glacier. The Skorpios cruises, with M/S *Skorpios I* (79 passengers) and M/S *Skorpios II* (150 passengers) offer Saturday departures for weekly cruises from September through April. The safe, peaceful six-day trip through southern Chile's fiords is an incomparable experience. The scenery includes mountains, icebergs, the channels, island valleys, fiords, and small fishing villages.

PRACTICAL INFORMATION FOR
PUERTO MONTT, CHILOÉ, AND THE CANAL REGION

HOTELS. PUERTO MONTT. Perez Rosales. *Expensive.* Av. Varas 447 (252–571). Of rustic design, its balconies were carved by Chilean artists to represent typical scenes of the "Chilote" people who live along the channels of the Reloncavi Gulf. Five floors, large luxurious sitting room, big dining rooms beautifully decorated and with fireplaces, bar, private supper rooms, beauty parlor, barber shop, commercial shops. 52 double rooms with small sitting room, one three-bed room, and one six-bed room. Puerto Montt is a must for the tourist. A clean city on the sea, it has a great panoramic view of the Reloncaví Gulf, Tenglo Island, and several volcanoes. Its seafood is famous all over the country, especially "centollas."

Hotel Colina. *Moderate.* Talca 81 (253–502). Comfortable 55-room hotel facing port. Good restaurant and bar.

RALUN. Hotel Ralun. *Deluxe.* (252–100). An impressive and beautiful resort in front of the Reloncaví fjord. The hotel is located 60 miles from Puerto Montt and offers accommodations for over 60 guests in large cabins and twin-room motel-type facilities. The resort features tennis, horses, boating, fishing, and conference facilities for groups up to 25. Surroundings are incomparably beautiful, and reminiscent of the Norwegian fjord country.

CHILOÉ. Hosteria Ancud. *Expensive.* (2340). A rustic, solid building with sitting room, bar, dining room, 12 singles and 12 doubles, each with private bath. The region is famous as a tourist attraction because of the many picturesque towns found on the Island of Chiloé. Its forests and mountains are much admired.

Hosteria Castro. *Expensive.* (2301). A modern building with bar, sitting room, dining room, 12 singles and 12 doubles with private baths, plus an extra 12-bed room. In the same region as the Hosteria Ancud.

Unicornio Azúl. *Moderate.* Avda. Pedro Montt 228 (2359). A new hotel with 18 rooms with private bath, bar and restaurant.

MAGALLANES

Chile's southern province of Magallanes is centered around industry and agriculture. Great herds of sheep are there, which are shipped to London and other European cities. The production from oil fields supplies Chile with almost one-third of the petroleum consumed in the country. Seals and whales in the area are used to provide a large source of revenue. An interesting 4-day, 3-night tour can be arranged from Punta Arenas to Tierra del Fuego, with visits to ranches, oil fields and a tour of Punta Arenas. Punta Arenas is an important seaport and cattle and industrial region. Oil is found in several nearby fields, and the area offers many attractions to the enterprising tourist. The first oil-production platform went on flow in 1979.

Punta Arenas

The city's attractions include Cerro La Cruz, from which the city and the Strait can be seen; racing tracks, golf course, and tennis courts at the Club Hípico; an ice skating rink and indoor stadium for sports fans; a zoo at the Pudeto Artillery Regiment; and the María Behety Municipal Park. Its Salesiano Regional Museum is filled with information on the culture of the Yagane, Ona, and Alacalufe Indians.

Four miles from Punta Arenas, atop the Patagonian Andes, are ski slopes that feature runs more than a mile long that drop 1,200 feet. More information is available from Santiago's Club Andino de Chile. Also nearby are fox farms, Seco (Dry) River, Loreto Mine, and the historic site of Fort Bulnes where the first settlers managed to survive. Boat trips can be made to the islands of Magdalena, Marta, and Contramaestre.

PRACTICAL INFORMATION FOR PUNTA ARENAS

HOTELS. Cabo de Hornos. *Expensive.* Plaza M. Gamero 1025 (222–134). Seven-story building with 150 deluxe rooms, each with private bath and telephone. Large reception hall, restaurant, bar, Winter Garden, laundry and valet service, garage.

Los Navegantes Hotel. *Moderate.* Jose Menéndez 647 (224–677). Fifty new and comfortable rooms.

CHILEAN PATAGONIA

A paved road now leads from Punta Arenas through 150 miles of Patagonian wilderness to Puerto Natales. At the 140-km marker, the new **Hostal Estancia Rio Penitente** offers rustic luxury on a working sheep ranch. In Puerto Natales, the small, modern **Hotel Eberhard,** Puerto Montt 25, is the best. Beyond Puerto Natales an all-weather road links the Milodon Cave and Torres del Paine National Park, which are both worth a visit. Within the park, the **Hosteria Pehoe** offers comfortable accommodations and spectacular dining-room views across Lake Pehoe.

Chile's Patagonia remains a frontier for adventure travel—fishing, white-water rafting, mountain climbing, and wildlife photography.

EASTER ISLAND

Chile's mysterious Easter Island lies 2,355 miles due west from the Chilean coast. The island, alone amid over 1,000,000 sq. miles of empty Pacific, is called *Rapa Nui,* or "Navel of the World," by its 2,000 plus Polynesian residents.

Easter Island is a vast outdoor museum where over 600 giant stone statues have intrigued visitors for centuries. Almost every part of the triangular shaped 45 square mile island's volcanic landscape is dotted with the strange statues.

The island's lone town is Hanga Roa where the airstrip and main hotel are located. Accommodations are limited and reservations may be made by writing the hotel's U.S. representative: Hotel Hanga Roa, c/o LARC, Box 1435, Dundee Fl. For reservations at other hotels or guest houses contact a Santiago travel agent.

A second famous Chilean island is located within the Juan Fernandez archipelago 403 mi. west of Valparaiso. The isle is now officially known as Robinson Crusoe Island and is now home to 800 Chilean fishermen who offer increasingly frequent visitors rustic lodging and often spectacular seafood meals featuring the world's largest lobsters. The island may be reached by charter flights from the Chilean mainland. For scheduled service contact Turismo COCHA in Santiago.

ANTARCTICA

Chile is fast becoming the major gateway for tourist travel to Antarctica, the Straits of Magellan, Beagle Channel, Cape Horn, South Georgia, and the Falkland and South Orkney islands. Punta Arenas and Puerto Williams are the gateway cities for air and sea departures to the white continent. Travel is offered during the Austral summer, from November through March.

Leader in cruises to Antarctica is **Society Expeditions,** 3131 Elliot Ave., Suite 700, Seattle, WA 98121. Society's cruises feature luxury expedition ships, each complete with a fleet of outboard Zodiacs that permit landings on the Antarctic mainland and offshore islands. Fourteen scheduled departures from Puerto Williams and Punta Arenas for cruises of 10 to 21 days.

Air travel tours to Chile's Lt. Marsh Antarctic Base is also offered via Chilean military aircraft with accommodations in Antarctica's only hostelry—the 35-room **Hotel Estrella** Polar. Contact Travcoa World Tours, 875 N. Michigan Ave., Chicago, IL 60611, or one of the listed travel agencies in Santiago.

COLOMBIA

Emerald of the Spanish Main

by
EARL M. HANKS and TOM QUINN

This beautiful country, the only South American republic with a sea view of both the Pacific and the Caribbean, never fails to dazzle visitors with its soaring green mountains, lush jungles, fertile deltas, quiet Indian villages, and bustling ultra-modern cities. It has beaches on both coasts, water-skiing on tropical lagoons, snow-skiing in the Andes, and fishing in mountain lakes and the deep blue sea. Colombia is big vertically as well as horizontally, with altitudes ranging from sea level to 18,000 feet. Within a few days, one can enjoy deepsea fishing, Andean mountain climbing, swimming, snorkeling, and a visit to the heart of a tropical jungle.

Even in Europe it would be hard to find a place like the 16th-century walled city of Cartagena, which combines the charm of quaint narrow streets and balconied houses with the amenities of a glittering beach resort. But if you tire of the lazy life under the palm trees, Bogotá, Colombia's exhilarating 8,700 foot-high capital, is less than one hour away by jet. In contrast to this modern sophisticated capital, there are Amazon villages where primitive Indians practice age-old rites. Colombia's weather ranges from equatorial jungle heat to the eternal snows of mountaintops, with a broad span of temperate climate in between.

There are over 30 million Colombians, mostly of European stock, with a strong Indian mestizo flavor. The country is intensely Spanish, inhabited by a people of deep and ancient culture and proud that its capital is known as the "Athens of America," because of its many institutes of learning. It's a mecca for shopping because the quality of merchandise is high and prices, thanks to a favorable exchange rate, are low. Bargains in emeralds, leather goods, and gold jewelry are astounding.

Since Colombia has a centralized government whose main institutions are concentrated in the capital, all roads lead to Bogotá. Along them travel visitors and Colombians alike intent on seeing historic sites linked to the birth of the country. Bogotá is the home of the Presidential Palace where Bolívar once lived. *La Candelaria,* formerly called "Barrio de los Príncipes" (Suburb of the Princes), was the scene of the social, cultural, and architectural development of the city of Santa Fé de Bogotá during the Spanish colonization and domination (1550–1810).

But all roads lead out of Bogotá as well. They enable you to trade the capital's climate of a year-round April for July warmth on the Caribbean coast or in low-lying towns along the Magdalena River. If you prefer winter to spring, there are the snow-covered slopes of El Ruiz near Manizales. If you prefer the past to the present, then it's not far from Bogotá to Tunja in old Boyacá, once the seat of Indian empires rich in gold, emeralds, and huge temples, later becoming a center for colonial art that was expressed in magnificently decorated churches. In the San Agustin archeological zone, sporadic government-sponsored digging has revealed hundreds of monolithic statues (some humorous, some grim) dating from 555 B.C. If you prefer wilderness to civilization, try the primitive beaches of San Andres Island or the great plains, known as the *Llanos,* spreading out from Villavicencio. Or if you just want to go hunting and fishing, there is Leticia in the Amazon jungle. For loftier forms of amusement, there are the film festivals, local primitive carnivals, fairs—and beauty contests that can be found in Cartagena, Cali, Manizales, and Ibagué.

Capsule Colombian History

Long before the discovery of America, the Colombian territory was inhabited by natives of different races, temperaments, and languages. Among the principal groups were the Chibchas, who lived in the mountainous interior, and the Caribs, who lived along the northern coast. Most advanced of Colombia's pre-Colombians, though, were the Chibchas, excellent goldsmiths skilled in the arts of weaving and pottery. It was they who gave birth to the legend of El Dorado—the "gilded one"—with their custom of anointing their chief every year and rolling him in gold dust, which he then washed off with a ceremonial bath in Lake Guatavita.

The Chibchas had given up this custom long before the first Europeans landed on the shores of what is now Colombia, but the legend lingered on. It drove a host of adventurers to the New World and, while they did not find El Dorado, they founded New Granada, a colony that once comprised the territory of what is now Colombia, Ecuador, Panama, and Venezuela. They included the Spanish and Italian sea captains—among them Columbus, Alonso de Ojeda, Juan de la Cosa, Rodrigo de Bastidas, and Amerigo Vespucci—who sailed into the Caribbean during the late 15th and early 16th centuries. These and other explorers founded the coastal cities of Colombia and those of the interior, which still exist and thrive: Santa Marta in 1525, Cartagena in 1533, Bogotá in 1538, and others. An effort had been made by Ojeda to found a settlement at Cartagena as early as 1500, but the Spaniards were driven off by fierce Indians and the effort was abandoned.

From the 16th Century to the beginning of the 19th, Spain governed Colombia through a system of viceroys, *presidentes,* and *oidores,* but as early as 1781 movements toward independence from the mother country were under way. The seeds of revolt were first sown in the Santander town of Socorro, where the Spaniards had to give way to demands for tax reform that led to the face-losing flight of the Spanish "royal visitor" from Cartagena. They came into full harvest when declarations of independence from Spain were made in Bogotá on July 20, 1810, and in Cartagena on November 11, 1811.

But declarations were not enough. Unable to raise troops in Cartagena, Simón Bolívar left for Jamaica in 1814 and the city fell to the Spanish after an epic siege. Five years went by before Bolívar dealt a crushing blow to the Spaniards of New Granada at the decisive Battle of Boyaca on August 7, 1819, when he donned a tattered uniform to lead 2,000 patriots to victory. The Spanish viceroy fled Bogotá when news of the defeat reached the capital 75 miles away. The life of the new republic began under the presidency of Bolívar, the great Liberator, and the vice-presidency of Francisco de Paula Santander, revered as "the man of laws." But Santander was far more popular than the Liberator, and Bolívar was discredited. He was forced to leave his Bogotá palace and go into hiding under a bridge. Dampness and discouragement aggravated the tubercular condition that already plagued him and finally caused his death in Santa Marta. This marked the end of *Gran Colombia*, a union of Colombia, Venezuela, and Ecuador that broke up in 1830. Colombia suffered another territorial loss in the 20th Century when Panama was established as a separate republic in 1903.

Following independence, a number of civil wars broke out in Colombia during the 19th century for administrative, political, and religious reasons. This often blood-drenched period saw a continuous struggle for power by the Liberal and Conservative parties. The Conservatives finally gained power in 1880 and held it until 1930, a period of unbroken rule that did little to allay the bitterness of the Liberals. Political strife in Colombia was not limited to the harmless "palace revolutions" that occurred elsewhere in Latin America during this period. In 1948, for example, a civil uprising broke out in Bogotá triggering sporadic nationwide violence for 10 years. The police fought the army and farmers streamed into the capital to pillage and burn, leaving much of the city in ashes.

Perhaps the Colombians have recognized that politics in their country is too deadly a game to be played as it is elsewhere. The political and administrative features of the government were consolidated with the Constitution of 1886, and since then have been amended several times. The last amendment, in 1957, established a unique system of alternating the presidency and all other elective and appointive offices in the nation on a 50–50 basis between the Liberal and Conservative parties for a period of 16 years. This agreement led to a four-year term for Alberto Lleras Camargo, one of the leading figures in the Organization of American States, who then stepped aside for a Conservative, Guillermo Leon Valencia. Carlos Lleras, a Liberal, was President for the 1966–1970 period; and Misael Pastrana, a Conservative, held the office until 1974. In that year, the 16-year period came to an end, and a straight election was held, won by the Liberal candidate, Alfonso Lopez Michelsen, a law professor. The system of parity in appointing ministers to the cabinets, as well as governors and mayors continued until 1978. Julio Cesar Turbay Ayala, a Liberal, was President from 1978 to 1982. Belisario Betancur, a Conservative, was elected President in 1982. Virgilio Barco, Liberal president elected in May 1986, will go down in history for his heroic stance against narcotics traffic. He was succeeded by Liberal Party's Cesar Gaviria, elected in 1990 for a four-year term.

Coffee and Main Industries

Against this changing political background, the Colombian economy has developed steadily. Coffee is still the mainstay of the nation's export trade, for the high quality of Colombian coffee—the country ranks second only to Brazil as a producer—keeps it in demand. Colombia exports consumer goods such as textiles, leather items, and flowers, and manufactures cement and pharmaceuticals. Heavy industry took a big stride forward with the development of the El Cerrejon coal mine, the largest in South America. Over the past few years, Colombia has become Latin America's third largest crude petroleum exporter, behind Mexico and Venezuela. U.S. Occidental Petroleum's extensive oil discovery in 1983 resulted in the construction of a new $2 billion petrochemical complex in Cartagena. It was built in cooperation with such multinationals as Hoechst, BASF, and Shell.

The Arts

Though the country is industrializing, it has not turned its back on the arts. From prehistoric times to the present, there have been artists in Colombia. The first ones carved the shapes of birds and animals into the rocky sides of mountains and painted on the walls of caves. Later, other unknown civilizations carved great stone statues to honor departed leaders. And the Chibchas on the plateau of Bogotá fashioned hammered gold breastplates, necklaces, and diadems that are still marvels today. Then European influence was injected into this pre-Colombian art and, during the colonial era, rococo churches sprouted in the country's principal towns and cities with frescos by painters like Arce y Ceballos.

The 19th century saw a flowering of Colombian painters with Epifanio Garay, Andres Santamaria, Eugenio Zerda, Domingo Moreno Otero, and Roberto Pizano, an interpreter of charming local scenes. Major sculptors have included Romulo Rozo, Tobon Mejia, Ramon Barba, Hena Rodriguez, Josefina Abarracin, and Archila.

Colombian art, however, has come into its own, particularly in modern times. Sculpture and painting are combined by Ramirez Villamizar, for example, who uses layers of plywood to paint in bas-relief. Among the modern masters are Santiago Martinez Delgado, whose Bolívar mural in Bogotá is worth seeing, and Gonzalo Ariza, who studied in Japan with Foujita and has used Oriental style to interpret local subjects. Proudly nationalistic, he even stirred *campesinos* in country villages to create original ceramics.

As far as major painters are concerned, Colombia's Big Three today are Alejandro Obregón from Barranquilla, Enrique Grau from Cartagena, and Fernando Botero of Medellin (it's no accident that they come from three of the country's most interesting provincial cities).

Obregon first rocketed into the limelight when he painted a huge mural devoted to the labors of the working class in the Hotel El Prado in Barranquilla. The setting was none too apt; the controversy stirred by this painting ended only when it was painted over. But Obregon remained close to the roots of Colombian life with his scenes of *corridas* (bullfights), the Andes, and harbor life. One of his most famous works is a painting of a pregnant woman killed during a political riot.

Grau began at the same time as Obregon in the early 1950s, but he fell under the influence of Bernard Buffet's school of sordidness and lost hope.

Since then, his palette has brightened in his paintings of life a generation ago that are highly appreciated by Colombians.

Youngest of the trio is Botero, who paints satyrs and madmen in a style reminiscent of Goya's later years. But his still lifes of Colombian fruits are more pleasant. There is a particularly famous one in Bogotá's Jockey Club.

Among sculptors, Edgar Negret's bright-orange abstract iron bars can be seen decorating Bogotá's public buildings. Old master Rodrigo Arenas Betancur, at 70 years of age, has turned to lyrical, realistic representations of the pioneer spirit of the Americas. Most of Arenas Betancur's work can be seen in Medellin. Upcoming artists to watch for include Maria de la Paz Jaramillo with her signature tango dancers, and Dario Morales's stunning, superrealistic nudes.

Music and Dance

Music and dance are as important as art in Colombian life. Dance rhythms vary as one moves around the country. Melodious African-style *porros* and *merecumbés* on the northern coast are part of Caribbean tradition, but these dances are more stately than those of the Dominican Republic or Jamaica, perhaps because the influence of Africa is felt less strongly. In the Andes to the south, music descends from the mournful airs of the Incas, but here again, there is a distinct Colombian quality in *bambucos, joropos,* and *guabinas.* Most popular of all Afro-Colombian music and dances is the *cumbia,* in which the girl holds a lighted candle while dancing. The cumbia is also popular in the Chocó region, but there it has a slightly different rhythm.

Villancicos, Christmas carols sung everywhere during the nine days of *novena* parties that traditionally precede Christmas, are closely related to the songs sung by medieval Spanish troubadours. Carols are heard in pageants, on the street, in churches, and around Christmas cribs in homes where the holy family is always shown in a *pesebre,* a homemade moss-covered mountain scene of tiny villages, magi on camels, shepherds, and flocks.

Recently some folk dance troupes have gained prominence and the best are those headed by Delia Zapata, Sonia Osorio, and Toto La Momposina. They perform at coffee, sugar, and tobacco festivals where they rely heavily on frequent changes of costumes (this is a good opportunity to see some of the most picturesque native styles of dress, hats, and hairdos). Delia Zapata is from Chocó and specializes in coastal dances. Her *cumbia* is very well done, for she manages to catch both the spiritual and earthy aspects of this dance. Sonia Osorio was born in Barranquilla, became a ballerina in Vienna, and now interprets everything from *bambucos* to *mapalés.*

Colombian dances are likely to be accompanied by orchestras playing instruments you have never seen before. Around Tolima, there are unusual violins and guitars, the most popular being the *tiple,* a many-stringed kin to the guitar. Its softness and sweetness make it a favorite of serenaders for it adds a gentle, though primitive, quality to music. All professional local bands use the Indian flute or *flauta,* because it is part and parcel of Colombia's best-loved dance: the Caribbean *cumbia.* They also never fail to have a *raspa,* a grooved gourd that can be rubbed, scratched, or simply rapped. Marimba virtuosos are scarce, but there are still enough to keep local marimba music alive.

You are bound to hear serenaders in Colombia, where they usually work in groups of two or three. There are also several large local groups.

COLOMBIA

CARIBBEAN SEA

Guajira
Peninsula

Providencia Island
San Andres Island

Santa Marta
Salgar
Puerto Colombia
Barranquilla
Cartagena

Riohacha
GUAJIRA
Taganga
Valledupar

MAGDALENA
San Jacinto

GULF OF
DARIEN

Montería
CORDOBA

BOLIVAR

NORTE
DE
SANTANDER

VENEZUELA

PAN AMERICAN HIGHWAY

ANTIOQUIA

Magdalena River

Cúcuta

Bucaramanga

SANTANDER

ARAUCA

River

Quibdó

CHOCO

Medellín

Manizales

Manizales

CALDAS

CUNDIN-
AMARCA

Tominé
Lake

Paipa
Tópaga
Mongui
Tunja
Sogamoso
Zipaquirá
Guatavita

Tota
Lake

BOYACA

Meta

VICHADA

PACIFIC OCEAN

Armenia

VALLE

Ibagué
TOLIMA

BOGOTÁ

Villavicencio

River

Buenaventura

Buga
Palmira
Cali

Flandes
Melgar
Girardot

Fusagasugá

META

Guaviare

Popayán

CAUCA

HUILA

Neiva

Patía River

Tumaco

San Agustín

NARINO

Pasto

Garzón

Florencia

VAUPES

Mitú

Ipiales

CAQUETÁ

ANDES MTNS

ECUADOR

PAN AMERICAN HIGHWAY

Putumayo River

AMAZONAS

BRAZIL

PERU

◆ ARCHEOLOGICAL SITE

SCALE
0   150 Miles
         250 Kilometers

Amazon River

Leticia

FACTS AT YOUR FINGERTIPS

WHAT IT WILL COST. Colombia is one of the few countries in South America where costs are relatively stable.

A first-class hotel will run under $65 a day per person and one can have three meals in Colombia for $30–$40. A taxi ride in the city will cost a few dollars.

SOURCES OF INFORMATION. Two sources of information in New York City: the **Colombian Government Tourist Office** at 140 East 57th St., New York, NY 10017 (212–688–0151) and **Avianca Airlines,** 6 West 49th St., New York, NY 10020 (212–246–5241, 800–327–9899 for reservations). There are Colombian Consulates and Avianca Offices in major cities.

WHEN TO GO. Since Colombia is a tropical country with its capital lying less than 800 miles north of the Equator, climate is very largely a matter of altitude. Temperatures range from an average of about 83 degrees F. along the Caribbean coast to a chilly 55 degrees F. average (in the 40s at night, about 75 degrees at noon) in the capital city, perched in the Andes at an altitude of 8,700 feet.

Although seasons as such do not exist, in general, there can be rainfall in October and November (afternoons) and April and June. The dry season usually runs from December–March. In the coastal area, the dry season is mid-December through to April and July–September.

Rainfall, however, is never excessive, except in such coastal areas as Chocó, where rainfall averages an inch a day. It also rains in Bogotá.

WHAT TO TAKE. With climate in Colombia depending pretty largely on the altitude, what a traveler brings with him will depend on where he intends to go in the country. On the coast the climate is tropical, so sport shirts and slacks for men and cotton dresses for women are recommended. In the better hotels jackets and ties for men and dresses for women are expected at meals. In Bogotá, the days are mild and nights chilly. Pants suits or separates and a coat are fine for women; a fall-type suit for men. Don't forget your raincoat!

SPECIAL EVENTS. Colombia celebrates the following holidays: *New Year; Epiphany; St. Joseph's Day; Holy Thursday; Good Friday; Labor Day; Ascension Day; Corpus Christi; Sacred Heart; Saints Peter* and *Paul; Independence Day; Battle of Boyacá; Assumption; Columbus Day; All Saints' Day; Independence of Cartagena; Immaculate Conception;* and *Christmas.* By recent decree, most holidays falling on a weekday have been transferred to the following Monday.

Cartagena celebrates its independence from Spain on *November 11* with a week of merrymaking, parades and dancing, ending with the election of the National Beauty Queen, who is Colombia's representative to international beauty contests. It also sponsors weeks devoted to folklore and music. Its Film Festival, held in *May,* is internationally recognized.

Barranquilla's carnival season, famous throughout the hemisphere, is held the week before *Ash Wednesday.*

International tennis matches are scheduled there in *March* and international fishing competitions are held in *May* and *November.*

In *July,* Santa Marta, oldest European-founded city on the South American continent, presents a "Fiesta del Mar" with regattas, beauty contests, waterskiing exhibitions, and street dances. In late *May* or early *June,* the Flower Festival is held in Medellín, which, incidentally, is the "orchid capital of the world."

The Folklore Festival, in Ibagué, is usually held in the last week of *June.* This is Colombia's largest folklore event, and includes auto races, horse shows, shooting contests and art shows, as well as the traditional dance and music events.

Many other Colombian cities have pageants and parades. Manizales has its *feria* the second week of *January,* coinciding every two years with its International Coffee

Queen contest. Cali celebrates its fair from *December 25* to *January 1.* Sonsón has a corn festival and Neiva a *bambuco* festival.

Bogotá has bullfights most of the year, but the principal season, during which outstanding Colombian, Venezuelan, Spanish, and Mexican *toreros* appear, is in *December* and *February.* Outstanding *corridas* also take place during the Cali and Manizales *ferias* late in *December* and *January,* respectively.

A national agricultural and cattle fair is held during the first week of *August.* Independence Day *(July 20)* and the anniversary of the decisive battle of Boyacá *(August 7)* are usually occasions for showy military parades.

Bogotá's plush Colón Theater presents ballet, opera, drama and music, with international and local groups. The open-air Media Torta presents music, plays, folk dances Sunday afternoons and holidays. Free. The Community Players of Bogotá, an amateur theatre group, gives frequent performances in English.

TRAVEL DOCUMENTS AND CUSTOMS. U.S. and Canadian visitors need a valid passport, and a visa, or tourist card, which will be issued at any Colombian consulate upon presentation of round-trip tickets, valid passport, and two passport-size photos. Citizens of the U.K. only need a passport.

A 15-day Transit Card, obtained from airlines, or Colombian consulates with no photographs required, permits transit through Colombia to a third destination. e.g. Miami/Bogotá/Lima. The traveler must have a valid passport in order to obtain the Transit Card.

Four-hundred cigarettes, 50 cigars, or up to one pound of tobacco, and two bottles of liquor allowed duty free. No other restriction on personal effects. There is a $30 airport tax on international flights and a 5,000 peso (about $10) tax on domestic flights.

HOW TO GET THERE. By air. From the U.S.: To Bogotá—*Avianca* non-stop from New York, Miami, Los Angeles and Panama; *American Airlines* from Miami, New York, and Panama; *LADECO* from Miami. *Air Panama* non-stop from Panama. *Aerolineas Argentinas* non-stop from Miami. To Barranquilla— *Avianca* from New York and Miami. *American* from Miami. From Panama, *LACSA* and *COPA*. To Cartagena— *Avianca* from New York and Miami. *COPA* from Panama. To Medellín— *Avianca* from New York and Miami. *SAM* and *COPA* from Panama. To Cali— *Avianca* and *American* from New York, Miami and Panama. To San Andres— *Avianca* from Miami. From Mexico to Bogotá— *Avianca* and *Varig.*

From Europe: *Avianca* from Frankfurt, Paris and Madrid to Bogotá and Barranquilla; *British Airways* from London; *Iberia* from Madrid; *Lufthansa* from Frankfurt; *VIASA* from Rome, Milan, Paris, Amsterdam and London via Caracas.

Regional: *Intercontinental de Aviacion, Avianca, SAM, Satena,* and *Aces.*

Flying hours to Bogotá from: New York 5; Miami 2.5; San Juan 3; Paris 11; London 12; Panama 1; Lima 3; Santiago 6; Lisbon 10; Madrid 10; Rome 14; Quito 1; Rio 8; Bueno Aires 7.

By ship. The following maritime companies regularly serve Colombian ports with both passenger and combination passenger-freight vessels: From Europe *French Line, Italian Line, Pacific Steam Navigation, Royal Netherlands SS Co.* and *Linea "C."*

There is weekly passenger service between Leticia, Colombia and Iquitos, Peru via regular passenger service on The *M/V Amazonas,* a specially-constructed, thatch-roofed riverraft with a total of 29 cabins, some of which are air-conditioned and with community baths and facilities. There is an air-conditioned dining room and separate lounge and an outside bar with a covered deck. The *M/V Amazonas* sails every Saturday afternoon from Leticia, and arrives Iquitos on Tuesday morning. She departs Iquitos every Wednesday afternoon and arrives Leticia Saturday morning. The rates are $495 per person sharing a double, air-conditioned cabin and $250 per person in a non-air conditioned cabin. For further details contact: South America Reps, Box 39583, Los Angeles, Ca 90039. (818) 246–4816 inside California, (800) 423–2791 outside California.

By car. Since the road through the Darién Gap, which lies in southern Panama and northwestern Colombia, has not been completed as part of the Pan American Highway system, it is impossible to drive one's car into Colombia from Panama at the present time. Vehicles must be freighted from Panama to one of Colombia's Caribbean or Pacific ports.

By bus. TEPSA buses connect with several other South American countries out of Pasto. There are second-class buses from Maracaibo to Santa Marta and Cartagena.

CURRENCY. Monetary unit is the peso, currently exchanged at approximately 620 to the American dollar. U.S., U.K., and Canadian money is changed at hotels, banks, shops, and travel agencies. There is usually a fee for such exchange. When leaving, upon presentation of official exchange receipts, you can convert your pesos (up to $60) back into U.S. dollars.

Prices, unless noted otherwise, are in U.S. dollars.

HOTELS. Generally speaking, Colombia's hotel standards stand up well in comparison with those of other hotels throughout South America. A few of its top-notch establishments rival the finest on the continent and service is excellent. In the face of constantly increasing tourist business, the hotels of the capital and the Caribbean area are often short of space. It is advisable to reserve well in advance. A 15 percent tax is added to hotel bills throughout the country to help promote tourism. Hotel and restaurant rates are subject to change, but you may use these guidelines based on double occupancy: *Deluxe,* $80 and up; *Expensive,* $65 and up; *Moderate,* $40 and up; *Inexpensive* rates are lower. Rates quoted are for room only, no meals.

RESTAURANTS. In the capital the hours are very Spanish indeed: you'll be sitting down to an *early* dinner at 9 P.M. There's a grand choice of restaurants, ranging from *Inexpensive* (less than $8), *Moderate* ($8–$15), *Expensive* ($15–$25), to *Deluxe* (over $25) per person.

Colombian Food and Drink. Colombians rarely drink alcoholic beverages with dinner. However, there are several good wines produced in Colombia: *Santo Tomás,* a full-bodied red wine, and *Vino Moriles,* a Chianti-like wine made locally under a Domecq patent.

The Colombian liquors are "aguardiente" and rum, both extracted from sugar cane. *Viejo de Caldas, Buc, Medellín, Añejo,* and *Cundinamarca* rums are worth mentioning.

While you should avoid eating unpeeled fruit, uncooked vegetables, and salads, be sure to try some of the following regional dishes:

Viudo de Pescado (fish stew), cooked in holes dug in the ground and covered with hot rocks, is a favorite in the Magdalena River region.

Frijoles (kidney beans), prepared in Antioquia and Caldas; *Arepas* (corn griddle cakes), of common use in Antioquia, Caldas, Santander, and Valle. *Peto* (soup), made out of a special white corn with milk. *Lechona,* a special dish prepared with suckling pigs, principally in warm climates. *Tamales* is a preparation of corn dough, meats, and vegetables cooked and wrapped in banana or wild leaves. Taste *Ajiaco,* a stew that is prepared with chicken, corn on the cob, and different varieties of potatoes. *Sancocho* is a soup that can be prepared with a base of fish or chicken, and includes potatoes, yuca, and plátano.

The rolls served with dinner are unique and excellent in Colombia. *Mogollas* are whole-wheat muffins with raisin-flavored centers. *Roscón* is a sugar-sprinkled bun filled with guava jelly. *Almojábanas* are corn muffins that are enriched with cottage cheese. *Yuca* bread is made with yuca (cassava) starch and cottage cheese. *Arepas* are corn griddle cakes made with white or yellow corn flour. *Obleas* are like giant Hosts, an unsalted wafer spread with the sugar-and-milk paste called *arequipe*. *Empanadas* is pastry folded to hold a paste of chopped meat, egg, and capers. Tiny salted baked "creole" (yellow) potatoes are favorite appetizers, and highly peppered mashed avocados serve as a dip. With breakfast there are *buñuelos,* golden balls of maize flour and cheese.

TIPPING. Taxi drivers do not expect tips. Porters at airports and hotels are usually given 200 pesos per each piece of luggage. In many restaurants, bars, and cafes, a 10 percent service charge is added to the bill. If not, a 10 percent tip is suggested. At a favorite spot where you want a choice table, 15 percent is advisable. Hotel maids or clerks are seldom tipped. Locker room attendants at private clubs do not expect tips.

ELECTRIC CURRENT. A few years ago all of Colombia was converted to 110 volts, 60 cycle alternating current. If you carry sophisticated electronic equipment, it is wise to bring along a stabilizer.

USEFUL ADDRESSES. Colombia Government Tourist Office: Barranquilla—Apdo. Aereo No. 36–16; Cucuta—Apdo. Aereo No. 800; Santa Marta—Apdo. Aereo No. 50–64; San Andres—Apdo. Aereo No. 110. **Tourist Information Centers:** Bogotá—Eldorado Airport; Calle 28 # 13A–15; Cartagena—Casa Del Marquez De Valdehoyos; Medellín—Turantioquia, Calle 49, 43–52.

Embassies: U.S.A.: Calle 38, 8–61; Canada: Calle 76, 11–52, 4th fl., both in Bogotá. Great Britain: Calle 98, 9–03, 4th fl. (Apartado Aereo 4508) Bogotá; Calle 11, 1–07, Rm. 410, Cali; Carrera 44, 45–57, Barranquilla; Calle 52, 49–27, Medellín.

Tour information. **Aviatur offices:** Bogotá—Av. 19, 4–62; Barranquilla—Carrera 54, 72–96 (453–312, 456–897); Cartagena—El Laguito, Centro Commercial, Pierino Callo, Local 5, Plazoleta Piso 2 (801–001, 800–81); Medellin—Carrera 49, 55–25, Edificio El Parque (420–345). **American Express offices:** Bogotá—Carrera 10, 27–91, Local 128 (283–2955); Cartagena—Carrera 4, 7–196, Bocagrande; Cali—Carrera 3, 8–13.

Automobile Club: Av. Caracas 14 No. 46–72, Bogotá; AAA Representative in Colombia: Allen and Mary Lowrie, Ltda., Carrera 7, No. 19–29, 3rd Floor, Bogotá. Tels: 2432546, 2432457.

The **International Association for Medical Assistance for Travelers (IAMAT)** is represented in Bogotá by the Clinica Samper, Carrera 16 No. 93–38.

The **National Institute for Natural Resources (INDERENA)** is at Diagonal 34 No. 5–18.

The **Hertz Rent-A-Car** system has offices in Bogotá at the Hotel Tequendama, Hotel Bogotá Hilton, Hotel La Fontana, and Eldorado Airport.

Avis has offices in Bavaria Building in Bogotá Hotel, Bogotá Plaza, Hotel Belvedere, and at the airport.

Protestant Churches: St. Alban's Episcopal Church, Carrera 4 No. 69–06 (all services in English). St. Paul's Episcopal Church, Calle 51 No. 6–19 (all services in Spanish). Union Church of Bogotá, Cra. 4 No. 69–06 (all services in English).

Catholic Church: Colegio de Nuestra Señora del Buen Consejo, Calle 104 with Cra. 19 (all services in Spanish). There is an 11 A.M. mass in English at the chapel of the Gimnasio Moderno, CRA 9A No. 74–50.

Synagogues: Ashkenazi: Synagogue Bet David Meier, Cra. 16A No. 28–33. Sefardi: Synagogue Maguen Ovadia, Calle 79 No. 9–66. Conservative: Asociacion Israelita Montefiore, Cra. 20 No. 37–54. Synagogue Adat Israel, Cra. 7–A No. 94–20.

SECURITY. A state of siege has been in effect in Colombia off and on for the last 40 years. At press time the State Department recommended that visitors exercise caution in some parts of the country, which it listed as dangerous due to guerrilla and narcotics activity. The terrorist assassinations and bombings that flared up in 1989 have decreased, the department stated, but Colombia continues to experience random criminal and political violence. You may want to check the current safety of your destinations in Colombia with the State Department before you leave or at the U.S. Embassy in Bogotá or the Consulate in Barranquilla once in Colombia. You should always carry your passport with you and we encourage you to register at the embassy in Bogotá on arrival in case your passport is ever lost.

Specifically, the State Department listed the following places as unsafe for travel: the area east of the Andes (except the city of Leticia and adjacent tourist areas); all of Antioguia Department; most of the north coast (except for the major tourist areas such as Santa Marta, Barranquilla, Cartagena, and Capurgana); the Magdelina Medio region; rural Valle de Cauca departments; and the Uraboa region in the northwest.

How do you stay out of trouble in Bogotá? The same way you stay out of trouble in any other large city: by taking certain ordinary precautions. Gentlemen should carry their wallets in their inside coat pocket; and ladies should use a clutch purse which can be held firmly under the arm. Valuables should be left in the hotel in a safety deposit box, and the door to the hotel rooms should be locked even when you are in the room. When taking a taxi, both rear doors should be locked and the windows closed.

Some areas to be avoided are the southern sections past the Bolívar Square and the Presidential Palace, as well as the cable car station to the Shrine of Monserrate. Carrera 10, which is given over exclusively to bus traffic, is a favorite spot for pickpockets and purse-snatchers.

A special tip: The local lottery ticket salesmen have a special trick which is to rush past you as if they were going to a fire and "accidentally" let fall a sheaf of tickets. If you, as a polite visitor, stop to pick up the fallen tickets and return them to the vendor, he will immediately launch into a lengthy spiel that the incident is a sure sign that you are destined to be the big winner of that particular lottery. While he is delivering his sales pitch, you will probably be surrounded by a crowd of curious spectators; and one of them just might be after your billfold or handbag. Therefore, curb your courteous instincts and ignore the fallen tickets.

HOW TO GET AROUND. By air. Colombia, faced with the extremely difficult problem of transport in a country which is almost as vertical as it is horizontal, has developed one of the best air transportation systems in the world.

Avianca, owned by private Colombian citizens, is the oldest airline in the Americas and second oldest anywhere. It operates daily flights connecting all important cities of Colombia, including those of the Caribbean coastal area. Avianca offers a "Know Colombia" airpass which permits travel to as many as 10 cities in 30 days, without stopping at the same city twice, except for connections. The airpass must be purchased outside of Colombia and costs $250 if San Andres and Leticia are not included. The cost to include San Andres and Leticia is $365.

Other airlines conducting internal flight operations: *SAM, Aces, Satena,* plus *Helicol,* an Avianca subsidiary, for short helicopter flights.

Avianca and *SAM* operate daily flights from Bogotá, Barranquilla, and Cartagena to San Andres island. At San Andres bicycles and dune buggies can be rented. There are boat trips to Johnny Cay and the Aquarium.

By car. A good highway connects Santa Marta on the east with Cartagena, crossing the Magdalena River by a recently opened automobile bridge and passing through Barranquilla en route. The brand-new Trans-Caribbean Highway, four-laned most of the way, has now placed Barranquilla only five hours away from the border with Venezuela. Northeast of Santa Marta, in the Guajira Peninsula, roads are usually passable except during rainy periods. *Avis, Hertz, National, General, Budget,* and *Dollar* have car rental offices, but city driving is not recommended.

By bus. Highway transportation is maintained between the coastal cities and the capital and other cities of the interior, but much of the highway is rutted. Modern buses and mini-buses provide transportation between coastal towns and cities. Taxis are plentiful with rates at about $.35 per mi.; from the airport 500 pesos are added to the fare; on Sunday and evenings, 150 more, or total of 650 pesos are added. Hourly rate about 1,200 pesos. There are also shared taxis, sold on seat availability basis. City bus fares are approximately 25 US cents.

The Magdalena River is the main artery of Colombia and although passenger service on it has been suspended, the traveller would be wise to inquire about it when making arrangements to visit Colombia.

We strongly urge the ladies to hold on to their purses; men, carry your wallets in your inside coat pocket. The street urchins are adept at snatching.

SPORTS. Water Sports. Fishing is excellent the year round for marlin, sailfish, tarpon, dolphin, and tuna. A license is required, obtainable from INDERENA, the National Institute for Natural Resources (see Useful Addresses for location). International fishing competitions are held in Barranquilla in May and November.

There is good skindiving at El Rosario Islands off Cartagena. Check with local authorities beforehand, since sharks and barracuda swim in these waters. Beaches along the north coast are of white sand shelving gently into the water and swimming is the most popular sport. Fishing and skindiving are excellent in the clear waters off San Andres Island and Santa Marta. Water skiing, boating, and pedal boats are common pastimes at El Rodadero, Puerto Galeón and Hotel Irotama.

Sailing and water skiing are popular at Los Lagartos and at the Bogotá Yacht Club on Lake Tominé near the city. Water skiing on River Cauca, Cali, and at Lake Sochagota in Boyaca. Trout fishing in mountain lakes may be arranged locally.

Tennis is a very popular sport among *costeños* and an international tournament is held each March at the Country Club in Barranquilla.

Because of import restrictions rental equipment for the above sports is not readily available; visitors wanting to participate should bring their own gear.

Hunting and Mountain Climbing. For the more active sportsman, the Sierra Nevada, which begins some 30 miles east of Santa Marta, offers an experience in mountain climbing with peaks that go up to nearly 19,000 feet.

Hunting for ducks along the coast may be arranged. Also, there is hunting for jaguar, tapir, and other animals. Also available by arrangement are safaris into the *Llanos* or the Amazon basin to established hunting camps. *Jaguar Safaris S.A.,* Apartado 1280, Medellín, specializes in safaris. **(See also "Adventure Vacations" chapter.)**

Golf. In Bogotá, visitors may play golf at the *Bogotá Country Club* (two 18-hole courses), *Los Lagartos,* and *San Andres* by arranging for guest cards at their hotels or tourist agencies. All three clubs have *tennis* courts. New *El Rincon Club,* very exclusive, with Trent Jones Course. By invitation only.

Golf is also available on presentation of a guest card at the Cali Country Club (18 holes), Medellín Country Club (18), El Rodeo Golf Club in Medellín (18), El Centro Country Club in Barrancabermeja (18), Bucaramanga Country Club (18), Barranquilla Country Club (18), Cartagena Country Club (9), Barranquilla Country Club (18), and Lagos de Caujaral, overlooking the CBB, a striking 18-hole course designed by Joe Lee. The Gaira Golf Club (8 with 8 more planned) 5 min. from Rodadero in Santa Marta.

Spectator Sports. Bullfights in almost all cities, but in particular: Dec. and Feb., Bogotá; Dec. 26–Jan. 2, Cali; Jan. 1–6, Cartagena; Jan. 1–13, Manizales; Feb. 2–24, Medellín. Cockfights: Bogotá, Barranquilla, Cartagena, Santa Marta, Valledupar. International contests at Cartagena in early Jan.; Valledupar in late Apr.-early May; national contests in Popayan in mid-Oct. Polo: Bogotá, where international matches are often held. Horse races: In Bogotá on Thurs., Sun., and holiday afternoons, with paramutuel betting. Soccer: In most cities late Jan. through Dec. every Thurs. and Sun.

Baseball is extremely popular on the coast, and the Professional International Baseball Championships are held each December and January.

Exploring Colombia

BOGOTÁ

Anyone who still thinks of South America in terms of siestas and som-breros had better check his ideas at his port or airport of embarkation be-fore he comes to Bogotá. Lying though it does only a few degrees from the Equator, Colombia's capital can take on the air of a northern city.

Like most cities all over the world, Bogotá is not immune to the unfortu-nate phenomena of pickpockets and purse-snatchers. It is a very good idea to leave your passports, air tickets, the bulk of your travelers' checks and other valuables in a safety deposit box in the hotel. Gentlemen should keep their wallets in their inside coat pocket and *not* in a hip pocket; ladies should use a clutch purse which can be held firmly under the arm. Strolling south of the Bolívar Square and the Presidential Palace is discouraged, and visitors should be especially careful in the area near the cable car sta-tion to the Shrine of Monserrate.

Politically, numerically, commercially, and culturally, it is the first city of Colombia. It lies 750 miles inland from the Caribbean in a long flat valley surrounded by the peaks of the eastern Andes at an altitude of 8,700 feet. Over 6 million people live in Bogotá's Special District (similar to the District of Columbia).

Civilization came to this valley long before the arrival of Europeans. Originally, the valley was covered with the waters of a lake that disap-peared in prehistoric times, leaving rich bottom lands that supported the farming communities of the Chibcha Indians, some of the greatest crafts-men of early South America.

The Chibchas' fame as goldsmiths had spread far beyond their lofty pla-teau and, by the time it reached the lowlands, it became another version of the legend of El Dorado. It was in pursuit of this legend that Gonzalo Jimenez de Quesada set out from Santa Marta, on the northern tip of the continent, in 1536. At the head of a Spanish army and eager to duplicate the prowesses of Cortes in Mexico and Pizarro in Peru, he decided to thrust his way into the heart of the continent along the Magdalena River. Though he lost half his army at the start when his rafts overturned, he was determined to continue. He marched a ragged crew hundreds of miles along the river's banks through jungle terrain, harassed by Indians and plagued by insects. The decimated army was near desperation when it en-countered some Indian salt traders and Jimenez de Quesada realized that his goal was near. He climbed the Andes and reached the plateau shortly before the arrival of two other bands of European adventurers. He outpar-leyed them both, then took on the Chibchas who were no match for him. On August 6, 1538, he named his conquest Santa Fe de Bogotá, in honor of Bacatá, the Chibcha Indian village the conquistadores discovered there.

And then Gonzalo Jiménez de Quesada, who is believed by some au-thorities to have served as a model for Cervantes' Don Quixote, set about to build a city. While he was not up to the standard of Pizarro in Lima as a town planner, he did seek beauty. He picked the site for his city, nestling against the Andes for protection against the wind, and he encouraged colonists.

Yields on the rich lake-bottom land of the plateau were high enough to enable hacienda owners to accumulate enough wealth to lure some of Spain's greatest artisans to Bogotá. When a farmer received a land grant with the seal of the King of Spain, a skilled carpenter or cabinet-maker would accompany him on his trip. As a result, fine architecture sprang up very quickly after the Spanish conquest and Bogotá homes were aristo-cratically furnished.

The results of this workmanship are visible today in the architecture, carved altars, statues of saints and oil paintings in Bogotá's older churches. While there are several churches going back to the early 17th century, few homes and haciendas of that period have survived. However, there are sev-eral 18th-century houses: the manor house of Santa Bárbara hacienda in Usaquén, the Marqués de San Jorge mansion, and the house standing at the center of the Los Laureles hacienda. These buildings all display the hand-carved ceiling beams and the sculptured doorways that marked the great architecture of colonial New Granada. Then, after independence, 19th-century romanticism took over and left Bogotá with Greek columns and cornices. The next stage in the 1880s was gingerbread Victorian, of which some quaint examples remain. By the 1930s, Bogotá was in early modern, then it switched to the California split-level ranch house current today.

All this can be viewed from the Hotel Tequendama or the Bogotá Hil-ton, between the uptown and downtown sections. Here, the city's architec-tural layers are within easy distance, beginning with the nearby charming San Diego Church. And the view is certainly one of contrasts. Before 1948, Bogotá was not much more than a large town. Today, its growing pains are illustrated by narrow colonial streets running parallel to four-lane thoroughfares and glass-sheathed skyscrapers rising beside one-story shacks. Yet, while the center of Bogotá is a jumble of styles, contemporary city planning becomes apparent in its outlying sections. Working-class dis-tricts and factories are concentrated in the south and west, while the better shops and the homes of the more moneyed are in the north. Embassies and private mansions line the terraced sides of mountains along the main road running north out of Bogotá toward Venezuela. These residential dis-tricts are worth seeing if only for their gardens that flourish in this climate of perpetual spring.

The Plaza de Bolívar, around which the original town of Bogotá grew, is at the heart of what used to be downtown, and around it spreads what is left of the old quarter, with its narrow streets and massive mansions boasting barred windows, carved doorways, and tiled roofs extending over the sidewalks. Worth the visitor's attention in this area are: the Museum of Colonial Art, with numerous paintings and sculptures by masters of the Spanish Colonial period (open Tuesday–Saturday, 9:30 A.M.–6:15 A.M.; Sundays and holidays, 10 A.M.–5 P.M.; entrance fee: 100 pesos); Presidential Palace (if only to enjoy its handsome exterior and the colorful changing of the guard, daily at 5). Collectors would be interested in the coin museum (Casa de la Moneda) located in one of Bogotá's most beautiful examples of Spanish-American architecture. Among its coins are some used during the Colonial period, in the shape of bars bearing the royal seal. There are coins whose gold content was secretly reduced by the King of Spain, and some made by revolutionaries from empty cartridges. Most unusual of all are coins for use in leper colonies (open Monday–Friday, 9–12 A.M., 2–6 P.M.; entrance free). The Luis Angel Arango Library and Chamber Music Concert Hall is a striking example of modern architecture and a leading cultural center of the city, with art exhibits, concerts, and lectures (open Monday–Friday 9 A.M.–9 P.M.; Saturday, 8 A.M.–9 P.M.; Sunday and holidays, 8 A.M.–6 P.M., entrance free). Other museums and sites include the Mansion of the Marquis of San Jorge, a museum of pre-Colombian pottery; Museum of Popular Arts and Traditions, a restored former cloister, with courtyards, fountains and arches; Santa Clara Church and Museum, 17th century, with Spanish-Moorish style altars and ceiling; and the Cathedral and El Sagrario Chapel, containing one of the country's leading collections of paintings by Gregorio Vasquez de Arce y Ceballos.

On leaving Bolívar Square, walk along Carrera 7, which will bring you to the 16th-century San Francisco Church, with an incredibly elaborate main altar; La Tercera Church, mid-18th century (with all altars carved in natural mahogany); and finally to the highlight of any visit to Bogotá— the Gold Museum.

The collection is housed in an especially designed building, a fine example of contemporary Colombian architecture. There are some 50,000 pre-Colombian gold pieces, including anthropomorphic stylization, necklaces, pendants, nose rings, diadems, pectorals, as well as such utilitarian items as needles, ceremonial objects, etc. By weight alone, the collection is worth some $200 million. You will be overcome by the dazzling finale to your tour! Upstairs is Colombia's most valuable collection of emeralds, among them the world's largest unpolished gem-type stone. (Tuesday–Saturday, 9–4; Sunday and holidays, 9–12; entrance fee: 250 pesos.)

Next, visit the Quinta de Bolívar, the Liberator's country estate, built in 1800, and acquired by the government in 1820. It was given to Simón Bolívar in gratitude for his services. You will see the tiny bed where he slept and the small furniture used by this mighty but delicately boned man. Some of his documents are preserved, as well as weapons, clothes, maps, medals, and other objects that belonged to him. Surrounding the building is a lovely garden. The paved walk to the house is outlined by shinbones of countless cattle, to prevent slipping when it is raining. (Open Tuesday–Sunday., 10–6; entrance fee: 250 pesos.) Just past the villa is the station of the Monserrate funicular and cable car, linking the city with the summit of the mountain, affording splendid views. (Cable car daily, funicular Sun. and holidays only.)

Continuing in the same direction, you can visit the recently opened Planetarium and Museum of Natural History. You can attend demonstrations of celestial phenomena and visit the six halls, containing a collection of Colombia's flora and fauna. Close by is the Bullring and Bullfight Museum; San Diego Church, a fine example of colonial architecture; Museum of Modern Art, with an excellent permanent collection and temporary exhibits of the works of Colombian and foreign modern artists (daily 10–7); and, finally, the National Museum, housed in a 19th-century fortress/prison. This museum has archeological, ethnographic, historic, and artistic collections. They include huge statues carved by the mysterious Indians of San Agustin, an exhibit of elements in the daily life of the Chocó Indians, the work of Colombian painters, and mementos of Colombia's independence era (Tuesday–Saturday., 9:30–6:30; Sunday and holidays, 11–5; entrance fee: 250 pesos).

Also housing interesting collections are the Hierba Buena Literary Museum, with a display of manuscripts tracing Colombia's literary movements, and the Theological Seminary Museum, grouping works of religious art; until recently the former was a hacienda and its fields have been worked for centuries. As for the Theological Seminary Museum, it is a modern brick building with a tranquil view of the Bogotá *sabana* and a collection of ornate, heavily gilded church ornaments of solid silver and

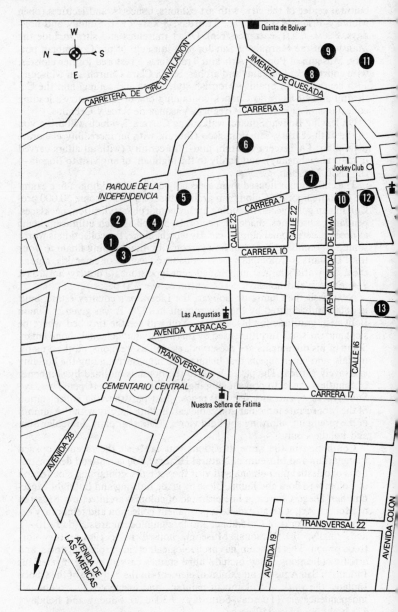

Points of Interest

1) National Museum
2) Bullring
3) Church of San Diego
4) Natural History Museum and Planetarium
5) Biblioteca Nacional

6) Universidad Jorge Tadeo Lozano
7) Las Nieves Church
8) Las Aguas Church
9) Universidad de Los Andes
10) La Tercera Church
11) Le Media Torta
12) La Veracruz Church

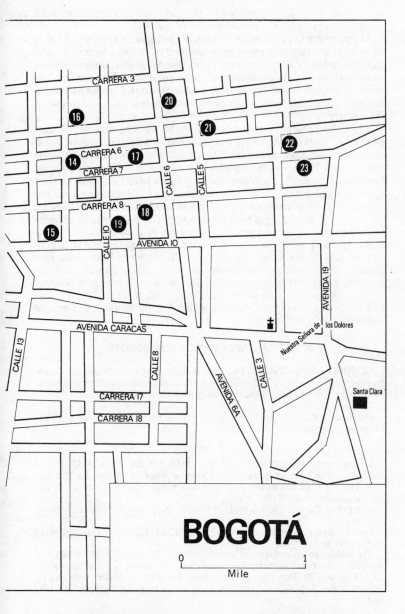

BOGOTÁ

0 _____ 1

Mile

13) La Capuchina Church
14) Basilica Primada
15) Church of San Juan de Dios
16) Casa de la Moneda (mint)
17) Colonial Art Museum
18) Church of Santa Clara
19) Colombian Academy of History
20) Nuestra Señora Del Carmen

21) Santa Barbara Church
22) Rosario University
23) La Cruces Church

portraits of early bishops painted by the great artists of their day. Both these buildings lie on the northern edge of the city.

As one roams the city, its human landscape becomes apparent. During its early years, Bogotá's population consisted of Indians, Spaniards, and mestizos, whose differences were easily distinguishable. Indian women wore long black skirts, fringed shawls, rope-soled shoes, and braided hair while Indian men dressed in calf-length white trousers, Panama hats beribboned in black, and blanket-like capes known as *ruanas*. They still do in the country.

While these costumes may occasionally be worn by visiting villagers even today, most Bogotanos are as conformist in their dress as New Yorkers. Men wear London-inspired dark suits and light raincoats, while women wear Paris, Rome, and New York fashions. Influenced by what they see on local TV programs, the Bogotanos have lost much of their aggressive individuality of the past. Since the old Indian-Spaniard mix has seen the addition of new ingredients from as far afield as Africa or Sweden, the more pronounced types tend to disappear. There is a process of Bogotanization pouring newcomers into some sort of giant mold that seems to turn out neat and fashionably dressed citizens. At the bullfights, at concerts or plays in the Colón Theater, or at the soccer stadium, Bogotanos display their fashion consciousness. They also display fashion-consciousness in the architecture and decoration of their homes, whether in the working-class south or the aristocratic north of the city. On Sundays and holidays, certain main streets are closed to traffic and given over to pedestrians, joggers, and bikers.

PRACTICAL INFORMATION FOR BOGOTÁ

GETTING AROUND BOGOTÁ. Taxis in Bogotá are metered and are recommended. Bogota has a very high theft rate, so if you do choose to walk or take public buses, wear a money belt rather than carry a purse or wallet.

HOTELS. For definitions of price categories, see "Facts at Your Fingertips" earlier in this chapter.

Deluxe

Bogotá Royal, Av. 100 No. 8A–01, (218–9911, 218–3261); fax 2183362; telex 43201 Royal Co.). Site of World Trade Center with special facilities for businessmen. Three fine restaurants and an elegant discotheque. Excellent location in garden-like setting north of city.

Charleston, Carrera 13, No. 85–42 (571–100). Very elegant; 32 suites, midtown location.

Casa Medina, Carrera 7A, No. 69A–22 (217–0288). Recently restored, Bogotá's most exclusive new hotel.

Tequendama Intercontinental, Carrera 10, No. 26–21, Box 6812 (282–9066). Top flight hotel member of the Intercontinental chain. 800 rooms, two excellent restaurants. One on 17th floor offers entertainment, but at an exorbitant cover charge. 24-hour coffee shop. Good shops. Ten blocks from major business district, near park.

Expensive

Bacatá, Calle 19, No. 5–20, Box 16815 (243–2210). Recently enlarged. Large repeat clientele. First-class rooms. In downtown area. 230 rooms.

Bogotá Plaza, Modern hotel, beautiful location in front of the famous Barraquer clinic. 50 rooms, restaurant.

Cosmos 100, Av. 106, No. 21A–41. 137 rooms, cafeteria, bar, restaurant, conference rooms. Located in the northern residential suburbs.

Dann Norte, Carrera 15 and Calle 111 (284–0100, toll free 9800–12225; fax 282–

3108, telex 42038 Danbo). Good location in north of city, near exclusive Unicentro Shopping Center.

El Presidente, Calle 23, No. 9–45, Box 12475 (284–1100). Funky location. Good for the budget-minded. Restaurant, coffee shop, bar. 160 rooms.

Los Urapanes, Carrera 13, No. 83–19 (218–1188). 32 rooms, private and cozy. European-style bar and restaurant.

Moderate

Hotel Centro Internacional, Carrera 13, No. 38–97, Box 3117. 42 rooms near the U.S. embassy.

Hotel Nueva Granada, Av. Jimenez, No. 4–81. 109 rooms near the old Bogotá section. Restaurant, bar, conference room.

Le Mirage, Carrera 15, No. 102–12 (256–1955). 6 very cozy, small rooms.

Las Terrazas, Calle 54, No. 2–12 (255–5777). Family-type hotel in residential area. Bar, restaurant. 33 rooms.

RESTAURANTS. For definitions of price categories see "Facts at Your Fingertips."

Hotel Dining Rooms

Tequendama: Monserrate Dining Room, rooftop, provides topnotch food and music for dancing. *Expensive.* **El Virrey** is a pleasant coffee shop. *Moderate.* **La Cascada** coffee shop is open 24 hours. *Inexpensive.*

Hotel Cosmos's rooftop restaurant has the best view in town and international cuisine. *Expensive.* **Bogota Plaza** restaurant is famous for culinary festivals based on typical foods of Latin American countries. *Expensive.*

Bacata: Specialty is Pineapple Surprise with chicken. **Continental:** European cuisine; Italian specialties. A special treat. **Dann:** Superior international cuisine. All three are *moderate.* **Presidente:** International cuisine. *Inexpensive.*

Typical Colombian

Noches de Colombia, Carrera 15, No. 97–65. Folklore groups provide constant entertainment. *Expensive.*

Casa Vieja, Avda. Jimenez 3–73. Also, **Casa Vieja del Claustro,** Carrera 3, 18–60 (Closed Sundays); and **Casa Vieja de San Diego,** Carrera 10, 26–50. **Restaurante La Yanuba,** Calle 122 No. 2–17, Carrera 11 No. 75–19, and Carrera 7 No. 17–01. Sun-filled garden and verandah dining. Great for Sunday lunch. **El Zaguan de las Aguas,** Calle 19, 5–62. Nice colonial dwelling. All *moderate.*

Museum of Popular Arts and Traditions, Carrera 8, 7–21. Basic Colombian cuisine. Lunch only. *Moderate.*

Spanish

Pajares Salinas, Carrera 10, 96–08 (uptown) and Calle 21, 6–43 (downtown). Delicious food. *Expensive.*

International

La Fragata, Carrera 13, 27–98. Specializes in seafood. *Deluxe.*

Chez Stefan, Carrera 18 No. 82–10; owned and operated by the best chef in town; serves *only* French food; excellent. *Expensive.*

Classic de Andrei Restaurante, Calle 75 No. 4–31. Exotic trout and jumbo shrimp specialties prepared by its Rumanian owner-chef. *Expensive.*

Eduardo's, Carrera 11, 89–43. Jet-set rendezvous, superb food. *Expensive.* Downtown branch at Calle 13, No. 8–66 has same high standard. Lunch only. *Expensive.*

Casa San Isidro, on Monserrate mountain, overlooking the city. Specializes in French food. *Expensive.*

Pimm's, Carrera 15, 82–46. Best onion soup in town. Informal. *Moderate.*

Tony Roma's, Calle 93 No. 13–85. World famous ribs. *Moderate.*

Mexican

Tacos, Carrera 15, No. 83–21. Authentic. *Inexpensive.*

Others

Barracuda, Calle 93 No. 12–18. Charcoal seafood and differently cut beef. *Expensive.*

Cream Helado, Carrera 14, 31–49. Cozy atmosphere, nice clientele. Try *arroz con pollo* or great hamburgers, milk shakes. *Inexpensive.* **Refugio Alpino,** Calle 23, 7–49. Small. Good food. Plain atmosphere. **El Museo,** Calle 37, 7–49. Excellent food and exhibition of the best of Colombia's artists. All *moderate.*

Chalet Suizo, Carrera 7 No. 21–51, centrally located. **Chesa,** Calle 23 No. 7–39, fine Swiss food, and the tea shop downstairs has pastries to make your mouth water. *Moderate.*

In the northern residential areas some good restaurants are: **Amberes, Cafe Imperial, Tramonti,** (all three *expensive*), and **Sandrick's** *(moderate).* Fried chicken like mother used to make.

El Portico, 10 miles from city. Charming. Excellent steaks. Playground equipment for youngsters, llama cart rides. Bullfighting ring for amateurs. *Expensive.*

Chicanos, Carrera 11 No. 79–50. Mexican food with Colombian touches. *Moderate.*

Mister Ribs, Avenida 82 No. 9–52, delightful atmosphere, impeccable service and spare ribs with a local sauce you'll never forget. *Moderate.*

Trafalgar Square, Carrera 13 No. 81–17, watering hole for foreign press, located in fashionable Calle 82 enclave with its exciting neon jungle of smart little bars and restaurants. *Moderate.*

For Chinese food: **Chop Suey,** Calle 101, No. 35–88. Good food and excellent atmosphere. **Hong Kong,** Calle 23, No. 5–98, is also good. Both *moderate.* **Mandarin,** Calle 100 No. 17–56; expensive, but best Chinese food in town.

Nihokan. Calle 90 No. 11A–31. Somewhat expensive; but, if Japanese food is your passion, this is your place.

SHOPPING. Because Colombia is considered a developing country, you may bring many of its locally made products into the U.S. duty free under the GSP plan.

Fine emeralds may be purchased from **Kawai,** located at Carrera 7, 24–89 (Colpatria building). The emeralds and jewelry are guaranteed. Exclusive designs. Also **W. F. Bronkie,** Carrera 9, 74–08, office 1203 (and at El Caribe Hotel in Cartagena), owned by a North American mining engineer. Other fine jewelry shops in Bogotá are **H. Stern** at Bogotá Hilton and Airport (duty free)—ask for free local "charm" and booklet. **Joyeria Bauer, Joyeria Enrique Lievano,** and **Sterling Joyeros.** Sterling Joyeros offers a free visit to their factory where you can see how emeralds are cut, polished, and mounted.

You'll find excellent leatherwork. The Colombians also have a way with straw, called *toquilla* and *iraca* and with *agave,* a tough native fiber from which they make hats, shoes, handbags, even umbrellas. **Artesanias de Colombia** offers a range of handcrafted articles in Bogotá as well as Medellín, Cucuta, Pitalito, and San Andres.

Men strike it rich in Colombian shops. Beautiful linen shirts cost as little as $25. You can get a made-to-measure suit in silk or wool for $100 and up. Top-quality shoes and hats are as low as $40. You'll find these plus accessories at the **Men's Shop** in the Hotel Tequendama, and at **Unicentro Shopping Center.**

Unicentro is also a leader for women's fashions. Which leads us to one of the unique buys of Colombia: the famous *ruana,* the striking native poncho, hand woven from hand-carded Colombian wool. An oil in the wool of native flocks makes these colorful garments almost impermeable to rain, and they're as warm as toast. Average price is only $30 to $40, depending on quality and style. **Almacen Tropicana** has a shop within Hotel Tequendama that offers the best buys in hand-loomed wool *ruanas* and artifacts.

Antique-lovers may browse in **Medina's** on Carrera 7 and Calle 50, at **Cancino Sisters** on Plaza Bolívar and at **Jaime Botero's** at Calle 10 No. 2–57, where both authentic antiques and reproductions are offered for sale in a lovely home called

La Toma de Agua, constructed in 1650. It's one of the finest examples of Spanish colonial architecture in Bogotá.

If you're an admirer of pre-Columbian artifacts and jewelry, you'll find the real thing here along with some very skillful imitations. Don't turn your back on the latter. Fashioned by hand, they make excellent souvenirs of this fascinating country, and you can actually find small charms and objects in 18 carat gold for $30 and up. For authentic pre-Columbian artifacts, check out the **Roca Gallery,** Calle 90 No. 15–17 Suite 302, owned by a knowledgeable Peruvian, Gerardo Roca. If you're lucky, he may invite you to his home to see his fantastic private collection of artifacts from the Tumaco culture. Genuine artifacts (complete with authenticity certificate) are also available at **Galeria Cano** in the Bavaria Building and in the lobby of the Bogotá Hilton. If you are pressed for time and wish to do your shopping in one spot, practically all of the shops listed above operate in the **Unicentro Shopping Center,** one of the largest in South America. If you're in town on a Sunday or a holiday, you might look over the local flea market on Carrera 3 between Calles 19 and 24. You just might pick up a real bargain.

NIGHTLIFE. Arrecifes, Av. 19, No. 123–42, provides an intimate atmosphere at its nightly show. **Tierra Colombiana** (near Hotel Tequendama) offers first-class Colombian floorshow. **La Casa del Gordo,** Carrera 16, No. 90–34, has a comedy review, restaurant, and dancing show. **Lloyd's Pub,** Carrera 14A between Calles 94 and 95, with a lively old English atmosphere, is where the foreign press meets. Discotheque **Keops** (*expensive*) is a membership club, but just show your passport or tourist card and you'll get in.

Liveliest night spots in addition to the Tequendama's **Monserrate Room** (*expensive*) and Calle 82's plethora of bars and taverns (**City Rock Cafe, Up & Down Club, Pipeline, Friday's**) can be found in the Calera Road that serpentines up the mountain behind the city: **Colors, Massai, Casa Brava, Tramonti** (all *moderate*).

EXCURSIONS FROM BOGOTÁ

Bogotá is the starting point of a number of side trips. The shortest and most famous is a trip from the eastern edge of town by funicular railroad or cable car to the venerated shrine on the peak of Monserrate. There is a splendid view of the city and the valley in which it lies.

Half an hour to the south are the Tequendama Falls, where great plumes of water splash through a sundered mountain landscape somewhat reminiscent of the Grand Canyon.

The artificial lake of Tominé, one and half hours to the northeast of Bogotá, was made in 1967. The waters cover the old town of Guatavita, but a new town called Guatavita la Nueva was built to replace it. Guatavita la Nueva is set in beautiful countryside, and its colonial-style architecture should be especially interesting to the visitor.

The Salt Cathedral of Zipaquirá is 31 miles north of Bogotá and is probably the favorite tourist spot in the country surrounding the city. It lies in the depths of a salt mine worked far beyond recorded history by the Chibcha Indians. Upon this mine an empire was built, as the Chibchas used their salt monopoly to dominate neighboring tribes in this inland region weeks away from the sea. And they converted this salt into gold. A morning's visit to the Salt Cathedral can be followed with lunch at the Liberator Inn just outside the mine or at the Funzipa Restaurant, located in an old salt-processing plant. The stately cathedral, where 10,000 people can worship, is well worth the effort.

Or else, 40 minutes to the west, there is the Archeological Park at Facatativa, fortress of the Zipa Indians, who left a number of still-undeciphered hieroglyphics inscribed on boulders.

You can take two- or three-day tours out of Bogotá on fine highways into the beautiful State of Boyacá. One covers Tunja-Sogamoso-Lake Tota and the Spanish colonial villages of Tópaga and Monguí, plus the mineral springs of Paipa and the native handicraft centers at Duitama, Nobsa, and the gardens of Tibasosa. Another tour includes the above, plus the Castille-like Villa de Leyva, the Sáchica olive groves, the 16th-century monastery of Santo Ecce Homo, and Ráquira with its traditional pottery makers and other craftsmen. There's an interesting market in Sogamoso on Tuesdays.

Beyond this, there are interesting trips to be made to a number of small towns and villages on the way to the *tierra caliente,* the hot country along the Magdalena River or to the bucolic valley of Tenza in southeastern Boyacá. Visitors may arrange trips to a ranch where fighting bulls are bred.

CENTRAL COLOMBIA

TUNJA

The city of Tunja, the capital of Boyacá, is steeped in Indian lore. This pre-Colombian civilization was deeply religious and transformed its ample supply of gold and emeralds into idols. Then the Spaniards came to the blue mountains of Boyacá under Captain Gonzalo Suarez Rendón and ordered the Indians to collect their precious idols inside their temples. The story goes that one temple full of gold was burned when two Spanish soldiers upset a torch, touching off its straw.

Boyacá boasts the greatest emerald mines of the Western Hemisphere at Muzo, Coscuez, Chivor, and Somondoco. According to another local legend, the Indians hid one mine from the Spanish for a hundred years. Then a Castillian horseman found a green rock under his horse's hoof. It turned out to be emerald matrix and he was able to trace it back to the secret mine. But Boyacá has other gems as well: colonial churches and shrines, great haciendas, fruit plantations, trout-filled lakes, and Shangri-la valleys covered with wheat fields, olive groves, and willow forests.

Tunja was an Indian religious center and it clung to its sacred role as it moved into the colonial era. Among its outstanding churches and seminaries are San Laureano, begun in 1566; the College, dating back to 1612; and the Tunja Cathedral that bears the date of 1598. Rendon built a home and settled in Tunja; this home is now open to the public (daily except Monday, 8:30–12:30 and 1:30–5), as is the home of the King's Scrivener Don Juan de Vargas (daily, 8:30–12:30; 1:30–5). San Ignacio Church is an important museum of religious art.

THE BOYACÁ AREA

Around Boyacá, there are other charming colonial towns besides Tunja. You reach them on roads that run through ranchlands and past lakes where Indian kings are said to have created the El Dorado legend by diving into lakes clad only in gold dust. Along the roads, you also see Boyacá women weaving straw hats or the wool *ruanas* worn by most Colombian mountaineers. Sogamoso has a museum that stands on the site of a great Temple of the Sun, overlooking the Conchucua Spring used by Indian priests in their rituals. Monguí offers a temple and an old convent with paintings by Arce y Ceballos, one of Colombia's greatest colonial artists. As for Chiquinquirá, its basilica and shrine draw thousands of pilgrims, for the Virgin is said to have appeared here. Villa de Leyva, a gem of colonial architecture, is located in an arid valley in which olive groves, wheat fields, and pepper trees are reminiscent of Spain. Boyacá also lures visitors with its hot sulphur springs at Paipa and nearby Lake Tota, with boating and trout fishing. Six miles from Paipa is the "Pantano de Vargas," situated at the site of one of the most important battles of the war for independence. The monument, largest of its type in Latin America, was built in honor of the battle by the sculptor Rodrigo Arenas.

West of Bogotá

A line drawn southwest of Tunja passes through Bogotá and then to Girardot, a favorite river vacation spot with its passionately tropical atmosphere punctuated by flamingo trees and blooming bougainvillea.

Across the Magdalena River at Girardot, is Flandes, a Tolima town, and many visitors make the crossing for a shot of Tolima rum that is more like a cannon shot in its impact.

Around Melgar, there are a number of resorts up in the cooler coffee country in the hills. Melgar is tiny but delightful, and a favorite weekend spot for Bogotá's diplomatic colony. Then there is Fusagasugá which also has a big Bogotá clientele, but the climate here at 6,000 feet is cool and can be rainy. Yet Fusagasugá is a good starting point for excursions by car into the 11,000-feet-high Andes. Along the road, giant ferns soar to 20-foot heights. As you climb higher, the eternal mists are brightened only by the candles placed by truck drivers in roadside shrines. A splash of color is provided on this trip by the orchid-like blossoms of *siete cueros* trees. Great bird-watching here, too!

Skipping back to Girardot and then to the northwest, there is Ibagué, best known as Colombia's music center and the home of a handsome modern country club considered to be an architectural gem. There are fine choral groups in Ibagué offering a folklore festival with excellent orchestras. From Bogotá, you can take an excursion that lasts about five days and includes the area of the Magdalena River, the center of the Andes Mountain chain, and the coffee production zone of the Manizales and Armenia.

Manizales offers an eclectic range of pastimes. There must be few places in the world that can display water-skiing, snow-skiing, and bullfighting within such a short radius. The skiing goes on at nearby El Ruiz, a peak 18,000 feet tall, and the road up from Manizales through green coffee plantations is an experience in itself. By the time you reach the snow line, the air has become quite rarified. Manizales also boasts an exciting *feria,* where the biggest attraction is the program of bullfights when the world's greatest *toreros* come to the city.

PRACTICAL INFORMATION FOR CENTRAL COLOMBIA

HOTELS. For definitions of price categories, see "Facts at Your Fingertips." **ARMENIA. Hotel Zuldemayda, Hotel Izcay, Hotel Palatino,** and **Hotel Maitama.** All centrally located and *moderately* priced.

BOYACÁ. Best are the **Suescún Hacienda** in Sogamoso at km. 4 Via Sogamoso, Box 063 (271–1251), a comfortable hotel, very popular with high Bogotá society, and **Pozo Azul,** Box 0032, on Lake Tota. In Duitama you can stop at **San Luis de Ucuenga,** km. 7 Duitama Hwy., Box 1043 (tel. in Bogotá 218–0374), a charming little inn built in a restored colonial *hacienda.* The above hotels are all *inexpensive.*

At Paipa Hot Springs is the pleasant tourist hotel, **Sochagota,** *Expensive* (tel. 211, 212, 213). Very posh, picturesque; all services. Some suites have private thermal baths.

Hospederia Duruelo, in Leyva. *Moderate.* Calle 44 No. 17–61 (tel. in Bogotá 245–1470). New and charmingly furnished and located on the brow of a hill overlooking the tile roofs of the town. Bar; restaurant; TV room; conference room. Excellent food. 66 rooms. Meals included.

The delightful **Hosteria del Molinos de Mesopotamia,** *Moderate.* Calle del Silencio (tel. 987–320–235). A restored 17th-century inn in Villa de Leyva.

Panorama Lago, *Moderate.* Box 5 (276–382). 25 rooms, restaurant, thermal water pool, sauna, water sports.

GIRARDOT. Lagomar El Peñon, *Deluxe.* Vereda Portachuelo, Box 450 (6981/4). Recently inaugurated complex offering practically anything the visitor would want. Lake with water skiing and other aquatic sports; tennis; horseback riding; swimming pool; casino; good dining room and poolside snack bar. All meals included.

Tocarema, Carrera 5A, No. 19–41 (3862, 3914, 3915) and **Bachue,** Carrera 8, No. 18–04 (226–791/95) are family-style hotels; have local atmosphere. Both *inexpensive.*

IBAGUE. Ambala, *Moderate.* Calle 11, No. 2–60, Box 1144 (63–8822). 140 air-conditioned rooms. Swimming pool and conference room for 210 persons. Very attractive.

MANIZALES. Las Colinas, Carrera 22, No. 20–20 (tel. 842–009). 65 rooms, bar, dining room with so-so food. **Carretero.** 100 rooms, bar, very good food. Both *moderate.* **Europa.** 13 rooms, comfortable but poorly located. *Inexpensive.*

MELGAR. Guadaira, charming hotel with large pool. *Moderate. Inexpensive* hotels are **Malachi,** km. 89, Via Melgar (tel. in Bogotá 245–4328) and **Sumapaz.**

MARIQUITA (near Manizales). **Las Acacias.** More motel than hotel; has 30 rooms; large swimming pool; dining room; bar, pleasant gardens. *Inexpensive.*

RESTAURANTS. For definitions of price categories, see "Facts at Your Fingertips." **GIRARDOT.** In nearby **Flandes** there are several rustic restaurants specializing in a sort of bouillabaisse called *viudo de pescado.* The most interesting of these is the houseboat restaurant down on the shore of the Magdalena. Many roadside stands offer a wide variety of goodies; they are not, however, recommended for tummy-pampering visitors. The three restaurants of the **Lagomar El Peñon** are all excellent. All range from *moderate* to *inexpensive.*

MANIZALES. The Hotel Las Colinas' dining room is not very inspired. You'd do better at **Caballo Loco, Mac's, Virrey,** and **Parador Turistico El Peñon.** All *moderate,* and all serve both International and typical Colombian food.

CAJICA. A 30-minute ride north of Bogotá. Typical Colombian restaurants, with particular recommendation for **Andres Carne De Res,** km. 25.

CALI AND ENVIRONS

There's a *feria* between Christmas and New Year's Day at Cali and this is the best time to visit Colombia's other big city. Despite its size, memories of the past remain, such as Cañasgordas, a colonial ranch house, where relics of Cali's last Royal Sheriff are preserved. Visitors can still see high canopied beds reached by ladders, a Hapsburg-style altar in a private chapel where a resident priest said masses a century ago for the Royal Sheriff's family, and an intriguing Moorish system of rainwater canals that surround the house and supply both water and air-conditioning somewhat in the way of the Alhambra in Spain. You can visit the 150-year-old Hacienda El Paraiso, a romantic museum, formerly the home of the author of *Maria.* There is a changing exhibit of local artists in the Museo de la Tertulia, near the Inter Continental Hotel. The Museum of Natural Sciences might also interest you. But Cali's best known attraction is its women, the descendants of those old ranching families, who are some of the most exquisitely beautiful in all of South America.

Nature is rewarding around Cali and offers a large variety of tropical birds in their natural habitats, including the *mirla,* which has the power of looking glum and talking.

Nearby Towns

There are two charming towns, Buga and Palmira, near Cali in the Cauca Valley. Buga is a tranquil little place tucked away in blue hills with a hospitable population that delights in opening its homes and gardens to visitors. Palmira offers the attraction of a green sea of sugar cane at harvest time, when it draws its visitors.

Then, on the rail line from Palmira, there are the red-tiled roofs and white-domed churches of Pereira (it can be reached by car, too, over a spaghetti of turns, but it's best to fly). Pereira is a young town as Colombian cities go—it is only a century old—but it has grown rapidly.

East of Cali to the Magdalena River country, there is the much-more ancient Neiva, founded in 1550 by *conquistadores* who came for its gold. Today, it raises cattle and comes to life very colorfully during its four yearly fairs: in January, April, June, and October. Travelers to colonial Neiva use it as a base for a trip that leads to one of Colombia's most memorable experiences: a visit to the San Agustin Valley where heroic-sized statues are strewn across what must once have been sacred ground in a forgotten empire. These statues share some Mayan characteristics and one theory holds that they were the work of Mayans who emigrated to the south. But the statues also have some kinship with the mysterious giants of Easter Island and their enigma makes them all the more impressive. In addition, a trip to San Agustin's Archeological Park offers an excursion to "El Estrecho" (The Narrows), a source of the Magdalena, and to a town that makes an ideal return address for letters home, called Hobo. Also in the area, at Gigante, is a giant ceiba tree covering the central square, that is supposedly over 1,000 years old. About an eight-hour drive on an unpaved road from San Agustin, or four hours from Popayan, is located the archeological site known as "Tierradentro," with its interesting necropolis of geometrically painted underground tombs.

Holy Week in Popayan

Wandering south in the direction of the Ecuadorean border, you encounter another impressive heritage of the past at Popayan, an early center of Spanish-American culture and learning. Plan your visit to Popayan during Holy Week, when scions of leading families shoulder heavy platforms bearing antique statues resplendent in jewels and velvet, strangely lifelike in their candlelit setting. Dressed in the robes of medieval penitents, the men parade past the torches of spectators in processions that end in colonial-era churches. During Holy Week of 1983, Popayan suffered a devastating earthquake that left this colonial jewel almost in total ruins; however, thanks to donations from Colombian and international entities, it has been practically rebuilt.

PRACTICAL INFORMATION FOR CALI AND ENVIRONS

HOTELS. For definitions of price categories, see "Facts at Your Fingertips."
BUENAVENTURA. Hotel Estacion. *Moderate.* Calle 2, No. 1A–08 (39–35/36). One of the most delightful hotels in Colombia. Colonial-style building; pool; discotheque; bar. 72 rooms.

BUGA. Guadalajara. *Moderate.* Calle 1, No. 13–33, Box 234 (72–611). A quality establishment, radiant with tropical flowers.

CALI. Intercontinental. *Deluxe.* Av. Colombia, No. 2–72 (823–225). Best in the city. 364 rooms; two restaurants; rooftop supper club; pool. Golf and tennis privileges arranged with a private club.

Dann. *Moderate.* Av. Colombia 1–40, Box 6100 (822–866, 823–230). New modern hotel, convention facilities. Downtown area.

Petecuy. *Moderate.* Carrera 9A, No. 15–33, Box 6662 (823–055). Located in market area, so can be noisy and unsafe. 140 air-conditioned rooms.

Aristi. *Inexpensive.* Carrera 9, No. 10–04, Box 152 (822–521, 822–516). Centrally located. Renovated, rooftop pool. Authentic pre-Columbian idols or burial jars sold inexpensively.

NEIVA. Matamundo. *Moderate.* Carrera 5 salida al sur, Box 459 (727–778). New, but resembling old colonial mansion. Flowering gardens, pool. **Hotel Plaza,** *Inexpensive.* Calle 7, No. 4–62 (723–980/6). On main square of city. Large pool, bar.

PEREIRA. Hotel Melia. *Expensive.* Carrera 13, No. 15–73 (350–770). Modern 10-story building with pool, discotheque, and bar. 138 rooms. Good Spanish restaurant. **Soratama.** *Inexpensive.* Carrera 7A, No. 19–20 (38–809). 83 rooms; bar; restaurant; located on central square overlooking controversial nude statue of Simón Bolívar.

POPAYAN. Monasterio. *Inexpensive.* Calle 4 betwwen Carrera 9 and 10 (21–91/93). An utterly charming, remodeled 17th-century convent with restaurant, bar, and swimming pool. 50 rooms.

SAN AGUSTÍN. Osoguaico. *Inexpensive.* Carretera Parque Arqueologico, Box 896 (73–069). 21 rooms, none with private bath; camping facilities; good dining room, one specialty of which is baked guinea pig. **Yalconia.** *Inexpensive.* Carretera Parque Arqueologico, Box 896 (73–013/01). The jumping-off place for viewing San Agustín's magnificent monoliths.

TIERRADENTRO (near Neiva). **Albergue de San Andres.** *Inexpensive.* (Call tourist office in Popayan, 22251.) Only seven rooms, each with private bath; open-air dining terrace; swimming pool but climate hardly conducive to bathing; horses for rent for visiting the archeological sites.

RESTAURANTS IN CALI. For definitions of price categories see "Facts at Your Fingertips."

The two restaurants of **Hotel Intercontinental Cali** have international and local dishes. The brand-new **El Campanario,** excellent international fare in charming atmosphere. **El Hostal** has international cuisine. **Don Carlos** is one of the best restaurants in Colombia's South, popular for Italian meals. All four are *moderate.* Other recommended restaurants include **Embajada Antioquena** for local cuisine, and **La Brasserie and Rotisserie,** both located in the Hotel Intercontinental; **Los Girasoles** for International food; and **Muelle 7** for seafood. All *moderately* priced.

THE PACIFIC AREA

Colombia changes when one moves from these inland regions across the Andes to the Pacific Coast. Midway along this coast lies Buenaventura, the country's busiest harbor, which is mainly a port of entry. There is not much to induce a traveler—unless he's a commercial traveler—to linger here.

Near the Ecuadorean border on the Pacific, Tumaco is still undeveloped, but has long beaches of fine sand with a steady supply of Pacific breakers for surfing. Besides swimming and surfing, the Pacific offers superlative offshore fishing and the big marlin are out there awaiting the fisherman who is willing to take them. Boats capable of reaching deep-sea grounds can be hired, but it's wise to bring your own gear. Tumaco itself is one of Colombia's newest towns. It was rebuilt a few years ago after a fire destroyed it. Gourmets know Tumaco for its giant shrimp, best eaten around a bonfire by moonlight on the beach with dinner music supplied by a local *murga,* a band of serenaders. That's the kind of tropical night that takes a long while to forget.

Pasto is also near the Ecuadorean border, but inland. It doesn't have the Pacific, but it does have Galeras, an active volcano, as well as the usual bargains found in frontier towns. It also offers unique woodwork: hand-carved tables, chairs, and trays and plates that are embossed with a latex-like sap that is dyed red or green then glued to an ivory or black background. The resulting geometric designs come from ancient Indian styles. There are some modern Indian tribes in villages near Pasto. They wear conical saucer hats that resemble those worn by Vietnamese farmers.

Still further south and looking right into Ecuador is Ipiales, in a valley bordered by three volcanoes. It draws pilgrims to its church, the Sanctuary of Our Lady of the Stones, perched seven stories above a gorge with a Gothic tower, arches, and buttresses in a tropical setting. Another local landmark is the Rumichaca Bridge, the feat of Inca engineers.

The valley around Ipiales is another stretch of Colombian cattle country. Here, the vaqueros dress in straw hats, cotton ponchos, leather chaps known as *zamarros,* and rope-soled sandals.

PRACTICAL INFORMATION FOR SOUTHWESTERN COLOMBIA

HOTELS. For definitions of price categories see "Facts at Your Fingertips." **IPIALES. Hostería Mayasquer.** *Moderate.* Carretera Panamericana, Box 696 (03984). Good, second class. 31 rooms overlooking Colombian-Ecuadorian border.

PASTO. Hotel Morasurco. *Moderate.* Av. de los Estudiantes, Box 954 (350–17/18). Two-and-one-half hour drive to Colombian-Ecuadorian border. 54 doubles, five suites. Tastefully decorated. Popular restaurant, bar, shops, convention hall.

TUMACO. Residencias La Sultana. *Inexpensive.* Calle Sucre (4381). 24 rustic rooms.

MEDELLÍN

The Caribbean coast and Bogotá usually are the main reasons for a trip to Colombia. But they certainly should not be the only reasons. During the nation's history, its spiny mountain topography led to the flourishing cities that developed a character of their own, isolated as they were as if on mid-ocean islands. These days, airlines and new roads and railroads have leapfrogged travel problems of the past, but towns and cities have retained much of their character. Since there is no stopping the steamroller of 20th-century life, it might not be a bad idea to see them before it is too late.

Colombia's second city has traditionally been Medellín, though it is now neck-and-neck with Cali for the title as both their populations hover over the 2 million mark. It lies in a mountain valley at 5,000 feet where airliners fly in and out in spectacular spirals. Though Medellín in central Colombia is the country's leading industrial beehive, you would never know it. Its prosperity is not expressed in soot and reeking chimneys, but in clean streets, flower-bedded boulevards, and magnificent residential quarters. It has a Convention Bureau, intent on promoting Medellín as "Latin America's Convention Capital."

Medellín is a sober, hard-working city that lets down its hair once a year during its annual flower festival, when it is turned into a bower and striking beauties parade through the streets under floral arches. Then Colombia's leading orchestras are flown in to keep staid Medellín dancing until all hours.

The best view of the city is from Nutibara Hill, which also has a restaurant. In 1972 the International Orchid Conference was held in buildings that are now a part of the Botanical Gardens. Over 150 years old, the buildings are being carefully reconstructed and house a reference library. The gardens exhibit a large variety of orchids and native flora. The Cathedral, built of 1,200,000 bricks, is considered the third-largest brick building in the world. Near the *Inter Continental Hotel* is the ultra-modern San Diego Shopping Mall, with quality shops. University City (for about 12,000 students) has some interesting art works and an Anthropological Museum. La Macarena, seating 10,000, has bullfights in February, on Saturday and Sunday. You will find the most complete collection of orchids in the world at El Ranchito, 10 miles from the city. The *Museo Folklorico Tejicondor* has exhibitions of handicrafts, costumes, rare musical instruments, frequent folk concerts, and dance groups (free, but check hours). "El Castillo" Museum, in the suburbs of El Poblado, is considered the most elegant place in Medellín. Beautiful gardens (open daily, 1–5 P.M.; free). Hacienda Fizebad, about one hour's drive out of Medellín, is the re-creation of a colonial village with magnificent gardens and a hacienda house, which is a veritable living museum. A favorite vacation spot for Medellín's large families is the fishing village of Tolu on the sparkling Morrosquillo Gulf. The fishing and swimming are wonderful—if you like children.

Turantioquia, the helpful local Tourist Information Office, operates delightful hotels outside of Medellín. En route to Cartagena in Caucasia, is the *Hosteria Horizontes,* a small hotel with pool, typical food and excellent service. *Santa Fe de Antioquia,* 47 miles from the city, is a colonial jewel. Of interest also are the open-air regional markets held on Friday and Saturday. You can stay at the *Mariscal Robledo,* a lovely colonial-style hotel. In La Pintada, 50 miles from the city, is the *Farrallones Motel,* a charming inn with a restaurant, pool, and spectacular views of the river, mountains, and valley.

PRACTICAL INFORMATION FOR MEDELLÍN

HOTELS. For definitions of price categories see "Facts at Your Fingertips."
Intercontinental Medellín. *Deluxe.* Calle 16 No. 28–51, Box 51855 (26–60–680). Best hotel in the city, beautifully located. 335 rooms; two restaurants; pool with poolside bar; lobby shops. Public rooms air conditioned. Well managed. Bullfighting ring for bull calves.
　　Amaru. *Expensive.* Carrera 50A, No. 53–45, Box 53100 (23–11–155 or 23–12–232). Modern hotel, centrally located, 93 rooms. Restaurant, convention facilities.
　　Nutibara. *Expensive.* Calle 52–A, No. 50–46, Box 1067 (31–91–11). Very good. 139 rooms. Located in active business and shopping district. Lovely pool, dining room, convention facilities. Gambling casino.
　　Veracruz. *Moderate.* Carrera 50, No. 54–18, Box 4266 (23–11–5511). Recently refurbished and expanding. 124 rooms. Small pool on the 11th floor, with panoramic view.
　　Inexpensive hotels include **Ambassador,** Carrera 50 No. 54–50 (315–311); **Hotel Europa Normandie,** Calle 53, No. 49–100; **Hotel Magestic,** Carrera 50 No. 55–14; **Hotel Cannes,** Carrera 50, 56–17.

　　RESTAURANTS. For definitions of price categories, see "Facts at Your Fingertips." **La Posada de la Montaña** is a must for any visitor! Exquisite, old hacienda recently converted into restaurant. Roofed dining area surrounds Spanish-tiled courtyard with lovely garden, fountain. Indoor dining also. Excellently prepared authentic regional dishes served on ceramic platters and colorful straw mats. Waitresses and waiters in regional dress. Background music. **Aguacatala** is an old wayside tavern, with very good typical cusines. At **Las Lomas** you will get excellent *paella, mariscos,* and other Spanish seafood. There are three branches of **Bremen-Manhattan,** known for German food. **Piemonte** serves Italian meat dishes. **La Yerra** has good Argentine-style food and **Monserrat** features fresh seafood. **Salvatore** has good Italian and European cuisine. International food served in **La Tranquera; El Mirador del Aburrá** is on a hill overlooking the city and serves excellent international cuisine. All range from *moderate* to *inexpensive.* For French food there is **La Bella Epoca** *(expensive),* located in the superb Torre Lavega estate and decorated with roaring twenties mementos. **La Madrileña** offers Spanish dishes. Its décor is great for bullfight aficionados. *Inexpensive.*

The **Hotel Intercontinental Medellín** has a top-floor supper club with excellent food and a spectacular view of the valley. Also a coffee shop with international food, poolside service. The **Hotel Nutibara** dining rooms are nice. Try also **Parador Tequendamita,** near Medellín; a small, informal inn. Marinilla (50 minutes from Medellín) will appeal to enthusiasts of the Colonial era and its **Camino Real Inn** specializes in "paisa" dishes. All *inexpensive* to *moderate.*

For local sausage and other regional specialties, there are several inexpensive *al fresco* cafes in the main square of the village of Envigado, about 15 minutes from downtown Medellín.

SHOPPING. In Medellín the **Centro Comercial San Diego** shopping center and **Exito** department stores offer a wide range of Colombian items.

NIGHTLIFE. In Medellín, there are four good nightclubs: **Grill de las Estrellas,** located in the Nutibara Hotel, **La Hosteria, Piamonte,** and **Fujiyama.** Discotheques: **Kevin's** and **Omega's.** And there is a casino in the same Nutibara Hotel. **Hotel Intercontinental Medellín** offers dining and dancing in the rooftop supper club.

THE CARIBBEAN COAST

The Caribbean coast of Colombia stretches from its juncture with Panama on the Gulf of Darién eastward to its boundary with Venezuela on the Peninsula of Guajira—approximately 1,200 miles of deeply indented coastline, curving sand beaches, modern port cities, and fishing villages. Beginning with the trio of cities that dominate the north coast, the visitor finds himself deep in an atmosphere reminiscent of the Spanish main, the Inquisition, and the 19th-century wars for independence.

CARTAGENA

One of the most fascinating cities of the Western Hemisphere, Cartagena de Indias, lies 15 minutes by air or two hours by highway west of Barranquilla on the Caribbean coast. A city of 850,000, Cartagena deals largely in platinum and timber from the headwaters of the Atrato and San Juan rivers, coffee from the Sierra Nevada, and oil products piped from Barrancabermeja, 335 miles up the Magdalena. An important industrial center is developing around the Mamonal area and its petro-chemical plants. The city was founded in 1533 by Don Pedro de Heredia, and for the most part still remains locked behind its massive walls on what once was an island. The city is no longer an island, since one of the two original entrances into its bay—Boca Grande—was blocked up by the Spaniards after the attack by Sir Edward Vernon in 1741. The other entrance—Boca Chica—is now the only passage into the bay from the sea, guarded by two ancient and derelict forts, San Fernando and San José. During the days when pirates of all nations harassed the Spanish Main, Cartagena was guarded by a massive chain stretched between these two forts. Launches run regularly to San Fernando, where there are facilities for picnicking and swimming.

Towering over all of the many forts that guarded the approaches to Cartagena is the powerful fortress of San Felipe de Barajas, 135 feet above sea level. Begun in 1657, it was captured and destroyed by the French in 1697. Between 1762 and 1769, it was converted into the impressive complex that it is today. A "sound-and-light" spectacle depicting the often bloody history of Cartagena is presented on Wednesday and Saturday nights against the backdrop of the fort.

After the interior of the country was settled, wealth of all kinds flowed into Cartagena for shipment to Spain, wealth which soon invited pirate attacks in spite of the sturdy defenses of the city. Cartagena was sacked by Martin Cote, by Sir Francis Drake, and by other freebooters, but an imposing fleet and powerful British army under Admiral Vernon failed before the city's stubborn resistance in 1741. Vernon was accompanied by a half-brother of George Washington in this attempt; Mount Vernon is named in his honor.

During the wars for independence, Cartagena was captured by Spanish loyalist troops under Pablo Morillo after a prolonged siege in 1815 which carved for it the title of "the Heroic City" or, as Colombians refer to it, "La Heroica." Simón Bolívar used Cartagena as his base in the Magdalena campaign in 1811.

Cartagena is divided by 17th-century walls into the "old" and "new" city. In the "old" city, houses are in the Iberian style: thick walls, high ceilings, central patios and gardens, and balconies. The streets are narrow and crooked, designed for protection during assault.

Other sites of interest to the visitor to Cartagena include the Paseo de los Mártires, a wide promenade flanked by busts of nine patriots executed by Morillo after he took the city; the Plaza Bolívar, with an equestrian statue of the Liberator in the center and flanked by the Palace of the Inquisition, a good example of colonial baroque architecture, which was built in 1776. It has a small Colonial Museum. Also noteworthy are the Cathedral (1575–1612); the Jesuit Church of St. Peter Claver (a well-to-do Spaniard who devoted his life to caring for the sick and aged among the black slaves imported from Africa to work on the construction of walls and forts), in which the body of the saint lies in a chest under the main altar; the restored 17th-century monastery of La Popa from which the best view of Cartagena is obtained; the bulwarks of Las Bovedas, now a variety of handicraft shops; the colorful and noisy market on the bay has recently been replaced by an ultramodern convention center accomodating 2,000 persons; and the restored Casa del Marques de Valdehoyos, where the Tourist Board is located.

November 11, the anniversary of the city's declaration of its independence from Spain, is the city's principal celebration and the population parades the streets in fancy dress and masks. Another feast of great popular participation is that of the Virgin of la Candelaria (Candlemas) on February 2, when pilgrims troop up the 500-foot height of La Popa bearing lighted tapers.

PRACTICAL INFORMATION FOR CARTAGENA

HOTELS. For definitions of price categories see "Facts at Your Fingertips." **Cartagena Hilton.** *Deluxe.* Apart. Aereo 1774 (650660/6). The one and only deluxe resort hotel operated on the Colombian Caribbean coast. 298 air-conditioned rooms, international cuisine at **Tinajera de Dona Rosa.** Music and dancing at **El Cangrejo.**

Capilla Del Mar. *Expensive.* Box 3939 (651140, 653866). Excellent French dining room. Coffee shop on terrace. Beauty and barber shops. Sauna. Beach. Pool. Revolving bar on 17th floor with spectacular view of bay and ocean. 189 rooms.

Caribe. *Expensive.* Carrera 1, No. 2–87, Box 1330 (650155). Completely renovated and once again open for business, this traditional hotel is probably the best located in Cartagena. Beach, bar, restaurant, swimming pool, marina, shops, even a small zoo.

Cartagena Real. *Expensive.* Ave. Malecon No. 10–150 (655555). Ideal location in Bocagrande section near restaurants, casinos, theaters, nightly entertainment.

Las Velas. *Expensive.* Calle 1, No. 1–160 El Laguito (650000). 18 floors with 95 rooms, many of them suites with kitchenettes. Good dining room; conference room; scenic swimming pool; bar on top floor offering a breathtaking view of the beach and the Caribbean. Casino.

Bahia. *Moderate.* Carrera 4 Bocagrande, Box 1629 (50316). 70 rooms, private bath and telephone, air-conditioned restaurant two blocks from beach and good value.

Barlovento. *Moderate.* Carrera 3 No. 6–23 (53965). Tourist-class hotel, 48 rooms. Private swimming pool. Dining room, watersport facilities.

El Dorado. *Moderate.* Ave. San Martin No. 4–41 Bocagrande. Wonderful location, private beach, restaurant, bar, swimming pool, shops. 180 rooms.

Hotel Flamingo. *Moderate.* Av. San Martin, No. 5–85 Boca Grande, Box 1104, (53160). 30 rooms.

Playa. *Moderate.* Carrera 2, No. 4–87 Av. San Martin (650552). Located in Bocagrande, close to the beach.

Hotel El Lago. *Inexpensive.* Calle 34, 11–15 (44192 and 46736). 104 rooms.

Resedencias Astoria. *Inexpensive.* Carrera 3, 8–96 (552237). Near beach. 12 rooms, all with private bath.

In **Monteria** (on route from Medellín to Cartagena). **Sinu.** *Moderate.* 66 air-conditioned rooms, good food, and inviting swimming pool.

RESTAURANTS. The **Capilla del Mar,** *Expensive,* is one of Colombia's great restaurants. Its owner, Pierre Daguet, is a French Gauguin-type expatriate painter. Try *Cazuela de frutos del mar,* a bouillabaisse of clams, oysters, squid and barracuda flavored with herbs, or lobster (Caribbean crayfish) thermidor. Closed Mon.

Also outstanding for seafood is the **Club de Pesca,** picturesquely situated in old Fort de San Sebastian. *Moderate.*

Costa Verde serves unusual seafood dishes. **Tinajero de Dona Rosa,** in the Hilton Hotel. International food and excellent entertainment. **Chef Julian.** Classical colonial restaurant with garden patio in rear. Lobster and jumbo shrimp specialties, as well as char-broiled steaks. **Trattoria Pietro** is the place to go for decor; also high-priced Italian meals. Daily specials. Closed Mon. **Marcel's** is a charming restaurant overlooking the sea. Fine French cuisine, Closed Wed. **Malecon 70** offers typical Colombian food and patio or indoor dining. **Grill & Discoteque Blowup** serves good seafood on the third floor. Nice view, too. Closed Monday. **El Bodegon** has outstanding soups, mouth-watering beef and sandwiches. Closed Tuesday. All of the above range from *moderate* to *inexpensive.*

Nautilius, with locations in Boca Grande and downtown. Superb seafood.

Cuban Sandwich. Super submarine sandwiches for only a couple of dollars.

La Piragua, Carrera 2, No. 8–13. Local seafood dishes. *Moderate.* **Restaurante de Doris.** Runs the gamut from typical Colombian foods to Arab dishes. *Moderate.*

NIGHTLIFE. In Cartagena: **Taberna La Quemada,** in the old walled city. A replica of a 17th-century English pub in a genuine Spanish colonial house, used in "Queimada," starring Marlon Brando. Terrific jazz sessions on weekends. **Zubiria** discotheque is very loud and very dark. Has modern American music, Latin music and great food. **Molino Rojo Disco, Aquarius** and **La Escollera** are others. **Hotel Capilla del Mar** has a basement discotheque with an all-girl orchestra, also a revolving bar, **Minerva,** on the 17th floor.

EXCURSIONS FROM CARTAGENA

A short distance by launch from Cartagena is **Bocachica** fortress, built in 1755. It is full of legend and history.

After 2½ hours' cruise on the open sea, one arrives at the unspoiled **Islas del Rosario,** a cluster of small islands where many residents of the coast and the interior have built villas and summer homes. Among the attractions of the archipelago are beautiful coral reefs and colorful tropical fish.

Two hours away from Cartagena is **San Jacinto,** where hammocks are made and one can see herds of purebred and beef cattle.

San Andres Island

One hour north by jet from Cartagena are the Colombian islands of San Andres and Providencia, possibly visited by Columbus on one of his voyages, popular among Colombians and other tourists because of their status as duty free ports, beautiful white beaches, rolling surf, and relaxed, informal atmosphere. The frequent *puentes* (holidays of three or more consecutive days) find hundreds of highland dwellers taking advantage of air excursion rates to visit them.

The island of San Andres was originally settled by Pilgrims at the same time another group landed at Plymouth Rock. The San Andres Pilgrims' ship was the *Seaflower.*

PRACTICAL INFORMATION FOR SAN ANDRES ISLAND

HOTELS. For definitions of price categories, see "Facts at Your Fingertips."

Aquarium. *Deluxe.* Av. Colombia No. 1–19 (26932). Beautiful landscape, cozy restaurant, comfortable suites, air-conditioned, live entertainment.

Calypso Beach. *Expensive.* Av. La Colombia con Duarte Blum, Box 1717 (23558, 23957). In the heart of the island. Shopping center, 78 rooms, swimming pool, water-skiing equipment.

Casablanca. *Expensive.* Av. Costa Rica No. 1–40 (25950). 62 rooms. Spanish-style architecture; beach; swimming pool; restaurant; air-conditioning.

El Isleño. *Expensive.* Av. La Playa, Bahia (23990). All 42 air-conditioned rooms have terraces overlooking beautiful beach. Attractive porch and bar. Poor food.

Royal Abacoa. *Expensive.* Av. Colombia (26932). 52 air-conditioned rooms. Nice décor. Well operated. Cafeteria. Shops.

Hotel Tiuna. *Moderate.* Avenida Colombia, 3–59. One of the better new hotels on the beach.

RESTAURANTS. Of course seafood is the order of the day here. **El Velero** is tops for seafood. **La Bruja** in the Acuario hotel has the best atmosphere. **Parrillada Los Recuerdos** features local island food and good steaks.

BARRANQUILLA

Barranquilla is a modern industrial city of over a million inhabitants and Colombia's second port, although in recent years silting of its Magdalena River entrance has caused concern to port authorities. But this is now being solved by breakwaters and steady dredging at Bocas de Ceniza, where the Magdalena River joins the Caribbean Sea. The city, founded in 1721, is located 10 miles from the river's mouth on the west bank of the Magdalena and is the principal port of entry for visitors arriving either by plane or ship from the north. The city also boasts five universities.

Barranquilla normally holds little of interest for the tourist beyond hunting or fishing, of which there is an abundance in the area, or observing the busy port and lively activity in the streets. An impressive, modern cathedral is almost completed. It has walls of stained glass and doors with aluminum and brass and will seat 3,000 people. The municipal market, on the Caño de las Compañias, a side channel of the Magdalena, is vivid and noisy. There is also a zoo with an interesting collection of Colombian species.

Normally a lively, happy city, Barranquilla becomes in the week before Lent each year what its inhabitants call *una ciudad loca*—a "crazy city," in which crowds fill the streets day and night dressed in exotic costumes and masks. There are parades of floats and folklore dances and music, a battle of flowers, beauty contests, an aquatic festival, and finally, the night before Ash Wednesday, the burial of "Joselito Carnival," the spirit of the celebration, for another year. Also observed by the *Barranquilleros* is the annual feast of San Roque on August 16.

Fifteen miles from Barranquilla eastward to the Caribbean shore is the beach resort of Puerto Colombia. Once used as the port of Barranquilla when the Magdalena became heavily silted, Puerto Colombia now serves only for the recreation of residents and visitors. Other nearby resorts include Pradomar, Salgar, Sabanilla, Galerazamba, Santa Veronica, Puerto Caiman, and Punta Rocas. Bajo de Caja (20 miles from the city) has good fishing, miniature golf, and a beach restaurant with regional food and *cumbia* performances. There is a torchlight illumination at night. Eighteen miles southwest are the excellent thermal springs of Usiacuri.

PRACTICAL INFORMATION FOR BARRANQUILLA

HOTELS. For definitions of price categories see "Facts at Your Fingertips."
Cadebia. *Expensive.* Calle 75 No. 41D–75, Box 51546 (456144). Only five star hotel in Barranquilla. 110 rooms with tub, color TV; conference rooms, sauna, pool, shops, casino, supper club.

El Golf. *Expensive.* Carrera 59B No. 81–158, Box 5953 (456933). First-class hotel, 40 suites, dining room, swimming pool, gymnasium, golf course, sauna, shopping center.

El Prado. *Expensive.* Carrera 54 No. 70–10 (456533). Lots of Spanish colonial atmosphere but sadly run-down. 200 rooms, pool, tennis courts, tropical garden. Showers only.

Royal. *Expensive.* Carrera 54, No. 68–124 (453058). Near El Prado area. Bar. Restaurant. Discotheque. Pool. 74 rooms.

Caribana. *Moderate.* Carrera 41, No. 40–02 (414277). Good downtown location. 150 rooms. One of the best in its class. Restaurant.

Doral. *Moderate.* Calle 45 No. 44–52 (28660–5). Excellent location. Informal coffee shop and bar. 83 rooms.

Génova. *Moderate,* Calle 44, 44–66. Good location; pool and garden.

Majestic. *Inexpensive.* Carrera 53, No. 54–41 (20–150/531). Near El Prado, handy for buses. Popular with North Americans. Restaurant, pool. 46 rooms.

RESTAURANTS. Devis has excellent French cuisine. *Expensive.* **Monserrate** is noted for international food. **El Calderito,** Carrera 54, No. 72–125. Typical Colombian food, specially from the Caribbean. **Biblos** serves Lebanese specialties. **El Meson de Morgan** serves top-rate seafood, as does **Juan Carlos. Parrillada La LLanerita** boasts succulent steaks. All *moderate.* **Jardines de Confusio** is a top Chinese restaurant. *Expensive.*

SHOPPING. Gutfreiind Ltd. has fine handmade jewelry, rare brass stirrups, and pre-Colombian artifacts. **Gerald Khon** offers much the same items. At the airport you can buy tax-free liquor. Colombia's best rum, Ron Viejo de Caldas, in a beautiful straw cover, sells for about $5, but this price applies only if you are on your way out of the country.

NIGHTLIFE. The best discos in Barranquilla are: **La Torre de Babel, La Caja de Pandora,** and **Tiphany.**

SANTA MARTA

Fifty airline miles northeast of Barranquilla—15 minutes by plane or one and a half hours by highway—is Santa Marta, the "Pearl of the Americas," which was founded in 1525 by Rodrigo de Bastidas, an early *conquistador.* Santa Marta lies on a deep bay protected on both flanks by ancient forts. In spite of these, however, the city was sacked by pirates in the 16th and 17th centuries.

Santa Marta, with its deep water allowing ocean-going vessels to lie alongside its docks, is an important port, embarking bananas, brought to dockside by a railway from the plantations of various fruit companies along the base of the Sierra Nevada, and coal from recently discovered deposits, reputed to be the largest in the world.

This compact range of mountains, highest of which reaches 19,500 feet, is snow-covered the year around. Coffee plantations growing a fine grade of mild coffee are found on its flanks. It is possible to reach the summit on your own, but it is advisable to use local guides.

It was to Santa Marta in 1830 that Bolívar, the liberator of half the countries of South America, came penniless, his health broken, on his way to voluntary exile after his dream of a *Gran Colombia* had shattered on the petty political machinations of his colleagues. He was given refuge at the plantation of the Marquis de Mier y Benítez, called "San Pedro Alejandrino," where he died on December 17 at the age of 47. The plantation, now a national shrine, no longer shelters the hero's remains, which were removed to Caracas in 1842, but the simple room in which he died and his few belongings may still be seen. The plantation is three miles southeast of Santa Marta on the road to the Sierra Nevada.

Aside from the beautiful Bay of Santa Marta, points of interest in and near the city are Tayrona National Park (one hour away), with spectacular, tropical beaches; a marine biology center at Punta de Betin; the Rodadero and Gaira beach; the fishing villages of La Concha and Taganga; and the Cathedral and the Church of San Francisco. El Rodadero is a modern city, with high rise condominiums, shops, casino, a branch of the famous *Unicorn* nightclub, and a tree-lined promenade along the beach. You can charter fishing boats here, snorkel, water-ski, enjoy pedalo boats, and bowl. The Aquarium features sharks, sea lions, and large tropical fish. The Museo Arqueologico del Magdalena is new. Recent archeological digs in the Santa Marta area have revealed the only stone-on-stone, pre-Hispanic construction uncovered thus far in Colombia.

PRACTICAL INFORMATION FOR SANTA MARTA

HOTELS. For definitions of price categories, see "Facts at Your Fingertips." There is no hot water at the following hotels unless otherwise noted. **Irotama.** *Expensive.* Km. 14, Box 598 (34000/2/3/4). Secluded. 134 rooms. Between airport and El Rodadero. Lovely junior suite-type cottages and new complex of buildings (excellent for groups) a short walk away. Hot water. Carefully tended gardens. Gourmet, terrace, and informal beach dining. Some entertainment. Repeat clientele indicates continued fine service. Splendid large beach.

La Sierra. *Moderate.* Carrera 1 No. 9–47, Box 694 (227960). 74 rooms, some kitchen facilities, English-speaking personnel. Snackbar on beach. Friendly service. Better value than price indicates.

Tamacá Inn. *Moderate.* Carrera 2 No. 11–A–98, Box 50–32 (27015). Right on the beach at El Rodadero, about 15 minutes from Santa Marta. 72 rooms, air-conditioning. Excellent food and service. Informal atmosphere. Adjoining casino.

El Rodadero. *Inexpensive.* Calle 11 No. 1–29, Box 611 (227262, 227371). 45 modest rooms. Contact Allen & Mary Lowrie Travel Service in Bogotá (243–2546) for rental of apartments at El Rodadero, accommodating up to 6 persons.

Hotel Miramar. *Inexpensive.* Carrera 1, 18–23 (237215).

Santamar. *Inexpensive.* Km. 8 Via Aeropuerto, Box 5056 (237098). Hot water. Pool, tennis.

RESTAURANTS. The **Irotama** will fill your every need. There is terrace dining, a gracious dining room and beachfront, informal patio. Some entertainment. Terrific drinks. At El Rodadero, the **Tamacá** is best, with a wide selection. **Capri,** on the promenade, is a gathering spot for Americans. The Italian and international cuisine is superior and the drinks generous. **La Baraca** features Spanish cuisine. **La Casa de mi Abuela** is inexpensive for seafood and international dishes. **Pez Caribe** is a highly recommended seafood place. **La Brasa** is for typical Colombian meals. Informal. The specialty of **Pacabuy** is seafood, and it's excellent. All *inexpensive* to *moderate.*

SHOPPING. In the Santa Marta area, at Rodadero, there are two branch stores of the **Tropicana**—one next door to the Capri and the other at the Tamacá. Both have a fine selection of handmade rugs, macramé bags, *ruanas.* At the Tamacá you will also find exquisite jewelry and pre-Colombian artifacts. **Cocodrilo** and **Puerto Libre** sell local souvenirs.

NIGHTLIFE. In the Santa Marta area at Rodadero there is now the exclusive **La Escollera** disco with tropical setting and Caribbean dance music.

THE NORTHEAST

BUCARAMANGA

Bucaramanga, on the other side of the Andes, very near the Venezuelan border, is a provincial capital in a spectacular site hemmed on one side by sheer cliffs crumbling in great chunks. Bucaramanga was settled in the early days of Colombian colonization. The soldiers who accompanied the German adventurer Nikolaus Federmann on his search for El Dorado passed through here. They are responsible for the high proportion of blond, blue-eyed citizens seen here today.

An archeological museum, housed in a building where Bolívar lived for two months, contains excellent pre-Columbian pottery, jewelry, and textiles that lead some scholars to presume that the Incas reached this area. Then there are the oil paintings and wood carvings in graceful churches, and also murals in the Bucaramanga city club, where an artist placed the faces of several well-known society ladies above the figures of lightly clad nymphs.

Bucaramanga's eating habits are equally picturesque. One local specialty is fried or jellied ants: fried, they come in paper bags and one crunches them like peanuts; jellied, they resemble caviar. Another is *tinajo,* a seal-like animal that tastes like pork when roasted. Finally, there is armadillo, tasting somewhat like chicken.

It's worth noting that tourists are welcome to Bucaramanga's country club. There's golf and tennis during the New Year season, and a nationally celebrated costume party.

PRACTICAL INFORMATION FOR BUCARAMANGA

HOTELS. For definitions of price categories see "Facts at Your Fingertips." **Bucarica,** Carrera 19 and Calle 35, Box 1047 (23111/14). Best in town. 90 rooms, *moderate;* bears the name of an Indian cacique on whose lands the city was founded.

Hotel Chicamocha, Calle 34, No. 31–24 (43000). *Moderate.* Swimming pool, discotheque, excellent restaurant. Pleasant family atmosphere.

RESTAURANTS. The restaurant of the **Hotel Bucarica** is fairly good. *Moderate.*

La Carreta specializes in steaks served in an open patio under huge trees. *Moderate.* The private-membership **Club Campestre** has the best food in town, served in a flower-filled garden. *Moderate.* **Bambu** serves international food. *Moderate.* **El Everest,** about 10 minutes outside town; magnificent views. *Inexpensive.*

OTHER CITIES IN THE NORTHEAST

HOTELS. BARBOSA. Moncada. *Inexpensive.* (86001). Motel with 36 rooms grouped around a large swimming pool. Bar, restaurant.

CUCUTA. Hotel Arizona. *Moderate.* (31884). One of the city's shiny new hotels. 68 rooms; bar, pool, good restaurant.

Tonchala. *Moderate.* (22005/9). Best hotel in town. 200 rooms, 80 air-conditioned, with telephone. Bar, grill, swimming pool. Vacationers from the capital come to enjoy the near-equatorial heat.

Vasconia. *Moderate.* Calle 10, 3–51 (20278). Downtown. Air-conditioned. 38 rooms.

Hotel Tonchala's dining room is very good. For fine international food served in a strikingly designed building, try **Oasis** in the Hotel Arizona. Both *moderate.*

PAMPLONA. Cariongo. *Inexpensive.* Carrera 5, Calle 9 (2944, 2807). Good, fairly new. 84 rooms. Excellent food.

RIOHACHA (east of Santa Marta). **Apartahotel Las Delicias.** *Inexpensive.* Calle 1, 7–109 (72317). 50 air-conditioned rooms; restaurant, bar. **Gimaura.** *Inexpensive.* Gimaura Av. La Playa (72266). 41 rooms, all air-conditioned.

SAN GIL. Bella Isla. *Inexpensive.* (2573311 in Bogota, 2971/79 in San Gil). 73 rooms; bar; restaurant; conference room; swimming pool; striking view from terrace.

VALLEDUPAR. Sicarare. *Inexpensive.* Carrera 9, 16–04 (22137, 22138). 56 air-conditioned rooms; all services.

PITALITO. Calamo. *Inexpensive.* (60600/2). 24 rooms; bar, restaurant; swimming pool; located on central square of town and therefore noisy.

Timanco. *Inexpensive.* (60666). 22 rooms; bar; restaurant; swimming pool; snack bar; immense grounds with lake for boating; very friendly and helpful management.

THE PLAINS

On the eastern fringe of this part of Colombia, there is a unique experience awaiting the traveler who ventures over the mountains to the great plains known as the *llanos.* The capital of this region is Villavicencio, three hours by car or half an hour by air from Bogotá. Villavicencio is cooled by nearby mountains in the evening but the days are well-nigh equatorial. The great Orinoco has its source in this region and the handsome Guaitiquia adds its waters, too, to the beauty of these endless seas of grass.

The *llanos* are good hunting country, abounding in jaguar, boar, alligator, deer, puma, tapir, and enticing birds. Safaris here should be carefully and competently planned so that the hunter does not become the hunted, with venomous snakes or carnivorous piraña fish doing the stalking. Piraña fish can strip a steer to a skeleton in minutes and hard-bitten *llaneros* always take due precautions before driving a herd across a river—they send their least valuable animal in first. The *llaneros* of Colombia belong to the same race as cowboys anywhere. They can ride hard all day long and dance their *joropo* all night. The best time to see them is in December, when Villavicencio stages a song festival and a cattle fair.

PRACTICAL INFORMATION FOR VILLAVICENCIO

HOTELS. Del Llano. *Moderate.* Carrera 30 No. 49–77, Box 2143 (24409/24412). 45 air-conditioned rooms. **Villavicencio.** *Expensive.* Carrera 30 No. 35A–22 (tel. 9866 26807; fax 9866 26438). This 70-room hotel features a restaurant, bar, and pool.

THE AMAZON

And now we have circled around most of settled Colombia. But there is still unsettled Colombia: the Amazon. Leticia, a river port, can be reached by plane from Bogotá in less than two hours. Planes have transformed it from a junglebound trading post to an international tourist center. Brazil and Peru are within easy distance here and local agents can arrange a trip to the river Atacuari, the natural border between Peru and Colombia. You can camp with the Yagua Indians and observe their weapons, customs, and general living habits. A minimum three-day stay is mandatory in most towns.

The *pièce de résistance* of a stay in Leticia is a trip on the Amazon, preferably with a good boat. Here you'll see the manatees, aquatic mammals native to tropical Atlantic coastal waters, as well as the unique birds of the Amazon. Even if you don't see anything more exciting than parrots or monkeys on your river trip, you will not go home empty-handed. That is because Leticia is practically a warehouse of animals in demand throughout the world for zoos, film sequences, or collectors. An entire Amazon island called *La Isla de Los Micos,* actually a breeding farm for rhesus monkeys, can be toured or visited overnight.

PRACTICAL INFORMATION FOR LETICIA

HOTELS. Parador Ticuna. *Expensive.* Carrera 11 No. 6–11, Box 074 (7243). with 16 cottages in operation. Pool. Also recommended: **Anaconda.** *Moderate.* Carrera 11, No. 7–34/37 (7119). Air-conditioned; restaurant, bar. Multistory, but no elevator. **Colonial.** *Moderate,* Calle 17 No. 5–43 (9819 27164). Funky location.

ECUADOR

Small, Rich, and Majestic

by
EDUARDO PROAÑO and ALMA M. SCHACHT

Ecuador is a tiny land of remarkable and beautiful contrasts. Situated on the Pacific coast, with Colombia to the north and Peru to the east and south, Ecuador is only 104,510 square miles (roughly the size of Colorado). Yet, to the unsuspecting visitor, Ecuador has been a beautiful and charming surprise, and has become for many their favorite country in South America.

Geographic Overview

The mainland of Ecuador can be classified into three main geographic areas, or climatic zones. The territory of Ecuador also encompasses the Galápagos Islands, six hundred miles west of Ecuador in the Pacific Ocean, and these islands can be considered the fourth region, or climatic zone, of that country.

The Andes Mountains form the first main climatic zone of Ecuador, and roughly divide the country down the middle, with the coastal plain to the west, and the tropical rain forest to the east. The Andes, running continuously from the northern border of Colombia and south to the Peruvian border, are actually two ranges, the Eastern Cordillera and the Western Cordillera. A high-altitude, fertile valley runs between the two ranges, and is a patchwork quilt of fields and small towns, and larger urban areas, principally Quito, the capital of Ecuador, in the northern highlands, and Cuenca in the southern highlands. This Central Valley is actually a series of basins, separated east to west by lesser ridges, and drained by rivers which run either to the tropical rain forest to the east or the Pacific coast to the west. This Central Valley is also called the "Avenue of the Volcanoes" because it is lined on either side by over 30 volcano peaks, many of which are snow-capped, and most of which, fortunately, are extinct. In the north are Cayambe (18,991 feet); Antisana (18,713 feet); Pichincha (15,728 feet), which towers over Quito on the west; Iliniza (17,266 feet); and Cotopaxi (19,346 feet). In the south are Chimborazo (20,701 feet), the tallest mountain in the world if measured from the center of the earth; Tungurahua (16,456 feet); El Altar (17,450 feet); and Sangay (17,158 feet). Understandably, for both scenery and adventure, this area receives most of the tourism to mainland Ecuador. The "sierra" is almost equatorial, so there is little seasonal variation in temperatures or climate. Generally, the months of November through May are the rainy months, averaging five inches of rainfall during this period; however, unlike the Peruvian and Bolivian Andes, there is no marked difference between rainy and dry seasons, and there is some rainfall throughout the year. Because of this, the Ecuadoran sierra boasts rich and verdant countryside and scenery year-round. The average elevation of the valleys varies from 7,000 to 9,000 feet, and temperatures range from 45 degrees F. to 68 degrees F. Temperatures vary not by latitude but by altitude.

Along Ecuador's northern coast the land is covered by a dense rain forest, and southward, as rainfall decreases, the land becomes less wooded and quickly changes into a stark desert at the Peruvian border. In the middle of this coastal strip lies the Guayas lowland, where much of Ecuador's tropical agriculture is centered. Guayaquil (pronounced Wy-ah-keel), the country's largest city and leading port, is located here on the rich delta of the Guayas River. The northern coast is tropical rain forest, and the rainfall is almost constant throughout the year. As the forest thins farther to the south, one can begin to discern a distinct rainy season from December to June. Farther to the south, around Guayaquil, the amount of annual rainfall declines, and the rainy season shrinks from January to April. On the Peruvian border there is almost no rainfall at all. The altitude of this region rarely varies more than 1,000 feet, with the exception of a hilly area west of Guayaquil, which never exceeds 2,500 feet. Therefore the temperature remains a constant 70 to 90 degrees F., and has little or no seasonal variation.

The heavily forested eastern slopes of the Andes drop to sea level and from there commences the immense Amazon River basin. This is the beginning of the world's mightiest drainage system—the headwaters of the Amazon. This vast, tropical rainforest has been exploited for oil since 1972, with an average production of 250,000 barrels per day. Ecuador and Peru have been disputing the border in this area for years, with the rich oil deposits one of the main reasons for the continued dispute. Actually, over the years Ecuador has continuously lost territory in this area to Peru through a series of wars, the most costly of which occurred in 1941. The "Oriente" contains less than 3 percent of Ecuador's population. The Napo River is the principal river and is a major tributary of the Amazon.

Ecuador also offers an "extra" to geographers and visitors, the exotic Galápagos Islands—an important destination for scientists as well as for tourists. These mysterious volcanic Pacific islands, located approximately 600 miles off Ecuador's coast, are as curiously fascinating as any place on earth, with a flora and fauna unique in the world. It is here that Charles

Darwin found inspiration for his theory of the evolution of species, when he visited the islands during the voyage of *The Beagle* in 1835.

The islands are actually the peaks of a volcanic chain of mountains, and the vegetation varies greatly according to elevation. There is, however, a hotter, rainy season from January to April. From May to December a cooling fog and cloud cover (called "garua") comes in; still, one should not be fooled by the overcast and fog. Although the sun's heat is filtered, the burning ultra violet rays are not, and protective sun covering must be worn at all times. At sea level the temperature may fall to 60 degrees F. at night, and can drop even more at the higher altitudes on the mountains, so warmer clothing is required for nighttime. The vegetation is normally sparse and the terrain is barren and rugged at sea level; at higher altitudes, however, the mountains are covered with a rich, subtropical cloud forest.

The People of Ecuador

Ecuador's population is mainly a mixture of Indian and Spanish, called "mestizo," other European nationalities, and Africans (who compose about 2 percent of the total). In the highlands, the purer, indigenous Indian population is more evident in the provinces and less urbanized areas, while the greater European mix can be seen in the major urban areas. The coastal inhabitants are a mix of three cultures: European, Indian, and African, with the African mix predominantly in the north. The highest population densities are found in the Andes (known as "la Sierra") and along the coast. The remainder of the population is found in the Oriente and on the four inhabited islands of the Galápagos.

Capsule History

Ecuador has been occupied continuously since the dawn of recorded history. Archaeologists are studying one site on the coast that has been continuously occupied for more than 5,000 years. Many generations before the Inca Empire was established, the Caras and Quitus civilizations inhabited the land.

In the early years of the fifteenth century, the powerful neighboring Incas extended their empire northward, conquering the area near present day Quito and gaining control of the surrounding country. Just before the conquest of Peru by the Spaniards, however, the Inca Empire was in the throes of a debilitating civil war. The empire had been divided between two rival half brothers: Atahualpa, who governed the northern kingdom from Quito, and Huascar, who governed the southern kingdom from Cuzco, Peru. This division was short-lived, and the brothers soon were at war for total control, with Atahualpa emerging as victor, but not after great cost to both sides. Atahualpa then transferred his court to Cuzco, Peru, and for this reason Quito was spared much of the ravaging by the Spaniards that was inflicted on Peru. Early colonial history in Ecuador was not altogether peaceful, however, as rival conquistadors fought for control, and the period is characterized by a see-saw of assassinations and treachery. Eventually, most of the original conquistadors managed to eliminate each other, and the Spanish crown sent a wily priest by the name of Pedro de la Gasca to Quito, where the last of the Pizarro brothers, Gonzalo, was still entrenched. Gonzalo's garrison, not known for their nobility of spirit or loyalty, deserted him, and de la Gasca was able to execute him on the grounds of treason.

There followed almost 300 years of peace and prosperity in Ecuador as part of the greater Viceroyalty of Peru. The rich blend of highly skilled and trained Indian craftsmen with the heavily patronized ecclesiastical art gave birth to one of the richest and most spontaneous periods of art in the Americas, which was called the "Quito School," for its distinctive style. Much that remains of this precious colonial art is housed in churches, monasteries, convents, and museums of Quito.

Ecuador started its war for independence from Spanish rule on August 10, 1809. The decisive victory at the Battle of Pichincha in 1822, under the leadership of the national hero, Field Marshal Antonio Jose de Sucre, secured Ecuadoran independence. However, Ecuador did not immediately become an autonomous state. From 1822 through 1830 Ecuador was part of a turbulent union with Venezuela and Colombia called La Gran Colombia. Even after Ecuador seceded from the union in 1830, the country's history was marked by border disputes with Colombia and Peru. The border between Colombia and Ecuador was not finally settled until 1916, and the border with Peru is still under dispute.

Serious political unrest also plagued Ecuador for the first 100 years, with power shifting between democratically elected governments and various branches of the military. In 1988 Ecuador elected its third president since the end of the last military dictatorship in 1979. Despite its turbulent history, Ecuador has remained relatively safe and stable compared to its more troubled neighbors, Colombia and Peru. The country has been severely hurt by declining prices for its oil in the international market, and has not recovered fully from the economic losses following the 1987 earthquake and the destruction wreaked by the storms accompanying the "El Niño" current in the Pacific Ocean in 1983. Despite these serious economic setbacks, Ecuador has not suffered from the extreme inflation and economic chaos that characterizes some of the other South American countries.

Economy of Soil and Sea

Ecuador is primarily an agricultural country. The great percentage of her coastal people is engaged in raising bananas (Ecuador is the world's largest exporter), coffee, cacao, rice, and sugar. The sierra farmers raise corn, wheat, and potatoes. Cattle raising is increasing on both the coast and in the sierra, and the fishing industry is developing. Shrimp and tuna processing and packaging plants are now completed and operating profitably and Ecuador is now the world's largest exporter of shrimp. Balsa, the world's lightest wood, is also an important export, as are rubber and kapok. Another famous export is Ecuador's misnamed Panama hat (although sales are dwindling because of high prices). The hats, woven from Ecuador's superior "toquilla" straw, were inadvertently given the name of the country where they were first distributed in large quantities. Other typical handicrafts—rugs, blankets, shawls, ponchos, and tweed-like materials—are produced in great quantities. Mineral resources are reportedly vast, particularly rich oil reserves in the Oriente, the rainforest east of the Andes. Petroleum resources are being developed by PetroEcuador in the Oriente, in the Gulf of Guayaquil, and also in other provinces of the coast of Ecuador. Oil is the country's principal source of foreign exchange, with an average production of 250,000 barrels per day, mostly for export. Until the discovery of oil, agriculture was the source of 90 percent of Ecuador's exportation. This sudden shift in status to oil exporter (Ecuador is second only to Venezuela for oil exportation in South America) gave rise to growing affluence. The present oil glut and decline in oil prices is putting a strain on the country.

Despite the richness of the country and the industriousness of her people, Ecuador still has all the earmarks of an underdeveloped country. Population is increasing, and there is a restricting lack of capital for development. International loans and aid programs are currently under way, however, and considerable industrial progress has been made in recent years. Agriculture gets top priority, and production has increased, owing to modernized methods. As with many nations, inflation, devaluation of the local currency, and external debt are putting various stresses on the country's economy.

The Ecuadorian Way of Life

Though Ecuador has grown and developed to a great extent, it is still a tranquil country, especially outside of Quito and Guayaquil. There the majority of citizens rise at 7 A.M. every morning and have a light breakfast of coffee and bread.

Traditionally, the business day started at 8:30 A.M. and continued until 6:30 P.M., with a two-hour midday break. The midday meal was a large affair usually consisting of hot soup followed by rice and meat, salad and fruit. This tradition still exists in the smaller cities and towns, but in Quito and Guayaquil the government offices, banks, and larger companies are adopting a single work session of "9 to 5" with an hour or less for lunch. In the evening the family dinner is usually served at 7:30 P.M. If dining out, Ecuadorans generally prefer to dine later, with restaurants having their busiest hours from about 8:30 P.M. to 10:30 P.M. Quito has much less night life than Guayaquil, where citizens have arranged their social life to take advantage of the cooler, less humid, nights. In smaller towns, social life is centered in homes or private clubs. Movies are the most popular form of entertainment, and by 10 P.M. the great majority of Ecuador is quietly in bed.

Despite the Spanish emphasis, anyone traveling in the provinces soon realizes the majority of Ecuadorans are Indian and Mestizo. In fact, *Quechua,* the leading Indian language, is spoken by more than 10 percent of the country's population exclusively. Life in the tiny Indian village has changed little in centuries and is only now beginning to feel the effects of the 20th century.

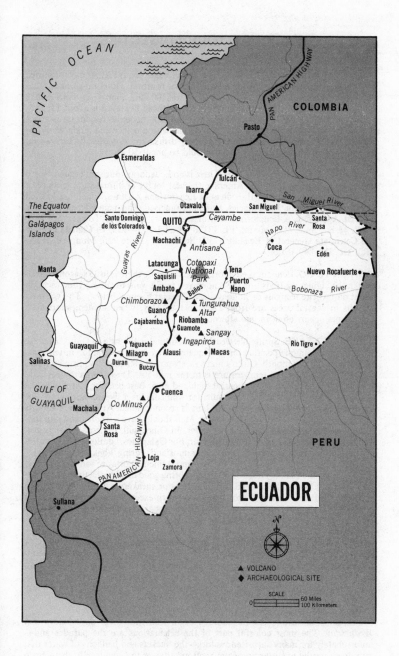

ECUADOR

▲ VOLCANO
◆ ARCHAEOLOGICAL SITE

SCALE
0 ___ 60 Miles
___ 100 Kilometers

FACTS AT YOUR FINGERTIPS

WHAT IT WILL COST. A visit to Ecuador averages about $20 per day for meals, $70 for lodging, and about $6 for each 100 miles of travel. Hotel rates range from about $20 for a double room in a tourist hotel to $100 for a double room in a deluxe hotel. Continental breakfast is about $2, and American breakfast is about $3. Dinner at an inexpensive restaurant is about $3 and at a moderate restaurant is about $6. A half-day sightseeing tour in a private car with a driver and guide would be about $50 for two ($25 per person). Evening drinks and domestic liquors would be about $4. Admission to a museum would be about $0.25.

SOURCES OF INFORMATION. There is no Ecuadoran tourist bureau in North America or Europe. In North America, the best source of information, outside of your travel agent, would be the offices of **Ecuatoriana Airlines,** which are located in New York, Miami, Los Angeles, and San Francisco. The main office is **Ecuador Tourist Agency,** c/o Ecuatoriana Airlines, Airport Executive Tower #2, 7270 N.W. 12 St., Suite 400, Miami, FL 33126 tel. 305/593–9955. **In Canada** contact the **Consulate General of Ecuador,** 1599 Stanley St., Suite 226, Montreal, H3A-1R3, tel. 514–849–0200.

WHEN TO GO. Ecuador is equatorial, and therefore there is little seasonal variation in the highlands. If visiting the Andes, you might want to choose your vacation based on favorite festivals or holidays (see "Special Events" below). The warmest months in coastal areas are from December to May, when sudden, short-lived downpours occur, often in late afternoon.

WHAT TO TAKE. Springlike weather year-round is the rule in Quito. Because of the capital's unique position on the Equator, there is little variation in temperature from month to month. Quito's highs rarely go over 80° and lows usually hover in the mid-40s. Average temperature is in the mid-50s. These temperatures hold true for most of the country's central highland area. Best bets for clothing in the sierra areas are dresses and woolen suits for women, plus a sweater and wrap. For excursions in the highlands, sports clothing is recommended. At major restaurants and hotels, a jacket is required for dinner. Men should have a woolen suit and topcoat. Raincoats are also needed in Ecuador. In Guayaquil, the coast, Galápagos, and the jungle, tropical wear is worn all year. For Galápagos, comfortable, summerweight clothing year round is the norm. For on-island touring, khakis or other lightweight cotton clothing are in order for men and women. Shorts are sometimes okay, depending on the island. The sun is strong, so bring good head protection. For walking, especially on the lava, good walking shoes or sneakers with rubber soles are recommended. No open-toed shoes should be worn except onboard boats. And, of course, bring your swimming wear. On ship, it's casual sport clothing. For the often cool evenings, a sweater or jacket is a good idea.

SPECIAL EVENTS. Highlights of an Ecuadoran visit are trips to the *ferias,* or special market days. The top attractions are the *ferias* of Otavalo, Ambato, Latacunga, Saquisili, Riobamba and Cuenca. Held once a week, they offer the visitor an excellent chance to observe true Indian life and pick up some excellent bargains. Full information on these colorful fairs and markets is contained in subsequent sections. Other special days of interest in Ecuador are:

January: *New Year's Day,* January 1. *Three Kings Day,* January 6.

February: *Carnival.* The Ecuadorans begin festivities three days before *Ash Wednesday.* The most colorful part of the celebrations are the parades and—unfortunately for many surprised visitors—the buckets and balloons of water that rain down on the unsuspecting from rooftops all over the country. Ambato Fruit and Flower Fair, held during Carnival. *Galápagos Day,* February 12.

March/April: *Semana Santa* (Holy Week). Very colorful and moving religious services all over Ecuador. *Holy Friday Processions* are very impressive.

May: *Battle of Pichincha Day,* May 24, commemorating the victory over the Spaniards at Quito.

June: *Corpus Christi* festivities, celebrated by Indians in highlands. Pujilí, a small town south of Quito, is especially noted for its festivities. *Fiesta de San Juan* (June 24, Otavalo) and *Festival de San Pedro & San Pablo* (June 28–29, in towns around Otavalo) are very lively, with street parties, sports competitions, and costumes. Also, commemoration of founding of Ecuador's Liberal Party.

July: *Bolivar's birthday,* July 24. *Founding of Guayaquil,* July 25.

August: *Primer Grito de la Independencia* (day recalling the first cry of independence of 1809), August 10.

September: First two weeks, *Festival of Yamor* in Otavalo—the most colorful of Ecuador's Indian celebrations. Native masks, costumes, dances.

October: Most popular holiday in Guayaquil is October 9, celebrating the city's independence. Parades, selection of the city's queen. *Columbus Day,* October 12.

November: *All Saints Day.* November 1. *Dia de los Muertos* (Day of the Dead), November 2. All citizens honor the dead, pay visits to cemeteries, refurbish graves of loved ones. *Dia de Cuenca* (Cuenca's Day), November 3. Latacunga celebrates its founding during the first two weeks of November. Its traditional festival of the *Mama Negra* is extremely colorful.

December: *Quito Holiday,* December 6, preceded by *Quito Fair,* bullfights, folklore exhibitions, sports events, carnival air, December 1–5. Impressive *Christmas Eve (La Noche Buena)* services. Costume pageants in Quito and Guayaquil. *Christmas Day,* December 25. *New Year's Eve,* December 31.

TRAVEL DOCUMENTS AND CUSTOMS. U.S., Canadian, and British tourists need a valid passport, a disembarkation card (filled out aboard the airplane or ship before arrival), proof of citizenship, and a return ticket or ticket for ongoing transportation out of the country. The disembarkation card must be returned upon departure. You will not be allowed to leave the country without it. Also, be sure your passport is valid for the duration of your planned stay in the country. You may be denied entry if there are only a few days remaining until your passport expires, and you may be denied permission to leave the country if your passport has expired during your visit. Visas are required for stays of longer than 90 days. 300 cigarettes or 50 cigars and one liter of alcoholic beverage are allowed duty-free. Travelers with portable computers should check with the Ecuadoran Embassy before attempting to bring them into the country. Exit and airport tax is $25.

GETTING TO ECUADOR. By air. There is excellent international air service to Ecuador. From New York: *Avianca* flies daily to Quito, *Ecuatoriana* four times per week, and *Viasa* once a week (via Caracas). From Miami: *American, Ecuatoriana, Saeta,* and *Avianca* have daily flights to Quito and Guayaquil, and both *Viasa* and *AeroPeru* have weekly flights. From Los Angeles: *Avianca* has three flights a week, and *Ecuatoriana* two. From Chicago: *Ecuatoriana* has two flights per week. *Viasa* has weekly flights from Houston and Toronto. From Europe: *KLM, Iberia, Lufthansa, Viasa,* and *Air France* provide service from Amsterdam, Frankfurt, London, Lisbon, Madrid, Milan, Oporto, Paris, Rome, and Zurich. From Central and South America and the Caribbean: *KLM, Iberia, Viasa, Avianca, Aerolineas Argentinas, AeroPeru, Lufthansa, Air France, Ecuatoriana,* and *Varig* provide service from Asunción, Aruba, Bogotá, Buenos Aires, Caracas, Curaçao, Lima, Mexico, Panamá, Rio, San José, San Juan, Santiago, and São Paulo.

By sea. There is no longer any passenger service to or from Ecuador on either regular passenger ships or passenger-carrying cargo boats.

By road. Ecuador's portion of the Pan American Highway is complete and bisects the country from the Colombian border at Tulcán south to Quito and on to Riobamba, Cuenca, Loja, and ends at Macará. The highway is completely paved, generally in good condition, and extremely scenic. A road to Huaquillas on the Peruvian border is open.

Bus service within Ecuador is plentiful and inexpensive, although buses in the provinces are usually extremely crowded and often primitive. Bus service between Quito and Guayaquil and from Quito to the main cities of the highlands is good. There are reserved seats.

By rail. There is no international railway service to Ecuador.

CURRENCY. The monetary unit is the *sucre*. Bills are issued in the following denominations: 5, 10, 20, 50, 100, 500, 1,000, and 5,000 sucres; the 10,000-sucre bill is due out soon. Coins in one, 5, 10, 20, and 50 sucres. Travelers checks and U.S. dollars are accepted for payment in most hotels and shops; however, travelers checks in U.S. dollars are easier to exchange than Canadian dollars or pounds sterling. Since early 1982, the sucre has suffered devaluations, and high inflation. Inflation has recently slid down to 40% from over 80%. Recently, the free-market rate for sucres has hovered at around 880 sucres to the U.S.$. Rates can, however, fluctuate substantially. Prices, unless noted otherwise, are in U.S. dollars.

HOTELS. Our selection of hotels in Ecuador follows the simple grading system: *Very Expensive,* $80 and up; *Expensive,* $46–$79; *Moderate,* $21–45; and *Inexpensive,* less than $20. Besides these categories, there are many more inexpensive possibilities; however, we are limiting inexpensive to clean, acceptable hotels with rooms with private baths. These categories apply to the main cities in Ecuador, but this differentiation quickly disappears to "best available" when outside of the main urban centers. "Best available" could be very quaint and comfortable, and at worst clean and acceptable. Reservations can be made for most luxury or superior hotels through one of the chains or through a reservations representation firm. One of the better tour wholesalers for South America can make reservations with inexpensive hotels, though there will probably be a service charge. Otherwise, the only way to make reservations with some moderate hotels and all inexpensive hotels is by correspondence, which is not very reliable.

Most hotel rates in Ecuador do not include breakfast or tax and service, so make sure you verify what the rates include when making your inquiries. A 10% service charge and 10% government tax is mandatory, and will be added to all of your hotel and restaurant charges, so you might as well take this into account from the very beginning.

Pensions, Guest Houses. If you find hotels impersonal, or are planning an extended stay in Quito, a pleasant and economic alternative are guest houses, known locally as *posadas* or *residenciales.* These are usually large, older houses refurbished to accommodate guests, and will often have a garden and TV room, and include cooking privileges. The friendly, more intimate atmosphere of most *posadas* makes them worth investigating.

Youth hostels do not exist per se, primarily because there are no huge waves of young people making annual summer migrations, as there are in Europe. One can always obtain clean, very basic accommodations in most cities for about $2 to $5 per night; however, you might have to share your room with another person, and the bathroom may be down the hall.

Roughing It. The climatic conditions in a good part of Ecuador are not conducive to camping due to low nighttime temperatures and a relatively high rate of precipitation all year round. In areas such as the Galápagos Islands, where the weather would be suitable for camping, camping is all but forbidden.

RESTAURANTS. Our restaurant grading system has three categories: *Expensive,* $20 per person and up (way up); *Moderate,* $10–$20 per person; and *Inexpensive,* $5–$10 per person. As many people have already discovered, moderate or inexpensive does not always exclude good food. Expensive restaurants might be charging for atmosphere, elegant decor, service, and gourmet cuisine, but very good, tasty food can be had in simple, unpretentious surroundings. Always be careful with foods that can be easily tainted, such as pork and shellfish, if you are not eating in one of the better restaurants, because refrigeration methods might be primitive. The cost of your meal will also naturally depend on how many "extras," especially alcoholic beverages, are consumed in addition to the main course.

Ecuadoran Food and Drink. Ecuadoran cuisine, especially in the large cities, is international, and Quito and Guayaquil offer a great variety of restaurants to choose from. Naturally, fresh fish from the Pacific coast is highly recommended. There is good French, Italian, German, and Continental cuisine, as well as typical Ecuadoran cuisine. If you want to sample some typical Ecuadoran dishes, try *Llapingachos* (ya-ping-ga'-chos), mashed potato and cheese cakes. *Ceviche* (say-vichi), a variety of marinated seafood with cilantro, onion, and hot peppers (slightly different from jalapeños), is known more as a Peruvian dish, but is popular in Ecuador as well. (Avoid the fish ceviche: it may be contaminated by some unpleasant, if not downright dangerous, parasites.) Also try *humitas,* a delicately flavored sweet-corn tamale, and *cuy,* baked guinea pig, a traditional Ecuadoran delicacy.

The rich coastal plains and the abundant tropical rain forest have blessed Ecuador with a wide variety of delicious fruits, many of which are not known outside of South America. A unique fruit juice called *naranjilla* (nah-rahn-hee'-ya) has a delicious flavor between citrus and peach. Best of the jungle fruits is *chirimoya* (chee-ree-moy'-a), with a sweet, custardlike pulp. *Mamey,* with red, sweet, squash-like meat, *pepinos,* which look like white and purple striped cucumbers, and Ecuadoran pineapples are all very sweet and juicy.

Like governments in most South American countries, the Ecuadoran government imposes heavy import duties on all luxury items, and this includes liquor and cigarettes. Ecuador has a very small national liquor industry, but has national vodka and gin. Therefore, in a country where everything else seems so economical, the consumption of alcoholic beverages could be costly. A cocktail of imported liquor will cost a minimum of $2 plus 20% tax and service. There are, however, some enjoyable local drinks which will surprise you with their low cost.

Beer! Ecuador has some of South America's finest brews. *Pilsener* and *Club* are the two top labels. A local drink, *canelaso,* is made with hot water, sugar cane spirits, lemon, and cinnamon. There is also an anise-flavored liquor called *aguardiente* which, when mixed with lemon, makes a drink called a *paico.* Imported Chilean wines are not as expensive as other wines, and are excellent. For any other liquors, we suggest that you stock up on your favorite flavors in the duty free shops before entering Ecuador.

TIPPING. Many restaurants, bars, and hotels automatically add 20% service charge to the bill. An additional modest gratuity (5% to 10%) is appreciated but not expected. Tipping to guides is $2 per person per day for a full day group tour. Drivers should be tipped about half that amount. On private tours, guides are tipped about $10 per day. Porters at the airport should be tipped a $.25 per bag, and hotel porters should be tipped $.50 per bag. Taxi drivers are independent, and need not be tipped.

BUSINESS HOURS AND HOLIDAYS. Shops are open from 9 A.M. to 5:30 P.M. Mon. through Fri., and close around noon on Sat., although there is an increasing trend among shops to stay open on Sat. The only shops open in Quito and Guayaquil on Sunday are those in the modern shopping centers. By law, pharmacies take turns providing service at night and on the weekends. (Hotel personnel are geniuses for finding open stores on Sun.) Government offices, post offices, and airline ticket offices are open Mon. through Fri. 9–5; banks generally 9:30–1:30. Airline ticket offices and some post offices are open 9–12 noon on Sat. Foreign consulates are generally open from 10 A.M. to 12 noon, and from 2 to 4 P.M. Mon. through Fri., but these hours may vary with each consulate. Consulates will also be closed on the national holidays of that country. Restaurants are usually open 6 days a week and dinner is usually served until 10:30 or 11 P.M., and some places will serve even later. It can be difficult to find restaurants open on Sundays. There are no required hours for closing drinking establishments, but they usually close about 4 A.M., if the crowd hasn't dispersed yet. If the crowd is very good, and the party persists, the 4 A.M. closing might even be suspended. Casinos usually close at 4 A.M.

National Holidays: Jan. 1 (New Year's Day), Jan. 6 (3 King's Day), Tuesday and Wednesday before Lent (Carnival, a movable feast), Holy Thursday and Good Friday before Easter (movable feasts), May 1 (Labor Day), May 24 (Pichincha Day), July 24 (Bolívar's Birthday), Aug. 10 (Independence Day), Oct. 12 (Columbus Day), Nov. 1 & 2 (All Saints & Souls Days), and Dec. 24 & 25 (Christmas Eve and Christmas Day). There are also local holidays in several towns, when the local municipalities and stores are closed: Guayaquil Day, Oct. 9; Cuenca Day, Nov. 3; and Quito Holiday, Dec. 6.

TELEPHONES. Long distance direct dialing is available only in the newest hotels: in Quito, the Alameda Real and Oro Verde; in Guayaquil, the Oro Verde and the Uni Centro. Otherwise, if you have a room with a telephone, you can place your call through the hotel operator. It is not possible at present to make collect calls from Ecuador! There are public telephone and telegraph stations in every city and town, although in the smaller towns the system is very primitive and unreliable. If you cannot find a public phone, most shops that have phones will let you make a local call for about 20 sucres (about 2 cents). Plan not to be able to communicate with the rest of the world when you are away from major urban centers. IETEL, Ecuador's telephone company, now has offices in Puerto Ayora and on San Cristóbal in the Galápagos Islands, but communication with the mainland can be difficult or impossible at times. Short wave radio can be used to communicate with an operator on the mainland, who can then relay messages for you; however, if you cannot be without daily communication with the world, forget the Galápagos Islands.

Most luxury, superior, and many moderate hotels have fax and telex which you can use for a fee; this is the most economical and dependable way of communication within and without Ecuador.

MAIL. A 5-gram air-mail letter takes about eight days to get to the U.S., and costs 200 sucres. Documents, packages, etc. can be sent via certified mail or, for more rapid and secure delivery, via a courier service such as DHL or Federal Express. There are frequent mail and communications strikes, and when there is no strike, mail is also sometimes "lost."

NEWSPAPERS. The *Miami Herald* may be purchased for about $2, and is usually available in the largest hotels on the afternoon of the same day of publication. The *Herald Tribune, New York Times,* and *Wall Street Journal* are usually available but may be several days old. The foreign editions of *Time* and *Newsweek* magazines are also available, although they too are usually a little stale. The principal local newspapers are: in Quito, *El Comercio, Hoy,* and *Ultimas Noticias;* in Guayaquil, *El Telegrafo, La Prensa,* and *El Universo.*

ELECTRIC CURRENT. 110 volts, 60 cycles, AC. Most electrical outlets are for 2-pronged plugs. Carry an adaptor if you have any 3-pronged appliances. If you are using sensitive electrical equipment such as portable computers, you should be aware that power surges and outages are common, and that many electrical systems are not grounded according to U.S. standards.

USEFUL ADDRESSES. Embassy of the United States, Ave. Patria and 12 de Octubre (562–890); **Embassy of the U.K.,** Avenida Gonzalez Suarez 111 (560–309). Both embassies are in Quito. **Canadian Consulate,** Av. 6 de Diciembre 2816 and Orton (564–795). **National Tourist Office (CETUR),** Reina Victoria 514 and Roca, Quito (527–002). **American Express Agents:** Ecuadorian Tours. In Guayaquil, 9 de Octubre 1900 y Esmeraldas, (207–111, 394–984). In Quito, Ave. Amazonas 339 y Jorge Washington, (560–488, 560–554).

HEALTH AND SAFETY. Although no inoculations are required for entry into Ecuador or return entry into the United States, the following are some recommended shots and inoculations: smallpox, typhoid, and gamma globulin against hepatitis. Dengué fever and malaria, including the chloroquinine–resistant falciparum malaria, are prevalent both along the coast and in the eastern jungles. Prophylactic drugs should be taken before, during, and for six weeks after a visit to these areas. Consult your doctor regarding the proper drugs and their possible side effects. If the symptoms of malaria (headache, shivering, high fever) appear, consult a qualified doctor *immediately.* Falciparum malaria, especially, can be extremely dangerous. Use insect repellent, and wear long-sleeved shirts, long pants, and socks as additional preventives. A good stomach remedy should be taken along. Visitors are also strongly urged not to drink the tap water in Ecuador. Safe bottled water is available, such as "sin gas" or carbonated "con gas." The top brands are *Guitig* (pronounced weetig) and *Manantial.* Uncooked vegetables or fruits should not be eaten unless they can be peeled. The high altitude of Quito and the sierra can be a problem for some. People with heart or pulmonary disorders should consult their physicians before traveling to these areas. Avoid alcohol, caffeine, and heavy or greasy foods at first, and rest upon arrival. Some find that a diet relatively higher in starches (pastas, potatoes, etc.) and relatively lower in protein helps ease the adjustment to the altitude. Also, many people find that eating a heavy meal at night makes it difficult for them to sleep afterward. Try to have your main meal at lunch and eat lightly at dinner.

If you observe the same safety precautions you would in any large city, there is very little danger to one's security in Ecuador. Quito is generally a safe city, although you should beware of pickpockets anywhere there are pressing crowds, especially the Old City. The area around the Church of San Francisco, including the main entrance to the church, is becoming increasingly risky. It is not advisable to walk around alone at night in the Old City, but with company or in taxis it is generally safe. In the more modern city, which is probably where you will spend most of your evenings—as this is where the greater concentration of restaurants and clubs is—simply using common sense should keep you out of trouble. Be more careful in Guayaquil, which is famous for its thieves and pickpockets. Crime is almost unknown in the provinces. Always follow the simple rules about not leaving valuables, cameras, airline tickets, or passports lying around your hotel room, where temptation might be too great. Such items should be kept in a hotel safe-deposit box, or in the hotel safe.

GETTING AROUND ECUADOR. Guayaquil, Quito, and Cuenca are linked by frequent domestic *air service* by *TAME, SAETA,* and *SAN.* Flights take about 40 minutes and cost around $22 round trip. There is frequent daily service among the three cities and several on Sunday. A number of small airlines serve the coast and eastern part of the country.

The Quito airport is about a 15-minute drive from the Hotel Quito ($2 per car), and the Guayaquil airport is on the edge of town, with taxis charging about $3 in daytime and $4 at night per car.

Some of the famous Quito/Guayaquil railroad was destroyed by flooding in 1983. The rails have been repaired except for a section between Riobamba and Alausi; Metropolitan Touring has arranged for this length to be covered by bus. Train trips are also available between Guayaquil/Riobamba and Riobamba/Cuenca. The remaining commercial trains in Ecuador are only for the most adventurous.

The Galápagos Islands are both a National Park and a wildlife preserve, so tourism there is regulated by the government. The basic source of information is: Superintendent, Galápagos National Park Service, Isla Santa Cruz, Isla Galápagos, Ecuador. The principal commercial agency covering this area is: Metropolitan Touring, Box 310, Sucursal 12 de Octubre, Quito, Ecuador. Access by sea is by two passenger vessels, and a couple of cargo ships. By air there are daily flights (except Sunday) by TAME airlines (Av. Amazonas 1354, Quito, 549–100, 524–023) and SAN airlines (Av. Colombia 442, 527–555). Within the archipelago travel is by local boats only, though interisland air service has been approved. All visits to any part of the National Park (97 percent of the land area and 7 million hectares of ocean) require permits and licensed guides. Accommodations are limited; at Puerto Ayora the very nice Hotel Galápagos, the Hotel Delfin, plus other small hotels, provide about 150 beds. There is one small hotel on Isabela and several hotels on San Cristobal. There are an increasing number of restaurants in the major ports. There are two limited campgrounds. Amenities such as sun lotion, film, etc., are unavailable or very expensive. For complete information, contact the Superintendent's office, or Metropolitan Touring (addresses above).

Taxis and rental cars are readily available in Quito and Guayaquil, as well as in other cities, for excursions to nearby areas. *Hertz, Budget, Dollar-Rent-a-Car,* and *Avis* have agencies.

SPORTS. Soccer, or *futbol,* is wildly popular in Ecuador, as it is in all Latin America. Most towns have a team and top games are played weekends in Quito's and Guayaquil's major stadiums.

Bullfights are featured in Quito's huge ring, during the Quito Days Festival in early December. Top Mexican and Spanish bullfighters often participate. There are also bull rings in Ambato and Riobamba.

Swimming, golf, and **tennis** are popular around Quito and on the coast at the new resorts. **Horseback riding** and **hiking** are extremely enjoyable in the sierra country, as are golf and tennis. There are excellent country clubs in Cuenca, Quito and Guayaquil; visitors are welcome through a local member. Golf fees are about $20.

The top new sporting attraction in Ecuador is **marlin fishing.** Several other game fish abound in Ecuadoran waters. Because the northwest-flowing Humboldt Current nearly touches Ecuador's coast from June to December, bringing cold water from the south, the offshore waters teem with hard-fighting, large coldwater game fish usually uncommon near the Equator. In the remaining months the current flows southward and the large game fish are replaced by great numbers of smaller species. Fair roads lead from Guayaquil to nearby Playas (60 miles) and Salinas (98 miles). First-class accommodations are available at both towns. Close by is the *Carnero Inn.* The depths off the Inn have already produced a 1,440-lb. black marlin, reputedly the second-largest ever landed. Four new world records have already been broken here. Two- to four-day trips, leaving daily. Several high-mountain lakes around Otavalo and Cuenca provide good fresh-water fishing.

Photographic safaris and sightseeing tours to the Oriente are also becoming popular. Several tour operators now offer three- to five-day jungle tours. Prices start at around $200 per person for three days in groups of over 26 persons, and go up to around $775 per person for private tours for two people for five days, four nights.

Mountain Climbing. Ecuador is famous among mountain climbers for its many rugged, snow-covered, volcanic peaks. Outfitters and guides are available in Quito and Riobamba. For renting equipment and information in Quito check out *Equipo Cotopaxi,* 6 de diciembre 1557. *Señor Camilo Andrade,* at Presidente Wilson 643, Apt. 135 (tel. 520–263), is one of Ecuador's most experienced climbers; he organizes and guides his own tours. He speaks several languages, including fluent English.

White-water rafting is just beginning to be promoted in Ecuador. *ExplorAndes,* Ave. Naciones 685, Quito (432–723), is now offering rafting trips for beginning and experienced rafters. Other tour companies will most likely soon follow suit, as there are some excellent rafting opportunities.

See also "Adventure Vacations" chapter.

Exploring Ecuador

QUITO

Quito, the capital of Ecuador, is scenically situated in a long, narrow valley at the foot of the slumbering volcano, Pichincha, and runs principally from the south to the north. The lush green fields on the hillsides surrounding Quito, the snow-capped volcano cones, and the brilliant sunlight only enhance the picturesque colonial sector in the south and the graceful, modern sector with broad parks and avenues in the north. Unfortunately, Quito is often considered just a stopping-off place en route to the Galápagos Islands, and this charming city is not given the time and attention it deserves. So often the unsuspecting visitor is heard expressing his delight in discovering Quito, as well as dismay for not having more time. A minimum of four days should be allowed for Quito, because the beauty of Quito lies not just in the city but also with the exciting excursions into the surrounding countryside.

Quito lies only 15 miles south of the equator; however, due to its altitude (9,250 feet) it has a mild, springlike climate all year. If the sun is shining, temperatures in the daytime can reach over 80 degrees F., but usually remain in the 70s. The evenings are cool, ranging from 40 to 50 degrees F. The heaviest rainfall is during the months of March through May, with light precipitation possible all year-round. Sometimes it will rain for several days, but usually for only a few hours in the later afternoon, at which time the climate can be chilly.

The oldest part of Quito is in the south, where the city was founded by the Spaniard Sebastian Benalcazar in 1534, on the site of the ancient Indian town of Shyris. The original city was established at the foot of "Cerro Panecillo" or Bread Roll Hill, which marks the southern terminus of the Quito valley. From here, the city sprawled in a northerly direction. Fortunately, in a stroke of wisdom, the government passed a law declaring the colonial sector a national monument, and banned both the destruction of any of the original colonial buildings and the construction of new buildings, and UNESCO has declared Old Quito a World Heritage Site. For this reason, the colonial sector is one of the best preserved in South America, and this is where one will be doing most of the sightseeing within Quito. A visitor once said, correctly, that Quito itself is a giant outdoor museum. Yet, unlike a museum, Old Quito is a living, breathing, vibrant part of the city, and still houses about 25 percent of its 1.5 million inhabitants. Traffic is choked along the narrow, cobblestone streets, so the best way to see Old Quito is on foot, either with a guide or on your own.

Exploring the Old City

A good starting place for a tour of Old Quito is the Plaza Independencia. This large square is often filled with people sitting around the central park, enjoying the sun and mild Quito air. The plaza is flanked on the south

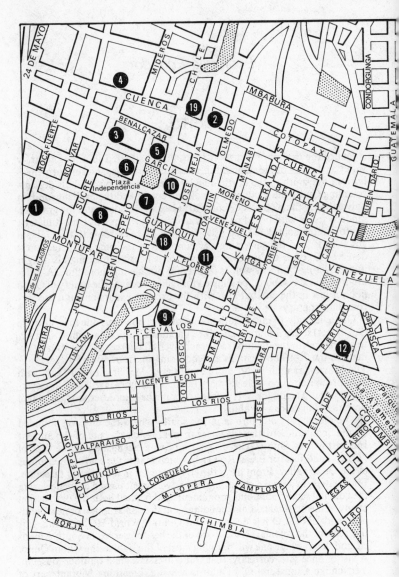

Points of Interest

1) Church of Santo Domingo
2) Museum of Colonial art
3) La Compañía Church
4) San Francisco Church
5) Palacio Presidencial
6) Cathedral
7) Palacio Municipal
8) Bolivar Theater

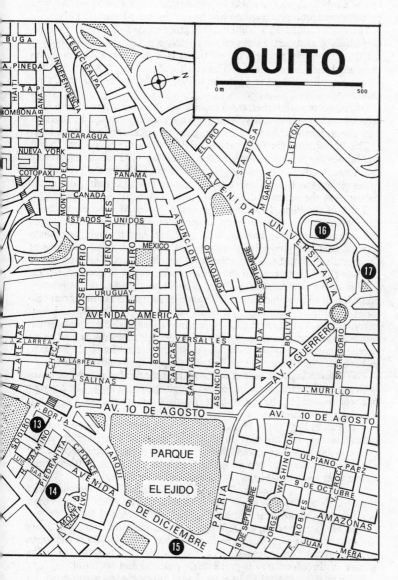

9) Coliseo de Deportes
10) Palacio Arzobispal
11) Sucre National Theater
12) Banco Central
13) Church of El Belen
14) Palacio Legislativo
15) Museo de la Casa de
la Cultura

16) Estadio University
17) Universidad Central
18) Convent and Museum of
San Agustin
19) Church and Monastery of
La Merced

by the Cathedral, on the north by the Archbishop's Palace, on the west by the Presidential Palace, and on the east by the Municipal Palace.

The city's Cathedral, a white-walled, green-domed structure, is a treasure chest of great art. Marks of the city's stormy political past show as mutilations on the outside wall, but the ageless, classic beauty still shines through. Inside is the tomb of Ecuador's national hero, Sucre, and the painting entitled "Descent from the Cross" by the Indian painter Caspicara.

On the northwest corner, the Archbishop's Palace is adorned with long arcades with a great variety of shops. This graceful colonnade, together with the elegant Archbishop's Palace, gives the square an impressive look.

The Presidential (or Government) Palace faces the Municipal Palace and houses the presidential offices. A huge mosaic of Orellana discovering the Amazon covers one wall on the ground floor. Under the present administration, tourists are sometimes permitted to visit certain parts of the palace. Ask the uniformed guards on duty if you can go in.

South of the Plaza Independencia, along Garcia Moreno Street, is La Compañía Church, famous for its copiously ornate interior. There are ten side altars, completely covered with gold-leaf, and a magnificent main altar of gold and gold gilt balconies. La Compañía is filled with one of the world's most outstanding collections of colonial art. The church, one of 86 in Quito, is considered the richest Jesuit temple in South America.

West of the Compañía is the Plaza of San Francisco and the Monastery and Church of San Francisco. This classic monastery is the first great religious building in South America. Founded by a cousin of the Spanish Emperor, Carlos V, the church developed into an unrivaled example of baroque art and architecture. World famous sculpture inside, as well as an excellent collection of works by the mestizo painter Miguel de Santiago in both the church and the monastery, attracts thousands annually.

The Church and Convent of San Agustin near the Independence Plaza is an impressive cloister that contains a high, carved ceiling. The convent has been restored by the government and made into a museum, and houses a collection of paintings by Miguel de Santiago.

Two blocks behind the Plaza San Francisco, next door to the Convent of las Clarisas, you can visit a typical daily market. There are no handicrafts or antiques, but a walk through the noisy stalls, where foods and plastics and other daily necessities are bought and sold, can be fascinating. Leave your valuables at the hotel, and watch out for thieves.

Southeast of the Plaza San Francisco is the Plaza Santo Domingo and the Church and Monastery of Santo Domingo. The Arch of the Virgin is a favorite "photo stop," presenting the classic colonial Quito.

The Monastery of Santo Domingo contains the oldest religious figure in Quito, the Virgin of Mercy, on its main altar. The Monastery (not open to women) has Quito's oldest clock, twin of Big Ben, built in 1817. The garden of the Monastery is particularly peaceful and beautiful.

Your walking tour of Old Quito should also include a stroll down La Ronda Street *(Calle Ronda)*, reputably the oldest street of Quito and certainly an authentic street of the 16th-century Spanish colonial period. The narrow cobbled street, and the heavy grilled doors and balconies, take the visitor back generations.

A short taxi ride from San Francisco Plaza are the Church, Monastery, and Cemetery of San Diego. The Monastery now houses a museum. (Admission: $0.25. Open daily 8–11 and 3–5.) The cemetery, with its flower vendors, numerous old family tombs and, from some locations, view of the city, is worth a visit.

At the end of your tour take a drive to the top of Panecillo Hill for an unequalled view of the city. It is recommended that the trip to Panecillo be made either in the early morning or late afternoon, in order to get the best views of the snow-capped volcanoes. During the day the sun heats the air surrounding the snow caps, and the cold air emanating from the ice caps creates a "hat" of atmosphere and cloud cover around each peak. Pickpockets and thieves are reportedly numerous on the stairs leading to the top of the hill. It's best to leave your valuables locked up at your hotel and take a taxi to the top.

Guapulo

Here is a storybook town if ever there was one. A world apart from the busy capital city, Guapulo is just a 10-minute walk into the valley below the Hotel Quito. The charming village, with its red-tile roofs and colonial architecture, sprang up around the monastery and church of the Virgin of Guadalupe in the late 17th century. A visit to the recently renovated monastery (now a naval college!) and church is well worth the walk down the steep cobbled steps. The church's pulpit, carved by the sculptor Menacho, is considered a masterpiece. Buses and taxis are available for the journey back to the city, for those who didn't come to the Andes to "get aerobic"!

The annual Fiestas of Guapulo take place in early September. Children's games, abundant food and drink stalls, and somewhat discordant marching bands are all part of this enchanting street festival.

Sangolquí

Not a typical tourist destination, Sangolquí nevertheless is a charming and interesting old neighborhood. Located a short distance southeast of Quito, on the Autopista del Valle de los Chillos, Sangolquí is a pleasant place to stop on the way to Pasochoa Park or other destinations south of Quito. Wednesday is market day, but wandering around any day for an hour or more is rewarding.

PRACTICAL INFORMATION FOR QUITO

GETTING AROUND QUITO. From the airport. Buses passing in front of the airport are en route to the downtown area if they are heading to your left as you look from the airport. (In other words, you must cross to the other side of the street to be pointed in the right direction). You can catch the right bus by asking "Centro?" There is no airport bus or limousine. A taxi should cost you about $2. Your travel agent can arrange to have you met by a bilingual guide, with a private car and driver for about $9 per person, based on two people sharing a car.

By bus. Quito has an extensive public bus transportation system, but the buses are often very crowded, and many are quite broken down. Beware of pickpockets on the public buses, which can be extremely crowded. Also, be prepared to jump off at your destination, as drivers will not always come to a complete stop.

By taxi. Taxis are very inexpensive. The average taxi ride within the city (for instance, from your hotel in the modern sector of Quito to the Old City) is about $1.50. Taxis are required to use meters. If the driver claims his meter is not working, agree on a price beforehand. If in doubt, ask an employee of the hotel what the taxi fare should be. Use only yellow taxis marked as members of cooperatives. There have been incidents in which drivers of "pirate" taxis have taken their passengers to remote areas and robbed them.

HOTELS. All major hotels are in the modern city, which is clean and relatively safe. The new city is also where the better restaurants, shops, airline ticket offices, consulates, embassies, and nightclubs are located. If you want to stay in the Old

City, there are some hotels and "pensiones," but bear in mind that the Old City is not as safe, particularly at night, and that even the best lodgings, recommended below, may not be as attractive as those in the new city. For definitions of price categories, see "Facts at Your Fingertips," earlier in this chapter.

The New City

Very Expensive

Colon Internacional, Av. Amazonas and Patria, Box 3103 (560–666). Well situated by the Parque El Ejido, with 415 nicely furnished rooms. Two restaurants, coffee shop, casino, two bars, swimming pool, gymnasium, sauna, barber shop, beauty parlor, valet service, laundry. (Telex 2542 HCOLON ED; Fax 563–903, Quito, Ecuador.)

Hotel Oro Verde, 12 de Octubre 1820, Box 21–565 (568–079; Telex 21017 HOV ED; Fax 569–189). Opened in late 1990, this is probably Quito's finest hotel. There are 247 rooms with full amenities, three restaurants, a bar, an indoor/outdoor pool, and a casino.

Hotel Quito, Best Western, Av. Gonzalo Suarez 2500 (230–300, 544–600; 800–528–1234 in U.S.; Telex 2223 WCUIO ED; Fax 567–284). The 230-room hotel has a spectacular view, pool, casino, sauna, rooftop restaurant and bar, coffee shop, beauty parlor, barber shop, and valet service. Recently redecorated rooms; lovely grounds.

Expensive

Alameda Real, Roca 653 & Av. Amazonas, Box 358-A (562–345, 564–217); Telex 22224 ALMEDA-ED; Fax 565–759. Centrally located near tour companies, shopping, and restaurants. This 150-room hotel was originally planned as a condominium project, and the rooms are all very large. There is a gourmet restaurant, coffee shop, cocktail lounge, barber shop, beauty parlor, valet service, laundry. (For U.S. reservations: Latin America Reservations Center (LARC Hotels), 800–327–3573. In U.K.: Steigenberger Reservation Service (SRS)).

Chalet Suisse, Av. Reina Victoria y Calama (562–700; Fax 563–966). Centrally located in the New City, its 53 rooms are slightly dilapidated, yet quaint. The restaurant is one of the best in Quito for beef. Casino, bar, valet service, small gym, sauna, and laundry.

Moderate

Hostal Los Alpes, Tamayo 233 y Jorge Washington (561–110, 561–128). Good restaurant; homey sitting room with fireplace, piano. Friendly.

Hotel Amaranta International, Leonidas Plaza 194 y Jorge Washington (238–385, 527–191). Suites with kitchen. Discounts for longer stays.

Hotel Ambassador, 9 de Octubre 1052 and Colón (562–054).

Hotel Tambo Real, Av. 12 de Octubre y Queseras del Medio, across from the American Embassy (563–822, 551–446). Single and double suites with kitchenette.

Inexpensive

Hostal Los Andes, Moros 146 y González Suárez (550–839). AE, DC, only.

Hotel Embassy, Wilson 441, Box 64-A (543–614, 561–990; telex 21181 TRA-HOT-ED). With good restaurant. Recommended.

Inca Imperial, Bogotá 219 (230–600). 45 quaint, clean rooms with private bath. Coffee shop and bar.

The following are small, pleasant *pensiones* (all are *Inexpensive*): **La Posada del Maple,** Juan Rodríguez 148 y 6 de diciembre (544–507). Breakfast included. **Hotel Residencia Cumbres,** Baquedano 148 y 6 de diciembre (560–850). **El Taxo,** Foch 909 y Cordero (232–593). Operated by one of Ecuador's leading musicians.

The Old City

Inexpensive

Hotel Casino Real Audiencia, Bolivar 220 y Guayaquil on the Plaza Santo Domingo (512–711, 510–590). 40 rooms, private bath, bar, restaurant, cafeteria. The best in the Old City.

Hotel Viena Internacional, Flores 610 and Chile (519–611, 213–605). Two blocks from the main plaza. Clean, safe, and pleasant, though noisy. Cash only.

RESTAURANTS. Quito is justifiably noted for its fine restaurants. For definitions of price categories see "Facts at Your Fingertips." Most restaurants are open from 12–3 and 7–11, and accept American Express, Diners Club, Visa and MasterCard. On Sundays you may want to dine at a hotel dining room, as many private restaurants are closed.

Expensive

Very popular eating places are **El Conquistador** in the Hotel Colón and **El Techo del Mundo** in the Hotel Quito.

For international cuisine try **Delmónicos,** Mariano Aguilera 331 (544–200); **El Limonar,** Juan Rodriguez 228 (541–253), closed all day Sat. and Sun. evening; or **Lafite,** La Nina 559 y Juan Leon Mera (231–266).

For French cuisine, try **Rincon de Francia,** Roca 779 y 9 de Octubre (554–668); **La Maison Marabac,** Baron Von Humboldt 209 y San Ignacio (238–397); **La Belle Epoque,** Whimper 925 between Av. 6 de Diciembre y Diego de Almagro (233–163); or **La Marmite,** Mariano Aguilera 287 y Almagro (237–751).

For good Italian food, try **Via Margutta,** Gral. Salazar 1093 between 12 de Octubre y Tamayo (563–691); **La Gritta,** Santa Maria 246 between La Rabida y Reina Victoria (567–628); or **Trattoria del Veneziano,** Roca 562 y Juan Leon Mera (523–085).

Excellent Spanish food is available at **Paella Valenciana,** Av. Republica y Diego de Almagro; **La Vieja Castilla,** Pinta 435 y Amazonas (566–979); and the **Costa Vasca,** 18 de Septiembre 553 y Paez (564–940).

For steaks try **Shorton Grill,** Calama 216 y Diego de Almagro (523–645); **La Terraza del Tartaro** (with a wonderful view of Quito), penthouse, Veintimilla 1106 y Av. Amazonas (527–987); and **El Toro Partido,** Veintimilla 878 y Amazonas (236–551). Italian seafood is the specialty at **Marina Yate,** Calama 369 y Juan León Mera (526–158).

Moderate

The coffee shops in the Hotel Quito, **Cafe Cayambe,** and the Hotel Colon, **Cafe Colón,** offer a wide variety of meals. The Cafe Colón is the only restaurant in town open 24 hours a day.

For good seafood, try **Su Cebiche,** Juan Leon Mera 1232 y Calama (526–380) or **La Jaiba,** Reina Victoria 870 y Colon (543–887). **Las Redes** serves traditional seafood plates at Av. Amazonas 845 y Veintimilla (525–691).

There are only a few restaurants that specialize in typical Ecuadoran dishes. **La Choza,** Av. 12 de Octubre 1821 y Cordero (230–839), serves excellent traditional Ecuadoran food, as does **La Ronda,** Belo Horizone 400 y Diego de Almagro (540–459). The **Equinoccio,** beside the Mitad del Mundo monument, is very good (533–741).

Inexpensive

Casa de Asia, Amazonas 5416 (241–373), serves delicious Korean and Japanese food in an informal, unpretentious ambience. For a vegetarian meal or a good breakfast, try the cafeteria at **The British Council,** Amazonas 1534 y Santa María (540–225). For an unusual, tasty pizza cooked in a brick beehive oven heated by wood, try **El Hornero,** at either Gonzalez Suarez 1070 (563–377) or Av. Amazonas 854 y Veintimilla (231–274). El Hornero delivers. Excellent barbecued ribs are found at **Adam's Rib,** Juan Leon Mera between 442 and Roca (563–196).

TRADITIONAL CAFES. The area around the Colón Internacional Hotel, Alameda Real, and Chalet Suisse is honeycombed with restaurants, shops, and cafes. Avenida Amazonas has several sidewalk cafes that are popular and inexpensive.

TOURIST INFORMATION. The National Tourist office is located at Reina Victoria 514 y Roca (527–002). Unfortunately, the staff is usually uninformed, and tourist brochures are often out of stock.

TOURS. Your best source for tourist information will be the tour companies, who will cheerfully supply you with information, even if you are not necessarily ready to sign up for any tours right away. (Ecuadorans are always helpful and courteous to strangers.) There are several very good tour companies in Quito. Prices will be about the same with all companies, but those listed here are the most experienced and provide excellent service. Most major tour operators also have offices in Guayaquil.

COLTUR de Quito, Paez 370 y Robles, Box 2771 (545–777, Telex 2302 COLTUR-ED). Besides offering tours in and around Quito, COLTUR has the most sophisticated radio equipment for communicating with the Galápagos Islands.

Ecuadorian Tours, Av. Amazonas 339 y Jorge Washington (560–488, 560–554). (Represented by American Express in the U.S., Canada, and Europe.) A very good, reliable operator for Quito and excursions around Ecuador.

Metropolitan Touring, Av. Amazonas 239, Box 310, Sucursal 12 de Octubre (560–550; telex 22482 METOUR-ED; Fax 593–2–564655). (Represented in U.S. by Adventure Associates, 13150 Coit Rd., Suite 110, Dallas, TX 75240, 800–527–2500, Fax 214–783–1286.) General sales agents of the *Santa Cruz* and the *Isabela II* in the Galápagos Islands. Also runs the Metropolitan Expreso train and the Flotel Orellana, the floating hotel in the eastern jungles. (All Galápagos, train, or Flotel trips can be booked at the same prices through any Ecuador tour company, or by your travel agent through one of their Ecuadoran tour companies' representatives.)

Wagon-Lits Turismo, Diego de Almagro 1831 y Alpallana, Box 8903 (235–110, 237–135; telex: 22763 VALEJO-ED). Offers a variety of tours for the adventurous as well as the not so adventurous.

Nuevo Mundo, Av. Amazonas 2468 y Mariana de Jesus, Box 402–A (552–816, 552–617; telex 22749 NMUNDO-ED; Fax 5932–552916). Member of several international nature conservancy organizations. Well-known for adventurous expeditions for those who like some comfort in their adventure. Hiking, horseback trips through the Andes, mountain climbing, jungle trips, and Galápagos, as well as some off-beat tours around Quito and some of the Andean towns.

Angermeyer's Enchanted Expeditions, Foch 769 y Av. Amazonas (231–713, 569–960; telex 2656 HUFCO-ED; Fax 569956). Offers tours of the Galápagos, and well-organized adventure tours into the jungles, to national parks and nature reserves, and hiking and mountain climbing expeditions.

Kleinturs, Shyris 1000 y Holanda, Box 617-A (430–345, 432–178; telex 21378 KLEIN-ED; Fax 442–389). Offers tours of Quito and the surrounding areas, hiking, mountain climbing, jungle exploring, and the Galápagos, as well as visits to indigenous communities.

ExplorAndes, Av. Naciones Unidas 685, ground floor (432–723, 434–669; Fax 441–587). Specializes in trekking and jungle tours, and is the only operation currently offering white water rafting trips in Ecuador.

Orientgal, Av. Amazonas 816 y Veintimilla (501–418, 501–419; telex 21220 GALSAM-ED; Fax 501419). Specializes in jungle and mountain tours for the adventurous.

Quasar Nautica, Av. Naciones Unidas 685, 9th floor, Box 69 (446–996, 448–786; telex 2220 YAGUA-ED; Fax 436625). Office in U.S.: Tumbaco, 25205 E. Marion Ave., Box 1036, Punta Gorda, Fla. 33950, 800–247–2925. Galápagos tours in modern boats, including tours for experienced scuba divers.

La Selva, 6 de Diciembre 2816, Box 635 (suc. 12 de Octubre) (550–995, 554–686; telex 22653 JOLEZ-ED; Fax 563814). U.S. office: Tumbaco (listed under Quasar Nautica, above). Manages an excellent jungle camp-hotel on the Rio Napo with private cabins with bath. Excursions into the surrounding jungle, fishing, birdwatching. Contact directly for brochures and detailed information.

Note: Prices quoted on tours listed below are approximate in U.S. dollars, and are per person, basis two people sharing a private car with a driver and bilingual guide, except where noted otherwise. Group tours are usually about half the price.

Quito Scenic Tour: Drive through the residential area, past the House of Culture, the Legislative Palace, and Alameda Park. Visit San Agustin Monastery, Independence Plaza, and La Compañía Church. Drive past San Francisco Church and Monastery. Tour ends with a visit to Panecillo Hill. $20 per person ($11 per person on group tour via motorcoach).

Country Scenic Tour: A short visit to the beautiful Guayllabamba Valley and the town of Calderón, where the famous bread dolls are made. $27 per person ($13 per person in group).

Quito Colonial Tour: Visit the Colonial Art Museum, the Church of La Merced with its treasury of art, and the museums of the Ecuadoran House of Culture. $27 per person ($14.50 per person in group).

MUSEUMS. Some of the finest art of the colonial period came from Quito, and the collections today are magnificent. Besides the priceless art in the churches, monasteries, and convents, there are also some very fine art museums and galleries. The **Casa de la Cultura Ecuatoriana,** Av. 12 de Octubre and Patria (565–808), has good murals, and an exhibition that traces the Ecuadoran culture from independence to modern day. There is a good art collection in conjunction with this exhibit, together with rare books and an unusual exhibit of musical instruments. Open Tues.–Sat., 9–6; Sun 10–2. Free. **The Museum of Colonial Art,** Calle Cuenca and Calle Mejia (212–297), has an excellent collection; moreover, the building itself is particularly lovely. Open Tues.–Fri. 8:30–5; Sat. and Sun., 10–2:30. Costs./50. There are good collections of religious art from the colonial period at the **Museum of the Monastery of Santo Domingo.** The best archeological collection is housed on the 5th floor of the **Central Bank** (Banco Central del Ecuador), 10 de Agosto y Briceno, which also houses an art gallery on the 6th floor. Open Tues.–Fri., 9–5 and weekends, 10:30–3. Costs./50 (about 10¢). **The Municipal Museum,** Espejo 1147 and Benalcazar (214–018), contains paintings and sculptures of the 16th and 17th centuries. Open Tues.–Fri. 8 A.M.–6 P.M. The **Jacinto Jijon y Caamano Museum** is a private collection of archeological objects, religious paintings, portraits, uniforms, and other items of interest. The museum is located in the library building of the Catholic University, Ave. 12 de Octubre y Carrion. Open Mon.–Fri. 9–4. Costs./25. The **Museo Camilo Egas,** Venezuela 1302 y Esmeraldas, has changing art exhibits (514–511), Tues.–Fri., 10–1 and 3–5:30; Sun. 10–2. Free. Please note that all of the exhibits are identified with Spanish captions only.

PUBLIC EVENTS. From Dec. 24 (Noche Buena) to New Year's Eve (El Año Viejo) the streets of Quito are filled with people. Political satire is performed by clowns dressed as old women, or as soldiers armed with clubs stuffed with rags. Displays, often political satires, are mounted along Avenue Amazonas on New Year's Eve, then burned for the arrival of the New Year. Dec. 6 is the culmination of the Festival of the foundation of Quito and ends a whole week of celebration. Carnival and the processions on Good Friday (both movable feasts) are worthwhile.

MUSIC, DANCE, AND STAGE. Plays, concerts, and ballet are regularly scheduled in Quito's Sucre National Theater, the theaters of the Casa de la Cultura, and other halls throughout the city. All productions are in Spanish. An English-language group, "The Pinchincha Players," presents plays in English several times a year.

SPORTS. (See also "Facts At Your Fingertips.") The most important **bullfights** are performed the first week of December. **Soccer,** the ultimate spectator sport in South America, is played Saturday afternoons and Sunday mornings at Atahualpa stadium.

SHOPPING. Excellent bargains of many kinds are available in Quito's fascinating shops and the country's many Indian markets. Some caution is advised when buying antiques, for one of Ecuador's most thriving industries is the creating of "colonial and pre-Columbian" paintings and carvings.

Though it is not illegal to buy any of the pre-Columbian or colonial art, pottery, silver, furniture, etc., sold in Quito's many antique stores, it *is* illegal to take these artifacts out of the country. Such pieces may be confiscated by customs officials upon departure, and fines or jail sentences may be imposed on offenders.

Wood carvings and Indian textiles make excellent buys, as do silver and 18-karat gold jewelry. Woolen rugs and blankets and handloomed textiles are also popular with visitors. Inquiries will uncover prizes from the Oriente country—genuine aboriginal art and native weapons. Avoid all items decorated with feathers, which the Amazonian Indians take from threatened species of jungle birds; avoid buying black coral also, which is in danger of rapidly becoming extinct.

Bargaining is the rule rather than the exception in all of the country's smaller shops. A few stores around the major hotels have fixed prices—but don't be timid about attempting to lower the price anywhere.

Best bet for bargain hunters are the weekly Indian markets in the smaller towns. Prices there haven't been pushed up by too many free-spending tourists—and there are great bargains in handicrafts, woven goods, and souvenirs. In Quito, the best shopping areas are around Amazonas and Juan León Mera avenues, starting from the Colón Internacional Hotel and going north. There are many shops selling tourist items in Old Quito, but few offer merchandise of good quality.

The most popular shop for Ecuador's unique handicrafts and Panama hats is **Folklore** on Avenida Colón 260 and in the Colón Internacional Hotel and Hotel Quito. High-quality handicrafts are available at **La Bodega** (Juan León Mera 614), **Central Artesenal** (Juan León Mera y Baquedano 804), **Galeria Latina** (Juan León Mera 823), and **El Aborígen** (Jorge Washington 536 y Juan León Mera). For an excellent and large selection of dolls, paintings, prints, masks, jewelry, and clothes from Cuenca, visit **El Tucán** (Amazonas 301 y J. Washington). Two artisans' cooperatives have large selections and inexpensive prices, although quality appears to have been at times sacrificed. They are **Ocepa** (J. Washington 252 and Amazonas) and **Productos Andinos** (Robles 800 or Urbina 111). **H. Stern** has branches in the hotels **Colón International** and **Intercontinental Quito** with a full line of locally made silver and gold jewelry.

The studio, museum, and workshop of Oswaldo Guayasamin, world-known painter, are at Bosmediano 543 y Jose Carbo (446–455). The paintings, sculptures, and handcrafted jewelry displayed here are for sale.

Libri Mundi is an excellent bookstore, with many items in English and French, maps, guidebooks, and picture books of Ecuador and the Galápagos. Their main shop is at Juan León Mera 851 y Veintimilla, with a branch in the Colón Internacional Hotel. **El Caracol, CCI,** and **CCNU** are three large shopping centers clustered around Amazonas at Naciones Unidas. With each center so close to another, it should be possible to find whatever is needed in one of these giant malls.

NIGHTLIFE. Quito may not be famous for its nightlife, but Ecuadorans love to dance, and there are plenty of nightclubs and dance bars here. **Serseribó Salsoteca** (Veintimilla y 12 de octubre) is currently a popular place in Quito to dance salsa, as is **Gato Son** (Carvajal y Aldana; **Blues** (La Granja 112 y Amazonas; open Tues.–Sat.) plays 70s rock, salsa, and pop. **Ñucanchi Peña** (Av. Universitaria 496) has many live bands with ethnic flavor each night. Most major hotels have their own discos; rarely do discos open before 9:30 P.M.

EXCURSIONS FROM QUITO

(For where to get tours described below see section on Tours in "Practical Information for Quito," above.)

EQUATORIAL MONUMENT

Fifteen miles north of Quito (usually a half hour by car) stands the globe-topped monument that marks the equator. Although there's really nothing spectacular about the granite monument, built in 1936, or the actual spot geographers call 0°00'00", most visitors greatly enjoy the sensation of crossing the equator a dozen or so times and having their pictures taken with one foot in the Northern Hemisphere and the other in the Southern. A huge tourist center is being built in the Equatorial Monument area. A whole village has been developed to include shops, restaurants, library, museum, bank, post office, and church. A highly recommended restaurant is the Equinoccio. A private car tour to the monument, based on two passengers, is about $20 per person, but this is one tour you can easily do on your own for less by hiring a taxi to take you there. Near the Equatorial monument are the ruins of Rumicucho, a fortress built by the people who occupied the area before the Incas. If a visit to the ruins is included, price per person is $27.

BAÑOS

Approximately 90 miles from Quito lies Baños, famous for its wonderful thermal baths and popular with pilgrims who visit Baños each year to solicit miracles from the Nuestra Señora de Santa Agua. The route from Quito to Baños follows the Avenue of the Volcanoes and affords fantastic views of numerous volcanoes, waterfalls, and lush vegetation. The town itself is beautiful and tranquil, set in a valley and completely surrounded by mountains, many of which are active volcanoes. Excellent walks and hikes can be taken around the outskirts of town and into Sangay National Park. Local travel agencies can recommend hikes and excursions; horses can also be rented. Baños is a jumping-off point for many self-organized jungle trips, and is therefore a good place to meet other travelers and form tour groups.

The following hotels are recommended: **Hotel Sangay,** a great place for families, has a swimming pool, sauna, tennis and raquetball courts, and color TV (Plazoleta Ayora 101, 740–490 or 740–056). *Moderate.* **Villa Gertrudis** is a charming establishment, almost 50 years old. It was built by Germans and still retains a European air. The price includes three meals (Av. Montalvo 2075, 740–441 or 740–442). *Moderate.* **Casa Nahuazo** is a pleasant bed-and-breakfast on the outskirts of town (Via al Salado, 740–419). *Inexpensive.*

Good restaurants include the following: **Le Petit Restaurant** serves wonderful French dishes and is often very lively (Eloy Alfaro 246 y Montalvo, 740–936. Closed Mon.). *Moderate.* **Café Cultura** is run by Danes and has fairly sophisticated international food, if a limited menu (Av. Montalvo at Santa Clara, 740–419). *Inexpensive.* **Regiue's** has an extensive menu and serves good German breakfasts (Av. Montalvo across the street from Parque Infantil Baños, 740–641. Closed Tues.). *Inexpensive.* There are also several fun bars on the main street.

If you prefer to visit Baños via organized tour, these are also available. Two-day tours include a stay in one of Baños' charming guest houses, a visit to one of the neighboring markets, two lunches, breakfast, and dinner, at a cost of $212 per person.

INDIAN MARKETS

A highlight of any trip to Ecuador is a visit to at least one of the lively and colorful Indian markets held in almost every town throughout the sierras. Each town has its weekly market day when early in the morning Indians from miles around pour into town with produce and crafts to buy, sell, and trade. The markets listed below are within a few hours' drive from Quito, both north and south.

The Otavalos

The powerful land of the Taihuantinsuyo (the Inca Empire, or, in Quechua, "The Four Corners of the World") was never able to fully conquer the territory just north of Quito known as the *Imbabura*. This was the land of the Caranqui people, a race with a philosophy of life that defied time. It is now the land of their descendants, the proud Otavalo Indians. The Otavalos (or "Otavaleños") are a handsome race and wear a distinctive, traditional costume that sets them apart from any other Indian race. The men wear their hair long, with one single pigtail down the back. They wear crisp, white linen pants, white shirts, straw sandals, dark, wool ponchos, and fedora hats. The women wear dark blue wrap skirts, with hand-woven belts tightly cinched around the waist, brightly hand-embroidered white blouses with delicate, handmade lace ruffles on the neck and sleeves, and a dark headdress, worn tight around the face, long in back, or wrapped up like a turban. The most distinctive aspect of the women's dress is the row upon row upon row of strands of gold beads wrapped around the neck. The beads were real gold in ancient times, and the present-day, gilt glass versions are still a symbol of wealth.

The Otavalo Indians are famous for their weavings and other crafts, which can be purchased in Quito, but are better bargains in their own territory.

The Saturday Otavalo Market is one of the best of all of the Indian markets in Ecuador for handicrafts, jewelry, and antiques. It starts early, about 5:30 A.M., with the livestock corner doing a brisk business in chickens, squealing pigs, braying donkeys, mooing cows, and squeaking guinea pigs. The food stands buzz with activity as the Otavalos breakfast and gossip with friends. By 11 A.M. many of the stands are packing up to go home. Therefore, regardless of a *very* early start, the Saturday tour from Quito hardly gives this market enough time to do it justice. Because of the market's early start, we recommend a two-day trip, spending Friday night in one of the hotels or converted haciendas in or near Otavalo. This will assure better bargains as well, since you will arrive when it is still a buyer's market, well ahead of the busloads of tourists arriving on the Saturday tour. (The Otavalos, like many Indians, have the superstition that if they make the very first sale of the day, then they will have a good market day.)

The two-day tour also gives greater attention to this very worthwhile area north of Quito. It includes a stop in Calderon, a town known for its quaint "bread-doll" figurines; San Antonio de Ibarra, known for its excellent wood carvings; and a stop at one of the weaving towns for a look at the rural Indian life and a visit to one of the homes, where you can appreciate the simple way of life, and see the dyeing, spinning, and weaving process. Lunch and overnight accommodations are usually arranged at the Hosteria Chorlavi or the Parador Cusin, both quaint haciendas from colonial times and loaded with charm. Less charming or comfortable, but also clean and acceptable are the Otavalo, Chipacan, and Ajavi hotels.

A one-day Otavalo tour with lunch costs $90 per person for a private car with a driver/guide or $31 per person via motorcoach. Rates go down for larger groups. A two-day tour in a private car with two lunches, breakfast, and dinner is $199 per person. Try to visit Otavalo on Saturday in order to visit the indigenous markets. If arrangements are made to stay in the Hosteria La Mirage, a new hotel in Cotocachi with elegant rooms, a Jacuzzi, zoo and horseback rides for the children, and an outstanding restaurant, the price for two people with private car is $237 ($149 for seat-in-car motorcoach tour) per person.

If you are not able to arrange your trip to Quito to include a Saturday, a trip to the Otavalo Indians during the week is also highly recommended, although it will not be market day. A full-day tour, with lunch, via private car with driver and guide ($80), will include a visit to Calderon, San Antonio de Ibarra, and include a stop at one of the weaving towns to visit the Indians in their homes so you can see their way of life and cottage industry, and, perhaps, purchase their weavings directly from them.

Other Indian Markets

South of Quito lies the incredibly scenic Machachi Valley and the start of the "Avenue of the Volcanoes." This beautiful valley is literally trimmed on either side by volcano peaks, many of them snow-capped. Here some other towns also hold colorful markets, which are also well worth visiting.

Ambato's main market day is Monday. The town itself is not particularly attractive since it was rebuilt following a devastating earthquake some years ago, but the market is busy and bustling. Because the fair doesn't get under way as early as Otavalo's, visitors may leave Quito early Monday morning and arrive in Ambato at the height of the trading. The bright, noisy market offers the visitor a chance to see colorfully dressed Indians spread among the markets in the city's six squares. The most popular buy is the area's renowned "Persian knot" rugs. Best spot for lunch on market day is the Hotel Villa Hilda. After lunch, tours take visitors to the nearby Salasca Indian territory for a look at rural Indian life in the highlands.

A full-day Monday Ambato market tour with lunch costs $83 (seat-in-car is $34).

Latacunga offers a Saturday market and a smaller one on Tuesdays, good substitutes for those who can't spare the time necessary to visit Otavalo. Latacunga is an easy 54-mile drive from Quito, and several one-day tours are available. The market is beside the rushing Cutuche River and draws Indians from the surrounding countryside for the weekly trading and bargaining sessions. Native handicrafts, leather goods, and textiles are the best buys. Ten miles from Latacunga are Pujili and Salcedo. Both have Sunday markets, although the one in Pujili is the more interesting of the two.

Saquisilí is located 68 miles south of Quito and 17 miles from Latacunga and offers a colorful Indian market—one of the largest Indian markets in Ecuador—every Thursday. You may visit Saquisilí in a day from the capital, and the incredibly scenic drive is as satisfying as the market itself. Rolling meadows, valleys of tiny Indian settlements, and a drive along the very edge of Cotopaxi make the trip memorable. Also check for occasional, extremely colorful religious processions at Saquisilí. Additionally, take time to visit and photograph the unique cemetery.

A full-day market tour with lunch costs $72 per person for Latacunga, Pujilí, or Saquisilí. Unlike Otavalo, these markets are mainly for the people of the region, rather than for tourists. Some vendors do have stalls for weavings and straw baskets, but don't expect the variety found in Otavalo.

If visiting the markets in the Latacunga area, a lovely place to eat lunch is **La Cienega,** a hacienda converted to hostería and restaurant. The beautiful main building is reached by a drive lined by enormous old eucalyptus trees and is surrounded by carefully tended flower gardens and green fields.

COTOPAXI NATIONAL PARK

You might want to take a full-day field trip, with a hardy boxed lunch, to the Cotopaxi National Park, south of Quito via the Pan American Highway. This recently created national park includes well-protected slopes and gorges with lovely dwarf wildflowers, lichens, and birds unique to this zone. The hike up to the snowline, where the view is spectacular, is only for the physically fit, and those with heart or breathing problems should avoid the drive up to the top altogether, as some people are bothered by the altitude even while sitting in the car.

A full-day trip, any day, with boxed lunch costs $69. A two-day trip to the National Park includes a stay at the beautiful hacienda, La Cienega, and costs $190 per person.

SANTO DOMINGO, TINALANDIA, AND THE SUBTROPICAL FOREST

A thrilling drive (blood-curdling if using public transportation) over the western cordillera and down the steep mountain slopes on the western side, passing numerous waterfalls and plunging streams into ever greener valleys, takes you to the frontier-like town of Santo Domingo de los Colorados. The town was once a tourist attraction because of the Colorado Indians—the men with hair plastered with paprika paste into a bright red, bow-shaped affair, and women naked from the waist up. While Colorado Indians in native dress are rare these days, the region is still a haven for bird and butterfly enthusiasts. Hotel Tinalandia, a rambling, ramshackle affair, is still a popular destination for offbeat honeymooners, golfers, and family groups. On the 18-hole golf course, grazing cattle and native birds compete with man-made hazards, and there are endless walks in the subtropical forests of the hacienda. Cost is $40 per person per night, which includes three meals. Reservations can be made through most travel agencies.

Pasochoa Andean Forest

A 45-minute drive from Quito, this 400-hectare park is one of the last examples of the Andean forest that once covered the region. The forest is home to more than 100 species of birds and a myriad of orchids, bromeliads, ferns, and other plants and trees. You may visit the park on your own; however, an experienced guide will provide much interesting information. Guide service can be arranged at Av. America 5653 y Vozandes (459–013 or 447–341). Public transportation is not available; unless you have a vehicle, it may be easier to arrange a day tour through one of the recommended travel agencies (see "Tours" in the Quito section above). Pasochoa is open seven days a week and entrance fee is about $1.

THE ECUADORAN ORIENTE

The word Oriente often confuses the newly arrived visitor to Ecuador. The word doesn't refer to the Far East and the Orient of the Pacific, but rather to the vast rainforest that lies to the east of the Andes.

About a quarter of Ecuador's land is included in the Oriente, but only a sparse population of an estimated 80,000 people live in the rugged, isolated jungle area. Geographically the Oriente is composed of the lower eastern slopes of the Andes and the jungle lowlands of the upper Amazon tributaries. The Oriente is laced with large, fast-running rivers that are often dangerous because of heavy, sudden flood rains, many rocks, rapids and other obstructions. The Oriente today is still virtually undeveloped and in many parts barely explored. These conditions however are changing fast because of recent oil discoveries, with a new network of roads and an airport facilitating travel into the Oriente.

Tours into the Jungle

For visitors who have only the time or the desire to sample just a taste of the Oriente, several photographic safaris are available from Quito to the jungle's edge. Tours leave from Quito via Ambato for an inspiring descent of the eastern Andean slopes through lush semitropical forestlands, the Salasaca Indian territory, deep gorges spanned by delicate bridges, past great waterfalls, fields of wild orchids and jungle flowers to the very edge of civilization and the small, prosperous town of Baños.

From Baños, several morning excursions to surrounding areas may be made on tours that return the same day to Quito via Ambato and Latacunga. Adventurous and experienced travelers who enjoy hiking and camping can form groups and contract guides in both Baños and Misahuallí for jungle expeditions. Many local guides are available; however, those who speak English and have a minimum of ecological awareness are, at present, few and far between. Good guides can be found, but be sure to question them closely before making a deal to make sure they won't be killing or trapping animals and will respect conservation principles. For travelers with limited vacation time, a preplanned trip is probably the better bet.

By Plane and Canoe

TAME, a military-run Ecuadoran airline, and Icaro offer regular flights to Lago Agrio and Coca. Aeroamazonico offers chartered plane service to several of the area's most important outposts. In addition, there are some mission planes available for hire. Travel is also available by motor canoes along the rivers.

A trip down one of the Oriente's rivers (most accessible are the Napo and Aguarico) is a fascinating adventure. Here is the true jungle with a swift, clear, fast-running river cutting into a five-story high jungle crammed with animal life and vegetation. In addition to the very comfortable *Jaguar Hotel* in Santa Rosa, there are typical lodges in the area of Ahuano and Santa Rosa. *La Misión Hotel,* in Coca, is new and has a decent restaurant (553–674; fax 564–675). A few guest houses without sanitation are available at Puerto Napo and other villages. Best bets for overnight accommodations are the scattered Army posts and many riverbank settlers' homes. For the Spanish-speaking traveler, a cordial welcome is always the rule along the main rivers. In emergencies an evening may be spent with the river Indians who will usually provide shelter and hot fish stew in return for any small gift. The Indians along the main riverbanks are normally friendly. If not traveling with a tour, check on the situation before going too deep into the jungle. Occasional clashes between colonists and the Indians can make it risky to go into some areas.

The Flotel Orellana and Other Metropolitan Tours

One way to "do" the Amazon in relative comfort is by floating hotel, the "Flotel" *Orellana*. This three-deck boat was until recently navigated on the Napo River, and will by press time have been transported to the less trafficked Aguarico River. Highly knowledgeable naturalist guides and a well-run operation make a jungle cruise aboard Metropolitan Touring's vessel a fascinating yet relaxing vacation adventure. The company plans to reduce the Flotel's carrying capacity from 56 to 40 passengers, presumably to reduce environmental impact. The new itinerary for the Flotel was still in the planning stages; however, years of experience as Ecuador's largest travel agency make it likely that the operation will run smoothly and according to plan. Three- and four-day itineraries are to be offered. Both include trips to the Sacha Pacha Scientific Research Station (still being developed), and the Cofán Indian Community, where visitors are invited to a "typical" dinner. Short to moderate-length hikes and river trips via dugout canoe form part of each day's itinerary. Price is approximately $140 per person per night (includes round-trip airfare from Quito).

As part of an ecologically conscious program being developed by Metropolitan, the *Iripari Lodge* was being built near Iriparicocha Lake, the largest lake in the Ecuadoran Amazon. The site will consist of 20 small, rustic cabins. Activities will be more flexible here, and tailored to the desires of the individual: guests can stroll, walk, or hike vigorously along a series of boardwalks and paths surrounding the lodge—either alone or with their guide. The "canopy trail," a boardwalk suspended high in the air, was being built to allow closer observation of one of the most active zones in the rainforest: the upper canopy. Programs of three and four nights are available; cost is about $150 per person per night.

The main attraction of the Imuya area is a series of lakes, each reportedly with a diverse ecosystem. The jungle lodge being built here consists of 10 double rooms, with shared dining and bathing facilities. The minimum stay is two nights; the lodge can also be booked as an extension to either the Iripari or Flotel programs. Cost is approximately $150 per person per night.

The yacht *Manati* is designed to explore, in relative luxury, the beautiful lakes along the Lagartococha River. This 20-passenger, steel-hulled yacht has air-conditioning, hot water, carpeting, sun deck, and reading room. Aboard the yacht, you may still see river dolphins and manatees, in addition to a profusion of colorful birds and chattering monkeys. Cost is about $165 per person per night (includes airfare from Quito). Reservations for all of the above tours can be made through Metropolitan Touring or other travel agencies (see "Tours" in the Quito section above).

La Selva and Safari Adventures

A visit to the La Selva Lodge, 60 miles and two hours downriver from Coca, is an unforgettable experience. Individual adventures can be tailor-made for insect and bird enthusiasts, among others. Short, long, or even overnight hikes can be arranged. The idea here is to provide good food (delicious desserts for lunch and dinner do put on the pounds), a flexible itinerary, and amenities such as crisp, clean white sheets that are changed daily. There are 16 cozy bamboo cabins, which usually keep out the rain when it bursts down upon the encampment in a furious nighttime downpour. Each cabin has a private bathroom and cold shower. There is no electricity in the rooms; however, a small generator provides power for dining room and bar. Its hum is barely audible and does not detract from the muted roar of jungle beasts as they press closer and closer upon the lodge as night descends.

La Selva's owners are now planning safari-like expeditions of the jungle surrounding their lodge. Campers will hike through the primary forest, arriving each afternoon to a new campsite—where tents will have been erected, the stew put on the fire, and the wine chilled. Visitors will have every opportunity to "become one" with the rainforest and its creatures in these luxurious wilderness camps. These trails should offer even more opportunities to see birds and animals than those closer to the lodge. A subtle screening process is supposed to group individuals of like interests. Cost is estimated at $1,200–$1,500 for a seven-night adventure. For more information contact La Selva (see "Tours" in the Quito section above; see "Adventure Vacations" chapter for other adventures).

OVERLAND BETWEEN QUITO AND GUAYAQUIL

One of the most unforgettable overland experiences in South America is the rail trip between Quito and Guayaquil. Not for the fainthearted, the switchbacks and turns on this route are enough to make a mountain climber dizzy. The best way to make the journey is on the Metropolitan Touring's Expreso Coach Car. Attached to the regular passenger train, this bright red car has pullman seats, wide windows, bathrooms, bar, and restaurant. These cars operate between Quito and Riobamba, in the central highlands, and Alausi and Guayaquil. A 50-mile stretch between Riobamba and Alausi has not been repaired since the El Niño floods of 1982–1983, but is bypassed in a first-class bus as part of the tour.

Probably the best way to give an idea of the trip is to reproduce the stations on the ticket, with altitudes:

Altitude in Feet	Station	Miles from Guayaquil	Altitude in Feet	Station	Miles from Guayaquil
15	Durán (Guayaquil)	0	10,379	Luisa	142
20	Yaguachi	14	9,020	Riobamba	150
42	Milagro	21	11,841	Urbina	170
100	Naranjito	31	10,346	Mocha	178
300	Barraganeta	43	9,100	Cevallos	186
975	Bucay	54	8,435	Ambato	196
4,000	Huigra	72	8,645	San Miguel	219
4,875	Chunchi	76	9,055	Latacunga	227
5,925	Sibambe	81	10,375	Lasso	239
8,553	Alausi	89	11,653	Cotopaxi	250
9,200	Tixán	95	10,118	Machachi	263
10,626	Palmira	103	9,090	Aloag	266
10,000	Guamote	112	9,891	Tambillo	273
10,388	Cajabamba	132	9,375	Quito	288

After scanning the elevations and then examining the geography between Guayaquil and Quito, one begins to appreciate the magnitude of the challenge construction engineers accepted when this road was planned. The obstacles before the builders were formidable. From the sea-level left bank of the Guayas River the track extends out 54 miles over flat savanna lands. At the 54-mile mark, the road begins a dizzy climb to 10,600 feet within the next 50 miles. To accomplish this, the track climbs at a 5.5 percent gradient along such engineering triumphs as "Devil's Nose"—a double switchback zigzag cut out of solid rock.

After a brief stop for both man and machine to catch their breath, the train starts out again, climbing even higher to Urbina at 11,841 feet above sea level. Urbina lies at the foot of snow-capped Mt. Chimborazo, which towers another 10,000 feet above the tracks and presents probably the most spectacular view seen from any train window anywhere in the world. As you continue your journey, you pass 309 bridges, tunnels, and bends. Mt. Cotopaxi, at 19,200 feet, the highest volcano in the world, looms against the bright, clear blue mountain sky. After crossing, climbing, and descending these Andean ranges, a final descent is made to Quito, where a tired but probably satisfied group of rail veterans disembark.

Listed below is a brief summary of the trip from Guayaquil to Quito with the most important stops identified. Best, however, is to take the trip in the opposite direction to get the most spectacular scenery in daylight. An advance reservation is needed because the trip is extremely popular and space is very limited. One-way fare is about $6.

Leave Guayaquil at 6 A.M. First stop is Yaguachi, a small village 14 miles from Guayaquil. First important stop is Milagro, where scores of Indian women greet the train with native fruits and *allullas* (a small, tasty, cookie-like bread). At the 54th mile of the journey the train arrives at Bucay, where a larger engine is often connected for the steeper grades ahead.

From Bucay the trip becomes spectacular, as the lush tropical fields pass by and the Andean ascent begins. The train climbs through the Chanchán River gorge to the small village of Huigra.

The most breathtaking segment of the journey starts an hour from Huigra. After inching along a steep canyon ledge high above the Chanchán River, the engine begins the slow pull up the Nariz del Diablo (Devil's Nose), which consists of a series of zig-zags that climb 1,000 feet in the gorge above the river. Tunnels, bridges, and steep cliffs highlight the arduous climb up the perpendicular ridge. The air cools and the tropics fade to a green haze far below.

Next, a series of small Indian mountain villages pass by—Chanchán, Subambe (where connections may be made for another train to Cuenca), and on to the once-popular mountain resort village of Alausí, where bus connections to Quito are possible.

At the 103-mile mark, the train stops in Palmira, and here on the crest of the Andes, in the clear stimulating air, many of the towering peaks of the Ecuadoran highlands appear.

The rarefied atmosphere seems to put Chimborazo, Tungurahua, Sangay, Altar, and Carihuairazo almost within reach. The train soon leaves for Guamote and continues past the shores of Lake Colta and into the agricultural oasis of the Cajabamba Valley.

After Cajabamba, dusk usually begins to conceal the dramatic scenery and the train pulls into Riobamba. Many travelers choose to stay here overnight before continuing on to Quito. Riobamba, the capital of Chimborazo Province, is a city of graceful stone colonial-style buildings. At night the sky glows with the reflection from Sangay volcano and its ashes often cover Riobamba's cobbled streets. Saturday is market day, and leather goods, baskets, sandals, and Indian wares are very reasonable. The tiny, intricate Tagua carvings are a favorite buy. Try the Andean specialty, baked guinea pig, at the large open-air restaurants.

From Riobamba the line climbs to its highest point, Urbina Pass, and for 26 miles crosses a succession of towering ridges to Ambato, an important town of 45,000 inhabitants, impressively situated at the base of towering Chimborazo. Ambato is an important road junction and home of one of Ecuador's best-known Indian markets.

From Ambato the line skirts the mighty volcano Cotopaxi to Latacunga, another important city of 25,000 inhabitants. Latacunga is dominated by the perfect-coned Cotopaxi, which is 18 miles from the city but still manages to dwarf everything in sight. On a clear day the sharp-eyed can see nine volcano cones from the town. Several tours are operated from Quito to Latacunga for the Saturday Indian market.

The only stop of interest after leaving Latacunga is Machachi, where one of Ecuador's top brands of mineral water is bottled. From the Machachi springs the train descends into the basin where Quito lies, and the final 25-mile run to the capital is rapid.

Bus connections for Quito can be made at either Riobamba (4 hours) or Ambato (2½ hours).

You may want to combine your scenic Andean train trip with an Amazon river journey on the Flotel Orellana or a cruise of the Galápagos Islands by either boat or plane from the port city of Guayaquil. Also, connections can be made in Alausi to continue on the train to Cuenca, in the southern Sierra. Metropolitan Touring or other local travel agencies can provide information on comprehensive tours combining these diverse adventures.

If you are in a hurry to get from one city to the other, you can hire a taxi from your hotel and make the trip for about $100 (for two) along the Pan American Highway (fairly good condition) in about seven or eight hours.

Expreso Metropolitan Train Tours

There are several tours designed to incorporate the scenic train ride with visits to Indian markets and handicraft centers located along the route. Metropolitan Touring offers packages which combine travel by both train and *autoferro,* an air-conditioned, refurbished school bus which has been refitted to ride the rails.

The Quito–Riobamba–Quito tour departs Tuesdays, Thursdays, and Saturdays via train.

Included are train tickets, a stop at Latacunga Indian market en route, all meals, services of a guide, overnight accommodations at a hotel in Riobamba, and return motorcoach transportation Riobamba to Quito, with stops at the major weaving centers of Ambato and Guano. The price is $133 per person based on double occupancy.

The Quito–Riobamba–Guayaquil tour departs Tuesdays and Saturdays via train. Day one includes a stop at the handicrafts market in Latacunga, and continues on to Riobamba for dinner and an overnight stay. The next day begins with a short bus ride to Alausi to board a train to Durán (Guayaquil), a breathtaking trip in which the elevation descends from over 80,000 feet to sea level in just 90 miles. Cost is $242 based on double occupancy.

The Quito–Riobamba–Cuenca tour begins with a trip to the Latacunga Indian market and continues on to Riobamba for the night. On day two you will board an *autoferro* for a visit to the Incan ruins at Ingapirca. The third day is spent touring the charming city of Cuenca and the lovely Gualaceo Valley. Tours depart from Quito on Tuesdays, Thursdays, and Saturdays and cost $399 per person, based on double occupancy.

GUAYAQUIL

Ecuador's largest city is the magnificent natural port of Guayaquil, claiming a population of two million. Guayaquil is the country's commercial as well as financial center. The tropical city lies on the heavily wooded banks of the chocolate-colored Guayas River, 12 miles from the Gulf of Guayaquil. The Guayas teems with ships, small boats, and native dugouts. Hyacinths that drift atop the water add a dash of color to the busy river. The river, navigable for the largest of ocean vessels, makes this one of the Pacific's most important and best-protected ports. Approximately 85 percent of Ecuador's exports flow through the port of Guayaquil and down the Guayas River to the outside world.

Rich in history, Guayaquil was the scene of one of South America's most historic meetings. The date was August 9, 1822, when the two greatest Latin American heroes of liberation—Bolívar and San Martín—met to decide the fate of Guayaquil. The negotiations were secret and most of what happened remains unknown to this day. After the crucial meeting, San Martín left Ecuador, and Guayaquil was incorporated into Gran Colombia.

Visitors to Guayaquil are usually just passing through—spending a day or possibly two before leaving for the Galápagos Islands. The city itself is not "visitor friendly," although its inhabitants are outgoing and open and certainly enjoy their city. It is, however, rather dirty, and streets and buildings are frequently poorly maintained. Crime is a serious and growing problem. Guayaquil is Ecuador's city of industry. Oil and sugar refineries, cement mills, breweries, and several other factories line the crowded river banks.

Several tours of the city are available (about $15 per person for two people sharing a private car) usually including sightseeing to: San Carlos fort, Municipal Tower, City Museum, Government Palace, La Rotonda (a colonnade commemorating the Bolívar-San Martín meeting), main docks, Colón Park (where the city was founded), Santo Domingo Church, and the general cemetery or "White City," which is one of South America's most striking burial grounds, with elaborate tombs and monuments. Most visitors visit *El Mirador* for a panoramic view of the city.

From Guayaquil several excursions are available for the visitor seeking a resort of sporting atmosphere. Most popular nearby destination is Playas (also known as Villamil), a resort town with beaches, a casino, and excellent fishing. A two-night tour of Playas and nearby beaches costs $90 and includes transportation, hotel accommodations, three breakfasts, and two dinners.

A second popular destination is Salinas, a popular resort located 98 miles west of Guayaquil on a half-moon bay with a long, if sometimes dirty, sand beach, an adequate hotel, and gambling casino. At Punta Carnero, a very attractive place to stay, is the fine and well located 45-room Carnero Inn. The blue waters of the Pacific Ocean abound with black, blue, and striped marlin, sailfish, amberjack, albacore, corbina, wahoo, dolphin, and roosterfish. Sport fishermen fight for these prizes year-round, but the biggest catches are usually made November through May. Pesca-Tours will charter day trips for two to six people. The price for one boat is $250, or $300 for a more luxurious model. Make arrangements through PescaTours in Guayaquil (Box 487, 443–365; fax 443–142) or in Salinas

(772–391). A one-day tour to Salinas for two in a private car is $127 per person (or $40 for three to five people). A two-days tour may prove more interesting as it includes a trip to several beach communities north of Salinas and a visit to the Museum of Valdivia. For those who speak Spanish it can be considerably cheaper to hire a taxi for one-day excursions.

Off Manta, a port 130 miles north of Guayaquil accessible by a fair road or air, big game saltwater fish are plentiful and the area is still relatively unknown to sport fishermen. Local commercial fishermen, using primitive hand-lines from small dugout canoes, annually catch thousands of marlin. However, there are several Ecuadoran and foreign companies fishing for tuna and marlin with modern boats and equipment. Accommodations, as well as charter boats, should be arranged in advance in Guayaquil for Manta and the other northern Ecuadoran ports and resorts.

A final port worth mentioning is Esmeraldas, reached by road and air from Quito and Guayaquil. Rough transport on small freighters or working fishing boats is sometimes available from Guayaquil, as well. An oil tanker and banana-loading center, Esmeraldas is gaining tourist interest because of the Atacames, Castel Novo, and Sua hotels, situated on beautiful beaches, with palm trees.

Comfortable motorcoaches make the 200-mile trip between Quito and Guayaquil every day. The ten-hour trip stops in San Domingo de los Colorados, where tourists may stay overnight, continuing their journey on the following day (about $25 to $35).

PRACTICAL INFORMATION FOR GUAYAQUIL

TAXIS. Although taxis in Guayaquil do not have meters, they are required to post a schedule of rates. The taxis tend to be rather battered. For safety, travel only in taxis that carry the logo of a taxi cooperative.

BUSES. Not recommended. Buses in Guayaquil are, if anything, even more run down than those in Quito. Be extremely cautious to avoid pickpockets and purse-snatchers.

HOTELS. There are few hotels below the expensive level in Guayaquil that are recommendable. Most have neither private baths nor a steady supply of water. For definitions of price categories see "Facts at Your Fingertips" earlier in this chapter.

Very Expensive

Grand Hotel Guayaquil, Boyaca between Clemente Ballen y Av. 10 de Agosto, Box 9282 (329–690, 529–918; telex 3394 GRANDH-ED; Fax 327251). 180 rooms, restaurant, 2 bars, 24-hour coffee shop, squash courts, pool, gym, sauna.

Oro Verde, 9 de Octubre y Garcia Moreno, across from the American Consulate (327–999; telex: 3744 HOROVE-ED; fax 329–350). The most luxurious hotel; under Swiss management. 225 rooms, casino, pool, gymnasium, sauna, 3 restaurants, coffee shop, bar, barber shop, beauty shop, valet service, laundry. (For reservations in the United States call 800–223–1230.)

Uni Hotel, Clemente Ballen 406 y Chile, Box 563 (328–352; telex: 43773 UNICEN-ED). 120 rooms. Three restaurants, coffee shop, 2 bars, casino, gym, sauna, Jacuzzi, shopping center attached. (For reservations in the United States call 800–223–5652.)

Expensive

Hotel Boulevard, Av. 9 de Octubre 432, Box 7524 (308–888, 306–700; telex 3661 HOCABO-ED; fax 300–354). 60 rooms. Cocktail lounge, restaurant.

Hotel Ramada, Malecon y Orellana, Box 10964 (312–200; telex: 42760 RAMADA-ED; fax 322–036). 110 rooms, restaurant, bar, coffee shop, pool, sauna, steam room, casino, beauty shop.

Moderate

Hotel Sol y Oriente, Aguirre 603 y Escobedo, Box 5875 (325–500; telex: 3091 HOSORI-ED; fax 329–352). 55 rooms. Centrally located, with restaurant, coffee shop, sauna, gift shop.

RESTAURANTS. The restaurants in the Uni, Continental, Oro Verde, and Ramada Hotels are all excellent. For international cuisine and seafood, try **Juan Salvador Gaviota,** Av. Boloña 603 y La Décima, Cdla. Vieja Kennedy (395–621), closed Sun.; also **Barandua Inn,** Circunvalacion Norte 528B (387–366); and **La Posada de las Garzas,** Circunvalacion Norte 536 y Ira (Primera) (383–256). **Los Ajos,** V.E. Estrada 712 y Ficos (382–831), serves excellent Spanish food. All the above restaurants are *Expensive.*

For typical Ecuadoran meats try **Restaurante La Tablita,** Ebanos 126 y V.E. Estrada (388–162) or **La Parrillada del Ñato,** Av. V.E. Estrada y Laureles (387–098). Try **El Cangrejo Criollo,** Quito 4860 y Oriente (346–066) or **El Parado Rústico,** Av. Carlos Luis, Plaza Dañin, Cdla. Nueva Kennedy (396–632) for some of the famous crabs from the area. All these restaurants are *Moderate.*

Tasty seafood is served at **El Taller,** Quisquís 1313 y Los Ríos (393–904). Antiques from the Peña district of old Guayaquil provide the perfect setting in which to enjoy the regional cuisine. *Inexpensive.*

CUENCA

In the southern highlands, about a 30-minute flight from Guayaquil and about a 45-minute flight from Quito, lies the third largest city of Ecuador. Cuenca has long been isolated in the Andes-rimmed Pucarabamba Valley in the south of the country and, gratefully, has also been overlooked by the normal tourist traffic. Cuenca's great charm lies in the purity with which its quaint colonial style has been preserved in its pastoral pace, cobblestone streets, and predominantly colonial buildings. To add to the appeal of this little-known city, Cuenca is surrounded by deep green, velvety hills and some of the most beautiful countryside in Ecuador.

Cuenca also boasts an interesting local market. Held on Thursdays and Sundays in the Plaza Rotary, it is here where "toquilla" straw hats, erroneously called Panama hats, are marketed. Ceramics, straw goods, and embroidered clothing are also specialties, though the hundreds of townspeople and Indians from the countryside sell almost everything imaginable. Thousands of others come to buy, trade, and socialize in a kaleidoscope of sights, sounds, and colors. A separate plaza is used for the toquilla straw hats and straw goods used to make them. Although Sunday is the main market day, a trip here on Thursday can be equally rewarding. Even the regular public market, which operates daily, is quite interesting and colorful.

Parque Abdon Calderon is the center of town, where the New Cathedral is located, built over a period of 82 years (1886–1967), with floors of Italian marble, pillars of Ecuadoran marble, and hand-carved choir chairs of native wood. The Old Cathedral faces the new, and its towers are said to have been used by the French Geodesic Mission as points of reference in measurement of the meridian arc. The town's finest museums include the Modern Art Museum at Av. Sucre and Talbot and the Museo de las Conceptas, a restored convent which houses religious statuary, furnishings, and art. Also worthwhile is the CIDAP museum, halfway down the stairs at the foot of Calle Hermano Miguel.

Outside of Cuenca

Ingapirca is Ecuador's only major Incan ruin, about two hours northeast of Cuenca in the province of Cañar. The stone fortress consists of one main round palace with low walls radiating from it, and has great views of the surrounding valleys. It is reached by traveling along the Pan American Highway through several small towns, including Biblián, with its castle-like church tucked into the hillside. A full-day Ingapirca tour with lunch costs about $40. Guides are sometimes available in the museum on site.

PRACTICAL INFORMATION FOR CUENCA AND ENVIRONS

HOTELS. For definitions of price categories see "Facts at Your Fingertips." **Hotel El Dorado.** *Expensive.* Av. Gran Colombia y Luis Cordero, Box 5001 (831–390); telex 8580 GIVASA–ED). One block from the main plaza, with 90 rooms, 2 restaurants, disco, sauna. (For reservations in the United States call LARC, 800–327–3573.) **Hosteria Uzhupud.** *Moderate.* 25 miles outside Cuenca, Box 1268, Cuenca (821–853). Old hacienda with a pool, sauna, restaurant, horseback riding, tennis. Also 10 *posada* rooms (*Inexpensive*), pleasant but with shared bathrooms. **Hotel Crespo.** *Moderate.* Calle Larga 7–93 Luis Cordero, Box 221 (827–857, 831–837). Lovely old hotel with good restaurant. Ask for a room with a view of the river, or stay in the hotel's no-frills annex (829–989). *Inexpensive.* The owner of the hotel can arrange special horseback trips into Cajas National Park for fishing, or into the jungle to visit one of the Indian tribes.

RESTAURANTS. El Jardín, Presidente Córdva 7–23 (824–883), is Cuenca's best restaurant. French cuisine. *Moderate.* The restaurant of the Hotel La Laguna is very good and specializes in Swiss and French cooking. **La Cantina,** Borrero y Pres. Cordova (no phone) serves typical food and drink. Open after 6 P.M.; closed Sun. *Moderate.* **Café El Carmen,** Sucre y B. Malo (no phone), serves good coffee, teas, and cakes; closed Sun. *Inexpensive.* The restaurant of the Hotel Crespo is good and has a lovely view. The Hotel El Dorado has a good coffee shop. *Inexpensive.*

SHOPPING. Cuenca is a center for crafts. Many of the best shops for traditional crafts, including baskets, weavings, woolen sweaters and capes, and marzapan figures, are found on Gran Colombia and around the main plaza. Some of the better shops include **Ocepa** (Pasaje Hortencia Mata), **Productos Andinos** (Gran Colombia 8–74), **Atahualpa Folklore** (L. Cordero y Muñoz Dávila), and **Le Tucán** (Gran Colombia 7–88). **Artesa** (Luis Cordero 6–96), has an extensive collection of ceramics produced in Cuenca. **Kinara** (Sucre y L. Cordero), next door to the Old Cathedral, carries modern fashions made of the locally woven, traditional textiles, as well as handmade jewelry and crafts. **Dsignos,** on Pasaje Hotencia Mata, also carries modern jewelry and pottery based on typical, regional designs.

Cuenca is famous worldwide for its fine jewelry, and 18-karat gold and silver which are all excellent buys here. There are many fine stores located on Gran Colombia between General Torres and Mariano Cueva, and most reputable shops will provide, upon request, a certificate guaranteeing your satisfaction.

As home of the misnamed Panama Hat, Cuenca has several firms that manufacture and sell this straw head wear. Some of the finest hats sell for hundreds of dollars and are so finely woven they look like silk. Two highly recommended shops are the *Ortega* brothers, at Benigno Malo 10–32 or Vega Muñoz 9–33. Either can arrange for you to visit the factory, where the selection is greatest.

GALÁPAGOS ISLANDS

The Spanish called them the "Encantadas," the "Enchanted Islands." Six hundred miles off the coast of South America and lying just south of the equator are the cluster of large volcanic islands and smaller islets that are known today as the Galápagos Islands. They are perhaps best known as the site where Charles Darwin made scientific observations which eventually led to his theory of evolution as outlined in *The Origin of Species.* Darwin visited the islands as part of his round-the-world voyage with the ship *Beagle.*

The Galápagos were first sighted by the Spanish Bishop, Thomas de Berlanga, on March 10, 1535, when unfavorable winds and ocean currents carried his ship to the islands. It is believed that the Incas, and possibly one of the Inca rulers, discovered the islands long before Berlanga arrived. They would have traveled on the big, square-sailed, ocean-going rafts which pre-Columbian traders and warriors used to journey from the tip of Chile up to Central America and possibly the North American coast.

The islands were claimed for Ecuador in November 1831 by General Jose de Villamil. A military expedition under the command of Colonel Ignacio Hernandez took possession of the islands on February 12, 1832. Hernandez established the first colony on Floreana Island and became the islands' first Governor General. At first the colony flourished, but political problems on the mainland and the decision to send political prisoners, criminals, and prostitutes to the new colony led to its disintegration. By 1842 the colonists moved to San Cristobal Island, and gradually the remaining prison colony disintegrated.

On July 20, 1959, the islands (with the exception of designated areas reserved for colonization) were declared a National Park by the government of Ecuador. The Charles Darwin Foundation for the Galápagos Islands was founded in Belgium in the same year. Its purpose was to preserve the animals and plants of the islands. In 1979 the United Nations designated the islands a World Heritage Site.

The Islands

The Galápagos Islands (also called the Archipelago of Colón) are volcanic in origin and encompass five large islands, eight small ones, 42 islets, and 26 rocks. Carried by winds and ocean currents, plants, animals, seeds, and birds have made their way to the islands. Over the course of thousands of years, these species diverged from their ancestors until now many of them are classified as distinct species. Some, such as the flightless cormorant, are found nowhere else on earth.

The Galápagos are also home to a distinctly odd mixture of polar and tropical creatures: penguins and flamingos, sea lions and iguanas, boobies and albatross are found here, at least at certain times of the year. This mixture is possible because the islands, so close to the equator, are cooled for most of the year by the Humboldt Current, which flows north along the South American coast from the Antarctic until it reaches Ecuador, where it swings west, directly toward the Galápagos.

The wildlife on the Galápagos is the main attraction for the visitor. Perhaps nowhere else on earth can you swim with seals, penguins, and brilliantly colored fish and feel so much a part of their world. You can watch

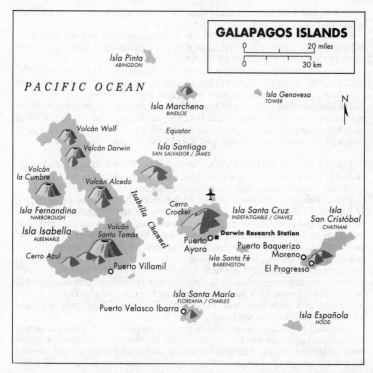

GALAPAGOS ISLANDS

0   20 miles
0   30 km

PACIFIC OCEAN

Isla Pinta
ABINGDON

Isla Genovesa
TOWER

Isla Marchena
BINDLOE

N

Volcán Wolf

Equator

Volcán Darwin

Isla Santiago
SAN SALVADOR / JAMES

Volcán
la Cumbre

Volcán Alcedo

Isla Fernandina
NARBOROUGH

Cerro
Crocket

Isla Santa Cruz
INDEFATIGABLE / CHAVEZ

Isla
San Cristóbal
CHATHAM

Isla Isabella
ALBEMARLE

Volcán
Santo Tomás

Darwin Research Station

Puerto
Ayora

Puerto Baquerizo
Moreno

Cerro Azul

Isla Santa Fé
BARRINGTON

El Progresso

Puerto Villamil

Isla Santa María
FLOREANA / CHARLES

Puerto Velasco Ibarra

Isla Española
HOOD

the courtship rites of the booby and frigatebirds close up, see the famous
Darwin finches, and feel that you are an accepted visitor rather than an
unwelcome and frightening intruder.

When visiting the islands, observe park regulations about staying on
marked paths, carrying out all trash, and not disturbing the wildlife.

Though there are no extremes of weather in the Galápagos, the best
months to visit are generally May–June and November–December. From
January to mid-May it is generally hotter, more humid, and rainier.
Stronger winds and rougher seas arise between July and September.

PRACTICAL INFORMATION FOR THE GALÁPAGOS ISLANDS

GETTING TO THE ISLANDS. Tours to the Galápagos can be booked in advance through any travel agent in the United States or Canada, or by writing directly to one of the travel agents listed here. If you are planning to travel as part of
a group and wish to reserve an entire boat, begin planning at least a year in advance.
The same advice applies if you are traveling independently during mid-December
to mid-January, or July through mid-September.

If you are unable or unwilling to plan so far in advance, you can still get to the
Galápagos, but there is no guarantee that the boat you prefer will have space available (not all boats will accept passengers who are not part of a charter group). Most
travel agencies offer individual, last-minute bookings, or can help you get a space
through another agency.

Some yachts offer special trips for divers. An increasing number of boats are now
equipped with air compressors, and some of those without compressors try to bring
enough tanks to allow divers one dive each day.

Most travelers get to the Galápagos by air. TAME and SAN offer flights from
Quito and Guayaquil to Baltra every Monday through Saturday. Round-trip flights

from Quito cost $367 and from Guayaquil, $324. The cost of air fare is *not* included in any charter or tour prices for the Galápagos.

Some boats occasionally offer tours out of Guayaquil. The one-way trip takes two days. Check with your travel agent if you are interested in booking on these tours, as they are not available all the time.

Transportation between islands is limited. The Galápagos National Institute (IN-GALA) offers interisland boat runs for passengers not on tours. Interisland flights have been approved but are unlikely to begin in the near future.

The National Park charges a $40 visitor fee upon arrival. This fee is not included in the cost of any of the charters and is subject to change without notice. Visitors must have their passports with them. Be sure to ask the officials to stamp your passport with the special park stamp, which looks like a Galápagos tortoise.

TOURS IN THE GALÁPAGOS. The bigger boats have fixed itineraries approved by the National Park and offer three, four, or seven nights at sea. The longer tours may include the passage to or from Guayaquil.

The *Galápagos Explorer* and smaller yachts generally offer seven nights at sea, all spent in the Galápagos. With advance planning, the smaller yachts can be chartered for special groups for shorter or longer tours, and they can usually adapt their itineraries to suit the interests of their passengers better than larger boats. Prices vary considerably according to ship, length of tour, number of passengers (in the case of the small yachts), and type of berth (in the case of the bigger ships). Deposits are required and, in general, are fully refundable with 60 days' notice.

For the big ships, depending on the type of berth, prices range from around $450 up to $700 per person for a three-night tour, and from around $1,000 up to $1,500 per person for a seven-night tour. The *Isabela II* costs $1,750 per person, double occupancy, for the seven-night tour.

Individual yachts are chartered on a per-boat per-week basis. Price per person varies according to the number of people who actually travel. Depending on the boat, prices vary widely. The deluxe *Nortada* carries 10 passengers and charters for $19,800 a week (seven nights). The more economical *Golondrina* carries 8 passengers and costs $5,200 per week.

For individuals planning to travel on the small yachts without a charter group, prices range from $350 for a three-night tour, to over $1,000 for the seven-night tour. Yachts offering diving facilities will charge around $150 more per person per week.

WHAT TO PACK. Visitors to the Galápagos should pack comfortable, lightweight cotton clothing, good walking shoes or sneakers, a sweater or jacket, and a swimsuit. Visitors should also bring a sun hat, one or two bottles of sunblock (the sun is very intense this close to the equator and is, in addition, reflected off the water), motion sickness pills, snorkeling equipment, and at least twice the amount of film you expect to need (you can always take unexposed rolls home with you). Besides the $40 park fee, carry enough money to cover the costs of soft drinks, beer, and alcohol consumed on board, tips to the guide and crew (or cabin attendants on the larger boats), and souvenirs. The larger boats have boutiques or shops on board, and many of the yachts sell their own T-shirts.

STAYING ON THE ISLANDS. Make reservations for hotels in the islands through your travel agent or by writing to the hotel in care of the post office on the island (i.e., Hotel Galápagos, Puerto Ayora, Santa Cruz, the Galápagos, Ecuador).

SANTA CRUZ

Expensive

Hotel Galápagos. The nicest hotel on the islands, with gardens, private shore, comfortable cabins, and a good restaurant. Next door to the Darwin Research Station.

Moderate

Hotel Delfin. Comfortable, pleasant hotel with good restaurant and private beach. It is rather isolated from town, and can only be reached by boat.

Inexpensive

Hotel Lobo del Mar. Fifteen new rooms, restaurant.
Hotel Sol y Mar. Situated on the waterfront, with restaurant and friendly staff.

SAN CRISTOBAL

The island is just opening for tourists with several SAN flights each week. Facilities for tourists are more limited than on Santa Cruz.

Expensive

Gran Hotel San Cristobal, new hotel with air-conditioning, private beach, and restaurant. Special packages are offered through SAN and tourist agencies for room, meals, and day trips: three days, $324; five days, $395.

TOUR AGENCIES. Besides the tour agencies listed under the tours section in Quito, the following have offices on Santa Cruz Island and can help you book the type of cruise which best fits your budget and itinerary. Both of them can provide radio contact with the rest of the world in an emergency.

Coltur. Across from the Port Captain's office, or aboard the *Capitanía*.

Isbella. Located in the SAN office, across from Pelican Bay. Long distance, collect calls can be made via shortwave radio from this office.

FRENCH GUIANA

Land of Wild and Primitive Beauty

French Guiana's forest, dense and mysterious, is watered by a fan of
rivers spreading out from south to north: the Maroni/Marouini System
along the Suriname border, Mana, Sinnamary, Approuague, Comté, and
Oyapock. A trip up any of these rivers by motorized dugout canoe is far
from a luxury cruise, but it's a travel experience that's hard to beat for
sheer exoticism. Fortunately, tourism in French Guiana has developed significantly over the past few years, and arranging trips to these destinations
is now possible.

Some of the greatest explorers of history explored the Guiana coast. Columbus was here in 1498. So was Alphonse d'Ojeda, Jean de las Cosa, and
the Italian navigator whose name came to stand for the whole New World:
Amerigo Vespucci. Such soldiers of fortune as Sir Walter Raleigh and
Laurence Keyms penetrated the steaming jungles of Guiana in search of
a legendary El Dorado. In 1598, the latter found not gold—but the
French, already ensconced and extracting dyes from the dark trees of the
tropic forest.

In 1604 the French contingent was reinforced by de la Ravardière and
a group of colonists. Several other French companies followed, leaving
the province of Normandy for richer virgin territory between the Orinoco
and the Amazon. There *was* gold in the soil of Guiana, though no golden
city existed, and there was sugar, spice, bauxite, and endless stretches of
forest whose trees promised an inexhaustible supply of timber, oil of rosewood, and other gums.

The rich land was coveted. The Dutch seized it from the French, but
Admiral d'Estrées recaptured it for France in 1676. Although the French
had to give up the rich prize between the Amazon and the Oyapock by

the treaty of Utrecht in 1713, they held onto what is now French Guiana, the western *arrondissement* of Saint Laurent du Maroni that borders Suriname and the eastern *arrondissement* of Cayenne that borders Brazil.

The *département*—originally a colony—is the site of a two-phase development boom. It started in 1964, when France established headquarters of her space exploration program on the sandy coastland of Kourou, 26 miles northwest of Cayenne, the capital. An instant town was created here, with ultra-modern facilities. The site was ideal for rocketry because it is less than 5° north of the Equator (as against Cape Canaveral's 28°), which means the rotating speed of the earth is much faster, so the same propulsion will lift 24 percent more hardware than in Florida. Visitors can arrange excursions to the space center; inquire at the Syndicat d'Initiative (address below) about this and about excursions to the Iles du Salut as well.

Then during the last eight years the French government has launched a plan for the economic development of French Guiana, with various income-producing programs, such as cattle raising, commercial fishing, forestry, and ore prospecting included.

There are 114,000 French Guianese, according to the 1990 census, many of whom are young. Some 50,000 Guianese live in Cayenne and the surrounding suburbs. The population is composed of French officials and businessmen, indigenous Guianese (largely black and Amerindian), French Creoles, and a number of Chinese. There are also settlements of immigrants from Southeast Asia, including the H'mong and other mountain tribes from Laos and Vietnam, who have set up communities where they maintain their culture and ethnicity. French culture has flourished under the hot equatorial sun, and the government boasts that French Guiana has the lowest illiteracy rate in South America, a claim disputed by Argentina.

French Guiana is rapidly joining the mainstream of international tourism. At one time its only identifiable tourist attraction was the Devil's Island prison complex; however, due to careful planning on the part of the French Government, the country is now accessible to the adventurous traveler. In addition to the Salut Islands, Centre Spatial Guyanais, and Cayenne, French Guiana offers visitors a pre-Columbian archaeological site, river trips by *pirogues* (dugout canoes), excursions into the amazonian forest, nature hikes, and ecological outings to the breeding grounds of giant sea turtles. All these natural attractions are inextricably linked to the beautiful flora and fauna of tropical South America.

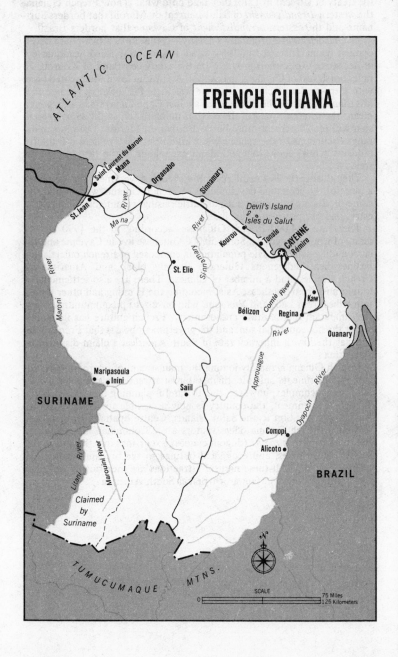

FRENCH GUIANA

ATLANTIC OCEAN

Saint Laurent du Maroni
Mana
Organabo
Sinnamary
St. Jean
Mana River
Devil's Island
Isles du Salut
Kourou
Tonate
CAYENNE
Rémire
St. Elie
Maroni River
Sinnamary River
Comté River
Kaw
Bélizon
Regina
River
Ouanary
Maripasoula
Inini
Saiil
Approuague
River
Oyapoch River
Comopi
Alicoto
SURINAME
BRAZIL
Litani River
Marouini River
Claimed
by
Suriname

TUMUCUMAQUE   MTNS.

SCALE

0   75 Miles
                              125 Kilometers

FACTS AT YOUR FINGERTIPS

WHAT IT WILL COST. A couple visiting French Guiana should expect to spend $250 to $300 a day for first-class hotel accommodations, meals, and a sightseeing tour of the capital by local taxi.

SOURCES OF INFORMATION. There is no branch of the Guiana Office of Tourism in the United States. Tourist information can be obtained from **Agence Regionale de Developpement Tourisme,** 12 rue Lallouette, 97300 Cayenne, tel. 30–09–00.

WHEN TO GO. Best weather is from July to December. There are short rain showers Dec.-Feb.; drizzles in Mar. and heavy, long rainstorms Apr.–July. Average temperature is only 80 degrees, but the humidity makes it rather more sticky than this would indicate.

WHAT TO TAKE. Modest beachwear is preferred. Take a sun block, sunglasses, a sun hat, and mosquito repellant, and an umbrella. If you plan to go into the forest, you'll need body-covering clothing, comfortable walking shoes or preferably boots (there *are* snakes as well as insects). A light poncho or raincoat is recommended. Camera-toters should include zoom and flash in their gear, for shooting in the dark-shadowed jungle. Binoculars are a must for bird-watching and wildlife viewing.

SPECIAL EVENTS. Throughout the country, the **Carnival** celebrations are the most important of the year. In Guiana they run from mid-January to Mardi Gras (February or March, depending on the year). Up to the Saturday before Mardi Gras, every weekend the people dance Friday nights, Saturday nights until dawn, and Sunday nights until midnight. Saturday mornings at about 5, groups of masqueraders, coming out of the dance halls, parade out, dancing, into the city streets, especially in the capital, to the music of Creole orchestras before separating and going home to rest. Every Sunday, in the afternoons, from 4:30 to 7 P.M. groups of *touloulou* (disguised or masked individuals), young and old, male and female, fill the principal arteries of Cayenne and other towns, showing themselves off to the crowds of spectators on the sidewalks. The touloulou go on foot. At about 6 each Sunday evening, the touloulou en masse dance to an orchestra placed on a trailer in the principal streets of the cities, especially Cayenne, Saint Laurent, and Kourou. And at about 7, the crowd disperses until the following Sunday. The crowds can number from 10,000 to 15,000 people counting the spectators and rubberneckers who follow the touloulou.

From the Friday before Mardi Gras to Ash Wednesday, Cayenne, Saint Laurent, Kourou, and the other towns are celebrating nonstop. It is a time of unrestricted merrymaking. Public and private balls, important parades of touloulous in the streets until the wee hours and on Saturday and Sunday afternoons. Monday afternoon the parade of touloulous is made up of married couples, disguised and followed by a grand procession, also disguised, whether stylishly or modestly.

On the Mardi Gras the joy is at its peak. It is the last day of Carnival. On Ash Wednesday everyone in the city wears black and white, and weeps for Vaval, the King of Carnival who must die. In the afternoon, there is a long parade, with Vaval at the rear. Finally the effigy, the symbol of the King of Carnival, is burned with great pomp in the most beautiful square in Cayenne, the Place des Palmistes, in front of an enormous crowd, of all of Cayenne. The burial takes place late that night marking the end of Carnival.

A ballroom specializing in traditional Carnival is Soleil Levant (Nana), 35, route de la Madeleine (31–35–93). Every Saturday and Sunday night from 9 P.M. until morning. Women in costume get in free. Men are not obliged to dress up, and pay full entrance price. Entrance: 50 francs, U.S. $6.

Besides Carnival, the **feasts** to honor the patron saint of a community, organized by the different municipalities, are interesting. The most popular is the one in Cayenne, around October 15. It lasts 1–2 weeks and is very lively due to the different ethnic, cultural, folkloric, and sporting clubs of the city, who set themselves up in temporary barracks on the Place des Palmistes. Many sporting events and cultural shows take place there. The main attraction of this feast remains the Grand Ball presided over by the Mayor surrounded by his guests and all of the country.

The other patron saint feasts, in alphabetical order are: *Apatou,* August 20; *Camopi,* July 14; *Iracoubo;* August 27; *Kaw-Regina,* November 26–30; *Kourou,* November 25; *Mana,* July 14; *Ouanary,* first weekend in October; *Rémire,* September 8; *Roura,* August 8; *Saint Laurent du Maroni,* August 15; *Saint Georges de L'Oyapock,* end of August; *Sinnamary,* September 16–18; *Tonate,* June 24.

Religious feasts: The French Guianese, mostly Catholic, have parades in the streets with statues of saints from the Cathedral of Cayenne, built in the 19th century. Among the most famous feasts are Easter (March–April) and Christmas.

In Cacao, a village in the Roura community (65 km from Cayenne) and in the village of Javouhey, Mana community (not far from Mana by car), the Asian refugees who arrived in French Guiana around 1970, the H'mongs, dress in their beautiful traditional Laotian costumes to celebrate their New Year in the streets.

TRAVEL DOCUMENTS. A valid passport is required, plus a return or onward ticket. Visas are not needed by citizens of the European Community (EC), the United States, or Canada. All others should check at the nearest French consulate.

An international certification of vaccination for yellow fever is required for stays of longer than 2 weeks. Malaria prophylaxis is recommended for any length of stay.

HOW TO GET THERE. Air France flies direct from Miami and San Juan to Cayenne's airport several times a week. Daily connections can also be made from Martinique or Guadaloupe. *Cruzeiro do Sul* offers flights to Suriname and Brazil.

Cayenne is a port of call for ships of the *Compagnie Générale Maritime,* and many of the larger cruise lines call at Devil's Island during their Amazon and South American cruises.

CURRENCY. French Guiana is an integral *département* of France. The French franc is the standard currency. At press time, there were 5 French francs to the U.S. dollar.

Prices, unless noted otherwise, are in U.S. dollars.

HOTELS. Hotels in this chapter are divided into the following categories based on double occupancy: over $75, *Expensive;* $35 to $75, *Moderate;* below $35, *Inexpensive.* All hotels are European plan.

RESTAURANTS. Most visitors will be surprised at how wonderful French Guiana's food is. French and Continental cuisine is the most popular in cosmopolitan restaurants, but there is a great deal of variety. Antillian-Guyanese (sometimes called Creole) and Asian food are also very popular.

Price categories, in U.S. dollars, are based on a three-course dinner for two, excluding drinks, tax, and tips: *Expensive,* $75 and up; *Moderate,* $35 to $75; and *Inexpensive,* under $35.

TIPPING. Most restaurants and hotels add a 15% service charge. Normally, in local Creole areas, a tip is accepted, but not necessarily expected, especially in outlying areas.

TELEPHONE AND MAIL. Overseas calls can be made directly from French Guiana and telegraph and fax services are available. French telephone cards are used instead of coins in most public telephones and can be purchased at all post offices and many stores. A $15 card buys about ten minutes on a United States call.

A letter weighing less than 5 grams going air mail to the United States will need $.75 in stamps, and will take between 5 and 10 days to reach New York from Cayenne. The main post office is on Route de Baduel and is open Mon. through Fri. 8 A.M. to 6 P.M. and Sat. 8 A.M. to 12:30 P.M. A branch office, Cayenne Ceperou, is located in the center of Cayenne and is open Mon. through Sat. 7:30 to noon and Tues. and Fri. afternoons from 3 to 5. For postal information call 31–22–25.

NEWSPAPERS. You can get up-to-date editions of English-language newsmagazines at the drugstore near La Place des Palmistes on the main street of Charles de Gaulle, at the Librairie Guyanaise on Ave. d'Estrées (31–53–16), and at the Librairie A. Jean Charles in the middle of blvd. Jubelin (30–31–32).

Local newspapers include: *France Guyana* for 80 cents; *Télé 7 Jours,* a weekly with radio and TV information for $1; and *La Presse de Guyane,* edited by the local assembly with administrative information, for 40 cents.

ELECTRIC CURRENT. 220 volts, 50 cycles. Bring an adapter for electrical appliances.

USEFUL ADDRESSES. Air France, Place de Palmistes, tel. 30–27–40, and **Air Guyane,** 2 Rue Lalouette, tel. 31–72–00, Cayenne and Rochambeau Airport; **Syndicat d'Initiative,** tel 31–29–19; **Institut Pasteur,** Av. Louis Pasteur. **Police,** at Prefectural Office, Rue Charles de Gaulle tel. 31–10–17. **Botanical Gardens,** Av. André Aron at Av. de la Republique. **British Consulate,** Rue Lalouette, B.P. 664. Nearest **US Consulate:** 14 Rue Blenal, B.P. 561, 76200 Fort de France, Martinique, FWI; tel. 71–94–93.

HEALTH. Bottled water from France is advisable; available in the hotels. There are two hospitals and three private clinics in Cayenne. Hospitals also in Kourou and one in St. Laurent du Maroni; dispensaries in all communes.
Malaria medication should be taken for any length of stay.

HOW TO GET AROUND. *Budget, Avis, Hertz,* and *Takari* rental cars, as well as taxis, are available in Cayenne and at Rochambeau Airport. The hotels or the Syndicat d'Initiative can help with this. Small buses operate along the coast. Into the interior one travels by plane or dugout canoe. There are about 200 miles of hardtop roads along the coast, and a daily bus trip each way between Cayenne and St. Laurent via Kourou, Sinnamary, Iracoubo in the west near the Suriname border.

TOURS. For information on well-organized excursions to the interior, Salut Islands, or Kourou, contact: *Guyane-Excursions,* B.P. 349, 97381 Kourou, tel. 32–05–41; *Havas Voyages,* Rue Christophe Colomb; *Sinnarive Tours,* tel. 34–56–56.

SPORTS. Firearms brought in by visitors must be declared at Customs. Canoes may be rented for hunting waterfowl along the rivers. There is fishing in the ocean from rocks or canoes. Swimming around Ile de Cayenne. For visiting the interior, a guide is a must, and also required is a special permit from the Prefecture in Cayenne. Water skiing and tennis are available in Cayenne.
River Safaris. A river safari offers a myriad of exhilarating experiences: visiting Indian, Creole, Bush Negro, and H'mong villages; mild white-water rapids; teeming jungle wildlife; and overnight stays in hammocked carbets and camps. The safaris are provided by expert guides and equipment is available from local tour operators.
See also "Adventure Vacations" chapter.

CAYENNE

Approaching by air or sea, you will sense grandeur as soon as you glimpse the Iles du Salut and the verdure-clad crags of the island of Cayenne, the territory's capital. This city of 50,000 has been laid out with the unerring French instinct for urban planning, which has resulted in the handsome promenades of the Place des Palmistes and the Place des Amandiers. Curiosities of the capital include the official residence of the Prefect, built in the 18th century by the Jesuit fathers. Also, not far from the island's Rochambeau Airport, is found one of the most exotic small zoos in existence, noted for its collection of magnificent tropical birds. A taxi will take you along the coast for an interesting tour of the summer homes of Cayenne's leading citizens, and it is just a few miles to the jungle where superb groves of bamboo meet overhead to form cool archways of golden green.

Cayenne is the hub of all activity, center for sea bathing, cockfighting (very popular, although illegal), and fishing, and point of departure for hunting safaris. The local museum is worth visiting, particularly noteworthy is the butterfly and insect collection. You will notice the giant double palms of the Place des Palmistes, a species unique to French Guiana.

PRACTICAL INFORMATION FOR CAYENNE

HOTELS. For definitions of price categories see "Facts at Your Fingertips." Be sure to reserve hotel rooms far in advance during space launches. The famous **Montabo Hotel** is now closed, although it is hoped that it will reopen under new management. The leading hotel is **Novotel Cayenne.** *Expensive.* Rue de Montabo, 3 km. out of town, 15 km. from airport. 100 air-conditioned rooms with private baths. Swimming pool, tennis courts, rental cars. European plan.

Hotel Le Polygone. *Expensive.* In Matoury, 8 km. from Cayenne, 4 km. from airport. 32 air-conditioned rooms. Pool, restaurant, covered tennis court. European plan (30–54–00).

Hotel Phigarta. *Expensive.* 47 bis rue François Arago (30–66–00).

Hotel Amazonia. *Moderate.* 28 Ave. du General de Gaulle (31–00–00). Central location, air-conditioned, clean, friendly atmosphere.

Central Hotel. *Moderate.* Angle des rues Becker et Mole (31–30–30). Central location, opened in 1990, 35 rooms.

Hotel Neptima. *Moderate.* 21 rue Felix Eboue (30–11–15).

RESTAURANTS. For Creole dishes try: **Le Cric-Crac,** *Expensive,* Route de Remire (35–63–90); **Le Grillardin,** *Expensive,* Matoury (35–63–90); **Le Paradis des Amis,** *Expensive,* 5 rue Mole (31–06–88); **Restaurant le Tatou,** *Expensive,* 35 avenue President Monnerville (31–12–12).

For French and Continental dishes try: **L'Angelique,** *Expensive,* Novotel (31–74–00); **Bar Restaurant Des Palmistes,** *Expensive,* Place de l'Esplanade (31–00–50); **La Belle Epoque,** *Expensive,* 88 rue Lallouette (30–20–19); **Le Saloon,** *Inexpensive,* 21 rue Christophe Columb (31–13–33).

For Asian food try: **Le Cap St. Jacques,** *Moderate,* 71 rue Vermont Polycarpe (31–47–26); **Le Chateau D'Asie,** *Moderate,* 21 rue Lieutenant Brasse (31–73–91); **La Riviere Des Parfums,** *Moderate,* 10 rue Justin Catayee (31–79–54).

There are also a number of restaurants featuring North African and Indonesian cuisine, as well as native dishes of crocodile, tapir, and iguana.

MUSEUMS AND HISTORIC SITES. The **Franconie Museum,** in the center of town, on Ave. de Gaulle, in the house of deputy Alexandre Franconie. Created in 1901, it contains the country's historic documents dealing with gold-prospecting, Boni and Indian handicrafts, prints, drawings, and sculptures.

The **Ceperou Fort,** built around 1643 by Charles Poncet de Brétigny, is located on Place Léopold Héder, formerly Place de Grenoble. This fort was the first settlement in Cayenne. Not very far away, facing the sea, you can see at the edge of the military quarter Loubère, the first barracks in the country, built by the governor De Ferolles in the 17th century and reconstructed in 1968 by Colonel Loubère.

The **Hall of the Prefecture,** former Jesuit convent and former Governor's Palace at the time of the colonial empire is located on Place Grenoble, was constructed between 1749 and 1752.

On the Place de Grenoble you can see the **Montravel Fountain,** named after the governor Tardy de Montravel in 1867. The **Place des Palmistes** is nearby, nicknamed "la Savane" by the people of Cayenne. Governor Laussat, in about 1822, decided to plant the giant palm trees which came from the Guisambourg commune. The feast of Cayenne's patron saint is held here each year.

In the center of the Place des Palmistes stands the monument to Felix Eboué, erected in 1957. Felix Eboué, born in Cayenne in 1884, colonial administrator and governor-general of French Equatorial Africa during World War II, is buried in the Panthéon in Paris in acknowledgement of his services to France.

The **Cayenne Market** on the Place du Coq, rebuilt in 1909–1910, is a very interesting sight, rich in colors and smells. Open on Tuesday, Wednesday, Thursday, Saturday morning, and Friday afternoon. The fish market flourishes every morning and is very animated.

The **Zoo**, Société Civile Agricole, previously mentioned, is near Rochambeau Airport on route PK 29, Route de Montsinery (31–73–06). This display of the wildlife of French Guiana in microcosm is well worth the visit.

SHOPPING. Within the past few years a great many new boutiques have opened, offering a wide range of merchandise. Good buys are basketry, hammocks, pottery, wood sculpture, and gold jewelry. You can find locally crafted items, made by the Boni and Amerindian people, such as moderately priced wood sculptures made by the Bonis, originally from Africa and now settled in the Haut Maroni region; baskets and small works of basketry; pottery and hammocks made by the Indian groups of the area (Wayana, Galibis, Palikours, Oyampis, Arawaks and Emerillons).

You can also find animal hides, tanned locally, and items made from alligator skin such as wallets, handbags, and briefcases, all at good prices as compared to Paris or New York. Before buying, however, check if any of these items are made from hides of endangered species. By all means, do *not* be tempted to buy any framed giant butterflies, many of which are unique to the area, or pictures made from the wings of rare butterflies. Even guides plead with tourists not to make such purchases in an attempt to halt the killing of these exquisite creatures.

In the center of Cayenne, stores of all kinds line the principal shopping streets which are the Avenue de Gaulle, rue Lallouette, rue François Arago. Particularly noteworthy are:

La Galerie Tropicale, Avenue de Gaulle for local items; **Boutique de la Bergerie,** at the corner of Avenue de Gaulle and rue François Arago (31–01–62), local and imported items including magnificent color postcards with Guyanese subjects and Guyanese slides; **Arouman,** 22 rue Lallouette (31–45–05), locally crafted items, butterflies, and sculpted wood.

For **jewelry** look for gold and precious stones from Brazil. Shops of note: **Richard Ho A Sim,** Ave. de Gaulle and rue Cataye (30–08–09), jewelry, gold; **Tresor Nature,** 62 rue Lallouette (31–52–17), gold nuggets, precious stones, gold jewelry. Outside of Cayenne, in Sinnamary there is **Paulin Clet,** 3 rue de L'Ouvrier (34–50–69) for filigree jewelry, nuggets; and in Saint Laurent, **Van Genderen Egbert Bijouterie,** 17 rue Victor Hugo (34–12–94).

Handicrafts from Latin American countries such as Peru and Amazonian Brazil can be found in stores in Cayenne and Kourou. In Sinnamary town, you can buy a Guyanese specialty of the community—flowers made from the feathers of the native birds, such as the ara. Contact the convent of the nuns of Sinnamary and also the *Maison de L'Artisanat* (the House of Crafts), rue du Calvaire, tel. 34–55–66. For the feather flowers, contact the Franciscan nuns on rue Bononse Vernet, tel. 34–50–23.

In Cayenne, French **perfumes** are available at: **Jean Elie Lydie,** 75 Avenue de Gaulle (30–28–60); **Parfumerie Muriel,** 7 rue Lieutenant Becker (31–28–11) for well-known French perfumes and beauty products; **Parfumerie Rose Helene,** 46 bis, rue Francois Arago (30–10–55), and 60 Avenue de Gaulle (31–03–01).

MUSIC AND DANCE. From time to time there are local orchestral concerts organized under the direction of Novotel, on the weekends. Call 30–38–88 for information.

The Academy of Dance is at 2 rue Remparts, tel. 30–19–92. Lessons in classical, modern and jazz dance.

MOVIE THEATERS. Eldorado, Place des Palmistes (31–03–00). Daily from noon to midnight. **Rex,** 36 rue Christophe Colomb (31–26–96). Three times daily.

NIGHTLIFE. Some nightclubs in Cayenne are Club 106, Avenue de Gaulle and Beguine Club Place Schoelcher I (30–06–11), in the town.

Local nightclubs for dancing include BBC on Lotissement Jean Gilles, phone: 31–50–94; Moucaya Club-RN2 Pk. 8 Matoury, phone: 35–65–71; Le Penitencier, adjacent to the Montabo Building (31–27–75); and Le Chat Noire, PK 3, Route de Larivot (31–91–55). Very popular during Carnival season.

The local folk-dance clubs are worth visiting, but you should be accompanied by a native Guyanese or else someone who has lived in Cayenne for a long time. Go to the Tourists' Information Bureau of the city in question or the Office of Tourism. Some of the well-known folklorical groups are: Buisson Ardent, Balourou, Wapa. The dances that are open to the public are usually held on one Saturday of each month, from 9 P.M. until morning. There are also recitals on drums made from wood from the Amazon forest.

There is also nightlife to be found in the very picturesque quarter called Rot Bo Crique, which means "on the other side of the creek" especially in the part of the quarter nicknamed "Chicago." This part has French bistro-style bars and discotheques with music; and is primarily for adults. Most places are open from 9 P.M. until morning.

OUTSIDE CAYENNE

There are a number of interesting excursions from Cayenne. Fort Diamant, built in 1652, is the New World's best-preserved example of a genuine feudal castle. Fort Trio with its double tower is another monument of European military architecture transplanted to America.

Twenty-six miles from Cayenne is Kourou, a complete new town built for the staff of France's Space Exploration Center. St. Laurent du Maroni, farther away on the border with Suriname, is a colonial town on the River Maroni. Small but bustling, it faces the former town of Albina on the Suriname side of the river. Ferry crossing has been suspended since 1986 due to the Suriname civil war. Sentenced prisoners were shipped here from France and assigned to various points within the colony, including the notorious complex known as Devil's Island (see below). Several of the old prison buildings still stand and have been converted into housing for local Guianese. Safaris depart from here up the wide Maroni/Marouini River to the outpost of Maripasoula and beyond. It is an exhilarating trip over mild white water, passing Boni and Indian villages en route.

The "Tour de l'ile" excursion will enable you to appreciate the magnificent scenery of French Guiana's rugged coast, swift rivers, and dense forests. The Montagne de Mahury provides hikers with a rare opportunity to climb among the orchid-draped trees of an equatorial forest to the three lakes of Mount Rorota. Most impressive—and most rugged—of all are the river trips into the heartland of the luxuriant interior province of Inini. These trips, where you can make overnight stops in rustic shelters in the jungle, are splendid for pioneering types. Inquire at Takari Tours for details.

You may visit Iracoubo with its melancholy tombs of France's political deportees. The church's interior is decorated with murals by an inmate of the prison. Then there are the lovely Iles du Salut and Devil's Island, which brings us back to the spectre that still haunts French Guiana. The jungle, which is gradually taking over the many prison cells and support buildings, is a beautiful place for picnicking and strolling, with poignant reminders of the past. The island complex has comfortable lodgings and restaurants at Auberge des Iles du Salut, making it popular for a one-day or overnight excursion. Daily ferry departs Kourou 8:30 A.M. and returns at 5 P.M.

For detailed information on the tour possibilities, contact one of the travel agencies listed at the front of this chapter. Although tours are well organized, their frequency depends on the number of tourists able to travel.

PRACTICAL INFORMATION FOR OUTSIDE CAYENNE

KOUROU

HOTEL. The Hotel des Roches. *Expensive.* On the beach; there is a pool and restaurant. Early risers may view the luxuriant scarlet ibis flying up from their night perches along the swampy banks of the Kourou River.

RESTAURANTS. Restaurant Edouard Le Thym. *Expensive,* Hotel des Roches (32–02–66). **Le Viet-Huong,** *Moderate,* rue du Temple (32–10–30); **Au Vieux Mont-martre,** *Expensive,* rue du Gal de Gaulle (32–13–33); **Le Colibri,** *Expensive,* place de l'Europe (32–18–45); **Milk Bar la Cage,** *Inexpensive,* Hotel des Roches, (32–02–77).

USEFUL ADDRESSES. *Air France,* Place Republique (32–10–50); *Takari Tours* (31–19–60); *Pharmacy Belrose Aline,* Simarouba (32–14–00).

ENTERTAINMENT. There is a movie theater on Allée des Tamanoirs, **Urania** (32–05–50). There are nightclubs in the new part of town and also in the Old City. One is **La Palace,** 20 rue de Gaulle (32–09–28).

SAINT LAURENT DU MARONI

HOTELS. There are several small hotels. Two are the **Star,** *Moderate,* rue Thiers (34–10–84); and **Le Toucan,** *Moderate,* Blvd. du Gal de Gaulle (34–10–07). The hotel/restaurant **L'Acararouany,** between St. Laurent and Mana (34–17–20), is excellent for viewing mammoth sea turtles laying eggs.

RESTAURANTS. Chez Philo, *Moderate,* 29 Cite Hibiscus (34–11–22); **Trois Et-oiles,** *Moderate,* Place Verdum (34–20–49).

USEFUL ADDRESSES. *Post Office,* Av. du Gal de Gaulle (34–11–94); *Hospital Andre Bouron,* Av. du Gal de Gaulle (34–10–37); *Pharmacie Centrale,* rue du Gal de Gaulle.

ENTERTAINMENT. The movie theater is in the center of town, **Le Toucan,** rue Schoelcher (34–12–36). For nightlife try **Le Toucan,** Blvd. de Gaulle (34–10–07).

SINNAMARY

HOTELS. Eldo Grill. *Moderate,* (34–51–41); **Sinnarive Motel,** *Moderate* (34–56–66).

RESTAURANT. Eldo Grill. *Moderate.* (34–51–41).

PARAGUAY

The Landlocked Island

by
ROBERT KAPLAN and LORRIE KLINE

Robert Kaplan and Lorrie Kline, residents of Princeton, NJ, were U.S. Peace Corps volunteers in Paraguay and lived in Asunción and the Interior. They have also traveled extensively through Brazil, Argentina, Chile, and Uruguay.

A century ago travelers to South America described Paraguay in glowing terms, enamored by both the lush vegetation of the countryside and the warm hospitality of its people. Today, however, this small landlocked nation is usually seen as little more than a curious footnote en route to South America's more glamorous hot spots. As a result of their relatively few encounters with outsiders, Paraguayans still greet visitors with a natural friendliness, which makes it a pleasure to explore Asunción and the interior, and to trace the country's rich history and traditions.

Travel in Paraguay today is even more attractive in light of several recent developments. Due to the devaluation of the guaraní, Paraguayan handicrafts—intricate laces, embroidered clothing, leather goods, and colorful woven blankets and hammocks—are affordable to even the most budget-conscious tourist. Paved roads now extend into formerly inaccessible areas and form circuitous routes for easy touring. Finally, the rapidly progressing restoration of the Jesuit Reductions is uncovering a fascinating historical picture of that unique colonial experiment.

Two Banks of the Paraguay River: The Fierce and the Fertile

Although depicted in the early nineteenth century by British and Spanish cartographers in largely arbitrary shapes and sizes, Paraguay has occupied an area the size of California since 1935. The Paraguay River, running from north to south, divides the country into two distinct regions: the inhospitable Chaco to the west and the fertile Paraná Plateau to the east. The Chaco region, also referred to as the "Green Hell" because of its insupportably high temperatures and humidity, encompasses two-thirds of the country's area but accounts for a negligible percentage of its population. Seen from the air, the Chaco appears as a thick green carpet blemished only by the straight red lines of the unpaved dirt roads seemingly leading nowhere. Since there are few towns here, current national maps of Paraguay denote little more than cattle ranches, military forts, and even water wells.

The new "Transchaco" road, presently under construction (470 of its 800 kilometers are already fully paved), hopes to connect Asunción with Bolivia and Argentina as a future route to the Pacific Ocean. When completed this may change the face of the Chaco, but until then the area remains largely an unconquered frontier, the domain of hearty opportunists, wealthy foreigners, and the outposts of the military government. Sportsmen still hunt a species of prehistoric wild pig, which was thought extinct until recently, and a steady stream of furs, pelts, and paws finds its way to Asunción, much to the chagrin of conservationists.

In stark contrast to the otherwise untamed quality of the Chaco are the Mennonite settlements, the most notable being Filadelfia (450 kilometers from Asunción), a thriving agricultural community founded in the 1920s. Of the nomadic peoples who were once the sole inhabitants of this expansive territory, 50,000 pure-blooded Indians remain, many of whom are exploited as a labor source for the numerous cattle ranches or for the Mennonite farms.

The eastern region of Paraguay consists of the Paraná Plateau, a low plain 300 to 600 meters above sea level stretching between The Paraguay and Paraná rivers and composed of low rolling hills and wide, flat grasslands. Occasionally, one is surprised by a taller string of hills (although they never even reach 800 meters); there is evidence that some of these hills are the necks of ancient volcanoes that have been extinct for several million years. Small rivers and streams abound throughout the region, and there are many small waterfalls. Unfortunately, what was once the spectacular series of waterfalls known as Los Saltos de Guairá, on the Paraná River, is now but an expansive man-made lake, their once unbridled power recently rechanneled by the Itaipú Hydroelectric Dam. The thick but fast receding forests of Paraguay are resplendent with flora and fauna, much of which remains uncataloged.

It is this fertile plain of eastern Paraguay which has attracted agricultural settlement from the sixteenth century onward. The vestiges of many early communities still exist, seeming to have remained virtually unchanged over the past century—an impression bolstered by the common sight of farmers cultivating their fields with hoe, machete, and oxen. Settlement efforts continue to this day, reaching ever farther into the hinterland as new generations abandon the exhausted, overly-parceled land of their ancestors for areas of virgin forest. Many parts of the eastern region have been electrified in recent years, although almost exclusively along major routes. Running water has been extended into some 140 rural communities in the last 15 years.

The Paraguayan People

After suffering two devastating wars, Paraguay remains relatively underpopulated, claiming only 4.5 million inhabitants, or about 11 persons per square kilometer in the eastern region and, of course, a much lower population density in the Chaco. Approximately 650,000 people live in the capital city of Asunción; no other population centers even approach that size, although there are numerous small cities (30,000 to 50,000) scattered throughout the interior.

The population is relatively homogeneous, considered to be 95 percent *mestizo*—a mixture of Spanish and Indian blood. Both Spanish and the Indian language Guaraní are officially recognized as the national languages, and 75 percent of the population is bilingual. While a visitor to Paraguay will hear Guaraní spoken on the streets of Asunción, and it is the language of preference of people living in the interior, some Asunción elite never learn to speak it. The majority of Paraguayan music is sung in Guaraní, and even a few books and plays are written in it; however, few Paraguayans are literate in that language.

The Jesuit/Guaraní Republic

Paraguay was originally inhabited by the nomadic Guaraní Indians, who had spread throughout much of central South America as far east as the coast of southeast Brazil, west to the Andean foothills and the Inca Empire, and north to the Amazon River. Towns with Guaraní names still dot the continent and, along parts of the Amazon River, Tupi-Guaraní speaking Indians can still be found. Paraguay is the only country that has retained Guaraní as its most widely spoken language.

In 1535 Pedro de Mendoza founded a small settlement at Buenos Aires but hostile Indians there soon forced him to abandon it. Before leaving, however, he sent Juan de Ayolas on an expedition up the Paraná River, seeking a route to Peru. On August 15, 1537 a member of his expedition, Juan de Salazar de Espinosa, after encountering peaceful Guaraní Indians, founded Asunción on the eastern bank of the Paraguay River near its confluence with the Pilcomayo River. When Lima, Peru became the viceroyalty over all Spanish holdings in South America in 1543, Asunción was designated capital of the provinces of Paraguay and Río de la Plata. It was from Asunción, then, that the Spaniards pushed northwest toward Peru to establish a settlement at Santa Cruz in Bolivia, east to settle the Paraguayan interior, and south to successfully reestablish a settlement at Buenos Aires in 1580. In 1617, Asunción lost jurisdiction over the Río de la Plata province to the new settlement of Buenos Aires. One hundred fifty years later, in 1776, the tables were turned even further as Asunción became subjugated under Buenos Aires, capital of the newly created Viceroyalty of Río de la Plata.

Failing to find gold or silver in the Paraguay or Río de la Plata provinces, the Spanish Crown devoted little effort to developing these regions. Nevertheless, both Spain and Portugal granted permission to the recently founded Society of Jesus to send missionaries to South America, and in 1609 Jesuit priests began organizing the Guaraní Indians into self-sufficient missions known as "Reductions." In the usage of the period a "reduction" signified a "gathering together." The Jesuits "reduced" the Indians for the three-fold purpose of evangelization, cultural development, and protection from Spanish and Portuguese colonists. The threat from colonists was real. Brazilian *bandeirantes* or frontiersmen constantly threatened the Reductions, seeking to sell captured Indians into slavery (which was legal in the Portuguese colony). Spanish law, on the other hand, expressly prohibited the enslavement of indigenous peoples. Nonetheless, because the Spanish Crown was so distant and communications so problematic, the law was rarely enforced. In fact, abuses, perpetrated by the overseers of Indian day laborers, were the rule rather than the exception.

Each highly organized Christian community, gathering roughly 3,000 Indians under the paternal guidance of two or three Jesuits, worked extensive agricultural holdings. Primary crops included sugar cane, cotton, wheat, rice, tobacco, and indigo along with *ka'a,* a distinctive herb used to make the tea known as *yerba maté.* (This "Jesuit Tea" was of such high quality that the Spanish Crown restricted its trade for fear that it would replace teas produced elsewhere in South America.) In addition, the Jesuits trained the Indians in a variety of practical skills such as masonry, carpentry, blacksmithing, wood-turning, and agricultural techniques as well as in more artistic endeavors such as calligraphy, sculpture, painting, and music. Their large choral and instrumental groups were said to have rivaled those in Europe.

All Jesuits were expelled from the continent in 1766. In Paraguay this meant leaving behind the thirty settlements they had founded and the approximately 100,000 Indians then living and working there. Under civil authorities the Reductions quickly declined; some Indians scattered for jobs as tradesmen in the cities, while others less fortunate were enslaved or killed. Many of the once magnificent churches became elaborate quarries for the unrestrained pilfering of stones until the structures inevitably collapsed under their own weight. Today only eight Reductions lie within Paraguayan borders due to territorial losses incurred in the War of the Triple Alliance. These remaining ruins are fascinating and excellent small museums. Several Reductions are now being restored, and many contain artwork of the Reduction Era. Today, some are tourist attractions worth visiting.

Prosperity in Isolation

Paraguay achieved independence from Spain without violence in May 1811, and later that year the first national government was created. In 1814, Dr. José Gaspar Rodriguez de Francia was named "Supreme Dictator of the Republic" for a term of five years by a thousand-member Congress. Only two years later, however, a new Congress elevated him to "Perpetual Dictator." No further Congress met until Francia's death in 1840.

It was through the efforts of this unique man that Paraguay was able to fight off Argentinian annexation attempts, and his introduction of two harvests per year allowed the new nation to become self-sufficient in agriculture. Indeed, since Francia decreed complete isolation for Paraguay, forbidding people to enter or leave and bringing all external trade to a standstill, the country was forced to meet all of its own needs. It is sometimes maintained that this isolation entrenched the Guaraní language in Paraguayan culture and built the strong sense of nationalism that has characterized the country since that period.

At Dr. Francia's death, the public coffers were full, owing to the dictator's scrupulous austerity. However, his omnipotence allowed no governmental infrastructure to be created. After two provisional governments, the presidency finally passed to Carlos Antonio Lopez in 1841 and the task of building a governmental system with legislative, judicial, and executive branches was begun. Lopez carried the country out of isolation and used the treasury's resources to contract foreign experts (primarily British) to construct the railroad, the ironworks, and many fine public buildings, many of which still stand today. It was during the twenty years of the Lopez presidency that Paraguay achieved its preeminence, boasting an impressive fabrics industry, both military and merchant marine forces, a profusion of schools, and a strong economy with a stable currency. Carlos Antonio Lopez is considered to have been a benevolent dictator who was able to build upon the successes of the brutal but honest Francia regime to promote the public good and, in the process, amass a personal fortune.

Adapting to New Frontiers

Upon Carlos Antonio Lopez's death in 1862 his son and vice-president, General Francisco Solano Lopez, rose to the presidency. During his first years in office, development of the country's infrastructure continued with the stringing of the first telegraph lines in Latin America. The year 1865, however, marked the advent of the infamous War of the Triple Alliance, which pitted Brazil, Argentina, and Uruguay against Solano Lopez's Paraguay. Despite considerable financing on the part of British banks, it took the allies over five years to achieve victory; the war ended in 1870 with the death of Solano Lopez in the far north of Paraguay. The republic's prospects for further progress had been dealt a crushing blow. Eighty percent of the male population had lost their lives, leaving only 14,000 men and 180,000 women. During the eight years of occupation following the war, the country's remaining reserves were appropriated by the victors to pay back war debts. Additionally, over 150,000 square kilometers of Paraguayan territory were annexed (an area roughly equal to the eastern third of modern Paraguay). The beautiful Iguazu Falls, once well within Paraguayan domain, passed to Brazil, and Argentina came away with the province of Misiones as well as a good portion of the Chaco. The section of the Chaco retained by Paraguay was named after U.S. President Rutherford B. Hayes, who arbitrated the land dispute recognizing Paraguayan rights to the territory.

In the following decades, Paraguay began the arduous process of rebuilding its population and its economy. However, another severe setback was dealt in 1932 as the beleaguered nation entered yet another brutal war, this time with Bolivia over the long-disputed Chaco. After having lost access to the Pacific Ocean in the Pacific War in 1883, Bolivia shifted its sights eastward, seeking an outlet to the Atlantic Ocean via the Paraguay-Paraná River. Rumors of gas and petroleum deposits only served to heighten the dispute over the Chaco territory, finally leading to war in 1932. Known as the "Chaco War," this conflict was fought under extremely inhospitable conditions, with tenuous communication and supply links for both armies. After three years of fierce fighting and tremendous losses on both sides, a peace treaty was signed in 1935. Paraguay retained the bulk of the disputed territory and Bolivia was granted only a small section of the northern Chaco with a virtually useless port on the Paraguay River several hundred kilometers north of Asunción. The Chaco War to this day remains vivid in the national memory; the soldiers who lost their lives there remain symbols of modern-day patriotism.

Nineteen years and 10 presidents later, General Alfredo Stroessner seized power in 1954 in what was expected to be just another short-lived coup. Instead, Stroessner ruled the country for over 34 years, exceeding the mere quarter century of "Perpetual Dictatorship" by Francia. Although his government enjoyed widespread support throughout Paraguay, it was often criticized for corruption and suppression of dissent. A brief military coup on February 2, 1989 left General Andrés Rodríguez as provisional president of the country. His promise to reinstitute genuine democracy resulted in his election as Constitutional President for a four-year term that began May 1, 1989.

Economy: The Post-Itaipu Years

The Paraguayan economy is based primarily on agriculture and livestock, together comprising one-third of the gross domestic product and employing almost 50 percent of the workforce; cotton and soybeans alone account for over two-thirds of the country's exports. Twenty-seven million hectares (66.7 million acres) are concentrated in the hands of less than 2,000 large landowners, while a remaining two million hectares (nearly five million acres) are worked by over 110,000 peasant farmers.

After experiencing the second highest growth rates in the Americas during the 1970s (primarily due to construction of the Itaipu Hydroelectric Dam with Brazil), Paraguay entered into a recession in 1981 from which it seemed to be recovering in 1984 and 1985 with record harvests of both cotton and soybeans. The country's terms of trade, however, have deteriorated since 1984, with the price of its two major crops falling more than 25 percent on world markets. This situation has, however, considerably improved over the past few years with better prices on the world market for those crops. In 1989, average increases of 16 percent in cotton, 15 percent in soybeans, and 40 percent in wheat crops were reached.

The 71 percent devaluation of the guaraní on the open market in 1985 (while the official import/export rate has held constant) posed a serious problem for policy-makers and the population at large. Although pursuing "outward oriented growth," promoting exports and discouraging imports, the government feared that hyperinflation and uncontrollable currency devaluation would be the result of allowing the guaraní to find equilibrium on the floating market. Therefore, the regime had established multiple official exchange rates which it could control more easily. The negative effects of this policy were lower prices to the farmer, a tax on exports, and a lively black market on both imports and exports. This situation ended in July 1988 when nearly all import/export went into the floating market and only two official exchange rates continued to apply for government transactions. Currently, all transactions are now made on the "free" floating exchange market, thus favoring exports with a convenient, steady exchange rate.

The Itaipu Dam ("sounding rock" in Guaraní) is the largest hydroelectric dam in the world, with eighteen turbines that will by 1992 generate 12,600 megawatts which will be shared equally by Paraguay and Brazil. Since half of the electricity generated by one turbine can fulfill Paraguay's present energy needs, the country will become a large exporter of electricity to Brazil. Once the project lured thousands of Paraguayans to the border city of Ciudad del Este; now, with construction nearly complete, increasing numbers are having to move back to the farmlands they abandoned. Another smaller, but nevertheless important hydroelectric dam is already under construction lower on the Paraná River at Yasyretá ("Moon Country"), this time with Argentina.

There is little industry in Paraguay excepting beverages, dairy, canned meats, and candy as well as some textiles, produced mainly for domestic consumption but also for export. Most products found in stores, whether in Asunción or deep in the Interior, are produced in Brazil and Argentine and, more recently, Taiwanese goods, are increasingly widespread.

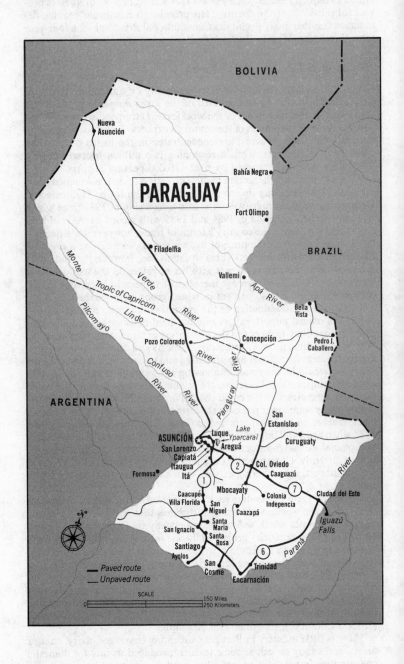

FACTS AT YOUR FINGERTIPS

WHAT IT WILL COST. Paraguay is exceedingly affordable to the tourist due to the devaluation of the guaraní against the dollar. Even though the inflation rate climbed to 40 percent in 1985, prices are still quite cheap. While the "tourist season" is from June to August, there is no corresponding hike in hotel or restaurant rates during these months.

A traveler can expect to pay under $35 for a moderately priced hotel room (double occupancy). Even the most expensive restaurant is affordable at about $12 for a three-course dinner for one, excluding drinks and tip; a tasty $4–$5 lunch is easily found in any of the numerous inexpensive restaurants.

For after dinner entertainment a few dollars quite suffices—movies cost about $2.50, as do concerts and mixed drinks, and taxis are cheap.

Generally, outside of Asunción, prices are even lower, although the range of accommodations and food establishments is much more limited.

SOURCES OF INFORMATION. Paraguay has no tourist offices in other countries. The country does, however, operate a small embassy in both the U.S. and the U.K. **In the U.S.:** Ambassador Marcos Martinez Mendieta, Massachusetts 2400 NW, Washington, DC (202–483–6960). **In the U.K.:** Chargé D'Affaires, Graciela F. De Jauregui, Braemar Lodge Cornwell Garden, London SW7.

Paraguayans living in the U.S. have organized **Associations of Paraguayans** in both New York and Washington, D.C., which may be able to provide information.

WHEN TO GO. Classified as subtropical, Paraguay can be very hot and very humid in the summer (Dec. 21–March 21), occasionally reaching 108° F but with temperatures usually ranging between 75° at night and 95° at mid-day. Winter temperatures can fall as low as 32° F and the dampness can make it quite uncomfortable. Usual winter temperatures, however, range between 45° at night and 75° during the day, making it generally the most pleasant time to visit. In any case, a visitor should come prepared for both cold and hot weather; abrupt changes in temperature are not uncommon, at times falling 20° in 30 minutes! Paraguay experiences spectacular lightening storms in all seasons that may cripple normal daily activity. Storm drainage is so poor that within minutes a fine city avenue becomes a small river, whereas in the interior a country lane becomes a muddy impasse or is simply barricaded by local officials in an attempt to avoid the rapid degeneration of this humble infrastructure. All in all, nature is not a force which can be taken for granted in Paraguay.

WHAT TO TAKE. Dress is informal but neat. In summer a short-sleeved cotton shirt and lightweight slacks for men and cotton skirts and blouses for women will be most appropriate. For a visit in June or July a sweater or a coat may be needed for a few days but warm weather apparel will also be desired. Locally made lightweight shirts and blouses, however, are inexpensive and excellent souvenirs so you may choose to augment your wardrobe after arriving. An umbrella is always advisable since it may rain in any season; a bathing suit will help you survive any extra-hot days.

SPECIAL EVENTS. February: *Fiesta de San Blas,* Patron Saint of Paraguay (3rd); an official holiday throughout the country, but the best festivities are in Itá (37 kilometers from Asunción). Carnival festivities with parades and water balloons kick off Lent in all the major towns. **March and April:** *Easter Week* brings furious preparation in the interior and much of Asunción passes Good Friday through Easter Sunday with their relatives in the country—consequently, most everything in Asunción is closed. **May:** *Independence festivities* cover two days (14th and 15th) of military and student parades in Asunción and all the major cities. **June:** *National holiday* celebrating the anniversary of the Peace Treaty ending the Chaco War (12th); all Chaco War veterans who can muster the strength march in the capital or in the nearest large town to their home. *San Juan* (23rd and 24th) is celebrated with dances of the *kambá* and testing of the faithful, who walk barefoot across a bed of hot coals. **August:** *Anniversary of the founding of Asunción (15th),* with parades and festivities in Asunción. **October:** *Octoberfest* at the Club Aleman in Asunción on the first Saturday of the month. **November:** *All Saints Day* (1st), a deeply religious day observed with visits to the cemetary by all. The second Saturday in November is *Octoberfest* in Colonia Independencia, near Villarrica. **December:** *Day of the Virgin of Caacupé* (8th), celebrated by a pilgrimage from all parts of the country to Caacupé (approximately 60 kilometers from Asunción), where masses and other Catholic religious rites are taken.

TRAVEL DOCUMENTS AND CUSTOMS. Citizens of the U.S., Canada, and the U.K. need only a valid passport and a tourist card ($3), purchased upon arrival. Visas are required for stays over 90 days. No health certificates or immunizations are required. "Reasonable quantities" of tobacco and alcohol are permitted duty-free.

A $7 (cheaper if paid in local currency) airport tax is levied on all international flights.

GETTING TO PARAGUAY. By air. From the U.S. and Europe. Several airlines fly regularly from the U.S. and Europe to Asunción—*LAP* (Paraguayan) is the most economical and flies direct from Miami and from Frankfurt and Madrid via Rio and São Paulo; *Varig* (Brazilian), from New York and Miami as well as several points in Europe via Rio, São Paulo, and Iguazú Falls; *LAB* (Bolivian), from Miami via La Paz (Fridays); *American* (considerably more expensive) from Miami via Panama, Lima, and La Paz.

From within South America: From Buenos Aires—many flights offered by *LAP, Aerolíneas Argentinas,* and Iberia; from Montevideo—*LAP* or *Pluna;* from Santiago—*Ladeco* and *LAP;* from Rio, São Paulo, or Iguazú Falls—*Varig* and *LAP;* from Lima and La Paz—*American, LAP,* and *LAB.*

By train. From Buenos Aires—modern train while in Argentina, then switch to wood-burner at the Paraguayan border (very slow but recommended for the durable, adventurous traveler).

By bus. From Buenos Aires—Brújula, Nuestra Señora de Asunción (Brújula also connects Asunción with the Argentinian city of Córdoba, as well as others along the west bank of the Paraguay River); from Montevideo—COIT, several times a week; from Rio, São Paulo, or Iguazú—Pluma, as well as COIT and Rapido Iguazú from Curitiba and Iguazú Falls.

CURRENCY. The official currency of Paraguay is the guaraní. There are no official exchange rates and all transactions are made on the "free" floating market, which has been sticking at around 1.2 guaranies (Gs) for $1. The *cambio* houses on Calle Palma in Asunción give a slightly better rate than the cambio men on the street and will also exchange traveler's checks for a very small fee. Five paper notes range between 100 and 10,000 guaranies. Four stainless steel coins cover denominations between one and 50.

Prices, unless noted otherwise, are in U.S. dollars.

HOTELS. In Asunción there is a wide variety of hotels covering the entire spectrum of both cost and comfort. The interior of the country offers less variety, but adequate and plain accommodation is generally the rule. Throughout this chapter all hotels, whether in Asunción or the interior, have been classified according to price for double occupancy accommodations, as follows: *Super Deluxe,* $120 and up; *Deluxe,* $75–$120; *Expensive,* $45–$75; *Moderate,* $30–$45; and *Inexpensive,* under $30. Rates generally include Continental breakfast except as noted. If you are planning a trip from June to August you are advised to make reservations well in advance for hotels in the *Deluxe* and *Expensive* categories.

There are many small Residenciales (boarding houses) for under $4 per person; these are strictly no frills and offer only common bathrooms.

ROUGHING IT. There is camping at the Botanical Gardens (about seven kilometers out of Asunción), at Casa Grande Camping (45 kilometers east of Asunción on Ruta II near Lake Ypacaraí), and at Westfalia Camping in Asunción (Ave. General Santos and José Felix Bogado). The fee is about $3 per tent. Camping is also permitted in the National Parks of Ybycuí and Cerro Cora.

RESTAURANTS. Restaurants have been classified along the following lines: *Expensive,* $14 and up; *Moderate* $8–$14; and *Inexpensive,* under $8. Prices are for a three-course meal for one person not including drink or tip.

Paraguayan Food and Drink. If you're a beef-eater the Paraguayan *parrillada,* with its assortment of grilled steaks, sausages, and innards, is a must. Parrilladas, typically characterized by outdoor dining, are a fancier, citified approximation of the beloved Paraguayan *asado* (barbecue), the traditional meal for all celebrations throughout the country. No asado is complete without *mandioca* (cassava), a fibrous tuber sometimes jokingly referred to as Paraguayan bread because of its integral role in the national diet. In addition to copious quantities of meat, the traditional asado also features *sopa paraguaya* (a type of corn bread made with onions and cheese) or *chipa guazú* (sopa paraguaya made with fresh corn); both are delicious when served hot! Chipa, by far the most popular of the corn bread variations, is made with cornmeal, cassava flour, and cheese—a favorite snack (again, best when fresh out of the oven). Chipa is also served as the traditional Easter fare; tons of chipa are prepared and stockpiled in every household on the Wednesday before Easter, to be eaten during the holy days through Easter Monday.

Surubí, a large catfish, is a very popular dish in Asunción as well as in other riverfront locales. Fish soup is widely available and highly recommended. Other popular soups include *bori-bori,* made with chunks of meat, vegetables, and the small cheese and corn balls that give the soup its name, and *soyo,* a ground beef soup flavored with a variety of different vegetables.

Empanadas with a variety of fillings such as meat, chicken, ham, cheese, and corn are popular snacks throughout the day, as are *croquetas* (breaded balls of chicken, beef, or pork). In finer restaurants, *palmitos* (palm hearts), considered to be one of the country's foremost delicacies, should not be missed. Once a major export, lack of timely foresight has made palmitos an increasingly rare and costly item, though still affordable to the tourist.

At both mid-morning and mid-afternoon, or basically whenever two or more Paraguayans get together, it's time to bring out the *tereré* (a refreshing cool drink made from yerba maté). Served from a *guampa* (usually a cow's horn, but acceptable alternatives include specially crafted wooden goblets or the nearest available plastic cup), and drunk through a metal straw called a *bombilla,* this custom originated in the Chaco War and is unique to Paraguay. The drinking of tereré is both an important social function and a necessary relief from the heat. The hot *maté,* (tea), popular throughout the "southern cone," is also for many a daily ritual, most commonly shared around dawn and again in late afternoon. Indeed, in every rural Paraguayan household elder family members enjoy the quiet morning hours before sunrise taking maté together around a modest kitchen fire before beginning another long day in the fields. No round of tereré or maté is truly complete without the addition of one or more traditional herbs, *yuyos* (pronounced jóo-joes). Used for medicinal purposes, or at times merely to refresh a "hot stomach," each yuyo has its specific properties well-known to virtually all Paraguayans, even young children. On a visit to the yuyo section of Asunción's Mercado 4, feel free to ask the robust middle-aged women vendors about the use of each yuyo; you may be surprised at the wealth of information you receive.

The several Paraguayan beers are quite good and are sold in 600 milliliter bottles. There are several brands of *caña,* a local rum made from sugar cane, as well as several national wines (produced for the most part by German immigrants). Their quality ranges from undrinkable to good. Old Cottage is a local brand of Scotch whisky.

TIPPING. No service charge is added to the bill but it is customary to leave a 10 percent tip in the better hotels and restaurants. Taxi drivers also expect a small tip. Tip airport and hotel porters $.40 per suitcase.

BUSINESS HOURS AND HOLIDAYS. Most shops and offices are open from 7:30 A.M. until noon, then close until 3:00 or 3:30 P.M. for siesta, reopening until 6:30 or 7:30 P.M. Saturday is a working day until noon. Banking hours are 8:45 A.M.

to 12:15 P.M., Mon.–Fri. Government offices operate from 7:00 A.M.–noon, Mon.–Sat.

National Holidays are Jan. 1 (New Year's Day); Feb. 3 (San Blas, Patron Saint of Paraguay); Mar. 1 (Heroes Day); Holy Thursday and Good Friday; May 1 (Labor Day); May 15 (Independence Day); June 12 (Chaco Armistice); Aug. 15 (Founding of Asunción); Dec. 8 (Virgin of Caacupé); Dec. 25 (Christmas Day).

TELEPHONES AND MAIL. Operator-assisted telephone service links all major towns and many minor ones, while direct-dialing within the country, though still rare, is becoming more common. International connections must all be operator-assisted, whether made from a hotel, private telephone, or one of several ANTEL-CO offices in Asunción or in the interior. Pay phones for local calls, costing about 13¢ (buy your *ficha* in the nearest street kiosk or commercial establishment), are located throughout Asunción and are now utilized in a handful of large towns in the Interior.

Mail service to the U.S. and Europe usually takes one week, although unexplained delays may occur. A five-gram letter to the U.S. costs about 35¢ through the Central Post Office, usually slightly more when mailed at the hotel or from the Interior. Urgent correspondence may be sent by courier service, provided by DHL Internacional, Haedo 105, office 117; and Interdoc Paraguay, corner of Estrella and J. E. O'Leary 409.

NEWSPAPERS. The English language *Buenos Aires Herald* is available daily at the newsstands on the Main Plaza in Asunción. Occasionally one can find a copy of *The New York Times,* but don't count on it. There are several Paraguayan Spanish-language dailies: *Hoy, ABC Color, Patria,* and *Diario* in the morning, and *Ultima Hora* in the afternoon. The Paraguayan Ecumenical Conference publishes a good newspaper every two weeks, *El Sendero.*

ELECTRIC CURRENT. Paraguay runs on 220 volts, 50 cycle current. Transformers are available, as are converter plugs (standard outlets receive only the continental European plug). The better hotels have both.

USEFUL ADDRESSES. U.S. Embassy and Consulate, 1776 Avenida Mariscal Lopez (corner of Kubitschek), phone 213–715, open 8 A.M.–5 P.M. (Consulate open 8–11:30 A.M.). **British Embassy,** Edificio Seguros Patria, fourth floor, corner of Presidente Franco and Juan O'Leary, 496–067/8, open 8 A.M.–5 P.M. **National Tourist Office,** Palma 468, 491–230, open Mon.–Sat. 7 A.M.–noon and Mon.–Fri. 4:30–6:30 P.M. **Brazilian Consulate** (for visas) is located on the seventh floor of the Banco do Brasil in the Main Plaza, corner Nuestra Señora de Asunción, 444–088, open Mon.–Fri. 8 A.M.–noon. The Argentine Consulate, España y Perú, 213–320/5, open Mon.–Fri. 7–11 A.M.

HEALTH AND SAFETY. In general there are few health risks to the tourist visiting Paraguay. Although parasitic infections, hepatitis, Chagas Disease, tetanus, and tuberculosis are common in the countryside, the casual visitor is unlikely to come in contact with them. The U.S. Department of Public Health has no formal vaccination recommendations. However, the extra-cautious tourist may want to be inoculated against typhoid, tetanus, and gamma globulin, which will increase resistence to hepatitis. Malaria has been completely eradicated but there are occasional cases brought in by Brazilians. Tap water and salads are safe in Asunción but bottled water (usually carbonated) is readily available. In the interior it is probably safer to drink only bottled water.

There is very little petty crime in Paraguay and it is perhaps one of the safest countries to visit in Latin America. Nevertheless, in the last few years, as the nation's economy has declined, there have been occasional reports of pickpocketing in Asunción. The border town of Ciudad del Este, on the other hand, has been the victim of more crime, and car theft could perhaps be considered epidemic in that city.

GETTING AROUND PARAGUAY. By air. *L.A.T.N.* and *TAM* connect Asunción to Concepción, Pedro Juan Caballero, and San Pedro every day except Sunday. Flights to Puerto Casado and Vallemi run Monday through Friday and TAM flies to Olimpo and Bahía Negro Tuesdays and Thursdays. All flights run about $50, with some as low as $25; TAM is consistently a few dollars cheaper than L.A.T.N. L.A.T.N. also provides an Air Taxi service: $167 an hour in a single engine plane carrying up to five passengers, or $267 in a two engine plane. The pilot will wait for one hour for free while you sightsee; successive hours cost $8.50.

By train. The wood-burning steam engines leaving every Tuesday and Friday pull passenger trains the 370 kilometers from Asunción to Encarnación for $3. The ride is very slow (averaging about 12 hours for the entire journey and on occasion as long as 18 hours due to frequent minor derailings), and a bit uncomfortable, but provides a wonderful opportunity to see beyond the facade of modernization presented along the main highways. There is a dining car with a complete menu but no sleeping facilities beyond the benches themselves. For the less hardy traveler a shorter ride, perhaps to the Botanical Gardens or Aregua, would be most enjoyable—a train going as far as Ypacaraí runs daily except Sundays and holidays at 12:15P.M.

By bus. Since this mode of transportation is the most utilized among Paraguayans, an extensive network of buses covers all of the country. While many bus lines are infamous for their interminable stops and their elaborate efforts to round up passengers, convenient *directo* buses connect the more major cities such as Ciudad del Este, Villarrica, and Encarnación with Asunción. Fares are quite inexpensive (under $8).

By car. Cars can be hired in Asunción by the day or week. The most economical, a VW Beetle, costs about $195 a week and includes 100 kilometers per day free mileage. Fuel prices are the most expensive in South America. An International Driver's License is required. You can rent cars from: National Câr Rental, Yegros and Cerro Corá (491–379); Hertz-Diesa SA, Avda. Eusebio Ayala km 4,5 (605–708); and Rent A Car, Palma 503 (492–731).

By boat. Riverboat services link Asunción with points farther north on the Paraguay River. Every Tuesday the boat goes to Concepción and Bahia Negra, 48 riverhours north of Concepción. You can make the voyage on deck or in an air-conditioned cabin, depending on your taste. Even the Executive Suite is eminently affordable.

NATIONAL PARKS. Paraguay has established six national parks to preserve the country's rich flora and fauna, some of which have come close to extinction. Three of the parks are in the Oriental region, and the remaining three are in the Chaco. Unfortunately, only two parks are equipped with administrative staff, nature trails, and camping areas making them accesible to the general public.

Ybycuí ("Sand"), the best organized and equipped National Park, is located southeast of the capital 15 kilometers beyond the town of the same name and 151 kilometers from Asunción. In addition to the reconstructed 1850s Iron Foundry, the 5,000-hectare park boasts many cascading waterfalls emptying into natural pools that are excellent for bathing, and lush subtropical forest with nature trails exhibiting a wide variety of trees, orchids, ferns, and philodendrons. If the visitor is quiet and lucky he may be able to see and hear the monkeys. The best way to take advantage of this beautiful park is to make a day trip, perhaps on a slow Asunción Sunday.

Far in the northeast corner of Paraguay and 35 kilometers west of Pedro Juan Caballero is the **Cerro Corá National Park** commemorating the site of the last battleground of the War of the Triple Alliance (where Mariscal Lopez was killed). The park contains several ecosystems—both high and low canopy forest, savannahs, swamps, several small streams, and a river. Innumerable statues as well as a towering monument pay homage to the courage of Paraguayan soldiers who fell with Solano Lopez in the Battle of Cerro Corá. The park supervisor and his staff are very accommodating to visitors. Cerro Corá National Park can be reached most easily by flying from Asunción to Pedro Juan Caballero (about $25), then by bus or taxi to the park.

SPORTS. As might be expected, **soccer** is the national sport of Paraguay and there are leagues at the professional and inter-city levels along with countless neighborhood soccer teams which play more informally, although competition is no less earnest. Play is top-notch and aggressive; the agile Paraguayans have literally been playing soccer all their lives. Some top Paraguayan players have been contracted to play for professional soccer teams in the U.S.

In the Paraguayan countryside **volleyball** is second only to soccer, and is usually played between two- or five-man teams for small amounts of money; the action can become very intense.

Horse racing, or perhaps more accurately, betting on horses, is another favorite pastime and practically every town, regardless of size, boasts a primitive, short, straight horse track. On a more organized level, the Asunción Jockey Club sports a 2,000 meter oval track; races are held every weekend at noon. **Cockfights** are also enjoyed in the interior.

Tennis tournaments, at private sports clubs, are held several times a year. **Hunting and fishing** are the biggest participant sports. **Golf** is available in Asunción at both the 18-hole Asunción Golf Club and the 9-hole Yacht & Golf Club. In Ciudad del Este, golf is available at the 18-hole Paraná Country Club.

See also "Adventure Vacations" chapter.

Exploring Paraguay

ASUNCIÓN

Fallen from its position as one-time colonial capital of southern South America, Asunción is now simply the capital of a small country. Yet despite its humbled status, here one finds extraordinary monetary wealth, exhibiting itself in the whimsical building of lavish replicas of Versailles, the U.S. White House, and *Gone With the Wind*'s Tara. Poverty and malnutrition seem to coexist peacefully with highly sophisticated medical equipment and fancy French restaurants. Classical post-Independence buildings stand next to virtually unoccupied glass and steel skyscrapers and sleek Mercedes maneuver impatiently around vintage yellow trolley cars.

Unfortunately, few traces of the first centuries of the city's life still remain today. Complaining that Asunción had been founded by "barbaric Spaniards," Paraguay's first president, Dr. Francia, undertook a campaign to create a "real city" out of what he perceived to be 300 years of growth without order or culture. Under his jurisdiction many public buildings, among them the original cathedral, were demolished, and the city's layout was considerably modified as the streets themselves both appeared and disappeared. Carlos Antonio Lopez took up the call; the years of his presidency were characterized by a proliferation of both private and public construction projects, including such fine public buildings as the Government Palace, the Legislative Palace, and the Lopez Theater (today housing the Internal Tax Division). Continuing his father's work, Francisco Solano Lopez initiated construction on the Pantheon of Heroes. However, the intervening years of the War of the Triple Alliance followed by eight long years of Brazilian and Argentinian occupation brought not only a halt to further construction efforts but also an unrestrained pillaging of existing structures. The city's development was successfully resumed after the restoration of Paraguayan sovereignty; the Municipal Theater, the Police Department, and the Military College all date to the 1880s. Claiming only a little over 40,000 inhabitants at the turn of the century, Asunción already began straining the limits of its boundaries. The substantial expansion which ensued involved the opening of several new barrios as well as the subsequent development of a system of public transportation to service these new "outlying areas." The city's first electric trams started down the tracks in 1913. By the 1950s Asunción's population had grown to over 200,000 and the following three decades have witnessed a tripling of the population to today's 650,000 people, which includes many of European and Asian descent as well as Brazilians and Argentines. As both the political and economic capital of Paraguay, in truth all roads do lead to Asunción.

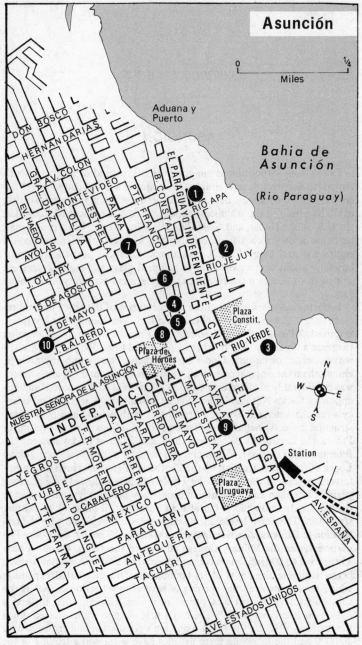

Asunción

0 .... 1/4
Miles

Aduana y
Puerto

*Bahia de
Asunción*

(Rio Paraguay)

Plaza
Constit.

Plaza de
Héroes

Plaza
Uruguaya

Station

Points of Interest

1) Government Palace
2) Estatua del Mcal. López
3) Catedral
4) Biblioteca Municipal
5) Teatro Municipal
6) Casa de la Independencia
7) Calle Palma
8) Panteón de los Héroes
9) Museum of Fine Arts and
   National Archives
10) Iglesia de la Encarnación

Walking Tour

The best place to start a tour of downtown Asunción is the Zodiac Restaurant (Calle 14 de Mayo near El Paraguayo Independiente). This 13th-floor overlook affords a splendid view of the city—the bay and port district, the many lush plazas, the erratic skyline—as well as the seemingly desolate stretches beyond the city limits. Many of the city's skyscrapers were built during the 1970 boom years.

Leaving the Zodiac and turning right on Calle 14 de Mayo brings you to the Casa de la Independencia, where in 1811 Paraguayan nationalists plotted independence from the Spanish Crown. Built in 1772, it stands today as one of the city's few well-preserved examples of colonial architecture and now houses a museum furnished with articles of the period. One block away is the popular Calle Palma, which is lined with many fine shops frequented by Asunción's elite. The numerous exchange houses nearby are the best places to change money since they offer a slightly better rate than the cambio men on the street. From here, head toward Av. Colón, where the best deals on Paraguayan handicrafts can be found—if you don't feel like walking, jump on one of the old yellow trolley cars. Turning right on Colon brings you once again to Calle El Paraguayo Independiente. Across the street to the left is the Customs House and, walking through it, the port.

Continuing up El Paraguayo Independiente, you will find the architectural pride of Asunción, the classic Government Palace overlooking the bay. Originally conceived by President Carlos Antonio Lopez as a personal residence for his son Francisco Solano, construction of the Palace remained unfinished until after the War of the Triple Alliance. Since its completion in 1890 the Palace has served as the executive office building. A little farther past the Palace (the Zodiac again towering to your right) lies Constitution Plaza, flanked by the former Military College, the Legislative Palace, and the National Cathedral. Practically overtaking the Legislative Palace from behind is the shanty-town La Chacarita. Once a menacing settlement of swamp-side squatters, La Chacarita is now a legitimate community, provided with running water, electricity, a high school, and a soccer stadium. Beside the cathedral is an interesting Museum of Paraguayan History, while close to the plaza, on the corner of Alberdi and El Paraguayo Independiente, is the ornate Main Post Office, which was recently restored. Walk up Calle Chile beside the Central Police Station and past the Municipal Theater and Library on your right (on Pte. Franco) to Calle Palma, where you will find the Ministry of Public Finance and an extensive window display of artifacts and photographs from the Chaco War. At this juncture your attention will undoubtedly be attracted by the Plaza de Héroes, dominated by the pink-domed Pantheon. Perpetually guarded by two soldiers in complete dress uniform, the Pantheon houses the remains of several Paraguayan heroes: President Carlos Antonio Lopez; his son and the principal hero of the War of the Triple Alliance, Francisco Solano Lopez; commander of the Paraguayan forces in the Chaco War, José Felix Estigarribia; and two unknown soldiers killed in battle during the Chaco War. Modeled after the Invalides in Paris, construction of the Pantheon was begun during the War of the Triple Alliance but was not completed until 1937.

The Plaza de Héroes and the adjacent Plaza de Independencia form the heart of modern-day Asunción. These brilliantly flowered plazas with their benches beneath exotic trees provide the perfect resting place for the weary traveler. Here, too, you may climb into a high wooden chair to have your shoes shined or resoled and have your picture taken by photographers using dated box-camaras. Macá Indians meander through the plazas selling brightly colored braided belts and headbands, as well as bows and arrows for children. On Saturday mornings there is often a band, and artisans gather to sell their wares.

Passing by the Museum of Fine Arts and the National Archives as you follow Mariscal Estigarribia (the continuation of Palma) you will arrive in the Plaza Uruguaya. This lively plaza is a favorite spot among locals to bring or prepare lunch or for drinking *tereré* (the refreshing cold maté drunk through a metal straw called a *bombilla*) and is visited almost daily by Argentine or Paraguayan charlatans selling elixirs and miracle cures. The porticoed train station facing onto the plaza was built in 1861 during the presidency of Carlos Antonio Lopez. Some of the wood-burning old steam engines are still functioning, today pulling modern passenger cars. A short ride on the train, 15 minutes to the Botanical Gardens or an hour to the lovely town of Aregua ("from the past" in Guaraní) on the shores of Lake Ypacaraí, or a longer trip for the more adventurous traveler, are all well worth it.

Also worth a visit is the beautiful Gran Hotel del Paraguay, the former residence of the Irishwoman Eliza Lynch, mistress of Solano Lopez. Located on Calle de la Residenta, a thirty-minute walk from the Plaza de Héroes, the well-kept grounds abound with tropical vegetation and the hotel itself features many nineteenth century paintings; the dining room features a decorative hand-painted ceiling.

A bus or taxi ride down Avenida Mariscal Lopez is a must. This beautiful shaded avenue is lined with many fine homes as well as foreign embassies and government buildings. At the corner of Avenida Kubitschek is the U.S. Embassy on the right; on the left, a replica of *Gone With the Wind*'s Tara. About a kilometer farther on the right is the Recoleta Cemetery, where the rich of Asunción are laid to rest, often in quite original and elaborate mausoleums.

Perhaps the best tourist attraction is not a tourist attraction at all but the city's principal produce market. Strictly speaking, Mercado 4 on Av. Pettirossi is much more than a produce market; the anticipated selection of fruits, vegetables, and live chickens is almost lost in a sea of innards, sides of beef, canned goods, shoes, wicker baskets, traditional herbs, and rarer items. Possibly the most bustling spot in Asunción, the market overflows onto several blocks, frequently bringing traffic to a standstill. Morning hours are especially active, with daily movement beginning hours before dawn; however, a colorful visit is guaranteed even for the late-sleeper.

About seven kilometers from the center of town is the suburb of Cacique Lambaré, where the resort hotel and casino Itá Enramada is located. Above the resort complex towers Cerro Lambaré, a rather unique monument atop the hill paying tribute to Paraguay's greatest statesmen: Carlos Antonio Lopez, Francisco Solano Lopez, and Bernardino Caballero. Dr. Francia is conspicuous by his absence. The hill also provides a sweeping view of the river slightly south of Asunción.

PRACTICAL INFORMATION FOR ASUNCIÓN

GETTING AROUND ASUNCIÓN. From the airport. A taxi ride costing about $13 is the most convenient way to make the 15 kilometer trip from the Silvio Pettirossi International Airport to downtown Asunción, but city buses also run quite frequently ($.25) and are fine if you don't have a lot of baggage.

The downtown area is small enough that walking is usually the easiest way around. However, for trips out of the center or if you are in a hurry, the following forms of transportation are available.

By bus. Colorful city buses, many with hardwood floors and framing, ply extensive routes throughout the city. A short ride might be fun but avoid the rush hours when the buses will be uncomfortably packed with passengers. Fare: $.25.

By tram. Yellow trolley cars operate during business hours and offer a pleasant ride through the center of town and then out into the suburb of Las Mercedes. Fare: $.15.

By taxi. Cabs wait at the 24-hour taxi stands scattered throughout the city and are very inexpensive (under a dollar for a typical trip). Drivers expect a 10 percent tip.

HOTELS. There are plenty of hotels in Asunción to cater to the desires of every visitor. Most hotels are located in the downtown area, with a few exceptions. Reservations are generally not needed except during the peak months of June to August, when you should book as far in advance as possible if planning to stay in a Super Deluxe, Deluxe, or Expensive hotel. Breakfast is usually included, except at the Hotel Excelsior (as noted). Definitions of price categories are given in the "Facts at Your Fingertips" section earlier in this chapter.

Super Deluxe

Excelsior, Calle Chile 980 (a few blocks from Main Plaza) (495–632). 175 rooms, 14 stories. The most expensive hotel in Paraguay, its excellent facilities include a swimming pool and sauna, 24-hour room service, king-size beds, the Excelsior Bar and La Cascada Restaurant, the Golden Room for large receptions, a mini shopping center, a hairdresser, laundry and dry cleaning service, and car rental. The clientele is mainly European or American. Breakfast is not included in the price. English is spoken.

Hotel del Yacht y Golf Club Paraguayo, 8 miles southeast of Asunción (near Itá Enramada) (36–117/135) New, modern accommodations in a country club setting on the shores of the Paraguay River. All comforts; many sports including golf on a 9-hole course.

Deluxe

Cecilia, Estados Unidos 341 corner Mariscal Estigarribia (210–365/7). 38 Luxurious rooms equipped with color television and Frigibar. Sixth floor swimming pool and gymnasium, excellent restaurant. Clientele mostly European. English is spoken.

Chaco, Caballero corner Mariscal Estigarribia (492–066). 72 lavishly furnished rooms (color television, Frigibar, etc.), many with balconies. Conference rooms, small roof-top swimming pool, excellent restaurant. Fully air-conditioned. Clientele primarily European and Japanese businessmen. English is spoken.

Hotel Guaraní, Oliva and Ind. Nacional (491–131), facing on main plaza. Recently renovated, with 172 rooms, convention facilities, swimming pool, restaurant, several small shops, a theater, and a casino. International clientele. English is spoken.

Husa, Calle 15 de Agosto 420 corner Estrella (493–760). 64 air-conditioned rooms with color television. Close to Main Plaza. Facilities include a rooftop swimming pool, excellent restaurant and bar, and a large reception room. Clientele mostly Japanese and European. English is spoken.

Ita Enramada, Box 1878 (33–041). On the shores of the Paraguay River about seven kilometers from downtown Asunción, this hotel/casino complex sports a large swimming pool, tennis courts, and sauna in addition to the casino and 150 luxuriously furnished rooms. There are several conference rooms and two excellent restaurants. Free bus service to town. European clientele. English is spoken.

Expensive

Armele, corner Ave. Palma and Colón (444–455). 225 air-conditioned rooms, many with balconies and good view of the Bay and Chaco. Located near the port on Ave. Colón, a major shopping area. The Cristal Salon Restaurant located on the 11th floor affords a splendid view. Clientele mostly Brazilian and Argentine.

Gran Hotel del Paraguay, De la Residenta 902 (200–052). Twenty blocks from Main Plaza. Formerly the elegant residence of Madam Lynch, Irish mistress of Solano Lopez. The grounds are fantastic. 76 fully equipped rooms (air-conditioner, Frigibar), a few rather cramped. Large swimming pool, tennis courts, conference rooms, comfortable sitting room with mammoth fireplace. Clientele mostly German. English is spoken.

Hotel Internacional de Asunción, Ayolas and Gral. Diaz (496–587). New city hotel. Comfortable, modern, and conveniently located.

Paraná, 25 de Mayo corner Caballero (444–236). 102 air-conditioned rooms with color television and Frigibar. Located between the Main Plaza and the Plaza Uruguaya. Restaurant and convention facilities (250 persons). Clientele mainly Brazilian and Argentine. Under new management.

Premier, 25 de Mayo corner Curupayty (23–881). Seven stories perched on a hill about 10 blocks from Main Plaza. 42 rooms with air-conditioning and Frigibar. Small swimming pool, restaurant. Mostly Brazilian and Argentine.

Moderate

Asunción Palace, Ave. Colón 415 corner Estrella (492–151). Formerly the spacious residence of Venancio Lopez (brother of Francisco Solano Lopez). 45 plainly furnished rooms, some with balconies overlooking Ave. Colón. All rooms air-conditioned and with telephone (no television). Clientele is Argentine and Brazilian.

Hotel de la Paz, Ave. Colón 350 (490–786). 35 rooms with air-conditioning and Frigibar (no television). Staff unaccommodating. Clientele is Argentine and Brazilian.

Renacimiento, Calle Chile 388 corner Estrella (445–165). 48 rooms with air-conditioning and Frigibar. Color television extra. Pool, sauna, snack bar, restaurant. Looks onto Main Plaza and the Pantheon of Heroes. Clientele is Argentine and European. Some English spoken.

Señorial del Paraguay, Ave. Mariscal Lopez 475 (24–304). 15 blocks from the Main Plaza and faces onto the elegant Av. Mariscal Lopez. 50 air-conditioned rooms. Swimming pool, restaurant. Clientele mainly European.

Inexpensive

Azara, Av. Azara 860 (449–754). 15 air-conditioned rooms with private bath. Breakfast included, small swimming pool. Central location. Clientele is European and Argentine.

La Española, Calle Luis A. de Herrera 142 (449–280). A few blocks from Main Plaza. 35 plain rooms with air-conditioning, private bath. Clientele is Argentine, Brazilian, and Asian.

El Lapacho, Av. Brasilia 158 (200–721). One block from U.S. Embassy. Air-conditioned rooms and private bathrooms. Small swimming pool, relaxing atmosphere. Clientele is U.S. Peace Corps volunteers and Europeans.

Stella D'Italia, Cerro Corá 933 (448–731). 8 clean, plainly furnished rooms with private bathroom and air-conditioning. Centrally located. Clientele Argentine and Brazilian; U.S. Peace Corps often occupy cheaper rooms with common bathrooms.

Budget Accommodations. Ypoa, Azara 1161 (23–276). About eight blocks from Main Plaza. $7 double occupancy. All rooms have a fan; some, a private bathroom. 20 rooms. Clientele is Asian and U.S. Peace Corps volunteers. Breakfast extra.

Camping. Westfalia Camping on the way to Lambaré (about eight kilometers from downtown) has camping facilities including toilets and showers for about $3 per tent. About 45 kilometers from Asunción, going east on Ruta II near Lake Ypacaraí, is Casa Grande Camping. Basic facilities. Camping is also permitted in the Botanical Gardens.

RESTAURANTS. Asunción sports a large variety of cuisines to suit your palate. Restaurants are generally open from 11:30 A.M.–3 P.M. for lunch and from 7 P.M.–midnight for dinner. Reservations are rarely necessary unless you need tables for a large group. Dress is always informal. For definitions of categories see "Facts at Your Fingertips" earlier in this chapter.

International Fare

La Cascada. *Expensive.* Calle Chile 980 in the Excelsior Hotel (495–632). Wide range of meats, fish, and chicken. Nicely decorated, 32 tables. Open every day.

Jaguar. *Moderate.* Caballero corner Mariscal Estigarribia in the Chaco Hotel (492–066). Extensive menu (English and Spanish), excellent service, delicious food. Put together your own appetizer choosing from the assortment on the hors d'oeuvres cart. 20 tables. Open every day.

La Preferida. *Moderate.* 25 de Mayo corner Estados Unidos in the Hotel Cecilia (210–641). Large menu and superb food. Equipped to serve 40 tables; can also handle large groups (make reservations). Open every day.

Restaurant del Gran Hotel del Paraguay. *Moderate.* De la Residenta 902 (200–051). Worth a trip even if you aren't staying here. You may dine outside and there is live music and dancing occasionally. Wednesday is Hindu Night, with curry that is not spicy but good. Spacious. Short Hours: 12–2 P.M. for lunch, 8–10 P.M. for dinner. Open every day.

Tayi Poty. *Moderate.* 8 km. from Asunción in the casino of the Hotel Itá Enramada (33–041/49). Excellent International cuisine with live music, dancing, and folk arts nightly (except Sundays).

El Molino. *Inexpensive.* Ave. España, 382 (25–351). Near Caballero Park. Although billed as a bakery (which is excellent), dinners here are superb. Wide variety of fish, meats, chicken, and pasta—probably Asunción's best culinary value. Diners sit on the second floor balcony overlooking the bakery. Open every day.

Restaurant Zodiac. *Inexpensive.* 14 de Mayo 150, 13th floor (no phone). Eat on the terrace, with a great view of the city. Open daily 10 A.M.-midnight.

Traditional

San Roque. *Inexpensive.* Eligio Ayala corner Tacuary (446–015). One block from the Plaza Uruguaya. Ceiling fans, waiters in black tie and white jacket. This popular, very inexpensive restaurant is a relic from another time. Features meats, fish soup, and chicken. There is also an air-conditioned room in the back. Opens at 7 A.M. every day except Sunday, when it opens at 10 A.M. Credit cards not accepted.

Spanish

Taberna Española El Antojo. *Expensive.* Ayolas 631 (441–743). Paella is the specialty but seafood is also prepared quite tastily. Open every day.

La Taberna Taurina. *Moderate.* Pdte. Franco 583 (492–090). Great atmosphere and excellent food. Order several small plates or a large meal. American Express cards (only) accepted.

Italian

Buon Apetita. *Inexpensive.* 25 de Mayo corner Constitución (950–523). Eat inside or outside on the patio. Tastefully decorated, excellent food. Credit cards not accepted.

Otelo. *Inexpensive.* Villa Morra Shopping Center (605–832). Excellent Italian dishes and pizzas. Very attentive service. Also, the bar is quite nice.

Pizza

Mastropiero. *Inexpensive.* Ave. Gral. Genes 1372 (600–160). 110 varieties of pizza. Excellent.

La Rosca. *Inexpensive.* Pdte. Franco 547. Excellent pizza and other Italian dishes.

Chinese

Celestial. *Inexpensive.* Louis A. de Herrera 919 (203–631). Good food, nice atmosphere. Service may be slow. No credit cards accepted.

Taipei. *Inexpensive.* Brasil 976 (23–858). Good food. No credit cards accepted.

Parrillada (grills)

Ave. Brasilia, near its intersection with Ave. España, may almost be called Parrillada Row. Here you will find **La Maracana, Tayi Poty, La Paraguaya, La Paraguayita** (the most popular), and **E. Cencerro.** Every night around 10 o'clock the street is lined with cars. All of these restaurants are inexpensive. No reservations are necessary and most accept credit cards.

German

Bayern Stuben. *Moderate.* Sucre 2689, near Denis Roa (64–202). Excellent German food served at long, pub-style tables in this lovely German home setting.
Restaurant Munich. *Moderate.* Eligio Ayala 163 (447–604). Sit on the back patio under the beautiful pink blossoms of Santa Rita.

French

Talleyrand. *Expensive.* Mariscal Estigarribia 932 (441–163). Intimate. Nicely decorated, excellent food.

Restaurant/Shows

Jardin de la Cerveza. *Moderate.* Ave. Argentina corner Castillo (600–752). Good show.
Yguazu. *Moderate.* Choferes del Chaco 1334 (601–008). Good show.

Cafeterias. For a quick, inexpensive meal try one of the several cafeterias near the Main Plaza. Both the **Lido Bar** and the **Bar Victoria** (located on Calle Chile but on opposite corners of the Plaza) serve a cheap, filling lunch or dinner once you find a seat. A bit fancier are the **Pergola del Bolsi** (corner of Estrella and Alberdi) and **Bar Asunción** (Estrella and 14 de Mayo). Both these cafeterias also have full-service dining rooms where they charge a bit more. **Anahi** (Pdte. Franco and Ayolas) serves good food, but is most popular for its ice cream. For baked goods and pastries, try **Wagner German Bakery** (Pdte. Franco 820) or **The French Bakery** (Villa Mora Shopping). **Di Trevi** (Palma 573), a new Italian coffee shop downtown, is worth trying.

There are many *copetines* (neighborhood eating spots) throughout the city serving good, basic fare for $1. No frills but not dangerous!

Bars. Da Vinci, Estrella corner J.E. O'Leary, **San Marcos,** Oliva corner Alberdi, and **Restaurant Zodiac** (13th floor), 14 de Mayo 150, are all nice bars to relax and talk with friends at any hour of the day. At night, also try the **Liverpool Pub** (run by a Chilean), Pdte. Franco 564—two pool tables and a video screen.
Chopperia Maes. Caballero corner Comuneros (492–342). Set in the old Hotel Terraza near the train station and overlooking the Chacarita and the bay. Sit on the terrace and enjoy Belgian beer and snacks. Opens at 6 P.M. nightly.

TOURIST INFORMATION. The **National Tourist Office** at Palma 468 offers brochures and other tourist information in both Spanish and English. Open Mon.–Sat. 7 A.M.-noon, Mon.–Fri. 4:30–6:30 P.M. Phone 491–230. In addition, **information booths** in the airport and the bus terminal are staffed during the day, and the reception desks at the better hotels can provide a lot of useful information and set up tours.

TOURS. Several companies operate guided tours of the city. *Chaco Tour,* Montevideo 1447 (84–453); English-speaking guide is extra. *Inter-Tours,* Mariscal Estigarribia 1097 (211–747), price includes English-speaking guide. *Lions Tour,* Alberdi 454 (490–278); English-speaking guide is extra. Prices are based on a two-person minimum.
City Tour including plazas, parks, monuments, old and new buildings (approx.

two and one-half hours, twice daily). Chaco Tour—$20 per person; Inter-Express—$33 per car (up to three in a car); Lions Tour—$20 per person.

Tour to the Botanical Gardens and Visit with Maká Indians (approximately two and one-half hours, twice daily). Chaco Tour—$15 per person; Inter-Express—$30 per car.

Asunción at Night Tour consisting of transportation to a restaurant/show and dinner (three hours). Chaco Tour—$25 per person; Inter Express—$25 per person; Lions Tour—$25 per person.

MUSEUMS AND SIGHTS. There are about a dozen small museums in Asunción; admission is usually free (hours are not always adhered to). The following are probably the best.

Bogarin Museum, beside the cathedral (a low, white colonial building), Ave. Independencia Nacional and Cnel. Bogado (no phone). Open 8–11 A.M. Mon.-Sat. Founded by Asunción's first Archbishop, Juan Sinforiano Bogarin, the museum displays indigenous art from Franciscan Reductions as well as relics from the War of the Triple Alliance and the Chaco War.

La Casa de Independencia, 14 de Mayo and Pdte. Franco (93918). Open Mon.-Sat. 7:30–11:30 A.M. The house where Paraguayan revolutionaries declared independence on May 14, 1811, now restored and decorated with furniture of the period.

The Natural History Museum, in the Botanical Gardens (290172). Open Mon.-Fri. 7:30–11:30 A.M. and 1:30–5 P.M. Extensive collection of Paraguayan animal life.

The Fine Arts Museum, Mariscal Estigarribia and Iturbe (447–716). Open Mon.-Fri. 7–11 A.M. and 3–5 P.M. Four rooms displaying paintings; one of the rooms is devoted to caricatures done by Paraguayan artist Miguel Acevedo just before World War I. The museum's Centro de Artes Visuales, Aviadepres del Chaco and Mcal. Lopez, has an exhibition of Paraguayan handicrafts. Open 9 A.M.–noon and 4–8 P.M. Mon.-Sat.

Ethnological Museum, Ave. España corner Mompox (no phone). Open Mon.-Fri. 7–11 A.M. Artifacts from the Indian tribes that populated Paraguay before the arrival of the Spanish.

Museum of General Bernardino Caballero, Caballero Park (no phone). Open Mon.-Fri. 7–11 A.M. Personal objects of ex-President Caballero.

Contrary to rumor the Government Palace is not open to visitors. You may, however, enter the **Legislative Palace** (on Constitution Plaza) and see the Chambers where the 72 Deputies and the 36 Senators meet.

Don't miss the grand **Lopez Theater,** occupying a full block on Calle Yegros between Eligio Ayala and Cnel. Bogado. Today it serves (somewhat absurdly) as the Internal Tax Division but the generously pillared alcove with its chandeliers, two winding staircases, and ample balconies in the main room make it quite easy to imagine what the theater must have been like in its heyday.

The **Train Station,** built in 1861, on Plaza Uruguaya was the first in South America and remains unchanged.

PARKS AND GARDENS. The Botanical Gardens, located in the suburb of Trinidad, were once the expansive grounds of the personal estate of Francisco Solano Lopez. The park now contains a small and somewhat depressing zoo that houses many animals perhaps unfamiliar to the foreigner, as well as the Museum of Natural History, and an 18-hole golf course.

Other parks in the city itself that may be worth a visit are **Parque Carlos Antonio Lopez,** set on a hill overlooking the city and the river, and **Parque Bernardino Caballero,** at the foot of Calle Estados Unidos (about seven blocks from the Plaza Uruguaya). The latter park sports a Municipal swimming pool as well as a small waterfall; it is a favorite place for cyclists and joggers.

SPORTS. The ten Division I **soccer teams** in Asunción compete Sundays year-round and the best game is always played in the Defensores del Chaco Stadium located in the suburb of Sajonia. Seats are inexpensive; avoid the cheapest "popular" section in favor of the "galeria" ($4) or the best seats in the house, "preferencia" ($8).

Horses are run every weekend at the Hipodromo Jockey Club, Avda Eusebio Ayala, km. 4.

There are usually **tennis tournaments** in progress at any one of the several Asunción Tennis Clubs.

Golf can be enjoyed at the Asunción Golf Club, 18 holes (Jardin Botánico, tel. 290–251). Also at the Yacht y Golf Club del Paraguay, 9 holes (near Itá Enramada, tel. 36–117/29).

MUSIC, DANCE, AND STAGE. The **music of Paraguay,** characterized by the delicate yet versatile "Paraguayan Harp," is appreciated throughout the world. Frequently considered to be the quintessence of Paraguayan culture, the harp was actually introduced into Paraguay in the late seventeenth century by Jesuit priest Anton Sepp, who wrote of the Guaraní Indians' seemingly instinctive mastery of even extremely complex baroque compositions. Today, Paraguayan music, accompanied by harp and guitar, is quite different from the baroque music of that period. The *"Mandu'ará" (Souvenir) Series* featuring modern Paraguayan folk music runs once a week for two months in the winter, and then again in the summer.

For aficionados of more **classical music,** the *Asunción Symphonic Orchestra* (OSCA) holds concerts from March through November in the Asunción Municipal Theater. Call 448–820 for more information.

There are five **theater companies** that perform plays and musicals (usually in Spanish) from March through November. The three major theaters in Asunción are: *Teatro Municipal Dr. Ignacio A. Pane,* corner Pdte. Franco and Alberdi (448–820 for the secretary, 445–169 for tickets); *Teatro Arlequin,* next to the Villa Morra Shopping Center, (605–107); and *Teatro de las Americas,* in the Paraguayan/American Cultural Center, Ave. España 352 (24–772). The several Cultural Centers in Asunción often offer concerts or plays; watch the newspapers.

ART GALLERIES. Several Asunción galleries display paintings, wood carvings, and pottery by Paraguayan artists.

Artesania Indigena, Calle Coronel Bogado, near the cathedral in San Lorenzo. Open Mon.–Fri., 8 A.M.–noon and 3–6 P.M. Wide selection of indigenous tribal art, much of it from the Chaco. Informative staff. Recommended.

Artesano Raity, Calle Pai Perez 778 (25–285). Open Mon–Sat. 8 A.M.–noon, Mon.–Fri. 3–6 P.M. Wide selection of Paraguayan art, also sports a small Art History Museum. Recommended.

Casa de Artesano Artesania Kuarayhy, Calle Juan O'Leary near Pdte. Franco (448–522). Open Mon.–Fri. 8 A.M.–noon, 3–6 P.M. Musical instruments, pottery, tapestries, etc.

Galeria Artesanos, Calle Cerro Corá corner 22 de Setiembre (27–853). Open Mon.–Fri. 8 A.M.–noon and 4–8 P.M. Paintings by Paraguayan and other Latin American artists.

SHOPPING. Once in Paraguay you may find it impossible to resist a buying spree. Prices for both national and imported manufactured goods are among the lowest in South America. Excellent buys in particular can be found on cameras and other electronic goods. Asunción is the clearinghouse for items made throughout the country—an attractive assortment of traditional handicrafts is available at remarkably low prices. In general, there is little room for bargaining.

The most well-known of Paraguayan handicrafts is *ñandutí* (spider's web), an intricate lace-work unique to this country. Traditionally made with hand-spun white silk or cotton thread, manufactured threads of varying colors are now being increasingly used. The finer the thread the more delicate the workmanship; quality will generally be reflected by price. Each design represents a local plant or animal, or very occasionally a traditional legend.

A type of embroidery work known as *Ao Po'i* (which means, literally, "narrow clothing"), adorns both men's and women's clothing along with tablecloths, place mats, and the like. Some stores, such as **Catedral Confecciones,** Eligio Ayala 189, and **Ao Po'i Raity,** Tte. Fariña 631, specialize in the craft; you can choose from their extensive selection on hand, or, equally affordable, order the style and colors to your fancy.

Woodcrafts include carvings, woodburning, and turned items such as *guampas* (for drinking maté), wine goblets, and mortar and pestle sets. Look for the excellent carved statuettes made by Zenon Páez. **Behage,** located on Ayolas 222 between Palma and Pdte. Franco, specializes in woodcrafts.

Leather goods, both tooled and untooled, are of fine quality, rivaling those found in Argentina but more reasonably priced. Other traditional crafts include colorful cotton hammocks and blankets (warning: colors may not be colorfast), women's crocheted tops, and wickerwork—the latter perhaps too cumbersome to take home but tempting anyhow. Harps and guitars are sold principally along Avenida Aviadores del Chaco on the way to Luque. Quality ranges from poor to excellent.

Many tourist shops offer the entire range of the above handicrafts. The best buys can be found in the Permanent Expositions on Avenida Colón between Pdte. Franco and El Paraguayo Independiente and along Avenida Pettirossi near Avenida Perú. The gallery **Artesano Raity,** Calle Paí Perez 778 (25–285), is worth a visit for its small museum. In addition, you can find just about anything in the many shops and street displays located along the Calles Palma and Estrella.

NIGHTLIFE. Asunción is not known for an exuberant nightlife, and the city usually closes by 1 A.M. You can hear good Paraguayan music as well as the music of other Latin American countries at **Nivel 10** Av. Meal. Lopez, San Lorenzo, which has a fairly young clientele (20s and 30s) and is inexpensive. Among the restaurant shows are: **Restaurant Show El Jardin de la Cerveza,** Avda. Argentina y Castillo (600–752); **Don Folklore,** Hernandarias 1142 (441–126); and **Yguazu Restaurant Show,** Choferes del Chaco 1334 (601–008). All are moderately priced.

Among the several discotheques—dress informally but neatly—is **DaVinci,** Estrella corner of O'Leary (23–620). A bit out of the city center are: **Caracol Club,** Gral. Santos corner El Porvenir (32–848); **Capricorinio** Club, Legion Civil Extranjera 585 (621–143); **Blue Moon Pub,** San Jose and José Berges (no phone); and **Musak Mall Discoteca,** Ocampos corner Bertoni (605–813).

CASINOS. The casino at the resort hotel **Itá Enramada** operates every day all year round from 9 P.M.–around 4 A.M. Roulette, blackjack, and slot machines are among the many games of chance played. A bus makes the 15-minute trip from the center of town to the casino (and vice versa) every 30 minutes starting at 9 P.M. Jacket and tie not required. In town, the Casino at the **Hotel Guaraní** (441–306) is open daily from 1:30 P.M to 6 A.M.

THE CENTRAL CIRCUIT

Life for the Paraguayan living in Asunción is understandably different from life for the small farmer living in the countryside. Although large mechanized farms do exist, the vast majority of Paraguayan farmers still plow their fields with oxen and weed with a hoe. Even the very smallest of streams are gathering places for the women of the family to wash clothes, and crude brick kilns and sugar cane presses (used for preparing refreshing *mosto* or sugar cane juice) dot the landscape.

For the traveler with little time to spend in Paraguay, the 250-kilometer Central Circuit day trip provides the perfect opportunity to get a taste for the interior of this predominantly rural country. The Circuit passes first through rolling pastoral landscape interspersed with small towns, some centuries-old. Later, the road climbs into a string of hills, affording striking scenic panoramas over the countryside below. This excursion is best traveled by car—rented in Asunción—but planned bus tours are also available from major tourist agencies.

To start the Circuit, drive down Avenida Mariscal Lopez to the neighboring city of San Lorenzo, where you can check out the gothic cathedral. Once in this busy town follow signs to Encarnación (Ruta I). After leaving San Lorenzo behind, traffic thins and small farms dominate the scenery. Look for signs advertising *Pan de Miel* (molasses bread), sold in many places along the highway.

Thirty kilometers from San Lorenzo is the small town of Itá ("Rock"), known for the numerous pottery workshops located there; you will see displays lining the street. People are very friendly and quite willing to show visitors their workshops.

Continuing on another 10 kilometers you will arrive in Yaguarón (founded in 1539), with its traditional Franciscan church, typical of the churches built in the early eighteenth century. Despite its humble exterior, the church sanctuary is lavishly decorated with excellent wood carvings. The confessionals, among other relics, were taken from the Jesuit Reduction in Santa Rosa after the Jesuits were expelled from the continent. Paraguay's "Supreme Dictator," Dr. Francia, spent his childhood in Yaguarón and his restored home near the church is now a museum.

The first leg of the Circuit ends in Paraguarí (15 kilometers from Yaguarón). Dominated by a large military installation, it was from this base that Alfredo Stroessner launched his coup in 1954 to seize power. Look carefully for a small sign to Chololó and Piribebuy, since the left turn onto the second leg of the circuit is easy to miss. The road to Cholol0 (onomatopoeic Guaraní for the sound of a waterfall) winds quickly into the "Cordillera de los Altos" (which, in truth, is not very high) and there are many fine views of the landscape below.

The Chololó Falls restaurant, overlooking the falls, is a good place for lunch after a refreshing dip in the stream. If you prefer more energetic swimming, you may continue on two kilometers to the turnoff for Pirareta ("Fish Country") Falls, then about 10 kilometers over an unpaved road from the main highway. After lunch, head on through Piribebuy to the junction with Ruta II, the East-West Highway, now being widened to four lanes. Ten kilometers to the left is Caacupé ("Behind the Forest").

The Blue Virgin, sculpted by an Indian in gratitude for having been saved by the Virgin Mary from certain death, is housed in Caacupé. Each year on December 8th thousands of faithful Catholics flock to the town for the Feast of the Immaculate Conception to fulfill promises to the Virgin made during the year. Most pilgrims walk to attend the celebrations, some coming from as many as several hundred kilometers away; buses also enter the city, transporting the less hardy. In the center of town towers the impressive basilica; an ambitious project to commemorate the religious zeal of the country under construction now for 43 years. Pope John Paul II visited this sanctuary in May 1988, and one of the many stained-glass windows in the domed cathedral will bear his likeness to commemorate this visit.

Not part of the Circuit but nearby and worth a visit is the village of Tobatí ("Kaolin," from which the best bricks in Paraguay are made). Along the 15-kilometer cobblestone road leading to Tobatí are many brick ovens (olerías) and some interesting natural rock formations. The church in town is Franciscan; although it cannot compare to the one in Yaguarón, its interior is of distinctively Peruvian influence. By far the main attraction in Tobatí is the workshop and store of master woodcarver Zenon Páez. Following in the footsteps of his father and grandfather, Señor Páez originally specialized in the carving of saints. However, in recent years the talented artisan and his sons have considerably expanded their repertoire to include a host of other intricately carved animals and bird statuettes, oxcarts with up to six oxen, and a chess set illustrating figures from the War of the Triple Alliance. The fine workmanship of these items has made Señor Páez one of the best known artisans of Paraguay; General Stroessner had consistently chosen Páez's works as gifts for visiting dignitaries.

Once back in Caacupé, continue on toward Asunción. As you climb past the National School of Agronomy, majestic eucalyptus trees line your path; the crest of the hill affords a stunning view of Lake Ypacaraí. Coming to the bottom of the hill watch for signs to San Bernardino, eight kilometers from Ruta II. Originally founded by German settlers in 1881, San Bernardino today is a popular resort for the wealthy. Although the lake is now polluted, the town is still quite attractive and, indeed, "San-Ber" has become a euphemism for the good-life in Paraguay. There are several good hotels and restaurants and even a casino.

Back on Ruta II, pass through the town of Ypacaraí ("Water, Sir?") where the railroad tracks cross on their way to Villarrica and Encarnación. The next town of interest is Itaugua, the home of the distinctive art known as *ñandutí*. While the exact origins of this craft remain a mystery, evidence has been found linking it to the Jesuits. In recent decades, ñandutí has played an increasingly important role in the economy of Itaugua, as the surrounding farmland has long been over-spent from centuries of intensive agricultural production. In 1942, the citizens of Itaugua were issued a proposal offering them title to virgin land in the department of Caaguazú. Although attractive, this proposal was nonetheless rejected by the population on the grounds that the town's close proximity to Asunción affords a reliable market for the sale of their centuries-old craft, thereby freeing them from their dependence on agriculture. Along with the delicate lace which has made Itaugua famous, other handicraft items such as leather goods, pottery, and gaily colored cotton blankets and hammocks are also available in the town's many tourist shops; prices are usually quite reasonable. Most store owners are willing to demonstrate how ñandutí is made to interested tourists, so ask for the fascinating show.

After Itaugua there is little else of interest along the more crowded 30-minute stretch ahead, so you may want to turn right at the Military College just before the town of Capiatá, following an alternate route to Asunción. After passing by Paraguay's sole international communications dish, the road continues into the sleepy ceramics town of Aregua ("From the Past"), enjoying a picturesque hilltop setting overlooking the lake. Just a short distance separates Aregua from Luque, an attractive suburb of Asunción, and then a few more kilometers on a four-lane highway completes the Central Circuit as you return to Asunción.

PRACTICAL INFORMATION FOR THE CENTRAL CIRCUIT

HOW TO GET THERE. The best way to see the Central Circuit is by rental car. Tourist Agencies also offer a seven-hour guided tour for about $30. The trip can be made by public buses but problematic bus connections will necessitate a lot of extra time to make the trip. (See "Facts at Your Fingertips" for details.)

HOTELS. For definitions of price categories see "Facts at Your Fingertips" earlier in this chapter. **CHOLOLÓ FALLS. Parador Chololó.** *Inexpensive.* Overlooking the Chololó Falls (0531–242).

SAN BERNARDINO. Hotel Casino San Bernardino. *Deluxe.* Just before San Bernardino, on the lake (0512–391/2/3/4/5/6/7). **Condovac.** *Deluxe.* Modern condominium hotel in town, with the popular Champagne Restaurant (0512–761/5). **Hotel Acuario.** *Moderate.* Just before town (0512–375). **Hotel del Lago.** *Inexpensive.* In town, on the lake, historic (0512–201).

RESTAURANTS. There are many small restaurants in each town with basic fare costing approximately $5–$6. Fancier restaurants include:

CHOLOLÓ FALLS. Parador Chololó. *Inexpensive.* (0521–242). Beef and chicken dishes.

CAACUPÉ. Edelweiss. *Inexpensive.* One kilometer east of Caacupé on the highway. International fare. **Hotel Uruguayo.** *Inexpensive.* Eligio Ayala corner Asunción (222). Excellent and abundant food, all you can eat.

SAN BERNARDINO. Restaurant at the **Hotel Casino.** *Moderate* (0512–391). Wide selection, good food. **Siddharta.** Located in an attractively restored old warehouse. Bar with music at night, very nice. **Champagne Restaurant,** at the Condovac Hotel. *Moderate* (0512–761). Very good International cuisine is served here.

THE SOUTHERN CIRCUIT

For the traveler with more time in Paraguay the Southern Circuit is recommended. This 900-kilometer tour, featuring the remaining Jesuit Reduction sites, provides an excellent opportunity to learn about this unique colonial experiment as well as to see a good portion of Paraguay's rich agricultural heartland. Of the seven Reductions, four have developed interesting museums, and all seven missions have undergone considerable restoration of the prolific works of art realized by the Indians under Jesuit tutelage and of the seventeenth-century Indian dwellings. Of the churches once the center of mission life, only one has survived to this day, and it, unfortunately, is in ruins. The remains of the spectacular church of Trinidad have in recent years been considerably reconstructed, offering the twentieth-century visitor a glimpse of its former glory. While the entire tour can be done in a hectic two days, three days or more would make it more relaxed and enjoyable, also enabling a visit to the spectacular Iguazú Falls and the mammoth Itaipu Dam.

The Missions

The trip begins following the first leg of the Central Circuit, then continues south from Paraguarí. Kilometer 165 (from Asunción) is the site of the vacation spot called Villa Florida, popular for its clear blue waters and beautiful sandy beaches. The Tebicuary River here formed the northern boundary of the region granted to the Jesuits for evangelization of the Guaraní Indians, and indeed, today, the river forms the division between the departments of Paraguarí and Misiones. The northernmost Reduction, however, lies 66 kilometers farther south at San Ignacio. As you proceed toward San Ignacio, a stop in San Miguel (kilometer 178) is recommended for the purchase of fine quality woolen goods, peculiar to this village along with colorful cotton blankets and hammocks.

The first of the many Jesuit communities, the mission at San Ignacio—also known as San Ignacio Guazu ("Big")—was founded in 1609. A visit to the Museum of San Ignacio is an excellent introduction to your tour of the ruins. There is reason to believe that the museum building itself, a restored Jesuit house, is the oldest in Paraguay; its thick earthen walls serve as a natural form of insulation, keeping the interior cool in summer and warm in winter. Among the many restored statues exhibited is one of the town's patron saint, San Ignacio, and one of the Christ Child as Judge. The more keen-eyed observer may detect Guaraní faces on some of the angels; even more significant Indian influence can be seen in the portrayal of Satan as a woman, as the devil in traditional Guaraní mythology was also female. In the main plaza of town is a statue of San Roque Gonzalez, the founder of several missions. This Jesuit priest was martyred in 1628 in modern-day Brazil, killed by a tomahawk at the hands of hostile Indians. Despite subsequent incineration of his body, the martyr's heart remained miraculously intact and can be seen today in the Capilla de los Mártires in the Colegio Christo Rey in Asunción.

Just southeast of San Ignacio is a dirt lane passing through rolling farmland for 10 kilometers to the village of Santa María. The museum of Santa María, housed in a carefully restored Indian dwelling (facing the plaza) features an interesting display of over 50 statues. In addition, the church of Santa María is adorned by a statue of the Virgin Mary over six feet tall. The original church was renowned as a cultural haven, housing an organ and a nine-bell bell tower, and offering concerts performed by the resident Indians. On the outskirts of town is a spring protected during the Jesuit period; today, in addition to providing drinking water for nearby residents, it is used to feed several shallow cement pools where women wash clothes.

Back to Ruta I and again heading south, the next town, Santa Rosa, also owes its founding to the Jesuits (1697). This attractive community with its tree-lined plaza flanked by Indian houses and a red-brick bell tower still retains much of its traditional appearance. Around the turn of the century, as in San Ingacio and Santa María, the original church was destroyed. The smaller Loreto Chapel, its sanctuary embellished by numerous frescoes, escaped disaster and today exhibits many astonishing wooden statues as well as an eighteenth century Parish Register. Many Indian houses still standing serve as dwellings even today. For a glimpse inside, visit one of the local shops.

Turning off Ruta I at Kilometer 257, continue another 22 kilometers on the recently asphalted highway to the Yasyretá Dam Construction Project to the Reduction site of Santiago (1672). A modern reproduction of the museum in San Ignacio, the Santiago museum exhibits over 60 restored wooden sculptures. Another item of interest is the wooden altar of the church featuring a representation of the baptism of Christ, the sole remaining painting from the Reduction period.

Continuing 50 kilometers more on Ruta I, then another 28 kilometers on another paved road south, is the final site of the Reduction San Cosme y Damian. Here the Colegio is well preserved and, again, restored statues fill the rebuilt church. It was in this Reduction, originally located slightly farther south, that Jesuit Buenaventura Suarez conducted his studies of the satellites of Jupiter and wrote his famous treatise, *The Lunar Influences During a Century,* published in Europe. A sundial is all that remains to suggest its former reputation in astronomy.

Ruta I comes to an end 370 kilometers from Asunción in the city of Encarnación, the birthplace of General Stroessner. This city was also originally founded as a Jesuit mission (1615) by Jesuit Roque Gonzalez, who later founded Posadas, Argentina, on the opposite bank of the Paraná River. A bridge connecting the two cities was inaugurated in early 1990. Unlike many other Reductions, Encarnación continued to prosper after the departure of the Jesuits. Sadly, a typical disinterest in historical artifacts doomed all traces of the former Reduction to obliteration.

Continuing on past Encarnación 28 kilometers northeast on paved Ruta VI is the tiny village of Trinidad, once the site of the most impressive church of all those constructed under the Jesuits. Measuring 58 meters long and 11 meters high, and topped by a huge dome, construction on the church was begun in 1706 and completed shortly before the expulsion. Today the buildings are being carefully reconstructed and the wooden and stone sculptures restored. The frieze depicting angels playing the clavichord, the harp, and other European instruments is enchanting and the profusely carved wooden doors at the side of the church are a marvelous illustration of Guaraní influence in otherwise predominantly European architecture. Among other remarkable achievements here, the Indians worked the renowned bell foundry and manufactured organs and harpsichords as well as operating a sugar factory and an oil mill.

The Jesús Reduction, built on a hill located only nine kilometers from Trinidad, is simply a ruin of an unfinished work. When the Jesuits were expelled, the civil administrator promised the Indians living there that they would be able to complete construction on the church within a year. There are signs that work was in fact carried on for a short time under Franciscan priests; nonetheless, the church remained unfinished. In that the visitor can still see the mission at Jesús virtually as it stood in 1768, it is considered by some to be one of the more interesting sites, offering a fascinating lesson on Jesuit Era construction.

Iguazú Falls and Itaipu Dam

The newly paved Ruta VI crosses the approximately 270 kilometers of fertile, hilly countryside between Encarnación and Ciudad del Este. Only a few years ago this road sliced through thick forest but today, nature has been beaten back and rapid development of the land along the route is under way. Many small towns line the highway, populated by German, Japanese, Russian, and Brazilian as well as Paraguayan homesteaders. The border town, Ciudad del Este, plagued by rapid population growth during the Itaipu years, is now a dirty frontier-town of 100,000 people dominated by black market trade. Consequently, the city's many commercial establishments offer some of the best buys on manufactured goods. Only 20 kilometers due north is the Itaipu Hydroelectric Project, the world's largest hydroelectric dam. Both Paraguay and Brazil offer bus tours to their respective sides of the dam and each country's Visitor Center shows an informative movie. To enter Brazil, cross over the 500-meter "Friendship Bridge," the longest single span bridge in the world; the awe-inspiring Iguazú ("Big Water") Falls are only 30 minutes away by car or city bus.

Ruta II runs west from Ciudad del Este once again through lush, hilly farm-country. A few kilometers before Caaguazú ("Big Forest") is Señor Juan Pio Rivaldi's fishery (watch carefully for his sign). This amiable philosopher/farmer will gladly show visitors his fishery, probably unique in Paraguay.

At the *Cruce Internacional* (the so-called International Crossroads) of Col. Oviedo, only 45 kilometers after Caaguazú, the traveler has a few options: south toward Villarrica (40 kilometers), north to San Estanislao (90 kilometers), or straight ahead to Asunción (134 kilometers). The road south before returning to Asunción offers the most interesting side trip.

Halfway to Villarrica look for the sign to Yataity ("Palm Field"), famous for the *ao po'i* (embroidered clothing) made here. Women are eager to demonstrate their art: elaborately embroidered shirts, dresses, and tablecloths. Much of the ao po'i made in Yataity is also sold in nearby Villarrica, where several shops specialize in that handicraft. Before reaching Villarrica, a few kilometers farther south of Yataity is Mbocayaty ("Coconut Field") and the crossroads for Colonia Independencia (23 kilometers) to the East. Nestled among the string of hills is Ybytyruzu, a colony founded in 1917 by Germans who had left their homeland. Today a wide variety of agricultural goods are produced in this region, including yerba for maté and grapes for the national wines. More German and some British immigrants arrive every year, and the foreign influence is so substantial—notable in the architecture, lifestyle, and farming techniques—that you may forget where you are. An overnight stay in Hotel Tilinski is recommended; it is a comfortable hotel with simple rooms and hearty food, perfect for a relaxing holiday.

Seven kilometers south of Mbocayaty is Villarrica (population 50,000), the picturesque capital of the department of Guairá. The birthplace of many of Paraguay's major artists, musicians, and poets, Villarrica is often touted as the cultural capital of Paraguay. Indeed, until recently several small weekly magazines were published here—a notable achievement in this country so dominated by its capital city. A quick tour by *kaxapé* (horse drawn taxi) can be an enjoyable way of taking in the city's sights, which include the two cathedrals, a small university, numerous well-kept plazas, and a spacious nineteenth-century train station. There is also a small, well-stocked though rather disorganized museum behind the Cathedral that exhibits artifacts from Villarrica's past.

After returning to the Cruce Internacional from Villarrica, Ruta II to the west completes the Southern Circuit on its trek back to the capital. Fifty kilometers west of Col. Oviedo the route crosses the Yhaguy River ("Shaded Water") in the pleasant village of Itacurubí ("Pebble"); this small river is packed to capacity on summer weekends, attracting people from as far away as Asunción.

The next town, Eusebio Ayala, is sometimes referred to as "Chipa Town" for the cheesy corn/cassava bread that is ritually bought by almost all who pass through. The visitor interested in the War of the Triple Alliance might want to make a quick trip to Vapor Cue Park, 28 kilometers northeast of Eusebio Ayala just past Caraguatay. Seven warships (among them three *Ironsides*) sailed up the Yhaguy River during the war to escape the marauding armies. Today, three boats have been reconstructed but the intervening years have seen the river dwindle to its present unnavigable state, trapping the ships where they were abandoned and sunk over a hundred years ago.

Continue west on Ruta II, following the third leg of the Central Circuit described above.

PRACTICAL INFORMATION FOR THE SOUTHERN CIRCUIT

HOW TO GET THERE. The best way to see the Southern Circuit is by rental car. The **Lions Tours Agency** offers an excursion along one side of the circuit, to one of the Jesuit Reductions, Trinidad (near Encarnación). The agency tour takes an entire day, returning along the same route ($125 per person, two person minimum). A tour of the entire Southern Circuit, including a visit to Trinidad, Iguazú Falls, and Itaipu Dam, runs three days and costs $283 per person, minimum two persons. The trip can also be made using public buses—plan to spend extra time but much less money.

HOTELS. For definitions of price categories see "Facts at Your Fingertips" earlier in this chapter. **VILLA FLORIDA. Hotel Las Mercedes.** *Moderate.* On the main hwy (083–220). Resort with cabins. **Hotel Nacional de Turismo.** *Moderate.* On the main hwy (083–207). **Centu Cué.** *Inexpensive.* On the river (083–219). The most popular resort.

AYOLAS. Hotel Nacional de Turismo de Ayolas. *Moderate.* Fairly new, with swimming pool and tennis courts (072–2271).

ENCARNACIÓN. Novohotel. *Expensive.* Ruta 1, km 361 (071–4222/5). **Hotel Paraná.** *Inexpensive.* Mariscal Estigarribia 1416 (071–4440). **Hotel Viena.** *Moderate.* Caballero 568 (3486). **Hotel Tirol.** *Moderate.* Twenty kilometers north of Encarnación on Ruta VI (071–2388). Price includes three meals, good food. 3 swimming pools, beautiful setting. Belgian-run. Highly recommended.

CIUDAD DEL ESTE. Hotel Acaray. *Moderate.* Casino, swimming pool (061–2555). **Hotel Catedral.** *Inexpensive.* Carlos Antonio Lopez 642 (061–2380). **Hotel Santo Domingo.** *Moderate.* Emiliano R. Fernandez corner Emerito Miranda (061–2534). **Hotel Executive.** *Moderate.* Av. Gral. Adrián Jara corner Curupayty (061–8981). **Hotel Munich.** *Moderate.* (061–2371).

VILLARRICA. Hotel Ybytyruzu. *Inexpensive.* Avda. C.A.Lopez corner Dr. Botrell (2390). Thirty kilometers east of Villarrica, in Colonia Independencia, is **Hotel Tilinski.** *Inexpensive.* Price includes three meals, all you can eat (240).

RESTAURANTS. VILLA FLORIDA. Restaurant of the **Hotel de Turismo.** *Inexpensive* (083–207). **Pensión Sirena** (across from the toll booth). *Inexpensive.* Looks dilapidated but serves the best fish.
ENCARNACIÓN. Try the restaurants of any of the hotels listed above.
CIUDAD DEL ESTE. Executive. *Inexpensive.* Gral. Adrian Jara y Curupayty (061–8981).
VILLARRICA. El Refugio. *Inexpensive.* Gral. Díaz near Melgarejo. Hearty plain food. **El Tirol.** *Inexpensive.* Carlos A. Lopez (in front of the Shell station). **Hotel Ybytyruzu.** *Inexpensive.* Carlos A. Lopez corner Dr. Botrell.
COL. OVIEDO. Parador Internacional. *Inexpensive.* One kilometer west of the Cruce Internacional. Hearty food.

SPORTS. VILLA FLORIDA. Fishing trips can be arranged through the hotels. Both Inter-Express Travel Agency and Lions Tour in Asunción can arrange complete excursions if you advise them two months in advance. Inter-Express, Yegros 690, Asunción, Paraguay, S.A.; Lions Tour, Alberdi 454, Asunción, Paraguay, S.A. *Scotty's sport fishing* (Box 1834, Asunción, 660–504) organizes the best fishing tours to Ayolas, Villeta, and other fine angling spots.

CONCEPCIÓN AND VALLEMÍ

There are a few remaining trips that may be of interest to the tourist.
A voyage up the Paraguay River to Concepción or, for the more adventurous, to Vallemí (with connections to Bahía Negra or Corumbá, Brazil) is fascinating for the picture of riverside life it presents. The more heavily traveled route to Concepción through flat, lush lowlands offers good opportunities for bird-watching but farther north the river grows narrower and the banks more hilly. Small villages and a wide assortment of wildlife can be seen, as well as Indian settlements. Vallemí, far to the north of Concepción, is the site of one of the largest cement factories in South America.

PRACTICAL INFORMATION FOR CONCEPCÍON

HOW TO GET THERE. The steamer leaves Asunción every second Friday for Concepción ($54 executive class) and continues on to Vallemí ($92 executive class). Daily plane service connects both Concepción and Vallemí to Asunción for a quicker return trip ($22 Asunción-Concepción, $29 Asunción-Vallemí).

HOTEL. Hotel Frances. *Inexpensive.* Av. Pte. Franco corner A. Lopez (tel. 031–383).

RESTAURANT. Candilejas Restaurant. *Inexpensive.* Try the surubí.

WHAT TO SEE. Old-fashioned market, beautiful Palo Santo (wooden) goblets, mortar and pestle sets, etc.

FILADELFIA

The arduous trip to Filadelfia, the largest of the Mennonite Colonies, in the heart of the Chaco, is a must for bird lovers. The lowlands area of the Chaco which comprises most of the seven-hour journey is resplendent with bird life; the merest roadside puddle attracts all manner of fowl, making for quite spectacular displays. Attentive bird-watchers may catch a glimpse of the South American ostrich which, generally scorning the waterholes, can be seen running between clumps of trees.

The community of Filadelfia itself is interesting for the picture it presents of an "other" Paraguay, where blond hair and fair skin are the rule. Pay a visit to the co-op there, which produces meat and dairy products for sale all over the country.

PRACTICAL INFORMATION FOR FILADELFIA

HOW TO GET THERE. The Nueva Asunción (NASA) bus company runs a 7-hour-long bus trip from Asunción to Filadelfia twice daily (approximately $10). Stel Turismo also runs a daily (except Sun.) 6–7-hour bus service (approximately $10).

HOTEL. Hotel Florida. Av. Hindenburg ((tel. 091–258). *Inexpensive.*

RESTAURANTS. Estrella and **Girasol,** both *inexpensive.*

WHAT TO SEE. Ask at the hotel for tours to surrounding Mennonite farms and Indian settlements.

PERU

Andean Time Warp

by
MICHAEL L. SMITH

Michael L. Smith is a freelance reporter and writer who has been covering Peru for the past 11 years. He writes frequently for The Washington Post *and* Newsweek International. *He has lived in Lima since 1974.*

A full moon rises over jagged mountain peaks to cast a shimmering light down on the majestic jewel setting of the Machu Picchu citadel while clouds rise up out of the humid canyons below. A Pacific sunset refracts to a peach-toned glow on the colonial plaza in front of San Francisco church and monastery in Lima and transports the viewer back to a more pious era. A sunrise in the valley of Huaylas catches the snowcapped peaks of Huascarán, Huandoy, and Chopicalqui with a brilliance which wipes the sleep out of the bleariest eyes of an early riser.

These are just a few of the snapshots which Peru yields to the hundreds of thousands of visitors who come to this Andean country each year. Peru is a country which offers a rare blend of landscapes and wildlife, millennia of history and culture, and a people proud of what it has to offer. It has the capacity to startle, bewilder, and captivate visitors and Peruvians alike.

There is a continuity back to pre-Hispanic cultures, a sense of community and family which has been enriched by the Spanish tradition. The family and the hometown—even when it has been left generations ago—give roots to Peruvian culture.

This ongoing permanence can be felt everywhere. The complex terraces of the Andean cultures, like those of the southern Colca River valley near Arequipa, are still in use—some of them date from 2,500 years ago! Archaeologists have calculated that it would have taken 10,000 people working for forty years to have built them. That is an enormous accomplishment considering that the valley at its peak held 70,000 inhabitants. The churches and chapels which are scattered around Lima, major cities, and small provincial towns alike testify to an otherworldly devotion which forged an earthy resignation to harsh social conditions and today still forms the backbone of hope. In the sun-drenched region of Ica, south of Lima, the well-preserved haciendas, or plantation houses, of the aristocratic families which once lorded over the valley are now open for visitors. Here is where the vineyards produce the grapes to make pisco, a distinctive brandy used in the world-famous pisco sour, and in an improving variety of wines.

As with the landscapes and historic sites, Peru is a converging flow of races, nationalities, and cultures. The majority of its 22 million inhabitants can trace their lineage back to the pre-Columbian cultures, which have given fame to Peru, or to the Spaniards who brought their sword, crown, and cross to this part of the New World. These two racial and ethnic groups have been mixing since the Conquest, giving birth to a new breed, the *mestizo*. But other nationalities have also contributed to Peru's diversity, though less than in other South American countries, like Argentina and Brazil, which were closer to Atlantic ocean routes. The Spaniards brought Negro laborers to work on the coastal haciendas. In the nineteenth century, Chinese coolies replaced the blacks as a source of cheap labor. Other nationalities—Jews and Arabs, Italians and Britons, Germans, Swiss, Japanese, and Americans, to name just a few—have also pitched in, frequently making a new home in the most inhospitable places, like the jungle frontier towns of Oxapampa and Pucallpa, or at the forefront of risk capital ventures in Lima business.

The Pacific, Andes, and Amazon

Few countries have such imposing physical barriers as Peru. Indeed, most Peruvians believe that the country has yet to integrate into a single nation. Along its 1,400 miles of Pacific coastline, there is a narrow band of some of the driest desert in the world—resembling a vast lunarscape—and the barren western slopes of the Andes, broken by forty-three valley oases. Although near the equator, there is nothing tropical about the coast because the chilly Humboldt current which flows up out of the depths of the Peru-Chile Trench supercharges the air with humidity, but without rainfall. Instead, the coast has six months of dense overcasting, called *neblina*.

Until this century, these valleys were worlds unto themselves, frequently more connected to the communities upstream and to Europe than to Lima or the rest of the country. For decades, the local economies were dependent on growing commodities like sugar cane and cotton. But in the past few years there has been a broad swing to fresh vegetable and fruit produce for Peruvian consumers and abroad. The coast has climatic conditions similar to Southern California, with the advantage of a year-round growing season. Table grapes, olives, and asparagus are just now being exported to New York.

The Pacific Ocean has been an abundant natural resource that has often been misused or ignored by Peruvians. In the early 1970s, Peru claimed to be the largest fishing country in the world, catching 13 million tons of fish, most of which was processed into fishmeal for livestock feed. But over-fishing and shifts in ocean conditions ended those boom days. Now the trend is toward fish for human consumption, exotic protein concentrates, and other high-tech uses for the ocean. But you can still see the traditional fishermen, coming back from a day tending their lines, nets, and traps to supply Peru's excellent seafood cuisine in Lima restaurants.

The Andes divide Peru like a spinal column running the length of the country. Snowcapped peaks tower up over 20,000 feet above sea level. From the depths of the Peru-Chile Trench just off the Peruvian coast to the peaks of the Andes is a difference in altitude of over 40,000 feet within a distance of 500 miles. Few serviceable roads penetrate the interior. This geographical isolation has kept many local customs, crafts, and life-styles alive over the centuries. More than three million Peruvians still live in their peasant communities. Today, modern aircraft and heavy-duty trucks and communication media have helped unite the country more than ever before.

The Andes contain immense mineral wealth: Peru could supply the world with copper, lead, zinc, silver, and other metals for the next 100 years. Uranium has also been discovered. The ancient Peruvian cultures discovered metalworking independently, using bronze for utilitarian articles and reserving fine crafts techniques for the gold and silver artifacts which today grace museum and private collections around the world. Unfortunately, the Spanish conquerors melted down most of the finest examples of this art form into coins and ingots.

But to tap Andean riches has required enormous feats of engineering. In the pre-Columbian epoch, civilization was built on irrigation canals and terracing to ration out scarce water supplies. Today, the Nor-Peru oil pipeline, which pumps crude over the Andes from the jungle to the coast, matches the technical prowess that was necessary to build the Central Railway a century ago, a feat that made Peru's mineral wealth accessible for the first time. The railway is still the highest standard-gauge railway in the world, reaching 15,688 feet above sea level at the Ticlio pass on its way from Lima to the Sierra market town of Huancayo and the mining center of Cerro de Pasco.

Although Peru is roughly equivalent to the size of the West Coast states of California, Oregon, Washington, and Nevada combined, the usable farmland is only as big as Connecticut and Massachusetts, so the available land has to be put to good use. The Andean peasant has learned how to do that, even if it has been just to survive. Under extremely hard conditions and with few resources, he has developed techniques like terracing, control of ecological levels according to altitude, and diversity of crops to guarantee that food is produced.

Finally, the vast Amazon basin spreads out for hundreds of thousands of square miles. The rivers themselves and airplanes provide the best transport system. Iquitos, the largest city in the Peruvian jungle, is not connected by land to the rest of the country. There are still tribes in the Peruvian Amazon who live as they did before the Spanish came, but oil crews, gold prospectors, river merchants, military detachments, and missionaries are slowly reducing virgin jungle. There are wildlife and nature reserves, like the Manu National Park in Madre de Dios, which are conserving one of the world's unique natural habitats.

The pioneer spirit lives on in the Amazon foothills, pushing eastward out of overcrowded, overworked Sierra into the Peruvian frontier. The fastest growing regions in the country are the footholds in the jungle: rice farmers in Tarapoto who are getting yields on a par with Japan; the lumbering town of Pucallpa, which has turned into a major staging area for the conquest of the Amazon; and the coffee, cocoa, and tropical fruit growers of San Ramon, who are pushing back the wilderness with bulldozers and machetes. Agriculture is initially precarious in these new enclaves and, if done incorrectly, can be extremely harmful ecologically, but Peru's twenty-first century lies in a rational use of renewable resources found in the rainforests and marshlands of the Amazon.

Ancient Worlds

It is a credit to the pre-Columbian cultures that they mastered these coastal valleys, mountain slopes, and jungle foothills much more competently than their current-day heirs. Man first arrived in this part of the Americas some 20,000 years ago, before agriculture had been discovered or animals domesticated. (These achievements were not attained until between 6000 and 4000 B.C.) An advanced civilization, the Chavín, appeared as the first consolidation of a Pan-Andean culture, providing a unity among the thousands of mountain and coastal enclaves of advancement.

The next Pan-Andean culture was the Wari, which expanded from the central Sierra in Ayacucho between A.D. 900 and 1200, when Europe was in the depths of the Dark Ages. It was also a period in which urban centers and crafts, based on an expansive market system, grew and prospered despite the geographic limits on trade. Archaeologists and historians are still puzzled by the downfall of this empire. It may have been due to a sharp shift in climatic conditions, which decimated the finely tuned agricultural system needed to support the Wari expansion. Finally, the Incas stormed out of Cuzco to conquer the largest empire yet seen in South America. Between these Pan-Andean cultures, there were regional cultures and kingdoms which made exquisite contributions.

Archaeological remains are found throughout Peru. Indeed, the main problem is to carry out the necessary investigations before the sites are tampered with or looted. Each year more discoveries add to the inventory of historical finds. In 1985, an expedition led by the explorer Gene Savoy came across another "lost kingdom," this one named Gran Vilaya, located 400 miles north of Lima near the Marañon river. Under dense rain forest vegetation, the group found an immense—120 square miles—complex, densely covered by stone urban complexes and terracing on a jungle-covered plateau 9,000 feet above sea level. Archaeologists have only had hints of this ancient civilization because a thick jungle canopy, heavy cloud cover, and the inaccessibility of much of the eastern slopes of the Andes have shrouded it. Savoy recently found large stone tablets at the site, which he believes contain examples of a formal writing style, which would be the first writing found associated with an ancient Peruvian culture. The University of Colorado has begun an archaeological dig at Gran Pajaten, a previously known fortification which was apparently the outpost of this newfound kingdom. It will tap just a small corner of this mysterious jungle kingdom.

The Sword and the Cross

The arrival of the Spanish *conquistadores* in 1532 dealt a severe blow to the Andean world, a rupture in two millennia of self-sustained development. The Americas were incorporated into an alien feudal order in which the natives were chattel. For the Andean people, this was equivalent to "the world being turned upside down," as a native legend expressed it. Knowledge of land use, crops, and water management were lost in oblivion, throwing the delicate balance of existence out of kilter. Nearly fifty years of war and civil wars, which pressed many natives into military service, disrupted social organization. Famines and European diseases like smallpox devastated the population. Once the Spanish had emptied the Inca treasures into furnaces to be sent back to Spain, another means was found to extract wealth from the Andes. In 1545, silver was discovered in the town of Potosi, in what is today Bolivia. Soon the Indians were organized into forced labor gangs to serve in the silver mines, and shortly after the mines of Huancavelica, which produced quicksilver for the processing of silver ore. Few survived the ordeal. Forced labor was also used to supply help for the Spaniards' landholdings, public projects like churches and monasteries, and many a whim. The most amazing building accomplishments of the Andean culture fell into disuse and were abandoned to the sands and vegetation.

In 1780, Tupac Amaru II, who traced his lineage back to the Incas, led a rebellion against the Spanish crown and this system of exploitation. It had enormous reverberations throughout the old Inca empire and sent shock waves from Buenos Aires to Bogotá. Thousands of Indians rose up in arms to join Tupac Amaru and his fellow conspirators. Thousands died in the most brutal repression since the Conquest itself. But the seeds of dissidence were planted. Today, Tupac Amaru is regarded as a forerunner of continental independence.

As the oldest and most entrenched seat of royal authority in South America, Lima was the last major city to feel the winds of independence which swept through the continent at the beginning of the nineteenth century. The heavy bloodshed of the Indian revolts had also taken its toll and even the most liberal thinkers of the viceregal court in Lima feared another uprising. In 1821, the Argentine patriot General José de San Martín arrived from Chile with his army to change the balance of power in favor of new ideas, but it would take the brilliant strategist and statesman Simon Bolívar and his field marshal Antonio José de Sucre to defeat the royal army at the battle of Ayacucho in 1826 and wipe out the last threat to independence.

Although Peru was in theory a republic, it suffered from political instability up through the twentieth century. Military strongmen, or "caudillos," and fragile civilian governments alternated in power. The War of the Pacific (1879–84) between Peru, Bolivia, and Chile ended with a humiliating defeat for the two northern countries and the annexation by Chile of Arica and Antofagasta, which had belonged to Peru and Bolivia. It took Peru well into the twentieth century to recover from the economic losses of this conflict; psychological scars persist. No freely elected government since 1911 was able to hand over power to a civilian successor because of military coups d'etat, especially when reform-minded parties seemed ready to touch vested interests. For the vast majority of Peruvians, the new values espoused by the frequently amended and aborted constitutions did not translate into any significant change in the way they lived, unless it was a change for the worse.

Then, in 1968, a military government broke radically with tradition. Under the leadership of General Juan Velasco, left-wing officers convinced the rest of the armed forces to back a set of radical changes, including a redistribution of landholdings which wiped out the "hacienda" system which had exploited the peasants and workers for centuries. The experiment in authoritarian reform was also plagued by economic mismanagement, which caught up with it in the late 1970s. However, the period set loose social forces which would unleash lasting change in the way Peruvians view themselves, their country, and the world.

By any standard, Peru today is enjoying the most vigorous surge of democracy in its 160 years of independence. In 1980, the Peruvian electorate restored Fernando Belaúnde, who had been overthrown by the military twelve years before, to the presidency in a symbolic act of justice. Picking up on many ventures which had been thwarted in his first presidential term, Belaúnde was able to serve out his five-year term and pass on his office to a freely elected successor, Alán García, who just barely met the age requirement for the presidency, thirty-five. García leads the American Popular Revolutionary Alliance (APRA), the oldest party organization in the country which, for fifty years, had been kept out of government by military coups and civilian plotting. But the Garcia government quickly lost popularity in the face of extreme inflation and growing leftist insurgencies. In June 1990, Alberto Fujimori, an independent politician of Japanese descent, defeated famed novelist Mario Vargas Llosa to become president. He soon embarked on a program to eliminate hyperinflation and radically reform the economy, to make Peru more attractive to both foreign and domestic investors.

For a country that seemed to have its past carved in granite andpatriarchal manners for centuries, Peru is intensely living its present and has embarked on changing its future. The past thirty years have brought Peru into a new era in which all the national ingredients are being remixed into new definitions: the recent urban migrant intent on bootstrapping a new life in Lima, the Sierra peasant who left bartering behind a few years ago and buys a big Volvo diesel truck to deliver his produce to the markets in Lima, and the Lima businessman who has just woken up to the profits to be made by exporting designer clothes made from Peru's fine cotton fiber to Bloomingdale's and Marshall Field in the United States.

A country and culture which has been a cradle of world civilization and fueled European empires with its wealth is shaking off four hundred years of missed opportunities and seeking its roots. The foreign visitor and the Peruvian alike are just discovering what Peru is to become.

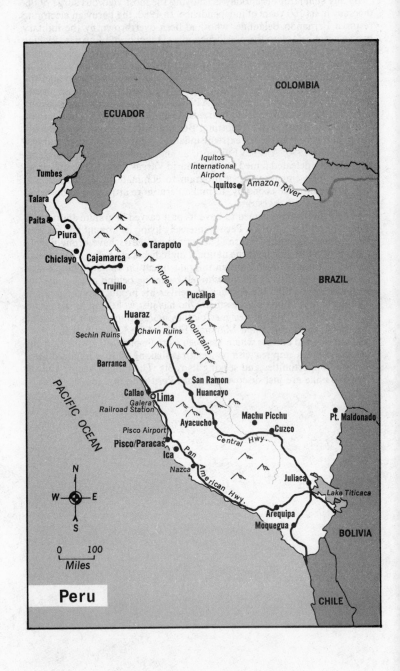

Peru

FACTS AT YOUR FINGERTIPS

WHAT IT WILL COST. In the past few years prices in Peru have gone up and down in the wake of the country's economic roller coaster. In July 1985, President García took office and installed an economic recovery program, which cut inflation and restored value to the nearly worthless local currency. In the two years that followed Peru became even more costly for tourists, and Lima became known as one of Latin America's most expensive cities. But in mid-1987 inflation resumed, followed by a deep recession the next three years. After taking office in July 1990, President Alberto Fujimori imposed a harsh economic "shock" program aimed at eliminating hyperinflation. The shock brought monthly inflation below 10%, but it also left the dollar undervalued, returning Peru to its place among Latin America's most expensive tourist destinations. A possible devaluation of the local currency, and/or increased demand for dollars by a growing economy, could rapidly make Peru more affordable. If inflation returns, as is always possible, the quick and constant rise in prices often leaps ahead of the dollar exchange rate, which moves in fits and starts against the local currency. So be aware that, though Peru is still moderately priced for tourists, prices could rise or fall again at almost any time, and prices quoted in this book are subject to change throughout 1992.

At press time, a sumptuous meal for two, without wine, costs about $35, a room at an expensive hotel runs about $100. Cities with tourist attractions, such as Lima, Cuzco, and Arequipa, tend to be more expensive than the rest of the country.

SOURCES OF INFORMATION. The **Peruvian Consulate** in Washington, DC is at 1700 Massachusetts Ave. NW; at 52 Sloan St., SW 1 in London; and at 170 Laurier Avenue in Ottawa.

WHEN TO GO. Peru has temperate to tropical weather, depending on the region, all year round, so there is no real optimum time to visit the country. In the Andes, rainy season is from Dec. through Mar. and it can be chilly all year round. On the central and southern coast, the Peruvian "summer" months, which coincide with Sierra rainy season, burn off the gray overcasting, make Lima a brighter spot, and give perfect beach weather. In Lima the temperature ranges from 55° to 80° F. In Cuzco, it ranges from 32° to 75°F. For those who like to avoid the package-tour rush, the peak tourism season is late-June through early-Sept., with a smaller rise in traffic in Dec. and Jan.

WHAT TO TAKE. Once prone to somber attire, Peru has become increasingly fashion conscious and inclined to accept casual sports clothes, even at evening meals in restaurants. However, there are still a few business clubs and formal gatherings which require a tie and jacket or evening dress. During winter months (June–Sept.) in Lima, a jacket or wrap are needed, especially at night. In summer months, a windbreaker or sweater may be needed for cool ocean breezes in the late afternoons. In Cuzco, or anywhere else in the Andes, one should be prepared for nippy nights all year round. Light rain gear should be taken. Showers are generally brief and concentrated in the afternoons. At Machu Picchu in the jungle foothills a shower can fall at any time. A visit to Lake Titicaca can be frigid. The Amazon is always hot and humid so summer clothes are best. Shorts are acceptable.

SPECIAL EVENTS. The most colorful occasions are organized around patron saints' days of cities, towns, and even parishes; these are also excuses for pageants full of drama, revelry, and Andean traditions. **January:** *Lima's 357th anniversary* in third week; *folk festival* in Huaraz (20). **February:** *Carnival* celebrated in the provinces, though in more humble fashion than in Brazil. Cajamarca is especially colorful. Two weeks of *folk festivities* in Puno. **March:** *wine festival* in Ica. **April:** *Easter*—Holy Week inspires processions and festivities throughout the country, especially picturesque in Tarma and Ayacucho, where streets are paved with flowers. **June:** the *Qoylluruth'y festivities* in Quispicanchis, Cusco (18–19), with fascinating peasant festivities; Iquitos and its *annual open-house; Intiraymi festivities* in Cusco. **July:** *Independence Day* (28–29). **August:** Arequipa *celebrates founding.* **September:** *Spring festival* in Trujillo. **October:** *Our Lord of the Miracles* congregates hundreds of thousands of faithful in Lima streets; *bullfighting season* starts. **December:** scores of special religious celebrations in preparation for Christmas in provincial towns.

TRAVEL DOCUMENTS AND CUSTOMS. For U.S., Canadian, and U.K. visitors, only a valid passport and return passage need be shown to migration officials at the point of entry to be issued a 60-day tourist visa. This visa may be extended twice, 30 days each time. A $15 airport tax must be paid on leaving Peru. It is against the law to remove pre-Columbian and colonial articles from the country. If a replica of a ceramic or painting is purchased, be sure to carry the receipt on leaving. Customs permits two cartons of cigarettes or its equivalent, 3.5 liters of alcoholic drinks, and gifts up to $300 per person.

GETTING TO PERU. By air. From the United States: *American* flies from Miami direct, and from other points in the United States via Miami; *Aero Peru* flies from Miami direct or via Panama and Guayaquil; *Faucett* flies from Miami direct or via Iquitos; *LAN Chile* flies from New York and Miami; *Aerolineas Argentinas* flies from Los Angeles; *Air Panama* flies from Miami via Panama; *Avianca* flies from Los Angeles via Bogotá; *Ecuatoriana* flies from Chicago, New York, Los Angeles, and Miami via Quito or Guayaquil; *Varig* flies from Los Angeles.

From Canada: *Canadian Airlines* flies non-stop from Toronto.

From Europe: *KLM, Lufthansa, Iberia, Avianca, Viasa, Aereoflot, Air France, Cubana,* and *Alitalia* all fly to Peru from various European cities.

Flying hours to Lima from: New York 7; Miami 5; Los Angeles 4.5; San Juan 5; Paris 13; London 13; Panama 3; Bogotá 2; Santiago 4; Buenos Aires 6; Quito 2; Rio 6.

By car. The Pan-American Highway provides a convenient route north to Ecuador and south to Chile and beyond.

By bus. *Ormeño, TEPSA,* and *Roggero* coaches can take passengers south to Santiago, Chile and on to Buenos Aires, Argentina. There is also regular service to Ecuador and north.

CURRENCY. Peru's currency has been undergoing steady changes as a result of four-digit inflation. Small-denomination bills and most coins were removed from circulation during 1988 and replaced with larger bills. Currently circulating are inti bills of 1,000, 5,000, 10,000, 50,000 100,000, 500,000, 1,000,000 and 5,000,000. The Fujimori government planned to introduce a new currency, called the "nuevo sol," beginning in 1991. Under the plan, which had not gone into effect at press time, six zeros were to be dropped from the inti, so that a 1,000,000 inti note would be equal to 1 nuevo sol. The plan also called for coins to be reintroduced. It is likely that old intis would remain in circulation for at least a year after the nuevo sol is introduced.

The government has done away with a multitiered system of exchange rates that had confused tourists and Peruvians alike. Currently there are just two exchange rates and no restrictions. Tourists deal at the bank rate and the slightly higher parallel market rate. Both fluctuate daily depending on demand. The bank rate is mainly for official transactions such as credit card purchases. Dollar exchanges are handled at the parallel rate. Both rates are published daily in newspapers.

Tourists can exchange their dollars for intis at most banks, at exchange houses that dot major cities, or with the hundreds of street-side currency traders who gather in key business and tourist zones. But tourists are cautioned that dealing with these money changers poses risks of receiving counterfeit bills or of outright robbery.

Upon arrival at the Lima airport, tourists should exchange just what they think they will need for the next few hours and then check with their hotel on the best exchange sites. Most tourist restaurants and stores will accept dollars as payment but at a slightly lower exchange rate.

Traveler's checks are traded at about 2% less than face value. Major credit cards are generally accepted but ask first to make sure. For instance, American Express cards have limited use, mainly for hotels and a few restaurants.

Final Note: The financial aspects of Peruvian travel can change at any moment. Be sure to check the various exchange rates, traveler's check, and credit card levels before leaving home.

ACCOMMODATIONS. The selection of hotels and other lodgings follows the following pricing system: *Super Deluxe,* $100 or more; *Deluxe,* $75–$100; *Expensive,* $50–$75; *Moderate,* $20–$50; and *Inexpensive,* under $20. Taxes have changed frequently in the past several years. As this edition goes to press, taxes were 30% for rooms rated deluxe and above and 18% for other lodgings. Taxes have already been figured into the pricing system. Be aware that all prices quoted are those available at press time, and a number of economic factors could cause fluctuations throughout 1992. Visitors are advised to look into the current situation before departure. Just a handful of hotels, which are listed below, remain suitable in decaying central Lima. Most of the finer lodgings are now situated in the suburbs. In Lima, most hotels do not include breakfast. In the provinces, you are more likely to receive continental breakfasts. The "Hostales Residenciales" differ little from hotels and are sometimes better. Hostels, frequently under family management, offer an attractive and inexpensive alternative to hotel fare and may include breakfast. Other types of lodging, like pensions, are not recommended unless you have personal references from someone who has used the facilities recently. During peak tourist seasons, it is wise to make reservations in advance. Outside major cities, hotels can change management without notice; there is no way to predict the quality of the service. Check with your travel agent for up-to-date information. The state-owned hotel chain ENTUR PERU operates 41 moderately priced hotels and hostels in many out-of-the-way towns, as well as main cities. Some are excellent lodgings while others are the best available in otherwise austere surroundings. Reservations may be made through a travel agency or by going to the ENTUR PERU Lima office, 1358 Javier Prado Oeste, San Isidro (72–1928 for information; 42–8626 for reservations).

ROUGHING IT. Camping is accepted in the provinces for hikers, for instance on the Inca Trail between Cuzco and Machu Picchu, and in most beach areas outside Lima. At some areas, like the Paracas National Park, there are designated areas. Equipment may be rented at adventure tourism agencies. Campers and vans can also be rented. It is advisable to camp in groups of four or more to avoid being a target for robbery.

RESTAURANTS. Our grading system has three categories: *Expensive,* over $20; *Moderate,* $10–20; and *Inexpensive,* under $10. Prices are per person for dinner, excluding drinks, tax, and tip. Some restaurants add a small cover charge. Restaurant taxes, too, have been in a state of flux. Most recently, *Expensive* eateries were adding a tip and service charge of 25% to the bill, while other restaurants charged 15%–18%. The visitor is well advised to feast his heart out in Lima. Fine restaurants in a variety of styles are readily available. In the provinces, except for a few hotels, select restaurants, and local delicacies which may not be to a visitor's taste, the standard fare is filling but bland. Many restaurants have specialties of the day, called *menús,* which are less expensive than ordering à la carte. For Peruvians, lunch time can last from 1 to 3 P.M. in the afternoon, if there is no rush. Dinner may be as early as 7 P.M., but formal meals will not start until 9 P.M. Breakfasts are light—fruit juice, coffee, and milk, with toast or fresh baked bread—but most restaurants can come up with something more filling.

Be aware that all prices quoted are those available at press time and are subject to change as the government implements new economic policies. Visitors are advised to check prices upon arrival.

Peruvian Food and Drink. The three key ingredients of Peruvian Creole cuisine are *ají* (a native chili pepper), *ajo* (garlic), and lemon. The *ají* and lemon have distinctive flavors that separate Peruvian cooking from other Latin American cuisine. The chili pepper is hot and spicy, but does not burn the roof of your mouth as the Mexican ones do. Most restaurants understand that foreigners may not tolerate spicy foods and can lower the octanes of *ají*-based dishes. The lemon is acidic and biting. These three ingredients are used with special abandon with the seafood. *Ceviche* is raw shellfish and fish which have been marinated in lemon juice. The side dishes of corn on the cob and sweet potato are to put out the fire. For those who wish to avoid a spicy entree, you can try *conchitas a la parmesana,* broiled scallops. *Corvina,* or sea-bass, is considered the best Peruvian saltwater fish. Trout can also be found. Shellfish, or *mariscos,* are served in a variety of ways, in sauces with fish or as a dish unto themselves. *Langostinos* (shrimp) are especially savory, but they must be in season to be served in restaurants. Most of the meat is imported from Argentina and Uruguay and is first-class. A delicious Peruvian sauce *à la Huancaina,* made with eggs and cheese, is often served with a meat dish, though it traditionally accompanies a boiled potato entree. Peruvians have a highly developed sweet tooth and the desserts tend to be sweeter than most Americans or Europeans prefer. Keep your portions small. For instance, *suspiro a la Limeña* is made from sweetened condensed milk and lemon and served in small portions. *Lucuma* (a small, brown, nutty-flavored fruit) and *chirimoya* (custard apple) are often used in making desserts. *Mazamorra morada* is a deep purple pudding made from purple maize. Peruvian beer is stout and twice as alcoholic as standard American types. The Cusquena and Arequipena brands are reputedly the best, followed by Pilsen. Be careful of overdrinking in Cuzco or elsewhere in the Sierra because the altitude increases the punch of the already high alcoholic content. Peruvian wines have been getting better over the past decade and are a fine accompaniment to Creole food. Try Ocujaje and Tacama brands, which come from vineyards in Ica. Finally, part of Peru's fame rests on the pisco sour, made from a native grape brandy, lemon, sugar, egg white, and nutmeg. It is an extremely potent drink so do not be deceived by its sweetness.

TIPPING. On all hotel and restaurant bills, 15% to 25% tax and service charge have already been included. However, for exceptional attention you might want to add another 5%. Porters should get the equivalent of 25 cents per bag. Taxi drivers do not expect tips.

BUSINESS HOURS AND HOLIDAYS. Shops are generally open from 10 A.M.– 8 P.M., Mon. through Sat. Some stores shut down from 1–3 P.M., in a modified "siesta" schedule. Bank hours are from 9:15 A.M.–1 P.M., except for the Jan.–Mar. summer period when hours are moved up, 8:30 A.M.–12:30 A.M. Main bank branches also offer afternoon hours.

Time. Peru is on Eastern Standard time, except from January through March when clocks move one hour ahead.

National holidays. Jan. 1 (New Year's Day); Easter; May 1 (Labor); June 29 (St. Peter and St. Paul); July 28–29 (Independence); Aug. 30 (Saint Rosa of the Americas); Oct. 8 (Miguel Grau—National Hero's Day); Nov. 1 (All Saints'); Dec. 8 (Immaculate Conception); Dec. 25 (Christmas).

TELEPHONES. Direct-dial, long-distance phone service is available in most of Peru, except for downtown Lima and a few provincial cities that still have antiquated switching equipment. For operator-assisted calls abroad dial 108. Dial 107 to call other Peruvian cities. Peru is undergoing a major expansion of its telephone service, so there may be some changes in the phone numbers listed here. Consult the *Peru Guide* monthly magazine for the latest numbers. At peak hours, however, you may just get busy signals. Public telephones require the use of tokens, called "rin," which are readily available at most newsstands and stores. They sell for the equivalent of 2 cents apiece.

MAIL. The Peruvian postal service is excruciatingly slow, erratic, and prone to loss. Use it only for the picture postcard or letter home. For important documents use the services of a courier: Giant Express, Las Orquideas 2772, San Isidro (40–8148), with branches throughout Lima; or DHL, 3355 Av. Republica of Panama, San Isidro, (41–8686, 40–5209). The post office is located one block from the Plaza de Armas, to the left as you face the government palace. Open 8 A.M.–6 P.M. Mon.–Sat., and Sun. mornings.

NEWSPAPERS. Lima's Spanish-language daily paper *El Comercio* is the nation's leading paper and carries the most complete and orderly listings of cultural and economic information pertinent to tourists. Exchange rates and the times and locations for shows and events can easily be followed, even by people who cannot read Spanish. There is an English-language weekly, *The Lima Times,* which is available at most newsstands in and near tourist hotels. It contains a page of cultural events and other activities, with dates, times, and addresses. In hotel lobbies, you can get copies of *The New York Times, The Wall Street Journal, The Miami Herald* and *The International Herald Tribune* on sale with one or two days' delay. *Time* and *Newsweek* are available weekly, along with other international magazines. The handy, monthly *Peru Guide* is available free at most hotels. The Peruvian press in Lima is lively and competitive, with no government censorship. The main morning papers are the standard-size *El Comercio* and the tabloids *La Republica* and *Expreso*. The most prestigious weekly news magazines are *Caretas* and *Si*.

ELECTRIC CURRENT. Peru runs on 220 volt current, 60 cycle A.C. Some hotels have special outlets for 110 volt current.

USEFUL ADDRESSES. The **U.S. Embassy** is located at 1400 Inca Garcilazo de la Vega Avenue, downtown Lima (33–8000), but the **Consulate** is at 346 Grimaldo del Solar, Miraflores (44–3621). The **British Embassy** is at the corner of Arequipa Avenue and Natalio Sanchez, Plaza Washington, Lince (33–4738). The **Canadian Embassy** is at 132 Libertad, Miraflores (44–4015). The **Peruvian Tourist Office** has an information booth at 1066 Jiron de la Union (32–3559) in downtown Lima. Open 9 A.M.–6 P.M., Mon.–Fri., and Sat. mornings. Also at the Lima airport (52–4416), open daily 8:30 A.M.–2:30 P.M. and 9 P.M.–2 A.M. Another source of help is the **South American Explorers' Club,** 146 Portugal Avenue, Brena (31–4480). The **International Association of Medical Assistance for Travelers** (IAMAT) is located at the Clinica Anglo-Americana, 400 Alfredo Salazar, San Isidro (40–3570, ask for administration).

HEALTH. Peru was in the throes of a serious cholera epidemic in 1991, which had taken more than 1,100 lives and sickened 150,000 at press time. To avoid the disease, drink only bottled beverages and do not accept ice in drinks. Some first-class hotels do give tap water special purification treatment; ask the management. Avoid buying food from street vendors and most quick-order food stalls and shops—sanitary standards are especially low in these places. For further information on cholera, contact the U.S. Department of Health and Human Services, Centers for Disease Control, Atlanta, GA 30333 (404–332–4559).

Also see special indications for adjusting to the altitude in the Cuzco section. Yellow fever shots are recommended for travelers to Peru's jungle zones. Malaria is also present in some jungle areas. Tourists to these areas should seek competent medical advice about vaccinations before leaving home. Most major hotels have a doctor on call. The following clinics have 24-hour emergency service and usually an English-speaking staff member on duty: *Clinica Anglo-Americana,* 400 Alfredo Salazar (40–3570); *Clinica Internacional,* 2475 Av. Washington, downtown Lima (28–8060).

SECURITY. Peru has been plagued by a growing leftist guerilla insurgency since 1980, increasing crime due to the recession, and severe transportation problems. Airline, train, and bus companies suffer from a shortage of foreign exchange to purchase replacement equipment and spare parts, and Peru's road system, especially in the highlands, is deteriorating. The result is that Peru, perhaps more than any other Latin American nation, has become increasingly difficult for tourists. Unfortunately, foreigners have been victimized by the political violence, and travelers are strongly advised to check their travel plans with a reputable travel agency and with their embassy in Lima. The U.S. State Department has issued warnings urging tourists to avoid rural emergency zones, which are mostly in the central highlands and the Upper Huallaga Valley, as well as the areas near Huaraz and Pucallpa. Travelers should avoid hiking the Inca Trail, and use extra caution when visiting in and around Cusco and Macchu Pichu.

Despite the above, tourists can have a safe and relatively carefree vacation if they adhere to some basic rules. Pickpocketing and petty theft are the most common sorts of crime confronting tourists. Do not carry more cash than necessary. All valuables should be left in a hotel safety deposit box. Gold and valuable jewelry should not be worn on the street. Purses, cameras, and other bags should be held by straps over the shoulder and retained in place with an arm. Avoid getting loaded down with shopping bags because it will be hard to keep track of them all. Pickpockets and snatch-and-run thieves are attracted to tourist sites, like the Cuzco main square or the Lima airport. Avoid dealing with anyone who calls up or stops you in the hotel lobby offering tourist services. Try to travel by day if you go by bus outside of Lima. Like other Latin American countries, Peru has been fighting against the international cocaine trade and sometimes a visitor may be approached in the streets and offered cocaine. It may be a pusher or an undercover policeman. In either case, the best advice is to turn around and head in the opposite direction. The U.S. State Department has issued formal warnings to all travelers to avoid any contact with drugs while in Peru. The government enforces a harsh law prohibiting all possession and use of drugs. Sentences are from 15 years to life. There is no bail and consulates can only recommend a good lawyer.

Note: Unknown to most visitors, there are places which are banned for taking pictures, especially when off the beaten tourist track. Military barracks, airstrips, large industrial plants, and mines are some of them. Before taking a snapshot of a quaint old fort, first look to see if there is a guard to ask if it is permitted. This will avoid a prolonged session with security police.

A Final Warning. Peru is a developing country undergoing major changes, in effect, reaching for adulthood as a nation. This may not have much bearing for a visitor who has come to see the sights and enjoy a well-deserved vacation. The travel industry does its best to shield visitors from the traumas of inefficiency and discomfort. But when things go bad, they can be extremely trying. An overbooked plane flight or a discourteous customs agent can set off a chain reaction of mishaps which may seem to put in danger the whole outing. In those situations, it is best to dig deeply into your reserves of patience. Once the episode is over, a visitor will find that Peruvians go out of their way to make up for the inconvenience. For all plane flights, be sure to reconfirm your reservations 24 hours before departure, no matter what other provisions have been made. This is an advantage of working through a reputable travel agency in Peru. Another tip is to travel light in the provinces—hand luggage only—to avoid long delays at baggage counters.

GETTING AROUND PERU. By air. Two domestic airlines (both with main offices on Plaza San Martín), the state-owned *Aeroperu* (Lima 32–2995, 31–7626, airport 52–2065) and the private *Faucett,* (Lima 33–6364, Miraflores 45–7649, airport 51–9711), provide regular, though not luxurious flights to most provincial cities, with Lima as the transport hub. The new *Aero-Chasqui* (Nicolas de Pierola 611, office 301, Lima 27–5471, 27–5758) also provides service to some outlying cities. *Aero-Condor,* Juan de Arona 781, San Isidro (42–5663, 41–1354), and *Aeroica,* Nicolas de Píerola 677, office 102, Lima (273–292) provide side trips over the Nazca lines though prices can be steep.

By train. Peru's railways offer an interesting and breathtaking means of getting to know the country and some of its most spectacular scenery. One line, the highest standard-gauge railway in the world, leaves Lima and goes to the central Sierra city of Huancayo. Another line starts out in the southern city of Arequipa and goes up to Lake Titicaca and then over to Cusco. A narrow-gauge line runs from Cuzco down to Machu Picchu and then further into the jungle of Quillabamba. For schedules call the state railroad company *Enafer* (27–6620, 28–9440).

By bus. There are many bus services offering routes to practically anywhere in the country, though it is wise to check the quality of the coaches before buying a ticket. Bus companies are listed in the telephone directory under "Transportes Terrestres." Many tourism agencies also provide package visits to provincial sights, which can eliminate some of the hassle of traveling by land.

By Colectivo. These passenger cars and vans cover most of the same routes as buses. They charge two to three times as much, but travelers arrive at their destinations more comfortably and more rapidly. Seats fill quickly, so purchase tickets a few days ahead of time if possible. Companies are listed in the telephone directory under "Transportes Terrestres."

By car. The *Peruvian Touring Club,* 699 Cesar Vallejo, Lince (40–3270) provides excellent services, with detailed maps and advice. The Panamerican Highway runs the length of the coast and the central Lima stretch is a four-lane expressway. Good highways link the Callejón de Huaylas with the coast, Huancayo to Lima, and Cuzco with the outlying districts. The rest of Peru's road system is only for the most adventurous, preferably equipped with four-wheel drive.

Rental cars. There are several car rental agencies operating in Lima and most major cities. However, if you are planning to take a trip off the main roads, you should not tell the counter attendant because most agencies will refuse to rent because of the extra wear and tear on the vehicles.

BEACHES. Peru's Pacific coast is impressive, with enormous stretches of sand and pebble beaches. Surfing conditions are excellent and several world championships have been held in Peru. Ocean temperatures are shockingly frigid, due to the influence of the Humboldt current, but refreshing on a scorching day. Several resort hotels, especially in Paracas in the south and Punto Sal in the north, are available all year round. It is also possible to rent beach houses for longer periods of time, but during the summer months they are extremely scarce.

FLORA AND FAUNA. Peru is a major gene pool for the world. Peru gave mankind the potato and corn (which also originated in Mexico). Scientific investigators are looking into plants to see how they can be used. For instance, quinua, which has fed the Andean Indian for over two thousand years, has been found to have the highest and most complete form of vegetable protein. Practically every type of ecological environment is found in Peru, from tropical rain forest to glacial plateau, with the corresponding flora and fauna for each niche. There are increasing opportunities for specialized tourists to experience a firsthand encounter with Peru's wildlife and flora, from orchid-hunting to bird-watching.

SPORTS. Like every country south of the Rio Grande, Peru is mad about **soccer,** called *fútbol* in Spanish. Peru fielded World Cup teams in 1970, 1978, and 1982. The professional playing season lasts all year, with regional or metropolitan leagues, followed by national championships usually culminating in Dec. or Jan. Amateur leagues abound. Because full-size fields are limited and expensive to maintain, many Peruvians play *fulbito* on a small field roughly the size of a tennis court. Teams have five to seven players each. Women's volleyball is the second most popular spectator sport. Peru frequently competes in world finals and in 1988 won the Silver Medal in the World Olympics in South Korea. There are active amateur and professional leagues, and top players are frequently hired to play in the United States, Europe, and Japan. Public sports facilities are scarce and in heavy use, frequently involving extended waiting lists. Many private clubs will allow foreigners who are visiting Peru briefly to use their facilities free or for a small charge. For instance, the *Lima Cricket and Football Club,* 200 J. Vigil, Magdalena del Mar (61–1423), offers clay tennis courts, squash, a swimming pool, and other sports. At a few clubs, golf is also available. Inquire with club management for these privileges.

Martial sport. There are scores of training centers for all varieties of Oriental martial sports.

With an ocean at Peru's doorstep, it is easy to see why ocean sports like **yachting, wind surfing, surfing,** and **skin diving** have a big following. **Deep-sea fishing,** especially in the north, and **trout fishing** in the Andes, are also possible. Consult with travel agencies or the specific sports federations for details.

Another adventure sport is **hang-gliding.** The Peruvian coast offers unique conditions for practicing this sport. **Mountaineering** (Andinism, as it has been tagged here), **trekking, canoeing, kayaking,** and **rafting** are growing in popularity, due to the unique advantages which Peru offers for these activities. **River sports** can be done on the Marañon, Huallaga, Santa, Apurimac, Vilcanota-Urubamba, and Colca rivers, though some stretches of these streams should be tackled only by world-class white-water experts and even on the tamer streams a guide should accompany the expedition. Close to Lima, there are one-day rafting expeditions to the Cañete river.

See also "Adventure Vacations" chapter.

Exploring Peru

LIMA

For many visitors to Peru, there is a gnawing urge to get beyond Lima, which they see as a place to rest up and shower after a long international flight before boarding a domestic flight to the marvels of Cuzco and Machu Picchu or to the steamy charms of the Amazon. But for those who take the time and look in the right places, they can gain a unique insight into the country and grasp the triple watersheds which nourish the Peruvian experience: the Andean world, the Spanish tradition, and the modern experience. Lima is, in effect, the crucible in which these sources are mixed.

Lima is the door to the rest of the country and can give a sense of what the whole country is like without actually visiting it. A stroll through Lima's shops can produce intricately modeled *retablos* (manger scenes) from the Sierra region of Ayacucho, the subdued painted pottery of the Amazon jungle, or carved devils' masks from Lake Titicaca. Lima nights are filled with the whining tunes of Andean music from Huancayo or Cajamarca and the seductive *marineras* from northern Trujillo. The museums house the relics of Paracas, Chavin, and Wari cultures. What's more, true *Limeños* are hard to find in Lima, because the majority of Lima's inhabitants are first or second generation descendants of provincial migrants.

Lima was originally called the "City of the Three Kings," because it was founded on that religious feast day, the Epiphany. To commemorate that founding, the coat of arms awarded by the King of Spain carries three crowns. Lima has also been called the "Garden City," for the time when it was surrounded by a pastoral setting of orchards and fields. Modern critics less sympathetic to its charms called it "Lima the Horrible" because at its worst it seemed to condense all that was wrong with the country.

For most of its four and one-half centuries of existence, Lima has seemed to deny that it belonged to the rest of Peru, which was vastly Indian, deeply rooted in a non-Occidental culture, and handicapped by geographical obstacles which could only be overcome through austere sacrifice. Lima was an administrative center for the Spanish Empire; when Peru gained its independence from the motherland, little changed. Lima remained a remote decision-maker in the lives of most Peruvian provincials and the seat of economic and political power. Lima started as an extension of a vast world empire and then aspired to be a European capital transplanted to South America.

Pattern out of Chaos

In 1535, the Spanish Conquistador Francisco Pizarro, acting like a true urban planner, took a blank sheet of drafting paper and drew up the city of Lima, a tight grid of streets and plazas with 117 blocks on the left bank of the Rimac River. For centuries, his successors seemed to follow his example with an orderly growth. However, the urban explosion of the past thirty years has outstripped the capacity of more recent urban planners.

Both housing developers and squatters have overrun the area with a patch-work of suburbs, shantytowns, and satellite cities. Underneath it all, there is still a pattern. Residents, from the upper-class districts to the most humble neighborhoods, still want their main square or park as a social focal point, a place for a church, a public school, a police station, and a health post or clinic.

Fifty years ago, Lima was a city with half a million inhabitants and an urban infrastructure which had been installed, for the most part, twenty years before. Today, Lima holds more than seven million souls, a full third of the nation's 22 million people. Most Lima residents are provincial migrants and their offspring who came to the capital seeking a better life. Even under optimum conditions, it would have been difficult to keep up with the population growth—paving streets; providing drinking water, sewage disposal facilities, and electricity; and providing education, health, and other services.

Downtown Lima is no longer the social hub of the city. Although during business hours Lima is still bustling because of its concentration of public offices and connected activities, in the evening it loses its vigor. The middle class which has come into its own since the 1950s has moved to the "suburbs," residential developments in traditional areas like Miraflores and newer zones like San Borja, Santiago de Surco, and La Molina, which even a decade ago were cornfields or dairy stables on the southern outskirts of the central city. These residential neighborhoods have their tree-lined streets, parks, and shopping centers, just like any self-respecting American suburb. The new business districts are now San Isidro and Miraflores, where high-rise office buildings are shooting up, shopping centers are opening, and businessmen congregate to trade.

Bootstrap Suburbs

But parallel to this middle-class shift has come another urban phenomenon: provincial migrants who came to find what was lacking in their home-towns. These new arrivals moved into vacant terrain, usually sand dunes or wasteland way to the south, east, and north. Ringing Lima, these settlements have been inappropriately named shantytowns. They may have started out as makeshift dwellings but they are permanent and aspire to the same status and public services that the middle-class neighborhoods have.

First, the squatters put up poles, reed mats, and plastic sheeting for shelter to stake their claim on the land. Later, as money permits, come bricks, cement, ironwork doors and windows, a first floor, then a second, and maybe a small store or workshop facing the street. On the drive in from the airport, which is usually a visitor's first exposure to Peru, a newcomer might be impressed by the barren, treeless landscape, the dusty, rudimentary streets, and, why not say it, the misery. What is not evident at first sight is how the inhabitants' tremendous industry, discipline, and drive have transformed the first shacks into ongoing communities; the same forces will eventually transform them into the equivalent of middle-class neighborhoods.

Some of these shantytowns have evolved into cities themselves. Villa El Salvador was founded in the early 1970s and today holds over a quarter million inhabitants. Investigators have located communities which started out with huts twenty years ago and today are homes and streets indistinguishable from housing developments built along traditional lines.

Lima is afflicted by a bad case of inner-city decay and urban sprawl. Serious efforts during the 1980s to reverse this trend have met with limited success, but the city fathers keep trying. The central and municipal governments, private foundations, corporations, and neighborhood associations have all contributed to rescue the best of the city. Major investments have been made in renovating pre-Hispanic, Colonial, and Republican historic sites. A few streets in downtown Lima have been declared off-limits to all but essential traffic. (Pizarro never foresaw the traffic needs of mass transit and autos when drafting narrow streets to his city.) Even among the most impoverished neighborhoods a sense of community has been born. In the southern cone of Lima, residents have planted over a million trees in the sand dunes.

Ironically, Lima has become more like the rest of the country in this chaotic, turbulent process of massive urbanization in three short decades, less than the time needed by the Spanish to consolidate their conquest of the Inca empire. The capital Pizarro founded to mark the conquest of the Inca empire, which banned the presence of natives except when they came as servants or by special dispensation, has finally been retaken by the vanquished's descendants.

A Search for Roots

When Pizarro came down from the Andes in triumph to found the seat of royal authority in South America in 1535, he found a prosperous community of natives living in the Rimac River Valley. Extensive irrigation networks made most of the land yield crops or fruit. To the south, the ceremonial site of Pachacamac, which was undoubtably the most important religious center of the Andean world since before the age of Christ, lent importance to the Rimac River Valley as a final stopoff for the final leg of the pilgrimage to hear the Pachacamac oracle. The Incas had left the shrine untouched during their conquests and had even incorporated it into their own religion.

Those who climb to the top of the main ceremonial site, only a twenty-minute drive from downtown Lima, cannot help being impressed by the magical view: the Pacific Ocean stretching out to the western horizon, the surf-laced arch of the bay, the rich coastal plain green under cultivation, and the foothills of the Andes rising up like jagged teeth to the east. When Pizarro's brother Hernando first arrived at the adobe step pyramid, he was surprised not to find vast stores of treasures, having heard of Pachacamac's importance. He was shown the disappointingly modest temple of the oracle and the view.

Although the Lima region has been inhabited on a permanent basis for at least four thousand years, there are few visible signs of this presence. Today, visitors can find vestiges of the pre-Columbian cultures in Lima. In the residential districts of San Isidro and Miraflores, there are two *huacas*—pyramids made out of adobe bricks, and other pre-Hispanic sites which were popularly assumed to be burial grounds—which were probably important in agricultural rites for valley inhabitants. These huacas have been restored and small site museums are open to the public. Other huacas are scattered around Lima, like one near the Park of Legends, a zoo-amusement park in the district of San Miguel. The coastal pre-Columbian cultures built with adobe, not in stone as in the Andes or Central America, because the lack of rainfall made adobe an alternative and, in fact, the only cheap building material available. Wind and moisture erosion, abuse, and other damage have erased the most striking features, reducing most sites to mounds.

A Lima humorist once said, half-jokingly, that archaeology in Peru is like oil in Texas—you just have to turn over the topsoil to strike paydirt.

Indeed, Peru is an archaeologist's dream come true. Although the Spaniards shipped gold and silver back to the crown, other objects which are just as highly prized today were left behind or were already buried under the sands. In Lima's countryside museums you can find an excellent sampling of those treasures. The pre-Columbian Peruvians were some of the finest weavers in the world, leaving behind a whole gamut of techniques. They also mastered the art of ceramics, but without the pottery wheel. Much of what we know about their existence and culture has been deciphered from these remains.

Lima can provide a good overview of all these manifestations of the pre-Hispanic world in its museums and private collections. The most didactic presentation is at the National Museum of Archaeology. Some of the best-preserved collections are in private hands—the Amano Museum is highly recommended for a visit. Peruvian archaeologists are still envious of pre-Columbian collections which have been taken out of the country by foreign investigators and arts traders. The huge, newly opened National Museum, though still mostly empty, is intended to give Peru's archaeological treasures the comprehensive and noble style of display they deserve.

The Colonial Heritage

The Plaza de Armas is the radius from which authority stretches out in Lima and Peru. The realms of the Catholic church, municipality, and national government share the Plaza. Most of the present buildings on the square date from 1920 on. Only on the corner between the Presidential Palace and the Cathedral is there a modest balconied structure which remains from colonial times; ironically, a fast-order restaurant now functions on the first floor. During the 1950s, a future-minded mayor decided to remove much of the Plaza's garden and trees to put down concrete for more parking space, spoiling the city's central "patio." Huge stretches of asphalt now give the Plaza de Armas a less leisurely and socially appealing appearance.

The Cathedral houses the crypt of Francisco Pizarro. But even that fact has had to be wrenched out of a murky past of legend and myth. Only in 1985, after a prolonged controversy and investigation which required American forensic expertise—and even a fencing master's guidance—were the real remains of Pizarro identified. Pizarro was killed in 1541 by conspirators of a rival band of conquistadores who resented his control over the Inca riches. He put up a fierce fight against tough odds, just as he had against the Inca army. He was buried in an unmarked niche in the Cathedral, as was the custom in that age.

But at the start of the twentieth century, the Peruvian government wanted to honor the legendary Spanish adventurer and in the rush to meet the ceremony's deadline insufficient care was placed in making sure that they had the right corpse. An "impostor" occupied Pizarro's crypt for seventy-five years. Finally, during a major restoration of part of the Cathedral, more bones were found where historical archives said that Pizarro's remains should have lain. It dawned on some specialists that an error had been made, but few authorities wanted to recognize that the wrong Pizarro had been the recipient of honors and visits by thousands of tourists. Finally, a U.S.-Peruvian team was able to reconstruct the exact circumstances of Pizarro's death, use Carbon-14 methods to date the disputed remains, and finally single out saber wounds on one set of bones and skull to permit positive identification.

Every weekday at the Presidential Palace there is a changing of the guard ceremony with full military pomp and circumstance. Though the

Palace itself was built this century after a fire damaged the previous building, there is a fig tree in an interior patio allegedly planted by Pizarro himself. Another yet unproven belief from colonial times is that there is an intricate system of underground passages which connects the Palace with the Cathedral and other churches in the downtown area. Facing the Cathedral, the Lima City Hall often has art exhibits or music festivals either in its facilities or on the Plaza itself. In the third week of January, each year, the city government pulls out all stops to celebrate the anniversary of its founding.

Within what is called *Lima cuadrada,* or the Lima grid, you will find most of the historical sites that date from colonial times. The original streets of old Lima acquired names that harked to the shops or residents along them. Names like Blue Powders (*Polvos Azules,* named after a special dye brought from Europe and distributed at a store on this street), Tailors, and Scribes are still used by the stubborn to identify streets. Polvos Azules, alongside the Rimac River between the Presidential Palace and the Central Post Office, is today a hurly-burly street vendors' market, which does have some handicraft stalls. The rest of the merchandise is black market contraband, tax-evading Peruvian goods, and products from the shantytowns' cottage industries.

As Lima was the seat of royal authority in South America, it was also the center of church authority. From it, missionaries set out to convert the "pagan" masses of Andean peasants. Back to Lima came its wealth. Because the Church has had continuity over the centuries and been less prone to seeing its centers of worship deteriorate, many more of its colonial structures have endured through earthquakes, civil wars, and foreign occupations. The most impressive churches are the San Francisco complex and San Pedro Church. The Casa de Osambela near the Plaza de Armas has recently been restored and frequently houses art exhibits.

Adobe and Quincha

The traditional construction material through Colonial and Republican times was adobe and *quincha,* a kind of plasterboard made out of reed matting and stucco. Both materials were—and are—cheap to produce and amazingly resilient to earthquakes and tremors since they bend and shift with the earth movements. They crack and crumble instead of shattering and collapsing. A drawback, however, is that they require consistent maintenance. Unless colonial buildings are held by public institutions or culturally minded private owners, landlords are not inclined to sink their money into keeping the old quarters in perfect condition, especially since many of them have been subdivided into tenements. In the past fifty years there has also been a shift toward bricks, concrete, and reinforced steel in new construction, which means that skilled labor for adobe and quincha techniques is becoming scarce. However, in the past decade there has been a revival of interest in alternative building methods and in the colonial heritage, which has meant that scores of buildings are being slowly returned to their past glory.

The Spaniards taught Indian craftsmen how to work stone and wood to adorn their churches and residences. But the Andean craftsmen rose above simple repetition of the baroque and rococo styles which were dear to the hearts of viceroys and courtesans. They infused their creations with an Andean sense of dimension and proportion. Altars, archways, and pulpits give testimony to their painstaking talents in the guise of modest crafts. A similar style also evolved in colonial paintings in which Christ, saints, archangels, and devils took on the trappings of viceregal-Andean Peru. Most of these Andean artists remain nameless today.

Another colonial structure which survives is the fortress Real Felipe in the port city of Callao. It was built in the mid-1700s to defend the viceregal capital from marauding English and Dutch buccaneers. It replaced fortifications which were destroyed by an earthquake and tidal wave. It is a formidable construction and during the War of Independence royalist troops held out for eighteen months of siege by the patriots. Lima itself was surrounded by fortifications which were pulled down in 1869 as a forewarning of the coming urban expansion.

The Plaza de Armas and the other main Lima square, Plaza San Martín, named after the Argentine patriot who came to the aid of Peruvian liberals in 1821, are connected by the Jiron de la Union. Up to the 1950s, it was the chic place to stroll and chat in the cafes in the evenings. Now it has been transformed into a pedestrian mall. The Plaza San Martín is the commercial heart of the downtown area. The Nicolas de Píerola Avenue, nicknamed *La Colmena* (The Beehive), crosses it. The Union-Colmena axis has plenty of shops, restaurants, and other attractions.

The Republican Continuance

Lima was founded so that the capital would be near the ocean, making it easier to ship any conquered wealth back to the metropolis via Panama. Pizarro, however, turned the city away from the ocean by placing it well inland. But no city can deny its roots, and the drift of Lima has been away from the downtown district toward the ocean and the southern suburbs. San Isidro was once a district of country houses for Lima's well-off classes and of fields to produce food for the capital. Miraflores, Barranco, and Chorrillos were small resort towns for summer weekends.

But in the past half century these districts became the core of Lima and the preferred residential neighborhoods of the middle class, with their gardens, parks, and tree-lined boulevards. Recently, residences were followed by high-rise apartment buildings, office towers, shops, boutiques, plush restaurants, and breezy cafes. Several tasteful shopping galleries give a chance to see what is available. The expressway, alternatively called the Paseo de la Republica or *el Zanjón* (the Ditch, because it runs below the normal ground level), was built in the late 1960s to connect the downtown district with the southern boroughs.

Nightlife is centered in Miraflores and another former beach resort, Barranco. During the weekends, Miraflores's Central Park takes on a festive atmosphere. Artists set up street markets for portraits, copies of colonial painting, and landscapes. A nearby bazaar also sells trinkets and crafts. The pizza parlors, cafes, restaurants, theaters, and movie houses buzz. In many ways, Lima still has the customs of a small town: it is possible to meet almost anyone you know strolling around or drinking coffee in Miraflores, just as a half-century ago the Jiron de la Union would have been the rendezvous.

Barranco, on the other hand, has kept part of its quaint taste of the late nineteenth century. The tracks of the trolley cars which used to bring summer bathers to the neighborhood until the 1960s can still be seen on a main street. A strong community effort has preserved many of the old buildings and banned high-rise apartments. Barranco is the haunt of artists, writers, intellectuals, and just plain revelers in a night of song and atmosphere. There is an active circuit of small restaurants and cafes which offer live performances of music, poetry, and drama, as well as exhibits of paintings and sculptures. One treasure of the community is the Bridge of Sighs, *El*

Puente de los Suspiros, which crosses a steep pathway down to the ocean shore. The tree-lined lane is closely tied to *criollo,* guitar music, poetry, bittersweet romance, and nostalgia.

Creole music is a vibrant vestige of Lima's bygone eras. Musicians frequently gather in *peñas,* special Creole restaurants, to sing the classics and improvise new ones in a bohemian atmosphere which can sometimes last until the wee hours of the morning. The mainstay of Creole music is the *vals,* but aside from the three-beat cadence there is nothing Viennese about it. The *marinera* and the *tondero* are more native musical forms which originated with coastal dance forms. These are usually danced with a white handkerchief in each partner's hand and waved to the beat. Creole music has also been enriched by black rhythms and there are many black groups which dance and perform at the *peñas* and tourist attractions. A distinctive Afro-Peruvian instrument is the *cajón,* quite literally a crate, which gives a hoarse, muted rhythmical accompaniment to the guitars. The instrument, however, has evolved and is now made by craftsmen out of cured wood.

While Creole music is an echo from the coast, Andean music, like the *huayno* and *mulizas,* has come to Lima with all the provincial migrants. There are thousands of distinctive forms and styles of this music, which is cultivated by Lima clubs and social associations from each region and district in the Sierra. But the music is only part of the pageant, as the music is meant to go with the dances. The dances themselves are dramatic reenactments of important events and may require elaborate, colorful costumes.

Sandwiched Between Sea and Sierra

The Bay of Chorrillos stretches all the way from the port of Callao on the north to Friar's Leap near Chorrillos on the south. Off Callao lie two islands, San Lorenzo and El Fronton, which was a maximum security prison, a Peruvian Alcatraz. Several of Lima's best restaurants are located on the beaches of Miraflores, Barranco, and Chorrillos. Although the weather does not always invite people to take a dip in the ocean, the salty air does stir up an appetite and Peruvian cuisine can satisfy it. Sunsets on the Pacific horizon are spectacular, Lima's overcasting permitting.

The Herradura cove, farther south of the Friar's Leap, was the favorite beach of pre-1960s Lima. A trolley line used to connect the cove to downtown Lima and the rest of the city, but the only thing remaining from that old piece of history is the narrow tunnel through a hill leading back to Lima. Herradura has several restaurants, but it is best for drinking a couple of beverages and watching the surf.

At the other extreme of Lima's waterfront is Ancon, a beach resort. It is still favored by Limeños who rent or own apartments there for the summer. During the winter, however, the town goes dead and there are few restaurants for day outings.

When winter (a usage which is stretching the definition to its limits) sets in, Lima is locked in by perennial overcasting (*neblina*) and heavy humidity. This climate has been known to send foreign residents into a state of depression, a kind of ongoing anticlimax because the body chemistry senses that a rainstorm should set in. The remedy for this malady, which also strikes native Limeños as well, is an excursion to Chosica, just fifteen miles up the Central Highway. Restaurants with recreational facilities, clubs, and parks offer sunny skies and clear Sierra air because the town is well up the Rimac River Valley. A trip to Chosica also shows how close the Andes really are to Lima because the valley narrows and the highway starts hugging the slopes to wind its way up.

PRACTICAL INFORMATION FOR LIMA

GETTING AROUND LIMA. From the airport. Stepping out of the baggage area of the Lima international airport can be a bewildering experience, if there is no one waiting to meet a visitor. Seemingly hundreds of people press in on incoming passengers. Lima still has a small-town attitude toward international travel: greeting a friend or relative is a major event. Despite improvements in security screening at the airport in late 1990, the State Department reported at press time that specialists still found inadequate adherence to international aviation security standards. In addition, there are hotel reps, tour organizers, and taxi drivers, all trying to make a buck. Keep your calm. Taxis to hotels cost $13–$20. Do not accept the first driver who approaches; have a look at the car first to make sure it's in good condition. A bus service to hotels, *Trans Hotel* (51–8011/airport, 46–9872/Miraflores), which is located directly in front of the airport exit, costs about $5, but is slower. Trans Hotel can also pick up travelers at their hotels to go to the airport.

By taxi. VW "bugs" with red-and-white "taxi" stickers on the windshield or roof-light are a convenient, though cramped, means of getting around Lima. Other model cars, including vintage models, charge slightly more. Taxis do not use meters. Fares start at the equivalent of $1 and should be agreed on before starting. Hotel taxis (black sedans) have more expensive rates, by trip and hour, which are posted in hotel lobbies. Charges go up 50% after midnight and on holidays.

By bus. Public transport in Lima relies almost exclusively on buses, but they are usually overcrowded, uncomfortable, and sometimes unsafe. There are hundreds of routes, some run by cooperatives, others by private owners, and still others by public companies. It is extremely cheap, 10 cents a fare. A visitor is wise to stick with the large, yellow, state-run (Enatruperu) buslines until he knows the city well. A mistake can leave a passenger stranded.

By colectivo. There are two main routes: one starts from near the corner of Avenidas Wilson and Nicolas de Piérola, downtown, and leaves for the airport when it has a full passenger load. The fare is about 20 cents. A second runs from near the Riviera Hotel downtown, and the Miraflores shopping district. A third route goes to the winter resort town of Chosica, 30 kilometers up the Central Highway. The departure point is across from Parque Universitario on Nicolas de Pierola, near Plaza San Martín.

Car Rentals. All agencies have airport offices. *Avis,* Sheraton Hotel (32–7245), *Hertz* (42–1566), Jiron Ocoña 262, downtown Lima; 550 Rivera Navarrete, San Isidro; 340 Pardo Avenue, Miraflores. *National* (23–2526), 449 Espana Avenue, downtown Lima; 319 Diez Canseco, Miraflores (44–2333). *Budget* (44–4546), Civic Center next to the Sheraton Hotel, 514 Corpac, San Isidro (41–1129); the Saga shopping complex, San Isidro. *Dollar Rent-a-car,* (44–4920), La Paz 430, Miraflores; 333 Mexico Avenue, La Victoria.

HOTELS. Lima has excellent hotels, suited to a range of tastes and budgets. Those in downtown Lima are close to museums and colonial churches, but can be noisy. Those in San Isidro and Miraflores are generally newer, in more pleasant settings, and near evening entertainment and the better shopping centers. See "Facts at Your Fingertips" earlier in this chapter for definitions of price categories.

Super Deluxe

Cesar's, corner of La Paz and Diez Canseco, Miraflores (44–1212). A swank 150-room hotel which pioneered the move to residential neighborhoods. Air-conditioned. A rooftop restaurant and bar, "La Azotea," with marvelous view. Pool and sauna. At press time, the hotel was in the process of building 58 more rooms, each equipped with an extra-large bath.

Sheraton, 170 Paseo de la Republica, downtown Lima (33–3320). A 490-room air-conditioned hotel centrally located and in the Sheraton's best international standard. Shopping gallery, three restaurants, tennis courts, pool, and sauna.

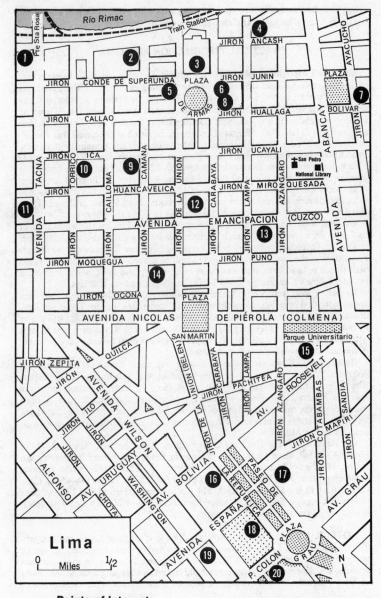

Points of Interest

1) Church of Santa Rosa
2) Church of Santo Domingo
3) Palacio de Gobierno
4) San Francisco Church
5) Palacio Municipal
6) Palacio Arzobispal
7) Congreso
8) Cathedral
9) Church of San Augustin
10) Municipal Theater
11) Church of Las Nazarenas
12) La Merced Church
13) Trinity Church
14) Church of Jesus Maria
15) San Marcos Universidad
16) Civic Center
17) Palacio de Justicia
18) Museum of Italian Art
19) U.S. Embassy
20) National Museum of Art

Deluxe

Bolívar, Plaza San Martín, downtown Lima (27–6400). This air-conditioned, 350-room hotel is the preferred of jaded foreign correspondents. Guests get a taste for what Lima was like 50 years ago. Excellent restaurant and legendary pisco sour.

Crillon, 589 Nicolas de Píerola, downtown Lima (28–3290). An air-conditioned, 515-room, full-service hotel with the "Skyroom" restaurant as an added plus. Folk music and dance every night.

Diplomat, 290 Alcanflores, Miraflores (44–1199). A 130-room luxury hotel. Restaurant open 24 hours. Piano bar.

El Condado, 465 Alcanfores, Miraflores (44–3614). Nicely done with 69 air-conditioned rooms, some with sauna. Two restaurants.

El Pardo, 420 Pardo Avenue, Miraflores (47–0348). New, 120 rooms, restaurant, and pool.

Maria Angola, 610 La Paz, Miraflores (44–1280). Small with 70 rooms but one of the most stylish lodgings in Lima. An excellent restaurant, Los Faisanes, on the basement floor.

Expensive

Apart-Hotel Los Galgos, 329 Alcanfores, Miraflores (46–0986). Offers 24 suites with kitchenette.

Ariosto Hostal Residencial, 769 La Paz, Miraflores (44–1416). Convenient alternative to a full-service hotel. Conference room. Fax and telex available. 75 rooms.

Exclusive, 550 San Martín, Miraflores (44–1919). 42 rooms.

Hotel Libertador, 500 Los Eucaliptos, San Isidro (41–6492). Offers 52 rooms with access to sports facilities of nearby country club.

Hotel Residencial Ritz, 2599 Salaverry Avenue, Magdalena del Mar (40–1595). 26 suites with kitchenette. Continental breakfast included.

Jose Antonio, 398 28 de Julio, Miraflores (45–6870). New; 56 rooms and restaurant.

La Hacienda, 511 Av. 28 de Julio, Miraflores (44–4346). New; 57 rooms and piano bar. Conference room and sauna.

Resort and Convention Hotel Pueblo Inn, Kilometer 11, Central Highway, Chaclacayo (91–0876/Chaclacayo, 35–0777/Lima). Removed from urban hassles in the Sierra foothills, this 172-room hotel is an experience unto itself. Meticulously modeled after an Andean village, it offers two restaurants, sports and recreational facilities, including pool, sauna, and tennis courts. Sunday barbecue is Lima attraction.

Riviera, 981 Inca Garcilaso de la Vega, downtown Lima (28–9460). A traditional hotel of the business district, 185 rooms, restaurants.

Moderate

El Doral, 486 José Pardo, Miraflores (47–6305, 47–3233). 36 rooms, some with kitchenette; pool.

El Marquez de San Isidro, 461 Chinchón, San Isidro (42–0311). Breakfast included.

El Plaza, 850 Nicolas de Píerola, downtown Lima (28–6270). Modern facilities with 56 air-conditioned rooms and restaurant in downtown area.

Garden, 450 Rivera Navarrete, San Isidro (42–1771). 53 rooms and restaurant, located in a new business district.

Gran Hotel Miraflores, 151 28 de Julio, Miraflores (47–9641). Recently remodeled with 81 rooms and restaurant.

Hostal Beech, 165 Libertadores, San Isidro (40–5595). Run by an American expatriate, 22 rooms, favored by frequent travelers to Peru. Breakfast included.

Hostal Granada, 323 Huancavelica, downtown Lima (279–033). 20 rooms.

Hostal La Esperanza, 350 Esperanza, Miraflores (444–909).

Hostal Polonia, 6599 República de Panama, Miraflores (45–6590). 33 rooms and restaurant.

Hostal Regina, 1421 Av. Dos de Mayo, San Isidro (22–1708).

Hostal San Martin, 882 Nicolas de Píerola, downtown Lima (28–5337). Fourteen air-conditioned rooms on Plaza San Martin.

Sans Souci, 2670 Arequipa, San Isidro (22–6035). 24 rooms.

Savoy, 224 Cailloma, downtown Lima (28–3520).

Las Suites, 466 Grau, Miraflores (47–6415). Air-conditioned suites with kitchenettes.

Suite Service, 111 Grimaldo del Solar, Miraflores (441–712).

Suites Larco, San Martin and Larco, Miraflores (46–1461). 14 suites with kitchenettes.

Inexpensive

Continental, 196 Puno, downtown Lima (27–5890). 100 rooms and restaurant.

Hostal Armendariz, 375 Av. Armendariz, Miraflores (453–239).

Hostal El Ovalo, 1110 Pardo, Miraflores (46–5549). 20 rooms in a quiet neighborhood.

Hostal Miraflores, 5444 Petit Thouars, Miraflores (45–8745). 40 rooms.

Hostal Renacimiento, 52–54 Parque Hernan Velarde, Lima (31–8461). Nicely restored colonial building on a quaint sidestreet between downtown and San Isidro. Breakfast included.

Hostal Residencial Collacocha, 100 Coronel Andres Reyes, San Isidro (42–3900).

Hostal Residencial Colonial Inn, 310 Comandante Espinar, Miraflores (46–6666). 14 rooms and restaurant.

Hostal Residencial La Castellana, 222 Grimaldo del Solar, Miraflores (444–662).

Hostal Residencial San Francisco, 340 Ancash, downtown Lima (28–3643). 36 rooms, but always crowded with European backpackers.

Hostal Residencial San Isidro Inn, 1765 Juan Pezet, San Isidro (41–5073). 30 rooms and restaurant.

Hostal Roma, 315 Jiron Ica, downtown Lima (27–7576). Clean, well run. In big demand on backpacking circuit.

Hostal Senorial Miraflores, 567 José Gonzales, Miraflores (45–9724). 30 rooms and restaurant. Nice garden.

Hostal Torreblanca, 1453 José Pardo, Miraflores (479–998). 14 rooms, breakfast included.

Pension Alemana, 4704 Arequipa, Miraflores (45–6999). Breakfast included.

Youth Hostels. Youth Hostel, Casimiro Ulloa 328, Miraflores (46–5488). $4 for members of the Youth Hostels Federation; $5 for nonmembers.

RESTAURANTS. Lima has a taste for varied and delicious food. Practically all restaurants offer seafood and Creole cuisine, but a few throw in briny air and surf with their dishes. Besides Creole dishes, there are regional specialties from the northern and southern coasts (Trujillo and Arequipa) and the Andes. International cuisine is also available for the less adventurous.

The large Chinese community in Peru has created a taste for their distinctive food, slightly savored with a Spanish accent. Chinese cuisine, served at *chifas,* is a weekly must for most Peruvians. Chifas are usually closed on Mon. Japanese restaurants are also available.

For the American who longs for his country's contribution to world cuisine, there are a number of American-style restaurants offering everything from southern-fried chicken to pizza.

Finally, several hotels—Cesar's, Crillon, Bolívar, Sheraton, and Plaza—all have restaurants and cafes which can be recommended on their own right. You don't have to be a guest there to take a shot at their cuisine.

For definitions of price categories, see "Facts at Your Fingertips."

Creole

Los Condes de San Isidro. *Expensive.* 290 Paz Soldán, San Isidro (22–2557). A former colonial hacienda house converted to a unique eating experience.

Jose Antonio. *Moderate.* 200 B. Monteagudo, San Isidro (61–9923). An excellent intro to local cuisine.

El Otro Sitio. *Moderate.* 317 Sucre, Barranco (772–413). On weekends, folk and Creole music enliven the meals. Offers popular Creole buffet.

Las Trece Monedas. *Moderate.* 536 Ancash, downtown Lima (27–6547). A colonial residence turned restaurant. Best option is lunch.

Los Balcones de Barranco. *Moderate.* 294 Grau, Barranco (45–4961). One of several great places to dine in this relaxing seaside suburb.

Bar Cordano. *Inexpensive.* Ancash and Carabaya, in downtown Lima, across from Desamparados train station. Turn-of-the-century atmosphere.

Las Tejas. *Inexpensive.* 340 Diez Canseco, Miraflores (44–4360). Shishkebabed beefheart *(antecuchos)* and other Creole delicacies. You can watch your food being prepared if there is a table available near the entrance.

Meson de Los Angeles. *Inexpensive.* Alemeda de los Descalzos, Rimac (27–2425). Lunches and dinners in a restored Franciscan monastery.

1900. *Inexpensive.* 1030 Unión, downtown Lima (23–3590). Formerly housed the U.S. Embassy and historical monument, now a handicrafts arcade with convenient restaurant in patio.

International

Carlin. *Expensive.* 646 La Paz, Miraflores (44–4134). Upscale but meets the highest cuisine standards.

La Carreta. *Expensive.* 740 Rivera Navarrete, San Isidro (405–424). A classy steakhouse, rustic yet elegant.

Meson Real. *Expensive.* 500 Av. Camino Real, San Isidro (22–0813). Steakhouse near Lima's swankiest shopping center.

Pabellon de Caza and Bwana Grill. *Expensive.* 1196 Alonso de Molina, Monterrico, 100 yards from the Gold Museum (37–9533). You pay for the decor, but the food does not let you down.

The Steak House. *Expensive.* 642 La Paz, Miraflores (44–3110). For the steak-and-potatoes crowd.

El Suche. *Expensive.* 646 La Paz, Miraflores (455–592). Nice scene for couples; salad bar and piano music.

Bavaria. *Moderate.* 220 Diagonal, Miraflores (46–5144). As the name implies, strong on German food.

Blue Moon. *Moderate.* 2526 Pumacahua, Lince (70–1190). A bit out of the way, but worth the search.

Café Paris. *Moderate.* 722 Nicolas de Píerola, downtown Lima (32–3059). Good service, also serves up good Creole food.

Casa Vasca. *Moderate.* 734 Nicolas de Píerola, downtown Lima (23–6690). Spanish cuisine.

Cheese and Wine. *Moderate.* El Alamo shopping gallery, corner of La Paz and Diez Canseco, Miraflores (no phone). Cozy little corner with cheese fondues and wine.

La Creperie. *Moderate.* 635 La Paz, Miraflores (44–1800). Lives up to its name, as well as French cuisine in general.

L'Eau Vive. *Moderate.* 370 Ucayali, downtown Lima (27–5612). A restored Republican house, with service provided by singing nuns. Inexpensive lunches available.

La Ermita. *Moderate.* 340 Baja de los Banos, Barranco (671–791). Dine on delicious seafood in a comfortable loft setting surrounded by trees and plants.

Los Faisanes. *Moderate.* 610 La Paz, Miraflores (44–1280). Fast becoming a preferred restaurant. Located on the basement floor of Maria Angola Hotel.

Granja Azul. *Moderate.* Near El Pueblo Hotel, Kilometer 11, Central Highway (35–2606). Eat all the barbecued chicken you can for set price.

La Parrillada. *Moderate.* Next to the Hotel Bolivar and Plaza San Martín. Fine steak and baked potatoes.

La Pizzería. *Moderate.* 322 Diagonal, Miraflores (46–7793). A perennial favorite for leisurely lunch or dinner, more than a pizza parlor.

El Puente. *Moderate.* 343 Baja de los Banos, Barranco (67–1886). Near Bridge of Sighs, in restored house near the sea.

Raimondi. *Moderate.* 110 Jiron Miro Quesada, downtown 27–7933). So well-known there's no street sign. Interior of ornately carved wood. Extensive menu; good food.

Rincon Gaucho. *Moderate.* Parque Salazar, Miraflores (47–4778). Dine on savory Argentine beef from a table overlooking the Pacific.

El Rodizio. *Moderate*. Corner of Av. Santa Cruz and Ovalo Gutierrez (45–0889). Brazilian-style meats.

San Tropéz. *Moderate*. 100 Tudela y Varela, San Isidro (40–3087). Unpretentious place with fine eating.

La Tranquera. *Moderate*. 285 José Pardo, Miraflores (47–5111). Argentine beef and rustic gaucho atmosphere.

Valentino. *Moderate*. 215 Manuel Bañon, San Isidro (41–6174). Strong on Italian and French, but multilingual.

Oriental

El Dorado. *Moderate*. 2450 Arequipa, 18th floor, San Isidro (22–1080). Chifa with a magnificent night view of Lima.

Fuji. *Moderate*. 4090 Paseo de la República, Miraflores (40–8531). Japanese.

Izakaya. *Moderate*. 2704 Aviacion, San Borja (75–1586). Japanese.

Lung Fung. *Moderate*. 3165 República de Panama, San Isidro (22–6382). The Emperor of the chifas.

Matsuei Sushi. *Moderate*. 236 Canada, La Victoria (72–2282). Japanese.

Mi Casa. *Moderate*. 150 Augusto Tamayo, San Isidro (40–3780). Japanese.

Shanghai, *Moderate*. Av. San Luis 1988, San Borja (35–9132). Spicy Szechuan.

Chinatown. *Inexpensive*. 379 Manuel de Pino, Lince (72–2253). Quality Chinese meals in plain but comfortable refurbished house.

Seafood

La Costa Verde. *Expensive*. Barranquito Beach, Barranco (67–8218). On the beach. The desserts are worth the meal.

La Rosa Naútica. *Expensive*. Espigon No. 4, Costa Verde, Miraflores (47–0057). An art-deco restaurant on a pier.

El Salto del Fraile. *Expensive*. Herradura Beach, Chorrillos (42–6622). A cliffside perch.

La Caleta. *Moderate*. 126 D. Derterano, San Isidro (42–3835).

Don Beta. *Moderate*. 667 Jose Galvez, Miraflores (469–465). One of the best seafood joints in town.

El Rincon del Pescador. *Moderate*. 598 Nicolas de Píerola. A quiet, comfortable place to eat good seafood amid the bustle of downtown Lima (24–1706).

Todo Fresco. *Moderate*. 110 Miguel Dasso, San Isidro (40–7955).

American-Style/Fast Food

Bon Beef. *Inexpensive*. 395 Camino Real, San Isidro (419–061). The closest you'll come to a McDonald's or Burger King in Peru.

Kentucky-Fried Chicken. *Inexpensive*. 4310 Arequipa, Miraflores (45–6616); 1650 Javier Prado, San Isidro (40–5195); and corner of Benavides and Artesanos, Surco (47–0016).

Pizza Hut. *Inexpensive*. 202 Comandante Espinar, Miraflores (47–0984).

Cafes and Bars. Lima is European in its approach to casual eating. Sidewalk cafes and the like are always well-populated. Talk can range from business to politics and the soccer championship. The cafes also tend to attract the foreign crowd as well.

The Brenchley Arms. *Moderate*. 174 Atahualpa, Miraflores (45–9680). English-style, English-speaking pub. Serves top-notch lamb chops.

Johann Sebastian Bar. *Moderate*. 3rd block of Schell, Miraflores. Drinks and classical music in a dimly lit room.

La Sueca. *Moderate*. 759 Larco, Miraflores (45–9733). For the pastry-and-chat crowd, preferred by Europeans.

Vivaldi. *Moderate*. 258 Ricardo Palma, Miraflores (47–1636). Up-market cafe which also serves good food.

Domino. *Inexpensive*. Pasaje Boza, downtown Lima. Near the Plaza San Martín. German atmosphere and also an inexpensive lunch.

D'Onofrio. *Inexpensive.* 147 Miguel Dasso, San Isidro and 401 Lima, Miraflores (45–0402). Serves snacks and ice cream treats.

Haiti. *Inexpensive.* 160 Diagonal, Miraflores (47–5052). A social hub of Miraflores. Stick to coffee, beer, and sandwiches, because the cooking is strictly greasy-spoon.

Indianopolis. *Inexpensive.* 110 Jose Pardo, Miraflores (45–7431). Also serves meals in a moderately-priced restaurant.

Quattro D. *Inexpensive.* 408 Angamos, Miraflores (47–1524). Italian ice cream, deserts, and espresso coffee.

La Tiendecita Blanca. *Inexpensive.* Larco 111, Miraflores (45–9797). Popular rallying point with good pastries.

TOURIST INFORMATION. The state tourist agency Foptur has a tourist information office in nearly every state capital and major city. The main office is in Lima at Andres Reyes 320, telephone 41–4700, 70–0781, 70–1978. Lima information booths are at the airport (524–416), and downtown at 1066 Jiron de la Union (Belen) (323–559).

TOURS. Although repeating common sense advice, use the services of an established tourism agency for sightseeing tours in Lima. Many individuals may offer to show you the sights, but there is no guarantee that they will live up to their promises. Lima is a sprawling city in which streets frequently change names and good directions are hard to come by. That is just one reason for using an agency, which can relieve the tension from a first reconnoiter of the city. The leading agencies for sightseeing are:

CBS Tours, 274 Miguel Dasso, San Isidro (70–4090).

Condor Travel, 677 Nicolas de Píerola, 2nd floor, downtown Lima (28–9845).

Dasatour, 331 José del Llano Zapata, 9th floor, Miraflores (41–5045).

Explorandes, 159 Bolognesi, Miraflores (45–0532).

Huron Travel Agency, 780 Camaná, office 510, downtown Lima (28–6314).

Lima Tours, 1040 Unión, downtown Lima (27–6720). New offices at Los Rosales 436, San Isidro (42–0750), and Jose Pardo 392, Miraflores (46–4991).

Receptour, Rufino Torrico 889, near Hotel Crillon, downtown Lima (31–2022).

Turicentro, 497 José Pardo, Miraflores (46–1773).

MUSEUMS AND SIGHTS. Lima has fine museums and private collections that are open to the public. There is no single museum that can give a visitor an elementary appreciation of the breadth and range of Peru's cultural wealth. Museums have limited space and were not originally designed for exhibition. Some of the most striking pieces are locked away in storage, to be rotated periodically. Security concerns also mean that gold and silver pieces cannot be displayed openly. In 1983, the National Archeology Museum was robbed of its most prized gold pieces. The best advice is to combine visits to a larger museum with two or three private collections, like the Gold and the Amano museums, to get a comprehensive view. Unless otherwise stated, most museums charge small admission fees.

National Anthropology and Archaeology Museum, Plaza Bolívar, Pueblo Libre (63–5070), Daily, 9 A.M.–6 P.M. A survey of pre-Columbian cultures.

National Museum of History, Plaza Bolívar, Pueblo Libre, adjacent to the Archeology Museum (63–2009), Mon.–Sat., 8:30 A.M.–6 P.M.; Sun., 10 A.M.–5 P.M. Both South American patriots San Martín and Bolívar lived in this house during the War of Independence. Furniture, paintings, and restoration display the ambience of the period.

Amano Museum, Retiro 160, Miraflores (41–2909), Mon.–Fri., 2–5 P.M. By appointment only, with guided tour. A fine private collection, especially of Chancay textiles. Not to be missed.

Rafael Larco Herrera Archeology Museum, 1515 Bolivar, Pueblo Libre (61–1312), Mon.–Sat., 9 A.M.–1 P.M.; 3–6 P.M. Sun. 9 A.M.–1 P.M. Huge private collection of pre-Hispanic ceramics and textiles, including erotic pottery.

Gold Museum, 7th block of Prolongación Primavera Avenue, Monterrico (35–2917), daily noon–7 P.M. A private collection of pre-Columbian gold and silver which has been exhibited around the world. Also a weapons display on the main floor.

Museum of Art, 125 Paseo de Colón, downtown Lima (23–4732), Tues.–Sun., 9 A.M.–6 P.M. Three thousand years of art, antiques, and culture on exhibit.

Museum of the Inquisition, 528 Junin, downtown Lima, Mon.–Fri., 9 A.M.–7:30 P.M.; Sat. 9 A.M.–4:30 P.M. Free. A quirky little museum on the "art" of getting confessions out of heretics. Excavations and mannequins show torture techniques. Also site of first Congress, with fine carved roof beams and ceilings.

Museum of the Central Reserve Bank, Jiron Lampa 271, intersection with Ucayali, downtown Lima (27–6250), Tues.–Sat., 10 A.M.–5 P.M.; Sun., 10 A.M.–1 P.M. Small but solid display of pre-Columbian pottery and gold, with an art gallery. Coins from those first minted by the Spanish crown to modern day medallions.

Numismatic Museum, Banco Wiese, 2nd floor, 245 Cusco, downtown Lima (27–5060, ext. 553), Mon.–Fri. 9 A.M.–1 P.M. Free. Coins from colonial times to the present.

Peruvian Health Sciences Museum, 270 Junin, downtown Lima (27–0190), Mon.–Sat., 9 A.M.–5 P.M. Pre-Columbian medical and surgical practices explained. Can also arrange to prepare pre-Columbian meals if there is a minimum of 15 people.

National Museum of Peruvian Culture, 650 Alfonso Ugarte, downtown Lima (23–5892), Mon.–Sat., 9:30 A.M.–1:30 P.M. Displays the way popular culture has manifested itself over three thousand years.

Contemporary Folk Art Museum, 163 Seco Olivero, downtown Lima, Tues.–Fri., 2:30–7 P.M.; Sat., 8:30 A.M.–noon. A surprisingly well done intro to the folk art traditions of Peru. Some handicrafts on display are on sale in museum shops.

National Museum, 2465 Javier Prado Ave., San Borja (37–7822, 37–7776), Tues.–Fri. 9 A.M.–7 P.M., Sat.–Sun. 10 A.M.–7 P.M. Newly opened in the expansive building that once housed the fisheries ministry. The collection is still incomplete.

Other private collections. Gold collection belonging to Mrs. Elsa Cohen has been recently relocated to first-floor mezzanine of Banco Wiese, 245 Cuzco, downtown Lima (275–060). Open during banking hours. Enrico Poli collection of pre-Columbian gold and ceramics, Lord Cochrane 466, Miraflores (22–2437). All of these collections may be seen by appointment. There is no guarantee that English is spoken, but visitors are welcome. Each collection is the result of a lifetime dedication to Peruvian culture.

CHURCHES AND HISTORICAL SITES. Lima has little gems of 16th-, 17th-, and 18th-century architecture, stone- and wood-work. **The Cathedral,** Plaza de Armas. Daily 10 A.M.–1 P.M., 2–5 P.M. A Museum of Religious Art is also open to the public. The crypt of Francisco Pizarro is on display. Most of the Cathedral's facade dates from this century, having been seriously damaged by several earthquakes, but parts of its interior go back centuries. **San Francisco,** corner of Lampa and Ancash. Daily 10 A.M.–1 P.M., 3–6 P.M. Visit the church, chapels, monastery, and colonial catacombs. A major restoration in progress has uncovered striking colonial fresco paintings. Sevillan tilework was brought to Lima as ballast in Spanish galleys which took gold bullion back to the metropolis. **San Pedro,** corner of Azangaro and Ucayali. Daily 7 A.M.–12:30 P.M., 6–8 P.M. Well preserved with exquisite chapel and patio built by the Jesuits. **Jesus Maria,** corner of Camaná and Moquegua. Daily 7 A.M.–1 P.M., 3–7 P.M. **San Agustin,** corner of Ica and Camaná. Daily 8:30 A.M.–noon, 3:30–5:30 P.M. Under reconstruction due to earthquake damage, but parts of it can be seen. **La Merced,** corner of Unión and Miro Quesada. Daily 7 A.M.–12:30 P.M., 4–8 P.M. Convent daily 8 A.M.–noon, 3–5:30 P.M. The oldest church in Lima, originally founded in 1534. **Santo Domingo,** first block off Camaná near the post office. Daily 7 A.M.–1 P.M., 4–8 P.M. Monastery and tombs Mon.–Sat. 9:30 A.M.–12:30 P.M., 3:30–5:30 P.M. Sun. and holidays open mornings only. Original site of the first university in the Americas, San Marcos. Also the resting place of Santa Rosa, the first saint in the New World, and Saint Martín de Porras, the first saint of African descent in the Americas. **Las Nazarenas,** corner of Huancavelica and Tacna. Under restoration at press time. Daily 7–11:30 A.M., 4:30–8 P.M.

Convent of Los Descalzos, Alameda de los Descalzos, Rimac. Daily 8 A.M.–1 P.M., 3–6 P.M. The convent with its fine collection of colonial paintings, chapels, and cloisters is located on a picturesque though badly maintained park and dates from colonial times. Another colonial park, the *Paseo de Aguas,* can be seen at the same time. The convent also houses a restaurant.

There are colonial houses which have been opened to the public, either as historic relics, museums, public offices, or tourist attractions. **Casa de Aliaga,** 224 Unión. Can be visited only through Vista Tours (27–6624). The oldest house in the Americas continually inhabited by its owners. **Casa Pilatos,** 390 Ancash. Mon.–Fri. 8:30 A.M.–4:30 P.M. Houses of the National Institute of Culture. **Museum of the Viceroyalty and Quinta Presa,** Rimac, across the Rimac River from the Plaza de Armas. A colonial mansion recently restored. **Casa de Osambela,** Conde de Superunda 298, downtown Lima, two blocks from the Plaza de Armas. A large colonial house recently restored. Frequently opened for art exhibits, normally Mon.–Sat. 11 A.M.–7 P.M.

Real Felipe Fortress and Military Museum, Callao (29–0532), Tues.–Sat. 9:30 A.M.–2 P.M., about $1. Massive fortification which played a key role during Spanish rule and War of Independence.

ARCHAEOLOGICAL SITES. Although Lima's pre-Columbian ruins are less impressive than those elsewhere in the country, an effort has been made to preserve and reconstruct them. All sites are open Tues.–Sun., 10 A.M.–5 P.M., and cost about $2 to enter. Tours are available to most of them.

Cajamarquilla, 15 kilometers east of Lima off the Central Highway. Pre-Inca ruins under restoration.

Puruchuco, 8 kilometers east of Lima off the Central Highway. Restored pre-Inca ruins with small site museum.

Pachacamac, 31 kilometers south of Lima off the Panamerican Highway, Lurin, The most important religious center in the pre-Hispanic Andean world. Small site museum.

Huaca Huallamarca, corner of El Rosario and Nicolas de Rivera, San Isidro. Huaca Juliana, Gral. Borgoño and Ayacucho, near 46th block of Arequipa, Miraflores. Both these sites have been restored, including native plants from the pre-Columbian period. Small site museums are open.

PUBLIC EVENTS. Changing of the Guard, at the Presidential Palace on the Plaza de Armas, has evolved into a ritual. The crack army unit performs a modified, syncopated goosestep to a full military band. The ceremony usually takes place between noon and 1 P.M., but can vary because of protocol visits. Photos of the event must be taken from the far side of the street running in front of the government palace. Security troops prohibit tourists from crossing the street to the building's fence. **Roving ministrels and players** can frequently be seen playing on the passageways leading to the Plaza de Armas or at the Plaza San Martin. Some of them are excellent musicians and mimes. However, be wary of pickpockets who like to prey on bystanders. The city government frequently organizes **open-air concerts** at the Plaza de Armas or at the acoustic shell at the Campo de Marte park; other concerts are held at the acoustic shell at the Salazar park, at the end of Larco Ave. in Miraflores, overlooking the Pacific Ocean. Check newspapers for daily listings.

PARKS. Park of Legends, Pueblo Libre between Marina and Venezuela avenues, near the Catholic University. Tues.–Sun, 9 A.M.–5 P.M. Fee: about $1. Wildlife from Peru's three geographic regions in re-creations of their natural settings. A couple of lions and elephants marooned from a traveling circus add a little African flavor. The **Parque del Olivar** in San Isidro was originally an olive grove which was absorbed but not digested by Lima's urban growth. Some of the olive trees date from the 1600s. **Japanese Park,** next to the Ministry of Transportation, Av. 28 de Julio, downtown Lima. Open Tues.–Sun., 10 A.M.–7 P.M. A garden of South American and Japanese plants. A children's theater program is offered on some weekends.

BEACHES. The beaches in the immediate Metropolitan Lima area tend to be overcrowded and unsanitary during the Jan.-Mar. bathing season, but just 15 miles south of Lima beaches are less packed, except on weekends. Be sure to check surf conditions because some beaches have dangerous undertows. Among the nicest are the resort towns of Ancon to the north and Santa Maria to the south. "El Silencio" beach, 30 kilometers south of Lima, sports the briefest bikinis west of Rio, and Punta Hermosa nearby is a favorite surfing beach. It should be remembered that with an equatorial sun it is extremely easy to get burned. Large-brimmed hats, sun screens, and cautious exposure are recommended. It is also possible to camp at most beaches outside Lima.

SPECTATOR SPORTS. Bullfighting season starts in late Oct. and ends in early Dec., when a highly coveted award for matadors, the *Escapulario de Nuestro Señor de los Milagros,* is awarded. The bullfights are at the Plaza de Acho in Rimac, just over the Rimac River from Abancay Ave. They start at 3 in the afternoon, with three bullfighters killing two bulls each. The seats in the shade *(sombra)* are in great demand and must be bought ahead of time ($20 and up). The bullfighting season includes the world's finest matadores, and also is one of Lima's most sought-after social occasions. Sometimes, the president and the full cabinet can be seen in the stands. Other bullfights are frequently staged, though they are not as prestigious as the Nov. season at Acho. Consult with a travel agency for dates and advance tickets. There is also a bullfighting museum at the Acho Plaza which is open to the public, Mon.–Fri. 9 A.M.–1 P.M., 3–6 P.M. and Sat.–Sun. 9 A.M.–1 P.M.

The National Stadium is located only five blocks from the Sheraton Hotel, on the Paseo de la República. Most major outdoor sports events, including football, are staged here. Some international football matches are also held at the smaller but more modern stadium of Alianza Lima, on the corner of Abtao and Isabel la Catolica, La Victoria.

Horse Racing. Lima has a first-class horse racing track in the suburb of Monterrico. There are races on Tues., Thurs., Sat., and Sun. Betting is legal at the racetrack and there are authorized brokers. Lima Tours offers a night at the races with dinner at the clubhouse twice a week. Peru is also world famous for the breeding of the *Caballo de Paso,* a horse which is trained for a distinctive, leg-raising gait. There are frequent exhibitions of the breed. Foreigners are allowed into the members-only clubhouse if they show their passports.

GALLERIES. There is an active art community, as might be expected from the society which has felt the crosscurrents of European, Andean, and Oriental cultures in a unique way. Among the main art galleries in Miraflores are **Galeria 715,** 216 Benavides; **Galeria Moll,** 1150–8 Larco; **Galeria Trapecio,** 743 Larco; **Galeria 9,** 474 Benavides; **Galeria Forum,** 1150 Larco; and **Galeria Equus,** 501 Colon. In San Isidro, you'll find **Galeria Borkas,** 851 Las Camelias, while in Barranco there is **Galeria Praxis,** 689 San Martín.

SHOPPING. Lima has the advantage that handicrafts and other articles are assembled from all the regions of the country which have generated their own styles. Many shops have moved away from the clichéd tourist souvenirs to products of artistic beauty and usefulness. There are scores of handicraft markets on Marina Avenue, San Miguel, on the way to the airport. It's good for browsing just to see what kind of fare is available. In downtown Lima, Nicolas de Píerola (Colmena) and Unión avenues are lined with tourist shops. The state handicrafts promotional agency, **Artesanias del Peru,** Basadre 610, San Isidro, offers a wide selection of items. Fairs and exhibitions are organized regularly throughout the year and offer a great opportunity to meet many of the craftsmen who make the articles on sale. Check *The Lima Times* or other newspapers for the latest information.

There are several specialty shops which are highly recommended for their outstanding selection and attention to the public: **Los Alamos,** 991 Lurigancho, Zarate, Mon.-Sat. 10 A.M.–6 P.M., specializing in antique and utilitarian handicrafts, with quality weavings and ceramics. **Las Pallas,** 212 Cajamarca, Barranco. **Antisuyo,** 460 Tacna, Miraflores, specializing in Amazon handicrafts. **La Gringa,** 522 La Paz, Miraflores. **Kuntar Huasi,** 182 Ocheron, Miraflores, specializing in high-quality crafts from throughout the Andes. **Poco a Poco,** 712 Nicolas de Pierola, downtown Lima and 425 Juan de Arona, San Isidro. **Huamanqaqa** 1041-A Union, downtown Lima, with some of the biggest name craftsmen in Peru. **Silvania Prints,** 714 Nicolas de Píerola, Lima; 905 Conquistadores, San Isidro; Cesar's Hotel lobby, 463 La Paz, Miraflores. Unique designs in fabric and articles drawn from pre-Columbian motives.

A shopper can save wear and tear on shoes by going to shopping galleries. Among the most conveniently located are: **1900,** 1030 Union (or Belen), Lima; **El Alamo,** 5th block of La Paz, Miraflores; and **El Suche,** 6th block of La Paz, Miraflores.

Alpaca Yarn, Fabric, and Wear

In the past decade, Peru's alpaca industry has taken a leap forward in preparation and design. Products are now being exported to designers and shops in the United States and Europe. Buying a cut of cloth here can mean major savings and compensate for the cost of a tailor or seamstress when back home. Yarn is also available. Specialty shops include: **Alpaca 111**, 859 Larco, Miraflores, **Alphaka Fashions** and **Alphaka Boutique**, both located in El Suche gallery, 463 Alcanfores, Miraflores, and **Helen Hamann**, Tacna 370, Miraflores, and at the Gold Museum.

Silver Jewelry and Tablewear

Fine filigree work and flatware, traditional, classical, and modern design, are available in most shops. It's worth more than the money. Specialty shops include: **H. Stern**, in lobbies of the Bolívar, Sheraton, and Cesar's, as well as at the airport. **Camusso**, 782 Rivera Navarrete, San Isidro, has a wide selection of tableware. **Vicky's**, 783 Nicolas de Pierola and 160 Ocona, downtown Lima. **Joyeria Vasco**, 3440 Paseo de la Republica, San Isidro. **A. Johari**, 851 Union, downtown Lima. **Equus**, 501 Colon, Miraflores, is an art gallery but carries a permanent exhibition of unique silver jewelry which combines folk art techniques and imaginative design.

Antiques

Bargains can be found in many of Lima's antique shops, which have furniture, household items, and other objects from the past century. Many Peruvians just do not appreciate what they have in hand. Most shops can help prepare larger purchases for shipping. The better antique shops are: **Alcanfores**, 674 28 de Julio, Miraflores; **Atelier in Roma**, 306 Diez Canseco, Miraflores; **Casa Mas**, 814 Union, downtown Lima; **C. Iturriarte**, 511 La Paz, Miraflores; **Galeria del Arte Pardo**, 356 Pardo, Miraflores; **Miriam's Antiques**, 465–102 Alcanfores, Miraflores; **Nisa**, 195 Monte Grande, Chacarrilla; **Status Antiques**, 179 Merino, San Isidro; **Porta 725**, Av. Porta 725, Miraflores.

NIGHTLIFE. There is a folklore show at the **Hotel Crillon's Skyroom** every night. **The Sheraton** has international performers at its main restaurant most evenings. **The Bolívar** also has folk music during dinner. **Berimbau**, 100 Berlin, Miraflores, (450–498), features Brazilian music and shows. **Satchmo Jazz Bar**, 538 La Paz, Miraflores (44 1753) is the "in" place of the moment. Jazz and Latin American progressive music are its strong points, plus good food. Reservations are a prerequisite.

Peñas are where you can hear the coastal music called criollo, or Creole. The places open late and keep going with festive fervor until exhaustion sets in. The best performers sing, play, and dance in several penas a night. Check the papers for locations and showtimes. In Miraflores, the best places are: **La Casa de Edith**, 250 Ignacio Merino, Miraflores (41–0612); **Sachun**, Av. del Ejercito 657 (41–0123); **La Palizada**, 800 Ejercito, Miraflores (41–0552).

Barranco has become one of Lima's most enchanting evening destinations. An artists' enclave has grown up around this seaside suburb's tastefully restored 19th-century mansions and homes, which now house a variety of peñas, bars, jazz clubs, dinner theaters, and restaurants. The entertainment circuit includes **Karamanduka**, 135 Sanchez Carrion (47–3237), **La Casona**, 329 Grau (77–1838), **La Casa de Florentino**, 689 Grau (77–1838), **La Estación**, 112 Pedro de Osma (67–8804), **El Buho Pub**, 315 Sucre, **Nosferatu**, 203 Zepita, unpretentious pub in interesting location offering quiet folk music, and **La Taberna**, 268 Grau.

Discotheques: Keops, 131 Camino Real, one of Lima's newest discos and popular among younger set. **Percy's**, TODOS shopping center, San Isidro. **Disco Salsa**, 120 Pardo, Miraflores (45–9331). **Red & Blue**, 28 de Julio 151, in Gran Hotel Miraflores (47–9641, extension 1312). **Midnight**, Miguel Dasso 143, San Isidro (40–8221).

The capital also has a wealth of theaters with offerings ranging from European orchestras to dinner theater. The hot sounds of salsa music are also extremely popular here, and Lima has several "salsadromos" to prove it. Check newspapers for locations and times.

CUZCO

The Fountainhead of the Incas

Cradled in a high Andean valley, Cuzco seems to surge up from the earth. The houses made from orange-hued adobe bricks with their pottery shingles match the deep red clay tones of the soil, contrasting with the vibrant greens of mountainsides. In the old core of the city, the colonial-period houses and mansions are made with the stones of volcanic rock, granite, and limestone which the Incans themselves quarried to build their palaces and temples. The foundations have not been moved, even by earthquakes. The Inca past seems to spring from the bedrock. Looming over the church spires, on a hill over the city, is the monumental Sacsayhuaman fortress. The narrow, cobblestoned streets wind their way along the hillsides.

Although Cuzco has changed, grown, and adapted to welcome the tens of thousands of tourists who come each year, its roots are deeply embedded in its history. Cuzco was the fountainhead of the Inca Empire, the most important seat of colonial power outside Lima, and a pole of development once Peru stepped into the twentieth century. It has retained a spiritual, almost mythical importance as craftsmen and artists have labored to preserve some of Peru's greatest achievements, from the humblest crafts to native arts, from the distinctive festive music to architectural marvels.

Cuzco is also a perfect jumping-off point for seeing Peru's diverse attractions in the southern region. The untamed Amazon jungle, filled with exotic wildlife and flora, gold-miners, and primitive native tribes, is only a half-hour flight from the snowcapped Andes. There is also a train to Lake Titicaca and the picturesque city of Arequipa, framed by three volcanos. But the *Cusqueños* themselves, the proud descendants of the Incas, are convinced that once you have seen the "Imperial City" itself, everything else will be an anticlimax. Like the Incas before them, who divided their reign, called Tawantinsuyo, into four quadrants—Chichasuyo (the northern conquests), Antisuyo (the Amazon jungle), Contisuyo (the far southern conquests), and Collasuyo (the high steppes of Lake Titicaca and beyond)—Cuzco was the central spoke or, as the Incas themselves called it, the navel of the universe.

Navel of the Universe

"The Peru that was conquered was the last advanced civilization completely isolated from the rest of mankind," writes John Hemming in his fine book, *The Conquest of the Incas*. This story has fired the imagination of novelists, playwrights, and historians (Hemming's book is highly recommended reading for those who wish to sense the full sweep of this chronicle. It is published in paperback by Penguin and is available at ABC, Epoca, and El Pacifico bookstores in Lima, and by Harcourt, Brace in the U.S.). It has also given rise to legends. Spanish speakers on both sides of the Atlantic still say *"Vale un Perú"* (it's worth a Peru) to describe something of incalculable value.

When the Spaniards, fresh from the plundering of the Aztec Empire in Mexico, set foot on the northern marches of the Inca Empire in 1532, the Incas ruled over an area which stretched almost 3,000 miles and included the present-day countries of southern Colombia, Ecuador, Peru, Bolivia, the northern half of Chile, and northeastern Argentina. South America had never seen a kingdom as large, powerful, or wealthy. In less than one hundred years, the small regional power of Cuzco swallowed up older kingdoms and cultures in an astute combination of cultural absorption, military force, and diplomacy. The territorial expansion required an enormous administrative bureaucracy and economic leverage to hold it together, especially since this far-stretching empire had never been united under single rule before.

Akin to the Romans in the Mediterranean centuries before, the Incas were builders, organizers, law-givers, administrators, warriors, and statesmen par excellence, but only tapped the innovations and cultural achievements of their subjugated peoples. They implanted in the Andes a new *lingua franca,* Quechua, which is still spoken by millions of peasants and can be heard in the streets of Lima and Quito. An elaborate system of royal highways along the dorsal spine of the Andes, including awe-inspiring suspension bridges, was created and maintained. A state religion, involving sun worship, was imposed to bolster the power of the trans-Andean kingdom. The long-standing communal ownership of the land found a counterpart in a central government which made provisions for poor harvests and natural disasters, as well as retaining for the state religion and the Inca a share of the produce and labor. This characteristic has led some specialists to think that the Incas established a primitive welfare state bordering on socialism. The Incas did make the condition of being subjected to a distant power beneficial to all but the most intransigent fiefdoms. Commerce flourished, the regional economy became more stable, and the arts and crafts were promoted.

This social and economic maturity under the Incas took place in a geographical environment—the rugged, barren Andes with isolated narrow valleys—which was more adverse than other centers of civilization, like the Mediterranean basin or the broad river plains of Egypt, Mesopotamia, India, and China. It also explains why the Andean world has always favored communal efforts—group survival over individual advancement.

A Quest for Fortune

Francisco Pizarro stumbled onto this vast culture following a dynastic dispute between two half-brothers, Atahualpa and Huascar. The Incas did not choose their leaders for hereditary reasons and on the death of each of the eleven Incas before Atahualpa and Huascar there had been power struggles among clans and families. Atahualpa had won out after an extended civil war, and his main army was still consolidating its victory when the first contact with the Europeans was made. The Empire had also felt the first ravages of European illnesses, like smallpox, which had probably been the cause of death for Huayna Capac, the previous Inca ruler, his heir-apparent, and a good part of the professional Inca army stationed near Quito in 1527.

Pizarro and his small group of adventurers, initially 150 men, took enormous risks, spurred on by the glimpse of gold, silver, and other wealth. In November 1532, Pizarro captured Atahualpa, in a daring act of treachery, in the northern town of Cajamarca. Seven months later, he executed the Inca after receiving a legendary ransom for the Inca's life, though the gold and silver could also have been tribute to buy time for Atahualpa's armies to rescue him.

Pizarro marched into Cuzco in November of the following year and crowned a puppet Inca, named Manco Inca. The plundering of the wealth stored in Cuzco and other administrative centers was begun. The Incas and their allies did not give up easily, though. Manco Inca himself rebelled against his new sovereigns after he had been subjected to abuses and extortion. In 1536, both Lima and Cuzco were in danger of being overrun by regrouped Inca armies. However, the Inca resistance, which could mass thousands of combatants, never seemed to acquire the tactics or weapons necessary to win sustained victories against the Spanish army. For instance, the Inca armies did not effectively use the bow and arrow and rarely ambushed Spanish columns in the narrow Andean passes. The conquistadores were superiorly armored and armed, mounted on horses, and were able to fight on their own terms. As in Mexico, cultural shock seemed the most devastating weapon in the Spaniards' arsenal. Although members of the Inca families opposed the Spanish for another fifty years, taking refuge in the lower reaches of the Vilcabamba Valley and giving rise to the legend of the "Lost City of the Incas," the fate of the Empire was sealed. Just as the Incas had played off regional rivalries to conquer the Andean world, the Spanish did the same, turning one Inca faction against another, fiefdoms against the central empire, servant classes against the masters.

Pizarro himself died in 1541 as a result of the spiraling greed set off by his conquest when a rival faction of Spaniards in Lima made a grab for fortune. In fact, the feuding and civil wars among the Spanish over the spoils of conquest seemed frequently to leave open the possibility of the Incas being able to expel them, at least temporarily. In 1568, Francisco de Toledo, the first great Spanish viceroy, arrived to consolidate the Conquest and put the new crown possessions in order. For the next 250 years, Spain held sway over the Andes.

That does not mean that the descendants of the Incas and other Andean cultures accepted their plight passively. The last Inca, Tupac Amaru, was executed in 1572 after his capital in exile was occupied by Spanish troops. The Spaniards had to put down a series of Indian rebellions, the most threatening one taking place in 1781 under Tupac Amaru II, who traced his lineage back to the last Inca. At one point, Tupac Amaru's ragged army threatened to capture Cuzco. Finally, however, he was defeated, captured, tried, and then drawn and quartered in the main square of Cuzco. The unrest continued into the twentieth century, as peasants organized to reclaim their ancestral lands which had been snatched from them by Creole landowners. In 1969, the Peruvian government started a major land reform program which corrected many of the injustices started back in the sixteenth century.

Stone Legends and Living History

Unlike in Mexico, however, the Spaniards did not completely destroy the native capital of the Incas. Although the Conquest, sieges, civil wars, and earthquakes have taken their toll on the Incas' splendid grasp of architecture and masonry, which was a privilege reserved for the royalty, the Inca structures have endured far better than the Spaniards' own constructions. Their remains can be seen in the foundations of the oldest colonial buildings. Around the Plaza de Armas, there are many streets and walls which remain from Inca times, especially the Callejon Loreto, located between what were once the House of the Women of the Sun (Aclla Huasi) and the Palace of the Serpents (Amaru Cancha) and today running beside the Church of the Company of Jesus. The Inca foundations are visible in

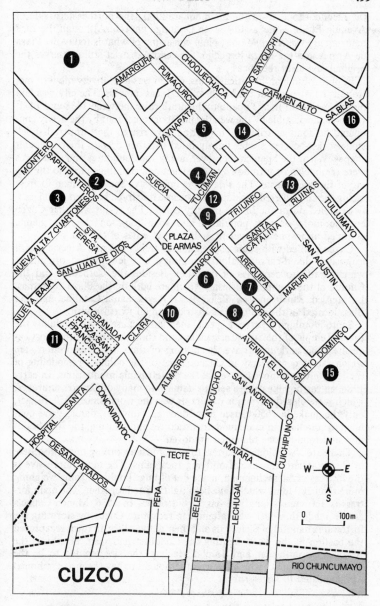

CUZCO

Points of Interest

1) Sacsayhuaman Fortress
2) Archaeological Museum
3) Santa Teresa
4) Palace of the Admiral
   (Regional Historical Museum)
5) Nazarenas
6) La Compania
7) Santa Catalina
8) Amarukancha
9) Cathedral
10) La Merced
11) San Francisco Church
12) Casa del Almirante
13) Hatunrumiyoc
14) Amarucata Ruins
15) Santo Domingo (Corikancha)
16) San Blas

the neighborhood from the main square along the northeastern side of Avenida El Sol as far as the Santo Domingo church. Although the Inca main square was a broad open plain consisting of what is today the Plaza de Armas and the Plaza Regocijo, the central district still conserves the original layout of the Incas.

In pre-Columbian historical terms, Cuzco was a relatively modern metropolis constructed at the height of the Incas' powers. The city was laid out by Pachacuti Inca Yupanqui, the ninth ruler, between 1438 and 1471. It was made possible by the wealth and labor forces sent by the newly conquered fiefdoms as tribute. This period gave rise to the "Imperial-style" stonework—beveled stones tightly fitted together despite their irregular shapes. When the Spanish took over, many Inca buildings and structures were remodeled or torn down to construct new buildings more to the liking of European taste. The side of the impressive Sacsayhuaman fortress facing the city suffered considerably because its carved boulders could easily be rolled down the hill to the city below. The result was that Cuzco became more densely populated and soon took on the unhygienic, cramped atmosphere prevalent in European cities of the era.

Cuzco is filled with some of the finest churches in Latin America, with exquisitely hand-carved pulpits, paintings, and jewel-inlaid ornaments which testify to centuries of devotion. Besides the Cathedral and the Church of the Company of Jesus, which are both on the Plaza de Armas, La Merced, San Francisco, Belen de los Reyes, Santa Catalina, and San Blas, located in the craftsmen's district, are all worth a visit.

Santo Domingo deserves a special mention because it was originally the Incas' Temple of the Sun (Coricancha) and contains some of the most exquisite stonework to survive the passing of time. In a restoration step which raised controversy in Cuzco, some of the colonial remodeling of the temple was removed to reveal the pre-Hispanic foundations. In early 1986, an earthquake caused serious damage to many of Cuzco's churches, which were closed for major repairs. It was the worst since 1950; in fact, only the quake in 1650 caused more damage. However, damage was confined to colonial and more modern structures and housing; the Inca buildings and foundations remained unmoved.

There are also colonial quarters to see for just absorbing the atmosphere in Cuzco. There are several outlying Inca ruins. The most impressive is the fortress of Sacsayhuaman, made out of huge boulders, some weighing more than 300 tons, which have been tightly fitted together. The main fortress is 360 meters long and has 21 buttresses. In 1536, Manco Capac's armies made their last, vain attempt to recapture Cuzco by storming the fortress. A handful of Spaniards and their native allies, in turn, recaptured the bastion in the worst fighting the Conquest had seen. Nearby is the Kkenko amphitheater and Tambo Machay, the site reputed to be the Baths of the Inca but which is currently thought to have been a ceremonial site dedicated to water rites.

The Sacred Valley of the Incas

An excursion to the Sacred Valley of the Urubamba (also called Vilcanota) River is a must. Here the wealthiest Inca families had their country estates, a first experiment with private property in the Inca Empire. Although the circuit, which has excellent highways to most sites, can easily be made in one day, this does not leave much time for lingering, for seeing some of the archaeological sites which are away from the roads, or simply for taking in the view. The town of Urubamba offers several hotels which allow the more inquisitive visitor to reside in the area without daily trips back to Cuzco.

Normally, tours drive to Pisac, thirty kilometers from Cuzco, and then go fifty-seven kilometers down the valley through the towns of Calca, Urubamba, Yucay, and Ollantaytambo. However, there are several sites upriver from Pisac which are less frequented by tourists, like the towns of Piquillacta, Andahuaylillas, and Urcos. Oropesa is also on the return route to Cuzco on this circuit.

The town of Pisac, dating from colonial times, has a Sunday market which has become a favorite of tourists. Above the town there are Inca ruins, including a stone fortress, with an impressive view of the valley. In Calca, there are more Inca ruins and the thermal springs of Machachanca and Minasmoqo. Yucay was another Inca country estate.

Ollantaytambo, forty-five miles from Cuzco, was a favorite residence of the Incas, with its terraces running up the steep slope to the top where a carved stone throne allowed the ruler a magnificent view of his holdings. Many of the buildings in the town itself date from Inca times. Walking through the village's narrow streets can give you a gut feeling of what it must have been like at the height of the Empire. On the way back from the Sacred Valley, a visit to Chinchero, another picturesque town with a pleasant lake nearby on a high plateau, is also worthwhile. There are also archaeological ruins.

The social foundation of the Inca Empire and the Andean world in general is the *ayllu,* the village community which is a tightly knit network of kinship bound together by family allegiances and the worship of local spirits. This trait has continued until this day, and it can be seen in the communities around Cuzco. For instance, the women of each community wear a distinctively styled hat. Each community has its own festive ceremonies, though most have merged with celebrations of the Catholic church. Many times a visitor is fortunate to be present for some of their colorful, gay occasions, like weddings, baptisms, and saints' days, which fall outside most touristic calendars. Dancing is round the clock to the eerie harmonies of Andean music, fueled by a heavy dose of liquor and enthusiasm. To this day, the communities are still ruled by the three pillars of Inca law: *ama sua, ama qella, ama llulla* (don't rob, don't be idle, and don't lie).

Machu Picchu: A Jewel in the Mist

Since Hiram Bingham "discovered" Machu Picchu in 1911, the site has captured the imagination of much of the world and is, perhaps, the single feature which people commonly identify with South America.

Machu Picchu was not really the "Lost City of the Incas" because most of the Indian residents of the zone knew about the site when Bingham arrived to "discover" it. Nor was it the site of the Incas' last refuge before the advance of the Spanish armies. In fact, the last Inca rulers probably withdrew from Machu Picchu once the Spanish gained control of the upper Urubamba River and the citadel may have been occupied by the Spaniards for several years before it was abandoned. The last Incas withdrew to the neighboring Vilcabamba region, which was more inaccessible and more easily defended but allowed them to raid the Spaniards' extended supply lines between Cuzco and Lima.

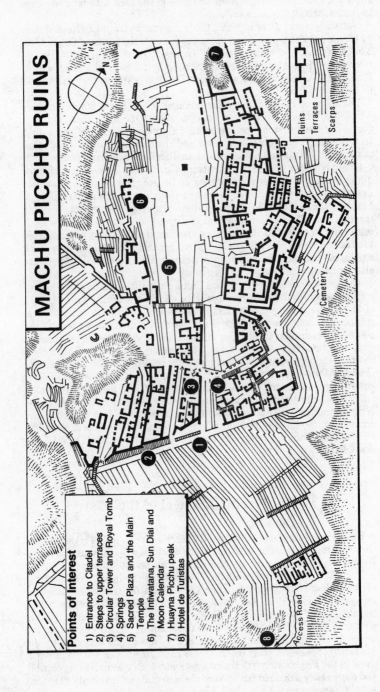

MACHU PICCHU RUINS

N

Ruins
Terraces
Scarps

Cemetery

Access Road

Points of Interest

1) Entrance to Citadel
2) Steps to upper terraces
3) Circular Tower and Royal Tomb
4) Springs
5) Sacred Plaza and the Main Temple
6) The Intiwatana, Sun Dial and Moon Calendar
7) Huayna Picchu peak
8) Hotel de Turistas

Machu Picchu was a flourishing ceremonial and agricultural site, probably the gateway to the jungle marches of the Empire. The central buildings were erected with the polished stoneworks of the Cuzco Imperial style, though the site was probably occupied well before the Incas started their expansion. It was closely associated with the earth cult revolving around the coca leaf, which was a privilege of the Inca royal family and priests. The Spanish and, later, Sierra land and mine owners, used coca to increase the output of their undernourished laborers. It originated on the eastern slopes of the Andes, in the Amazon foothills, requiring cool breezes and plenty of rain. Its cultivation, for largely illegal trafficking as cocaine, has now spread from Bolivia to Colombia.

Since the Yale Expedition started hacking down the overgrowth and digging out Machu Picchu in 1912, there have been extensive excavations and investigations, but it has continued to yield new finds. Around the river bend from the citadel, archaeologists have recently found a whole cliff face, a mile and half long, filled with agricultural terracing, aqueducts, warehouses, and ceremonial sites. Killapata, as it has been named, was a last purification site on the pilgrimage route to the religious center of Machu Picchu. A gravesite has also been found which may yield the male mummies that seemed so conspicuously absent from Machu Picchu when it was originally excavated. As a ceremonial center, Machu Picchu was serviced by the *mita*—regional labor donated to the state or official religion—and the *agllawasi*—female laborers specialized in crafts.

Stepping up to the Past

The easiest way to get to Machu Picchu is to take the daily tourist train that leaves early in the morning, climbs onto a broad fertile Andean plateau, and then descends into the Urubamba Valley. It arrives at Machu Picchu station before noon. A cafeteria-style lunch is available at the Machu Picchu hotel. It takes about two hours to stroll through the ruins and climb to a prominence above the citadel for a panoramic view.

Visitors should learn to take the tour guides' version of Machu Picchu with a grain of salt. Many of the colorful descriptions of the buildings and their uses have come from the Yale Expedition's original hypotheses about the citadel and been mixed with tradition, legends, and fancy. However, many of these hypotheses have since been surpassed as further research has filled in the holes over which Bingham's imagination leaped.

Machu Picchu itself needs no such embellishment. After the hair-raising ascent in a bus along hairpin turns up the steep cliffs, the first glimpse of the citadel is breathtaking. Machu Picchu does not owe its reputation to colossal dimensions. No single building is more than three stories high, though some structures take advantage of the slope to build up complexes in tiers. Rather, it is a beautiful jewel in an equally beautiful setting, perfectly proportioned to the contours of the mountain, at times appearing to be suspended in the mist, a shrouded apparition out of the past.

For those lucky enough to spend the night at a comfortably equipped tourist hotel (reservations should be made well in advance at ENTUR-PERU offices in Lima or a travel agency) on top of Machu Picchu, there is a special magic to the ruins under starlight or the moon. Equally impressive is the view of the citadel at dawn. For the most athletic, a climb up Huayna Picchu, the towering sugarloaf peak facing the citadel, or up to Inti Punku, the gateway of the Inca Trail at 2,600 meters above sea level, can provide rare panoramic views. Both of these trips take about two hours each, with regular rest periods, so they are difficult to fit into the routine day trip to Machu Picchu.

The hardest way to get to Machu Picchu, but probably the most rewarding, is to take the Inca Trail starting from Km. 88 on the Machu Picchu
rail line, 22 kms past the Ollantaytambo station. It takes three to five days
and should not be attempted by the unprepared or short-winded. The trail
passes through or near many Inca ruins which can rival Machu Picchu
in some respects. The scenery is striking. In Cuzco, there are adventure
tourism agencies which specialize in organizing these outings for experts
and novices.

A SPECIAL WARNING: Tourists are strongly cautioned not to hike the trail
in groups of less than four due to an increasing number of robberies in isolated areas.
Incidents of injury are rare but two Dutch tourists hiking together were slain along
the trail in late 1988.

PRACTICAL INFORMATION FOR CUZCO

GETTING TO CUZCO. There are daily flights to Cuzco from Lima (1,170 kilometers or 725 miles), as well as air connections with Juliaca, Arequipa, and Puerto
Maldonado. Tourists must pay a $5 airport tax on leaving Cuzco. Airline offices
in Cuzco are: *Aeroperu,* 600 Sol (23–3051) and *Faucett,* 567 Sol (23–3151). In addition, *Lloyd Aereo Boliviano,* 180 Portal Mantas (22–2990), has weekly direct flights
between La Paz and Cuzco.

There is also a train connection to Puno and Arequipa, which has some great
scenery. An attempt to drive to Cuzco is not recommended for the normal traveler.

Unfortunately, the nation's prime tourist destinations of Cuzco, Puno, and Arequipa occasionally become flight bottlenecks due to large numbers of travelers and
grounded flights during the summer rainy season. Passengers are sometimes bum-
ped and entire flights are cancelled. It is extremely important to be sure you have
a valid ticket and to reconfirm your flight with the airline one day ahead. This rule
also applies to return portions of round-trip tickets. When problems arise, work
closely with one of the travel agents listed in this book or with another reputable
company. They can usually find another flight or a satisfactory alternative means
of travel. But there are no guarantees, and there could be a wait of a few hours
to a few days.

HOW TO GET AROUND. The points of interest in Cuzco are concentrated in
the old sector of the city, and maps showing them are readily available. **Taxis** are
the most reasonable means of transport in Cuzco. Fares range from $2 to $6 to
the airport, more if there is luggage. Rides within the city cost about $2. Taxi drivers
frequently offer their services as guides for charges which vary with time and distance.

Car Rental. *Avis,* 459 Sol (22–4871). The main tourist circuits around Cuzco
have excellent roads and clear road signs, which makes touring by car feasible.

A SPECIAL WARNING: When going to high altitudes, like Cuzco or elsewhere
in the Sierra, a first day should be spent relaxing, allowing the body to adjust gradually to the lesser amount of oxygen. Cuzco is at 3,400 meters (11,155 feet) above
sea level, which can produce a shock when coming from Lima. Most hotels offer
"mate de coca" (coca tea) on checking in. It has no adverse side effects and really
does relieve some of the effects of altitude sickness (called *soroche* in Spanish). Rest
two or three hours minimum before venturing for even a stroll, though a full two
weeks is needed for the body to adjust completely to the altitude. Eat lightly and
avoid consuming alcohol on the first day. (Liquor seems to have twice the effect
in the Andean heights; even beer, which is twice as strong as the brews consumed
in the United States, can carry a wallop.) Otherwise, soroche will set in and ruin
the whole trip with headaches, body pains, troubled breathing, and even worse side
effects. In severe cases, oxygen should be administered. Riding up to the Sierra (for
instance, taking the train from Arequipa to Lake Titicaca and then to Cuzco or
taking a car or bus elsewhere) allows a more gradual adjustment to the heights.
Altitude sickness varies greatly from person to person. Children tend to feel it more
severely but adjust quickly. Be on the conservative side in measuring how it affects

you personally. An overexertion can ruin your outing. Once soroche hits you, the only definitive cure is to go down to a lower altitude.

HOTELS. In the past 15 years, Cuzco's hotels have undergone major renovations and expansions. Several new hotels, like the Libertador, have been constructed. These have been made while trying to conserve the city's unique atmosphere and historical monuments. Though central heating may not be necessary to weather the nights, many visitors may find it a welcome comfort. For definitions of price categories, see "Facts at Your Fingertips" earlier in this chapter.

Expensive

El Dorado, 395 Sol (23–2573, 42–0166/Lima). 75 rooms, central heating, restaurant, and snack shop. A stone's throw from the Plaza de Armas.
Libertador, 400 San Agustín (23–1961, 42–0166/Lima). One of the finest hotels in Cuzco, 131 rooms with restaurant, snack shop, central heating, and handicraft shops. Formerly called the House of Four Busts (*Cuatro Bustos*).
Picoaga, 344 Santa Teresa (22–7691, 28–6314/Lima). 70 rooms with central heating, restaurant, and snack bar.
Royal Inka II, 335 Santa Teresa (23–1067). A recently opened luxury hotel, among Cuzco's best. Central heating; bar and restaurant.
Savoy, 954–Sol (22–4322, 47–8188/Lima). 132 rooms with two restaurants, coffee shop, and central heating. It has its shortcomings on cuisine.

Moderate

Alhambra 2, 596 Sol (22–4899). 26 rooms with restaurant and snackbar. Cozy atmosphere.
Conquistador, Santa Catalina 149 (22–4461), 28 rooms.
Cuzco, 150 Heladeros (22–4821, 28–3320/Lima). 107 rooms, restaurant, and coffee shop. The oldest major hotel in Cuzco, spacious but chilly.
Royal Inka, Plaza Regocijo (23–1067).
San Agustín, 390 San Agustín (23–1001, 44–2066/Lima). 77 rooms, 2 restaurants.

Inexpensive

El Arqueologo, 425 Ladrillos (23–2569).
Garcilaso, 233 Garcilaso (23–3031). 27 rooms.
El Solar, 162 Plaza San Francisco (232–451).

Outside Cuzco

URUBAMBA. Alhambra 3. *Moderate.* (224076, make reservations at the Alhambra 2 in Cuzco, see above). 31 rooms, swimming pool. **Vacation Center of Urubamba.** *Inexpensive.* Urubamba Highway, Kilometer 70 (22–7191). 35 bungalows with restaurant, snack bar, and swimming pool. **Hostal Naranhachayoc.** *Inexpensive.* Kilometer 69.
MACHU PICCHU. Reservations should be made through your travel agent or the offices of ENTUR PERU in Lima (72–1928). **The Hotel Turistas.** *Moderate.* 31 rooms, including Continental breakfast, with central heating, restaurant, and coffee shop.

RESTAURANTS AND CAFES. All the major hotels in Cuzco have adequate to good restaurants, though prices will tend to be a bit steeper than at restaurants on the streets. For definitions of price categories see "Facts at Your Fingertips."
El Bucaro. *Moderate.* In Alhambra 2. Nightly shows.
Chef Victor. *Moderate.* 115 and 139 Portal de Panes.
Mesón Alhambra. *Moderate.* 163 Portal de Panes.
Chez Maggy. *Moderate.* 365 Procuradores. Pizzas baked in wood-burning oven. Music on weekends.
Mesón de Espaderos. *Moderate.* 105 Espaderos.
Pizzería La Mamma. *Moderate.* 177 Portal Escribanos.
El Trattoria. *Moderate.* 185 Portal Escribanos. The best restaurant in Cuzco, so it's crowded at meal times.

Café Varayoc. *Inexpensive.* 142 Espaderos. Nice atmosphere and good pizza.
Pucara. *Inexpensive.* 309 Plateros. Café-bar.
Quinta Eulalia. *Inexpensive.* 384 Choquechaca. Lunch only.
El Truco. *Inexpensive.* 247 Plaza Regocijo. Nightly shows.

TOURIST INFORMATION. Portal Belen 115, on the Plaza de Armas. Mon.-Fri. 8:30 A.M.–5:30 P.M., Sat. 8:30 A.M.–12:30 P.M. (23–7364). Airport, until noon. A $10 ticket purchased at any of the following sites is good for entrance to all: Cathedral, San Blas church, Santo Domingo church (Koricancha), Regional History Museum, Museum of Santa Catalina, Religious Art Museum, Tambo Machay, Puka Pukara, Sacsayhuaman, Ollantaytambo, Pisac, Chinchero, and Piquillacta.

TOURS. CBS Tours, 171 Ayacucho (22–3410).
Condor Travel, 164 Heladeros (22–5921).
Dasatour, 373 Plateros (22–3341).
Lima Tours, 567 Sol (22–8431).
Receptour, Hotel Libertador, San Agustín 400 (22–3981).

Adventure Tourism. Trekking and rafting are available in and around Cuzco, with specialized agencies which can remove some of the discomfort and risks involved. Equipment can also be rented. The Inca Trail, from near the Ollantaytambo train station to Machu Picchu, is a lifetime experience for those with well developed legs and strong lungs. However, it should not be tried on a lark. It is a minimum three-day hike and the only options, should you have any troubles, are to turn back or continue. Rafting can be done on the Urubamba River or on the Tambopata River.
Apu Expediciones, 236 Portal de Carnes (235–408).
Expediciones Mayuc, 354 Procuradores (23–2666).
Explorandes, 372 Procuradores (23–3292).
Hirca Ventures, 230 Garcilaso (22–7051).
Manu Nature Tours, 627–B Sol, office 401 (23–4793).
Peruvian Andean Treks, 575 Pardo (22–5701).
Southern Cross Adventures, Portal Panes 123, office 301 (23–9447).

MUSEUMS AND SIGHTS. Archeology Museum, House of Jeronimo Cabrera, Plaza de las Nazarenas, (23–3210), Mon.–Fri., 8 A.M.–noon, 3–6 P.M. A collection of pre-Inca and Inca artifacts. The prize display features turquoise miniature figures from Piquillacta. At press time, temporarily closed for renovation.
Museum of Religious Art, corner of Hatunrumiyoc and Herrajes (22–2781), Mon.–Sat. 9 A.M.–12:30 P.M., 3–5:30 P.M.; Sun. 3–5:30 P.M. The Diocese of Cuzco has pooled its finest examples of paintings and other artwork for this display.
Regional History Museum, Cuesta del Almirante (just behind the Cathedral) (22–3245), Mon.–Sat. 9 A.M.–noon, 3–6 P.M.; Sun. 3–6 P.M. Antiquities and artwork which portray Cuzco's history are housed in the Palace of the Admiral.
Museum of Santa Catalina, Plazoleta Santa Catalina, Mon.–Sat. 9 A.M.–noon, 3–6 P.M. Religious art from the convent's collection. There is also a church and convent which may be seen.

CHURCHES, CONVENTS, AND COLONIAL BUILDINGS. Most churches dating from the colonial founding had to undergo major, even total renovation after the 1650 earthquake, which coincided with a stylistic maturity among Andean architects, stonemasons, and carpenters. Many of the churches have convents or monasteries which are worth visiting, though not all are open to tourists.
The **Cathedral** and the **Church of the Company of Jesus.** Both churches are on the Plaza de Armas. The entranceway of the Company of Jesus is one of the finest examples of stonework in the New World and was copied by parish churches in Cuzco. Although the cathedral is still undergoing repairs from a 1986 earthquake, it is open to the public. **La Merced,** on Marquez street and only a block from the main square, is where many of the conquistadores are buried. **San Francisco,** located on the Plaza San Francisco three blocks west of the main square, has fine examples of stonework. **San Pedro,** located six blocks west of the main square near the Machu Picchu train station and the market, is in the stoneworking style of the Company of Jesus church. **San Blás,** three blocks east of the main square on Carmen

Bajo, has an impressive carved pulpit. The church itself is an example of the more humble, native building techniques using adobe for parish churches. **Santo Domingo,** on Santo Domingo street one block off El Sol Avenue, is a colonial church superimposed over the Inca foundation of the Koricancha, or Temple of the Sun, showing a marked contrast between the two styles. **San Cristóbal** is located on the hillside above Cuzco on the way to Sacsayhuaman. This church was endowed by Paullu, the last puppet Inca and a Christian convert who led the Inca faction which sided with the Spaniards. The stone walls with niches were part of Paullu's quarters. Other churches which you might want to visit are **Santa Ana** in the northeastern neighborhood of Carmenca, **Santa Teresa** across from the Archeological Museum, and the **Convent of the Nazarenes** two blocks east of the main square up Tucuman street near the Regional Historical Museum.

HISTORICAL SITES. Most of the points of interest belonging to the pre-Columbian period have several different spellings because, until this century, Quechua was an oral language and Spanish speakers and writers frequently deformed place names. Recently the revival of indigenous pride has led to the revising of many names to conform to systematic linguistic standards. For instance, Sacsayhuaman is alternatively called Sacsahuaman, Sacsaihuaman, Saqsaywaman, or, for humorous effect for tourists, "saxy woman." The terms in this section are the most commonly used. **Sacsayhuaman.** Originally commissioned by the great Inca Pachacuti, like the rest of pre-colonial Cuzco, it also served as a parade ground for his victorious armies. The three zigzag terraced walls stretch for 400 yards and originally stood 50 feet high. It was crowned by three tall towers and other structures, since destroyed. Across the parade ground, there is another stone defensive position. **Kkenko** temple and amphitheater is 2 kilometers from Sacsayhuaman. **Puka Pukara,** an Inca way station (tambo) which has often been confused with a fortress, is 6 kilometers beyond Kkenko. **Tambo Machay,** popularly known as the Baths of the Inca, is nearby and well preserved.

Piquillacta, a town dating from the 8th century, and **Pumi Ccolca,** an aqueduct-turned-Inca-gateway, are located 32 kilometers south of Cuzco.

Oropesa and **Andahuaylillas,** both on the road to Puno, have beautiful colonial churches, with the advantage that they are off the beaten tourist path.

The Urubamba Valley: Pisac, Yucay, Urubamba, and Ollantaytambo provide a natural circuit for a day trip. These can also be combined with **Chinchero.** The total distance is about 113 kilometers.

SHOPPING. Shopping for local handcrafts and souvenirs can be one of the most enjoyable experiences in Cuzco. The city is full of shops. Vendors ply their wares on the streets as well. There are also markets in Cuzco, Pisac, Chinchero, and other villages, usually on Sunday, the traditional day for Andean peasants to trade agricultural produce and other articles. The Pisac market—and to a lesser degree, the Chinchero one—have become increasingly targeted at tourists, but still they are worth seeing.

Another option is to go straight to the craftsmen themselves. In Cuzco, renowned folk artists have opened their workshops to the public. These can be visited through organized tours or on individual initiative, though a smattering of Spanish is necessary. Special tours can also be arranged to see craft-specialized communities, like weavers.

Alpaca 111, 472 Ruinas.

Arte Peru, 295 Portal de Confiturías, on Plaza de Armas. This is the state-run handicrafts promotion agency.

Artesanías y Decoraciones Santo Domingo, 261 Santo Domingo. Antiques.

Cerámica y Artesanía Ruíz Caro, 387 Triunfo.

Josefina Olivera, 501 Santa Clara and 334 Plateros.

THE SOUTHERN REGION

At 12,530 feet above sea level on Lake Titicaca, the crystalline sky, turquoise waters, and geometrical shapes of the landscape seem to confirm the Indians' belief that God took mankind out of the lake and placed him in this world of almost abstract, even cruel beauty. But this one provincial vision's claim to uniqueness is contradicted repeatedly from the high steppes of the *Altiplano* to the idyllic setting of Arequipa and down to the stark stretches of Pacific desert coast—each such pocket of life is convinced that God has saved special blessings for its provincial enclave. And each of them is probably partially right.

LAKE TITICACA

Lake Titicaca is the world's highest navigable lake and has shaped life among the high-cheekboned, dark-skinned people who inhabit its shores and islands. When dry land is not enough, it is also possible to create artificial habitats. The Uro Indians live on floating reed islands in the lake. The reeds, called *totora* in the local language, are also used for the distinctive boats which are used to ply the placid but frigid waters. The women are accomplished embroiderers. It takes a three-and-a-half-hour boat ride to get to the islands under normal conditions. In 1986, the lake's water level rose to its highest level this century, scattering the islands from their traditional moors.

The Indians on Tequile Island, about twenty-five kilometers by boat from Puno, have made their vivid color schemes and weaving designs part of the regional folk art and their island one of the most prosperous points in the region. The brilliant color choice of the Indians seems to compensate for the bleak, wind-swept steppes which fill the Titicaca horizons. On the neighboring Amantani Island, the inhabitants are expert basket weavers.

Puno is proud of its Indian heritage and has kept up a strong folklore and music, in its more unfiltered forms. There is a seemingly endless cycle of festivals and saint days which are celebrated with dances and music. The "devils' masks," carved and painted wooden disguises for these rites, are invaluable pieces of folk art. At the southernmost part of the lake, the Indians have maintained a separate ethnic identity from the Quechua-speaking Indians to the north. These speak Aymara, and share community ties with the Bolivian Indians who speak the same language. At both places the Indians put visitors up in their own homes. There are pre-Columbian ruins on both islands.

Sillustani, about thirty-two kilometers from Puno, provides some of the best ruins in the region. These consist of circular stone towers, called *chullpas*, which overlook Lake Umayo. These were probably built under Inca rule, but archaeological evidence seems to point towards a Pan-Andean architectural trend in which these circular structures were the vogue. During Spanish times, many were destroyed because these impressive structures were associated with idolatry.

Another living remnant of Inca times lies just ten kilometers outside Puno. The town of Ichu is actually an Indian community which traces its roots back to pre-Columbian Ecuador. The Incas frequently transplanted conquered peoples to other regions as a means of breaking local resistance. These *mitimaes* of Ichu are Siris, who have kept their ethnic identity.

Temperatures can fall well below freezing at night so travelers should go well equipped for cold weather. The high altitudes also mean that it is extremely easy to get sunburned.

AREQUIPA

Arequipa is the Peruvian city that has conserved its colonial architecture most rigorously. Although it has grown to be the second most important city in the country, it has not lost its distinctive personality. The colonial buildings are made out of *sillar,* a soft, white volcanic rock which is found in abundance in the region. It also gives Arequipa its nickname, the "White City." Three volcanoes—Misti, Chachani, and Pichu Pichu, sometimes capped in snow and puffing steam against the azure Sierra sky—tower over Arequipa. The city lies 7,800 feet (2,380 meters) above sea level.

With its independent spirit, the city has fought to salvage the architectural heritage found in churches, convents, and colonial mansions. Some buildings have been turned into shopping malls or offices. For instance, the colonial residences of the Casa del Moral and the Casa de Tristán del Pozo are regional headquarters for commercial banks. Others are academic centers or museums. But the star in Arequipa's crown is the Convent of Santa Catalina. It was founded in 1579 and remained a self-enclosed world unto itself for nearly 400 years. It was restored and opened to the public in 1970.

Part of Arequipa's charm lies in its natural setting in the valley of the Chili River, an oasis in the midst of the dry, southern Sierra. The colonial mill Sabandía, eight kilometers outside Arequipa, is a popular pleasure spot. Another colonial center is the Casa del Fundador, a restored mansion ten kilometers into the countryside.

One hundred forty kilometers from Arequipa, the Colca River Valley is an enclave out of the Andean past. There are sixteen well-preserved churches and chapels. The colorfully dressed Indians have also kept up cultivation on the pre-Columbian terraces, which line the valley walls, and archaeological ruins are readily visible throughout the valley. Farther down the river, the waters have gouged out the deepest canyon in the world, up to 13,100 feet (4,000 meters) from the riverbed to the top of the cliff face.

Arequipa also offers adventure tourism opportunities, from white-river kayaking and rafting to birdwatching (the lagoons of Mejia are one of the few resting places for migratory birds on the Pacific coast).

DESERT OASES

In the six hundred miles between Arequipa and Lima, there is almost nothing but one of the driest deserts in the world (less than two millimeters of water wrung from the mist over twenty years). But even that impression can prove false. At Paracas, a wind-swept peninsula protruding into the Pacific Ocean, the waters and shores teem with life. In the tidal pools on both sides of the peninsula pink flamingos can frequently be seen resting on their migratory flights. On the nearby Ballestas Islands off the Bay of Paracas are the natural habitats of sea lions, penguins, and thousands of sea birds. The sea lions come right up to the excursion boats which visit the islands each day. The most fearless tourist can jump into the ocean to swim with them. On the mainland, condors can frequently be seen glid-ing on the sea winds or perched on the cliffs overlooking the ocean.

Paracas

Paracas means "big winds." These start softly in the mornings and build up force as the day passes until they are overpowering. The complex inter-action between wind and ocean, sun and land has made this one of the most unique wildlife habitats in the world. It has also transformed the land, turning it into a kind of lunarscape under an equatorial sun. The winds have carved the land into strange shapes.

The earliest Andean people also found shelter here. The Paracas culture (1000 B.C. to 300 B.C.) is derivative of the Chavín culture, but its unique manifestations set it apart: fine weavings in geometrical designs and vi-brant colors which have been preserved for thousands of years by the dry coastal climate. There is a museum displaying some of the mummies and artifacts found at Paracas. Some of the finest examples of weaving are in museums in Lima.

Nazca Lines

But nature is not the only marvel which has been working in the desert sands. Farther south on a large barren plain are the mysterious Nazca Lines, which have bewildered archaeologists, historians, and mathemati-cians this century. The Nazca Lines are markings or drawings which stretch for several miles. Some thirty drawings depict animals and birds, like a monkey with a coiled tail, a hummingbird fluttering in flight, or an owl. Others form geometrical shapes. Still others are complex knots of lines which seem to have been precisely measured and laid.

There are scores of theories which try to explain why a pre-Columbian culture would trace huge patterns in the sands which they would not nec-essarily be able to see themselves. The lines show an understanding of so-phisticated mathematics and surveying techniques. The most eccentric in-vestigators insist that the Nazca Lines show the presence of extraterrestrial beings, a kind of landing strip for flying saucers, but other theorists point to more rational schemes—a huge map of the Sierra or a celestial calendar.

Should you have the privilege of seeing the Nazca Lines from the air (flights can be arranged from Lima, Paracas, Ica, or Nazca), you will no-tice that the valley countryside around Nazca looks as if it has been pock-marked by aerial bombardments. These holes are what is left by the *huaqueros* who rob the pre-Columbian graves. The ceramics found in buri-al grounds are highly prized in the world antiquity market. The Nazca culture (A.D. 100 to A.D. 800) would apply its distinctive artistic perspective to polychromatic ceramics. The paintings depict daily life (much as Greek ceramics did about the same time in the Mediterranean) and many special-ists believe that the patterns contain a primitive pictographic writing. In any case, these ceramics give an unparalleled perspective of the world be-fore the coming of the Europeans, from the customs of hanging mummi-fied heads on a man's belt as trophies of valor to wildlife in the region. The Nazca culture also made painstaking use of the scarce water sources. Today, the city is crossed by underground canals build by the Nazca cul-ture. These waterworks—and the ceramics—are this culture's monu-ments.

Ica

Another oasis in the desert is Ica, which lies in a broad valley surrounded by impressive sand dunes. Here are Peru's finest vineyards for wine and pisco. Visits can be arranged to Tacama, Ocucaje, or Vista Alegre haciendas, which give a rare insight into the way Peru used to be. Outside Ica is Huacachina, which has been a quaint vacation spot since the beginning of the twentieth century. Its oasis waters were considered to produce medicinal cures. Today, the tranquil setting will eliminate a case of anxiety.

PRACTICAL INFORMATION FOR THE SOUTH

HOW TO GET THERE. Arequipa, 634 miles (1,020 kilometers) south of Lima, is connected to the capital **by air** by *Faucett* and *Aeroperu,* and Puno, 840 miles (1,351 kilometers) southeast, is serviced daily by Aeroperu via the airport at Juliaca, 30 miles north. Tourists must pay a $5 airport tax when leaving Arequipa. An interesting route is to fly to either Arequipa or Cuzco and take the **train** to the other city, which requires a stopover in Juliaca or Puno. With special tourist class coaches, the trip is scenic, comfortable, and recommended over trying to follow the same route by highway. The cost is about $15, though using a sleeping car can cost another $30. Shortages of spare parts have recently made train travel between Puno and Arequipa uncertain. Check well in advance to make sure the train is operating.

The Lake Titicaca **ferry** to Bolivia goes to the town of Guaqui, where a train or bus route to La Paz and beyond is available. The cost is about $30 and includes a berth and two meals. The trip takes 12 hours. A quicker alternative is to take a **hydrofoil** leaving from the town of Juli, 85 kilometers south of Puno.

The cities of Ica and Nazca may be reached only by highway. Ica is 190 miles (305 kilometers) south on the Panamerican highway and Nazca lies another 90 miles farther south. You may also charter a small plane in Lima which can also overfly the Nazca Lines. Pisco and neighboring Paracas are 150 miles (243 kilometers) south of Lima, just off the Panamerican highway.

A SPECIAL WARNING: Buses to Ica and Nazca have been the targets of highwaymen. On an average of once a month, armed thieves board the buses as passengers and force the buses to stop in isolated stretches along the route. Although injuries have been rare, tourists are urged to work with tourist agencies at finding a safer means of travel.

HOTELS. For definitions of price categories see "Facts at Your Fingertips" earlier in this chapter.

LAKE TITICACA. Hotel Isla Esteves. *Moderate.* Puno (724). 126 rooms with central heating; includes Continental breakfast. Located on an island in the lake, 40 kilometers from the Puno airport, with a breathtaking view. Reservations through ENTUR (42–8626 in Lima). **Hostal Sillustani.** *Inexpensive.* 195 Lambayeque (792) (276–720 in Lima). 25 rooms and restaurant. **Hotel de Turistas.** *Inexpensive.* San Roman 158, Juliaca (366). 40 rooms, including Continental breakfast. Reservation information with ENTUR (42–8626).

AREQUIPA. El Conquistador. *Moderate.* 409 Mercaderes (21 8987). **Maison Plaza.** *Moderate.* 143 Portal San Agustin (21–8929). **El Portal.** *Moderate.* Portal de Flores 116 on the main square (21–5530). 55 rooms. **Posada del Puente.** *Moderate.* Bolognesi 101 (21–7444). **Presidente Hotel.** *Moderate.* 201 Pierola (21–3642). **Tourist Hotel.** *Moderate.* Plaza Bolívar, Selva Alegre (21–5110). 94 rooms with central heating and Continental breakfast, swimming pool, and restaurant. Located in the middle of a pleasant park. **Crismar.** *Inexpensive.* Moral 107 (21–5290). 60 rooms. **Jerusalem.** *Inexpensive.* Jerusalem 601 (22–2502). 108 rooms.

ICA. Hotel Las Dunas. *Expensive.* Panamerican Highway kilometer 300 (42–4180 in Lima, 23–1031 in Ica). Two swimming pools, tennis courts, golf course, horseback riding, and other facilities make it a favored holiday resort. Within easy reach of Paracas and Nazca. **Hotel Turistas of Ica.** *Moderate.* Avenida Los Maestros (233–320). 56 rooms. Swimming pool. **Hostal el Carmelo.** *Inexpensive.*

Panamerican Highway kilometer 301, Ica (23–2191). 32 rooms in quaint old hacienda house.

PISCO. Hotel Paracas. *Moderate,* Ribera del Mar (46–4865/Lima). 100 rooms, dated facilities. On the beachfront, but not recommended for bathing. Tennis courts, swimming pools, and minature golf. The Sunday buffet is legendary for its seafood and desserts—all you can eat for $15 per person—and many Lima residents drive down for the weekly event.

NAZCA. Hotel de la Borda. *Expensive.* km. 447 (reservations in Lima, 40–8430). **Hotel Turistas.** *Moderate.* Jirón Bolognesi (tel. 60). 32 rooms, including Continental breakfast. Swimming pool.

RESTAURANTS. The best option is to stick with hotel restaurants in most of the southern region. However, in Arequipa, a visitor may want to make a visit to the *picanterías,* famous for the spicy food of the region. Try *cuy* (an Andean type of guinea pig). The *rocoto relleno* (stuffed pepper) should only be tasted by those with jaded pallets since it is reputed to be able to burn through leather. Arequipa also has excellent shrimp when in season, which can be served in a thick broth called *chupe.* In Ica, be sure to sample the local wines and piscos. *Iqueños* also make a special sweet called *teja,* which is sugar-covered fruit or nuts. In Puno, there are plenty of freshwater fish, such as trout.

THE NORTHERN CIRCUIT

TRUJILLO

On the flat river plains of Trujillo, amid the green fields of sugar cane, a huge beige mound rises 160 feet into the air, blocking out the view of the Pacific Ocean. It is the Pyramid of the Sun, built more than a thousand years ago by the pre-Columbian inhabitants of the fertile valley. It is 600 feet long and 400 feet wide at its base. Archaeologists have calculated that 50 million adobe bricks were required to put up a mountain where none existed. The people who constructed it, the Mochica, were a fierce, warlike culture which served its numerous gods human sacrifices.

But specialists have wondered why a culture should venerate high places. The answer may lie a few hundred miles away in the majestic Cordillera Blanca, the snowcapped mountain range which forms the dorsal spine of South America. If a god should wish to inhabit this earth, he would, no doubt, pick these cragged, inaccessible summits, shrouded in a sacred white mantle of snow and ice. More than the sparse rains, these mountains provide the Pacific coast with water to irrigate their fields. At times, they rumble, letting loose landslides and earthquakes. They inspire awe even to the modern eye.

Today, this once sacred mound casts its shadow on Trujillo, the third largest city in Peru. It was founded in 1534 by the first conquistadores. Its nickname is the "City of Eternal Spring" because the sun shines year-round. It is a city that still feels strong ties to the land because it grew into its present form under the auspices of sugar cane. Though King Sugar has been dethroned in the world markets, Trujillo is still dependent on the cooperatives which produced it.

There is something of a country gentleman in the city's atmosphere. The city is famous for its old colonial houses with iron gratings and balconies, like the Casa del Mayorazgo, the Casa Urquiaqa, the Casa Ganoza (today converted to an art gallery), and the Casa Bracamonte, which are all clustered around the Plaza de Armas. Its cathedral, four churches, and convent can rival the highest standards of baroque religious architecture and ornamentation.

Trujillo can trace its roots back beyond the Conquest because the valley was one of the great breeding grounds of civilization in the Americas. The pyramid-building Mochica culture (A.D. 100 to A.D. 800) was one of the regional kingdoms which unfolded in the first millennium after Christ. Like the Nazca culture to the south, the Mochica (or Moche) developed a distinctive ceramics style, using molds in the shape of animals, plants, and humans, many of them done with a touch of humor and irony which escaped the utilitarian patterns of craftsmen. They also painted their daily lives and habits on the pottery and wall frescos, giving archaeologists invaluable evidence of the past. The Mochica were also excellent weavers. The Moche culture was eventually overrun by the Huari culture which came out of the central Andes, as the Incas would 600 years later.

With the downfall of the Pan-Andean Empire of the Huari culture, the Chimú culture (A.D. 1200 to A.D. 1460) established its regional hold over the northern coast. It eventually evolved into an empire which stretched from the present-day border of Ecuador to Lima. It did not exert that much influence in the Sierra. When confronted by the Inca war machine, it quickly accepted a role as vassal.

The Chimú culture consolidated the trend toward true cities and also created the supreme example, its capital, the adobe city of Chan Chan, the largest urban center in the New World. Although some specialists have calculated that the city could have quartered over a quarter million people, it was really a vast labyrinth-mausoleum housing mummies, households, and riches for veneration. Probably no more than 10,000 people actually inhabited Chan Chan at one time. It expanded over nearly eight square miles (twenty square kilometers) and was meticulously planned, with broad boulevards, aqueducts, reservoirs, gardens, and palaces. One of the excavated palaces had 500 rooms and was surrounded by a wall fifty feet high. Typical of the coast, it was constructed out of adobe, which means that over the centuries this amazing example of urban planning has deteriorated under the wind, infrequent rains, and scavengers. However, archaeological excavations have been able to uncover magnificent wall friezes and fresco paintings. According to legend, some of the walls were covered with gold leaf because the Chimú were excellent metalworkers, especially with gold and silver. After their conquest by the Incas, Chimu craftsmen were taken back to Cuzco to ply their trade for the new overlords.

In addition to the Pyramid of the Sun (and the smaller Pyramid of the Moon) just south of Trujillo and Chan Chan, other archaeological sites, like the Dragon *Huaca* (meaning sacred place) and the Emerald *Huaca*, are also open to the public.

Huanchaco is the fishing port twelve kilometers east of Trujillo where the fishermen still use *cabellitos de totora* (little reed horses) to ride the waves out into the ocean. Trujillo's preferred beaches are Buenos Aires and Las Delicias, nearby.

CHICLAYO, PIURA, AND TUMBES

Further north, the twentieth-century city of Chiclayo is a bustling commercial and agricultural center which was the center of the other pre-Columbian cultures that rivaled the Mochica-Chimú cultures in the Trujillo Valley. The Brunning Museum is well worth a visit since it has the best archaeological collection outside of Lima. The gold display is impressive. There are many pyramids and archaeological ruins throughout the region, most of which have been studied only superficially.

Still farther north along the Panamerican Highway lies Piura, a proud, independent city which has set its sights on building on the high-quality

Pima cotton which is grown in its fields. But Piura also claims to be the first Spanish city founded in Peru. On landing on the fringes of the Inca Empire in 1532, Pizarro established San Miguel de Piura as his first base of operations. It was eventually lost in the desert sands during the wars of conquest, but the *Piuranos* still feel their bonds to that ghost town. The Catacaos community, just outside Piura, is an example of how communal efforts have raised the inhabitants above poverty. The residents are famous for their utilitarian pottery and basket weaving.

In Tumbes, the climate starts to turn truly tropical. A popular beach resort, the Punta Sal Club Hotel, is trying to rescue the great tradition of Hemingway's Cabo Blanco deep-sea fishing haunts.

THE NORTHERN SIERRA

The Callejón de Huaylas (*callejon* literally means "alleyway") is one of the most majestic mountain ranges in the world. On one side of the valley lies the snowless Cordillera Negra (soaring to 16,000 feet above sea level) and on the other the Cordillera Blanca. The glaciated peaks and the pastoral setting of the valley have earned it the reputation of being the "Andean Switzerland." The Huascaran peak rises up to 22,205 feet (6,768 meters) above sea level, and there are more than thirty other peaks which surpass 6,000 meters. More than 1,300 square miles of the Cordillera Blanca have been declared a national park and are available for hiking, camping, mountaineering, and other adventure sports. The glacier-fed Santos river is also used for canoeing and rafting. The river must bore its way through the mountains, forming the narrow Cañón del Pato (Duck Canyon), to reach the Pacific Ocean.

Huaraz

The main valley town is Huaraz, at 10,000 feet (3,052 meters) above sea level. Its peaceful atmosphere masks a tragic past. In 1970, an earthquake racked the valley, shaking loose a mudslide which enveloped most of the town of Yungay and its 30,000 inhabitants. Today, the palm trees which shaded the main square can still be seen in a rubble-littered field, along with the top of the church spires. The town has been relocated in a more secure site. In the whole region, 80,000 lives were lost and a major reconstruction effort was mounted by governments from around the world. The earthquake also meant that most of the structures dating from colonial times were destroyed or seriously damaged, which has eliminated one of the charms of the region. However, the peasants still build their houses as they always did.

The Sierra above the Callejón de Huaylas was also the birthplace of the first Pan-Andean culture, named after the main temple, Chavín de Huantar. Stone monoliths and buildings with intricate carvings, coding in important events, gods, and beliefs, testified to a theocratic civilization. There is a museum in Huaraz which displays many examples of these stone figures, though the most striking examples are in Lima's National Archeological Museum or at the temple site. The Chavin culture's influence stretched as far south as Paracas and covered most of the Central Andes and the northern coast. To visit Chavin de Huantar, located a *long* sixty-four kilometers and seven hours southeast of Huaraz, means spending a night at the Tourist Guesthouse (Albergue) near the site.

The Callejón de Huaylas is a haven for outdoor sports enthusiasts. There are over 600 miles of hiking trails which vary in difficulty. It is also possible to ski on the Andean glaciers. Because the Cordillera Blanca is so close to highways and urban centers like Lima and Huaraz, which provide it an economical base of operation, it has become a world attraction for mountain climbers who want to take a crack at expert-level climbing. For the more sedate, at least three sites—Lake Llanganuco, Lake Parón, and the Puya Raimondi (a wildlife and flora reserve)—are accessible by car or tourist bus. But just taking the top-of-the-world view can make anyone break out in a sweat. There are also hot springs for those who have overexerted.

Cajamarca

Although Cajamarca, farther north in the Andes and 9,022 feet (2,750 meters) above sea level, cannot claim such a dramatic natural backdrop, it is perhaps the region which has withstood the arrival of the twentieth century without losing its colonial past to urban blight and remodeling. The city has six fine churches and chapels dating from the seventeenth and eighteenth centuries. Two blocks south of the main square, within a former convent, are Inca ruins said to contain the room which the Inca Atahualpa offered to fill with gold and silver to ransom his life from Francisco Pizarro. It is more likely that this is where he was held imprisoned.

Six miles east of Cajamarca, there are thermal baths which were reputed to be used by the Incas, but the archaeological ruins date from several hundred years before the Incas conquered the region. There are two other archaeological sites close by—Cumbemayo and Ventanillas de Otuzco. Excursions outside of Cajamarca will also give the visitor a chance to see the splendid countryside.

PRACTICAL INFORMATION FOR THE NORTHERN CIRCUIT

HOW TO GET THERE. Both *Aeroperu* and *Faucett* have daily flights to the coastal cities of Trujillo, Chiclayo, Piura, and Tumbes. There is a $5 tax on leaving the airport in Trujillo. All four cities may also be reached by taking the *Panamerican Highway:* Trujillo 354 miles (570 kilometers), Chiclayo 485 miles (649 kilometers), Piura 652 miles (1,050 kilometers), and Tumbes 839 miles (1,350 kilometers). There are three flights a week on Aeroperu to Cajamarca. The city can also be reached easily by road 137 miles (221 kilometers) up from the coast town of Pacasmayo. Huaraz is 133 miles (414 kilometers) north of Lima and the highway link from the coastal town of Paramonga is one of the best in Peru. There are no passenger flights to Huaraz. Buses to Huaraz have had the same robbery problems as buses to Ica and Nazca. Check with travel agents on the best way to reach the region.

HOTELS. For definitions of price categories see "Facts at Your Fingertips" earlier in this chapter.
TRUJILLO. Hotel el Golf. *Moderate.* Manzana J-1, Urbanización El Golf (24–2592/Trujillo, 44–4155/Lima). 120 rooms. Swimming pool, tennis and squash courts, and discotheque. **Hotel de Turistas.** *Moderate.* Independencia 485, Plaza de Armas (23–2741, 42–8626/Lima-Entur). Refurbished colonial mansion, one of the finest tourist hotels. 54 rooms. Continental breakfast. Restaurant and snack shop. **Hotel Opt Gar.** *Inexpensive.* Grau 595 (24–2192/Trujillo, 47–8760/Lima). 66 rooms with restaurant and snack shop.
CHICLAYO. Hotel de Turistas. *Inexpensive.* Salaverry Avenue, Urbanización Patazca (23–4911). 129 rooms including Continental breakfast. Restaurant and snack shop.
PIURA. Hostal Vicus. *Inexpensive.* Guardia Civil B-3 (32–2541). 24 rooms. **Hotel Turistas.** *Inexpensive.* Libertad 875 (31–1161, 32–5920). 33 rooms including Continental breakfast, restaurants, and snack shop.
TUMBES. Punta Sal Club Hotel. *Moderate.* Panamerican Highway Kilometer 1245 (22–2093). 18 bungalows and restaurant. The cost of lodging includes three meals a day. On the ocean. The hotel is 60 kilometers south of Tumbes.

HUARAZ. Hotel de Turistas. *Moderate.* Centenario, block 10 (72–1640, 42–8626/Lima). 60 rooms with heating and Continental breakfast. **Hostal Andino.** *Inexpensive.* Pedro Cochachin 357 (72–1662/Huaraz, 45–9230/Lima). 38 rooms and restaurant. A well-run hotel with a great view of the snowcapped mountains. **Hostal Colomba.** *Inexpensive.* 210 Francisco de Zela (72–1501). 30 rooms and restaurant. **Hotel de Turistas de Monterrey.** *Inexpensive.* 7 kilometers north of Huaraz (no phone, make reservations with Hotel de Turistas in Huaraz, above, or 42–8626 in Lima). 24 rooms, restaurant, hot spring baths.

CAJAMARCA. Hostal Laguna Seca. *Inexpensive.* Baños del Inca (tel. 05 in Cajamarca, 46–3270 in Lima). 23 rooms. **Hotel de Turistas.** *Inexpensive.* Lima 773, on Plaza de Armas (tel. 2470 in Cajamarca, 42–8626 in Lima). 60 rooms with heating and Continental breakfast. One of the finest examples of spacious, old-fashioned hotels run by ENTUR PERU.

RESTAURANTS. On the northern coast, the regional delicacies include roast kid and, of course, seafood prepared in a variety of ways. In the Sierra, the cheese and other dairy products are tasty and fresh. Trout is also served, fresh from the stream. Stick to the hotel restaurants.

THE AMAZON JUNGLE

There are three separate choices for exploring the marvels of the Peruvian Amazon: Iquitos, Puerto Maldonado, and Manu National Park. A fourth, Pucallpa, has unfortunately become a center of guerrilla activity. All of them offer the same attractions, packaged in slightly different forms. An excursion means being exposed to a tropical rain forest with its exotic flora and fauna, sensing firsthand the surging power of the Amazon River or one of its tributaries, and meeting a native Indian community.

Near Iquitos, over a century of hunting has almost eliminated large animals from the area. In Puerto Maldonado and Manu Park, it is still possible to see monkeys, giant river otters, and black caimans. Otter, capybara, tapir, monkeys, jaguars, over 400 species of birds—like toucans, parrots, hummingbirds—and snakes, like the boa constrictor, also inhabit the forests. The more developed the area visited, the harder it is to see rare species.

Most Indian communities around large settlements such as Iquitos changed their life-styles decades ago, accepting such conveniences as store-bought clothes, shotguns, radios, and sewing machines. Most have left behind their traditional attire. However, when a tourist boat comes to the village, arrangements have usually been made for them to take out their old costumes. Many communities, however, have kept up their crafts as a means of entering into a cash economy. For instance, jungle pottery and embroidery is beautifully designed and made. In more remote areas there still exist Indian tribes that have not been contacted by Western society. These and all other Indians in the area are under strict government protection and cannot be visited without special permits.

The most developed tourist facilities for Amazon tourism are in Iquitos in the northeast jungle. The city has several good hotels and a variety of jungle lodges which put the visitor in the middle of the tropical rain forests.

The Amazon River is over a mile wide at that point, an enormous flowing ocean which is deceptively powerful. It is continually remaking its course to the Atlantic Ocean, dissolving islands, turning oxbow bends into lakes, and sweeping away riverfront settlements. It is teeming with life, from freshwater dolphins to the feared piranha. On its shores, there is abundant wildlife and flora as well, though you will need a good set of binoculars to see them.

Iquitos

Iquitos is a town which has gone through several boom times. The heydays of the rubber barons in the early twentieth century made the sleepy jungle outpost into a boom town. But that phase soon passed and it slipped back into hibernation. In the early 1970s, petroleum was discovered in the northeastern jungle, making Iquitos an important staging area for exploration and development. Although vast deposits of crude were never found, oil has given a sustained shove to the city. Today, 270,000 people reside in Iquitos, which makes it the largest city in the Peruvian Amazon.

Manu National Park

Manu National Park's 1.5 million hectares are located in the Madre de Dios jungle east of Cuzco. The park, nearly the size of Massachusetts, is more difficult to reach than Iquitos or Puerto Maldonado. However, it offers one of the best opportunities for viewing Amazonian rainforest wildlife. Some of the most important research on Amazonian ecology has taken place at the biological station at Cocha Cashu in the park. Transport inside the park is almost entirely by river canoe with outboard motors. Revenue from the $10 entrance fee goes to pay guards, maintain trails, and protect against poachers, loggers, and settlers. Manu can be reached by plane from Cuzco, or by road and outboard canoe.

Madre de Dios

The third option is a sidetrip to Puerto Maldonado, farther south in the Madre de Dios jungle. This can easily be tagged on to a trip to Cuzco since it is only a half an hour flight from the Imperial City. Puerto Maldonado is a small settlement with a rough-and-tumble tilt. The Tambopata Candamo Wildlife Reserve was expanded from 5,500 to 1.7 million hectares in 1990. Several tourist companies are developing lodges and camping facilities in or near the park. The Heath River Plains Sanctuary (100,000 hectares) is at present virtually inaccessible, although there are projects to develop tourist facilities in the area.

You can also pan for gold in the riverbed. Gold-bearing silt washed out of the Andes over the centuries has been gradually deposited on the riverbeds and horseshoe bends (both in the current river course and in the old ones). Thousands of men brave the jungle wilds to pan for gold dust while several large international mining companies have also placed their bets on making a major find.

However, visitors should be forewarned that because Madre de Dios is one of the least developed regions of Peru, a stay there could be considered "roughing it." For example, electrical power can be interrupted at any time.

PRACTICAL INFORMATION FOR THE AMAZON

SPECIAL PREPARATION. If you are planning to spend a couple of days in the jungle or take an outing on an Amazon river, make sure you take a good sunscreen and insect repellent with you since there are no drugstores along the way. These are best brought from home since local products are usually expensive and/or ineffectual. In the evenings, your lodging should also have mosquito netting. Wearing long-sleeved shirts and trousers made out of lightweight fabric may seem odd in the tropics, but it fights off the sun and the insects. Rain slickers with pants are advisable, especially for travel by canoe. Maintain strict sanitary precautions and drink only bottled water and beverages. Carry a roll of toilet paper with you as well. Cholera, yellow fever, dengue fever, and malaria are present in some Peruvian jungle areas. This should not pose a significant problem if tourists adhere to travel precautions made available by their governments and seek competent medical advice before leaving. A pair of binoculars is a must.

HOW TO GET THERE. *Faucett* has direct weekly flights between Iquitos and Miami. Iquitos is serviced by *Aeroperu* and Faucett daily. Puerto Maldonado receives daily flights from Aeroperu, and Faucett flies there three times a week. It is impractical to try to reach these destinations by land. Manu Park is reached by small plane or by rough road and outboard canoe from Cuzco. Be sure to check with your embassy on the advisability of travel.

HOTELS. For definitions of price categories, see "Facts at Your Fingertips" earlier in this chapter. We recommend dining at the hotel restaurants.

IQUITOS. Acosta I and **II.** *Expensive.* 252 Calle Ricardo Palma (23–1983, 23–2904). 40 air-conditioned rooms and swimming pool. **Amazonas Hotel.** *Expensive.* Abelardo Quiñonéz Kilometer 2 (23–5731, 23–1091/Iquitos, 40–4559/Lima). 121 rooms and 7 suites with air-conditioning. Swimming pool, restaurants, and shopping center. **Amazon Bungalows.** *Moderate.* Carretera Pampa Chica 1940 (23–2913). 22 rooms in a vacation center setting. **Hostal Ambassador.** *Inexpensive.* Pevas 260 (23–3110). 25 rooms. **Hostal Maria Antonieta.** *Inexpensive.* Prospero 616 (23–4761). 33 rooms. **Hostal Safari.** *Inexpensive.* Napo 118 (23–5593). 22 rooms. **Hotel Turistas.** *Inexpensive.* Malecón Tarapaca (42–8626 in Lima). 73 rooms on the riverfront. One restaurant.

Jungle Lodges. Before laying out money for several days in an Amazon jungle, first check with a reputable travel agency in Lima. Once you are taken by riverboat to a jungle lodge, the only way back is on the one you came on. If you have bought a package tour, the agency will already have guaranteed services.

Amazon Lodge. Two hours from Iquitos on Yanayacu creek. 165 Putumayo, Iquitos (23–3032). Camino Real, San Isidro, Lima (41–9194).

Amazon Safari Camp. 40 minutes from Iquitos on the Momon River. 196 Putumayo, Iquitos (23–3931). 661 Colmena, office B, Lima (28–7813).

Amazon Sinchicuy Lodge. 132 Putumayo, Iquitos (23–3110, 23–8684). 714 Cailloma, office 505, Lima (46–3838, 46–3684).

Amazon Village. On the shores of the Momon River. 167 Miguel Dasso, San Isidro, Lima (45–9713).

Anaconda Lodge. 45 min. from Iquitos on the Nanay River, office in Iquitos at 133 Putumayo (23–6918).

Explorama Lodge. Two-and-a-half hours from Iquitos on Yanamono Creek. 350 Ave. de la Marina, Iquitos (23–5471). 851 Camaná, office 1501, Lima (24–4764).

Explornapo Camp. On the shores of the Napo river. 150 Putumayo, Iquitos (23–5471). 851 Camaná, office 1501, Lima (24–4764).

Jungle Amazon Inn. 311 Yavari, Iquitos. (23–2249). 732 Garcilaso de la Vega, Lima (40–8068).

MANU NATIONAL PARK. Manu Lodge. *Moderate.* Sol 627–B, Of. 401, Cuzco (23–4793). Built in 1988 by Manu Nature Tours. **Expediciones Manu.** *Moderate.* Procuradores 372, Cuzco. Organizes camping trips. Several other lodges are being built near the park, get details from a travel agent.

PUERTO MALDONADO. Albergue Cuzco Amazonico. *Inexpensive.* 15 kilometers outside Puerto Maldonado (47–7193, 46–2775/Lima). 30 rooms, 15 minutes down the Madre de Dios river. **Explorer's Inn,** outside Puerto Maldonado (235–342/Cuzco, 31–6330/Lima). 24 rooms. Located in the Tambopata wildlife preserve. **Hotel Turistas,** Leon Velarde (no number), Puerto Maldonado (tel. 29, 42–8626 in Lima). 16 rooms.

URUGUAY

The Purple Land

by
RAFAEL SARDÁ

A native of Uruguay, Rafael Sardá spent over 30 years with the Organization of American States in Washington, DC, as chief of visitor services and the speakers bureau in the department of public information, then as public relations director for the OAS Museum of Modern Art of Latin America. Most recently he was cultural and information officer at the OAS office in Montevideo.

There is nowhere quite like Uruguay. It was once referred to as the "Switzerland of South America" because of the nation's wealth, unique institutions, and political stability during the first half of the century. This, together with its population (almost all of European descent), makes Uruguay an atypical South American country. Uruguay is today more accurately described as "another Riviera." The country's spectacular 200-mile coastline is the site of many resorts, particularly the world famous Punta del Este.

Uruguay, as the second-smallest South American country (72,172 square miles), might be described as a big city with a large ranch that spreads over gently rolling hills (none above 2,000 feet), with very few trees native to the land. Most are newly planted in a remarkable reforestation program.

Uruguay's climate is temperate, subject to swift variation. In winter—June through August—the temperature sometimes dips as low as 23°F., but averages about 58°F. Summers—December through February—average about 85°F, and are tempered by Atlantic breezes. Along the coast, people wear light sweaters in the evenings, even on days when it has been very hot. Well-distributed rainfall is about 40 inches yearly at Montevideo and 10 more inches in the north.

Uruguay means "River of Birds." The country's vast prairies are often covered with purple flowers and a dark soil rich in potash that grows the world's most superior grasses for cattle and sheep. Only 8 percent of the land is farmed, while 90 percent is used for grazing. There are some sierras, none very high, and no mountains.

Montevideo, the southernmost point of the nation, fans out from the center into the hinterland. All roads lead to or from Montevideo. It has the nation's largest university, about half the secondary schools, half the newspapers, with 90 percent of the circulation, half the radio stations, half the doctors, and two-thirds of the hospital beds. Moreover, Montevideo has almost half the population.

This leaves about 100,000 working ranchers and farmers and their families who provide Montevideo's 1,450,000 residents with all the food they need. Fruits, vegetables, and rice are grown in the south and east, grain in the west. Cattle and sheep ranching are concentrated in the north central plateau, although these activities are found everywhere outside Montevideo. Livestock is a major export.

History

Uruguay was inhabited by seminomadic and sometimes warlike Indians, the *Charruas*, until late in the colonial era. The Portuguese were the first Europeans to settle here and founded the city of Colonia in 1680. In 1726, Spain established a fortress in Montevideo and the two European countries vied for control of the area. After a series of wars, Spain won possession of the whole region in 1726.

When Napoleon moved into Spain in 1808, Buenos Aires declared the Spanish Vice-Royalty autonomous. However, Montevideo still had loyalties to Spain and resisted Buenos Aires' control.

In 1811 José Gervasio Artigas, captain of the Spanish forces in the interior of Uruguay, mobilized Creoles and natives to fight with Buenos Aires for Latin American independence. He took Las Piedras and besieged Montevideo in the winter of 1811. After Portuguese troops moved into Uruguay, an agreement was reached between the conflicting forces and the siege of Montevideo was lifted.

Artigas then organized an exodus of all wishing to join him in an area north of Salto on the west bank of the Uruguay River. About one-fourth of the nation's estimated 60,000 population joined him in what has been compared to the Boer trek in South Africa. Paysandú was one of several communities almost completely abandoned by this force of about 13,000 civilians and 3,000 troops.

Influenced by the young U.S. federal republic and its new constitution, Artigas became the leader of a federal form of government in opposition to Buenos Aires and its desire to control the Plata River area under a centralist form of government. Artigas drove Buenos Aires forces from Uruguayan soil in 1815 and held together a federated area of what is now Uruguay and northern Argentina.

Driven out of Uruguay by a Portuguese army from Brazil in 1816, Artigas fell back to Northern Argentina, where he continued to fight Buenos

Aires' central government. He was finally beaten and forced to flee to Paraguay in 1820. Uruguay became a province of Portugal once again, until it was annexed by Brazil in 1824.

Thirty-three Uruguayan exiles—known as the "33 Orientales"—returned to Uruguay in 1825, and led a successful revolt against a strong Brazilian occupation force. Uruguay's independence was declared and signed in the Cabildo Building in Montevideo on August 25, 1825, and its first constitution on July 18, 1830, a date which gives the name to the main downtown avenue in the capital city. Fructuoso Rivera, a former Artigas lieutenant, joined the "33" under Juan Antonio Lavalleja and others to vote union with Argentina. This meant war between Argentina and Brazil, fought on Uruguayan soil and adding to the nation's potential for battle monuments. Britain, wanting peaceful commerce in the area, negotiated a peace in 1828 in which all concerned recognized Uruguay as an independent republic. From 1828 to 1872, civil war was frequent in Uruguay between two political forces, the *Colorados* and the *Blancos*. The Colorados were the dominant group over the Blancos, who were mostly ranchers. In 1872, the latter group needed peace to ship their beef to Europe and the two factions were able to reach an agreement by dividing the country into areas of influence. This was a major step towards political stability and the last decades of the 19th century were years of relative peace.

Democratic Growth

José Batlle y Ordóñez became president in 1903 and made Uruguay mostly what it is today—essentially a mixed socialist-capitalist economy, an urban cradle-to-grave welfare state. He served twice as president, 1903–1907 and 1911–1915, and dominated the nation's politics until his death in 1929. He had the combined physical features of a judge, professor, and "Kentucky colonel"—and he had a mental insight into political problems that were to label him one of Latin America's first and greatest reformers, although some feel he did too much for the urban proletariat and too little for the rural peasants. He knew what democracy was and how to obtain it. He emancipated women and gave them the right to vote, thus making Uruguay the first country in Latin America to do so. He also broke relations between church and state, making this also a "first" in Latin America, and built an advanced system of free public education as well.

In his climb to the presidency, he enlisted the middle class, which had been enlarged by European immigrants. Instead of starting his own reform party, he started his own newspaper and shaped the disordered Colorado Party into his own image. He cited both his Colorado and Blanco parties in demanding honest elections and civic responsibility. His first term of office was spent mostly in putting down another bloody civil war with the Blancos.

During four years in Europe between terms, he was impressed with Switzerland's executive council, social legislation, and state-operated industries as a cure for Uruguay's problems. From the editorial page of his *El Día* newspaper, he fashioned his ideas for a new Uruguay during his second term. For better government, he obtained a modified national council, a limited proportional representation in congress, direct presidential election, and complete separation of church and state. For labor, he instituted an eight-hour work day, minimum wages, old-age pensions, and other benefits. For small industrialists, he secured high tariffs to counter what he regarded "foreign economic imperialism." For rural workers who would provide the production to pay for these benefits, he offered little but rural schools. For women, he obtained a divorce law and arranged for education.

"The modern state unhesitatingly accepts its status as an economic organization," he explained. "It will enter industry when competition is not practicable, when control by private interests vests in them authority inconsistent with the welfare of the state, when a fiscal monopoly may serve as a great source of income to meet urgent tax problems, when the continued export of national wealth is considered undesirable." And then he showed just what he meant. He brought the government into insurance, utilities, railroads, banking, meat processing, tourist hotels, and even a "pawn shop."

Gabriel Terra, leader of the conservative faction in the Colorado Party, reversed Uruguay's democratic development in 1933 by installing himself as virtual dictator in collusion with the army. His regime, however, was unable to still the democratic forces that had become a national heritage.

A nine-man National Council replaced the president as executive head of the government on March 1, 1952. The Colorados had been consistently defeated at the polls; so they finally agreed to a system that would give them at least a minority voice in the government.

Until 1966, Uruguay inaugurated a new president every year, to serve as the nation's ceremonial head and preside at the nine-member National Council meetings.

Uruguay's unique elector system placed the government's executive power in the council, composed of six from the winning party and three from the losing party. The first four runners took one-year turns at the council presidency during the council's four-year tenure. Now all this has changed again. As a result of national elections in November 1966, Uruguay returned to its former system of a single executive administration, the people having disposed of the former nine-man National Council by vote.

In 1972, an urban guerilla group (the M.L.N. Tupamaros), was defeated by the military after almost seven years of overt action. A year later, in June 1973, sectors of the army and the navy led a successful coup. With the help of the president Juan Maria Bordaberry, the Armed Forces dissolved the Congress, and the military started to rule the nation.

After losing a plebiscite in 1980, and pushed by popular discontent, the military-led government started to bring the country back to a democratic, freely elected government, and political figures began to appear as candidates for the presidency. Many meetings were held between the military and civilians until a pact was agreed upon and signed at the headquarters of the Navy Club, which became known as "El Pacto del Club Naval." From that time on the race was on for the presidency, with leading candidates of the two old parties, the Blancos and the Colorados, as well as the Frente Amplio (Broad Front), a coalition of many different types. For the first time in all those years, elections were held, and Dr. Julio Maria Sanguinetti of the Colorado Party won the presidency, bringing forth a new congress of senators, congressmen, etc., all elected at that time, and who are now governing the nation.

Sanguinetti's government has been fairly successful in controlling the military and slowing Uruguay's economic decline. In December 1986 the Parliament voted an amnesty for human rights violators during the military period. But this measure has been very controversial and more than half a million Uruguayans have signed a petition to repeal the law. Finally, the decision was upheld in a plebiscite which took place in April 1989. In the presidential elections of November 1989, Sanguinetti's Colorado Party suffered its worse defeat in history. Luis Alberto Lacalle, the grandson of long-time Blanco party leader Luis Alberto de Herrera, was elected President of Uruguay for a five-year term. President Lacalle's main undertaking has been to eliminate government deficit-raising taxes and to reduce government spending.

The Arts

Literature, art and related subjects are organized on the intramural level for the joy of all and great prestige of none in particular. It is the enduring emphasis on the individual and his equality in the national society that characterizes the Uruguayan.

This affinity for the individual and democracy perhaps began with José Pedro Varela, the father of Uruguay's extensive public education system. While visiting the U.S., he came under the constructive influence of Horace Mann, noted U.S. educator, and Domingo Faustino Sarmiento, Argentine statesman-educator. Varela and Sarmiento returned to South America together in 1868—Sarmiento to become president of Argentina and Varela to inspire the formation of the Society of the Friends of Popular Education in his native land. Uruguay's middle-class society, responsible citizenship, and advanced democracy stand today as living monuments to the Uruguayan who did so much for education in just 11 years, before death stilled his boundless energies at the age of 34.

One big exception to Uruguay's intramural type culture is José Enrique Rodó (1872–1917). One of Latin America's several great writers, Rodó exerted considerable political influence with his magic pen. In his *Ariel,* he aroused the fear of many Latins against the U.S., then extending the "big stick" policy of Teddy Roosevelt about the Caribbean. He appreciated such virtues as freedom, education, and dignity in the U.S., but he thought these too mixed with materialism. He wanted a united Latin America that could stand together against the stronger U.S.

A group of novelists covered the taming of the gaucho from wild primitive to reluctant cowboy. Others captured the gaucho's folk songs and music. The latter resulted in Uruguay's national dance, the "pericon," a triple-time round dance resembling the French minuet.

Musical concerts are held often and are well attended. But Uruguay's top composer, Eduardo Fabini (1883–1951), is little known beyond the land. The national symphony orchestra has been compared well with large symphonies in the world and it has broadcast programs across the Plata River to sophisticated Buenos Aires. In summer the best musical performances are given free on open-air stages in different parts of the city.

The first native Uruguayan painter of note was Juan Manuel Blanes (1830–1901), who recorded on canvas much of his nation's rich history, as well as scenes depicting the life of the people in the country and rural activities. Blanes had two sons, Juan Luis (1855–1895), and Nicanor. Juan Luis became the country's first important sculptor, but died very young, while Nicanor became an important painter whose paintings depicted much of military life. Pedro Blanes Viale (1879–1926), was an impressionist who has two well-known historical scenes hanging in the Legislative Palace (Congress Building) and at the National Museum of Fine Arts. Pedro Figari (1861–1938), although he only started to paint after turning fifty years old, became one of the best artists of the nation with his colorful works of life in Montevideo in the nineteenth century. Rafael Barradas (1890–1928) was a well-known draftsman who moved to Spain, where he became one of the pioneers of the modern art movement. Joaquin Torres-García (1874–1949) has become the most internationally known of all Uruguayan artists. He lived in Spain, Italy, France, and New York during his younger years, returned to Uruguay in 1934, and became the leader of the constructivist movement. He founded a workshop, which still operates today, where many of the contemporary artists of Uruguay spent their formative years. His life became the basis for an excellent documentary prepared by the Organization of American States and the University of Texas. Together with Figari's, his works have commanded high prices at art sales and auctions held in New York and Europe.

Sculptors have also played a very important role in Uruguay's artistic life. Two of the leading ones have been José Belloni (1880–1965) and José Luis Zorrilla de San Martín, son of the great writer and poet, Juan Zorrilla de San Martín. Belloni is the author of three outstanding works that have become tourist landmarks in Montevideo. One, the covered wagon, is located at the park by the football stadium; the second, the Stage Coach, can be found at Prado's Park; and the third, El Entrevero, a group of gauchos fighting on horseback, is located in the heart of downtown. Zorrilla's two most important works are the statue of the Gaucho, also in downtown Montevideo, near the City Hall, and foremost, the obelisk commemorating the centenary of the first constitution, a beautiful work with three figures on its base, located at the crossroads of Artigas Boulevard and 18 de Julio Avenue.

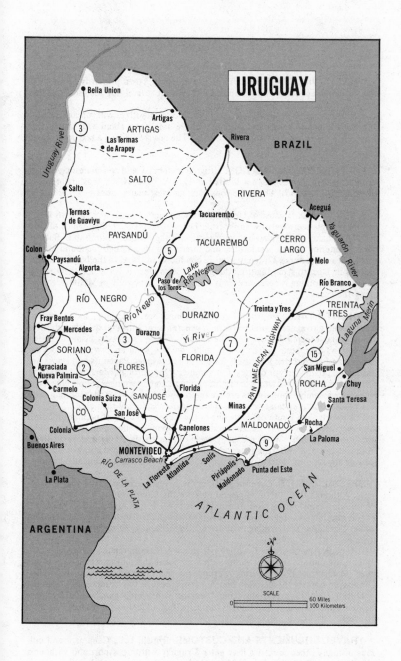

URUGUAY

Bella Union

Artigas

Rivera

BRAZIL

Uruguay River

3

ARTIGAS

Las Termas de Arapey

SALTO

Salto

RIVERA

Termas de Guaviyu

Tacuarembó

Aceguá

PAYSANDÚ

TACUAREMBÓ

CERRO LARGO

Yaguarón River

Colon

5

Melo

Paysandú

Algorta

Lake Río Negro

Paso de los Toros

Río Branco

RÍO NEGRO

Río Negro

DURAZNO

TREINTA Y TRES

Fray Bentos

Mercedes

3

Durazno

Yi River

7

Treinta y Tres

Laguna Merín

SORIANO

FLORES

FLORIDA

PAN AMERICAN HIGHWAY

15

Agraciada

2

San Miguel

Chuy

Nueva Palmira

Florida

ROCHA

Carmelo

Colonia Suiza

SAN JOSÉ

Minas

Santa Teresa

CO

San José

Canelones

MALDONADO

Rocha

Colonia

1

9

La Paloma

Buenos Aires

MONTEVIDEO

Carrasco Beach

La Floresta   Atlantida   Solís

Piriápolis

Punta del Este

La Plata

RÍO DE LA PLATA

Maldonado

ATLANTIC OCEAN

ARGENTINA

N

SCALE

0   60 Miles

100 Kilometers

FACTS AT YOUR FINGERTIPS

WHAT IT WILL COST. The Uruguayan economy, based primarily on the land and virtually dependent on oil importation, was hit severely by the oil crisis; this led to a general rise in prices.

A first-class hotel in Montevideo such as the Victoria Plaza will run around $70 to $100, while a decent room in an inexpensive hotel costs about $25. Lunch and dinner run $5–$10 and $10–$15 respectively. The bus is $.25, and a taxi costs about $1.50 in Montevideo.

SOURCES OF INFORMATION. Uruguay's embassy and consulates have tourist information. The embassy is located at 1918 F Street N.W., Washington, DC 20006 (202–331–1315). There are consulates in most major cities.

WHEN TO GO. Because of Uruguay's beaches and climate, most tourists come here in the relatively warm weather from Dec. to Apr. The chilling winds of July and Aug. make Montevideo uncomfortable and the beaches undesirable. But the nation's interior resorts, scenic sites, and interesting places might be found attractive all year. Of course, Uruguay is more conducive to travel in the better weather months of Dec. to Apr. Light clothing and sports wear is better for this season, but warmer clothing is necessary from June to Sept., especially in Montevideo and along the coast.

WHAT TO TAKE. Winter in Uruguay requires heavy clothing, and overcoats, scarves, and gloves are advisable. Men, in general, wear suits and ties, though there are irregular exceptions now (e.g. the casino). Women's dress is fashion-minded and follows European patterns—fur coats, woolen suits and sweaters, cocktail dresses, and at least one long dress for evening occasions. Pantsuits and slacks are less favored than skirts or dresses. For summer (Dec. through Mar.) in town, summer dresses or skirts with tops are right, although among younger people blue jeans and various combination outfits are common. For evening wear, have a long skirt and blouse, and a sweater or shawl too, as it may suddenly turn cool.

For resorts, like Punta del Este, one of the smartest and most popular in South America, men wear sport jackets, trousers, or Bermuda shorts, and no ties, even for formal occasions. Women usually wear caftans by day, long dresses at night. Both sun hats and rain wear are good to have along for both men and women. Blue jeans of any type are worn by young people and old as well for any and all occasions.

SPECIAL EVENTS. *Carnival Week* is the gayest occasion of the year in Uruguay. Although this "fiesta" is official only for the Mon. and Tues. preceding Ash Wednesday, many offices close during Carnival Week, although all shops are open. People masquerade, sing, dance, and parade through the streets of Montevideo. Fun makers, including many foreign visitors, crowd the hotels, clubs, casinos, and discotheques.

Although American and Brazilian pop music have been replacing the tango and other Latin dances, Carnival bursts with traditional Uruguayan music. One of the most remarkable events during Carnival is the "llamadas," when the Afro-Uruguayan community parades, dancing to the beat of the "tamboriles" (drums).

During *Holy Week,* officially called "Semana de turismo," gauchos in traditional cowboy outfits gather at Prado Park to compete in a giant *doma* (rodeo) that lasts all week.

TRAVEL DOCUMENTS AND CUSTOMS. British, U.S., Canadian, and citizens of many other countries may enter Uruguay with a passport and without a visa for a period of 90 days, and although the stay can be extended easily, tourists should make certain that the period covered is not three months but 90 days by calendar. No vaccinations are required to enter Uruguay from any country. It is wise for travelers to carry their passports with them for identification purposes. 400

cigarettes, 50 cigars, or 500 grams of tobacco, 2 liters of alcoholic beverages, and 5 kilos of food stuffs are allowed duty free. No other restrictions on personal effects in limited quantities.

HOW TO GET THERE. This country is well connected with others by air, boat and bus. *Pan American* and *Varig* airlines have several flights weekly from the U.S. direct to Montevideo. *LAN-Chile Airlines* has flights between Miami, New York, and Montevideo. *Cruzeiro do Sul* flies from Brazil. *Lineas Aereas Paraguayas* from Asunción and Lima, *Lloyd Aereo Boliviano* from La Paz, and *Avianca* from Miami and Bogotá.

Passengers from Europe might consider *Iberia, PLUNA,* (Uruguay's airline), *Air France, KLM, Varig, Lufthansa,* and *Scandinavian Airlines,* which all have flights to Montevideo. Embarcation tax is $9.

From Buenos Aires, there are many different ways to reach Montevideo. *Aerolineas Argentinas,* PLUNA, and *Aereo Uruguay* have shuttle services almost every hour from 7 A.M. to 9 P.M., or even later during the summer. *Aliscafos* is a hydrofoil company with runs to Montevideo. *Vapor de la Carrera* has an overnight boat trip sailing from each city at 10 P.M. and reaching either Montevideo or Buenos Aires by 7 A.M. the following morning; staterooms, a restaurant, and dancing are on board. *BuqueBus* and *Bus de la Carrera,* a combination of bus and boat services, and several other companies, provide services between the two countries.

Overland travel is becoming popular with travelers between Brazil and Uruguay. ONDA and T.T.L. bus lines operate comfortable buses between the two neighboring countries. Montevideo is 14 hours from Pôrto Alegre, Brazil. Many budget-minded Brazilians find a pleasant vacation in traveling to Montevideo by bus, then returning from either Montevideo or Buenos Aires by boat. The recently established bus line COIT has two departures weekly for Asunción and Iguazú Falls, plus excursions, on new Mercedes-Benz buses. Hostess and bar service. A new bus service links Montevideo and Buenos Aires through daily trips over the new bridges between Uruguay and Argentina, and weekly trips to Santiago, Chile.

CURRENCY. The new peso (N$) is the monetary unit in Uruguay. Notes of 50, 100, 200, 500, 1,000, 5,000, 10,000, 20,000, and 50,000 each are printed in different colors for easy identification. Coins for 100, 200, and 500 pesos are used (5 and 10 peso coins have almost no value). The exchange rate has been on the increase for a year or so, and runs about 1,500 new pesos to one dollar and will continue to go higher. There is *no* black market. Banks, as well as all exchange agencies, will exchange your dollars at the current day rate, with only a few cents difference among them. It is hard to cash traveler's checks, which are not always accepted.

Prices, unless noted otherwise, are in U.S. dollars.

HOTELS. In Montevideo, rates are based on double occupancy and categories determined by price: *Expensive,* $70 and up; *Moderate,* $30–$70; *Inexpensive,* $30 and under. Most resort hotels in Punta del Este are expensive by South American standards and must be reserved in advance from Dec. to Mar. Deluxe accommodations are from $100 single. Many of the country's fine, small resort hotels are available for less than $20 per night and apartments for about $50 a day, accommodating up to three persons. A 22 percent V.A.T. is added to all hotel bills.

RESTAURANTS. Uruguayan national dishes are built around beef, mixed salads and wine, but Italian pasta is also very popular. Good food is a national pastime here, and part of the population can afford a good appetite.

Besides those places known as excellent restaurants, a healthy, good-tasting, economical lunch or dinner can be had anywhere along the main street or in the downtown area.

Although lunch for the average Uruguayan means a three-course meal at home during the two-and-one-half hour noontime break, any of the sidewalk cafes, called "bars," will serve you an excellent steak sandwich ("chivito"), grilled ham and cheese ("sandwich caliente"), or tuna fish, turkey or club sandwich ("Olímpicos") for about $3, including a beer or Coke.

As an attractive alternative, you might order a "cóctel con preparación," a drink with at least half a dozen hors d'oeuvres included in the price. Keep in mind that imported whisky is expensive; you can settle for a local one at half the price. A "cóctel con preparación" with local whisky costs about $5.

Dinner is generally late; no restaurant will serve it before 8 P.M., and local people usually wait until 9:30 or 10 o'clock. However, around 5 or 6 P.M., local tea rooms get crowded. A meal for two with wine at an *expensive* restaurant costs about $20–$30 per person; at a *moderate* one: $10–$15.

TIPPING. Hotels and restaurants bill guests with extra charges ranging from about 10 percent, which are supposed to be tips but are actually what they consider wages for their service employees. These people expect another 10 percent on top of the bill. These extra charges are usually distributed among all workers but elevator operators on a point system. Figure $.80 or $1 for two pieces of luggage at the airport and other points of arrival and departure, 10 percent for taxis and $.30 for theater ushers. At airports and hotels tip in dollars a little bit less than you would at home.

BUSINESS HOURS AND HOLIDAYS. Normal business hours in Uruguay are 9 A.M. to 7 P.M. with a two-hour lunch break from noon to 2 P.M. Government offices and banks have a seasonal schedule. They are open from 8 A.M. to 1:30 P.M. in the summer; noon to 6:30 P.M. in the winter.

National Holidays: New Year's Day, Jan. 1; Three Kings Day, Jan. 6; Carnival (the three days before Lent begins); Semana de Turismo (Holy Week); Landing of the 33, April 19; Labor Day, May 1; Birth of Artigas, June 19; Constitution Day, July 18; Independence Day, Aug. 25; Columbus Day, Oct. 12; All Souls Day, Nov. 2; Dia de la Familia (Christmas), Dec. 25.

TELEPHONES. Local telephone service is adequate and operated by ANTEL, the government-run company. The entire country is equipped with direct dialing by area codes, and can be reached at once. There is also direct dialing to most countries in the world. Area code numbers are listed in all telephone books at hotel information services. According to the season in the United States, the time in Uruguay is one, two, or three hours later than in the eastern part of the United States. To call the United States dial 001 first, then the area code and number. Each minute costs about $5.

MAIL. Letters may be posted at any of the various post offices or letter-boxes. Airmail costs from N$.25 and takes five to six days for delivery. Hotels generally will sell you the necessary stamps.

TELEGRAMS AND CABLES. Charges for telegrams inside Uruguay and to Argentina and Chile are nominal. Cables can be sent worldwide through Telégrafo Nacional. Antel's TELE CENTER in Montevideo at San Jose Street 1102 (91–16–85) is open 24 hours a day for international fax, telex, telegrams, and long-distance calls.

ELECTRIC CURRENT. Uruguay runs on 220-volt current.

USEFUL ADDRESSES. *American Consulate and Embassy,* Calle Lauro Müller 1776 (40–90–50). *British Embassy,* Marco Bruto 1073 (72–35–97). *International Association for Medical Assistance for Travelers (IAMAT),* Avenida Italia 2484 (404364–409011). *Ministerio de Turismo,* Avenida Agraciada 1409, 6th floor. *Correo Central* (Central Post Office), corner of Misiones and Buenos Aires. *Bueme's Travel,* Colonia 979 (91–96–03).

The British Hospital, Avenida Italia 2440 (80–00–20), with English-speaking doctors, nurses, and staff.

The *Tourist Information Center,* Plaza Libertad (90–52–16), is open from 8 A.M. to 8 P.M. on weekdays, and from 8 A.M. to 2 P.M. on weekends.

One block from Victoria Plaza is *JET-MAR Travel Services,* the leading agency in Montevideo, with a staff able to assist in English, German, Italian, French, and Portuguese. Address: Plaza Independencia 725 (91–90–19).

HEALTH AND SAFETY. For American tourists visiting Uruguay there is no need for an international vaccination certificate. Uruguay does not have any contagious diseases. The offices of the Pan-American Health Organization in Uruguay informs, however, that anyone who has spent more than 5 days in Brazil prior to coming to Uruguay should be vaccinated for yellow fever. If you wish to contact the PAHO in Montevideo, call 44–455.

Uruguay, a peace-loving country, has no terrorism and no threat of bombings. While the drug problem spans the world, it is a small matter in Uruguay, and those dealing with drugs are dealt with severely by authorities. For example, anyone found selling marijuana is sent to jail, and those found smoking it are sent to rehabilitation centers or hospitals. Foreigners trafficking hard drugs have been caught a few times at Montevideo International Airport and some nightclubs, and have been sent to jail and dealt with according to Uruguay's laws.

Children begging on the streets, something completely unheard of a few years ago, has started to be a common sight in some areas of Montevideo. However, these children are not thieves, and will not attempt to steal your purse or bag. Usually they will ask you for a "monedita," meaning coin.

Uruguay is a safe country for tourists, and there is no reason to feel uneasy in any area of the country you choose to visit. Particularly safe are downtown Montevideo, Pocitos, Carrasco, and the resorts such as Punta del Este. All of the capital cities in the interior are also safe, and most people living here still don't even lock the doors of their homes. In Montevideo robberies have increased in the last couple of years but rarely, if ever, has a tourist visiting the city been the victim of a purse-snatching or had anything stolen from his or her hotel room. Still, it is important to exercise proper caution in these matters. All places where tourists would go—stores, restaurants, etc.—are perfectly safe day or night.

If you do ever need police assistance, dial 999.

HOW TO GET AROUND. Every place the visitor might wish to see in Uruguay may be reached by either plane, bus, boat, or car. There are several bus companies (with fixed rates) under government supervision. Some buses are air-conditioned. Cars rent for about $30 to $85 a day.

Unfortunately, in January of 1988 the government-owned and -operated rail system was closed. Originally built in the late 1800s by the British, this rail system had been poorly maintained and had provided increasingly inadequate service.

There are no scheduled boat lines along the principal rivers, but the Uruguayan River is navigable for pleasure boats or freight (no passenger ships) from Colonia to Salto, and the Río Negro, flowing across the country from northeast to northwest, is navigable to the port of Mercedes, an important rail hub.

PLUNA (Primeras Lineas Uruguayas de Navegación Aerea) Colonia 1021 (92–14–14/18 and 98–06–06), is an Urguayan airline with daily flights to all major points within the country.

Three bus lines—CITA, Pza. Cagancha (91–04–19 and 98–37–90), COT, Sarandi 699 (91–22–66); and ONDA, Plaza Cagancha (92–02–00 and 98–35–70)—provide comfortable travel throughout Uruguay. Buses enable the traveler to see more of the beautiful landscape, and also connect at Brazilian and Argentinian border points.

Cars are available for rent from *Avis, Hertz, Punta Car,* and *Rent-a-Car.* Rates range from about $21 daily, plus $.25 per km, for a FIAT 147—to $50 for a BMW 520 daily, plus $.55 per km.

Exploring Uruguay

MONTEVIDEO

Uruguay has no medieval history or regal colonial past, like that of Peru and Mexico, to provide it with ancient ruins or colonial monuments of great splendor. However, it is a pleasant place to relax and get to know the country, especially in the good weather from December to March.

Montevideo is well laid out for the tourist to explore. One might start at the port and customs area and cover the Old City, with its remnants of 19th-century and beautiful early 20th-century architecture. Since about three-fourths of Uruguay's extensive foreign trade is funneled through Montevideo, much of this area involves businesses related to shipping, banking and commerce. Almost all the nation's 73 banks are in this area—an industry probably resulting from the nation's political stability and efficient banking practices.

About five blocks in any of three directions from the waterfront, one finds the first of many combination parks and monuments. One is Plaza Zabala, with a monument to Bruno Mauricio de Zabala, the Buenos Aires governor who brought seven families here and founded Montevideo in 1726. The spot is marked by an outstanding piece of architecture, the Palacio Taranco, built by a wealthy merchant in French style and filled with its original imported furniture, marble floors, statuary, draperies, clocks, and paintings by prominent European artists of the period. At present, the Ministry of Education and Culture is responsible for its preservation and runs it as a center for cultural activities. One of the reception rooms has been transformed into a small auditorium that can hold up to 140 people, where the best of opera, chamber and recital concerts, plays, and ballet are offered from March to December.

The late 19th- and early 20th-century atmosphere of the city is evident four blocks up Rincon Street at Plaza Matriz, or Plaza Constitucion, as it is often called. This is the heart of the Old City. Standing face to face across the Plaza is the old Cathedral, seat of the Catholic hierarchy, and the Cabildo Building, where the constitution was signed in 1830. The Cabildo contains an outstanding museum dedicated to the history of the city, beautifully presented, with the best paintings, sculptures, antique furniture, old clocks, and a replica of the old Montevideo bastion. Open in the afternoon for tours, which can be conducted in English, French, and Spanish.

From this plaza, you can see the Río Plata to the right, as well as the walls and gun emplacements that once protected the city from foreign foes. The British stormed this bastion in 1806 and held Montevideo for several months. Their breakthrough occurred near the site of the present Anglican church, another symbol of British influence in Uruguay's early economic development.

From Plaza Matriz, two blocks eastward stands the big gate that was once part of the wall, which opens onto Plaza Independencia. This blends the old with the new and marks the colonial era from the republican one.

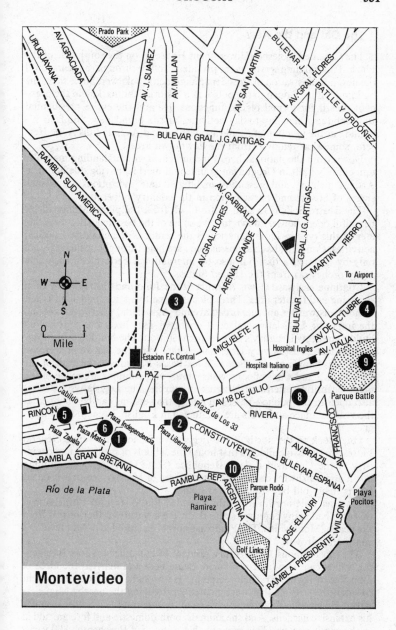

Montevideo

Points of Interest

1) Museum of Natural History
2) City Hall and Pre-Columbian and Colonial Arts Museum
3) Legislative Palace
4) Military Hospital
5) Cathedral
6) Solís Theater
7) Gaucho Statue
8) Hospital de Niños
9) Centenario Stadium
10) Museo de Artes Plasticas y Visuales

The Old and the New

The Casa de Gobierno (Government House) is on the south side of the Plaza. This building served as the president's office through the years, until the new administration of President Sanguinetti took over. Since then, the building has been open to the public as a historic landmark, and the president uses it for formal official functions. He and the entire presidential staff conduct their day-to-day activities at the brand new "Edificio Libertad" at the junction of Boulevard Artigas and Avenue Luis A. de Herrera, somewhat removed from the downtown area.

Down from the national hero's monument is an outstanding mausoleum, entirely built in Uruguayan granite and marble, paying due honor to Artigas' memory, and presenting, in different date inscriptions, the various stages of his life and participation in the country's liberation.

The Teatro Solís is located half a block from the plaza. Montevideo's beautiful opera house, known to have some of the best acoustics for a theater of this type in Latin America, is the center of the country's musical activities. Concerts, ballets, operas, etc., are held throughout the year, not only by national artists but also by international performers, including many orchestras from the United States.

Continue eastward down Avenida 18 de Julio and through the main shopping and theater area. Three blocks down this street and slightly left or northeastward is another broad avenue, Agraciada, where you will find the imposing Legislative Palace (Congress). This luxurious century-old building reflects Uruguay's democratic tradition. The building's most important feature is its very large hall, which joins the Senate and House chambers, known as the "Salón de los Pasos Perdidos" (the Hall of the Lost Steps), and whose floors, walls, stairs, and columns are made of the many beautiful varieties of Uruguayan marble. The Legislative Palace is also open to the public—passes to attend the sessions can be obtained at the visitors' office and tours are conducted in English, French, and Portuguese.

One block to the north of the Legislative Palace on Avenue General Flores are the two buildings that house the schools of medicine and chemistry of the Universidad de la Republica (State University). Continuing north and northwest one reaches an old area of Montevideo that is noted for its many old but still splendid homes.

Another mile northward is the so-called Prado. In mid-19th century, this area had many country estates that were a warm-weather retreat from the heat of Montevideo. The Prado has now been enfolded in Montevideo's continuing growth.

The most famous 19th-century resident of this area was José Buschental, a financier who built a 175-acre estate here and married the niece of Don Pedro II, the Brazilian emperor. He brought fish from the Orient to stock the streams that were created by dredging the nearby Miguelete River. He brought flowering plants from throughout the world to beautify his extensive gardens. And the animals, both domestic and foreign, added to the exotic scenery. This area now has a statue of Buschental, 800 varieties of roses, and is known as Prado Park, Montevideo's oldest.

Picking up at the broad intersection of 18 de Julio and Agraciada, travel two blocks eastward to find another plaza symbolic of Uruguayan life. Plaza Cagancha, which contains a column to liberty. Across the intersection and to the left on 18 de Julio is the Ministry of Foreign Relations, a beautiful palace from the late 19th century.

The Famous Gaucho

Three blocks farther down the road is an apex that steers 18 de Julio slightly to the left. Here is the famous gaucho on his horse, one of the two best examples of Uruguayan sculpture. Zorrilla de San Martín was at his best in freezing into bronze the true character of the gaucho: his dashing courage, threatening smile, and enduring freedom.

Another plaza four blocks down 18 de Julio marks another of Uruguay's historical mileposts. This one is named for the 33 brave ones who returned to their native land and expelled the Brazilians.

Down a few blocks is the University of the Republic's main building, which houses the schools of law and social sciences. Next to it stands the National Library building. Schools of engineering and architecture occupy more modern buildings in other parts of the city. With a passion for politics, university students are a serious group, and the professions they later practice are a tribute to their intellectual energies. Many also hold full-time jobs. The university is renowned for its education in medicine and architecture.

This wide avenue finally ends at Parque José Batlle y Ordóñez, a park that introduces the visitor to the man who created the contemporary phase of Uruguayan history. The park contains the 75,000-seat Centenario Stadium, built in 1930 to mark the nation's 100th anniversary of the signing of the constitution, and houses the first Soccer World Cup. The British introduced soccer here in the last century, then the Uruguayans took it from there and made it a national institution. Uruguay has won two Olympic gold medals and two World Championships. Also in the park is Belloni's famous bronze statue of the covered wagon, which reminds one of the covered-wagon days on the western frontier of the U.S. This life-size statue depicts six oxen hauling the covered wagon and a gaucho directing the oxen.

The third interesting travel route in Montevideo is the riverfront drive, called the "Rambla." This drive begins in the port area and runs along a wide sidewalk by the waterfront, clear to Miramar beach, some 12 miles linking all the beaches along the city's coast. The first of these beaches is Ramírez, very popular because of its proximity to downtown. Right at its waterfront stands the "Parque Hotel Casino," one of the two casinos in Montevideo open year-round. Along the beach is Rodó Park, named for one of Latin America's greatest literary figures. This park, with its artificial lake and small boats, is surrounded by beautiful eucalyptus, paradise, palm, and ombú trees. And the park, of course, has a statue of Rodó. The cluster of amusement facilities and refreshment stands gives the park a festive atmosphere. The beach and park are designed eventually to form a large waterfront recreation area. At the park, on the riverfront, there is an open-stage theater where ballet performances, concerts, and stage plays are offered mostly during the summer.

In conformity with this plan, an excellent municipal golf course adjoins the park as one continues along the drive. On Sunday afternoon, golfers must abandon the links so that young lovers may hike along the fairways and old people rest on green, shaded lawns.

Eight blocks along the Rambla is the small beach of La Estacada. Continue four more blocks to see the ornate skyline of Pocitos Beach. This is still part of the residential area of Montevideo, and in warm weather residents of Montevideo line the beach.

PRACTICAL INFORMATION FOR MONTEVIDEO

GETTING AROUND MONTEVIDEO. There are taxi stands all over the city and taxis can also be flagged or called for. Taxis in Uruguay are very inexpensive and comfortable. The cars are black and yellow with a lighted sign on the roof. Montevideo also has a public transportation system and buses go from one end of the city to the other; but a taxi is probably the easiest choice for the tourist.

HOTELS. For definitions of price categories see "Facts at Your Fingertips."

Downtown Area

Expensive

Victoria Plaza. Plaza Independencia 759; 90–05–39. 357 air-conditioned rooms and 22 suites; garage free of charge; car rentals; restaurant; bar; convention facilities.

Moderate

Columbia Palace. Reconquista 470; 96–00–01. 150 rooms and 5 suites; bar; restaurant; Finnish sauna; convention facilities.

International. Colonia 823; 92–00–01 and 92–00–02; fax 92–12–42. 95 air-conditioned rooms; bar and restaurant; convention facilities; garage.

Parque Hotel. Gonzalo Ramirez 2067; 49–71–11. 86 rooms and 4 suites; garage; bar; restaurant; casino; convention facilities.

Inexpensive

Embajador. San José 1212; 92–00–09. 68 air-conditioned rooms and 2 suites; coffee shop and bar; garage.

Europa. Colonia 1341; 92–00–45. 64 air-conditioned rooms and 8 suites with color TV and individual freezer; bar; restaurant; garage.

Gran Hotel América. Río Negro 1330; 92–03–92. 90 rooms; bar.

Lancaster. Plaza Cagancha 1334; 92–01–54. 80 air-conditioned rooms; bar; convention facilities.

Beach Area

Expensive

Hosteria del Lago. Arizona 9637; 61–22–10, 61–29–49, and 61–29–21; fax 61–28–80. 60 air-conditioned suites overlooking a lake; swimming pool; tennis court; garage; restaurant; bar; convention facilities.

Moderate

Casino Hotel Carrasco. Rambla Rep. de México (no street number); 61–05–11. 100 rooms, some overlooking the beautiful Carrasco Beach; bar, restaurant and gambling casino.

Oceania. Mar Artico 1227, 60–04–44. 26 air-conditioned rooms and 4 suites; restaurant; discotheque; convention facilities.

There are several lower-priced hotels in Montevideo for those adventurous tourists not expecting first-class service or bilingual staff.

RESTAURANTS. In the Pocitos residential district, 10 minutes by taxi from downtown Montevideo, is one of the best restaurants in town, **Doña Flor,** Bvar. Artigas 1034 (78–57–51). offering first class French cuisine in an elegant atmosphere.

For U.S. or European dishes, the **Victoria Plaza** has excellent food at reasonable prices. **Del Aguila,** Buenos Aires 694 (95–99–05), across the plaza and adjoining the Teatro Solís, provides the Uruguayan elite and foreign visitors good food at higher prices. For the budget traveler, there is good food at reasonable prices at **Morini's** half a block off the Plaza Independencia Ciudadela 1229 (95–97–33). But wherever in Montevideo one sees a spit turning in what is called *parrilladas,* and here one can get good beef with a good salad at incredibly low prices. The best parrilladas are at *El mercado del puerto,* in the Old City area next to the port. Here, in an iron building that served as a market in the 19th century, are many small restaurants that serve traditional Uruguayan food in a charming atmosphere. **El Palenque,** Perez Castellanos 1579 (95–47–04), and **La Proa,** Peatonal Pérez Castellanos y Yacaré (95–42–58), are two good ones.

One could not leave Montevideo without having dinner at the **Panoramico,** Soriano 1375 (92–08–25), located on the very top floor of the Municipio (City Hall) in the heart of the city. The excellent food and service is matched by a spectacular view of the city. Also in town are **La Suiza,** Soriano 939 (91–13–70), famous for the fondues; and **Club Aleman (Deutscher Klub),** Paysandu 935, 4th floor (91–74–96) for good German food.

Along the beach route, before reaching Rodó park, another outstanding restaurant is **Bellini,** San Salvador 1644 (41–29–87), where excellent Italian cuisine is served. In Pocitos are several places that have good cocktail hours such as **Cafe de la Paix,** Blvr. España 3000, overlooking the beach. Reaching Carrasco you will find **Dakel's,** Gabriel Otero 6438, serving German cuisine. On top of the Cerro de Montevideo hill, you will find the **Parador del Cerro,** Camino de la Fortaleza (31–13–14), a pleasant restaurant overlooking the city and its bay.

TOURS. For the visitor who has two or three days in Uruguay, there are several musts. A city tour with a guide would be desirable; otherwise, see the central area of the Old City and part of the New City by foot. The ornate Legislative Palace is a must, along with at least one of the major parks. And it is essential to take a taxi ride, a half-hour or an hour trip, along the Rambla drive and metropolitan beach area. A trip to Uruguay is not complete without visiting Punta del Este, especially in season. And a ride to a good cattle ranch, not further than 80 miles from Montevideo, can easily be arranged. To arrange for a tour guide or cattle ranch visit, contact *CEPLATUR,* Minas 1483, first floor (41–49–46). A taxi drive from downtown along the Rambla as far as Carrasco costs approximately $7 to $8. Drivers will figure the cost by the figure on the meter and an official chart they carry and must show the passenger.

MUSEUMS. The **Museo Histórico Nacional** (National Historical Museum) is located at Rincón 437 with an annex at Zabala 1469 (95–1051). These, residences of General Fructuoso Rivera and General Juan Antonio de Lavalleja in their times, contain 20 rooms displaying distinct steps in the nation's history. The **Museo de Historia Natural** (Natural History Museum), at Buenos Aires 652 (90–4114), displays in 10 sections Uruguayan fauna and flora, also archaeological objects and fossils. Other museums are the **Museo Nacional de Bellas Artes** (National Fine Arts Museum) in Rodó Park (41–6317); and the **Museo Oceanografico y de Pesca** (Oceanography and Fish Museum) at Rambla República de Chile 4315, which is located on the beach at Puerto Buceo. The **Military Museum,** on top of Montevideo Hill, has a collection of colonial Spanish uniforms and guns (31–1154); **Museo Romantico,** 25 de Mayo 428, has paintings and antique Spanish furniture; **Museo Precolombino,** Mateo Vidal 3249, has excellent Indian art, fossils. **Pre-Columbian and Colonial Museum,** in the City Hall building, has a good collection of Indian art from various primitive cultures of the continent. In the downtown area, the **Museo del Gaucho y de la Moneda,** Avda 18 de Julio 998, sports a collection of silver and gold objects ranging from swords to coins.

ART GALERIES. Many young Uruguayan painters, sculptors, and ceramists have won distinction in international art circles. Their works are shown in art galleries in Montevideo and Punta del Este. In Montevideo, **Galeria Bruzzone,** Bartolome Mitre 1373, and **Galeria Aramayo,** Mercedes 918, offer the best works and are worth a visit.

HORSE RACING. There are two main tracks: **Hipodromo de Maronas** (Sat., Sun. afternoon); **Las Piedras** (Thurs., Sat., Sun.). Entrance fees range between $.30 and $.75 (depending on the area chosen). Minimum betting ranges, respectively, between $.30 and $1.50.

SHOPPING. Because Uruguay is considered a developing country, you may bring many of the locally made products that you buy there into the U.S. duty free.

There are several items that should be in the luggage of every departing visitor. The best buy is a suede or antelope jacket, for both men and women. Some claim the amethyst jewels here, along with those of Siberia, are the best in the world, and they are moderately priced.

The same claim is made for Uruguayan nutria furs, with additional claims that the hair is longer, thicker, softer, and better colored than others. In any event the price is much less than elsewhere. And seal furs, from the estimated half-million seals on an island off of Punta del Este, are also popular with tourists. A Uruguayan specialty is a variety of gift items made from the hide of unborn calves *(nonato)*. Antiques and paintings can also be very good buys.

Montevideo also has some interesting flea markets selling handicrafts and antiques. Try Villa Biarritz Plaza and Zabala Plaza every Saturday morning, and Tristan Narvaja Street every Sunday morning. No tourist should leave Uruguay without buying, at bargain prices, some sweaters, skirts, ponchos, scarves, etc. The best places are the main three stores of the traditional *Manos del Uruguay,* the first co-op shop of wool goods, and the fancier Knit and Fashion Know located at Sarandí Street and Juan Carlos Gomez next to the Cabildo. In Montevideo the co-op stores are located at San José Street and Paraguay, behind the Solís Theatre in the Old Town Section, and across the street in a beautiful restored early 19th-century house.

Also, to enhance your own home or to bring gifts to friends, there are many beautiful things made of Uruguayan agate. In the rough or polished, you will find items from beautifully-set rings, earrings, and necklaces to ashtrays, paper knives, cigarette boxes, coasters, clocks, etc., all at very reasonable prices. One place to buy them is at *Cuarzos del Uruguay S.R.L,* Sarandi 604 (95–92–10), on the Plaza Matriz. *El Taller,* the studio and workshop of artist Zina Fernandez at Julio Herrera Street and Soriano, is also worth visiting.

Once a year, all through December, Uruguayan artists and craftsmen gather at *La Feria del Libro y del Grabado.* There, you will find beautiful ceramic works, as well as drawings and engravings.

NIGHTLIFE. This is not one of Uruguay's tourist attractions or an attraction for Uruguayans, for that matter. But there are several places where the visitor may relax, without expecting too much. There are popular and attractive discotheques in the Carrasco area, some with good floor shows. The best discotheque is **Zum Zum,** near the Panamerican Bldg. There are several dinner-dance places in Montevideo, but these come and go.

The Montevideo hotels have good bars, and the **Victoria Plaza** provides music for listening and sometimes for dancing.

CASINOS. Casinos, operated and controlled by the government, are found at the **Parque Hotel** in Montevideo, the **Hotel Carrasco** in Carrasco, **Hotel Casino** and its annex, both in Atlántida, and the **Hotel Argentino** in Piriapolis.

EXCURSIONS FROM MONTEVIDEO

Traveling east along the beaches, the air becomes cooler. The last so-called metropolitan beach is at Carrasco-Miramar, the most fashionable residential section of Montevideo, nine miles from downtown, whose streets are shaded by big trees—mainly pines and eucalyptus—and lined with large, beautiful homes. The beautiful beach is lined with small sand dunes banked by incessant winds. In contrast to the many modern brick houses with colorful tile roofs is the old Hotel Casino Carrasco, a French Renaissance-type building, restored and kept in perfect condition and open year-round as a hotel and as the second casino of Montevideo. Carrasco's International Airport lies three miles from Carrasco's center, about twelve miles from downtown Montevideo.

Beyond Carrasco, the highway becomes the *Ruta Interbalnearia* and turns somewhat inland, linking the entire Uruguayan coastline and its many beautiful white sand beaches, with branches off the highway into the resorts. While still within the limits of the department (state) of Montevideo, there are Lagomar, Solymar, and El Pinar beaches, joined themselves by yet another waterfront road. Once entering the department of Canelones, you'll come to Atlántida, thirty-five miles from Montevideo and surrounded by beautiful forests of pine and eucalyptus. This beach resort also has a casino, golf course, movies, restaurants, and fine fishing; a brand new port for sport boats will be built soon. Between Atlántida and the next important resort, Piriápolis, there are La Floresta, Salinas, Solís, and many other small resorts, all with lovely beaches and accommodations. Passing the second toll booth you enter the department of Maldonado and on to Piriápolis. Its large, excellent Hotel Argentino offers an indoor pool for year-round swimming, sauna, etc. Piriápolis, with its horseshoe-shaped bay, also has plans for building a port geared to pleasure boats. Well-planned, tree-lined streets stretch inland toward the high hills or low sierras that surround the area. Foremost is the Pan de Azucar (Sugar Loaf), with a huge cross on top of it that can be visited inside; the view from here, inside or out, is fantastic. Hill climbing is a popular sport; one of the prime attractions is San Antonio, where a small chapel dedicated to St. Anthony attracts pilgrims in June. Also near Piriápolis is Punta Fria, noted for its rock gardens. There is a brand new highway running along the shoreline from Punta Fria to Barra de Portezuelo, ending at the Intercoastal Highway a couple of miles from the airport at Laguna del Sauce, where daily shuttle flights, several times a day, fly to and from Buenos Aires, as this is the airport serving the internationally-known resort of Punta del Este.

EASTERN URUGUAY

Punta del Este

Punta del Este has, of course, become world famous as an international jet set beach resort, as the site of movie festivals and as a place for international conferences, such as the Meeting of Presidents of the Western Hemisphere nations and Assemblies of the Inter-American Development Bank. This resort on a peninsula, eighty-five miles from Montevideo, draws wealthy vacationers from Argentina, Brazil, Chile, Paraguay, the United States, and European countries. Argentines, mainly, own some of the most spectacular homes in the area in sections such as Lugano, San Rafael, and Pinares. Modern high-rises, apartment buildings, hotels, and homes are set among tall pine trees and facing long stretches of white sand beaches, divided at the tip of the peninsula. Entering Punta del Este area is Playa Mansa, or the "calm water" beach, and on the other side, running along to San Rafael and the former fishing village of La Barra, today a very sought-after area, is Playa Brava, or "agitated" beach. People there enjoy a December to March average temperature of 75°F., while enjoying two excellent golf courses in Punta del Este and another at Club del Lago a few miles before coming to the peninsula. You'll also find fishing, yachting (centered around the Yacht Club), waterskiing, wind surfing, polo, and horse shows. Social life is very active in Punta del Este, with dinner and cocktail parties starting near midnight and ending at dawn. Many art galleries have openings and shows presenting the works of Uruguay's outstanding artists. Some of the finest international cuisines can be found in Punta del Este's many restaurants. The Cantegrill Country Club offers tennis courts, swimming pools, theater, residential bungalows, etc. Off the shore of Punta del Este across the port is Isla Gorriti, formerly known as Green Island, a peaceful, beautiful haven of pine trees, beaches, and restaurants (there are two). Small craft from the port constantly make the crossing for tours, taking fifteen minutes for the trip. On the Brava side of the beach, farther out to sea is Isla de Lobos, or Sea Wolf Island. While tourists can not go ashore, it is fascinating to visit this huge colony of seals and sea wolves.

Maldonado

From Punta del Este, you can drive along the coast passing La Barra, Manantiales, and other beaches, reaching Jose Ignacio, another resort famous for its lighthouse. The town of Maldonado, capital of the department, is only three miles from the center of Punta del Este and has some fine examples of colonial architecture, much of it restored, such as the old City Hall—converted today to the Casa de la Cultura, seat of the cultural center, art school, music school, etc. The old Cuartel de Dragones, with its over 100-year-old chapel, cathedral, and Museum of American Art, can be visited before you continue on to the city of Rocha.

Rocha and La Paloma

Rocha is located to the northeast, 115 miles (185 km) from Montevideo. The capital city of the department of the same name is several miles from the Atlantic Ocean and can be reached by bus or car. As you run along the highway, palm groves stretching from sand dunes will show you the unusual beauty of the countryside. Right from Rocha, along Highway 15, you reach La Paloma, a lovely resort where a port for cruise and cargo ships is being built. Ten miles to the east you'll find La Pedrera, a charming fishing village now turned into a small resort.

Battle Monuments

Beyond Rocha, on the highway to Porto Alegre, Brazil, is the reconstructed fortress of Santa Teresa, which has been converted into a museum. This fortress, built by the Portuguese when they held this area in the 1750's, is part of a national park lined with palm trees and featuring a bird sanctuary and freshwater pools for swimming. Two miles away on the coast is La Coronilla, where people can fish in the ocean for sharks and among the rocks for black corvina and skates (the latter weighing up to 100 pounds).

Another old fortress at San Miguel, near the Brazilian border town of Chuy, has also been adapted to a national park. The park has many plants and animals, both foreign and domestic. There is a museum at the fortress and good surf-bathing at nearby Barra del Chuy. There are accommodations in San Miguel Park at the San Miguel Inn near the fortress.

PRACTICAL INFORMATION FOR EASTERN URUGUAY

HOTELS. For definitions of price categories see "Facts at Your Fingertips" earlier in this chapter. **PUNTA DEL ESTE.** (Maldonado's area code is 042.) **L'Auberge.** *Expensive.* Barrio el Golf (8–35–37). Very exclusive; 30 excellent air-conditioned rooms in a Swiss-style building; bar; coffee shop; French restaurant.

San Rafael. *Expensive.* Rambla Batalle Pacheco (8–21–61/5). Overlooking the beach; 150 rooms; gambling casino; bar; coffee shop and restaurant; convention facilities; swimming pool.

Alhambra. *Moderate.* Calle 28 No. 573 (4–00–94).

Amsterdam. *Moderate.* El Foque 759 (4–26–82).

La Capilla. *Moderate.* Viña del Mar y Blvd. Artigas (8–40–59). 40 rooms (some with air-conditioning); swimming pool; tennis court; bar and famous restaurant **Troika.** Open all year-round.

Castilla. *Moderate.* Calle 18 No. 933 (4–41–35).

Champagne. *Moderate.* Gorlero 828 (4–52–76).

Charrua. *Moderate.* Calle 27 No. 617 (4–14–02).

Marbella. *Moderate.* Calla 31 No. 623 (4–18–14).

Palace. *Moderate.* Gorlero Av. and 11th. St. (4–19–19). 60 colonial decorated rooms; coffee shop and bar; restaurant.

Azul. *Inexpensive.* Gorlero 540 (4–01–06). 25 rooms, coffee shop.

Embajador. *Inexpensive.* Parada 1 (8–10–08). 30 rooms, coffee shop.

Playa Hotel. *Inexpensive.* Av. Cont. Gorlero y Risso (8–22–31/2); 50 rooms; coffee shop.

LA PALOMA. Cabo Casino Sta. Maria. *Inexpensive.* On the beach, with casino (0473–6151/52).

Hotel Portobello. *Inexpensive.* On the beach (0473–6159). 47 rooms.

LA CORONILLA (near Rocha). **Costas Del Mar** (0472–011) and **Parador La Coronilla Hotel** (0472–04), both on the beach and *Inexpensive.*

LA PEDRERA. La Pedrera. (0472–034). *Inexpensive.* On the beach.

RESTAURANTS. To enjoy the best French cuisine, atmosphere, service with French-speaking staff, and elegance, the choices are **La Bourgogne** at Avenida Pedragosa Sierra, and, a couple of blocks away on the same avenue, **La Tabla del Rey Arturo.** Along Roosevelt Avenue is **Bungalow Suizo.** Almost at the entrance to the peninsula by water's edge is **El Club de Pesca.** There are several **Paradores** restaurants along the same route before reaching Punta del Este, all with informal atmosphere and good food. At the peninsula itself, the most exclusive—open only to members and guests—is the Yacht Club. For seafood, try **Mariskonea.** Italian food can be found at **Catari's** at the Palace Hotel at the end of Avenida Gorlero, Punta del Este's main drag. At the San Rafael beach, besides the hotel-casino of the same name there is an excellent restaurant and hotel at **La Capilla,** also open year-round; it is located next to the church, which provides some of the most delightful services in the area. Another must at the fishing village of La Barra is **La Posta del Cangrejo.** Owned by the same people who run Montevideo's Doña Flor, it offers fantastic food and an indoor/outdoor setting; especially pretty are the terraces with tables under beach umbrellas, overlooking the rocks, the sand, and the ocean. The proprietors of the Punta del Este Doña Flor also own San Rafael's **Doña Flor.** The Posta del Cangrejo has been host to celebrities such as Julio Iglesias and many American and European artists in its Mediterranean-type hotel.

The English-speaking traveler should always remember that only in the more pretentious restaurants and hotels is English understood. Tourists not speaking Spanish should learn a few restaurant words before going to the more popular and locally patronized restaurants.

CASINOS. There are two casinos in Punta del Este: **Hotel-Casino San Rafael** and **Nogaró.**

BOATING. Motorboat rental is available at **Lanchas Tuttie,** Puerto Punta del Este (4–25–94) for daily excursions to Isla de Gorriti and Isla de Lobos.

THE INTERIOR

Uruguay's interior unfolds unique scenery and sites for visitors. Much of this area was opened by the Pan American Highway, which stretches from the Brazilian border town of Acegua southwestward across Uruguay to Montevideo, then westward to Colonia, across the Plata River from Buenos Aires.

A trip to Colonia brings into view some of the nation's richest farming area, rolling hills, neat towns, and varied scenery. Santiago Vazquez, on the banks of the Santa Lucia River, is famous for what is known elsewhere as fish-fries, made from fish weighing up to 75 pounds that are caught from the river. The concentration of pleasure craft reflects the popularity of boating in this area. Two hours out of Montevideo and a small distance from the Pan American Highway is "Colonia Suiza," settled by immigrants from Switzerland more than a century ago. This little tourist resort features Swiss-style entertainments, clean and comfortable hotels, fine cheeses, and quiet rest in beautiful surroundings. Nearby are "Colonia Valdense" and "Nueva Helvecia," noted for fine fruits, vegetables, cheese, and quaint, locally manufactured music boxes. Colonia Valdense, founded by evangelical followers of Peter Waldo (12th-century French religious leader), retains many of the customs and practices of its ancestors.

COLONIA

Colonia del Sacramento, about two-and-a-half hours by car from Montevideo, is a hub of traffic toward Buenos Aires and up the Uruguay River. A hydrofoil operates to Buenos Aires three times daily. This 17th-century Portuguese settlement retains more of its colonial atmosphere than other Uruguayan communities. Old houses with barred windows line narrow cobblestone streets. Sights to see include the historic parochial church, municipal museum, viceroy's mansion, and the lighthouse. San Carlos, a warm-weather resort, is four miles from Colonia. The community's bull ring (Plaza de Toros) stands in ruins as a memory of bullfights that attracted many Argentines from across the river before the sport was outlawed a half-century ago.

PRACTICAL INFORMATION FOR COLONIA

HOTELS. COLONIA DEL SACRAMENTO. Hotel Mirador. *Expensive.* (0522–2004). First-class hotel with excellent restaurant, bar, swimming pool, casino.

Posada del Gobernador. *Inexpensive.* Av. Roosevelt (0522–2918, 3018). Good hotel with excellent restaurant in an old colonial building in the heart of the historical area.

COLONIA SUIZA. Hotel Nirvana. *Expensive.* (0522–4081). Countryside hotel with 120 rooms. Tennis court, swimming pool, restaurant, bar.

RIVER COUNTRY

Fifty miles (81 km) north of Colonia is the picturesque river port of Carmelo, a popular yachting center and resort area. The sheltered waters of a stream flowing into the Uruguay River, Arroyo de las Vacas, form a sort of naturally endowed yacht basin catering to craft from rowboat to luxury dimensions. Historically, Carmelo has the ruins of a Jesuit orphanage, where José Artigas was elected leader of the revolutionary movement in 1811.

Continuing 18 more miles (29 km) up the Uruguay River you come to Nueva Palmira, a port of call for river steamers. Another 12 miles is La Agraciada, where the famous 33 patriots landed from Argentina and organized a Uruguayan force that expelled Portuguese occupation troops. A statue to General Lavalleja, group leader, is on the beach. The livestock and resort center of Mercedes lies 30 miles up from the point where the Río Negro flows into the Uruguay River. This can be reached by the road from Colonia or from Montevideo, 186 miles (299 km) away. Yachting and fishing are popular here in warm weather. Paysandú, on the Uruguay River 299 miles (481 km) from Montevideo, is a popular fishing area for the dorado game fish.

Uruguay has two new links with Argentina and the rest of South America. Two bridges cross the Uruguay River; one of them connecting the villages of Fray Bentos (Uruguay) and Puerto Unzue (Argentina), by the name of Gral. San Martin, and another one connecting Paysandú, a northern city in Uruguay, with Colón, in Argentina. The latter is called Gral. Artigas Bridge.

These two important engineering constructions, along with the Salto Grande hydroelectric power plant, have become a very interesting feature of the new Uruguay, and a different way to reach other countries overland.

Traveling along Highway 3 past Mercedes, Fray Bentos, Paysandú, and Salto, there are three excellent spots for tourism known as "termas," where natural thermal water is used year-round in swimming pools and whirlpool baths. Hotels and private bungalows provide comfortable accommodations. Slightly northeast from the city of Paysandú you find the first of these spots, called Las Termas de Guayabos. Farther up Highway 3 are Termas de Guaviyu in the department of Salto; near the capital city of the department of the same name are a small cluster of several termas. Finally, in the department of Artigas in the northern tip of Uruguay, a few miles eastward from Highway 3, are Las Termas de Arapey, the largest of them all.

For beautiful scenery and interesting sites, travel north via national route No. 5 from Montevideo through Florida, Durazno, and the surrounding valley of the Yi River, and Tacuarembó to the Brazilian border town of Rivera, from where it is easy to continue on to São Paulo, Brazil. Although the area is not heavily populated, this trip through almost the country's dead center can be made by bus or car.

From Montevideo, the traveler soon picks up a variety of interesting scenery, which includes the vineyards providing the good wines (consumed with even better steaks), dairy and poultry farms, and fields of alfalfa, corn, and tobacco. At Florida, 78 miles (126 km) from Montevideo, one enters the city through a historically important display of smooth stone. Here, the Uruguayan patriots declared their independence and freedom from foreign domination August 25, 1825. There is good fishing on the Santa Lucia River, which flows by the city. Nearing Durazno on the banks of the Yi River, the so-called "purple land" of Uruguay comes into view. This scenery was made famous by William Henry Hudson in what is perhaps the best travel literature yet done on Uruguay, *The Purple Land.* This book, first released in 1885, was one of Theodore Roosevelt's favorites and perhaps induced him to travel to South America. The nearby hydroelectric plant of Rincon del Bonete produces power from Uruguay's largest artificial lake, stocked with many varieties of fish for the attention of increasing tourists. Plenty of game and fowl are found at Tacuarembó, 279 miles (449 km) from Montevideo. Visitors here enjoy the caves about 10 miles distant in this hill country. Rivera lies 73 miles (118 km) beyond, on the Brazilian border, spread over two hills that feature a park, Plaza International, the Cunapiru Dam, and the pleasant aspects of good relations with Brazilians living in the adjoining community of Santa Ana do Livramento. The international boundary line is like a main street in other communities, and both nationalities walk back and forth freely.

The Pan American Highway, running northeast from Montevideo, is one of the country's newest and best-paved roads; it starts as Highway 8 at the outskirts of Montevideo and leads you to Minas, capital of the department of Lavalleja, named for the leader of the 33 patriots, along some of the most spectacular scenery in the sierras. Some tourists find Minas, about 75 miles (121 km) from Montevideo, to be a nice change from the beach resorts. It features mineral deposits, beautiful marble ranging from pure white to black, mineral springs used for baths, excellent drinking water, nearby caves, and the equestrian statue of Lavalleja. The mineral water of Minas is also used in the excellent beer that Uruguay produces.

PRACTICAL INFORMATION FOR THE RIVER COUNTRY

HOTELS. All hotels in the interior are *inexpensive.* **MERCEDES. Hotel Brisas Del Hum,** Gimenez 766 (05352–633).

FRAY BENTOS. Fray Bentos Hotel, Paraguay St. (0532–358). **Plaza Hotel,** corner 18 de Julio and 25 de Mayo (0532–363).

PAYSANDÚ. Grand Hotel, corner 18 de Julio and 19 de Abril (0722–3400/4200/4600). **Nuevo Hotel Paysandú,** corner L.A. de Herrera and Leandro Gomez (0722–3062, 3063).

SALTO. Gran Hotel, 25 de Agosto, No. 5 (0732–3250/3251); **Los Cedros,** Uruguay 665 (0732–3984/3985); and **Concordia,** Uruguay 749 (0732–2263/2735).

URUGUAY'S LAST FRONTIER

Instead of continuing northward to Melo and the border town of Aceguà, Brazil, most people prefer to turn off at Treinta y Tres and travel northeastward to the border town of Río Branco. Treinta y Tres, 200 miles (322 km) from Montevideo, can also be reached by rail. Travelers along this route see what was Uruguay's last frontier that has now been recorded in its folklore. It was here that cattle roamed unattended until the wandering gauchos would come along with their baggy trousers, boleadoras, guitars, and *maté* (tea) to camp along a stream. One of the most important words in the Uruguayan vocabulary developed here: *estancia* ("to be located"), the word for ranch. When the ranges were finally fenced in, the adventurous gaucho began to disappear. But, like his counterpart in Argentina and Brazil, he is remembered in the nation's songs and dances. Some modern gauchos still ply their trade and retain the customs of their forebears, but they are bucking the twentieth century.

VENEZUELA

Where the Andes Meet the Caribbean

by
HILARY BRANCH

A resident of Venezuela for over three decades, Hilary Branch is a freelance writer whose work has appeared in the World Environment Report, The Daily Journal, *Caracas's English-language newspaper, and* Ve Venezuela, *the local tourist magazine which she edited for many years.*

In store for travelers to Venezuela is a land as rich and exciting in natural beauty as in cultural contrasts. The country rewards bold spirits with discovery and delight, from the arid Guajira Peninsula in the west where tribesmen raise cattle and weave bright tapestries, to the eastern Orinoco Delta where Warao craftsmen carve wooden animals and dugout canoes, and from the southern forests of Amazonas Territory peopled by the Stone-Age Yanomami, to the steel and aluminum mills of Ciudad Guayana, Venezuela's capital of heavy industry on the great Orinoco River.

Three destinations top most tours. Charter flights direct from the United States and Canada bring tourists the easy way to Margarita Island's beaches; in Mérida the world's longest and highest cablecar system makes scaling the snowy Andes swift and unforgettable; and for many passengers on the daily jet to Canaima, a view of Angel Falls is the high point of Venezuelan adventure. But for travelers who want to get off the beaten track, the interior of this country of 352,143 square miles (566,950 sq km) unfolds fascinating panoramas. A dozen new specialty travel agencies are filling the demand for adventure treks and photo safaris. They provide the private flights, permits, and equipment that enable outsiders to go places normally inaccessible, such as the Orinoco headwaters, Los Roques Archipelago, or the *Llanos* (pronounced Yah-nos), vast plains which are home to millions of birds and animals, comparing favorably to Africa in variety and quantity of fauna, if not in big game.

Cloud forests, coral islands, rivers, mountains, jungles, and caves make up 35 national parks covering 9.5 percent of the country. Most of this area of 30,800 square miles (49,588 sq km) is virgin, undeveloped. The largest park, Canaima, is the size of Belgium and stretches from the diamond-strewn Caroní River to Brazil and Guyana; the borders of the three nations meet atop Mt. Roraima, a giant mesa that inspired Conan Doyle's fantastic tale of *The Lost World*.

No longer on the list of most expensive destinations, the country is combating economic recession in a number of ways, not the least of which is tourism promotion. With the currency devalued many times, a meal for two at a first-class restaurant, excluding wine, costs less than $25, while a ride on the modern Metro halfway across Caracas costs less than $.25. The low cost of gasoline, subsidized at less than 50 cents a gallon, and the excellent network of freeways that crisscross the country help to make Venezuelans among the most mobile people in Latin America. Since the opening of a road to Amazonas Territory, branch highways now link every part of Venezuela.

Oil still brings Venezuela a multibillion-dollar income and prosperity is seen in lavish restaurants and nightclubs, in four-story shopping pyramids, and in glass and concrete office blocks, topped by the fifty-six-floor Parque Central towers. And, of course, in the spic-and-span new Metro whose efficiency seems little less than miraculous to delighted *Caraqueños.*

Generous and usually relaxed people, there is nothing stuffy about Venezuelans. Irrepressible in their love for repartee, quick to anger and just as quick to smile, they approach life with optimism and casualness in everything except three matters: motherhood, democracy, and honor—a slur implying lack of respect can lead to big problems, especially if it is an official's character that is in question. Since 1958, favored by a relatively high standard of living, the nation has enjoyed one of the most stable democracies in Latin America, where almost 90 percent of the population votes in presidential elections (voting is obligatory).

Venezuela has welcomed wave after wave of immigrants: refugees from war-torn Europe, political exiles from dictatorships in Spain and later Argentina, Chile, and Haiti, and landless peasants from Colombia, Portugal, and Spain. As many as 10 percent of the country's 20 million inhabitants are foreign-born. Illegal immigration by Colombians has resulted in certain problems at the border crossing for tourists not equipped with return fares.

Indian Heritage

And what of Venezuela's original inhabitants? The Carib- and Arawak-speaking Indian groups today are a small minority. Numbering only 140,000 in some twenty-eight ethnic groups, they live in the remoter parts of the country, protected to some extent by the inaccessible or inhospitable nature of the Orinoco's delta, the rain forests spreading south to Brazil and west to Colombia, and the semi-desert home of the partly acculturated Guajiro Indians on the Guajira Peninsula. The Motilones or Barí, who defended their hills west of Lake Maracaibo with lethal aim for 450 years, are now "tame."

While it is true that no tribe in Venezuela built stone temples, Indian culture has contributed much to the country's social makeup, folklore, food, and art. An Indian fertility goddess, María Leonza, is still worshiped with a pantheon of lesser notables in the hills near Chivacoa (between Valencia and Barquisimeto) in a mixture of Catholic and pagan rites. In Caracas, her followers heap flowers on the pedestal of her statue on one of the busiest freeways near the Central University. Riding a tapir and carrying a man's pelvis aloft, the naked Indian Princess is an astonishing sight.

But it is in the practical arts that the surviving tribes contribute most to Venezuelan culture. Dugout canoes, skillfully hollowed from single tree trunks, some as long as 36 feet, are as yet unsurpassed as river craft. The hammock is an Indian invention and no Venezuelan beach-goer, hunter, or hiker travels without one. They come in many sizes and materials and the best are made by Indian women starting with palm leaf fiber or wild cotton. And no Venezuelan woman raises her family without cornmeal cakes or *arepas,* a word taken from the Cumanagoto for maize. In the less fertile jungles, *casabe,* or flat cakes made of manioc meal (yuca), continue to be the best and simplest way of conserving food, a difficult thing to do in the hot country. Then again, Christmas is not Christmas in Venezuela without the tamale-style *hallaca* in its Indian banana-leaf wrapping.

The Indians' knowledge of plants, such as the Strychnos lianas used in making curare, has led to valuable medical applications. Curarine is employed as a muscle relaxant in surgery today.

The Conquest

Indian houses built on stilts along Lake Maracaibo gave rise to Venezuela's name when mapmaker Amerigo Vespucci was reminded of "Little Venice" and its canals. Vespucci sailed to the New World with Alonso de Ojeda in 1499, the year after Columbus had claimed Venezuela for Spain on his third voyage. In the years that followed, the conquistadors made incredible explorations overland and upriver in fruitless searches for gold. To pay his debts, Charles V mortgaged Venezuela to the German banking house of Welser in 1528, but the German fortune hunters had no better luck. Sir Walter Raleigh, the piratical favorite of England's Queen Elizabeth I, also forayed up the Orinoco in the vain hope of finding El Dorado.

With no treasure to plunder, the Spaniards eventually turned to the land, subjugating the Indians as slave labor for large haciendas. Francisco Fajardo, the son of a Spanish nobleman and a Guayquerí Indian, was given men and arms by the governor of Margarita to settle the coast of Caracas in 1559. He was a natural choice for cementing peaceful Indian relations and was able to establish a farm in the valley of the Caracas Indians, where eight years later Diego de Losada founded the town of Caracas. Today only the names of the resisting tribes remain—the Caracas, Teques, Mariches, Cumanagotos, Tamanacos, and their slain heroes Guaicaipuro, Manaure, and Mara. Even Fajardo was betrayed and executed.

By the end of the sixteenth century, twenty towns had been established. But the cost in Indian lives was appalling. From Cumaná to Maracaibo along the Venezuelan "slave coast," which was heavily settled by Carib tribes, the entire native population of several million was wiped out. (South America had about fifty million inhabitants in the fifteenth century; of these, scarcely two million survived the Conquest.) The landowners then imported Negro slaves to work cacao and tobacco. The Africans intermingled early with the Spanish Creoles and surviving Indians, producing a racial fusion that is apparent in two-thirds of today's population.

Independence and Bolívar

The Venezuelans developed independent habits early on. The provincial government in Caracas, administered from Spain, ran its affairs pretty much as it pleased, as did the six other Venezuelan provinces. Attempts to bring the colony to heel only encouraged resistance to Spanish economic and political controls, and there were uprisings in 1749, 1797, and 1806. In 1810, when Spain was invaded by Napoleon, the Creoles in Caracas took advantage to depose the governor and, with patriot leaders from the provinces, set up a National Congress. On July 5, 1811, independence was declared; the day is still celebrated as Venezuelan Independence Day, although the patriots' struggle had just begun.

After the collapse of the first republic, leadership of the revolution passed to Simón Bolívar, who was to liberate Peru, Bolivia, Ecuador, Colombia, and Venezuela. Simón Bolívar was born in Caracas of wealthy Venezuelan parents in 1783. Orphaned at an early age, he spent many years studying and traveling in Europe, where he was inspired with a mission to free his people from Spanish rule.

Bolívar played an active role in the 1811 independence movement and was second in command to Francisco de Miranda under the short-lived first republic. Then followed ten years as war leader before the Venezuelan patriots finally trounced the Spanish forces on June 24, 1821, at the Battle of Carabobo. Although Bolívar went on to greater glories, his dream of uniting Venezuela, Ecuador, and Colombia into "Gran Colombia" was a failure. Regionalism triumphed with the determination of the local elite to rule their own countries. Hounded by jealousies, ill with tuberculosis, and almost penniless, Bolívar retreated to private life. Ironically, it was a Spaniard in Santa Marta, Colombia, who gave him refuge. He died on December 17, 1830, a disillusioned man. In 1842 his remains were transferred to Caracas, where today they repose in the National Pantheon.

Foundations of Modern Democracy

Venezuelans, however, did not achieve real economic or social independence for another 125 years, as a succession of unsavory dictators and a small, landed aristocracy ruled during the nineteenth and early twentieth centuries. From 1908 to 1935, power was held by the most brutal dictator of them all, Juan Vicente Gómez, a semi-literate bandido. It was during the Gómez tyranny that the first generation of modern leaders, known as the "generation of 1928," rebelled. Jailed and then exiled, these young rebels returned to Venezuela after Gómez's death to become an important political force during the transitional period under Eleazar López Contreras and Isaías Medina Angarita. Rómulo Betancourt, founder of Acción Democrática (AD), one of the two leading political parties, headed a popular revolution in 1945 with a group of young military officers. In 1948, novelist Rómulo Gallegos (author of "Doña Bárbara") of AD became the first democratically elected president.

But the military had not lost its taste for power; within nine months the government fell to yet another dictator, Major Marcos Pérez Jiménez. A spendthrift who used oil wealth to build some of the continent's flashiest public works—including a horse racetrack and mountaintop hotel—Pérez Jiménez jailed or exiled most of the country's democratic leaders. His rule lasted until he was overthrown on January 23, 1958. Venezuela was at last able to undertake a series of far-reaching reforms.

Elected president, Rómulo Betancourt completed a five-year term and in 1964 turned his sash over to another AD leader, Raúl Leoni, in the country's first democratic change of government. Alternating in power, the Social Christian party (COPEI) ascended with Rafael Caldera who was president from 1969 to 1974. Succeeding Caldera was Carlos Andrés Pérez of AD, who served 1974–1979. After an absence of two terms (decreed by law), in which office was held by Pres. Luis Herrera of COPEI and Pres. Jaime Lusinchi of AD, Pérez returned to the presidency in 1989.

Social Problems

Adding to the fact that 90 percent of the country's inhabitants are crowded into one tenth of the land (the northern Andean and coastal belt) is a yearly population growth of 3 percent and massive migration from rural to urban areas.

Four of every five Venezuelans today reside in cities. In the Federal District of Caracas, more than half the population live in the poverty belt of *ranchos*, or huts, which rings the capital. Although many of these communities, called *barrios*, have water, roads, electricity, and schools, a rising crime rate accompanies the large floating population and high index of broken or incomplete families.

All these factors contribute to the overstraining of public services. Many problems can be traced to the long reign of dictators who had no thought for schools or hospitals even as late as the 1950s. For example, in 1948 there were only 20,000 high school students, a figure which today has increased 20 fold. Because four of every 10 Venezuelans are under 15 years old, pressure is enormous on the state educational system. Some schools work in two shifts, morning and afternoon. Low teaching standards, early dropouts, and an illiteracy rate of 10.5 percent are all problems.

Public hospitals have long waiting lines and sometimes no sheets. Policemen and judges are underpaid. The prison system is overburdened and four-fifths of all prisoners await sentencing, sometimes for years. Virtually all prisoners are from underprivileged groups and crime is on the rise, reflecting the problem of unemployment. Officially the jobless rate is around 10 percent (1990), but union estimates put the figure at 25 percent, and almost 40 percent of the population must support itself by 'under-ground' or informal economic activities. Of those who do have jobs, one in every four works for some state enterprise, ministry, or government bureau.

Economic Concerns

The 1990s should mark the turning point for an economy which shrank steadily during the previous decade, ending with 80 percent inflation and riots. Trouble started with the collapse of oil prices and Venezuela's inability to pay heavy foreign debts to the tune of $36 billion. In 1983 the bolívar stood at Bs.4.29 to the U.S. dollar; by early 1991 it had been devalued to Bs.53 to the U.S. dollar.

A severe adjustment program introduced by the Pérez administration caused the gross domestic product to fall 8.3 percent in 1989. However, the economy began to show signs of a turnaround in 1990, as GDP rose 4.4 percent, international reserves were increased by almost $5 billion, and the balance of payments deficit was turned into a surplus. Much of this growth was due to an oil windfall of almost $4 billion, the result of the Persian Gulf crisis.

Agriculture, which had enjoyed vigorous growth during the mid-1980s, began to decline again as subsidies were removed and import restrictions

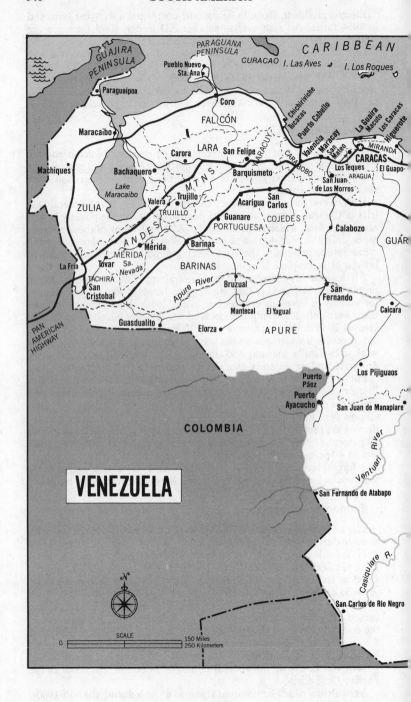

GUAJIRA PENINSULA

PARAGUANA PENINSULA

CARIBBEAN

CURACAO   I. Las Aves   I. Los Roques

Pueblo Nuevo
Sta. Ana

Coro

Paraguaipoa

Chichiriviche
Tucacas

La Guaira Macuto
Los Caracas
Higuerote

Maracaibo

FALCÓN

Puerto Cabello

LARA

Valencia Maracay

MIRANDA

Carora

San Felipe

San Mateo

CARACAS

Machiques

Bachaquero

Lake Maracaibo

ARACUY

CARABOBO

Los Teques

El Guapo

ZULIA

Barquismeto

San Juan
de Los Morros

ARAGUA

M.T.N.S

Valera Trujillo

Acarigua

San
Carlos

TRUJILLO

Guanare

COJEDES

Calabozo

ANDES

PORTUGUESA

GUÁR

Mérida

MERIDA

Barinas

Sa.
Nevada

La Fria

Tovar

BARINAS

TACHIRA

Apure River

Bruzual

San
Fernando

San
Cristobal

Caicara

Guasdualito

Mantecal El Yagual

Elorza

APURE

PAN
AMERICAN
HIGHWAY

Puerto
Páez

Los Pijiguaos

Puerto
Ayacucho

San Juan de Manapiare

COLOMBIA

Ventuari River

VENEZUELA

San Fernando de Atabapo

Casiquiare R.

San Carlos de Rio Negro

N

SCALE

0   150 Miles
         250 Kilometers

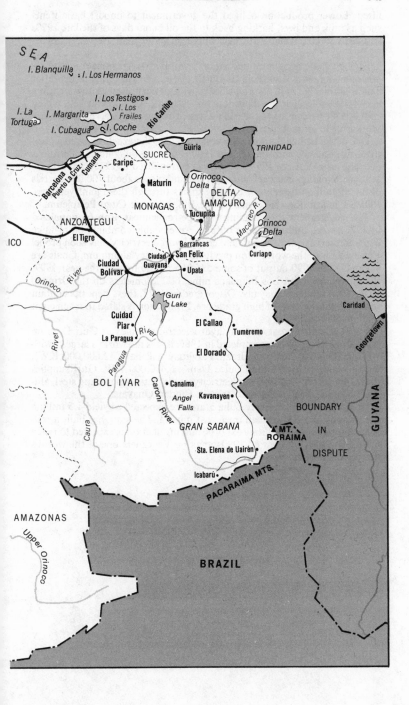

lifted. Lower production obliged the government to import basic items such as milk and beef, harking back to the oil boom days of the late 1970s and early 1980s, when Venezuela imported more than 70 percent of its food.

Big new finds of light crudes and a "conservative" revaluationof oil reserves have raised Venezuela to fourth place in world crude terms (after Saudi Arabia, Kuwait, and the USSR), with proven reserves now standing at over 58 billion barrels. This does not count the Orinoco tar belt, which contains 44 percent of the world's extra-heavy crude reserves, which are too costly to extract at present.

One of the United States's oldest oil suppliers, Venezuela enjoyed a positive trade balance with the U.S. in 1990. The state oil company Petroleos de Venezuela, S.A., or PDVSA (oil was nationalized in 1975), has 50 percent participation in six refineries abroad and places about 700,000 barrels of its 1.9 million barrels per day of exports through these joint ventures. PDVSA is also the sole owner of the U.S. oil giant Citgo Petroleum.

The government is expanding state petrochemical, iron (nationalized in 1975), steel, and aluminum output. An enviable combination of huge bauxite reserves, plentiful gas, and cheap hydroelectricity may soon propel Venezuela into the world's top producer of primary aluminum. Goals are to double the 1990 output of some 595,966 metric tons by the year 1997. Bauxite comes from Los Pijiguaos mine, 600 kilometers up the Orinoco River from Ciudad Guayana. Discovered in 1977, these deposits contain some 500 million tons of high grade ore. Production is slated to reach eight million tons in 1997.

Venezuela also boasts a giant hydroelectric complex at Guri Dam on the Caroní River. When completed in 1986, it was the world's largest, with 10,300,000 KW (Itaipu in Brazil/Paraguay will have 12,600,000 KW), which outstrips by far the Coulee Dam's 6,490,000 KW. Guri supplies three-quarters of Venezuela's electricity needs, besides powering steel, aluminum, and other heavy industries in Ciudad Guayana.

Coal deposits in Guasare, Zulia State, are expected to yield 1.5 million metric tons in 1991 through open cast mining. The state has built a railroad and seaport to facilitate exports, and production is expected to reach 6.5 million tons by the mid-1990s, making Venezuela one of the world's top coal exporters.

FACTS AT YOUR FINGERTIPS

WHAT IT WILL COST. Devaluation has made Venezuela a very attractive destination for the tourist, whose dollars now buy considerably more than they did in 1982. Moreover, inflation has been kept relatively low until now. Thus the best hotel in Caracas costs $170 a night (for a double) and in Mérida $40. *Haute cuisine* dining in Caracas will cost roughly $20 a person (without drinks); in Maracaibo the finest food costs half as much. Light eaters can save money by lunching on a French roll with ham "a la plancha" (grilled) at any coffee shop; top it off with fresh orange juice and delicious expresso coffee and pay $1.10. Drinks run about $1.50 for the very good national rum; double for imported whisky. Excellent beer for 60 cents (half if bought in the can), but a bottle of French wine at a restaurant may cost $12. A nightclub tour of Caracas costs $40, including dinner, drinks, and show. In general, entertainment is inexpensive and tickets to plays or bullfights rarely cost as much as $15. Movies are $1.15 (half price on Mon.). But the best news of all for the traveler is the low cost of transportation. Most taxi rides within Caracas clock between $1.50 and $3, and drivers will chauffeur clients by the day for $38, the same price as a drive-yourself Ford. Top-grade gasoline is still less than 50 cents a gallon. And plane fares, like many essential goods and services, are government-controlled. A border-to-border journey (3 flights) from Colombia (San Antonio) to Brazil (Santa Elena de Uairén) runs about $160.

SOURCES OF INFORMATION. The Corporación de Turismo de Venezuela, working in conjunction with Venezuelan consulates and embassies, supplies some tourist brochures. **In the U.S.** Embassy: 1099 30th St. N.W., Washington, DC 20007 (202–342–2214). Consulates: Suite 402, 111 Water St., Baltimore, MD 21217 (301–962–0362/63); 545 Boylston St., 6th floor, Boston, MA 02116 (617–266–9355); Suite 750, 20 N. Wacker St., Chicago, IL 60606 (312–236–9655); Suite 303, Newmarket at Head House Sq., Philadelphia, PA 19147 (215–923–2905); Suite 1500, 2700 Post Oak Blvd., Houston, TX 77056 (713–961–5141); 1101 Brickell Ave., Suite 901, Miami, FL 33131 (305–577–4210); 1006 World Trade Center, New Orleans, LA 70130 (504–522–3284); 7 East 51st St., New York, NY 10022 (212–826–1682); Suite 220, 455 Market St., San Francisco, CA 94105 (415–512–8340). **In Canada.** Embassy: Suite 400, 2055 Peel St., Montreal, H3A 1V4 (514–842–3417/18). Consulates: Suite 703, 2 Carlton St., Toronto, ONT M5B 1J3 (416–977–6809/11). **In the U.K.** Embassy: 1 Cromwell Rd., London SW7 2HR (071/581–2776). Consulate: Bellow Lodge, 56 Grafton Way, London, WIP 5LB (071/387–6727).

VIASA, the national carrier, actively promotes tourism abroad. **In the U.S.:** 18 East 48th St., New York, NY 10017 (212–486–4360); Suite 600, 1101 Brickell Ave., Miami, FL 33131 (305–358–3900); 3800 Buffalo Speedway, Houston, TX 77098 (713–877–8223). **In Canada:** Suite 530, 102 Bloor St. West, Toronto, ONT M5S 1MB (416–968–7524). **In the U.K.:** 19–20 Grosvenor St., London W1X 9FD (071–629–1223).

AVENSA, now an international line, has offices **in the U.S.** at: 40 W. 57th St., Suite 1515, New York, NY 10019 (212–956–8500); Kennedy Airport, New York (718–244–6858); and 800 Brickell Ave., Suite 1109, Miami, FL 33131 (305–381–8001).

The 800-page *Guide to Venezuela,* by Jan Bauman and Leni Young, is a fascinating, invaluable traveler's companion. It is published by Gráficas Armitano (02–342565) in Caracas; look for it in hotel bookshops ($20). Call the Venezuelan-American Chamber of Commerce, Torre Credival, 2a Av. de Campo Alegre, Caracas (02–263–0833), for their practical guide to *Living in Venezuela* ($21).

WHEN TO GO. Venezuela's sunny climate, particularly in Caracas, is so pleasant that many foreigners who come to work for a "few months" end up staying years. There is a dry season from about mid-Dec. to May when many trees lose their leaves and burst into brilliant yellow, pink, scarlet, or blue blossoms. The rains often start in late May, turning the plains green with new grass. By July the countryside is splendid in its lushness, and by Aug. many rivers are in full flood. Temperatures vary with altitude from an average of 85°F. near sea level in Maracaibo, to 74°F. in Caracas at 3,000 feet, and 57°F. in Mucuchies at 9,000 feet. But even at the beach or in the jungle, nights tend to cool off pleasantly as trade winds freshen the air.

WHAT TO TAKE. For mountain travel, including Caracas with its nearby Mt. Avila and Colonia Tovar, take a sweater or a jacket. Caracas is a sophisticated city and does not look approvingly on splashy "cruise line" attire. Shorts are not worn outside beaches and clubs, except by joggers, but slacks are common and pantsuits acceptable at night. For expensive dining or clubbing, men should wear jacket and tie. At beach resorts, casual clothes and a wrap or sweater may be needed for air-conditioned buildings and breezy evenings. Take a mask for snorkeling and a hat for the sun. If you are going to rough it in the Interior, bring a cloth hat, lightweight trousers, sweatshirt, long-sleeved shirts to keep off insects, sneakers and socks, plastic rain gear, insect repellent, and flashlight. Do *not* bring firearms.

SPECIAL EVENTS. Depending on the region, towns celebrate their patron saint's day with fireworks, religious processions, street dances, bulldogging, and contests including climbing a greased pole. Colorful customs blend cultural sources from Africa, Spain, and pre-Columbian America. Some fiestas blossom into large regional events with bullfights, cattle fairs, and beauty contests, as in Mérida (*Feria del Sol,* 3d week in Feb.), San Cristóbal in January, and Maracaibo (*Feria de La Chinita,* mid-Nov.).

January: *Feast of the Three Kings* (6) brings out the entire town of San Miguel de Boconó, Trujillo State, for costume parades, street dances, and a procession bearing the infant Jesus. *La Feria de San Sebastián* (3d week) is a 4-day explosion of sports, bullfights, and fairs in San Cristóbal, Táchira State. *San Sebastian's Day,* (20) transforms the seaside town of Ocumare, Aragua State, into a 4-day party with choir, drums, fireworks, and cockfights.

February/March: *Carnaval* is not the time for a business trip since all work stops a week before Ash Wednesday amid a mass exodus for the beaches. In Caracas, water throwing is a hazard; also chancy are costume balls where women masked as "negritas" take the initiative (and some turn out to be men!). For parades, calypsos, and a great time, go to El Callao, Bolívar State, or Carúpano, Sucre State; Valencia also has a lively parade (and better hotels); in Colonia Tovar a mock funeral ends Carnival German-style.

March/April: *Easter.* Blessing of the Palms in Plaza Bolívar and Plaza Chacao, Caracas. In El Hatillo, south Caracas, villagers act out the Passion drama starting on Holy Thursday. Nazarene pilgrims dressed in purple gather at Santa Teresa Church in downtown Caracas. In the Andes, passion plays are acted out in Capacho, La Parroquia, and La Punta near Mérida. In Ureña, Táchira State, and in La Cejita, Trujillo State, robed and hooded penitents or "encapuchados" go on their knees to mass. In many town squares, a life-size dummy of Judas, sometimes stuffed with rockets, is mocked and set afire on Easter Sunday.

April: In San Fernando de Apure, a mid-month *Alma Llanera Fair* combines a cattle show with bulldogging, barbecues, and harp contests. Venezuela's national dance, the *joropo,* is from the Llanos, as is the national dress, the *liquiliqui* ("leeky-leeky"). On April 22 in Barquisimeto, Lara State, a national horse fair draws buyers from afar.

May: *The May Cross* (3–15). Processions and maypole dances usher in the planting season when the Southern Cross rides high. Bailadores and Lagunillas, Mérida State; Boconó and Jajo, Trujillo State.

June: *Corpus Christi,* 9 weeks after Easter, releases Devil Dancers in grotesque masks who perform outside the churches of San Francisco de Yare in Miranda State, Naiguatá on the central littoral, Turiamo, Chuao, Cata, and Cuyagua on the coast of Aragua State, and Patanemo on the Carabobo coast. June 23–25: In coastal villages from Patanemo to Curiepe, Miranda State, the Feast of St. John the Baptist is a 3-day workout of big drums, the *mina* and *curveta,* which keep crowds dancing in the streets far into the night. June 24: commemorations take place at Carabobo Battlefield, 18 miles west of Valencia, where patriots sealed independence in 1821.

June 28–29: in Guatire, near Caracas, the *Parranda de San Pedro*, led by townsmen with top hats and blackened faces, celebrates St. Peter's Day.

August: In Ciudad Bolívar, the *Orinoco Fair* (5–8) combines a songfest, calypso bands, horse races, and fishing contests. August is the time for feasting on *sapoara* fish, which ascend the Orinoco to spawn in such large schools that you can hear the fish pass. Mid-August: in Táriba, Táchira State, a week of bullfights in honor of the Virgin of Táriba.

September: Pilgrims gather in Guanare, Portuguesa State, on the day of the patroness of Venezuela, *La Virgen de Coromoto* (8), at a shrine built where she appeared first in 1651. Also on September 8, *La Virgen del Valle* in Margarita attracts thousands of grateful devotees who have made her church one of Venezuela's richest. September 23–24: In Maparari, Falcón State, the Dance of the Turas (flutes) honors Our Lady of Mercy in a half-pagan rite.

October: *Columbus Day* (12) is "Dia de la Raza" celebrating Amerindian origins. In Chivacoa, Yaracuy State, followers of the Maria Lionza cult converge on the sacred site of Quivallo.

November: Maracaibo turns out for the week-long *Feria de La Chinita* (18) honoring the Virgin of Chiquinquirá; parades, bands, fairs.

December: The birth of Christ is celebrated in many traditions, led by the elaborately costumed *Pastores* (shepherds). In Mariara, Carabobo State, on the 1st Sun. in December, half the male dancers dress as shepherdesses. Also, the *Pastores* dance on the 2nd Sat. in Limón near Maracay and on Christmas Eve in San Joaquín near Valencia. In the Andes, San Miguel de Boconó is famous for its costumed *Pastores*, who are joined by *Payasos* (clowns) on January 4–6. On December 27 the black saint San Benito is paraded through the towns of Mucuchíes in Mérida State, and Gibraltar and Bobures, south of Lake Maracaibo (where the *Los Chimbangueles* festival lasts through New Year's Eve).

Caracas at Christmas resounds to strident *gaita* music of Zulia State, which has displaced carols; Santa Claus and reindeer have almost, but not quite, usurped the place of creches or *nacimientos*. Also on the wane is roller skating to the Midnight Mass or *Misa del Gallo* (rooster). Following this, boys in eastern Venezuela used to turn gasoline-soaked coconuts into flaming footballs.

TRAVEL DOCUMENTS AND CUSTOMS. With a passport (valid for at least 6 months), 60-day *tourist cards* are issued by Venezuelan consulates and carrier airlines serving Venezuela upon purchase of a return ticket, and are renewable for another 60 days. One-year tourist visas are issued only by consulates. Smallpox vaccinations are sometimes asked for at the discretion of the consul. Tourists should *not* apply for *transeunte* (transient) visas; these give the right to engage in business and the holder must obtain a tax clearance to leave the country. Travelers already abroad have reported snags in getting tourist cards for ongoing journeys to Venezuela, denied on grounds that the traveler is not in his country of origin, so get cards before leaving the United States or Canada.

Persons entering Venezuela may bring in duty-free 400 cigarettes and 50 cigars, 2 liters of liquor, items for personal use, and new goods up to Bs. 5,000 in value (about $100), if declared and accompanied by receipts. Plants, fresh fruits, and pork are prohibited. Firearms will be confiscated if not covered by consular permit.

Departing tourists pay an airport tax of Bs.530 on international flights, Bs.40 on local flights, and an additional Bs.10 for each suitcase.

Automobiles. Vehicles may be imported for a maximum of 6 months by tourists with documents validated beforehand by a Venezuelan consulate in the country of embarkation; request detailed information about requirements (bond) before deciding to take a car.

GETTING TO VENEZUELA. By plane. National carriers are *VIASA, Avensa, Aeropostal,* and *Aereotuy.* Other scheduled airlines serving Caracas (Simón Bolívar Int'l Airport in Maiquetía) include *Aerolíneas Argentinas, Aeroperu, Air Canada, Air France, Air Panamá, Alitalia, Avianca, British Airways, Ecuatoriana, Iberia, KLM, Lacsa, Lan Chile, Lufthansa, Swissair, TAP,* and *Varig.* Direct Caribbean flights by: *American Airlines* from Puerto Rico; *Aeropostal* from Aruba, Curacao, Trinidad, Barbados, Grenada, Cuba, Martinique, Puerto Rico, and Santo Domingo; *Air Aruba* from Aruba; *Air France* from Martinique; *ALM* from Curacao; *Avensa* from Aruba and Bonaire; *BWIA* from Trinidad; *Dominicana* from Santo Domingo;

Liat from Barbados and St. Lucia; *Viasa* from Puerto Rico. *Pan Am* and *Lacsa* also serve Maracaibo. *Lloyd Aereo Boliviano* flies from Caracas to Manaos, as well as La Paz and Santa Cruz.

By sea. Cunard's *Countess* sails the Caribbean between San Juan and La Guaira, in the winter season. The S.S. *Victoria* makes weekly circuits between San Juan and La Guaira, as does the *C Line*.

A **car ferry** crosses between Curaçao and Venezuela. The *Almirante Brion,* carrying up to 40 cars and 1,200 passengers, leaves at 11 P.M. on Mon. and Fri. from La Vela de Coro, Falcón State. Fares are about $80 round-trip per car and $65 per passenger. Ferries del Caribe in Coro (068–510–554 or 511–956).

By land. Express buses link Cúcuta in Colombia with Caracas: *Aerobuses de Venezuela* (02–545–0315); *Expresos Los Llanos* (02–545–0428); *Union Transporte San Cristobal* (02–541–4218). There is no road open to Guyana, but the Gran Sabana route to Santa Elena de Uairen continues to Brazil and there is a bus to Boa Vista leaving daily at 8 A.M. from Santa Elena.

CURRENCY. The monetary unit is the *bolivar* (Bs.). Paper money comes in bills of 10, 20, 50, 100, and 500. Coins: 5 *céntimos*—a coin about the size of a U.S. penny, called a *puya* or a *centavo;* 25 céntimos—a coin slightly smaller than a dime, called a *medio;* 50 céntimos—called a *real,* about the size of a nickel; 1 *bolivar* (100 céntimos), the size of a quarter; 2 bolivars—slightly larger than a quarter; 5 bolivars—called a *fuerte,* about the same size as a U.S. half dollar. 1, 2, and 5 bolívar bills have recently become available as well.

At press time the floating exchange rate for the dollar stood between Bs.50 and Bs.52. The best rates are given by exchange houses. In Caracas, among others: Agencia Wallis, 325525, Av. Miranda, Campo Alegre; Confinanzas, 922202, Local PA-C1, east end C.C. Paseo Las Mercedes; Italcambio, 5 branches in Maiquetía, Valencia and Caracas—Altamira, 261–6567, Av. Roche opposite Teatro Altamira; Turven, 951–1557, next to Cine Broadway, Chacaito.

Prices in this chapter, unless noted otherwise, are in U.S. dollars.

HOTELS. Accommodations in Venezuela range from 5-star hotels of the international chains in Caracas, Valencia, Maracaibo, Barquisimeto, and Cuidad Guayana to hostels in country *pueblos.* The price categories used in this chapter are for two people in a double room: *Super Deluxe,* about $150; *Deluxe,* $70; *Expensive,* $40; *Moderate,* $24; *Inexpensive,* $16 and under. Rates for singles are about 75% of the cost of a double room. Foreign tourists must now pay a 10 percent tax on hotel rooms.

Reservations should be made 10 weeks in advance, with payment, for popular destinations such as Margarita and Mérida. Beach resorts and Canaima are completely booked during winter months, Carnival, and Easter holidays. Prepaid reservations for over 300 hotels may be made through Fairmont Reserv-Hotel (02–782–8433, telex 21232 FAINT–VC; fax 2–7824407).

RESTAURANTS. Our listing of restaurants is keyed by price per person, based on a three-course meal and 10 percent service charge, without alcoholic beverages. *Expensive,* $13 and up; *Moderate,* $6–$12; *Inexpensive,* $5 and under.

Venezuelan Food and Drink. Simple and hearty staple foods include fried *plátanos* (cooking bananas), *caraotas negras* (black beans), and *hervido,* a soup with chunks of chicken, beef, vegetables, or roots. It is the use of such roots as yuca, yam, sweet potato, ocumo (tannia), and apio that give the distinctive flavor to many popular dishes. Try the special *crema de apio.* Another good and economical ribsticker is *sancocho,* a cross between a stew and an hervido, with large pieces of beef, potato, cabbage, corn, and pumpkin. *Parrillada,* either grilled Argentine-style in thick churrasco steaks or *criollo,* marinated in thin strips, is a favorite standby with fried yuca and *arepitas* or corn *bollos.* Fresh fruit juices are fabulous, made on the spot at most *areperas.* Ask for *jugo natural* (unprocessed) or *batido* (a fruit-shake); these are made from orange, mango, bananas, watermelon, *parchita* (passion fruit), *lechosa* (pawpaw), etc., and cost about 50 cents.

TIPPING. In most restaurants 10% is added to the check but it is customary to leave another 10% on the table. Tip bellboys, chambermaids, hairdressers, guides, and drivers of excursion vehicles. Taxi drivers are not usually tipped much unless they carry suitcases (about Bs.20 for two).

BUSINESS HOURS AND HOLIDAYS. Banks are open Mon.-Fri., 8:30 to 11:30 A.M. and 2 to 4:30 P.M.; they have the custom of closing the Mon. after religious holidays falling between Tues. and Fri. Consulates often work only mornings. Post offices work through lunch, 8 A.M. to 6 P.M. Shops usually are open 9 A.M. to noon and 2 or 3 to 6 P.M. or later; supermarkets, 8 A.M. to 1 P.M. and 3 to 8 P.M. Most government offices and private companies work from 8 A.M. to 5 P.M. with an hour for lunch; do not rely on appointments later than 4 P.M. or on Fri. afternoons. Travel agencies and airline offices (except at the airport) are closed Sat.

National Holidays. All except essential services stop on: Jan. 1; Carnival Mon. and Tues.; Apr. 19—Proclamation of Independence; Easter Thursday and Good Friday; May 1—Labor Day; June 24—Battle of Carabobo; July 5—Independence Day; July 24—Bolívar's Birthday; October 12—Columbus Day *(Día de la Raza);* December 24–25—Christmas. Religious holidays are observed by schools, some businesses, and banks (on the following Mon.); these include Mar. 19—St. Joseph; Ascension (movable); Corpus Christi (movable); Aug. 15—Assumption; Nov. 1—All Saints; Dec. 8—Immaculate Conception; Dec. 17—the day Bolívar died. When holidays fall on Thurs. or Tues., an extra day is often taken to make a "puente" or 4-day weekend. Little official business gets done 2–3 days before the big holidays of Carnival, Easter, or New Year's; at Christmas, some companies go on collective vacations and government offices finish early ("horario corrido" from 7:30 A.M. to 3:30 or 4 P.M.).

TELEPHONES AND TELEX. Local calls: direct dialing to all numbers in Venezuela, except from pay phones. Pay phones operate with 25 céntimo, 50 céntimo, and 1 bolivar coins. Try pharmacies or Metro stations for reliable pay phones. For information, dial 103 or 510144 (for new numbers); for long-distance information, dial 100—check the phone book for area codes. For Caracas calls from the airport dial area code 02 and number. In the cities and most airports a CANTV office gives public long-distance phone service. In Caracas: CANTV, 284–7923, Nivel 5, Centro Plaza, Los Palos Grandes (open 8 A.M. to 9:30 P.M.); and CANTV in El Silencio, 418644, on large interior plaza of Simón Bolívar South Tower (open 24 hours). Telex service (information 524711) is given by these offices and by CANTV in Ciudad Comercial Tamanaco, Chuao (959–0979). Translation services, as well as telex and fax, are available in most of the big hotels. CANTV has a telex service (529089); private ones include Trans Fax (740231) and Archivos del Este (348451–53).

International calls: The time in Venezuela is the same as U.S. Eastern Daylight Saving Time from May to Oct.; from Nov. to Apr., Venezuelan time is one hour ahead of Eastern Standard. There is direct dialing to major cities abroad from most, but not all, exchanges in Caracas. For person-to-person calls, try the overseas operator (dial 122), though you may not get through.

Emergencies: The U.S. Embassy (02–285–3111, 285–2222) has a list of legal interpreters and registered attorneys who can speak English. In extreme emergency, the embassy can provide advice at any hour. In Caracas a 24-hour doctor service for medical emergencies is provided by Centro Móvil de Medicina (02–483–7021 and 412439).

MAIL AND CABLE. Within Venezuela, and even within cities, mail is slow (two weeks). For faster mail to the United States and Europe, the "Expreso Internacional" service is worth the extra money. Registered mail or "correo certificado" is reliable. For bulky envelopes or urgent papers, businessmen use delivery services: national—Aerocav (02–225511); overseas—DHL (987–0111 and 263–2211) has express centers in the Tamanaco Hotel (208–7293) and Caracas Hilton (571–2322, ext. 4324). RECEI (951–3106) works with Federal Express. Domesa also hand delivers (715058, 545–0411). Messenger services offering immediate delivery in Caracas include Mensajeros Radio (782–1422) and Express 24 (781–8979).

Telegrams. IPOSTEL post offices in Caracas which send international cables include: Carmelitas, Av. Urdaneta; Edificio Sur, Centro Simón Bolívar, 1st floor; Sabana Grande, Edif. Cedíaz, Av. Casanova; Chacao, Av. Miranda near Libertador underpass; Unicentro El Marqués. For telegrams by telephone, call 462–4055 from 8 A.M. to 8 P.M.

NEWSPAPERS. *The Daily Journal* has good international and business coverage and a useful classified section. The Caracas Hilton and Tamanaco Hotel bookshops have recent airmail editions of the *New York Times* and the *Miami Herald*. In Spanish, *El Universal* leads in financial coverage, *El Nacional* in the arts, and *El Diario* in opposition politics; two new morning papers, *Reporte de la Economia* and the pink-hued *Economia Hoy,* cover business and economics, while the afternoon *El Mundo* gives the latest headlines and entertainment. Newsmagazines from the U.S., Britain, and Europe are available at leading newsstands.

ELECTRIC CURRENT. 110 volts, 60-cycle AC current, single phase, is the standard, although 220 hookups are made for heavy electrical equipment.

USEFUL ADDRESSES (in Caracas). Embassies: U.S.—Av. Miranda, La Floresta, 285–3111 or 285–2222 (Mon.-Fri. 8 A.M. to noon and 1 to 5 P.M.; passports 8 A.M. to 3 P.M.). Canada—Torre Europa, Av. Miranda, Chacaito, 951–6166 (Mon.–Thurs. 7:30 to 4:30 and Fri. 7:30 to 1 P.M. Great Britain—Torre Las Mercedes, Av. La Estancia, Chuao, 751–1022 (Mon.-Fri. 8:30 A.M. to 12:30 P.M., 1:30 to 3 P.M.).
Tourist Bureau: Corporación de Turismo de Venezuela, 37th floor, Torre Oeste, Parque Central, 507–8815 (8:30 A.M. to 12:30 P.M., 2 to 5 P.M.); some posters and brochures, but no maps. Venezuelan-American Chamber of Commerce, 10th floor, Torre Credival, 2nd Av. Campo Alegre at Av. Miranda, 263–0833 (Mon.-Fri. 9 A.M. to noon, 2 to 6 P.M.); knowledgeable assistance in many spheres. Venezuelan American Association of University Women, Qta. Vaauw, Tr. 6, Altamira, Caracas, 329312; art shows, cultural and educational programs, social work. Sociedad Conservacionista Audubon, La Cuadra section of Paseo Las Mercedes, Caracas, 913813 (Mon.-Fri. 9 A.M. to 12:30 P.M. and 2:30 to 6 P.M.); good bookshop and information on nature; monthly lectures (free); off-the-track excursions and treks (membership about $15).

HEALTH AND SAFETY. Although tap water in cities is purified, the house tanks in which it is stored may not be so pure and visitors staying a short time are advised to drink bottled water, especially at the start of the rains (May–June). Also, stay away from salads and ice cubes to avoid microbial upsets. Yellow fever has not been registered in Venezuela for some years but malaria is endemic in the Amazonas Territory at elevations under 2,000 feet, where the *Anopheles* mosquitoes live. The Health Ministry, which carries out annual anti-malaria campaigns to spray all dwellings in these areas, urges travelers to use mosquito nets and take a preventive pill such as Maloprim twice weekly or Fansidar once weekly. Warnings are also made against bathing in slow-moving streams and lagoons in low country where reeds may harbor the snail vector of a blood parasite causing bilharzia.
Health care in Venezuela has improved dramatically since 1938, when life expectancy was 35 years; it is now 70 years. There are many U.S.- and U.K.-trained specialists on the staffs of a dozen or so excellent private clinics in Caracas: Clínica El Avila, Transversal 6, Altamira (208–1111) and Policlínica Metropolitana, Calle A-1, Caurimare (987–2222) are two. Both have 24-hour emergency service.
Venezuelans and visitors alike are required to carry identification at all times; always have your passport at hand. If stopped by a police check, never show signs of impatience. As in any big city, stay away from dark streets and do not walk alone at night. When on planes or buses, do not accept packages from strangers, even for a few moments; since the increase of drug traffic, Venezuela has become a major cocaine route and laws treat possession of an ounce the same as a kilo. When at the beach, do not leave belongings unattended.

GETTING AROUND VENEZUELA. By plane. Avensa's 10-day Airpass for unlimited travel costs $185 ($93 for children). It's available to foreigners only; for information call 562–3022, ext. 1128. Passes are sold by Avensa in Caracas (Esq. El Conde) and at airports in Maiquetía, Maracaibo, Porlamar, and Barcelona; or abroad by Avensa and some 30 international air carriers, including Viasa, Pan Am, BA, KLM, and Air France. *Avensa* (02–563–3366) serves not only the bigger cities in Venezuela but also Margarita, Canaima, and Mérida, the star tourist destinations. *Aeropostal* (02–575–2511) goes daily to the Llanos and Puerto Ayacucho in the Amazonas Territory. *Aereotuy* (02–71–62–31, fax 72–52–54) flies from Ciudad Bolívar to Sta. Elena in a circle over the fabulous "tepui" country of the Gran Sabana. Flying from Aeropuerto Caracas in Charallave, *CAVE* (02–724–312) serves Margarita, Calabozo, and Valle La Pascua.

Plane rentals. In a country where ranchers, prospectors, and missionaries fly to remote strips, airtaxis are a standard service at the airports of Ciudad Bolívar and Puerto Ayacucho (see area information). With offices in Caracas, CAVE, Aereotuy, and Aeroejecutivos are only three of many air services which offer national (and international) charters. Some others are: Charter Ejecutivo (02–924–002), Renta-charter (02–261–7480, radio contact 335 at 283–6055), and Aeroservicios Waica (02–918042, telex 27996 ASCARVC). Depending on the destination, from a coral isle to a jungle strip, such companies can provide turbo props, jets, helicopters, and 4-seaters.

By bus. The hub of Venezuela's extensive network of long distance and express buses which run day and night is the Nuevo Circo Terminal at Av. Fuerzas Armadas and Av. Bolívar in Caracas (La Hoyada metro station). The many lines which serve major destinations including Margarita and the Colombian border are supplemented by "por puesto" cars (pay by the seat) which leave as soon as they are full. Bus tickets, bought at the booths of some 40 lines, are cheap (Caracas to Maracaibo costs $11) and should be bought 2 days in advance, especially during national holidays, when there is an enormous crush of passengers (you should also beware of pickpockets). The Nuevo Circo bus station is a dirty and dangerous spot; there have been accusations of police harassment of foreigners there, so be on your guard.

By car. Excellent roads are accompanied by good road maps issued by oil subsidiaries, such as Lagoven and Maraven, sold at gas stations. Driving requirements for foreigners: valid license from country of origin, medical certificate obtained from Colegio de Médicos offices (Bs.50), and third party insurance for the vehicle. For more information and documents needed to import a car temporarily, ask the Touring & Automóvil Club de Venezuela, planta baja, Centro Integral Santa Rosa de Lima, Av. Principal con Calle A, Santa Rosa de Lima, Caracas (02–910639 and 914448).

Car rental. Major companies, with branches around the country are: Aco (02–918511); Avis (02–263–2444); Budget (02–283–4333); Briauto-Ford (02–262–0769); Fiesta El Rosal (02–951–3616); Hertz (02–715332, telex 21283); National (02–239–1134, fax 239–4119). Although most charge by the day, plus a kilometer rate and insurance, some offer special monthly and weekly rates. The daily base rate is about $40. Most companies require hirers to be over 25 and hold credit cards.

SPORTS. Three "B's" are big in Venezuela: **baseball, basketball,** and **boxing.** The national sport is baseball; the kid's league, Los Criollitos, draws over 200,000 boys aged 5 to 18. The best go on to play professionally for teams such as the Caracas Lions, La Guaira Sharks, and Zulia Eagles. The champion of these teams defends Venezuela in the Caribbean Series. Greater glory crowns the half dozen Venezuelan stars in the U.S. big leagues: shortstop David Concepción, home run champion Tony Armas, rookie of the year for 1985 Ozzie Guillén, utility man Luis Salazar, and infielders Manny Trillo and Andy Galarraga.

Horse racing. A fourth "B"—betting—rates No. 1 for racing addicts. There are racetracks in Ciudad Bolívar, Maracaibo, Punto Fijo, and Barquisimeto, as well as the heavily attended tracks of Valencia and Caracas.

Cockfighting, *pelea de gallo,* is a betting sport, and is popular in the smaller towns. Enthusiasts risk large sums to acquire and train birds for a fight which may last no more than 3 minutes. In the plains, *toros coleados* or **bulldogging** competitions enliven periodic fairs, the aim being to throw the bull to the ground by twisting its tail. **Bullfighting** in the Spanish tradition has its season from Nov. through Mar. with *corridas* led by the world's best matadors. Tickets for the sunny bleachers at bullrings in Caracas, Valencia, Mérida, and San Cristóbal start at $5.

Some of the best **deep-sea fishing** in the world, particularly white marlin, is recorded off the central coast of Venezuela. Foreign fishermen may enter several local tournaments: in Feb. sailfish off Puerto Cabello, in Sept. white marlin off Macuto, and in Nov. kingfish off Falcón—some of these fish have been known to jump as high as 16 feet. In one year (1978) six different world records were registered—for white and blue marlin, sailfish, barracuda, and tarpon. Day-long sportfishing costs about $500 (max. 5 people) in a 42' vessel with all equipment, bait, meals, and beer. For rental of yachts, sailboats, and houseboats, contact Linda Sonderman at Alpi Tour (see below), who represents fully crewed charter craft, including sailboats and yachts up to 80 feet for as many as 10 passengers, at costs ranging from $500 to $1,500 a day, including meals and excursions. Also, leaving from the central coast are crewed fishing yachts at about $400 a day for four fishermen, organized by Yachting Tours (031–944300, ext. 188, fax 031–944318). Intervac, based in the Melia Hotel (031–965555), has boats for various budgets and destinations as far as Margarita, Aruba, or Grenada.

Scuba diving and snorkeling along coasts and reefs provide endless underwater sport. Three national parks conserve maritime environments: Los Roques, 90 miles north of La Guaira, Morrocoy Park on the western coast, and Mochima Park on the eastern coast; in each, fishing boats can be hired for a day's sport. (Spearfishing is prohibited.) For information on scuba services, write Mike Osborn, Submatur, Apartado 68512, Caracas 1062A (02–782–2946 or 042–84082).

TREKS AND ADVENTURE TOURS. Venezuela is blossoming into a major destination for bold travelers who want to explore remote rain forests and "Lost World" mesas, tropical rivers and coral islands, and who are fit enough to hike and camp. The dry season peak, Jan. to the first rains in May, is the best time for hiking and bird-watching. Rain forests are most impressive in the wet season, June to Oct., and this is a good time for river travel since waters are high. But avoid the Llanos during the wet season, because these low plains may be flooded. (The simplest way to fend off insects is to wear a long-sleeved shirt and tuck trouser legs into socks.) In the tropics a hat is a must on walks and boat trips. Other standard equipment: plastic rain cape, track shoes, jersey, windbreaker, acrylic blanket or sleeping bag for cool jungle nights, flashlight, repellent, and sun block.

Reached by a spectacular river route from Canaima in well-organized treks, Angel Falls tops the list of adventure destinations. Veteran guide *Rudy Truffino* pioneered expeditions 30 years ago. By motorized dugout, Rudy's 4-day river trips, from July to November when the falls are full, are offered at about $520 a person for groups of 5–8, but can be tailored for more days or for fewer people (no children under 12). All equipment is provided. More difficult treks to the top of Auyantepui can also be planned. Truffino, Apartado 61879, Caracas 1060A (02–661–9153). If you speak Spanish, more economical group treks to Angel Falls, Camarata Mission, and Kavak Cave are offered by local outfits such as the Kamaracoto Indian guides of *Excursiones Churum-Vena* (information 02–7312034) and *Excursiones Canaima* (reservations 02–545–7920 or write Brígida Contreras, piso 11, Peinero a Dr. Díaz, Caracas). These outfits offer trips from May through Oct. at a cost of about $250 a person, for groups of 6 or more.

Alechiven, S.A., Centro Comercial Siglo XXI, Local A–18, Nivel Plaza, La Vina, Valencia (041–211828 or 041–212660, fax 041–217018). Edith Rogge leads canoe, boat, and trekking trips for groups ranging from 4 to 10 persons, to Angel Falls, Auyan-Tepui, Kamadac Falls and the Kavac Canyon, and the Piedra del Cocuy, at the border of Venezuela, Colombia, and Brazil. Alechiven also has a special 16-day excursion that follows the route of the 19th-century German explorer Alexander Von Humboldt up the Orinoco River, aboard its own 70-foot riverboat. Prices average $120 per day, per person, including transfers and hotel on the last night in Caracas.

Alpi Tour, Torre Centro, Parque Boyacá, Los Dos Caminos, Caracas (02–283–1433/6677), telex 24354; fax 284–7098. U.S. mail to: M–491, Jet Cargo, Box 020010, Miami, FL 33102–0010. Amazonas wilderness camps by charter plane: Yutajé (exc. August); new camp at Caño Santo, Bolívar State, Hato Las Nieves; Caura River excursion and hike to Para Falls. Bass fishing in the Cinaruco River; bone fishing and scuba diving in Los Roques atoll. Pilot Linda Sonderman makes light plane trips (min. 4 passengers for single- or twin-engine plane). The approximate cost of a trip involving a light plane will be about $200 per person, per day. A one-day trip to Los Roques including sailing costs $100, and a 3-bedroom house in Morrocoy National Park with full service and boat costs $90 per day per person. Alpi Tour charters planes from 4 to 30 seats, and has a fleet of sailboats, houseboats, and yachts for hire, based along the coast from Morrocoy to Mochima.

Candes Turismo, Edif. Roraima, Av. Miranda, Campo Alegre, Caracas (02–263–3033, telex 23330 CANDES). Special adventures for nature lovers include a bird-watching tour; a 3-day horseback trip to Tisure Páramo in the Andes; and rainy or dry season sojourns in Hato Altamira, a ranch abounding in waterfowl, monkeys, capybara, and cayman. Candes lists over three dozen tours, from Coro in the west to the Orinoco Delta in the East, at prices averaging $100 a day.

Happy Tours, Hotel Inter-Continental Guayana, Ciudad Guayana, Estado Bolívar (086–227748, fax 223257, telex 86238). Leaving from the hotel's Caroni dock, river trips to Llovizna Falls (1½ hrs.). One-day trips to Spanish Forts on the Orinoco, for $50 with barbecue; 4-day trip by launch to Curiapo and the Indian missions in the Orinoco Delta, sleeping in hammocks, $200 a person (min. 6). Angel Falls flyover by charter or commercial flight.

Lost World Adventures, with an office in Atlanta (U.S. toll-free 1–800–999–0558), is an American outfit whose directors combine 30 years field experience in Venezuela. The company offers comfortable tours and strenuous treks: relaxing in a Caribbean hideaway, mountain biking in the Andes, and trekking through the Roraima formation. Also, world-class deep-sea and freshwater fishing; bird watching. Costs average $135 a day per person, all inclusive. Bilingual guides.

Montaña, Apartado Postal 645, Mérida (074–631740 tel. or fax). Providing all equipment for tenting and climbing, this American-run agency shows backpackers the high altitude páramos, lagoons, and glaciers of beautiful Sierra Nevada National Park. Walks, horseback trails, 2–4 days; Mérida, Mucuchíes, and ascent of Mount Bolívar, 9 days. Other tours include mountain biking in the Andes, canoe trips up the Caura River to Para Falls in Bolívar state, and Mount Roraima. Costs average $100 per day from Mérida, all inclusive. Bilingual guides throughout.

Morgan Tours, Edif. Roraima, Av. Miranda, Campo Alegre, Caracas (02–261–7217, telex 23516 MORGNVC, fax 261–9265). Morgan tailors itineraries for 'tough' or 'soft' adventure, from Roraima to leisure beaches. Bird watching in the Andes, Henri Pittier National Park, and the plains. Photo safari on the 250,000-acre reserve of Piñero Ranch where protected habitats harbor tapirs, tayras, howler monkeys, giant otters, ocelots, foxes, and an amazing variety of birds. Reserve well in advance for 'tough' expeditions such as Humboldt's Orinoco passage by dugout (13 days), or the hike-and-dugout crossing from El Dorado to Angel Falls (11 days); these require special preparations. Costs from $80 to $175 a day per person, all inclusive from hotel pick-up.

Selva Tours, Edif. Mayupa, Av. Bolivia, Puerto Ordaz, Estado Bolívar (086–225537, telex 86171), Hotel Rio Orinoco, Ciudad Bolívar (085–48743, fax 42844), or Puerto Ayacucho (048–22122). Jungle tours in the Amazonas Territory, 1 to 7 days, by dugout or jeep run from $75 a day. A popular "Lost World" route explores the Gran Sabana by jeep, returning by plane from Sta. Elena de Uairén. River trips to Angel Falls with English-speaking guide run from May–Oct. for about $300.

Tobogan Tours, Av. Río Negro, Puerto Ayacucho, T.F. Amazonas (048–21700 fax 048–21600). River travel by powered dugouts, *curiara* or *falca,* some over 30 feet long, is exciting, fun, and leisurely. For a first adventure, Pepe Jaimes recommends 4 days (3 nights in a hammock) to the foot of Mt. Autana by way of the Orinoco and Sipapo rivers. Costs about $70 per day per person in groups of 7 to 12, from Puerto Ayacucho.

Turismo Colorama C.A. Local # 53, Centro Com. Bello Campo, Caracas (02–261–7732, fax 262–1828). 4-day jeep tour through the Gran Sabana, famous for its waterfalls and tablemountains, for $324. Daily flights from Caracas to Puerto Ayacucho in the Amazon Territory to travel up the Orinoco and see local indian communities, 3 days for $255 including air fare. Beach excursions include Los Roques Archipelago, Paria Peninsula, or Morrocoy; $75–$110 per day.

Turven Tropical Travel Services, lado Cine Broadway, Calle Real de Sabana Grande, Chacaito, Caracas (02–951–1372; telex 21213, fax 951–1176). From San Fernando de Apure, charters whisk guests to Hato El Cedral deep in the Llanos for ranch-style music and food as well as a spectacular array of dry-season birds. Or fly into Las Nieves camp in southern Bolívar State for hiking. Fly over Angel Falls on your way to Camarata Mission, then hike up to Kavac canyon and river. $125 a day includes flights.

Venezuela Autentika, Edif. Galerías Bolívar, Of. 22A, Sabana Grande Blvd., Caracas (02–717328, fax 725030). Discover the eastern coast near Paria Peninsula, where pelicans nest on cliffs and cottages nestle by idyllic Medina Beach. Great base for jeep rides to water buffalo ranch, cacao and coffee plantations, and Guácharo Caves. Or, by river craft, seek the wildlife on the *caños* or creeks of the Gulf of Paria. About $60 a day per person from Carúpano.

Venguides, piso 7-Oficina A, Edificio Galipan "A", Av. Francisco Miranda, El Rosal; write Aptdo. 80572, Caracas (02–951–6211, fax 951–6544, telex 24714 BVENC-VC). Tailoring services for upscale travelers, Venguides offers door-to-door itineraries from hotel pick-up to jungle landing. Explore Caribbean coves, cloud forests, a ranch on the vast plains (great for bird and animal watching, Oct. through May), bass fishing in Guri Lake, or camping by one of the remote, dark rivers of Amazonas Territory. Costs vary with air charter and destination.

See also "Adventure Vacations" chapter.

Exploring Venezuela

CARACAS

Taxis cut corners as if there were no mañana. Pedestrians bargain with street vendors for avocados, limes, and mangoes in string bags. Graffito in aerosol letters on a building cautions "I love you, M, but I won't wait in line." Salesmen and secretaries break for a potent black *cafecito* at the corner *arepera*. The proprietor is Portuguese, his coffee machine makes Italian espresso, and many of his clients speak with accents of Spain, Argentina, Colombia, France, the United States, and even Japan. At the long counter the Portuguese butters hot corn patties or *arepas* as he fills orders for "arepa con pollo" . . . if not chicken, then cheese, tuna, ham, eggs, beans, shrimp, shark . . . you get the picture. An old woman enters and silently accepts a coin; she will return tomorrow—her lucky number never came up. The state lottery agency down the street lures players with six-digit prizes. Hoping to cheat inflation, thousands of Venezuelans play the lottery and the Sunday "5 & 6" racing pool for a weekly pot of twenty million bolívars or more.

It is Monday in cosmopolitan Caracas. On the freeway drivers watch with envy as private planes take off from the air club beside the crowded *autopista*. The air club took over a sugar plantation before the city overtook it in turn. The red tile roofs of colonial Caracas have all but disappeared in the march of apartment blocks and office towers. The capital, with nearly four million people, has doubled in population since 1960 as a whole generation arrived from plains and hills to claim jobs and schools, the newcomers throwing a ring of shanties around the city. Almost half the dwellings in Caracas are now *ranchitos*. But in time, brick by brick, owners convert shacks into solid structures and neighborhood cooperatives lay water lines and sewers.

Due to its rapid growth, Caracas is a hodgepodge of styles. The modern architecture is often innovative, as in the *"cubo negro"* or Centro Banaven, which is a black, glass-sided box; or ambitious, as in the 457-foot-wide "Poliedro," the geodesic dome which is Caracas's largest arena. There is some neoclassic architecture, such as the nineteenth-century Capitol and the twentieth-century Fine Arts Museum, and some heavy neogothic. But little is to be seen of the charming colonial dwellings except in La Pastora district and in former country houses such as the Quinta Anauco, now the Colonial Museum.

The hub of business, finance, and government, the capital spills over a long, narrow valley in the coastal mountains. Although four- and eight-lane speedways cut the length of the valley, traffic jams are still notorious in Caracas. It can take an hour to get to Maiquetía Airport by the seventeen-and-a-half-mile expressway.

At 3,000 feet above sea level, Caracas has one of the world's best climates, with an average temperature of 75°F. Days can reach 90°, but nights are distinctly cool and in December and January dip to 54°F. The rainy

Points of Interest

1) Plaza Bolívar
2) El Capitolio
3) Biblioteca Nacional
4) Municipal Theater
5) Basilica de San Pedro
6) National Theater
7) Simón Bolívar Twin Towers
8) San Francisco Church
9) El Panteon Nacional
10) El Calvario Park
11) Cathedral
12) Bolívar's Birthplace
13) Miraflores Palace
14) Cuadra Bolívar
15) La Pastora Church
16) Nuevo Circo Bullring
17) San José Church

Caracas

0   1

Mile

SAN AGUSTIN   DEL SUR

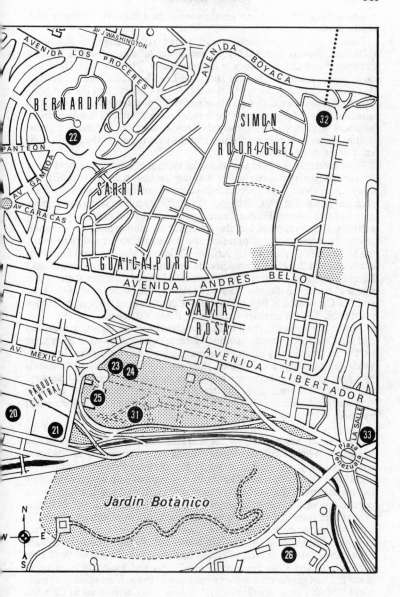

18) Candelaria Church
19) Airbus Terminal
20) Museo de los Niños
21) Museo de Arte
   Contemporáneo
22) Museo de Arte Colonial
23) Museo de Ciencias Naturales
24) Museo de Bellas Artes
25) Teresa Carreno Cultural Complex

26) UCV—University City
27) Nuevo Circo Bus Terminal
28) Carmelitas Post Office
29) Concejo Municipal
30) Boulton Historical
   Museum
31) Los Caobos Park
32) Teleférico Terminal
33) Centro Capriles

season is June through October; showers, although heavy, alternate with sunny spells.

Due to the topographical blocks of the Avila range on the north (Naiguatá Peak is over 9,000 feet) and lower hills in the south, the city has spread east and west from its historic center, Plaza Bolívar. Here, Caracas was founded in 1567 by Diego de Losada, who called it Santiago de León de Caracas. The old Cathedral, Town Council, and Foreign Ministry or Casa Amarilla all face Plaza Bolívar, a pleasant shady square with benches, flocks of pigeons, and the fine equestrian statue of Simón Bolívar, who was born only a block away. Nearby also are the Capitol, the presidential offices in Miraflores Palace, and the twin towers of the Simón Bolívar Center in El Silencio.

Now replacing the twin towers as the symbol of modern Caracas is the concrete city-within-a-city called Parque Central, with its two fifty-six-story skyscrapers. Built over sixteen years, the office and apartment complex was finished in 1986. Designed for 10,000 people in seven condominiums and two towers, Parque Central encompasses not only shops, supermarkets, and restaurants, but also schools, a swimming pool, a convention center for international congresses, the Anauco Hilton residential hotel, the Museum of Contemporary Art, the Children's Museum, and ministerial offices including the Corporación de Turismo. A pedestrian bridge links Parque Central to the new Teresa Carreño Cultural Complex with its theater and concert halls, the National Gallery, the Museum of Fine Arts, and Los Caobos Park. Beyond this bower of mahogany trees, once a coffee plantation, lies the circular fountain of Plaza Venezuela.

Across the autopista from Plaza Venezuela are the Botanical Gardens and the Central University campus. Here, art was conceived as an organic part of architecture by master designer Carlos Raul Villanueva. In courtyards and buildings are a stained glass wall by Ferdinand Léger, murals by Léger and Mateo Manaure, sculptures by Antoine Pevsner, Jean Arp, and Henry Laurens, and, in the Aula Magna auditorium, acoustic "clouds" by Alexander Calder. The 400-acre university city is frequented by about 60,000 people a day.

The great fountain with colored lights in Plaza Venezuela is part of the urban renewal undertaken by the Caracas Metro. The first line of the handsome subway with its elegant French cars was opened in 1983 and completed six years later, covering 21 km. between Propatria in the west and Palo Verde in the east. The stations along this east-west line are now fed by modern "Metrobuses," which run north and south along routes connecting with residential neighborhoods. As promised, the Metro is changing the face of Caracas. When entire avenues were torn up, the architects and landscapers, close behind, converted the commercial high street of Sabana Grande into a pedestrian boulevard of shops, popular sidewalk cafés, potted plants, and chess tables; cars are banned between the Radio City theater and Chacaito; people of all ages and nationalities come to savor the best cappuccino and conversation in town, from midday to midnight. "Meet you at the Gran Café" is how dates often start in Caracas.

For many, an evening on the town begins with beer and *tapitas* (those sizzling seafood snacks popular in Madrid) in one of Sabana Grande's crowded, relaxed bars. Small and large, Italian, Spanish, or Venezuelan, family-style restaurants with good food abound between Casanova Avenue and Solano López. However, the star zone for "big time" dining and clubbing glitters between Chacaito and the Tamanaco Hotel, encompassing El Rosal, Las Mercedes, and Chuao districts. On four or five streets jammed with cars on Saturday night, new restaurants vie with old favorites as the "in" places, with parking attendants, subdued lighting, and live music. An island between the freeway and the air club, the inverted pyramid housing the CCCT shopping and office center in Chuao hums louder after dark than in the day. Its upstairs movie theaters and downstairs fast-food eateries and nightclubs draw many of the 13,000 cars rolling into the CCCT daily. Other ultra-modern centers with elegant boutiques, jewelers, record stores, restaurants, and hairdressers are Paseo Las Mercedes, Concresa, Plaza Las Américas, and the Centro Comercial Chacaito, the one which started the trend in the swinging sixties.

PRACTICAL INFORMATION FOR CARACAS

GETTING AROUND CARACAS. From the airport. Taxis are plentiful at Maiquetía airport and travelers may prepay rides to Caracas according to their destination. Staff at the taxi fare booth, on the main concourse in the airport, will help you select one of six zones with set prices, from about $10 for the closest (Plaza Bolívar) to $15 for the farthest, about 22 miles (El Hatillo). Nighttime fares have a 20¢ surcharge; luggage is about 50 cents per piece.

In general, **taxis** are metered and rides are cheap; tipping is not the rule. For 24-hour pickup service to airport (approx. $10), reserve through Taxi Móvil, 752–6433; Taxitour, 749411; Tele Taxi, 752–4155; UTAC, 575–0053.

Buses and **por puestos** go everywhere in the city for less than Bs.10. Airport por puestos and the **Maiquetía bus service** (Organización UCAMC, 573–0612) leave day and night from Av. Sur 17, west of Parque Central, below Av. Bolívar. Buses to the coast leave from the Nuevo Circo terminal and from Av. Solano López, east end, near Centro Comercial Chacaito.

The efficient **Metro**, opened in 1983, runs east-west, from Petare to Propatria, and from Silencio to Caricuao. Air-conditioned cars on rubber wheels whiz a million passengers daily for fares as low as Bs.7.

HOTELS. Caracas accommodations range from 5-star hotels of international chains such as the Caracas Hilton, largest hotel on the continent, and the Tamanaco, pearl of the Inter-Continental chain, to pensions. Most of those listed here are located in midtown or east Caracas, convenient to restaurants and transportation. For definitions of price categories see "Facts at Your Fingertips" earlier in the chapter.

Super Deluxe

Caracas Hilton, Av. Mexico, (574–1122 or 800–HILTONS in U.S., telex 21171). 905 rooms and suites, 3 restaurants, penthouse Cota 808 nightclub, convention and banquet facilities for more than 5,000, pool, 2 tennis courts, gym and sauna, beauty salon and barber shop, boutiques, car rental, travel agency, secretarial and translation service. Convenient for sightseeing, government business, museums, and concerts.

Eurobuilding, Calle La Guairita, Chuao (959–1133, fax 922069). Plush new 473-room hotel in modern business complex with all services, plus disco, nightclub, recreation-sports club, and pool. Also 180 residential suites. Overlooking CCCT shopping center, but not an easy location if you prefer to explore on foot.

Tamanaco Inter-continental, Av. Principal Las Mercedes (924522, reservations 208–7000). East Caracas's favorite business hotel. Well-located in the lively restaurant, shopping, and nightclub district. 600 rooms, 3 restaurants, and Naiguatá nightclub. Tennis courts, pool, gym, sauna, convention and banquet facilities for 2,000, travel agency, bank, car rental, shops, beauty salon, barber shop.

Deluxe

Anauco Hilton, Edificio Anauco, Parque Central (5734111 or 800–HILTONS in U.S.). Large, comfortable, well-equipped split-level apartments for up to 4 people. Bar, restaurant, access to Caracas Hilton pool, 2 meeting rooms for 100 people each. The hotel forms part of the Parque Central complex with its enormous convention facilities, museums, shops.

Aventura Caracas, Av. Sorocaima, above the Centro Médico, San Bernardino

(51–40–11, telex 27359). Comfortable, modern 85-room hotel near town center. Restaurant, bar, convention hall, car rental, Jacuzzi, gym, pool, spa club.

CCT Venantur, Centro Ciudad Comercial Tamanaco, Chuao (959–1544/1644, fax 261–4122). Attached to a high-class shopping center with movies, nightclubs (hotel guests may enter free). 8 floors have 161 rooms, 4 meeting rooms, restaurants. Small pool, 2 tennis courts. Convenient for east Caracas business.

Lincoln Suites, Av. Solano between Los Jabillos and Jerónimo, Sabana Grande (725503, fax 978–1497). New, convenient hotel run by Venantur. 40 double rooms, 88 junior suites with refrigerator and central air-conditioning.

Paseo Las Mercedes, Av. Principal, Las Mercedes (910444; fax 921797; telex 23127). Part of shopping center with movie theater, restaurants, and nightclub. Popular for its good location in the east and easy transportation. 197 rooms, restaurant, small pool, meeting rooms.

President, Av. Valparaiso, Los Caobos (708–8111, fax 782–6458; telex 29037 PARDO VC). Attractive new tower with 165 rooms, Italian restaurant, piano-bar, pool, Jacuzzi. Sabana Grande area.

Expensive

Avila, Av. George Washington, San Bernardino (515128, telex 21637). Set among lovely gardens at the foot of Mt. Avila, this gracious hotel with 117 rooms has long been a favorite. Pleasant dining room near the pool, piano bar, convention facilities, and shops. Near Cota Mil highway.

Coliseo, Av. Casanova at Coromoto, Sabana Grande (727916). Modern, busy hotel. Nerone Restaurant. Midtown.

Continental Altamira, Av. San Juan Bosco, Altamira (261–6019, fax 262–2163; telex 24367). Good value in residential east. 80 rooms, restaurant, pool.

El Condor, 3rd Av. Las Delicias, Sabana Grande (729911; fax 72–86–21). Busy, 37 rooms and 36 suites. Banquet facilities for 200, excellent Italian restaurant.

La Floresta, Av. Luis Roche, Plaza Altamira Sur (284–4111). Pleasant, residential hotel, 84 rooms.

Tampa, No. 9 Av. Francisco Solano, Sabana Grande (723771; telex 24403). Convenient, commercial, 134 rooms. Rugantino restaurant.

Moderate

Campo Alegre, 2d Calle, Campo Alegre at Calle Paéz de Chacao (328028). New 56-room hotel near crowded Chacao.

City, Av. Bolivia, Los Caobos (782–7501). 48 rooms.

Crillon, Av. Libertador at Las Acacias (716912; fax 716911). Commercial hotel with 80 rooms on busy thoroughfare. Swiss Chalet restaurant. Near Sabana Grande.

El Cid, Av. San Felipe, La Castellana (987–8511). Good residential hotel with 52 small apartments, east Caracas.

El Conde, Esquina El Conde (811171). Traditional downtown hotel 1 block from Plaza Bolívar. 130 rooms, restaurant, bar, patronized by politicians and journalists.

King's Inn, Calle Olimpo, Sabana Grande (782–7033). 53 modern rooms near Metro and Plaza Venezuela.

Kursaal, Av. Casanova, Sabana Grande (722922). Long established hotel in busy midtown. 89 rooms.

Grand Galaxie, Av. Baralt, Truco a Caja de Agua (839011/44; telex 26319). 68 modern rooms, 3 blocks north of Urdaneta, downtown.

Las Americas, Calle Los Cerritos, Bello Monte (951–7596). 72 rooms in hotel near Chacaito, much in demand. Rooftop pool.

Luna, Calle El Colegio, Sabana Grande (725851). Standard lodgings but very convenient. Midtown.

Montpark, Calle Los Cerritos near Casanova (951–5520). 48 rooms.

Plaza Catedral, Esq. La Torre, Plaza Bolívar (563–7022). Tastefully remodeled with 78 rooms. In the heart of old Caracas.

Plaza Palace, Av. Los Mangos, Las Delicias de Sabana Grande (724821). On a side street off restaurant area. 84 rooms.

Savoy, Av. Solano at 2d Av. Las Delicias, Sabana Grande (721971). Convenient 95-room hotel run by Cumberland Hotels.

Inexpensive

Altamira, Av. F. J. Sosa, opposite Teatro Altamira (314284). 80 rooms.

Bruno, Prolongación Sur, Av. Las Acacias (781–8324). Near Sabana Grande. A business hotel with 105 rooms.

Canaima, Abanico a Maturín (561–1366). Downtown. 60 rooms, some without air-conditioning.

Escorial, Calle El Colegio, Sabana Grande (719621). 34 rooms.

Madrid, Calle Chacaito, Bello Monte (711160). Small family hotel.

Plaza Venezuela, Av. La Salle, Los Caobos (781–7811). Standard accommodations on a main avenue in midtown.

Waldorf, Av. Industrial, San Bernardino, block south of Av. Urdaneta (571–5543). Older downtown hotel with 34 rooms, restaurant.

Beach Hotels

Macuto Sheraton. *Super Deluxe.* Caraballeda (031–944300/8 or 800–325–3535 in U.S.; fax 031–944318). Resort hotel and conference center with 543 rooms, 3 restaurants, nightclub, 2 pool areas, theater, shops, and beauty salons. Car rental. Marina. Guests may use luxurious Caraballeda Golf Club facilities. Reservations in Caracas (02–781–1508, 781–7631).

Meliá Caribe. *Deluxe.* Caraballeda (031–945555; fax 031–941509). 300 rooms. Modern resort hotel with all facilities. Swimming pool, restaurants, discotheque, shops, car rental. Reservations in Caracas (729314; telex 21549).

Bahía by the Sea. *Moderate.* Av. La Playa and Costanera, Los Corales (031–942417). 40 rooms, restaurant, pool, near beach.

Fioremar. *Moderate.* Urbanización Caribe, Caraballeda (031–941743). 25 family-style rooms near beach.

Hotel Macuto. *Moderate.* Av. La Playa, Macuto (031–44561). Popular weekend hotel in seaside district of fish bars. 70 rooms, pool. Poor swimming on the beach.

Las Quince Letras. *Moderate.* Av. La Playa, Macuto (031–45821). 79 rooms in a tower, 5-minute walk from public beach. Famous seafood restaurant.

Riviera. *Moderate.* Calle San Bartolomé, Macuto (031–44313). 28 rooms opposite beach in the old town. Restaurant, *tasca* bar, Jacuzzi, kid's park.

Royal Atlantic. *Moderate.* Av. Principal del Caribe, Caraballeda (031–91250). In classy district, 2 blocks from beach. 20 rooms, pool, restaurant.

RESTAURANTS. Reflecting the principal stock in Caracas's ethnic pot, the most popular dining spots are Italian pasta houses, Spanish seafood centers, *criollo* or Venezuelan specialty restaurants and Argentine parrilla steak houses. High society eats in elegant (jacket and tie) French restaurants with European chefs, some of the best being found at the leading hotels. The Hilton's *Rotisserie* is famous; the *Tamanaco's* informal poolside buffet lunch is great value. Fashionable dining hours are between 9 and 11 P.M.; however, don't go out too late, as few restaurants are open beyond 11:30. Most restaurants are closed one day a week, usually Sunday or Monday.

Other nationalities account for Arabian, Hungarian, Chinese, and Japanese restaurants. Indeed there is such a wide variety and great number of restaurants that the following list is only a sampling. Outside Caracas, ask for the best *pollo a la parrilla* (chicken barbecue), Italian or Chinese restaurant.

For definitions of price categories, see "Facts at Your Fingertips."

All expensive restaurants, and most moderate ones, accept credit cards. There's a 10 percent service charge and it is usual to tip the waiter another 5–10 percent.

Caraqueños have taken to fast food with gusto, and McDonald's in El Rosal is only the latest of many hamburger and pizza palaces. The CCCT shopping center in Chuao, which draws 13,000 cars on a Sat., is popular for its fast-food eateries touting everything from tacos to bratwurst. But none of these foreign delights displaces Venezuela's original home-grown arepa, the flat corncake served hot with your choice of fillings, from fresh white cheese to shrimp and avocado, and best accompanied by delicious tropical fruit juices. To mention only three areperas (also offering standard menu): **Doña Arepota,** Edificio Doral, Av. Mexico at Bellas Artes metro station near the Hilton (572–6545); sidewalk tables, open 24 hours. **El Granjero,** Av. Rio de Janeiro, Las Mercedes (916619); in fashionable restaurant area, open all night. **La Sifrina,** Av. Blandin, near Plaza de La Castellana (336569); "in" place in east Caracas, open 24 hours.

Venezuelan

La Atarraya. *Moderate.* Plaza El Venezolano near Casa Natal (5458235). Lively atmosphere, balcony serenades at night, picturesque setting.

Dama Antañona. *Moderate.* No. 14 Jesuitas a Maturín, downtown (563–5639). Charming 150-year-old house. Recommended for lunch but not for dinner, as the quality of food and service diminishes at night, when there are few customers. Try the Sunday *criollo* breakfast.

Doña Bárbara. *Moderate.* Plaza Henry Clay near Teatro Nacional (541–1351). Downtown meeting place of lawyers, politicians. Salads, *sancochos,* shrimp, steak.

El Portón. *Moderate.* No. 18 Av. Pichincha, El Rosal (716071). Arepas and *hallaquitas* accompany *ternera* (roast veal) and other specialties.

Zaguán de Un Solo Pueblo. *Moderate.* 3rd Trans., Los Palos Grandes, near Av. Roche (284–1236). Hearty Venezuelan music and food.

Jaime Vivas. *Inexpensive.* Edificio Manaure, Calle San Antonio, near Gran Café, Sabana Grande (714761). No frills.

Anglo-American

Café L'Attico. *Moderate.* Upstairs at Qta. Palic, Ave. Roche above Plaza Altamira (261–2819). Try Sunday brunch . . . waffles, hash browns, muffins.

Lee Hamilton Steak House. *Moderate.* No.30 Av. San Felipe, La Castellana (325227). Mecca of the head lettuce and roast beef. Large portions.

Weekends. *Moderate.* Av. San Juan Bosco at 2d Transv., Altamira (261–3839). Ultramodern, 2-story restaurant serving pastries and short-order fare. Very trendy.

French

Chez Antoine. *Expensive.* No. 4–09, Calle Trinidad, Las Mercedes (917712). More emphasis on food here than on fashion.

L'Entrecote. *Expensive.* Av. Tamanaco, El Rosal (951–0189). Old tradition, new locale offers fish, fowl, and beef.

Gazebo. *Expensive.* Av. Janeiro and Av. Trinidad, Las Mercedes (925568). High on cuisine, cachet, and coin. There's a classy delicatessen.

Patrick's. *Expensive.* Calle Trinidad at Paris, Las Mercedes (916641). Garden atmosphere, nouveau cuisine.

Primi. *Expensive.* Av. Principal La Castellana, 1½ blocks above Av. Miranda. Inventive cuisine under a glass roof.

Bistrot de Jacques. *Moderate.* Av. Principal de Las Mercedes, near Av. Orinoco (918108). New, small, for the knowledgeable gourmet.

Le Coq d'Or. *Moderate.* Calle Los Mangos, Las Delicias de Sabana Grande. (710891). New locale for old favorite. Small—make reservations.

Jardin des Crepes. *Moderate.* Calle Madrid between Trinidad and New York (914193). Pleasant balcony, salad bar, crepes both salty and sweet.

El Parque. *Moderate.* Ed. Anauco, Parque Central (573–7013). Breezy tables at exit of art museum.

Italian

Da Emore. *Expensive.* Centro Com. Concresa, Prados del Este (979–0264). Great antipastos, 5-course dinners. Reservations needed.

Da Pippo. *Moderate.* Av. San Felipe, La Castellana (337730). Popular east Caracas spot.

Da Sandra. *Moderate.* Av. Solano, Sabana Grande (726546). Intimate atmosphere, excellent food.

La Taberna del Cubo. *Moderate.* Centro Banaven (Cubo Negro), Chuao (926212). Said to be the one and only cantina Italiana. Live music.

Da Guido. *Inexpensive.* No. 8 Av. Solano, Sabana Grande (710937). Satisfying fare for the whole family.

Vecchio Mulino. *Inexpensive.* No. 17 Av. Solano, Sabana Grande (712695). Spacious, popular, pleasant.

Seafood

Since Venezuela enjoys a Caribbean cornucopia of fish, shrimp, and lobster, and since Spaniards are expert seafood cooks, it is no surprise that many of the best seafood houses are Spanish. Most are *moderate.*

Barba Roja, Av. Tamanaco, El Rosal (333072). Piano-bar.

El Barquero, Av. Roche at 5th transversal, Altamira (284–0910).

Bogavante, Av. Venezuela near Pichincha (718624). Live music.

Casa Juancho, Av. San Juan Bosco, lower Altamira (323794).

La Cebolla, Av. Venezuela, El Rosal (951–3381). Live music, open to 3 A.M.

Dena Ona, Av. Tamanaco No. 52, El Rosal (337658).

La Fonda de Las Mercedes, Calle Veracruz, Las Mercedes (913553).

La Jaiba. *Moderate.* Av. Principal del Bosque, parte Alta de la Av. Libertador (731–0329).

El Mar, Av. Venezuela at Mohedano, El Rosal (330231).

Taberna Mi Tasca, Av. Solano at Los Manquitos, Sabana Grande (718364).

Torre Vieja, Calle Madrid between Trinidad and New York (922460). Tascas and music by lamplight.

Steak Houses

If you like charcoal-grilled beef, you can't go wrong with a *churrasco* at any of these popular restaurants. *Inexpensive* to *moderate.*

Alfi's, basement, Centro Comercial Chacaito (725567). Delicious prime ribs.

Buffalo Station, Av. La Trinidad, Las Mercedes (912357). It's buffalo and good.

El Caney, Av. Trinidad between Paris and Madrid, Las Mercedes (911641).

El Carrizo, Av. Blandin, La Castellana (329270). Faithful clientele.

La Estancia, Av. Principal, La Castellana at 1st Tr. (331937).

Hereford Grill, Calle Madrid, Las Mercedes (929664).

La Mansion, Av. Tamanaco, El Rosal, behind Edificio Galipan (333455).

Maute Grill, Av. Rio de Janeiro at New York, Las Mercedes (910892).

Shorthorn Grill, Av. Libertador, El Bosque (711052). Tried and true.

TOURIST INFORMATION. The **Corporación de Turismo de Venezuela** offices are in the Torre Oeste, 37th floor, Parque Central (507–8611); open 8:30 A.M. to 12:30 P.M., 2 to 5 P.M. Mon.-Fri. Corpoturismo also has an airport office in Maiquetía (031–552747) open 6 A.M. to midnight every day, and a tourism library in Parque Central. For special interests such as diving, birding, or hiking, inquire through local clubs, some of whose members will speak English. A sample: Cariaquáticos (scuba), 752–8542; Audubon de Venezuela (nature), 912813; Centro Excursionista de Caracas (hiking), contact M. Pap 284–6808. Other groups specialize in climbing, spelunking, hunting, fishing, and flying. Check the Living Section of the *Daily Journal.*

TOURS. In pullmans and minibuses, tours offer an introduction to Caracas, a complicated city where a car is a necessity except for downtown. All companies offer **Caracas ½ day** and **Colonial Caracas** for about $10 per person; a **Night Tour** with dinner, show, and drink for $25–$40. A popular day trip is to **Colonia Tovar,** a mountain village; the cost of about $30 includes lunch at a German restaurant. For best rates, book 2–3 days ahead so as to make a minimum of 6 people.

Candes, Caracas Hilton lobby, 571–0987, day tours to coast, cloud forest, museums, Colonia Tovar; average cost $40. *Happy Tours,* Of. 206, Centro Capriles, Plaza Venezuela (782–3342 and 781–5022). *Latin Tours,* 4th floor, Torre Maracaibo, Av. Libertador (722707/03). *Rally Tours,* 7th floor, Edif. Galipan-B, Av. Miranda, Chacao (951–1408; for information at any hour call 283–9411, ext. 180). *Servicios Colectivos Especiales* offer hotel pick-up for a varied list of 25 trips at bargain prices (283–1198, 284–3111, ext. 672).

SIGHTS. Historic Center. A walk in the heart of old Caracas is a pleasure now that streets around Plaza Bolívar are closed to traffic and the Metro whisks you downtown in 12 minutes from Chacaito. Start at the gilt-domed *Capitol,* 483–1235 (9 A.M. to noon and 3 to 6 P.M. except Mon.), with its lovely gardens and fountain. Built in 1874 in a record 114 days, legislative chambers at the south end may be visited during sessions (483–3644, Senate secretary). State occasions are held in the Salón Elíptico, 413719, where the 1811 Independence Act is kept in a crystal ark; impressive ceiling murals of Carabobo Battle are by M. Tovar y Tovar.

San Francisco Church on Av. Universidad facing the Capitol, is one of the oldest (1575) in the country. Here, at age 30, Bolívar received the title of "Liberator" and command of patriot forces. Outside the church stands a venerable kapok tree, the *ceiba de San Francisco.* Next to the church is the *Palace of Academies* (414306), housed in the old Franciscan cloisters; the History Academy archives contain Francisco Miranda's papers and 1,200 volumes on Bolívar. The adjacent *National Library* (483–2058), is open 8:30 A.M. to 8 P.M. weekdays and 8:30 A.M. to 4:30 P.M. on Sat. The block ends with the *Palace of Justice* where the Supreme Court meets.

Continue to *Plaza Bolívar,* always full of greenery, people feeding pigeons, and tourists admiring the fine equestrian statue of Bolívar by Tadolini (1874); the Banda Municipal plays Thurs. and Sun. at 6 P.M. There is a reading room under the north end (818136). On the west side of the square, ask to see the patio of the colonial *Casa Amarilla* (818521), now the seat of the Foreign Ministry but once the royal prison, and later the presidential palace. On the north is the Federal District *Government House* (810911), where there are periodic exhibitions. On the south side is the Town Council or *Palacio Municipal* (545–6706), where a Museum of Caracas displays deeds signed by city founder Diego de Losada, early maps, and the unique miniatures of 1920s slice-of-life in Caracas by Raul Santana. The Declaration of Independence was signed July 5, 1811, in the adjoining chapel (open Mon.–Fri. 9 A.M. to noon and 2:30 to 4:30 P.M.; weekends 10:30 A.M. to 6 P.M.). The *Cathedral* (824063), rebuilt in 1674, stands where Caracas's first church was raised in 1595 on the east side of the Plaza Mayor, as it was then called; it features paintings by Rubens, Murillo, and Michelena, and the tomb of Bolívar's parents and wife, who died of yellow fever within months of their marriage (open daily 6:30 A.M. to noon and 3 to 7 P.M.).

Bolívar's birthplace, the *Casa Natal* (545–7693), is a block east at Plaza San Jacinto (Tue.–Fri. 9 A.M. to noon and 2:30 to 5:30 P.M.; Sat., Sun., and holidays, 10 A.M. to 1 P.M., 2 to 5 P.M.). This faithfully reconstructed, elegant residence where Simón Bolívar was born July 24, 1783, displays the family bed plus Bolívar's library and files. Next door, the *Museo Bolivariano* (545–9828), contains weapons, maps, books, and relics of the independence era. The *Cuadra Bolívar* (483–3971), same hours, was once the summer home of the Bolívar family where Simón conspired with other youths to free the colony. Today its high walls enclose tranquil gardens, patios, a kitchen, and a stable. 8 blocks due south of Plaza Bolívar on Av. Sur 2 at Esq. Bárcenas.

Miraflores Palace (810811, visits ext. 293), Av. Urdaneta, 1 block west of Av. Baralt. The presidential offices occupy a nineteenth-century mansion built by Gen. Joaquín Crespo. No photographs allowed, but visits by groups may be arranged for Sun. mornings.

Venezuelan presidents reside officially in *La Casona,* in eastern Caracas, at the foot of Av. La Carlota. Until the 1940s, La Carlota was a sugar hacienda including the present air club. The restored manor house, modernized with a pool, council room, and barracks, has beautiful gardens, 7 patios, fountains, and a fine painting collection. For a tour with bilingual guide, call (Protocol, 284–6322) 2 weeks ahead with passport number. No camera or bags. The band plays during the changing of the Presidential Guard at 6 A.M. and 6 P.M.

MUSEUMS. Arte Colonial (518517), Av. Panteón, San Bernardino (Tues.–Sat., 9 to 11:30 A.M. and 2 to 4:30 P.M.; Sun., holidays, 10 A.M. to 4:30 P.M.). Not to be missed is this graceful, garden-sheltered residence called Quinta Anauco, where the Marquis del Toro lived. The colonial era comes to life in flower-scented patios, kitchen, household, and sunken bath fed by a brook.

Arte Contemporáneo (573–4602), Parque Central next to Anauco Hilton (Tues.–Sun. 10 A.M. to 6 P.M.); 3-level museum showing the best in modern art, both local and foreign.

Arte La Rinconada (606–6648), at entrance to race track, El Valle (Tues.–Fri. 10 A.M. to 5 P.M.; Sat.–Sun., 10 A.M. to 3 P.M.). Three floors of art exhibitions.

Banco Central (829821/31/41), Esq. Carmelitas, Av. Urdaneta. (weekdays 8:30 A.M. to 11:30 A.M. and 2 P.M. to 4:30 P.M.). A collection of Bolívar's medals, gold sword, jewels. Mezzanine.

Bellas Artes (571–1813), Plaza Morelos, near Caracas Hilton (Tues.–Fri. 9 A.M. to noon and 3 to 5:30 P.M.; Sat., Sun., and holidays, 9:30 A.M. to 5 P.M.), and the **Galería de Arte Nacional** (571–3519), house collections by top Venezuelan talent, past and present; also foreign shows. In the patios and gardens are works by Calder, Moore, and Arp. **Ciencias Naturales** (571–1265), opposite Galería National (same hours); archaeology, African art, birds of Venezuela, dioramas.

De Los Niños (573–4112), Edif Tacagua, Parque Central (Wed.–Sun., 9 A.M. to noon and 2 to 5 P.M.). At the Children's Museum, guides lead kids and adults through 5 levels of fun plus learning about perception, sound, radio, TV; admission 60 cents adults, 30 cents children. Closed Mon. and Tues.

Historical Museum of Boulton Foundation (563–1838), Torre El Chorro, 11th floor, Av. Universidad (Mon.–Fri. 8:30 A.M. to 4:30 P.M.; Sat.–Sun. 9:30 A.M. to 1:30 P.M.). History through the collection by one family of antiques, paintings, and books.

Histórico Militar (410808), La Planicie (Sat.–Sun. 10 A.M. to 4 P.M.); the hilltop Defense Ministry displays uniforms, arms, and battle plans of Independence wars.

Michelena (825853), Esq. Urapal, La Pastora (Tues.–Thur. and Sat.–Sun. 9 A.M. to noon and 3 to 5 P.M.); charming little house where nineteenth-century painter Arturo Michelena lived and worked.

Petare (215363), Calle Lino Clemente, 2 blocks south of Plaza Sucre, Petare (Tues.–Sun. 9 A.M. to 5 P.M.); a visit to the restored colonial house with popular and folk art exhibits provides an opportunity to explore Petare's narrow streets, restored church (1760), Casa de Cultura Lira (218858, located a block before the museum), and Capilla del Calvario with carved statues.

Transporte (341621 and 342234), Parque del Este, eastern annex (Sat., Sun., and holidays 10 A.M. to 5 P.M.; Wed. for kids 9 A.M. to 6 P.M.); steam engines, planes, fine old machines.

PARKS AND ZOOS. Avila National Park, with its tropical forest, trails, and clear streams, is also a hiker's challenge, rising to the peak of Naiguatá at 9,071 feet. Permits are issued by rangers at park guardposts on the Avila for a small fee. Instituto Nacional de Parques offices are on Av. Rómulo Gallegos by the Parque del Este Metro Station (284–3266). Since the Avila park is huge (210,500 acres) and in places quite wild, it is important to start any excursion early, and never go alone. Take a hat to shield yourself from the sun and a good windbreaker for high climbs. Some enthusiasts camp out. At Los Venados, a former coffee hacienda where rangers have their headquarters, there are shelters with barbecue grills and a Visitors Center (810690) with library, museum, infirmary, and cafetería. A road to Los Venados for 4-wheel-drive vehicles starts from Av. Peñalver, Cotiza. Regular weekend hikes are led by the Club de Excursionistas de Caracas; call Jesus Pereira (751–1974).

Botanical Gardens (662–9254), at the Plaza Venezuela entrance to UCV (Mon.–Sun. 8 A.M. to 5 P.M.). 170 acres, some planted with succulents, marsh plants, 300 kinds of palm trees; a natural stand of forest with vines and orchids. There is an arboretum with 80 species, and a Botanical Institute. The National Herbarium has 120,000 pressed plants. No picnicking and no public facilities.

Caricuao Zoo (431–2045), at western end of Autopista del Este (Francisco Fajardo), about 12 miles from Plaza Venezuela (Sat.–Sun. and holidays 9 A.M. to 5 P.M.; midweek for school visits only). Spacious (1,200 acres) but still unfinished park with over 160 kinds of birds and animals; monkeys, peacocks, and ibis run free. Kiosks for picnics, snack bar.

Los Próceres Promenade and Officers' Club, reached from Santa Mónica or Av. Nueva Granada, are part of an imposing parade ground complex honoring Venezuela's founding fathers which leads to the military academy. The luxurious *Circulo Militar* (662–3111), open to visitors Mon.–Fri. 8 A.M. to 4 P.M., provides members with gym, pool, theater, chapel, horses, rowing lake, jogging track. Visitors may use the restaurant, poolside snack bar.

Los Caobos Park, Plaza Venezuela to Museo de Bellas Artes, is full of mahoganies which used to shade coffee bushes. An exhibit hall, Módulo Venezuela (Tues.–Sun. 9 A.M. to noon, 2 to 5 P.M.), is run by Corpoturismo. The fountain with maidens carved by Narváez used to be in Plaza Venezuela.

Parque del Este and Planetarium (284–3266), Av. F. Miranda (Tues.–Sun. and holidays, 8 A.M. to 6 P.M.). 200 well-kept acres, a favorite outdoor spot for thousands of families on weekends; joggers may enter at 5:30 A.M. Aviary, terrarium, monkey island, ponds with herons, scarlet ibis and cayman, boating lagoon; replica of Columbus's ship, the *Santa María*. The Humboldt Planetarium (349189), run by the Navy, gives shows on Sat. at 5 P.M., Sun. at noon, 3, 4, and 5 P.M.; also astronomy, navigation courses on weeknights.

Pinar Zoo (461–7794), is reached by Av. Guzmán Blanco (Cota 905) or Av. Paez, El Paraiso (Tues.–Sun. 9 A.M. to 5:30 P.M.). The zoo is small but crowded with life—lions, tigers, and animals for children to touch such as donkeys, rabbits, and goats.

MUSIC AND DANCE. Besides Caracas's full stage program of music, dance, theater, and opera, there are some free events. The band concerts in Plaza Bolívar are traditional on Thurs. and Sun. at 6 P.M. The Metro's cultural department promotes presentations by various groups at subway stations; the Venezuelan Symphony Orchestra did a stint at 5 P.M. in La Hoyada station, rotating with the UCV choir and little theater groups.

Many fine musicians, three orchestras, and the national opera give a wide range of recitals and concerts, from Bach to jazz. Check daily papers for times. Advance tickets may be bought for some theaters at Don Disco record shop, Plaza Chacaito (718056).

Ateneo, Plaza Morelos, opposite Caracas Hilton (573–4622). Concert hall for 300; Rajatabla Theater (572–6109), for drama group, seats 150.

Aula Magna, Universidad Central (619811–30, ext. 2505); a modern hall with 3,000 seats and acoustic "clouds" by Alexander Calder. Sun. concerts at 11 A.M. by Venezuelan Symphony Orchestra (except Aug.-Sept.).

Cantv, Av. Libertador opposite Colegio de Ingenieros Metro station (500–8346); plays and recitals at the telephone company auditorium.

Concha Acústica, top end Av. Caurimare at Chaura, Colinas de Bello Monte (751–0710). Very occasional shows in outdoor amphitheater.

Electricidad de Caracas, Av. Vollmer, San Bernardino (574–9111); modern concert hall offers good music at low price (about $2).

Estudio Mata de Coco, Av. Blandin, La Castellana (261–9398); Latin pop and rock stars, folk singers, and modern dancers often play to sold-out houses in this 1,300-capacity stage-cum-night club.

Museo del Teclado, mezz., Edif. Tacagua, Parque Central (572–0713); collection of rare harpsichords and pianos is open Tues.–Sun. 10 A.M. to 12:30 P.M. and 2 to 4 P.M.; concerts Mon. and Wed. at 8 P.M.

Teresa Carreño Cultural Complex, opposite Caracas Hilton (571–7691). Box office 573–4600 (Mon.–Fri. noon to 7 P.M.; Sat.–Sun. 9 A.M. to 5 P.M.). Costly new performing arts center with a concert hall for 400, home of the National Youth Orchestra; 2,500-seat Ríos Reyna Hall with electronic controls for 50 sets, computer-modulated acoustics. The Venezuelan Symphony Orchestra plays here. Telephone reservations, Diners Club accepted; 507–1555 (Mon.–Fri. 8 A.M. to 5:45 P.M.); guided tours 571–1213.

THEATER. In addition to these cultural centers, a dozen theaters put on plays. The Caracas Playhouse presents 4 productions a year in English (for information call F. Jacomé, 661–9606). Check *El Universal* for Spanish plays. A sample of theaters:

Juana Sujo, Alberto Paz y Mateos, the Nuevo Grupo's two theaters on Prolongación Av. Los Manolos, Las Palmas (782–1621/1117). **Las Palmas,** Av. Las Palmas near Libertador (782–2468). **Teatro Municipal,** Esq. Municipal opposite south Twin Tower downtown (483–4630); prestigious, handsome, old (1880s) theater where many operas and ballets are given. **Teatro Nacional,** Esq. Cipreses, Av. Este 10, downtown (415956); rival of the Municipal as fine old-style theater, built in 1905. **Santa Sofía,** Centro Comercial Santa Sofía, El Cafetal (987–5334), theater hall in east suburb. **Rafael Guinand,** Centro Plaza, Tr. 1, Los Palos Grandes. **Rajatabla,** Ateneo, opposite Caracas Hilton (572–6109); top-notch.

ART GALLERIES. Private galleries, like public, are popular on weekends; hours are generally Tues.–Sat. 10 A.M. to 1 P.M. and 3 to 7 P.M.; Sun. 10 A.M. to 1 P.M., except where noted. **Acquavella,** Torre El Bosque, Av. Principal del Bosque (713689); leading figurative painters including Héctor Poleo. **Artehoy,** Av. El Empalme, El Bosque (718647); new talents. **Cesar Rengifo,** Calle California, Las Mercedes (912445). Tues.–Sat. 11:30 A.M. to 6:30 P.M.

Durban, Calle Madrid, Las Mercedes (924231); Mon.–Fri. 9 A.M. to 7 P.M.; Sat.–Sun. 11 A.M. to 3 P.M.; collectives by up and coming painters. **Espacios Cálidos,** Ateneo, opposite Caracas Hilton (573–4622); photography, painting galleries. **Estudio 1,** locale CL5, near Sala Plenaria, Edif. Mohedano, Parque Central (572–2196); Mon.–Fri. 9:30 A.M. to 1 P.M. and 2 to 5 P.M.; Jesús Soto, the founder of the kinetic art movement, has a small outlet here, also representing other painters. **Felix,** Transversal 3 at Av. 6, Altamira (261–4517); artists outside the establishment. **Galería Artehoy,** Av. Empalme, El Bosque (731–0443); small, well established. **Lynn's,** Av. 3 between Tr. 6–7, Los Palos Grandes (283–5237); Haitian and Venezuelan primitives. **Mendoza,** Edif. Las Fundaciones, Av. Andrés Bello (571–7120); daily 9 A.M. to 12:30 P.M. and 3 to 6 P.M.; Sun. 11 A.M. to 1 P.M.); the best all-round shows, bookshop, twice-yearly auctions. **Petare Museum of Popular Art,** Calles Guanche and Lino Clemente (215363); in the conserved colonial center of the former village of Petare, this attractive gallery shows local talent, often naive painters. **Sala Rómulo Gallegos,** Av. Luis Roche, Altamira, near Tr.3 (285–2644); handsome quarters for exhibits in new cultural center. **Tigana Art,** Centro Com. Quinso, Av. Rio de Janeiro, Las Mercedes (911079); shows by regional artisans. **Yakera,** Av. Andrés Bello between Tr. 1–2, Los Palos Grandes (283–8153); excellent indigenous art—carvings, basketry, and weaving.

HORSE RACING. The Rinconada Hippodrome in El Valle (606–6111), is said to be one of Latin America's most beautiful tracks. A favorite project of dictator Pérez Jiménez, who fled the country a year before its opening in 1959, it has stables for 2,000 horses, training grounds, an equine swimming pool, and laboratories. Thoroughbred races are held every Sat. and Sun. from 1 to 6 P.M. Entrance to Tribunes A and C costs Bs.10. Formally dressed visitors (jacket and tie for men) head for Tribune B. The upper-tier Jockey Club restaurant is for members only.

Most of the weekly $2 million in bets comes from the nationwide network of a million "5 & 6" fans who eagerly follow race results on radio and TV to learn whether their racing form or *cuadro* has accurately predicted the winners in five or six selected Sunday races.

SHOPPING. Many of Caracas's sophisticated shops are now in modern shopping complexes known as "centros comerciales." Today these are less stocked with imports since devaluation has put foreign goods beyond local shoppers' purses. It is a buyer's market for fine clothing, tailored suits, elegant well-made shoes, and jewelry.

Gems, gold. At the CCCT shopping center in Chuao, there are four jewelers and a gold-diamond dealer. *Diamoro,* 3rd floor, Of. A–310 Torre A, CCCT (959–0624), sells gold ingots (.999) at NY closing price plus a small commission. *Muzo Gemologists,* Nivel C-1, Torre A, CCCT (929361), specializes in gemstones and has a fine collection of rough stones and crystals. *Roca Hermanos,* Nivel Uno (959–1730), represents Rolex and also displays pre-Columbian quartz idols. *Fischbach,* Nivel C-1 (959–3704), is a jeweler long known for good design and setting. *Retzignac,* also Nivel C-1, is representative for Baume & Mercier, Piaget. *H. Stern* sells fine gems at outlets in the Tamanaco (927313) and Hilton (571–0520).

Jewelry wholesalers hang together in a downtown building, Edificio La Francia, whose 9 stories off Plaza Bolívar hold some 80 gold workshops and gem traders; profit margins are low so buys are attractive.

Since alluvial gold is found in Venezuela, nuggets or *cochanos* are made into pendants, rings, and bracelets. Wholesale merchants do a brisk business selling watches, silver, and gold (you pay by weight) downtown at the Edificio La Francia on the southwest corner of Plaza Bolívar. There is a wide selection and good prices.

Devil masks are much sought after for colorful souvenirs. Used in ritual dances marking Corpus Christi (usually in early June), they are made of brightly painted papier maché. A good place to find these and other uniquely Venezuelan things is *El Taller de La Esquina,* Nivel Galería, Paseo Las Mercedes (926308), which carries an astonishing variety of crafts: Guahibo pottery, carved wooden birds from Trujillo State, and miniature ceramic villages from the Andes. If you haven't been to the old village of El Hatillo on the southern outskirts of Caracas (via La Trinidad), the trip is worthwhile just to buy crafts at *Hannsi's,* Calle Bolívar (963–7184).

Artesanía Amazonas, Calle Paris at the corner of New York, a few blocks from Paseo Las Mercedes, is a small shop with baskets, carved jaguar benches, necklaces of peccary teeth, and masks, all flown in from southern Venezuela.

In rainbow-colored wools, **Guajiro tapestries** are sold in many souvenir shops. The gay designs of birds and flowers are made up as cushions and wall hangings, each one unique. *Pablo's* display on Av. Rio de Janeiro a block before Cada, Las Mercedes, has good prices on these as well as many kinds of *chinchorros* or hammocks. Those made of hand spun wild cotton or *moriche* palm fiber, again the secret of Indian artisans, cost more than factory-woven hammocks but last a lifetime.

Undoubtedly the master **hammock and basket** weavers are the Warao Indians of the Orinoco Delta. The *Yakera Gallery,* on Av. Andrés Bello between Tr. 1 and 2 in Los Palos Grandes, is the main outlet for Warao art, including the charming **animals and birds** carved from ultra-light sangrito wood. While in Los Palos Grandes, visit *Plaza Souvenirs* and *Artesanía Plaza* in the Villa Mediterranea sector of Centro Plaza shopping center.

NIGHTLIFE. Caracas nightlife is loud, brassy, flashy, and vigorous. Things usually warm up after 10:30 and continue until 4 A.M. Remember that night clubs in Caracas require jackets (not all require ties). The Hilton's **Cota 880** restaurant-nightclub offers two bands and a superb view of the city. Other evening spots are meccas for dancers who love rhythm and flashing lights. Most frequented are: **Poems** and **Memory**—large, plush dance clubs on Av. Venezuela, El Rosal; **Magic Club** in Las Mercedes; **Feelings** on Av. Tamanaco, El Rosal, which is known for its authentic Latin atmosphere, product of the best "salsa" music; and **Gypsy** under the Paseo Las Mercedes shopping center, a suave club where guests of the nearby Tamanaco often drop in. Hotel guests may also visit the select club **1900. My Way,** an emporium of dance, music, games, TV rooms, and restaurant in the CCCT, mezzanine, Chuao. Also in the CCCT, Nivel C, is **Winners** nightclub.

Two popular night spots in Altamira are: **The Place** on Tr. 3 opposite Galería Felix, an intimate restaurant-bar with band; and **La Guacharaca,** in Torre Central, Av. Luis Roche, a club with entertainers (reservations 261–5701). Live shows are what makes evenings click at the **Fango Cafe-Concert,** Av. Trinidad at Madrid, Las Mercedes (921509); and **Madison Pub,** Av. Principal, Bello Campo (332931).

La Cebolla, Ave. Venezuela, El Rosal (951–3381), with its live music, wooden tables, tasty bar snacks called *tapas,* and hearty Catalán food, is one of the largest Spanish 'tascas,' where a good time includes dancing until 3 A.M. Also, **La Taguara de Lorenzo,** Av. Tamanaco, El Rosal (951–1711), where roast kid may precede live music and dancing.

Jazz followers go to **La Menta,** a basement bar in Torre Phelps, Plaza Venezuela, to **Scape's,** a new spot in Torre Polar, Plaza Venezuela (574–3694), and to **Juan Sebastian,** a restaurant-cum-club on Av. Venezuela, El Rosal (951–5575), where the resident jazz quintet plays until 3 A.M.

Sidewalk Cafes, on Sabana Grande's traffic-free boulevard, not only provide some of the best coffee in the world, but also animated conversation far into the night, with accompaniment by strolling musicians, children, and peddlers. Best known is the *Gran Café* at the corner of Calle Acueducto (719502).

EXCURSIONS FROM CARACAS

La Guaira

Ten minutes from Caracas's international airport at Maiquetía is the busy port of La Guaira, a colonial delight steeped in history. Plaza Vargas, with its statue of José María Vargas, a *Guaireño* who was Venezuela's third president, is a good place from which to begin explorations. Plaza Vargas is bounded by Calle Bolívar running between the shore road and the mountain. Lined by the cool and cavernous warehouses of another century's trade and by one- and two-story houses with their colonial windows and red-tiled roofs, the street funnels the sea breezes like voices from a more gracious age.

One of the most important old buildings is the Casa Guipuzcoana, on the main shore road. Built in 1734, it was the largest civic structure of the colony, housing first the Basque company which held a trading monopoly for 50 years, then the Customs. Restored as a cultural center, it is now the Vargas District Town Hall.

The Boulton Museum (031–25921), a tall house with an ample wooden balcony, stands behind the Casa Guipuzcoana. Inside is a treasury of maps, paintings, pistols, documents, and miscellanea collected by the family of John Boulton, which has occupied the house for over 140 years. The young Englishman who came to Venezuela in 1826 at age 20 soon became a leading exporter of coffee, cacao, tobacco, and indigo, bringing in return flour, oil, brandy, and china. Open Tuesday through Friday 9:30 A.M. to 1 P.M. and 3 to 6 P.M.; Saturday and Sunday, 9 A.M. to 1 P.M.

Macuto

Macuto has been the seaside town favored by presidents since Guzmán Blanco had a railway built from Caracas in the 1880s (not even the track remains today). The presidential residence, La Guzmania, is on Plaza Andres Mata, named for the writer who brought the doves here. Closed to traffic, the Paseo Macuto is a tree-shaded walk where beach-goers enjoy their ease and eating (lovely on weekdays).

The Reverón Museum (Tuesday through Saturday 8 A.M. to noon and 2 to 5 P.M.; Sunday, 10 A.M. to 3 P.M.), beside the Quince Letras Hotel, preserves the seaside refuge of Macuto's wild genius Armando Reverón (1889–1954) whose light-filled paintings hang in the National Gallery. He made not only stuffed dolls for use as models, but also benches, spoons, and painting tools.

Beaches

Breakwaters, changing rooms, and lifeguards are essentials at the half-dozen public beaches (open 8 A.M. to 5 P.M. daily) strung along an otherwise rocky coast from Macuto east to Los Caracas. The nicest and least crowded *balnearios* are also the farthest away. From west to east: Macuto, Camurí Chico, Macuto Sheraton, Naiguatá, and Los Angeles. Swimming is prohibited on all "wild" beaches because of dangerous currents. The coast road, however, with its spectacular succession of mountains and breakers, is a superb drive, again on weekdays only (order a *pargo,* red snapper, at any of the seaside restaurants). Between Los Caracas, a workers' vacation resort, and Higuerote are 50 miles of undeveloped coast with no facilities. Parts of the road are unpaved, making it passable only by four-wheel drive vehicles, and there are some streams still without bridges, but lovely panoramas alternate with good beaches in Todasana, La Sabana, and Chuspa.

Miranda State

Miranda State, curving around the Federal District, covers a large part of metropolitan Caracas. Definitely worth a visit for its charming houses, plaza, church, and craft shops is El Hatillo, once a separate village (like Petare, which has also been restored).

Los Teques, state capital about 15 miles west of Caracas on the Pan American Highway, is now a bedroom city, along with San Antonio de Los Altos. The mountains around Los Teques were once the territory of the Teques Indians, whose heroic chief Guaicaipuro, killed by Spaniards in 1568, is portrayed in a bronze statue on Plaza Guaicaipuro. If you want to visit the hilly hideout of IVIC, the national scientific research station at Km 21, before Los Teques, and see its archaeology collection and artworks by Soto, Marisol, and Otero, call 746554.

Colonia Tovar

Forty miles west of Caracas over the mountains is a "Black Forest" village. For 100 years after the colony's founding in 1843, the Bavarian immigrants were isolated on their farms here. Today the route is a pleasant excursion (1½ hours by car) on weekdays, but jammed on Sundays. At 5,860 feet, Colonia Tovar is a cool mountain resort, very popular for its hearty German food, sausages, flowers, vegetable gardens, and homemade jams. Daily por puestos to Colonia Tovar leave Caracas from the terminal at Plaza Catia and also on Av. Lecuna opposite the Nuevo Circo.

San Mateo

A 20-mile paved road winds from Colonia Tovar down to join the Caracas-Valencia highway at La Victoria. A few miles west in the fertile Aragua valley is San Mateo, the centuries-old hacienda of the Bolívar family, where Simón grew up and read with his freethinking tutor. To this sugar plantation he brought his young Spanish bride (Bolívar, 18, never remarried after she died of yellow fever within six months of their wedding). Now restored as the San Mateo Historical Museum and Bolívar Ingenio or sugar mill (Tuesday through Sunday, 8 A.M. to noon and 2 to 5 P.M.), the hacienda is also famous as the site where a young patriot, Antonio Ricaurte, blew up the armory, the enemy, and himself in 1814.

Guatopo

Guatopo, 40 miles south of Caracas on the Santa Teresa-Altagracia road, is Miranda State's National Park. Heavily forested, Guatopo's slopes rise to nearly 5,000 feet, giving birth to many streams feeding Guanapito and Lagartijo reservoirs. At Agua Blanca, an old sugar mill, there are shelters, picnic grates, and bathing pools. For bird watchers, botanists, and bug hunters, this is a favorite sanctuary. Information about hikes and camping can be obtained at La Macanilla ranger station, located 25 miles south of Santa Teresa on the highway that crosses the park. The park guards will issue permits and direct you to nature trails.

MARGARITA AND LOS ROQUES ARCHIPELAGO

Now a major target for international sun-seekers, Margarita Island (373 square miles) has long been a favorite resort of Venezuelans for its lovely beaches, picturesque towns, colonial churches, and forts. Together with the smaller, undeveloped islands of Cubagua and Coche, it forms the state of Nueva Esparta (population 200,000). Another 70 islands, mostly uninhabited, are grouped administratively as Federal Dependencies. The islands closest to Margarita are Los Frailes, Los Testigos, La Blanquilla,

Los Hermanos, and La Tortuga. Venezuela even owns a tiny island 300 miles north of Margarita, Isla de Aves, opposite Dominica. Anyone lucky enough to explore the archipelagoes of Los Roques or Las Aves will dream for months of turquoise waters, dazzling beaches, coral reefs. . . .

Margarita (a name which means "pearl" in Greek) was a prized Spanish possession. The year after Columbus landed on the mainland in 1498 and reported Indians wearing pearls, an expedition to Cubagua plundered 80 pounds of pearls. In the "pearl stampede" unleashed by these fortune seekers from Santo Domingo, Spaniards founded Nueva Cadiz, the first settlement in South America in 1500 on Cubagua. But like the Indians, who were brutally enslaved as pearl divers, Nueva Cadiz was short-lived. Its foundations can still be seen but otherwise the island is barren and Nueva Esparta's pearl beds largely destroyed.

Spanish forts built to protect Margarita from pirates, and colonial churches dating back to 1570, compete for the visitor's time with free port shopping in Porlamar, beaches, water sports, island hopping, and now dog racing at the Magic Isle amusement center near Pampatar.

Exploring Margarita

Old Porlamar, founded in 1536, has been swamped by the boom in shops and commercial hotels since the area became a free port. In the current recession, however, imports have dwindled and the selection is rather poor. Most shops are concentrated between Calle Igualdad and Calle Zamora, higher priced goods on Av. 4 de Mayo and Av. Santiago Mariño. A shopping mall, Boulevard Guevara, links Plaza Bolívar and the market, in itself a lively center for fresh foods and dry goods. Many taxi and por puesto lines start west of the market; also from Plaza Bolívar. Four blocks east of shady Plaza Bolívar is the Francisco Narvaez Contemporary Art Museum, named after the sculptor whose works are found on the shopping mall and in the Bella Vista Hotel grounds.

You should start exploring Margarita from Pampatar. On the way, stop at the sixteenth-century church in Los Robles, home of the golden Virgin of El Pilar. Pampatar bay is dominated by the fort of San Carlos de Borromeo built of coral rock in 1664–84. Opposite it is the colonial church of Santísimo Cristo, with a curious bell tower. The seascapes and views of the coast are splendid from El Vigía Morro past Pampatar.

Near Pampatar a giant amusement park, the Magic Isle, has been built by the national racing institute. A novelty attraction is evening greyhound racing, held Thurs.-Sun. at 8 P.M. Only canodrome in Venezuela, the dog track with its 400 greyhounds and air-conditioned kennels, is managed by a U.S. company. Big daytime draws are a huge Ferris wheel and a giant roller coaster. Cockfights are held at the Gallera Monumental.

Just outside Porlamar is El Valle,, site of a great annual pilgrimage on the feast day (Sept. 8) of the Virgin of the Valley. El Valle was Margarita's first capital, founded in 1529. Today it is a sales center for souvenirs and crafts, from hammocks to dolls. From here, take the sierra road 7 miles to La Asunción, capital of Nueva Esparta State. The mountain route climbs into El Copey National Park, giving spectacular views of island, sea, and even the mainland, before dropping down to Castillo Santa Rosa, which dominates La Asunción. The seventeenth-century fort had dungeons and tunnels to the San Francisco Convent, now the Government House, and to the sixteenth-century Cathedral. Even older than Asunción (1565), nearby Santa Ana dates back to 1530. A charming, shady town, it is noted for a very handsome church. Many of its trees are the blue-flowering *guayacán* or lignum vitae, one of the hardest woods known.

If you rent a car, you can circle Margarita, making side trips to beaches such as Guacuco's, Cardón, and El Tirano. Playa El Agua, near the island's northern tip, is famous for its fine sands, gentle surf, and coconut palms. Head north to Manzanillo, a fishing village and beach, then follow the highway down the southwest coast to wild Guayacán and Puerto Viejo before reaching the picturesque bay of Juangriego.

Oysters abound among the mangroves of La Restinga Lagoon, a national park in the narrow waist which joins Margarita's populous east to the western mountains of Macanao Peninsula. Boatmen take bathers miles through mangrove canals to the Restinga barrier reef on La Guardia Bay. Dry and hot, Macanao Peninsula has scattered fishing villages, mostly without tourist facilities. However, a paved road around the peninsula makes an interesting drive.

PRACTICAL INFORMATION FOR MARGARITA ISLAND

GETTING TO MARGARITA. By air. Margarita has an international airport 18 miles southwest of Porlamar. *Viasa* flies direct from New York; foreign charters come from the U.S. and Canada; *Aeropostal* stops on its Trinidad run. Internal flights, as many as 12 daily by *Avensa* and Aeropostal, link Margarita with Maiquetía, Cumaná, Carúpano, Güiria, Tucupita, Ciudad Guayana, Maracaibo, Acarigua, Valencia, and Barcelona. Airport taxis to Porlamar ($10) may be scarce, but rental agencies abound.

By bus. Express coaches leave Caracas—some driving through the night to catch the early ferry from Puerto La Cruz to arrive by mid-morning at the Porlamar bus terminal in Centro Comercial Bella Vista. *Expresos Camargui* (02–541–0364), recommends purchasing tickets 2 days in advance. Also *Union Conductores Margarita* (02–545–0124). Fare of $10 includes ferry. Total trip time is 13 hours.

Ferries. Three lines serve Margarita from Puerto La Cruz and Cumaná; all are crowded on long weekends and holidays. *Conferry* makes 6 crossings daily from Puerto La Cruz and 2 from Cumaná with passengers and up to 150 cars per ferry. Reservations should be pre-paid for both ways; return fare for car is about $20, for passengers about $8. In Margarita the Conferry office is opposite Bella Vista Hotel (095–616780). In Caracas, Torre Banhoriente, Av. Acacias at Casanova (02–781–6688 and 782–8544); Puerto La Cruz, Los Cocos terminal (081–660468); Cumaná (093–661903). Three *Gran Cacique* vessels speed to Margarita from Puerto La Cruz (081–692301) in a little over 2 hours, at 7 A.M. and 1 P.M., carrying up to 350 passengers but no cars. *Naviarca* (Naviera Rassi C.A.) crosses in 4 hours from Cumaná (093–26230), stopping at Araya Peninsula. The two-deck ferries carry 60 cars. No credit cards and no reservations, but you can buy your ticket a day ahead.

GETTING AROUND. Cheap buses and por puestos go from Porlamar to all towns in the northeastern half of the island where the popular beaches and most hotels are located. To explore the west, Macanao Peninsula, and La Restinga Lagoon, a car is best. Rentals at airport, from 6:30 A.M.: *Avis* (095–691023); *Miami* (095–691183); *Hertz* (095–691074); *Miky Movil* (095–691128); *National Car* (095–691171); *Budget* (095–691047); *Rojas Rental* (095–691142).

HOTELS IN MARGARITA. For definitions of price categories, see "Facts at Your Fingertips." **PORLAMAR. Bella Vista.** *Expensive.* Av. Santiago Mariño on the beach (095–617222 and 02–782–8433 in Caracas). 320 carpeted rooms, piano bar, disco, 2 pools, shops, waterskiing. **Concorde.** *Moderate.* Bahia El Morro (095–613333). 24 stories, 500 carpeted rooms, disco, restaurant, tennis, pool, and beach; reservations in Caracas (02–751–9211/9855).

Margarita International Resort. *Moderate.* Av. Bolívar, (095–611667, telex 95536). New tower with pool, playground, tennis, 110 apartments; $55 for 2 bedroom flat.

Torre Margarita Venantur. *Deluxe.* Av. Mariño at Av. 4 Mayo (095–619633, 02–979–3246; telex 28707). 104 new suites for 2–4 people, pool, restaurant, transport to beaches. **Aguila Inn.** *Moderate.* Calle Narvaez near Bella Vista bus terminal (095–665845, telex 81267). 90 modern rooms near shopping. **For You.** *Moderate.*

Av. Santiago Mariño (095–612911). 300 yards from beach, modern, 90 rooms, fridge, room service, bar, restaurant, shops; excursions arranged; reservations in Caracas (02–321074). **Boulevard.** *Moderate.* Calle Marcano near Plaza Bolívar (095–610522). New, 44 rooms, pool. **El Farallón Suites.** *Moderate.* Calle Malavé/Av. Marcano (095–616722). 42 modern suites with fridge, restaurant; guests use Bella Vista beach and pool. **Le Parc.** *Inexpensive-Moderate.* Calle Guillarte (095–612653). Clean, 77-room motel on outskirts, pool, playground, veranda restaurant. **Los Pinos.** *Moderate.* Calle Los Pinos/Av. San Francisco (095–612211). 92 rooms, restaurant. **Maria Luisa.** *Moderate.* Blvd. Raul Leoni (095–610564). 42 new rooms, restaurant, near beach, pleasant. **Caribbean.** *Moderate.* El Morro Bay (095–610731). 60 rooms across from beach, pool, restaurant, disco. **Evang.** *Inexpensive.* Calle Fraternidad (095–616868). 29 comfortable rooms, fridge, downtown.

PAMPATAR. Puerto Esmeralda. *Moderate.* Playa del Angel (095–78536; for reservations in Caracas, 02–7817986-Incret). 108 suites, pool, restaurant. **Chalets de Caranta.** *Moderate.* Bahía de Pampatar (095–78963). 12 modern 2-story units sleeping six, kitchen, terrace, on the beach; good outdoor seafood restaurant El Caney de Caranta. **Aparthotel Pampatar.** *Inexpensive.* Calle Cristo (095–78144). 25 basic housekeeping units across street from beach; reservations in Caracas (02–461–5772).

PUNTA CARDON. Playa Cardón. *Moderate.* Bahía del Tirano (095–48242). 2-story wooden hotel built on bluff, 45 rooms with balcony facing sea breeze; short walk to beach; good seafood restaurant; reservations in Caracas (02–333771/3).

PLAYA EL AGUA. Hostería El Agua. *Inexpensive.* Via Manzanillo (095–610680). 15 comfy rooms in a low building, 100 yards from the beach. **Shangrila.** *Inexpensive.* Via Manzanillo (095–48413). 8 cabin-style rooms, 5 minutes from the beach.

JUANGRIEGO. Residencias Juan el Griego. *Moderate.* Av. Jesús Rafael Leandro (095–55933, reservations only in Caracas 02–716077, telex 27060 VIVSA). Centrally air-conditioned, 12-story block near beach, fully furnished apartments for 4, kitchen, pool, disco, tennis court, pizzería. **Residencias Clary's.** *Inexpensive.* Calle Mártires (095–55037). 6 pleasant rooms over manager's quarters and 7 units in rear; small restaurant with good seafood opposite.

LA GALERA BAY. Motel La Galera. *Inexpensive* (095–55151). 6 clean cabins. **Posada del Sol.** *Inexpensive* (095–55354). 12 cabins with 2 bedrooms each, stove, refrigerator. **Chalets Flamingo.** *Moderate.* Vía Playa Caribe (095–55341). 32 rooms and suites, pool. Not on beach.

RESTAURANTS. For definitions of price categories see "Facts at Your Fingertips." In Margarita, where Porlamar's hotels provide the best international menus and disco dancing, many small, *inexpensive* restaurants serve good fresh fish and local dishes. Some of the better ones are **El Chipi** on Calle Cedeño, **La Casa de Rubén**, **L'Ete** (French), **La Loba** (Italian), **La Pimienta** (Spanish), **La Talanquera** (steak), and **Martín Pescador** (seafood)—all on Av.4 de Mayo.

Nightclubs in Porlamar are headed by the Hotel Concorde's **Stella Maris.** Other spots with live music are: **Casa Blanca**, Calle Jesus María Patiño; and **Fandango Tasca**, Av.4 de Mayo. **Pimenton, Soho Pub,** and **Wladimir's** offer food and shows.

COCHE AND CUBAGUA

Coche and Cubagua, south of Margarita, are reached from Punta de Piedras. A ferry goes about 9 miles to San Pedro, Coche's only town. Fresh water is piped to Coche and Margarita from the mainland. The island which produces fish and salt is hilly and suffered less from the earthquake and tidal wave which wiped out Cubagua in 1541. Excavations on Cubagua revealed Spanish pillars, foundations of Nueva Cadiz, and large, buried pots filled with pearls. Cubagua, 5 miles long, is smaller than Coche and has no water. In early 1991, negotiations were underway to lease the island of Cubagua to an international resort company that proposed to build a tourist complex there.

LOS FRAILES

Los Frailes Archipelago, off Margarita's northeast coast, is a group of 8 islands bare of life except for birds. Snorklers and bird watchers go over for the day by fishing boat from Puerto Fermín.

LA BLANQUILLA AND LOS HERMANOS ISLANDS

Some 70 miles north northwest of Margarita, these islands lie in crystal clear waters. Their white coral beaches, coves, and reefs of unspoiled beauty are compared by those who know to the Virgin Islands of 30 years ago. La Blanquilla, inhabited by one or two fishermen, has a landing strip. Morgan Tours and Alpi Tour in Caracas fly visitors in for the day, about 1½ hours from Caracas by twin engine craft. No shelter for overnighting. Motorsailers make the crossing overnight from Puerto La Cruz. Inquire with **Yachts, Marina Americo Vespucio,** El Morro Tourist Complex (081–813393); the cost of a 4-day sail to La Blanquilla is $100 a day per passenger (min. 6). **Intervac** (031–945555, ext. 385 Melia Hotel) runs exploring and fishing trips from Caraballeda on the central coast to Blanquilla. Trips start at three days, and cost from $500 for four people.

LA TORTUGA

About 125 miles northeast of La Guaira, La Tortuga is only one hour's flight from Caracas by small plane. Pilot Linda Sonderman of Alpi Tour describes La Tortuga in one word: "magnificent." The price tag for a day on La Tortuga, by air charter from Caracas, is about $200, all-inclusive, per person (group of five).

LOS ROQUES ARCHIPELAGO

Los Roques Archipelago, 90 miles north of La Guaira, curves in a great necklace of coral islands around a central lagoon in what is Venezuela's largest group of islands—40 with names, 300 coral keys and outcrops unnamed and uninhabited. Los Roques was made a National Park in 1972. Gran Roque, the biggest island, has a pueblo and airstrip. Fishermen depend on their small craft known as *peñeros.* Well-heeled visitors arrive on their planes or yachts. The archipelago's wealth of birds, fish, lobster, and turtles has been famous for centuries. Although the lobsters have been overexploited, like the green turtle, they are still available in season, Oct. to Mar. Before the arrival of Europeans, Indians came from the mainland in dugouts to harvest the turtles and their eggs at mating season, the booby chicks at breeding time, and maybe even the fat black lizards which are found only here. These early inhabitants left behind huge mounds of queen conch shells (the *botutos* are still a favored food of *Roqueños*), pottery vessels, and clay deities. Archaeological excavations on Dos Mosquises in 1982–1986 uncovered vessels, pots, shell tools, adornments (and a skeleton) of these early navigators. There is a marine biology station on Dos Mosquises run by the Fundación Científica Los Roques (02–326771).

PRACTICAL INFORMATION FOR LOS ROQUES ARCHIPELAGO

GETTING TO LOS ROQUES. Today, through most of the leading tour agencies (see *Treks and Adventure Tours* in "Facts at Your Fingertips"), a visitor with $100 can get to once-inaccessible keys (and back, reluctantly) on 6-, 8-, or 12-seater private planes. Regular flights are now operated by Aereotuy (02–716231, fax 725254) on turbo-props departing Maiquetía Tues. through Sun. at 8 A.M. and returning at 6 P.M. Besides day-long swimming and snorkeling excursions, the airline can also arrange stays on Gran Roque for $80 per day which includes food, lodging, boat rides, and bonefishing. *CAVE*, a charter line, operates flights to Los Roques for a day of sunning or boating; Thurs. to Sun., $85. Call Diadema tours (02–724856/8, fax 724556).

Good news for those wishing to stay longer: houseboats and even houses are rented. Consult Linda Sonderman at *Alpi* (02–284–1344/6677) or Miguel Arjona (02–941–8498, telex 02–29287), who can arrange packages for 4 to 5 people.

THE CARIBBEAN COAST

Along the ribbon of Venezuela's 1,730-mile seacoast, broad sandy stretches alternate with rocky shores where mountains plunge steeply into the Caribbean, sheltering hideaway bays. Many of these are popular bathing spots; some lack roads even today and so have no visitors. A few, such as Tucacas, Cata, Choroní, Higuerote, and Lecherías, combine picture-postcard beaches with hotels and good roads. These are very crowded in the high season, from the year-end holidays to Carnival and Easter, when city people take advantage of the dry season and fresh winds to camp out on the beaches. (Belongings and tents are never left unattended to avoid theft.) Below, some of the main points of interest along the coast are reviewed, traveling from from west to east.

ZULIA STATE

Maracaibo, capital of Zulia State, is one of the few cities where Indians retaining their culture may be seen. Stoutly independent, western Zulia was long isolated before the Rafael Urdaneta bridge was built in 1962, spanning the five-mile neck of Lake Maracaibo. The waters of the lake, largest in South America (5,400 square miles), grow saltier each year because of dredging done to allow passage of large oil tankers. A forest of oil derricks on the lake is only a small part of Zulia's network producing 60 percent of Venezuela's oil and gas. Now, since vast forests and wetlands south of the lake have been converted into farms and dairy pastures, Zulia also leads in milk production. Unfortunately, pesticides, sewage, and oil have contaminated the lake and it is not fit for bathing.

Venezuela's largest city after Caracas, sprawling Maracaibo has over a million inhabitants, who are called *Maracuchos*. The city's distinctive personality comes from a mingling of oil executives, ranchers, and on-the-go merchants, with Italian and Colombian immigrants (many of the latter illegal), fishermen, and nomad Guajiros. Despite the heat (median 86°F.), Maracuchos are active and aggressive in business, preferring to make money instead of talking about politics. A thriving cultural life supports a Fine Arts Center, art shows, and music festivals. A week-long *Feria* in mid-November honors La Chinita, a tiny painted picture of the Virgin of Chiquinquirá which appeared miraculously in 1749 on a bit of driftwood salvaged by a woman who lived at a spot today called El Milagro, by the lake.

Guajira Peninsula

The longest and widest beaches are in the west on the desolate Guajira Peninsula which borders the Gulf of Venezuela. Near the Paraguaipoa road, hard flat sands and shallow waters are playgrounds for the Guajiro Indians who live in both Venezuela and Colombia. Men ride bicycles through the water's edge and children splash with abandon while women in long flowing *mantas* walk calmly into the waves. The Guajiros not only herd cattle, goats, and sheep in the arid scrubland, but also engage in a certain amount of the smuggling which has long supported border trade with Maicao in Colombia. Today this is a truly dangerous occupation since the growth of cocaine traffic. The "wild west" frontier is not recommended for tourists.

The Guajiro market at Los Filúos, just outside Paraguaipoa, is a fascinating, teeming event held every Monday, well worth the sixty-mile drive from Maracaibo. Hundreds of Indians converge at dawn, arriving by burro and by battered trucks over the rough peninsula trails, to buy meat, plantains, and dry goods and to barter horses and goats. By noon, all trading finished, the stalls are empty. It is possible to buy here some of the brightly woven belts and saddlebags which are the pride of Guajiro men, or straw hats, calabash bowls, hammocks, and other artifacts. The floor-length mantas worn by the women are often made of polyester nowadays instead of cotton. The men, who wear little more than a shirt and loincloth, are excellent weavers and cattlemen. Guajiro society, organized in family clans, is matriarchal; a man may pay many cows to marry the bride of his choice. In the Chichamaya dance, it is the woman who pursues the man and the woman who wears the clan sign painted on her arm.

Quite famous now is Guajiro tapestry artist Luis Montiel, whose biggest piece, considered the most important craftwork in Latin America, is the sixty-six-foot by twenty-two-and-a-half-foot theater curtain for Maracaibo's Centro de Bellas Artes. His workshop, Taller Mali Mai, may be visited from 5 A.M. to 5 P.M.; to find it, take a left turn for Yaguasirú some four miles along the Los Filúos-Maicao road.

Sinamaica Lagoon, midway between Maracaibo and Paraguaipoa, has a large community of houses built on stilts. These "palafitos" have scarcely changed in the 500 years since they inspired Spanish geographer Ojeda to baptize the coast "Little Venice" or Venezuela. The lake-dwellers here are Paraujano Indians and mestizos who use reeds to make roofs, room-dividers, and sleeping mats. Boat tours of Sinamaica to El Barro village, where there is a tourist restaurant, leave from Puerto Mara on Río Limón and from Puerto Cuervito (see the Wednesday morning floating market), south of Sinamaica village.

Maracaibo

The Basilica of Chiquinquirá rises west of the eight-block-long Paseo de Ciencias park filled with sculptures. At the east end is Plaza Bolívar, flanked by the modern Municipal Council, the eighteenth-century Casa Morales where Spain's last general in Venezuela surrendered in 1823 (now seat of the Academy of History, open Mon.–Fri. 8 to 11:45 A.M. and 2:30 to 5:45 P.M.), and the Government House or Palacio de las Aguilas, named for its rooftop eagles. A remnant of old Maracaibo with its narrow streets and low houses in a rainbow of colors survives around Santa Lucia Church. Close by are the Guajiro crafts stalls on Calle 96 at Av. El Milagro and Turismo del Trópico souvenirs, Av. El Milagro at Calle 93. The old Central Market on Plaza Baralt has been restored as a cultural center while a larger Mercado de las Pulgas (flea market) now spreads several blocks south of Calle 100. From the docks by the market, a ferry service of *flechas* or launches leaves hourly for the eastern shore of Lake Maracaibo (from 5:30 A.M. to 6 P.M.), crossing in fifteen minutes.

The Centro de Bellas Artes is on Calle 68A in Bella Vista, not far from the Hotel del Lago. It offers something for everyone: a painter's flea market the first Sunday of each month, concerts on Thursdays at 8:30 P.M., plays in English by the Maracaibo Players. The theater curtain donated by the Players is the famous twenty-two-color Guajiro tapestry made by Luis Montiel. More Guajiro weaving, rugs, cushions, as well as fine hammocks and baskets, are sold at the Center's Taller Mali Mai showroom (Mon.–Fri. 9 A.M. to noon and 2 to 6 P.M.; Sat. 9 A.M. to noon).

San Carlos Fortress

San Carlos Fortress, on an island at the entrance to Lake Maracaibo, saw action against foreign ships as recently as 1903, but for most of its 300 years the fort held Venezuelan prisoners. Cells within its double walls were last used in the 1930s by dictator Gómez. The twenty-five-minute trip by ten-passenger launch from El Moján, north of Maracaibo, makes a good excursion. There are no facilities but plenty of sun and sandy beaches and a village on stilts rising over the dry sands on the point.

Machiques and Tukuko Mission

Machiques and Tukuko Mission, west of Lake Maracaibo, formed a double spearhead in the very recent opening of virgin lands fiercely defended by the Motilon and Yucpa tribes until the mid-1950s. Machiques, seventy-seven miles south of Maracaibo, is today a dairy center where a million quarts of milk are processed daily into cheese, butter, and dried milk. Deep in former Yucpa territory, which is now lush, though largely cleared, cattle country, the Capuchin base of Tukuko is reached by a little-traveled road branching from Machiques thirty miles to the southwest. While ranchers fought the Indians with guns, planes, and fire, the priests pacified them with airdrops of food and presents. In the land struggle, however, many of the Indians retreated farther into the Perijá mountains or died. The mission boarding school receives 300 children. Besides a crafts display, there is a shop stocked with baskets, arrows.

From Machiques south to La Fría (150 miles), the route—crossing lands stripped of forest—is hot, empty, and with few services.

No one has been able to explain the cause of almost permanent lightning over the mouth of the Catatumbo River; the noiseless flashes are seen from as far away as Maracaibo and San Antonio.

PRACTICAL INFORMATION FOR ZULIA

HOTELS. For definitions of price categories see "Facts at Your Fingertips." **MARACAIBO.** Most of Maracaibo's hotels offer efficient, highrise lodgings for businessmen, mainly in the center. **Del Lago.** *Deluxe.* Av. El Milagro (061–912022, fax 061–914551). On the lake shore, 364 well-appointed rooms in the hotel and new tower annex, pool, gym, sauna, jogging path, restaurants, bar, convention-banquet facilities; shops, car rental, travel agency; an Inter-Continental Hotel. Reservations in Caracas (02–208–7243). **El Paseo.** *Deluxe.* Av. El Milagro at Av. 2 (061–919744). New 12-story tower with 54 suites each with 3 double beds and divan; small pool, cafeteria, tower-top Girasol Restaurant. **Kristoff.** *Expensive.* No. 68–48 Av. 8 (061–72911). 327 rooms and cabins with pool, piano bar, restaurants, shops. **Maruma.** *Deluxe.* Av. Circunvalación No. 2 (061–349011). Near industrial zone, 180 rooms, pool, playground, tennis, basketball, shopping center with bank, car rental, convention facilities. **Delicias.** *Moderate.* Av. 15 at Calle 70, Las Delicias (061–76111). 8-story hotel with 108 rooms, pool, restaurant. **Cantaclaro.** *Moderate.* No.125 Calle 86A (061–222944). A Cumberland hotel, 70 rooms, restaurant. **Presidente.** *Moderate.* Av. 11 at Calle 68 (061–83133, fax 061–82485). Apart-hotel with

54 rooms, kitchen, fridge, laundry, restaurant, pool. **El Boulevard.** *Inexpensive.* Calle 75 at Av. 14A (061–78385). 40 rooms, TV, restaurant. **Ejecutivo Ven.** *Inexpensive.* Calle 89 N.15–44 (061–513215). 33 rooms downtown.

MACHIQUES. Motel Tukuko. *Inexpensive.* Calle Santa Teresa (063–71343). 20 rooms, soda fountain, bar, restaurant.

CABIMAS. Cabimas Internacional. *Deluxe.* Av. Andrés Bello, sector Ambrosio (064–45692, fax 064–44302). On east shore of lake with great view, a businessman's haven, 127 rooms and suites, La Terraza restaurant by pool, discotheque, banquet-convention facility for 400, bank, car rental agency; 45 minutes by car from Maracaibo; also, a helicopter service can take you to Maracaibo (8 minutes).

FALCÓN STATE

Colonial Coro

Whitewashed walls sparkle in the sun while in the shady parks of this truly charming colonial town a constant breeze stirs. One of the earliest settlements in South America and first capital of the Province of Venezuela, Coro was founded in 1527 at the base of the Paraguaná Peninsula, and its Arawak name means "wind." East winds continue to form the *médanos* or dunes which cover the narrow isthmus, now a national park. Here it is common to see camels crossing the sands carrying tourists from Los Médanos Hotel.

When the first gold seekers failed to find El Dorado, Coro nearly died; its aqueduct built in Indian times dried up. But fortunes improved in the 1700s when Coro became chief supplier for Bonaire and Curaçao, only sixty-five miles distant. Since trade was reserved for the royal monopoly, all the food, tobacco, hides, and mules which Coro exported were contraband and highly profitable. The goods were shipped from the port of La Vela de Coro, a few miles east. Still standing in the now quiet port is the old customs house, a handsome 2-story building (early 1600s) now occupied by a marine biology school.

Leaving La Vela de Coro at midnight on Mon. and Wed., the 3,000-ton "Almirante Brion" ferry sails for Curaçao and Aruba. Drivers wishing to take cars on the ferry should be at Muaco Dock at 6 P.M. Ferrys del Caribe recommends booking a week in advance; consult their offices (weekdays only) about requirements for vehicle insurance and police clearance—Coro (068–510554), La Vela de Coro (068–78328).

The capital of Falcón State, Coro (population 140,000) today prospers on farming, raising onions and melons with irrigation. But the way is being prepared for tourism. Several eighteenth-century houses have been beautifully restored. Most are near the Plaza de San Clemente with its old chapel and a wooden cross made of Cují so hard it is called ironwood; it is said the cross was used at the first mass held by Ampíes in 1527. Santa Ana, now Coro's Cathedral, was one of the first two churches in Venezuela, along with La Asunción in Margarita, both begun in 1538.

The Casa del Sol, so named for the sun design on its door, at Calle Zamora and Federación (Mon.–Fri. 8 A.M. to noon and 2 to 6 P.M.); opposite, the two-story Arcaya House with its roofed balcony contains a Ceramics Museum exhibiting not only colonial and pre-Columbian pottery but many dinosaur fossils (Tue. 9 A.M. to noon, Wed.–Fri. 4 to 7 P.M., Sat.–Sun. 10 A.M. to 1 P.M.). Farther down Calle Zamora is the House of the Iron Windows, much photographed for its superb baroque doorway (Sat., Sun., and holidays, 7 to 11 A.M. and 2 to 4 P.M.). Next to it is the Casa del Tesoro, whose name means "treasure house" because beneath it runs one of the secret tunnels where colonists once hid valuables from marauding pirates. The spacious cloisters of a former convent, also on Calle Zamora, now house the fine Diocesan Museum of colonial furniture, art, bells, and religious objects of gold and silver (Tues.–Sun. 10 A.M. to 1 P.M. and 3 to 6 P.M.; cost is Bs. 5).

Santa Ana, Moruy, and Pueblo Nuevo

More colonial houses on the peninsula, conserved by the near-desert climate and by generations of occupants, are located some thirty-five miles north of Coro in the villages of Santa Ana (see the fortress-like church), Moruy, and Pueblo Nuevo—where each house is painted a different color.

From the thorny brush of eastern Paraguaná, home to more goats than people, to the modern avenues, supermarkets, and oil refineries on the west coast, the distance is only twenty-five miles, but culturally the gap is more on a scale of light years. In Santa Ana, women still turn goat's milk into cheese and milk fudge, the delicious *dulce de leche coriano;* in Cardón and Amuay, engineers refine crude in huge cracking towers. None of the gardens and palm trees existed before the oilmen came here forty years ago; Punto Fijo now has 70,000 people. In the north, the peninsula is a wilderness of cactus where sandy tracks lead to dazzling salt beds and to Cape San Román, where pelicans feed off fishermen's nets and shell collectors on rocky shores between cliffs find treasures such as the rare music volute. Shelling is also good on the gentle west coast beaches of Villa Marina and El Pico. On the east coast, bathers head for the beaches of Adícora, Supí, and Buchuago, protected from the rough sea breakers by coral reefs. These beaches have few facilities.

Morrocoy: Shore and Marine Park

Beach-goers, following a good road east through Falcón State, come next to the fabulous Morrocoy National Park. Some 155 miles from Caracas, Morrocoy is a favorite destination not only for snorkelers, divers, and water skiers, but for bird watchers as well. Here is a naturalist's delight of four ecosystems: the thirty-odd keys and coral reefs; the mangroves which form impenetrable havens for nesting frigate birds and the rare coastal crocodile; a hilly point with deciduous trees and fauna such as howler monkeys, crab foxes, anteaters, and ocelots; and salt flats nurturing wading birds—scarlet ibis, pink flamingos, crested herons, cormorants, and thousands of ducks. A levee crosses seven miles over the flats to Chichiriviche (five hotels), launching point for the northern keys.

Tucacas, at the park's eastern edge, is an untidy old town. But it boasts a new resort complex, port facilities, and a yacht-ferry. A bridge links Tucacas with camping grounds on Punta Brava island, where there is parking for motor homes. Fishermen with open boats take parties to any one of the keys; passengers pay upon return, prices begin at about $10 and increase according to the distance to the keys. A professional diving instructor, Mike Osborn, has his headquarters at Submatur, Calle Ayacucho No. 6 (042–84082 or 042–84679. In Caracas, 02–782–2946, fax 781–6773). He rents scuba gear, gives NAUI courses, and leads diving parties. A day's snorkeling, including equipment and lunch, costs about $15 a person in groups of 4 to 20. Submatur also makes charter diving trips by sailboat from Tucacas to Las Aves and Los Roques islands. Beach trippers take ice chests, picnics (no fires permitted), and hammocks to the keys. Midges (tiny, biting insects) are bothersome in rainy or windless months, August into December, so windward beaches are the most popular. (Avoid "beaching" on public holidays because of large crowds.)

Continuing along the palm-lined coast to the east are sketchily developed balnearios (beaches open for swimming), where for a small fee bathers can use basic facilities and sling hammocks.

PRACTICAL INFORMATION FOR FALCÓN

HOTELS. For definitions of price categories see "Facts at Your Fingertips" earlier in this chapter.

CORO. Caracas. *Inexpensive.* Calle Toledo No. 17 (068–512465). 14 rooms around the central patio of a converted 200-year-old house, in the colonial district. **Miranda.** *Inexpensive.* Av. Josefa Camejo, near airport (061–516732). 86 rooms in spacious grounds, pool, play area, restaurant, bar, car rental.

PARAGUANA PENINSULA. Although the Peninsula has wonderful beaches and unfailing sunshine, there is no tourist development. *In Adícora,* on the east coast, cottages can be rented from their owners; **Ramón Torres** offers 7 basic cabins. On the west coast: **Motel Cardón.** *Inexpensive.* Av. de la Costa by Miramar Club (069–404095). 30 rooms overlooking the busy gulf with its fishing and tanker traffic; La Casona restaurant next door. Like Cardón, *Punto Fijo* is a refinery town: **Villa Real.** *Expensive.* Av. Coro No. 75 (069–450213). 110 rooms and 34 apartments on 5 floors, cafeteria closes at 3 P.M., bar open till 1 A.M. **Presidente.** *Moderate.* Av. Peru (069–453710). 4-story hotel with 51 rooms, restaurant-bar open until 2 A.M., room service.

CHICHIRIVICHE. Although offering visitors to Morrocoy National Park adequate lodgings, Chichiriviche is not attractive in itself. **La Garza.** *Moderate.* On main road (042–86126). Breezy 3-story hotel with 72 rooms, pool, restaurant. **Mario.** *Moderate.* On main road (042–86114). 92 rooms with balcony, restaurant, pool, hairdresser, disco, 40 lockers for snorkeler's gear. Two-meals-a-day plan also available. Reservations in Caracas (02–682–9197). **Parador Manaure.** *Inexpensive.* Calle La Marina 1 (042–86121). 24 rooms, with or without meals; 18 apartments. **Náutico.** *Inexpensive.* By cement plant (042–86024). Old lodge for divers, 20 rooms, home cooking.

TUCACAS. Good news is the first resort in the area, **Morrocoy Conjunto Náutico Residencial.** *Deluxe.* Tucacas–Coro Highway west (042–84806; Caracas 02–9590322). A time-sharing resort with 600 suites, the first part of an ambitious plan to transform the area. Low buildings with suites for 2 to 7 people surround dreamy pool; salon for 1200, restaurants; live entertainment; marina for 600 yachts; island excursions. Reservations through tour agencies only.

Tucacas. *Expensive.* Av. Morón–Coro (042–84343). 12 modern 3-bedroom apartments. **Gaeta.** *Moderate.* Calle Ayacucho (042–84414). 18 rooms in a 4-story central hotel. **Manaure.** *Moderate.* Av. Silva (042–84611/2). 45 rooms in town.

CARABOBO, LARA, AND ARAGUA STATES

Puerto Cabello

The coast road passes a huge petrochemical complex at Morón, which marks the boundary of Carabobo State, whose many industries are served by Puerto Cabello. The large natural port is often busier than La Guaira. Stroll along the harborside Paseo Malecón, a park with fountains and cannon, and explore the street behind it, named Calle de Los Lanceros for the patriots who won over this Spanish stronghold by way of the mangroves at the rear, carrying only lances and swimming part of the way. The narrow street, closed to traffic, is flanked by balconied colonial houses. The port's colonial San Felipe Fort, built in 1732, is today surrounded by a naval base. The navy runs a launch across the channel to the fort, and visitors may ride over free. The Malecón also gives onto the large new Marina del Caribe with space for 250 yachts.

A road leads from Puerto Cabello around the harbor to the Naval Base, where the guard issues passes to visit San Felipe Fort. Two fine beaches lie three and seven miles east of Puerto Cabello. The long sandy curve of Quizandal, on the way to the Naval Base, is popular on weekends (showers, soda fountain, dance band). But of greater beauty is an island, fifteen minutes away by open boat (less than $2; the ferryman returns to pick up bathers at a set hour). Isla Larga has dazzling beaches, emerald sea, and two underwater wrecks of World War II cargo ships, now coral-encrusted playgrounds for fish and snorkelers. This is a camper's paradise except during the windless months of Dec. and Jan., when "no-see-um" midges bite at night.

At the end of the shore road (the route returns to the coast again in Miranda State) is Patanemo Bay, a wide crescent beach fringed by coconut groves. There are several resort developments planned here but in the meantime bathers and campers are happy with the present spartan facilities.

The Central Axis: Barquisimeto-Valencia-Maracay

To continue east, drivers must go by the Puerto Cabello-Valencia route, which leads by excellent expressways to the industrial parks and agricultural valleys of Lara, Carabobo, and Aragua States. The cities of Barquisimeto, Valencia, and Maracay form the axis of light industry in these central states. After Caracas and Maracaibo, they are the country's largest cities, with populations of 700,000, 1,100,000, and 810,000 respectively.

Venezuela's only public railway takes people and cargo from Puerto Cabello to Barquisimeto, seventy-seven miles, at an average twenty miles an hour. The train leaves Puerto Cabello at 6 A.M. and 4 P.M., stopping at two stations on the coast, El Palito and Morón. Fast-growing capital of Lara State, dubbed the "music capital" for its many singers and folk bands, Barquisimeto has opened a fine cultural center, the Museo de Barquisimeto, in a restored 1918 mansion on Carrera 15. Ten rooms for exhibitions, including an archaeology collection, surround a colonnaded courtyard where an old chapel is the stage for films, music, and folklore events. When in Barquisimeto, relax in the new fifty-acre Bararida Park on Av. Los Abogados, popular for its zoo, gardens, playgrounds, and boating lagoon.

Historic buildings in Valencia are clustered around the colonial center. The Cathedral on Plaza Bolívar was founded in 1580, rebuilt in 1767, and later added to. A block southeast on Calle Páez is the house of José Antonio Páez, first President of Venezuela; the house is open as a museum. On the same Calle Páez, 4 blocks west, is the State Capitol, housed in a former Carmelite convent built in 1772.

Valencia also boasts the Museo de la Cultura, an ambitious glass and concrete structure with four gallery wings around a central core for theater and conference hall. It is built by the Cabriales River in the downtown Parque Metropolitano (open Tuesday through Friday, 9 A.M. to noon and 2 to 5 P.M. Saturday and Sunday, 10 A.M. to 3:30 P.M.). The Ateneo de Valencia, Av. Bolívar (041–53845), with a full program of plays, films, and exhibitions, has long been the city's artistic focus; open daily 9 A.M. to noon and 3 to 6 P.M.

Besides a race track and a monumental bullring, the second largest in the New World after Mexico City's, other points of interest include a tropical Aquarium with a good collection of fresh-water fish and electric eels, anacondas, and river dolphins. The clear water of the dolphin pool allows a close look at these unusual mammals, which inhabit the Orinoco and many turbid rivers of the Llanos. Paseo Cuatricentenario, vía Valencia-Guataparo (041–89222); open Tues. to Sun. 10 A.M. to 5 P.M.

Carabobo Battlefield, twenty miles from Valencia, surrounds an impressive monument to Independence heroes who defeated the royalist troops here. A scale model of the battle and a diorama show what happened here on June 24, 1821. Soldiers dressed in red patriot uniforms guard the Tomb of the Unknown Soldier. The diorama is open Wednesday, Saturday, and Sunday.; the park daily 6 A.M. to 6 P.M. except Monday.

When Valencia was founded in 1553, the year after Barquisimeto, Lake Valencia was twice as big as its present twenty-mile length. Paleontologists, who have unearthed fossils of mastodons, prehistoric sloths, armadillos, early horses, and tapirs, estimate that the lake's level was once fifty-six feet higher. As evidence that the area was later home to a thriving Indian culture stands a hill covered with petroglyphs; the track to this Parque Piedras Pintadas turns west off the Guacara-Vigirima road, crosses the Tronconero River, and, near a tiny schoolhouse, veers north through cornfields towards the hills. Because there are no signs, ask a local inhabitant to guide you.

The shrinking lake, which is today the target of earnest conservation efforts because it has no outlet but many inlets contaminated by industries (swimming is not recommended), is best seen from Punta Palmita on Cabrera Peninsula, a mile or so west of Maracay.

Valencia and Maracay offer beach explorers convenient midway hotels. Since there is no road along the coast between Caracas and Puerto Cabello, drivers take two mountain routes from Maracay to reach either Choroní or the palm-fringed crescent bays of Cata and Cuyagua. These roads cross the Cordillera de La Costa through luxuriant cloud forest. Here, in some 430 square miles, the Henri Pittier National Park protects an astonishing variety of fauna and flora, including over 400 different bird species. Scientists from all over the world come to study the natural history of the high, cool jungle known as Rancho Grande Cloud Forest.

Cata Bay

The crescent beach bordering an idyllic bay sports a private apartment tower, eight new duplex cabins for hire, and a simple restaurant. Fishermen provide boat rides to the eastern point and Catita Bay. Campers may sling hammocks between the palms or pitch a tent on the sands. Three miles back from the sea is old Cata village, once part of a cacao plantation; the cacao pods are harvested up the valley. Lovely Cuyagua beach, eight miles to the east, is still "wild." Surfers like the rough water, but swimmers are wise to stay close to shore.

Choroní

Only thirty miles long, the route from Maracay to charming Choroní village is a series of hairpin bends rising through the gorgeous mountain forest of Pittier Park. Until the road was paved in 1979, Choroní's beauty was well guarded (even today the trip takes nearly an hour-and-a-half) and travelers gave thanks for a tiny German-run hostel. Now, without changing the face of the village, first-class lodgings have been made in two walled houses restored by the Cotoperix Club. Fishermen supply fresh red snapper and kingfish for guests' suppers; farmers bring pawpaw, pineapple, coffee, and chocolate. Since guests come only with advance reservations, the Cotoperix hotel is part of Choroní's secretive tradition. Playa Grande beach is 400 yards east of the port, Puerto Colombia; its sands are golden, its sea is green. The peace here is disturbed just once yearly, when the Carnival crowds descend.

PRACTICAL INFORMATION FOR LARA, CARABOBO, AND ARAGUA

HOTELS. For definitions of price categories, see "Facts at Your Fingertips" earlier in this chapter.

Lara State

BARQUISIMETO. Barquisimeto Hilton. *Deluxe.* Carrera 5 (051–536022). Splendid businessman's refuge in the suburb of Nueva Segovia, large pool, 2 tennis courts, kids' playground, and shops complement 138 rooms, meeting halls, 3 restaurants, and nightclub; secretarial services, car rental.**Hostería Obelisco.** *Moderate.* Av. Libertador at city entrance (051–422233). Comfortable 88-room motel with pool, bar, restaurant; crowded.**Principe.** *Moderate.* Carrera 19 con Calle 23 (051–312244). Popular downtown hotel with 150 rooms in 3 towers, swimming pool, bar, restaurant, soda fountain open until 1 A.M.; car rental. **Gran Hotel Barquisimeto.** *Inexpensive.* Av. Prolongación 20 (051–420511). 53 rooms, swimming pool open to non-guests, restaurant. **Mesón de la Campana.** *Inexpensive.* Near Obelisco (051–423732). Basic lodgings in a 64-unit motel with pool open to non-guests; popular grilled beef restaurant.

Carabobo State

PALMA SOLA. Canaima. *Inexpensive.* On the beach (042–71571). 41 rooms in 35 cabins without air-conditioning, but plenty of breeze, restaurant.
PUERTO CABELLO. Caribe Suites. *Moderate.* Av. Salom (042–615556). 90 modern rooms, air-conditioned, near the airport, restaurant. **Cumboto.** *Inexpensive.* On the beach before the port (042–69211). 74 rooms in run-down 2-story building (repairs are announced); beach not recommended but there is a pool and open-air restaurant.
LAS TRINCHERAS. Las Trincheras Hotel Spa. *Moderate.* Half mile from Valencia-Pto, Cabello tollway (041–669795). 58 new rooms at hot springs famous for curative waters; 3 thermal pools open 7 A.M. to 10 P.M. (Bs.40); massages.
VALENCIA. Intercontinental Valencia. *Deluxe.* Av. Juan Uslar, La Viña (041–211033). Modern high-rise building with 173 rooms and suites; Cabriales restaurant is meeting place for executives; good buffet, pool-side restaurant-bar, banquet facilities, plus bilingual service. **Stauffer Valencia.** *Deluxe.* Av. Bolívar, El Recreo (041–222440, fax 222639). New 200-room tower in shopping center, Swiss Chalet restaurant, bar. **Ucaima Suites.** *Expensive.* Ave. Boyacá next to La Viña shopping center (041–227011). 75 suites, kitchenette with fridge, 1 to 3 bedrooms; pool, tennis court, restaurant. **Don Pelayo.** *Moderate.* Av. Díaz Moreno (041–80679). New commercial tower downtown with 120 rooms and a presidential suite, restaurant, piano bar, and tasca bar. **Hotel 400.** *Inexpensive.* Av. Bolívar 113 (041–210533). 38 rooms in a converted residence. **Le Paris.** *Inexpensive.* Av. Bolívar 125 (041–227122). Old-style family hotel with shady garden, 120 rooms on 3 floors, restaurant.

Aragua State

MARACAY. Byblos. *Expensive.* Av. Las Delicias (043–415111). Modern 87-room tower, restaurant, nightclub. **Maracay.** *Moderate.* Las Delicias (043–416211, telex 43274). Spacious grounds with 157 rooms, pool, gym; guests may use stables and golf course, now run by private clubs, at a discount rate. **Italo.** *Moderate.* Av. 6, Urb. La Soledad (043–22897/9). 66 rooms near town center, renowned restaurant with Italian food (closed Sun.). **Pipo.** *Moderate.* Av. El Castaño (043–413111). In the cooler part of town, this comfortable new hotel with 120 rooms and suites caters to honeymooners; pool, gym, Turkish baths, Italian restaurant. **Wladimir.** *Inexpensive.* 27 Av. Bolívar Este (043–24998/9). 38-room business hotel with good Italian restaurant (closed Sun.).
OCUMARE DE LA COSTA. Montemar. *Inexpensive.* Block from the sea, no phone. Modest 2-story building with 22 air-conditioned rooms. **Playa Azul.** *Inexpensive.* Also near the bay, no phone. 12 rooms, restaurant nearby.

CATA. Aventura Cata. On Cata bay; reservations in Caracas (02–509–0111). New duplex cabins for 60 people; complete cabin for 7 costs about $40; kitchenettes, no restaurant. **Carmil.** *Inexpensive.* No phone. 13 primitive cabins; run-down.

CHORONÍ. Club Cotoperix. Puerto Colombia; by reservation only, in Caracas (02–951–7741). 2 beautifully restored old houses enclosed within high walls (no sign); 20 comfortable rooms, leafy patios. The price of about $50 a night includes all food and drinks, boat rides to neighboring Chuao bay, barbecue on the beach, and excursion through cacao plantation and Pittier Park. Truly lovely environment, the best of local cuisine, plus folk music, entertainment, some English-speaking staff. **Hotel Alemania.** *Inexpensive.* On the main street in Choroní, no phone (reservations in Caracas 02–986–2698). Very modest and clean, 8 rooms, restaurant.

COLONIA TOVAR. Freiburg. *Moderate.* (033–51313). 8 rooms and 7 cottages for 2–4, restaurant, meeting room (no credit cards). **Selva Negra.** *Moderate.* (033–51808). Oldest and best, 37 rooms, good restaurant, blooming gardens near church. **Alta Baviera.** *Moderate* (033–51333). 11 mountaintop cottages with stunning view, fireplace, restaurant (breakfast, dinner included). **Bergland.** *Moderate.* (033–51229). 3 rooms, 7 heated cabins, kids' park; price includes breakfast, dinner. **Drei Tannen.** *Inexpensive.* (033–51246). 7 heated rooms and 2 apartments, restaurant, surrounded by pines; price includes breakfast, dinner. **Kaiserstuhl.** *Inexpensive* (033–51132). 26 rooms in the village center, a German and an English-style restaurant.

EASTERN COAST: ROUTE OF THE SUN

Venezuelans call the highway which runs for more than 350 miles from Caracas to Cumaná and beyond the Route of the Sun. Major resorts with clubs and hotels are transforming the sweeping sandy shores and mangroves of Higuerote and Puerto La Cruz into holiday centers. But there are three national parks—Tacarigua, Mochima, and Paria—protecting lagoons, islands and peninsulas, as well as many isolated beaches beyond Cumaná still scarcely touched. The highway has all services as it is the major artery not only for coastal cities but also for oil towns in southern Anzoátegui and more distant industries of Bolívar State.

MIRANDA STATE

Marinas and seaside developments are converting Carenero, Higuerote, and Rio Chico into weekend magnets for thousands of Caraqueños. Mangrove thickets have been cleared and shallows dredged for water-skiers. In Carenero, two yacht clubs and three marinas service a small fleet of pleasure craft. Fishermen run a ferry service to Buche Island for bathers and campers who are not members of the yacht set. Inland, this lush tropical region of Miranda is known as Barlovento (although it is not marked as such on maps). It is dotted with villages first settled by runaway slaves. Today such communities as Birongo and Curiepe generate big crowds with three-day drum festivals celebrating the May Cross, the Feast of St. John on June 22–24, and St. Peter on June 27–29.

The national park of Laguna de Tacarigua protects a great shallow lagoon, habitat of flamingos, pelicans, frigate birds, ibis, and storks. A spit of land with unspoiled beaches separates the lagoon from the sea. Jeeps drive for mile after mile on the hard, damp beach at the waves' edge, as far as the hamlets of Machurucuto and Boca de Uchire at the head of another lagoon, Unare, in Anzoategui State.

PRACTICAL INFORMATION FOR MIRANDA

HOTELS. HIGUEROTE. Barlovento. *Inexpensive.* Av. Barlovento (034–21161). 28 plain rooms with fan, restaurant, pool; at last report neglected (no credit cards). **Campomar.** *Inexpensive.* Via Caucagua-Higuerote (034–41322). 67 rooms, 4 miles before Higuerote, open-air restaurant by the pool. **Mar-Sol Viera.** *Inexpensive.* Plaza Miranda (034–21034). 20 air-conditioned rooms on 3 floors, restaurant opens onto the esplanade.

TACARIGUA DE LA LAGUNA. Club Miami. *Moderate.* On the long palm-fringed beach, no phone. Its 9 cabins and 6 apartments are an old favorite; rate includes three meals; access by car across the neck of the lagoon is sometimes chancy; there is a ferry (about $4); also a landing strip; information (02–7521771).

ANZOATEGUI STATE

Barcelona and Puerto La Cruz

The old fishing port of Píritu, its popular beach, and the solid, seventeenth-century church above the town are well worth exploring. Nearby is the capital of Anzoátegui State, Barcelona, another seventeenth-century town where the past is kept alive in museums and monuments. A statue in the Plaza Boyacá portrays General Anzoátegui, hero of Boyacá battle which decided Colombia's freedom. (Miranda and Sucre states are also named after independence leaders.) The city's oldest house stands on one corner of the plaza. Built in 1671, it has been restored as the Museo de la Tradición, and is open every day 8 A.M. to noon and 3 to 6 P.M.

Barcelona and Puerto La Cruz, six miles away, have 455,000 inhabitants. Barcelona's international airport is the gateway for fun-in-the-sun charter flights bringing thousands of escapees from the winter cold of Canada and the U.S. to luxury hotels such as the Doral Beach in El Morro and the Meliá in Puerto La Cruz.

An ambitious beach resort by any standard, El Morro Tourist Complex is taking shape between Barcelona and Puerto La Cruz. The 2,000-acre tract of canals, marinas, houseboat lots, golf courses, and shopping centers is still unfinished after years of investment adding up to $1 billion. Original plans were for 15,000 hotel rooms and the same again in apartments and houses in two sectors: the sea-level Aquavilla, interlaced with canals, and El Morro, a peninsula overlooking Pozuelos Bay, where a ring of islands forms part of Mochima National Park. It is said that blueprints for the complex inspired Mexican officials in the early 1970s to build Cancun. One hotel, the deluxe Doral Beach Villas, now offers 900 rooms in thirty-two villas (said to be South America's largest hotel, along with the Caracas Hilton).

Both the Doral Beach and the Meliá Puerto La Cruz are very well set up for water sports and excursions with nearby marinas. Beaches are free of undertow and rough breakers, fabulous reefs on the islands contain thirty-five species of coral, and the Caribbean is crystal clear during the rains (July-November). Rental of craft for deep-sea fishing costs less than $5 an hour per person (group of four); Sunfish cost $12. A day-long outing to an island such as Chimana, Plata, or Borracha in a *peñero* runs about $60 per boat (bring a picnic).

From the Meliá beach seven miles out to sea, and from El Morro peninsula in the west almost to Cumaná in the east, the sea and all its islands are part of Mochima National Park. Over half the park's 360 square miles are maritime.

PRACTICAL INFORMATION FOR ANZOATEGUI STATE

HOTELS. For definitions of price categories, see "Facts at Your Fingertips" earlier in this chapter.

BOCA DE UCHIRE. Shangri-La. *Inexpensive.* On the beach. Reservations in Caracas (02–284–5135 and 719233). A pleasant 10-room house and 4 double cabins; good restaurant.

PUERTO PIRITU. Casacoima. *Moderate.* Av. Urachiche (081–411072). Simple 4-story buildings with 96 rooms, restaurant, pool; near public beach.

BARCELONA. Barcelona. *Inexpensive.* Av. 5 de Julio (081–771065). 70 rooms in town center.

EL MORRO-LECHERIA. Doral Beach Villas. *Expensive–Deluxe* (081–812222, telex 81307). Reserve 6–8 weeks in advance during peak periods, Caracas (02–781–1444). An ambitious development with 1,300 rooms and suites with kitchenettes in 32 beach villas; pool-side cafeteria, (formal dress) restaurant; among the many facilities of this resort are gym, sauna, Jacuzzi, shops, beauty parlor, car rental, and all water sports; explosub shop (ext. 1206) also rents kayaks, Sunfish, yachts, and snorkeling gear. **Pueblo Viejo.** *Expensive.* Complejo Turístico El Morro (081–2812952). Five seaside villas with fully equipped flats for 2 to 6, including kitchen. **Hostería El Morro.** *Moderate.* Ave. Américo Vespucio (081–811312). 149 rooms and suites, restaurant, bar, pool, beach.

PUERTO LA CRUZ. Meliá Puerto La Cruz. *Deluxe.* Paseo Colón (081–691311). Reservations in Caracas (02–729314). A 12-story resort with 231 rooms, adult pool, children's pool and playground, gym, sauna, Turkish bath, shops; near the Margarita ferry terminal; all water sports and excursions to islands nearby from the Marina El Morro. **Rasil Puerto La Cruz.** *Deluxe.* Calle Monagas at Paseo Colón (081–21184). New tower with 312 rooms, 34 suites; also cabins. Sauna, pool, tennis, shops, restaurants. **Gaeta.** *Moderate.* Paseo Colón (081–691816). 50 air-conditioned rooms, restaurant. **Riviera.** *Moderate.* 33 Paseo Colón (081–22039). 74 rooms in 8-floor hotel, centrally located. **Neptuno.** *Inexpensive.* Paseo Colón (081–691273). 2 floors, 31 rooms; the oldest but preferred by many; restaurant.

SUCRE STATE

Along the most beautiful coast in Venezuela, the forty-seven-mile drive from Puerto La Cruz to Cumaná pauses at two gems of beaches, Playa Arapito and Playa Colorada, before rising to the crest of the park, giving spectacular views of the Santa Fe Gulf, jutting peninsulas, and islands set in a sea mirroring the sun's rays. A short side road dips to Mochima village, launching point for boat trips to the tranquil fjord and beaches of Mochima National Park.

Cumaná to Güiria

History buffs will enjoy proud Cumaná (population 269,000), capital of Sucre State, where a fortified Spanish castle, museums, churches, and graceful colonial houses recall the heritage of the continent's first settlement, dating back to 1521. Fort San Antonio commands a panorama over the Gulf of Cariaco, treeless Araya Peninsula, and even distant Margarita Island. But a fort on Araya, Castillo de Santiago, built in 1665, was Venezuela's most costly and important structure; it was erected to protect valuable salt beds, the world's biggest at the time of their discovery in 1499.

Launches cross to Araya and its beaches in thirty minutes from Cumaná, but Araya has little else than sun, sand, and salt. Cumaná, like Puerto La Cruz, is a terminal for ferry services to Margarita, the fastest being the "Gran Cacique," crossing in eighty minutes.

Near the beach in San Luís district is a new crafts center, the Villa Artesanal, displaying a profusion of hammocks, baskets, rag dolls, chairs, *cuatros* or four-string guitars, and other local instruments. But for Sucre's famous handmade cigars and local coffee, the downtown market is the place to go, every day from 5 A.M. to noon.

Supplying the canneries of Cumaná and Marigüitar, the Gulf of Cariaco contains some of the richest fish breeding waters found anywhere. In Marigüitar on the gulf, inhabitants delight in painting bright murals on their houses, a custom also followed in Cariaco. At the head of the gulf, Cariaco is an old town set in fertile land. In the next thirty miles are a string of beaches deserted except on major holidays: Saucedo, La Esmeralda, Escondido, and Bahía de Patilla, west of the lively cacao and coffee port of Carúpano. The town is famous for its Carnival parades and dances, one of the two colorful celebrations in Venezuela (the other is in El Callao). A beautiful surfing beach, Puerto Santo, lies east of Carúpano.

Beyond the small port of Río Caribe, with its impressive red-domed church and friendly swallows, the route leaves the coast and enters verdant cacao country where Spanish moss festoons great shade trees. No roads penetrate the hills of Paria Peninsula, now a national park. However, there is a 5-mile side road (Puipuy) to Medina Beach, a half-moon bay of fine sand on the north coast.

Before ending at Güiria, the route passes wetlands occupied by water buffalo farms. Beyond Güiria, the tougher traveler may explore distant beaches using fishing boats which go to Macuro. (*Warning:* Lacking immigration facilities, this is not a legal route to Trinidad.)

PRACTICAL INFORMATION FOR SUCRE STATE

HOTELS. For definitions of price categories see "Facts at Your Fingertips" earlier in this chapter.

CUMANÁ. Los Bordones. *Expensive.* Av. Universidad, on the beach (093–653622, fax 093–652408). Family hotel of 115 rooms built on a breezy coconut plantation, large and small pool, restaurant, pool-side soda fountain, bar; all rooms have balconies over the sea. **Cumanagoto.** *Moderate–Expensive.* Av. Universidad (093–653355, fax 081–652043). Pleasant 4-story hotel built around large pool, 166 rooms all overlooking the sea, open-air restaurant among palm trees between pool and beach, also indoor rotisserie, bar with live music at night; kids' pool and playground, horseback riding. **Minerva.** *Moderate.* Av. Cristobal Colón (093–662700). 7-story hotel with 130 rooms, small pool, 2nd story restaurant with panorama of Cariaco Gulf and Araya Peninsula. **Gran Hotel.** *Inexpensive.* Av. Universidad (093–662611). Convenient 41-room hotel, a block from Los Uveros beach; restaurant. **Villamar.** *Inexpensive.* Av. Universidad on Playa San Luís (093–22147). 37 modest rooms on 2 floors.

SAN ANTONIO DEL GOLFO. Cachamaure. *Inexpensive.* On good beach 30 miles from Cumaná (093–93045/662470). A new government-built resort with 30 privately-run double cabin units (maximum 6 people each), kitchen, fridge; restaurant, soda fountain, folk music on weekends; also attractive camping and picnic areas; many fishing boats for trips.

CARUPANO. Victoria. *Inexpensive.* Facing the port (094–39776). 45 rooms, pool, restaurant, discotheque; near Conferry's office. **Lilma.** *Inexpensive.* No. 161 Av. 3 (094–39341). 44 rooms on 2 floors in town, restaurant.

RIO CARIBE. Mar Caribe. *Moderate.* On the coastal highway (094–61491). Colonial-style government-built hotel has 20 rooms, swimming pool open to non-guests (Bs. 10), restaurant, soda fountain; fishing vessels can be hired for up to 10 passengers to the beaches near and far.

PLAYA MEDINA. Hotel Playa Medina. *Expensive.* Reservations through Encuentros, Viajes y Turismo, 34 Av. Independencia. Carupano (tel. and fax, 094–312067). Rate includes three meals daily, drinks, and a half-day excursion to nearby buffalo ranch. Take a boat ride to Paria's cliffs or join a tour to Guácharo Cave. Either way, 8 charming cottages make a perfect haven.

GÜIRIA. The end of the road. Gran Puerto. *Inexpensive.* Calle Pagallos; 20

rooms on 2 floors, restaurant; another 14 rooms are located two blocks away (no credit cards).

FROM MONAGAS TO THE DELTA

Fascinating Guácharo Cave

No visitor to the Oriente should miss Guácharo Cave with its fascinating oilbirds. The cave has been famous since 1799, when naturalist Baron Alexander von Humboldt reported the existence of thousands of cave-dwelling *guácharos*—large, night-flying relatives of the nightjar and whip-poorwill—and named them *Steatornis caripensis*. Still the largest known colony of these birds, estimated at 10,000, their numbers are far less today than in Humboldt's time, when every June the nestlings were harvested by Indians and missionaries for their fat, which was then rendered to make lamp oil. Flying out at dusk to eat palm and laurel fruits, the guácharos navigate by echo location, using rapid-fire clicks. They have a wing span of over three feet.

The cave, declared World Sanctuary of the Guácharo, is protected by a 38,000-acre National Park of forested limestone mountains. A small museum and a canteen mark the entrance to the cave, open daily from 7 A.M. to 5 P.M. Each party is assigned a guide (who will expect a tip) for the two-hour tour. Special permission is needed to go farther than 3,300 feet. No cameras, flashlights, or bags of any kind are allowed. Take a jacket because it is quite cool inside.

Described by speleologists as one of the world's most complete and beautiful caverns, Guácharo Cave has six miles of majestic halls and deep galleries. The first hall, named after Humboldt, is 130 feet high and 1,470 feet long. It is here that the speckled reddish-brown birds live. Besides oil-birds, the complex fauna include pink fish, rodents, spiders, crickets, and centipedes. Geologically, nearly all phenomena found elsewhere in caves are present here. Speleologists say that in the deeper halls crystals form incredible displays.

The nearest hotels to the cave are a few miles down the road in Caripe.

Monagas State

Monagas's history as an oil state began as early as 1891 when the Guanoco Asphalt Lake was exploited; development of the eastern oilfields came in the 1920s (drillers and rigs were shipped in via the San Juan River on the Gulf of Paria). Today, although vast new deposits are being tapped west of Maturín in El Furrial, agriculture is on the rise.

A new resource, the pine tree, is turning the empty plains of southern Monagas and Anzoátegui into a land of "green gold." Surprisingly, the Honduras pines adapt well to the hot, semi-arid plains where the government has planted half a million acres since 1969. These industrial planta-tions are said to be twenty times more valuable for pulp and paper than if they were natural forests. To visit the pine forests in Chaguaramas, call Proforca (02–781–5342); for the plantations near Temblador, call Corp. Forestal Guayamure (02–782–1955).

Maturín

Sixty miles from the Guácharo Cave is Maturín, a pleasant city of 276,000, with many shade trees, boulevards, and modest hotels. Maturín, founded as a mission settlement in 1760, was supplied via the San Juan River from the Gulf of Paria and was long cut off from the rest of the country. A road from El Tigre was opened by oil companies in the 1950s. It is halfway along this route that the village of Aguasay stands out as the home of some of Venezuela's finest hammocks. The famous *chinchorros de curagua* are woven out of lace-fine fiber from a bromeliad, a relative of the pineapple plant. The artisans, all women, will sell directly from their homes.

From Maturín to Temblador and east to Tucupita is a flat run of 130 miles. (Or, by taking a fork south of Chaguaramas to the Orinoco through the pine forests, drivers can cross by ferry to Ciudad Guayana.)

Delta Amacuro

The least visited area of Venezuela, the Delta Amacuro Federal Territory (16,000 square miles), is a world of islands, canals, and jungle where transportation and most communications depend on rivers. The huge fan of the Orinoco's many mouths spreads out from the river's widest point, thirteen-and-a-half miles, near the town of Barrancas. Two main arteries, the Macareo and the Rio Grande, embrace hundreds of *caños* or channels which together bear an astounding 1,110 billion cubic meters of water a year into the Atlantic. Silt carried down from the Andes and plains on the Orinoco's 1,300-mile journey to the sea has added some 600 square miles to the Delta in the past century.

The Orinoco's fresh, turbid waters meet the equatorial ocean current coming from Africa in a spectacle few tourists ever see. The first white traveler, Christopher Columbus, was amazed: "Never have I read nor heard of so much sweet water within a salt ocean." His son Ferdinand reported, "A mountain range of waves seized our two ships so that we feared for their safety." The mouth of just one *brazo,* or arm, the Rio Grande, is over twelve miles wide, and there are seventy others.

The cliffs for which Barrancas is named are made of sediment thrown up during the June to September rains, when the swollen Orinoco rises some eight meters. The state development agency, Corp. Venezolana de Guayana, built a fifty-mile dike in 1968 to close off the Caño Mánamo, reclaiming over two million acres for agriculture.

Tucupita

The levee-top road linking the capital, Tucupita (pop. 50,000), brought new life to the territory. Stock raising, including water buffalo, prospers on reclaimed land and new crops include rice and *manaca* palms famous for their delectable hearts. Although the dike cuts off navigation upstream to Barrancas, Tucupita is still a river town where most of the action is in the port. Tucupita's one-story houses with interior patios and tin or asbestos-cement roofs keep out little of the steamy heat, averaging nearly 85°F. There are two gas stations and two modest hotels.

For the last sixty years, Capuchin padres have made Tucupita their base for missionary work, setting up schools in remote Delta communities of Warao Indians. Araguaimujo, the closest mission, is eight hours from Barrancas by dugout with outboard motor; other posts are two days away.

Guests may find free lodging at the missions, but should bring their own food since supplies are all shipped in by river.

Natives of the Delta are the Warao Indians, numbering 15,000 of the territory's 80,000 inhabitants. Skilled navigators, fishermen, and weavers, the Warao build villages on stilts of *moriche* palm trunks and use palm fiber for making hammocks and baskets whose beauty has been seen in U.S. exhibitions. White wood carvings of animals, insects, birds, fish, snakes, and freshwater dolphins reveal the rich variety of Delta fauna, the Warao's "animal brothers."

PRACTICAL INFORMATION FOR MONAGAS AND THE DELTA

GETTING THERE. By plane. *Avensa* turbo props link Tucupita daily with Anaco, Maiquetía, Güiria, and Porlamar; the airfield has no car rentals but taxis meet all flights. Maturín has 4 daily flights from Maiquetía, others via Porlamar, Cuidad Bolívar, and Puerto Ordaz. **By bus.** Expresos de la Costa buses leave Caracas at 7 A.M. and 10 P.M. daily for the 11-hour run to Tucupita via Maturín. Por puestos charge by the seat and go from Tucupita as far as Ciudad Guayana.

HOTELS AND RESTAURANTS. For definitions of price categories see "Facts at Your Fingertips" earlier in this chapter.

CARIPE. Hotel El Samán. *Inexpensive.* Av. Chaumer No. 29 (092–51183). At west end of town, 30 rooms with bath, scrupulously clean; good restaurant open 8 A.M. to 10 P.M. **Caripe.** *Inexpensive.* Calle Guzman Blanco (092–51246). 6 rooms, restaurant; 5 miles from the cave. **El Guácharo.** *Moderate.* Ave. Principal (092–51218, fax 51501). On 7 acres of land, this remodelled hotel is the area's largest. Also has a restaurant, convention room, and a pool.

MATURÍN. Several business hotels to choose from: **Chaima Inn.** *Moderate.* Blvd. del Sur, opp. IUPEM (091–26817). Bar, restaurant, pool, 95 rooms. **Emperador.** *Inexpensive.* Av. Bolívar (091–23927). 72 new rooms. **Friuli.** *Inexpensive.* Calle 30 (091–27450). 45 rooms, restaurant. **Hostería Juanico.** *Inexpensive.* Blvd. del Sur (091–39082). 97 rooms in a motel with small pool, restaurant. **Mallorca.** *Inexpensive.* Av. Las Palmeras (091–39675). 70 rooms. **Perla Princess.** *Moderate.* Av. Juncal (091–27271, fax 414008). 94 rooms, new.

TUCUPITA. Amacuro. *Inexpensive.* 23 Calle Bolívar (087–21057). 31 air-conditioned rooms with bath. **Delta.** *Inexpensive.* Calle Pativilca (087–21219). A hostel with air-conditioning, baths. **Pequeña Venecia.** *Inexpensive.* San Salvador, via El Sierre (087–21558). Plain, but fine view of the Orinoco.

GETTING AROUND THE DELTA. Organized tourism now exists in Tucupita, but with a hammock and mosquito net, plus cash (forget credit cards), those who want to rough it can go a long way into the Delta by paying passage on the bongos which transport produce, finding shelter at villages or missions. Photo hunters and basket buyers hire craft and navigator for river forays. Bargain with any of the dugout owners near the river gas pump; price, roughly $50 a day, varies with distance and time. Also, ask the padres at the Capuchin Mission to recommend guides. River excursions can be made from La Horqueta, up the road from Tucupita. The hearts of palm canning center here is run by Warao Indians. The journey to Pedernales at the mouth of Caño Mánamo takes 8 hours. Pedernales (pop. 5,000), some 25 miles from Trinidad, is the center of the Delta's shrimp and fishing industry. Curiapo, at the ocean outlet of Rio Grande, is a picturesque village on stilts, once a rubber center.

For travel beyond the Delta, ask at the Trinidad-Tobago consulate, Edif. Antonieta, Calle Mariño 12, Tucupita.

TOURS. The best way to see the Delta's islands and Indian communities is to go with those who know them. **Mánamo Tours,** Calle Dallacosta No. 22, Plaza Bolívar, Tucupita (087–21156), organizes 3-day river trips in motorized bongos; you sleep in hammocks in the native community of San Francisco de Guayo and explore as far as Curiapo. Costs for river travel are about $50 per person per day, minimum three persons; 3-day advance notice. **Wek'ta Tours,** Hotel Basil, Centro Cívico Puerto Ordaz, Estado Bolívar (086–222723/10, fax 22703), also specializes in Delta travel, flying groups to Tucupita and making 4- to 6-day trips to northern communities in La Barra de Cocuima and Pedernales at the Dragon's Mouth.

CRAFTS. The superb baskets and hammocks of palm fiber and a Noah's ark of carved animals bound for souvenir shops throughout Venezuela originate in the Delta. The talented Warao artisans run a row of stalls on a small plaza a few blocks north of Tucupita's cathedral. Also, *Foto Rodriguez,* 17 Calle Petión, has a good selection.

THE ANDES

The Venezuelan Andes rise directly south of Lake Maracaibo to the snowy heights of the Sierra Nevada de Mérida where four peaks soar over 16,000 feet. The *Transandina* road winds through Trujillo, Mérida, and Táchira states toward Colombia. From the east, looping in hairpin bends, it climbs spectacularly to the foggy (or snowy) Paso del Aguila at an inhospitable 13,146 feet, where a bronze condor marks the heroic passage of Bolívar's forces on foot and horseback in 1813. The Andean routes in Trujillo State are a succession of lovely vistas, verdant coffee hills, and farming villages, from Biscucuy, Boconó, and Burbusay to Escuque, La Puerta, La Mesa de Esnujaque, and Timotes.

On the way up from subtropical Valera, the changes are swift and fascinating. Tile-roofed hamlets cling to hillsides, gardens of begonias and fuchsias give way to willow trees, brooks rush through cabbage patches, and, at 10,000 feet, stony fields sprout with wheat. Colder and higher still, the treeless mist-veiled *páramo* is a botanist's dream of wild flowers in red, blue, magenta, and white. The banner of the Andes is the yellow-flowering *frailejón* of which there are no less than forty-five species in Venezuela. Its furry leaves look like rabbit ears and have been used to stuff mattresses.

Just beyond the pass, the Transandina is joined at Apartaderos by the Barinas-Santo Domingo route from the Llanos. Nearby, the glacial lagoons of Sierra Nevada National Park (760 square miles) attract many hikers and campers. Some hire horses at the park's entrance (where a roadside hostel serves steaming hot chocolate). Deep, dark, and clear, Laguna Mucubají mirrors the Andean sky, intensely blue at this altitude (11,614 ft.). Afternoons, however, tend to be foggy and walkers to Laguna Negra, an hour higher, would do well to start early. Still farther are Laguna Los Patos and La Canoa. Trout in many high lakes and rivers draw fishermen in the season from March to September.

From Apartaderos, a cluster of souvenir shops and hostels heated against the cold, the road twists steeply down the Chama Valley, pausing at villages with Indian names—Mucuchíes, Moconoque, Mucurubá.

Among the charms of the Andes are the quiet, courteous mountain people. Weather-beaten and sturdy, they wrest a hard living from wheat, potatoes, and dairy cows, plowing slopes where even oxen walk precariously. The women knit sweaters, weave woolen blankets and ponchos, here called *ruanas,* make arepas of wheat, and bake *mantecado* cakes. Red-cheeked children sell flowers by the road, or hold up fat puppies for sale. A large white breed, the Mucuchíes, is favored locally as a watchdog.

Fervent Catholics, *Andinos* observe holy days with street processions and songs. In La Punta, the Dance of the Vassals celebrates La Candelaria's day, February 2. In Bailadores, Boconó, Jajo, and other villages dances are performed by costumed men on May 15, the day of San Isidro Labrador. July 16 is the Fiesta del Carmen, observed widely throughout the Andes. In San Rafael de Mucuchíes, the patron saint's day is October 24. December is the month of San Benito; dances and processions are held in Mérida City on the 12th, in Timotes, La Mesa de Esnujaque from the 15th to the 24th, and in Mucuchíes on the 28th and 29th. The new year opens with the procession of the Christ Child, La Paradura del Niño, on January 1 and 2.

In the heart of the Andes is Mérida, a handsome city founded in 1558 and now spreading up the valley between two high sierras. *Merideños* call the peaks of the Sierra Nevada the Five White Eagles. They are: La Corona—pairing Humboldt (16,213 feet) and Bonpland (16,020 feet) peaks, La Concha (16,148 feet), La Columna—the name for Bolívar (16,427 feet) and Espejo (15,633 feet) peaks, El Toro (15,600 feet), and El León (15,550 feet) Just 8° north of the equator, snow blankets the highest peaks in July and August. Near their crown, remnants of beautiful glaciers such as Timoncitos persist. The "Eagles" can be seen from Mérida's Park of the Five Republics. Here is the first monument ever erected to Bolívar (1842), and a bit of soil from each of the countries he liberated.

At 5,332 feet above sea level, Mérida's climate is benign by day, chilly at night. Capital of Mérida State, this city of 275,000 people lies some 100 miles from Valera (population 196,000) and 160 miles from San Cristóbal (population 365,000). These are the three largest Andean cities. With its panorama of peaks, dignified Cathedral, modern university campus, twenty-one parks, zoo, colonial museum, market, fabulous cablecar, and many hotels, Mérida is the mecca for Andean travelers.

West of Mérida, the route follows the Chama gorge. It drops to Lagunillas and Estanques, hot and low (1,450 feet) before rising for the final switchbacks from Tovar and Bailadores up to chilly Páramo La Negra in Táchira State. Often wrapped in afternoon fog, the moor-like páramo blooms into an Andean flower show in October and November.

The descent to San Cristóbal is through a chain of hamlets and coffee plantations. At a pleasant 2,700 feet above sea level, San Cristóbal is a thriving mountain city twenty-seven miles from the Colombian border. Every January the San Sebastian Fair draws thousands to sports events, cattle shows, horse races, and bullfights. Many of the steep streets are closed for dances and processions. With its Memorial Bull Ring, sports stadium, velodrome, and fair grounds, San Cristóbal is a lively place. Bicycle racing, the local passion, is practiced every weekend at the velodrome. Adding an impressive note of modernity to the old city (founded in 1561) is the double-tower Civic Center and Town Hall opened in 1986 on Parque Bolívar.

PRACTICAL INFORMATION FOR THE ANDES

HOW TO GET THERE. By plane. Daily flights by jet from Maiquetía, Barquisimeto, Maracaibo, and Valencia to both Merida and San Antonio; one daily flight from Barquisimeto to Valera. San Cristóbal is served by the airport of San Antonio, the border town nearest Colombia; La Fría, a 1½-hour drive north; and the new airport of Santo Domingo, an hour south.

By bus. Although several express coach and por puesto lines go from Caracas's Nuevo Circo terminal to the Andes, most leave at night. The trip to Mérida takes at least 12 hours. From Mérida on, tickets should be bought 2–3 days in advance. As many as 6 lines serve San Cristóbal's terminal and San Antonio on the border (some continue through to Cúcuta in Colombia). The following go to Mérida and San Cristóbal, but not on the same itinerary: Expresos Alianza (02–545–0113) also serves Cúcuta, Maracaibo, and Barquisimeto; Expresos Los Llanos (02–545–0428); Expresos Mérida (02–541–1975); Expresos Occidente (02–545–3993); Union Transporte San Cristóbal (02–541–4218).

HOTELS. For descriptions of price categories see "Facts at Your Fingertips" earlier in this chapter.

Trujillo State

TRUJILLO CITY. Trujillo. *Moderate.* Av. Carmona, upper end Av. Independencia (072–33646, fax 072–33942). Popular state-run hotel. 32 rooms, pool, restaurant. **La Paz.** *Moderate.* Calle 15 at Av. Carmona (072–34864). All suites, with dining area, refrigerator. **Valle de los Mukas.** *Inexpensive.* Calle Arismendi (072–33184). 8 rooms with hot water, around a patio restaurant.
VALERA. Camino Real. *Moderate.* Av. Independencia (071–51704). New, 70 rooms, color TV, telephones. **Albergue Turístico Valera.** *Inexpensive.* Av. Independencia behind the Ateneo (071–55016). 19 rooms on a very noisy street, restaurant. **Motel Valera.** *Inexpensive.* Ave. Maya-Bolivar (071–57937). Pleasant, "u"-shaped motel with 93 rooms, open-air restaurant.

ISNOTU. Albergue Turístico. *Inexpensive.* Off Plaza Bolívar (071–62336). New hillside complex has 12 rooms with 3 to 6 beds, hot water, restaurant.
LA PUERTA. Guadalupe. *Moderate.* At entrance to village (071–83825, fax 83703). A long-established family hotel, 33 rooms, gardens, playground, cabins, good food. **Valeralta.** *Moderate.* Transandean highway via La Mesa (071–83925). 16 rooms and 8 cabins surrounded by trees (altitude 8,500 ft.), dining room; nearby is a good eating place, *Mesón Cascada Comboco*, by a stream.
LA MESA DE ESNUJAQUE. Tibisay. *Moderate.* Av. Bolívar (071–86034). 17 cabins for 2–8 people, set in ample gardens; restaurant, bar. **El Remanso.** *Inexpensive.* Transandean highway (071–86278). 3 cabins, 20 rooms, playing grounds, restaurant. **Miraflores,** *Inexpensive,* in the village (071–86045). 25 comfortable rooms in cabins, bar-restaurant in colonial house; an acre of gardens.
BOCONÓ. Hostería Jardin. *Moderate.* Carretera Boconó-Flor de Patria (072–52480). The newest spot in Boconó, a motel with 40 rooms surrounded by pastures, restaurant; pool (closed Mon.) is open to nonguests (Bs. 20); lively Sat. night music. **Campestre La Colina.** *Inexpensive–Moderate.* Puente El Zumbador (072–52695). 31 rooms, 5 cabins are popular mountain get-away with gardens, restaurant. **Vega del Rio.** *Inexpensive.* Near Boconó river, via La Guayabita (072–52992). Green gardens are the setting for 24 rooms, outdoor restaurant in 4 pavilions.

Mérida State

SANTO DOMINGO. Moruco. *Moderate.* On the highway (073–88070). Very attractive chalet-style hotel and cabins in landscaped gardens; 23 rooms, kids' park, horseback riding; good restaurant serves homegrown vegetables. **Trucha Azul.** *Moderate.* On main road (no phone). 14 rooms, 4 cabins, well-known for its restaurant. **Los Frailes.** *Moderate.* 15 minutes from Santo Domingo. Reservations in Caracas (Hoturvensa 02–562–3022, fax 02–562–3475). The monastery-style buildings are beautifully furnished with brass beds, colonial-style furniture, and real antiques; unremarkable food but a good place from which to organize mountain walks on foot or horseback. **Santo Domingo.** *Inexpensive.* At east end of town (073–88144). 19 cabins and main building are a family standby; dining room; horseback riding.
TIMOTES. Las Truchas. *Inexpensive.* On Transandean highway (071–89158). 10 rooms and 26 cabins for 3 to 8 people, no utensils in cabins, dining room.
APARTADEROS. Parque Turistico. Apartaderos. *Moderate.* Carretera Mérida (074–81004, tel. and fax). 45 heated rooms, Italian restaurant. Altitude 10,500 ft. **Sierra Nevada.** *Moderate* (no phone). 130 rooms, restaurant, bar.
MUCUCHÍES. Los Conquistadores (formerly El Faro). *Moderate.* Av. Carabobo (074–81089). 42 rooms, restaurant. **Los Andes,** *Inexpensive,* Calle Independencia No. 42 (074–81151). A typical Andean townhouse attractively converted with 5 rooms sharing 2 baths; very good restaurant.
MÉRIDA CITY. Pedregosa. *Expensive.* Av. Próceres (074–630525, fax 074–639936; in Caracas 02–261–4547, 02–261–5571). Lovely grounds with 25 large cabins and a main building, playground, horseback riding, restaurant. **Park.** *Moderate.* Calle 37, parque Glorias Pátrias (074–634866, fax 074–634582). 125 rooms, 6-story hotel, good views of mountains, restaurant, cafeteria, discotheque. **Prado Rio.** *Moderate.* Av. Milla, in east (074–520775). 57 rooms and cabin units in ample gardens;

restaurant, pool open to nonguests (closed Tues.). **Princesa.** *Moderate.* El Valle (074–443950). 60 units and cabins, modern and attractive, playground, baby-sitter service, horseback excursions. **Caribay.** *Moderate.* Av. 2 near the airport (074–636451, fax 074–637141). 80 modern rooms, restaurant, nightclub. **Chama.** *Moderate.* Av. Bolívar at Calle 29 (074–521011, telex 74171). 63 rooms in renovated downtown hotel. **La Terraza.** *Moderate.* Av. Chorros de Milla (074–441133, fax 448237). Plain 150–room hotel, restaurant, sauna, pool. **Belensate.** *Moderate.* La Punta, west Mérida (074–691150, fax 074–691659). 56 rooms, 7 cabins, restaurant, gardens, small zoo, all in a quiet residential neighborhood, convenient to airport. **Mucubají.** *Inexpensive.* Av. Universidad (074–447080). 64 rooms near the University, restaurant; no credit cards. **Teleférico.** *Inexpensive.* Plaza de las Heroinas Merideñas (074–527370). New, plain, 4-story hotel with 18 rooms, restaurant; near the cablecar terminus. **Valle Grande.** *Inexpensive.* San Javier Valley, 5 miles from city of Merida (074–443011, tel. and fax). Mountain setting for 3–story hotel with 30 rooms plus 31 cabins, each with fireplace and unstocked kitchen; excellent restaurant, golfito, horses.

JAJÍ. Posada de Jají. *Inexpensive.* On main Plaza (no phone). Charming inn with 4 double and triple rooms, good restaurant, live music group on Sun. **Fonda Jaguani.** *Inexpensive.* Also on the Plaza. 5 rooms upstairs over the restaurant; no credit cards.

TOVAR. Hostería Sabaneta. *Inexpensive.* Carrera 3 (075–72204). A motel with 28 rooms, small kids' park, restaurant. **La Posada de Mariño.** *Inexpensive.* El Amparo, via Laguna Blanca, on the way to Zea. A high country inn with 21 rooms, restaurant with Andean food.

BAILADORES. HotelVel. *Inexpensive.* Av. Bolívar (075–70136). Well-run 2-story mountain hotel with 20 rooms, garden, restaurant, 4 cabins, piano bar, discotheque, kids' park, and ponies.

Táchira State

LA GRITA. Hotel de Montaña. *Inexpensive.* 4 miles above La Grita (077–82938). Busy local resort with 24 rooms in cabins for 2 to 12 people, restaurant, discotheque and live music on weekends.

SAN CRISTÓBAL. El Tamá. *Moderate.* In Los Pirineos district (076–554335). A 10-story hotel with 112 rooms, restaurant, bar, car rentals, olympic pool. **Horizonte.** *Inexpensive.* Av. 5 at Calle 7 (076–430011). 84 rooms and suites in 10-story business hotel. **El Jardín.** *Inexpensive.* Av. Libertador 48 (076–431555). 80 rooms in plesasant 3-floor structure, cabins; restaurant. **Las Lomas.** *Inexpensive.* Av. Libertador (076–435775). 68-unit motel; small pool, restaurant. **Korinu.** *Moderate.* Carrera 6 bis, near bus terminal (076–449866). 4-story hotel with 70 rooms, restaurant. **Palermo.** *Inexpensive.* Av. Libertador (076–439738). 2-story hotel with 40 rooms, pool, restaurant, and disco.

UREÑA. Aguas Calientes. *Moderate.* 4 miles from Ureña (076–86291). A hot springs resort, convenient for travelers to Colombia; each of the 31 rooms has a solarium with 3 kinds of thermal waters; non-guests may use the attractive pool.

SAN JUAN DE COLON. Las Palmeras. *Inexpensive.* On highway to La Fria (077–93201). 27 rooms and 3 suites, pool (closed Wed.); the restaurant offers the best food between San Cristóbal and Lake Maracaibo.

WHAT TO SEE. All routes in the Andes are scenic and nearly every village has its old church, historic building, or nearby nature spot.

But topping all sights is Mérida's **Teleférico** or cablecar ascending to a literally breathtaking 15,633 feet atop Pico Espejo. This is 853 feet higher than Switzerland's Matterhorn. The ride up takes an hour from Mérida (at 5,174 feet), or longer if visitors snack or rest at the 3 intermediate stations. The top station has a canteen serving sandwiches and hot chocolate. Venezuelans love to see the snow here, and for many this is their only glimpse. But when it is not snowing, very early on a clear day you can see from Pico Espejo to the plains in the south and Sierra de Cocuy in Colombia. To the east, Pico Bolívar, Venezuela's highest, looms through swirling clouds in all its 16,427-foot grandeur. It is topped by a bronze bust of Bolívar. The Teleférico is in service Wed. to Sun., from 7:30 A.M.; the last car goes up at noon. Plan an early start, not only to get the best photo weather before clouds close in but also to avoid lines. Make reservations as soon as you arrive in Mérida;

the Teleférico is tremendously popular, especially during school holidays. For information (074–525080 and 521997). Cost is about $4 for adults, children up to 10, students half price. Jackets and gloves can be rented at the station but don't forget warm shoes. (A note to romantics: there is *no* skiing on Pico Espejo.)

Hikers wishing to climb **Pico Bolívar** and other peaks should enquire for guides at the Teleférico, or contact Montaña Treks (074–631740) or Casa del Montañista (074–525696), which provides equipment, horses, and English-speaking personnel.

Los Aleros is a make-believe village of the past peopled by Andeans of the present; the old widow and her young bridegroom, the highwayman, the herb curer . . . all are players in a stage set by a local dreamer and antiques collector, Alexis Montilla. On 18 acres near Tabay east of Mérida, Montilla takes sightseers in three ancient buses around his detailed miniature village. Silent films are shown. 8 A.M.– 6 P.M. Entrance fee about $3.

Jají, a showcase village 22 miles northwest of Mérida on the Azulita road, sparkles with whitewash, varnish, and flowers. The picturesque church and plaza and the surrounding houses and streets were done over by the government as a tourist attraction. A 5-room inn, the Posada de Jají, is big in value, *inexpensive,* with good food. The Feast of St. Michael Archangel is celebrated here on Sept. 24.

The 3-domed **Observatory** of the Astrophysical Institute (CIDA) sits on a granite ridge behind the Paso del Aguila where a hostel, Páramo Aguila, offers lodging, food, and a fire at night. The road to the observatory turns off west, above Apartaderos, and passes Llano del Hato village perched at 11,516 feet. The Observatory conducts daily guided tours for Bs.50 at 10 A.M., 2, 3:30, 7, and 10 P.M. during school holidays (the longest covers 3rd weekend in July through 2nd weekend in Sept.). Otherwise, CIDA is open one Saturday night per month (074–791893).

Trout Lagoons. In Santo Domingo there is a trout hatchery which supplies restaurants as far away as Caracas. But of great beauty in their chilly isolation on the *páramos* of Mérida State are as many as 200 trout-stocked lakes and lagoons, most near the high peaks. Small and clear, wide and green, or deep and black, all are icy cold. Most are unvisited except by die-hard anglers; wind and near-freezing temperatures when the sun goes in keep most locals away. (Jan. to Mar. is the sunniest time for camping.) Catches in the high lakes are reported at 15 lbs. and over. Guides live in hamlets around Santo Domingo and Los Frailes and nearest to Laguna de los Patos, Laguna Negra, La Canoa, and La Carbonera. Three lakes near Piñango village are reached by jeep track from the Paso del Aguila. Lagunas Say-Say, Pogal, Montón, and Rollal are reached from Mucuchíes, 1–2 hours by mule. Yearly licenses for the season Mar. 15 to Sept. 30 can be obtained from the Ministerio de Agricultura y Cría (MAC) in Mérida, Av. Urdaneta opposite Banco Regional Los Andes (074–632576). Hours are 8 A.M. to noon and 1:30 to 5. Bring a Bs.2.50 fiscal stamp.

Trujillo and The Virgin of Peace. Trujillo, its long, one-way streets squeezed in a narrow gorge, is the historic and cultural capital of the mountain state of the same name which is known for its excellent pineapples and coffee. Browse through the *Centro Histórico,* a colonial house converted into a museum. Here, on June 15, 1813, Bolívar proclaimed "war to the death" to enemies of the struggling republic. Some of the original furnishings are preserved, including the bed Bolívar slept in. Also, paintings, coins, arms (open daily 8 A.M. to noon and 3 to 6 P.M.; Sun. until noon).

Southwest of Trujillo, off the Sabaneta road, the gigantic concrete statue of the Virgin Mary was raised in 1983 as a monument to peace. The same height as New York's Statue of Liberty (150 feet), the *Virgen de la Paz* was designed by Manuel de la Fuente and built on a rocky outcrop 4,300 feet above sea level. Internal stairs and an elevator lead to windows at three levels—knees, waist, and eyes. From the top lookout you can see not only Valera, 10 miles away, but on clear days, Lake Maracaibo and the Andean peaks. On foggy days when mist wraps the statue's feet, the locals like to say the "Virgin is in Heaven."

Valera and Isnotú. Valera is the commercial center of Trujillo State and starting point for the Transandean Highway and for three other interesting mountain routes. Isnotú, 9 miles northwest, is famous as the birthplace of José Gregorio Hernández (1864–1919), a self-denying doctor widely revered as a modern-day saint. Most of his devotees among the poor and middle-class pray to him for cures. Postcards and little statues of the modest doctor in his felt hat are seen throughout Venezuela. Since his death as victim of one of Caracas's first traffic accidents, his reputation as a miracle worker has grown. A simple memorial chapel and a small museum in Isnotú draw thousands of pilgrims.

Boconó. For almost 400 years after its founding in 1549 in the mountains of eastern Trujillo, Boconó had no road; its isolation was ended only in 1935. Today a 1½ hour drive from the state capital, this pleasant "garden town" is a center for coffee, vegetable, and flower cultivation and crafts such as weaving, pottery, and basketry. The Sat. market on Calle 5 displays a rich variety of local produce.

When driving north of Boconó, take the 2-mile turnoff to lovely *San Miguel Valley* to see the renowned church with its yard-thick walls and brightly painted (circa 1760) reliefs of St. Michael and his guardian angels. San Miguel Church (open 9 to 11 A.M. and 2 to 5 P.M., except Tues.) is the center of fiestas celebrated Jan. 4–6, the "Romerías de los Pastores y Payasos," when costumed shepherds and masked clowns lead street processions.

A rough road leading from Boconó provides access to a new national park covering 100,000 acres of Páramo Guaramacal, refuge of the threatened spectacled bear.

Jajó. From Boconó southwest to Niquitao, a steep road leads hardy Andean explorers up the Río Burate Valley, where the 13,000-foot mountain called La Teta (the teat) de Niquitao rises. The road reaches tiny Las Mesitas by a ford, and crosses the Páramo de Tuñame to Jajó, a farm village charming in its whitewashed simplicity. Jajó is a few miles from the Transandean Highway and the hotels of La Puerta.

THE LLANOS

One of the great physical features of the continent, the *Llanos,* or plains, curve in a band some 600 miles long from the Orinoco Delta westward into Colombia. Lying south of the coastal mountains, the plains are crossed by many streams and big rivers, all draining into the Orinoco. This vast interior covers almost a third of Venezuela but is home to only 9 percent of the population. Through irrigation from reservoirs such as the huge Embalse de Guárico, mechanized farming produces most of the nation's rice, sorghum, cotton, and corn in the upper plains of Barinas, Cojedes, Portuguesa, and Guárico States. Calabozo is a busy agricultural center some 165 miles south of Caracas. Eighty-three miles farther is San Fernando, capital of Apure, the flattest state of all. From here south, cattle range freely on grasslands of huge unfenced *hatos,* or ranches, which are reached by private plane. Continuing south to a ferry over the Orinoco, today the San Fernando-Puerto Páez road is largely paved.

Parched by merciless sun the first half of the year and flooded by rain-swollen rivers from June to September, the low Llanos are ruled by extremes. In the dry season (December to April), tough *Llaneros* mount wiry horses to round up cattle for market. As rivers dry up, many cows and other animals in Apure die of thirst while millions of wading birds, ducks, and storks compete for the fish trapped in shrinking ponds. When thunderstorms announce the first rains, the plains burst into new green grass. Like the kiss of the legendary princess, rain brings life to frogs, small reptiles, and even certain species of fish which survive beneath the baked mud in a state of suspended animation called aestivation. Again the Llanero must go out to rescue cattle, but now he poles a boat through flooded lowland.

Rivers such as the San José, Aguaro, and Guárico, and reservoirs such as Las Majaguas, Playa de Piedras, and Camatagua, lead many anglers off the beaten track for some of the best sport fishing on the continent. The famed peacock bass known as *pavón* is found in many Llanos rivers, along with six-foot catfish, laolao, palometa, cachama, morocota, coporo, curbinata, and the fang-toothed aymara. In clear-running rivers, swimming is safe, but the turbid streams are avoided for their fierce piranhas, here called *caribes* (which means "meat-eater" and is the root not only

of Caribbean, after the Carib Indians, but also "cannibal"). Other enemies
to be feared in slow waters are electric eels and stingrays. Then again, the
Orinoco and many tributaries harbor the gentle manatees and rare fresh-
water dolphins which, like their sea cousins, play in groups.

Like Africa, the plains have an astonishing wealth of wildlife, even after
four centuries of ranching and hunting. Probably more different animal
and bird species can be seen in one day on a Llanos reserve than anywhere
else in the Americas or Africa, except in a zoo. One ranch in the upper
Cojedes plains, Hato Piñero, where hunting has been banned since 1950,
has classified no less than 300 species of birds, fifty mammals, and twenty
reptiles. These include the giant otter, tapir, jaguar, ocelot, monkeys, armadillos, anteaters, porcupine, sloth, deer, fox, peccary, agouti, water
opossum, capybara, coati, crocodile, anaconda, cayman, turtles, and more.
The roster of birds is usually headed by the superb scarlet ibis, followed
by pink flamingo, spoonbill, herons, egrets, hoatzin, jabiru stork, toucans,
parrots, hummingbirds, kingfishers, trogons, bitterns, crakes, gallinules,
anhingas, guans, curassows, and birds of prey such as the harpy eagle.

PRACTICAL INFORMATION FOR THE LLANOS

GETTING THERE. By plane. Daily *Avensa* or *Aeropostal* jets link Maiquetía
with San Fernando de Apure, Barinas, Guanare, and Acarigua. Other agricultural
centers such as Calabozo and Valle de la Pascua are served from the Aeropuerto
del Centro (02–574–7713) in Charallave by *CAVE* (02–952–1940 or 02–952–1806).
The airline runs a bus from Caracas, leaving from the east parking lot of the CCCT
shopping center (by Cada supermarket) at 6 A.M. and 3 P.M.

By road. From Maturín in the east to San Cristóbal in the west, 770 miles of
highway crosses the upper plains. It carries heavy bus and truck traffic, as well as
por puesto cars running between bus terminals at all major points.

HOTELS. Accommodations in the farming and oil towns consist of undistin-
guished commercial hotels, all air-conditioned, most with restaurant; some motels
have swimming pools and are busy on weekends. For definitions of price categories
see "Facts at Your Fingertips" earlier in this chapter.

Apure State

SAN FERNANDO DE APURE. Gran Hotel Plaza. *Moderate.* Plaza Bolívar
(047–21255). The best and newest, 50 rooms, restaurant, bar. **Boulevard.** *Inexpensive.* Paseo Libertador (047–23122). 30 rooms, restaurant, bar. **La Torraca.** *Inexpensive.* Paseo Libertador (047–22887). 47 rooms, restaurant, bar.

Guarico State

CALABOZO. Aristón. *Inexpensive.* Carrera 11 (046–74598). Relatively new,
clean, with bar-restaurant. The **Venezia.** *Inexpensive.* Next door (046–72564). Also
rather new, with busy restaurant.
SAN JUAN DE LOS MORROS. Capital of Guárico State and gateway to the
Llanos, a pretty town spread at the foot of spectacular humpback hills, the *morros,*
or points. **Santa Mónica.** *Moderate.* Entrance on Route 2 (046–311111, in Caracas
510144). A pleasant motel with restaurant, pool. **Los Morros.** *Moderate.* Northern
entrance to town (046–35490). 40 rooms, restaurant. **Ana.** *Inexpensive.* Also on the
route (046–36126).

Cojedes State

SAN CARLOS. Capital of Cojedes State, center of fertile cattle and farm lands;
visit the historic colonial house, La Blanquera, restored as a cultural center. **Central.** *Inexpensive.* Ave. Bolívar in center (058–32469). 41 rooms, restaurant.

Portuguesa State

ACARIGUA. Prosperous farm center with much new growth. **Las Majaguas.** *Moderate.* Calle 28 (055–41360). New, 29 rooms with pool, restaurant. **Miraflores.** *Inexpensive.* On highway (055–47026). Attractive motel, 42 rooms, pool, restaurant. **Payara.** *Inexpensive.* On highway to Guanare (055–214611). 150 rooms, restaurant, pool; popular.

GUANARE. Capital of Portuguesa State. A quiet old town, founded in 1591; cathedral, several restored colonial houses, cultural centers; famous for its shrine of the patron saint of Venezuela, the Virgin of Coromoto, who appeared on Sept. 8, 1652 to an Indian chief. **Coromoto.** *Moderate.* Ave. Miranda (057–55342). New, 76 rooms, restaurant, pool. **Portuguesa.** *Moderate.* Ave. 23 de Enero (057–55171). 48 rooms, soda fountain, small pool. **La Gondola.** *Moderate.* Plaza Miranda (057–53682). 34 rooms, good Italian restaurant, convenient.

Barinas State

BARINAS. The growing state capital thrives on farming and cattle. In colonial days Barinas, founded in 1576, was the largest town after Caracas and was a renowned exporter of tobacco and indigo to Europe. Visit Government House, formerly home of the Marqués de Boconó and now the largest surviving colonial home. Best hotels are run by Italians. **Bristol.** *Moderate.* Ave. 23 de Enero (073–20698). 69 modern rooms and suites, restaurant, disco, car rental, shops. **Valle Hondo.** *Moderate.* Ave. 23 de Enero (073–23677). Also new, 6 stories, 92 rooms, restaurant, bar, convention room. **Los Guasimitos.** *Inexpensive.* On highway by Santo Domingo bridge (073–24189). Motel with 80 units, pool, steak restaurant, open all night.

NATURE RESERVES. Aguaro-Guariquito National Park covers 2,300 square miles between 2 tributaries of the Orinoco. Lacking any facilities for visitors, it remains a reserve for the hundreds of thousands of fish, birds, and animals in its marshes, gallery forests, creeks, and pools. The road from Las Mercedes to Cabruta runs along the east border.

Hato El Frío, a private ranch of over 300 square miles, is located near Mantecal some 80 miles west of San Fernando de Apure. Besides 40,000 head of cattle, the ranch raises capybara, locally called *chiguire* (largest member of the rodent family), whose herds number 30,000. At a biological station one of the studies concerns the Orinoco crocodile, a severely endangered species. To arrange for group visit, call Científica La Salle (02–782–8155 or 782–8711, ext. 228). The fee covers 2 days, a biologist guide, and beds for 6 in a rural cottage.

Hato El Piñero in Cojedes State, where animals have bred freely since hunting was banned four decades ago, today teems with an astonishing array of fauna, including endangered animals such as the giant otter, jaguar, and crocodile. Bounded by 4 rivers and the 2,000-foot hills of the Baul Massif, the working ranch maintains a reserve with four ecosystems: grassy plains, deciduous forest, gallery forest, and mountain savanna. At a biological station, visiting scientists study some of the nearly 400 species of animals and birds and 30 species of fish. El Piñero is internationally cited as an example of how man, cattle, and wild fauna can flourish under wise management. Naturalist groups of 2 to 20 are escorted by jeep and on foot around the 300-square-mile ranch. Cost, including all food (no alcohol) and transportation is about $150 day. Groups of 10 to 12 visitors are preferred; call Morgan Tours, Venguides, or Hato Piñero in Caracas (02–916676, 916854).

More and more ranches are remodeling to offer travelers the best of Llanos music (the *joropo*), food (such as *ternero,* roasted veal), and comfort, along with dry season wildlife. Most reservations are taken through tour agencies. (See *Treks and Adventure Tours* in "Facts at Your Fingertips.") Such nature lodges include Hato Macanillal, Hato El Cedral, Campamento Las Garzas, Hato Buenaventura, and Hato Bayona.

BOLÍVAR STATE—THE GUAYANA HIGHLANDS

There's no way to put on paper the magic of the Guayana Highlands of Bolívar State, an ancient plateau stretching down to Brazil. Here, clouds wrap table mountains, and clear waters foam over a myriad of falls in a camper's paradise. Vertical mesas, or *tepuys,* which tower over the grassy savanna, are remnants of one of the world's oldest geological formations, the Guayana Shield. Part of this area, known as the *Gran Sabana,* or Great Savanna, forms Canaima National Park, the world's third largest. Its area of 11,500 square miles is greater than New Jersey and Delaware combined.

Mount Roraima, the tallest mesa, inspired Sir Arthur Conan Doyle's fantasy about prehistoric monsters atop a "Lost World," and the name has stuck. Long inaccessible, it was first scaled in 1884 by two English naturalists who traveled two months through British Guiana to reach it. Today a road to Brazil passes near Roraima and many trekkers scale the 9,000-foot mesa in two days.

But the glory of the park is Angel Falls on Auyantepuy, or Devil's Mountain. Angel Falls towers not only as the world's tallest (at 3,212 feet, it's twice as high as the Empire State Building) but as high spot on any air tour of Venezuela. Avensa jets land daily at Canaima camp downstream. Struck by the beauty of more waterfalls, lagoons, and pink beaches, visitors often call Canaima "a corner of Eden." Several guides run river trips to the foot of Angel Falls in a canyon deep in Auyantepuy. The falls were put on the map by an American pilot, Jimmie Angel, who landed on the huge mesa in 1937 looking for gold. His plane may be seen today in a park by the Ciudad Bolívar airport.

Gold and diamonds are found, in fact, in many tributaries of the Caroní and Paragua rivers. Diamond prospecting is a case of every man for himself and the fever is highest in the dry season. At rumors of a new strike thousands of miners converge, setting up primitive towns overnight. The towns which outlive the *bulla* help to settle new areas of the sparsely populated state—Santa Elena de Uairén in the 1940s following discovery of the 154-carat "Barrabás" stone, Icabarú in the 1950s, Guaniamo in the 1970s. The gold rush centers of the nineteenth century, El Callao and El Dorado, are seeing new exploitation spurred by high gold prices.

The treasure of El Dorado fame eluded Sir Walter Raleigh twice. On a 1595 expedition he was turned back at the Caroní by rains but wrote a best-seller, *The Discoverie of the Large, Rich and Bewtiful Empyre of Guiana;* the second failure in 1618 cost the life of his son to Spanish guns and his own head to King James's wrath.

Ironically, Guayana's true riches do not lie in gold but in iron and bauxite. Not one but three mountains of iron, the most famous being Cerro Bolívar (discovered in 1947), add up to two billion tons of reserves. Bauxite reserves discovered in 1977 at Los Pijiguaos promise 200 million tons. Converting raw materials into national wealth is the job of the regional development agency, Corporación Venezolana de Guayana. CVG's first step in 1961 was to forge the towns of Puerto Ordaz and San Felix at the confluence of the Orinoco and Caroní Rivers into a new city. Ciudad Guayana, today the hub of heavy industry, is now Venezuela's fifth largest city with nearly half a million inhabitants. From docks on the Orinoco, ocean-going ships load iron ore and briquettes, steel pipes and wire, aluminum and ferro-alloys for the world markets. All this is made possible by cheap hydropower from giant Guri Dam, only fifty miles up the Caroní River. The 500-foot-high dam can produce ten million kilowatts of power.

Ciudad Bolívar

The historic trading center of Ciudad Bolívar is the capital of Bolívar State. The 95,200 square miles of the state cover a quarter of Venezuela but have less than 5 percent of the population. Located 270 miles upstream from the sea, Ciudad Bolívar overlooks the Orinoco from a rocky promontory. Its picturesque waterfront was long the starting point for explorers, missionaries, and merchants heading upriver to the vast plains of Apure and forests of the Amazon Territory. Today a city of 285,000, the old port conserves the flavor of colonial roots, independence battles, and export heydays of rubber, chicle, *sarrapia,* or tonka beans, copaiba oil, palm fiber, hides, and cattle. Although airplanes and jeeps have taken over from riverboats for travel to the interior, "CB" remains the center for gold and diamond prospectors who buy supplies here and sell nuggets and rough stones to international buyers and jewelers.

It was formerly called Angostura (meaning "narrows") because here the great Orinoco is only two-thirds of a mile wide. But its waters are over eighty feet deep and can rise another thirty-five during the August peak, carrying rains from over two-thirds of Venezuela and a quarter of Colombia. A few miles from Ciudad Bolívar the beautiful Angostura Bridge arches across to Anzoategui State. The name Angostura also identifies the famous bitters, first decocted here in 1824 from the bark of a tree, used locally against fevers, and later made in Trinidad.

A patriot stronghold, Angostura was capital of the struggling republic from 1817 until the triumph of Independence in 1821. Here Bolívar gathered arms from the Antilles and veterans from England, Ireland, and Germany for his foreign legions. A Scot, Andrew Roderick, printed the republic's first newspaper, the *Correo del Orinoco,* or "Orinoco Mail," in a house on the waterfront which is today one of the city's several museums.

PRACTICAL INFORMATION FOR BOLÍVAR STATE

HOW TO GET AROUND. By plane. *Avensa* and *Aeropostal* jets link Maiquetía with Ciudad Bolívar and Puerto Ordaz (Ciudad Guayana) 6 times a day. From Ciudad Guayana, jets fan out to Porlamar, Barcelona, Maracaibo, and Valencia. From Cuidad Bolívar, Avensa flies to Canaima, Aeropostal to Maturín, and *Aereotuy* (085–25907) to Caicara, Los Pijiguaos, and Puerto Ayacucho. Cuidad Bolívar is the base for Aereotuy's exciting Gran Sabana route to Santa Elena de Uairén, skimming tablelands and dark rivers on the way to Camarata Mission, Urimán, and Icabarú. Ask about Aereotuy's day excursion to Kavac Canyon to view Angel Falls.

By bus. Interstate pullman lines such as *Expresos de Guayana* (02–545–4952) and *Expresos de Oriente* (02–545–3040) go all the way from Caracas to Ciudad Bolívar, Ciudad Guayana, and El Dorado (16 hours). The Ciudad Bolívar bus terminal on Ave. República at Ave. Sucre, like the air terminal, is communications hub for the entire region. A small Turismo office supplies information. Por puestos go out of state to Tucupita, El Tigre, and even Margarita, and cover every town in the state to the Brazilian frontier. From Santa Elena de Uairén a Brazilian line goes daily to Boa Vista. From San Félix (Ciudad Guayana), buses cross the Orinoco by ferry for Maturín.

Plane rentals. For a flying visit to Gran Sabana missions of Cavanayen and Camarata, charter an air-taxi at the CB airport: *Comeravia* (085–23255), *Aeroból* (085–26279), *Rutaca* (085–24010), and *Transmandu* (085–21462). The last 3 give daily service to gold and diamond mines (about ½ hour); a seat may cost $60.

Jeep rentals. 4-wheel-drive vehicles may be rented at Puerto Ordaz airport from *Hertz* (086–223917); *Budget* (086–591692); *ACO* (086–591711); *Rasil* (086–

591746); and *National Car* (086–222225), which also has an airport office in Ciudad Bolívar (085–27090). Advance reservation is essential for jeeps, up to a month ahead during the peak holiday seasons of Dec.–Apr. and Jul.–Aug. Credit card required.

Ciudad Bolívar

HOTELS. For definitions of price categories see "Facts at Your Fingertips" earlier in this chapter. Two new hotels fill a need for first-class facilities.

Rio Orinoco Venantur. *Expensive.* 1½ miles from Cd. Bolívar off highway to the Angostura Bridge (085–42011, telex 85268; Caracas fax 02–9781497). New 5-story hotel on the banks of the Orinoco; 125 double rooms, 2 pools, restaurant, bar/disco, shops, jogging path, pedal-boats, on 28 acres of grounds.

Laja Real. *Moderate.* Av. Jesús Soto opposite airport (085–27911, fax 085–28778, telex 85112). 12 acres of gardens, pool, convention rooms, terrace soda fountain, restaurant, bar. 73 rooms. Big pool is open to non-guests.

Also on the waterfront, right downtown: **Gran Hotel Bolívar.** *Moderate.* Paseo Orinoco (085–20100/02). Distinguished old hotel, 70 rooms, good restaurant, nearby parking.

Also in airport vicinity: **Da Gino.** *Moderate.* Av. Jesus Soto (085–28367). 31 modern rooms, good Italian restaurant. **Don Salo.** *Inexpensive.* Av. Bolívar at Táchira (085–29919–20). 36 rooms, restaurant, bar, good value. **Valentina.** *Inexpensive.* No. 55 Av. Maracay (085–22145). 36 rooms in converted residence, Italian restaurant. **Florida.** *Inexpensive.* Av. Táchira (085–27942). A few spartan rooms, tasty Italian fare. **Táchira.** *Inexpensive.* No. 27 Av. Táchira. 38 pleasant rooms, good restaurant.

RESTAURANTS. Germania, *Moderate,* Av. Táchira opp. airport. Pleasant outdoor tables, music, German specialties, English tea. **Gran Paella,** *Inexpensive,* 12 Av. Vidal (085–22743). International menu, good antipastos. **Mirador,** *Inexpensive,* Paseo Orinoco (085–21604). Grilled steak and fresh Orinoco fish—curbinata and sapoara. **Rancho de Doña Carmen,** *Inexpensive,* Calle Pichincha (085–23190). Venezuelan and Guyanese specialties—takari (curry), merey (cashew fruit) in syrup.

CIUDAD GUAYANA

HOTELS. The following hotels are in Puerto Ordaz, catering largely to businessmen. The exception is the **Inter-Continental Guayana.** *Deluxe.* Punta Vista Park (086–222244/280, fax 085–222253). Half the 205 rooms have a view over Cachamay rapids; convention rooms, pool, tennis, gym, restaurant, bar with music, pier for river excursions.

Rasil. *Moderate.* Centro Cívico Puerto Ordaz (086–223405, fax 085–227703). 312 rooms and suites; convenient; noisy bar, discotheque. **Dos Rios.** *Moderate.* Calle Mexico (086–229188). 72 rooms, gardens, pool, restaurant, bar. **Embajador.** *Inexpensive.* Calle La Urbana (086–225511). Modern, 80 rooms, restaurant, bar. **Guayana.** *Inexpensive.* Ave. Las Américas (086–227375). 30 rooms. **Tepuy.** *Inexpensive.* Carrera Upata (086–220102). 46 rooms. **Saint Georges.** *Inexpensive.* Calle La Urbana (086–229411). 32 rooms, restaurant, bar.

RESTAURANTS. Downtown spots such as **La Cucciara, La Forchetta di Oro, Key Club, Mario's, El Embajador,** and **El Churrasco** are popular for satisfying fare at *moderate* prices. **La Romanina** and **Paolo's,** *expensive,* are posh, with arctic airconditioning. In Alta Vista, two popular spots are **Café Salto Angel** and **Café Continental.**

GUAYANA HIGHLANDS

SOURCES OF INFORMATION AND TOURS. Corp. Venezolana de Guayana, Edificio CVG, Alta Vista, Ciudad Guayana (086–226155). The CVG library and Information Dept. (086–222714) give an overview of tourism facilities as well as CVG industries. Most plants provide tours for the public on weekdays (call for hours—best times are 8 A.M. and 1 P.M.). Sidor, the giant steel complex, has 500 acres of roofed plants and is still expanding. The output of Alcasa (086–222753) and Venalum (086–222977) is being enlarged to 750,000 tons of primary aluminum.

Guri Dam, officially called Represa Raul Leoni, with its artificial lake covering 1,600 square miles, is a major attraction for engineers and tourists, and is located 60 miles south of Ciudad Guayana. Built in stages over 21 years, when completed in 1986 Guri was the world's second largest dam, with 10 million kilowatt capacity. The dam's operator, Edelca (086–229411) conducts free bus tours; get a pass at Guri Visitors Center and check tour times. There is a restaurant and a hotel open to visitors. **Hotel Guri,** at the dam. *Inexpensive.* (086–229411). 58 rooms, pool.

Cerro Bolívar, the iron mountain which inspired Puerto Ordaz's founding in 1952 as an iron port for US Steel, is worked by CVG's Ferrominera del Orinoco (iron was nationalized in 1975). Passes to visit the terraced 1,800-foot-high iron deposit may be obtained from Ferrominera in Puerto Ordaz (086–221584) or from the mine administration in the company town, Ciudad Piar, 30 miles south of Guri.

Adventure Tours and Guides. With more rivers than roads and more mountains than towns, the Guayana region is wide open for treks. A crop of "adventure" firms now makes reaching the top of Roraima or the foot of Angel Falls without hassle a reality for foreigners, who need bring no special equipment. (See *Treks and Adventure Tours* in "Facts at Your Fingertips" section for addresses and phone numbers.)

Mt. Roraima treks (10–12 days), covering a lot of the Gran Sabana by jeep for $75 to $100 a day according to services and party. *Lost World Adventures* organizes hikes to the summits of Roraima or Auyantepui (the "Devil Mountain" of Angel Falls); provides all food and equipment; English-speaking leaders. *Morgan Tours* arranges treks for parties of 2 and up by plane, jeep, or foot, with guide and cook. *Wek'ta Tours,* (at the Rasil, 086–223405) takes groups of 4 to 8 hiking up Roraima or Auyantepui, or boating on the Yuruani or the Caura (Para Falls). *Happy Tours* in Ciudad Guayana goes camping to Kavanayen Mission by jeep (4 persons, 4-day minimum). A jeep circle of the Gran Sabana's many waterfalls, with a look-in at gold mines and a return trip by air from Santa Elena, is offered for groups by *Selva Tours. Alechiven,* based in Valencia, offers a 10-day trekking ascent of the Auyantepui.

Getting on the **rivers** can be more exciting, if less active. Starting with the *Selva Tours* fishing excursions to Guri Lake, by the day, longer trips can be arranged to go up the dark, swift Paragua River for 3–4 days, stopping at a diamond dredge and Uraima rapids.

WHAT TO SEE. Ciudad Bolívar. Great view of city and river from small hilltop fort of El Zamuro. The Jesús Soto Modern Art Museum on Ave. Germania, named after Venezuelan founder of kinetic art, has changing shows. Quinta San Isidro, on Ave. Táchira, is a beautifully conserved colonial country house where Simón Bolívar lived in 1818–19. Surrounding Plaza Bolívar are the restored Cathedral of Nuestra Señora de lasNieves (popular religious festivities are held on Aug. 5), the eighteenth-century Government House, and the colonial school famous as site of the 1819 Angostura Congress. The Correo del Orinoco Museum is on the riverside Paseo Orinoco, a busy street with crowded shopping arcades and old two-story houses. Gold nuggets, or *cochanos,* and diamonds are worked by craftsmen here into earrings and necklaces. One workshop, the Taller de Diamantes Universal Guayanesa, is in the arcade called Paisaje Guayana. Ask at the old Gran Hotel Bolívar for others.

Ciudad Guayana. Before the dark waters of the Caroní River join the muddy Orinoco, they spread 4 miles wide in a series of cataracts around islands. Alongside Cachamay cataracts stretches a pretty park; adjacent Loefling Park has a small zoo of capybaras, giant otters, and deer. Access to lovely Llovizna Falls and Park near Macagua I power plant is by way of San Felix (take the road towards El Pao mine). Hours of 9:30 A.M. to 3 P.M. (no picnics) also apply to the Spanish ruins of La Concepción Mission, the first (1724) of the Caroní Missions. From the road junction the distance is 20 miles to El Pao. Passes are issued on weekdays for touring the mine, really a mountain of iron. Ore trains from El Pao unload at Palua docks in San Félix.

Los Castillos. One hour down the Orinoco from Puerto Ordaz are two colonial forts. The higher of the two, San Diego de Alcalá, dates from 1747 and, with its star-shaped design, commands land and water. The smaller and lower, Fort San Francisco, was built in 1678–81. The forts controlled all river traffic until 1943. There is a road from San Félix, 25 miles, to the Castillos. Excursions by river (half day, very sunny) leave from the Inter-Continental's pier. (See *Treks and Adventure Tours* in "Facts at Your Fingertips" for agencies and addresses.)

Canaima and Angel Falls. A few minutes downstream from the world's highest falls, Avensa's jet lands every morning at bewitchingly beautiful Canaima, framed by majestic tepuys, savanna, and forest. The sherry-dark waters of the Carrao here thunder over the Hacha Falls' seven cataracts into quiet Canaima lagoon, which is ringed with pink sands. Good swimming, boating, and excursions from a few hours to several days, run by the Hermanos Jiménez—they do 4-day river trips for about $150 a person to Angel Falls, minimum group 6. Alechiven (041–211828, 041–212660) runs an 8-day tour to Angel Falls in dugout canoes, starting from the Pemom Indian village of Kamarata. Costs approximately $120 per person per day, including transfer and hotel last night in Caracas. Canaima camp, run by Hoturvensa, accommodates 160 in simple cabins; plentiful food. Avensa offers 3 days/2 nights, including boat ride, meals, and flight, for about $350 per couple from Ciudad Bolívar; additional night, $50. Canaima is usually full on holidays and weekends. Reservations for vacation times should be made 2 months in advance through Hoturvensa (02–562–3022), fax 562–3475); in the U.S., through a travel agent or Avensa (212–956–8500, 305–381–8001).

Ucaima Camp. Above Hacha Falls is "Jungle Rudy" Truffino's charming base on the banks of the Carrao. Comfortable cabins, $75 a day with meals. The atmosphere is intimate; guests come from all over the world. Rudy's mid-week trips to Angel Falls leave early on Mon. (July–Nov.) and cost about $520 per person for groups of 5–8, including pickup from Canaima, 3 nights on excursion (cots), and 2 nights in Ucaima Camp.

Kavak Falls, which lie south of the vast mesa of Auyantepui, are now on Aereotuy's turbo-prop route. Leaving from Ciudad Bolívar at 9 A.M. every day except Mon., Aereotuy flies over Angel Falls on the way to Kamarata Valley. An hour's hike leads into a narrow gorge or *cueva* with a stream falling from above. Take swim suit, change of shoes and clothes, windbreaker, and plastic bags to protect your camera.

Paragua River. Sixty miles south of Ciudad Piar and the iron mines of Cerro Bolívar is the old river port of La Paragua, founded in 1770. River trips can be arranged to Isla Casabe diamond dredge or to Uraima Falls, 4–5 hours upstream. With its private airfield, Hato El Burro is a good base for seeing Guri, Kavac, or the Paragua, guided by multilingual experts (Ackermann 02–782–0797).

On the **road to Brazil** through the Gran Sabana, credit cards and traveler's checks are of less use than new tires, spare gas, and food for picnics. Starting from the Caroní ferry crossing at Paso Caruachi (6 A.M. to 6 P.M.), the route winds east through low hills to **Upata,** founded in 1762 by Capuchin missionaries. A dairy and farming center then and now, Upata grew rich in the nineteenth-century gold rush through a monopoly on ox and mule trains to the mines of El Callao. Among inexpensive hostels are the *Comercio,* Calle Ayacucho No. 25–1 (088–21156), known for good Italian food, and the large *Andrea* (088–22211), at the Upata exit.

The tiny town of **Guasipati** was once state capital of the "gold province" called Yuruari during the stampede of 1850–90, and its cemetery holds the graves of many men who met violent deaths. On its main street there is a good coffee house by the plaza, and a new modest motel, the *Reina* (088–67357). Today gold is mined in **El Callao** by the state enterprise Minerven, producing some 400 pounds a month. In the old days prospectors poured into every tributary of the Yuruari and Cuyuni, taking out as much as 55 tons of gold during the peak years of 1874–88. As a legacy of the Negro miners who came from Trinidad, English lingers today in the calypsos which make El Callao's Carnival the liveliest in Venezuela. For a look at gold crushers and the cyanide flotation process, ask at Minerven office in El Peru (086–691780).

Tumeremo, founded in 1788 as the last of the Caroní missions, still has the air of a frontier town. Here is the last air service (4 Aeropostal flights a week from Ciudad Bolívar), bank, CANTV telephone service, premium gas, spare parts, and ice before Santa Elena de Uairén, 257 miles south. Bus and jeep services to Santa Elena leave every morning, often bypassing El Dorado. An inexpensive hotel on the plaza is the *Central* (088–71264). The ill fame of sultry **El Dorado** as a prison town is fading in the light of gold strikes since high prices have re-started old mines. This is the end of the line for buses from Caracas such as Expresos de Oriente which cover the 600 miles in 16 hours. Lodgings can be found at cheap new hotels, and at a riverside tourist camp with garden, *Campamento Turístico El Dorado,* 8 rooms run by Londoner Richard Coles. The penal colony is actually not in El Dorado but some miles beyond the Cuyuni River bridge.

Straight and hot, the road tunnels through the lush Imataca Forest Reserve to km 88, San Isidro, the last gasoline, food, and Santa Elena jeep stop, now a gathering place for gold miners including English-speaking Arecuna Indians from Guyana. At La Clarita, km 85, there is a hostel.

The entrance to **Canaima National Park,** shortly after San Isidro, is marked by the mammoth "Virgin's Rock." From here, the ascent to the cool plateau of the Gran Sabana is so steep it is called "La Escalera," the stairway. The road was opened as recently as 1973. Heavy rains erode the loose, sandy (and extremely infertile) soils, making road engineers' work a misery but at the same time feeding gorgeous waterfalls. Off the 40-mile detour to **Cavanayen Mission** there are two spectacular falls reached by rough jeep tracks: Aponguao Falls (Chinak-Meru), 370 feet high, and Torón, about 300 feet. Each deserves an early start in the day. A chain of massive table mountains crowned by dramatic clouds dwarfs the Catholic mission in Cavanayen valley. During school holidays the padres allow visitors to stay overnight for a few dollars at the stone boarding school. *Chivaton* camp, 11 miles before Cavanayen, offers basic lodging.

Between here and Santa Elena there are splendid camping sites by streams (the water is quite safe for drinking) and more lovely waterfalls—dropping west below the road are **Kama Falls** (160 feet) and **La Laja,** about the same height. The cataracts at the Yuruani River, however, are the haunt of merciless blackflies. A 4-wheel-drive track leading to **Roraima and Kukenam** mesas, looming in the east, takes off beyond San Francisco de Yuruaní, a Pemón settlement. Jeeps penetrate almost to the foot of Mt. Roraima in the dry season (Dec.-Apr.), but even then electric storms justify the Indian name for the mountain as Great Mother of Streams, whose waters flow into 3 basins: the Orinoco by way of the Caroní, the Amazon in Brazil, and the Essequibo in Guyana. Trekkers usually hire guides at Paraitepuy, an Indian village reached by a 15-mile jeep track ($12 a day).

Nine miles from Brazil, **Santa Elena** is a growing frontier town complete with hospital, army post, gas station, bank, air service, and telephone office. Its first inhabitant arrived in 1923, built a house on the banks of the Uairén, and called the place Elena after his daughter. Many of the 27 children of founder Lucas Fernández Peña today raise cattle, run shops, or work gold around Santa Elena. Mines still produce gold and diamonds in Icabarú, at the end of the road 70 miles west. New lodgings such as *La Nona* on the road entering town, and the *Friedenau's* five cabins in Cielo Azul district, are nicer than the crowded *Hotel Las Fronteras* on Calle Urdaneta. Life is springing up in pioneer farms around El Paují and tourist camps such as *Cantarrana* near Icabarú. *Camp Shailili-Kó,* opened in 1986 in a lovely wooded spot before El Paují, has 10 cabins with beds for 40; ample food, excursions to El Abismo Canyon overlooking Brazil; great hiking and birding. For Shailili-Ko reservations, including air charter, call Ana Ponte (02–752–6767, 751–5009). Outside Icabarú, *Villa Tranquila* offers six comfortable cabins with bath, in a well-run camp by a river. Reservations in Caracas through Venguides (02–951–6211, fax 951–6544).

AMAZONAS FEDERAL TERRITORY

Just one hour by jet south of Caracas is Puerto Ayacucho, capital of the Amazonas Federal Territory (70,200 square miles), whose forests, rivers, and mountains stretch south to Brazil, half a degree from the equator. The territory occupies one-fifth of Venezuela but has scarcely 80,000 inhabitants and 180 miles of roads; it is still little known away from the rivers which afford access. Here are the headwaters of the great Orinoco River which runs over 320,000 square miles of Venezuela and Colombia through

2,000 tributaries. The Orinoco has the peculiarity, however, of feeding some of its water into the Amazon basin via the Casiquire River which connects the two great river systems. This canal was first recorded by Alexander Humboldt, the famous German explorer, who reached here in 1800.

A dozen different Indian tribes, each with its own culture and language, make the forests and rivers their home. The Makiritare, or Yekuana, are masters of river navigation and the art of hollowing dugout canoes (curiaras and bongos) from tree trunks, some eighteen yards long. The Piaroa build superb conical houses, or *shuruatas,* twelve yards high and thatched with palm. The Sanemá have no chiefs and no one gives or takes orders. The Yanomami, who move freely over the Brazilian border, have only recently learned about missionaries; many have never seen white men.

This land of "Green Mansions" typified by W.H. Hudson has long fascinated and frustrated foreign travelers. Lack of communications and prohibitions against visiting Indian territory without an armful of permits have dampened tourism. Gradually, this is changing. A road now links Puerto Ayacucho, at the northwest corner of the territory, with Caicara in Bolívar State, and work is going ahead on a 185-mile road to San Juan de Manapiare, also from Caicara. The tourist camp at Yutaje in the Manapiare Valley is popular with fly-in weekenders; even remoter camps run specialized tours.

Puerto Ayacucho is a river port of 24,000 inhabitants situated some 570 miles from the Orinoco's mouth. The Atures and Maipures rapids here interrupt all river navigation. Goods bound for the upper Orinoco must be trucked forty miles south of the rapids to Samariapo. Colombia borders the west bank of the Orinoco until the Atabapo River.

Hot and dusty in the dry season (December through April) and hot and muggy in the rains (May through November), there is little to distinguish Puerto Ayacucho from other tropical trading posts. Founded in 1924, it has a shady Plaza Bolívar surrounded by the Town Hall, state and Indian Affairs offices (ORAI), and Salesian church and school. There is an Ethnological Museum, movie theater, an old hotel of note, and several modest restaurants. The water is clean and the government health service has eradicated yellow fever and smallpox. But malaria is on the rise and travelers to jungle destinations should take antimalaria pills such as chlorquine and paludrine, two doses before arrival and two doses weekly. Tropical disease control is studied at CAICET, a research center.

PRACTICAL INFORMATION FOR AMAZONAS TERRITORY

GETTING THERE. All traffic, ground, air, or river, goes through Puerto Ayacucho. **By air.** Daily *Aeropostal* and *Avensa* jets from Maiquetia, via San Fernando de Apure. Twice-weekly flights by *Aereotuy* from Ciudad Bolívar-Caicara. **By road.** Por puestos and buses cover the Caicara route daily. Four-wheel-drive vehicles using the new Llanos road from San Fernando de Apure cross the Orinoco on the ferry or *chalana* between Puerto Páez and El Burro. **By river.** Orinoco ferries haul goods, people, and cars up from Ciudad Guayana, Ciudad Bolívar, and Cabruta. Depending on high or low water, the journey can take up to 3 days. The ferry is uneventful and cheap at $30 for car plus passengers from Cabruta, but provides no food.

GETTING AROUND. To see the Puerto Ayacucho environs, a group of 4 is ideal for hiring a jeep plus guide. Nearby sights include Piaroa villages of Raya, Gavilan, and Carinaguita and Guahibo communities at Mirabal, Coromoto, and Cerro Pintado, the latter named for an enormous rock bearing a prehistoric carving of a serpent. The petroglyph is 50 yards long and has a sister snake on a rock west of the Orinoco, in Colombia. A jeep is also needed to reach cool bathing spots on the green

Cataniapo River and in the Jungle Toboggan Park with its natural slide and rock pools. **Jeep rentals** from: *Tour Amazonas* opposite the Obelisco, Ave. 23 de Enero (048–21337); credit card required. *Turisur,* No. 17 Ave. 23 de Enero (048–21993); Visa credit card. About $40 a day.

Six-seater **air taxis** go regularly to Maroa and San Carlos de Rio Negro near Brazil, to San Fernando de Atabapo and San Juan de Manapiare, as well as to San Fernando in Apure State and Caicara in Bolívar. For charters by the hour, contact *Aguaysa* (048–21443) or *Transporte Aéreo Wayumi* (048–21635).

Boats or dugouts, from small curiaras to large bongos, can be hired by arrangement for a day's excursion up the Orinoco, from Samariapo to Isla Ratón, where there is a large Salesian Mission. How much this costs will depend on bargaining, but $50 should go a long way. From Puerto Ayacucho docks, launches cross to the Colombian side; for less than $2 anyone may go for the day after registering at the Guardia Nacional dock post. Launches also regularly take passengers down to Puerto Páez at the mouth of the Meta River opposite Puerto Carreño, a busy Colombian port.

Although its dangers are greatly exaggerated by moviemakers, the Amazonas Territory is far enough from civilization to make credit cards impractical and even banks have been known to balk at traveler's checks. Cash will avoid hang-ups.

HOTELS AND RESTAURANTS. Puerto Ayacucho. One hotel of note—**Gran Amazonas.** *Moderate* (048–21962). Air-conditioning, pool, patio restaurant. **Maguari.** *Inexpensive.* Calle Evelio Roa (048–21120). Aging but air-conditioned, 16 rooms; restaurant with plain food. Other lodging: the **Autana, Aeropuerto, Tobogan.** Other *inexpensive* restaurants: **Rio Negro** on Ave. Amazonas, **El Rincon de Apure** on airport road.

Camturama. *Expensive.* Located on the banks of the Orinoco at Garcita rapids (048–22574). The kind of hotel/camp this area has long needed. 60 doubles in Indian-style, round, thatched-roof houses (air-conditioned). Swimming in the river or in a gigantic pool. For tour packages, contact Caracas agencies such as Diadema (02–724856/8, fax 724556).

Toucan Resort. *Expensive.* (048–22601). Well-run guest house north of Puerto Ayacucho where 16 doubles serve as base for trips by river or to Indian villages. (Contact Alpi Tours.)

TOURIST INFORMATION AND TOURS. The Amazonas Territory, long a mystery to tourists and travel agents alike, is at last open to adventure tours. In Puerto Ayacucho, Pepe Jaimes of **Tobogan Tours,** Av. Rio Negro (048–21700), handles groups as large as 50, from 1 to 10 days, combining travel by plane, jeep, and *falca*—large dugout with outboard motor. The star excursion, or Estrella Tour, to vertical Mt. Autana goes by dugout up the Orinoco, Sipapo, and Autana rivers, 4 days, and provides all food and camping gear. Each tourist is given his own hammock and shown how to sling and use it.

Selva Tours (Av. Orinoco, 048–22122), from its branch office, arranges private flights to jungle lodges near San Juan de Manapiare and river trips on the Orinoco for 1 to 4 days. Prices run approximately $100 a day per person (min. 4) for river expeditions, more when charter flights are required.

Venguides (02–951–6211, telex 24714 BVENC VC) flies those with more money than time from Caracas to the Amazonas and "Lost World," stopping at Yutaje camp, Piaroa communities in Guanay Valley, and Cacurí Mission, before heading on to Canaima and points east in a spectacular week-long circle, at a price tag of about $200 per day.

Alechiven (041–211828) runs tours to Puerto Ayacucho and San Carlos de Rio Negro, then upriver to San Simon de Cucuy to see the famous Cucuy rock at the border of Venezuela, Colombia, and Brazil. Costs approximately $125 per day per person.

For a less strenuous vacation, Yutajé Camp in the Manapiare Valley appeals to families who prefer bed, bath, cabin, and sit-down meals. Built and run year-round by an Italian, José Raggi, the camp has a 5,000-foot airstrip and accommodations for about 30. Lots of birds, howler monkeys, treks through woods, great bass fishing, waterfalls, lagoons with otters, freshwater dolphins. **Alpi Tours** (02–283–1433, fax 284–7098), flies groups from Caracas to Yutajé, 5 degrees from the equator, at a cost of about $400 a person (3 days/2 nights), all inclusive. Alpi's Linda Sondermann reports that the beautiful jungle base of Caño Santo in the Manapiare Valley has reopened with new lodgings, including some 2-room *churuatas* with private baths. Guests here can sleep in hammocks. From Puerto Ayacucho by commercial plane, the 3-day package runs $350 a person (min. 4).

(See *Treks and Adventure Tours* in "Facts at Your Fingertips" for addresses as well as "Adventure Vacations" chapter for other tours.)

CRAFTS. From the many tribes of the Orinoco headwaters come handsome baskets and *wapas,* or trays, masks, blowpipes, feather and bead adornments, rings made of jet, carved body stamps, and jaguar stools of hardwood. The **Artesanía Amazonas** shop at the airport has a good supply. An early Friday morning **crafts market** in Puerto Ayacucho attracts hundreds of Indian artisans to the plaza fronting the **Museo de Etnología,** which has its own good shop.

TOURIST VOCABULARIES

TEN-MINUTE SPANISH

Glossary of often used terms and phrases

ENGLISH	SPANISH	PHONETIC PRONUNCIATION
Good morning (afternoon) (evening).	Buenos días (buenas tardes), (buenas noches).	Boo-*ennohs dee*-ahs (boo-*eh*-nahs *tahr*-dehs) (boo-*en*-nahs *no*-ches)
I don't speak Spanish.	No hablo español.	Noh *ah*-bloh ehs-pahn-*yohl*
I don't understand.	No comprendo.	*No kohm-prehn*-doh
How are you?	?Cómo está usted?	*Koh*-moh ehs-*tah* oohs-*teh*?
Very well, thank you.	Muy bien, gracias.	*Mooee* bee-*ehn*, grah-*see*-ahs
Where are you going?	?A dónde va usted?	Ah-*dohn*—deh *vah* oos-teh?
When are you returning?	?Cuando volverá usted?	Koo-*ahn*-doh vohl-veh-*rah oos*-teh?
Many thanks.	Muchas gracias.	*Moo*chahs *grah*-see-ahs
Please.	Por favor.	pohr fah-*vohr*
No, (yes).	No. (sí).	*Noh, (see)*
Don't mention it.	De nada.	*Deh nah*-dah
To the right.	A la derecha.	Ah la deh-*reh*-chah
To the left.	A la izquierda.	Ah lah ees-key-*ehr*-dah
Do you have a match?	?Tiene usted un fósforo?	Tee-eh-*neh* oos-*teh* oon *fohs*-foh-roh?
Can you tell me?	?Puede usted decirme?	Poo-*eh*-deh oos-*teh* deh-*seer*-meh?
I think so.	Creo que sí.	*Kreh*-oh deh see
I don't think so.	Creo que no.	*Kreh*-oh-keh noh
More slowly, please.	Más despacio, por favor.	Mahs dehs-*pah*-see-oh, pohr fah-*vohr*
Repeat, please.	Repita, por favor.	Reh-*pee*-tah, pohr fah-*vohr*
Pardon me.	Perdóneme.	*Pehr-doh*-neh-meh
I don't know.	No sé.	Noh *seh*
Do you know?	?Sabe usted?	*Sah*-beh oos-*teh*?
Goodbye.	Adiós.	Ah-dee-*ohs*
Come here, please.	Sírvase venir acá.	*Seer*-vah-seh veh-*neer* ah*kah*
It doesn't matter.	No importa.	Noh eem-*pohr*-tah
Next week.	La semana próxima.	Lah seh-*mah*-nah *prok*-see-mah
Yesterday.	Ayer.	Ah-*yehr*
Don't forget.	No se olvide.	Noh seh ohl-*vee*-deh
Call me ('phone me).	Llámeme (por teléfono).	*Yah*-meh-meh (pohr teh-*leh*-foh-noh)
What do you wish?	?Qué desea usted?	Keh deh-*seh*-ah oss-*teh*?
The gentleman	El señor	Ehl sehn-*yohr*
The lady	La señora	Lah sehn-*yor*-ah
The young lady	La señorita	Lah sehn-yohr-*eetah*
Monday	lunes	*loo*-nehs
Tuesday	martes	*mahr*-tehs
Wednesday	miércoles	mee-*ehr*-koh-lehs
Thursday	jueves	who-*eh*-vehs
Friday	viernes	vee-*ehr*-nehs
Saturday	sábado	*sah*-bah-doh
Sunday	domingo	doh-*meen*-goh

614

Black	Negro (masc.)	*Neh*-groh
	Negra (fem.)	*Neh*-grah
Red	Rojo (masc.)	*Roh*-hoh
	Roja (fem.)	*Roh*-hah
Blue	Azul	Ah-*zool*
White	Blanco (masc.)	*Blahn*-koh
	Blanca (fem.)	*Blahn*-kah
Green	Verde	*Vehr*-deh
Yellow	Amarillo (masc.)	Ah-mah-*ree*-yoh
	Amarilla (fem.)	Ah-mah-*ree*-yah
Zero	Zero	*Seh*-roh
One	Uno	*Oo*-noh
Two	Dos	Dohs
Three	Tres	Trehs
Four	Cuatro	Koo-*ah*-troh
Five	Cinco	*Seeng*-koo
Six	Seis	*Say*-ees
Seven	Siete	See-*eh*-teh
Eight	Ocho	*Oh*-choh
Nine	Nueve	Noo-*eh*-veh
Ten	Diez	Dee-*ehs*
Eleven	Once	*Ohn*-seh
Twelve	Doce	*Doh*-seh

TEN-MINUTE PORTUGUESE

Glossary of often-used terms and phrases

ENGLISH	PORTUGUESE	PHONETIC PRONUNCIATION
Good morning (afternoon) (evening) (or good night).	Bom dia (boa tarde), (boa noite).	vone dee'-uh (bo'-uh tar'-dee) (boh'-a noy'-te)
I don't speak Portuguese.	Nao falo portugues.	now faw'-loo Por'-too-gays
I don't understand.	Nao compreendo.	now comb-pree-en'-doo
How are you?	Como está?	comb-ooess-taw'
Very well, thank you.	**Man's answer:** Muito bem, obrigado.	Mwee'-too bain, oh-bree-gaw'-doo
	Lady's answer: Muito bem, obrigada.	Moo'-ee-too baying, oh-bree-gah' da
Where are you going?	Onde vai?	On'-djee vie'?
When are you returning?	Quando volta?	Kwahn'—doo vohl'-ta?
Many thanks.	Muito obrigado. (Lady-Muito obrigada.	Moo'-ee-too oh-bree-gah'-doo (Lady-Moo'-ee-too oh-bree-gah'-da)
More slowly.	Mais devagar.	My'-ees de-va-gahr'
Pardon me.	Desculpe-me.	Dis-kool'pe me
I don't know.	Nao sei.	Nah'-oong say
Do you know?	O senhor (a senhora), a senhorita), (voce) sabe?	oo se-nyohr (a se-nyor'-a), (a se-Nyoh-ree'-ta) (Voh-say') sah'-be?
Today	Hoje	Oh'-jee
Tomorrow	Amanha	Ah-mahn-yah'
Yesterday	Ontem	On'—tain
This week	Esta semana	Es'-ta se-mah'-na
Next week	Apróxima semana smana	se-mah'-na
Don't forget.	Nao se esqueca.	Nah'-oong se is-kay'-sa
All right.	Muito bem.	Moo'-ee-too baying
See you later.	Até logo.	A-tay' loh'-goo
Goodbye.	Adeus.	A-day'-oos
Come here, please.	vehna ca, por favor.	Vayng'-ya kah, poor fah-vohr'
It doesn't matter.	Nao tem importancia.	Nah'-oong tayng eem-poortahn see-a
Let's go.	Vamos.	Vah'-moos.
Very good. (bad).	Muito bem (mal).	Moo'-ee-too bayng (mah'-l)
Where can I change my money?	Onde posso trocar meu dinheiro?	Ohn-de po'-ssoo troo-kahr' may'-oo-dee-nyay'-roo?
Monday	Segunda-feira	Se-goon'-da fay'-ra
Tuesday	Terca-feira	Tayr'-sa fay'ra
Wednesday	Quarta-feira	Kwahr'-ta fay'-ra
Thursday	Quinta-feira	Keen'-ta fay'-ra
Friday	Sexta-feira	Ses'-ta fay'-ra
Saturday	Sábado	Sah'ba-doo
Sunday	Domingo	Doh-meeng'-goo
Black	Preto, negro	Pre'-too, nay'-groo
White	Branco	Brahng'-koo
Red	Vermelho	V-mel'-yoo
Green	Verde	Vayr'-de
Blue	Azul	A-zool'
Yellow	Amarelo	A-ma-re'-loo
One	Um (uma)	Oong (oom-a)
Two	Dois (Duas)	Doys (Doo'-as)
Three	Tres	Trays
Four	Quatro	Kway'-troo
Five	Cinco	Seeng'-koo
Six	Seis	Say'-ees

Seven	Sete	Se'-te
Eight	Oito	Oy'-too
Nine	Nove	Noh'-ve
Ten	Dez	Dayz
Eleven	Onze	Ohn'-zay
Twelve	Doze	Doh'-zay

Index

Fodor's Travel Guides

U.S. Guides

Alaska
Arizona
Boston
California
Cape Cod, Martha's
  Vineyard, Nantucket
The Carolinas & the
  Georgia Coast
The Chesapeake
  Region
Chicago
Colorado
Disney World & the
  Orlando Area
Florida
Hawaii

Las Vegas, Reno,
  Tahoe
Los Angeles
Maine, Vermont,
  New Hampshire
Maui
Miami & the
  Keys
National Parks
  of the West
New England
New Mexico
New Orleans
New York City
New York City
  (Pocket Guide)

Pacific North Coast
Philadelphia & the
  Pennsylvania
  Dutch Country
Puerto Rico
  (Pocket Guide)
The Rockies
San Diego
San Francisco
San Francisco
  (Pocket Guide)
The South
Santa Fe, Taos,
  Albuquerque
Seattle &
  Vancouver

Texas
USA
The U. S. & British
  Virgin Islands
The Upper Great
  Lakes Region
Vacations in
  New York State
Vacations on the
  Jersey Shore
Virginia & Maryland
Waikiki
Washington, D.C.
Washington, D.C.
  (Pocket Guide)

Foreign Guides

Acapulco
Amsterdam
Australia
Austria
The Bahamas
The Bahamas
  (Pocket Guide)
Baja & Mexico's Pacific
  Coast Resorts
Barbados
Barcelona, Madrid,
  Seville
Belgium &
  Luxembourg
Berlin
Bermuda
Brazil
Budapest
Budget Europe
Canada
Canada's Atlantic
  Provinces

Cancun, Cozumel,
  Yucatan Peninsula
Caribbean
Central America
China
Czechoslovakia
Eastern Europe
Egypt
Europe
Europe's Great Cities
France
Germany
Great Britain
Greece
The Himalayan
  Countries
Holland
Hong Kong
India
Ireland
Israel
Italy

Italy 's Great Cities
Jamaica
Japan
Kenya, Tanzania,
  Seychelles
Korea
London
London
  (Pocket Guide)
London Companion
Mexico
Mexico City
Montreal &
  Quebec City
Morocco
New Zealand
Norway
Nova Scotia,
  New Brunswick,
  Prince Edward
  Island
Paris

Paris (Pocket Guide)
Portugal
Rome
Scandinavia
Scandinavian Cities
Scotland
Singapore
South America
South Pacific
Southeast Asia
Soviet Union
Spain
Sweden
Switzerland
Sydney
Thailand
Tokyo
Toronto
Turkey
Vienna & the Danube
  Valley
Yugoslavia

Wall Street Journal Guides to Business Travel

Europe   International Cities   Pacific Rim   USA & Canada

Special-Interest Guides

Bed & Breakfast and
  Country Inn Guides:
Mid-Atlantic Region
New England
The South
The West

Cruises and Ports
  of Call
Healthy Escapes
Fodor's Flashmaps
  New York

Fodor's Flashmaps
  Washington, D.C.
Shopping in Europe
Skiing in the USA &
  Canada

Smart Shopper's
  Guide to London
Sunday in New York
Touring Europe
Touring USA